WOMEN'S AMERICA

Refocusing the Past

WOMEN'S AMERICA

Refocusing the Past

EIGHTH EDITION

Edited by

Linda K. Kerber
University of Iowa

Jane Sherron De Hart
University of California, Santa Barbara

Cornelia Hughes Dayton
University of Connecticut

Judy Tzu-Chun Wu
University of California, Irvine

New York   Oxford
Oxford University Press

Oxford University Press is a department of the University of Oxford.
It furthers the University's objective of excellence in research,
scholarship, and education by publishing worldwide.

Oxford   New York
Auckland   Cape Town   Dar es Salaam   Hong Kong   Karachi
Kuala Lumpur   Madrid   Melbourne   Mexico City   Nairobi
New Delhi   Shanghai   Taipei   Toronto

With offices in
Argentina   Austria   Brazil   Chile   Czech Republic   France   Greece
Guatemala   Hungary   Italy   Japan   Poland   Portugal   Singapore
South Korea   Switzerland   Thailand   Turkey   Ukraine   Vietnam

For titles covered by Section 112 of the US Higher Education
Opportunity Act, please visit www.oup.com/us/he for the
latest information about pricing and alternate formats.

Published by Oxford University Press
198 Madison Avenue, New York, New York 10016
http://www.oup.com

Library of Congress Cataloging-in-Publication Data
Women's America / edited by Linda K. Kerber, University of Iowa, Jane Sherron
De Hart, University of California, Santa Barbara, Cornelia Hughes Dayton, University
of Connecticut, Judy Tzu-Chun Wu, Ohio State University. -- Eighth edition.
     pages cm
   ISBN 978-0-19-934934-0
  1. Women--United States--History--Sources. 2. Women--Employment--United States--
History--Sources. 3. Women--Political activity--United States--History--Sources.
4. Women--Health and hygiene--United States--History--Sources. 5. Feminism--United
States--History--Sources. I. Kerber, Linda K.
   HQ1426.W663 2015
   305.40973--dc23

                                                                        2014033991

Printing number: 9 8 7 6 5 4 3 2

Printed in the United States of America
on acid-free paper

For our teachers

Annette Kar Baxter (1926–1984)

Mary Maples Dunn

Lilia Fernández

Estelle Freedman

Susan Hartmann

John Atlee Kouwenhoven (1909–1990)

Gerda Lerner (1920–2013)

Peggy Pascoe (1954–2010)

Susan Porter Benson (1943–2005)

Leila J. Rupp

Anne Firor Scott

Christine Stansell

Eleanor M. Tilton (1913–1994)

Teaching Workshop in Women's History (UCLA)

and

our own cohorts of pioneering women's historians

and, of course,

the present and future generations of women's and gender history scholars

ILLUSTRATIONS

CONTENTS

xi

PREFACE

To our readers:

Twenty-seven years ago, writing the preface for the second edition of *Women's America*, we observed that in the few years since the first edition, "an extraordinary amount of new scholarship has appeared, changing the way in which professional historians address the major issues in the field. . . . The pace of scholarly development is so rapid that comparisons can appropriately be made to scientific fields, which are expected to change overnight, rather than to the leisured pace of traditional history." That observation is even truer today, as the history of women in the United States reaches out to embrace changing understandings of gender and to engage comparisons with other national histories.

Recognizing the wider range of new scholarship, this eighth edition of *Women's America* includes some 23 new items, many on subjects new to these volumes, with enhanced coverage of women's transnational contacts and activities; sexual choices and dilemmas, including transsexuality; and women's lives in the West, the Midwest, and the South. Even more than all previous editions, *Women's America* gives fresh attention to the challenges of citizenship and its grounding in the law, now in global context.

We have written a new, more succinct Introduction, reflecting on the book's purposes and its readers' questions in the 32 years since *Women's America* was first published. We continue to offer an account of different stages in historians' inquiries into the history of women and gender in the United States. In it, we explain key terms and concepts, such as feminism, the social construction of gender, and intersectionality (the understanding that categories of difference, of race, ethnicity, class, able-bodiedness, sexual expression, culture, nationality, religion, and historical memory intersect and define one another). We give a few examples of how mainstream ideas about proper gender roles and women's and men's differing sexual drives have changed dramatically over the four centuries of U.S. history. For example, today, sex (male/female) is increasingly seen as a spectrum. We stress that varied activism aimed at improving women's lives, expanding rights, and fulfilling goals of liberation occurred continuously throughout the nation's history—and sometimes in unexpected places and ways. The introduction contains tips on using the book and a roadmap in terms of the book's major themes. Here and throughout the book, we invite students to join us in asking how we can find equality in an American society shaped, like all human societies, by differences. Repeatedly we encourage students to ask their own questions and to embark on their own research, especially by doing local and oral histories.

Recognizing the richness of new scholarship on the twentieth century, and wanting to accommodate the different shapes of upper-division courses, *Women's America* now gathers its essays, documents, and images into five chronological sections. Part I: Early America, 1600–1820, and Part II: America's Many Frontiers, 1820–1880, retain the same temporal bounds as previous editions, although new readings have been added. We introduce a new bridge section, Part III: Modern America Emerges, 1880–1920. In the two-volume version, Part III appears in each volume. Instructors of *early* U.S. women's history can use Part III to extend their course to the passage of women's suffrage, if they wish to. Instructors of *modern* U.S. women's history can extend their course back to the late nineteenth century. A new Part IV: A Transforming World, 1920–1945, focuses on women's history from suffrage to the end of World War II. Part V: A Transforming World, 1945–2014, includes emerging scholarship along with some key primary sources on the decades since World War II.

For instructors perhaps the most salient innovation is that that the materials in each Part are now arranged in thematic clusters, such as Workplace and Household Scenes, Sexuality and the Body, Gender and the Armed Forces. These vary in each part, but reflect six core themes of *Women's America*: *family/household/sexuality, labor/economy/class, race/ethnicity/religion, law and citizenship, women's activism,* and the *global context of U.S. women's history.* And don't forget the two Photo Essays, each of which ranges over the full sweep of U.S. history, offering a running commentary on visual materials relating to the broad themes of Women in Public and Adorning the Body. These images and text can serve as independent readings and as supplements to other items in *Women's America*. We have also added a list of illustrations to the volume's table of contents so that all visual materials can be better identified by readers.

ACKNOWLEDGMENTS

We are delighted to welcome Judy Tzu-Chun Wu to our quartet of editors. And although the best part of the collaboration is meeting in person, we are grateful for the many means of electronic communication that carry our daily exchanges—Dropbox, e-mail, SKYPE—that enable the rich, three- and four-way conversations among us.

We are lucky to have had the advice of nearly seven users of previous editions, who offered their advice anonymously to Oxford University Press.

We are grateful for the good counsel of friends and colleagues as we prepared this edition. Among them are Alexis Boylan, Judith Carney, Catherine Denial, Estelle Freedman, Allison Horrocks, Omar Jimenez-Valerio, Katherine Marino, Stephanie McCurry, Micki McElya, Tracy McQueen, Daniel Rivers, Terri Snyder, Amy Sopcak-Joseph, Lisa Wilson, and Sharon Wood. Karissa Haugeberg shared her deep knowledge of the history of reproductive rights and pitched in at crucial moments. We benefitted from the ideas and advice of students in Lisa Wilson's classes at Connecticut College and Dayton's at the University of Connecticut. We are especially grateful to Mike Limberg and Philip Moore, who assisted Nina Dayton at the University of Connecticut, and to law librarians Druet Cameron Klughmand and Noëlle Sinclair at the University of Iowa College of Law.

James Boster unflaggingly cheered us on and was a fount of invaluable computer know-how. We are grateful to archivist Jenny Gotwals at the Schlesinger Library for the History of Women in America at the Radcliffe Institute. We thank Brian Wheel, Brianna Provenzano, and Taylor Pilkington of Oxford University Press; India Gray and Christian Holdener for shepherding the manuscript through copy-editing; and our thoughtful agent, Anne Borchardt.

Linda K. Kerber
Jane Sherron De Hart
Cornelia Hughes Dayton
Judy Tzu-Chun Wu

INTRODUCTION

Linda K. Kerber
Jane Sherron DeHart
Cornelia Hughes Dayton
Judy Tzu-Chun Wu

. . . all men are created equal.

—Declaration of Independence, 1776

No State shall . . . deny to any person within its jurisdiction equal protection of the laws.

—Fourteenth Amendment to the U.S. Constitution, 1868

Equality of rights under the law shall not be denied or abridged by the United States or by any State on account of sex.

—Proposed Equal Rights Amendment
Submitted to the states, 1972; failed to be ratified, 1982

Recalling that discrimination against women violates the principles of equality of rights and respect for human dignity, . . . [signers of this convention agree] to embody the principle of the equality of men and women in their national constitutions . . . and to ensure, through law and other appropriate means, the practical realization of this principle.

—UN Convention on the Elimination of Forms of Discrimination Against
Women, Entered into force, 1981. Not ratified by the United States.

The first edition of *Women's America* was published in 1982, in the midst of intense national debate about what equality means. At the time, women of all ages were deeply engaged in or by the women's liberation movement of the 1960s and 1970s, challenging the many dimensions of unequal treatment of women and men that pervaded American law and cultural practices. They wanted to know why most women worked in jobs in which their coworkers were generally women and in which their wages were substantially lower than the wages of men who did roughly similar work. They wanted to know why women could not be hired as police officers or firefighters. They wanted to know why women were regularly excluded from professional training—medical and law schools generally had strict quotas that held women to 10 percent of the class. They wanted to know why only 2 percent of military officers could be women. On college campuses they wanted to know why they were so frequently discouraged from fields of study marked as "men's fields"—for example, mathematics, engineering, and astronomy. They wanted to know why men's sports teams were generally funded from student fees but

1

women's sports teams had to hold bake sales to raise their own funds for travel to competitions.

And they wanted to know why they learned so little in courses in literature, political science, and history about women's experiences. When they examined the indexes of high school and college textbooks, they found the witches of seventeenth-century Salem, Massachusetts; a few women reformers scattered throughout the 1800s and 1900s; and Ethel Rosenberg, executed for treason in 1953. (Among the reasons that President Dwight Eisenhower offered for refusing to commute her sentence was, as he wrote in a letter to his son John, "if there would be any commuting of the woman's sentence without the man's then from here on the Soviets would simply recruit their spies from among women."[1]) Virtually everything else of consequence in the past seemed to have been accomplished by men. Could that really be true?

The first edition of *Women's America* was a result of young women's demands for their own history.

When they searched the past for evidence of changing relations between men and women, inquirers found that the practices of silencing women as authors, lawmakers, and voters that European settlers had brought to the American colonies contrasted with traditions among the many indigenous American groups where women were important storytellers, religious leaders, and clan elders. Scanning the history of American politics, they found that the promise of equality has been central to American identity since the founding of the nation. But equality can be a complex and elusive concept. It is tangled with the hierarchies of race, class, religion, and sexual identity. In the new nation, adult women, whatever their class or perceived racial heritage, were barred from voting and holding political office, but class and race privilege gave some the power of mastery over household dependents—enslaved persons, servants, and children. After the passage of the Nineteenth Amendment to the Constitution in 1920, adult women were entitled to suffrage, but if they were black and lived in the segregated South they were generally excluded from the polls. Women in Japanese and Japanese-American families living in California and other states in the 1910s and 1920s were acutely aware of the unjust Alien Land laws that barred Asian-origin residents (who were ineligible for U.S. citizenship) from owning the land they tended as proficient farmers. Throughout the nineteenth and twentieth centuries, long before women's liberation took form in the 1960s, women in these and countless other communities all over the continent protested and worked against inequalities that riled them. Once you start looking for evidence of their activities, you find a great deal.

In response to student demand, some faculty invented new courses: others, like Anne Firor Scott at Duke University, "bootlegged women's history into the two-semester introductory American History course." The very earliest such courses were offered in the early and mid-1960s. "Women's history," Scott observed, "developed in close association with women's activism."[2] In the 1970s new courses were flooding into the curricula—in history, literature, philosophy, sociology, and other fields—and in the same decade women's studies programs took root, stressing interdisciplinary methods and knowledge. But none of these changes came easily. College and university faculties, accustomed to defining what was appropriate for students to learn, were generally slow to appreciate the compliment that was being paid. The new courses and programs were sometimes denounced as "feminist propaganda"—or as overtly political or inappropriately polemical.

Women's studies programs, like the African American studies initiated a few years before, were typically the result of protracted negotiations; in extreme cases these came about only after sit-ins and other disruptive protests.[3]

The 8th edition of *Women's America* appears at another time of anxiety about the meanings of equality in the twenty-first century. Some of the inequalities with which women have long struggled have been eliminated; others have emerged. What changes would you count as eliminating inequalities? What do you see as new and persisting problems?

As we seek to retrieve the history of women's experience, we are strengthened by the work that women and their male allies have done to protect historical records. Women activists in the nineteenth century self-consciously created an historical archive. Fearing that women would be denied knowledge of their own history and predicting that pioneering campaigners on behalf of women's rights would die before their experiences had been recorded, Elizabeth Cady Stanton and Susan B. Anthony energetically collected evidence of some of the women's movements of their own time. The rich collection of documents that they published—six large volumes, entitled *History of Woman Suffrage*—was intended to be "an arsenal of facts" for the next generation of activists and historians.[4] But, starting in the early twentieth century, most writers of history ignored it. "[I]f women were doing any thinking . . . ," the historian Mary Beard acidly observed in 1946, "it is difficult to find out [from college textbooks] . . . what it was."[5] In 1933 she edited a documentary collection, *America through Women's Eyes*, in which she argued that an accurate understanding of the past required that women's experiences be analyzed with as much care as historians devoted to the experiences of men. Despite the existence of these documents, books that treated women's history were rare.[6]

STAGES IN WOMEN'S HISTORY

The historian Gerda Lerner suggested that the writing of women's history can be arranged in stages of development, each stage more complex and sophisticated than the last, but all useful and necessary.[7] The first stage she called *"compensatory history,"* in which the historian seeks to identify women and their activities. In the 1970s, some historians began to search for women whose work and experiences deserved to be more widely known. The accomplishments of these women ranged from feats of exploration and endurance to scientific discoveries, artistic achievements, and humanitarian reforms. They included such pioneers as Amelia Earhart, the pilot whose solo flight across the Atlantic in 1933 dramatically demonstrated women's courage and daring; Alice Hamilton, the social reformer and physician whose innovative work in the 1920s on lead poisoning and other toxins made her a world authority on industrial disease and a strong critic of American industries; Maria Goeppert-Mayer, the brilliant theoretical physicist whose research on the structure of the atom and its nucleus won her the Nobel Prize; and Zora Neale Hurston, the novelist and folklorist who mastered African American folk idiom and depicted independent black women.

One result of this early search for women in the historical record was the publication of *Notable American Women*, five volumes of fascinating biographies of over 2,200 remarkable individuals.[8] This project inspired many people to collect the neglected histories of other women—by searching family papers, store accounts, and business records that had been archived or thought of as men's history; and by eliciting oral histories of many women whose experiences had been deemed trivial. In this work, amateur historians and professionals, newcomers and long-time practitioners, students and the friends they recruit, make important contributions.[9] We hope that you may be inspired to add to the histories we tell here.

"The next level of conceptualizing women's history," in Lerner's taxonomy, is *contribution history*." In this stage, historians describe women's contribution to events, arenas, and themes that storytellers of the nation's past had already determined important. The main actors in the historical narrative remain men; women are subordinate, "helping" or "contributing" to the work of men. If the tone of "compensatory history" is delighted discovery of previously unknown women, the tone of contributory history can often be reproachful: how is it that men did not acknowledge women's help? Still, the work of contributory history can be very important in connecting women to major movements in the past: the women of Hull House in Chicago, such as Jane Addams, "contribute" to Progressive reforms; the women in cotton factories in Lowell, Massachusetts, are an important part of the story of early industrialization. Another example is the grassroots, behind-the-scenes activism of Ella Baker, a key civil rights organizer who worked with black ministers as well as the student movement. People know of Martin Luther King, Jr. but less frequently of Baker, Fannie Lou Hamer, Anne Moody, and others who were crucial to the mobilizing around racial justice and human rights in the 1950s and 1960s.[10]

Once major examples of women's "contributions" were identified, familiar historical narratives were no longer reliable. Lerner saw rewriting historical narratives as a third stage in the development of women's history—one that was more transformative than stages one and two. Things we thought we "knew" about American history turn out to be more complex than we had suspected. For example, most textbooks suggest that frontier lands meant opportunity for Americans—"a gate of escape from the bondage of the past." But it was white men who more readily found on the frontiers compensation for their hard work; many pioneering women found only drudgery. (In fact, white women were more likely to find economic opportunity in cities than on the frontier.) When the United States acquired Texas and New Mexico in 1848, the inhabitants, who were mostly indigenous and Mexican, experienced the changes as encroachment and loss of political control. But not all outcomes were negative. For example, as there was virtually no divorce in Mexico, women trapped in unhappy marriages often welcomed the opportunities offered by the U.S. courts.[11]

Over a decade after Gerda Lerner identified these phases of studying women's history, Joan Wallach Scott and others argued for the importance of using gender as an analytical category that helps reveal power relationships.[12] Gender refers to the socially constructed nature of sex roles. One example of this is that earlier in U.S. history (but not among all groups or with one understanding) concepts of womanhood or manhood were understood as biologically determined and unchanging. As Supreme Court Justice David Brewer put it in 1908, "The two sexes differ in the structure of the body, in the functions to be performed by each, in the amount of physical strength, in the capacity for long continuing labor . . . , [in] the self reliance which enables one to assert full rights, and in the capacity to maintain the struggle for subsistence." Woman's "physical structure and a proper discharge of her maternal functions" place her at a disadvantage in that struggle, he continued, and justify legislation to protect her.[13] The assumption that men are self-reliant and that women are not, that men struggle for subsistence and women do not, that women nurture their children and men cannot, reflects the ways in which Justice Brewer and most of his generation understood the implications of being male or female.

More recent thinking about gender challenges biologically essentialist understandings of maleness and femaleness, asserting instead that normative understandings of masculinity and femininity are socially defined ideas projected onto perceived biological differences. It also makes it easy to grasp that, as a social construction, gender has history. Gender practices and ideas about gender change over time and space. Historians ask how the concepts of womanhood and manhood were created, sustained, contested, and altered.

Historians also argue that gendered differences exemplify broader power hierarchies. These social differences and hierarchies have been *systemically created* over time. Economics, law, politics, religion—each has been permeated by assumptions, practices, and expectations that are deeply gendered (as well as shaped by understandings of race, class, and what is understood to be able-bodied).[14] These are so widely shared and so much a part of the ordinary, everyday experience that they acquire an aura of naturalness, rightness, and even inevitability. Common sense dictates that "this is simply the way things are." The price of comprehending the world in this way—whether in the past or in the present—is that it obscures the workings of systems in which economic, political, and cultural forces interact and reinforce each other in ways that benefit some groups and disadvantage others.

Just as historians have argued that gender is a social construction, scholars find that concepts of sex and sexuality change over time. In her study of transsexuality, Joanne Meyerowitz points out that biological differences between men and women are not always clearly distinct. Some people are born with characteristics of more than one sex, as traditionally defined. Furthermore, among experts and medical researchers, understandings of sex difference have not been static. In recent decades, people who desire to alter their sex have been able to do so through surgery and taking hormones. The multiplicity of approaches and the regulations established to reinforce sex differences suggest that the boundaries between male and female can change over time.[15]

And of course sexuality has its own history. Concepts of sexual feelings and behavior, including attitudes toward how erotic desire should be expressed, with whom, and where, vary among cultural groups and, in mainstream Euro-American society, have morphed over time. In the seventeenth century, for example, women were believed to be more lustful and carnal than men. Female sexuality was seen as a source of power and corruption to be feared and controlled. By the nineteenth century, sexuality was redefined. Women—at least white, native-born, middle- and upper-class women—were viewed as having weaker sexual desires than men. Sensuality was attached to working-class and "darker" women—who, so the assumption went, "invited" male advances.[16]

In addition to highlighting women, gender, sex, and sexuality, scholars of women also emphasize the importance of an intersectional approach to studying women. *Intersectionality* reminds us that categories of difference intersect and mutually define one another.[17] In other words, the category of "woman" has different meanings depending on the race, class, citizenship status, sexuality, and able-bodiedness of an individual.

Differences among women are multiple. Differences of culture, nationality, and historical memory are exacerbated by distinctions of race, class, ethnicity, ability, and sexual preference. Each of these differences carries with it implications of hierarchy. As Martha Minow writes, "Women are compared to the unstated norm of men, 'minority' races to white, handicapped persons to the able-bodied, and 'minority' religions to 'majorities.'" Difference is not a neutral term: "A short person is different only in relation to a tall one."[18]

How can we find equality within a society shaped—like all societies—by differences? That is a challenge we continue to face. We may find it helpful to think about two forms of law that coexist in Anglo-American legal tradition. There is "law"—the rules that are understood to apply to every person on the same terms, whatever their sex. When two coworkers do the same job, their wages should be the same. As one judge famously observed in comparing the wages of a maid and a janitor, "dusting is dusting is dusting."[19] And there is a parallel system that we call "equity"—in which courts search for outcomes that have equal impact even though the specifics may be different. What is equal treatment of two coworkers when one can become pregnant and the other cannot? Is maternity leave best understood as vacation leave, sick leave, or something else entirely? What is equality when one partner does the work of maintaining the household and the other does not? In the 1970s, full-time employed women packed an additional twenty-five hours of work—housework and child care—into evenings and weekends each week. While there is evidence that men are doing considerably more than they used to, the gender disparity in housework persists in the twenty-first century, not only in the United States but throughout the world.[20]

Although one provision (Title VII) of the 1964 Civil Rights Act squelched employers' routine habit of limiting certain jobs to one sex (see pp. 745–746), most men and women workers are still employed in occupations where substantial majorities of their coworkers are the same sex. The following statistics reveal how difficult it is to effect structural changes in the labor market. Barely 5 percent of the chief executives at large corporations are women. Historically, once a form of work has been identified with women, it has invariably become associated with low pay and minimal prestige. The overwhelming majority of women are employed in the retail, clerical, and service sectors of the economy. In 2013, for every dollar earned by men, women earned seventy-eight cents; this pay gap has not changed much for the past decade.[21] Finally, juxtapose these facts about the opposite ends of the economic spectrum in the United States: (a) women make up nearly two-thirds of those who hold minimum wage jobs; and (b) a survey of the 2014 graduates of an elite university revealed that among those who had accepted job offers, 19 percent of men and only 4 percent of women were destined to receive the highest starting salaries ($90,000 or more).[22] Much as we would like to think that women and men now occupy level playing fields, the evidence presented here reflects a persistent, societal devaluing of women's work. Why is this so?

HOW TO READ *WOMEN'S AMERICA?*

Women's America invites you to join the continuing expansion of our knowledge by exploring the field of U.S. women's history. Our book offers both *primary sources* (materials that were created during the historical period being studied, e.g., diaries, newspaper articles, letters, government records, photographs), and *secondary sources* (articles or books published by scholars who study history). We encourage you to read both *primary* and *secondary* sources with a critical eye. As you read, ask questions:

- Who wrote or created these sources?
- When and why did they create them?
- How did the historical and legal contexts of their time shape what they recorded and what they did not record? What might we learn from the silences in historical documents and historical writing?
- What assumptions informed these writings?
- Using the primary and secondary sources in this volume, what questions do you think require further research? What subjects do you think have been neglected? When do you see parallels and applications to your communities?

The changing interpretations of the past are referred to as *historiography*—or the history of history writing. Scholars' interpretations vary, based not only on the information they gather, but also on the subtlety of their analysis, the cultural context in which they work, and, to some extent, their own life experiences. That is why we use endnotes—to place the evidence where readers can see it and assess whether the author's interpretations are reasonable and persuasive. You can advance women's history by evaluating previous interpretations, asking new questions, and thinking creatively about sources.

Women's America also encourages you to hone and demonstrate your skills at analyzing images. We have placed visual sources throughout the book—mostly photographs, but also engravings, prints, and posters. Some appear in the essays and documents they are relevant to; for example, in Ruth Milkman's essay on the sexual division of labor during World War II, you will find a photograph of the Women's Airforce Service pilots who named their plane *Pistol Packin' Mama*. Others are grouped in the two Photo Essays, each of which provocatively addresses a big theme over the centuries. Women in Public offers examples of women who placed themselves in the public eye, sometimes risking serious attack. Adorning the Body considers the meanings of appearance. Each image in the book is itself a historical document, adding to what we learn from texts. Each is accompanied by some reflections, to which much can be added by you. With a modest amount of investigation, readers of this book have discovered a great deal about individual images—their creators, the circumstances of their creation, the response or backlash after the image circulated. We hope that scrutinizing these images will prompt you to raise your own questions.

MAJOR THEMES IN *WOMEN'S AMERICA*

Women's America seeks to capture the burgeoning and rich field of U.S. women's history by focusing on six main themes.

- *Family/household/sexuality*: how women and girls are situated in relation to their familial roles and household responsibilities, as well as women's experiences of sexuality and reproduction.
- *Labor/economy/class*: women's engagements in both unpaid and paid labor; women's secondary status within the dominant economy; and the class positions and divisions among women.

- *Race/ethnicity/religion*: how these categories of difference have an impact on women's experiences, identities, and their relationships to one another.
- *Law and citizenship*: how laws, including those governing marriage, reproduction, work, and taxation, shape the choices open to women and men; how changing definitions of citizenship affect women's national identity and their rights and obligations.
- *The global context of U.S. women's history*: how women's lives are intertwined with peoples and developments around the world, including migrations, trade, diplomacy, and war.
- *Women's activism*: how women of diverse backgrounds have been present in virtually all social, cultural, and political movements whether or not these were specifically focused on women; how U.S. women's activism has been in dialogue with allies in other countries and places.

Women's activism has often been described using the metaphor of a wave. The first wave commonly refers to the campaign for women's rights, including suffrage, that stretched from the 1840s to 1920. The second wave describes the women's liberation movement of the 1960s and 1970s. The third wave is used to capture feminist activism of the 1990s and onward. To speak of waves is to oversimplify. Important political work by and on behalf of women occurred outside the so-called wave periods. *Women's America* challenges the wave metaphor by presenting a broad understanding of women's activism.

What are some useful ways to think about feminism? The term came into use in the United States around 1910 when women were engaged in the fight for suffrage and a wide range other reforms. Historian Linda Gordon has offered this definition: "Feminism is a critique of male supremacy, formed and offered in the light of a will to change it, which in turn assumes a conviction that it is changeable."[23] Some of the outspoken women and change agents who appear in this book recognized themselves as feminists; others did not. U.S. history has been populated not by one feminism but by many feminisms.

We invite you to study women's history critically, to take part in a bold enterprise that can eventually lead us to new histories and new pathways of historical investigation. Let's think creatively together about the treasure trove of historical materials presented here. We encourage you to seek out new sources that await discovery in libraries, digital databases, auction houses, museums, family keepsakes, and people's memories.

NOTES

1. Stephen E. Ambrose, *Ike's Spies: Eisenhower and the Espionage Establishment* (New York, 1981; reprint 2012), pp. 182–83.

2. Anne Firor Scott to Linda K. Kerber, May 17, 2009, e-mail communication. Scott first offered such a course at a 1971 University of Washington summer session; her syllabus for GIS 468, "The Search for the American Woman," is in the Mary Aikin Rothschild Papers, Sophia Smith Collection, Smith College, Northampton, Mass. Scott would teach women's history at Duke for the rest of her career.

3. For primary documents that chronicle the founding of a women's studies program at Harvard University (late in the game), including the "propaganda" charge by Harvey C. Mansfield, professor of government, see *Yards and Gates: Gender in Harvard and Radcliffe History*, ed. Laurel Thatcher Ulrich (New York, 2004), pp. 299–302.

4. Elizabeth Cady Stanton, Susan B. Anthony, and Matilda Joslyn Gage, eds., *History of Woman Suffrage*, vol. 1 (New York, 1881), pp. 7–8.

5. Mary R. Beard, *Woman as Force in History: A Study in Traditions and Realities* (New York, 1946), pp. 59–60.

6. For one of the rare ones, see Eleanor Flexner, *Century of Struggle: The Woman's Rights Movement in the United States* (Cambridge, Mass., 1959).

7. Gerda Lerner, "Placing Women in History: Definitions and Challenges," *Feminist Studies* 3 (1975): 5–14; reprinted in Gerda Lerner, *The Majority Finds Its Past: Placing Women in History* (New York, 1979), pp. 145–59. Lerner's essay on the Seneca Falls Convention appears in *Women's America* on pp. 221–227.

8. Edward T. James, Janet Wilson James, and Paul Boyer, eds., *Notable American Women: A Biographical Dictionary*, vols. 1–3: *1607–1950* (Cambridge, Mass., 1971); Barbara Sicherman and Carol Hurd Green, eds., *Notable American Women: A Biographical Dictionary*, vol. 4: *The Modern Period* (Cambridge, Mass., 1980); Susan Ware and Stacy Braukman, eds., *Notable American Women: A Biographical Dictionary*, vol. 5: *Completing the Twentieth Century* (Cambridge, Mass., 2005).

9. For other models, see Barbara Bennett Peterson, ed., *Notable Women of Hawaii* (Honolulu, 1984); Linda K. Kerber, "The 40th Anniversary of *Roe v. Wade*: A Teachable Moment," *Perspectives on History* 50 (October 2012): 65–67; Nicola Foote, Frances Davey, and Kristine De Welde, "Teaching and Researching *Roe vs. Wade*: Responding to Linda Kerber's Call for Historical Action Through a Service-Learning Undergraduate Project," *Perspectives on History* (forthcoming, 2015); and "Weaving Women's Words: Seattle Stories," online at the Jewish Women's Archive, http://jwa.org/communitystories/seattle.

10. Barbara Ransby, *Ella Baker and the Black Freedom Movement: A Radical Democratic Vision* (Chapel Hill, N.C., 2005); Anne Moody, *Coming of Age in Mississippi* (New York, 1968); Chana Kai Lee, *For Freedom's Sake: The Life of Fannie Lou Hamer* (Athens, 1999). Learn why the Ella Baker Center for Human Rights in Oakland, Calif. took her name, and see one of the many biographical accounts available on the web, http://ellabakercenter.org/.

11. Johnny Faragher and Christine Stansell, "Women and Their Families on the Overland Trail to California and Oregon, 1842—1867," *Feminist Studies* 2 (1975): 150–66; Omar S. Valerio-Jiménez, "New Avenues for Domestic Dispute and Divorce Lawsuits Along the U.S. Mexico Border, 1832–1893," *Journal of Women's History* 21 (Spring 2009): 10–33.

12. Joan Wallach Scott, "Gender: A Useful Category of Historical Analysis," *American Historical Review* 91 (Dec. 1986): 1053–75.

13. *Muller v. Oregon*, 208 U.S. 412.

14. On able-bodiedness, see Barbara Young Welke, *Law and the Borders of Belonging in the Long Nineteenth Century United States* (New York, 2010), and Kim E. Nielsen, *A Disability History of the United States* (Boston, 2012).

15. Joanne J. Meyerowitz, *How Sex Changed: A History of Transsexuality in the United States* (Cambridge, Mass., 2002). See the related essay, pp. 615–629.

16. For an overview, see John D'Emilio and Estelle Freedman, *Intimate Matters: A History of Sexuality in America*, 3rd ed. (Chicago, 2012).

17. Kimberle Crenshaw, "Demarginalizing the Intersection of Race and Sex: A Black Feminist Critique of Antidiscrimination Doctrine, Feminist Theory and Antiracist Politics," *University of Chicago Legal Forum* (1989): 139–67; Crenshaw, "Mapping the Margins: Intersectionality, Identity Politics, and Violence Against Women of Color," *Stanford Law Review* 43 (July 1991): 1241–99; Evelyn Brooks Higginbotham, "African American Women's History and the Metalanguage of Race," *Signs* 17 (Winter 1992): 251–74.

18. Martha Minow, "The Supreme Court—1986 Term. Foreword: Justice Engendered," *Harvard Law Review* 101 (1987): 13. Minow points out that "'minority' itself is a relative term. . . . Only in relation to white Westerners are [people of color] minorities."

19. *Equal Employment Opportunities Commission v. Rhode Island*, 549 F. Supp. 60, 66 (1982).

20. Statistics on these matters are reliably kept by the Organisation for Economic Co-Operation and Development (OCED), a nonprofit sponsored by 34 developed countries that collaborate in comparing common policy experiences and identifying good practices. In 2014, the OCED reported that U.S. women spend an average of 126 minutes per day in routine housework; men spend 82 minutes. See http://www.oecd.org/gender/data/balancingpaidworkunpaidworkandleisure.htm.

21. Claire Cain Miller, "Pay Gap Shrinks, but is Still Stubborn," *New York Times*, Sep. 19, 2014, p. B4. See also the American Association of University Women, "The Simple Truth about the Gender Pay Gap" (2014), http://www.aauw.org/research/the-simple-truth-about-the-gender-pay-gap. There is great variability among regions. In 2012, in Washington D.C., women earn 90 percent of what men earn; in Wyoming they earn 64 percent. The gaps are greatest for women of color; Hispanic women earned 53 percent of what white men earned.

22. Claire Cain Miller, "An Elusive Jackpot," *New York Times*, June 8, 2014, p. BU1; The White House, "The Impact of Raising the Minimum Wage on Women," March 2014 Report, http://www.whitehouse.gov/sites/default/files/docs/20140325minimumwageandwomenreportfinal.pdf. David Madland and Keith Miller, "Raising the Minimum Wage Would Boost the Incomes of Millions of Women and Their Families," Center for American Progress, Dec. 9, 2013, http://americanprogress.org/issues/labor/news/2013/12/09/80497/raising-the-minimum-wage-would-boost-the-incomes-of-millions-of-women-and-their-families. Starting salaries: Rebecca D. Robbins et al., "The Class of 2014 by the Numbers," *Harvard Crimson*, Commencement 2014 issue, Senior Section, http://features.thecrimson.com/2014/senior-survey/. For a perceptive essay on the origins of this pattern, see pp. 128–139.

23. Linda Gordon, quoted in Nancy F. Cott, "What's in a Name? The Limits of 'Social Feminism'; or, Expanding the Vocabulary of Women's History," *Journal of American History* 76 (Dec. 1989): 826.

I

EARLY AMERICA

1600–1820

GENDER FRONTIERS

KATHLEEN M. BROWN
The Anglo-Indian Gender Frontier

The first American women were Native American women. The religious, economic, and political roles that they played in their own societies prior to the arrival of Europeans indicate that Europeans and Native Americans held dramatically different ideas about what women and men should be and should do. The difficulties that Europeans had in understanding the alternative gender realities to which they were exposed tells us how strong is the impulse to view established gender definitions in one's own culture as natural rather than socially constructed. Kathleen M. Brown calls this chasm of understanding a "gender frontier." How did Pocahontas and her father, Powhatan, try to cross those divides to reach common understandings or alliances? If you were assigned to do research in the vast area of Indian women and gender relations before and during contact with visiting and colonizing Europeans, what questions and sources would you pursue?

On a January evening in London in 1617, Pocahontas, daughter of a powerful Virginia *werowance* (paramount chief), sat in attendance with James I and Queen Anne to watch the pageantry of Ben Jonson's masque *The Vision of Delight* unfold. Pocahontas had traveled a long way for this performance. Nine years earlier, as a young girl, she had participated in the first Anglo-Indian contact on the mainland the English called "Virginia." Now, as an adult, she continued the encounter by traveling to London with an entourage of Algonquian-speaking Indians. After making a favorable impression on their royal hosts, the Virginia Algonquians had been invited to join the annual Twelfth Night festivities. One Virginia Company investor noted that Pocahontas and her Indian escort Uttamatomakkin were "well placed" at the masque, meaning that they were not only well positioned for viewing the spectacle but could easily be seen by other spectators. Seated next to the king and queen, the two visitors became part of the glittering display presented to other guests on this evening of costumed entertainment, an integral part of *The Vision of Delight*.[1]

Part of the appeal of Pocahontas for curious London notables was her reputed transformation to English gentility. The daughter of an Indian werowance . . . [and] a recent convert to Christianity, Pocahontas had relinquished her Indian name, Matoaka, and taken the new name Rebecca. She also spoke English, impressing her hosts with her fluency. Her marriage to English man John Rolfe and the birth of their son completed her [perceived] conversion. . . .

In contrast to Pocahontas, Uttamatomakkin, the trusted councillor of her father who accompanied her to the masque, retained his

Excerpted and slightly revised by the author from "The Anglo-Algonquian Gender Frontier" by Kathleen M. Brown in *Negotiators of Change: Historical Perspectives on Native American Women*, ed. Nancy Shoemaker (London: Routledge, 1995), pp. 26–48, and ch. 2 of *Good Wives, Nasty Wenches, and Anxious Patriarchs: Gender, Race, and Power in Colonial Virginia* (Chapel Hill: University of North Carolina Press, 1996). Reprinted by permission of the author and publishers. Notes have been edited and renumbered.

Indian dress and stubbornly refused to give ground in conversations with English ministers about Christian theology. He remained a skeptic about English symbols of royal authority, moreover, and persisted in judging the English by Indian standards of generosity in gift giving. When James I failed to offer a gift at their meeting, Uttamatomakkin doubted that he was king of the English. . . . Uttamatomakkin was appalled that James lacked the manners and wealth to treat visiting strangers appropriately. When he returned to Virginia, he fulminated against the shortcomings of the English.[2]

With their visit to London in 1616–1617, Pocahontas and Uttamatomakkin traveled along an Anglo-Indian gender frontier they had actively participated in making. During the early English voyages to Roanoake and Jamestown Island, English male adventurers, accompanied by few English women, confronted Indian men and women in their native land. In this cultural encounter, the gender performances of Virginia Algonquians challenged English gentlemen's assumptions about the naturalness of their own gender identities. In the responses of both groups to the other came exchanges, new cultural forms, discoveries of common ground, painful deceptions, bitter misunderstandings, and bloody conflicts.[3]

In both Indian and English societies, differences between men and women were critical to social order. Ethnic identities formed along this "gender frontier," the site of creative and destructive processes resulting from the confrontations of culturally-specific manhoods and womanhoods. In the emerging Anglo-Indian struggle, gender symbols and social relations signified claims to power. Never an absolute barrier, however, the gender frontier also produced sources for new identities and social practices.[4]

In this essay, I explore in two ways the gender frontier that evolved between English settlers and the indigenous peoples of Virginia's tidewater. First, I assess how differences in gender roles shaped the perceptions and interactions of both groups. Second, I analyze the "gendering" of the emerging Anglo-Indian power struggle. While the English depicted themselves as warriors dominating a feminized native population, Indian women and men initially refused to acknowledge [these] claims to military supremacy, treating the foreigners as they would subject peoples,

cowards, or servants. When English warrior discourse became unavoidable, however, Indian women and men attempted to exploit what they saw as the warrior's obvious dependence upon others for the agricultural and reproductive services that ensured group survival.

The indigenous peoples who engaged in this struggle were residents of Virginia's coastal plain, a region of fields, forests, and winding rivers that extended from the shores of the Chesapeake Bay to the mountains and waterfalls near present-day Richmond. Many were affiliated with Powhatan, the werowance who had consolidated several distinct groups under his influence at the time of contact with the English. Most were Algonquian-speakers whose distant cultural roots in the Northeast distinguished them from peoples further south and west where native economies depended more on agriculture and less on hunting and fishing.[5] Although culturally diverse, tidewater inhabitants shared certain features of social organization, commonalities that may have become more pronounced with Powhatan's ambitious chiefdom-building and the arrival of the English. . . .

English gender differences manifested themselves in primary responsibilities and arenas of activity, relationships to property, ideals for conduct, and social identities. Using plow agriculture, rural Englishmen cultivated grain while women oversaw household production, including gardening, dairying, brewing, and spinning. Women also constituted a flexible reserve labor force, performing agricultural work when demand for labor was high, as at harvest time. While Englishmen's property ownership formed the basis of their political existence and identity, most women did not own property [unless] they were no longer subject to a father or husband.[6]

. . . Early seventeenth century, advice-book authors enjoined English women . . . to maintain a modest demeanor. Publicly punishing shrewish and sexually aggressive women, communities enforced this standard of wifely submission as ideal and of wifely domination as intolerable. The sexual activity of poor and unmarried women proved particularly threatening to community order; these "nasty wenches" provided pamphleteers with a foil for the "good wives" female readers were urged to emulate.[7]

How did one know an English good wife when one saw one? Her body and head would be modestly covered. The tools of her work, such as the skimming ladle used in dairying, the distaff of the spinning wheel, and the butter churn reflected her domestic production. When affixed to a man, as in community-initiated shaming rituals, these gender symbols communicated his fall from "natural" dominance and his wife's unnatural authority over him.[8]

Advice-book authors described men's "natural" domain as one of authority derived from his primary economic role. A man's economic assertiveness, mirrored in his authority over wife, child and servant, was emblematized by the plow's penetration of the earth, the master craftsman's ability to shape his raw materials, and the rider's ability to subdue his horse. Although hunting and fishing supplemented the incomes of many Englishmen, formal group hunts . . . remained the preserve of the aristocracy and upper gentry.

The divide between men's and women's activities described by sixteenth- and seventeenth-century authors did not capture the flexibility of gender relations in most English communities. Beliefs in male authority over women and in the primacy of men's economic activities sustained a perception of social order even as women marketed butter, cheese and ale, and cuckolded unlucky husbands.

Gender roles and identities were also important to the Algonquian speakers whom the English encountered along the three major tributaries of the Chesapeake Bay. Like indigenous peoples throughout the Americas, Virginia Algonquians invoked a divine division of labor to explain and justify differences between men's and women's roles on earth. . . . Tidewater Indians described several creator gods, including a malevolent deity named Okeus, who appeared to worshippers as a hunter-warrior. With the right side of his head shaved so that hair would not catch in his bowstring and the left side grown long—a style adopted by Indian men—Okeus epitomized the virility of the Indian bowman.[9]

Although the English collected little information about female deities from the Indian men they questioned, they did take note of at least one goddess. The Patawomeck werowance Iopassus described a divine woman who lived along the road traveled by dead Indians as they approached the home of their creator, a giant hare god. She "hath alwaies her doores open for hospitality," related Iopassus, "and hath at all tymes ready drest greene *Uskatahomen* and *Pokahichary*," an Indian delicacy made from bruised unripe corn and walnut milk. The consummate Indian hostess, this goddess provided "all manner of pleasant fruicts" and stood in "readines to entertayne all such as do travell to the great hares howse." For the Patawomecks and perhaps for other Virginia Algonquians as well, goddesses set the standard for gracious entertainment and unlimited hospitality.[10]

. . . Indian women's tasks centered on cultivating and processing corn, which provided up to 75 percent of the calories consumed by residents of the coastal plain. In addition, women grew squash, peas, and beans and tended the fires needed for cooking stews and cakes. Women also were responsible for providing much of the material culture of daily life, including clothing, jewelry, and domestic tools and furnishings like pots, baskets, and bedding. Indian women appear to have been active in housebuilding. Their practice of maintaining their own homes, providing kinsmen with basic household necessities, transporting belongings, and building winter houses makes it likely that women provided much of the labor of household construction.[11] . . . Bearing and raising children and mourning the dead rounded out the range of female duties. All were spiritually united by life-giving and its association with earth and agricultural production, sexuality and reproduction. Lineage wealth and political power passed through the female line. Among certain peoples, women may also have had the power to determine the fate of captives, the nugget of truth in the much-embellished tale of Pocahontas's intervention on behalf of Captain John Smith.[12]

Indian women were responsible not only for reproducing the traditional features of their culture, but for much of its adaptive capacity as well. As agriculturalists, women must have had great influence over decisions to move to new grounds, to leave old grounds fallow, and to initiate planting. As producers and consumers of vital household goods and implements, women may have been among the first to feel the impact of new technologies, commodities, and trade. And as accumulators of lineage property, Indian women may have been forced to change strategies as subsistence opportunities shifted.

Indian men assumed a range of responsibilities that complemented those of women. Men cleared new planting grounds of trees. During the spring and summer months, they periodically left villages to fish and hunt, providing highly valued protein. After the final corn harvest, whole villages traveled with their hunters to provide support throughout the winter. Women carried furnishings, cooking implements, and other belongings, setting up temporary winter headquarters. Men's pursuit of game shaped the rhythms of village life during these cold months, just as women's cultivation of crops determined feasts and the allocation of labor during the late spring and summer.[13]

Indian men's social and work roles became distinct from women's at the moment of the *huskanaw*—a male rite of passage—and remained so until the men were too old to hunt or go to war. Young boys chosen by priests to participate in the ceremonial test of manhood endured a physical and psychological trial of several weeks. The English were under the impression that many boys did not survive the ordeal in the woods, which may have included the near-starvation, drug-induced hallucinations, and frequent beatings that later-seventeenth-century observers described. Those who withstood the journey's harrowing approximation of social and physical death began their lives as men with all memories ritually (if not actually) erased. According to Spelman, women attended these ceremonies carrying funeral accoutrements and mourning loudly for the "death" of their young boys. Men departed from the event "merily," having witnessed the ritual male birthing of a new generation of hunters and warriors.[14]

During the prime of manhood, the period of greatest divergence in gender roles, men continued to live in households with women and children. Higher-status men, including local werowances, were recorded by English men as eating separately from the women of the household. In extremely wealthy homes, such as those of polygynous regional werowances, women served meals to seated men. When ordinary men needed to adopt a more virile identity, they may have slept away from women and children, even leaving the village. By ritually separating themselves from women through sexual abstinence, hunters periodically became warriors, taking revenge for killings or initiating their own raids. This adult leave-taking reenacted the separation celebrated in the huskanaw, in which young boys left their mothers' homes to become men.[15]

Men's hunting and fighting were associated with life-taking, with its ironic relationship to the life-sustaining acts of procreation, protection, and provision. Whereas earth and corn symbolized women, the weapons of the hunt, the trophies taken from the hunted, and the predators of the animal world represented men. Men displayed their status as hunters by wearing bucks' antlers on their heads, claw earrings, bears' teeth necklaces, and snake and weasel skin headdresses. The ritual use of *pocones,* a blood-colored dye, also reflected this gender division. Women anointed their bodies with pocones for sexual encounters and ceremonies celebrating the harvest; men wore it during hunting, warfare, or the ritual celebrations of successes in these endeavors.[16]

The exigencies of the winter hunt, the value placed on meat, and intermittent warfare among native peoples may have been the foundation of male dominance in politics and religious matters. Women were not without their bases of power in Algonquian society, however; their important roles as agriculturalists, reproducers of Indian culture, and caretakers of lineage property kept gender relations in rough balance. Indian women's ability to choose spouses motivated men to be "paynefull" in their hunting and fishing. These same men warily avoided female spaces in which menstruating women may have gathered. By no means equal to men, whose political and religious decisions directed village life, Indian women were perhaps more powerful in their subordination than English women.[17]

Even before the English sailed up the river they renamed the James, however, Indian women's power may have been waning, eroded by Powhatan's chiefdom-building tactics. A "goodly old-man, not yet shrincking," with gray hair and weather-beaten-skin, Powhatan was probably in his seventies when the English met him. During the last quarter of the sixteenth century, perhaps as a consequence of early Spanish forays into the region, he began to add to his inherited chiefdom, coercing and manipulating other coastal residents into economic and military alliances. Powhatan also subverted the matrilineal transmission of political power by appointing his kinsmen to be werowances of villages recently consolidated into his chiefdom. The central military force under his command created opportunities for male recognition in which acts of bravery, rather than matrilineal property or political inheritance, determined privileges. . . . [Powhatan extracted] tribute for promise[d] protection or non-aggression [from him]. He [was thus] appropriating corn, the product of women's labor, from the villages he dominated. He also communicated power and wealth through conspicuous displays of young wives. Through marriages to women drawn from villages throughout his chiefdom, Powhatan emblematized his dominance over the margins of his domain and created kinship ties to strengthen his influence over these villages. With the arrival of the English, the value of male warfare and the symbolism of corn as tribute only intensified, further strengthening the patriarchal tendencies of Powhatan's people.[18]

Conquest seemed justifiable to many English because Native Americans had failed to tame the wilderness according to English standards. Writers claimed they found "only an idle, improvident, scattered people . . . carelesse of anything but from hand to mouth." Most authors compounded impressions of sparse indigenous populations by listing only numbers of fighting men, whom they derided as impotent for their failure to exploit the virgin resources of the "bowells and womb of their Land." The seasonal migration of native groups and the corresponding shift in diet indicated to the English a lack of mastery over the environment, reminding them of animals. John Smith commented, "It is strange to see how their bodies alter with their diet; even as the deare and wild beastes, they seem fat and leane, strong and weak."[19]

The English derision of Indian dependence on the environment and the comparison to animals . . . contained implicit gender meanings. Women's bodies, for example, showed great alteration during pregnancy from fat to lean, strong to weak. English authors often compared female sexual appetites and insubordination to those of wild animals in need of taming. Implicit in all these commentaries was a critique of indigenous men for failing to fulfill the responsibility of economic provision with which the English believed all men to be charged. Lacking private property in the English sense, Indian men, like the Gaelic Irish, appeared to the English to be feminine and not yet civilized to manliness.[20]

For many English observers, natives' "failure" to develop an agricultural economy or dense population was rooted in their gender division of labor. Women's primary responsibility for agriculture merely confirmed the abdication by men of their proper role and explained the "inferiority" of native economies in a land of plenty. [John] Smith commented that "the land is not populous, for the men be fewe; their far greater number is of women and children," a pattern he attributed to inadequate cultivation. Of the significance of women's work and Indian agriculture, he concluded, "When all their fruits be gathered, little els they plant, and this is done by their women and children; neither doth this long suffice them, for neere 3 parts of the yeare, they only observe times and seasons, and live off what the Country naturally affordeth from hand to mouth." In Smith's convoluted analysis, the "failure" of Indian agriculture, implicitly associated in other parts of his text with the "idleness" of men and the reliance upon female labor, had a gendered consequence; native populations became vulnerable and feminized, consisting of many more women and children than of "able men fitt for their warres."[21]

English commentators reacted with disapproval to seeing women perform work relegated to laboring men in England while Indian men pursued activities associated with the English aristocracy. Indian women, George Percy claimed, "doe all their dru[d]gerie. The men takes their pleasure in hunting and their warres, which they are in continually." Observing that the women were heavily burdened and the men only lightly so, John Smith similarly noted "the men bestowe their times in fishing, hunting, wars and such manlike exercises, scorning to be seene in any woman like exercise," while the "women and children do the rest of the worke." Smith's account revealed his discomfort with women's performance of work he considered the most valuable.[22]

The English were hard pressed to explain other Indian behavior without contradicting their own beliefs in the natural and divinely-sanctioned characteristics of men and women. Such was the case with discussions of Indian women's pain during childbirth. . . . Many English writers claimed that Indian women gave birth with little or no pain. Their relatively easy labor appeared to contradict Judeo-Christian traditions in which all women, as products of an original and single divine creation, paid for the sins of Eve. The belief that

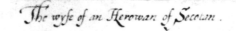

Carolina Algonquin woman, drawing by John White, 1585.
This portrait of an Algonquin woman was drawn at her home settlement during the summer of 1585 by John White, the official artist of the English expedition to Roanoke. His drawings are rare representations of Algonquin life before extensive European contact. The woman, who looks skeptically at the viewer, is the wife of a leading male chief or counselor. Her body is decorated with gray, brown, and blue tattoos on the face, neck, arms, and legs. Women's tattoos simulated elaborate necklaces and other ornamentation; men used body paint for ceremonial purposes. (Courtesy of the British Museum. See also Paul Hulton, America 1585: The Complete Drawings of John White *[Chapel Hill: University of North Carolina Press and British Museum Publications, 1984].)*

indigenous women were closer to nature than English women—which implied that English women had labor pains because they were civilized—allowed the English to finesse Indian women's seeming exemption from Eve's curse.[23]

The English were both fascinated and disturbed by other aspects of Native American society through which gender identities were communicated, including hairstyle, dress and make-up. The native male fashion of going clean-shaven, for example, clashed with English associations of beards with male political and sexual maturity, diminishing Indian men's claims to manhood in the eyes of the English. . . . It probably did not enhance English respect for Indian manhood that female barbers sheared men's facial hair.[24]

Most English writers found it difficult to distinguish between the sexual behavior of Chesapeake dwellers and what they viewed as sexual potency conveyed through dress and ritual. English male explorers were particularly fascinated by indigenous women's attire, which seemed scanty and immodest compared to English women's multiple layers and wraps. John Smith described an entertainment arranged for him in which "30 young women came naked out of the woods (only covered behind and before with a few greene leaves), their bodies al painted." Several other writers commented that Native Americans "goe altogether naked," or had "scarce to cover their nakednesse." Smith claimed, however, that the women were "alwaies covered about their midles with a skin and very shamefast to be seene bare." Yet he noted, as did several other English travelers, the body adornments, including beads, paintings, and tattoos, that were visible on Indian women's legs, hands, breasts, and faces. Perhaps some of the "shamefastness" reported by Smith resulted from Englishmen's close scrutiny of Indian women's bodies.[25]

For most English writers, Indian manners and customs reinforced an impression of sexual passion. Hospitality that included sexual privileges, for instance sending "a woman fresh painted red with *Pocones* and oile" to be the "bedfellow" of a guest, may have confirmed in the minds of Englishmen that Indians were licentious. Smith's experience with the thirty women, clad in leaves, body paint, and buck's horns and emitting "hellish cries and shouts," undoubtedly strengthened the English association of Indian culture with unbridled passion: "they solemnly invited Smith to their lodging, but no sooner was hee within the house, but all these Nimphes more tormented him than ever, with crowding, and pressing, and hanging upon him, most tediously crying, *love you not mee.*"[26] Such incidents left the English with a vivid impression of unconstrained sexuality that in their own culture could mean only promiscuity. . . .

Although the dominant strand of English discourse about Indian men denounced them for being savage and failed providers, not all Englishmen shared these assessments of the meaning of cultural differences. Throughout the early years of settlement, male laborers deserted military compounds to escape puny rations, disease and harsh discipline, preferring to take their chances with local Indians whom they knew had food aplenty. Young boys like Henry Spelman, moreover, had nearly as much to fear from the English, who used him as a hostage, as he did from his Indian hosts. Spelman witnessed and participated in Indian culture from a very different perspective than most Virginia chroniclers. While . . . John Smith described Indian entertainments as horrible antics, Spelman coolly noted that Patawomeck dances bore a remarkable resemblance to the Darbyshire hornpipe. . . .

. . . After a period of homesickness provoked him to escape his duties as a hostage among the Powhatans, Spelman returned to live in relative security among [the group he was assigned to live with,] the Patawomecks. He formed close bonds with the Patawomeck werowance and at least one of his children, whom he could reputedly quiet better than any other person in the werowance's household.[27]

Even among men more elite and more widely traveled than Spelman, a lurking and disquieting suspicion that Indian men were men like the English disrupted discourses about natural savagery and inferiority. Smith, the only Jamestown leader of yeoman background, often explained Indian complexions and superior resistance to the elements as a result of conditioning and daily practice rather than of nature. Indian women had trained their children from early infancy to endure cold river baths, Smith believed, thus enabling their sons (although presumably the same could have been said of daughters) to withstand physical discomforts in later life: "They are very strong, of an able body and full of agilitie, able to endure to lie in the woods under a tree by the fire, in the worst of winter, or in the weedes and grasse, in Ambuscado in the Sommer."[28] . . .

English leaders at Jamestown also created areas of common ground with Algonquians through exchanges of gifts, shared entertainments, and feasts. The need to deal with Indians on Indian terms and in Indian ways enhanced the overlap between the two cultures during the first two years of English settlement. Drawn into Indian cultural expressions despite himself, Smith gave gifts when he would have preferred to barter. . . . Despite flamboyant rhetoric about savage warriors lurking in the forests like animals, Smith soon had English men learning to fight in the woods. He clearly thought his manly English, many of whom could barely fire a gun, had much to learn from their Indian opponents.[29] . . .

Most English writers did not dwell on these areas of similarity and exchange, but emphasized the "wild" and animalistic qualities of tidewater peoples. Descriptions of Indian warfare, sexual behavior, and religion inspired fear and supported English claims to dominance and superiority. As much as animals fell below humans in the hierarchy of the natural world, so the Indians of English chronicles inhabited a place that was technologically, socially, and morally beneath that of the civilized English. Through depictions of feminized, impotent, male "naturalls," English men reworked Anglo-Indian relations, portraying themselves as the "naturally" dominant men of gender relations. In so doing, they contributed to an emerging male colonial identity that was deeply rooted in English gender discourses.

The gendering of Anglo-Indian relations in English writing was not without contest and contradiction, nor did it lead inevitably to easy conclusions of English dominance. Englishmen incorporated Indian ways into their diets and military tactics, and Indian women into their sexual lives. Some formed close bonds with Indian companions, while others lived to father their own "naturall" progeny. . . . Colonial domination was a complex process involving sexual intimacy, cultural incorporation, and self-scrutiny.

The Englishmen who landed on the shores of Chesapeake Bay and the James River were not the first European men that Virginia Algonquians had seen. During the 1570s, Spanish Jesuits established a short-lived mission near the James River tributary that folded with the murder of the clerics. The Spaniards who revenged the Jesuit deaths left an unfavorable impression upon local Chickahominy, Paspegh, and Kecoughtan Indians. [In addition,] at least one English ship also predated the 1607 arrival of the Jamestown settlers; its captain was long remembered for killing a Rappahannock river werowance.[30]

The maleness of English explorers' parties and early settlements undoubtedly raised Indian suspicions of bellicose motives. Interrogating Smith at their first meeting about the purpose of the English voyage, Powhatan was apparently satisfied with Smith's answer that the English presence was temporary. Smith claimed his men sought passage to "the backe Sea," the ever elusive water route to India which they believed lay beyond the falls of the Chesapeake river system. . . . The explanation may have initially seemed credible to Powhatan because the English expedition consisted only of men and boys. Frequent English military drills in the woods and the construction of a fort at Jamestown, however, may have aroused his suspicions that the English strangers planned a longer and more violent stay.[31]

Equipped with impressive blasting guns, the English may have found it easy to perpetuate the warrior image from afar; up close was a different matter, however. English men were pale, hairy, and awkward compared to Indian men. They also had the dirty habit of letting facial hair grow so that it obscured the bottom part of their faces where it collected food and other debris. Their clumsy stomping through the woods announced their presence to friends, enemies, and wildlife alike and they were forced, on at least one very public occasion, to ask for Indian assistance when their boats became mired in river ooze. Perhaps worst of all from the perspective of Indian people who valued a warrior's stoicism in the face of death, the Englishmen they captured and killed died screaming and whimpering. William Strachey recorded the mocking song sung by Indian men sometime in 1611, in which they ridiculed "what lamentation our people made when they kild him, namely saying how they [the Englishmen] would cry whe, whe."[32]

Indian assumptions about masculinity may have led Powhatan to over-estimate the vulnerability of Smith's men. The gentlemen and artisans who were the first to arrive in Virginia proved to be dismal farmers, remaining wholly dependent upon native corn stores during their first three years and partially dependent thereafter. They tried, futilely, to persuade Indians to grow more corn to meet their needs, but their requests were greeted with scorn by Indian men who found no glory in the "woman-like exercise" of farming. Perhaps believing that the male settlement would always require another population to supply it, Powhatan tried to use the threat of starvation to level the playing field with the English. During trade negotiations with Smith in January 1609, Powhatan held out for guns and swords, claiming disingenuously that corn was more valuable to him than copper trinkets because he could eat it.[33]

When Powhatan and other Indian peoples reminded Smith of his dependence upon Indian food supplies, Smith reacted with anger. In his first account of Virginia, he recalled with bitterness the scorn of the Kecoughtan Indians for "a famished man": they "would in derision offer him a handfull of Corne, a peece of bread." Such treatment signified both indigence and female vulnerability to the English, made worse by the fact that the crops they needed were grown by women. At Kecoughtan, Smith responded by "let[ting] fly his muskets" to provoke a Kecoughtan retreat and then killing several men at close range. The survivors fell back in confusion, allowing the image of their god Okeus to fall into English hands. After this display of force, he found the Kecoughtan "content" to let the English dictate the terms of trade: Kecoughtan corn in exchange for copper, beads, hatchets, and the return of Okeus. The English thus used their superior weaponry to transform themselves from scorned men into respected warriors and to recast the relationship: humble agriculturists became duty-bound to produce for those who spared their lives.[34]

Powhatan's interactions with Englishmen may also have been guided by his assessment of the gender imbalance among them. His provision of women to entertain English male guests was a political gesture whose message seems to have been misunderstood as sexual license by the English. . . . Powhatan may also have believed that by encouraging English warriors' sexual activity, he might diminish their military potency . . . Ultimately, Powhatan may have hoped that intimacy between native women and English men would lead to an integration of the foreigners and a diffusion of

the threat they presented. . . . Powhatan's gesture, however, only reinforced the English rationale for subjugating the "uncivilized" and offered English men an opportunity to express the Anglo-Indian power relationship sexually with native women.[35]

Indian women were often more successful than Powhatan in manipulating Englishmen's desires for sexual intimacy. At the James River village of Appocant in late 1607, the unfortunate George Cawson met his death when village women "enticed [him] up from the barge into their howses." Oppossunoquonuske, a clever *werowansqua* of another village, similarly led fourteen Englishmen to their demise. Inviting the unwary men to come "up into her Towne, to feast and make Merry," she convinced them to "leave their Armes in their boat, because they said how their women would be afrayd ells of their pieces."[36]

Although both of these accounts are cautionary tales that represent Indians literally as feminine seducers capable of entrapping Englishmen in the web of their own sexual desires, the incidents suggest Indian women's canny assessment of the men who would be colonial conquerors. Exploiting Englishmen's hopes for colonial pleasures, Indian women dangled before them the opportunity for sexual intimacy, turning a female tradition of sexual hospitality into a weapon of war. Acknowledging the capacity of English "pieces" to terrorize Indian women, Oppossunoquonuske tacitly recognized Englishmen's dependence on their guns to construct self-images of bold and masculine conquerors. Her genius lay in convincing them to rely on other masculine "pieces." When she succeeded in getting Englishmen to set aside one colonial masculine identity—the warrior—for another—the lover of native women—the men were easily killed. . . .

. . . Algonquians tried to maneuver the English into positions of political subordination. Smith's account of his captivity, near-execution, and rescue by Pocahontas was undoubtedly part of an adoption ritual in which Powhatan defined his relationship to Smith as one of patriarchal dominance. Smith became Powhatan's prisoner after warriors easily slew his English companions and then "missed" with nearly all of the twenty or thirty arrows they aimed at Smith himself. Clearly, Powhatan wanted Smith brought to him alive. Smith reported that during his captivity he was offered "life, libertie, land and women," prizes Powhatan must have believed to be very attractive to Englishmen, in exchange for information about how best to capture Jamestown: After ceremonies and consultations with priests, Powhatan brought Smith before an assembly where, Smith later claimed, Pocahontas risked her own life to prevent him from being clubbed to death by executioners. It seems that Smith understood neither the ritual adoption taking place nor the significance of Powhatan's promise to make him a werowance and to "for ever esteeme him as [he did] his son Nantaquoud."[37]

After returning Smith to Jamestown, Powhatan showered him with gifts of food and entreaties to take up his kingdom as a subordinate werowance. Although interested in both the land and the corn, Smith wanted to avoid making gestures of obeisance. Upon a subsequent visit to Powhatan, the werowance assured Smith he would receive his due but that "he expected to have all these [Smith's] men lay their armes at his feet, as did his subjects." Smith demurred at the implied subordination, claiming that only an enemy of the English would expect them to disarm. Powhatan again repeated his offer to Smith, urging the adoptive relationship upon him. Pronouncing him "a werowanes of Powhatan, and that all his subjects should so esteeme us," Powhatan integrated Smith and his men into his own chieftancy, declaring "no man account us strangers nor Paspaheghans, but Powhatans, and that the Corne, weomen and Country, should be to us as to his owne people."[38] . . .

That Smith's rejection of Powhatan's claims to benevolent fatherhood was not simply an attempt to retain the upper hand but also a refusal to accept the implied obligation of the relationship as Indians perceived it became evident only much later, during Smith's final conversation with Pocahontas in 1617. Having been in England for nearly six months, Pocahontas was surprised to see Smith for the first time only near the end of her stay [there]. According to Smith's account, she upbraided him for his rudeness and failure to reciprocate the hospitality the Algonquians had shown him. After "remembr[ing] [Smith] well what courtesies shee had done," she focused on Smith's betrayal of her father. "You did promise Powhatan what was yours should bee his, and he the like to you," Smith recalled her saying. "You called him father being in his land a stranger, and by the same reason so must

I doe you." Recounting the words with which the two men had become fictive kin, Pocahontas noted that Smith had failed to do for her, a stranger to his land, what her father had done for him. Also, he had reneged on his promise to share with Powhatan all that was his. . . .[39]

With false modesty and calculated deference, Smith demurred that a king's daughter should call him father. Pocahontas, he noted, responded angrily, taunting Smith, asking him how it was that in the safety of his own country he should fear being called father when he had shown no qualms about invading Powhatan's country, causing "feare in him and all his people (but mee)." Pocahontas insisted: "I tell you then I will [call you father], and you shall call mee childe, and so I will bee for ever and ever your Countrieman." With this remark, Pocahontas recast the politics and the meaning of her conversion to Englishness. No longer simply the adoption of a new language, strange religion, and foreign manners, Pocahontas's transformation implied mutual obligations that originated with the promises exchanged by Powhatan and Smith. She interpreted her Englishness as a consequence of the relationship between the two men, through which Smith as well as the daughter of Powhatan should have been transformed.[40]

Despite her fashionable English dress and hat, Pocahontas held Smith to an Indian standard of reciprocity and exchange. By transferring the burden of obligation to Smith, she challenged depictions of Powhatan's daughter as indebted to the English for the gift of civilization. Her words, undoubtedly altered somewhat by the self-serving Smith, nonetheless suggest that her own view of her conversion was considerably more complicated than either Smith or the Virginia Company would ever understand.

The first decade of encounter between English and Indian peoples wrought changes in the gender relations of both societies. Contact bred trade, political reshuffling, sexual intimacy, and warfare, [and, for the indigenous, unfamiliar illnesses and a spike in deaths due to diseases spread by Europeans]. The very process of confrontation between two groups with male-dominated political and religious systems initially may have strengthened the value of patriarchy for each.

The rapid change in Indian life and culture had a particularly devastating impact upon women. Many women, whose office it was to bury and mourn the dead, may have been relegated to perpetual grieving. Corn was also uniquely the provenance of women; economically it was the source of female authority, and religiously and symbolically they were identified with it. The wanton burning and pillaging of corn supplies, through which the English transformed their dependence into domination, may have represented to indigenous residents an egregious violation of women.

English dominance in the region [especially after 1644] ultimately led to the decline of the native population and its way of life. As a consequence of war, nutritional deprivation, and disease, Virginia Indians were reduced in numbers from the approximately 14,000 inhabitants of the Chesapeake Bay and tidewater in 1607 to less than 3,000 by the early eighteenth century. White settlement forced tidewater dwellers farther west, rupturing the connections between ritual activity, lineage, and geographic place. [Indigenous] priests lost credibility as traditional medicines failed to cure new diseases, while confederacies such as Powhatan's declined and disappeared. Uprooted tidewater peoples also encountered opposition from piedmont [inland] inhabitants upon whose territory they encroached. Ironically, the destruction of Powhatan's carefully nurtured political institutions and of Indian societies themselves opened up opportunities for individual women to assume leadership over tribal remnants by the mid-seventeenth century.[41]

The English, meanwhile, emerged from these early years of settlement with gender roles more explicitly defined in English, Christian, and yeoman terms. This core of English identity proved remarkably resilient, persisting through seventy years of wars with neighboring Indians and continuing to evolve as English settlers imported Africans to work the colony's tobacco fields. Initially serving to legitimate the destruction of traditional Indian ways of life, this concept of Englishness ultimately constituted one of the most powerful legacies of the Anglo-Indian gender frontier.

NOTES

1. Philip L. Barbour, *Pocahontas and Her World: A Chronicle of America's First Settlement* (Boston, 1970), 176–176, 179.
2. John Smith, *The Generall Historie of Virginia, New-England, and the Summer Isles . . .* (1624), in *The*

Complete Works of Captain John Smith (1580–1631), ed. Philip L. Barbour, 3 vols. (Chapel Hill, N.C., 1986) (hereafter, *CWJS*), II, 261.
3. For "performances" as used here, see Judith Butler, "Gender Trouble," in Linda J. Nicholson, ed., *Feminism/Postmodernism* (New York, 1990), 336–339.
4. For analyses of economic, linguistic, and religious "frontiers," see James Merrell, "'The Customes of Our Country': Indians and Colonists in Early America," in *Strangers Within the Realm: Cultural Margins of the First British Empire*, ed. Bernard Bailyn and Phillip D. Morgan (Chapel Hill, N.C., 1991), 117–156. In no way separate or distinct, the gender frontier infiltrated other frontiers we usually describe as economic, social, or cultural. See Kathleen M. Brown, "Brave New Worlds: Women's and Gender History," *William and Mary Quarterly*, 3rd ser., 50 (April 1993), 311–328.
5. See, for example, Ben C. McCary, *Indians in Seventeenth Century Virginia* (Williamsburg, Va., 1957); Helen C. Rountree, *The Powhatan Indians of Virginia: Their Traditional Culture* (Norman, Okla., 1989), 17–31, 151–52; Helen C. Rountree, *Pocahontas's People: The Powhatan Indians of Virginia through Four Centuries* (Norman, Okla., 1990); G. Melvin Herndon, "Indian Agriculture in the Southern Colonies," *North Carolina Historical Review* 44 (1967), 283–297; and Nancy Oestreich Lurie, "Indian Cultural Adjustment to European Civilization," in *Seventeenth-Century America: Essays in Colonial History*, ed. James Morton Smith (Chapel Hill, N.C., 1959), 40–42. The groups under Powhatan's mantle of authority included the Pamunkey, Kecoughtan, Mattaponi, Appamattuck, Rappahannock, Piankatank, Chiskiack, Werowocomoco, Nansemond, and Chesapeake.
6. Among the most useful accounts of English agriculture are Joan Thirsk, ed., *The Agrarian History of England and Wales*, 6 vols. (Cambridge, 1967), vol. 4; K. D. M. Snell, *Annals of the Laboring Poor: Social Change and Agrarian England, 1660–1900* (Cambridge, 1985); and Ann Kussmaul, *Servants in Husbandry in Early Modern England* (Cambridge, 1981).
7. See Susan Dwyer Amussen, *An Ordered Society: Gender and Class in Early Modern England* (New York, 1988), ch. 2; William Gouge, *Domesticall Duties* (London, 1622); Richard Brathwait, *The English Gentlewoman* (London, 1631); Gervase Markham, *Country Contentments or the English Housewife* (London, 1623). For the terms "good wives" and "nasty wenches," see John Hammond, *Leah and Rachel, or the Two Fruitfull Sisters* (London, 1656).
8. Martin Ingram, "Ridings Rough Music, and the 'Reform of Popular Culture,' in Early Modern England," *Past and Present* 105 (Nov. 1984), 78–113; D. E. Underdown, "Taming of the Scold: The Enforcement of Patriarchal Authority in Early Modern England," in *Order and Disorder in Early Modern England*, ed. Anthony Fletcher and John Stevenson (New York, 1985), 116–136.
9. Smith, *Generall Historie*, in *CWJS*, II, 121–125; William Strachey, *The Historie of Travell into Virginia Britania*, ed. Louis B. Wright and Virginia Freund (London, 1953), 89, 103 (hereafter, *HTVB*); Rountree, *Powhatan Indians*, 135–138; Charles Hudson, *The Southeastern Indians* (Knoxville, Tenn., 1976), 148–149.

10. *HTVB*, 103. The dearth of information about female goddesses may have resulted from the relative uninterest of English Protestants and their habit of talking mainly to Indian men.

11. Edwin Randolph Turner III, "An Archaeological and Ethnohistorical Study on the Evolution of Rank Socieites in the Virginia Coastal Plain" (Ph.D. diss., Pennsylvania State University, 1976), 182–187; Rountree, *Powhatan Indians*, 45–54, 63–65, 90; Rountree, *Pocahontas's People*, 88. For primary accounts of Algonquian agriculture and women's work, see Henry Spelman, *Relation of Virginea*, in *Travels and Works of Captain John Smith*, ed. Edward Archer and A. G. Bradley, 2 vols. (Edinburgh, 1910) (hereafter *TWJS*), I, cvii, cxi–cxii; and John Smith, *Map of Virginia . . .*, in *CWJS*, I, 157–159.

12. Rountree, *Powhatan Indians*, 84, 86, 88 n. 2.

13. Smith, *Generall Historie*, in *CWJS*, II, 118, 178; *HTVB*, 81; Spelman, *Relation of Virginea*, in *TWJS*, I, cvii; Rountree, *Powhatan Indians*, 32–35.

14. Smith, *Generall Historie*, in *CWJS*, II, 124–125, 178; Spelman, *Relation of Virginea*, in *TWJS*, I, cvi.

15. Smith, *Generall Historie*, in *CWJS*, II, 124–125; Rountree, *Powhatan Indians*, 88, 94; J. Leitch Wright, Jr., *The Only Land They Knew: The Tragic Story of the American Indians in the Old South* (New York, 1981), 8–14; Hudson, *Southeastern Indians*, 148–156, 258–260.

16. Hudson, *Southeastern Indians*, 259; Smith, *Generall Historie*, in *CWJS*, II, 147–148, 155.

17. *HTVB*, 83, 84.

18. Ibid., 40, 44, 57 (description of Powhatan), 62, 65–69; Spelman, *Relation of Virginea*, in *TWJS*, I, cxiv.

19. John Smith, *The Proceedings of the English Colony in Virginia . . .* (London, 1612), in *CWJS*, I, 257; *HTVB*, 24; Smith, *Map of Virginia*, in *CWJS*, I, 162–163.

20. V. G. Kiernan, "Private Property in History," in *Family and Inheritance: Rural Society in Western Europe, 1200–1800*, ed. Jack Goody et al. (Cambridge, 1976), 361–398.

21. Smith, *Generall Historie*, in *CWJS*, II, 114; Smith, *Map of Virginia*, ibid., I, 146–148.

22. George Percy, *Observations by Master George Percy, 1607* (1607), in *Narratives of Early Virginia, 1606–1625*, ed. Lyon Gardiner Tyler (New York, 1907) (hereafter, *NEV*), 18; Smith, *Map of Virginia*, in *CWJS*, II, 162, 164. See also David D. Smits, "'The Squaw Drudge': A Prime Index of Savagism," *Ethnohistory* 29 (1982), 281–306.

23. John Smith, *Description of Virginia and Proceedings of the Colonie* (London, 1612), in *NEV*, 99; Anne Laurence, "The Cradle to the Grave: English Observation of Irish Social Customs in the Seventeenth Century," *The Seventeenth Century* 3 (Spring 1988), 66–75; Jo Murphy-Lawless, "Images of Poor Women in the Writings of Irish Men Midwives," in *Women in Early Modern Ireland*, ed. Margaret MacCurtain and Mary O'Dowd (Edinburgh, 1991), 291–303.

24. Smith, *Generall Historie*, in *CWJS*, II, 173. For the deeper reverberations of different clothing and naming practices, see James Axtell, *The European and the Indian: Essays in the Ethnohistory of Colonial North America* (New York, 1981), 45, 47–55, 57–60.

25. Smith, *Proceedings of the English Colonies*, in *CWJS*, I, 235–236; Thomas Hariot, *A Briefe and True Report of the New Found Land of Virginia* (London, 1588; reprint, New York, 1903), E2–E3; Percy, *Observations*, in *NEV*, 12; Smith, *Map of Virginia*, in *CWJS*, I, 161.

26. Smith, *Proceedings of the English Colonies*, in *CWJS*, I, 236.

27. Spelman, *Relation of Virginea*, in *TWJS*, I, cviii, cxiv.

28. Smith, *Map of Virginia*, in *CWJS*, I, 160.

29. John Smith, *A True Relation of Such Occurences and Accidents of Note, as Hath Hapned in Virginia . . .*, in *CWJS*, I, 54–55, 85.

30. James Axtell, *Beyond 1492: Encounters in Colonial North America* (New York, 1992), 104; Rountree, *Powhatan Indians*, 142; Rountree, *Pocahontas's People*, 15–18.

31. Smith, *True Relation*, in *CWJS*, I, 39, 91.

32. Axtell, *Beyond 1492*, 101; *HTVB*, 86.

33. Rountree, *Powhatan Indians*, 89; Smith, *Proceedings of the English Colonies*, in *CWJS*, I, 246.

34. Smith, *Proceedings of the English Colonies*, in *CWJS*, I, 248. See ibid., II, 247, for allusions to English dependence in Powhatan's speech to Smith. See Smith, *Proceedings of the English Colonies*, in *CWJS*, I, for Smith's admission of dependence on native corn supplies. For Smith on the engagement with the Kecoughtan, see *Generall Historie*, ibid., II, 144–145.

35. See Axtell, *Beyond 1492*, 31–32, 39, 45, and 102, for the claim that, whereas Europeans stressed sharp distinctions between Europeans and non-Europeans, Indians tended to stress the similarities.

36. *HTVB*, 60, 64.

37. Smith, *True Relation*, in *CWJS*, I, 45; Smith, *Generall Historie*, ibid., II, 147–151.

38. Smith, *True Relation*, in *CWJS*, I, 61–67.

39. Smith, *Generall Historie*, in *CWJS*, II, 260–262.

40. Ibid., 261; Peter Hulme, *Colonial Encounters: Europe and the Native Caribbean, 1492–1797* (London, 1986), 146–147, 151–152, 156.

41. Hudson, *Southeastern Indians*, ch. 8; Timothy Silver, *A New Face on the Countryside: Indians, Colonists, and Slaves in South Atlantic Forests, 1500–1800* (New York, 1990), 72, 74–83, 87–88, 91, 102; Alfred W. Crosby, *Ecological Imperialism: The Biological Expansion of Europe, 900–1900* (Cambridge, 1986), 195–216; Wright, *Only Land They Knew*, 24–26; Peter Wood, "The Changing Population of the Colonial South," in Peter Wood et al., eds., *Powhatan's Mantle: Indians in the Colonial Southeast* (Lincoln, Nebr., 1989), 38, 40–42. See Martha McCartney, "Cockacoeske, Queen of the Pamunkey: Diplomat and Suzeraine," in ibid., 173–195; Robert Steven Grumet, "Sunsquaws, Shamans, and Tradeswomen: Middle Atlantic Coastal Algonqian Women during the Seventeenth and Eighteenth Centuries," in *Women and Colonization: Anthropological Perspectives*, ed. Mona Etienne and Eleanor Leacock (New York, 1980), 43–62.

JENNIFER L. MORGAN
"Some Could Suckle over Their Shoulder": European Depictions of Indigenous Women, 1492–1750

Of all the women who crossed the Atlantic east to west between 1492 and 1800, four-fifths made the journey from African homelands. They were fully one-third of the Africans compelled to embark on the infamous Middle Passage. White European women were a small proportion of female migrants—forced or voluntary—because of the insatiable demand of New World planters, especially in Brazil and the Caribbean (then referred to as the West Indies), for laborers to harvest profitable crops like sugarcane. These taskmasters were not averse to using girls and women as laborers.* Thus, while middling-status European women were likely to experience the hope, anxiety, and exhilaration that could come with establishing a homestead in a new land, far more African women were fated to associate the American continent with severe trauma, ongoing despair, and cultural loss.

The merchant capitalists, investors, and planters who promoted New World colonization had little compunction about subjecting poor, uneducated European working men, women, and children to a host of exploitative, coercive labor systems. But they forced upon the eight million Africans carried off in the transatlantic slave trade even more degrading conditions—both on slave ships and on American plantations. How did they justify this behavior to themselves? We cannot point simply to racism, because a concept of race as a biologically heritable set of traits congealed only in the nineteenth century. In the sixteenth century, educated Europeans believed that all humans descended from a common ancestor and thus shared a common humanity. "Race" was used mostly to indicate national origin or lineage. Skin color was not seen as an immutable marker of difference; many believed one's complexion would change according to how close one lived to the equator. Jennifer Morgan's essay forces us to grapple with how Europeans and Africans alike called into being the categories of blackness and whiteness.

To understand the process, Morgan argues, we must pay attention to Europeans' depictions of women's bodies and sexuality in the travel narratives of the time. The narratives' authors, European adventurers of the sixteenth to eighteenth centuries, can be thought of as early ethnographers in that they engaged in the close description of human cultures. Travelers to Africa borrowed tropes (i.e., significant themes or motifs) from earlier accounts written about indigenous American women. How did European depictions of African women change between the

---

*Jennifer L. Morgan, "Slavery and the Slave Trade," in *A Companion to American Women's History*, ed. Nancy A. Hewitt (Malden, Mass.: Blackwell, 2002), pp. 20–34.

Excerpted from the introduction and "'Some Could Suckle over Their Shoulder': Male Travelers, Female Bodies, and the Gendering of Racial Ideology," ch. 1 of *Laboring Women: Reproduction and Gender in New World Slavery* by Jennifer L. Morgan (Philadelphia: University of Pennsylvania Press, 2004). Reprinted by permission of the author and publisher. Notes have been edited and renumbered.

1550s and the 1770s? Do you agree that these imaginary presentations amounted to "porno-tropical writings"? Does Morgan convince you about their boundary-making power? Morgan's analysis helps us understand not only the impact of these texts and their accompanying pictures on English readers, but also the enduring legacy they created for African and African-descended women and men in the Americas.*

Ideas about black sexuality and misconceptions about black female sexual behavior formed the cornerstone of Europeans' and Euro-Americans' general attitudes toward slavery.[1] Arguably, the sexual stereotypes levied against African-American women in the nineteenth and twentieth centuries were so powerful because of the depth and utility of their roots. Before they came into contact with enslaved women either in West Africa or on American plantations, slaveowners' images and beliefs about race and savagery were indelibly marked on the women's bodies. . . . For European travelers, both those who settled in the Americas and those who did not, the enslavement of African laborers required a sense of moral and social distance over those they would enslave. They acquired that distance in part through manipulating symbolic representations of African women's sexuality. In so doing, European men gradually brought African women into focus—women whose pain-free reproduction (at least to European men) indicated that they did not descend from Eve and who illustrated their proclivity for hard work through their ability to simultaneously till the soil and birth a child. Such imaginary women suggested an immutable difference between Africans and Europeans, a difference ultimately codified as race. . . .

Prior to their entry onto the stage of New World conquests, women of African descent lived in bodies unmarked by what would emerge as Europe's preoccupation with physiognomy—skin color, hair texture, and facial features presumed to be evidence of cultural deficiency. Not until the gaze of European travelers fell upon them would African women see themselves, or indeed one another, as defined by "racial" characteristics. During the decades after European arrival to the Americas, as

various nations gained and lost footholds, followed fairytale rivers of gold, traded with and decimated Native inhabitants, and ignored and mobilized Christian notions of conversion and just wars, English settlers constructed an elaborate edifice of forced labor on the foundation of emerging categories of race and reproduction. The process of calling blackness into being and causing it to become inextricable from brute labor took place in legislative acts, laws, wills, bills of sale, and plantation inventories just as it did in journals and adventurers' tales of travels. Indeed, the gap between intimate experience (the Africans with whom one lived and worked) and ideology (monstrous, barely human savages) would be bridged in the hearts and minds of prosaic settlers rather than in the tales of worldly adventurers. . . . I turn here to travel narratives to explore developing categories of race and racial slavery. . . .

The connections between forced labor and race became increasingly important. . . . A concept of "race" rooted firmly in biology is primarily a late eighteenth- and early nineteenth-century phenomenon. . . . As travelers and men of letters thought through the thorny entanglements of skin color, complexion, features, and hair texture [over the course of the sixteenth and seventeenth centuries], they constructed weighty notions of civility, nationhood, citizenship, and manliness on the foundation of the amalgam of nature and culture. Given the ways in which appearance became a trope for civility and morality, it is no surprise to find gender located at the heart of Europeans' encounter with and musings over the connection between bodies and Atlantic economies.

In June 1647, Englishman Richard Ligon left London on the ship *Achilles* to establish himself as a planter in the newly settled colony

---

*A set of the illustrations analyzed by Morgan appears in an earlier version of this essay, "'Some Could Suckle over Their Shoulder': Male Travelers, Female Bodies, and the Gendering of Racial Ideology, 1500–1770," *William and Mary Quarterly*, 3rd ser., 54 (Jan. 1997): 167–92 (accessible online in some college libraries via the database JSTOR).

of Barbados. En route, Ligon's ship stopped in the Cape Verde islands for provisions and trade. There Ligon saw a black woman for the first time. He recorded the encounter in his *True and Exact History of Barbadoes*: she was a "Negro of the greatest beauty and majesty together: that ever I saw in one woman. Her stature large, and excellently shap'd, well favour'd, full eye'd, and admirably grac'd . . . [I] awaited her comming out, which was with far greater Majesty and gracefulness, than I have seen Queen Anne, descend from the Chaire of State." Ligon's rhetoric must have surprised his English readers, for seventeenth-century images of black women did not usually evoke the monarchy as the referent. . . .[2]

[But] over the course of his journey, Richard Ligon came to another view of black women. He wrote that their breasts "hang down below their Navels, so that when they stoop at their common work of weeding, they hang almost to the ground, that at a distance you would think they had six legs." In this context, black women's monstrous bodies symbolized their sole utility—the ability to produce both crops and other laborers.[3] It is this dual value, sometimes explicit and sometimes lurking in the background of slaveowners' decision-making processes, that would come to define women's experience of enslavement most critically. . . .

As Ligon penned his manuscript while in debtors prison in 1653, he constructed a layered narrative in which the discovery of African women's monstrosity helped to assure the work's success. Taking the female body as a symbol of the deceptive beauty and ultimate savagery of blackness, Ligon allowed his readers to dally with him among beautiful black women, only to seductively disclose their monstrosity over the course of the narrative. Ligon's narrative is a microcosm of a much-larger ideological maneuver that juxtaposed the familiar with the unfamiliar—the beautiful woman who is also the monstrous laboring beast. As the tenacious and historically deep roots of racialist ideology become more evident, it becomes clear also that, through the rubric of monstrously "raced" African women, Europeans found a way to articulate shifting perceptions of themselves as religiously, culturally, and phenotypically superior to the black or brown persons they sought to define. In the discourse used to justify the slave trade, Ligon's beautiful Negro woman was as important as her "six-legged" counterpart.

Both imaginary women marked a gendered. . . . whiteness on which European colonial expansionism depended. . . .[4]

Travel accounts produced in Europe and available in England provided a corpus from which subsequent writers borrowed freely, reproducing images of Native American and African women that resonated with readers. Over the course of the second half of the seventeenth century, some eighteen new collections with descriptions of Africa and the West Indies were published and reissued in England; by the eighteenth century, more than fifty new synthetic works, reissued again and again, found audiences in England.[5] Both the writers and the readers of these texts learned to dismiss the idea that women in the Americas and Africa might be innocuous or unremarkable. Rather, indigenous women bore an enormous symbolic burden, as writers from Walter Raleigh to Edward Long used them to mark metaphorically the symbiotic boundaries of European national identities and white supremacy. The conflict between perceptions of beauty and assertions of monstrosity such as Ligon's exemplified a much larger process through which the familiar became unfamiliar as beauty became beastliness and mothers became monstrous, all of which ultimately buttressed racial distinctions. Writers who articulated religious and moral justifications for the slave trade simultaneously grappled with the character of a contradictory female African body—a body both desirable and repulsive, available and untouchable, productive and reproductive, beautiful and black. By the time an eighteenth-century Carolina slaveowner could look at an African woman with the detached gaze of an investor, travelers and philosophers had already subjected her to a host of taxonomic calculations.

Europe had a long tradition of identifying Others through the monstrous physiognomy or sexual behavior of women. Armchair adventurers might shelve Pliny the Elder's ancient collection of monstrous races, *Historia Naturalis*, which catalogued the long-breasted wild woman, alongside Herodotus's *History*, in which Indian and Ethiopian tribal women bore only one child in a lifetime. They may have read Julian's arguments with Augustine in which he wrote that "barbarian and nomadic women give birth with ease, scarcely interrupting their travels to bear children." . . . Images of female devils included sagging breasts as part of the iconography of danger and monstrosity. The medieval wild woman, whose breasts dragged on the ground when she walked and could be thrown over her shoulder, was believed to disguise herself with youth and beauty in order to enact seductions. . . .[6]

Writers . . . easily applied similar modifiers to Others in Africa and the Americas in order to mark European boundaries. According to *The Travels of Sir John Mandeville*, "in Ethiopia and in many other countries [in Africa] the folk lie all naked . . . and the women have no shame of the men." Furthermore, "they wed there no wives, for all the women there be common . . . and when [women] have children they may give them to what man they will that hath companied with them." Deviant sexual behavior reflected the breakdown of natural laws—the absence of shame, the inability to identify lines of heredity and descent. This concern with deviant sexuality, articulated almost always through descriptions of women, is a constant theme in the travel writings of early modern Europe. . . . Indeed, Columbus used his reliance on the female body to articulate the colonial venture at the very outset of his voyage when he wrote that the earth was shaped like a breast with the Indies composing the nipple; his urge for discovery of new lands was inextricable from the language of sexual conquest.[7]

Richard Eden's 1553 English translation of Sebastian Münster's *A Treatyse of the Newe India* presented Amerigo Vespucci's 1502 voyage to English readers for the first time. Vespucci did not use color to mark the difference of the people he encountered; rather, he described them in terms of their lack of social institutions ("they fight not for the enlargeing of theyr dominion for asmuch as they have no Magistrates") and social niceties ("at theyr meate they use rude and barberous fashions, lying on the ground without any table clothe or coverlet"). Nonetheless, his descriptions are not without positive attributes, and when he turned his attention to women his language bristled with illuminating contradiction:

> Theyr bodies are verye smothe and clene by reason of theyr often washinge. They are in other thinges fylthy and withoute shame. Thei use no lawful coniunccion of mariage, and but every one hath as many women as him liketh, and leaveth them agayn at his pleasure. The women are very fruiteful, and refuse no laboure al the whyle they are with childe. They travayle in maner withoute

payne, so that the nexte day they are cherefull and able to walke. Neyther have they theyr bellies wimpeled or loose, and hanginge pappes, by reason of bearinge manye chyldren.[8]

The passage conveys admiration for indigenous women's strength in pregnancy and their ability to maintain aesthetically pleasing bodies, but it also illustrates the conflict at the heart of European discourse on gender and difference. It hinges on both a veiled critique of European female weakness and a dismissal of Amerindian women's pain. Once English men and women were firmly settled in New World colonies, they too would struggle with the notion of female weakness; they needed both white and black women for hard manual labor, but they also needed to preserve a notion of white gentlewomen's unsuitability for physical labor. . . .

Despite his respect for female reproductive hardiness, at the end of the volume Vespucci fixed the indigenous woman as a dangerous cannibal:

> There came sodeynly a woman downe from a mountayne, bringing with her secretly a great stake with which she [killed a Spaniard.] The other wommene foorthwith toke him by the legges, and drewe him to the mountayne. . . . The women also which had slayne the yong man, cut him in pieces even in the sight of the Spaniardes, shewinge them the pieces, and rosting them at a greate fyre.

Vespucci later made manifest the latent sexualized danger inherent in the man-slaying woman in a letter in which he wrote of women biting off the penises of their sexual partners, thus linking cannibalism—an absolute indicator of savagery and distance from European norms—to female sexual insatiability.[9]

The label "savage" was not uniformly applied to Amerindian people. Indeed, in the context of European national rivalries, the indigenous woman became somewhat less savage. In the mid to late sixteenth century, the bodies of women figured at the borders of national identities. . . .

In "Discoverie of the . . . Empire of Guiana" (1598), [Sir Walter] Ralegh stated that he "suffered not any man to . . . touch any of [the natives'] wives or daughters: which course so contrary to the Spaniards (who tyrannize over them in all things) drewe them to admire her [English] majestie." Although he permitted himself and his men to gaze upon naked Indian women, Ralegh accentuated the restraint they exercised. In doing so, he used the untouched bodies of Native American women to mark national boundaries and signal the civility and superiority of English colonizers in contrast to the sexually violent Spaniards. Moreover, in linking the eroticism of indigenous women to the sexual attention of Spanish men, Ralegh signaled the Spaniards' "lapse into savagery."[10] . . .

[Visual depictions of Native women were always in flux]. . . . [E]arly volumes of Theodor de Bry's *Grand Voyages* (1590) depicted the Algonkians of Virginia and the Timucuas of Florida as classical Europeans: Amerindian bodies mirrored ancient Greek and Roman statuary, modest virgins covered their breasts, and infants suckled at the high, small breasts of young attractive women. . . .

In the third de Bry volume, *Voyages to Brazil*, published in 1592, the Indian was portrayed as aggressive and savage, and the representation of women's bodies changed. The new woman is a cannibal with breasts that fell below her waist. She licks the juices of grilled human flesh from her fingers. . . . The absence of a suckling child in these . . . depictions . . . signified the women's cannibalism—they consumed rather than produced. Although women alone did not exemplify cannibalism, women with long breasts came to mark such savagery in Native Americans for English readers. As depictions of Native Americans traversed the gamut of savage to noble, the long-breasted women became a clear signpost of savagery in contrast to her high-breasted counterpart . . .[11]

English travelers to West Africa drew on American narrative traditions as they too worked to establish a clearly demarcated line that would ultimately define them. Richard Hakluyt's collection of travel narratives, *Principal Navigations* (1589), brought Africa into the purview of English readers. *Principal Navigations* portrayed Africa and Africans in both positive and negative terms. . . . In response, Hakluyt presented texts that, through an often-conflicted depiction of African peoples, ultimately differentiated between Africa and England and erected a boundary that made English expansion in the face of confused and uncivilized peoples reasonable, profitable, and moral. . . .[12] [To] write of sex was also to define and expand the boundaries of profit through productive and reproductive labor.

The symbolic weight of indigenous women's sexual, childbearing, and childrearing practices moved from the Americas to Africa and continued to be brought to bear on England's literary imagination in ways that rallied familiar notions of gendered difference for English readers. John Lok's account of his 1554 voyage to Guinea, published forty years later in Hakluyt's collection, . . . described all Africans as "people of beastly living." He located the proof of this in women's behavior: among the Garamantes, women "are common: for they contract no matrimonie, neither have respect to chastitie." This description of the Garamantes first appeared in Pliny, was reproduced again by Iulius Solinus's sixth century *Polyhistor* and can be found in travel accounts through the Middle Ages and into the sixteenth and seventeenth centuries. . . .[13]

William Towrson's narrative of his 1555 voyage to Guinea, also published by Hakluyt in 1589, further exhibits this kind of distillation. Towrson depicted women and men as largely indistinguishable. They "goe so alike, that one cannot know a man from a woman but by their breastes, which in the most part be very foule and long, hanging downe low like the udder of a goate." This was, perhaps, the first time an Englishman in Africa explicitly used breasts as an identifying trait of beastliness and difference. He went on to maintain that "diverse of the women have such exceeding long breasts, that some of them will lay the same upon the ground and lie downe by them."[14] Lok and Towrson represented African women's bodies and sexual behavior in order to distinguish Africa from Europe. Towrson in particular gave readers only two analogies through which to view and understand African women—beasts and monsters. . . .

. . . After Hakluyt died, Samuel Purchas took up the mantle of editor and published twenty additional volumes in Hakluyt's series beginning in 1624.[15] . . . [including] a translation of Pieter de Marees's *A description and historicall declaration of the golden Kingedome of Guinea*. This narrative was first published in Dutch in 1602, was translated into German and Latin for the de Bry volumes (1603–1634), and appeared in French in 1605. Plagiarism by seventeenth- and eighteenth-century writers gave it still wider circulation. Here, too, black women embody African savagery. De Marees began by describing the people at Sierra Leone as "very greedie eaters, and no lesse drinkers, and very lecherous, and theevish, and much addicted to uncleanenesse; one man hath as many wives as

Women in Africa, engraving by Theodor de Bry, 1604.
Appearing in a much-reproduced travel narrative, this engraving purported to show representative examples of women's clothing and personal decoration in four regions of western Africa. (Women in Africa, *from* Verum et Historicam Descriptionem Avriferi Regni Guineaa, *in* Small Voyages, *vol. 6, by Theodor de Bry [Frankfurt am Main, 1604], p. 3. Courtesy of the John Work Garrett Library, Johns Hopkins University.)

hee is able to keepe and maintaine. The women also are much addicted to leacherie, specially, with strange Countrey people . . . [and] are also great Lyers, and not to be credited." As did most of his contemporaries, de Marees invoked women's sexuality to castigate the incivility of both men and women. Women's savagery does not stand apart. Rather, it indicts the whole: all Africans were savage. The passage displays African males' savagery alongside their access to multiple women. Similarly, de Marees located evidence of African women's savagery in their sexual desire. . . .

[He] further castigated West African women: they delivered children surrounded by men, women, and youngsters "in most shamelesse manner . . . before them all." This absence of shame (evoked explicitly, as here, or implicitly in the constant references to nakedness in

other narratives) worked to establish distance. Readers, titillated by the topics discussed and thus tacitly shamed, found themselves further distanced from the shameless subject of the narrative. De Marees dwelled on the brute nature of shameless African women. He marveled that "when the child is borne [the mother] goes to the water to wash and make cleane her selfe, not once dreaming of a moneths lying-in . . . as women here with us use to doe; they use no Nurses to help them when they lie in child-bed, neither seeke to lie dainty and soft. . . . The next day after, they goe abroad in the streets, to doe their businesse."[16] . . .

De Marees goes on to inscribe an image of women's reproductive identity whose influence persisted long after his original publication. "When [the child] is two or three monethes old, the mother ties the childe with a peece of cloth at her backe. . . . When the child crieth to sucke, the mother casteth one of her dugs backeward over her shoulder, and so the child suckes it as it hangs."[17] Frontispieces for the de Marees narrative and the African narratives in de Bry approximate the over-the-shoulder breast-feeding de Marees described, thereby creating an image that could symbolize the continent . . .

The image, in more or less extreme form, remained a compelling one, offering in a single narrative-visual moment evidence that black women's difference was both cultural (in this strange *habit*) and physical (in this strange *ability*). The word "dug," which by the early seventeenth century meant both a woman's breasts and an animal's teats, connoted a brute animality that de Marees reinforced through his description of small children "lying downe in their house, like Dogges, [and] rooting in the ground like Hogges" and of "boyes and girles [that] goe starke naked as they were borne, with their privie members all open, without any shame or civilitie.[18] . . .

As Englishmen traversed the uncertain ground of nature and culture, African women became a touchstone for physical and behavioral curiosity both within Africa and in the Americas and Europe. Fynes Moryson wrote of Irish women in 1617 that they "have very great Dugges, some so big as they give their children suck over their Shoulders." But it is important that he connects this to being "not laced at all," or to the lack of corsetry.[19] While nudity—a state in which the absence of corsetry is certainly implicit—is constantly at play in descriptions of African women, the overwhelming physicality of the image is disaggregated from culture and instead becomes part of African female nature; something no amount of corsetry would set right . . .

African women's Africanness became contingent on the linkages between sexuality and a savagery that fitted them for both productive and reproductive labor. . . . [D]escriptions of African women in the Americas almost always highlighted their fecundity along with their capacity for manual labor. Erroneous observations about African women's propensity for easy birth and breast-feeding reassured colonizers that these women could easily perform hard labor in the Americas; at the same time, such observations erected a barrier of difference between Africa and England. Seventeenth-century English medical writers, both men and

women, equated breast-feeding and tending to children with difficult work, and the practice of wealthy women forgoing breast-feeding in favor of sending their children to wet nurses was widespread. English women and men anticipated pregnancy and childbirth with extreme uneasiness and fear of death, but they knew that the experience of pain in childbirth marked women as members of a Christian community.[20] . . .

. . . By about the turn of the seventeenth century, however, as England joined in the transatlantic slave trade, assertions of African savagery began to be predicated less on consumption and cannibalism and more on production and reproduction. African women came into the conversation in the context of England's need for productivity. Descriptions of these women that highlighted the apparent ease and indifference of their reproductive lives created a mechanistic image. . . . Whereas English women's reproductive work took place solely in the domestic economy, African women's reproductive work embodied the developing discourses of extraction and forced labor at the heart of England's design for the Americas. . . .

By the eighteenth century, English writers rarely used black women's breasts or behavior for anything but concrete evidence of barbarism in Africa. In *A Description of the Coasts of North and South-Guinea*, begun in the 1680s and completed and published almost forty years later, John Barbot "admired the quietness of the poor babes, so carr'd about at their mothers' backs . . . and how freely they suck the breasts, which are always full of milk, over their mothers' *shoulders, and sleep soundly in that odd posture." William Snelgrave introduced his New Account of Some Parts of Guinea and the Slavetrade* with an anecdote designed to illustrate the benevolence of the trade. He described himself rescuing an infant from human sacrifice and reuniting the child with its mother, who "had much Milk in her Breasts." He accented the barbarism of those who had attempted to sacrifice the child and claimed that the reunion cemented his goodwill in the eyes of the enslaved, who, thus convinced of the "good notion of White Men," caused no problems during the voyage to Antigua.[21] . . .

Eighteenth-century abolitionist John Atkins similarly adopted the icon of black female bodies in his writings on Guinea. "Childing, and their Breasts always pendulous, stretches them to so unseemly a length and Bigness that some . . . could suckle over their shoulder." Atkins then considered the idea of African women copulating with apes. He noted that "at some places the Negroes have been suspected of Bestiality." . . . The evidence lay mostly in apes' resemblance to humans but was bolstered by "the Ignorance and Stupidity [of black women unable] to guide or controll lust." Abolitionists and anti-abolitionists alike accepted the connections between race and black women's monstrous and fecund bodies . . .

The visual shorthand of the sagging-breasted African savage held sway for decades . . . When William Smith embarked on a voyage to map the Gold Coast for the Royal Africa Company in 1727, he was initially uninterested in ethnography. His first description of people comes more than halfway through the narrative when he writes "but before I describe the Vegetables, I shall take Notice of the Animals of this Country; beginning with the Natives, who are generally speaking a lusty strong-bodied People, but are mostly of a lazy idle Disposition." His short description, followed by a section on "Quadrepedes," is organized primarily around accusations of polygamy and promiscuity in which "hot constitution'd Ladies" are put to work by husbands who treat them like slaves. As the narrative continues, his ethnographic passages, while always brief, are also always organized around sexually available African women. In Whydah, for example, the reader encounters female Priests inclined to whoredom, and he tells of an anomalous Queen in Agonna who satisfies her sexual needs with male slaves, hands down her crown to the resulting female progeny and sells any male children into slavery.[23] . . .

One of a very few English women in late eighteenth-century West Africa, abolitionist Anna Falconbridge . . . noted that women's breasts in Sierra Leone were "disgusting to Europeans, though considered *beautiful* and ornamental here." But such weak claims of sisterly sympathy could hardly interrupt 300 years of porno-tropical writing. By the 1770s, Edward Long's *History of Jamaica* presented readers with African women whose savagery was total, for whom enslavement was the only means of civilization. . . . Long used women's bodies and behavior to justify and promote the mass enslavement of Africans. By the time he wrote, the Jamaican economy was fully invested in slave labor and was contributing more than half of the profits obtained by England from the West Indies as a whole. The association of black people with beasts—via African women—had been cemented: "Their women are delivered with little or no labour; they have therefore no more occasion for midwifes than the female oran-outang, or any other wild animall. . . . Thus they seem exempted from the course inflicted upon Eve *and her daughters.*"[24] If African women gave birth without pain, they somehow side-stepped God's curse upon Eve. If they were not Eve's descendants, they were not related to Europeans and could therefore be forced to labor on England's overseas plantations with impunity. . . .[25]

When [Richard] Ligon arrived in Barbados and settled on 500-acre sugar plantation with 100 slaves, his notion of African beauty—if it had ever really existed—dissolved in the face of racial slavery. He saw African men and women carrying bunches of plantains: "Tis a lovely sight to see a hundred handsom Negroes, men and women, with every one a grasse-green bunch of these fruits on their heads . . . the black and green so well becoming one another." Here in the context of the sugar plantation, where he saw African women working as he had never seen English woman do, Ligon struggled to situate African women as workers. Their innate unfamiliarity as laborers caused him to cast about for a useful metaphor. He compares African people to vegetation; now they are only passively and abstractly beautiful as blocks of color. Ligon attested to their passivity with their servitude: They made "very good servants, if they be not spoyled by the English."[26]

But . . . he ultimately equated black people with animals. He declared that planters bought slaves so that the "sexes may be equall . . . [because] they cannot live without Wives," although the enslaved choose their partners much "as Cows do . . . for, the most of them are as near beasts as may be." Like his predecessors, Ligon offered further proof of Africans' capacity for physical labor—their aptitude for slavery—through ease of childbearing. "In a fortnight [after giving birth] this woman is at worke with her Pickaninny at her back, as merry a soule as any is there."[27] In the Americas, African women's purportedly pain-free childbearing thus continued to be central. When Ligon reinforced African women's animality with descriptions of breasts "hang[ing] down below their Navels," he tethered his narrative to familiar images of black women that—for readers nourished on Hakluyt and de Bry—effectively naturalized the enslavement of Africans . . .

By the time the English made their way to the West Indies, decades of ideas and information about brown and black women predated the actual encounter. In many ways, the encounter had already taken place in parlors and reading rooms on English soil, assuring that colonists would arrive with a battery of assumptions and predispositions about race, femininity, sexuality, and civilization. Confronted with an Africa they needed to exploit, European writers turned to black women as evidence of a cultural inferiority that ultimately became encoded as racial difference. Monstrous bodies became enmeshed with savage behavior as the icon of women's breasts became evidence of tangible barbarism. African women's "unwomanly" behavior evoked an immutable distance between Europe and Africa on which the development of racial slavery depended. By the mid-seventeenth century, what had initially marked African women as unfamiliar—their sexually and reproductively bound savagery—had become familiar. To invoke it was to conjure a gendered and racialized figure that marked the boundaries of English civility even as she naturalized the subjugation of Africans and their descendants in the Americas.

NOTES

1. Deborah Gray White, *Ar'n't I A Woman? Female Slaves in the Plantation South* (New York and London: W.W. Norton, 1985), 29–46; Barbara Bush, *Slave Women in Caribbean Society, 1650–1838* (Bloomington: Indiana University Press, 1990), 11–12.

2. Richard Ligon, *A True and Exact History of the Island of Barbados* (London, 1657), 12–13.

3. Ligon, *True and Exact History of Barbados*, 51.

4. Kim F. Hall, *Things of Darkness: Economies of Race and Gender in Early Modern England* (Ithaca, N.Y.: Cornell University Press, 1995), 29–61.

5. Anthony J. Barker, *The African Link: British Attitudes to the Negro in the Era of the Atlantic Slave Trade, 1550–1807* (London: Frank Cass, 1978), 22.

6. Pliny the Elder, *Natural History*, 10 vols., trans. H. Rackham (Cambridge, Mass., Harvard University Press, 1938–63), 2: 509–27; Herodotus, *The History*, trans. David Grene (Chicago: University of Chicago Press, 1987), 4, 180, 191; Elizabeth A. Clark, "Generation, Degeneration, Regeneration: Original Sin and the Conception of Jesus in the Polemic Between Augustine and Julian of Eclanum," in *Generation and Degeneration: Tropes of Reproduction in*

Literature and History from Antiquity to Early Modern Europe, ed. Valeria Finucci and Kevin Brownlee (Durham, N.C.: Duke University Press, 2001), 30; Richard Bernheimer, *Wild Men in the Middle Ages: A Study in Art, Sentiment, and Demonology* (Cambridge, Mass.: Harvard University Press, 1952), 33–41, 34.

7. *The Travels of Sir John Mandeville: The Version of the Cotton Manuscript in Modern Spelling*, ed. A.W. Pollard (London: Macmillan, 1915), 109, 119; Sharon W. Tiffany and Kathleen J. Adams, *The Wild Woman: An Inquiry into the Anthropology of an Idea* (Cambridge: Schenkman, 1985), 63.

8. *A Treatyse of the Newe India by Sebastian Münster (1553)*, trans. Richard Eden (microprint) (Ann Arbor, Mich., 1966), 57.

9. Münster, *Treatyse*, trans. Eden, quoted in Louis Montrose, "The Work of Gender in the Discourse of Discovery," *Representations* 33 (1991): 1–41, 4, 5.

10. Ralegh, "The Discoverie of the large rich and beautifull Empire of Guiana," in Richard Hakluyt, *The Principal Navigations, Voyages, Traffiques & Discoveries of the English Nation*, 12 vols. (1598–1600; reprint Glasgow, 1903–5), 10, 39; Karen Robertson, "Pocahantas at the Masque," *Signs* 21 (1996): 561.

11. Theodore de Bry, ed., *Grand Voyages*, 13 vols. (Frankfurt am Main, 1590–1627); Bernadette Bucher, *Icon and Conquest: A Structural Analysis of the Illustrations of de Bry's Great Voyages*, trans. Basia Miller Gulati (Chicago: University of Chicago Press, 1981).

12. Emily C. Bartels, "Imperialist Beginnings: Richard Hakluyt and the Construction of Africa," *Criticism* 34 (1992): 517–38, 519.

13. "The second voyage [of Master John Lok] to Guinea . . . 1554," in Richard Hakluyt, *The Principal Navigations, Voyages, Traffiques, and Discoveries of the English Nation*, 12 vols. (London, 1598–1600), 6: 167, 168; Barker, *African Link*, 121.

14. "The first voyage made by Master William Towrson Marchant of London, to the coast of Guinea . . . in the yeere 1555," in Hakluyt, *Principal Navigations*, 6: 184, 187.

15. Samuel Purchas, *Hakluytus Posthumus, or Purchas His Pilgrimes: Contayning a History of the World in Sea Voyages and Land Travells by Englishmen and Others*, 20 vols. (1624; reprint Glasgow: J. MacLehose and Sons, 1905).

16. De Marees, "Description and historicall declaration of the golden Kingdome of Guinea," in *Purchas His Pilgrimes*, 6: 251, 258–59. This testimony to African women's physical strength and emotional indifference is even more emphatic in the original Dutch. In the most recent translation from the Dutch, the passage continues: "This shows that the women here are of a cruder nature and stronger posture than the Females in our Lands in Europe." Pieter de Marees, *Description and Historical Account of the Gold Kingdom of Guinea*, trans, and ed. Albert van Dantzig and Adam Jones (1602; reprint Oxford: Oxford University Press, 1987), 23.

17. De Marees, "Description and historicall declaration of the Golden Kingdome," 259.

18. De Marees, "Description and historicall declaration of the Golden Kingdome," 261. *Oxford English Dictionary*, 2nd ed., 1989.

19. Fynes Moryson, *Shakespeare's Europe: A survey of the Condition of Europe at the end of the Sixteenth Century, Being unpublished chapters of Fynes*

Moryson's Itinerary, 2nd ed. (1617; reprint New York: Benjamin Blom, 1967), 485.

20. Jordan, *White over Black*, 39; Marylynn Salmon, "The Cultural Significance of Breastfeeding and Infant Care in Early Modern England and America," *Journal of Social History* 28 (1994): 247–70; Linda Pollock, "Embarking on a Rough Passage: The Experience of Pregnancy in Early Modern Society," in *Women as Mothers in Pre-Industrial England*, ed. Valerie Fildes (New York: Routledge, 1990), 45.

21. Barbot, *A Description of the Coasts of North and South-Guinea, in A Collection of Voyages*, ed. A. Churchill (London, 1732), 36; William Snelgrave, "Introduction," *A New Account of Some Parts of Guinea and the Slave Trade* (1734; reprint London: Cass, 1971).

22. John Atkins, *A Voyage to Guinea, Brazil, and the West-Indies* (1735; reprint London: Cass, 1970), 50, 108.

23. William Smith, *A New Voyage to Guinea* (London, 1744), 142–43, 195, 208.

24. Anna Maria Falconbridge, *Two Voyages to Sierra Leone, During the Years 1791–2–3, in Maiden Voyages and Infant Colonies: Two Women's Travel Narratives of the 1790s*, ed. Deirdre Coleman (London: Leicester University Press, 1999), 45–168, 74, emphasis in the original; Edward Long, "History of Jamaica, 2, with notes and corrections by the Author" (1774), Add. Ms., 12405, p364/f295, p380/f304; Robin Blackburn, *The Making of New World Slavery: From the Baroque to the Modern, 1492–1800* (London: Verso, 1997), 527–45.

25. Early modern European women were so defined by their experience of pain in childbirth that an inability to feel pain was considered evidence of witchcraft. Lyndal Roper, *Oedipus and the Devil: Witchcraft, Sexuality and Religion in Early Modern Europe* (London: Routledge, 1994), 203–4.

26. Ligon, *True and Exact History of Barbadoes*, 44, 47, 51.

27. Ligon, *True and Exact History of Barbadoes*, 47, 51.

EUROPEAN SETTLERS: GENDER PUZZLES, GENDER RULES

MARY BETH NORTON

An Indentured Servant Identifies as "Both Man and Woeman": Jamestown, 1629

The story that Mary Beth Norton tells is one that demonstrates that gender is a social as well as a biological construction. It is very rare that a newborn is hermaphrodite, or intersexed, displaying "some combination of 'female' and 'male' reproductive and sexual features." Later in life, hormonal abnormalities may mask clear distinctions between male and female. In our own time, "sexual reassignment" surgery is generally performed while an intersexed child is an infant; for adults, hormonal treatments, sometimes accompanied by surgery, can be used to clarify the gender identity of an individual.*

In one seventeenth-century Virginia community, the presence of a person who dressed as a man and also as a woman, who behaved alternately like a woman and like a man, and whose physical formation was vulnerable to multiple interpretations was deeply disconcerting. How did T. Hall's neighbors respond to gossip that this person's sex was unclear? What authority did women claim in assessing the situation? What authority did men claim? What does the struggle to mark T. Hall's gender identity suggest about the structure of community life and the roles of men and women?

On April 8, 1629, a person named Hall was brought before the General Court of the colony of Virginia. Hall was not formally charged with a crime, although witnesses alluded to a rumor about fornication. Yet Hall's case is one of the most remarkable to be found in the court records of any colony. If no crime was involved, why was Hall in court?

Hall had been reported to the authorities for one simple reason: people were confused about Hall's sexual identity. At times Hall dressed as a man; at other times, evidently, as

---

* Suzanne Kessler, "The Medical Construction of Gender: Case Management of Intersexed Infants," *Signs: Journal of Women in Culture and Society* 16 (1990): 3–26. For other interpretations of the Hall case, see Kathleen Brown, "'Changed . . . into the fashion of a man': The Politics of Sexual Difference in a Seventeenth-Century Anglo-American Settlement," *Journal of the History of Sexuality* 6 (1995): 171–93; and Elizabeth Reis, *Bodies in Doubt: An American History of Intersex* (Baltimore: Johns Hopkins University Press, 2009), 10–16, 22, 29.

Excerpted from the prologue to sec. 2 of *Founding Mothers and Fathers: Gendered Power and the Forming of American Society* by Mary Beth Norton (New York: Alfred A. Knopf, 1996). Reprinted by permission of the author and publisher. Notes have been edited and renumbered. For transcripts of the court records in the Hall case see H. R. McIlwaine, ed., *Minutes of the Council and General Court of Colonial Virginia, 1622–1632, 1670–1676* (Richmond, Va.: Colonial Press/Everett Waddey, 1924), 194–195, via www.archive.org.

a woman. What sex was this person? Other colonists wanted to know. The vigor with which they pursued their concerns dramatically underscores the significance of gender distinctions in seventeenth-century Anglo-America. The case also provides excellent illustrations of the powerful role the community could play in individuals' lives and of the potential influence of ordinary folk, both men and women, on the official actions of colonial governments.

The Hall case offers compelling insights into the process of defining gender in early American society. Hall was an anomalous individual, and focusing on such anomalies can help to expose fundamental belief systems. Since in this case sex was difficult to determine, so too was gender identity. Persons of indeterminate sex, such as the subject of this discussion, pose perplexing questions for any society. The process through which the culture categorizes these people is both complex and revealing. The analysis here will examine the ways in which seventeenth-century Virginians attempted to come to grips with the problems presented to them by a sexually ambiguous person.[1] . . .

Describing my usage of personal pronouns and names is essential to the analysis that follows. The other historians who have dealt with the case have referred to Hall as "Thomas" and "he," as do the court records (with one significant exception). Yet the details of the case, including Hall's testimony, make such usage problematic. Therefore the practice here shall be the following: when Hall is acting as a female, the name "Thomasine" and the pronoun "she" will be used. Conversely, when Hall is acting as a male, "Thomas" and "he" are just as obviously called for. In moments of ambiguity or generalization (as now) "Hall," or the simple initial "T" will be employed (the latter as an ungendered pronoun).

Thomasine Hall was born "at or neere" the northeastern English city of Newcastle upon Tyne.[2] As the name suggests, Hall was christened and raised as a girl. At the age of twelve, Thomasine went to London to stay with her aunt, and she lived there for ten years. But in 1625 her brother was pressed into the army to serve in an expedition against Cadiz. Perhaps encouraged by her brother's experience (or perhaps taking his place after his death, for that expedition incurred many casualties), Hall subsequently adopted a new gender identity.

Thomas told the court that he "Cut of[f] his heire and Changed his apparell into the fashion of man and went over as a souldier in the Isle of Ree being in the habit of a man."[3] Upon returning to Plymouth from army service in France, probably in the autumn of 1627, Hall resumed a feminine identity. Thomasine donned women's clothing and supported herself briefly by making "bone lace" and doing other needlework. That she did so suggests that Thomasine had been taught these valuable female skills by her aunt during her earlier sojourn in London.

Plymouth was one of the major points of embarkation for the American colonies, and Hall recounted that "shortly after" arriving in the city Thomasine learned that a ship was being made ready for a voyage to Virginia. Once again, Hall decided to become a man, so he put on men's clothing and sailed to the fledgling colony. Thomas was then approximately twenty-five years old, comparable in age to many of the immigrants to Virginia, and like most of his fellows he seems to have gone to the Chesapeake as an indentured servant.

By December, Hall was settled in Virginia, for on January 21, 1627/8, a man named Thomas Hall, living with John and Jane Tyos (T's master and mistress), was convicted along with them for receiving stolen goods from William Mills, a servant of one of their neighbors. According to the testimony, Hall and the Tyoses had encouraged Mills in a series of thefts that began before Christmas 1627. Some of the purloined items—which included tobacco, chickens, currants, a shirt, and several pairs of shoes—were still in the possession of Hall and the Tyoses at the time their house was searched by the authorities on January 14. Although Thomas Hall is a common name (indeed, John Tyos knew another Thomas Hall, who had arrived with him on the ship Bona Nova in 1620), a significant piece of evidence suggests that T and the man charged with this crime were one and the same. William Mills had difficulty carrying the currants, which he piled into his cap during his initial theft. Since that was clearly an unsatisfactory conveyance, when Mills was about to make a second foray after the desirable dried fruits he asked his accomplices to supply him with a better container. Thomas Hall testified that Jane Tyos then "did bring a napkin unto him and willed him to sowe it & make a bagg of it to carry currants." It is highly unlikely that an ordinary male servant would have had better seamstressing skills than his mistress, but Thomasine was an expert at such tasks.[4]

Although thus far in Hall's tale the chronology and the sequence of gender switches have been clear—for T specifically recounted the first part of the tale to the Virginia General Court, and the timing of the thefts and their prosecution is clearly described in court testimony—the next phase of the story must be pieced together from the muddled testimony of two witnesses and some logical surmises.

A key question not definitively answered in the records is: what happened to raise questions in people's minds about Hall's sexual identity? Two possibilities suggest themselves. One is that John and Jane Tyos, who obviously recognized that Hall had "feminine" skills shortly after T came to live with them, spoke of that fact to others, or perhaps visitors to their plantation observed Hall's activities and drew their own conclusions. Another possibility is that, after traveling to Virginia as a man, Hall reverted to the female clothing and role that T appears to have found more comfortable. The court records imply that Hall did choose to dress as a woman in Virginia, for Francis England, a witness, reported overhearing a conversation in which another man asked T directly: why do you wear women's clothing? T's reply—"I goe in weomans aparell to gett a bitt for my Catt"—is difficult to interpret and will be analyzed later. In any event, a Mr. Stacy (who cannot be further identified) seems to have first raised the issue of T's anomalous sexual character by asserting to other colonists that Hall was "as hee thought a man and woman." Just when Mr. Stacy made this statement is not clear, but he probably voiced his opinion about a year after T arrived in the colony.

In the aftermath of Mr. Stacy's statement, a significant incident occurred at the home of Nicholas Eyres, perhaps a relative of Robert Eyres, who had recently become John Tyos's partner. "Uppon [Mr Stacy's] report," three women—Alice Longe, Dorothy Rodes, and Barbara Hall—scrutinized Hall's body. Their action implied that T was at the time dressed as a woman, for women regularly searched other women's bodies (often at the direction of a court) to look for signs of illicit pregnancy or perhaps witchcraft. They never, however, performed the same function with respect to men—or anyone dressed like a man. Moreover, John Tyos both then and later told Dorothy Rodes that Hall was a woman. Even so, the female searchers, having examined Hall, declared that T was a man. As a result of the disagreement between Tyos and the women about T's sex, T was brought before the commander of the region, Captain Nathaniel Basse, for further examination.[5]

Questioned by Mr. Basse, T responded with a description of a unique anatomy with ambiguous physical characteristics. (The text of the testimony is mutilated, and the remaining fragments are too incomplete to provide a clear description of T's body.) Hall then refused to choose a gender identity, instead declaring that T was "both man and woeman." Captain Basse nevertheless decided that Hall was female and ordered T "to bee putt in weomans apparell"—thus implying that T was, at that moment at least, dressed as a man. The three women who had previously searched T's body were shaken by the official ruling that contradicted their own judgment; after being informed of the commander's decision, they reportedly "stood in doubte of what they had formerly affirmed."

John Tyos then sold Hall, now legally a maidservant named Thomasine, to John Atkins, who was present when Captain Basse questioned T. Atkins must have fully concurred with Mr. Basse's decision; surely he would not have purchased a female servant about whose sex he had any doubts. Yet on February 12, 1628/9, questions were again raised about T, for Alice Longe and her two friends went to Atkins's house to scrutinize Thomasine's body for a second time. They covertly examined her while she slept and once more decided that the servant was male. But Atkins, though summoned by the searchers to look at his maid's anatomy, was unable to do so, for Hall's "seeming to starre as if shee had beene awake" caused Atkins to leave without viewing her body.

The next Sunday, the three women returned with two additional female helpers.[6] On this occasion, the searchers had the active cooperation and participation of John Atkins, who ordered Thomasine to show her body to them. For a third time the women concluded that Hall was a man. Atkins thereupon ordered his servant to don men's clothing and informed Captain Basse of his decision.

By this time not only Hall but also everyone else was undoubtedly confused. Since Hall was now deemed to be male, the next curiosity-seekers to examine T's body were also male.

One of them was Roger Rodes, probably the husband of Dorothy, who had joined in all the previous searches of Hall's body. Before forcefully throwing Thomas onto his back and checking his anatomy, Roger told Hall, "thou hast beene reported to be a woman and now thou art proved to bee a man, i will see what thou carriest." Like the female searchers before them, Roger and his associate Francis England concluded that T was male.

A rumor that Hall "did ly with a maid of Mr Richard Bennetts called great Besse" must have added considerably to the uncertainty. Hall accused Alice Longe, one of the persistent female searchers, of spreading the tale. She denied the charge, blaming the slander instead on an unnamed male servant of John Tyos's. If the story was true, what did it imply about Hall's sexual identity? Whether Hall was male or female would obviously have a bearing on the interpretation of any relationship with Bennett's maid Bess. Clearly, Virginians now had reason to seek a firm resolution of the conflict. Since Captain Basse, the local commander, had been unable to find an acceptable solution, there was just one remaining alternative—referring the dilemma to the General Court.

That court, composed of the governor and council, was the highest judicial authority in the small colony. The judges heard from Hall and considered the sworn depositions of two male witnesses (Francis England and John Atkins), who described the events just outlined. Remarkably, the court accepted T's own self-definition and, although using the male personal pronoun, declared that Hall was "a man and a woman, that all the Inhabitants there may take notice thereof and that hee shall goe Clothed in mans apparell, only his head to bee attired in a Coyfe and Crosecloth with an Apron before him." Ordering Hall to post bond for good behavior until formally released from that obligation, the court also told Captain Basse to see that its directives were carried out. Since most court records for subsequent years have been lost (they were burned during the Civil War), it is impossible to trace Hall's story further.

What can this tale reveal about gender definitions and the role of the community in the formative years of American society? Six different but related issues emerge from the analysis of Hall's case.

First, the relationship of sexual characteristics and gender identity. All those who examined T, be they male or female, insisted T was male. Thus T's external sex organs resembled male genitals. Roger Rodes and Francis England, for example, pronounced Thomas "a perfect man" after they had "pulled out his members." Still, T informed Captain Basse "hee had not the use of the mans parte" and told John Atkins that "I have a peece of an hole" (a vulva). Since T was identified as a girl at birth, christened Thomasine, and raised accordingly, T probably fell into that category of human beings who appear female in infancy but at puberty develop what seem to be male genitalia. Such individuals were the subjects of many stories in early modern Europe, the most famous of which involved a French peasant girl, Marie, who suddenly developed male sex organs while chasing pigs when she was fifteen, and who in adulthood became a shepherd named Germain. It is not clear whether early Virginians were aware of such tales, but if they understood contemporary explanations of sexual difference, the narrative of Marie-Germain would not have surprised them. Women were viewed as inferior types of men, and their sexual organs were regarded as internal versions of male genitalia. In the best scientific understanding of the day, there was just one sex, and under certain circumstances women could turn into men.[7]

What, then, in the eyes of Virginia's English residents, constituted sufficient evidence of sexual identity? For the male and female searchers of T's body, genitalia that appeared to be normally masculine provided the answer. But that was not the only possible contemporary response to the question. Leaving aside for the moment the persons who saw T as a combination of male and female (they will be considered later), it is useful to focus on those who at different times indicated that they thought T was female. There were three such individuals, all of them men: Captain Nathaniel Basse, who ordered T to wear women's clothing after T had appeared before him; John Atkins, T's second master, who purchased Thomasine as a maidservant and referred to T as "shee" before bowing to the contrary opinion of the female searchers and changing the pronoun to "him"; and, most important of all, T's first master, John Tyos.

It is not clear from the trial record why Captain Basse directed T to dress as a woman, for T asserted a dual sexual identity in response to questioning and never claimed to be exclusively female. Perhaps the crucial fact was T's admission that "hee had not the use of the mans parte." Another possibility was that Mr. Basse interpreted T's anatomy as insufficiently masculine. As was already indicated, the partial physical description of T included in this portion of the record survives only in fragmentary form and so is impossible to interpret, especially in light of the certainty of all the searchers.

John Atkins acquired T as a servant after Captain Basse had issued his order, and he at first accepted Thomasine as a woman, referring to how "shee" seemed to awaken from sleep. Yet Atkins changed his mind about his servant after he and the five women subjected T's body to the most thorough examination described in the case record. It involved a physical search by the women, then questioning by Atkins, followed by an order from Atkins to Hall to "lye on his backe and shew" the "peece of an hole" that T claimed to have. When the women "did again find him to bee a man," Atkins issued the directive that contradicted Captain Basse's, ordering T to put on men's clothes. For Atkins, Hall's anatomy (which he saw with his own eyes) and the women's testimony were together decisive in overriding his initial belief that T was female, a belief presumably based at least in part on his presence at Mr. Basse's interrogation of T.

Unlike Atkins, John Tyos had purchased T as Thomas—a man. And for him the interpretive process was reversed. After just a brief acquaintance with Thomas, John and his wife learned that he had female skills. Approximately a year later Tyos "swore" to Dorothy Rodes that Hall "was a woman," a conclusion that contradicted the opinion of the female searchers. It also seemingly flew in the face of what must have been his own intimate knowledge of Hall's physical being. The lack of space in the small houses of the seventeenth-century Chesapeake is well known to scholars.[8] It is difficult to imagine that Tyos had never seen Hall's naked body—the same body that convinced searchers of both sexes that T was male. So why would Tyos insist that T was Thomasine, even to Dorothy Rodes, who forcefully asserted the contrary? The answer must lie not in T's sexual organs but in T's gender—that is, in the feminine skills and mannerisms that would have been exhibited by a person born, raised, and living as a female until reaching the age of twenty-two, and which would have

been immediately evident to anyone who, like John Tyos, lived with T for any length of time.

Thus, for these colonists, sex had two possible determinants. One was physical: the nature of one's genitalia. The other was cultural: the character of one's knowledge and one's manner of behaving. The female and male searchers used the former criterion, John Tyos, the latter. John Atkins initially adopted the second approach, but later switched to the first. Nathaniel Basse may have agreed with Tyos, or he may have refused to interpret T's anatomy as unambiguously as did the searchers: it is not clear which. But it is clear that two quite distinct tests of sexual identity existed in tandem in early Virginia. One relied on physical characteristics, the other on learned, gendered behavior. On most occasions, of course, results of the two tests would accord with each other. Persons raised as females would physically appear to be females; persons raised as males would look like other males. Hall acted like a woman and physically resembled a man. Thus in T's case the results of the two independent criteria clashed, and that was the source of the confusion.

Second, the importance of clothing. Many of the key questions about Hall were couched in terms of what clothing T should wear, men's or women's. Captain Basse and John Atkins did not say to T, "you are a man," or "you are a woman," but instead issued instructions about what sort of apparel T was to put on. Likewise, although the General Court declared explicitly that Hall was both male and female, its decision also described the clothing T was to wear in specific detail. Why was clothing so important?

The answer lies in the fact that in the seventeenth century clothing was a crucial identifier of persons. Not only did males and females wear very different garb, but persons of different ranks also were expected to reveal their social status in their dress. In short, one was supposed to display visually one's sex and rank to everyone else in the society. Thus, ideally, new acquaintances would know how to categorize each other even before exchanging a word of greeting. In a fundamental sense, seventeenth-century people's identity was expressed in their apparel. Virginia never went so far as Massachusetts, which passed laws regulating what clothing people of different ranks could wear, but the Virginia colonists were clearly determined to uphold the same sorts of rules.[9]

Clothing, which was sharply distinguished by the sex of its wearer, served as a visual trope for gender. And gender was one of the two most basic determinants of role in the early modern world (the other was rank, which was never at issue in Hall's case—T was always a servant). People who wore skirts nurtured children; people who wore pants did not. People who wore aprons could take no role in governing the colony, whereas other people could, if they were of appropriate status. People who wore headdresses performed certain sorts of jobs in the household; people who wore hats did other types of jobs in the fields. It is hardly surprising, therefore, that Virginians had difficulty dealing with a person who sometimes dressed as a man and other times as a woman—and who, on different occasions, did both at the direction of superiors. Nor, in light of this context, is it surprising that decisions about T's sexual identity were stated in terms of clothing.[10]

Third, the absence of a sense of personal privacy throughout the proceedings. To a modern sensibility, two aspects of the case stand out. First, seventeenth-century Virginians appear to have had few hesitations about their right to examine the genitalia of another colonist, with or without official authorization from a court and regardless of whether that activity occurred forcibly, clandestinely, or openly. The physical examinations were nominally by same-sex individuals (women when T was thought to be female, men when T had been declared to be male), with one key exception: John Atkins joined the women in scrutinizing the body of his maidservant. A master's authority over the household, in other words, extended to the bodies of his dependents. If a master like Atkins chose to search the body of a subordinate of either sex, no barrier would stand in his way.

Second, Hall seems not to have objected to any of the intrusive searches of T's body nor to the intimate questioning to which T was subjected by Captain Basse and the General Court. Hall too appears to have assumed that T's sexual identity was a matter of concern for the community at large. Such an attitude on Hall's part was congruent with a society in which the existing minimal privacy rights were seen as accruing to households as a unit or perhaps to their heads alone. Subordinates like Hall neither expected nor received any right to privacy of any sort.

Fourth, the involvement of the community, especially women, in the process of determining sexual identity. One of the most significant aspects of Hall's story is the initiative taken throughout by Hall's fellow colonists. They not only brought their doubts about Hall's sex to the attention of the authorities, they also refused to accept Captain Basse's determination that Hall was female. Both men and women joined in the effort to convince Virginia's leaders that T was male. Nearly uniformly rejecting T's self-characterization as "both" (the only exception outside the General Court being Mr. Stacy), Virginians insisted that Hall had to be either female or male, with most favoring the latter definition. They wanted a sexual category into which to fit T, and they did not hesitate to express their opinions about which category was the more appropriate.

Women in particular were active in this regard. Three times groups of women scrutinized T's body, whereas a group of men did so only once. After each examination, women rejected T as one of their number. Because of the vigorous and persistent efforts of female Virginians, Hall was deprived of the possibility of adopting unambiguously the role with which T seemed most comfortable, that of Thomasine. Here Hall's physical characteristics determined the outcome. Accustomed to searching the bodies of other females, women thought T did not physically qualify as feminine—regardless of the gendered skills T possessed—and they repeatedly asserted that to any man who would listen. For them, T's anatomy (sex) was more important than T's feminine qualities (gender).

Male opinion, on the other hand, was divided. The three male searchers of T's body—Roger Rodes, Francis England, and John Atkins—agreed with the women's conclusion. Other men were not so sure. John Tyos and Nathaniel Basse thought T more appropriately classified as a woman, while Mr. Stacy and the members of the General Court said T displayed aspects of both sexes. It seems plausible to infer from their lack of agreement about T's sex that men as a group were not entirely certain about what criteria to apply to create the categories "male" and "female." Some relied on physical appearance, others on behavior.

Moreover, the complacency of the male searchers can be interpreted as quite remarkable.

They failed to police the boundaries of their sex with the same militance as did women. That T, if a man, was a very unusual sort of man indeed did not seem to bother Rodes, Atkins, and England. For them, T's physical resemblance to other men was adequate evidence of masculinity, despite their knowledge of T's feminine skills and occasional feminine dress. That opinion was, however, in the end overridden by the doubts of higher-ranking men on the General Court, who were not so willing to overlook T's peculiarities.

Fifth, the relationship among sex, gender, and sexuality. Twice, and in quite different ways, the case record raises issues of sexuality rather than of biological sex or of gendered behavior. Both references have been alluded to briefly: the rumor of Thomas's having committed fornication with "greate Besse," and T's explanation for wearing women's clothing—"to gett a bitt for my Catt."

A judgment about T's body would imply a judgment about T's sexuality as well. Yet was it possible to reach a definitive conclusion about T's sexuality? If T were Thomas, then he could potentially be guilty of fornicating with the maidservant Bess; if T were Thomasine, then being in the same bed with Bess might mean nothing—or it could imply "unnatural" acts, the sort of same-sex coupling universally condemned when it occurred between men. The rumor about Bess, which for an ordinary male servant might have led to a fistfight (with the supposed slanderer, Tyos's servant), a defamation suit, or a fornication presentment, thus raised perplexing questions because of T's ambiguous sexual identity, questions that had to be resolved in court.[11]

T's phrase "to gett a bitt for my Catt," as reported by Francis England, was even more troubling. What did it mean, and was that meaning evident to England and the members of the General Court? As an explanation for wearing female apparel, it could have been straightforward and innocent. One historian reads it literally, as indicating that Hall wore women's clothing to beg scraps for a pet cat. Hall might also have been saying that because T's skills were feminine, dressing as a woman was the best way for T to earn a living, "to get a bit (morsel) to eat." But some scholars have read erotic connotations into the statement. Could T, speaking as a man, have been saying that wearing women's clothing allowed T to get close to women, to—in modern slang—"get a piece of pussy" by masquerading as a female?[12]

There is another more likely and even more intriguing erotic possibility. Since Hall had served in the English army on an expedition to France, T could well have learned a contemporary French slang phrase—"pour avoir une bite pour mon chat"—or, crudely put in English, "to get a penis for my cunt." Translating the key words literally into English equivalents (bite=bit, chat=cat) rather than into their metaphorical meanings produced an answer that was probably as opaque and confusing to seventeenth-century Virginians as it has proved to be to subsequent historians.[13] Since much of Francis England's testimony (with the exception of his report of this statement and the account of his and Roger Rodes's examination of T's anatomy) duplicated John Atkins's deposition, England could have been called as a witness primarily to repeat such a mysterious conversation to the court.

If T was indeed employing a deliberately misleading Anglicized version of contemporary French slang, as appears probable, two conclusions are warranted. First, the response confirms T's predominantly feminine gender, for it describes sexual intercourse from a woman's perspective. In light of the shortage of women in early Virginia, it moreover would have accurately represented T's experience: donning women's garb unquestionably opened sexual possibilities to Thomasine that Thomas lacked. Second, at the same time, Hall was playing with T's listeners, answering the question about wearing women's apparel truthfully, but in such an obscure way that it was unlikely anyone would comprehend T's meaning. In other words, Hall was having a private joke at the expense of the formal and informal publics in the colony. Hall's sly reply thus discloses a mischievous aspect of T's character otherwise hidden by the flat prose of the legal record.

Sixth, the court's decision. At first glance, the most surprising aspect of the case is the General Court's acceptance of Hall's self-definition as both man and woman. By specifying that T's basic apparel should be masculine, but with feminine signs—the apron and the coif and cross-cloth, a headdress commonly worn by women at the time—Virginia officials formally recognized that Hall contained elements of both sexes. The elite men who sat as judges thereby demonstrated their ability to transcend the dichotomous sexual categories that determined the thinking of ordinary Virginians. But their superficially astonishing verdict becomes explicable when the judges' options are analyzed in terms of contemporary understandings of sex and gender.

First, consider T's sexual identity. Could the court have declared Hall to be female? That alternative was effectively foreclosed. Women had repeatedly scrutinized T's anatomy and had consistently concluded that T was male. Their initial determination that T was a man (in the wake of Mr. Stacy's comment that T was both) first brought the question before Captain Basse. Subsequently, their adamant rejection of Captain Basse's contrary opinion and their ability to convince John Atkins that they were correct, coupled with the similar assessment reached by two men, were the key elements forcing the General Court to consider the case. A small community could not tolerate a situation in which groups of men and women alternately stripped and searched the body of one of its residents, or in which the decisions of the local commander were so openly disobeyed. Declaring T to be female was impossible; ordinary Virginians of both sexes would not accept such a verdict.

Yet, at the same time, could anyone assert unconditionally that Hall was sexually a man? Francis England, Roger Rodes, John Atkins, and the five female searchers thought so, on the basis of anatomy; but John Tyos, who was probably better acquainted with T than anyone else, declared unequivocally that Hall was a woman. And T had testified about not having "the use of the mans parte." Hall, in other words, revealed that although T had what appeared to be male genitalia, T did not function sexually as a man and presumably could not have an erection. To Captain Basse and the members of the General Court, that meant that (whatever T's physical description) Hall would not be able to father children or be a proper husband to a wife.

. . . The ability to impregnate a woman was a key indicator of manhood in seventeenth-century Anglo-America. Childless men were the objects of gossip, and impotence served as adequate grounds for divorce. A person who could not father a child was by that criterion alone an unsatisfactory male. T had admitted being incapable of male orgasm. Given that admitted physical incapacity and its implications,

declaring Hall to be a man was as impossible as declaring T to be a woman.[14]

Second, consider T's gender identity. In seventeenth-century Anglo-America, as in all other known societies, sexual characteristics carried with them gendered consequences. In Hall's life history those consequences were especially evident, because what T did and how T did it were deeply affected by whether T chose to be Thomas or Thomasine.

Whenever Hall traveled far from home, to France in the army or to Virginia, T became Thomas. Men had much more freedom of movement than did women. Unlike other persons raised as females, Hall's unusual anatomy gave T the opportunity to live as a male when there was an advantage to doing so. Even though T seemed more comfortable being Thomasine—to judge by frequent reversions to that role—the option of becoming Thomas must have been a welcome one. It permitted Hall to escape the normal strictures that governed early modern English women's lives and allowed T to pursue a more adventurous lifestyle.[15]

Thus whether T chose to be male or female made a great difference in T's life. As Thomas, Hall joined the army and emigrated to the colonies; as Thomasine, Hall lived quietly in London with an aunt, did fancy needlework in Plymouth, and presumably performed tasks normally assigned to women in Virginia. T's most highly developed skills were feminine ones, so T was undoubtedly more expert at and familiar with "women's work" in general, not just seamstressing.

It was, indeed, Hall's feminine skills that convinced some men that T was female; and those qualities, coupled with Hall's physical appearance, must have combined to lead to the court's decision. T's gender was feminine but T's sex seemed to be masculine—with the crucial exception of sexual functioning. Given T's sexual incapacity, all indications pointed to a feminine identity—to Thomasine. But Virginia women's refusal to accept T as Thomasine precluded that verdict. On the other hand, the judges could not declare a person to be male who had admitted to Captain Basse an inability to consummate a marriage. Ordinary men might possibly make a decision on the basis of physical appearance alone, but the members of the General Court had a responsibility to maintain the wider social order. If they said Hall was a man, then Thomas theoretically could marry and become a household head once his term of service was complete. That alternative was simply not acceptable for a person of T's description.

So, considering sex (incompletely masculine) and gender (primarily feminine), the Virginia General Court's solution to the dilemma posed by Hall was to create a unique category that combined sex and gender for T alone. Unable to fit Hall into the standard male/female dichotomy, the judges preferred to develop a singular definition that enshrined T's dual identity by prescribing clothing that simultaneously carried conflicting messages.

The court's decision to make Hall unique in terms of clothing—and thus gender identity—did not assist the community in classifying or dealing with T. After the verdict, Virginians were forced to cope with someone who by official sanction straddled the dichotomous roles of male and female. By court order, Hall was now a dual-sexed person. T's identity had no counterpart or precedent; paradoxically, a society in which gender—the outward manifestation of sex—served as a fundamental dividing line had formally designated a person as belonging to both sexes. Yet at the same time it was precisely because gender was so basic a concern to seventeenth-century society that no other solution was possible.

Hall's life after the court verdict must have been lonely. Marked as T was by unique clothing, unable to adopt the gender switches that had previously given T unparalleled flexibility in choosing a way of life, Hall must have had a very difficult time. T, like other publicly marked deviants—persons branded for theft or adultery or mutilated for perjury or forgery—was perhaps the target of insults or assaults. The verdict in T's case, in its insistence that T be constantly clothed as both sexes rather than alternating between them, was therefore harsh, though it nominally accorded with T's own self-definition. Hall's identity as "both" allowed movement back and forth across gender lines. The court's verdict had quite a different meaning, insisting not on the either/or sexual ambiguity T had employed to such great advantage, but rather on a definition of "both" that required duality and allowed for no flexibility.

It is essential to re-emphasize here what necessitated this unusual ending to a remarkable case: the opinions and actions of the female neighbors of John Tyos and John Atkins. Captain Nathaniel Basse, confronted with basically the same information that the General Court later considered, concluded that Hall should be dressed and treated as a woman. In a sexual belief system that hypothesized that women were inferior men, any inferior man—that is, one who could not function adequately in sexual terms—was a woman. Thus, charged the women at an Accomack cow pen in 1637, John Waltham "hade his Mounthly Courses as Women have" because his wife had not become pregnant.[16] Undoubtedly the General Court's first impulse would have been the same as Captain Basse's: to declare that T, an inferior man, was female and should wear women's clothing. But Virginia women had already demonstrated forcefully that they would not accept such a verdict. Hall's fate therefore was determined as much by a decision reached by ordinary women as it was by a verdict formally rendered by the elite men who served on the General Court.

NOTES

1. Anthropologists have been in the forefront of the investigation of the various relationships of sex and gender. A good introduction to such work is Sherry Ortner and Harriet Whitehead, eds., *Sexual Meanings: The Cultural Construction of Gender and Sexuality* (New York: Cambridge University Press, 1981). . . . For an account of how contemporary American society handles sexually ambiguous babies at birth, see Suzanne J. Kessler, "The Medical Construction of Gender: Case Management of Intersexed Infants," *Signs*, XVI (1990), 3–26.

2. Unless otherwise indicated, all quotations and details in the account that follows are taken from the record in the case, *Va Ct Recs*, 194–95.

3. The expedition in which Thomas took part was an ill-fated English attack on the Isle de Ré during the summer of 1627. The troops who futilely tried to relieve the French Protestants besieged in the city of La Rochelle embarked on July 10, 1627; most of them returned to Plymouth in early November.

4. *Va Ct Recs*, 159, 162–64 (quotation 163). Yet it is possible that the Thomas Hall in this case was the other man, the one who came to Virginia in 1620. For him, see Virginia M. Meyer and John F. Dorman, eds., *Adventurers of Purse and Person Virginia 1607–1624/5*, 3d ed. [Richmond: Order of First Families of Virginia, 1987]. The Virginia muster of 1624/5 (ibid., 42) lists Thomas Hall and John Tyos as residents of George Sandys's plantation in James City. . . .

5. Little can be discovered about the three women. . . .

6. The two newcomers were the wife of Allen Kinaston and the wife of Ambrose Griffen. . . .

7. The best discussion of the one-sex model of humanity and its implications is Thomas Laqueur, *Making Sex: Body and Gender from the Greeks to Freud*

(Cambridge, Mass.: Harvard University Press, 1990). See 126–30 for an analysis of Marie-Germain.

8. See Lois Green Carr et al., *Robert Cole's World: Agriculture and Society in Early Maryland* (Chapel Hill: University of North Carolina Press, 1991), 90–114, on "the standard of life" in the early Chesapeake.

9. See *Mass Col Recs*, IV, pt 1, 60–61, IV, pt 2, 41–42. . . .

10. Laqueur observes, in *Making Sex*, 124–25, that "in the absence of a purportedly stable system of two sexes, strict sumptuary laws of the body attempted to stabilize gender—woman as woman and man as man—and punishments for transgression were quite severe." A relevant recent study is Marjorie Garber, *Vested Interests: Cross-Dressing and Cultural Anxiety* (New York: Routledge, 1991).

11. A good general discussion of the colonists' attitudes toward sexuality is John D'Emilio and Estelle B. Freedman, *Intimate Matters: A History of Sexuality in America* (New York: Harper & Row, 1988), 1–52, especially (on the regulation of deviance) 27–38.

12. Brown interprets the statement literally in her "Gender and the Genesis of Race and Class System," I, 88. The suggestion that the phrase might have meant "earning a living" is mine, developed after consulting the *OED* (s.v. "bit"). Katz speculates that T's phrase had the erotic meaning suggested here, though he recognizes that such an interpretation is problematic (*Gay/Lesbian Almanac*, 72).

13. I owe the identification of the probable French origin of this phrase to Marina Warner and, through her, to Julian Barnes, whom she consulted (personal communication, 1993). My colleague Steven Kaplan, a specialist in the history of early modern France (and scholars he consulted in Paris), confirmed that "bite" and "chat" were used thus in the late sixteenth century and that the interpretation appears plausible.

14. On the importance of marital sexuality in the colonies: D'Emilio and Freedman, *Intimate Matters*, 16–27.

15. See, on this point, Rudolf M. Dekker and Lotte C. van de Pol, *The Tradition of Female Transvestism in Early Modern Europe* (London: Macmillan, 1989).

16. Susie M. Ames, ed., *County Court Records of Accomack-Northampton, Virginia, 1632–1640* (American Legal Records, VII) (Washington, D.C., 1954), p. 85.

LAUREL THATCHER ULRICH
Three Inventories, Three Households

One of the greatest barriers to an accurate assessment of women's role in the community has been the habit of assuming that what women did was not very important. Housekeeping has long been women's work, and housework has long been regarded as trivial. Laurel Thatcher Ulrich shows, however, that housekeeping can be a complex task and that real skill and intelligence might be exercised in performing it. The services housekeepers perform, in early as well as in contemporary America, are an important part of the economic arrangements that sustain the family and need to be taken into account when describing any community or society. Note the differences Ulrich finds between rural and urban women, and between middle-class and impoverished women.

By English tradition, a woman's environment was the family dwelling and the yard or yards surrounding it. Though the exact composition of her setting obviously depended upon the occupation and economic status of her husband, its general outlines were surprisingly similar regardless of where it was located. The difference between an urban "houselot" and a rural "homelot" was not as dramatic as one might suppose.

If we were to draw a line around the housewife's domain, it would extend from the kitchen and its appendages, the cellars, pantries, brewhouses, milkhouses, washhouses,

Excerpted from ch. 1 of *Good Wives: Image and Reality in the Lives of Women in Northern New England, 1650–1750,* by Laurel Thatcher Ulrich (New York: Alfred A. Knopf, 1982). Reprinted by permission of the author and publisher. Notes have been edited and renumbered.

and butteries which appear in various combinations in household inventories, to the exterior of the house, where, even in the city, a mélange of animal and vegetable life flourished among the straw, husks, clutter, and muck. Encircling the pigpen, such a line would surround the garden, the milkyard, the well, the hen-house, and perhaps the orchard itself—though husbands pruned and planted trees and eventually supervised the making of cider, good housewives strung their wash between the trees and in season harvested fruit for pies and conserves.

The line demarking the housewife's realm would not cross the fences which defined outlying fields of Indian corn or barley, nor would it stretch to fishing stages, mills, or wharves, but in berry or mushroom season it would extend into nearby woods or marsh and in spells of dearth or leisure reach to the shore. Of necessity, the boundaries of each woman's world would also extend into the houses of neighbors and into the cartways of a village or town. Housewives commanded a limited domain. But they were neither isolated nor self-sufficient. Even in farming settlements, families found it essential to bargain for needed goods and services. For prosperous and socially prominent women, interdependence took on another meaning as well. Prosperity meant charity, and in early New England charity meant personal responsibility for nearby neighbors. . . .

. . . For most historians, as for almost all antiquarians, the quintessential early American woman has been a churner of cream and a spinner of wool. Because home manufacturing has all but disappeared from modern housekeeping, many scholars have assumed that the key change in female economic life has been a shift from "production" to "consumption," a shift precipitated by the industrial revolution.[1] This is far too simple, obscuring the variety which existed even in the preindustrial world. . . .

. . . Beatrice Plummer, Hannah Grafton, and Magdalen Wear lived and died in New England in the years before 1750. One of them lived on the frontier, another on a farm, and a third in town. Because they were real women, however, and not hypothetical examples, the ways of their households were shaped by personal as well as geographic factors. A careful examination of the contents of their kitchens and chambers suggests the varied complexity as well as the underlying unity in the lives of early American women.

Let us begin with Beatrice Plummer of Newbury, Massachusetts.[2] Forgetting that death brought her neighbors into the house on January 24, 1672, we can use the probate inventory which they prepared to reconstruct the normal pattern of her work.

With a clear estate of £343, Francis Plummer had belonged to the "middling sort" who were the church members and freeholders of the Puritan settlement of Newbury. As an immigrant of 1653, he had listed himself as a "linnen weaver," but he soon became a farmer as well.[3] At his death, his loom and tackling stood in the "shop" with his pitchforks, his hoes, and his tools for smithing and carpentry. Plummer had integrated four smaller plots to form one continuous sixteen-acre farm. An additional twenty acres of salt marsh and meadow provided hay and forage for his small herd of cows and sheep. His farm provided a comfortable living for his family, which at this stage of his life included only his second wife, Beatrice, and her grandchild by a previous marriage. . . .

The house over which Beatrice presided must have looked much like surviving dwellings from seventeenth-century New England, with its "Hall" and "Parlor" on the ground floor and two "chambers" above. A space designated in the inventory only as "another Roome" held the family's collection of pots, kettles, dripping pans, trays, buckets, and earthenware. . . . The upstairs chambers were not bedrooms but storage rooms for foodstuffs and out-of-season equipment. The best bed with its bolster, pillows, blanket, and coverlet stood in the parlor; a second bed occupied one corner of the kitchen, while a cupboard, a "great chest," a table, and a backless bench called a "form" furnished the hall. More food was found in the "cellar" and in the "dairy house," a room which may have stood at the coolest end of the kitchen lean-to.[4]

The Plummer house was devoid of ornament, but its contents bespeak such comforts as conscientious yeomanry and good huswifery afforded. On this winter morning the dairy house held four and a half "flitches" or sides of bacon, a quarter of a barrel of salt pork, twenty-eight pounds of cheese, and four pounds of butter. Upstairs in a chamber were more than twenty-five bushels of "English" grain—barley, oats, wheat, and rye. (The Plummers apparently reserved their Indian corn, stored in another location, for their animals.) When made into malt by a village specialist, barley would become the basis for beer. Two bushels of malt were already stored in the house. The oats might appear in a variety of dishes, from plain breakfast porridge to "flummery," a gelatinous dish flavored with spices and dried fruit.[5] But the wheat and rye were almost certainly reserved for bread and pies. The fine hair sieves stored with the grain in the hall chamber suggest that Beatrice Plummer was particular about her baking, preferring a finer flour than came directly from the miller. A "bushell of pease & beans" found near the grain and a full barrel of cider in the cellar are the only vegetables and fruits listed in the inventory, though small quantities of pickles, preserves, or dried herbs might have escaped notice. Perhaps the Plummers added variety to their diet by trading some of their abundant supply of grain for cabbages, turnips, sugar, molasses, and spices. . . .

Since wives were involved with early-morning milking, breakfast of necessity featured prepared foods or leftovers—toasted bread, cheese, and perhaps meat and turnips kept from the day before, any of this washed down with cider or beer in winter, with milk in summer. Only on special occasions would there be pie or doughnuts. Dinner was the main meal of the day. Here a housewife with culinary aspirations and an ample larder could display her specialties. After harvest Beatrice Plummer might have served roast pork or goose with apples, in spring an eel pie flavored with parsley and winter savory, and in summer a leek soup or gooseberry cream; but for ordinary days the most common menu was boiled meat with whatever "sauce" the season provided—dried peas or beans, parsnips, turnips, onions, cabbage, or garden greens. A heavy pudding stuffed into a cloth bag could steam atop the vegetables and meat. The broth from this boiled dinner might reappear at supper as "pottage" with the addition of minced herbs and some oatmeal or barley for thickening. Supper, like breakfast, was a simple meal. Bread, cheese, and beer were as welcome at the end of a winter day as at the beginning. . . .

Preparing the simplest of these meals required both judgment and skill. . . . The most basic of the housewife's skills was building and regulating fires—a task so fundamental that it must have appeared more as habit than craft. Summer and winter, day and night, she kept a few brands smoldering, ready to stir into flame as needed. The cavernous fireplaces of early New England were but a century removed from the open fires of medieval houses, and they retained some of the characteristics of the latter. Standing inside one of these huge openings today, a person can see the sky above. Seventeenth-century housewives did stand in their fireplaces, which were conceived less as enclosed spaces for a single blaze than as accessible working surfaces upon which a number of small fires might be built. Preparing several dishes simultaneously, a cook could move from one fire to another, turning a spit, checking the state of the embers under a skillet, adjusting the height of a pot hung from the lug-pole by its adjustable trammel. The complexity of firetending, as much as anything else, encouraged the one-pot meal.[6]

The contents of her inventory suggest that Beatrice Plummer was adept not only at roasting, frying, and boiling but also at baking, the most difficult branch of cookery. Judging from the grain in the upstairs chamber, the bread which she baked was "maslin," a common type made from a mixture of wheat and other grains, usually rye. She began with the sieves stored nearby, carefully sifting out the coarser pieces of grain and bran. Soon after supper she could have mixed the "sponge," a thin dough made from warm water, yeast, and flour. Her yeast might have come from the foamy "barm" found on top of fermenting ale or beer, from a piece of dough saved from an earlier baking, or even from the crevices in an unwashed kneading trough. Like fire-building, bread-making was based upon a self-perpetuating chain, an organic sequence which if once interrupted was difficult to begin again. Warmth from the banked fire would raise the sponge by morning, when Beatrice could work in more flour, knead the finished dough, and shape the loaves, leaving them to rise again.

Even in twentieth-century kitchens with standardized yeast and thermostatically controlled temperatures, bread dough is subject to wide variations in consistency and behavior. In a drafty house with an uncertain supply of yeast, bread-making was indeed "an art, craft, and mystery." Not the least of the problem was regulating the fire so that the oven was ready at the same time as the risen loaves. Small cakes or biscuits could be baked in a skillet or directly on the hearth under an upside-down pot covered with coals. But to produce bread in any quantity required an oven. Before 1650 these were frequently constructed in dooryards, but in the last decades of the century they were built into the rear of the kitchen fireplace, as Beatrice Plummer's must have been. Since her oven would have had no flue, she would have left the door open once she kindled a fire inside, allowing the smoke to escape through the fireplace chimney. Moving about her kitchen, she would have kept an eye on this fire, occasionally raking the coals to distribute the heat evenly, testing periodically with her hand to see if the oven had reached the right temperature. When she determined that it had, she would have scraped out the coals and inserted the bread—assuming that it had risen enough by this time or had not risen too much and collapsed waiting for the oven to heat.[7]

Cooking and baking were year-round tasks. Inserted into these day-by-day routines were seasonal specialities which allowed a housewife to bridge the dearth of one period with the bounty of another. In the preservation calendar, dairying came first, beginning with the first calves of early spring. In colonial New England cows were all-purpose creatures, raised for meat as well as for milk. Even in new settlements they could survive by browsing on rough land; their meat was a hedge against famine. But only in areas with abundant meadow (and even there only in certain months) would they produce milk with sufficient butterfat for serious dairying.[8] Newbury was such a place.

We can imagine Beatrice Plummer some morning in early summer processing the milk which would appear as cheese in a January breakfast. Slowly she heated several gallons with rennet dried and saved from the autumn's slaughtering. Within an hour or two the curd had formed. She broke it, drained off the whey, then worked in a little of her own fresh butter. Packing this rich mixture into a mold, she turned it in her wooden press for an hour or more, changing and washing the cheesecloth frequently as the whey dripped out. Repacking it in dry cloth, she left it in the press for another thirty or forty hours before washing it once more with whey, drying it, and placing it in the cellar or dairy house to age. As a young girl she would have learned from her mother or a mistress the importance of thorough pressing and the virtues of cleanliness. . . .

The Plummer inventory gives little evidence of the second stage of preservation in the housewife's year, the season of gardening and gathering which followed quickly upon the dairy months. But there is ample evidence of the autumn slaughtering. Beatrice could well have killed the smaller pigs herself, holding their "hinder parts between her legs," as one observer described the process, "and taking the snout in her left hand" while she stuck the animal through the heart with a long knife. Once the bleeding stopped, she would have submerged the pig in boiling water for a few minutes, then rubbed it with rosin, stripped off the hair, and disemboweled it. Nothing was lost. She reserved the organ meats for immediate use, then cleaned the intestines for later service as sausage casing. Stuffed with meat scraps and herbs and smoked, these "links" were a treasured delicacy. The larger cuts could be roasted at once or preserved in several ways.[9] . . .

Fall was also the season for cider-making. The mildly alcoholic beverage produced by natural fermentation of apple juice was a staple of the New England diet and was practically the only method of preserving the fruit harvest. With the addition of sugar, the alcoholic content could be raised from five to about seven percent, as it usually was in taverns and for export. . . .

Prosaic beer was even more important to the Plummer diet. Although some housewives brewed a winter's supply of strong beer in October, storing it in the cellar, Beatrice seems to have been content with "small beer," a mild beverage usually brewed weekly or bi-weekly and used almost at once. Malting—the process of sprouting and drying barley to increase its sugar content—was wisely left to the village expert. Beatrice started with cracked malt or grist, processing her beer in three stages. "Mashing" required slow steeping at just below the boiling point, a sensitive and smelly process which largely determined the success of the beverage. Experienced brewers knew by taste whether the enzymes were working. If it was too hot, acetic acid developed which would sour the finished product. The next stage, "brewing," was relatively simple. Herbs and hops were boiled with the malted liquid. In the final step this liquor was cooled and mixed with yeast saved from last week's beer or bread. Within twenty-four hours—if all had gone well—the beer was bubbling actively.[10]

... A wife who knew how to manage the ticklish chemical processes which changed milk into cheese, meal into bread, malt into beer, and flesh into bacon was a valuable asset, ... [though some men were too churlish to admit it]. After her husband's death, Beatrice married a man ... who not only refused to provide her with provisions, [but insisted on doing his own cooking]. He took his meat "out of ye pickle" and broiled it directly on the coals, and when she offered him "a cup of my owne Sugar & Bear," he refused it. When the neighbors testified that she had been a dutiful wife, the Quarterly Court fined him for "abusive carriages and speeches." Even the unhappy marriage that thrust Beatrice Plummer into court helps to document the central position of huswifery in her life.[11] ...

Beatrice Plummer represents one type of early American housewife. Hannah Grafton represents another.[12] Chronology, geography, and personal biography created differences between the household inventories of the two women, but there are obvious similarities as well. Like Beatrice Plummer, Hannah Grafton lived in a house with two major rooms on the ground floor and two chambers above. At various locations near the ground-floor rooms were service areas—a washhouse with its own loft or chamber, a shop, a lean-to, and two cellars. The central rooms in the Grafton house were the "parlour," with the expected featherbed, and the "kitchen," which included much of the same collection of utensils and iron pots which appeared in the Plummer house. Standing in the corner of the kitchen were a spade and a hoe, two implements useful only for chipping away ice and snow on the December day on which the inventory was taken, though apparently destined for another purpose come spring. With a garden, a cow, and three pigs, Hannah Grafton clearly had agricultural responsibilities, but these were performed in a strikingly different context than on the Plummer farm. The Grafton homelot was a single acre of land standing just a few feet from shoreline in the urban center of Salem.[13]

Joshua Grafton was a mariner like his father before him. His estate of £236 was modest, but he was still a young man and he had firm connections with the seafaring elite who were transforming the economy of Salem. When he died late in 1699, Hannah had three living children—Hannah, eight; Joshua, six; and Priscilla, who was just ten months.[14] This young family used their space quite differently than had the Plummers. The upstairs chambers which served as storage areas in the Newbury farmhouse were sleeping quarters here. In addition to the bed in the parlor and the cradle in the kitchen, there were two beds in each of the upstairs rooms. One of these, designated as "smaller," may have been used by young Joshua. It would be interesting to know whether the mother carried the two chamber pots kept in the parlor upstairs to the bedrooms at night or whether the children found their way in the dark to their parents' sides as necessity demanded. But adults were probably never far away. Because there are more bedsteads in the Grafton house than members of the immediate family, they may have shared their living quarters with unmarried relatives or servants.

Ten chairs and two stools furnished the kitchen, while no fewer than fifteen chairs, in two separate sets, crowded the parlor with its curtained bed. The presence of a punch bowl on a square table in the parlor reinforces the notion that sociability was an important value in this Salem household. Thirteen ounces of plate, a pair of gold buttons, and a silverheaded cane suggest a measure of luxury as well—all of this in stark contrast to the Plummers, who had only two chairs and a backless bench and no discernible ornamentation at all. Yet the Grafton house was only slightly more specialized than the Newbury farmhouse. It had no servants' quarters, no sharp segregation of public and private spaces, no real separation of sleeping, eating, and work. A cradle in the kitchen and a go-cart kept with the spinning wheels in the upstairs chamber show that little Priscilla was very much a part of this workaday world.

How then might the pattern of Hannah Grafton's work have differed from that of Beatrice Plummer? Certainly cooking remained central. Hannah's menus probably varied only slightly from those prepared in the Plummer kitchen, and her cooking techniques must have been identical. But one dramatic difference is apparent in the two inventories. The Grafton house contained no provisions worth listing on that December day when Isaac Foot and Samuel Willard appeared to take inventory. Hannah had brewing vessels, but no malt; sieves and a meal trough, but no grain; and a cow, but no cheese. What little milk her cow gave in winter probably went directly into the children's mugs.

Perhaps she would continue to breast-feed Priscilla until spring brought a more secure supply. . . . Trade, rather than manufacturing or agriculture, was the dominant motif in her meal preparations.

In colonial New England most food went directly from processer or producer to consumer. Joshua may have purchased grain or flour from the mill near the shipbuilding center called Knocker's Hole, about a mile away from their house. Or Hannah may have eschewed bread-making altogether, walking or sending a servant the half-mile to Elizabeth Haskett's bakery near the North River. Fresh meat for the spits in her washhouse may have come from John Cromwell's slaughterhouse on Main Street near the Congregational meeting-house, and soap for her washtubs from the soap-boiler farther up the street near the Quaker meetinghouse.[15] Salem, like other colonial towns, was laid out helter-skelter, with the residences of the wealthy interspersed with the small houses of carpenters or fishermen. Because there was no center of retail trade, assembling the ingredients of a dinner involved many transactions. Sugar, wine, and spice came by sea; fresh lamb, veal, eggs, butter, gooseberries, and parsnips came by land. Merchants retailed their goods in shops or warehouses near their wharves and houses. Farmers or their wives often hawked their produce door to door.[16] . . .

In such a setting, trading for food might require as much energy and skill as manufacturing or growing it. One key to success was simply knowing where to go. Keeping abreast of the arrival of ships in the harbor or establishing personal contact with just the right farmwife from nearby Salem village required time and attention. Equally important was the ability to evaluate the variety of unstandardized goods offered. An apparently sound cheese might teem with maggots when cut.[17] Since cash was scarce, a third necessity was the establishment of credit, a problem which ultimately devolved upon husbands. But petty haggling over direct exchanges was also a feature of this barter economy.

Hannah Grafton was involved in trade on more than one level. The "shop" attached to her house was not the all-purpose storage shed and workroom it seems to have been for Francis Plummer. It was a retail store, offering door locks, nails, hammers, gimlets, and other hardware as well as English cloth, pins, needles, and thread. As a mariner, Joshua Grafton may well have sailed the ship which brought these goods to Salem. In his absence, Hannah was not only a mother and a housewife but, like many other Salem women, a shopkeeper as well.

There is another highly visible activity in the Grafton inventory which was not immediately apparent in the Plummer's—care of clothing. Presumably, Beatrice Plummer washed occasionally, but she did not have a "washhouse." Hannah did. The arrangement of this unusual room is far from clear. On December 2, 1699, it contained two spits, two "bould-ishes," a gridiron, and "other things." Whether those other things included washtubs, soap, or a beating staff is impossible to determine. . . .

But on any morning in December the washhouse could . . . have been hung with the family wash. Dark woolen jackets and petti-coats went from year to year without seeing a kettle of suds, but linen shifts, aprons, shirts, and handkerchiefs required washing. Laundering might not have been a weekly affair in most colonial households, but it was a well-defined if infrequent necessity even for transient seamen and laborers. One can only speculate on its frequency in a house with a child under a year. When her baby was only a few months old, Hannah may have learned to hold little Priscilla over the chamber pot at frequent intervals, but in early infancy, tightly wrapped in her cradle, the baby could easily have used five dozen "clouts" and almost as many "belly bands" from one washing to another. Even with the use of a "pilch," a thick square of flannel securely bound over the diaper, blankets and coverlets occasionally needed sudsing as well.[18]

Joshua's shirts and Hannah's own aprons and shifts would require careful ironing. Hannah's "smoothing irons" fitted into their own heaters, which she filled with coals from the fire. As the embers waned and the irons cooled, she would have made frequent trips from her table to the hearth to the fire and back to the table again. At least two of these heavy instruments were essential. A dampened apron could dry and wrinkle while a single flatiron replenished its heat.

As frequent a task as washing was sewing. Joshua's coats and breeches went to a tailor, but his shirts were probably made at home. Certainly Hannah stitched and unstitched the tucks which altered Priscilla's simple gowns and petticoats as she grew. The little dresses which the baby trailed in her go-cart had once clothed her brother. Gender identity in childhood was less important in this society than economy of effort. It was not that boys were seen as identical to girls, only that all-purpose garments could be handed from one child to another regardless of sex, and dresses were more easily altered than breeches and more adaptable to diapering and toileting. At eight years of age little Hannah had probably begun to imitate her mother's even stitches, helping with the continual mending, altering, and knitting which kept this growing family clothed.[19]

In some ways the most interesting items in the Grafton inventory are the two spinning wheels kept in the upstairs chamber. Beatrice Plummer's wheel and reel had been key components in an intricate production chain. The Plummers had twenty-five sheep in the fold and a loom in the shed. The Graftons had neither. Children—not sheep—put wheels in Hannah's house. The mechanical nature of spinning made it a perfect occupation for women whose attention was engrossed by young children. This is one reason why the ownership of wheels in both York and Essex counties had a constancy over time unrelated to the ownership of sheep or looms. In the dozen inventories taken in urban Salem about the time of Joshua Grafton's death, the six nonspinners averaged one minor child each, the six spinners had almost four. Instruction at the wheel was part of the almost ritualistic preparation mothers offered their daughters.[20] Spinning was a useful craft, easily picked up, easily put down, and even small quantities of yarn could be knitted into caps, stockings, dishcloths, and mittens.

. . . [A] cluster of objects in the chamber over Hannah Grafton's kitchen suggests a fanciful but by no means improbable vignette. Imagine her gathered with her two daughters in this upstairs room on a New England winter's day. Little Priscilla navigates around the end of the bedstead in her go-cart while her mother sits at one spinning wheel and her sister at the other. Young Hannah is spinning "oakum," the coarsest and least expensive part of the flax. As her mother leans over to help her wind the uneven thread on the bobbin, she catches a troublesome scent from downstairs. Have the turnips caught on the bottom of the pot? Has the maid scorched Joshua's best shirt? Or has a family servant returned from the wharf and spread his wet clothes by the fire? Hastening

down the narrow stairs to the kitchen, Hannah hears the shop bell ring. Just then little Priscilla, left upstairs with her sister, begins to cry. In such pivotal but unrecorded moments much of the history of women lies hidden.

The third inventory can be more quickly described.[21] Elias Wear of York, Maine, left an estate totaling £92, of which less than £7 was in household goods—including some old pewter, a pot, two bedsteads, bedding, one chest, and a box. Wear also owned a saddle, three guns, and a river craft called a gundalow. But his wealth, such as it was, consisted of land (£40) and livestock (£36). It is not just relative poverty which distinguished Elias Wear's inventory from that of Joshua Grafton or Francis Plummer. Every settlement in northern New England had men who owned only a pot, a bed, and a chest. Their children crowded in with them or slept on straw. These men and their sons provided some of the labor which harvested barley for farmers like Francis Plummer or stepped masts for mariners like Joshua Grafton. Their wives and their daughters carded wool or kneaded bread in other women's kitchens. No, Elias Wear was distinguished by a special sort of frontier poverty.

His father had come to northern New England in the 1640s, exploring and trading for furs as far inland in New Hampshire as Lake Winnipesaukee. By 1650 he had settled in York, a then hopeful site for establishing a patrimony. Forty years later he died in the York Massacre, an assault by French and Indians which virtually destroyed the town, bringing death or captivity to fully half of the inhabitants. Almost continuous warfare between 1689 and 1713 created prosperity for the merchant community of Portsmouth and Kittery, but it kept most of the inhabitants of outlying settlements in a state of impecunious insecurity.[22]

In 1696, established on a small homestead in the same neighborhood in which his father had been killed, Elias Wear married a young widow with the fitting name of Magdalen. When their first child was born "too soon," the couple found themselves in York County court owning a presentment for fornication. Although New England courts were still sentencing couples in similar circumstances to "nine stripes a piece upon the Naked back," most of the defendants, like the Wears, managed to pay the not inconsequential fine. The fifty-nine shillings which Elias and Magdalen pledged the court amounted to almost half of the total value of two steers. A presentment for fornication was expensive as well as inconvenient, but it did not carry a permanent onus. Within seven years of their conviction Elias was himself serving on the "Jury of Tryalls" for the county, while Magdalen had proved herself a dutiful and productive wife.[23]

Every other winter she gave birth, producing four sons—Elias, Jeremiah, John, and Joseph—in addition to the untimely Ruth. A sixth child, Mary, was just five months old when her father met his own death by Indians in August of 1707 while traveling between their Cape Neddick home and the more densely settled York village. Without the benefits of a cradle, a go-cart, a spinning wheel, or even a secure supply of grain, Magdalen raised these six children. Unfortunately, there is little in her inventory and nothing in any other record to document the specific strategies which she used, though the general circumstances of her life can be imagined.

Chopping and hauling for a local timber merchant, Elias could have filled Magdalen's porridge pot with grain shipped from the port of Salem or Boston. During the spring corn famine, an almost yearly occurrence on the Maine frontier, she might have gone herself with other wives of her settlement to dig on the clam flats, hedging against the day when relief would come by sea.[24] Like Beatrice Plummer and Hannah Grafton, she would have spent some hours cooking, washing, hoeing cabbages, bargaining with neighbors, and, in season, herding and milking a cow. But poverty, short summers, and rough land also made gathering an essential part of her work. We may imagine her cutting pine splinters for lights and "cattails" and "silkgrass" for beds. Long before her small garden began to produce, she would have searched out a wild "sallet" in the nearby woods, in summer turning to streams and barrens for other delicacies congenial to English taste—eels, salmon, berries, and plums. She would have embarked on such excursions with caution, however, remembering the wives of nearby Exeter who took their children into the woods for strawberries "without any Guard" and narrowly avoided capture.[25] . . .

. . . The Wears probably lived in a single-story cottage which may or may not have been subdivided into more than one room. A loft above provided extra space for storage or sleeping. With the addition of a lean-to, this house could have sheltered animals as well as humans, especially in harsh weather or in periods of Indian alarm. Housing a pig or a calf in the next room would have simplified Magdalen's chores in the winter. If she managed to raise a few chickens, these too would have thrived better near the kitchen fire.[26]

Thus, penury erased the elaborate demarcation of "houses" and "yards" evident in yeoman inventories. It also blurred distinctions between the work of a husbandman and the work of his wife. At planting time and at harvest Magdalen Wear undoubtedly went into the fields to help Elias, taking her babies with her or leaving Ruth to watch them as best she could.[27] A century later an elderly Maine woman bragged that she "had dropped corn many a day with two governors: a judge in her arms and a general on her back."[28] None of the Wear children grew up to such prominence, but all six of them survived to adulthood and four married and founded families of their own. Six children did not prevent Magdalen Wear from remarrying within two years of her husband's death. Whatever her assets—a pleasant face, a strong back, or lifetime possession of £40 in land—she was soon wed to the unmarried son of a neighboring millowner.[29]

Magdalen Wear, Hannah Grafton, and Beatrice Plummer were all "typical" New England housewives of the period 1650–1750. Magdalen's iron pot represents the housekeeping minimum which often characterized frontier life. Hannah's punch bowl and her hardware shop exemplify both the commerce and the self-conscious civilization of coastal towns. Beatrice's brewing tubs and churn epitomize home manufacturing and agrarian self-sufficiency as they existed in established villages. Each type of housekeeping could be found somewhere in northern New England in any decade of the century. Yet these three women should not be placed in rigidly separate categories. Wealth, geography, occupation, and age determined that some women in any decade would be more heavily involved in one aspect of housekeeping than another, yet all three women shared a common vocation. Each understood the rhythms of the seasons, the technology of fire-building, the persistence of the daily demands of cooking, the complexity of home production, and the dexterity demanded from the often conflicting roles of housekeeper, mother, and wife.

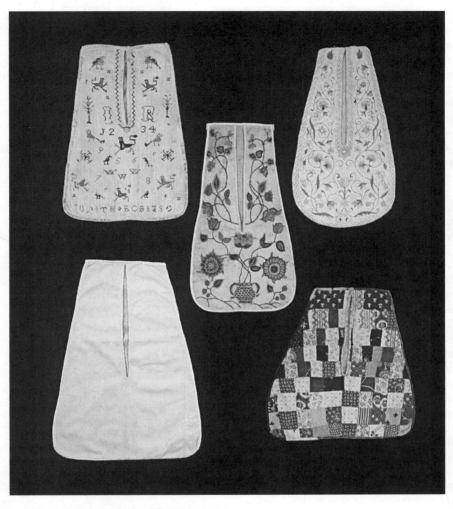

Pockets, sewn and embroidered 1720–1830.
Laurel Thatcher Ulrich suggests that the pocket, not the spinning wheel, is the best icon for colonial European women. Pockets were tied around the waist, and hidden between the skirt and the petticoat. They were handy for carrying small objects on one's daily circuit. Women typically made their own pockets—sometimes in a plain style and sometimes embroidered or pieced. Here are five examples ranging in date from roughly the 1720s to the 1820s. Clockwise from top left: Pocket with lions, made by Judith Robinson, Pennsylvania, 1780–1820; Pocket with flowers and vase, New England, 1720–1750; Floral pocket, Britain, 1737; Pieced pocket, New York, probably Albany, ca. 1810; White pocket, New York, Scotia area, 1780–1820. (Courtesy of the Colonial Williamsburg Foundation.)

The thing which distinguished these women from their counterparts in modern America was not, as some historians have suggested, that their work was essential to survival. "Survival," after all, is a minimal concept. Individual men and women have never needed each other for mere survival but for far more complex reasons, and women were essential in the seventeenth century for the very same reasons they are essential today—for the perpetuation of the race. . . . Nor was it the narrowness of their choices which really set them apart. Women in industrial cities have lived monotonous and confining lives, and they may have worked even harder than early American women. The really striking differences are social.

. . . [T]he lives of early American housewives were distinguished less by the tasks they performed than by forms of social organization which linked economic responsibilities to family responsibilities and which tied each woman's household to the larger world of her village or town.

For centuries the industrious Bathsheba has been pictured sitting at a spinning wheel—"She layeth her hands to the spindle, and her hands hold the distaff." Perhaps it is time to suggest a new icon for women's history. Certainly spinning was an important female craft in northern New England, linked not only to housework but to mothering, but it was one enterprise among many. Spinning wheels are such intriguing and picturesque objects, so resonant with antiquity, that they tend to obscure rather than clarify the nature of female economic life, making home production the essential element in early American huswifery and the era of industrialization the period of crucial change. Challenging the symbolism of the wheel not only undermines the popular stereotype, it questions a prevailing emphasis in women's history.

An alternate symbol might be the pocket. In early America a woman's pocket was not attached to her clothing, but tied around her waist with a string or tape. (When "Lucy Locket lost her pocket, Kitty Fisher found it.") Much better than a spinning wheel, this homely object symbolizes the obscurity, the versatility, and the personal nature of the housekeeping role. A woman sat at a wheel, but she carried her pocket with her from room to room, from house to yard, from yard to street. The items which it contained would shift from day to day and from year to year, but they would of necessity be small, easily lost, yet precious. A pocket could be a mended and patched pouch of plain homespun or a rich personal ornament boldly embroidered in crewel. It reflected the status as well as the skills of its owner. Whether it contained cellar keys or a paper of pins, a packet of seeds or a baby's bib, a hank of yarn, or a Testament, it characterized the social complexity as well as the demanding diversity of women's work.

Notes

1. [See] William H. Chafe, *Women and Equality: Changing Patterns in American Culture* (New York: Oxford University Press, 1977), p. 17; . . . and Nancy F. Cott, *The Bonds of Womanhood* (New Haven and London: Yale University Press, 1977), p. 21.

2. Unless otherwise noted, the information which follows comes from the Francis Plummer will

and inventory, *The Probate Records of Essex County* (hereafter *EPR*) (Salem, Mass.: Essex Institute, 1916–1920), II: 319–22.

3. Joshua Coffin, *A Sketch of the History of Newbury, Newburyport, and West Newbury* (Boston, 1845; Hampton, N.H.: Peter E. Randall, 1977), p. 315.

4. Abbott Lowell Cummings, *The Framed Houses of Massachusetts Bay, 1625–1725* (Cambridge, Mass., and London: Harvard University Press, 1979), pp. 29–32.

5. Darrett B. Rutman, *Husbandmen of Plymouth* (Boston: Beacon Press, 1967), pp. 10–11. . . . *Records and Files of the Quarterly Courts of Essex County, Massachusetts* (hereafter *ECR*) (Salem, Mass.: Essex Institute, 1911–1975), III:50; . . . Massachusetts Historical Society (hereafter MHS) *Collections*, 5th Ser., I:97; and Jay Allen Anderson, "A Solid Sufficiency: An Ethnography of Yeoman Foodways in Stuart England" (Ph.D. diss., University of Pennsylvania, 1971), pp. 171, 203–04, 265, 267, 268.

6. Cummings, *Framed Houses*, pp. 4, 120–22; . . . Jane Carson, *Colonial Virginia Cookery* (Charlottesville: University Press of Virginia, 1968), p. 104. . . .

7. Carson, *Colonial Virginia Cookery*, pp. 104–06.

8. Anderson, "Solid Sufficiency," pp. 63, 65, 118; . . . New Hampshire Historical Society Collections, V (1837), p. 225.

9. Anderson, "Solid Sufficiency," pp. 99–108, 120–32.

10. Sanborn C. Brown, *Wines and Beers of Old New England* (Hanover, N.H.: University Press of New England, 1978). . . .

11. *ECR*, IV:194–95, 297–98.

12. Unless otherwise noted, the information which follows comes from the Joshua Grafton will and inventory, Manuscript Probate Records, Essex County Probate Court, Salem, Mass. (hereafter Essex Probate), vol. CCCVII, pp. 58–59.

13. "Part of Salem in 1700," pocket map in James Duncan Phillips, *Salem in the Seventeenth Century* (Boston: Houghton Mifflin, 1933), H-6.

14. Sidney Perley, *The History of Salem, Massachusetts* (Salem, 1924), I:435, 441.

15. Phillips, *Salem in the Seventeenth Century*, pp. 314, 317, 318, 328; and James Duncan Phillips, *Salem in the Eighteenth Century* (Boston: Houghton Mifflin, 1937), pp. 20–21.

16. [See] Karen Friedman, "Victualling Colonial Boston," *Agricultural History* XLVII (July 1973): 189–205, and . . . Benjamin Coleman, *Some Reasons and Arguments Offered to the Good People of Boston and Adjacent Places, for the Setting Up Markets in Boston* (Boston, 1719), pp. 5–9.

17. . . . *The Salem Witchcraft Papers*, ed. Paul Boyer and Stephen Nissenbaum (New York: Da Capo Press, 1977), I:117–29.

18. [See] . . . e.g., *Province and Court Records of Maine* (hereafter *MPCR*) (Portland: Maine Historical Society, 1928–1975), IV:205–06; . . . and Essex Probate, CCCXXI:96. . . .

19. Susan Burrows Swan, *Plain and Fancy: American Women and Their Needlework, 1700–1850* (New York: Holt, Rinehart and Winston, 1977), pp. 18–19, 34–38.

20. "Letter-Book of Samuel Sewall," MHS *Collections*, 6th Ser., I:19. . . .

21. Unless otherwise noted, the information which follows comes from the Elias Wear will and inventory, Manuscript Probate Records, York County Probate Court, Alfred, Me., . . . II:26.

22. Charles Clark, *The Eastern Frontier* (New York: Alfred A. Knopf, 1970), pp. 67–72.

23. *MPCR*, IV:91–92, 175, 176, 206, 263, 307, 310.

24. Maine Historical Society *Collections*, IX: 58–59, 457, 566; MHS *Collections*, 6th Ser., I:126–65, 182–84, 186–89. . . .

25. Cotton Mather, *Decennium Luctuosum* (Boston, 1699), reprint Charles H. Lincoln, ed., *Narratives of the Indian Wars* (New York: Charles Scribner's Sons, 1913), pp. 266–67.

26. Richard M. Candee, "Wooden Buildings in Early Maine and New Hampshire: A Technological and Cultural History, 1600–1720" (Ph.D. diss., University of Pennsylvania, 1976), pp. 18, 42–48. . . .

27. . . . MHS *Proceedings* (1876), p. 129. Also see *ECR*, II: 372–73, 22, 442. . . .

28. Sarah Orne Jewett, *The Old Town of Berwick* (Berwick, Me.: Old Berwick Historical Society, 1967), n.p. . . .

29. Sybil Noyes, Charles Thornton Libby, and Walter Goodwin Davis, *A Genealogical Dictionary of Maine and New Hampshire* (Portland, Me.: Southworth-Anthoensen Press, 1928), pp. 726, 729.

CAROL F. KARLSEN

The Devil in the Shape of a Woman: The Economic Basis of Witchcraft

Puritan ministers stressed the equality of each soul in the eyes of God and the responsibility of each believer to read the Bible. They urged women as well as men toward literacy and taking responsibility for their own salvation. One distinguished minister, Cotton Mather, writing at the end of the seventeenth century, observed that since women came close to the experience of death in repeated childbirth, their religiosity was likely to be greater than that of men. In being "helpmeets" to their husbands, women were encouraged to strengthen their ability to be competent and capable. There was much in Puritan thought that could be appealing to women.

But, as we have seen in the case of Anne Hutchinson, the Puritan community was unforgiving to women who failed to serve the needs of godly men in their strictly hierarchical community. Lurking in their imagination—as it lurked throughout the Judeo-Christian tradition—was the cautionary biblical story of Eve, who, by her disobedience, brought evil into the world. (Puritans paid no attention to other elements of that complicated tale: Eve's disobedience, after all, was in quest of Knowledge; the biology of birth is reversed, with Eve emerging from Adam's body.) Witchcraft prosecutions were rare in English colonies outside of New England; there, they occurred individually or in small clusters, numbering under 100 until the famous outbreak in and near Salem, Massachusetts, in 1692, during which nearly 200 people, three-quarters of whom were women, were accused, and 13 women and 6 men were executed. Carol F. Karlsen argues that in early colonial New England culture, an older view of women as a necessary evil had been only superficially superseded by a new, Protestant view of women as a necessary good. Note that fear of women-as-witches was endemic at this time in Europe, where between 1450 and 1750 roughly 90,000 trials occurred, including 3,000 in the British Isles.

Excerpted from "The Economic Basis of Witchcraft," ch. 3 of *The Devil in the Shape of a Woman: Witchcraft in Colonial New England* by Carol F. Karlsen (New York: W. W. Norton, 1987). Reprinted by permission of the author and publisher. Notes have been edited and renumbered and tables renumbered.

In her essay, Karlsen provides in-depth, biographical profiles of several women who faced accusations both prior to and during the Salem witch-hunt. This research technique led her to make a startling and truly innovative discovery involving the category of "inheriting women." Her findings help to answer a frequently asked question: even though everyone in the society believed that witches existed and supernatural forces were operating in their lives, why did neighbors and aquaintances launch accusations against particular persons?

Anthropologists have long understood that communities define as witches people whose behavior enacts the things the community most fears; witchcraft beliefs, wrote Monica Hunter Wilson, are "the standardized nightmare of a group, and . . . the comparative analysis of such nightmares . . . [is] one of the keys to the understanding of society."* Have witch-hunts (using the word metaphorically) occurred in your lifetime or the lifetimes of your parents or grandparents?

Most observers now agree that witches in the villages and towns of late sixteenth- and early seventeeth-century England tended to be poor. They were not usually the poorest women in their communities, one historian has argued; they were the "moderately poor." Rarely were relief recipients suspect; rather it was those just above them on the economic ladder, "like the woman who felt she ought to get poor relief, but was denied it."[1] This example brings to mind New England's Eunice Cole, who once berated Hampton selectmen for refusing her aid when, she insisted, a man no worse off than she was receiving it.[2]

Eunice Cole's experience also suggests the difficulty in evaluating the class position of the accused. Commonly used class indicators such as the amount of property owned, yearly income, occupation, and political offices held are almost useless in analyzing the positions of women during the colonial period. While early New England women surely shared in the material benefits and social status of their fathers, husbands, and even sons, most were economically dependent on the male members of their families throughout their lives. Only a small proportion of these women owned property outright, and even though they participated actively in the productive work of their communities, their labor did not translate into financial independence or economic power. Any income generated by married women belonged by law to their husbands, and because occupations open to women were few and wages meager, women alone could only rarely support themselves. Their material condition, moreover, could easily change with an alteration in their marital status. William Cole, with an estate at his death of £41 after debts, might be counted among the "moderately poor," as might Eunice Cole when he was alive. But the refusal of the authorities to recognize the earlier transfer of this estate from husband to wife ensured, among other things, that as a widow Eunice Cole was among the poorest of New England's poor. . . .

Despite conceptual problems and sparse evidence, it is clear that poor women, both the destitute and those with access to some resources, were surely represented, and very probably overrepresented, among the New England accused. Perhaps 20 percent of accused women . . . were either impoverished or living at a level of bare subsistence when they were accused.[3] Some, like thirty-seven-year-old Abigail Somes, worked as servants a substantial portion of their adult lives. Some supported themselves and their families with various kinds of temporary labor such as nursing infants, caring for sick neighbors, taking in washing and sewing, or harvesting crops. A few, most notably Tituba, the first person accused during the Salem outbreak, were slaves. Others, like the once-prosperous Sarah Good of Wenham and Salem, and the never-very-well-off Ruth Wilford of Haverhill, found themselves reduced to abject poverty by the death of a parent or a change in their own marital status.[4] Accused witches came before local magistrates requesting permission to sell family land in order to support themselves, to submit claims against their children or executors of their former husbands' estates for nonpayment of the widow's lawful share of the estate, or simply to ask for food and fuel from

---

* Quoted in Carol F. Karlsen, *The Devil in the Shape of a Woman* (New York: W. W. Norton, 1987), p. 181.

the town selectmen. Because they could not pay the costs of their trials or jail terms, several were forced to remain in prison after courts acquitted them. The familiar stereotype of the witch as an indigent woman who resorted to begging for her survival is hardly an inaccurate picture of some of New England's accused.

Still, the poor account for only a minority of the women accused. Even without precise economic indicators, it is clear that women from all levels of society were vulnerable to accusation. . . . Wives, daughters, and widows of "middling" farmers, artisans, and mariners were regularly accused, and (although much less often) so too were women belonging to the gentry class. The accused were addressed as Goodwife (or Goody) and as the more honorific Mrs. or Mistress, as well as by their first names.

Prosecution was a different matter. Unless they were single or widowed, accused women from wealthy families—families with estates valued at more than £500—could be fairly confident that the accusations would be ignored by the authorities or deflected by their husbands through suits for slander against their accusers. Even during the Salem outbreak, when several women married to wealthy men were arrested, most managed to escape to the safety of other colonies through their husbands' influence. Married women from moderately well-off families— families with estates valued at between roughly £200 and £500—did not always escape prosecution so easily, but neither do they seem, as a group, to have been as vulnerable as their less prosperous counterparts. When only married women are considered, women in families with estates worth less than £200 seem significantly overrepresented among convicted witches—a pattern which suggests that economic position was a more important factor to judges and juries than to the community as a whole in its role as accuser.[5]

Without a husband to act on behalf of the accused, wealth alone rarely provided women with protection against prosecution. Boston's Ann Hibbens, New Haven's Elizabeth Godman, and Wethersfield's Katherine Harrison, all women alone, were tried as witches despite sizable estates. In contrast, the accusations against women like Hannah Griswold of Saybrook, Connecticut, Elizabeth Blackleach of Hartford, and Margaret Gifford of Salem, all wives of prosperous men when they were accused, were simply not taken seriously by the courts.[6] . . .

Economic considerations, then, do appear to have been at work in the New England witchcraft cases. But the issue was not simply the relative poverty—or wealth—of accused witches or their families. It was the special position of most accused witches vis-à-vis their society's rules for transferring wealth from one generation to another. To explain why their position was so unusual, we must turn first to New England's system of inheritance.

Inheritance is normally thought of as the transmission of property at death, but in New England, as in other agricultural societies, adult children received part of their father's accumulated estates prior to his death, usually at the time they married.[7] Thus the inheritance system included both pre-mortem endowments and post-mortem distributions. While no laws compelled fathers to settle part of their estates on their children as marriage portions, it was customary to do so. Marriages were, among other things, economic arrangements, and young people could not benefit from these arrangements unless their fathers provided them with the means to set up households and earn their livelihoods. Sons' portions tended to be land, whereas daughters commonly received movable goods and/or money. The exact value of these endowments varied to a father's wealth and inclination, but it appears that as a general rule the father of the young woman settled on the couple roughly half as much as the father of the young man.[8]

Custom, not law, also guided the distribution of a man's property at his death, but with two important exceptions. First, a man's widow, if he left one, was legally entitled "by way of dower" to one-third part of his real property, "to have and injoy for term of her natural life." She was expected to support herself with the profits of this property, but since she held only a life interest in it, she had to see that she did not "strip or waste" it.[9] None of the immovable estate could be sold, unless necessary for her or her children's maintenance, and then only with the permission of the court. A man might will his wife more than a third of his real property—but not less. Only if the woman came before the court to renounce her dower right publicly, and then only if the court approved, could this principle be waived. In the form of her "thirds," dower was meant to provide for a woman's support in widowhood. The inviolability of dower protected the widow from the claims of her children against the estate and protected the community from the potential burden of her care.

The second way in which law determined inheritance patterns had to do specifically with intestate cases.[10] If a man died without leaving a will, several principles governed the division of his property. The widow's thirds, of course, were to be laid out first. Unless "just cause" could be shown for some other distribution, the other two-thirds were to be divided among the surviving children, both male and female.[11] A double portion was to go to the eldest son, and single portions to his sisters and younger brothers. If there were no sons, the law stipulated that the estate was to be shared equally by the daughters. In cases where any or all of the children had not yet come of age, their portions were to be held by their mother or by a court-appointed guardian until they reached their majorities[12] or married. What remained of the widow's thirds at her death was to be divided among the surviving children, in the same proportions as the other two-thirds.

Although bound to conform to laws concerning the widow's thirds, men who wrote wills were not legally required to follow the principles of inheritance laid out in intestate cases. Individual men had the right to decide for themselves who would ultimately inherit their property. . . . [T]he majority seem to have adhered closely (though not always precisely) to the custom of leaving a double portion to the eldest son. Beyond that, New England men seem generally to have agreed to a system of partible inheritance, with both sons and daughters inheriting.

When these rules were followed, property ownership and control generally devolved upon men. Neither the widow's dower nor, for the most part, the daughter's right to inherit signified more than access to property. For widows, the law was clear that dower allowed for "use" only. For inheriting daughters who were married, the separate but inheritance-related principle of coverture applied. Under English common law, "feme covert" stipulated that married women had no right to own property—indeed, upon marriage, "the very being or legal existence of the woman is suspended."[13] Personal property which a married daughter inherited from her father, either as dowry or as a post-mortem bequest, immediately became the legal possession of her husband, who could exert full powers of ownership over it. A married daughter who inherited land from her father retained title to the land, which her husband could not sell without her consent. On her husband's death such land became the property of her children, but during his life her husband was entitled to the use and profits of it, and his wife could not devise it to her children by will.[14] The property of an inheriting daughter who was single seems to have been held "for improvement" for her until she was married, when it became her dowry.[15]

This is not to say that women did not benefit when they inherited property. A sizable inheritance could provide a woman with a materially better life; if single or widowed, inheriting women enjoyed better chances for an economically advantageous marriage or remarriage. But inheritance did not normally bring women the independent economic power it brought men.

The rules of inheritance were not always followed, however. In some cases, individual men decided not to conform to customary practices; instead, they employed one of several legal devices to give much larger shares of their estates to their wives or daughters, many times for disposal at their own discretion. Occasionally, the magistrates themselves allowed the estate to be distributed in some other fashion. Or, most commonly, the absence of male heirs in families made conformity impossible. In all three exceptions to inheritance customs, but most particularly the last, the women who stood to benefit economically also assumed a position of unusual vulnerability. They, and in many instances their daughters, became prime targets for witchcraft accusations.

Consider first the experience of witches who came from families without male heirs. . . . [T]hese histories begin to illuminate the subtle and often intricate manner in which anxieties about inheritance lay at the heart of most witchcraft accusations.

KATHERINE HARRISON

Katherine Harrison first appears in the Connecticut colonial records in the early 1650s, as the wife of John Harrison, a wealthy Wethersfield landowner.[16] Her age is unknown[17] and her family background is obscure. We know that she called John, Jonathan, and Josiah Gilbert, three prominent Connecticut Valley settlers, her cousins, but her actual relationship to them is ambiguous.[18] . . . She may have been the daughter or niece of Lydia Gilbert, who was executed as a witch in Hartford in 1654, but we can be reasonably certain only that the two women were members of the same Connecticut family.[19] . . .

It has been said that Katherine Harrison was first tried as a witch in October 1668.[20] If so, then she must have been acquitted, because she was indicted in the Court of Assistants in Hartford on 25 May 1669, on the same charge.[21] The jury was unable to agree upon a verdict, however, and the court adjourned to the next session. Meantime, Harrison was supposed to remain in jail, but for some reason she was released in the summer or early fall, and she returned home to Wethersfield. Shortly thereafter, thirty-eight Wethersfield townsmen filed a petition, complaining that "shee was suffered to be at libertie," since she "was lately prooved to be Deaply guiltie of suspicion of Wichcrafte" and that "the Juerie (the greater part of them) judged or beleaved that she was guilty of such high crimes" and "ought to be put to death." Among the petition's signers were several of the town's most prominent citizens, including John Blackleach, Sr., who had "taken much paines in the prosecution of this cause from the beginninge," and John Chester, who was then involved in a legal controversy with Harrison concerning a parcel of land.[22] When the Court of Assistants met again in October, all of the jury members found her guilty of witchcraft.[23]

The Hartford magistrates, however, were reluctant to accept the verdict. Perhaps remembering how accusations had gotten out of hand during the Hartford outbreak seven years before, they put Harrison back in prison and appealed to local ministers for advice on the use of evidence. The response was ambiguous enough to forestall execution.[24] At a special session of the Court of Assistants the following May, the magistrates reconsidered the verdict, determined that they were not able to concur with the jury "so as to sentance her to death or to a longer continuance in restraynt," and ordered Harrison to pay her fees and leave the colony for good.[25]

If witnesses testifying against her in her 1669 trial can be believed, Katherine Harrison's neighbors had suspected that she was a witch sixteen or eighteen years earlier. Elizabeth Simon deposed that as a single woman, Harrison was noted to be "a great or notorious liar, a Sabbath breaker and one that told fortunes"—and that her predictions frequently came to pass. Simon was also suspicious of Harrison for another reason: because she "did often spin so great a quantity of fine linen yarn as the said Elizabeth did never know nor hear of any other woman that could spin so much."[26] Other witnesses testified to the more recent damage she did to individuals and their property. Harrison was also a healer, and although many of her neighbors called upon her skills, over the years some of them came to suspect her of killing as well as curing.[27] Or so they said in 1668–69; she was not formally accused of any witchcraft crimes until after her husband's death.

John Harrison had died in 1666, leaving his wife one of the wealthiest, if not *the* wealthiest woman in Wethersfield. In his will he bequeathed his entire estate of £929 to his wife and three daughters. Rebecca, age twelve, was to have £60, and his two younger daughters, eleven-year-old Mary and nine-year-old Sarah, were to have £40 each. The remaining £789 was to go to his widow.[28] Unlike many widows in colonial New England, Katherine Harrison chose not to remarry. Instead she lived alone, managing her extensive holdings herself, with the advice and assistance of her Hartford kinsman, Jonathan Gilbert.

In October 1668, not long after her adversaries began gathering their witchcraft evidence against her, Harrison submitted a lengthy petition to "the Fathers of the Comonweale" asking for relief for the extensive vandalism of her estate since her husband's death. Among other damage, she spoke of oxen beaten and bruised to the point of being "altogether unserviceable"; of a hole bored into the side of her cow; of a three-year-old heifer slashed to death; and of the back of a two-year-old steer broken. Her corn crop was destroyed, she said, "damnified with horses, they being staked upon it," and "30 poles of hops cutt and spoyled." Twelve of her relatives and neighbors, she said, including Jonathan and Josiah Gilbert, could testify to the damage done. The response of the court went unrecorded, but there is no indication that provision was made for the "due recompense" Harrison requested or that her grievances were even investigated.[29]

The Court of Assistants also seems to have been unsympathetic to another petition Harrison submitted in the fall of 1668, in which she complained that the actions of the magistrates themselves were depleting her estate.[30] Indeed, the local court had recently fined her £40 for slandering her neighbors, Michael and Ann Griswold—a fine greatly in excess of the normal punishment in such cases.[31] The exact circumstances of the incident are unknown, but the Griswolds were among Harrison's witchcraft accusers, and she apparently considered Michael Griswold central in the recruiting of additional witnesses against her, for she said that "the sayd Michael Griswold would Hang her though he damned a thousand soules," adding that "as for his own soule it was damned long agoe." Griswold, a member of Wethersfield's elite, but not as wealthy as Harrison, sued her for these slanderous remarks and for calling his wife Ann "a savadge whore."[32] Besides levying the fine, the court ordered Harrison to confess her sins publicly.[33] She made the required confession, but she appealed the exorbitant fine.

Harrison's petition, which she filed within the month, was a peculiar mixture of justification for her actions, concession to the magistrates' insistence on deference in women, determination in her convictions, and desperation in her attempt to salvage her estate. Acknowledging herself to be "a female, a weaker vessell, subject to passion," she pleaded as the source of her frustration and anger the vicious abuse to which she had been subjected since her husband's death. She admitted her "corruption," but pointed out that it was well known that she had made "a full and free confession of [her] fault" and had offered "to repaire the wound that [she] had given to [the Griswolds'] names by a plaster as broad as the sore, at any time and in any place where it should content them." At the same time, she indicated Michael Griswold for being less interested in the reparation of his name than in her estate and did not hesitate to call the fine oppressive, citing the laws of God and the laws of the commonwealth as providing "that noe mans estate shal be deminished or taken away by any colony or pretence of Authority" in such an arbitrary manner. In her final statements, however, she returned to a more conciliatory stance: "I speake not to excuse my fault," she said, "but to save my estate as far as Righteousness will permit for a distressed Widow and Orphanes."[34]

Fear of losing her estate is a recurring theme in the records of Harrison's life during this period. Almost immediately after her husband's death in 1666, she petitioned the court to change the terms of her husband's will. Arguing that the bequests to the children were "inconsiderate" (by which she probably meant inconsiderable), she asked that the magistrates settle on her eldest daughter £210, and £200 on each of her younger daughters, reserving the house and lot for herself during her lifetime.[35] Since her husband had left her full ownership of most of his estate, she could simply have given her daughters larger portions, but she must have felt that the court's sanction rendered the inheritances less vulnerable. Several months later, she appealed directly to Connecticut's governor, John Winthrop, Jr., requesting that Hartford's John and Jonathan Gilbert, and John Riley of Wethersfield, be appointed overseers of her estate.[36] Winthrop must not have granted her request, because in 1668 Harrison signed over the rest of the estate she had inherited from her husband to her daughters and appointed Jonathan and John Gilbert her daughters' guardians.[37] By the following year, her neighbors reported, she had "disposed of great part of her estate to others in trust."[38]

In June 1670, Katherine Harrison moved to Westchester, New York, to begin her life anew. Her reputation for witchcraft followed her, however, in the form of a complaint, filed in July by two of her new neighbors, that she had been allowed to resettle in Westchester. Noting that suspicion of her in Connecticut "hath given some cause of apprehension" to the townspeople, in order to "end their jealousyes and feares" a local New York magistrate told her to leave the jurisdiction.[39] Harrison refused. Before any action could be taken against her, her eldest daughter was fortuitously betrothed to Josiah Hunt, a son of Thomas Hunt, one of the men who had protested her presence in Westchester. The elder Hunt became a supporter and appeared in court on her behalf, with his son and three other influential men. Though she was required to give security for her "Civill carriage and good behaviour," the General Court of Assizes in New York ordered "that in regard there is nothing appears against her deserving the continuance of that obligacion shee is to bee releast from it, and hath Liberty to remaine in the Towne of Westchester where shee now resides, or any where else in the Government during her pleasure."[40]

Evidently Harrison continued to live with recurring witchcraft suspicion, but after 1670 there is no further evidence of official harassment.[41] Early in 1672, she reappeared in Hartford to sue eleven of her old Connecticut Valley neighbors, in most cases for debt, and to release her "intrusted overseer" Jonathan Gilbert from his responsibilities for her estate (although he continued to act as guardian to her two younger daughters).[42] A month later, she signed at least some of her remaining Wethersfield land over to Gilbert.[43] After that, she fades from view. She may have returned to Connecticut for good at that time, for some evidence suggests that she died at Dividend, then an outlying section of Wethersfield, in October 1682.[44]

SUSANNA MARTIN

Born in England in 1625, Susanna North was the youngest of three daughters of Richard North. Her mother died when Susanna was young and her father subsequently remarried. The family migrated to New England in or just prior to 1639, the year in which Richard North was listed as one of the first proprietors of Salisbury, Massachusetts. Susanna's sister Mary had married Thomas Jones and was living in Gloucester by 1642. Of her sister Sarah we know only that she married a man named Oldham, had a daughter named Ann, and died before the child was grown. In August 1646, at the age of twenty-one, Susanna married George Martin, a Salisbury man whose first wife had recently died. In June of the following year, she gave birth to her son Richard, the first of nine children. One of these children, a son, died in infancy.[45] . . .

Early in 1668, less than a year after the birth of her last child, Susanna Martin's father died, leaving a modest estate of about £150. As the only surviving children, the then forty-three-year-old Susanna and her sister Mary anticipated receiving a major portion of the property, to posses either immediately or after the death of their stepmother, Ursula North. They were disappointed. According to the will probated shortly after he died, Richard North had voided all previous wills and written a new one—*nearly two decades* before his death. In this document, dated January 1649, he left all but £22 of his estate directly to his wife. Twenty-one pounds was to be divided among Mary Jones, Susanna Martin, and Ann Bates (Sarah Oldham's daughter). Susanna's share was 20 shillings and the cancellation of a £10 debt George Martin owed his father-in-law. Listed as witnesses to this will were Thomas Bradbury of Salisbury and Mary Jones's daughter, Mary Winsley.[46] But the will raised problems. In 1649, Ann Bates was still Ann Oldham (she did not marry Francis Bates until 1661) and the Mary Winsley listed as witness to the will was still Mary Jones, at most eleven or twelve years old

when it was allegedly written.[47] Despite the obvious irregularities, Thomas Bradbury and Mary Winsley attested in court that this was indeed Richard North's last will and testament.

Whether Susanna Martin and her sister saw or protested this will when it was probated cannot be determined. Susanna, at least, may have had more pressing concerns on her mind. In April 1669, a bond of £100 was posted for her appearance at the next Court of Assistants "upon suspicion of witchcraft." That was the same day that George Martin sued William Sargent for slandering his wife. According to George Martin, Sargent had not only said that Susanna "was a witch, and he would call her witch," but also accused her of having "had a child" while still single and of "wringing its neck" shortly after. George Martin also sued William Sargent's brother Thomas for saying "that his son George Marttin was a bastard and that Richard Marttin was Goodwife Marttin's imp."[48] . . .

Meanwhile, the magistrates bound Susanna Martin over to the higher court to be tried for witchcraft. Although the records have not survived, she must have been acquitted, because several months later she was at liberty. In October 1669, George Martin was again bound for his wife's appearance in court, not for witchcraft this time but for calling one of her neighbors a liar and a thief.[49]

By April 1671, George and Susanna Martin (Susanna's sister Mary Jones would later join them) were involved in what would become protracted litigation over the estate of Susanna's father. Ursula North had died a month or two before, leaving a will, dated shortly after her husband's death, that effectively disinherited her two stepdaughters by awarding them 40 shillings apiece. She left the rest of the original North estate first to her granddaughter, Mary Winsley, and secondarily to Mary and Nathaniel Winsley's only child, Hepzibah.[50]

The exact sequence of the numerous court hearings that followed is less clear. Evidently, Susanna and George Martin initiated legal proceedings against Mary and Nathaniel Winsley in April 1671, for unwarranted possession of the North estate. . . . In October 1672, the General Court responded, giving Susanna Martin liberty to sue for her inheritance a second time at the local level.

In April 1673, the recently widowed Mary Jones and George Martin, acting for his wife, sued Nathaniel Winsley "for withholding the inheritance of housing, lands and other estate ... under color of a feigned or confused writing like the handwriting of Mr. Thomas Bradbury and seemingly attested by him, and Mary Winsly." The court declared the case nonsuited, and again Susanna Martin appealed to the General Court, requesting that the case be reheard at the local level. The General Court consented in May 1673, and the following October, Susanna and George Martin instituted proceedings against the Winsleys for the third time. Again the county court decided for the defendants, and the Martins appealed to the Court of Assistants. For a while it looked as though things were finally going their way. The higher court, which "found for the plaintiff there being no legall prooffe of Richard North's will," ordered that "the estate the said North left be left to the disposall of the county court." ...

[In 1674] Susanna, George, and Mary appealed a final time to the General Court, this time for "a hearing of the whole case" by the highest court itself. The magistrates agreed to hear the case, remitting the usual court fees, as they had done before, on the basis of Susanna's pleas of poverty. But in October 1674, after "perusall of what hath binn heard and alleadged by both parties," the court found for Nathaniel Winsley.[51] In what Susanna Martin and Mary Jones believed was a flagrant miscarriage of justice, they had lost what they considered their rightful inheritances.

For almost the next two decades, Susanna Martin's name rarely appears in the public records of the colony. Her sister Mary died in 1682, followed by her husband George in 1686.[52] Early in 1692, she was again accused of witchcraft, this time by several of the possessed females in Salem. They claimed that her apparition "greviously afflected" them, urging them to become witches themselves. Summoned before the court as witnesses against her were eleven men and four women, all old neighbors of the now sixty-seven-year-old widow.[53]

Unnerved by neither the agonies of the possessed or the magistrates' obvious belief in her guilt, Martin insisted that she was innocent. To Cotton Mather, she "was one of the most impudent, scurrilous, wicked Creatures in the World," who had the effrontery to claim "that she had lead a most virtuous and holy life."[54] Years of living as a reputed witch had left Martin well-versed on the subject of the Devil's powers. "He that appeared in sam[uel]s

shape, a glorifyed saint," she said, citing the Bible in her own defense, "can appear in any ones shape." She laughed at the fits of her young accusers, explaining: "Well I may at such folly." When asked what she thought the possessed were experiencing, she said she did not know. Pressed to speculate on it, she retorted: "I do not desire to spend my judgment upon it" and added (revealing what must have been her long-standing opinion of the magistrates' bias), "my thoughts are my own, when they are in, but when they are out they are anothers."[55] ...

Susanna Martin was found guilty of witchcraft and was one of five women executed on 19 July 1692. One week later, another Salisbury woman was indicted on the same charge. She was Mary Bradbury, the now elderly wife of the man Susanna Martin believed had written her father's "will" nearly twenty-five years before. Mary Bradbury was sentenced to hang too, but friends helped her to escape. No explicit connection between the accusations of the two women is discernible. Rumors circulated, however, that because Thomas Bradbury had friends in positions of authority, there had been little real effort to capture his fugitive wife.[56] ...

These ... short histories ... suggest the diverse economic circumstances of witches in early New England. ... The ... women featured in these histories were either (1) daughters of parents who had no sons (or whose sons had died), (2) women in marriages which brought forth only daughters (or in which the sons had died), or (3) women in marriages with no children at all. These patterns had significant economic implications. Because there were no legitimate male heirs in their immediate families, each of these ... women stood to inherit, did inherit, or were denied their apparent right to inherit substantially larger portions of their fathers' or husbands' accumulated estates than women in families with male heirs. Whatever actually happened to the property in question—and in some cases we simply do not know—these women were aberrations in a society with an inheritance system designed to keep property in the hands of men.

These ... cases also illustrate fertility and mortality patterns widely shared among the families of accused witches. A substantial majority of New England's accused females were women without brothers, women with daughters but no sons, or women in marriages with no children at all (see Table 1). Of the 267 accused females, enough is known about 158 to identify them as either having or not having brothers or sons to inherit: only 62 of the 158 (39 percent) did, whereas 96 (61 percent) did not. More striking, once accused, women without brothers or sons were even more likely than women with brothers or sons to be tried, convicted, and executed: women from families without male heirs made up 64 percent of the females prosecuted, 76 percent of those who were found guilty, and 89 percent of those who were executed.

These figures must be read with care, however, for two reasons. First, eighteen of the sixty-two accused females who had brothers or sons to inherit were themselves daughters and granddaughters of women who did not. It appears that these eighteen females, most of whom were young women or girls, were accused because their neighbors believed that their mothers and grandmothers passed their witchcraft on to them. Therefore they form a somewhat ambiguous group. Since they all had brothers to inherit, it would be inaccurate to exclude them from this category in Table 1, yet including them understates the extent to which inheritance-related concerns were at issue in witchcraft accusations. At the same time, the large number of cases in which the fertility and mortality patterns of witches' families are unknown (109 of the 267 accused females in New England) makes it impossible to assess precisely the proportion of women among the accused who did not have brothers or sons.

Table 2 helps clarify the point. It includes as a separate category the daughters and granddaughters of women without brothers or sons and incorporates the cases for which this information is unknown. Although inclusion of the unknowns renders the overall percentages meaningless, this way of representing the

TABLE 1. Female Witches by Presence or Absence of Brothers or Sons, New England, 1620–1725 (A)

Action	Women without Brothers or Sons	Women with Brothers or Sons	Total
Accused	96 (61%)	62 (39%)	158
Tried	41 (64%)	23 (36%)	64
Convicted	25 (76%)	8 (24%)	33
Executed	17 (89%)	2 (11%)	19

available information shows clearly the particular vulnerability of women without brothers or sons. Even if *all* the unknown cases involved women from families *with* male heirs—a highly unlikely possibility—women from families without males to inherit would still form a majority of convicted and executed witches. Were the complete picture visible, I suspect that it would not differ substantially from that presented earlier in Table 1—which is based on data reflecting 60 percent of New England's witches and which indicates that women without brothers and sons were more vulnerable than other women at all stages of the process.

Numbers alone, however, do not tell the whole story. More remains to be said about what happened to these inheriting or potentially inheriting women, both before and after they were accused of witchcraft.

It was not unusual for women in families without male heirs to be accused of witchcraft shortly after the deaths of fathers, husbands, brothers, or sons. Katherine Harrison [and] Susanna Martin . . . exemplify this pattern. So too does elderly Ann Hibbens of Boston, whose execution in 1656 seems to have had a profound enough effect on some of her peers to influence the outcome of subsequent trials for years to come. Hibbens had three sons from her first marriage, all of whom lived in England; but she had no children by her husband William Hibbens, with whom she had come to Massachusetts in the 1630s. William died in 1654; Ann was brought to trial two years later. Although her husband's will has not survived, he apparently left a substantial portion (if not all) of his property directly to her: when she wrote her own will shortly before her execution, Ann Hibbens was in full possession of a £344 estate, most of which she bequeathed to her sons in England.[57]

Similarly, less than two years elapsed between the death of Gloucester's William Vinson and the imprisonment of his widow Rachel in 1692. Two children, a son and a daughter, had been born to the marriage, but the son had died in 1675. Though William Vinson had had four sons (and three daughters) by a previous marriage, the sons were all dead by 1683. In his will, which he wrote in 1684, before he was certain that his last son had been lost at sea, William left his whole £180 estate to Rachel for her life, stipulating that she could sell part of the lands and cattle

TABLE 2. Female Witches by Presence or Absence of Brothers or Sons, New England, 1620–1725 (B)

Action	Women without Brothers or Sons	Daughters and Granddaughters of Women without Brothers or Sons	Women with Brothers or Sons	Unknown Cases	Total
Accused	96 (36%)	18 (7%)	44 (16%)	109 (41%)	267
Tried	41 (48%)	6 (7%)	17 (20%)	22 (26%)	86
Convicted	25 (56%)	0 (0%)	6 (13%)	12 (27%)	45
Executed	17 (61%)	0 (0%)	2 (7%)	9 (32%)	28

if she found herself in need of resources. After Rachel's death, "in Case" his son John "be Living and returne home agayne," William said, most of the estate was to be divided between John and their daughter Abigail. If John did not return, both shares were to be Abigail's.[58] . . .

In other cases, many years passed between the death of the crucial male relative and the moment when a formal witchcraft complaint was filed.

. . . Mary English of Salem was charged with witchcraft seven years after she came into her inheritance. Her father, merchant William Hollingworth, had been declared lost at sea in 1677, but at that time Mary's brother William was still alive. Possibly because the younger William was handling the family's interests in other colonies, or possibly because the father's estate was in debt for more than it was worth, the magistrates gave the widow Elinor Hollingworth power of attorney to salvage what she could. With her "owne labor," as she put it, "but making use of other mens estates," the aggressive and outspoken Mistress Hollingworth soon had her deceased husband's debts paid and his wharf, warehouse, and tavern solvent again.[59] She had no sooner done so, however, than she was accused of witchcraft by the wife of a Gloucester mariner.[60] Though the magistrates gave little credence to the charge at the time, they may have had second thoughts later. In 1685, her son William died, and Elinor subsequently conveyed the whole Hollingworth estate over to Mary English, who was probably her only surviving child.[61]

Elinor Hollingworth had died by 1692, but Mary English was one of the women cried out upon early in the Salem outbreak. Her husband, the merchant Philip English, was accused soon after. Knowing their lives were in grave danger, the Englishes fled to the safety of New York. But as one historian of witchcraft has pointed out, flight was "the legal equivalent of conviction."[62] No sooner had they left than close to £1200 of their property was confiscated under the law providing attainder for witchcraft.[63]

Not all witches from families without male heirs were accused of conspiring with the Devil after they had come into their inheritances. On the contrary, some were accused prior to the death of the crucial male relative, many times before it was clear who would inherit. . . . [O]ne of these women . . . was Martha Corey of Salem, who was accused of witchcraft in 1692 while her husband was still alive. Giles Corey had been married twice before and had several daughters by the time he married the widow Martha Rich, probably in the 1680s. With no sons to inherit, Giles's substantial land holdings would, his neighbors might have assumed, be passed on to his wife and daughters. Alice Parker, who may have been Giles's daughter from a former marriage, also came before the magistrates as a witch in 1692, as did Giles himself. Martha Corey and Alice Parker maintained their innocence and were hanged. Giles Corey, in an apparently futile attempt to preserve his whole estate for his heirs, refused to respond to the indictment. To force him to enter a plea, he was tortured: successively heavier weights were placed on his body until he was pressed to death.[64]

What seems especially significant here is that most accused witches whose husbands were still alive were, like their counterparts who were widows and spinsters, over forty years of age—and therefore unlikely if not unable to produce male heirs. Indeed, the fact that witchcraft accusations were rarely taken seriously by the community until the accused stopped bearing children takes on a special meaning when it is juxtaposed with the anomalous position of inheriting women or potentially inheriting women in New England's social structure.

Witches in families without male heirs sometimes had been dispossessed of part or all of their inheritances before—sometimes long before—they were formally charged with witchcraft. Few of these women, however, accepted disinheritance with equanimity. Rather, like Susanna Martin, they took their battles to court, casting themselves in the role of public challengers to the system of male inheritance. In most instances, the authorities sided with their antagonists. . . .

. . . The property of women in families without male heirs was vulnerable to loss in a variety of ways, from deliberate destruction by neighbors (as Katherine Harrison experienced) to official sequestering by local magistrates. In nearly every case, the authorities themselves seem hostile or at best indifferent to the property claims of these women. One final example deserves mention here, not only because it indicates how reluctant magistrates were to leave property in the control of women, but because it shows that the property of convicted witches was liable to seizure even without the benefit of an attainder law.

Rebecca Greensmith had been widowed twice before her marriage to Nathaniel Greensmith. Her first husband, Abraham Elsen of Wethersfield, had died intestate in 1648, leaving an estate £99. After checking the birth dates of the Elsens' two children, three-year-old Sarah and one-year-old Hannah, the court initially left the whole estate with the widow. When Rebecca married Wethersfield's Jarvis Mudge the following year, the local magistrates sequestered the house and land Abraham Elsen had left, worth £40, stating their intention to rent it out "for the Use and Benefit of the two daughters."[65] The family moved to New London shortly after, but Jarvis Mudge died in 1652 and Rebecca moved with Hannah and Sarah to Hartford. Since Rebecca was unable to support herself and her two daughters, the court allowed her to sell the small amount of land owned by her second husband (with whom she had had no children) "for the paing of debts and the Bettering the Childrens portyons."[66]

Sometime prior to 1660, Rebecca married Nathaniel Greensmith. During the Hartford outbreak, Rebecca came under suspicion of witchcraft. After Nathaniel sued his wife's accuser for slander, Nathaniel himself was named. Both husband and wife were convicted and executed.[67]

Respecting Nathaniel's £182 estate, £44 of which was claimed by the then eighteen-year-old Sarah and seventeen-year-old Hannah Elsen, the court ordered the three overseers "to preserve the estate from Waste" and to pay "any just debts," the only one recorded being the Greensmiths' jail fees. Except for allowing the overseers "to dispose of the 2 daughters," presumably to service, the magistrates postponed until the next court any decision concerning the young women's portions. First, however, they deducted £40 to go "to the Treasurer for the County."[68] No reason was given for this substantial appropriation and no record of further distribution of the estate has survived.

Aside from these many women who lived or had lived in families without male heirs, there were at least a dozen other witches who, despite the presence of brothers and sons, came into much larger shares of estates than their neighbors would have expected. In some cases, these women gained full control over the disposition of property. We know about these women because their fathers, husbands, or other relatives left wills, because the women themselves wrote wills, or because male relatives who felt cheated out of their customary shares fought in the courts for more favorable arrangements.

Grace Boulter of Hampton, one of several children of Richard Swain, is one of these women. Grace was accused of witchcraft in 1680, along with her thirty-two-year-old daughter, Mary Prescott. Twenty years earlier, in 1660, just prior to his removal to Nantucket, Grace's father had deeded a substantial portion of his Hampton property to her and her husband Nathaniel, some of which he gave directly to her.[69]

Another witch in this group is Jane James of Marblehead, who left an estate at her death in 1669 which was valued at £85. While it is not clear how she came into possession of it, the property had not belonged to her husband Erasmus, who had died in 1660, though it did play a significant role in a controversy between her son and son-in-law over their rightful shares of both Erasmus's and Jane's estates. Between 1650 and her death in 1669, Jane was accused of witchcraft at least three times by her Marblehead neighbors.[70] . . .

Looking back over the lives of these many women—most particularly those who did not have brothers or sons to inherit—we begin to understand the complexity of the economic dimension of New England witchcraft. Only rarely does the actual trial testimony indicate that economic power was even at issue. Nevertheless it is there, recurring with a telling persistence once we look beyond what was explicitly said about these women as witches. Inheritance disputes surface frequently enough in witchcraft cases, cropping up as part of the general context even when no direct link between the dispute and the charge is discernible, to suggest the fears that underlay most accusations. No matter how deeply entrenched the principle of male inheritance, no matter how carefully written the laws that protected it, it was impossible to insure that all families had male offspring. The women who stood to benefit from these demographic "accidents" account for most of New England's female witches.

The amount of property in question was not the crucial factor in the way these women were viewed or treated by their neighbors, however. Women of widely varying economic circumstances were vulnerable to accusation and even to conviction. Neither was there a direct line from accuser to material beneficiary of the accusation: others in the community did sometimes profit personally from the losses sustained by these women . . . , but only rarely did the gain accrue to the accusers themselves. Indeed, occasionally there was no direct temporal connection: in some instances several decades passed between the creation of the key economic conditions and the charge of witchcraft; the charge in other cases even anticipated the development of those conditions.

Finally, inheriting or potentially inheriting women were vulnerable to witchcraft accusations not only during the Salem outbreak, but from the time of the first formal accusations in New England at least until the end of the century. . . . The Salem outbreak created only a slight wrinkle in this established fabric of suspicion. If daughters, husbands, and sons of witches were more vulnerable to danger in 1692 than they had been previously, they were mostly the daughters, husbands, and sons of inheriting or potentially inheriting women. As the outbreak spread, it drew into its orbit increasing numbers of women, "unlikely" witches in that they were married to well-off

and influential men, but familiar figures to some of their neighbors nonetheless. What the impoverished Sarah Good had in common with Mary Phips, wife of Massachusetts's governor, was what Eunice Cole had in common with Katherine Harrison. . . . However varied their backgrounds and economic positions, as women without brothers or women without sons, they stood in the way of the orderly transmission of property from one generation of males to another.

NOTES

1. Alan Macfarlane, *Witchcraft in Tudor and Stuart England: A Regional and Comparative Study* (New York, 1970), pp. 149–51. See also Keith Thomas, *Religion and the Decline of Magic* (New York, 1971), pp. 457, 520–21, 560–68.

2. See Trials for Witchcraft in New England (unpaged), dated 5 September 1656 (manuscript volume, Houghton Library, Harvard University, Cambridge, Mass.).

3. Relying on very general indicators (a married woman who worked as a servant, a widow whose husband had left an estate of £39, and so forth), I was able to make rough estimates about the economic position of 150 accused women. Twenty-nine of these women seem to have been poor. . . .

4. For Abigail Somes, see *The Salem Witchcraft Papers: Verbatim Transcripts of the Legal Documents of the Salem Witchcraft Outbreak of 1692*, 3 vols., eds. Paul Boyer and Stephen Nissenbaum (New York, 1977), 3:733–37 (hereafter cited as *Witchcraft Papers*). For Tituba, see *Witchcraft Papers* 3:745–57. Documents relating to Ruth Wilford are in *Witchcraft Papers* 2:459; 3:961; *The Probate Records of Essex County, Massachusetts, 1635–1681*, 3 vols. (Salem, 1916–20), 3:93–95 (hereafter cited as *Essex Probate Records*).

5. Most families in seventeenth-century New England had estates worth less than £200. However, since only a very small proportion of convicted witches who were married seem to have come from families with estates worth *more* than £200, it seems reasonable to conclude that married women from families with less than £200 estates were overrepresented among the accused. Nearly all of the convictions of married women from families with estates worth more than £200 occurred during the Salem outbreak. . . .

6. For accusations against Hannah Griswold and Margaret Gifford, see Norbert B. Lacy, "The Records of the Court of Assistants of Connecticut, 1665–1701" (M.A. thesis, Yale University, 1937), pp. 6–7 (hereafter cited as "Conn. Assistants Records"); and *Records and Files of the Quarterly Courts of Essex County, Massachusetts*, 9 vols. (Salem, 1912–75), 7:405; 8:23 (hereafter cited as Essex Court Records).

7. This discussion of the inheritance system of seventeenth-century New England is drawn from the following sources: *The Book of the General Lawes and Libertyes Concerning the Inhabitants of the Massachusetts*, ed. Thomas G. Barnes (facsimile from the 1648 edition, San Marino, Calif., 1975); *The Colonial*

Laws of Massachusetts. Reprinted from the Edition of 1672, with the Supplements through 1686, ed. William H. Whitmore (Boston, 1887); John D. Cushing, comp., *The Laws and Liberties of Massachusetts, 1641–91: A Facsimile Edition*, 3 vols. (Wilmington, Del., 1976); *Massachusetts Province Laws, 1692–1699*, ed. John D. Cushing (Wilmington, Del., 1978); *New Hampshire Probate Records; Essex Probate Records: A Digest of the Early Connecticut Probate Records*, vol. 1, ed. Charles W. Manwaring (Hartford, 1904) (hereafter cited as *Conn. Probate Records*); Marylynn Salmon, *Women and the Law of Property in Early America* (Chapel Hill, 1986); George L. Haskins, "The Beginnings of Partible Inheritance in the American Colonies," in *Essays in the History of American Law*, ed. David H. Flaherty (Chapel Hill, 1969); Edmund S. Morgan, *The Puritan Family: Religion and Domestic Relations in Seventeenth-Century New England* (1944; reprint New York, 1966).

8. See Morgan, *The Puritan Family*, pp. 81–82.

9. Barnes, *Book of the General Lawes*, pp. 17–18. . . .

10. Since only a small proportion of men left wills during the colonial period, intestacy law played a significant role in determining inheritance practices. See Salmon, *Women and the Law of Property*, p. 141.

11. Barnes, *The Book of the General Lawes*, p. 53.

12. Young women officially came of age in New England when they reached 18; young men when they reached 21.

13. William Blackstone, *Commentaries on the Laws of England*, 4 vols. (Oxford, 1765–69), 1:433.

14. Once widowed, a woman who inherited land from her father (or who had bought land with her husband in both of their names) could make a will of her own, as could a single woman who came into possession of land. . . . See Salmon, *Women and the Law of Property*, pp. 144–45 and passim.

15. Evidence suggests that in seventeenth-century New England, daughters of fathers who died relatively young (and possibly most sons) did not normally come into their inheritances until they married. If daughters had received their shares when they came of age, we would expect to find probate records for single women who died before they had the opportunity to marry. Though there are many existing intestate records and wills for single men who died in early adulthood, I have located only one record involving a young, single woman.

16. Wethersfield Land Records (manuscript volume, Town Clerk's Office, Town Hall, Wethersfield, Conn.) 1:19, 38.

17. Given the ages of her children, Katherine Harrison had to have been between her late twenties and her mid-fifties when she was first accused of witchcraft in 1668. I suspect that she was in her forties.

18. See Wethersfield Land Records 2:149; Katherine Harrison to John Winthrop, Jr., undated letter (probably early 1667), and Katherine Harrison's Testimony, undated document (probably October 1669), in the Winthrop Papers, Massachusetts Historical Society, Boston (hereafter cited as Winthrop Papers). . . .

19. Samuel Wyllys Papers: Depositions on Cases of Witchcraft, Assault, Theft, Drunkenness and Other Crimes, Tried in Connecticut, 1663–1728 (manuscript volume, Archives, History and Genealogy Unit, Connecticut State Library, Hartford, doc. 15) (hereafter cited as Wyllys Papers).

20. See Sherman W. Adams and Henry R. Stiles, *The History of Ancient Wethersfield*, 2 vols. (New York, 1904), 1:682; and Lacy, "Conn. Assistants Records," p. 12.

21. Lacy, "Conn. Assistants Records," p. 13.

22. Petition for the Investigation of Katherine Harrison, Recently Released after Imprisonment, Signed by John Chester and Thirty-Eight Other Citizens of Wethersfield (Manuscript Collections, Connecticut Historical Society, Hartford [hereafter cited as Petition for the Investigation of Katherine Harrison]) (emphasis mine). See also Order about Katherine Harrison's Land, in the Winthrop Papers. . . .

23. Lacy, "Conn. Assistants Records," pp. 13–14, 18–19.

24. "The Answers of Some Ministers to the Questions Propounded to Them by the Honored Magistrates," dated 20 October 1669, Samuel Wyllys Papers, Supplement: Depositions on Cases of Witchcraft Tried in Connecticut, 1662–1693, photostat copies of original documents from the Wyllys Papers, Annmary Brown Memorial Brown University Library, Providence, R.I. . . .

25. Lacy, "Conn. Assistants Records," p. 23. . . .

26. Wyllys Papers Supplement, p. 11.

27. Depositions submitted against Harrison in 1668 and 1669 are in the Wyllys Papers, docs. 6–17; Wyllys Papers Supplement, pp. 46–63. . . . For Harrison's response to these accusations, see Katherine Harrison's Testimony, Winthrop Papers.

28. Manwaring, *Conn. Probate Records* 1:206.

29. "A Complaint of Severall Greevances of the Widdow Harrison's," Wyllys Papers Supplement, p. 53.

30. "The Declaration of Katherine Harrison in Her Appeal to This Court of Assistants," dated September 1668, in Connecticut Archives, Crimes and Misdemeanors, 1st ser. (1662–1789) (manuscript volume, Archives, History and Genealogy Unit, Connecticut State Library, Hartford), vol. 1 (pt. 1):34 (hereafter cited as Crimes and Misdemeanors).

31. Connecticut Colonial Probate Records 56:80; Records of the Colony of Connecticut, Connecticut Colonial Probate Records, County Court, vol. 56, 1663–77 (Archives, History and Genealogy Unit, Connecticut State Library, Hartford, 56:79–81 (hereafter cited as Connecticut Colonial Probate Records).

32. Ibid., pp. 78–79. For the Griswolds as accusers, see Katherine Harrison's Testimony, Winthrop Papers.

33. Connecticut Colonial Probate Records 56:80.

34. "The Declaration of Katherine Harrison," Crimes and Misdemeanors, 1 (pt. 1):34.

35. Manwaring, *Connecticut Probate Records*, p. 206.

36. Katherine Harrison to John Winthrop, Jr., "Letter," Winthrop Papers.

37. Wethersfield Land Records 2:149.

38. Petition for the Investigation of Katherine Harrison.

39. See "The Cases of Hall and Harrison," in *Narratives of the Witchcraft Cases, 1648–1706*, ed. Charles Lincoln Burr (New York, 1914), pp. 48–49.

40. Ibid., pp. 48–52.

41. See Samuel D. Drake, *Annals of Witchcraft in New England* (New York, 1869), pp. 133–34.

42. Connecticut Colonial Probate Records 56:118; Wethersfield Land Records 2:249.

43. Wethersfield Land Records 2:210.

44. See Gilbert Collection.

45. See Joseph Merrill, *History of Amesbury, Including the First Seventeen Years of Salisbury....* (Haverhill, Mass., 1880), pp. 11–13, 28; *Vital Records of Salisbury...* (Topsfield, Mass., 1915), pp. 151, 415.

46. *Essex Probate Records* 2:125–27.

47. James Savage, *A Genealogical Dictionary of the First Settlers of New England*, 4 vols. (Boston, 1860–62), 1:138; 4:483.

48. See *Essex Court Records* 4:129, 133.

49. *Essex Court Records* 4:184, 187, 239.

50. *Essex Probate Records* 2:223–24.

51. See *Records of the Governor and Company of the Massachusetts Bay in New England*, 6 vols., ed. Nathaniel B. Shurtleff (Boston, 1853–54), 5:6, 26–27.

52. Savage, *Genealogical Dictionary* 2:566.... When he died, George Martin left an estate valued at £75, most of which he left to Susanna "during her Widowhood."

53. See *Witchcraft Papers* 2:549–79.

54. Cotton Mather, *The Wonders of the Invisible World* (1693; facsimile of the 1862 London edition, Ann Arbor, Mich., 1974), p. 148.

55. *Witchcraft Papers* 2:551.

56. *Witchcraft Papers* 1:115–29.

57. Ann Hibbens' will is reprinted in *New England Historical and Genealogical Register*, vol. 6 (1852), pp. 287–88.

58. See *Witchcraft Papers* 3:880–81.

59. *Essex Probate Records* 3:191–93.

60. *Essex Court Records* 7:238.

61. *New England Historical and Genealogical Register*, vol. 3 (1849), p. 129.

62. Marion L. Starkey, *The Devil in Massachusetts* (New York, 1949), p. 185.

63. *Witchcraft Papers* 3:988–91.

64. For Martha and Giles Corey and Alice Parker, see *Witchcraft Papers* 1:239–66; 2:623–28, 632–33; 3:985–86, 1018–19.

65. Manwaring, *Conn. Probate Records* 1:7–8.

66. *Records of the Particular Court of Connecticut, 1639–1663, Collections of the Connecticut Historical Society*, vol. 22 (1928), p. 119.

67. Ibid., p. 258.

68. Manwaring, *Conn. Probate Records* 1:121–22.

69. Norfolk Deeds (manuscript volume, Registry of Deeds, Essex County Courthouse, Salem, Mass.), 1:116, 154.

70. *Essex Probate Records* 1:314–16; 2:160; *Essex Court Records* 1:199, 204, 229; 2:213; 3:292, 342, 413.

ANN M. LITTLE
Captivity and Conversion: Daughters of New England in French Canada

Ann Little's essay introduces us to the geopolitics of the second half of the colonial period. Protestant England and Catholic France, along with their independent-minded Indian allies, engaged in a succession of imperial wars involving North American territory from the late seventeenth century through the Seven Years' War of 1756–63. In 1700, English settlers far outnumbered the 15,000 French soldiers, missionaries, fur traders, and habitants (farmers) clustered chiefly in settlements along the St. Lawrence River. However, the English occupied only a narrow sliver along the eastern seaboard, while the French claimed authority (and established mutually advantageous relations with native groups) from Louisiana to Canada along the Mississippi River and around the Great Lakes. It was not at all clear if one European power (France, Spain, or England) could gain ascendancy over the continent as a whole.

The author takes us on a detective's journey to recover the voices of and find out what happened to the children, teenagers, and grown women who were

Excerpted from Ann M. Little, "'A Jesuit will ruin your Body & Soul!': Daughters of New England in Canada," ch. 4 of *Abraham in Arms: War and Gender in Colonial New England* by Ann M. Little (Philadelphia: University of Pennsylvania Press, 2007). Reprinted by permission of the author and publisher. Notes have been edited and renumbered.

captured from New England towns and farms in wartime raids by Abenaki allies of the French. On arrival in Canada, English girls were typically schooled at Ursuline convents in New France's principal northern towns, Montreal, Québec (City), and Trois Rivières. Finding these New England women in the thorough records kept by French notaries—baptisms, marriages, deaths—means that they converted to Catholicism. Letters exchanged with their birth families in New England confirm that a high proportion of them chose not to be redeemed or ransomed so as to return to their onetime homes.

A good way to assess the author's evidence is to construct a list or table profiling the life courses of the captives who stayed. What do you find are the most compelling factors explaining why New England women remained in New France?

In the 1690s in the midst of the first war with New France, English depictions of frontier warfare and captivity shifted dramatically from identifying Indians as the primary danger to New England to portraying the French and their Catholicism as the chief threat to the New England way. While Indians were still formidable opponents in the battle, in New England they came to be feared more as agents of the French than as actors in their own right . . . Even more threatening . . . were European enemies who had studied the tactics of their Native allies so well. French Catholics proved more successful than Indians at encouraging English people to cross cultural borders and live among them for the rest of their lives. European Catholics were perhaps even more disturbing than Indian enemies because they were not all that different from English Protestants. They dressed the same, they did the same work, they ate the same food, they worshipped the same God—and thus they could be plotting and scheming just about anywhere and at any time. . . . Thus New Englanders began to worry less about Indian captivity and more about the vulnerability of captives in the hands of dedicated missionaries like the Jesuits, Ursulines, Sulpicians, and the Sisters of the Congregation of Notre Dame. Captivity narratives began to discuss the dedicated efforts that French priests and nuns made to convert their English prisoners of war, a theme that was . . . a feature of the genre through the Seven Years' War (1756–63).[1]

What was perhaps additionally disturbing about French successes in getting and keeping English captives is that the majority of the captives were New England's daughters, sisters, wives, and widows. While male captives always comprised the majority of New Englanders in captivity (mostly as prisoners of war, sometimes as adopted captives), female captives were vastly more likely to remain in Canada, convert to Catholicism, and marry.[2] This apparent danger to female captives jibed with long-standing puritan fears of women's greater vulnerability to spiritual corruption, as well as their specific susceptibility to the seductions of Catholicism. The sensually rich experiences of the Mass were believed to be powerfully attractive to unlearned, undisciplined women, as they had already proved to be to the Indians living in the French mission villages like Odanak (St. Francis), Kahnawake, La Montaigne, and Lorette.[3] Girls and women who remained in Canada became the focus of a great deal of familial and cultural anxiety in New England, as they lived lives that openly rejected the faith, language, and laws of their fathers. The following pages offer some explanations for their decisions to stay in Canada, choices that so baffled, wounded, and disturbed their families and communities in New England.

While for a time they were the subjects of intense diplomacy and worry on the part of their families and New England officials alike, these girls and women have been largely forgotten in the histories of the northeastern borderlands. This is partly because they did not write narratives about their experiences the way returned captives did, but it may also be due in part to their families' shame of daughters or sisters who stayed in Canada even when they were free to return to New England, and even in the face of parental and brotherly pleading and admonitions to come home. Because these women chose to remain in Canada, the sources for understanding their motivations and their lives in Canada are very thin. Furthermore, once these girls and women decided to remain in Canada, their New England families apparently had very little to say about them. . . . [M]ost New England families evidently disinherited and turned their backs on their disobedient daughters. . . .

Why is it that the usually prolific, expansive, and furious New England writers like Cotton Mather had so little to say about these girls and women who did not come home? Perhaps the shame and anger they felt both at being bested by the French, as well as because of their daughters' defiance, explains why these women's stories have been largely deleted from the family histories of New England.

New England's paranoia about the designs of the French and their successful alliances with Indians emerged in local writings and publications as early as King Philip's War (1675–78). Reports on the war's progress on the Maine and western Massachusetts frontiers note the presence and influence of the French among the Indians. By the time of the first war with New France, the English came to see the French as their major—if not yet their only—rivals for the control of North America.[4] The clear success of the French in creating political and diplomatic alliances with Indians (particularly with the Eastern Abenaki and the mission Iroquois) made a formidable European foe truly frightening to the English living in the northeastern borderlands at the end of the seventeenth century.

Fear and loathing of the French as enemies went hand-in-glove with the strong anti-Catholicism that was a foundational part of New England's sense of its historical and religious mission. Because religion and nationalism were so intertwined for English Protestants in the early modern era, it is impossible to separate New Englanders' fears of French political and military victories and their fear of being compelled to embrace Catholicism. . . . New England was founded by people who were especially zealous adherents to several versions of reformed Protestantism. They and their descendants believed that warfare and Indian captivity in the northeastern borderlands were evidence, variously, of God's disfavor or his willingness to test their faith. New Englanders who saw Indian warfare as an opportunity to test and prove their faith were even more willing to see wars against Catholic New France as an extension of Christ's struggle against the Devil for worldwide dominations.[5]

. . . [A]nti-Catholicism in Old and New England was . . . a strongly gendered phenomenon. Ever since the struggles between Elizabeth and Mary Queen of Scots for the English throne in the 1560s and 1570s, Protestant propagandists had effectively linked Catholicism with femininity and claimed that this feminization was both the cause and result of political and spiritual corruption. By the seventeenth century, xenophobia and misogyny were knit into the fabric of transatlantic English nationalism. All English people were in theory united by their collective struggle against the "Scarlet Whore of Babylon," the foreign and feminized Roman church.[6]

With King William's War under way (1688–97), New England writers and publishers of the 1690s produced some of its first virulently anti-French and anti-Catholic books and pamphlets. . . . [The Puritan minister] Cotton Mather was one of the most enterprising purveyors of this propaganda. . . . Mather's books and other contemporary pamphlets show that both the Roman empire and the Church of Rome represented despotic power in the minds of New Englanders and stood only for the power to compel people of the true faith to worship false gods.[7]

. . . [W]e cannot dismiss Mather's fears as mere paranoia, as the French had purposefully and determinedly sought to bring their religion to the Indians. Led chiefly by the energetic Catholic Reformation orders of the Jesuits and the Ursulines, religious men traveled down the St. Lawrence River to the Great Lakes, up to Hudson's Bay, and down the Mississippi to spread their faith, and they established successful Indian missions throughout New France and its borderlands from modern-day Maine and Nova Scotia westward to Ontario, Michigan, and the Mississippi River valley. Religious women established schools in Québec, Montreal, and Three Rivers that served as vital centers for the preservation and transmission of French language and culture as well as religion. The work of these French men and women stood in direct contrast to the distinctly underfunded efforts of the English to convert Indians and establish "praying towns." Only a minority of English ministers and settlers expended any efforts whatsoever on preaching to and converting Native Americans. . . .[8]

Cotton Mather agreed with other frontier observers that New England had failed grievously in its neglect of the souls of the Indians, and he argued that King William's War was in part God's punishment of New England for failing their duty to spread the gospel as energetically as French priests had brought their religion to the New World: "This is the Vengeance of God upon you, because you did no more, for the Conversion of those Miserable Heathen." But Mather's concern about Protestant missionary work was not simply for fear of the Lord's judgment; he also saw how French missionary work had paid off in their strong military alliances with the Eastern and Western Abenaki in particular. "Had we done, but half so much as the French Papists have done, to Proselyte the Indians of our East, unto the Christian Faith, instead of being, Snares and Traps unto us, and Scourges in our Sides, and Thorns in our Eyes they would have been, A wall unto us, both by Night and Day." Mather supports this observation with the claim that English captives of the Indians had been told by their captors that "had the English been as careful to Instruct us, as the French, we had been of your Religion!" While at other times in the same book Mather scorns the close association between the French and the Indians, disdaining the "Frenchified Indians" and "Indianized French" that were the result of such New World alliances, in the end he recognizes the advantage of their cooperation and blames New England for not reaching out to the Indians. "[I]f the Salvages had been Enlightened with The Christian Faith, from us, the French Papists could never have instill'd into them those French Poisons."[9]

. . . Mather played a key role in introducing explicitly anti-Catholic themes to captivity narratives with the publication of Hannah Swarton's story in 1697. Even amidst her difficult removes with the Indians after her capture from Casco in 1690, she reports, "yet I dreaded going to Canada, to the French, for fear lest I should be overcome by them, to yield to their Religion; which I had Vowed unto God, That I would not do. But the Extremity of my Sufferings were such, that at length I was willing to go, to preserve my Life." Like many New England captives who were brought to Canada, she was relieved to receive the hospitality of the French and gloried in eating familiar foods and dressing in European clothing once again. But this was the danger of consorting with the French— their way of life was so comfortable to English captives, especially after months or even years

with the Indians, that it made captives all the more susceptible to seduction by "popery." After being taken to Québec and so "kindly Entertained" and "courteously provided for . . . so that I wanted nothing for my Bodily Comfort, which they could help me unto," she was inevitably cast into a conflict that caused her intense spiritual discomfort. (Many readers might have assumed that as a woman, she was naturally more easily seduced by creature comforts that appealed to her carnal nature.) But Swarton, as we hear her through Mather's pen, was all too aware of the dangers that faced her: "Here was a great and comfortable Change, as to my Outward man, in my Freedom from my former Hardships, and Hard hearted Oppressors. But here began a greater Snare and Trouble to my Soul and Danger to my Inward man." Her mistress in Québec, and several priests and nuns "set upon me . . . to perswade me to Turn Papist." Swarton, through Mather's narrative, claims that they sometimes used scriptural arguments, "which they pressed with very much Zeal, Love, Intreaties, and Promises," and sometimes "Hard Usages," even threatening to send her "to France, and there I should be Burned, because I would not Turn to them." This kind of rhetoric served two purposes: it would stir up the emotions of the New England reading public to hear of the allegedly barbarous methods of French proselytizers, but it also gave Swarton and Mather the opportunity to demonstrate the steadfastness of her faith and prove herself a worthy model for other New Englanders to emulate . . . Through her ordeal [Swarton] . . . was comforted by Psalm 118:17–18, "I shall not Dy but live, and Declare the works of the Lord.". . .[10]

. . . The gaping hole in Swarton's narrative of triumph over French priestly designs is the fact that Swarton's own daughter Mary remained in Montreal after she herself returned to New England. She and Mather end her narrative with an earnest request for the "prayers of my Christian Friends, that the Lord will deliver" her [daughter]. Captured with her mother when she was fourteen, at the age of twenty-two Mary married an Irish fellow convert, John Lahey (more often rendered in the French records as Jean LaHaye) in 1697, the same year Mather published her mother's narrative. They presented eleven children for baptism over the next twenty years, three of whom had New England-born godmothers, Christine Otis, Freedom French, and Mary

Silver. As eloquent as Mather and Swarton are about her heroic efforts to resist conversion, they are silent about the decision her daughter made to become a French *bonne femme* instead of an English goodwife.[11]

As Swarton's narrative and personal experiences with captivity suggest, children (and especially daughters) were more vulnerable to the various cultural and religious conversions that might be required of them in captivity. Elizabeth Hanson was grateful when she was purchased by the French in 1725, whom she reports "were civil beyond what I could either desire or expect." "But," she reports with some alarm, "the next Day after I was redeemed, the Romish Priests took my Babe from me, and according to their custom, they baptized it." The priests explained that "if it died before [baptism], it would be damned, like some of our modern pretended reformed Priests." Hanson, a Quaker, worked in an insult aimed at other Protestants in her discussion of priestly intervention. Significantly, Hanson also reports that the priests gave her daughter a new Catholic name: "Mary Ann Frossways" (actually Françoise, or French).[12]

The captivity narrative of John Gyles, published in 1736, nearly fifty years after his boyhood capture and captivity among the Maliseet (Eastern Abenaki) in 1689, illustrates how completely French Catholics had replaced Indians as the enemies of New England and highlights particular fears of the vulnerability of children to conversion. After his initial capture, his Indian "master" shows him to a Jesuit missionary, who Gyles says "had a great mind to buy me. . . . I saw the Jesuit shew him Pieces of Gold, and understood afterward, that he tendered them for me." The politics of the mid-eighteenth century surely shaped his memories of 1689, as he reports a great deal of anxiety about conversion. "The Jesuit gave me a Bisket, which I put into my Pocket, and dare not eat; but buried it under a Log, fearing that he had put something in it, to make me Love him: for I was very Young, and had heard much of the Papists torturing the Protestants &c. so that I hated the sight of a Jesuit."

Fear of being made to "love" a priest may also reflect other dangers Catholic clergy represented in the minds of English people: their sexual ambiguity, and the possibility that they may replace English mothers and fathers, as Indian men and women had for many captives. Just as Catholicism itself was suspect because of its allegedly feminized nature and its

greater appeal to women, so priests were often held in suspicion by Protestants as "unnatural" or feminized men. Men who lived intimately together and shunned marriage were suspect in a culture that elevated heterosexuality to a near-sacrament and regularly depicted Catholicism as a shield for all manner of sexual improprieties. Additionally, New Englanders may have feared that French priests (or nuns) might offer their captive children another alternative family. . . .

A poignant moment in Gyles's narrative suggests that priests might represent both of these kinds of danger, sexual and familial, at the same time. The last time Gyles saw his mother alive, he told her that he might be sold to a Jesuit, and he reports that she reacted with great alarm: "Oh! my dear Child! If it were GOD's Will, I had rather follow you to your Grave! Or never see you more in this World, than you should be Sold to a Jesuit: for a Jesuit will ruin you Body & Soul!". . .[13]

. . . [W]e have almost no direct testimony from captives who remained in Canada. What little evidence we have of these people, their lives in Canada, and their reasons for remaining there comes from their slight communications with their New England families and their chance encounters with other captives who returned to New England to author narratives of their captivity among the Indians and the French. The numbers and demography of those who remained in Canada speak powerfully to the notion that their fates were not accidental. While they were always in the minority of those taken during the border wars (approximately 392 of 1,579 total captives, or less than a quarter of the captive population), girls and women were much likelier to remain in Canada, convert to Catholicism, marry French men, and (presumably) fill Canada's need for European housewifery. Of ninety-five captives taken between 1689 and 1755 who can be reliably traced through the Canadian notarial records, sixty-five (nearly 70 percent) were girls and women. While overall only about one captive in twenty stayed in Canada, female captives were nearly seven times as likely to stay in Canada as their male peers. . . . [A] bare majority of the female captives who remain in Canada were abducted as children; almost a third of them were adolescents or adults—a few women were even married mothers or widows in their thirties and forties. . . .[14]

What made these (mostly) girls and young women remain in Canada? More than half of them (thirty-four out of sixty-five) were taken into captivity before their thirteenth birthday, many of them as very young children. These captives, who frequently lost all memories of their English families and mother tongue, were the most easily assimilated into Canadian life. William Pote tells the sad story of Rachael Quackenbush, whom he saw while in prison in Québec during King George's War (1744–48). "This Child had been with ye French Ever since she was Taken with her Parents which is about 18 months. There was her Father & mother, Grandfather and Grandmother In this prison. They Endeavour'd to make her speak with ym, But she would not Speak a word Neither in Dutch nor English." Even for those captive girls who remembered their families and their native language, after spending several years in Canada, learning French, converting to Catholicism, and marrying a French man, it may have been simply unimaginable to return to a home a family they no longer knew nor remembered well. However, twenty of these captives were adolescents or adults when taken into captivity, young women who were almost fully grown and fully acculturated as English-speaking Protestants, and who would have been unlikely candidates to forget their native language and homeland. The choices of these twenty women are difficult to untangle, although given their age, it is appropriate to call their remaining in Canada a choice. [By the time they were free to return to New England], many of these older captives—especially the older teenagers—had probably adapted to life in Canada and perhaps had already converted to Catholicism. Many may have met a French man they fancied ... Some of them may have resented or disliked their natal families; surviving court records indicate that at least one of them was eager to escape an abusive home in New England, as we will see.[15] ...

There are some broad economic and legal facts that might have made New France a more attractive place for women. In stark contrast to the English common law tradition, French Canadian laws governing the "communauté de biens," or the "marriage community" of husband and wife, followed the Custom of Paris, which said that except for wealth in land owned by either partner prior to marriage, husbands and wives owned marital property equally. Although husbands were designated "masters of the community," neither husbands nor their wives could sell, mortgage, or alienate their joint property without the written consent of the other.... Upon the death of either spouse, the widow or widower inherited half of all real and personal property, as well as half the debts; the other half of the property and debts went to the children. Thus, women in French Canada were not economically disenfranchised in marriage as were their sisters in the English colonies. We will never know the extent to which French marital laws were major factors in these women's decisions to turn their backs on New England. However, these property laws may be indicative of a culture that was generally more welcoming and tolerant of women as economic producers and decision makers. This autonomy might have been especially attractive to former captives, as many of them would have spent significant time among Indians before they were purchased by French masters, and they may have come to expect the authority over family resources exercised by their Indian mothers.[16]

Beyond this legal framework, it is clear that New France had very good reasons to want to recruit and retain New England girls and women in the late seventeenth and early eighteenth centuries. French agricultural settlements in the St. Lawrence River valley had long suffered from an imbalanced sex ratio and they were desperate for women trained in European housewifery skills like dairying, baking, and working with textiles (spinning, knitting, weaving, and sewing). Censuses of seventeenth-century New France are unreliable and vary greatly, but they indicate that the scarcity of women was a problem in colonial New France. One historian has put the overall percentage of women among French immigrants to Canada at 12.3 percent for the seventeenth century....[17]

Women skilled in European housewifery would have made the lives of male habitants more comfortable, to be sure, but these skills were also central to European identity in a place that was dominated by other people and other cultural ways. Indians in the colonial northeastern borderlands did not keep cows or consume dairy products; they did not bake European bread; and they did not produce their own thread or cloth. Furthermore, in the later seventeenth century, French officials came to see that the more obvious fruits of marriage might be important to the colony's political future. Observing the rapidly increasing English population along the Atlantic seaboard and in the Connecticut and Hudson River valleys, Canadian officials concluded that recruiting and retaining women with strong bodies and European skills was not just a personal convenience for male habitants; it was a political necessity if the French were going to best their rivals for the control of North America.[18]

Officials in New France spent considerable money and energy recruiting French women for Canadian settlement or, alternatively, training Indian girls to become like French wives and mothers, and religious women played a key role in these efforts in the 1670s and 1680s. Teaching not just French girls but English captives and Indian girls and women in their convent schools, the nuns instructed them in academic subjects, religion, and women's domestic skills that were in such scarce supply in early New France. This dedication to girls' education resulted in a literacy rate higher among French women than men before the British conquest, although in the end few Indian girls and women crossed over to become French housewives—the majority of Native women trained in French schools assumed Indian ways when they returned to their villages and married there. . . .[19]

One of the most striking things about the treatment of English female captives in Canada was the attention and personal involvement of the colony's highest officials. Governor of Montreal (1698–1703) and then governor general of New France from 1703 to his death in 1725, Philippe de Rigaud, Marquis de Vaudreuil, was a powerful central player in the politics and diplomacy of the first two intercolonial wars. Thus it is revealing that he took a personal interest in several female captives during his governorship, even bringing some of them into his household and looking after their educations. He was the godfather of Mary Silver when she was baptized in 1710 among the Sisters of the Congregation of Notre Dame in Ville-Marie (near Montreal), and he placed Mary Scammon among the Ursulines in Three Rivers in 1725. . . . [T]he girls and women that Vaudreuil took such a personal interest in were high-status captives. In order to preserve diplomatic relations, he would have had a strong interest in ensuring these young women's health and happiness as much as possible, given their circumstances. However, the measures he took—putting them into convent schools and witnessing their baptisms and

marriages—doubtlessly served to bind them closer to their adopted home. Other officials of New France also served as godfathers and witnesses at the marriages of English captives, as the notarial records are full of references to "Intendants" performing these duties. In contrast, no New England governors ever expended equal funds or political capital to get these young women back.[20]

Vaudreuil's son Pierre de Rigaud, Marquis de Vaudreuil-Cavagnal, who was governor of Three Rivers and then Louisiana before he became governor general of New France in 1755, carried on his father's tradition of looking after English captives, especially the girls. He witnessed their baptisms, put them into convent schools, and took them into his home. He placed Jemima Howe's daughters Mary and Submit Phipps in the Ursuline convent school in Québec during the Seven Years' War with the instructions that "they should both of them together, be well looked after, and carefully educated, as his adopted children." When he brought Mary Phipps to France with him after the French capitulation in 1760, her mother reports that she was married there "to a French gentleman, whose name is Cron Lewis." Submit became so enthusiastic about her new faith that she refused to leave her convent. "[S]he absolutely refused," wrote her frustrated mother, "and all the persuasions and arguments I could use with her, were to no effect." Only because the younger Vaudreuil himself insisted that she be returned to her mother did Submit finally live up to her name, but she returned to her mother quite unwillingly. This very personal touch was doubtlessly influential in the lives of the young women taken in by the Vaudreuil family over a half-century, but perhaps more significantly, it suggests how important these girls and women were to their new country.[21]

Beyond this personal and official encouragement of English captives, the French crown also directly assisted their assimilation into Canadian society by offering naturalization and even cash payments to male and female captives alike. In 1702, Canadian officials secured two thousand livres of crown support for thirty-eight Catholicized English captives (twenty-one women and seventeen men). In May of 1710, Louis XIV naturalized twenty-eight male and thirty-eight female war captives, and again in 1713 he naturalized another thirty-four men and four women. . . .

The interest of government officials in the fates of these captive girls and women was important, but they relied heavily on Church officials to bring the young women over to French language, culture, and religion. While priests alone had the power to administer the sacraments of baptism and marriage that were so important to bringing ex-captives into Canadian society, much of the daily hard work of these multiple conversions was done by the nuns of Québec, Montreal, and Three Rivers through their convent schools. As we have seen, these female-run institutions were central to seventeenth-century efforts to bring Native girls and women into French society, so adding English girls to their lists of pupils required little adjustment on the part of the sisters who gloried in their evangelical work.[22]

We know that all of the captives who stayed to make lives in Canada were persuaded by this evangelism—or, at least that they accepted the necessity of converting to Catholicism in order to be naturalized. There is too little evidence on the religious opinions of former captives in Canada for us to generalize about their religious experiences. Renouncing Protestantism and converting to Catholicism was an enormous ideological leap, as religion and nationalism were so tightly bound to each other in New England. Even English families on the far borderlands of New England had a strong sense of the moral and intellectual superiority of English Protestantism versus their perceptions of the so-called despotism and corruption of French Catholicism, although they may not have appreciated the finer points of doctrinal difference. Nevertheless, many former captives may have become earnestly devout Catholics. . . . For those who had spent months or years among Indian families who were not living in mission towns, they may have felt a welcome familiarity upon seeing a cross, hearing European music sung, or taking communion again. Some might have come to Catholicism through the practice of Indian families who adopted them. . . .

While officials of both the church and the state clearly played an important role in acculturating English captives, the girls and women themselves established bonds with one another that appear to have eased their adoption into Canadian society. The fact that English captives created and maintained their own networks that lasted decades is further evidence that remaining in New France was a choice, not a fate, for most of them. Canadian notarial records show that ex-captives witnessed one another's baptisms, weddings, and children's baptisms; . . . these women were friends and neighbors who continued to support one another through their lives. . . .

We get only a haphazard picture of these networks through the captivity narratives of returned New Englanders . . . Susanna Johnson reports being approached by two ex-captives turned Ursuline nuns when Johnson and her sister as captives went to the Ursuline convent in Québec to visit Jemimah Howe's daughters, Mary and Submit Phipps. "We here found two aged English ladies, who had been taken in former wars." One of them was Esther Wheelwright (now La Mère Marie-Joseph de l'Enfant Jésus), and the other perhaps Sarah Davis, who took the name Marie-Anne Davis de Saint-Benoit. Mother Esther (as she called herself) was taken in the same 1703 raid on Wells, Maine, along with the Storer cousins Mary and Priscilla, including Priscilla's sister Rachael who also married a French man but settled in Québec rather than Montreal. Mother Esther too expressed interest in the English visitors to her convent, and she told Johnson that she had "a brother in Boston, on whom she requested me to call, if ever I went to that place." After she was redeemed and returned to New England, Johnson followed up on the connection. "I complied with her request afterwards, and received many civilities from her brother." Mother Esther, Mary St. Germaine, and other captives clearly had the connections to go home if they wanted to. They were interested in and affectionate toward their New England friends and families, but they had made their home in Canada. . . .[23]

[A]t least one of the women who stayed in Canada fled some of the more dramatic consequences of New England patriarchy. Abigail Willey (or Willy) stands out . . . because of her age and her marital status: taken in 1689 from Oyster River, New Hampshire, she was a married woman of 32 with two daughters who were about thirteen and eight. Her young daughters were prime candidates to stay in Canada, but why would someone of such a relatively advanced age, and with a husband and other children remaining in New Hampshire, choose baptism and (eventually) remarriage in New France? In a 1683 statement to the New Hampshire colony court, Abigail Willey outlined the harsh reality of her life as an English goodwife. She complained of her husband's chronic violence against her and her isolation as an abused woman: "I have for several years past lived and spent, without making my addresses to any in authority, with Stephen Willy, my husband, often suffering much by sore and heavy blows received from his hand, too much for any weak woman to bear." She also related his frequent threats "to take away my life by the evil disposition of his own mind, seeing that neither his own relations, neither my own natural brothers, dare countenance in any way of natural friendship [with Stephen]." Abigail Willey described herself, in short, as "the suffering subject of his insatial jealousy." Her claims in this petition were supported by an accompanying deposition by a neighbor, Joseph Hill, who one night heard Stephen Willey yell, "I will kill her or whore." (Perhaps Hill meant to indicate that Willey said either, "I will kill her," or "I will kill the whore.") He apparently went into the Willey home to intervene in the violent affair, and found "John Willy, his brother, standing between the said Stephen and his wife, to prevent them from danger."

She had not brought her situation to the attention of local officials and instead suffered for years in silence, perhaps because she believed herself to be the victim of the English courts as well as of her husband. An earlier experience before the bar was grievously humiliating: when Stephen Willey brought her before Judge Edgerly, Willey reports that her husband "at his own request procured of said judge the shameful sentence of ten strips, to be laid upon me at a post." The judge later reversed himself and cancelled the whipping, accepting a twenty-shilling fine instead. But then, when Willey went to visit her sister in Kittery, she reports "said judge sent after me as a runaway, to be procured; the second time to be dealt with according to law." . . . Clearly, she saw this English magistrate and English law as operating at the whim of her disreputable and abusive husband. Perhaps she chose to remain in Canada because she saw an opportunity to escape not just a despotic husband but a legal system that did not operate in her interest.[24]

Colonial Anglo-American women's historians have shown how difficult it was for woman to procure a divorce on any grounds other than desertion, [adultery,] or sexual insufficiency on the part of the husband. Catholic Canada was hardly a libertine's playground—in fact, divorce was nonexistent—but French Canadian women could claim greater economic self-sufficiency when their marriages broke down, and for a wider variety of reasons. There were two types of legal separation available to aggrieved couples: division of the marital property without physical separation, or a separation of bed and board in addition to the division of all assets. Of 149 petitions for separation in the seventeenth- and eighteenth-century St. Lawrence Valley, most were filed by wives, and most focused on the profligacy of the husband and his inability to manage domestic affairs, situations that were frequently linked to drunkenness and domestic violence. . . . New France, like New England, tolerated wife-beating, but evidence from separation petitions suggests that repeated spousal abuse, death threats, insanity, and venereal infection could gain wives a bed and board separation from men like Stephen Willey. The differences between the New France and New England legal systems are telling, with Canada offering women more flexibility and control in both happy and unhappy marriages. New France's legal tradition offered abused wives more economic rights and autonomy in marital separations than . . . New England.[25]

We know comparatively little of Willey's life in Canada and can glean only a few details from the notarial records that note her transformation from English wife and mother, to French servant, and eventually to wife of a Montreal habitant. Willey was baptized as a Catholic in 1693, took the name Marie Louise Pilman (presumably a transcription error, after her maiden name Pitman), and was described as a servant to Hector de Callières, a Montreal official; apparently even servitude was preferable to her life as an abused New England wife. Her husband Stephen's 1696 will made no mention of her name or her existence whatsoever; neither did he recognize or remember his two daughters in Canada. He died sometime in or before 1700; Mary Louise Pilman married Edouard de Flecheur in 1710 and was naturalized the same year, at the age of fifty-three. Her two daughters had preceded her in marriage to French men . . .[26]

English families used inheritances and inheritance law to compel their captive children and siblings to return to New England, although this tactic was used differently depending on the sex of the captive. Based on the fragmentary evidence available in wills and probate records, it appears that daughters' inheritances were more likely to be contingent upon their return to New England, while New England's captive sons were twice as likely to receive their inheritances without returning to New England. . . . The fact that female captives in Canada fared worse than their male counterparts when it came to their inheritances may be unsurprising, given the patriarchal nature of inheritance law in general: eldest sons reaped great privileges that eldest daughters did not. Furthermore, property ownership was itself a gendered phenomenon, because the law of coverture meant that Anglo-American women might easily spend the majority of their lives as *femes couverts*, and thus not as property owners. But even beyond this, evidence indicates that parents of children who remained in Canada of their own choice used the power of inheritance to communicate disapproval of their children's decisions, or to compel a return to New England, especially when it came to their daughters. . . . [T]he legal structures of Anglo-American society communicated very clearly whose work was valued and whose was not; and whose interests were directly represented and whose were not. We will never know to what extent the concepts of coverture versus the marriage community (in New France) influenced the thinking of captive girls and women, but it was a difference that they were likely aware of, especially those daughters who were threatened with disinheritance.

The way in which William and Mary Moore's parents' estate was settled in 1694 reveals a clear double standard of male and female captives' inheritance. Whereas brother William could receive his portion of the estate "provided said William be alive & demand it," sister Mary could receive hers only if she returned to New England: "if Mary More doo not return from captivity, then her redemption money and her portion to be equally devided among the rest of her brethren and sisters." . . . The language parents used could be very specific: daughters could not simply come home to claim their inheritance (like William Moore would have been permitted to); they had to renounce French law, language, and religion, and come home to stay. Joseph Storer wrote in his 1721 will: "I Give & Bequeath to my beloved Daughter Mary St. Germain Fifty pounds in good Contrey pay upon Condition that She return from under the French Government & Settle in New England.". . . Esther Wheelwright

was . . . disinherited by her mother's 1750 will, unless she "by the Wonder working Providence of God be returned to her Native Land and tarry & dwell in it."[27]

Captive sons fared much better. . . . Even when their claims on inheritance were disputed, returned male captives had good luck in court, especially with the help of a mother's testimony. William Hutchins, taken from Kittery, Maine, in 1705 when he was nine, was apparently presumed dead when the state ordered the division of his late father's estate in 1721, as he was left entirely out of the proceedings. When he returned to Maine in 1733 to claim his inheritance, . . . his brothers denied his identity, so he decided to sue them for his inheritance. Many neighbors testified that he was in fact the real William Hutchins; in the end his mother's judgment that "he is the first born of my Body" prevailed. Hutchins not only received an inheritance, he won the double portion due him as the eldest brother. Conveniently settled, he married a New England woman in 1734 and remained for some time in Kittery. Clearly, English male captives who remained in French Canada were still seen as legitimate heirs, by their families and by the courts, even decades after they had left New England. Their sisters were not so lucky. . . .[28]

The case of Mary Storer and her contested relationship with her English family bears close examination, both for what it suggests about the female captives who remained in Canada and for one family's reaction to this exercise of daughterly will and determination. The surviving correspondence of Mary Storer St. Germaine consists of nine letters to her eldest brother, Ebenezer, one letter each to her mother and another brother, five letters from her husband, Jean St. Germaine, to Ebenezer, and two letters from Ebenezer, one addressed to Mary, the other to her husband, a total of eighteen letters that span nearly thirty years, from 1725 to 1754. Read together, these letters offer valuable glimpses into family relationships in colonial New England. More importantly, they are almost the only direct words we have from a female captive who remained in Canada, and thus offer us some insight into the mind of one captive as she attempts to reconcile the English and the French sides of her family and her own identity. Mary's brother Ebenezer seems to have functioned as the go-between for his sister and the rest of their family in these letters, performing as the executor of not only his father's will but also his family's wishes regarding Mary in general.[29]

The correspondence begins twenty-two years after Mary was taken by the Indians, when both she and Ebenezer were middle-aged parents. Mary Storer was taken in the 1703 Abenaki raid on Wells, Maine, when she and her cousins Rachael and Priscilla Storer were taken in the same attack as Aaron Little-field and Esther Wheelwright. . . . [T]he Storer girls were teenagers: Mary was eighteen, Priscilla nineteen, and Rachael about sixteen. All three Storers were therefore young women at the time of their captivity, not children, which may have contributed to greater resentment among the Storer family of their daughters' choices. All three married French men and remained in Canada—Mary and Priscilla . . . lived near each other in Montreal the rest of their lives, and Rachael (baptized "Marie Françoise") settled in Québec with her husband, Jean Berger.

The occasion for what seems to have been a new or renewed epistolary relationship with Mary's brother Ebenezer was a visit she made to Boston in the late spring and summer of 1725, as the first letters she writes are posted from Newport, Rhode Island, where she was awaiting the ship that would return her to Montreal. These first letters, all but one addressed to Ebenezer, communicate her distress at having been so long separated from her birth family and indicate that like the Williams family, her family wanted to return her and her children to New England and thus to the Protestant faith. In her own handwriting and crude spelling, she assures brother Ebenezer, "my harte is alwais full of sorey and my eyes full of ters to think that I have toke sech a grate jorney to come to se my deare father and mother and had no coumforte to staye longe with them." In another letter she repeats the same sentiments in similar language: "[While] I am not with you my harte and tender love is alwaise with you I shall never for git what every good peple has sead to me becaus I know that is for my good and I pray to god onley that it maie be so an if I can sende one of my childrine I will." Another letter, which was probably intended for her brother Seth, a congregational minister in Watertown, Massachusetts, also gives thanks for some good counsel she received during her visit: "I had but a litel time with you

who I thought woulde show and teach me more then aney bodey [sir?] but what you have saide to me I will not forgett it and I hope god will in able me in all my aflections and that it may be for the best and good of my soule deare brother." Clearly, Mary's natal family had urged her to the Protestant fold, as well as tried to convince her to return to New England. Her notation to Ebenezer that "if I can sende one of my childrine I will" seems to indicate that the Storers were interested in taking in and evangelizing her Catholic children as well. . . .

Although Mary wrote that she understood that the Storer family's counsel to return to New England and to puritanism was "for the goode of my soule and bodey," she had no intention of remaining with them. Her continuing correspondence with Ebenezer suggests that she was adept at shifting between identifying with her natal family in Boston and with her husband and children in Montreal. Continuing to address herself to Ebenezer before her return home, she writes, "Dear brother it grievs me to thinke of my father and mother that I had soe litel time to staye with theme but I finde the time very longe with strangers and longe to be with my famelie." Thus by calling her natal family "strangers," as opposed to her "famelie" in Montreal, she makes it clear that her family of first allegiance was in Montreal, not in Boston. And while she implies that her Boston family are "strangers" to her, her emotional attachment to them was quite powerful immediately after her 1725 visit. "Deare brother I remember what you have saide to me I thanke you and all that has spoke for my goode." Then again using formulaic language, she writes, "I desier your prayers for me who is youre sister til death with a harte full of sorey and my eyes full of tears fearewell my deare brother and sister I remaine your loving and sorrowful sister," and signs herself, as she did through most of their correspondence, "Mary St. Germaine, Mary Storer," as though to signify her awareness of her two families and her two identities. With only a few notable exceptions, however, her married name was written above her maiden name.

. . . For eight years after her visit to Boston, Mary and Ebenezer continued to exchange letters every year or two, updating each other on family news and sending along formulaic but apparently warm good wishes. When Ebenezer sent news of their father's death, Mary [wrote]. . . "I pray to god to comforte us all wee are father les children [while] I am hear [in Montreal], you may beleive my harte love is with you all we are al the same blode you can not denie it."

. . . In a letter to her mother, she writes that Ebenezer told her, "my dear father maide his will that I [might?] be equal to my sisters you may believe my dear mother [while] I am far of[f] from you and my deare familei I belave that is not cappable to kep it frome me in conseonc that is for me who is youre [own] child." Regarding her father's command that she remove herself from "French government" in order to receive her inheritance, Mary then claims it is impossible for her even to visit Boston: "wee have a governer & he will nat give any permission to goe in [New] Ingland to our contre[y]," she writes, and names the merchant in Boston whom she had designated to receive and convey her inheritance. . . . [S]he signs her letter, "your dutifull daughter," a departure from her usual practice, and a maneuver that suggests an effort to recast herself as a properly obedient and submissive daughter.

There exists no letter of reply from Mary's mother, but brother Ebenezer's reply underscores the differences her New England family drew between Mary and her siblings. . . . Ebenezer does not promise [her] her inheritance, but he writes that he will remind their mother of her request, and assures Mary, "I know she will do any thing yt is proper & it be not against ye will of our Father deceas'd." The problem was that what Mary was requesting was clearly against her father's will. Joseph Storer had decreed that "if She doth not returne [to New England] Then I Give & bequeath to her the Sum of Tenn Shillings in Countrey pay." This paltry remembrance stood as a rebuke to Mary's resistance of her father's will, and her mother and brother were apparently willing to let the rebuke stand. Legally they could not have directly sent Mary St. Germaine her portion directly from her father's estate, but they could have chosen to give her her portion out of their own fortunes.

Perhaps not surprisingly, there is no record of Mary St. Germaine ever receiving her inheritance, and the surviving correspondence between her and her brother ceases for several years. Only in the autumn of 1739, nearly six and a half years since her last surviving letter to Ebenezer, Mary wrote to him, and the tone

of that letter suggests that she is still annoyed with him and his role in her non-inheritance. Whereas before she had always written him in English in her own hand, this letter appears to have been written by an amanuensis; it is also, significantly, written in French. She opens this letter with a standard, if cooler, salutation to Ebenezer, and then quickly announces the purpose of her letter: "I desire the favour to Let me hear from you & your family for as I have not heard any knews of mother I dont know whether she is on the Land of the Living which obliges me to adress my self to you to lett me hear from her." Notice how her language has changed since her fervent correspondence around the time of her father's death. . . . "If you still have any Love for me I hope you will not refuse me that Comfort," she adds, in further confirmation of her alienation from her natal family. She passes on news of her family, briefly reporting her children's marriages and sadly noting the death of her youngest son the previous year. We do not know if she ever received a reply. . . .

This may well have been the last letter Mary St. Germaine wrote to her brother Ebenezer, for the next letter in the collection is by her husband, Jean, dated eight and a half years after Mary's last letter. Like Mary's last letter, it too is written in French. Seven months after the fact, he wrote the man he addressed as his "very dear brother" to let Ebenezer know of his sister's death. "She died with all possible resignation to the will of God, that is to say as a perfect Christian, and as she had been here 39 years that we were together we had a blessed union and we never had a single difficulty. You know well my dear brother that her death is a great affliction to me, but I must submit to the will of our Creator, as it was he who gave me one of the best women in the world." . . .

Stories like that of Mary Storer St. Germaine show the effects that choices like hers had on the workings of patriarchal power within New England families. The Storer family was typical of other New England families, . . . who also went to great lengths to recover their daughters and save them from the twin evils of French government and Catholicism, or to punish them for their rejection of New England government and Protestantism, or both. Any captives who turned their backs on New England by converting to Catholicism and remaining in Canada represented a painful and shameful failure of the New England way, boys and men as well as girls and women. But New England communities and colonial governments actively courted the return of male ex-captives by offering them cash and jobs, whereas former female captives were offered little if any incentive to return. Instead, it was the government of New France that went out of its way to retain female captives from New England, especially in the years 1689–1713. Mary Storer St. Germaine's story demonstrates that New England families interpreted their daughters' conversion to Catholicism and marriage to French men and Indians as a rejection of New England patriarchal authority. Instead of dutiful obedience and submission to their fathers' (or brothers') household government, women like Mary Storer St. Germaine set themselves against New England's prescribed gender roles when they refused to come home and return to puritanism. While their own decision to abandon New England is no doubt part of the reason they have been written out of New England history, perhaps their families' shame and desire to forget these daughters are also responsible for the fact that so many of them have disappeared from the New England record.

NOTES

1. Frances E. Dolan, *Whores of Babylon: Catholicism, Gender, and Seventeenth-Century Print Culture* (Ithaca, NY.: Cornell University Press, 1999).

2. James Axtell, *The Invasion Within: The Contest of Cultures in Colonial North America* (New York: Oxford University Press, 1985), 287–301; Barbara E. Austen, "Captured . . . Never Came Back: Social Networks Among New England Female Captives in Canada, 1689–1763," and Alice N. Nash, "Two Stories of New England Captives: Grizel and Christine Otis of Dover, New Hampshire," both in *New England/New France, 1600–1850*, ed. Peter Benes (Boston: Boston University, 1992), 28–48; William Foster, *The Captors' Narrative: Catholic Women and Their Puritan Men on the Early American Frontier* (Ithaca, N.Y.: Cornell University Press, 2003).

3. On women's alleged vulnerability to the devil's blandishments, see Carol Karlsen, *The Devil in the Shape of a Woman: Witchcraft in Colonial New England* (New York: Norton, 1987), especially chs. 4 and 5; Elizabeth Reis, *Damned Women: Sinners and Witches in Puritan New England* (Ithaca, N.Y.: Cornell University Press, 1997).

4. For reports of French collaboration with the Abenaki during King Philip's War, see Henry Jocelyn and Joshua Scottow to Gov. John Leverett, September 15, 1676, Coll. S-888, misc. box 33/21, Maine Historical Society, Portland, Maine; *Documentary History of the State of Maine* (Portland, Maine: Lefavor-Tower, 1869–1916), 4:377–79.

5. Francis D. Cogliano, *No King, No Popery: Anti-Catholicism in Revolutionary New England* (Westport, Conn.: Greenwood Press, 1995), introduction and chs. 1–2.

6. Anne McLaren, "Gender, Religion, and Early Modern Nationalism: Elizabeth I, Mary Queen of Scots, and the Genesis of English Anti-Catholicism," *American Historical Review* 107 (June 2002): 739–67; Dolan, 6–27.

7. Cotton Mather, *Humiliations follow'd with Deliverances* (Boston, 1697), 30–31. He made the same historical argument a few years later in *Decennium Luctuosum: an History of Remarkable Occurences in the long war which New England hath had with the Indian Salvages, 1688–1698* (Boston, 1699).

8. Francis Jennings, *The Invasion of America: Indians, Colonialism, and the Cant of Conquest* (Chapel Hill: University of North Carolina Press, 1975), 228–53. On the praying Indians more generally, see Ann Marie Plane, *Colonial Intimacies: Indian Marriage in Early New England* (Ithaca, N.Y.: Cornell University Press, 2000).

9. Mather, *Decennium Luctuosum*, 81, 215–16.

10. Mather, *Humiliations follow'd with Deliverances*, 59–71; Emma Lewis Coleman, *New England Captives Carried to Canada* (Portland, Maine: The Southworth Press, 1925; reprint, Bowie, Md.: Heritage Books, 1989), vols. 1 and 2.

11. Mather, *Humiliations follow'd with Deliverances*, 72; Coleman, *New England Captives*, 1:204–08.

12. Elizabeth Hanson, *God's Mercy Surmounting Man's Cruelty* (Philadelphia, 1729), 34; Coleman, *New England Captives*, 2:163.

13. John Gyles, *Memoirs of Odd Adventures* (Boston, 1736), 4–5; Dolan, 85–93.

14. Alden T. Vaughan and Daniel K. Richter, "Crossing the Cultural Divide: Indians and New Englanders, 1605–1763," *American Antiquarian Society Proceedings*, 90 (April 16, 1980), 23–99; author's database compiled from the cases documented by Coleman, *New England Captives*, vols. 1 and 2.

15. William Pote, Jr., original ms. journal kept by him 1745–47 during captivity among the French & Indians, Ayer Collection, Newberry Library, Chicago, Ill., 15; Axtell, *Invasion Within*, 291–94; Laurel Thatcher Ulrich, *Good Wives: Image and Reality in the Lives of Women in Northern New England, 1650–1750* (New York: Oxford University Press, 1983), 208–13.

16. Louise Dechêne, *Habitants and Merchants in Seventeenth Century Montreal* (Montreal: McGill-Queens University Press, 1992), 240–49; Trevor G. Burnard and Ann M. Little, "Where the Girls Aren't: Women as Reluctant Migrants but Rational Actors in Early America," in *The Practice of U.S. Women's History: Narratives, Intersections, and Dialogues*, ed. Eileen Boris, Jay Kleinberg, and Vicki Ruiz (New Brunswick, N.J.: Rutgers University Press, 2007), 12–29.

17. Peter Moogk, "Manon's Fellow Exiles: Emigration from France to North America before 1763," in *Europeans on the Move: Studies on European Migration, 1500–1800*, ed. Nicholas Canny (Oxford: Clarendon Press, 1994), 236–60; Leslie Choquette, "French and British Emigration to the North American Colonies: A Comparative Overview," *New England/New France, 1600–1850*, ed. Peter Benes (Boston: Boston University, 1992), 49–59.

18. For evidence of the state's drive to bring more properly trained housewives into Canada, see, for example, the correspondence of Governor Frontenac and Minister Colbert, *Rapport de L'Archiviste de la Province de Québec* (Québec: Ls- A. Proulx, 1927), 7:44, 60, 65–66, 82 (1673–74); and the correspondence of Governor Frontenac and Intendant Bochart Champigny to the Minister, 8:351, 359, 377 (1697–98).

19. Leslie Choquette, "'Ces Amazones du Grand Dieu': Women and Mission in Seventeenth-Century Canada," *French Historical Studies* 17 (1992): 627–55; Clark Robenstine, "French Colonial Policy and the Education of Women and Minorities: Louisiana in the Early Eighteenth Century," *History of Education Quarterly* 32 (1992): 193–211; Natalie Zemon Davis, "Marie de l'Incarnation: New Worlds," in *Women on the Margins: Three Seventeenth-Century Lives* (Cambridge, Mass.: Harvard University Press, 1995), 63–139.

20. Coleman, *New England Captives*, 1:316–17, 330–31, 356–57, 425–35, 2:44–58, 147, 390–91; SC1 45X, Massachusetts Archives Collection, 51:212–13, and 72:13–15, Massachusetts State Archives, Boston; Ann M. Little, "The Life of Mother Marie-Joseph de L'Enfant Jesus, or, How a little English Girl from Wells became a Big French Politician," *Maine History* 40 (Winter 2002), 276–308.

21. Coleman, *New England Captives*, 2: 320–21, 391, 396; Bunker Gay, *A genuine and correct account of the captivity, sufferings & deliverance of Mrs. Jemima Howe, of Hinsdale in New Hampshire* (Boston, 1792), 16–18.

22. Coleman, *New England Captives*, 1:121–29; Choquette, "Ces Amazones du Grand Dieu"; Little, "Mother Marie-Joseph."

23. Susanna Johnson, *A Narrative of the Captivity of Mrs. Johnson, together with a Narrative of James Johnson*, 3rd ed. (Windsor, Vt., 1814; reprint, Bowie, Md.: Heritage Books, 1990), 89–90.

24. Coleman, *New England Captives*, 1:255–61; Nathaniel Bouton, ed., *Collections of the New Hampshire Historical Society*, vol 8 (Concord: McFarland & Jenks, 1866), 146–48; Ulrich also cites domestic violence as a reason why Willey might have wanted to remain in Canada, *Good Wives*, 209.

25. Cornelia Hughes Dayton, *Women Before the Bar: Gender, Law, and Society in Connecticut, 1639–1789* (Chapel Hill: University of North Carolina Press, 1995), ch. 3; Nancy Cott, "Divorce and the Changing Status of Women in Eighteenth- Century Massachusetts," *William and Mary Quarterly* 3rd ser., 33 (1976): 586–614; Peter Moogk, *La Nouvelle France: The Making of French Canada—A Cultural History* (East Lansing: Michigan State University Press, 2000), 229–33.

26. Coleman, *New England Captives*, 1:255–61.

27. Evidence taken from Coleman, *New England Captives*, vols. 1 and 2, passim. Specific cases from vol. 1: 234–35, 418–19, 431.

28. Coleman, *New England Captives*, 1:391–93.

29. Mary Storer Papers, Massachusetts Historical Society, Boston, Mass. All letters discussed below are in this collection.

The Trial of Anne Hutchinson, 1637

In 1989, in a solemn ceremony soaked with irony and bitter humor, the leaders of the Newport Rhode Island Congregational Church announced that injustice had been done more than 350 years before when Anne Hutchinson had been expelled from Boston's Congregational Church for blasphemy and perjury. The minister who took the initiative, and who coincidentally bore the same name as the John Wilson who had read the formal excommunication in the seventeenth century, thought that the Hutchinson affair raised questions that remained central to religion in the present: questions "of spiritual freedom, the role of women in the church, the issue of individual freedom versus being part of a covenant community, and the church-state issue." In a public ceremony, the president of the Rhode Island Conference of the United Church of Christ burned a copy of the writ of excommunication.*

The Antinomian heresy of 1637–38 threw the Puritan colony of Massachusetts Bay into turmoil for years and forced its leaders to reconsider the nature of their experiment. Antinomians placed greater emphasis on religious feeling than did orthodox Puritans. They tended to be suspicious (*anti*) of law (*nomos*) or formal rules and came close to asserting that individuals had access to direct revelation from the Holy Spirit. They criticized ministers who seemed to argue that it was possible to earn salvation by good deeds rather than leaving it to God freely to decide who was to be saved by their faith, a distinction between the "covenant of works" and a "covenant of faith" which they thought separated authentic Puritans from ones who remained too close to the Anglican Church.

One such Antinomian critic, clergyman John Wheelwright (Anne Hutchinson's brother-in-law) was tried in early 1637 for giving a controversial sermon, found guilty of sedition, and banished. The close relationship between church and state in early New England meant that such challenges to the majority's theological views were interpreted as threatening to established authority of all kinds.

One leading dissenter was Anne Hutchinson, a high-status, well-educated woman in her mid-forties who had migrated to the colony with her merchant husband in 1634, four years after its founding, and who commanded great respect for her competence as a midwife. At meetings held in her home after Sunday church services, she summarized, discussed, and criticized ministers' sermons. Initially attended by five or six women, the meetings became very popular; soon Hutchinson was holding separate gatherings for men and women. The women who followed Hutchinson were often those who respected her medical knowledge and shared her theological ideas. The men who attended were often those

* Madeline Pecora Nugent, "Apologizing to Anne Hutchinson," *Christian Century* 106 (Mar. 22, 1989): 304–5.

Excerpted from "Examination of Mrs. Anne Hutchinson before the court at Newton, 1637," in *The Antinomian Controversy, 1636–1638: A Documentary History*, ed. David D. Hall (Middletown, Conn.: Wesleyan University Press, 1968), pp. 312–16. Copyright © 1968 by David D. Hall. Reprinted by permission of the editor. Notes have been edited and renumbered.

who were critical of the colony's leadership on political and economic as well as religious grounds. Tensions were high in Massachusetts Bay through 1636 and 1637 as colonists violently attacked the Pequot Indians, decimating the tribe and capturing and enslaving the women and children. In a context in which pastor John Wilson linked the destruction of "barbarous Indians" with God's will, religious and political dissent seemed to merge easily. Rumor spread that criticism of the governor and council, the majority of ministers, and the Pequot War had been voiced in the Hutchinsons' house. This led to Anne's being grilled, first by a convocation of ministers and then, in November 1637, by the magistrates and legislators of the colony, in a court held in Newtown (now Cambridge).

The proceedings were not a trial in the contemporary sense with due process safeguards; instead they followed the format of the early modern magisterial examination, an inquisition without a jury. Hutchinson, who was pregnant, had no lawyer. Her trial was conducted by the governor of the colony, John Winthrop. (His house was directly across the path from the Hutchinsons' dwelling; he could not have avoided seeing the people coming and going to her meetings.) Winthrop was joined in his questioning by the deputy governor and other members of the legislature (called the General Court). Only very late in the interrogation did Anne make an incautious statement—that God had directly revealed things to her—which provided her judges with a rationale to convict her of heresy and sentence her banishment from the colony.

Hutchinson's secular trial was followed by a disciplinary hearing in the Boston church to which she belonged. This second trial covered much of the same ground as the first; one of the ministers present spoke for many of the men in the room when he declared: "You have stept out of your place, you have rather bine a Husband than a Wife and a preacher than a Hearer; and a Magistrate than a Subject." After the members voted to excommunicate her, pastor Wilson pronounced the judgment: "Forasmuch as you, Mistress Hutchinson, have highly transgressed and offended and forasmuch as you have so many ways troubled the Church with your Errors and have drawn away many a poor soul and have upheld your Revelations: . . . I command you . . . as a Leper to withdraw your self out of the Congregation." At this, Hutchinson rose, walked to the meetinghouse door, turned, and spoke directly to her accusers: "The lord judgeth not as man judgeth, better to be cast out of the Church then [than] to deny Christ."

After Hutchinson was exiled, at least ten more women were banished or excommunicated for being outspoken. Thus, a clear message was sent that explicit dissent by women was not to be tolerated in the Massachusetts Bay Colony. In Winthrop's memoir of the events, published in 1644, miscarriages suffered by Hutchinson and her closest colleague, Mary Dyer, were interpreted as evidence of God's "displeasure against their opinions and practices, as clearly as if he had pointed with his finger, in causing the two fomenting women in the time of the height of the Opinions to produce out of their wombs, as before they had out of their braines, such monstrous births as no Chronicle . . . hardly ever recorded the like."*

* Sandra F. VanBurkleo, "'To Bee Rooted Out of Her Station': The Ordeal of Anne Hutchinson," in *American Political Trials*, rev. ed., ed. Michael R. Belknap (Westport, Conn.: Greenwood Press, 1994), pp. 1–24; *The Antinomian Controversy, 1636–1638: A Documentary History*, ed. David D. Hall (quotes on pp. 214, 382–83, 388); and *Winthrop's Journal, "History of New England": 1630–1649*, vol. 1, ed. James Kendall Hosmer (New York: Charles Scribner's Sons, 1908), p. 251.

Hutchinson and her husband fled to Rhode Island, a colony with a policy of religious toleration. Several years later, they moved to Dutch territory north of what is now New York City. Widowed, Anne Hutchinson died in an Indian raid on her settlement, in 1643.

In reading this excerpt from Anne Hutchinson's 1637 trial, note the extent to which criticism of her religious and political behavior merges with the complaint that she is challenging gender roles. It will help to know that by "rule," Protestants of the era meant a biblical passage that stipulated how Christians should behave. What strategies did Hutchinson use to defend her actions and challenge the proceedings? Which points of the dialogue best reveal colonial leaders' fear of independent women?

NOVEMBER 1637

The Examination of Mrs. Ann Hutchinson at the Court at Newtown

Mr. Winthrop, governor. Mrs. Hutchinson, you are called here as one of those that have troubled the peace of the commonwealth and the churches here; you are known to be a woman that hath had a great share in the promoting and divulging of those opinions that are causes of this trouble, and to be nearly joined not only in affinity and affection with some of those the court had taken notice of and passed censure upon, but you have spoken divers things as we have been informed very prejudicial to the honour of the churches and ministers thereof, and you have maintained a meeting and an assembly in your house that hath been condemned by the general assembly as a thing not tolerable nor comely in the sight of God nor fitting for your sex, and notwithstanding that was cried down you have continued the same, therefore we have thought good to send for you to understand how things are, that if you be in an erroneous way we may reduce you that so you may become a profitable member here among us, otherwise (if you be obstinate in your course that then the court may take such course that you may trouble us no further) therefore I would intreat you to express whether you do not hold and assent in practice to those opinions and factions that have been handled in court already, that is to say, whether you do not justify Mr. Wheelwright's sermon and the petition.[1]

Mrs. Hutchinson. I am called here to answer before you but I hear no things laid to my charge.

Gov. I have told you some already and more I can tell you.

Mrs. H. Name one, Sir.

Gov. Have I not named some already?

Mrs. H. What have I said or done?

Gov. Why for your doings, this you did harbour and countenance those that are parties in this faction that you have heard of.

Mrs. H. That's matter of conscience, Sir.

Gov. Your conscience you must keep or it must be kept for you. . . . Say that one brother should commit felony or treason and come to his other brother's house, if he knows him guilty and conceals him he is guilty of the same. It is his conscience to entertain him, but if his conscience comes into act in giving countenance and entertainment to him that hath broken the law he is guilty too. So if you do countenance those that are transgressors of the law you are in the same fact.

Mrs. H. What law do they transgress?

Gov. The law of God and of the state.

Mrs. H. In what particular?

Gov. Why in this among the rest, whereas the Lord doth say honour thy father and thy mother.

Mrs. H. Ey Sir in the Lord.

Gov. This honour you have broke in giving countenance to them. . . .

Mrs. H. What law have I broken?

Gov. Why the fifth commandment.

Mrs. H. I deny that for [Mr. Wheelwright] saith in the Lord.

Gov. You have joined with them in the faction.

Mrs. H. In what faction have I joined with them?

Gov. In presenting the petition . . .

Mrs. H. But I had not my hand to the petition.

Gov. You have councelled them.

Mrs. H. Wherein?

Gov. Why in entertaining them.

Mrs. H. What breach of law is that Sir?

Gov. Why dishonouring of parents.

Mrs. H. But put the case Sir that I do fear the Lord and my parents, may not I entertain them that fear the Lord because my parents will not give me leave?

Gov. If they be the fathers of the commonwealth, and they of another religion, if you entertain them then you dishonour your parents and are justly punishable.

Mrs. H. If I entertain them, as they have dishonoured their parents I do.

Gov. No but you by countenancing them above others put honor upon them.

Mrs. H. I may put honor upon them as the children of God and as they do honor the Lord.

Gov. We do not mean to discourse with those of your sex but only this; you do adhere unto them and do endeavour to set forward this faction and so you do dishonour us.

Mrs. H. I do acknowledge no such thing neither do I think that I ever put any dishonour upon you.

Gov. Why do you keep such a meeting at your house as you do every week upon a set day?

Mrs. H. It is lawful for me so to do, as it is all your practices and can you find a warrant for yourself and condemn me for the same thing? [I]t was in practice before I came therefore I was not the first.

Gov. For this, that you appeal to our practice you need no confutation. If your meeting had answered to the former it had not been offensive, but I will say that there was no meeting of women alone, but your meeting is of another sort for there are sometimes men among you.

Mrs. H. There was never any man with us.

Gov. Well, admit there was no man at your meeting and that you was sorry for it, there is no warrant for your doings, and by what warrant do you continue such a course?

Mrs. H. I conceive there lyes a clear rule in Titus, that the elder women should instruct the younger[2] and then I must have a time wherein I must do it.

Gov. All this I grant you, I grant you a time for it, but what is this to the purpose that you Mrs. Hutchinson must call a company together from their callings to come to be taught of you?

Mrs. H. Will it please you to answer me this and to give me a rule for then I will willingly submit to any truth. If any come to my house to be instructed in the ways of God what rule have I to put them away?

Gov. But suppose that a hundred men come unto you to be instructed will you forbear to instruct them?

Mrs. H. As far as I conceive I cross a rule in it.

Gov. Very well and do you not so here?

Mrs. H. No Sir for my ground is they are men.

Gov. Men and women all is one for that, but suppose that a man should come and say Mrs. Hutchinson I hear that you are a woman that God hath given his grace unto and you have knowledge in the word of God I pray instruct me a little, ought you not to instruct this man?

Mrs. H. I think I may.—Do you think it not lawful for me to teach women and why do you call me to teach the court?

Gov. We do not call you to teach the court but to lay open yourself.

Mrs. H. I desire you that you would then set me down a rule by which I may put them away that come unto me and so have peace in so doing.

Gov. You must shew your rule to receive them.

Mrs. H. I have done it.

Gov. I deny it because I have brought more arguments than you have.

Mrs. H. I say, to me it is a rule.

Mr. Endicot. You say there are some rules unto you. I think there is a contradiction in your own words. What rule for your practice do you bring, only a custom in Boston.

Mrs. H. No Sir that was no rule to me but if you look upon the rule in Titus it is a rule to me. If you convince me that it is no rule I shall yield.

Gov. . . . . [T]his rule crosses that in the Corinthians.[3] But you must take it in this sense that elder women must instruct the younger about their business, and to love their husbands and not to make them to clash.

Mrs. H. I do not conceive but that it is meant for some publick times.

Gov. Well, have you no more to say but this?

Mrs. H. I have said sufficient for my practice.

Gov. Your course is not to be suffered for, besides that we find such a course as this to be greatly prejudicial to the state, besides the occasion that it is to seduce many honest persons that are called to those meetings and your opinions being known to be different from the word of God may seduce many simple souls that resort unto you, besides that the occasion which hath come of late hath come from none but such as have frequented your meetings, so that now they are flown off from magistrates and ministers and this since they have come to you, and besides that it will not well stand with the commonwealth that families should be neglected for so many neighbours and dames and so much time spent, we see no rule of God for this, we see not that any should have authority to set up any other exercises besides what authority hath already set up and so what hurt comes of this you will be guilty of and we for suffering you.

Mrs. H. Sir I do not believe that to be so.

Gov. Well, we see how it is we must therefore put it away from you, or restrain you from maintaining this course.

Mrs. H. If you have a rule for it from God's word you may.

Gov. We are your judges, and not you ours and we must compel you to it.

Mrs. H. If it please you by authority to put it down I freely let you for I am subject to your authority.

Notes

1. The petition the Antinomian party presented to the General Court in March 1637.

2. Titus 2.3, 4, 5.

3. 1 Corinthians 14.34, 35.

European Women and the Law: Examples from Colonial Connecticut

---

Marriage is an intimate relationship that is a result of private choice. But marriage is also a public act and has important social, political, and legal implications for both women and men. Indeed, deep into our own time, the law of marriage has shaped how men and women relate to each other and how they act in the world; when people want to change those relationships, they often begin by challenging the rules of marriage. If we want to understand the systems of gender in a culture, the rules of marriage are the place to begin.

Europeans were startled by the patterns of intimate relations among Native Americans. Although there were many differences among native cultures, marriage was generally situated within complex matrifocal systems of kinship in which husbands moved into the dwellings of the wife's kin; in which sisters and brothers remained close even in adulthood; and in which uncles and aunts could play important roles in the upbringing of nieces and nephews. In these kin networks, premarital sex, polygamy, marital separation, and divorce were not necessarily frowned upon, and there was often a space for a third gender or homosexual practice. For Europeans, such different rules of intimacy were signs of weakness and lack of civilization.

"Husband and wife are one person in law, that is, the very being or legal existence of the woman is suspended during the marriage, or at least is incorporated and consolidated into that of the husband; under whose wing, protection, and cover, she performs every thing; and is therefore called . . . *a feme covert.*" This understanding, known as *coverture*, was the foundation of the English law of domestic relations. When an Englishwoman married, her husband became the owner of all the movable things she possessed and of all the property or wages she might earn during their marriage. He also received the right to manage and collect the rents and profits on any real estate she owned; if they had a child, the child could not inherit the dead mother's lands until after the death of the father. (For more details of the system of coverture, see Kerber, pp. 110–117.)

All colonies placed in their statutes a law regulating marriage. This step reflected a concern that marriage be celebrated publicly in order to guard against bigamy. Connecticut did not forbid interracial marriage, but many other colonies did.

Early America was for the most part a divorceless society. South Carolina boasted that it granted no divorce until 1868. Most colonies followed the British practice of treating marriage as a moral obligation for life. Occasional special dissolutions of a marriage were granted by legislatures in response to individual petitions or by courts of equity, but these were separations from bed and board, which normally did not carry with them freedom to marry again.

The Puritan settlers of Massachusetts and Connecticut were unusual in treating marriage as a civil contract, which might be broken if its terms were not carried out. Connecticut enacted the earliest divorce law in the colonies. It made divorce available after a simple petition to the superior court under certain circumstances. People who did not fit these circumstances were able to present special petitions to the legislature.

Most petitioners for divorce in early America were women. What sorts of troubled marriages could women in colonial Connecticut exit by getting a judicial divorce? If you were a legislator, what grounds for divorce would you add? Scholars call the eighteenth and nineteenth centuries a period of "fault divorce." One spouse was seen as guilty of having breached the contract, while the other was innocent; thus, divorce due to incompatibility or irreconcilable differences was not available. Identify the language in the Connecticut statute that reflects this outlook.

AN ACT RELATING TO BILLS OF DIVORCE, 1667

Be it enacted . . . that no bill of divorce shall be granted to any man or woman, lawfully married, but in case of adultery, or fraudulent contract, or wilful desertion for three years with total neglect of duty; or in case of seven years absence of one party not heard of: after due enquiry is made, and the matter certified to the superior court, in which case the other party may be deemed and accounted single and unmarried. And in that case, and in all other cases aforementioned, a bill of divorce may be granted by the superior court to the aggrieved party; who may then lawfully marry or be married again.

Perhaps no statutes were more important to women in the first 250 years after settlement of the English colonies than the laws protecting their claims to dower. The "widow's dower" should be distinguished from the dowry a bride might bring with her into marriage. "The widow's dower" or the "widow's third" was the right of a widow to use one-third of the real estate that her husband held at the time of his death. She was also entitled to one-third of the personal property he had owned, after the debts were paid. It was an old English tradition that he might leave her more in his will, but he could not leave her less. If a man died without a will, the courts would ensure that his widow received her "thirds."

It is important to note that she only had the right to use the land and buildings. She might live on this property, rent it out, farm the land, and sell the produce. But she could not sell or bequeath it. If the real estate was simply the family home and her children were adults, she had a claim only to a portion of the house. After the widow's death, the property reverted to her husband's heirs, who normally would be their children, but in the event of a childless marriage was likely to revert to his brothers or nephews.

A contrasting situation existed in the community property jurisdictions, including Louisiana, New Mexico, and California. There, "dotal" property, or dowry that came with the bride, was intended to help with the expenses of the marriage; the husband could manage this property and spend its income, but at the end of the marriage it was restored to the wife or her heirs, thus keeping it in her own family line of succession. She also kept her own "paraphernalia"—personal clothing and other items—which she could trade as a merchant (without her husband's consent) and dispose of in her own will.

In the Connecticut statute, which follows, note the provisions protecting the widow's interests. Normally colonial courts were scrupulous about assigning the widow's portion. Observe, however, that widows could not claim dower in "movable" property, which might represent a larger share of their husband's wealth than real estate. As time passed and the American economy became more complex, it became increasingly likely that a man's property would not be held in the form of land. If the land were heavily mortgaged, the widow's prior right to her "third" became a barrier to creditors seeking to collect their portion of a husband's debts. By the early nineteenth century, courts were losing their enthusiasm for protecting widows' thirds. By the middle of the century, the married women's property acts began to reformulate a definition of the terms by which married women could claim their share of the property of wife and husband. But between 1790 and 1840, when the right to dower was more and more laxly enforced and the new married women's property acts had not yet been devised, married women were in a particularly vulnerable position. (See Keziah Kendall, pp. 242–244.)

AN ACT CONCERNING THE DOWRY OF WIDOWS, 1672

That there may be suitable provision made for the maintenance and comfortable support of widows, after the decease of their husbands, Be it enacted . . . that every married woman, living with her husband in this state, or absent elsewhere from him with his consent, or through his mere default, or by inevitable providence; or in case of divorce where she is the innocent party, that shall not before marriage be estated by way of jointure in some houses, lands, tenements or hereditaments for term of life . . . shall immediately upon, and after the death of her husband, have right, title and interest by way of dower, in and unto one third part of the real estate of her said deceased husband, in houses and lands which he stood possessed of in his own right, at the time of his decease, to be to her during her natural life: the remainder of the estate shall be disposed of according to the will of the deceased. . . .

And for the more easy, and speedy ascertaining such rights of dower, It is further enacted, That upon the death of any man possessed of any real estate . . . which his widow . . . hath a right of dower in, if the person, or persons that by law have a right to inherit said estate, do not within sixty days next after the death of such husband, by three sufficient freeholders of the same county; to be appointed by the judge of probate . . . and sworn for that purpose, set out, and ascertain such right of dower, that then such widow may make her complaint to the judge of probate . . . which judge shall decree, and order that such woman's dowry shall be set out, and ascertained by three sufficient freeholders of the county . . . and upon approbation thereof by said judge, such dower shall remain fixed and certain. . . .

And every widow so endowed . . . shall maintain all such houses, buildings, fences, and inclosures as shall be assigned, and set out to her for her dowry; and shall leave the same in good and sufficient repair.

HIDDEN TRANSCRIPTS
WITHIN SLAVERY

JUDITH A. CARNEY
The African Women Who Preceded Uncle Ben: Black Rice in Carolina

"When most of us think about the origin of rice, we think of Asia. But there is another species of rice whose history is less well known—a rice of African origin, *Oryza glaberrima*." So explains historical geographer Judith A. Carney. Until the 1970s, scholars assumed that the rice grown in England's southern mainland colonies was of Asian origin. Then, historian Peter Wood, in 1974, argued that the rice initially cultivated in the Carolina colony was *glaberrima* and that its success as an export crop was possible only because of the knowledge system of the many enslaved Africans charged with planting, weeding, harvesting, and milling it—especially women's knowledge.[*]

In colonial North America, "the most lucrative plantation system was not based on the crops we traditionally associate with slavery, such as cotton, sugar, and tobacco. Rather, it was based on rice, for which there was a considerable demand in Europe," Carney writes. But when the Carolina colony was first established by English planters in 1670, they were intent on growing sugar. The enslaved persons who accompanied them began cultivating rice in the subsistence plots where they grew provisions to feed themselves. Within a few decades, rice shifted from a local food crop to a plantation export crop. On the eve of the American Revolution, over the years 1768–1772, rice exports from South Carolina exceeded 66 million pounds annually. Already rice had become the first cereal to be globally traded.

Two points of orientation should help when reading Carney's essay. First, early European settlers in the Carolina colony (which later became North and South Carolina) and Georgia (founded in 1733) used the terms tidewater and low country to describe the territory along the rivers that ran to the Atlantic Ocean as far upstream as the fall-line—the point above which boats could not navigate. Second, rice growers in Carolina and Georgia worked under a task system, with enslaved women, men, and children assigned specific tasks they were expected to get done by the end of the day. Although they were not constantly supervised by

---

[*] Peter Wood, *Black Majority: Negroes in Colonial South Carolina from 1670 through the Stono Rebellion* (New York: Knopf, 1974)

white overseers, and although they managed to find time to grow a variety of African and other foods to either consume or take to market, they faced grueling physical requirements in rice cultivation, as you will see.

Carney's research tells us about one of many African food contributions to the Americas. To this day, rice retains its prominence in the foodways of many former plantation societies. Her essay reminds us, too, that although we tend to take the cultivation of food crops for granted, each one requires a body of information and skills—a system of knowledge—that is neither simple nor self-evident. Like the white women of free status in early New England colonies described by Laurel Thatcher Ulrich (see pp. 43–53), the female protagonists of Carney's essay brought a complicated skill set to the annual cycle of rice cultivation. But they and their African kinfolk did not profit or benefit from the hard physical labor they performed. As you read, see if you can list the preconditions and steps necessary to make rice into an export crop that enriched the white planters of this rice-growing region.

Over much of the northern portion of the West African rice region, rice has long been a woman's crop. . . . Wherever rice is grown in West Africa, women are involved. They display sophisticated knowledge in recognizing soil fertility by plant indicators, which reveal, for instance, soil impoverishment or recovery. Females are responsible for seed selection, sowing, hoeing, and rice processing. Seed selection in particular requires a sophisticated understanding of the specific demands made by diverse rice micro-environments, such as water availability, the influence of salinity, flooding levels, and soil conditions.

Women's expertise in African rice culture extended beyond knowledge of the crop's cultivation to include the processing of rice. . . . To what extent did the gendered knowledge systems of African rice culture diffuse to South Carolina? Did the institution of slavery reproduce any of the gendered forms of African cultivation and processing systems on Carolina rice plantations?

The hoe is the primary agricultural tool throughout the entire West African rice region. Indispensable to women's work in rice culture are a long- and short-handled version, the former used for field preparation and the latter for detailed work and weeding. Several colonial-period engravings and paintings of American rice plantations depict slaves, often females, carrying or working with the long-handled hoe. Its significance in field preparation continued after Emancipation [in 1863]. Written accounts of Carolina rice culture also mention the use of short-handled hoes, with handles four and eight inches in length, for detailed plot work.[1]

During the colonial period the use of hand tools predominated in southern agriculture. The clearing of forests resulted in fields full of stumps and roots, which could not be worked by draft animal traction. However, by the close of the period hoes were being replaced, as stump removal and decay facilitated the use of horse- and ox-drawn plows. The exception to this pattern occurred on Carolina rice plantations, where the use of hand tools continued into the antebellum period. Historian Lewis Gray calls the use of hoes in Carolina low-country agriculture the "West Indian method," which he claimed to be fixed in local custom rather than technological necessity. [The] method links the continuance of hoe agriculture in South Carolina to the system of planting in islands of the West Indies, such as Barbados, whence migrated some of the first European and black settlers to the Carolina low country. The West Indian tradition of using hand tools likely has its roots in West Africa.[2] . . .

As an agricultural implement the hoe actually played a minor role in eighteenth-century European farming systems, which relied principally on draft animal traction. Hoes were typically used for work in the corners of fields, on small parcels, or for specialized crops like grapes. In Africa, the hoe took on a preeminent role since much of the continent potentially favored for draft animal traction suffered adversely from trypanosome infection lethal to cattle. On no other continent but Africa does the hoe figure so centrally or take so many forms.[3]

Three cultivation techniques on Carolina plantations suggest African antecedents. Throughout West Africa women are the sowers of rice. On Carolina and Georgia rice plantations, sowing was typically the work of female slaves. The method of planting additionally reveals an African basis. Sowing usually involved dropping seeds onto the trenched ground and covering them with the foot. African antecedents are also evident in a second, though less common, method in which seeds are enveloped with marsh clay before planting. The technique is similar to one long used in West Africa, where women wrap seeds in cow dung and/or mud to protect them against birds, insects, and microbial parasites. The documentary *Family across the Sea*, which profiled many of the similarities in rice cultivation between South Carolina and Sierra Leone, filmed African women dropping the encased seeds in the soil for cultivation. In South Carolina and Georgia this method of sowing became known as open-trench planting.[4] . . .

Another technique in Carolina rice cultivation that indicates the transfer of a gendered knowledge system across the Atlantic relates to the method used for cultivating freshwater river floodplains. Rice cultivation in this environment is often a West African female farming system with transplanting practiced only in areas beset by high tides or when variability in the onset of precipitation delays the return of the flood. . . . [This was] one of the features distinguishing African from Asian rice systems. Tidal rice cultivation in South Carolina and Georgia developed on freshwater rivers and seldom involved transplanted seedlings, relying instead upon direct seeding of floodplains, as in Africa.[5]

Another group of techniques that testify to the transfer of female knowledge systems to the Americas relates to the manner of milling and cooking rice. For most of the colonial period rice was milled with a wooden mortar and pestle, with winnowing accomplished with fanner baskets. Thus until the advent of water-driven mechanical devices during the second half of the eighteenth century, rice milling was performed in the African manner with an upright wooden mortar and pestle. . . .

The processing of rice also involves the removal of the indigestible hulls or chaff, a process known as winnowing. In West Africa, winnowing occurs by placing the hand-milled rice, a mixture of grains and empty hulls, in circular and shallow straw baskets as much as two feet in diameter. During a breeze the grains and hulls are rotated inside and repeatedly tossed in the air. By tossing the grains and hulls up and down, the lighter chaff is carried off into the air, leaving the heavier husked grains inside the basket. Winnowing on South Carolina plantations followed the same method. The winnowing baskets, known on rice plantations as fanner baskets, were shallow disks with a raised lip about two feet across. They could hold about a pound of rice at a time.

Even the weaving style used in making fanner baskets displays an African origin. . . . The fanner baskets used for winnowing on Carolina and Georgia plantations [were always coiled and have been linked] to a tradition derived from the West African rice area. . . . Those marketed as folk craft by female African-American vendors in the Charleston area today are woven in the identical manner.[6] . . .

Methods of cooking reveal additional linkages to Africa. The characteristic way of preparing rice in the Carolina plantation kitchen favored grain separation, the way African dishes based on *glaberrima* rice are typically cooked. In South Carolina and elsewhere in the Americas this culinary tradition could be achieved with sativa rice by using medium- to long-grained varieties that tended not to clump together. Then the plate of rice was prepared so that it appeared "white, dry, and every grain separate." The method involves steaming and absorption, boiling rice first for 10–15 minutes, draining off excess water, removing the pan from direct heat so the grains can absorb the moisture, and leaving the pot covered for at least an hour before eating. Often the product was encased in a thick residue of crust on the inner edges of the pot: "Around the pot there is a brown rice-cake, in the center of which are the snow-white grains, each thoroughly done and each separate. Unless one has eaten rice cooked in this way, he knows nothing about it. The stuff called rice—soft and gluey—may do to paper a wall, but not to feed civilized man." This is the same manner in which rice is traditionally prepared throughout the West African rice region.[7] . . .

Despite the familiar logo of Uncle Ben on the converted rice marketed by that name in the United States, it was African women who perfected rice cooking. . . . They also developed the method of parboiling, another name for converted rice. In newly harvested rice,

which has not properly dried for milling, parboiling facilitates the removal of hulls. While
the steaming of rice in its hull improves nutritional value by concentrating vitamins in the
grain's center, parboiling causes the oils to migrate to the bran, a process that eases milling.
As partial cooking reduces storage loss from
mold, parboiled rice additionally confers superior keeping qualities.

For such reasons parboiling continued as a
method of rice preparation in some rural southern communities well into this century. The
method was undoubtedly known to the black
Texas rice farmers symbolized by Uncle Ben,
whose trademark was established when the
process was industrialized during the 1940s.[8]
Although the passage of time would divorce
the image of Uncle Ben from its historical context to mere product icon, his representation on
a well-known consumer product speaks to a
deeper social and cultural memory of the early
twentieth century, which associated black
Americans with rice culture. The method of
parboiling represents the diffusion of a female
knowledge system from Africa, which survived slavery in the cooking practices of their
free male and female descendants.

Thus more than the cultivation of rice
took root in the Americas. Rice culture embodied a sophisticated knowledge system that
spanned field and kitchen, one that demanded
understanding the diverse soil and water conditions of seed survival along with cooking
methods for consumption. The transformation
of rice from field grain to food depended on
yet another knowledge system perfected by
African women, that of milling the cereal by
hand. During the colonial period rice milling
involved a skilled tapping motion for removing hulls without grain breakage. This female
knowledge system served as the linchpin for
the entire development of the Carolina rice
economy. For without a means to mill rice, the
crop could not be exported.

The issue of milling on Carolina plantations raises one remaining and pertinent question. To what degree, if any, did the gender
division of labor characterizing African rice
cultivation reappear under slavery in South
Carolina? Since slavery could dissolve any pre-
existing pattern of work, what were the
broader implications of the transfer of a knowledge system both African and gendered? An
examination of the work cycle regulating life
on rice plantations illuminates these issues

while bringing attention to the colonial milling method, which involved use of the mortar
and pestle. The brutality of slave labor during
the colonial period vividly portrays the complexity of the demeaning shift of work that
blacks experienced under slavery.

Rice cultivation was arduous, requiring
slaves to labor under strenuous and insalubri-
ous conditions year-round. Slaves worked in
knee-deep water, which exposed them to ma-
laria, dysentery, and other waterborne diseases that in turn contributed to high mortality
rates. . . . During the hot and humid summers
of South Carolina and Georgia, where temperatures average over 90 degrees Fahrenheit,
slaves labored mightily to keep up with the
demands made upon their bodies. Partly to
avoid the summer heat, the slaves' day began
at sunrise on rice plantations. The pernicious
conditions of rice cultivation and slaves' presumed racial predisposition to working in heat
and humidity were captured by one planter
descendant, Duncan Heyward: "For there was
at that time in the province no white labor
which could perform the work of reclaiming
the river swamps. The white man could not
stand the summer heat, nor could he endure
working in the water. Negroes alone had to be
relied upon."[9]

The rice calendar involved year-round
work, and most of it was done completely by
hand. Only in the last decades of slavery were
animals brought into use for plowing and
transport of materials. Even the harvest was
carried out from the fields, typically in baskets
placed on the head. Slaves began preparing for
a new cycle of rice cultivation almost immediately after the harvest of the previous crop. The
agricultural calendar got under way with land
preparation from December to March. This involved burning the stubble from the previous
harvest, digging out ditches, and fortifying the
sides of canals that had slumped as well as removing excess mud from ditches. Slaves found
especially odious the strenuous work involved
in the digging, cleaning, and repair of ditches,
where they were forced to labor over vast acre-
ages with just their hands, buckets, and simple
tools. Then in the spring the fields were
cleared, leveled, and clods were broken apart
with hoes in preparation for cultivation.[10]

. . . The sowing of seed was staggered in
two planting periods, one from mid-March to
early April and the other in late May through
early June. The full moon regulated both sowing

periods because its stronger tides facilitated germination by spreading water over the entire field.[11] Sowing was immediately followed by the first of four protracted floodings. The first or "sprout flow" aimed at seed germination, a period that lasted between three to six days. Then the water was drained off to allow the cleaning of debris, which was followed by hoeing and weeding. Next came the second irrigation flow, known as the "point or stretch" flow. Water remained on the field for another three to seven days, after which hoeing and weeding again took place.

Over the period from mid-July through August the field was once more flooded, the "deep flow" lasting for about three weeks. Hoeing and weeding again followed the draining off of water before the fourth and final period of field flooding, the "lay by or harvest flow." This referred to the irrigation phase when the plant began to joint so that the stalks supported clusters of rice. Water now stayed on the field until the rice crop reached maturity. The staggered sowings of rice enabled the cultivation of two rice crops and, as in Africa, reduced the labor bottlenecks in hoeing, weeding, and harvesting. The cycle of rice cultivation spanned a period from six to seven months. Once ripened, the crop was harvested with a sickle, usually over a six- to eight-week period from late August or early September into October.

Evidence from archival and historical sources yields clues on the division of labor underlying rice culture in South Carolina and Georgia. These include reminiscences by planter descendants and elderly ex-slaves of the Depression-era Federal Writers' Project, planter records . . . , and drawings that depict slave labor in rice cultivation, such as those of Alice Huger Smith for Elizabeth Allston Pringle's 1914 plantation memoir. Such evidence indicates that female slaves composed the majority of "prime hands" on Carolina and Georgia rice plantations. Rice cultivation was characterized by a field labor force that was disproportionately female, with the less arduous artisanal "skilled" work such as making barrel staves for the crop's shipment, blacksmithing, and cooperage monopolized by male bondsmen.[12]

. . . [All of this evidence attests] to the necessity of revising conceptions of slavery that display a gender bias, such as those that undervalue agricultural and women's work by designating it as unskilled. . . .

. . . The institution of slavery meant that the preexisting gender division of labor that characterized production of a crop in Africa could be disassembled in the Americas to accord with the dictates of the market and requirements of the plantation owner. Early accounts, however, do reveal the contours of a gendered system of production. Writing about rice cultivation in Georgia during the colonial period, Johan Martin Bolzius noted that with the exception of milling, there was no difference in the labor demanded of male and female slaves. However, men usually repaired rice embankments and ditches while the sowing of rice was principally performed by women. The association of rice sowing with female labor continued throughout the antebellum period, as planter descendant Duncan Heyward remarked: "Women always did this work, for the men used to say this was 'woman's wuck,' and I do not recall seeing one of the men attempt it." . . . Women wielding long-handled hoes, the "human hoeing machine" as Frances Kemble described them at work in rice fields during the 1830s, provided crucial labor for land preparation and weeding. Following patterns established in West African rice culture, women typically performed the tasks of sowing, hoeing, and weeding on Carolina plantations.[13] . . . The expertise of female slaves in rice culture must have proved of [great] value for adapting the crop to new conditions in the Americas.

As the cultivation cycle drew to a close with harvest in late September or early October, rice milling got under way. The processing of rice dominated the agricultural calendar until the resumption of cultivation in March or April. Although the actual period of farming was concentrated in the months from mid-March through October, production of rice for international markets in fact demanded work every month of the year. Nor was rice the only plantation crop cultivated. Its agricultural calendar was superimposed upon the planting, weeding, and harvest of subsistence crops like corn, beans, potatoes, and greens. The work of slaves on rice plantations intensified even more from the mid-eighteenth century with the cultivation of an additional export crop, indigo. Over the same period plantation labor demands were increasing with the expansion of tidal rice cultivation, which necessitated swamp reclamation and the construction of irrigation infrastructure. Such factors strained the endurance of slaves on rice plantations and undoubtedly contributed to their abbreviated life expectancy.[14]

But no work was as demanding as the toil of the postharvest period. Once the crop was harvested, rice stubble required plowing-under, then burning. Next the land was hoed to break up the soil. Field embankments, ditches, and fences needed repair, the canals cleaning and digging. But most important, the international market demanded a crop already milled. Once harvested, rice required threshing, winnowing, and pounding prior to shipment overseas. During the months from December to May work on a rice plantation intensified. In 1765 one Charleston visitor commented on the "active" work pace of slaves during winter and spring, when the "crops of rice and indigo [were] brought to town and shipped off." But the activity involved a great deal more than harvesting and loading the ships. Millions of pounds of rice required processing before shipment and this fact set the pace for the season's activity. The work regime of a Carolina rice plantation was thus more rigorous and sustained throughout the year than that on comparable cotton or sugar plantations.[15]

The principal demand for the rice crop in the colonial era was in Catholic Europe, with peak market prices prevailing during Lent. Aiming production at this southern European market, planters sought to complete rice milling by early winter in time for the transatlantic voyage that would deliver the grain in February. . . .[16] But the goal of punctual delivery to Europe was often not met, as is evident from one Charleston merchant's complaint in January 1726 about the shortage of milled grain for loading his waiting vessels: "Here thirty seven barrels of Rice and two Chest of Dearé Skin Ship by me Richard Splatt on board the *Lovely Polly* Michael Bath Master bound for London on my proper account and . . . goes Consigned to Mr. William Crisp . . . that there is not rice to load the ½ of 'em."[17] . . .

A Carolina rice plantation during the colonial period represented a stark departure in the work rhythms known to slaves who grew rice in West Africa. Instead of signaling the end of an agricultural cycle, the harvest marked the prelude to even more grueling work routines associated with milling. No wonder that cases of barn burnings as acts of sabotage increased in the fall, when the huge rice harvest had been gathered from

thousands of acres and impatient planters were demanding that the crop be cleaned quickly and transported in heavy barrels to waiting ships. The intensified work effort required to process millions of pounds of rice by hand during the postharvest period brutalized slaves while transforming the colonial plantation system into a factory in the field.[18]

On the eve of the American Revolution exports of rice from South Carolina reached over sixty million pounds annually. This represented a staggering growth of the rice economy since 1700, when less than half a million pounds had been exported. The shift in rice cultivation from inland swamps to fertile floodplains had dramatically increased yields. Growing the crop with irrigation reduced the amount of weeding needed, which greatly improved labor productivity. From the first to the second half of the eighteenth century the per capita output of milled rice produced by slaves climbed from 2,250 pounds to an average that reached between 3,000 and 3,600 pounds.[19] But improved productivity scarcely ameliorated the work burdens facing slaves, for following the harvest, rice had to be milled. The exertions required by the rice harvest were negligible compared with the Herculean toil that awaited slaves milling the crop for export. For most of the eighteenth century this crucial step in preparing rice for export markets depended upon processing the crop by hand, with a mortar and pestle. . . .

. . . An examination of the milling process . . . reveals the effects of enslavement and mass production of rice on an African knowledge system, male and female identities, and slave culture. [On the one hand] active involvement in developing rice culture on Carolina plantations provided slaves the means to negotiate the conditions of their labor. But [on the other hand,] the very success of rice transfer to the low-country region resulted in one of the most profitable economies of the Americas, thereby consolidating planter power. With economic success, planters exerted greater control over slave lives. They made new claims on the bodies of enslaved persons, demands that tested human endurance. The expansion of the rice culture came at great cost to black lives.

. . . The method used in Africa to prepare rice for daily subsistence became transformed under slavery into a grueling labor regime in which millions of pounds of rice were processed in just a few months of the year. The story of this plantation crop and its milling, deeply rooted in West African culture and history, reveals the changing relationship of time, labor, and market that characterized the commodification of rice during the eighteenth century. The pounding of rice resonated through African communities as the heartbeat of daily life, the echo of cultural identity. Under slavery it was compressed into a seasonal activity, where each stroke of the pestle made inhuman demands on labor. . . .

The mortar was made by taking a tree trunk (usually cypress or pine), and using fire to burn a cavity or receptacle for placing the unmilled grain. With the mortar hollowed out to waist height, unprocessed rice was then milled with a wooden pestle (about one to one and a half meters long) that weighed between seven and ten pounds. Processing requires standing over the mortar, taking the pestle in hand and repeatedly lifting it up and down to remove the hulls that enclose the grain. . . . In recalling the process of making a mortar and pestle, an Alabama woman earlier this century drew attention to the steps involved in . . . [this skilled operation]:

> . . . [With the rice in the hollowed-out stump] we would take that maul [pestle] and beat it up and down on the top of the rice . . . Every once in a while we'd put our hands through it to see if all the husks, all the rice had gotten outa the husks . . . So a big windy day then we'd take that rice and spread a sheet out and then take it in a bucket and hold it up high. Let the rice fall down on the sheet and the husks would blow off. The wind would blow. We did that mo' one time to get all the husks and the rice was just as pretty and white as the rice you buy at the sto'.[20]

The processing of rice by hand with a mortar and pestle is known as pounding, which is really a misnomer, since the desire to obtain whole, in preference to broken, grains requires a skilled tapping and rolling motion, where loosening the pestle grip at the right moment prior to striking the rice minimizes grain breakage. This is a delicate operation that demands care and skill, especially when the objective is to produce white rice. Pounding by hand unfolds in two distinct stages. The first step takes off the grain's hull; the second step removes the bran and nutrient-bearing germ from the softer endosperm, which polishes or whitens the rice. Following each pounding, rice is winnowed to remove unwanted materials. . . .

The grade of rice produced by hand milling varied considerably with the skill level of the person carrying out the processing. An experienced person could obtain between 65 percent and 75 percent whole grains; half the rice might end up broken with a less-skilled, careless, or fatigued operator. While observers of rice processing during the colonial period commented upon the variability in the percentage of whole to broken rice with hand milling, the uneven quality was viewed as the result of worker apathy rather than of the brutal labor demanded by processing. . . . In fact, different rates of milled to broken rice among slaves probably had less to do with indifference than with the skill level and other plantation duties of individual slaves.[21]

Concern over obtaining a high percentage of whole grains from processing figure[d] prominently in planter concerns. In eighteenth-century world markets, as in those of the present day, broken rice sold at a much-reduced price. Merchant lists from the colonial period indicate that the export market favored "very clean, bright and whole grains." Higher market prices depended on milling the whole grains to remove the protein-bearing bran and then polishing them to whiteness. While this process reduced the nutritional value of white rice, it had the advantage of minimizing grain spoilage on long transatlantic voyages. Such market preferences required Carolina planters to separate milled rice production into three grades: whole grains, those partially broken, and small broken ones. . . . The broken rice, not as salable in international markets, was either sold at a lower price or reserved for local consumption.[22]

However, given the labor regimen facing rice plantation slaves in the eighteenth century, achieving a high percentage of whole grains with hand milling would have proved difficult. The abbreviated time period allotted for rice processing and the stress it placed on slave labor resulted in sacrificing quality for completion of the task. Slavery additionally forced men to process rice with the mortar and pestle. A skill of African women became with slavery male as well as female work due to the high demand for Carolina rice in international markets and the intensive labor required for its processing. Men's inexperience in milling rice with a mortar and pestle would have also resulted in a higher concentration of shattered grains. With slavery the division of labor characterizing

African farming systems dissolved, subjecting both male and female slaves to the radically different and demanding work regime of hand milling.

During the eighteenth century the percentage of broken rice likely remained high. Mortality rates kept the slave population from reproducing itself well into the century. Reliance on continuous slave imports from Africa meant males had to learn the skill upon arrival, the outcome resulting in high levels of broken rice. Differences in skill level between males and females directly imported from Africa partially explains some of the variability in quality of the output commented upon by numerous observers. For reasons such as these, planters deliberately sought slaves with expertise in rice culture. Women's skills in rice processing must have figured among the desired qualities in the unusual planter demand for female slaves on Carolina rice plantations. But slave markets could not always respond to such demands. Planters would take any able-bodied laborer, male or female, with or without previous experience growing rice, to complete their labor force.[23] . . .

Milling rice with a mortar and pestle was grueling, for the worker had to stand for hours at a time, repeatedly lifting a pestle that weighed as much as ten pounds to remove the hulls and bran. The task demanded strength and endurance as well as care and finesse. . . . [Women at the mortar and pestle] worked alone. Each one would have stood upright for hours at a time lifting the heavy pestle to meet a daily production quota. . . .

Since at least the 1750s the task of processing rice was divided into two sessions, morning and evening work, as Johan Martin Bolzius observed: "They [slaves] gather the rice, thresh it, grind it into wooden mills, and stamp [pound] it mornings and evenings." . . . Slaves worked late into the night during the winter months, beating the rice in large mortars to free the grain.[24] . . .

The pressures brought to bear on the slaves by market forces tested their physical endurance to its limits. Death was too frequently the result, as South Carolina scientist Alexander Garden noted in 1755: "Labour and the Loss of many of their lives testified the fatigue they underwent in Satiating the Inexpressible Avarice of their Masters . . . but the worst comes last for after the Rice is threshed, they beat it all in large Wooden Mortars to clean it from the

Women hulling rice with mortar and pestles, Sapelo Island, Georgia, between 1915 and 1934. (Courtesy of Georgia Archives, Vanishing Georgia Collection.)

Husk . . . [planters who work their slaves so much] often pay . . . dear for their Barbarity, by the Loss of many . . . Valuable Negroes."[25]

Technical progress on the second step of milling, removal of the inner skin of the rice grain or its bran, lagged until 1787 when Jonathan Lucas, the "Eli Whitney" of rice, invented a water-driven mill for polishing. The Lucas mill successfully husked the grain with minimal breakage and polished it to the desired whiteness. His machine achieved excellent results with the Carolina gold *sativa* variety then being planted in the colony. The tidal rivers used for irrigating rice fields during the spring and summer cultivation season served in the fall and winter as the source of water power for milling. With the diffusion of water mills throughout low-country rice plantations during the remaining decade of the century, slaves were for the most part finally relieved of the burden involved in processing the entire export crop by hand.[26]

Like all aspects of the plantation rice system, processing was "tasked," with each slave expected to deliver a fixed amount of polished rice daily until the plantation crop was completely milled. [Scientist] Alexander Garden provide[d] an early estimate of the amount of rice each slave was expected to clean: "Each Slave is tasked at Seven Mortars for One Day, and each Mortar Contains three pecks of Rice." [A peck weighed about eleven pounds.] While Garden placed the task as equal for men and women, later commentators like planter R. F. W. Allston, who drew upon family records, wrote that the daily task for milling differed between females and males, with six pecks required for men and four for women: "The method was, that each male laborer had three pecks of rough rice in a mortar, and each female two pecks, to pound before day or sun-rise; and the same at night, after finishing the ordinary task in the field." . . . Research on the Lowndes' rice plantation in South Carolina from the first decades of the nineteenth century show[s] that the daily task for an individual man working alone was one and one-half bushels while that for a woman was one bushel, approximately 67 and 45 pounds respectively.[27] . . .

By dividing processing into two daily work periods, before sunrise and after sunset, planters improved the "efficiency" of labor expended while intensifying it on a daily basis. Rice processing contributed to lengthening the number of days worked in rice cultivation during the calendar year. The addition of rice milling to a full day's plantation work starkly illustrates the dramatic rupture in labor relations slavery represented over the precapitalist agricultural system known in West Africa. A task performed daily by African women in less than an hour became transformed with commodity production into extended hours of daily toil by male and female slaves over an abbreviated period of the year.

The pounding of rice, the preparation of a food that signals daybreak and the re-creation of community life in West Africa, underwent a radical transformation on eighteenth-century rice plantations. As workers arose to the first of two pounding periods, the striking of the pestle represented a new conception of time and labor, calibrated by the dictates of planter and market. Commodity production transformed the mortar and pestle into a device that harnessed human arms to a measurement of rice required by planters for processing.

The pestle represented a powerful symbol of bondage for slaves on Carolina rice plantations as well as in other areas of plantation slavery in the Americas. . . . Only in areas of the Americas where slaves had escaped, as among rice-growing maroons of the Guianas, did the mortar and pestle reassert its African meaning. For Suriname's maroons, as in other free communities of blacks, the rhythms of food preparation still heralded the dawn of a new day. The striking of the pestle in a mortar became again the heartbeat of village life, a daily reminder of the significance of rice for daily culture. . . .[28]

During the period of slavery in the United States the market pressures to satisfy an increased international demand for rice shattered this aspect of African daily existence. Rice plantations ruptured and then transformed the traditional cultural associations of hand milling into an insatiable demand for labor that was forced to work faster to complete the processing of rice as quickly as possible. . . .

Women's indigenous knowledge, transmitted from one generation to another and from mother to daughter, forms a significant aspect of rice culture in West Africa. With enslavement, this knowledge crossed the Middle Passage and reemerged in the way rice was grown and processed and in the cooking styles that mark the African diaspora in the Americas. Among all the African crops that transferred to the New World, none proved as significant as rice in affirming African cultural identity. Rice became a dietary staple wherever blacks settled in environments amid social conditions favorable for its cultivation. Slaves as well as maroons adopted the crop, and their descendants planted it in freedom throughout tropical and subtropical America. . . .

In South Carolina, however, where rice became a plantation crop, slavery dismantled this gender division of labor as both men and women were forced to work in its cultivation and milling. The rice plantation economy necessitated the resolution of several problems associated with hand processing. Slavery shifted the temporal pattern of rice milling in Africa, characterized by women pounding the cereal for a short period of time each day of the year, to one that compressed milling into just a few months. The shift demanded that slaves spend grueling hours processing rice. Then, as the rice export economy placed ever greater demands on labor, rice processing required dissolving its African basis as a female responsibility so that both men and women processed the crop.

African knowledge of rice farming [especially women's knowledge] established, then, the basis for the Carolina economy. But by the mid-eighteenth century rice plantations had increasingly come to resemble those of sugar, imposing brutal demands on labor. Slaves with knowledge of growing rice had to submit to the ultimate irony of seeing their traditional agriculture emerge as the first food commodity traded across oceans on a large scale by capitalists who then took complete credit for discovering such an "ingenious" crop for the Carolina and Georgia floodplains. For this reason, the words "black rice" fittingly describe their struggle to endure slavery amid the enormity of the travail they faced to survive.

NOTES

1. Lewis Gray, *History of Agriculture in the Southern United States to 1860*, 2 vols. (Gloucester, Mass.: Peter Smith, 1958), 1:194–195; Leslie Schwalm, *A Hard Fight for We: Women's Transition from Slavery to Freedom in South Carolina* (Urbana: University of Illinois Press, 1997), p. 21.

2. Gray, *History of Agriculture*. 1:195; R. Berleant-Schiller and R. and L. Pulsipher, "Subsistence Cultivation in the Caribbean," *New West Indian Guide*, 60, nos. 1–2 (1986): 1–40.

3. See three essays in a special issue of *Cahiers ORSTOM*, série Sciences Humains, 20, nos. 3–4 (1984): H. M. Raulin, "Techniques agraires et instruments aratoires au sud de Sahara," pp. 339–58, esp. p. 350; F. Sigaut, "Essai d'identification des instruments à bras de travail de sol," pp. 360–67; and A. Lericollais and J. Schmitz, "La calebasse et la houe," p. 438.

4. Ibid. See the memoir of a plantation descendant: Theodore Ravenal, "The Last Days of Rice Planting," in David Doar, *Rice and Rice Planting in the South Carolina Low Country* (1936; Charleston: Charleston Museum, 1970), pp. 43–50, esp. pp. 49–50. And note this description: "Young men brought the clay water . . . while young girls, with bare feet and skirts well tied up, danced and shuffled the rice about with their feet until the whole mass was thoroughly clayed"; Elizabeth Allston Pringle, *A Woman Rice Planter* (1914; Cambridge, Mass.: Harvard University Press, 1961), pp. 11–12. *Family Across the Sea*, 57 minutes, directed by Tim Carrier, 1990, South Carolina ETV Commission.

5. See Doar, *Rice and Rice Planting*; R. F. W. Allston, "Essay on Sea Coast Crops," *De Bow's Review*, 16 (1854): 589–615, and Allston, "Memoir of the Introduction and Planting of Rice in South Carolina," *De Bow's Review*, 1 (1846): 320–357; Duncan Heyward, *Seed from Madagascar* (Chapel Hill: University of North Carolina Press, 1937), pp. 9–10.

6. Dale Rosengarten, "Social Origins of the African-American Lowcountry Basket" (Ph.D. dissertation, Harvard University, 1997), esp. pp. 273–311. These fanner baskets were woven from bullrush and sweet grass. On the Gullah tradition of fanner baskets, see Joseph Opala, *The Gullah* (Freetown, Sierra Leone: U.S. Information Service, 1987).

7. Karen Hess, *The Carolina Rice Kitchen: The African Connection* (Columbia: University of South Carolina Press, 1992), esp. pp. 2–26; Ntozake Shange, *If I Can Cook/You Know God Can* (Boston Beacon Press, 1998), pp. 33, 48–49; Jacob Motte Alston, cited in Charles Joyner, *Down by the Riverside* (Urbana: University of Illinois, 1984), p. 96.

8. For instance, elderly informants who lived in Oklahoma, descendants of Black Seminoles who settled there after their removal from Florida in the early 1840s, remember the method. Linda Salmon, pers. comm., March 20, 2000. Kate Sheehan, in Janice Jorgensen, ed., *Encyclopedia of Consumer Brands*, vol. 1 (Washington, D.C.: St. James Press, 1994), pp. 608–609.

9. Heyward, *Seed from Madagascar*, p. 55; Peter Wood, *Black Majority* (New York: Knopf, 1974); Peter Coclanis, *The Shadow of a Dream* (New York: Oxford University Press, 1989); William Dusinberre, *Them Dark Days* (Oxford: Oxford University Press, 1996).

10. Ira Berlin, *Many Thousands Gone: The First Two Centuries of Slavery in North America* (Cambridge, Mass.: Harvard University Press, 1998), p. 167.

11. On the rice calendar, see J. H. Easterby, "The South Carolina Factor as Revealed in the Papers of Robert F. W. Allston," *Journal of Southern History*, 7, no. 2 (1941): 160–172; Doar, *Rice and Rice Planting*; Daina L. Ramey, "'She Do a Heap of Work': Female Slave Labor on Glynn County Rice and Cotton Plantations," *Georgia Historical Quarterly* 82, no. 4 (1998), 707–734.

12. Schwalm, *Hard Fight*; Leigh Ann Pruneau, "All the Time is Work Time: Gender and the Task System on Antebellum Low Country Rice Plantations" (Ph.D. dissertation, University of Arizona, 1997), p. 15; Berlin, *Many Thousands Gone*, p. 168. Pringle's memoir can be found at www. http:// docsouth.unc.edu/fpn/pringle/pringle.html.

13. Bolzius, quoted in Klaus G. Loewald, Beverly Starika, and Paul Taylor, "Johan Bolzius Answers a Questionnaire on Carolina and Georgia," *William and Mary Quarterly*, 3rd ser., 14 (1957): 257; Heyward, *Seed from Madagascar*, p. 31; Frances Kemble, *Journal of a Residence on a Georgia Plantation in 1838–1839* (Athens: University of Georgia Press, 1984; orig. pub. 1863), p. 156. See Joyner, *Down by the Riverside*, p. 48, for a drawing by one planter descendant of women sowing rice in the African manner of covering the seed by foot. Elizabeth Pringle, one of the last Carolina planters, wrote in 1913 that among male laborers: "The hoe they consider purely a feminine implement"; *Woman Rice Planter*, p. 79. See also Schwalm, *Hard Fight*, 9, 23, 37.

14. Doar, *Rice and Rice Planting*, pp. 13–15; Joyner, *Down by the Riverside*, pp. 46–47. Indigo, planted on the higher lands behind the riverine rice fields, got under way in the 1740s but declined as a cash crop after the American Revolution. Joyce Chaplin, *An Anxious Pursuit: Agricultural Innovation and Modernity in the Lower South, 1730–1815* (Chapel Hill: University of North Carolina Press, 1993), pp. 191–208.

Indigo cultivation and dyeing diffused to West Africa from the Nile Valley circa a.d. 700–1100. See George Brooks, *Landlords and Strangers: Ecology, Society, and Trade in Western Africa, 1000–1630* (Boulder: Westview Press, 1993), p. 56. On female slaves and indigo dyeing in West Africa, see Claire Robertson and Martin Klein, "Women's Importance in African Slave Systems," in Robertson and Klein, eds., *Women and Slavery in Africa* (Madison: University of Wisconsin Press, 1983), pp. 3–28, esp. pp. 15–16.

15. Pelatiah Webster, "Journal of a Visit to Charleston, 1765," in H. Roy Merrens, ed., *The Colonial South Carolina Scene: Contemporary Views, 1697–1774* (Columbia: University of South Carolina Press, 1977), p. 221; Henry C. Dethloff, *A History of the American Rice Industry, 1685–1985* (College Station: Texas A&M Press, 1988), p. 23.

16. James Clifton, "The Rice Industry in Colonial America," *Agricultural History,* 55 (1981): 266–283, esp. pp. 280–281; M. Eugene Sirmans, *Colonial South Carolina: A Political History, 1662–1763* (Chapel Hill: University of North Carolina Press, 1966), pp. 107–108; Clifton, "The Rice Industry," pp. 280–281. Demand for rice expanded during the eighteenth century throughout Europe since it was used for brewing beer and to make paper.

17. Richard Splatt, Charles Towne, to William Crisp, London, January 17, 1726, quoted in Dethloff, *American Rice Industry,* p. 11.

18. Barn burnings, Peter Wood, pers. comm., August 31, 1999; Michael Mullin, *American Negro Slavery: A Documentary History* (Columbia: University of South Carolina Press, 1976).

19. Dethloff, *American Rice Industry,* p. 10; estimates appear in Coclanis, *Shadow,* p. 97.

20. Onnie Lee Logan, as told to Katherine Clark, *Motherwit: An Alabama Midwife's Story* (New York: Dutton, 1989), p. 9.

21. Converse Clowse, *Economic Beginnings in Colonial South Carolina, 1670–1730* (Columbia: University of South Carolina Press, 1971), p. 129; Gray, *History of Agriculture,* 1:278.

22. Merchant demand list of Josiah Smith, Jr., quotes Leila Sellers, *Charleston Business on the Eve of the American Revolution* (Chapel Hill: University of North Carolina Press, 1934), p. 68. On spoilage of cereal grains, see Dethloff, *American Rice Industry,* p. 35, and Carville Earle, *Geographical Inquiry and American Historical Problems* (Stanford: Stanford University Press, 1992), p. 114. On rice grades, see U. B. Phillips, *American Negro Slavery* (New York: D. Appleton, 1918), p. 90; Gray, *History of Agriculture,* 1:278.

23. On slave imports directly from Africa, see Berlin, *Many Thousands Gone,* pp. 313–315. On planter preferences for slaves familiar with rice growing with the shift to tidal production, see Daniel C. Littlefield, *Rice and Slaves* (Baton Rouge: Louisiana State University Press, 1981); and D. Richardson, "The British Slave Trade to Colonial South Carolina," *Slavery and Abolition,* 12 (1991), 135–172.

24. Loewald, Starika, and Taylor, "Johan Bolzius," p. 259; Berlin, *Many Thousands Gone,* p. 147.

25. Samuel G. Stoney, *Plantations of the South Carolina Low Country* (Charleston: Carolina Art Association, 1938), pp. 33–34.

26. Dethloff, *American Rice Industry,* p. 29; Chaplin, *An Anxious Pursuit,* p. 254. Mortar-and-pestle processing continued, however, with rice retained for plantation consumption. It also continued in areas where the main plantation crop was cotton but slaves planted rice as a provision crop. See Amelia Wallace Vernon, *African Americans at Mars Bluff, South Carolina* (Baton Rouge: Louisiana State University Press, 1993).

27. Correspondence between Alexander Garden, M.D., and the Royal Society of Arts, quoted in Wood, *Black Majority,* p. 79; Allston, "Memoir of the Introduction," p. 342; J. Drayton, *A View of South Carolina* (Columbia: University of South Carolina Press, 1972; orig. pub. 1802), p. 151; Pruneau, "All the Time," pp. 68, 97, 155.

28. Melville Herskovits and Frances Herskovits, *Rebel Destiny: Among the Bush Negroes of Dutch Guiana* (New York: McGraw-Hill, 1934), p. 185.

ANNETTE GORDON-REED

The Hemings–Jefferson Treaty: Paris, 1789

From 1787 to 1789, Sally Hemings lived in Paris, becoming familiar with the city, learning French, and earning wages. She had been only fourteen years old when she made the Atlantic transit from Virginia, accompanying eight-year-old Polly Jefferson whose father, Thomas, wished his youngest child to join him in France. Three years earlier, Jefferson had taken up his diplomatic post in France,

Excerpted from chs. 14–17 of *The Hemingses of Monticello: An American Family* by Annette Gordon-Reed (New York: W. W. Norton, 2008). Reprinted by permission of the author and publisher. Notes have been edited and renumbered.

arriving with his teenage daughter Martha (called Patsy) and Sally's older brother James. By the time Polly and Sally joined him, the diplomat was renting an elegant, twenty-four-room house known as the Hôtel de Langeac; it was on the Champs-Elysées at some remove from the city center.

Sally and her brothers were born slaves, the legal property of Virginia planter John Wayles whose daughter Martha became Thomas Jefferson's first and only wife. At the Wayles-Jefferson wedding in 1772, various enslaved Hemingses, including Sally, James, and their mother Elizabeth, were added to Jefferson's human assets. John Wayles was actually Sally's biological father as well as her master; Sally was therefore the half sister of Jefferson's wife. Sally and other Hemings women were at Martha Wayles Jefferson's deathbed in 1782, where Martha, weeping, asked her husband to promise not to remarry and impose a stepmother on their then-living four children. Afterward, the young Sally lived with, and attended, the Jeffersons' youngest daughters; thus, she in effect grew up alongside her nieces. What she thought about this situation, we do not know.

Sally was still a slave girl when she lived in Paris. She remained an enslaved person until several years before her death in 1835. But those who observed her in Paris would not have associated her with the strenuous, debasing, and exhausting field labor that many African-descended women had to endure on New World plantations. She undertook light household duties such as sewing; she accompanied Patsy and Polly on daytime urban promenades and to evening receptions and balls. She wore fine clothes, as circumstances dictated. She did not have her femininity denied her.

Annette Gordon-Reed's essay pivots on a dramatic and private agreement that Sally Hemings and Thomas Jefferson made just before Jefferson was to leave his post and return to Monticello, his beloved Virginia plantation. Being under French law gave the Hemings siblings the opportunity to claim free status; Sally, the teenager, understood it as an extraordinary moment of leverage.

Until very recently, major Jefferson biographers (except for Fawn Brodie) refused to believe that Thomas Jefferson, slave owner, founding father, and two-term president, had a sexual relationship, or, as Gordon-Reed calls it, a long-term, possibly loving concubinage arrangement, with Sally Hemings. Even before there was DNA evidence to support this, Gordon-Reed, a lawyer as well as a scholar, wrote a book carefully laying out the evidence, pro and con. Appalled by decades of scholarly obfuscations and willed ignorance about the agency of African Americans, she pointed out the curious disconnect between the popular appeal of the Hemings-Jefferson story in the 1970s and 1980s and the historians' vehement, sometimes irrational denials.*

What do you make of the author's suggestion that for Sally Hemings, being female was more at the core of her identity than being enslaved? Some skeptics will argue that the existence of the 1789 treaty rests on slim evidence—Hemings family lore and an inkwell. How do you assess Gordon-Reed's reasoning?

Postscript to the story told here: the child that Sally Hemings was carrying in 1789 did not survive. Later, at Monticello where they continued their relationship, she gave birth to seven children, five of whom survived infancy. For these children, Thomas Jefferson abided by the terms of the treaty of 1789.

---

* Annette Gordon-Reed, *Thomas Jefferson and Sally Hemings: An American Controversy* (Charlottesville: University Press of Virginia, 1997); Dinitia Smith and Nicholas Wade, "DNA Test Finds Evidence of Jefferson Child by Slave," *New York Times*, Nov. 1, 1998, p. A1.

When we think of the young Sally Hemings, . . . we acknowledge that she was born into a cohort—eighteenth-century enslaved black women—whose humanity and femininity were constantly assaulted by slavery and white supremacy. While the experiences typical to that cohort are highly relevant as a starting point for looking at Hemings, they can never be an end in themselves. For Hemings lived in her own skin, and cannot simply be defined through the enumerated experiences of the group—enslaved black females.

Taking account of the larger social context in which Hemings lived is essential. . . . There is . . . no one context to consult in regard to [her] . . . she had the multiple identities that are the normal part of the human makeup. The people and places she encountered gave her multiple personal contexts—the circle of her mother and siblings, her extended family, the larger enslaved community at Monticello, her community in Paris, Jefferson, his white family, and, finally, her own children. Those associations . . . shaped her inner life and outlook. . . .

Sally Hemings . . . spent her first fourteen years in a country that defined her as human chattel. In her fifteenth and sixteenth years, she was in a place (France) where a court would . . . transform her status, turning her into a legally recognized free person. Sometime between 1787 and 1789, this teenager learned the difference between law in Virginia and law in France. The power of the former could reenslave her, while the power of the latter could set her free. So she stood poised between the reality of life in the place of her birth and the moment when she had to decide whether to take the step toward freedom in a new land. She could make her journey alone or with her older brother, leaving not only slavery behind but also a large and intensely connected family in Virginia. . .

[The years in Paris were also the time when Hemings became Jefferson's "concubine."] How is it possible to get at the nature of a relationship between a man and a woman like Jefferson and Hemings when neither party specifically writes or speaks to others about that relationship or their feelings? Even written words can be quite deceptive and seldom tell the whole story, for people sometimes choose, for whatever reason, to tell a story of their lives that is rosier, or grimmer, than it actually was. In the absence of words, actions may be quite telling. An event in the life of Hemings's oldest sister Mary that took place at the same time that Hemings was in Paris dealing with Jefferson offers some insight into the varied nature of the veiled relationships between enslaved women and white men. . . .

[Due to mounting family debts, Jefferson was under pressure to hire out some of his slaves. Thus, in the late 1780s] Mary Hemings, Sally's oldest sibling, was hired out to a prosperous merchant named Thomas Bell . . . She moved, along with three of her children—Molly, Joseph, and Betsy—to Bell's home on Main Street [in Charlottesville]. . . .

We do not know the circumstances surrounding the origins of the Bell-Hemings connection: Did he notice her and lease her for the purpose of making her his concubine, or was it something that developed after the leasehold? In either event, things moved quickly, for her children were born soon after she was leased. However matters started, in Mary Hemings we get a rare sense, from her own actions, of an enslaved woman's preferences regarding her choice of mate and the course of her life. Not long after Jefferson returned from Paris, Hemings specifically asked to be sold to Bell. Jefferson complied with her request and gave Nicholas Lewis, still overseeing his affairs, "power to dispose of Mary according to her desire, with such of her younger children as she chose."[1] In an ironic twist on his practice of selling or buying slaves to unite them with family members from other plantations, Jefferson sold Mary Hemings to unite her to her white partner and their children. He knew the couple's situation very well, and he acted in deference not just to the wishes of an enslaved woman but also to the desires of the white father of her children.

Within the extremely narrow constraints of what life offered her—ownership by Thomas Jefferson or ownership by Thomas Bell—Mary Hemings took an action that had enormous, lasting, and, in the end, quite favorable consequences for her, her two youngest children, and the Hemings family as a whole. She found in Bell a man willing to live openly with her, and to treat her and their children as if they were bound together as a legal family. She must have seen that capacity in him during the early stages of their time together. Over the years she would be able to compare notes on her life with a white man with her youngest sister, whom she honored by giving her own youngest daughter the name Sarah (also called Sally), known by the time of her marriage, in the early 1800s, as Sarah Jefferson Bell.[2] . . .

... Both Hemings sisters had very firm internal understandings about how they might influence the course of their lives so that they could have what many of the women of their day, black and white, wanted—the ability, during their measured time on earth, to associate with a man who would take care of them and provide the best possible lives for their children with some chance of stability in an unstable world. Mary Hemings experienced firsthand what this instability meant. Although she found a place for herself with Bell, unlike her sister Sally, she experienced one of the harshest aspects of enslaved motherhood.... [F]our of her six children were taken from her. The liaison with Bell ensured that any new children she had would be protected. The contingencies of the lives of Sally and Mary Hemings were such that Jefferson and Bell, for whatever reason—their personalities, their feelings about the women involved—supported these sisters' aspirations. As a result both women, in their own way, achieved exactly what they wanted. That their very elemental desires as women were met in the context of slavemaster, black-white relationships is troubling because they mix something that seems almost sacred (the human desire for a secure family life) with something deeply profane (slavery). ...

The title ... [of] historian Walter Johnson's *Soul by Souls*[3] captures the enormity of slavery's inhumanity and suggests at least one way to go about illuminating it in the pages of history. Slavery was not just one, enormous act of oppression against a nameless, interchangeable mass of people. It was millions of separate assassinations and attempted assassinations of individual spirits carried out over centuries. When we encounter some of those spirits responding to their circumstances as human beings respond and using whatever means available to them to maintain or assert their humanity in the face of the onslaught, their individual efforts should not be minimized or ignored, because they could never alone have killed off the institution of slavery. That is far too heavy a load to place on people whose burdens in life were already almost unimaginably heavy....

PARIS, 1789

James and Sally Hemings had many months to contemplate their possible return to Virginia. Jefferson had, in fact, been preparing to go home long before he received official word that his request for a leave of absence had been granted; he had packed his bags to be ready to go on a moment's notice.[4] The Hemingses, as well as his daughters, were expected to return with him, and were likely as much on tenterhooks as he, for they, too, had to be ready to leave as soon as word arrived. When it was clear that return to America was imminent, Sally Hemings was pregnant, and her pregnancy created a problem that she and Jefferson had to address and sort out. [In a memoir recorded in 1873,] Madison Hemings, [a son of Sally Hemings,] described what happened:

> But during that time my mother became Mr. Jefferson's concubine, and when he was called back home she was enciente by him. He desired to bring my mother back to Virginia with him, but she demurred. She was just beginning to understand the French language well, and in France she was free, while if she returned to Virginia she would be re-enslaved. So she refused to return with him. To induce her to do so he promised her extraordinary privileges, and made a solemn pledge that her children should be freed at the age of twenty-one years. In consequence of his promises, on which she implicitly relied, she returned with him to Virginia.[5]

There is much to consider about this very simple, yet powerful, explanation of what happened between Sally Hemings and Thomas Jefferson in France. First, it could only have been a shorthand version of all that actually happened, all the words that passed between these two.... The stakes were extremely high for both, but highest for Hemings. She knew all too well what slavery meant, and she lived with the hard knowledge that, were she to return to Virginia, every child from her womb would follow her condition. In this moment and place, she was in the best position she would ever be in to walk away from *partus sequitur ventrem* [meaning the status of the child follows the status of the mother,] forever....

We cannot know what Hemings thought about abortion for herself or whether the thought of not keeping her baby even crossed her mind. She was away from the network of her mother and female siblings who could counsel her and, as far as we know, without a network of women of color to confide in and discuss a matter so personal....

Hemings's son described his mother as "implicitly" relying on his father, which goes to the mystery at the heart of Sally Hemings's life: Why would she trust Jefferson, and why would she, under any circumstances, return to Virginia with him? Trading immediate freedom for herself and her progeny for a life at Monticello with him and a promise of eventual freedom for her children was not an even exchange. There was something in the gap between those two conditions—some desired prospect on the other side of the ocean—that motivated her.

It is all too easy to ignore how being female shaped Hemings's desires and expectations and focus in on the thing that makes her so different from us today: she was born enslaved. By the time they were in France together, Jefferson had already helped set the terms for the development of Hemings's view of herself as a female. As the authority figure at Monticello, he sent a strong message to her when he acted to protect what he considered to be the femininity of Hemings and her female relatives, while failing to show similar concerns for other enslaved women on his plantations. Hemings watched every female go to the fields at harvest time, except her sisters, mother, and whatever white females were at the plantation.[6] She learned from all this that, in Jefferson's eyes, she was a female to be protected from certain things, when most women of her same legal status received no protection at all. . . .

Even without Jefferson's intervention, it is doubtful that Hemings thought being a slave was more at the core of her existence than being female; she could cease to be the one, never the other. Their numbers were still small when she was growing up, but there were free black people in Virginia, and their numbers would grow in the years after she returned to America.[7] The world sent her a very definite and hard message about enslavement at the same time as it conveyed another powerful message about what was to be her role in life as a woman—partner to a man and a mother. Those roles were tenuous because the law did not protect her in either of them. They were not, however, meaningless to her.

Having a child was perhaps the most serious matter that confronted women. Females who faced motherhood during Hemings's time—enslaved, free, black, white, and red—confronted the immediate issue of surviving the ordeal of pregnancy. They knew that even if they survived, at least some of their children would likely die because no society had figured out how to save its children from deadly childhood diseases that are of little import in the developed world today. The death of children was not the only stalker of slave mothers and potential mothers like Hemings. She and other enslaved women faced the added, unspeakable reality that they could be separated from their children by sale. Above all of slavery's depredations, the separation of children from their families crystallized the system's barbarity so clearly that slave owners claimed that it rarely happened or spent endless time talking about how loath they were to do it—just before they did it. . . . [S]eparation from children by sale . . . shaped . . . [enslaved women's] identities as women. Hemings, like other enslaved girls, must have dreamed of a future in which her motherhood would never be blighted by such a moment. . . .

Had Hemings never been in Paris, her choice of mates at Monticello would have been perhaps even more limited than that of other enslaved women on the plantation. Her racial background contributed to her identity and undoubtedly affected her views about who would be attractive as a companion and as father of her children. . . . In slavery and outside of it, members of Hemings's family—female and male—developed a practice of having children with, and marrying when that was available, people who looked something like themselves, which is what most people in the world tend to do.[8] Jefferson probably resembled Hemings more than the average male slave on the plantation did, in terms of hair texture, skin color, and eye color. This is not to say that she would never under any circumstances have welcomed a partner with skin darker than her own or tightly curled hair, as allowances must always be made for the vagaries of attraction. It is human beings we are dealing with, after all, and no one has devised a precise formula or foolproof predictor of personal taste, and black couples and families come in all shades.

Although Hemings was probably not thinking in strictly legal terms about the racial makeup of the child she was carrying in Paris when she was deciding whether to come home with Jefferson, Virginia statutory law on racial categorizations, as Jefferson noted many years later, would make all of her children by him legally white [Virginia law provided that a person who was seven-eighths white was to be considered white]. We know Hemings wanted to free her children from slavery, and Jefferson's actions show he wanted that as well. No one has ever said that Hemings thought it important to free them from blackness, too. However, that is exactly the route that three of her four children took when they left both slavery and the black community to live as white people. The one child of hers who did remain in the black community, Madison Hemings, married a woman who was fair-skinned enough that some of their children were able to pass into the white world. We do not know whether the Hemings-Jefferson offspring were raised to do that, but it would not be surprising, particularly given their father's stated values, if that was a part of a plan or at least a very strong hope. . . .

Under the circumstances of Hemings's life, given her society and her family history, what type of man would be most able to end slavery for her children along with all the problems associated with being a person with black skin in America? If not Thomas Jefferson, who? She may have thought him as good a white man as any other, perhaps even better in some ways. That was a judgment to ponder. . . .

Unlike the vast majority of her enslaved cohort back in Virginia, freedom was within . . . [Sally Hemings'] grasp [in Paris], and she ended up using the unique opportunity she possessed, not as an end in itself, but as a starting point for a discussion with the man who wanted to take her home with him. That Jefferson desired that at all, a further contingent element in Hemings's life, gave her leverage under their particular circumstances. Another man might not have cared enough to try to persuade her or would have dared her (and her brother) to do their worst: take their claim to the Admiralty Court. . . .

Hemings had not only her own observations of Jefferson to draw upon; a wealth of family history supplemented her knowledge. Whether she had had time in her young life to learn this fact about him or not, the truth is that few things could have disturbed the very thin-skinned, possessive, and controlling Jefferson more deeply than having persons in his inner circle take the initiative and express their willingness to remove themselves from it. To have this come from a young female, the kind of person he thought was supposed to be under the control of males, whether they were enslaved or not, was likely doubly upsetting. . . . This challenge was a far greater threat to his self-esteem and emotions than to his

wallet. He had great confidence in his ability to charm and in his capacity to bring people to his side and keep them there. . . .

[Furthermore,] Hemings knew how Jefferson viewed women, and implicitly understood that if she were paired with an enslaved man [at Monticello] she would have two men over her: her enslaved husband and Jefferson. She would be one step removed from the man who held power over both of them, and Jefferson would have no personal stake in her or the children she bore with another man. . . .

Like other enslaved people when the all too rare chance presented itself, Hemings seized her moment and used the knowledge of her rights to make a decision based upon what she thought was best for her as a woman, family member, and a potential mother in her specific circumstances.

Visitors to the Hôtel de Langeac toasted Jefferson as the "apostle of liberty" and made much of his progressivism in the face of those who wanted to maintain the status quo in society. Imagine the stir if a slave of the "apostle" had shown up at the Admiralty Court in Paris, forced there because he had refused her request for freedom. Jefferson's image, which he so assiduously cultivated throughout his entire public career, would have been left in tatters. . . . To have Jefferson, of all people, act in direct opposition to France's Freedom Principle so that he could keep control over a sixteen-year-old enslaved girl would have been a spectacle for the ages. The word "irony" does not even begin to approach doing the situation justice. If the court had gotten the chance to see her, all would have been revealed instantly. . . . That was an outcome to be avoided at all costs. . . . Aside from whatever he felt for her, the Parisian Admiralty Court and Jefferson's special position and reputation in France gave Sally Hemings latitude to say, "I will go home with you, but only on certain conditions."[9]

Jefferson may have pointed out to Hemings and her brother the potential problems they might face by remaining in Paris. . . . [But] by this time, whatever sense of entitlement [Sally] had as a Hemings had been added to all her experiences to date—traveling across an ocean, . . . learning a new language, . . . and being a handsomely paid employee. The last experience was probably the most important. She worked alongside other French servants at the Hôtel de Langeac and knew she could work elsewhere. The fashion of having African and mixed-race servants gave her an advantage if she sought work as a *femme de chambre*. . . .

And then there was Paris' small community of color. . . . Sally Hemings had a special reason for thinking of this community. She did not likely consider staying in France without thinking of what the future might hold in the way of marriage and companionship. Although only around a thousand gens de couleur lived in all of Paris, the vast majority of them, concentrated in a small number of neighborhoods, were males in their late teens and early twenties—exactly suitable for a young woman approaching her seventeenth birthday.[10]

. . . [H]ad Hemings decided to break away from Jefferson and start a new life with her brother, she would have had the chance to be the mother of children who were free at birth and she could have had a legal marriage and the social respectability that would elude her totally in Virginia living with Jefferson. None of her children would have felt compelled to leave her, one another, and their family history behind in order to escape the racism of nineteenth-century America. . . .

. . . With no opportunity for legal marriage, Sally Hemings . . . was operating without the benefit of any written rules. The plan for her life at Monticello with Jefferson . . . depended . . . upon Hemings's ability to hold Jefferson in some serious fashion over the years and, more importantly, the quality of his personal character and his willingness to remain committed to her. It is not all surprising, therefore, that Hemings and Jefferson talked [in Paris] of the very matters that were among the core issues addressed in the basic marriage contract for free couples in the world in which they lived: the treatment of the woman, the man's duties and obligations toward the children, and what the children would receive from the man when they became adults, questions that men and women in every type of society from time immemorial have had to address. That the two would be having sex was implicit in the understanding that Hemings was going to have more children and that provision would be made for them as well as the one about to be born—the particular one that Hemings most wanted: their freedom.

[For the past decade, I have traveled the country, speaking about Hemings and Jefferson. I do not recall a setting where this question was not asked explicitly or implicitly: "Did they love each other?"] The most intimate of situations, the one least likely to be observed by others—sexual compatibility—can . . . be a form of love. But in our Western culture (and some others, to be fair) sex is considered, if not exactly dirty or shameful, a somewhat guilty pleasure that must always be separated from more exalted love. This is especially true when a couple, like Hemings and Jefferson, for reasons of race, status, or gender are not supposed to be together, as if partners who do not have the imprimatur of law, society, and custom could never feel the emotion of love for one another. The invariable charge against such pairs is that they are inauthentic per se, because they are bound together purely for sex, rather than love.

[A] Jefferson great-granddaughter through the Hemings line told a . . . story about Hemings and Jefferson's origins in France when explaining why her great-grandmother gave up the chance for freedom and came back to Virginia, saying, "Jefferson loved her dearly."[11] In other words, she and other family members answered the questions why Hemings trusted Jefferson and came back to Virginia with him, by referencing her confidence in her knowledge of that fact, a confidence that allowed her to take what seems a breathtakingly large risk. . . .

Jefferson wanted Hemings to come back to Virginia with him, so much so that he took to bargaining with her about this. He well knew that in Virginia there were many other women, enslaved and not, who could satisfy any merely carnal impulses as soon as he returned to America. The problem was, however, that they would not actually have been Sally Hemings herself, a requirement that was evidently very important to him. Her siblings and other relatives seemed to have gauged this. . . . [T]heir attitude toward Jefferson after Hemings's return to Virginia is in perfect keeping with the idea that they believed he cared for her. If what had happened between them in France had been along the lines of more typical master-female slave sex, Hemings's expressed desire to stay in the country, especially after she became aware that she was pregnant, would have been exactly what Jefferson needed. He could have left her in Paris with her quite capable older brother, helped the pair financially, . . . thus ridding himself of a potentially embarrassing problem in a way that actually bolstered, instead of hurt, his image. History, and his philosophc friends of the moment, would have recorded that Jefferson (breathing the rarefied air of Enlightenment France) so identified with the Freedom Principle that he let go of two of his own slaves. He would have been a veritable hero.

Instead of doing that, Jefferson insisted on setting up an arrangement with a young woman that he knew could easily result in a houseful of children whose existence would be easily tied to him. . . . During the decades that followed their time in France, . . . this most thin-skinned of individuals persisted on his course, . . . having more children with her who were named in the same fashion as the older ones: for his important and favorite family members and his best friends.[12] . . . Jefferson continued on, guided by his own internal compass and, no doubt, his awareness that the woman being vilified in the press had given up to him a thing whose value he understood: her freedom. He knew very well that these people, really, did not know what, and whom, they were talking about.

If sex had been the only issue, it would have been a far simpler and more practical matter, for himself and his white family when they returned to Monticello, for Jefferson to have installed Hemings in one of his nearby quarter farms . . . and visited her there when the mood hit him. . . . Instead, Jefferson arranged his life at Monticello so that Hemings would be in it every day that he was there, taking care of his possessions, in his private enclave.

What most disturbed contemporary commentators about the arrangement at Monticello was not that the master had a slave mistress but that she was not sufficiently hidden away.[13] Hemings was a visible presence in his home when everyone knew that Jefferson had the resources to have her be someplace else. The racism and sexual hysteria this unleashed among white Americans was a thing to behold. . . . Yet, through all the talk during Jefferson's lifetime of his "Congo Harem," "Negro Harem," and "African Harem," only one woman's name emerged: Sally. Jefferson's enemies of the day could list each of Hemings's children, their order of birth and ages, what her duties were at Monticello, but they could never produce the name of another specific woman to be a part of his alleged seraglio.

From her side, it was Hemings who backed down from her decision to stay in France in return for a life at Monticello in which Jefferson would be a very serious presence. . . . [D]uring an almost twenty-year period of childbearing, she conceived no children during Jefferson's sometimes prolonged absences from Monticello as he acted as a public servant, indicating that she had no other sexual partners.[14] That could well have been at his insistence as much as her own personal desires. Still, the expectation of fidelity—on her part at least—suggests something about the nature of their relationship. . . . Hemings's connection to Jefferson, held together totally by whatever was going on between them, was her children's way out of slavery, so long as her children were his, too. She was apparently unwilling to do anything (as in having babies by other men) that might jeopardize that connection and bring the effects of *partus sequitur ventrem* back into her life.

Before Hemings died, she gave one of her sons as heirlooms personal items that had belonged to Jefferson, a pair of his eyeglasses, a shoe buckle, and an inkwell that she had kept during the nine years after his death. These artifacts—things she saw him wear and a thing he used to write words that would make him live in history—were seemingly all that she had left of him. Monticello and virtually all its contents were sold to pay debts or were in the control of his legal white family. These items were quietly passed down in the Hemings family until well into the twentieth century.[15] . . . Hemings's action, which at the very least exhorted her descendants to both remember Jefferson and her connection to him, indicate that she wanted them to know he meant something to her. She had, after all, lived with him for decades, and he had given her valued children whom he had let go to make their way in the world. . . . Jefferson had kept his promises to her.

. . . Working backward to 1789 from either her death in 1835 or Jefferson's death in 1826, one can say that sixteen-year-old Hemings's instincts about how she might best shape her future in the context of her particular circumstances and needs were as sound as her older sister Mary's instincts about Thomas Bell, developing at the same time on another continent. Hemings could not have known this as she treated with Jefferson at the Hôtel de Langeac, but at the end of her life she would be able to say that she got the important things that she most wanted.

NOTES

1. TJ to Nicholas Lewis, April 12, 1792, *The Papers of Thomas Jefferson*, ed. Julian P. Boyd et al., 35 vols. to date (Princeton, 1950–), 23:408.

2. Lucia Stanton, "Monticello to Main Street: The Hemings Family and Charlottesville," *Magazine of Albemarle County History* 55 (1997): 100.

3. Walter Johnson, *Soul by Soul: Life inside the Antebellum Slave Market* (Cambridge, Mass., 1999).

4. TJ to Andre Limozin, May 3, 1789, *Papers*, 16:86.

5. [Reproduced in] Annette Gordon-Reed, *Thomas Jefferson and Sally Hemings: An American Controversy* (Charlottesville: University Press of Virginia, 1997), 246.

6. Lucia Stanton, *Free Some Day: The African-American Families of Monticello* (Charlottesville, 2000), 105.

7. Philip D. Morgan, *Slave Counterpoint: Black Culture in the Eighteenth-Century Chesapeake and Lowcountry* (Chapel Hill: University of North Carolina Press, 1998), 665–66; "An Act to Authorize the Manumission of Slaves," Laws of Virginia, 1782, chap. 61.

8. Stanton, *Free Some Day*, 106; Lucia Stanton and Dianne Swann Wright, "Bonds of Memory Identity and the Hemings Family," in *Sally Hemings and Thomas Jefferson: History, Memory and Civic Culture*, eds. Jan Ellen Lewis and Peter S. Onuf (Charlottesville, 1999), 170–72.

9. Sue Peabody, "There Are No Slaves in France": *The Political Culture of Race and Slavery in the Ancient Régime* (New York: Oxford University Press, 1996), 101–3.

10. Pierre H. Boulle, "Les Gens de couleur à Paris à la veille de la Révolution" in *L'Image de la Révolution française*, ed. Michel Vovelle. Vol 1 (Paris: Pergamon Press, 1989), 160–61.

11. Stanton and Swann Wright, "Bonds of Memory Identity," 176.

12. Gordon-Reed, *Thomas Jefferson and Sally Hemings*, 196–201.

13. Ibid., 170–71.

14. Ibid., 100–2, 216.

15. Nellie Jones to Stuart Gibboney, July 29, 1938, Aug. 10, 1938; Stuart Gibboney to Nellie Jones, Aug. 1, 1938, Nov. 1, 1938, correspondence in the University of Virginia Library, Accession No. 6636-a-b, Box No. Control Folder, Folder Dates 1735–1961. Nellie Jones was Madison Hemings's granddaughter. She wrote to Gibboney, the then president of the Thomas Jefferson Memorial Foundation, offering to donate mementos that her great-grandmother Sally Hemings had saved and given to their son: a pair of his glasses, an inkwell, and a silver buckle.

Virginia Establishes a Double Standard in Tax Law

Tax policy was the site of one of the earliest and most significant interventions made by English colonial lawmakers to cordon off black women from white, practically and symbolically. In the 1643 law that follows, the Virginia Assembly made one of its first discriminations according to race. The provision clarified the tithing system—by which Anglican ministers in each parish would be paid. European colonists paid a variety of taxes based not on income but "per poll" (per person) or according to the property they owned. Given the scarcity of circulating coins or paper currency, taxes were typically paid in goods including foodstuffs. From 1643 forward, heads of household would be required to pay annually the designated amount for each male over fifteen in the household (whether free, indentured, or enslaved)—and for what other category of person? We can think of the distinction that the law silently made between "negro" and other women as a continuation, or a second act, in the process of sexual stereotyping described by Jennifer L. Morgan (pp. 24–33). The Virginia law not only placed an extra financial burden on free black families, but also broadcast the ruling class's dictum that African and African-descended women were assumed to be field laborers, thus denying their domesticity.

The 1643 statute was tested in the colony's lower courts. Would authorities permit any exceptions to be made? Two examples are given here. In the first case, white male colonist Francis Stripes had recently married; probably a neighbor or tax assessor complained to the court that Stripes had not been paying the proper tithe. In Susannah's case, we do not know how the petitioner made a living, but it was not necessarily as a farm laborer. What do you imagine she argued in her plea (which was likely made orally) to the bench of local gentlemen who served as justices? How did they justify their ruling to themselves and to her? The court clerk's omission of Susannah's surname reflected a common colonial tendency to erase the chosen identities of people of color.

Be it further enacted and confirmed That there be tenn pounds of tob[acco]o per poll & a bushel of corne per poll paid to the ministers within the severall parishes of the colony for all tithable persons, that is to say, as well for all youths of sixteen years of age as upwards, as also for all negro women at the age of sixteen years.

1671 case, Lower Norfolk County: It is the opinion and Judgement of the Court that francis Stripes ought to pay Leavyes and tythes for his wife (shee being a negro) It being according to Law; and therefore ordered that he pay the Same for the Last year past, as well as this present [year] and so for the future.

Assembly of Virginia, act 1, March 1643, in William Waller Hening, *The Statutes at Large: Being a Collection of All the Laws of Virginia, from the First Session of the Legislature, in the Year 1619*, 13 vols. (New York: R. & W. & G. Bartow, 1823), 1:242; Lower Norfolk County Order Book, 1665–75, vol. 73, and Charles City County Order Book, 1677–79, 216, reproduced in *The Old Dominion in the Seventeenth Century: A Documentary History of Virginia, 1606–1689*, rev. ed., ed. Warren M. Billings (Chapel Hill: University of North Carolina Press, 2007), p. 183. The cases are reprinted with the kind permission of the author and publisher.

1677 case, Charles City County: Upon the petition of Susannah a free Negro-Woman that she may be Exempted from paying Levyes, And Whereas the Worshipful Courte is informed of her strength and ability It is thereupon thought fit that she be not Exempted but pay Levyes.

"According to the condition of the mother . . ."

The North American system of slavery relied heavily on marking differences of status (slave or free)—by visible bodily difference (black or white). Free black people and enslaved mulattoes undermined the simplicity of these signals, displaying in their very beings the fact that it was power, not nature, that placed any particular individual in one status or another.

In defining slavery—a condition not then recognized in English law—colonial lawmakers faced the question of how to interpret the status of children born to parents who were not married to each other, and whose fathers were white and mothers were black. Might such offspring claim free status? Could white fathers be obliged to take responsibility for the children's upbringing? In Spanish colonies in Central and South America, a complex system of godparenting made it possible for white fathers to maintain a wide variety of relationships with their mixed-blood children.

The Virginia law of 1662 shows how English colonists settled the question (Maryland had passed a similar statute two years earlier). Along with other laws passed at mid-century, it marked a turning point—from a period when blacks' status was often ambiguous and freedom was not foreclosed to a long era in which the default assumption would be that African-descended persons were enslaved and had few opportunities to become free. The Latin phrase for the rule enshrined in the colonial slave codes was *partus sequitur ventrem*, meaning that the status of the child (slave or free) would follow the mother's status. How did the 1662 law conflict with traditional English inheritance practices? What do the statute's two sections reveal about how Virginia legislators wished to shape interracial sexual relations? (With regard to the second section, note that the usual fine for fornication was 500 pounds of tobacco.) What are the implications of the law for children whose fathers were free black men and whose mothers were enslaved?

Whereas some doubts have arrisen whether children got by any Englishman upon a negro woman should be slave or free, *Be it therefore enacted and declared by this present grand assembly,* that all children borne in this country shalbe held bond or free only according to the condition of the mother, *And* that if any christian shall committ fornication with a negro man or woman hee or shee soe offending shall pay double the [usual] fines. . . .

Assembly of Virginia, act 16, December 1691, in William Waller Hening, *The Statutes at Large: Being a Collection of All the Laws of Virginia, from the First Session of the Legislature, in the Year 1619,* 13 vols. (New York: R & W & G Bartow, 1823), 2:170.

> ### "For prevention of that abominable mixture . . ."

L ate in the seventeenth century, Virginia and Maryland lawmakers imposed harsh disincentives for whites and blacks who wished to marry such as Francis Stripes and his wife in the earlier document extract, stopping just short of an outright ban like the one that would later be enacted and would stand until the 1967 U.S. Supreme Court ruling in *Loving v. Virginia* (p. 670). What interracial relationships are omitted in Virginia's 1691 law? How would you characterize the legal status of mixed-race children born out of wedlock to free white women? Why did legislators think this set of laws would be self-enforcing?

[1691] . . . for prevention of that abominable mixture and spurious issue which hereafter may encrease in this dominion, as well by negroes, mulattoes, and Indians intermarrying with English, or other white women, as by their unlawful accompanying with one another, *Be it enacted* . . . that . . . whatsoever English or other white man or woman being free shall intermarry with a negroe, mulatto or Indian man or woman bond or free shall within three months after such marriage be banished and removed from this dominion forever. . . .

And be it further enacted . . . That if any English woman being free shall have a bastard child by any negro or mulatto, she pay the sume of fifteen pounds sterling, within one moneth after such bastard child shall be born, to the Church wardens of the parish . . . and in default of such payment she shall be taken into the possession of the said Church wardens and disposed of for five yeares, and the said fine of fifteen pounds, or whatever the woman shall be disposed of for, shall be paid, one third part to

their majesties . . . and one other third part to the use of the parish . . . and the other third part to the informer, and that such bastard child be bound out as a servant by the said Church wardens untill he or she shall attaine the age of thirty yeares, and in case such English woman that shall have such bastard child be a servant, she shall be sold by the said church wardens, (after her time is expired that she ought by law to serve her master) for five yeares, and the money she shall be sold for divided as is before appointed, and the child to serve as aforesaid.

[1705] *And be it further enacted*, That no minister of the church of England, or other minister, or person whatsoever, within this colony and dominion, shall hereafter wittingly presume to marry a white man with a negro or mulatto woman; or to marry a white woman with a negro or mulatto man, upon pain of forfeiting or paying, for every such marriage the sum of ten thousand pounds of tobacco; one half to our sovereign lady the Queen . . . and the other half to the informer. . . .

> ### A Massachusetts Minister's Slave Marriage Vows

A lthough Africans and African-descended people made up a much smaller proportion of the population and labor force in northern than in southern colonies, few white northerners took issue with the assumptions that undergirded the slave system. In fact, the merchants of Newport, Rhode Island, made

Assembly of Virginia, act 16, April 1691, in William Waller Hening, *The Statutes at Large: Being a Collection of All the Laws of Virginia, from the First Session of the Legislature, in the Year 1619*, 13 vols. (New York: R & W & G Bartow, 1823), 3:86–87; and Assembly of Virginia, ch. 49, sec. 20, October 1705 in Hening, *Statutes at Large*, 3:453.

enormous profits as the most active slave traders in the English colonies. For a gentleman, having one or two enslaved persons among his dependents was seen as a status symbol. Clergymen—who were respected for their learnedness, but were rarely wealthy—were sometimes presented with the gift of an enslaved youth or adult by their wealthy parishioners. By the eighteenth century, New England elites did not hesitate to encourage enslaved men and women to acculturate by embracing Christianity. Church records contain scattered entries for blacks—free and enslaved—receiving baptism, owning the covenant, marrying, having their children baptized, and being buried.

This is the "form of a Negro-Marriage" used by Congregational clergyman Samuel Phillips of Andover, Massachusetts, when enslaved men and women came to him, asking to be wed, during his sixty-year pastorate (1710–71). Similar vows were used in other churches. Read the vows aloud, and imagine what the marriage ceremony was like. How would you characterize the marriage contract that is being made? Which Christian rules is the Reverend Phillips selectively invoking? Some years later, in the famous *Jennison v. Walker* case that is often cited as ending slavery in Massachusetts, attorney Levi Lincoln confirmed and challenged the paradox at the core of these vows: "The master has a right to separate the Husband and wife—is this consistent with the law of nature[?] Is it consistent with the law of nature to separate what God has joined and no man can put asunder?"*

Minister: "You,—do now in the Presence of God, and these Witnesses, Take—: to be your Wife; Promising that so far as shall be consistent with the Relations which you now sustain, as a Servant, you will Perform the Part of an Husband towards her; And in particular, you Promise, that you will Love her: And that, as you shall have the Opportunity & Ability, you will take a proper Care of her in Sickness and Health, in Prosperity & Adversity: And that you will be True & Faithfull to her, and will Cleave to her only, so long as God, in his Providence, shall continue your and her abode in Such Place (or Places) as that you can conveniently come together:—Do you thus Promise?"

Then the same Vow was declared for the woman to agree to.

Minister: "I then agreeable to your Request, and with the Consent of your Masters & Mistresses,

do Declare, that you have Licence given you to be conversant and familiar together, as Husband and Wife, so long as God shall continue your Places of abode as aforesaid; and so long as you shall behave yourselves as it becomes Servants to doe: For you must, both of you, bear in mind, that you Remain Still, as really and truly as ever, your Master's Property, and therefore it will be justly expected, both by God and Man, that you behave and conduct yourselves, as Obedient and faithfull Servants towards your respective Masters & Mistresses for the Time being. . . ."

"I shall now conclude with Prayer for you, that you may become good Christians, and that you may be enabled to conduct as such; and in particular, that you may have Grace to behave suitably towards each Other, as also dutifully towards your Masters & Mistresses, not with Eye-Service, as Men-pleasers, but as the Servants of Christ, doing the will of God from the heart."

* "Brief of Levi Lincoln in the Slave Case Tried 1781," *Collections of the Massachusetts Historical Society*, 5th ser., 3 (1877): 441.

George E. Howard, *A History of Matrimonial Institutions* . . . (London, 1904), vol. 2, pp. 225–26, quoting George H. Moore, "Slave Marriages in Massachusetts," *Dawson's Historical Magazine*, 2nd ser., 5 (1869): 137. We have modernized spelling and expanded abbreviated words.

Living Through War and Revolution

Philadelphia Women Raise Money Door to Door

This broadside of 1780 announced a women's campaign to raise contributions for patriot soldiers. Organized and led by Esther DeBerdt Reed, wife of the president of Pennsylvania, and by Benjamin Franklin's daughter Sarah Franklin Bache, the campaign was large and effective. "Instead of waiting for the Donations being sent the ladys of each Ward go from dore to dore and collect them," wrote one participant. Collecting contributions this way invited confrontation. One loyalist wrote to her sister, "Of all absurdities, the ladies going about for money exceeded everything; they were so extremely importunate that people were obliged to give them something to get rid of them."* The campaign raised $300,000 in paper dollars in inflated war currency. Rather than let George Washington merge it with the general fund, the women insisted on using it to buy materials for making shirts so that each soldier might know he had received an extraordinary contribution from the women of Philadelphia. The broadside itself is an unusually explicit justification for women's intrusion into politics.

On the commencement of actual war, the Women of America manifested a firm resolution to contribute . . . to the deliverance of their country. Animated by the purest patriotism, they are sensible of sorrow at this day, in not offering more than barren wishes for the success of so glorious a Revolution. They aspire to render themselves more really useful; and this sentiment is universal from the north to the south of the Thirteen United States. Our ambition is kindled by the fame of those heroines of antiquity, who have rendered their sex illustrious, and have proved to the universe, that, if the weakness of our Constitution, if opinion and manners did not forbid us to march to glory by the same paths as the Men, we should at least equal, and sometimes surpass them in our love for the public good. I glory in all that which my sex has done great and commendable. I call to mind with enthusiasm and with admiration, all those acts of courage, of constancy and patriotism, which history has transmitted to us: The people favoured by Heaven, preserved from destruction by the virtues, the zeal and the resolution of Deborah, of Judith, of Esther! The fortitude of the mother of the Macchabees, in giving up her sons to die before her eyes: Rome saved from the fury of a victorious enemy by the efforts of Volumnia, and other Roman Ladies: So many famous sieges where the Women have been seen forgetting the weakness of their sex, building new walls, digging trenches with their feeble hands, furnishing arms to their defenders, they themselves darting the missile weapons on the enemy, resigning the ornaments of their apparel, and their fortune, to fill the public treasury, and to hasten the deliverance of their country; burying themselves under its ruins;

---

*Mary Morris to Catharine Livingston, June 10 [1780], Ridley Family Papers, Massachusetts Historical Society, Boston; Anna Rawle to Rebecca Rawle Shoemaker, June 30, 1780, in *Pennsylvania Magazine of History and Biography* 35 (1911), 398.

Excerpted from *The Sentiments of an American Woman* ([Philadelphia]: John Dunlap, 1780).

throwing themselves into the flames rather than submit to the disgrace of humiliation before a proud enemy.

Born for liberty, disdaining to bear the irons of a tyrannic Government, we associate ourselves to the grandeur of those Sovereigns, cherished and revered, who have held with so much splendour the scepter of the greatest States, The Batildas, the Elizabeths, the Maries, the Catharines, who have extented the empire of liberty, and contented to reign by sweetness and justice, have broken the chains of slavery, forged by tyrants in times of ignorance and barbarity. . . .

We know that at a distance from the theatre of war, if we enjoy any tranquility, it is the fruit of your watchings, your labours, your dangers. . . . Who, amongst us, will not renounce with the highest pleasure, those vain ornaments, when she shall consider that the valiant defenders of America will be able to draw some advantage from the money which she may have laid out in these. . . . The time is arrived to display the same sentiments which animated us at the beginning of the Revolution, when we renounced the use of teas, however agreeable to our taste, rather than receive them from our persecutors; when we made it appear to them that we placed former necessaries in the rank of superfluities, when our liberty was interested; when our republican and laborious hands spun the flax, prepared the linen intended for the use of our soldiers; when [as] exiles and fugitives we supported with courage all the evils which are the concomitants of war. . . .

Sarah Osborn, "The bullets would not cheat the gallows . . ."

S arah Osborn was eighty-one years old when Congress made it possible for dependent survivors of Revolutionary war veterans to claim their pensions. She testified to her own service as well as to her husband's in the following deposition, sworn before the Court of Common Pleas in Wayne County, New Jersey, in 1837. Osborn's husband was a commissary guard; like many thousands of women, Osborn traveled with him, cooking and cleaning for troops at a time when there was no formal quartermaster corps and in which cleanliness was virtually the only guard against disease. Her account tells of working when the army was at West Point in 1780; of the long expedition south, marching proudly on horseback into Philadelphia, and then continuing to Yorktown. Osborn is the only one of the "women of the army" who has left us a narrative of her experiences. At Yorktown she brought food to soldiers under fire. When she told George Washington that she did not fear the bullets because they "would not cheat the gallows," she was conveying her understanding that her challenge to royal authority was congruent with his; if the soldiers risked being hanged for treason, so would she.

[In the march to Philadelphia in 1781?] Deponent was part of the time on horseback and part of the time in a wagon. Deponent's . . . husband was still serving as one of the commissary's guard. . . . They continued their march to Philadelphia, deponent on horseback through the streets. . . . Being out of bread, deponent was employed in baking the afternoon and evening . . . they continued their march . . . [at Baltimore she] embarked on board a vessel and sailed . . . until they had got up the St. James River as far as the tide would carry them. . . . They . . . marched for Yorktown. . . . Deponent was on foot. . . . Deponent took her stand just back of the American tents, say about a mile from the town, and busied herself washing, mending, and cooking for the soldiers, in which she was assisted by the other females; some men washed their own clothing. She heard the roar of the artillery for a number

Excerpted from *The Revolution Remembered: Eyewitness Accounts of the American Revolution*, ed. John C. Dann (Chicago: University of Chicago Press, 1980), pp. 240–45.

Deborah Sampson, who served in the Fourth Massachusetts Regiment as Robert Shurtleff, painted by Joseph Stone, 1797.

In 1782, Deborah Sampson, who was already notable in her community of Middleborough, Massachusetts, for her height and strength, adopted men's clothing and the name of Robert Shurtleff. She enlisted for service with the Fourth Massachusetts Regiment. Like many young women from impoverished families, Deborah Sampson had been bound out to domestic service as a young teenager. When her term was up, she taught school briefly in Middleborough and joined the First Baptist Church there. She was expelled from the church before her enlistment. She served with her regiment in New York and possibly in Pennsylvania until she was wounded at a battle near Tarrytown, New York.

After her return to Massachusetts, Sampson married and bore three children. The fame of her exploits persisted. After a fictionalized biography was published by Herman Mann in 1797, she went on a wide-ranging speaking tour, perhaps the first American woman to undertake such an enterprise, and applied for the pensions to which her wartime service entitled her. These were awarded slowly and grudgingly, and she died impoverished in 1827. (Joseph Stone, Deborah Sampson [Gannett], 1797, oil on paper, later pasted on wood. Courtesy of the Rhode Island Historical Society.)

of days. . . . Deponent's . . . husband was there throwing up entrenchments, and deponent cooked and carried in beef, and bread, and coffee (in a gallon pot) to the soldiers in the entrenchment.

On one occasion when deponent was thus employed carrying in provisions, she met General Washington, who asked her if she "was not afraid of the cannonballs?"

She replied, "No, the bullets would not cheat the gallows," that "It would not do for the men to fight and starve too."

They dug entrenchments nearer and nearer to Yorktown every night or two till the last. While digging that, the enemy fired very heavy till about nine o'clock next morning, then stopped, and the drums from the enemy beat excessively. Deponent was a little way off in Colonel Van Shaick's or the officers' marquee and a number of officers were present. . . .

The drums continued beating, and all at once the officers hurrahed and swung their hats, and deponent asked them, "What is the matter now?"

One of them replied, "Are not you soldier enough to know what it means?" Deponent replied, "No."

They then replied, "The British have surrendered."

Deponent, having provisions ready, carried the same down to the entrenchments that morning, and four of the soldiers whom she was in the habit of cooking for ate their breakfasts.

Deponent stood on one side of the road and the American officers upon the other side when the British officers came out of the town and rode up to the American officers and delivered up [their swords, which the deponent] thinks were returned again, and the British officers rode right on before the army, who marched out beating and playing a melancholy tune, their drums covered with black handkerchiefs and their fifes with black ribbands tied around them, into an old field and there grounded their arms and then returned into town again to await their destiny. . . . The British general at the head of the army was a large, portly man, full face, and the tears rolled down his cheeks as he passed along.

Rachel Wells, "I have Don as much to Carrey on the Warr as maney . . ."

Rachel Wells was probably sixty-five years old when she wrote the following words. She had bought loan office certificates from the state of New Jersey during the Revolution: subsequently she had moved to Philadelphia, but returned to Bordentown, New Jersey, after the war. In an effort to curb speculation, the New Jersey legislature decided that only state residents had a claim on interest payments; Rachel Wells's claim on her money was turned down because she had not been in the state at the war's end in 1783. She appealed directly to the Continental Congress. Although her petition was tabled, it remains—despite its bad spelling—as perhaps the most moving witness to the Revolution left to us by a woman. What did Rachel Wells think had been her contribution to the Revolution? What did she think the government owed to her?

To the Honnorabell Congress I rachel do make this Complaint Who am a Widow far advanced in years & Dearly have ocasion of ye Interst for that Cash I Lent the States. I was a Sitisen in ye jersey when I Lent ye State a considerable Sum of Moneys & had I justice dun me it mite be Suficant to suporte me in ye Contrey whear I am now, near burdentown. I Leved hear then . . . but Being . . . so Robd by the Britans & others i went to Phila to try to

Rachel Wells, Petition to Congress, May 18, 1786, Microfilm Papers of the Continental Congress, National Archives, Washington, D.C., M247, roll 56, item 42, vol. 8, pp. 354–55.

get a Living . . . & was There in the year 1783 when our assembley was pleasd to pas a Law that No one Should have aney Interest that Livd out of jearsey Stats . . .

Now gentelmen is this Liberty, had it bin advertised that he or She that Moved out of the Stat should Louse his or her Interest you mite have sum plea against me.

But I am Innocent Suspected no Trick. I have Don as much to Carrey on the Warr as maney that Sett now at ye healm of government. . . . your asembly Borrowed £300 in gould of me jest as the Warr Comencd & Now I Can Nither git Intrust nor principall Nor Even Security. . . . My dr Sister . . . wrote to me to be thankfull that I had it in my Power to help on the Warr which is well enough but then this is to be Considerd that others gits their Intrust & why then a poor old widow to be put of[f]. . . . I hartely pity others that ar in my Case that Cant Speak for themselves. . . .

god has Spred a plentifull table for us & you gentlemen are ye Carvers for us pray forgit Not the Poor weaklings at the foot of the Tabel ye poor Sogers has got Sum Crumbs That fall from their masters tabel. . . . Why Not Rachel Wells have a Little intrust?

if She did not fight She threw in all her mite which bought ye Sogers food & Clothing & Let Them have Blankets & Since that She has bin obligd to Lay upon Straw & glad of that . . .

Grace Galloway, Loyalist

Because the Revolution was a civil war, each adult had to assume a political identity and maintain it with sufficient clarity to satisfy the local authorities. Women had an advantage. Because they were not being recruited into the conflicting armies, their political choices were less carefully scrutinized than those of men; they might even shift back and forth between enemy camps. One patriot complained that the British "were informed of every thing that passed among us and that Women were the most proper persons for that purpose."*

Despite the presence of women spies and informant, the belief that politics was somehow no part of the woman's domain persisted throughout the war, expressed even by women whose own lives were in fact directly dependent on political developments. Grace Growden Galloway reveals this cluster of contradictory traits. She was a formidable woman, and not surprisingly her biographers tend to describe her as "imperious." The daughter of one of the wealthiest and most powerful men in colonial Pennsylvania, she married another, Joseph Galloway, who became Speaker of the Pennsylvania Assembly in the decade before war broke out. It was not a happy marriage. In one of the poems she inscribed in her diary she warned:

Never get tied to a man
    for when once you are yoked
'Tis all a mere joke
    of seeing your freedom again.

---

*Testimony of Henry Livingston, Feb. 5, 1777, *Minutes of the . . . Committee . . . for Detecting and Defeating Conspiracies . . .* (New York, 1924), I:120.

Excerpted from "Diary of Grace Growden Galloway, Kept at Philadelphia . . ." *Pennsylvania Magazine of History and Biography,* 55 (1931), 50ff. See also Linda K. Kerber, *Women of the Republic: Intellect and Ideology in Revolutionary America* (Chapel Hill: University of North Carolina Press, 1980), pp. 49, 74–76.

When the war began, Philadelphia was in rebel hands. Joseph Galloway fled the city to join the British army stationed to the north. When the British occupied Philadelphia in 1777, he returned with them, serving as Superintendent of the Port and the Police, a role in which he could make life hard for rebels. When the patriots regained control early in 1778 he left again, taking the couple's daughter (and only surviving child) with him.

Grace grimly stayed on in occupied Philadelphia, hoping by her presence to maintain her claim not only to the city property on which they lived but other property—several thousand acres—that she stood to inherit from her father. In the meantime, as a leading male loyalist, Galloway was singled out by Pennsylvania's governing patriots. He was convicted in absentia for high treason and his property was confiscated. His wife's dower right in it was ignored. (Wives, on their husbands' deaths, were entitled to the use and income of one-third of land and buildings; being a convicted traitor was a political form of death.)

When her husband and daughter left with the British, Grace Galloway began a diary. It is a marvelously opinionated document in which she registered her emotions as well as the weather and the names of her visitors. Her spelling is often informal (e.g., "Embassell'd" for "embezzled") but her voice is clear. Despite her open scorn for the patriot cause (in the diary and in public), she was surprised when her house was seized along with other loyalists' property, and she was stunned when the patriots evicted her, refusing to honor her dower rights.

WEDNESDAY JULY 22, 1778

Was ill in ye morn. . . . sent for Mr. Dickinson last Night & he tole Me he wou'd look over ye law to see if I cou'd recover My own estate & this evening he came & he told Me I cou'd Not recover dower & he fear'd my income in My estate was forfeited likewise & ye no tryal wou'd be of service: but advised Me to draw up a peti'on to ye Chief Judge Mccean for the recovery of my estate & refused a fee in ye Politest Manner but begg'd I wou'd look on him as My sincere friend & told me he would do me any service to ye Utmost of his power & I think he behaves much better than Chew. So I find I am a beggar indeed I expect every hour to be turn'd out of doors & where to go I know not. No one will take me in & all ye Men keeps from Me. . . . But I am fled from as a Pestilence. Mrs Jones here in the morn: sent nurse to Parson Combs to desire him to [tell] Mr G of my unhappy situation.

MONDAY, AUGUST 10, 1778

Peggy Johns & Becky Redman came in ye Morn, Lewis sent Me word Smith had gave his honour not to Molest Me till the Opinion of ye executive council was known but in a short time after came Peel[e], . . . [and others] took Possession of my house. I was taken very ill & obliged to Lay down & sent them word I cou'd not see them; they went every Where below stairs & [one man] . . . offer'd to Me chuse My own bed chamber; but I sent them no Message but was very ill Up stairs. But between 2 & 3 o'clock the last went away. Peel[e] told Nurse now they had given [one] . . . Gentle Man possession they had nothing More to do with it. But they took the Key out of ye front parlor door & locked Me out & left the windows Open . . .

SUNDAY AUGUST 16, 1778 [THE COMING EVICTION HAS BEEN ANNOUNCED]

Mrs Redman & Mrs Montgomery drank tea here. I desired Mrs Montgomery to desire Mr McKean to drank tea with me or let me know when it Wou'd be Agreeable for me to Wait on him & I find [Samuel] Shoemaker . . . had been before me. The quakers all Assist her but they wou'd let me fall. I sent twice to Lewise for a sight of ye petition but he wou'd not let me see it & as I have No friends they treat me as they please. So much for Mr G [Galloway's] great friends. He has not one who will go out of ye way to serve him. I am in hopes they will let me have my Estate but that will be on my own

Account. No favour shown to J G [Joseph Galloway] or his Child: Nor has he a friend that will say now word in his favour. I am tired with sending after a set of men that allways keeps from me when I most need them. Am vex'd.

[Galloway was highly indignant when Charles Willson Peale (who later would be known as one of the greatest artists of the new nation) came to evict her.]

THURSDAY, AUGUST 20, 1778
[EVICTION DAY]

... Lewise sent me word that I must shut my doors & windows & if they wou'd come to let them Make a forcible Entry. Accordingly I did so & a little after 10 o'clock they Knocked Violently at the door three times. The Third time I sent Nurse & call'd out myself to tell them I was in possession of my own House & wou'd keep so & that they shou'd gain No admittance Hereupon which they went round in ye yard & Try'd every door but cou'd None Open. Then they went to the Kitchen door & with a scrubbing brush which they broke to pieces they forced that open, we Women standing in ye Entry in ye Dark. They made repeated strokes at ye door & I think was 8 or 10 Minuets before they got it open. When they came in I had ye windows open'd they look'd very Mad. Their was Peel[e], [Charles Willson Peale] Smith, ye Hatter, & a Col. Will, a pewterer in Second Street. I spoke first & told them I was Used ill: & show'd them the Opinion of ye Lawyers. Peel read it: but they all despised it & Peel said he had studyed ye Law & knew they did right. I told them Nothing but force shou'd get me out of My house. Smith said they knew how to Manage that & that they wou'd throw my cloaths in ye street: & told Me that Mrs Sympson & forty others [loyalist women] ware put out of ye lines in one day. . . . He . . . hinted that Mr G had treated people Cruely. I found the Villan wou'd say anything so I stop'd after hearing several insulting things. . . . In ye Mean While Peel & Will went over ye House to see Nothing was Embassell'd & Locking Up the things[. A]t last Smith went away & Mrs Irwin & he sat talking [in] ye Kitchen as they took my things to her House.

Peel went to the generals & asked for his Chariot & then returned & told me ye General was so kind as to let me have it & he, Mr Peel, was willing to Accommodate Me as well as he cou'd. I told him he Need not give himself the Troble for if I wanted ye Chariot I cou'd send to ye General myself. Just after ye General sent in his Housekeeper with His compliments & to let me know that I was wellcome to His Chariot & he wou'd have it ready any hour I pleased. I then Accepted of it & told her [that] I . . . after every Mortifying treatment [I] was tired & wanted to be turn'd out. Peel went Upstairs & brought down My Work bag & 2 bonnets & put them on the side table. At last we went in the Entry to sit. . . . Two of ye Men went out & after staying some time return'd & said they had been with the council & that they had done right [by ordering the eviction] & must proceed. I did not hear this myself but ye rest of ye Women did.

Mrs Craig asked for My Bed but they wou'd let Me Have Nothing & as I told them acted entirely from Malice: after we had been in ye Entry some time Smith & Will went away & Peel said ye Chariot was ready but he would not hasten me. I told him I was at home & in My own House & nothing but force shou'd drive me out of it. He said it was not ye first time he had taken a Lady by the Hand [he is] an insolent wretch. This speech was made some time in the room; at last he becon'd for ye Chariot for ye General wou'd not let it come till I wanted it & as the Chariot drew up Peel fetched My Bonnets & gave one to me ye other to Mrs Craig: then with [the] greatest air said come Mrs Galloway give me your hand. I answer'd I will not nor will I go out of my house but by force. He then took hold of my arm & I rose & he took me to the door. I then Took hold on one side & Look round & said pray take Notice I do not leave my house of My own accord or with my own inclination but by force & Nothing but force shou'd have Made Me give up possession. Peel said with a sneer very well Madam & when he led me down ye step I said now Mr Peel let go My Arm I want not your Assistance. He said he cou'd help me to ye Carriage. I told him I cou'd go without & you Mr Peel are the last Man on earth I wou'd wish to be Obliged to.

Mrs Craig then step'd into ye Carriage & we drove to her house where we din'd. It was neer two o'clock . . . Distress'd in ye afternoon when I reflected on the Occurences of ye day & that I was drove out of my house distitute & without any maintenance . . . Sent for Mr Chew. He came & told me I must sue them for a forcible Entry. I am just distracted but Glad it is over.

As litigation to recover her property continued, Grace Galloway's scorn for patriots was as vigorous and emphatic as any patriot castigation of the loyalists. "Nothing reigns here but interess[t]," she wrote of Philadelphia. But despite her pride and her assertiveness, she continued to define herself in private terms. "I . . . laughed at the whole wig [Whig—the name of the British opposition] party," she wrote on April 20, 1779. "I told them I was the happiest woman in town for I had been strip[p]ed and Turn'd out of Doors yet I was still the same and must be Joseph Galloway's Wife and Lawrxence Growdens daughter and that it was not in their power to humble Me."

Grace Galloway was a resentful woman to the end. Her husband, safely in London with their daughter, never asked her to join him. She boarded with Quaker friends, fending for herself with devalued Continental currency. The war seemed an intrusion into a private—and luxurious—world in which she had expected to enjoy her inheritance safely. She did not particularly love her husband, but she proudly claimed his identity. Though she made no secret of her hostility to the patriots or her admiration for the Crown, she failed to comprehend why she—a woman—should be expected to account for her views or why her views had any more significance than a preference for silver over pewter. Even in the midst of the struggle over the possession of her house, she persisted in serving tea, a beverage that patriots had given up at the time of the Boston Tea Party in 1773 and that marked her as a proud Loyalist. Galloway was not a stupid woman, but she failed to recognize that her political gestures went beyond merely private behavior, and she never came to terms with the invasion of the political world into her private and material life.

The United States was formed in a revolution that claimed that "it is the right of the people to alter or abolish" a government when they understand it to be destructive of their rights to "Life, Liberty and the Pursuit of Happiness" (quoting the Declaration of Independence). The British claimed that subjects owe permanent allegiance to the Crown; the patriots insisted that allegiance must be voluntary. Grace Galloway never consented to change her allegiance. What do her diary entries and the violence she experienced suggest about the nature of the Revolution? About her conception of womanhood?

LINDA K. KERBER
Why Diamonds Really Are a Girl's Best Friend: The Republican Mother and the Woman Citizen

---

A kiss on the hand may be quite continental
But diamonds are a girl's best friend
A kiss may be grand . . . but it won't pay the rental on your humble flat
Or help you at the automat . . .
> Jules Styne, 1950, sung by Carol Channing in the Broadway musical "Gentlemen Prefer Blondes"

"I expect to see our young women forming a new era in female history," wrote Judith Sargent Murray in 1798. Her optimism was part of a general sense that all possibilities were open in the post-Revolutionary world. The experience of war had given words like independence and self-reliance personal as well as

This essay has been prepared by the author for *Women's America*, 8th edition. It is drawn from *Women of the Republic: Intellect and Ideology in Revolutionary America* (Chapel Hill: University of North Carolina Press, 1980), chs. 7 and 9; *No Constitutional Right to Be Ladies: Women and the Obligations of Citizenship* (New York: Hill and Wang, 1998), introduction and ch. 1; and "Why Diamonds Really Are a Girl's Best Friend: Another American Narrative," *Daedalus* 141, no. 1 (Winter 2012), 89–100; all by Linda K. Kerber.

political overtones; among the things that ordinary people had learned from wartime had been that the world could, as the song played during the British surrender at Yorktown put it, turn upside down. The rich could quickly become poor; wives might suddenly have to manage farms and businesses; women might even, as the famous Deborah Sampson Gannett had done, shoulder a gun. Revolutionary experience taught that it was useful to be prepared for a wide range of unusual possibilities; political theory taught that republics rested on the virtue of their citizens. The stability and competence on which republican government relied required a highly literate and politically sophisticated constituency. Maintaining the republic was an intellectual and educational as well as a political challenge.

Murray herself, born into an elite family in Salem, Massachusetts, had felt the dislocations of the Revolution severely. Widowed, remarried to a Universalist minister of modest means, she understood what it was to be thrown on her own resources. "I would give my daughters every accomplishment which I thought proper," she wrote,

> and to crown all, I would early accustom them to habits of industry and order. They should be taught with precision the art economical; they should be enabled to procure for themselves the necessaries of life; independence should be placed within their grasp. . . . The SEX should be taught to depend on their own efforts, for the procurement of an establishment in life.[1]

The model republican woman was competent and confident. She could resist the vagaries of fashion; she was rational, independent, literate, benevolent, and self-reliant. Nearly every writer who described this paragon prepared a list of role models, echoing the pantheon of heroines admired by the fund-raising women of Philadelphia in 1780 (see pp. 110–111). There were women of the ancient world, like Cornelia, the mother of the Gracchi; rulers like Elizabeth of England and the Empress Catherine the Great of Russia; and a long list of British intellectuals: Lady Mary Wortley Montagu, Hannah More, Mary Wollstonecraft, and the historian Catherine Macaulay. Those who believed in these republican models demanded that their presence be recognized and endorsed and that a new generation of young women be urged to find in them patterns for their own behavior.

The Revolutionary years had brought some women close to direct criticism of political systems. Women had signed petitions, they had boycotted imported tea and textiles, they had made homespun and "felt nationly," as one young woman put it. In some places they had signed oaths of loyalty to patriot or loyalist forces. Rachel Wells bought £300 of government bonds to support the war and had a keen sense of her own contribution: "I did my Posabels every way . . . Ive Don as much to help on this war as Though I had bin a good Soger," she told the New Jersey legislature.[2]

Women were citizens of the new republic. They could be naturalized; they were required to refrain from treason on pain of punishment; if single, they paid taxes. Women could develop their own agendas; when Abigail Adams wrote the now-famous letter in which she urged her husband and his colleagues in the Continental Congress to "remember the ladies," she urged that domestic violence should be on the republican agenda: "Put it out of the power of our husbands to use us with impunity," she demanded. "Remember all men would be tyrants if they could."[3]

Expressions of women's desire to play a frankly political role were regularly camouflaged in satire, a device that typically makes new ideas and social criticism seem less threatening. (Think of the recent example of Jon Stewart's and Stephen Colbert's satirical political commentary on the Comedy Channel.) In 1791, for example, a New Jersey newspaper published a pair of semiserious satires in which women discuss the politics of excise taxes and national defense. "Roxana" expresses a feminist impatience:

> In fifty quarto volumes of ancient and modern history, you will not find fifty illustrious female names; heroes, statesmen, divines, philosophers, artists, are all of masculine gender. And pray what have they done during this long period of usurpation? . . . They have written ten thousand unintelligible books. . . . They have been cutting each other's throats all over the globe.[4]

Some years later, the students at Sarah Pierce's famous school for girls in Litchfield, Connecticut, prepared a "Ladies Declaration of Independence" for the Fourth of July. Alongside the frivolous phrasing is earnest comment on the unfilled promises of the republic. Less than ten years after that, Elizabeth Cady Stanton would use the same technique. "When in the Course of Human Events," the Litchfield declaration begins,

> it becomes necessary for the Ladies to dissolve those bonds by which they have been subjected

to others, and to assume among the self styled Lords of Creation that separate and equal station to which the laws of nature and their own talents entitle them, a decent respect to the opinions of mankind requires, that they should declare the causes which impel them to the separation.

We hold these truths to be self evident. That all mankind are created equal.

The Litchfield women wished to change "social relations." They complained about men who "have undervalued our talents, and disparaged our attainments; they have combined with each other, for the purpose of excluding us from all participation in Legislation and in the administration of Justice."[5]

As these young women understood, American revolutionaries had brilliantly and radically challenged the laws governing the relationship between ruler and ruled, subjects and the king. Republican ideology was antipatriarchal. It voiced the claim of adult men to be freed from the control of kings and political "fathers" in an antique monarchical system. "Is it in the interest of a man to be a boy all his life?" Tom Paine asked in *Common Sense*, the great political manifesto of the era.

But the men who modeled the new American republic after the war remodeled it in their own image. They did not eliminate the political father immediately or completely. George Washington quickly became the "Father of his Country"; at the Governor's Palace in Williamsburg, Virginia, the life-size portrait of George III was quickly replaced by a life-size portrait of George Washington in a similar pose. American revolutionary men understood that two major elements of prerevolutionary social and political life—the system of slavery and the system of domestic relations—directly clashed with the egalitarian principles of the Revolution. But they kept both systems in place. By embedding the three-fifths compromise and the Fugitive Slave Law in the federal Constitution of 1787, the founders actually strengthened and stabilized the system of slavery. And they left virtually intact the old English law governing relations between husbands and wives.

These codes (what we now call family law) are not well known nowadays, even by otherwise well-informed historians and lawyers. They were not written into the U.S. Constitution of 1787; unlike the fugitive slave clause or the three-fifths compromise, they were not publicly debated. White men—plantation masters, merchants, ministers, farmers, laborers, Northerners, Southerners—were differently situated in relation to slavery, so they had real reason to debate it. But every free man, rich or poor, whatever their race, benefited from the structures of traditional family law. They had no need to debate it. As a result, we have to search hard to find the details of the old law of domestic relations embedded in old state statutes, outdated treatises, and judges' reasoning in humdrum cases from state and local courts.

The old law of domestic relations began with the principle that at marriage the husband controlled the physical body of his wife. He had unfettered sexual access to her body. (There was no concept of rape within marriage in U.S. law until feminists put it there, beginning in the 1970s.) The system was known as *coverture*: a married woman was understood to be "covered" by her husband's civic identity, as though they were walking together under an umbrella that the husband held. She was absorbed by her husband's civil identity in much the same way that children were subject to their parents. At the moment of marriage, the husband gained "absolute title" to the personal property a wife brought to the marriage as well as ownership of whatever she earned during it. He gained extensive authority over the real estate she brought to the marriage or inherited (perhaps from her father) once married. It followed that he could easily pressure her into agreement with him on all other matters. As Tapping Reeve, author of the treatise on which large numbers of lawyers would rely through much of the nineteenth century, put it, she gained no advantage "in point of property" from marriage.[6]

The rules of coverture made it seem logical that husbands manage the property that wives brought to the marriage and earned during it. As long as she was married, an adult woman could not make a contract without her husband's permission, because she had no property with which to guarantee that she would honor her commitments. Since she controlled no property to convey, she could not make a will until after she was a widow. The father was the guardian of the children: the mother could not make choices—for example, to whom a child was to be apprenticed—that challenged the choices made by her husband.

When Tapping Reeve explained why it was logical that wives could not enter into contracts, he added the point that wives could not enter into contracts involving their own labor.

"The right of the husband to the person of his wife," Reeve observed, "is a right guarded by the law with the utmost solicitude; if she could bind herself by her contracts, she would be liable to be arrested, taken in execution [of her bond], and confined in a prison; and then the husband would be deprived of the company of his wife, which the law will not suffer." If a husband were banished from the realm, however, then his wife "could contract, could sue and be sued in her own name; for in this case. . . . he was already deprived of the company of his wife."[7]

The rules of coverture made it seem logical that husbands determine where the family would live. Deep into the twentieth century, Oklahoma, like many states, was still using the traditional wording: "The husband is the head of the family. He may choose any reasonable place or mode of living and the wife must conform thereto." That law was not repealed until 1988, and then only after six years of vigorous debate.[8]

By giving fathers responsibility for children born within marriage (that's why fathers in the early republic had custody of children in case of divorce, which was rare), but leaving to mothers the responsibility for children born outside marriage, the old law of domestic relations excused all fathers from serious responsibility for children born out of wedlock—a principle that was largely unquestioned in American law until the twentieth century. It also ensured that children born to a free father and an enslaved mother followed the condition of the mother into slavery, not only binding enslaved men and women to labor but also making them permanently vulnerable to the sexual appetites of their masters. (Thus Sally Hemings was born into slavery; Thomas Jefferson married her half-sister.)

Since married women did not control property, and since at the time of the Revolution there were property requirements for voting, it seemed to follow that married women should not vote. (The reasoning, for both propertyless men and women, was that they could be too easily pressured by propertied husbands or employers.) No one has yet found a reasonable explanation for why unmarried propertied women were not permitted to vote. And although men had long served on juries in England and the United States even if they were not qualified to vote, women were barred from juries. Even after women won the right to vote, it did not automatically follow that they could serve on juries or hold office. In many states, new statutes were required.

Coverture gave husbands property rights in their wives' "services." These services included the right to "consortium"—understood not only as housekeeping but also love, affection, companionship, and sexual relations. If a married woman were injured by the negligence of another person, her husband could sue for damages, which included a monetary estimate of his loss of consortium. If he were injured, she had no claim for the loss of his companionship and sexual relations. This imbalance between the sexes in marriage was rarely tested, but when it was, as in the case of major accidents, the impact was severe. Not until the early 1950s were married women successful in making such a claim—in Washington D.C. in 1950, in Iowa in 1951—yet it took until the 1990s for all states to recognize the claim.

Because the civil law treated husband and wife as one, it seemed to follow that they could not sue each other—a situation known as "interspousal tort immunity." Thus a husband could not be convicted of larceny for theft of his wife's property; to do so, explained one New York judge (presumably with a straight face), would be to sow "the seeds of perpetual discord and broil." Interspousal tort immunity also means that married women could not claim civil damages for assault and battery by their husbands or for which their husbands were at fault.[9]

The rules of coverture were taken to imply that a married woman could not have a nationality independent of her husband's. It seemed to follow that a foreign woman who married an American man was "deemed a citizen" at marriage, but an American woman who married a foreign man lost her U.S. citizenship. Marriage to a foreign man was ruled "as voluntary and distinctive as expatriation," according to the U.S. Supreme Court during World War I. (Once the United States entered World War I, hundreds of U.S. women who had married German men were forced to register as enemy aliens. See *MacKenzie v. Hare*, pp. 413–15.) American men have never put their own citizenship at risk by their marriages.

In return for submitting their bodies and property to their husbands, women were assured that, if widowed, they could expect an inheritance. If a man died without a will, the probate courts would ensure that his widow received her "thirds": he could leave her more, but not less. The widow's dower right was grudging: it allowed her *to make use of one-third of the real estate* that her husband held at the time of his death. It was generally recognized that this could well be less than the property she had brought to the marriage. She usually could not sell it (or, if woodland, could not cut down the trees to sell to support herself) and was required to pass it down unscathed to her husband's heirs. A widow was also usually entitled to claim outright one-third of the personal property her husband had owned, *after* debts were paid, and to claim outright her personal "paraphernalia"—her clothing and cooking pots and featherbed—suitable to her station, as judged by probate officers.

So finally we get to diamonds. The jewelry a woman had been given was the last asset vulnerable to being seized as payment for her late husband's debts. The diamonds about which Carol Channing sings are a reference to the jewelry—generally pearls or opals—of the old law. In the late nineteenth and early twentieth centuries, especially after the marketing campaigns that accompanied the opening of diamond mines in South Africa, valuable jewels came to carry an additional value when given as an engagement present. The jilted fiancée no longer needed to face the humiliation of soothing her aching heart with money awarded to her in a breach of promise lawsuit. She got to keep the diamonds.

Yet the fact of women's citizenship in a democratic republic contained deep within it an implicit challenge to coverture. The revolutionary republic had promised to protect "life, liberty and property," but under the old law a married woman was deprived of her property and had none to protect. Patriot men rarely spoke about this contradiction, but their actions speak for them. In England, the killing of a husband by a wife was *petit treason,* analogous to regicide, although the killing of a wife by a husband was murder. The penalties for *petit treason* were worse than those for murder. The concept was not much enforced in colonial America, but it remained in the statutes. It was the only element of the old law of domestic relations that legislators of the early republic eliminated. Legislators were conscious of what they intended; they carefully retained the concept of *petit treason* for the killing of a master by a slave. With that single exception, neither the Revolutionary government under the Articles of Confederation nor the federal government of

the Constitution directly challenged the legal system of coverture.[10]

Instead of revising the law to remove its coercive elements, jurists simply ensured that the coerced voices would not speak. Husbands were responsible for crimes committed by their wives in their presence or with their approval—except in the case of treason, a crime so severe that responsibility for it overrode the obligation to a husband. Another exception was in the event that a wife kept a brothel with her husband's knowledge, since keeping a brothel "is an offense of which the wife is supposed to have the principal management."[11]

That the system of marriage contradicted the basic tenets of revolutionary thinking was obvious. But women who named the contradictions invited extraordinary hostility and ridicule. Among the most persistent themes was the link of female intellectual activity and political autonomy to an unflattering masculinity. "There is a *sex of soul,*" announced the prominent Boston minister John Gardiner. "Women of masculine minds, have generally masculine manners.... Queen Elizabeth understood Latin and Greek, swore with the fluency of a sailor, and boxed the ears of her courtiers.... " A "mild, dove-like temper is so necessary to Female beauty, is so natural a part of the sex," reflected Parson Mason Locke Weems wistfully. "A masculine air in a woman frightens us."[12]

Selections from Mary Wollstonecraft's *Vindication of the Rights of Women* were published in the American press shortly after the book was published in London in 1792. She had borne one illegitimate daughter (Fanny Imlay) and lived with William Godwin before marrying him; after marriage she maintained lodgings in another house so that she could be free to write. Once her life history became generally known, it could be used to link intellectual women to political feminism and to aggressive sexuality, as one Federalist writer did in his bitter "Morpheus" essays, which ran in a Boston newspaper in 1802. In a dream sequence in "Morpheus," Wollstonecraft has arrived in America and sets out to teach its inhabitants wisdom.

> Women ... are entitled to all the rights, and are capable of all the energies of men. I do not mean merely mental examples. ... They can naturally run as fast, leap as high, and as far, and wrestle, scuffle, and box with as much success, as any of the ... other sex.

That is a mistake (said an old man). . . [W]omen always feebler than men[—why]?

Because (said MARY) they are educated to be feeble; and by indulgence . . . are made poor, puny, baby-faced dolls; instead of the manly women they ought to be.

Manly women! (cried the wag). Wheu! A manly woman is a hoyden . . . a strumpet.[13]

Thus political behavior, like abstract thought, continued to be specifically proscribed as a threat to sensual attractiveness.

Only the mother who promised to use her political knowledge to serve the republic was spared this hostility. The concept was a variant of the argument for the improved education of women that republicans such as Judith Sargent Murray and Wollstonecraft herself had demanded. It defended education for women not only for their autonomy and self-realization but also so that they could be better wives, rational household managers, and better mothers for the next generation of virtuous republican citizens—especially sons. In a widely reprinted speech, "Thoughts upon Female Education," originally given at the new Young Ladies Academy of Philadelphia, the physician and politician Benjamin Rush addressed the issue directly: "The equal share that every citizen has in the liberty, and the possible share he may have in the government of our country, make it necessary that our ladies should be qualified to a certain degree, by a peculiar and suitable education, to concur in instructing their sons in the principles of liberty and government."[14] The Republican Mother was an educated woman who could be spared the criticism normally directed at the intellectually competent woman because she placed her learning at her family's service. That she had the leisure and opportunity for study located her solidly in the middle class.

It was commonly believed that republican government was fragile and rested on the presence of virtuous citizens. The Republican Mother was also a Republican Wife.[15] She chose a virtuous man for her husband; she condemned and corrected her husband's lapses from civic virtue; she educated her sons for it. The creation of virtuous citizens required wives and mothers who were well informed, "properly methodical," and free of "invidious and rancorous passions." The word virtue was derived from the Latin word for man, with its connotations of virility. Political action was ideologically marked as masculine; as we have seen, if political voice required independent property holding, it was legally marked masculine as well. Virtue in a woman required another theater for its display. To that end, writers created a mother who had a political purpose and argued that her domestic behavior had a direct political function in the republic.

As one college orator put it,

Let us then figure to ourselves the accomplished woman, surrounded by a sprightly band, from the babe that imbibes the nutritive fluid, to the generous youth. . . . Let us contemplate the mother distributing the mental nourishment to the fond smiling circle . . . watching the gradual openings of their minds . . . see, under her cultivating hand, reason assuming the reins of government, and knowledge increasing gradually to her beloved pupils. . . . Yes, ye fair, the reformation of a world is in your power. . . . It rests with you to make this retreat [from the corruptions of Europe] doubly peaceful, doubly happy, by banishing from it those crimes and corruptions, which have never yet failed of giving rise to tyranny, or anarchy. While you thus keep our country virtuous, you maintain its independence.[16]

Defined this way, the educated woman ceased to threaten the sanctity of marriage; the intellectual woman need not be masculine.

The ideology of Republican Motherhood was deeply ambivalent. On the one hand, it was a progressive ideology, challenging those who opposed women in politics by the proposal that women could—and should—play a political role through influencing their husbands and raising patriotic children. Within the dynamic relationships of the private family—between husbands and wives, mothers and children—it allocated an assertive role to women. Those who shared the vision of the Republican Mother usually insisted upon better education, clearer recognition of women's economic contributions, and a strong political identification with the republic. This ideology could complement the "fertility transition" under way in the postwar republic, a rapid fall in birthrates that would continue into our own time, and that was first found in urban areas that had experienced commercial and industrial as well as political revolution. Free women, the historian Susan Klepp has recently suggested, "applied egalitarian ideas and a virtuous, prudent sensibility to their bodies and to their traditional images of self as revolutions inspired discussion and debate. . . . On the household level, restricted fertility and high rates of literacy or years of education were persistently linked: the higher the educational attainment of women, the lower fertility rates."[17]

The idea that a mother can perform a political function represents the recognition that a citizen's political socialization takes place at an early age, that the family is a basic part of the system of political communication, and that patterns of family authority influence the general political culture. Most premodern political societies—and even some fairly modern democracies—maintain unarticulated, but nevertheless very firm, social restrictions that seem to isolate the family's domestic world from politics. The willingness of the American woman to overcome this ancient separation brought her into the political community.[18] In this sense, Republican Motherhood was an important and progressive invention congruent with revolutionary politics and the demographic transition. It altered the female domain in which most women had lived out their lives; it justified women's claims for participation in the civic culture. The ideology was strong enough to rout commentators such as "Morpheus" by redefining female political behavior as valuable rather than abnormal, as a source of strength to the republic rather than an embarrassment. The ideology would be revived as a rallying point for many twentieth-century women reformers, who saw their commitment to honest politics, efficient urban sanitation, and pure food and drug laws as an extension of their responsibilities as mothers.

But Republican Motherhood flourished in the context of coverture. The old law of domestic relations hemmed it in at every turn. Republican motherhood could legitimize only a minimum of political sophistication and interest. It was an extension into the republic of conservative traditions, stretching back at least as far as the Renaissance, that put narrow limits on women's assertiveness.[19] Captured by marriage, which not only secured their intimate relations but also their relationship to the public authority, for most of their lives most women had no alternative but to perform the narrow political role they managed to claim for themselves. Just as white planters claimed that democracy in the antebellum South necessarily rested on the economic base of black slavery, so male egalitarian society was said to rest on the moral base of deference among a class of people—women—who would devote their efforts to service by raising sons and disciplining husbands to be virtuous citizens of the republic. The learned woman, who might very well wish to make choices as well as to influence attitudes, was a visible threat to this arrangement. Women were to contain their political judgments within their homes and families; they were not to bridge the world outside and the world within. The Republican Wife was not to tell her husband for whom to vote. She was a citizen but not really a constituent.

Restricting women's politicization was one of a series of conservative choices that Americans made in the postwar years as they avoided the full implications of their own Revolutionary radicalism. By these decisions Americans may well have been spared the agony of the French cycle of revolution and counterrevolution, which spilled more blood and produced a political system more regressive than had the American war. Nevertheless, the impact of these choices was to leave race equality to the mercies of a bloody century that stretched from the Civil War through Reconstruction and lynching into the civil rights movement of our own time. And the impact of these choices was also to leave in place the system by which marriage stood between women and civil society. When the revolutionary war made thousands of women widows, and hundreds of desperate military widows begged Congress for support, they found no one to listen when they claimed that they had served the nation's war effort. (See Rachel Wells' petition, pp. 113–114). But if they begged for recognition as wives and mothers who had been deprived , as one Congressman put it, "of their natural and civil protectors," women's pleas reached sympathetic ears. The unprecedented system of cash pensions developed in the decades before the civil war was distinctive in that for women marriage was the route to entitlement; "marriage," explains historian Kristin A. Collins, was "the source of legitimacy for women's citizenship." This practice continued to shape government programs for more than a century.[20] For most of the history of the United States, deep into the twentieth century, the legal traditions of marriage would be used to deny women citizens juries drawn from a full cross-section of the community, deny them control over their own property and their own earnings, sometimes deny them custody of their children, even deny them their rights as citizens should they marry a foreign man.

The 1960s and 1970s are distinctive for a remarkable shift in the way the law treats women's rights and obligations. Pressed by increasing public impatience with the ascriptive dependence of adult women on laws that disempowered women, legislatures and courts began to acknowledge that laws embodying gendered stereotypes harm not only women but also men and society as a whole. Indeed, they recognized that it is possible (something not imagined in the coverture regime) for men to be economically dependent on women, and therefore that it could be in men's interest for women to be independent civil actors.

Air Force Captain Sharron Frontiero had to press her argument all the way to the U.S. Supreme Court before she was authorized to draw a dependent's allowance for her husband in 1973. In a landmark decision, Justice William Brennan wrote in support of Frontiero: "Our nation has had a long and unfortunate history of sex discrimination . . . rationalized by an attitude of 'romantic paternalism,' which, in practical effect, put women, not on a pedestal but in a cage." (Frontiero v. Richardson, pp. 452–53). In a now classic series of opinions issued in the 1970s, the U.S. Supreme Court established the principle that laws based on gender stereotypes about the way men and women behave are unfair and unconstitutional. Ruth Bader Ginsburg argued these cases dazzlingly well as an attorney for the Women's Rights Project of the American Civil Liberties Union (ACLU). Even when stereotypes about women's or men's behavior might accurately predict what a majority of people will do, she argued, those individuals whose behavior does not conform to the stereotype ought not to be penalized. In 1975, Ginsburg argued Weinberger v. Wiesenfeld, leading the Supreme Court to agree unanimously that a Social Security law providing benefits to widows with small children, but not to similarly situated widowers, was based on the stereotype that imagined only bereft mothers, not bereft fathers. Many years later, in 1988, Ginsburg, now a U.S. Supreme Court Justice, would preside over the marriage of Jason Wiesenfeld, the little boy whose father had wanted to stay home and care for him.[21]

Laws that were once viewed as protective of women are now viewed as discriminating against them. It often startles people to learn that the Supreme Court did not regard discrimination on the basis of sex as a denial of the equal protection guaranteed of the Fourteenth Amendment (p. 289) until 1971, and then only very narrowly, in a case involving a teenager's cornet and a bank account worth $200. Other decisions followed in legislatures and in state and federal courts, reshaping the rules by which men and women make choices. It is no longer a reasonable defense against a charge of rape to claim that the victim dressed provocatively (although criminal charges of rape remain notoriously hard to prosecute successfully; the old suspicion of women's word remains). Discrimination on the basis of pregnancy, sexual harassment on the job, and exclusion from jobs on the basis that they are too harsh or dangerous: any of these actions can now count as a denial of equal protection.

It is now unreasonable to claim that women do not possess fully equal status, or that they lack the competence to make responsible choices. Nevertheless, while the legacy of coverture has been generally repudiated, it has not been eradicated. Distrust of women's claims to autonomy, cultural beliefs about the primacy of women's domestic obligations, and opinions about women's need to be protected from certain situations all reveal the lingering effects of coverture. Not until 1992 did the U.S. Supreme Court rule that as a general principle, "Women do not lose their constitutionally protected liberty when they marry."[22] As recently as the year 2000, dozens of state attorneys general called for passage of a new Violence Against Women Act, arguing that long-established laws against assault and battery have proven ineffective to protect women. As this volume goes to press, a grassroots movement among college women has revitalized the protections promised by Title IX (pp. 750–51) and the President of the United States has named sexual violence on campus as one of the key challenges facing the nation.

An antique story about how the world works, a story grounded in English legal practice and continued in the great narrative that we Americans have told ourselves about how we came to be what we are, continues to lurk in American law and practice. In that story, a husband could not kill his wife—that would be murder—but the only other guarantee she had was that he could not thrust her out naked into the world. She had her paraphernalia—her petticoats and her cooking pots. And the last thing he could take from her in order to pay his debts was her jewels—the diamonds that she could keep as her best friend. Those diamonds still gleam, but few among us know quite why.

NOTES

1. Murray's newspaper essays were reprinted in a collected edition, *The Gleaner* (Boston, 1798). These comments appear in vol. III, pp. 167–68, 189. See also Sheila L. Skemp, *First Lady of Letters: Judith Sargent Murray and the Struggle for Female Independence* (Philadelphia, 2009).

2. "Rachel Wells Petition for Relief," Nov. 15, 1785, New Jersey Archives, Trenton.

3. Abigail Adams to John Adams, Mar. 31, 1776, *Adams Family Correspondence* (Cambridge, Mass., 1963), I:370.

4. *Burlington (N.J.) Advertiser*, Feb. 1, 1791.

5. Miss Pierce's School Papers, 1839, Litchfield Historical Society, Litchfield, Conn.

6. Tapping Reeve, *The Law of Baron and Femme, Parent and Child, Guardian and Ward, Master and Servant* . . . (New Haven, Conn., 1816; Burlington, Vt., 1846), 37.

7. Ibid., ch. viii, pp. 98–99.

8. *Revised Laws of Oklahoma, 1910* . . . (St. Paul, Minn.: The Pioneer Co., 1912), I:837; Chris Casteel, "Husband-Wife Law Won't Stand, Opinion Advises," NewsOK, July 18, 1986, via www.newsok.com; *Annual Review of Population Law* 15 (1988): 81.

9. *Longendyke v. Longendyke*, 44 Barb. 366 (1863) (quotation at 369).

10. See, for example, "An Act for Annulling the Distinction between the Crimes of Murder and Petit Treason," Mar. 16, 1785, in Asahel Stearns et al., eds., *The General Laws of Massachusetts* . . . (Boston, 1823), I:188.

11. Reeve, *Law of Baron and Femme*, ch. v, p. 73.

12. "The Restorator" on "Rights of Woman," *Mercury and New-England Palladium*, Sept. 16, 1801, p. 1; Parson Mason Locke Weems, *Hymen's Recruiting Sergeant* (Philadelphia, 1800).

13. [Timothy Dwight], "Morpheus, Part 2, No. 1," *Mercury and New-England Palladium*, Mar. 2, 1802, p. 1.

14. Benjamin Rush, *Thoughts upon Female Education, Accommodated to the Present State of Society, Manners, and Government* . . . (Boston, 1787), p. 6.

15. See Linda K. Kerber, "The Republican Mother: Women and the Enlightenment—An American Perspective," *American Quarterly* 28 (Summer 1976): 187–205; Jan Lewis, "The Republican Wife: Virtue and Seduction in the Early Republic," *William and Mary Quarterly*, 3rd ser., 44 (Oct. 1987): 689–721.

16. *New York Magazine*, May 1795, pp. 301–305.

17. Susan E. Klepp, *Revolutionary Conceptions: Women, Fertility, and Family Limitation in America, 1760–1820* (Chapel Hill: University of North Carolina Press, 2009), p. 14.

18. See Gabriel Almond and Sidney Verba, *The Civic Culture* (Princeton, N.J.: Princeton University Press, 1963), pp. 377–401.

19. Elaine Forman Crane emphasizes this dimension; see *Ebb Tide in New England: Women, Seaports, and Social Change, 1630–1800* (Boston, 1998).

20. "'Petitions Without Number': Widows' Petitions and the Early Nineteenth-Century Origins of Public Marriage-Based Entitlements," *Law and History Review*, 31 (2013): 1–60.

21. *Coral Gables* [FL] *Sun-Journal*, Sept. 16, 1998.

22. *Planned Parenthood of Pennsylvania v. Casey*, 112 S. Ct. 2791 (1992).

II

AMERICA'S MANY FRONTIERS

1820–1880

WORKPLACE AND
HOUSEHOLD SCENES

JEANNE BOYDSTON
The Pastoralization of Housework

Having read fiction and advice literature directed to women in the years before the Civil War, in 1966 the historian Barbara Welter identified a pervasive stereotype, which she called the "Cult of True Womanhood." Women were encouraged to cultivate the virtues of domesticity, piety, purity, and submissiveness. Home was referred to as women's "proper sphere" and understood to be a shelter from the outside world in which men engaged in hard work and cutthroat competition. Other historians agreed that men's and women's spheres of activity were separated and suggested that this separation was somehow linked to the simultaneous growth of capitalism and industrialization. Historian Gerda Lerner argued, by contrast, that stressing the shelter of home was a way by which middle-class women distinguished themselves from mill girls, and so maintained class boundaries.

How does Jeanne Boydston describe the relationship between home and work in antebellum America? How does she describe the relationship between women's work and men's work? What does she think were the uses of the ideology of separate spheres? How do the middle-class households described by Boydston differ from the households in which Harriet Jacobs and Rachel Davis lived (pp. 179–188)?

In the colonial period, family survival had been based on two types of resources: the skills of the wife in housewifery, and the skills and property of the husband in agriculture. Both sets of skills involved the production of tangible goods for the family—such items as furnishings, food, and fabrics. Both were likely to involve some market exchange, as husbands sold grain and wives sold eggs or cheese, for example. And both involved services directly to the household. By the early nineteenth century, however, husbands' contributions to their households were focused disproportionately on market exchange—on the cash they brought into the family—while their direct activities in producing both goods and services for the family had vastly decreased.

The meaning of this shift has often been misread, interpreted as an indication that households were no longer dependent on goods and services provided from within but had instead become reliant upon the market for their survival. . . . [But] consumerism was sharply curtailed by the amount of available cash. Choices constantly had to be made: to purchase a new cloak or try to refurbish the old one for another season, to hire a woman to help with the wash or lay aside some money to buy a house. In these patterns of mundane decisions lay the essential economic character of antebellum households: they were in fact "mixed economies"—economic systems that functioned on the bases of both paid and unpaid labor and were dependent upon both. They required paid labor for the cash to purchase some goods and services. Equally, they depended on unpaid labor in the household to process those commodities into consumable form and to produce other goods and services directly without recourse to the cash market. . . .

[The] antebellum era was the last period during which most adult women shared the experience of having been, at some point in their lives, paid household workers. To an extent never repeated, even middle-class wives were likely to have worked as hired "help" in their youth. . . . [It is therefore possible to make a rough calculation] of the cost to a family to replace the unpaid labor of the wife by purchasing it on the market.[1] . . .

In northeastern cities in 1860, a woman hired both to cook and to do the laundry earned between $3 and $4 a week. Seamstresses and maids averaged two-and-a-half dollars a week. On the market, caring for children was at the lower end of the pay scale, seldom commanding more than $2 a week. If we assume that a woman did the full work of a hired cook and child's nurse, and also spent even an hour a day each sewing and cleaning (valued at about three cents an hour apiece), the weekly price of her basic housework would approximate $4.70. Even if we reduce this almost by half to $3 a week (to allow for variations in her work schedule and for the presence of assistance of some sort), taken at an average, this puts the price of a wife's basic housework at about $150 dollars a year.[2] . . .

To this should be added the value of goods a wife might make available within the family for free or at a reduced cost. Among poorer households, this was the labor of scavenging. A rag rug found among the refuse was worth half a dollar in money saved, an old coat, several dollars. Flour for a week, scooped from a broken barrel on the docks, could save the household almost a dollar in cash outlay.[3] In these ways, a wife with a good eye and a quick hand might easily save her family a dollar a week—or $50 or so over the course of the year. In households with more cash, wives found

other ways to avoid expenditures. By shopping carefully, buying in bulk, and drying or salting extra food, a wife could save ten to fifty percent of the family food budget . . . this could mean a saving of from 40 cents to over $2 a week. Wives who kept kitchen gardens or chickens . . . could . . . produce food worth a quarter a week (the price of 1/4 bushel of potatoes in New York in 1851).[4]

But there was also the cash that working-class wives brought into the household, by their needlework, or vending, or by taking in boarders, running a grocery or a tavern from her kitchen, or working unpaid in her husband's trade. A boarder might pay $4 a week into the family economy. Subtracting a dollar and a half for food and rent, the wife's labor-time represented $2.50 of that amount, or $130 a year.[5] . . .

The particular labor performed by a given woman depended on the size and resources of her household. . . . Yet we can estimate a general market price of housework by combining the values of the individual activities that made it up: perhaps $150 for cooking, cleaning, laundry, and childrearing; another $50 or so saved through scavenging or careful shopping, another $50 or so in cash brought directly into the household. This would set the price of a wife's labor-time among the laboring poor at roughly $250 a year beyond maintenance. . . . In working-class households with more income, where the wife could focus her labor on money-saving and on taking in a full-time boarder, that price might reach over $500 annually. . . . These shifts in the nature of a wife's work, and in the value of that work, as a husband's income increased seems not to have been entirely lost on males, who advised young men that if they meant to get ahead, they should "get married."[6] . . .

But husbands were not the sole beneficiaries of the economic value of housework, or of its unique invisibility. Employers were enabled by the presence of this sizeable but uncounted labor in the home to pay both men and women wages which were, in fact, below the level of subsistence. The difference was critical to the development of industrialization in the antebellum Northeast.[7] . . . Occasionally, mill owners acknowledged that the wages they paid did not cover maintenance. One agent admitted: "So long as they can do my work *for what I choose to pay them*, I keep them, getting out of them all I can. . . . [H]ow they fare outside my walls

I don't know, nor do I consider it my business to know. They must look out for themselves."[8] . . .

Even when employers paid high enough salaries to provide present security for a family, they seldom provided either the income or the job security to ensure a household's well-being against the erratic boom-and-bust cycles of business and the unemployment consequent upon those cycles. . . . Women's unremunerated labor in the household provided the needed "safety net," enabling middle-class families to maintain some degree of both material stability and healthfulness in a volatile economic environment. . . . Put simply, a wife was a good investment for a man who wanted to get ahead.

THE PASTORALIZATION OF HOUSEWORK

The culture of the antebellum Northeast recognized the role of wives in the making of contented and healthy families. Indeed, the years between the War of 1812 and the Civil War were a period of almost unabated celebration of women's special and saving domestic mission. "Grant that others besides woman have responsibilities at home. . . ." wrote the Reverend Jesse Peck in 1857, "[s]till we fully accord the supremacy of domestic bliss to the wife and mother."[9] . . .

As recent historians have recognized, this glorification of wife and motherhood was at the heart of one of the most compelling and widely shared belief systems of the early nineteenth century: the ideology of gender spheres. An elaborate set of intellectual and behavioral conventions, the doctrine of gender spheres expressed a worldview in which both the orderliness of daily social relations and the larger organization of society derived from and depended on the preservation of an all-encompassing gender division of labor. Consequently, in the conceptual and emotional universe of the doctrine of spheres, males and females existed as creatures of naturally and essentially different capacities. As the Providence-based *Ladies Museum* explained in 1825:

Man is strong—woman is beautiful. Man is daring and confident—woman is diffident and unassuming. Man is great in action—woman i[n] suffering. Man shines abroad—woman at home. Man talks to convince—woman to persuade and please. Man has a rugged heart—woman a soft and tender one. Man prevents misery—woman

relieves it. Man has science—woman taste. Man has judgment—woman sensibility. Man is a being of justice—woman of mercy.

These "natural" differences of temperament and ability were presumed to translate into different social roles and responsibilities for men and women. Clearly intended by the order of nature to "shine at home," Woman was deemed especially ill-equipped to venture into the world of nineteenth-century business, where "cunning, intrigue, falsehood, slander, [and] vituperative violence" reigned and where "mercy, pity, and sympathy, are vagrant fowls."[10]

. . . [T]he ideology of gender spheres was partly a response to the ongoing chaos of a changing society—an intellectually and emotionally comforting way of setting limits to the uncertainties of early industrialization. . . . The traits that presumably rendered Woman so defenseless against the guiles and machinations of the business world not only served to confine her to the home as her proper sphere but made her presence there crucial for her family, especially for her husband. Even the most enthusiastic boosters of economic expansion agreed that the explosive opportunism of antebellum society created an atmosphere too heady with competition and greed to engender either social or personal stability. However great his wisdom or strong his determination, to each man must come a time

when body, mind, and heart are overtaxed with exhausting labor; when the heavens are overcast, and the angry clouds portend the fearful storm; when business schemes are antagonized, thwarted by stubborn matter, capricious man, or an inauspicious providence; when coldness, jealousy, or slander chills his heart, misrepresents his motives, or attacks his reputation; when he looks with suspicion on all he sees, and shrinks from the frauds and corruptions of men with instinctive dread.[11] . . .

Whatever the proclivities or ambitions of individual women, the presumed contrasts between the sexes permitted Woman-in-the-abstract to be defined as the embodiment of all that was contrary to the values and behaviors of men in the marketplace, and thus, to the marketplace itself. Against its callousness, she offered nurturance. Against its ambition, she pitted her self-effacement and the modesty of her needs. Against its materialism, she held up the twin shields of morality and spiritual solace. If business was a world into which only men traveled and where they daily risked losing their souls, then wherever Woman was, was sanctuary. And Woman was in the Home.

The contrast between Man and Woman melted easily into a contrast between "workplace" and "home" and between "work" as Man engaged in it and the "occupations" of Woman in the home. Most writers of prescriptive literature did acknowledge that women were involved in activities of some sort in their households. For example, T. S. Arthur worried that a woman would be unable to keep the constant vigilance required to be a good mother if she also had to attend to "the operations of the needle, the mysteries of culinary science, and all the complicated duties of housekeeping." His language is revealing, however: housework consisted of "mysteries" and "duties"; it was a different order of activity from the labor that men performed. Indeed, some observers cautioned that the wife and mother should deliberately stay clear of employments which might seem to involve her in the economy.... William Alcott was among this group. Noting that a woman "... has duties to perform to the sick and to the well— to the young and to the aged; duties even to domestic animals," Alcott nevertheless cautioned that "[v]ery few of these duties are favorable to the laying up of much property, and some are opposed to it. So that while we commend industry—of the most untiring kind, too—we would neither commend nor recommend strong efforts to lay up property." The advice was not only consistent with, but reflected a critical aspect of the ideology of spheres: to the extent that workers in the household identified themselves with the labor of the marketplace, the function of the home as a place of psychological refuge would be undermined.[12]

Thus, the responsibilities of wives in their households were generally described in the prescriptive literature less as purposeful activities required and ordered by the welfare of their individual families than as emanations of an abstract but shared Womanhood. As Daniel C. Eddy explained:

> Home is woman's throne, where she maintains her royal court, and sways her queenly authority. It is there that man learns to appreciate her worth, and to realize the sweet and tender influences which she casts around her; there she exhibits the excellences of character which God had in view in her creation.

Underscoring the essentially passive nature of women's functions, Eddy concluded: "Her life should be a calm, holy, beautiful walk."[13]

... The consequence of this conflation of ideology with behavior was to obscure both the nature and the economic importance of women's domestic labor. It was not only Woman-in-the-abstract who did not labor in the economy, but also, by extension, individual women. It was not only Woman-in-the-abstract, but presumably, real women who guided the on-going functions of the home through the effortless "emanations" of their very being, providing for the needs of their families without labor, through their very presence in the household. As romantic narrative played against lived experience, the labor and economic value of housework ceased to exist in the culture of the antebellum Northeast. It became work's opposite: a new form of leisure. ...

William Alcott's description of the wife's labors in *The Young Wife* provides a striking illustration of the pastoralization of housework in descriptions of the antebellum home:

> Where is it that the eye brightens, the smile lights up, the tongue becomes flippant, the form erect, and every motion cheerful and graceful? Is it at home? Is it in doing the work of the kitchen? Is it at the wash-tub—at the oven—darning a stocking— mending a coat—making a pudding? Is it in preparing a neat table and table cloth, with a few plain but neat dishes? Is it in covering it with some of nature's simple but choice viands? Is it in preparing the room for the reception of an absent companion? Is it in warming and lighting the apartments at evening, and waiting, with female patience, for his return from his appointed labor? Is it in greeting him with all her heart on his arrival?[14]

Clearly, Alcott was quite familiar with the types of work performed by women in their own families, and his description is all the more interesting on this account: cooking, baking, washing clothes, mending and darning, serving meals, building fires, attending to lamps—it is a surprisingly accurate catalogue. It is also incomplete, of course. Missing from this picture is the making of the soap that the wash might be done, the lugging and heating of the water, the tiresome process of heating and lifting cast-iron irons, the dusting and sweeping of rooms, the cleaning of the stove, and the making of the stocking and the coat now in need of repair.

Even the domestic tasks which Alcott acknowledges, however, are not to be contemplated as true work, a point which is made explicit in his identification of only the husband's employments as "labor." With "labor," indeed, the wife's activities have no truck, for there is no labor here to perform. . . . the food appears virtually as a gift of nature, and the compliant fires and lamps seem to light and tend themselves. . . . All is ordered, and the ordering of it is not only *not* burdensome or tiring, but the certain vehicle of good health and a cheerful disposition. Far from labor, housework is positively regenerating. . . .

The pastoralization of housework, with its emphasis on the sanctified home as an emanation of Woman's nature, required the articulation of a new way of seeing (or, more exactly, of *not* seeing) women as actors, capable of physical exertion. Most specifically, this applied to women as laborers, but the "magical extraction" of physical activity from the concept of Womanhood in fact proceeded in much larger terms and was most apparent in the recurrent celebrations of female "influence." Typically invoked as the female counterpart to the presumably *male* formal political power,[15] the concept of indirect womanly "influence" supplanted notions of women as direct agents, and thus as laborers. [In an article entitled "Woman's Offices and Influences," J. H. Agnew argued that] the contrast between presumably male "power" (physical as well as moral) and female "influence" could be drawn quite explicitly:

> We may stand in awe, indeed, before the exhibition of *power*, whether physical or moral, but we are not won by them to the love of truth and goodness, while *influence* steals in upon our hearts, gets hold of the springs of action, and leads us into its own ways. It is the *inflowing* upon others from the nameless traits of character which constitute woman's idiosyncracy. Her heart is a great reservoir of love, the water-works of moral influence, from which go out ten thousand tubes, conveying the ethereal essences of her nature, and diffusing them quietly over the secret chambers of man's inner being.

Woman does not herself *act*. Rather, she "gets hold of the springs of action." An idiosyncrasy in the human order, she is not so much a physical as an ethereal being. Agnew concluded: "Let man, then, exercise power; woman exercise influence. By this she will best perform her offices, discharge her duties." It is the crowning touch on the pastoralization of housework: the home is not the setting of labor, but of "offices" and "duties." Therefore, what is required

for the happy home is not a worker, but rather "a great reservoir of love."[16]

The pastoralization of household labor became a common feature of antebellum literature, both private and published. . . . [It] shaped much of the fiction of the period. In a piece entitled "The Wife" (published in the *Ladies' Literary Cabinet* in July of 1819 and included in *The Sketch Book* the following year), Washington Irving described the plight of a young couple forced by the husband's disastrous speculations to give up their fashionable life in the city and move to a modest country cottage. One might anticipate numerous headaches and a good deal of hard work in such a move, especially for the wife, but such was not the case for Irving's "Wife." Mary goes out to the cottage to spend the day "superintending its arrangement," but the substance of that process remains a mystery, for the packing and unpacking, cleaning, hanging of curtains, arranging of furniture, putting away of dishes, sorting of clothes, and adjusting of new domestic equipment which one might expect to be required under such circumstances remain undisclosed in the text. Indeed, all we learn is that, when next encountered by the narrator, Mary "seems in better spirits than I have ever known." Transformed into a creature who is far more sylvan nymph than human female, Mary greets her husband and the narrator "singing, in a style of the most touching simplicity. . . . Mary came tripping forth to meet us; she was in a pretty rural dress of white, a few wild flowers were twisted in her fine hair, a fresh bloom was on her cheek, her whole countenance beamed with smile—I have never seen her look so lovely." To complete the pastoral scene, nature has obligingly provided "a beautiful tree behind the cottage" where the threesome picnic on a feast of wild strawberries and thick sweet cream.[17] . . .

In both its briefer and its more extended forms in fiction and in exposition, in prescription and in proscription, the pastoralization of housework permeated the culture of the antebellum Northeast. Often, it was expressed simply as a truism, as when the Reverend Hubbard Winslow reminded his Boston congregation that "[t]he more severe manual labors, the toils of the fields, the mechanics, the cares and burdens of mercantile business, the exposures and perils of absence from home, the duties of the learned professions devolve upon man. . . ." [H]e considered women's occupations to be of a "more delicate and retired nature." That same year, the shocked and angered Congregational clergy of Massachusetts drew upon the same assumptions and the same imagery of Womanhood to denounce the abolitionist activities of Sarah and Angelina Grimké. Reminding their female congregants that "the power of woman is in her dependence," the clergy spoke of the "unobtrusive and private" nature of women's "appropriate duties" and directed them to devote their energies to "those departments of life that form the character of individuals" and to embodying "that modesty and delicacy which is the charm of domestic life. . . ."[18]

As we have seen, working class husbands appear to have embraced the view that paid labor was economically superior to unpaid labor. They shared, too, a tendency to pastoralize the labor of their wives. The speeches of early labor activists, for example, frequently invoked both the rhetoric of the ideology of spheres and pastoral images of the household, implying a sharp contrast between "the odious, cruel, unjust and tyrannical system" of the factory, which "compels the operative Mechanic to exhaust his physical and mental powers," with the presumably rejuvenating powers of the home. Discouraging women from carrying their labor "beyond the home," working men called upon women to devote themselves to improving the quality of life within their families. . . . [A]s William Sylvis put it, it was the proper work of woman "to guide the tottering footsteps of tender infancy in the paths of rectitude and virtue, to smooth down the wrinkles of our perverse nature, to weep over our shortcomings, and make us glad in the days of our adversity. . . ."[19]

African-American newspapers of the antebellum Northeast also reflected and reaffirmed the pastoral conventions of women's domestic labor. *The Rights of All* compared women to ornamental creatures of nature, "as various in decorations as the insects, the birds, and the shells. . . ." In 1842, *The Northern Star and Freeman's Advocate* approvingly reprinted an article from the *Philadelphia Temperance Advocate* in which wives were described as deities "who preside over the sanctities of domestic life, and administer its sacred rights. . . ." That this perception ill fit the experiences of those female readers whose home was also their unpaid workplace, as well as those women who worked for money in someone else's home, appears not to have disturbed the paper's editors. Rather than as a worker, Woman was represented as a force of nature—and presumably one intended for man's special benefit: "The morning star of our youth—the day star of our manhood—the evening star of our age."[20]

For both middle-class and working-class men, the insecurities of income-earning during the antebellum period struck at the very heart of their traditional roles as husbands and fathers. Particularly since the late eighteenth century, manhood had been identified with wage-earning—with the provision of the cash necessary to make the necessary purchases of the household. In the context of the reorganization of paid work in the antebellum Northeast, the growing dependency of households on cash, and the roller-coaster business cycles against which few families could feel safe, that identification faced almost constant challenge. And as it was challenged, it intensified.

By the antebellum period, the late-eighteenth century association of manhood with wage-earning had flowered into the cult of the male "breadwinner." A direct response to the unstable economic conditions of early industrialization, this association crossed the lines of the emerging classes, characterizing the self-perceptions and social claims of both laboring and middle-class men.

Among laboring men, the identification of manhood with wage-earning melded easily with the traditional emphasis on the "manliness" of the crafts. . . . General Trades' Union leader Ely Moore warned that the unchecked industrial avarice of employers would create a class of "breadless and impotent" workers. When they struck for higher wages in 1860, the shoemakers of Massachusetts linked the encroachments of capital with an attack upon their manhood; in the "Cordwainers' Song," they called upon each other to "stand for your rights like men" and "Resolve by your fathers' graves" to emerge victorious and "like men" to "hold onto the last!"[21] Gender also provided the language for belittling the oppressor, for working men often expressed their rage—and reaffirmed the importance of their own manhood—by impugning the masculinity of their employers. The "Mechanic" sneered at "[t]he employers and those who hang on their skirts."[22]

In the midst of the upheavals of the antebellum economy, however, it was not only employers who threatened the old artisan definitions of manhood. Because an entire way of life was being undermined, so the dangers seemed to arise from everywhere in the new social order—including from wage-earning women themselves. In fact, women seldom directly imperiled men's jobs. The young women who went to Lowell were entering an essentially new industry. Moreover, in their families and hired out on an individual basis, carding, spinning, fulling, and even, to some extent, weaving had long been a part of women's work. . . .

But if wage-earning women did not directly challenge men's jobs, their very presence in the new paid labor force may have underscored the precariousness of men's position as wage-earners. Particularly given the post-Revolutionary emphasis on the importance of women's remaining in the home to cultivate the private virtues, females who were visible as outworkers and operatives may have seemed to bespeak an "unnaturalness" in society—an inability of wage-earning men to establish proper households. Like the witches of the seventeenth century, wage-earning women became symbols of the threats posed to a particular concept of manhood—in this instance, a concept that identified male claims to authority and power with the status of sole wage-earner. As they grappled with the precariousness of their own positions, laboring-class men focused their anxieties on the women who were their wives, daughters, and sisters, as well as on the men who were their employers.

They expressed these anxieties in two forms. First, wage-earning men complained that women were taking jobs—and thus the proper masculine role—away from men. An 1836 report of the National Trades' Union charged that because women's wages were so low, a woman's "efforts to sustain herself and family are actually the same as tying a stone around the neck of her natural protector, Man, and destroying him with the weight she has brought to his assistance." Not uncommonly, working men suggested that women did not really need to work for money and castigated "the girl, or the woman, as the case may be, who being in a condition to live comfortably at home by proper economy" selfishly took work from the truly needy. In 1831, the *Working Man's Advocate* called upon "those females who . . . are not dependent on their labor for a living" to withdraw from paid work so that men might have the jobs.[23]

At the same time, working men organized to call for "the family wage"—a wage packet for the male "breadwinner" high enough to permit his wife and children to withdraw from paid work. As Martha May has pointed out, the family wage "promised a means to diminish capitalists' control over family life, by allowing workingmen to provide independently for their families." But the demand for the family wage also signalled the gendering of the emerging class system, and, in this, the gendering of early industrial culture. Identifying the husband as the proper and "natural" wage-earner, the family wage ideal reinforced a distinctive male claim to the role of "breadwinner." By nature, women were ill-suited to wage-earning, many laboring-class men insisted. The National Trades' Union called attention to Women's "physical organization" and "moral sensibilities" as evidence of her unfitness for paid labor, and the anonymous "mechanic" focused on "the fragile character of a girl's constitution, [and] her peculiar liability to sickness."[24] Presumably, only men had the constitution for regular, paid labor.

It is tempting to see in the antebellum ideology of spheres a simple extension of the Puritan injunction to wives to be keepers at home and faithful helpmates to men. Certainly, the two sets of beliefs were related. The colonists brought with them a conviction that men and women were socially different beings, so created by God and so designated in the order of nature. Both were meant to labor, but they were meant to labor at different tasks. Perhaps even more important, they were meant to occupy quite different stations in social life and to exercise quite different levels of control over economic life. . . . "Labor" may have been a gender-neutral term in colonial culture, but "authority" and "property" were masculine concepts, while "dependence" and "subordination" were clearly feminine conditions. . . .

The origins of the antebellum gender culture were as much in the particular conditions of early industrialization as in the inherited past, however. . . . [T]he specific character of the nineteenth-century gender culture was dictated less by transformations in women's experience than by transformations in men's. To be sure, the principle of male dominance persisted into the nineteenth century. . . . Social power in the antebellum Northeast rested increasingly on the ability to command the instruments of production and to accumulate and reinvest profits. From these activities wives were legally barred, as they were from formal political processes that established the ground rules for the development of industrial capitalism. While most men were also eliminated from the contest on other grounds (race, class, and ethnicity, primarily), one had to be male to get into the competition at all. . . .

. . . With the demise of the artisan system, and so of a man's hopes to pass along a trade to his sons, the practical grounds on which a laboring man might lay claim to the role of male head-of-household had altered. Increasingly, it was less his position as future benefactor of the next generation than his position as the provider of the present generation (that is, the "breadwinner") that established a man's familial authority.

For men of the emerging middle class, the stakes were equally high but somewhat different. Many of these were the sons and grandsons of middling farmers, forebears who, while not wealthy, had established their adulthood through the ownership of land, and whose role within the family had been centrally that of the "father." Their power residing in their control of inheritance to the next generation, these were men who might have been described with some degree of accuracy as "patriarchs." But by the second decade of the nineteenth century middling farms throughout much of the Northeast were scarcely capable of supporting the present generation; much less were they sizeable or fertile enough to establish patriarchal control of the family. Simultaneously, the emergence of an increasingly industrialized and urbanized society rendered the inheritance of land a less useful and less attractive investment in the future for sons. Even successful businessmen and professionals experienced diminishing control over their sons' economic futures. A son might still read the law with his father, but new law schools, like medical schools, foreshadowed the time when specialized education, rather than on-the-job training with his father or his father's friends, would offer a young man the best chance for success. . . .

Early industrialization preserved the principle of male dominance, then, but in a new form: the "husband" replaced the "father." Men claimed social authority—and indeed exercised economic control—not because they owned the material resources upon which subsequent generations would be founded, but because they owned the resources upon which the present generations subsisted. More important, they had established hegemony over the definition of those resources. In the gender culture of the antebellum Northeast, subsistence was purchased by wages—and men were the wage-earners.

Early industrialization had simultaneously redefined the paradigm that guided the social and economic position of women. . . . [T]he paradigm of womanhood shifted from "goodwife" to "mother"—that is, from "worker" to "nurturer." . . . [W]hat-ever cultural authority women gained as "mothers" was at the direct cost of a social identity in the terms that counted most in the nineteenth century—that is, as workers. As Caroline Dall noted in 1860, most Americans cherished "that old idea, that all men support all women. . . ." Dall recognized this to be "an absurd fiction," but it was a fiction with enormous social consequences. Even when women did enter paid work, their preeminent social identity as "mothers" (in distinct contrast to "workers") made their status as producers in the economy suspect: the predisposition to consider women "unfit" helped justify underpaying them.[25]

In all of this, the pastoralization of housework implicitly reinforced both the social right and the power of husbands and capitalists to claim the surplus value of women's labor, both paid and unpaid. It accomplished this by rendering the economic dimension of the labor invisible, thereby making pointless the very question of exploitation: one cannot confiscate what does not exist. Since the ideology of spheres made the non-economic character of housework a simple fact of nature, few observers in the antebellum Northeast felt compelled to argue the point.

The ideology of spheres did not affect all women in the same way, of course. Insisting that the domestic ideal was founded in the nature of Woman (and not in the nature of society), prescriptive writers saw its embodiments everywhere—from the poorest orphan on the streets, to the mechanic's daughter, to the merchant's wife. But their models transparently were meant to be the women of the emerging middle class. It was, after all, in the middle classes that women had presumably been freed from the necessity for labor that had characterized the colonial helpmate; there, that mothers and wives had supposedly been enabled to express their fullest capacities in the service of family formation. In celebrations of middle-class "Motherhood" lay the fullest embodiments of the marginalization of housewives as workers.

But if middle-class women were encased in the image of the nurturant (and nonlaboring) mother, working-class women found that their visible inability to replicate that model worked equally hard against them. As historian Christine Stansell has vividly demonstrated, the inability (or unwillingness) of working-class women to remain in their homes—that is, their need to go out into the streets, as vendors, washerwomen, prostitutes, or simply as neighbors helping a friend out—provided the excuse for a growing middle-class intrusion into working-class households, as reformers claimed that women who could not (or did not wish to) aspire to middle-class standards were defined as poor mothers.[26] . . .

In addition to its specific implications for women, the ideology of spheres, and the pastoralization of housework which lay at the heart of that ideology, both represented and supported larger cultural changes attendant upon the evolution of early industrial capitalism. The transition of industrialization was not purely material: it was ideological as well, involving and requiring new ways of viewing the relationship of labor to its products and of the worker to his or her work. In its denial of the economic value of one form of labor, the pastoralization of housework signaled the growing devaluation of labor in general in industrial America. Artisans were discovering, and would continue to discover, what housewives learned early in the nineteenth century: as the old skills were debased, and gradually replaced by new ones, workers' social claims to the fruits of their labor would be severely undercut. Increasingly, productivity was attributed, not to workers, but to those "most wonderful machines."[27] It was in part against such a redefinition that the craft workers of New York and the shoemakers of Lynn, Massachusetts, struggled.[28]

The denial of the economic value of housework was also one aspect of a tendency, originating much earlier but growing throughout the eighteenth and nineteenth centuries, to draw ever-finer distinctions between the values of different categories of labor, and to elevate certain forms of economic activity to a superior status on the grounds of the income they produced. As with housework, these distinctions were rarely founded on the actual material value of the labor in question. Rather, they were based on contemporary levels of power and wealth, and served to justify those existing conditions. An industrialist or financier presumably deserved to earn very sizeable amounts of money, because in accumulating capital he had clearly contributed more labor and labor of a more valuable kind to society than had, for example, a drayman or a foundry worker. . . .

Finally, the ideology of spheres functioned to support the emergence of the wage system necessary to the development of industrial capitalism. The success of the wage system depends upon a number of factors—among them the perception of money as a neutral index of economic value and the acceptance of the wage as representing a fair "livelihood." The devaluation of housework was a part of a larger process of obscuring the continuation of and necessity for barter-based exchanges in the American economy. In this, it veiled the reliance of the family on resources other than those provided through paid labor and heightened the visibility of the wage as the source of family maintenance.

But how did women respond to the growing devaluation of their contributions as laborers in the family economy? . . . [I]n their private letters and diaries, wives quietly offered their own definition of what constituted the livelihood of their families, posing their own perception of the importance of conservation and stewardship against the cash-based index of the marketplace and easily integrating the family's periodic needs for extra cash into their understanding of their own obligations.

Nevertheless, among the public voices affirming that Woman was meant for a different sphere than Man, and that the employments of Woman in the home were of a spiritual rather than an economic nature, were the voices of many women. In *Woman in America*, for example, Mrs. A. J. Graves declared: ". . . home is [woman's] appropriate sphere of action; and . . . whenever she neglects these duties, or goes out of this sphere . . . she is deserting the station which God and nature have assigned to her." Underscoring the stark contrast between Woman's duties in the household and Man's in "the busy and turbulent world," Graves described the refuge of the home in terms as solemn as any penned by men during the antebellum period: ". . . our husbands and our sons . . . will rejoice to return to its sanctuary of rest," she averred, "there to refresh their wearied spirits, and renew their strength for the toils and conflicts of life."[29]

Graves was not unusual in her endorsement of the ideology of spheres and of the pastoralization of housework. Even those women who most championed the continuing importance of women's household labor often couched that position in the language of spheres. No one more graphically illustrates this combination than Catharine Beecher, at once probably the most outspoken defender of the importance of women's domestic labor and one of the chief proponents of the ideology of female domesticity. . . . Beecher was clear and insistent that housework was hard work, and she did not shrink from suggesting that its demands and obligations were very similar to men's "business." In her *Treatise on Domestic Economy,* Beecher went so far as to draw a specific analogy between the marriage contract and the wage labor contract:

> No woman is forced to obey any husband but the one she chooses for herself; nor is she obliged to take a husband, if she prefers to remain single. So every domestic, and every artisan or laborer, after passing from parental control, can choose the employer to whom he is to accord obedience, or, if he prefers to relinquish certain advantages, he can remain without taking a subordinate place to any employer.

Nevertheless, Beecher regularly characterized women's work in the home as the occupation merely of administering "the gentler charities of life," a "mission" chiefly of "self-denial" to "lay up treasures, not on earth, but in heaven." This employment she contrasts with the "toils" of Man, to whom was "appointed the out-door labor—to till the earth, dig the mines, toil in the foundries, traverse the ocean, transport the merchandise, labor in manufactories, construct houses . . . and all the heavy work. . . ."[30]

Beecher's apparently self-defeating endorsement of a view that ultimately discounted the value of women's labor arose from many sources, not the least of which was her own identification with the larger middle-class interests served by the ideology of spheres. Beecher enjoyed the new standing afforded middle-class women by their roles as moral guardians to their families and to societies, and based much of her own claim to status as a woman on the presumed differences between

herself and immigrant and laboring-class women. For example, she ended an extended discussion of "the care of Servants" in *The American Woman's Home* with the resigned conclusion that "[t]he mistresses of American families, whether they like it or not, have the duties of missionaries imposed upon them by that class from which our supply of domestic servants is drawn."[31]

But, also like many women in antebellum America, Catharine Beecher was sharply aware of the power difference between males and females. It was a theme to which she constantly returned in her writings, especially in her discussions of women's rights. . . . In her *Essay on Slavery and Abolitionism,* Beecher was quite explicit about the reasons why a woman might cloak herself and her positions in the language of dependency and subordination:

> [T]he moment woman begins to feel the promptings of ambition, or the thirst for power, her aegis of defence is gone. All the sacred protection of religion, all the generous promptings of chivalry, all the poetry of romantic gallantry, depend upon woman's retaining her place as dependent and defenceless, and making no claims. . . .

It was much the same point that Elizabeth Ellet would later make in her *The Practical Housekeeper:* since men had many more alternatives than women, the smart woman made it her "policy" to create an appearance of domestic serenity.[32]

But it would be a mistake to read women's endorsement of the pastoralization of housework purely as a protective strategy. Women were not immune from the values of their communities, and many wives appear to have shared the perception of the larger society that their work had separated from the economic life of the community and that it was, in fact, not really work at all.

Those misgivings were nowhere more evident than in the letter that Harriet Beecher Stowe wrote to her sister-in-law, Sarah Beecher, in 1850. It was the first opportunity Harriet had had to write since the Stowes had moved to Brunswick, Maine, the spring before. Since her arrival with the children, she explained, she had "made two sofas—or lounges—a barrel chair—divers bedspreads—pillowcases—pillows—bolsters—matresses . . . painted rooms . . . [and] revarnished furniture." She had also laid a month-long siege at the landlord's door, lobbying him to install a new sink. Meanwhile, she had given birth to her eighth child, made her way through the novels of Sir Walter Scott, and tried to meet the obligations of her increasingly active career as an author—all of this while also attending to the more mundane work of running a household: dealing with tradespeople, cooking, and taking care of the children. From delivery bed to delivery cart, downstairs to the kitchen, upstairs to the baby, out to a neighbor's, home to stir the stew, the image of Stowe flies through these pages like the specter of the sorcerer's apprentice.

Halfway through the letter, Stowe paused. "And yet," she confided to her sister-in-law, "I am constantly pursued and haunted by the idea that I don't do anything."[33] It is a jarring note in a letter—and a life—so shaped by the demands of housework. That a skilled and loving mother could impart dignity and a sense of humane purpose to a family otherwise vulnerable to the degradations of the marketplace, Stowe had no doubt. But was that really "work"? She was less certain. In that uncertainty, to borrow Daniel Eddy's words, lay "a world of domestic meaning"—for housewives of the antebellum era, and for women since.

NOTES

1. See Luisella Goldschmidt-Clermont, *Unpaid Work in the Household: A Review of Economic Evaluation Methods* (Geneva, 1982).

2. See Edgar Martin, *The Standard of Living in 1860: American Consumption Levels on the Eve of the Civil War* (Chicago, 1942), p. 177; and Faye Dudden, *Serving Women: Household Service in Nineteenth-Century America* (Middletown, Conn., 1983), p. 149.

3. This is calculated on the basis of an average weekly budget for a working-class family of five, as itemized in the New York *Daily Tribune*, May 27, 1851. See also Martin, *Standard of Living*, p. 122.

4. New York *Daily Tribune*, May 27, 1851.

5. Martin, *Standard of Living*, p. 168.

6. Grant Thorburn, *Sketches from the Note-book of Lurie Todd* (New York, 1847), p. 12.

7. See Alice Kessler-Harris and Karen Brodkin Sacks, "The Demise of Domesticity in America," *Women, Households, and the Economy*, eds. Lourdes Beneria and Catherine R. Stimpson (New Brunswick, N.J., 1987), p. 67.

8. Quoted in Norman Ware, *The Industrial Worker, 1840–1860: The Reaction of American Industrial Society to the Advance of the Industrial Revolution* (New York, 1924; reprinted Gloucester, Mass., 1959), p. 77.

9. Jesse T. Peck, *The True Woman; or, Life and Happiness at Home and Abroad* (New York, 1857), p. 245.

10. *The Ladies Museum*, July 16, 1825, p. 3; Henry Ward Beecher, *Lectures to Young Men, on Various Important Subjects* (Boston, 1846). pp. 87, 91.

11. Peck, *The True Woman*, pp. 242–43.

12. *The Mother's Rule: or, The Right Way and the Wrong Way*, ed. T. S. Arthur (Philadelphia, 1856), p. 261; William A. Alcott, *The Young Wife, or, Duties of Woman in the Marriage Relation* (Boston, 1837), p. 149.

13. Daniel C. Eddy, *The Young Woman's Friend; or the Duties, Trials, Loves, and Hopes of Woman* (Boston, 1857), p. 23.

14. Alcott, *The Young Wife*, pp. 84–85.

15. For an excellent discussion of the concept of female "influence," see Lori D. Ginzburg, *Women and the Work of Benevolence: Morality and Politics in the Northeastern United States, 1820–1885* (New Haven, Conn., 1990).

16. J. H. Agnew, "Women's Offices and Influence," *Harper's New Monthly Magazine* 17: no. 3 (Oct. 1851):654–57, quote on p. 657.

17. Washington Irving, "The Wife," *Ladies Literary Cabinet*, July 4, 1819, pp. 82–84. Quotations are from Washington Irving, *The Sketch Book of Geoffrey Crayon, Gent.* (New York, 1961), pp. 34–36.

18. "Pastoral Letter of the Massachusetts Congregationalist Clergy" (1837) in *Up From the Pedestal: Selected Writings in the History of American Feminism*, ed. Aileen S. Kraditor (Chicago, 1968), pp. 51–52; Reverend Hubbard Winslow, *A Discourse Delivered in the Bowdoin Street Church* (Boston, 1837), p. 8.

19. *The Man*, May 13, 1835; *Life, Speeches, Labors, and Essays of William H. Sylvis*, ed. James C. Sylvis (Philadelphia, 1872), p. 120.

20. *The Rights of All*, June 12, 1829; *The Northern Star and Freeman's Advocate*, Dec. 8, 1842, and Jan. 2, 1843.

21. Moore is quoted in Sean Wilentz, *Chants Democratic: New York City and the Rise of the American Working Class, 1788–1850* (New York, 1986), p. 239. The "Cordwainers' Song" is printed in Alan Dawley, *Class and Community: The Industrial Revolution in Lynn* (Cambridge, Mass., 1976), pp. 82–83.

22. "A Mechanic," *Elements of Social Disorder: A Plea for the Working Classes in the United States* (Providence, R.I., 1844), p. 96.

23. Quoted in John Andrews and W. D. P. Bliss, *A History of Women in Trade Unions*, vol. 10 of *Report on Condition of Woman and Child Earners in the United States*, Senate Doc. 645, 61st Cong., 2d Sess. (Washington, D.C., 1911; reprint ed. New York, 1974), p. 48; "Mechanic," *Elements of Social Disorder*, p. 45; *Working Man's Advocate*, June 11, 1831.

24. Martha May, "Bread Before Roses: American Workingmen, Labor Unions and the Family Wage," in *Women, Work, and Protest: A Century of U.S. Women's Labor History*, ed. Ruth Milkman (Boston, 1985), p. 4; vol. 6 of *A Documentary History of American Industrial Society*, eds. John R. Commons et al. (New York, 1958), p. 281; "Mechanic," *Elements of Social Disorder*, p. 42.

25. Caroline Dall, *"Woman's Right to Labor"; or, Low Wages and Hard Work* (Boston, 1860), p. 57.

26. Christine Stansell, *City of Women: Sex and Class in New York, 1789–1860* (New York, 1986), pp. 193–216.

27. The phrase is from the title of Judith McGaw's study, *Most Wonderful Machine: Mechanization and Social Change in Berkshire Papermaking, 1801–1885* (Princeton, 1987).

28. See Wilentz, *Chants Democratic*; and Dawley, *Class and Community*, cited in n. 21 above.

29. Mrs. A. J. Garves, *Woman in America: Being an Examination into the Morals and Intellectual Condition of American Female Society* (New York, 1841), p. 156.

30. Catharine E. Beecher, *A Treatise on Domestic Economy, for the Use of Young Ladies at Home, and at School* (Boston, 1841), p. 26; Beecher, *An Essay on Slavery and Abolitionism, with Reference to the Duty of American Females* (Philadelphia, 1837), p. 128; Catharine E. Beecher and Harriet Beecher Stowe, *The American Woman's Home, or Principles of Domestic Science* (Hartford, Conn., 1975), p. 19.

31. Beecher and Stowe, *The American Woman's Home*, p. 327.

32. Beecher, *Essay on Slavery and Abolitionism*, pp. 101–2; *The Practical Housekeeper; a Cyclopaedia of Domestic Economy*, ed. Mrs. [Elizabeth] Ellet (New York, 1857), p. 17.

33. Harriet Beecher Stowe to Sarah Buckingham Beecher, Dec. 17 [1850], The Schlesinger Library, Radcliffe College, Cambridge, Mass.

STEPHANIE JONES-ROGERS
Mistresses in the Making

When masters spoke of their "family" they meant something very different than the meaning we now give that word. They meant an extended web of relations—not only their wives and children, brothers and sisters, nieces and nephews and cousins, but also apprentices bound to the household head for a term of years, and enslaved people bound for life. The buildings in which slaveowners lived were homes to the members of the masters' families but sites of oppression and often violence to the enslaved people who spent their lives there.

Families groom children for the lives that they are expected to lead. Slaveholding parents started to prepare their children early for an adulthood that involved the control of other people. In her careful reading of the correspondence of slaveowners and interviews with formerly enslaved people, Stephanie Jones-Rogers has found evidence of how girls were shaped for the roles that they were expected to play. The preparation of girls to be mistresses who demanded deference from the enslaved and were educated in a variety of punishments was as forceful as the preparation of boys to be masters. How does reading this essay alter your perception of the ways we tell stories about and histories of childhoods?

In 1847, Lizzie Anna Burwell was growing up in a slaveholding household in Lynesville, North Carolina. She, like many other girls in the region, loved flowers, and she often strolled through her parents' garden with Fanny, the enslaved female charged with her care. After spending so much time with Fanny, Lizzie Anna developed an intense bond with her, but one day something changed. Lizzie Anna became "vexed" with Fanny, so much so that she went to her father and demanded that he "cut Fanny's ears off and get her a new maid from Clarksville."[1]

During those walks through the garden, and perhaps while observing her parents interact with the enslaved people around them, Lizzie Anna learned how to be a slaveowner. She came to understand the obscene logic that made it perfectly acceptable to stroll through her family's garden enjoying the company of her enslaved caretaker in one moment, and threaten to mutilate her and buy another slave

Prepared especially for *Women's America*. Drawn from *Lady Flesh Stealers, Female Soul Drivers, and She-Merchants: White Women and the Economy of American Slavery*, by Stephanie Jones-Rogers, book manuscript in-progress, esp. chap. 1. Copyright 2014 by Stephanie Jones-Rogers.

to take her place in the next. In the comfort of her home, she recognized that she possessed the power to command others to do so, and her father did little to discourage her from believing that she did. In fact, he relayed the incident to his sister with an air of conviviality and amusement, which suggests that Lizzie Anna's aunt also accepted the logic underpinning her niece's behavior. All in all, Lizzie Anna was a mistress in the making, and the people around her were crucial to her development as such.

White southern girls like Lizzie Anna learned how to be mistresses and slaveowners through a learning process that spanned the years of their childhood and adolescence. During this time, white females practiced techniques of slave discipline and management, and decided what kind of slaveowners they wanted to become. Many of them decided that they wanted to be effective ones.

Slaveowning parents were critical to this learning process in two ways. Slaveowning parents gave enslaved men, women, and children to their young daughters as gifts on special occasions like birthdays and Christmas, and upon marriage—or for no reason at all.[2] They also bequeathed enslaved people to their daughters in their wills. And when they did so, their daughters came to value the crucial ties between slaveownership and autonomous and stable financial futures. Coupled with this, parents offered their daughters vicarious lessons on how to own and control enslaved people through their words and deeds. As young girls watched their parents interact with the enslaved people around them, they observed different models of slave mastery, and through a process of trial and error, they were able to develop styles of their own.

White southern girls grew up alongside the slaves their parents gave to them. They developed relationships of power with enslaved people. And through all of this, slaveownership became an important element of their identities, a fact that would shape their relationships with their husbands and communities once they reached adulthood.

Slave inheritances were essential aspects of white girls' development as slaveowners; these most frequently came from parents. Slaveowning parents thought very carefully about the kinds of property they would give to their daughters and one of their most critical considerations in this matter was the amount of control their daughters would have over the gift once married. Rosalie Calvert, for example, wrote to her father who lived in Belgium about her daughter's future inheritance. In her correspondence, Rosalie indicated that she and her husband were "presently thinking about giving her what is called here 'real property,' which is to say, lands or houses over which a husband has no power."[3] After the Revolutionary era, when primogeniture, or the practice of giving all property to a family's eldest son, fell out of favor, parents tended to give their daughters equal amounts of property; but they also gave them more slaves than land.[4] Young white girls came to expect these inheritances, and enslaved people anticipated these transfers of wealth too.

Enslaved people often knew that their owners would give them to their daughters well before the transfer of property took place. Bacchus White recalled that his owners "alwa's sed dat I wus to belon' to Miss Kathie." Agnes James's master had already chosen her as a gift to his daughter Janie Little, because, as Agnes remembered, "he give all his daughters one of us to have a care for dem." Cornelia Winfield "always knowed [she] wuz to belong to one of marster's daughters." But, for these enslaved girls born shortly before the Civil War broke out, freedom came before that transfer of ownership could take place.[5] Just as enslaved people came to anticipate the transition from one household to the next, young white girls did too.

As they planned out their daughters' futures, some slaveowning parents preferred to give their daughters female slaves, and they began doing so when they were only infants. Filmore Hancock's grandmother "was given to missus, as her own de day she was born." Remarkably, Filmore recalled, "old missus was only a year old den." Formerly enslaved people told of how a master "had women he gave to his daughters and men he give to his sons." Charity Bowery's first mistress "made it a point to give one of [her] mother's children to each of hers." Charity eventually belonged to her mistress's second daughter Elizabeth. An unnamed formerly enslaved woman told historian Frederic Bancroft that her owners gave her to their "daughter fer a present. Dey make *presunts* o' niggahs in *doze* days, dey did *dat*."[6]

Slaveowners often adhered to this inheritance practice over multiple generations too. Mrs. William Keller owned Sarah Thompson

Chavis, and she and Sarah gave birth to daughters around the same time. When Mrs. Keller's daughter Julia was still a young girl, she gave her Sarah's daughter Amy as a "daily gift."[7]

Slaveowners occasionally gave their female descendants human property in ritualized affairs, which shaped the young women's development as slaveowners. When these future slaveowners were just girls, elders would join the hands of their young heirs together with those of the slaves they were giving to them. After doing so, they would tell them that the enslaved people in question were their property forever.[8] "Drawing" ceremonies were sometimes held after the death of a slaveowner who wished to divide enslaved people equally among his or her heirs but had not stipulated who would receive whom by will. During these affairs, the potential legatees gathered to draw straws. Whichever straws they pulled determined which slaves (and sometimes other property) they received from their deceased loved one's estate. This is how Ora M. Flagg came to belong to her mistress, Julia Taylor: "[T]he old heads died. . . . Their children when they died drawed for the slaves. . . . The Taylors were relatives of the Scurlocks, and were allowed to draw, and Julia Taylor drawed my mother."[9] Another formerly enslaved person recalled a similar kind of drawing ceremony: "When my old mistress died she had four children. . . . When Christmas come we had to be divided out, and straws were drawn with our names on them. The first straw was drawn, you would get that darkey. . . . Miss Betsey drawed mother and drawed me. Everyone drawed two darkeis [sic] and so much money."[10] Occasionally, these kinds of estate divisions occurred when a slaveowner was still alive. Sallie Crane did not understand why her master's property was divided because "he wasn't dead nor nothin'," but she "fell to Miss Evelyn," his daughter.[11]

These affairs were not simply for show; the property transfers and acquisitions that took place became significant events in white girls' lives and these young women assumed partial responsibility for managing the enslaved people their parents and kinfolks gave them. Immediately upon transferal, enslaved men, women, and children took care of their new owners in whatever ways necessary. When Jennie Fitts was just a young person, her owner gave her to his daughter Annie: "Ise can membah whens de Marster takes me to Missy Annie and sez, 'Ise gibin you to Missy, You jest do what she tells you to.'" Taking her master's charge very seriously, Jennie attended to her young mistress's every need and want: "Ise wid Missy Annie alls de time and 'tend to her. Ise wid her night and day, Ise sleeps at de foot ob her bed. Ise keeps de flies off her wid de fan, gets her drink and sich, goes places fo' to get things fo' her. When she am ready to go to sleep, eber night, Ise rub her feet." From Annie's head to her toes, Jennie "sho tend to Missy." Jennie undoubtedly had to learn how to perform many of the tasks that her mistress asked her to perform. Conversely, her mistress had to develop some important skills too. Above all, Annie had to learn how to be a mistress and she thought very self-consciously about what kind of slaveowner she would be. Jennie often heard her young mistress say "Ise sho an goin' to take care ob my nigger." And by Jennie's measure, "She sho did."[12]

For white girls newly inducted into slaveowning communities, "the plantation was a school" where they learned how to be propertied women. Ownership and control went hand-in-hand within the context of slavery such that developing adeptness in techniques of management and discipline was an important aspect of white girls' development as slaveowning mistresses. Their parents taught them about the principles of slaveownership and they learned vicariously through their parents' continued engagement with enslaved people in their midst. Slaveowning parents also allowed their daughters to assume the roles of instructors and disciplinarians very early on.[13]

One of the most significant, yet seemingly innocuous, methods that white parents used to teach their daughters how to be slaveowners began when they compelled enslaved people to recognize them as such. Immediately upon the birth of their children, slaveowning parents forced enslaved people to use the salutations "master" and "mistress." Enslaved children began to learn this lesson very early and the process continued over the course of their childhoods. A formerly enslaved woman remembered such a lesson which took place shortly after she was purchased at auction and brought to her new owners' home as a little girl: "When we got to the house, my mistress came out with a baby in her arm and said, 'Well, here's my little nigger. Shake hands with me.' Then he [her master] come up and said, 'Speak to your young mistress,' and I said, 'Where she at?'

He said, 'Right there,' and I said, 'No, I don't see no young mistress, that's a baby.'"[14] Savilla Burell's owners taught her "to call chillum three years old Young Marster, and say Missie." Another formerly enslaved person recalled that "[w]hen your marster had a baby born in his family they would call all the niggers and tell them to come in and 'see your new marster.' We had to call them babies 'Mr.' and 'Miss,' too."[15]

Slaveowners' objective in requiring this kind of deference was simple. They wanted enslaved people to recognize the power their children possessed over them, even at the time of their birth. Enslaved people understood this too. George Womble asserted that his owner wanted the slaves he owned to hold "him and his family in awe" and at the birth of new members of his family, enslaved people were compelled to "go and pay their respects to the newly born white children on the day after their birth. At such time they were required to get in line outside of the door and then one by one they went through the room and bowed their heads as they passed the bed and uttered 'Young Marster' or if the baby was a girl they said: 'Young Mistress.'"[16]

Enslaved people paid a high cost if they failed to use the required salutations. Rebecca Jane Grant either could not or would not call her mistress's young son "Marster." One day, Rebecca's mistress wrote a note and asked her to deliver it to the clerk employed at the shop of a local storekeeper. The clerk prepared a package in accordance with the note's instructions and gave it to Rebecca to deliver to her mistress. When she returned, she quickly learned what was inside: "a cowhide strap about two feet long." Her mistress immediately pulled the whip out of the package and began to beat Rebecca. She did not know why her mistress was beating her until she exclaimed: "You can't say 'Marster Henry.' Miss?" Needless to say, Rebecca quickly responded: "Yes'm. Yes'm. I can say 'Marster Henry!'" She bitterly remarked to her interviewer: "Marster Henry was just a little boy about three or four years old. . . . [She] [w]anted me to say 'Marster' to him—a baby!"[17] When another formerly enslaved woman forgot to refer her mistress's eight- or nine-month-old daughter as "miss," her mistress put her "in a stock and beat" her. While she was in the stocks, the woman twisted her leg so that it broke. In spite of the excruciating pain that would likely come as a result of such an injury, her mistress continued to beat her until she was satisfied.[18] Teaching enslaved children to call their owner's offspring "master" or "mistress" also served to educate white slaveowning children in two significant ways; it taught them about the deference that all African-Americans, regardless of age, must show them, and it served to underscore their own superiority.

Slaveowners' daughters often grew up alongside enslaved children as playmates and companions; but these future slaveowners eventually came to realize that the African-American children they shared their days with were far more than that.[19] They came to know that these African-American children were their property and they treated them as such. White girls and the enslaved people around them underwent a mutual process of training, and both groups acquired knowledge about the differences between them. When Betty Cofer was born, her master's daughter Ella was only a little girl, but she nevertheless understood that this enslaved infant would live a life that was very different from her own. Ella "claimed" Betty as her slave shortly after her birth, and afterward they "played together an' grew up together." Betty became Ella's personal servant, waiting on her, standing behind her chair during meal times, and sleeping beside her on the bedroom floor.[20]

At age three, newly arrived in Georgia after having spent her earlier years in Britain, Sarah Kemble quickly grasped the distinction between slavery and freedom and some of the privileges accorded to those who were not in bondage. Sarah was the daughter of Pierce Mease Butler, scion of a wealthy Georgia white family, and famed actress-turned-writer Frances Anne Kemble. Kemble recorded an exchange between the young Sarah and Mary, an enslaved chambermaid who was charged with her care, in which Sarah told Mary that "some persons are free and some are not." She established her unbound status by saying, "I am a free person." She paused and waited for a reply. When she did not get one, she repeated her assertion: "I say, I am a free person, Mary—do you know that?" Finally, her chambermaid responded, "Yes, missis." And the little girl continued, "Some persons are free and some are not—do you know that, Mary?" And again Mary replied, but this time with her own understanding of the subject: "Yes, missis, *here* . . . I know it is so here, in this world." New to the plantation setting, Butler's and Kemble's daughter was discovering and understanding a fundamental distinction between herself and the woman her father owned, and she sought to communicate and reinforce that difference to her enslaved chambermaid. In this brief conversation, she drew the line between free and unfree; between the powerful and the disempowered. She placed herself on one side of it, ensured that Mary knew she was on the other, and implied that Mary must not cross it.[21]

Slaveowning girls also made their ability to claim other human beings as their own property thoroughly clear in their conversations with the enslaved people they owned. Sylvia Watkins said that her "young missis . . . allus called me her little nig." Neal Upson's mistress similarly referred to him as her "little nigger."[22] A formerly enslaved woman named Melinda recalled that her young mistress would frequently tell her "when I get big and get married to a prince, you come with me and 'tend all my chilens." When her young mistress grew up and later married Honoré Dufour, she did indeed take Melinda with her as she and her husband established their new household.[23] As little girls, privileged southerners imagined how enslaved people would fit into their lives, not as playmates or companions, but as property. And when they were old enough, they made those fantasies real.

Young white girls began to practice different management and disciplinary strategies and techniques with the enslaved people they owned, and this helped them develop and refine the skills of slave mastery they would need once they became mistresses of their own households. Most white slaveowning women were also mothers, and many of them taught their children about different strategies for slave management and discipline. Tines Kendrick's mistress owned all of the slaves and the land, and she was determined to manage her estate as she saw fit without her husband's interference. As a consequence, Tines said that her mistress's husband Arch, "didn't have much to say 'bout de runnin' of de place or de' handlin' of de niggers." Tines's mistress enlisted her son's help instead, and she taught him everything he knew about effectively operating a large estate and cruelly managing the slaves who worked it. Tines recalled that he "got all he meanness from old mis' an' he sure got plenty of it too."[24]

Lewis Cartwright refused to be whipped without a fight, and in a bizarre role reversal, his master asked his own mother to whip Lewis. Every time he tried to whip Lewis, he would fight him so much that he would have to stop. Constantly defeated, he began to have his mother whip Lewis because he knew that Lewis would not dare hit a white woman.[25] This may have been so, but it is quite possible that she was a more effective master, and her ability to command obedience from Lewis and other slaves reflected that.

On occasion, slaveowning mothers and daughters disciplined enslaved people together, bringing about trauma and disfigurement when they did. This is what happened to Henrietta King when she stole and ate a piece of her mistress's candy because she was hungry. Her mistress kept the people who labored in her home in a constant state of near starvation. When Henrietta was about eight or nine years of age, she was responsible for emptying her owners' chamberpots, and when she went to collect the pot in her mistress's room each morning she began to notice a piece of candy on the washstand. She knew her mistress left it there as a test to see if she would take it, and at first she resisted. But after several days Henrietta could no longer resist. One day, her mistress noticed that the candy was gone and questioned Henrietta about taking it. When she denied stealing it, her mistress commenced whipping her. Henrietta refused to remain still, so her mistress grabbed her by the legs and pinned her head under the rocker of her chair while her young daughter whipped Henrietta. For approximately an hour, her mistress rocked back and forth on Henrietta's head while her daughter beat her with a cowhide.

The beating crushed the bones in the left side of Henrietta's jaw, so much so that she could not open her mouth. The left side of her mouth constantly slid to the right side. Her mistress called a doctor in to examine her, and he determined that nothing could be done. Her face was irreparably damaged. After her mistress reckoned with what she had done, she would sit around and stare at Henrietta while she completed her tasks about the house. She never brutalized her again. But Henrietta and her disfigurement were disquieting, and so the decision was made to give her to a female cousin, who treated her kindly.

This one act of brutality profoundly affected Henrietta for the rest of her life. Because she could not chew, she was forced to consume "liquid, stews, an' soup." The teeth on the left side of her face never grew back. When children saw her disfigured face, they either laughed or cried. Adults would stare at her "wonderin' what debbil got in an' made [her] born dis way." Henrietta also had to contend with encounters with her mistress's descendants who apparently knew what happened to her. On one occasion, when she saw her former mistress's granddaughter in town, the young woman was so ashamed that she crossed the street and pretended that she did not see her.[26]

Not all slaveowning women endorsed the use of brutality against their slaves. As young girls practiced disciplinary and management techniques upon their slaves, slaveowning mothers might correct their children when they used tactics that displeased them. When Elsie Cottrell saw her daughter Martha abusing an enslaved adolescent, she interrupted her and said "Don't you know you will never have a nigger with any sense if you bump der heads against de wall?" Looking back on these events, her former slave Henry Gibbs believed that his mistress's daughter engaged in this practice because "[s]he was young and didn't know no better." But her mother wanted her to hone her methods of slave mastery in ways that preserved enslaved people's usefulness in the long run. As she acquired and refined this skill set, her mother molded and shaped her, making sure that she was equipped to manage, control and retain her human property for as long as possible and keep them in functional condition to labor for her, over her lifetime.[27]

Many women found their children to be agreeable pupils who easily absorbed their lessons in slave mastery; but others clashed with them over proper strategies for management and discipline. Mary Armstrong's mother belonged to a couple that she described as "the meanest two white folks what ever lived"; but in Mary's estimation, her mother's mistress was particularly cruel. "Old Polly" was the "devil if there ever was one," a woman who beat Mary's nine-month-old sister to death because she would not stop crying. Polly's daughter Olivia eventually came to own Mary. During one visit to Olivia's marital home, Polly tried to beat ten-year-old Mary. The enslaved woman retaliated by picking up "a rock 'bout as big as half your fist an' hit[ting] her right in the eye." Mary "busted the eyeball an' told her that was for whippin' my baby sister to death." When Mary told her young mistress what she had done to her mother, her mistress said,

"Well, I guess mamma has learnt her lesson at last." After years of watching her mother abuse and, in at least one case, murder the family's slaves, Olivia chose a different approach to managing the people she came to own as an adult. Although Mary described Olivia's parents as mean and cruel, she characterized Olivia in a starkly different way: "she was kind to everyone, an' everyone jes' love her." More profoundly, Olivia allowed Mary to defend herself against her own mother, something that may have created tension between them and altered their relationship thereafter.[28]

Of course, not all young slaveowning women diverged so significantly from the systems of management and discipline their mothers used. Some employed the same tactics, only milder in intensity. As Jennie Brown prepared for her upcoming marriage, her parents gave her a pick of their slaves. Elizabeth Sparks was among the ones she chose. Elizabeth was deeply relieved when Jennie selected her because she was "a good woman" who would "slap an' beat yer once in a while but she warn't no woman fur fighting fussin' an' beatin' yer all day." Jennie's mother was far more severe in the forms of punishment she used, beating slaves "with a broom or a leather strap or anythin' she'd git her hands on," without legitimate cause. Mistress Brown would also make Elizabeth's Aunt Caroline knit all day and well into the night, and if she dozed or if her body became limp as she drifted off into sleep, Jennie's mother would "come down across her haid [head] with a switch." Although Elizabeth clearly thought she could withstand her young mistress's disciplinary tactics, she suggested that it was only because she was still young and would have to learn how to be as brutal as her mother, something that would happen with age.[29]

As they learned how to be mistresses, white girls also trained enslaved people how to be the kind of servants that they would need later on. When Ellen Thomas and her mistress Cornelia Kimball were just young girls, Cornelia taught Ellen "the arts of good housekeeping, including fine sewing." Her training also involved being "blindfolded and then told to go through the motions of serving" so that she could "learn to do so without disturbing anything on the table."[30] Nancy Thomas recalled that she "was de special little girl fo' Mistress Harriett's daughter. Her name was Palonia. Even durin' dem days I would sew and knit. I had a little three-legged stool and I'd set it between Palony's legs, while she was settin' down. Den she'd watch me when I knitted. If I done somethin' wrong, she'd pinch my ear a little and say, 'Yo' dropped a stitch, Nannie.'"[31] As Nancy Thomas's testimony shows, Palonia was a mistress-in-the-making, responsible for overseeing Nancy's production and disciplining her when it diminished in quality. Palonia learned that Nancy was under her command and that as her "special little girl" she possessed the power to have Nancy do whatever she desired.

To be sure, enslaved people sometimes developed caring and loving relationships with their young owners. But no matter how amicable relations between young white girls and enslaved people may have been, these young slaveowners frequently articulated and exercised their power over them as mistresses-in-the-making. Some of these young girls and women enthusiastically assumed their roles as mistresses early in life, and some exhibited signs that they might evolve into brutal ones. When an unidentified woman spoke of the cruelties she suffered at the hands of her adult mistress, she included a telling account of similar suffering meted out by her mistress's daughter: "When we was little, she used to whip us and then make us kiss the switch. She was the meanest of the daughters."[32] As she interacted with the enslaved people around her, this young white girl was following her mother's footsteps of cruelty very closely.

What did it mean to young white girls to be given human beings as their own property or to expect to receive them during the course of their lives? How did witnessing slave punishments or hearing conversations about the value of enslaved human beings affect the relationships they cultivated with these individuals and to the institution as they matured? As the recollections and accounts above suggest, young white girls came to realize very early on that they could own and control other human beings. The ability to do so was integral to their identities as young white women in the slaveholding South.

Through wealth transfers from parents to daughters, white girls throughout the South became transformed. They were no longer just children who lived in southern households and communities filled with enslaved people who made a certain kind of lifestyle possible.

When their parents gave them enslaved people, they became slaveowners. Over the course of their lives, they grew up alongside the slaves they owned. In the process, they learned valuable lessons about the importance of owning property, how to be effective slaveowners, and when, if and how others would be involved with any aspect of their wealth in slaves.

When young slaveowning women married their husbands, they brought their slaves, and their ideas about how to control and manage them, into their new households with them. Yet few historians who explore the lives of married white women in the South focus on those who owned slaves. This tendency has much to do with prevailing assumptions about the ways that laws pertaining to marriage and property created legal and economic disabilities for married women. Coverture, for example, was a doctrine which stated that married women's legal and economic identities were subsumed into their husbands' upon marriage. During the period of coverture, married women's property and wages fell within the purview of their husbands' control. Furthermore, married women could not conduct legal or financial business in their own names, or without their husbands' consent. While coverture adversely impacted many women's lives, scholars discount the ways that kinship and communal networks, as well as the lifetime socialization of white girls in mastery and principles of slaveownership shaped the adult lives of others, their relationships with their spouses, and their decisions to circumvent the disabilities that coverture imposed.[33]

White parents raised their daughters with particular expectations related to owning slaves and, as a consequence, many of these women did not feel compelled to relinquish control over their slaves to spouses and male kin once they married. Instead, marriage marked a point at which their identities as slaveowners were fully realized, and many of them sought to manage and "master" their slaves, too. More profoundly, white slaveowning women's propertied status often formed the seed of marital conflicts, and their economic ties to slavery frequently influenced the internal order of their households and shaped their interactions with individuals beyond them.

In spite of the constraints of formal property laws, slaveowning women cultivated relationships of power with their slaves and found legal and extra-legal ways to protect their property from those who jeopardized their ability to control it. Women used various legal mechanisms such as separate estates, marital settlements, and separations in property to maintain control of their slaves before and after they married. But even slaveowning women who didn't secure control over their property with these mechanisms conducted themselves in ways that challenge scholars' assumptions about the sanctity of southern legal institutions and laws. The knowledge and skills that white females acquired as young people prepared them for these kinds of negotiations, challenges and conflicts. They valiantly fought to preserve their investments in slavery, and their former slaves tell us that in many cases, they were victorious. What is more, individuals in their communities routinely recognized and respected these women's choices.

NOTES

1. John A. Burwell ALS to Elizabeth T. Guy, Lynesville, N.C., April 30, 1847, Burwell-Guy Family Papers, William L. Clements Library, University of Michigan, Ann Arbor.

2. Jane Censer Turner, *North Carolina Planters and Their Children, 1800–1860* (Baton Rouge: Louisiana University Press, 1984), 105.

3. Rosalie Calvert to Henri J. Stier, November 9, 1817, in *Mistress of Riversdale: The Plantation Letters of Rosalie Stier Calvert, 1795–1821* (Baltimore: Johns Hopkins University Press, 1991), 325. Discussion of George Calvert's demand that his daughter Eugenia devise a marriage contract prior to receiving her inheritance appears on page 378.

4. Marylynn Salmon, *Women and the Law of Property in Early America* (Chapel Hill: University of North Carolina Press, 1986), 142, 158; Cara Anzilotti, *In the Affairs of the World: Women, Patriarchy, and Power in Colonial South Carolina* (Westport, Conn.: Greenwood Press, 2002), 74, 143; Turner, *North Carolina Planters and Their Children*, 107; Carole Shammas, *The History of Household Government in America* (Charlottesville: University of Virginia Press, 2002), 72.

5. Interviews with Bacchus White, in Charles L. Purdue, Thomas E. Barden, and Robert K. Phillips, eds., *Weevils in the Wheat: Interviews With Virginia Ex-Slaves* (Charlottesville: University of Virginia Press, 1976), 303; Interview with Agnes James, WPA Slave Narrative Project, South Carolina Narratives, Vol. XIV, Part 3, 8, *Born in Slavery: Slave Narratives from the Federal Writers' Project, 1936–1938*, http://memory.loc.gov/ammem/snhtml [hereafter cited as *Born in Slavery*]; Interview with Cornelia Winfield, WPA Slave Narrative Project, Georgia Narratives, Vol. IV, Part 4, 177, ibid.

6. Interview with "Uncle" Fil Hancock, WPA Slave Narrative Project, Missouri Narratives, Vol. 10, 148, *Born in Slavery*; Interview with Charity Bowery, in *Slave Testimony: Two Centuries of Letters, Speeches, Interview, and Autobiographies*, ed. John Blassingame (Baton Rouge: Louisiana State University Press,

1977), 261–67; Frederic Bancroft, *Slave Trading in the Old South* (Columbia: University of South Carolina Press, 1996; orig. pub. 1931), 292 (emphasis in original).

7. Interview with Amy Perry, WPA Slave Narrative Project, South Carolina Narratives, Vol. XIV, Part 3, *Born in Slavery*. I find that the phrase "daily gift" was peculiar to those raised in South Carolina and was used to refer to the gifting of slaves from a slaveowning parent to a child. For other examples, see interviews with Amos Gadsden and Jane Hollins, WPA Slave Narrative Project, South Carolina Narratives, Vol. XIV, Part 9, 291, *Born in Slavery*.

8. This method of property transferal was not legally binding without more formal documentation to support it, and some women learned this the hard way. See for example, *Goodwin v. Morgan*, 1 Stewart 278, January 1828, Ala.; *Irwin v. Morell*, Dudl. Ga. 72, July 1831; and *Carter v. Buchannon*, 3 Ga. 513, November 1847, in Helen Tunnicliff Catterall, ed., *Judicial Cases Concerning American Slavery and the Negro*, Vol. 3: *Cases from the Courts of Georgia, Florida, Alabama, Mississippi, and Louisiana* (New York: Octagon Books, 1968; orig. pub. 1932), 14, 18.

9. Interview with Ora M. Flagg, WPA Slave Narrative Project, North Carolina Narratives, Vol. XI, Part 1, 308, *Born in Slavery*.

10. Interview with unidentified enslaved person, *Unwritten History of Slavery: Autobiographical Accounts of Negro Ex-Slaves* (Nashville: Fisk University Social Science Institute, 1945), 117.

11. Interview with Sallie Crane, WPA Slave Narrative Project, Arkansas Narratives, Vol. II, Part 2, *Born in Slavery*.

12. Interview with Jennie Fitts, in *The American Slave: A Composite Autobiography, Supplement, Series 2*, Vol. 4: *Texas Narratives, Part 3*, ed. George P. Rawick (Westport, Conn.: Greenwood Press, 1979), 1351–2, digitized in *The African American Experience* (Greenwood Publishing Group). http://aae.greenwood.com/doc.aspx?fileID=RSW1&chapterID=RSW1-007-042&path=/primarydocenc/greenwood//.); this series is hereafter cited as *The American Slave*.

13. Ulrich B. Phillips, *Life and Labor in the Old South* (Boston: Little, Brown, 1929), 198–99.

14. Interview with unidentified formerly enslaved woman, in *Unwritten History*, 263.

15. Interviews with unidentified formerly enslaved person, *Unwritten History*, 150; and Savilla Burrell, *Before Freedom When I Just Can Remember*, ed. Belinda Hurmence (Winston-Salem: John F. Blair, 1989), 133.

16. Interview with George Womble, WPA Slave Narrative Project, Georgia Narratives, Volume IV, Part 4, 191, *Born in Slavery*.

17. Interview with Rebecca Jane Grant, in *Before Freedom When I Just Can Remember*, 57.

18. Interview with unidentified former slave, "Mistreatment of Slaves," WPA Slave Narrative Project, Georgia Narratives, Volume IV, Part 4, 303, *Born in Slavery*.

19. Nell Irvin Painter argues that white children often found themselves in situations under which they had to identify with either the enslaved or the enslaver. Furthermore, she argues that young girls often identified with slaves while young boys identified with slaveowners. See Painter, "Soul Murder and Slavery: Toward a Full Loaded Cost

Accounting," in *Southern History Across the Color Line* (Chapel Hill: University of North Carolina Press, 2002), 34–35. In my own research, while I found some cases that support Painter's assertion, many white slaveowning women did not identify with the slaves they owned.

20. Interview with Betty Cofer, WPA Slave Narrative Project, North Carolina Narratives, Volume XI, Part 1, 168, *Born in Slavery*.

21. Frances Anne Kemble, *Journal of a Residence on a Georgian Plantation, 1838–1839* (New York: Harper and Brothers, 1864), 22. Kemble was an actress, writer, and abolitionist whose publication of letters she wrote to Elizabeth Sedgwick caused an uproar in the United States and abroad. She deplored the institution of slavery and hoped that she could persuade her slaveowning husband that the system was wrong. He, on the other hand, hoped that Fanny's time on his plantation in Georgia would change her mind about slavery's injustice. With Kemble on one side of the slavery issue and Butler on the other, the couple soon separated and divorced. Butler retained custody of his two daughters until they reached twenty-one years old. Fanny and Pierce's youngest daughter, Frances Butler Leigh, became a staunch supporter of the Confederacy while their eldest Sarah supported the Union. One can only wonder whether Sarah's encounter with Mary shaped her stance on slavery in any way.

22. Interview with Sylvia Watkins, WPA Slave Narrative Project, Tennessee Narratives, Vol. XV, 76; interview with Neal Upson, Georgia Narratives, Vol. IV, Part 4, 55, *Born in Slavery*.

23. Interview with Melinda, *Mother Wit: The Ex-Slave Narratives of the Louisiana Writer's Project*, ed.

Ronnie Clayton (New York: Peter Lang, 1990), 167–68.

24. Interview with Tines Kendricks, WPA Slave Narrative Project, Arkansas Narratives, Vol. II, Part 4, 178–79, *Born in Slavery*.

25. Interview with J. L. Smith, WPA Slave Narrative Project, Arkansas Narratives, Vol, II, Part 6, 199, *Born in Slavery*.

26. Interview with Henrietta King, in *Weevils in the Wheat*, 190–92.

27. Interview with Henry Gibbs, *The American Slave, Supplement, Series 1*, vol. 8: *Mississippi Narratives*, 815.

28. Interview with Mary Armstrong, WPA Slave Narrative Project, Texas Narratives, vol. 16, Part 1, 25–27, *Born in Slavery*.

29. Interview with Elizabeth Sparks, WPA Slave Narrative Project, Virginia Narratives, Vol. XVII, 50–52, *Born in Slavery*.

30. Interview with Ellen Thomas, WPA Slave Narrative Project, Alabama Narratives, Vol. I, 376–77, *Born in Slavery*.

31. Interview with Nancy Thomas, in *The American Slave, Supplement, Series 2*, Vol. 9: *Texas Narratives, Part 8*, 3810.

32. Interview with unidentified formerly enslaved woman, in *Unwritten History of Slavery*, 279–80.

33. I explore these aspects of white slaveowning women's mastery in my forthcoming book manuscript, *Lady Flesh Stealers, Female Soul Drivers, and She-Merchants: White Women and the Economy of American Slavery*.

THAVOLIA GLYMPH
Women in Slavery: The Gender of Violence

The stereotypes of the gentle southern lady and the nurturing black "mammy" have long been a part of American stories and folklore. They figured in "Gone With the Wind," the epic film of 1939 which won ten academy awards, among them Best Supporting Actress to Hattie McDaniel, the first African American to win an Oscar. (McDaniel disapproved of the script but famously observed that she would "rather make seven hundred dollars a week playing a maid than seven dollars a week being one.") These stubborn stereotypes live on in our culture: where do you see them?*

*Molly Haskell, *Frankly, My Dear: Gone With the Wind Revisited* (New Haven, Conn.: Yale University Press, 2010), pp. 213–14. For the persistence of the mammy figure, see Michele McElya, *Clinging to Mammy: The Faithful Slave in Twentieth-Century America* (Cambridge, Mass.: Harvard University Press, 2007).

Excerpted from introduction and chs. 1 and 2 of *Out of the House of Bondage: The Transformation of the Plantation Household* by Thavolia Glymph (New York: Cambridge University Press, 2008). Reprinted by permission of the author and publisher. Notes have been edited and renumbered.

The lived experience of mistresses and their enslaved servants rarely matched the stereotype. Thavolia Glymph examines the oral histories of formerly enslaved men and women, court records, and the correspondence of slaveholders to document a society soaked in a culture of terror. She insists that we acknowledge what even many feminist historians have failed to see: privileged, white women were perpetrators of violence in routine fashion. In her essay in this volume, Jones-Rogers has shown how girls in slaveholding families learned to be powerful mistresses, whose untrammeled exercise of power, Glymph argues, "helped define their place in the world of slavery."

What are your responses to Glymph's question: "What did it mean to be a southern woman?"

"The word *home* has died upon my lips." Writing to her son late June 1865, Mary Jones summed up one outcome of the Civil War. Decades later, Katie Rowe remembered another. "It was de fourth day of June in 1865 I begins to live."[1] Without slaves to do the work of her home, Jones's world, her home, was dead. In that death, Katie Rowe saw life and a future to claim as her own. As a former mistress and a former slave, Jones and Rowe stood opposite each other in 1865. Once connected by the institution of slavery, they now faced a common task: to build new lives on the ground of freedom. Both were transformed. . . .

The story properly begins before the war, when enslaved and slaveholding women related to each other on the ground of slavery. For Mrs. Jones, the home that died was, whatever else, a workplace. Enslaved women mopped its floors, dusted its mahogany tables, made its beds, ironed, wet-nursed, and bathed and powdered their owners. In its yard and outbuildings—from kitchens, smokehouses, loom and weaving houses to spring and ice houses, wood sheds, dairies, and chicken houses—enslaved women scoured dishes, made biscuits and pies from scratch, churned butter, turned vegetables cultivated in gardens they worked and freshly-killed chickens into breakfast, supper, and evening meals, and fruits into jams and jellies. They washed damask tablecloths and every piece of clothing their owners wore, raised and fattened the poultry, and fetched wood.[2] They were expected to do these things in silence and reverence, barefooted and ill-clothed.[3] These expectations formed part of the legitimized violence to which they were subjected. The story ends with a transformed plantation household and the emergence of free black and white homes. In the transformed plantation household, former mistresses could no longer command labor or deference. In the new black homes, black women found some privacy and the space to live fuller lives. . . .

Historians have noticed and taken account of violence against slaves in the cotton, rice, sugar, and tobacco fields. Here it is easier to "see" because it took place in a "public" arena where cash crops were produced and came principally from the hands of men— masters, overseers, and slave drivers. Violence and power in the great house, the female side of domination, have not received nearly the commensurate attention. This neglect stems in part from the fact that violence in the household took place within a supposed private domain and came from the hands of women. We must remember that the plantation household was also a workplace, not a haven from the economic world, that it was not private or made so by the nature of the labor performed within it or the sex of the managers.

Home as a political figure and space comes into focus only when a key misconception is set aside: that the household is a private space. Once the public character of the plantation household comes into full view, so, too, does . . . a second misconception, that plantation mistresses wielded little or no power. Nothing could be further from the truth, which comes into focus when we notice that male dominance was not the controlling force within the plantation household. A third misconception interprets the aspirations and actions of black women on the basis of assumptions and questions that have framed the writing of the history of white women. Distinctions between modes of power are diminished. The fact that black and white women experienced different, and particular, modes of power within the plantation household becomes less visible. Just as plantation mistresses can be misconceived as more different than masters than the evidence shows, slave women can be misconceived as more like mistresses than the evidence shows.

If the authority of planter women is defined by the restrictions, legal and customary, imposed by white male authority, their power and violence disappear. On this view, the plantation household held freedom only for its male "white head."[4] Nothing bars the absurd conclusion that Mary Jones and Katie Rowe were equals by virtue of their femaleness. Indeed some scholars have challenged the idea of the southern lady that animated post–Civil War reminiscences, Lost Cause propaganda, and most historical studies prior to the mid-twentieth century. But their portrait generally depicts planter women as a silent abolitionist constituency and still, thus, as potent allies of slaves, and slave women in particular. Here were hardworking women so handicapped by patriarchy and paternalism that their lives more closely resembled those of enslaved women than the white men who were their fathers, husbands, and brothers; here were women who found in their own subjection the basis for an alliance with enslaved women.[5] Slaves rarely thought this. . . .

White women . . . owned slaves and managed households in which they held the power of . . . life and death, and the importance of those facts for southern women's identity—black and white—[was] enormous. In the antebellum period, white women were clearly subordinate in fundamental ways to white men, but far from being victims of the slave system, they dominated slaves.[6] . . . [My focus is] the female face of slave owners' power. . . . Once we acknowledge that white women wielded the power of slave ownership, then our culture's fascination with slavery's and mistresses' seeming elegance and "veneer of manners" becomes visible as a dodge and can be cleared away. Not only did white women's violence, and their ownership and management of slaves make it impossible for black people to see them as ideal models of a "kind and gentle womanhood," but they resulted in specific practices of resistance. . . . Contrary to most interpretations, violence on the part of white women was integral to the making of slavery, crucial to shaping black and white women's understanding of what it meant to be female, and no more defensible than masters'

violence. At the same time, white women's violence contradicted prevailing conceptions of white womanhood—and still does.

. . . [This work explores] the interplay of notions of domesticity and ideologies of race and slavery within the plantation household. Slaveholding women were called on to make their homes and themselves models of domestic virtue but depended on the work of slave women to accomplish these objectives. Southern prescriptive ideals asked them to "play the lady" *and* to be "domestic manager," and judged them according to both yardsticks. Accomplishing this required that they be both submissive and dominant. Their manners had to be perfect and their households had to demonstrate attention to order, punctuality, and economy. Failure threatened their status as ladies and the institution of slavery.

Success, in turn, depended on the cooperation of black women who notoriously refused to play their part. The ideology of domesticity required enslaved women to work for the plantation household as if their own interests were involved. Their failure to do so made it hard for mistresses to meet the emerging standards of domesticity. Mistresses couched black women's noncooperation as a refusal to be "better girls," in terms that suggested innate backwardness. This, not discontent under slavery, made them unalterably inefficient, slothful, and dirty. This was the source of their "misbehavior" and could be used to explain mistresses's violent responses and their inability to create the ideal domestic home, to be "better girls" themselves. Violence against enslaved women was thus justified. The disjuncture between these views and the fact that beds got made, meals cooked, clothes washed and ironing done, floors scrubbed, babies nursed, beds turned back, jams made, flies swatted, and much more is glaring but not unexplainable. In the end, black women's noncooperation defined and marked the failure of southern domesticity and simultaneously the defeat of its accomplice, the ideology of a gentle and noble white womanhood. . . .

Now, Missus Hodges studied 'bout meanness more'n [her husband] Wash [Hodges] done. She was mean to anybody she could lay her hands to, but special mean to me. She beat me and used to tie my hands and make me lie flat on the floor and she put snuff in my eyes. I ain't lyin' 'fore Gawd when I say I know that's why I went blind.[7]

. . . [Lulu] Wilson's description of [Mrs. Hodges] is the virtual antithesis of the paradigmatic good mistress with whom we have become so familiar. The "good" mistress dedicated her life to the never-ending task of managing her household and caring for her family and slaves in sickness and in health. Her comeliness was due in no small measure to her ability to satisfy all who depended on her, to manage a household rent by inequalities of race and gender with seeming equanimity. This ability was taught, of course, but it was also believed to be inherent in the very nature of white women, "racially naturalized," in today's shorthand. According to Kathleen Boone Samuels, "We were taught to speak very low and to be delicate in our ways." The mistress, as Maria Bryan put it, was a lady of delicacy and unmatched "gracefulness," as compared to the not-to-be envied "precision and primness of a northern fine lady, erect and stiff."[8]

. . . There have been other powerful and influential ideals of American womanhood but, arguably, none as coveted and admired.[9] Juxtaposing the claims of this ideal against the violence to which Wilson . . . [and others] testified brings to fuller view the literal as well as grammatical antagonism in the conjoined usage of the adjectives "delicate" and "slaveholding." The power of the plantation mistress is exposed . . . when we realize that in the American South, as elsewhere, the "domestic realm [w]as a site of power for women." It was also and therefore a site of struggle *between* women. For in the American South, no less than in more traditionally hierarchical societies, "rank could overcome the handicap of gender."[10] . . .

The testimony of former slaves is replete with bitter memories of violent acts committed by mistresses. As [historian] Norrece T. Jones writes, slaveholding women were "depicted frequently [by slaves and ex-slaves] as the most stringent and sadistic of the manor born." He describes the plantation household as a "war zone" where "spilling milk, breaking dishes, and a variety of other kitchen peccadilloes could and often did trigger barbaric responses from slaveholders throughout South Carolina."[11] . . .

In the enduring story of the Old South, mistresses gently ran households and nurtured their families, black and white. That they nonetheless engaged in violent behavior has confronted many historians with the vexing problem of what to call mistresses' violence, and how to explain it.[12] . . .

Mistresses were not masters, true. But when women slaveholders acted in the affairs of the household, a great deal of evidence says that they acted on their own authority, and not simply as their husbands' representatives. A great deal of evidence suggests that when black women resisted the plantation household, they resisted the authority that mistresses exercised.[13] . . .

In general, a silence surrounds white women's contributions to the basic nature of slavery, its maintenance, and especially, one of its central tendencies, the maiming and destruction of black life. With the silence goes an apparent reticence to probe mistresses' participation in the abuse of power even though slave ownership conferred that power. . . . The great house, whether a six-columned mansion or a rude house of four rooms, was a space of slavery and, thus, of domination and subordination. . . .

. . . If, "in the heat of the moment a mistress might strike out with whatever was handy," she nonetheless had to be preconditioned to this kind of response. She lived in a world in which actions of this kind were accepted as understandable if not laudatory "slips." She also lived in a world that denied to her witnesses, particularly the slaves among them, the recourse to restrain or retaliate. And finally, she lived in a world that did not construe her actions as damaging to her reputation as *compos mentis*.

All societies recognize a continuum of violence and advocate distinctions between legitimate and illegitimate violence, criminal homicide and justifiable homicide, random violence and coordinated violence. The slave South was no different. . . . The ruling classes of slave societies resorted to large-scale violence and brutality only in the last analysis. Their day-to-day domination depended more on their slaves' knowledge that their mistresses and masters *could* kill them but also subject them to the constant experience of "normal" violence. Ria Sorrell's memory of the pretty cruelties to which she was subjected haunted her long after emancipation. Her mistress "would hide her baby's cap an' tell me to find it. If I couldn't fin' it, she whipped me."[14] This kind of gratuitously perverse mental cruelty, with physical violence, reveals normative behavior in slave societies. . . . Such occasional or spontaneous acts of violence can be said to be "premeditated" in the important sense that their randomness and, sometimes, unpredictability were far more effective reminders of what could happen than sustained predictable assaults would be, not least because it left, more often than not, valuable labor power standing, if subdued.

In the end, white women's agency has been profoundly underestimated.[15] While conceding that slaveholding women internalized the social values of the Old South and reaped the rewards of slave labor, historians have been less clear about the role mistresses played in the construction of these values and in disciplining slaves. By the outbreak of the Civil War, slaveholding women had become, in fact if not in law, central partners in slavery's maintenance and management, more solidly members of the ruling class in their own right despite whatever civil and social disabilities they suffered because they were not men. . . .

Slavery, Delia Garlic concluded, "wuz hell." And it was as much hell in the plantation household, where mistresses were principal perpetrators of violence, as it was in the cotton, tobacco, sugar, and rice fields. Violence permeated the plantation household, where the control and management of slaves required white women's active participation and authorized the exercise of brute or sadistic force. Mistresses became expert in the use of psychological and physical violence and, from their perch in the household, influenced the construction of antebellum slave society in its gender and racial dimensions.[16]

Hellish punishment did not require large transgressions. The young female slave whose mistress beat her like a dog also suffered for her inability to go up and down a wooden staircase noiselessly. Her mistress called her a "black bitch" and threatened to kill her for going up the stairs "like a horse." On another occasion, her mistress called her a "nappy-head bitch" and, though sick, mustered enough strength to "try to hit me." Maria White's mistress beat the slaves in her household whenever their work displeased her. Austin Steward's mistress was "continually finding fault" and "frequently punished slave children herself by striking them over the head with a heavy iron key, until the blood ran." And even when not doing violence, she threatened violence. She "always kept by her side when sitting in her room," a cowhide whip, expecting, one imagines, to always find occasion to use it.[17]

Sometimes the punishments of hell required no transgressions at all on the slaves'

part. One mistress used the occasion of instructing her children in spelling to beat a female slave. "At every word them chillum missed," Harriet Robinson remembered, "she gived me a lick 'cross the head for it." Sarah Carpenter Colbert told her interviewer that her former mistress whipped slaves on a regular every-morning schedule; Hannah Plummer told how Caroline Manly, the daughter-in-law of North Carolina Governor Charles Manly, whipped her mother "most every day, and about anything, sometimes stripping her to her waist before beating her with a carriage whip." Jacob Branch's mother received a whipping every wash day.[18] . . .

Mistresses' violence against slave women in the plantation household ran along a continuum: Bible-thumping threats of hell for disobedience, verbal abuse, pinches and slaps, severe beatings, burnings, and murder. Frederick Douglass described one victim as "pinched, kicked, cut and pecked to pieces," with "scars and blotches on her neck, head and shoulders." The weapons mistresses took up against slaves ran the gamut from brooms, tongs, irons, shovels, and their hands to whatever was most readily available. Some mistresses did not leave the matter of choice of weapons to chance. The cowhide whip is ubiquitous in the slave narratives. It sat beside mistresses as they read to their children, knitted, or as they sat and rocked in their chairs doing nothing, as Frederick Douglass observed of "the psalm-singing Mrs. Hamilton," whose mistreatment of two slave women was common knowledge in the white community:

> She used to sit in a large rocking chair near the middle of the room, with a heavy cowskin . . . and I speak within the truth when I say, that those girls seldom passed that chair, during the day, without a blow from that cowskin, either upon their bare arms or upon their shoulders. As they passed her, she would draw that cowskin and give them a blow, saying, *"Move faster, you black jip!"* and, again, *"Take that, you black jip!"* continuing, *"If you don't move faster, I will give you more."* Then the lady would go on, singing her sweet hymns, as though her *righteous* soul were singing for the holy realms of paradise.

The cowhide whip, usually about three feet long, made from dried, untanned oxhide, was a weapon designed to cut the flesh and draw blood. Douglass described it "as hard as a piece of well-seasoned live oak" and "elastic and springy." The latter characteristic drew from its design: The whip was tapered from the part held by the hand to a point at the end. Douglass thought it was a more fearsome weapon than the more legendary cat-'o-nine tails.[19] . . .

Mistresses sometimes coupled physical violence with psychological violence. Slave children in the white household were introduced to these practices from an early age. The same hands, tongs, and shovels used in violence against adults were applied to children. Madison Jefferson said that his mistress pulled his hair so hard it came out and pinched his ears so hard that they bled. In addition to abusing enslaved children herself, she forced them to abuse each other. She had them "get a basin of water, and scrub each others faces with a corn cob . . . they bled under the affliction." He thought she looked for excuses to find fault with their work and to beat them, and that she took voyeuristic pleasure in observing their pain. Some evidence also suggests that slave-holding women who beat their slaves and/or were beaten by their husbands, in turn, abused their own children. . . .[20]

A kind of warring intimacy characterized many of the conflicts between mistresses and slave women in the household. The vision of a mistress dragging a slave woman into her house, or of a mistress and a household slave coming to blows in the mistress's kitchen, suggests one of the reasons we need not only to rethink relations between mistresses and slaves in the white household (and the image of mistresses as "ladies"), but also the very notion of that household as a space of domesticity apart from the public world of labor and labor disputes. . . .

Some mistresses, of course, neither beat their slaves nor delegated the task to others, rejecting the use of physical violence, sometimes using psychological tactics instead, or whipping, "as de las thing." A Wake County, North Carolina, mistress punished slaves variously by sending them to bed without supper, working them at night, or forcing them to memorize scripture and poems. But in the end, even if "once in a coon's moon," she used the whip.[21]

Overall, in narratives where slaves make explicit comparisons, mistresses are depicted as harder and crueler than masters. Mistresses emerge from these narratives not only as the principal actors in the violence that took place in the household, but as instigators inciting masters to violence. John Rudd was certain his

mistress pressed his master to cruelties, always "rilin' him up." Lucretia Heyward said that her master never whipped her but her mistress "cut my back w'en I don't do to suit her."[22]

Other slaves drew no such contrast between cruel masters and mistresses. According to Armaci Adams, they "was both hell cats." Yet, even in these mixed accounts, mistresses are named the more brutal and sadistic. Ria Sorrell's master whipped slaves, but Sorrell noted that he seemed to take no joy in it. Her mistress, on the other hand, was a "bad" person, "de pure debil," a woman who fed slaves as little as possible and "jist joyed whuppin' Negroes," especially when her husband was away. At such times, she "raised ole scratch wid de slaves."[23] . . .

Slavery gave mistresses the power to be hard and cruel in punishing and humiliating slaves, and the prerogative to be indifferent. It was the cruelty of indifference that Lucinda Hall Shaw specifically recalled. Hall knew neither where she was born nor who her parents were. As a child she lived on a small farm belonging to Reuben and Sara Humphries Hall along with three other slaves. Here she witnessed the fatal beating of a slave woman and the woman's burial on the spot where she had been tied to a post. She was then "jus' rolled" into a grave that "wuzn't nuthin but a hole in de groun." Decades later, the memory still gnawed at Shaw, for what happened next was, to her mind, as heinous as the beating. She recalled seeing something "shoveled in . . . dat I tho't I saw move." She immediately told her mistress who "tend lak she did't see nuthin' . . . she tol' me atterwards, dat de overseer whipped her so hard she birfed a baby."[24] . . .

Slave resistance sometimes arose in direct response to white women's abuse and in particular to the "nasty forms" it took.[25] The 1861 slave conspiracy at Second Creek, Mississippi, the record suggests, matured from just such circumstances. The testimony of the slaves called to explain why they had conspired to kill their owners is striking in this regard. The rebels had many grievances. The "whipping colored people would stop," for example. But one grievance stood out. The slave men stressed the abuse that their sisters, daughters, and wives had suffered at the hands of white women. The rebellion would rid their community of white women who "whips our children." They referred repeatedly to the water torture of a young female slave who was beaten and had water thrown on her by a group of young white women. For "drowning and beating Wesley's sister," they testified, the young women deserved to be punished. This, the slaves offered, explained the decision of Wesley and his father to join the conspiracy to overthrow slavery. . . .[26]

. . . Despite proslavery ideology, which held that slaves were members, albeit inferior ones, of one family, black and white, this notion could not be sustained where relations of slavery existed. Mistresses's management of household slaves made the distinction clear. . . .

Like slaveholding men, slaveholding women acknowledged the integral role of violence in the mediation and maintenance of slavery. . . . It is a record of the extraordinary recorded as ordinary, the ordinary language of power where "[e]xtreme acts of violence are depicted matter-of-factly because of their regularity." Lucille McCorckle penned just such an account: "Business negligently done & much altogether neglected, some disobedience, much idleness, sullenness, slovenliness. . . Used the rod."[27] Lizzie Neblett's account of how she handled a slave stands out for its banality. "I haven't even dressed Kate [a teenager] but once since you left," she informed her husband in a letter during the Civil War, "& then only a few cuts." One finds no sense of equivocation in either account, no suggestion of anything unusual. Nor does either account suggest that the women found punishing slaves particularly disagreeable or necessarily viewed it as men's work.[28] . . . There was a quality of ordinariness and a certain quality of casualness in the way mistresses talked about and meted out punishment. . . .

In admonishing daughters on proper etiquette, parents often used the occasion to provide instruction on the demeanor expected of slaveholding women in their relationships to slaves. The colonial Virginia patriarch, Colonel Daniel Parke, gave this advice to his daughter Lucy Parke: "Mind your writing and everything else you have learnt, and do not learn to romp, but behave yourself soberly and like a gentlewoman. Mind reading, and carry yourself so that everybody may respect you. Be calm and obliging to all the servants, and when you speak, do it mildly, even to the poorest slave." When she became the mistress of her own household, Lucy Parke ignored the advice.[29]

Upon her marriage to William Byrd II, Lucy Parke Byrd dominated her household in the ways her father had cautioned against. She used the lash (and other instruments) frequently and brutally. Her husband's objections ultimately carried no more weight than her father's admonitions. He, like her father, objected to the more brutal punishments she inflicted on slaves, especially women. He chastised her for burning a slave with a hot iron and beating her with tongs. . . . [Byrd] condemned his wife's brutality and her use of the lash when he thought she acted out of mean spiritedness, or when she exercised her authority in the presence of guests, just as he would have condemned a man of his class for like behavior. He did not, however, deny "her authority" to beat slaves in the absence of guests when he thought she was justified. Her determination "to show her authority before company" breached prevailing conventions and undermined "her authority" among the slaves. . . .[30]

Prescriptive literature that directly targeted mistresses sanctioned punishment from their hands but urged restraint. An article in the *Southern Planter* gave this advice to mistresses: "Never scold when a servant neglects his duty, but *always punish* him, no matter how mildly, for mild treatment is the best; severity hardens them. Be firm in this, that no neglect go unpunished. Never let a servant say to you, '*I forgot it.*' That sentence, so often used, is no excuse at all."[31] . . .

. . . Observing the systems of management available to their husbands and fathers, mistresses might easily have thought they were more vulnerable to clashes with slaves [that they could not win without help]. All but the smallest slaveholders used systems of management for crop production—overseers or slave drivers—which allowed them to get cash crops produced, and maintain a certain distance from their slaves. Charles Manigault had one of the most insulating systems. Manigault's factor, for example, oversaw the purchase and sale of slaves and supplies, and hired, fired, and oversaw the overseers, thereby providing Manigault with several layers of protection and distance from slaves. For elite men, the work of managing slaves was divided, parceled out to factors, overseers, drivers, and sons. This gave them an important advantage over mistresses. Slaveholding men might stroll, or invade, the slave quarters when they felt so inclined or ride out to check their fields, but those who had overseers and drivers were not required to so every day.[32] . . .

The distance that separated planters from intimate contact with their slaves was in other ways more often literal in comparison to that between mistresses and household slaves. Planters often spent months away from their plantations, and often from their town homes as well; their wives were much less mobile.[33] . . . Unlike European aristocrats, to whom they often compared themselves, slaveholders generally did not hire butlers or white female managers, or use slaves as household managers. . . .

By contrast, the work of mistresses was done at close quarters, on a daily and intimate basis. . . . Mistresses could and often did call upon and rely on the authority of their husbands, brothers, and fathers for assistance in managing slaves, to help settle scores, real and imagined. Yet this resort to masculine authority carried its own drawbacks. It undercut their own claims to authority over slaves within the household, marking them as poor and inefficient managers of the domestic space.[34] . . .

Memories of the injuries of enslavement stayed with black women, and their husbands and children into the twentieth century. Children born after emancipation were certainly not unaffected. Dave Lawson was born long after emancipation—his mother was only six months old herself in 1865. He grew up, however, with the knowledge of slavery passed on to him by others who had been enslaved. From them he learned, when he was "ole enough to lissn," about Luzanne, whipped "kaze she burnt de biscuits," and from Aunt Becky, why his grandmother and grandfather were hanged, both at the "same time an' from de same lim'" of an oak tree on a North Carolina plantation. The first time he heard the story he was unable to sleep for a week.[35]

Mandy Cooper left her story with her children. Like many parents, she found talking to her children about slavery difficult and put off doing so until they saw her back one day as she was bathing. She began to explain but the children "thought she was tellin' a big story," and made fun of her. Angry and pained, Mandy Cooper taught her children a lesson both unorthodox and painful. She had them strip to the waist, and struck each with a whip severe enough to draw blood. She finished her story and her son conveyed it to posterity in the 1930s.[36] . . .

The narratives of ex-slaves (and slaveholders) are "evidence" of the process by which terror was created and sustained on southern plantations and mistresses' role in its production. Slaveholding women's exercise of power over slaves helped define their place in the world of slavery. And this was not contradicted by their own vulnerability to violent acts committed by slaveholding fathers or husbands.

The scandal caused when Eliza Bird's husband "struck her down in the street," meaning to kill her, doubtless escaped neither the ears nor eyes of slaves nor, likely, the attempt of a drunken Georgia planter to "split" his wife's "head open" and kill her. Lewis Wallace's master was an alcoholic. When intoxicated, Wallace recalled, he would "grab old Missus by de hair of her head an' drag her up an' down de long front gallery." A slave named Peggy witnessed Thomas Powell beat his wife with a horsewhip and tried to intervene. Slaves talked about the mistress who died in childbirth along with her unborn child following a beating at the hands of her husband and noted that it was not the first time he had assaulted her and done so *publicly*, before their eyes. The last time, he had chased her around the house as he beat her with a whip.[37] . . .

A commonplace among slaveholders was that slaves saw and heard too much, about which they "talk too much." In these overheard conversations, and by way of neighborhood gossip and their own witness, slaves indeed saw, heard, and talked about masters who, forgetful of patriarchal standards, neglected their families, and committed adultery and other forms of spousal abuse.[38] . . .

Ultimately, mistresses found no shelter behind the curtains of the great house, not from slaves, not from the larger white public of which they were a part. Mary Culbreath was raped by the husband of one of her friends. The incident, remarkably, went to court, publicizing Culbreath's plight far beyond her home and neighborhood, where it had already caused great "excitement." Among those who took special notice were other white women in her community. Gertrude Thomas worried that the court might free the accused "to desolate the life of some other woman." Thomas's concern addressed the vulnerability of white women under supposed patriarchal protection. Culbreath's "insulted virtue," Thomas argued, required the defense of chivalrous men. The accused rapist, however, skipped town to avoid jail, leaving his wife and her friend, the rape victim, to face the consequences of his actions: the shame he had brought to two families and the embarrassed financial circumstance in which he left his wife and three children. A court levy against his already heavily mortgaged property left them further embarrassed and homeless.[39]

Mistresses turned out of their homes due to the fecklessness of their husbands, or who were victims of abuse, indeed may have kindled the greatest sympathy from slaves. But slaves also would have observed that they were not, as slaves were, without all protection or bereft of all civic capacity or rights. Despite the rule of patriarchy—and importantly because of it—white women found a judicial system that offered them some protection from errant husbands and, often enough, sympathetic judges willing to grant it. "A wife ill used, beaten and driven from her home by her husband, is entitled to the protection of the court, and will be allowed alimony, or the income of a settled property, for her maintenance until her husband received her home and treats kindly," the Court of Chancery ruled in a case.[40] . . .

Even though white women were generally required to make a clear case of "ill usage" on the part of their husbands, and "correct conduct" on their own part, in order to obtain alimony or access to their homes, the courts sought to ensure women's financial security even when they could not provide this kind of definitive evidence. This was especially true in cases involving the planter elite. But magistrates made it clear that they were not happy to see cases arising from the elites come before them. They were not above lecturing elite litigants on the impropriety of public airings of their domestic disputes. The court's position reflected its concern for the potential damage such cases could have on the stability of class and race relations. Unsavory behavior undermined elite power and authority, so the courts urged the elite to adjudicate in private charges of incontinence, adultery, or battery. Chancellor James emphasized in one case "how important it is for married persons to control their tempers." The significance of the case before him, extended, he wrote, to the "respectability of the parties litigant," and "the example it is to offer to the community."[41] In the community of slaves, the damage was most often already

done. Patriarchy stood exposed in new ways. Yet sympathy for the plight of white women among slaves could still only be limited.

In the end, mistresses's use of violence manifested the regular demands and challenges of slaveholding. It drew upon the certain knowledge that they acted on their own rights. Although there might be rules about when, and before whom, they could exercise their power, not all mistresses felt obliged to follow them. The violence and humiliation that marked white women's treatment of enslaved women raised implacable barriers between them and tempered the very meaning of womanhood in the South. What did it mean to be a southern woman? How, out of the bramble of hate and terror, subjection and fear, did white and black women of the South construct and reconstruct their identities, their notions of what it meant to be female, their ideas about citizenship and freedom? For these endeavors, what did it mean that mistresses might have limited legal rights to divorce and could be beaten by masters, but that they could own slaves whom they could beat? Or, that enslaved women had hand-sawed-up backs or backs that looked like chokeberry trees? The antebellum South was a world, ultimately, that neither white nor black women could easily abide. Enslaved women, [historian Elizabeth] Fox-Genovese writes, understood "that power was no abstraction: It wore a white male face." Yet, it was also the case that the antebellum South was a place where power could wear a white female face. And that made the common vulnerability of black and white women to white male power distinctly different in operation and meaning. Slaves interpreted the abuse mistresses meted out as deliberate and calculated. But even if they thought it unpremeditated or "petulant," it is hard to imagine how they would come to the conclusion that white women were their allies or women to be emulated. A sobering verdict came in the case of *State v. Montgomery*. A husband and wife, master and mistress, were tried "for killing a slave by undue correction. The husband was acquitted, but the wife was convicted, and sentenced to pay the fine . . . $214.28." As Frederick Douglass, who experienced violent and nonphysically violent mistresses, wrote: "To talk of *kindness* entering into the relation of slave and slaveholder is most absurd, wicked, and preposterous."[42]

NOTES

1. Mary Jones to Charles C. Jones Jr., June 26, 1985 in *Children of Pride: A True Story of Georgia and the Civil War*, ed. Robert Manson Myers (New Haven, Conn.: Yale University Press, 1972), p. 1275. Katie Rowe in *The American Slave: A Composite Autobiography, Oklahoma and Mississippi Narratives*, vol. 7 (Westport, Conn.: Greenwood, 1972), p. 284. Series hereafter cited by name of interviewee.

2. Elizabeth Fox-Genovese, *Within the Plantation Household: Black and White Women of the Old South* (Chapel Hill: University of North Carolina Press, 1988), pp. 137–138; John Michael Vlach, *Back of the Big House: The Architecture of Plantation Slavery* (Chapel Hill: University of North Carolina Press, 1993); Deborah Gray White, *Ar'n't I a Woman: Female Slaves in the Plantation South* (rev. ed., New York: W.W. Norton, 1999).

3. See, for example, Jacob Manson, *North Carolina Narratives*, vol. 15, pt. 2, p. 97.

4. Lee Ann Whites, *The Civil War as a Crisis in Gender: Augusta, Georgia, 1860–1890* (Athens: University of Georgia Press, 1995), p. 18.

5. This historiography has its modern roots in Anne Firor Scott's pioneering *The Southern Lady: From Pedestal to Politics* (1970; reprint, Charlottesville: University of Virginia Press, 1995) and Catherine Clinton's *The Plantation Mistress: Woman's World in the Old South* (New York: Pantheon Books, 1982). For more recent elaborations of the thesis, see, for example, Leslie A. Schwalm, *A Hard Fight for We: Women's Transition from Slavery to Freedom in South Carolina* (Urbana: University of Illinois Press, 1997); Brenda E. Stevenson, *Life in Black and White: Family and Community in the Slave South* (New York: Oxford University Press, 1996); and Marli F. Weiner, *Mistresses and Slaves, Mistresses and Slaves: Plantation Women in South Carolina, 1830–80* (Urbana: University of Illinois Press, 1998), pp. 123–24.

6. For an important corrective on this point, see White, *Ar'n't I a Woman?*, rev. ed., pp. 6–7.

7. Lulu Wilson in *The American Slave: A Composite Autobiography*, ed. George P. Rawick, *Texas Narratives*, Supplement Series 2, vol. 10, pt. 9 (Westport, Conn.: Greenwood, 1979), p. 4194.

8. Elizabeth R. Baer, ed., *Shadows on My Heart: The Civil War Diary of Lucy Rebecca Buck* (Athens: University of Georgia Press, 1997), p. xvii; Carol Bleser, ed., *Tokens of Affection: The Letters of a Planter's Daughter in the Old South* (Athens: University of Georgia, 1996), p. 20.

9. The most oft-cited example of this entrancement is Margaret Mitchell's *Gone With the Wind* (New York: Macmillan, 1936).

10. Quotes are from Ingrid H. Tague, *Women of Quality: Accepting and Contesting Ideals of Femininity in England, 1690–1760* (Suffolk, UK: Boydell Press, 2002), p. 97. My thinking about this question has benefited greatly from Amanda Vickery, *The Gentleman's Daughter: Women's Lives in Georgian England* (New Haven, Conn.: Yale University Press, 1998); Leonore Davidoff and Catherine Hall, *Family Fortunes: Men and Women of the English Middle Class, 1780–1850* (Chicago: University of Chicago Press, 2002); and Achille Mbembe, *On the Postcolony* (Berkeley: University of California Press, 2001), 26–27.

11. Jones, *Born a Child of Freedom Yet a Slave: Mechanisms of Control and Strategies of Resistance in Antebellum South Carolina* (Hanover, N.H.: University Press of New England, 1990), p. 116.

12. For mistresses, there were no equivalents to the publicly sanctioned outlets for violent impulses that existed for white men—such as duels, patrols, militia, and war. For a comparative perspective, see Hilary McD. Beckles, "Taking Liberties: Enslaved Women and Anti-Slavery in the Caribbean," in *Gender and Imperialism*, ed. Clare Midgley (Manchester: Manchester University Press, 1998), pp. 137–57; Beckles, "White Women and Slavery in the Caribbean," *History Workshop Journal* 36 (1993): 66–82.

13. Fox-Genovese draws the opposite conclusion that "the vast majority" of mistresses acted as "delegates of the master, or male authority" and that slave women's resistance in the household was a protest of the master's authority (*Within the Plantation Household*, pp. 102, 110, 135; note quote at p. 110).

14. Ria Sorrell, *North Carolina Narratives*, vol. 15, pt. 2, pp. 300–302, quote is at p. 302; Genovese, *Roll, Jordan, Roll*, pp. 333–34. See Joel Best, *Random Violence: How We Talk about New Crimes and New Violence* (Berkeley: University of California Press, 1999); Melanie Perrault, "'To Fear and to Love Us': Intercultural Violence in the English Atlantic," *Journal of World History* 17 (March 2006): 71–93.

15. As two studies of slave punishment that do not mention white women at all demonstrate, some scholars do not see white female power at all. See, for example, Stephen C. Crawford, "Punishments and Rewards," in *Without Consent or Contract, The Rise and Fall of American Slavery: Conditions of Slave Life and the Transition to Freedom: Technical Papers*, vol. 2, ed. Robert William Fogel and Stanley L. Engerman (New York: W.W. Norton, 1992), pp. 536–50; Charles Kahn, "An Agency Theory Approach to Slave Punishments and Rewards," in ibid., pp. 551–65.

16. Delia Garlic, *Alabama Narratives*, vol. 6, p. 129. On the need for studies of the psychological costs of slavery, see Deborah Gray White, *Ar'n't I a Woman? Female Slaves in the Plantation South* (1985; rev. ed., New York: Norton, 1999), pp. 9–10, and Nell Irvin Painter, "Soul Murder: Toward a Fully Loaded Cost Accounting," in *Southern History Across the Color Line* (Chapel Hill: University of North Carolina Press, 2002), pp. 15–39.

17. Clifton H. Johnson, ed., *God Struck Me Dead: Religious Conversion Experiences and Autobiographies of Ex-Slaves* (Philadelphia: Pilgrim Press, 1969), p. 154; see also pp. 155, 161. Maria White, *Mississippi Narratives*, Supplement Series I, vol. 10, pt. 5, p. 2277; Austin Stewart, *Twenty-Two Years a Slave, and Forty Years a Freeman* (1856; reprint, New York: Negro Universities Press, 1968), p. 17.

18. Harriet Robinson, *Oklahoma and Mississippi Narratives*, vol. 7, p. 271; Sarah Carpenter Colbert, *Alabama and Indiana Narratives*, vol. 6, p. 57; Lucretia Heyward, *South Carolina Narratives*, vol. 2, pt. 2, p. 279; Hannah Plummer, ibid., p. 180; Jacob Branch, *Texas Narratives*, vol. 4, pt. 1, p. 139.

19. Frederick Douglass, *My Bondage and My Freedom* (1855; reprint, New York: Negro Universities Press, 1969), pp. 103, 149–50, 150; White, *Ar'n't I a Woman?*, p. 50.

20. John W. Blassingame, ed., *Slave Testimony: Two Centuries of Letters, Speeches, Interviews, and Autobiographies* (Baton Rouge: Louisiana State University Press, 1977), p. 218; Carol Bleser, ed., *Tokens of Affection: The Letters of a Planter's Daughter in the Old South* (Athens: University of Georgia Press, 1996), p. 108. Mistresses' abuse of enslaved children tempers the view that they played a central and positive role in the socialization of enslaved children. For the latter view, see White, *Ar'n't I a Woman?*, pp. 52–53, and Weiner, *Mistresses and Slaves*, p. 82. On the abuse of slave children, see also Painter, "Soul Murder," pp. 22–25.

21. Valley Perry, *North Carolina Narratives*, vol. 15, pt. 2, p. 170.

22. John Rudd, *Indiana Narratives*, vol. 6, pt. 2, p. 169; Lucretia Heyward, *South Carolina Narratives*, vol. 2, pt. 2, pp. 279–81.

23. Charles L. Perdue, Jr., Thomas E. Barden, and Robert K. Phillips, eds., *Weevils in the Wheat: Interviews with Virginia Ex-Slaves* (Charlottesville: University Press of Virginia, 1976), p. 1; Ria Sorrell, *North Carolina Narratives*, vol. 15, pt. 2, pp. 300–301. On the brutality of masters, see, for example, Dave Lawson, *North Carolina Narratives*, vol. 15, p. 45.

24. Lucinda Hall Shaw, *Mississippi Narratives*, Supplement Series 1, vol. 10, pt. 5, p. 1927.

25. Quote is from Fox-Genovese, "To Be Worthy of God's Favor: Southern Women's Defense and Critique of Slavery," 32d Annual Fortenbaugh Memorial Lecture, Gettysburg College, 1993, p. 12.

26. Winthrop D. Jordan, *Tumult and Silence at Second Creek: An Inquiry into a Civil War Slave Conspiracy* (Baton Rouge: Louisiana State University Press, 1993), pp. 164–65, 167, 201–2, 276, 279, 281, 294, 298; quotes at pp. 165, 281, and 295, respectively. An end to beatings as a determinant of freedom struggles appears frequently in the slaves narratives. See, for example, William Moore Narrative, *Texas Narratives*, vol. 7, pt. 6, Supplement Series 2, p. 2770.

27. Saidiya V. Hartman, *Scenes of Subjection: Terror, Slavery, and Self-Making in Nineteenth-Century America* (New York: Oxford, 1997). Used the rod: quoted in Scott, *Southern Lady*, p. 37; see also Fox-Genovese, *Within the Plantation Household*, p. 136.

28. Neblett quoted in Drew Gilpin Faust, "'Trying to Do a Man's Business': Gender, Violence, and Slave Management in Civil War Texas," in Faust, *Southern Stories: Slaveholders in War and Peace* (Columbia: University of Missouri Press, 1992), p. 185. See also Drew Gilpin Faust, *Mothers of Invention: Women of the Slaveholding South in the American Civil War* (Chapel Hill: University of North Carolina Press, 1996), pp. 64–70.

29. Parke, quoted in David Hackett Fischer, *Albion's Seed: Four British Folkways in America* (New York: Oxford University Press, 1989), p. 320. See Clinton, *Plantation Mistress*, pp. 96–97; Scott, *Southern Lady*, pp. 4–21.

30. William Byrd, *The Secret Diary of William Byrd of Westover, 1709–1712*, eds. Louis B. Wright and

Marion Tinling (Richmond, VA: Dietz Press, 1941), pp. 34–35, 205, 494.

31. Ulrich B. Phillips, *American Negro Slavery: A Survey of the Supply, Employment and Control of Negro Labor as Determined by the Plantation Regime* (Baton Rouge: Louisiana State University Press, 1966), pp. 276–77; Cecelia, "Management of Servants," *Southern Planter*, III (August 1843), p. 175, as quoted in Eugene D. Genovese, *Roll, Jordan, Roll: The World the Slaves Made* (New York: Vintage Books, 1974), pp. 334–35.

32. Douglass, *My Bondage and My Freedom*, p. 83.

33. See, for example, Drew Gilpin Faust, "Culture, Conflict and Community: The Meaning of Power on an Antebellum Plantation," *Journal of Social History* 14 (Autumn, 1980): 84.

34. For an extended discussion of domestic space and southern domesticity, see Thavolia Glymph, *Out of the House of Bondage: The Transformation of the Plantation Household* (New York: Cambridge University Press, 2008), ch. 3.

35. Jones, *Born a Child of Freedom Yet a Slave*, 7, 57. Dave Lawson, *North Carolina Narratives*, vol. 15, pt. 2, pp. 44–50.

36. Fred Cooper, *Indiana Narratives*, vol. 6, p. 61.

37. Bird: Bleser, ed., *Tokens of Affection*, pp. 131, 282; Mary Ellison, "Resistance to Oppression: Black Women's Response to Slavery in the United States." *Slavery and Abolition*, vol. 1 (May 1983): 57–59. Lewis Wallace, *Mississippi Narratives*, Supplement Series 1, vol. 10, pt. 5, pp. 2165–66. Peggy: Joan E. Cashin, ed., *Our Common Affairs: Texts from Women in the Old South* (Baltimore: Johns Hopkins Press, 1996), p. 208. Mistress beaten: Dave Lawson, *North Carolina Narratives*, vol. 15, pt. 2, pp. 44–48.

38. Talk too much: Augustin L. Taveau to [Delpine Taveau], 7 October 1863, Augustine Louis Taveau Papers, Duke University. For additional examples, see Virginia Ingraham Burr, ed., *The Secret Eye: The Journal of Ella Gertrude Thomas, 1848–1899*, Introduction by Nell Irwin Painter (Chapel Hill: University of North Carolina Press, 1990), February 9, 1958, p. 160.

39. Burr, ed., *The Secret Eye*, July 23, 1852, p. 111; March 30, 1856, p. 145 (quotation). See also, February 9, 1858, p. 160.

40. *Harriet Devall, by her next friend, v. Michael Devall and others*, Cases Argued and Determined in the Court of Chancery of South Carolina (June 1809), pp. 78–81.

41. See, for example, Anonymous, Court of Chancery Cases, pp. 94–95. In this case, the social status of the plaintiff and defendant was specifically raised.

42. The chokeberry tree reference is from Toni Morrison, *Beloved* (New York: Signet, 1991), pp. 20–21. Fox-Genovese, *Within the Plantation Household*, p. 190; *State v. Montgomery*, Cheves 120, February 1840, in Helen Tunnicliff Catterall, ed., *Judicial Cases Concerning American Slavery and the Negro, 1926–1937* (1926; reprint, New York: Negro Universities Press, 1968), p. 377; Douglass, *My Bondage and My Freedom*, p. 436.

Eliza R. Hemmingway and Sarah Bagley, Testimony on Working Conditions in Early Factories, 1845

The textile factories of the first wave of industrialization might not have been built at all had their owners not believed they could count on a steady supply of cheap female labor. The history of industrialization as it affected both men and women needs to be understood in the context of the segmented labor market that women entered. Women were a major part of the first new workforce that was shaped into "modern" work patterns: long, uninterrupted hours of labor in a mechanized factory with little or no room for individual initiative.

One of the earliest mill towns was Lowell, Massachusetts, where factory owners began recruiting young, unmarried women to work in six textile mills in 1823. Rural young women already toiled at home at farm labor and also at "out-work," making goods that could be sold for cash. Compared to the work they had done at home, mill work at first seemed to pay well and to offer new opportunities. The Lowell mills developed a system of boardinghouses, which assured families that girls would live in wholesome surroundings. Letters sent home and fiction published by young women in the first wave of employment often testified to their pride in the financial independence that their new work brought.

Work in the mills was strictly segregated by sex: men were supervisors and skilled mechanics; women attended the spinning and weaving machinery. The daily earnings of almost all female workers depended on piece rates—the number of pieces or the output of the particular machine they tended. Their wages ranged from one-third to one-half that of men; the highest-paid woman generally earned less than the lowest-paid man. Employers responded to economic downturns in the 1830s either by lowering wages or by requiring more pieces per day. Mills established stricter discipline: workers who were insubordinate were fired; those who did not fulfill their yearlong contracts were blacklisted. But boardinghouse life meant that the factory women developed strong support networks; when their wages were cut and work hours lengthened in the 1830s, those who lived together came together in opposition to the owners and staged some of the earliest industrial strikes in American history. In 1836, 1,500 women walked out in protest, claiming their inheritance as "Daughters of the Revolution." One manifesto stated: "As our fathers resisted unto blood the lordly avarice of the British ministry, so we, their daughters, never will wear the yoke which has been prepared for us."*

*Thomas Dublin, *Women at Work: The Transformation of Work and Community in Lowell, Massachusetts, 1826–1860* (New York: Columbia University Press, 1979), p. 98.

Excerpted from "The First Official Investigation of Labor Conditions in Massachusetts," in *A Documentary History of American Industrial Society*, vol. 8, eds. John R. Commons, Ulrich B. Phillips, Eugene A. Gilmore, Helen L. Sumner, and John B. Andrews (Cleveland, 1910), pp. 133–42.

Women at textile machinery in a New England mill, photograph, ca. 1850.
Note the poor lighting and the absence of anything to sit on during the long hours at the machines.
(Courtesy of George Eastman House.)

In January 1845, led by the indomitable worker Sarah Bagley, the Female Labor Reform Association organized a petition drive throughout the region, which forced the Massachusetts legislature to hold the first public hearings on industrial working conditions ever held in the United States. On February 13, 1845, Eliza Hemmingway and Sarah Bagley had their chance to testify. What did they think it was important for the legislators to know?

. . . The first petitioner who testified was Eliza R. Hemmingway. She had worked 2 years and 9 months in the Lowell Factories . . . Her employment is weaving—works by the piece . . . and attends one loom. Her wages average from $16 to $23 a month exclusive of board. She complained of the hours for labor being too many, and the time for meals too limited. In the summer season, the work is commenced at 5 o'clock, a.m., and continued till 7 o'clock, p.m., with half an hour for breakfast and three quarters of an hour for dinner. During eight months of the year, but half an hour is allowed for dinner. The air in the room she considered not to be wholesome. There were 293 small [oil] lamps and 61 large lamps lighted in the room in which she worked, when evening work is required. These lamps are also lighted sometimes in the morning. About 130 females, 11 men, and 12 children (between the ages of 11 and 14) work in the room with her. . . . The children work but 9 months out of 12. The other 3 months they must attend school. Thinks that there is no day when there are less than six of the females out of the mill from sickness. Has known as many as thirty. She herself, is out quite often, on account of sickness. . . .

She thought there was a general desire among the females to work but ten hours, regardless of pay. . . . She knew of one girl who last winter went into the mill at half past 4 o'clock, a.m. and worked till half past 7 o'clock, p.m. She did so to make more money. She earned from $25 to $30 per month. There is always a large number of girls at the gate wishing to get in before the bell rings. . . . They do this to make more wages. A large number come to Lowell to make money to aid their parents who are poor. She knew of many cases where married women came to Lowell and worked in the mills to assist their husbands to pay for their farms. . . .

Miss Sarah G. Bagley said she had worked in the Lowell Mills eight years and a half . . . She is a weaver, and works by the piece. . . . She thinks the health of the operatives is not so good as the health of females who do housework or millinery business. The chief evil, so far as health is concerned, is the shortness of time allowed for meals. The next evil is the length of time employed—not giving them

time to cultivate their minds. . . . She had presented a petition, same as the one before the Committee, to 132 girls, most of whom said that they would prefer to work but ten hours. In a pecuniary point of view, it would be better, as their health would be improved. They would have more time for sewing. Their intellectual, moral and religious habits would also be benefited by the change. . . .

On Saturday the 1st of March, a portion of the Committee went to Lowell to examine the mills, and to observe the general appearance of the operatives. . . . [The Committee concluded:] Not only is the interior of the mills kept in the best order, but great regard has been paid by many of the agents to the arrangement of the enclosed grounds. Grass plats have been laid out, trees have been planted . . . everything in and about the mills, and the boarding houses appeared, to have for its end, health and comfort. . . . The [average hours of work per day throughout the year was 11½; the workday was longest in April, when it reached 13½ hours].

Maria Perkins Writes to Her Husband on the Eve of Being Sold, 1854

Because masters understood the connection between literacy and rebelliousness, slaves were rarely taught to read and write. This anguished letter from Maria Perkins is unusual because it was written by an enslaved woman. We do not know whether Perkins's husband Richard managed to persuade his master to buy her and keep the family together. If a trader did buy Maria Perkins or her child, the likelihood of permanent separation was great. Scottsville, mentioned in the letter, is a small town near Charlottesville; Staunton is some forty miles away.

Charlottesville, Oct. 8th, 1852
Dear Husband I write you a letter to let you know my distress my master has sold albert to a trader on Monday court day and myself and other child is for sale also and I want you to let [me] hear from you very soon before next cort if you can I don't know when I don't want you to wait till Christmas I want you to tell dr Hamelton and your master if either will buy me they can attend to it know and then I can go afterwards. I don't want a trader to get me they

asked me if I had got any person to buy me and I told them no they took me to the court houste too they never put me up a man buy the name of brady bought albert and is gone I don't know where they say he lives in Scottesville my things is in several places some is in staunton and if I should be sold I don't know what will become of them I don't expect to meet with the luck to get that way till I am quite heartsick nothing more I am and ever will be your kind wife Maria Perkins.

Maria Perkins to Richard Perkins, October 8, 1852, Ulrich B. Phillips Collection, Yale University Library, New Haven.

BETWEEN NATIONS AND ON THE BORDERS

LUCY ELDERSVELD MURPHY

Public Mothers: Creole Mediators in the Northern Borderlands

What did "westward expansion" look like for the people and their communities who were being expanded upon? Lucy Eldersveld Murphy's essay reminds us that the Midwest in what is now the United States was a borderland. In other words, it was a region in which multiple cultures, nations, and peoples met and coexisted. She highlights in particular the role of indigenous and Métis (mixed-race) women in navigating these migration streams and diverse cultures. Murphy argues that these women played important roles as what she calls "public mothers" in these multicultural and multiracial communities. In fact, these public mothers were crucial in fostering a Creole or local culture.

As you read this essay, think about how the portrayal of public mothers changes the ways in which we think about conquest and about Anglo-Franco-Indian relations. Why were some women better able to bridge cultural and racial divides? Is the evidence for this convincing? Why is it important to make the distinction between Métis and Creole? How might you rewrite the history of westward expansion by focusing on the roles of indigenous and Métis women?

On the northwestern shore of Lake Michigan's Green Bay, where the Menominee River flows into the lake along an old fur trade route, there is a city straddling the border of Wisconsin and Michigan. This city, and the county that surrounds it, are named for a woman of color: she was Marinette Chevalier, and the place name is Marinette. A Menominee, Ojibwe, and French Métisse (mixed-race woman) related to a prominent Ojibwe family, she married one fur trader, separated from him and then married another according to "the custom of the country," working side-by-side with each husband at the mouth of the Menominee River, a region in which many Indians spent part of their year.[1] She eventually separated from her

second husband, took over the management of the trading post with the help of her children, and became extremely successful in business and in cultivating warm relationships with the Indian people living in the area, many of whom were her kin.

When she was in her twenties, the War of 1812 clamped U.S. sovereignty onto this northern borderland region, and the Native people and fur-trade families were colonized by the United States. The conquering army built new forts and fortified older ones, enforcing control to be administered by a new judicial and legislative system. Although Marinette Chevalier and most of the other residents spoke French and/or Indian languages, the United States

Excerpted from "Public Mothers: Native American and Métis Women as Creole Mediators in the Nineteenth-Century Midwest," by Lucy Eldersveld Murphy, *Journal of Women's History* 14, no. 4 (Winter 2003): 142–65. Reprinted by permission of the author and publisher. Notes have been edited and renumbered.

imposed English as a new court language. Waves of immigrants from the eastern United States and even some from Europe swarmed into the Midwest, bringing different ideas about race, class, and gender. Before long, such people as Marinette Chevalier were minorities in their own communities. Yet when English-speaking immigrants began to move into the Menominee River area, they, like the local Indians and Métis people, became her customers, neighbors, and friends.

An essay in the Michigan Pioneer Society's 1877 yearbook recounting the history of Menominee County praised Marinette Chevalier. The Anglophone author chose not to dwell on her entrepreneurial experiences, but focused instead on another of her roles. According to the article, "Marinette died in 1863, highly honored by all the residents about the river. She was 72 years old when she died, and had been looked to as a mother by all the early settlers and Indians, for she had always been ready to assist the needy and comfort the distressed." Not only are her experiences remarkable, but also is the fact that the Anglo writer for the pioneer society noted and even celebrated this Métis woman, and that a city and county (now in Wisconsin) were named in her honor.[2]

While Marinette Chevalier's experiences were notable, they were not unique. Many other women whose lives spanned the transition to U.S. control of the Midwest worked to mediate between cultural groups, as did some of their brothers, sons, and husbands. During the nineteenth century, as the newcomers were changing the region's economy, landscape, and government to the detriment of many Creole people, some of these women both created connections and even transcended the prejudices of the Anglo "pioneers" to gain the praise of their neighbors.

Although many members of the old fur-trade families were what Canadians would call "Métis," that is, people of mixed Indian and white ancestry, others were not. Residents of these communities such as Green Bay and Mackinac also included Indians, whites, and people with African backgrounds. Rather than having an identical *ancestry*, they had in common a *culture* born in the Midwest, one that was in place before the United States took control of the region. For this reason, the word "Creole" is used here as a general term to describe the culture and the people who created

it, with the understanding that it may refer to any of the long-time residents connected to the old fur-trade culture who were Métis, Indian, Euro-, or African American. This article will discuss the roles of Creole women in multiethnic and changing communities. Some of them, I argue, found ways to mediate between cultural groups, by negotiating overlapping ideals of womanhood common to both Anglos and Native-descended people, serving their communities in roles as "public mothers."

In many ways, Creole women's experiences in the American Midwest mirrored those of women facing colonization in other parts of the world. For example, during the eighteenth and nineteenth centuries, West African coastal women, often operating as traders, served as social and cultural intermediaries, helped to create networks linking people of different ethnic groups, and facilitated cultural fusion in changing communities. In Senegal, African women traders married European men and helped to create a hybrid society in Saint-Louis and Gorée; their Euro-African daughters might be political as well as economic and social mediators. In Sierra Leone, women traders facilitated cross-cultural contact both as travelers and as vendors in the great markets. Their roles and activities, however, were frequently overlooked or misunderstood by foreign observers.[3]

Creole families in the American Midwest were initially formed when, during the seventeenth and eighteenth centuries, French Canadian and French fur traders traveled into the Great Lakes region in increasing numbers and married into Indian customers' families and communities. These mixed couples raised biracial children in bicultural households. Many of these mixed families eventually moved from the Indian villages into their own fur-trade towns and developed hybrid societies. Over fifty Creole communities were founded during the eighteenth century in the western Great Lakes and upper Mississippi Valley by Francophone men who married Indian women and raised Métis children. At least ten to fifteen thousand people called these communities home by the late 1820s. . . .[4]

Marinette Chevalier usually spent part of each year in the fur-trade town of Green Bay, known in French as LaBaye. Like her, thousands of people lived in culturally mixed communities and shared a syncretic culture. These people spoke French and various Indian languages, dressed, farmed, traveled, and celebrated in unique ways, and were not particularly loyal to the United States of America. People who had been born in the Great Lakes region, residents of towns such as Green Bay, Prairie du Chien, St. Louis, Vincennes, Detroit, and Mackinac, included French and Anglo-American fur traders and related workers, Indian wives, and some of their kin, and a wide variety of young and old Métis people, with a few African Americans.

It is important to understand these people in the context of colonization, as residents who lived in this part of the Midwest before it was annexed by the United States. During the eighteenth century, they had created communities with a regional culture that was a distinctive mix of their varied cultural heritages. Although they were not indigenous in the same sense that Indian peoples were, they were residents with a culture that was specific to the region, and strongly related to Indian culture. Their history parallels that of the Spanish-speaking Californios, Tejanos, and Hispanos of the nineteenth-century Southwest, people who were also colonized by the United States in the nineteenth century.[5] The people of midwestern fur-trade communities thought of themselves in cultural rather than racial terms, and they were keenly aware that they were being invaded and dominated by the culturally different Anglos of the United States. Both they and the Anglos understood them to be an ethnic group that pre-dated U.S. hegemony. In the early nineteenth century, the word "Creole" was used in the Mississippi Valley to convey this sense of a culture group created in the previous colonial era (although the word had other meanings in other contexts).[6] Other somewhat misleading terms such as "Canadians," "French" people, or "half-breeds" were sometimes used.

Creole culture combined Native American and Euro-American elements as mixed families negotiated lifeways and selected ideas and practices from their collective traditions. Wives' Indian-kin connections linked traders to friends and customers during the fur-trade era. Children tended to speak both French and at least one Native language. Native wives, who had grown up in societies that regarded farming as women's work, often continued to be very active in growing food, while white or Métis husbands might raise livestock, a practice

that was not customary in Indian communities. Dairying might be unpopular with Creole wives, but Indian maple sugaring expeditions became part of their Lenten season.[7]

Creole culture was complex and variable: the people who lived and created it were often bi- (or even tri-) cultural; they might be Ojibwe, Dakota, Potawatomi, Sauk, Pawnee, or members of other Native tribes, French, Scottish, English, African American, or any combination of the above. Practices and beliefs varied from one community or family or individual to another; there was change over time, presenting a real challenge to historians. . . .

The colonization of the Midwest by the United States and the immigration of large numbers of Anglo-Americans chiefly from New England and the Mid-Atlantic states caused profound social change. Such people as Marinette Chevalier faced a new political reality that altered membership of society's elite class, imposed new ruling families, and worked to demote many previously elite Creoles.

The transition to Anglo hegemony had the potential to constrict women's rights, and to stigmatize and marginalize Creoles. . . . The newly dominant society not only brought different gender ideals, but also tried to enforce those values with a legal system that constricted the rights of wives and rigidified the concept of marriage. While the *coutume de Paris* [a customary law code] as applied in New France (including the Midwest) had allowed wives to be co-owners of a couple's property and guaranteed widows at least half of the estate, U.S. hegemony imposed coverture on wives and did not protect widows from [the claims of their husbands'] creditors. Local norms recognized marriages that had been contracted "according to the custom of the country," but under the new regime these marriages were sometimes considered illegitimate. . . . Marinette Chevalier's second husband was one of thirty-six men charged with fornication by a new judge in nearby Green Bay because the couple had not formalized their union according to the legal system of the United States.[8]

In addition, Creoles experienced both cultural prejudice and racism on the part of the colonizers. Anglophone immigrants referred to themselves as "settlers," and, later, . . . "pioneers." They arrived intending to build farms, towns, and businesses, bringing with them cultural baggage that included ethnocentrism and devotion to a social hierarchy based upon race. Most wanted to believe that they were creating a new society where none had existed before, so they wrote essays for their "pioneer societies" congratulating themselves for having brought "civilization" to the "wilderness." In their letters and memoirs, they often felt the need to denigrate the established populations of Indians and Creoles.

"The Americans generally consider the Canadians as ignorant," remarked an Italian traveler in the region in 1828. For example, Henry Schoolcraft, an Indian agent and folklorist, wrote, "it is but repeating a common observation to say, that in morality and intelligence they are far inferior to the American population." Caleb Atwater, an agent sent to Wisconsin for an 1827 treaty, wrote that the Creoles of Prairie du Chien were "without even one redeeming virtue." Claiming exclusive ownership on the nationality "American," constructed in ethnic terms, said it all.[9]

For other newcomers, the striking and unsettling thing about the Creoles was their skin color. For example, J. H. Lamotte wrote to a friend in 1836 that the elite fur traders were "as fat, ragged and black as their great-grandfathers were (if they ever had any)." James Lockwood remembered noticing a bothersome disjunction of color and status, race and class, and being amazed at finding "nut-brown" Indian wives and biracial children among the elites of the community.[10] From the Anglos' point of view, the Creoles were people of color, neither Negro nor Indian, but also not white, a reason—added to their cultural "otherness"— that the new social system so often worked to marginalize them. . . . This same prejudice also presents a challenge to historians, because it caused Anglo writers to disparage, ignore, or minimize the experiences of Creoles.

Prejudicial attitudes also affected the literary traditions that neglected the activities and contributions of women. "Pioneer" writers recording their region's history, of course, usually assumed that women's experiences and efforts were unimportant, often to an absurd degree. When they were mentioned at all, women were frequently identified by their relationships to men, often not even by their names, a pattern even more pronounced in the representations of women of color. For example, a typical article about "James Allen Reed: First Permanent Settler in Trempealeau County and Founder of Trempealeau [Wisconsin]"

written in 1914 by a Dr. Eben D. Price stated: "During his army life Reed married a Potawatomi woman, by whom he had five children, Elizabeth, Joseph, Mary, Madeline, and James. Upon her death in 1830 he was married a second time to a Menominee mixed blood, widow of the trader, Russell Farnham. Two children, Margaret and John, resulted from this union. He later married the widow of Amable Grignon, whose son Antoine was the chief source of this biography."

Several pages later, the article states that "the widow Grignon . . . was a relative of the Sioux chief Wabashaw. Her relationship with the noted chief gave Reed great prestige among this band of Sioux." That Reed alone was considered to be the "first permanent settler" rather than, with one of his unnamed wives, as the first couple or the first family is equally typical. (For the record, the wives were Marguerite Oskache, Agathe Wood, and Archange Barret.)[11]

And yet biased Anglo writers praised such women of color as Marinette Chevalier. . . . [Why? I argue here that Creole women like Chevalier] did not act like ideal Anglo women. Anglo northeasterners might find them lacking in purity and submissiveness, and their religious participation did not always strictly conform to Protestant concepts of piety (partly because they were usually Catholic). They seemed, however, to possess many of the virtues of domesticity [and neighborliness that the Anglos associated nostalgically with] colonial-era hospitality [and] communalism.[12] [Simply put,] the pioneers were comforted by women of color who looked after their neighbors.

. . . Anglos' accounts are [often] our only written sources for Creole women. . . . [The accounts allow us to see,] in particular, elite Creole women—that is, those who were prominent, wealthy, and/or well-connected . . . [taking] on activities related to charity, hospitality, healing, and midwifery. They nurtured their neighbors, newcomers, travelers, kin, and fellow clan and tribal members. They came from Native and Creole traditions in which women's roles . . . could be at once public and private, social and political. Although political and economic roles for Creoles under the new regime were being constricted and the Anglo gender system being imposed was more restrictive than the systems of Creoles and Native Americans, some Creole women maintained quasi-public roles in transitional communities, because they were perceived by the newcomers as praiseworthy females doing motherly work. Although there are many instances of elite Creole men making connections and laboring to smooth intercultural relations, the role of Creole mediator [as reported by Anglos] is most evident in the actions of women.

Some Creole women reached out to their communities as healers—roles women could hold in Native communities—and as midwives, a trade women monopolized among Indians. Native and Métis women brought their knowledge of medicine, midwifery, and nurturing to the service of their neighbors. It is likely that bicultural women drew upon multiple medical traditions, making their range of treatment options greater than those available to people with access to only a single medical tradition. . . . Their efforts frequently brought them into the homes of neighbors who were culturally different, creating ties of respect and affection, and sometimes enhancing the healers' status and authority.

One such woman was Marianne LaBuche Menard, Prairie du Chien's midwife and healer, "a person of consequence," according to an 1856 pioneer writer who knew her in the early nineteenth century. She was a woman of French and African descent, a native of New Orleans who had thirteen children by three husbands. "She was sent for by the sick, and attended them as regularly as a physician, and charged fees therefor[e], giving them . . . 'device and yarb drink' [advice and herb drink] . . . she took her pay in the produce of the country, but was not very modest in her charges." After the U.S. army brought in a physician who would attend to civilians, many still preferred "Aunt Mary Ann," as she was called, and she sometimes cured people despaired of by the army doctor.[13]

During the mid-nineteenth century, an Ojibwe Métisse from Detroit came with her husband Louis Demarie to Chippewa Falls, Wisconsin. An Anglo neighbor wrote about Madame Demarie in 1875: "She was a woman of uncommon natural abilities, and with education and culture would have graced a high social position in any community. She was a born physician, and for many years the only one in the valley; and in making a diagnosis of disease, and her knowledge of the healing properties and proper application of many of the remedies used in the Materia Medica, exhibited extraordinary insight and skill in her

practice. She was frequently called to attend upon myself and family, and her prescriptions were simple, natural, and always efficacious."[14] Similarly, Josette DeRosier Duvernay Moon Robinson, another Ojibwe Métisse, cared for the sick and pregnant of Oceana County, Michigan, during the second half of the nineteenth century and delivered hundreds of babies. At the time of her death in 1904, an obituary in the Hart *Journal* stated, "Perhaps no other woman of Indian blood has been more respected and generally beloved than was Mrs. Robinson. . . . A woman of no literary education, yet she possessed much wisdom. . . . The sick and suffering always desired 'Grandma' Robinson as nurse, and she was never known to refuse aid whenever it was possible for her to render it. Every home in the township of Elbridge has welcomed her at their firesides and her death has caused more than usual mourning." Josette's daughter, Sarah Moon, also continued as a midwife.[15]

. . . Creoles expected prominent families to offer hospitality to travelers, particularly their own, but also to miscellaneous strangers. In doing so, they became the strangers' patrons but also served their communities by supervising the outsiders' behavior.

Marguerite LePage LeClaire, for example, was a Métisse related to a prominent Mesquakie (Fox) family and married to Potawatomi Métis interpreter Antoine LeClaire who was stationed for many years at Rock Island. She received a substantial land grant at the request of her Indian relatives at the time of the removal treaty of 1832, a grant which helped her family to become wealthy and prominent as founders of the city of Davenport, Iowa. Afterwards, according to a local historian in 1910, "delegations of the Sac and Fox Indians visited her place every year, where they were always made welcome, entertained as long as they wished to remain, and when leaving, always carried away as a free gift what necessaries they required—corn, flour, etc."[16] Anglo uneasiness about having Indians in town might be calmed by knowing that they were associates and relatives of Marguerite LePage LeClaire and that she was keeping an eye on them. Many other Creole women remained in touch with distant Indian communities, and welcomed, fed, and sheltered visitors. . . .

Creoles frequently offered hospitality not only to Native but also to non-Indian travelers and newcomers. Elizabeth Baird was one of Green Bay's hospitable Métisses six years after moving to Green Bay. . . . When Juliette Kinzie and her husband visited the town in 1830, . . . a party was thrown for them. "Everybody will remember that dance at Mrs. Baird's. All the people, young and old . . . were assembled. . . . Everybody was bound to do honor to the strangers by appearing in their very best [clothing]. It was to be an entertainment unequalled by any given before."[17] It is interesting that Kinzie remembered this party as being at *Mrs.* Baird's rather than as at the Baird home, or Mr. Baird's. . . .

In addition to gifts of lodging and food for sojourners, Creole giving benefited their neighbors as well, following Native tradition. Midwestern Indians valued generosity highly and expected elites to be the most giving of all. Reciprocity here was mixed with a heavy dose of communalism. Native people viewed wealth, in fact, as a sign of selfishness, a viewpoint that frustrated missionaries and agents trying to teach Native people acquisitiveness.[18]

Creoles adopted the Native sense of elite obligation, extending to neighbors the generosity they showed visitors. . . . Hononegah Mack [a HoChunk Winnebago] was known in northern Illinois for her hospitality and charity to everyone. When she died in 1847, her Anglo husband wrote: "In her the hungry and naked have lost a benefactor, the sick a nurse, and I have lost a friend who taught me to reverence God by doing good to his creatures. . . . Her funeral proved that I am not the only sufferer by her loss. My house is large but it was filled to overflowing by mourning friends who assembled to pay the last sad duties to her who had set them the example how to Live and how to Die." After her funeral, one Anglo man remarked to his neighbors, "The best woman in Winnebago County died last night." In later years, a forest preserve was named for her.[19]

A Trempealeau County, Wisconsin, pioneer in 1886 recalled a woman who, during the 1850s, epitomized for him the "twin traits [of] generosity and hospitality," one of James Reed's three invisible wives (probably Archange Barret). "Squaw though she was, she was an angel of mercy to the residents of Reed's Landing and Montoville. How distinctly I recall her commanding figure—going from house to house—not with words, for few could understand her broken French and native tongue—but with

well filled basket, and ready hand—tender as only a woman's is—to cheer the sick."[20] Although this Anglo writer racialized her as a "squaw," he viewed Archange Barret Reed's actions as appropriate, gendered behavior.

It is noteworthy that all kinds of people apparently referred to these women in kinship terms, as "Aunt," "Grandma," and "mother," and as elder relatives. . . . Métis people seem to have been traditionally viewed as kin by Indians ("all Indians called me sister," Elizabeth Baird recalled, looking back on herself as a young woman). Anglos did not necessarily think of Creoles in kinship terms, however, nor did Anglos consider their formally trained doctors as father, uncle, or grandfather figures. This sense of kinship that Anglos, Creoles, and Indians felt for such women as Menard, Chevalier, and DeRosier resulted from networks the women created in the community, demonstrating one way they successfully mediated among many groups. [I]t is also significant that people thought of them as older relatives. . . . "Mother," "Aunt," and "Grandma" are terms of deference, suggesting that these women of color likely derived some status and authority in their communities based not only on age but also from their ministrations to their neighbors.[21] . . .

. . . Creoles valued women and men who were community-minded, [and] they appreciated that public mothers did more than create personal links between themselves and other individuals. These women's actions had specific meaning for the community as a whole: their efforts served social welfare and educational functions, facilitated social control, provided inter-group diplomacy, promoted peace, and served to acculturate and assimilate newcomers into the community. . . .

. . . [Public mothers' roles in facilitating] diplomatic alliances [is vividly illustrated in the account of] a traveling Englishman who published under the pseudonym "A Merry Briton." [Ironically,] he did not understand what he was seeing. . . . [I]n 1841 [he] happened upon the home of Nancy McCrea and her husband Augustin Grignon, at a fur-trade center on Wisconsin's Wolf River consisting of a house and garden (including several acres of corn), with a number of Indian lodges nearby. The traveler entered the house uninvited, and observed "sundry pigeon-toed squaws, and mild-looking, half-breed girls, were busy preparing victuals about an immense fire-place."

Meanwhile, Augustin Grignon and another Creole man sat by a window working on account books, while "several Indians and half-breeds lounged about in various attitudes . . . smoking their tomahawk pipes." The Briton was greeted by Grignon, who made him welcome.[22]

At dusk, the Menominee chief Oshkosh, a kinsman of the Métis hostess Nancy McCrea, arrived with a number of companions and was warmly greeted by the family and other guests. After a meal consisting of "wild-duck stew, tea, and cakes," Oshkosh stood before the fireplace to make a long and formal speech in the Menominee language to the sizeable crowd. A member of the Grignon family translated the half-hour long presentation for the Briton. "The speech, from first to last, was in the declamatory style, and against whisky," he wrote. Another speech was clearly called for, and Nancy McCrea Grignon spoke up in the Menominee language. "Anon, old mother Grignon, a squaw of high and ancient family, with a crucifix round her neck, replied, in a nasal, whining voice: her speech was listened to with great attention." Unfortunately, we do not know what she said, as the Briton dozed off during the oration.[23]

McCrea . . . , the fur trader's wife, was clearly a person who connected people of different worlds. The daughter of a woman from an elite Menominee family and a Scottish fur trader, she spoke French and Menominee, and probably several other Indian languages.[24] Her role as public speaker in the simultaneously public and private arena of her home and the rapt attention of her family and guests testify to her significance in smoothing relations between the fur traders and Indian customers, between Creoles and Menominees, and between the extended Grignon family and the clan of Oshkosh. . . .

. . . [By the time of the Briton's visit, one longstanding arena of cross-cultural interaction was on the decline—marriage.] A look at 330 recorded marriages in Crawford County, Wisconsin, where Prairie du Chien is located, shows that exogamy—marriage to someone of another ethnic group—was declining as a proportion of all marriages. Exogamous marriages as a proportion of all marriages declined from 32 percent in the 1820s, to 24 percent in the 1830s, to 14 percent in the 1840s.[25] The relative decline in exogamy reduced opportunities for people to gain linguistic and cultural tools

needed to create alliances. Even so, many Creoles [as we have seen] responded to colonization by continuing to mediate, not only between Indians and Creoles, but also between these two groups and the immigrants. Indeed, the decrease in intermarriage in the face of surging Anglo immigration created a greater need for informal mediation within . . . [communities—mediation which public mothers provided. These women] had been reared observing negotiation and mediation, hearing [these approaches] praised, [and] perhaps even trained in [them].

No doubt Creole people attempted a variety of forms of negotiation, public mothering being only one of them. Probably there were some efforts that failed and others that succeeded but were not publicly lauded. Racism could cause failure. Rebecca Kugel has found, for example, that Creole women in Protestant mission schools aspired to leadership that could have allowed them to serve as intermediaries as teachers, missionaries, and interpreters, but the white Anglo missionaries tried to channel women of color into positions as domestic servants.[26] . . .

The behaviors of Creole public mothers, and the extent to which their efforts were appreciated and even valorized, teach us that they actively reached out to their communities, and that in doing so, they had found a middle ground among the various ideals of womanhood held by the region's people. . . . Their actions were in the best traditions of Native American, African American, Euro-American, and Creole women's activism. Although Creoles were frequently scorned for their cultural, ethnic, racial, and economic differences, some Creole women succeeded in reaching across the barriers by navigating the intersections of cultural ideals.

Notes

1. The terms "Native American," "Native," and "Indian" are used interchangeably in this article, following American Indian Studies' conventional usage.

2. "Menominee County," Report of the Pioneer Society of the State of Michigan vol. 1 (1877), 266; Beverly Hayward Johnson, *Queen Marinette: Spirit of Survival on the Great Lakes Frontier* (Amasa, Michigan: White Water Associates, 1995).

3. George E. Brookes Jr., "The *Signares* of Saint-Louis and Gorée: Women Entrepreneurs in Eighteenth-Century Senegal," in Nancy J. Hafkin

and Edna G. Bay, eds., *Women in Africa: Studies in Social and Economic Change* (Stanford: Stanford University Press, 1976), 19–44; and E. Frances White, *Sierra Leone's Settler Women Traders* (Ann Arbor: University of Michigan Press, 1987).

4. Jacqueline Peterson, "The People In Between: Indian-White Marriage and the Genesis of a Métis Society and Culture in the Great Lakes Region, 1680–1830" (Ph.D. diss., University of Illinois at Chicago, 1981), 133, 136. On intermarriage see Clara Sue Kidwell, "Indian Women as Cultural Mediators," *Ethnohistory* 39 (1992), 97–107; Sylvia Van Kirk, *Many Tender Ties: Women in Fur-Trade Society, 1670* (Norman: University of Oklahoma Press, 1980); Jennifer S. H. Brown, *Strangers in Blood: Fur Trade Company Families in Indian Country* (Vancouver, 1980); Tanis Chapman Thorne, *The Many Hands of My Relations; French and Indians on the Lower Missouri* (Columbia: University of Missouri Press, 1996); Susan Sleeper-Smith, *Native Women and French Men: Rethinking Cultural Encounter in the Western Great Lakes* (Amherst: University of Massachusetts Press, 2001); and Lucy Eldersveld Murphy, *A Gathering of Rivers: Indians, Métis, and Mining in the Western Great Lakes, 1737–1832* (Lincoln: University of Nebraska Press, 2000).

5. Rodolfo Acuña, *Occupied America: A History of Chicanos* (New York: Harper and Row, 1988); Antonia Castañeda, "Presidarias y pobladoras: Spanish-Mexican Women in Frontier Monterey, Alta California, 1770–1821" (Ph.D. diss., Stanford University, 1990); and Douglas Monroy, *Thrown Among Strangers; The Making of Mexican Culture in Frontier California* (Berkeley: University of California Press, 1990).

6. Les and Jeanne Rentmeester, *The Wisconsin Creoles* (Melbourne, Fla.: privately published, 1987), v–iii; Mary Gehman, *Women and New Orleans, A History* (New Orleans: Margaret Media, 1988), 10; "Creoles," *The Iowa Patriot*, 6 June 1839.

7. Peterson, "People In Between"; Murphy, *Gathering of Rivers*, 45–76.

8. Johnson, *Queen Marinette*, 32–33. Allan Greer, *The People of New France* (Toronto: University of Toronto Press, 1997), 69–71; James H. Lockwood, "Early Times and Events in Wisconsin," *Collections of the State Historical Society of Wisconsin* 2 (1856), 121–122, 176; Jacqueline Peterson, "People In-Between," 1; and Ebenezer Childs, "Recollections of Wisconsin since 1820," *Collections of the State Historical Society of Wisconsin*, 4:167.

9. Giacomo Constantino Beltrami, *A Pilgrimage in Europe and America* (London: Hunt & Clarke, 1828), 2:174; Henry R. Schoolcraft, *A View of the Lead Mines of Missouri* (New York: Charles Wiley, 1819), 39; Caleb Atwater, *Remarks made on a tour to Prairie du Chien in 1829* (Columbus, Ohio: Isaac Whiting, 1831), 180.

10. J. H. LaMotte to William Beaumont, 2 September 1836, Beaumont Papers, Missouri Historical Society; Lockwood, "Early Times," 110.

11. Wisconsin Historical Society, *Proceedings* 1914, 108, 112. Wives' names: Hansen, "Crawford County, Wisconsin Marriages, 1816–1848," *Minnesota Genealogical Journal*, vol. 1 (May 1984), 48, 54, 55; and Hansen, "Prairie du Chien and Galena Church Records, 1827–29," *Minnesota Genealogical Journal* 5 (May 1986), 18. Oskache may have been Ojibwe, according to the marriage record.

12. Laurel Thatcher Ulrich, *Good Wives: Image and Reality in the Lives of Women in Northern New England, 1650–1750* (New York: Alfred A. Knopf, 1982), 59–65; Barbara Welter, "The Cult of True Womanhood, 1820–1860," *American Quarterly* 18 (1966), 151–74; Mary P. Ryan, *Cradle of the Middle Class: The Family in Oneida County, New York, 1790–1865* (New York: Cambridge University Press, 1981), 210–18. Community studies of mid-western Anglo settlements emphasize the ways in which "pioneers" idealized "good neighborship." See John Mack Faragher, *Sugar Creek: Life on the Illinois Prairie* (New Haven: Yale University Press, 1979), 15–20; and Merle Curti, *The Making of an American Community* (Stanford, Calif.: Stanford University Press, 1959), 114–16.

13. Lockwood, "Early Times," 125–26.

14. Thomas E. Randall, *History of the Chippewa Valley* (Eau Claire, Wisc.: Free Press Print, 1875), 17–18.

15. *Oceana County History, 1880–1990*, vol. 1. (Hart, Mich.: Oceana County Historical Society, 1991), 425; and Paula Stofer, "Angels of Mercy, Michigan's Midwives," *Michigan History*, 73:5 (1989), 46. "Mrs. H. L. Robinson Dead," *The Journal* (Hart, Michigan), 22 April 1904, 1. Typescript copy in the possession of Susan Russick.

16. "Memoir of Antoine LeClaire, Esquire, of Davenport, Iowa," *Annals of Iowa*, v. 1 (1863), 144–47; and Harry E. Downer, *History of Davenport and Scott County, Iowa* (Chicago: S.J. Clarke, 1910), 394–405 (quotation, 400).

17. Juliette M. Kinzie, *Wau-Bun: The "Early Day" in the North-West* [1856] (Urbana: University of Illinois Press, 1992), 19.

18. Richard White, *The Middle Ground: Indians, Empires, and Republics in the Great Lakes Region, 1650–1815* (Cambridge: Cambridge University Press, 1991), 38, 97–104.

19. Stephen Mack to H. M. Whittmore, Pecatoni, Oct. 6, 1847, quoted in David Bishop and Craig G. Campbell, *History of the Forest Preserves of Winnebago County, Illinois* (Rockford: Winnebago County Forest Preserve Commission, 1979), 35.

20. John McGilvray to B. F. Heuston, June 18, 1886, Heuston Collection, Murphy Library, University of Wisconsin–La Crosse, Wisconsin State Historical Society, LaCrosse.

21. Elizabeth T. Baird, "O-De-Jit-Wa-Win-Wing; Comptes du Temps Passe," Henry S. Baird Collection, Box 4, folder 9, State Historical Society of Wisconsin, Madison, chap. 17.

22. Anonymous, *A Merry Briton in Pioneer Wisconsin* [1842] (Chicago: State Historical Society of Wisconsin, 1950), 69.

23. Ibid., 71–72.

24. Virginia G. Crane, "A Métis Woman of the Fox River Frontier: The Two Cultures of Sophia Grignon Porlier," paper presented at the "Women of the Midwest: History and Sources; A Women's History Outreach Conference," Madison, Wisconsin, 13 June 1997.

25. Hansen, "Crawford County, Wisconsin Marriages," 39–58.

26. Rebecca Kugel, "Reworking Ethnicity: Gender, Work Roles, and Contending Redefinition of the Great Lakes Métis," in R. David Edmunds, ed., *Enduring Nations: Native Americans in the Midwest* (Urbana: University of Illinois Press, 2008), 160–81.

MAUREEN FITZGERALD
Habits of Compassion: Irish American Nuns in New York City

Even before the potato famine of 1845, the population of Ireland was declining, pressed by harsh British policies and the attraction of American opportunity. In the 1840s alone, death and immigration decreased the Irish population by more than 20 percent, and nearly half of all immigrants to the United States in that decade were Irish. And more than half of Irish immigrants were women. They were "the only significant group of foreign-born women who outnumbered men," writes historian Hasia Diner, and "the only significant group of women who chose to migrate in primarily female cliques."*

In the following essay, Maureen Fitzgerald examines the distinctive shape of Irish women's migration and the creative work of the institutions they built. How does Fitzgerald describe the desirability of convent life for Irish American women? How did Irish American nuns "change the nature of convent life even as they embraced it"? How did nuns respond to urban poverty? In what ways did they claim power in the public sphere? How were these ways different from the ways claimed by Protestant women of the same generation?

On Monday morning, August 17, 1896, a simple black hearse pulled by a single horse traveled through the streets of New York City. The hearse carried the body of Sister Mary Irene Fitzgibbon and was followed by four hundred of the three thousand Catholic nuns active in the city.[1] Like Sister Irene, most of the sisters hailed from Irish backgrounds, the children of Irish famine refugees. Thousands of mourners, including Protestants and Jews as well as Catholics, watched from the sidewalks and followed the hearse as it passed by their workplaces and through their neighborhoods, until the procession was estimated at twenty thousand. Secular and Catholic newspapers alike marked her death with prominent articles; the *New York Times'* headline read simply "Sister Mary Irene Is Dead." The *Times* called her "the most remarkable woman of her age in her sphere of philanthropy," and other non-Catholic newspapers agreed. The *Herald* characterized the

massive yet simple procession that marked her death as unprecedented: "Never in the history of New York has such a tribute been paid."[2]

Over the weekend before 3,500 mourners paid their respects at the Foundling Asylum, Sister Irene's crowning achievement, an institution she had founded and then supervised for twenty-seven years. The Foundling Asylum housed an average of six hundred women and 1,800 infants at a time and also provided day care for working mothers, a maternity hospital for poor women, a children's hospital, and a shelter for unwed mothers. With an annual budget of $250,000 derived from *city taxes*, secured initially through Irish Catholic men's control of Tammany Hall, the Foundling Asylum was the largest institution of its kind in the country and the only one in New York City to guarantee care for all children and women who came to its doors, regardless of religion, race or ethnicity, marital status, or ability to pay for care.

*Hasia Diner, *Erin's Daughters in America: Irish Immigrant Women in the Nineteenth Century* (Baltimore: Johns Hopkins University Press, 1983), p. xiv.

Excerpted from the introduction and ch. 1 of *Habits of Compassion: Irish Catholic Nuns and the Origins of New York's Welfare System, 1830–1920,* by Maureen Fitzgerald (Urbana: University of Illinois Press, 2006). Reprinted by permission of the author and publisher. Notes have been edited and renumbered.

The tribute paid to Sister Irene, although remarkable in itself, becomes more so when we consider that Sister Irene Fitzgibbon is virtually unknown to historians of women in the United States. She was but one of approximately two thousand Catholic nuns then active in New York City charities and whose charitable work was dependent primarily or exclusively on public funding. . . .

In the United States between 1830 and 1900, Catholic women established 106 new foundations of women religious and grew to a collective workforce of approximately fifty thousand. In New York City alone, the number of women religious rose from eighty-two in 1848 to 2,846 in 1898, not only increasing their own numbers exponentially but also composing the majority of the church workforce. While men and women joined the church in New York City in relatively equal numbers at mid century, the number of nuns grew to almost triple that of the combined number of priests and brothers by 1898.[3]

Irish and Irish American women, moreover, changed the nature of convent life even as they embraced it. . . . They transform[ed] convents from institutions run by elite women to those composed of and administered by women who had been poor or were from the working class. Convents thus became a primary means through which working class Irish Catholic women gained public power [although not a public voice]. Moreover, convents provided the Irish Catholic working class with the means to articulate and make manifest its political agendas and social vision.

Irish Catholic nuns considered protecting women and children in their group from the ravages of poverty, dislocation, and racial oppression to be central to their work, and they often did so through direct confrontation with Protestant middle-class women. The most derided and vulnerable of Irish Catholic women in nineteenth-century America was the destitute mother with children; she became the archetypal image of a woman whose mothering in poverty necessitated drastic societal intervention. Because they viewed poverty in the nineteenth century, as [many do] today, as a moral problem with roots in particular cultures, Protestant reformers believed that the best strategy for eradicating it was to intervene in motherhood so as to alter the reproduction of moral traits associated with poverty. According to the logic of Protestant reformers,

Catholicism either exacerbated or was wholly responsible for the tendency toward dependency, and even alcoholism, evident in the behavioral patterns of the Irish Catholic poor. The sooner children could be removed from the influence of such a mother, community, and religion, the better. . . .

From the early 1850s through the mid-1870s, Protestant elite reformers removed tens of thousands of poor immigrant children from New York City streets and homes and sent them to Protestant homes in the Midwest. . . . The practice of taking urban poor children away from their natural parents rested on the normative belief that the American Protestant nuclear family, guided by the maternal devotion of the American woman, was the only proper setting for child-rearing in the American republic. . . .

A large workforce of Irish Catholic nuns in concert with a city political machine dominated by Irish Catholic men was able in the 1870s and 1880s to construct Catholic institutions that directly offset such programs. Sisters funded these institutions, moreover, through city taxes. In the name of the "parental rights" of the poor, nuns housed tens of thousands of children. . . . By 1885 they directly controlled most of New York City's public child-care system, rearing more than 80 percent of its dependent children while Jews and Protestants controlled 10 percent each. Nuns alone housed fifteen thousand children at a time; perhaps most important, they constructed a "revolving door" policy. They took children into their institutions at the initiation of poor parents, and on a temporary basis only, to be returned when parents themselves thought they were financially able to provide for them.[4] . . .

. . . After the Council of Trent in the early sixteenth century, all Catholic nuns were required to make solemn, lifelong vows and observe papal cloister or enclosure, thereby severely restricting their mobility, rights to property, and ability to transact business or interact directly with the larger populace. These contemplative orders, distinguished from "active" orders by enclosed status and a focus on prayer and meditation, were more likely to exist when and where wealthy women could bring sufficient dowries to convents to fund lifelong seclusion.[5]

In the late eighteenth century . . . Catholic women in Ireland and the United States began to form active "religious institutes" sanctioned by the pope but not regulated by the Vatican until the turn of the twentieth century. Because the women did not call themselves nuns but rather "sisters" or "women religious" and made annual, or what they termed "simple," vows, they were not subject to the same regulation of convent life that governed contemplative orders.[6] Catholic women transformed this opening into a cultural and political mechanism for collective organization and public authority. . . .

Irish Catholic women religious of the early nineteenth century were above all at the center of a nation that existed only in the imaginations of those committed to an Ireland free of British rule. . . . [T]hrough the Penal Laws instituted after Oliver Cromwell's conquest of the island in the seventeenth century, . . . Catholics in Ireland were legally barred from worship in Catholic churches, voting, holding public office, or passing on property to heirs. By 1750 Catholics owned only 5 percent of all the land in Ireland. The . . . [British], moreover, developed ideological rationales for colonization and Protestant rule that linked race to religion. The Irish were judged an inferior race over which dominion was justified because of the strength of Catholic "barbarism" among its people.[7] Although individual Irish people could avoid the worst effects of the Penal Laws by converting to Protestantism, few did. . . .

. . . Consider, for instance, Mother Mary Augustine, born Ellen McKenna, who joined the Sisters of Mercy in New York in 1849, approximately three years after a small contingent of the order had set off from their motherhouse in Dublin to establish themselves in the city. From the earliest days of her childhood McKenna was encouraged by her family to support the development of Catholicism as a gesture of solidarity with other Irish and against British colonialism.[8] . . .

Unlike most of the Irish peasantry who remained Gaelic-speaking, illiterate, and only nominally tied to the institutional church, for instance, Ellen McKenna was sent to school in Waterford at an early age. . . . Ellen McKenna's desire to enter a Catholic sisterhood was not an attempt to leave the world and its strife but rather an effort to play a leading role in shaping nationalist institutional Catholicism. The rise of institutional Catholicism in nineteenth-century Ireland was, perhaps above all, a cultural project in which Irish Catholic nationalists attempted to supplant the institutional structures of British colonialism with institutions of

their own. Education and charities, because they decreased dependence on British National Schools and the British Poor Laws, were as central to that [catholic] nationalist vision as the building of parishes. By 1840, although having a workforce of only 1,600 sisters (in a population of eight million), 81 percent of Irish Catholic convents had instituted facilities and programs for the poor, including sick and prisoner visitation, free schools, meal and clothing distribution, houses of industry, and visitation of workhouses among other activities. Of the convents in Ireland, 84 percent ran schools by 1864.[9] . . . Some men in religious orders oversaw the education and care of boys, especially older boys, but charities, as in New York, were to become the almost exclusive province of nuns.

Although from a prosperous family, Ellen McKenna nonetheless experienced the trauma and catastrophe of famine by the mid-1840s, and emigration proved her greatest burden and constant inspiration. When the famine struck just after her father died, she aided the impoverished until the McKennas' own poverty became so great that they were forced to emigrate. Ellen deemed that experience a political "exile" as coerced as a political deportation. And yet she "offered it up" as penance, invoking the forced exile of St. Columba from Ireland:

> Dear St. MacCartin, fearful was the sorrow
>   I offered at thy shrine as penance dread
> Upon this day, long, long ago, for Willville
>   And home, and hope, to seek strange lands
>   instead
> God, merciful and patient, oh! accept it—
>   This hard Columban penance—thus away
> From our sweet motherland, our native country,
>   To wear out life. Oh! aid me still, I pray.[10]

Ellen was no longer in Ireland but neither was she about to "wear out life." When her mother died in New York City in 1849, Ellen and her sister, Julia, both joined the Mercy Sisters in New York.

Called Sister Mary Augustine in religious life, Ellen worked immediately in the House of Mercy, the shelter for female famine migrants, where she interacted with thousands of starving Gaelic-speaking women who had fled peasant areas in western Ireland. At every point in her life thereafter she helped move the order into uncharted areas of charitable work, including the establishment of a home for destitute girls in 1860.

As mother superior of the order after the Civil War she also aggressively sought, and won, public funding through Tammany Hall, thereby enabling the order to branch out into work with children on an unprecedented scale. Ireland, however, was never far from her mind, nor were the British, whom she struggled to "forgive" as an act of charity. The continuing migration of the Irish to North America was for her a constant reminder of the deprivation and cultural losses the Irish were forced to endure and the responsibility she felt for re-producing that culture. As she characteristi-cally observed to another Sister of Mercy in 1878, "It grieves me when the children we bring up know little about [St. Patrick] and about St. Brigid, the glory of Irishwomen.[11] . . .

. . . By 1860 the Irish accounted for 1.6 of the 2.2 million Catholics throughout the United States, thereby dwarfing the French, German, and Anglo Catholic communities. The strength of Irish cultural and ecclesiastic power in New York City was premised in part on the proportion of the church's workforce that was Irish. Fifty-nine (55 percent) of 107 male clergy in 1845 were born in Ireland. By 1865, twenty-three of the thirty-two Catholic parishes in New York City were Irish, distin-guished from the rest by the English language spoken by priests.[12] The organization of the city's women religious also reflected Irish dominance as the Sisters of Charity, the Sisters of Mercy, and the Sisters of the Good Shep-herd, established in New York City in 1817, 1846, and 1859, respectively, became more Irish over time. Each existed outside parish struc-tures, in contrast to others such as the French Holy Cross Sisters and the German Sisters of Notre Dame that were attached, respectively, to French and German parishes. . . .

. . . Without a substantial middle class to foot the bill for churches, charities, and educa-tion, and with an ever-growing number of des-titute people from peasant backgrounds constituting the laity, the church was poor and resources were scarce. Prioritizing how best to use the resources of the community, especially its labor and funding, was a constant and un-resolved tension, and Catholic sisters were often at the center of such battles. . . .

Irish Catholic sisters had to contend with anti-Catholicism of all types, but anti-nun lit-erature and Protestant assumptions about nuns' victimization certainly framed their struggles through the century. . . . [T]he belief that convents were brothels for the use of priests, in which women were tortured and raped, was not limited to a fringe of nativist fanatics. The most popular American version of the immorality of convent life, that contrib-uted by Maria Monk in her *Awful Disclosures of the Hotel Dieu Nunnery of Montreal*, was pub-lished originally in 1836 and sold more than three hundred thousand copies by the Civil War, making it second only to *Uncle Tom's Cabin* in antebellum book sales.[13] . . .

Burning convents, avenging "escaped" nuns, and demanding convent inspection laws throughout the United States during the 1850s were all premised on an abhorrence of wom-en's public space, free from male control. . . . Irish Catholic sisters were . . . at the very least inscrutable. Their daily lives, dress, behavior, and value systems did not reflect a "true wom-anhood" in which domesticity and mother-hood rhetorically defined duties to family and nation. Nuns' "delusions" [e]voked . . . pity be-cause their commitment to Catholicism, through which they established independence from individual men, made them literally in-comprehensible as women.

Why then would Ellen McKenna choose life in a convent? When asked that question on applications for the Sisters of Mercy in New York, McKenna's cohorts were likely to state that they aspired to life in a sisterhood "for the greater Glory of God."[14] Yet such an assertion reveals relatively little about the reasons for the growth of convent life in nineteenth-century Ireland or why so many Irish women chose that life compared, for instance, to women in other Catholic cultures. . . . They, like Ellen McKenna, were likely to see opportunities and possibilities in the life of a religious that ren-dered other options less desirable.

At the heart of the choice was a willing-ness to make vows of chastity, poverty, and obedience. Making such vows seems a simple ritual on its surface, but each was made in the context of larger cultural shifts, and none was ever simple. . . . In the experience of women committed to life in a sisterhood the vows were not discrete but often in conflict. Negoti-ating their relative weight and balance in any situation or circumstance was at the heart of convent politics. . . .

Catholic women made vows of chastity in direct renunciation of the familial roles as wives, mothers, and daughters. The vows ena-bled nuns to cast themselves as special women sanctioned by the social and religious culture to live apart from the familial obligations most women were expected to honor. Nuns did not derive status because they were women but because they denied themselves the pleasures and fruits of the female body, especially sex and motherhood. And yet the vows were not only experienced as renunciation but also [paradoxically] as liberation. As Rose-Mary Reuther has [observed,] ... "Women dedicated to asceticism could count on the support of the Church in making decisions against their family's demands that they marry and bear children."[15] ...

Church leaders encouraged Irish Catholics to believe that a son or daughter's entrance into the church was a great honor for the family in general, yet Catholic parental resistance was often overt. When the founder of the New York convent of the Sisters of Mercy, thirty-year-old Mary O'Connor, decided to leave Dublin for New York in 1846, her mother beseeched the Dublin male hierarchy to interfere with her daughter's and the Mercy order's decision and convince her to stay in Ireland instead. ... [From the convent nun's point of view,] conflicts between parents and postulants were expected. ... [A]pplications for admission to orders asked explicitly if there was parental resistance to the women's entrance. ... [Convents often denied] entrance to a novice if they believed that aged parents were dependent on that woman's wages or relied on her caretaking for their health. ...

Among the most important reasons that so many Irish women chose to become women religious was that committing to a life of celibacy was not a radical break from the sexual patterns evident in much of Ireland. ... The rising rural middling classes increasingly ... plac[ed] enormous emphasis on consolidating land holdings. Instead of the rampant subdivision characteristic of peasants, only one daughter and one son in each family would be dowered or receive land. ... Few women in this class could marry in Ireland. ... Those deemed superfluous, moreover, such as a second or third daughter, understood from an early age that they would not be given a dowry and therefore had few options for marriage. As this pattern accelerated in the aftermath of the famine the proportion of people who remained unmarried in Ireland through most or all of their lives became very high by international standards despite high levels of emigration.[16]

Depopulation, not reproduction, was the organizing principle in gender and sexual relations in postfamine Ireland. One million deaths from starvation and disease and urgent emigration decreased Ireland's population from more than 8 million in 1841 to 5.8 million in 1861. By 1921 Ireland's population was at 4.3 million, roughly half the 1841 census. Subdivision and population growth were unthinkable, given their role in making the poor so vulnerable to the potato crop's failure and contributing to what all classes believed was the death of Ireland as they knew it.[17] For many, sex itself was the culprit in Ireland's ruin, and demonizing sexual behavior outside, or even inside, marriage became a critical foundation for Irish Catholic sexual culture.

Thus as the nineteenth century wore on the respectability of all Irish Catholic women was contingent upon maintaining a sexually chaste lifestyle. Unlike American Protestant middle-class culture, however, Irish Catholic dependence on Catholic ascetic tradition worked in tandem with cultural shifts to position mothers and wives on relatively low rungs of a hierarchy of sexual respectability. In the Irish Catholic schema, "virgins" and nuns came first; widows, second; and wives, because of their continuing sexual experience, third. Once a woman lost her status as a virgin in Irish Catholic society, even within marriage, she would never regain it, nor would her position as mother offset the loss of status entailed by heterosexual experience. Protestant women, in contrast, continued to be labeled as sexually "pure" so long as their sexual experience was contained within the institution of marriage. ...

For nuns, the vow of chastity was never only one of renouncing heterosexuality but always simultaneously a commitment to live in a community of women throughout one's lifetime and according to rules, and with cultural power, governing convent life. Women's ability, desire, and willingness to make a lifelong commitment to live and work with other women provided the social foundation of a sisterhood. Convent rules were often written with proscriptions against "particular friendships," meaning any attachment of particular nuns to each other that might interfere with the general harmony of community life, including exclusive attachments or favoritism, or friendships that led to sexual relations. ...

Lifelong and very close friendships in convents were not just tolerated but assumed

and encouraged. Sometimes two or three natural sisters would join the same sisterhood simultaneously. Women who could count
favorite aunts or cousins as role models often
followed them into convent life and sometimes
into the same convent. Friends often entered
convents together. . . . Sisters of Charity Irene
Fitzgibbon and Teresa Vincent together
founded and administered the Foundling
Asylum, their partnership/friendship providing the core of continuity through nearly three
decades of work and activism.[18] . . .

The vow of poverty was a complex and even
paradoxical one. . . . At base, the vow of poverty was not intended to impoverish women
religious but rather to encourage identification
with "Christ's poor" in their work and spiritual lives. At times that meant suffering
through very real poverty, but at other times
women religious risked their work with the
poor if they squandered or did not reproduce
the wealth they had. Nor did all women religious embrace the same kind of commitment
to poverty. Even within orders, poverty was
often an unequal experience. . . .

. . . [E]ntrance into a convent allowed
women the opportunity to collectivize wealth
with other women and apart from men.
Some who formed sisterhoods in pre-famine
Ireland were very wealthy. . . . Their collectivi-
zation of women's wealth made sisterhoods
perhaps the most powerful and rich female institutions in pre-famine Ireland. The act of
joining a sisterhood moved an individual's
wealth to the larger collective, and thus any individual lost their wealth as such. Yet through
that action women also removed wealth from
the control of men by placing it outside standard patriarchal inheritance structures. When
those who dedicated their wealth to the sisterhood died, relatives could not claim an inheritance; the property remained in the hands of the
present and future sisterhood.

The premise of sisterhoods' financial autonomy was augmented by the American legal
system; nuns maintained feme sole legal status
throughout their lifetimes. Married women of
the period, who were defined [as] feme covert,
or "covered" in marriage, generally did not
hold property individually; the property was
assumed to become their husbands'. . . .

Nuns, conversely, by virtue of their feme
sole status, could and did collectivize wealth,
incorporate institutions under exclusively

female control, derive revenue from business
transactions, sign contracts, and secure loans.
No men in the church, furthermore, had either
legal or cultural claims to such wealth. Their
collective financial and legal power thereby
enabled women religious to establish female-
run and female-owned public institutions at
a time when the most radical woman's rights
activists in Protestant America rarely lived
apart from marriage or owned property of
their own. Catharine Beecher herself, the chief
advocate of American marital domesticity,
noted in 1843 that Catholic nuns had means to
power that she did not. "The rich and noble
have places provided as heads of great establishments," she wrote, "where in fact they have
a power and station and influence which even
ambition might seek." That Catholic nuns
lived and worked in the public sphere in all-
female enclaves long before such organization
was perceived as a social or political possibility for Protestant middle-class women was for
Beecher self-evident. As an ambitious unmarried woman who spent her adult lifetime with
no clear channels through which to engage her
talents and education, Beecher lamented that
Protestant culture did not allow her to live and
work together with other women in a women's
community.[19]

Not all sisters shared equally in that
wealth and power. European orders, including
those of Irish origin, were divided into lay and
choir sisters, the latter the more wealthy postulants. At mid-century, poor women who entered sisterhoods would most likely make
vows as a "lay sister." Lay sisters were expected
to perform the tasks of domestic servants in
convents, thereby freeing the choir sisters for
"higher" pursuits. In the American context,
however, these distinctions quickly eroded,
both because there were so few wealthy women
with a requisite choir sister's dowry (approximately five hundred pounds) and because lay
sisters actively protested against this caste
system. . . .

. . . New York's Mercy lay sisters were successful in gradually winning the abolition of
outward indications of class status. In 1878
they were no longer required to wear a distinctive apron that set them apart from choir, and
by 1895 community records no longer referred
to any single member as choir or lay, even if
they were professed as such. Individual work
schedules of the New York Mercy Sisters show
that while some women worked consistently

in high-status or low-status jobs, such as academy teaching or kitchen work, there was often considerable flexibility in work assignments for women over a lifetime. One sister worked alternatively as a first- and fourth-grade teacher in the select school, a kitchen worker, and sewing worker in the boys' home over a ten-year period. Others alternated between sewing, kitchen, teaching, and administrative duties throughout their lifetimes.[20]

Poverty was understood broadly as an ascetic life, denying pleasure and comfort.... And yet freedom *from* the world, rather than *in* the world, allowed women public legitimacy in offering a critique of society.... As the Irish poor swelled the prisons in New York City and the Sisters of Mercy and Sisters of Charity undertook daily prison visitations, they frequently befriended men and women characterized as irredeemable by native-born Protestants. Catherine Seton, ... [one of] the Mercy Sisters, became attached to a young man who spent time variously at Sing Sing, the Tombs, and the city penitentiary. After his failed attempt at armed robbery, Mother Seton sent him $5 to aid in his escape and promised to care for his wife and children. When another of her protegés died, she inherited the tools he used for breaking and entering, including jimmies and pistols.[21] That such stories were included in the Mercy Sisters' published annals suggests an unwillingness to accept uncritically the notions of the native-born middle class about exactly what constituted criminality, respectability, or viciousness. In classic Irish fashion it also made for a good, funny story in the midst of tragedy.

For those orders committed to work with the poor in New York City and throughout the United States, financial pressures constantly vied with individual sisterhoods' efforts to keep their work and "mission" focused on those in poverty.... In the United States, all charitable sisterhoods had to devise a means of income capable of sustaining both the order itself and its charitable work. The most common strategy was to create an elite school in which tuition was charged and then use that tuition for the convent's upkeep and charities....

Until the mid 1840s, women formed and joined convents in the United States and Ireland with the understanding that women's orders were parallel, separate entities that coexisted with but were not subordinate to local or national male ecclesiastical structures. Convents and monasteries were subordinate to the pope and maintained hierarchies within their respective orders, but most were not subject to the bishops in the dioceses in which they worked. Between their foundation in New York in 1817 and 1846, for instance, New York's Sisters of Charity, like other local convents of the Sisters of Charity, was accountable to their motherhouse at Emmitsburg, Maryland. The motherhouse retained ultimate control of sisters who worked in any specific diocese, and the wishes of local bishops, priests, and laity were considered secondary to the demands and needs of the order at large. Within the motherhouse, a mother general was considered the head officer, followed by assistant mother, bursar, mistress of novices, and various grades of sisters, including professed sisters, novices, and postulants. In each city in which the sisters worked, moreover, internal convent hierarchies were replicated.[22] when nuns established institutions in which they lived apart from the main local convent, particular sisters, usually called sisters superior or head sisters, would be given ultimate charge of the specific institutions. Although the rationalization of the order allowed nuns in localities distant from the motherhouse to govern their own lives and activism in ways responsive to local contexts, they remained ultimately responsible to the motherhouse.

Motherhouse rule was the linchpin in convent autonomy, and through it sisters were able to control the kinds of work they did, their religious lives, and, most important, their ability to make vows of obedience to other women, not to men. Until 1846 the Sisters of Charity did not make vows of obedience to the church at large, but rather to the order to which they belonged, specifically to the mother superior and other female leadership. Obedience, moreover, was interpreted more broadly than simple subordination to specific people. It included the utilization of individual conscience to determine if a superior's actions were in accordance with the larger "mission" or apostolate of each distinctive sisterhood. Dedicating the order and collective lives of nuns to charity, for instance, and to a particular group in poverty—whether orphans, prostitutes, or unwed mothers—meant that those who made vows of obedience were dedicating themselves simultaneously to a religious lifestyle and a lifetime of work. A postulant would learn about the "spirit" or "mission" of the order through intensive study and contemplation of the reasons for the order's foundation, especially through writing by and stories about the founding superior.

When individuals or groups in a community felt that the superiors of an order took action that pitted their obligations to the mission against those to the convent's leadership, community discord could be great enough to induce the majority of professed sisters in the community to impede the reelection or encourage resignation of convent officers. . . .

On an individual level, women religious who rejected the tenor or politics of convent life could simply leave. Despite the dramatic "escapes" so vivid in anti-nun literature, no active orders were "enclosed," and therefore no women within them were barred from leaving at will. Sisters in active orders took yearly "simple vows," not lifelong vows, and therefore could leave convents without a formal repudiation of those vows. In practice, however, the system of novitiate, postulancy, and final profession, which lasted anywhere from three to five years, was expected to weed out those who either did not want to commit to the order for a lifetime or were considered unacceptable by the professed sisters, who would have the final vote in chapter meeting to recommend continuance or expulsion.

On both an individual and collective level, obedience demanded a selflessness that required extraordinary ascetic discipline. As Mother McKenna advised young Sisters of Mercy about to make their vows in 1873, that sacrifice was intended to benefit both the soul and others in the world:

> . . . I pray God that your heart and soul may be devoted to the poor, sick, and that serving the Lord in His poor, He may make you rich in graces and blessings. . . . Inch by inch this sacrifice is exacted by little trials, more galling than great ones. To say nothing when we would naturally say something sharp; to do simply as we are told, without objection or remonstrance, . . . to seem cheerful when the heart aches, to be kind in return for unkindness, . . .—these efforts will be sacrifices.

Yet Mother Augustine McKenna was also supremely conscious of the need to balance obedience against ambition and assertiveness, particularly when that ambition was in the name of others who needed her help. As the chief architect of the order's work with children, then Sister McKenna wrote out a separate

promise to herself and God in 1860 and placed it at the back of the book that held her original vows. She showed it to no one, but other Sisters of Mercy found it and buried it with her. Mother McKenna wrote [in part]:

> In the name of our Lord and Saviour, Jesus Christ, and under the protection of His Immaculate Mother, Mary ever Virgin, I, Sister Mary Augustine, for the love of his Sacred Heart, do resolve, but not vow, to suffer all the blame, shame, and humiliation, toil, trial, and trouble, that it may be God's will to permit, in order to establish a home for homeless children. I protest that, in all that concerns it, I rely solely on the assistance of God and the guidance of the Holy Spirit. . . . [23]

[When she wrote this, she knew that her proposal for moving into work with poor children would provoke the archbishop's anger.] As Mother McKenna's resolution suggests, obedience was hardly passivity. . . . Her obedience to the spiritual authorities above was constructed in such a way to ready herself for the worldly battles to come.

And yet few even in the Catholic community understood fully what either Mother McKenna or other sisters did and thought on a regular basis. Indeed, the single most salient political limitation affecting sisters' overall power in nineteenth-century America was their relative lack of public voice. Whereas white, Protestant, middle-class women increasingly legitimated their claims to public power through a set of rational discourses promoting their cause as women or as mothers, nuns were reluctant to promote their causes through public discourse.

The effect of that limitation was both far-reaching and paradoxical. The most powerful women in the church, including the founder of the Foundling Asylum, Sister Irene Fitzgibbon, demanded that they be treated, and nuns under their guidance should treat themselves, as "old shoe[s]."[24] Consistent with an ethic of ascetic selflessness, Sister Irene's pronouncements should not lead historians to assume that these ostensible "old shoes" lacked substantial power. And yet their reluctance to claim that power as such, especially in public and to the larger community, proved decisive in public arenas in which the Catholic hierarchy or Protestant native-borns contested that power. Women religious were thus most vulnerable when discussion of themselves or their work moved to public arenas. Nor did this limitation affect only nuns. Because they were the female leaders in the Irish Catholic community, their unwillingness to spar publicly with Catholic men or Protestant native-borns made the relative power of Irish Catholic women as a group, and the causes they championed, similarly vulnerable to their posture of collective selflessness.

Part of the reason that nuns nave remained virtually invisible in nineteenth-century women's history is that the measures, or signposts, of their public power do not fit the framework constructed for understanding the public power of Protestant middle-class and elite women during the same period. Nuns' strengths were centered in areas of Protestant female reformers' relative weakness. Both white and black Protestant middle-class women derived public power through associational organizations and claims to public voice, especially through their role as mothers. Nuns' effectiveness, however, was based on an ability to live together and organize themselves as large bodies of single women who lived apart from marriage and domesticity. Convents became powerful collectives for activist labor through the sisterhoods' combined labor power in educational and welfare institutions, their centuries-long apprenticeship traditions and systems in nursing, teaching, and charities, their feme sole legal status and accumulation of wealth under exclusively female control, and their freedom from mothering and the direct controls of husbands. It was a form of public organization for welfare work, moreover, that most Protestant women were unable to construct until the turn of the twentieth century.

Indeed, if we concentrate on the spectacular growth of Catholic convents in America through the late nineteenth century, the dominant narrative of Protestant women's work in social reform through the Progressive Era begins to take new shape. Although histories of "women's" constructions of nursing, teaching, and social work rarely acknowledge the influence of Catholic female traditions in these areas, the roots of these "professions" are nonetheless everywhere entwined with the work of nuns. Settlement work in particular is deemed an extraordinary departure from all tradition in that it allowed Protestant women to live together, apart from marriage and within immigrant neighborhoods, and from that base construct charitable programs. The parallels to convent life are so obvious that the compelling question is not whether the convent served as a model for settlement life but why this parallel goes unanalyzed. That such a connection is not thought conspicuously absent is made possible primarily by our construction of frameworks that render nuns historically invisible.

. . . The limits and threats to nuns' power, . . . , were also often distinct from those that threatened Protestant women. Over the course of [the 19th century] nuns' relative power to men in their group was threatened most directly by the rationalization of bishops' authority over religious orders in their dioceses. That process of rationalization, however, was uneven. . . . A critical factor determining whether or for how long nuns could deflect male control . . . was their ability to gain financial independence from the hierarchy. [T]he public funding of nuns' charitable work helped orders delay substantial loss of autonomy until the early twentieth century.

NOTES

1. Throughout this work I refer to Catholic women in religious institutes as "women religious," "sisters," and "nuns," thereby reflecting common usage but not canon law, which stipulated that only enclosed women religious be referred to as nuns.

2. *New York Times*, Aug. 17, 1896, 6; *New York Herald Tribune*, Aug. 18, 1896.

3. Mary Ewens, *The Role of the Nun in Nineteenth-Century America* (1971, repr. Salem, N.H.: Ayer, 1984), 86, 201, 252; *The Catholic Almanac for 1848* (Baltimore: F. Lucas, Jr., 1849), 180–81; *Hoffmann's Catholic Directory, Almanac and Clergy List* (Milwaukee: Hoffmann Brothers, 1898), 98–104.

4. A sizable literature on the availability of this option nationwide makes evident that poor parents used a variety of institutions to rear children temporarily through the Gilded Age period. See especially Patricia Kelleher, "Maternal Strategies: Irish Women's Headship of Families in Gilded Age Chicago," *Journal of Women's History* 13 (Summer 2001): 80; Timothy Hasci, *Second Home: Orphan Asylums and Poor Families in America* (Cambridge: Harvard University Press, 1997); Matthew Crenson, *Building the Invisible Orphanage: A Prehistory of the American Welfare System* (Cambridge: Harvard University Press, 1998).

5. Among the literature on Catholic sisters that has been critical to my understanding of their collective and distinctive histories are Carol K. Coburn and Martha Smith, *Spirited Lives: How Nuns Shaped Catholic Culture and American Life, 1836–1920* (Chapel Hill: University of North Carolina Press, 1999); JoAnn Kay McNamara, *Sisters in Arms: Catholic Nuns through Two Millennia* (Cambridge: Harvard University Press, 1996); and Diane Batts Morrow, *Persons of Color and Religious at the Same Time: The Oblate Sisters of Providence, 1828–1860* (Chapel Hill: University of North Carolina Press, 2002).

6. Two sophisticated studies of Catholic charities have put the development of Catholic charities in a national context and in relation to the larger welfare system: Mary J. Oates, *The Catholic Philanthropic Tradition in America* (Bloomington: Indiana University Press, 1995), and Dorothy M. Brown and Elizabeth McKeown, *The Poor Belong to Us: Catholic Charities and American Welfare* (Cambridge: Harvard University Press, 1997).

7. Kerby A. Miller, *Emigrants and Exiles: Ireland and the Irish Exodus to North America* (New York: Oxford University Press, 1985), 21–23; William V. Shannon, *The American Irish* (New York: Collier Books, 1963), 21.

8. [Mother Mary Teresa] Austin Carroll, *Leaves from the Annals of the Sisters of Mercy*, 4 vols. (New York: Catholic Publication Society, 1889), 3: 203–13.

9. Caitriona Clear, *Nuns in Nineteenth-Century Ireland* (Dublin: Gill and MacMillan, 1987), 101–105.

10. Carroll, *Leaves from the Annals*, 3:207.

11. Ibid., 3:216.

12. Carol Wittke, *The Irish in America* (Baton Rouge: Louisiana State University Press, 1956), 89; James Olson, *Catholic Immigrants in America* (Chicago: Nelson-Hall, 1987), 29; Jay Dolan, *The Immigrant Church: New York's Irish and German Catholics, 1815–1865* (Baltimore: Johns Hopkins University Press, 1975), 22.

13. Preface to Maria Monk, *Awful Disclosures of the Hotel Dieu Nunnery* (1836, repr. Hamden: Archon Books, 1962), 1.

14. Applications for the Sisters of Mercy of New York, Archives of the Sisters of Mercy, Dobbs Ferry, N.Y. (hereafter ASMNY).

15. Rosemary Ruether, "Mothers of the Church: Ascetic Women in the Late Patristic Age," in *Women of Spirit: Female Leadership in the Jewish and Christian Traditions*, edited by Rosemary Ruether and Eleanor McLaughlin (New York: Simon and Schuster, 1979), 72.

16. K. H. Connell, *The Population of Ireland, 1750–1845* (New York: Oxford University Press, 1950); Robert Kennedy, *The Irish: Emigration, Marriage and Fertility* (Berkeley: University of California Press, 1973); Hasia Diner, *Erin's Daughters in America: Irish Immigrant Women in the Nineteenth Century* (Baltimore: Johns Hopkins University Press, 1983), 6–29.

17. Miller, *Emigrants and Exiles*, 346.

18. Sister Marie De Lourdes Walsh, *The Sisters of Charity of New York, 1809–1959*, 3 vols. (New York: Fordham University Press, 1960), 3:64–88.

19. Catherine E. Beecher to Sarah Buckingham Beecher, Aug. 20, 1843, reprinted in *The Limits of Sisterhood: The Beecher Sisters on Women's Rights and Woman's Sphere*, edited by Jeanne Boydston, Mary Kelley, and Anne Margolis (Chapel Hill: University of North Carolina Press, 1988), 110, 239–40.

20. "Notes from the Annals of St. Catherine's Convent of Mercy," 1878, ASMNY; *Acts of Chapter, St. Catherine Convent, Madison Avenue, New York*, ASMNY; "Work Schedules," ASMNY.

21. Carroll, *Leaves from the Annals*, 171–72.

22. For the range of elective practices by convents in the United States, see Ewens, *The Role of the Nun*, passim.

23. Mother Mary Augustine McKenna to other Sisters of Mercy, 1873, reprinted in Carroll, *Leaves from the Annals*, 209, 215.

24. Sister Francis Cecilia Conway, "Notes on Foundling," Archives of the Sisters of Charity of New York at Mount St. Vincent. Sister Francis Conway worked with Sister Irene at the Foundling from 1890 to 1896.

INTIMACY AND DISCIPLINING BODIES

SHARON BLOCK

Lines of Color, Sex, and Service: Sexual Coercion in the Early Republic

A long tradition of describing northern society as "free" and southern society as "slave" has had the unfortunate effect of making distinctions seem far more clear in retrospect than they were in experience. Manumission was gradual and grudging in parts of the North where significant numbers of people were held as property. In Massachusetts, New Hampshire, and Vermont, many enslaved took their freedom by walking away from owners or bringing successful freedom suits based on the civil rights promised by the new state constitutions. However, other jurisdictions passed gradual emancipation laws that paid more attention to slave owners' property rights than to human rights. For example, by the 1780 Pennsylvania statute, all enslaved persons living at the time remained in bondage; all children born in the future to enslaved women were declared free but had to serve their mother's owner until the age of twenty-eight. This confusing legal landscape meant that African-descended people experienced a mixture of statuses—enslaved, indentured, free—throughout the first half of the nineteenth century.

Moreover, parental poverty, itinerancy, or perceived idleness could trigger laws allowing local officials to take children and place them in other households as indentured workers. Thus, in the early republic, youths of black, Indian, and white parents were regularly put out to bound labor. Burdened by their work, they were also vulnerable to the power and authority of their masters. This included, as we see in the essay that follows, vulnerability to sexual coercion—a term Sharon Block uses to mark a wider range of experience than is suggested by the simple term *rape*.* The essay that follows is based on a close reading of a Pennsylvania court record and on one of the great autobiographies of the nineteenth century, Harriet Jacobs's *Incidents in the Life of a Slave Girl*. Writing under a pseudonym after years as a fugitive, supported in her project by the abolitionist writer and editor Lydia Maria Child, Jacobs herself became invisible to historians. For many years her narrative was treated as fiction. Not until 1987, when historian Jean Fagan Yellin published an edition identifying virtually all the individuals and substantiating virtually all the

*Sharon Block explains that first names are used for all actors in incidents of sexual coercion because first names more easily distinguish men from women and eliminate confusion in identifying members of the same family.

Excerpted from "Lines of Color, Sex, and Service: Comparative Sexual Coercion in Early America" by Sharon Block in *Sex, Love, Race: Crossing Boundaries in North American History*, ed. Martha Hodes (New York: New York University Press, 1999). Reprinted by permission of the author and publisher. Notes have been edited and renumbered.

events, has it been possible to understand the narrative as nonfiction. It is compelling reading.[†]

In what ways did Rachel Davis and Harriet Jacobs try to avoid the power of their masters? In whom did they find allies? In what ways were the experiences of these young women similar? What difference did slavery make?

Rachel Davis was born a free white child in the Pennsylvania mountains in 1790. She was fourteen years old when she became an indentured servant to William and Becky Cress in Philadelphia County. By the time Rachel was fifteen, William had begun making sexual overtures to her. After months of continuing sexual assaults, William's wife, Becky, suspected that her husband was having a sexual relationship with their servant. Ultimately, Becky demanded that Rachel be removed from the house. William continued to visit Rachel at her new home, again trying to have sex with her. In 1807, Rachel's father found out what had occurred and initiated a rape prosecution against William, who was found guilty and sentenced to ten years in prison.[1]

Harriet Jacobs was born an enslaved black child in Edenton, North Carolina, in 1813. In 1825, she became a slave in James and Mary Norcom's household. By the time Harriet was sixteen, James had begun making sexual overtures toward her. After months of continuing sexual assaults, James's wife, Mary, suspected that her husband was having a sexual relationship with their slave. Ultimately, Mary demanded that Harriet be removed from the house. James continued to visit Harriet at her new home, again trying to have sex with her. In 1835, Harriet became a runaway slave, and spent the next seven years a fugitive, hiding in her free grandmother's attic crawl space.[2]

If we were to focus on the conclusions to these stories, we would frame a picture of the contrasting consequences for masters who sexually coerced black and white women: the master of the white servant was sent to prison, while the black slave imprisoned herself to escape her abuser. But these opposing ends tell only part of the story. Until their conclusions, both women engaged in nearly parallel struggles with masters, mistresses, and unwanted sexual overtures. This contrast between the laborers' similar experiences and their stories' opposing conclusions suggests that the practice

of sexual coercion and the classification of the criminal act of rape were differently dependent on status and race.

... Rachel had an opportunity for institutional intervention that was unequivocally denied to Harriet. Enslaved women in early America did not have access to legal redress against white men who raped them. While no colonial or early republic statute explicitly excluded enslaved women from being the victims of rape or attempted rape, many mid-Atlantic and Southern legislatures set harsh punishments for black men's sexual assaults on white women, thus implicitly privileging white women as victims of rape.[3] At the same time, enslaved people could only be witnesses against non-white defendants, so an enslaved woman could not testify against a white man who had raped her.[4] Accordingly, no historian has recorded a conviction of a white man for the rape of a slave at any point from 1700 to the Civil War, let alone a conviction of a master for raping his own slave. Rape in early America was a crime whose definition was structured by race.[5]

Even though the early American legal system segregated Rachel Davis and Harriet Jacobs into incomparable categories, their own presentations told nearly parallel stories of sexual coercion. In both women's stories, their masters attempted to control the parameters and meanings of sexual acts. Thus, rape in these situations was not just an act of power, it was also the power to define an act. Servants and slaves could not only be forced to consent, but this force was refigured as consent. At the same time, neither Harriet Jacobs nor Rachel Davis presented herself as an abject victim of her master's will.

Rather than a clear demarcation between the rape of slaves and the rape of servants, these narratives suggest that black and white laboring women interpreted and experienced a master's sexual coercion in strikingly similar ways. The parallels in these two stories, however, stopped at the courtroom door, where a racially

---

[†]Harriet A. Jacobs, *Incidents in the Life of a Slave Girl: Written by Herself*, ed. Jean Fagan Yellin (Cambridge, Mass.: Harvard University Press, 1987). Jean Fagan Yellin, *Harriet Jacobs: A Life* (New York: Basic Civitas Books, 2004).

based legal system ended the women's comparable negotiations of personal interactions.

CREATING MASTERY: THE PROCESS OF COERCION

How did a master sexually coerce a servant or slave in early America? A master did not have to rely on physical abilities to force his dependents into a sexual act. Instead, he might use the power of his position to create opportunities for sexual coercion, backing a woman into a corner where capitulation was her best option. A servant or enslaved woman often recognized this manipulation and tried to negotiate her way around her master's overtures rather than confront him with direct resistance. But that compromise came at a high price ... negotiation implied willingness, and a woman's willingness contrasted with the early American legal and social code that rape consisted of irresistible force. Despite its surface counterintuitiveness, it was precisely women's attempts to bargain their way out of sexual assaults that made these sexual encounters seem consensual.[6]

Both Harriet Jacobs and Rachel Davis drew direct links between their status and their masters' sexual assaults on them. Each explained how her master had forced her into situations where he could sexually coerce her without being discovered. Rachel described how William ordered her to hold the lantern for him one night in the stable, where he "tried to persuade me to something." In the most blatantly contrived incident, when they were reaping in the meadow, William "handed me his sickle & bad me to lay it down. He saw where I put it." Later that night, William asked Rachel,

where I put them sickles. I asked if he did not see—he said no, I must come & show him. I told him I cd go with my sister, or by myself. he said that was not as he bad me. I went. Before we got quite to sickles, he bad me stop—I told him I was partly to the sickles—he bad me stop—I did—he came up & threw me down. . . . I hallowed—he put his hand over my mouth . . . he pulled up my cloathes, & got upon me . . . he did penetrate my body. I was dreadfully injured.

According to Rachel's statement, William had forced her to accompany him into a dark field on a contrived search for a purposefully lost farm implement so that he could rape her. William's authority to control where she went and what she did was integral to his ability to force Rachel to have sex with him.

Harriet Jacobs was even more explicit about the connections between James Norcum's mastery and his ability to force her into sexually vulnerable positions. It seemed to Harriet that he followed her everywhere—in her words, "my master met me at every turn"—trying to force her to have sex with him. As William did with Rachel, James structured Harriet's work so that she was often alone with him. He ordered Harriet to bring his meals to him so that while she watched him eat he could verbally torture her with the consequences of refusing his sexual overtures. Harriet further recalled that "when I succeeded in avoiding opportunities for him to talk to me at home, I was ordered to come to his office, to do some errand." Tiring of Harriet's continued resistance, James ordered his four-year-old daughter to sleep near him, thus requiring that Harriet also sleep in his room in case the child needed attention during the night. James repeatedly used his position as a master who controlled his slave's labor to manipulate Harriet into sexually vulnerable situations.[7] Controlling a woman's daily routine, her work requirements, and her physical presence—in other words, control over her labor and her body—gave men in positions of mastery access to a particular means of sexually coercive behavior.

Each woman also recalled how she had challenged her master's right to force her into a sexual relationship. Rachel recounted how she had "resisted" and "cried" when William tried to pull her into a darkened bedroom after sending the rest of the servants to bed, and how she threatened that she would tell his wife what he was doing. When these forms of resistance did not end his overtures, Rachel tried to carry out her master's orders in ways that might prevent her own sexual vulnerability. Rachel's description of being raped in the dark field began by recollecting that she had suggested that William could find the sickle himself, and then offered to find it on her own or with her sister. Ultimately, William resorted to his position as a master—"he said that was not as he bad me"—and issued a direct order for Rachel to accompany him. Rachel portrayed an interactive relationship with William: she may not have been able to override her master's orders, but she forced him to change their content. Rather than sex in the bedroom while the other children slept and his wife was away, Rachel forced William to order her into the dark field, thereby disrupting his original attempts at a seamless consensual interaction.

rape only a crime if the women was not black

Harriet Jacobs's story contained similar efforts to avoid her master's sexual overtures that forced him to refigure his behavior. When Mary Norcum's suspicions made her husband revert to physical gestures instead of words to convey his sexual desires to Harriet, Harriet responded by letting "them pass, as if I did not understand what he meant." When James realized that Harriet could read, he wrote her notes that expressed his sexual intentions. But Harriet repeatedly pretended "I can't read them, sir." Overall, "by managing to keep within sight of people, as much as possible during the day time, I had hitherto succeeded in eluding my master." Harriet forced James into baldly claiming his right for sexual access as a privilege of mastery: according to Harriet, James began constantly "reminding me that I belonged to him, and swearing by heaven and earth that he would compel me to submit to him" because "I was his property; that I must be subject to his will in all things." Like Rachel Davis, Harriet Jacobs engaged in an exchange of maneuvers with her master where each tried to foil the other's plans and counterplans. Despite her master's legal property in her body, Harriet did not portray herself as utterly powerless. By playing into his image of her as too stupid to understand his signs and too illiterate to read his notes, Harriet used her own position as a slave to avoid her master's sexual overtures, forcing him to raise the stakes of his desires toward her.[8]

Because he did not receive unquestioned acquiescence from a servant or slave, a master had to create situations in which his laborers had little choice but to have sexual relations with him. Rachel's attempted refusal to go alone into a dark field with her master and Harriet's feigned ignorance of her master's intentions forced each man to modify his route to sexual interactions. By not consenting to a master's more subtle attempts at sexual relations, a servant or slave might force her master into more overtly coerced sexual acts. Ironically, this compelled a master to enact his laborer's interpretation of his overtures. Rather than the sexual offers that the masters first proposed, the men were forced to use coercion to carry out their sexual plans. Theoretically, a master could coerce through his physical prowess, but most masters did not have to rely exclusively on fists or whips to commit rape. Instead, they could rely on the strength of their mastery.

Beyond the unadorned physical power that could compel a woman into a sexual act, a master had an array of indirect means to force a dependent to have sex with him that simultaneously denied her resistance to him. . . . Harriet characterized her master as "a crafty man, [who] resorted to many means to accomplish his purposes. Sometimes he had stormy, terrific ways, that made his victims tremble; sometimes he assumed a gentleness that he thought must surely subdue." James promised Harriet that if she would give in to him sexually, "I would cherish you. I would make a lady of you." The possibility of a better life that transcended her racial and labor status was more than a bribe to induce Harriet's consent. It created a fiction that Harriet could voluntarily choose to have sexual relations with her master. By switching between the threats of physical harm and the gifts of courtship, James undercut the appearance of a forced sexual interaction. By theoretically allowing space for Harriet's consent to his sexual overtures, James was redefining coercion into consensual sexual relations.[9]

Similarly, William's verbal narration of consensual relations overlay his forceful attempts at sex. While he had Rachel trapped underneath his body, William told her that "he wd have the good will of me." William's modification of the classic legal description of rape as a man having carnal knowledge of a woman "against her will" verbally created a consensual act even as he used force to have sexual relations.[10] In the same incident, William called Rachel by her family nickname, telling her, "Nate you dear creature, I must fuck you." Even while forcing Rachel to have sex with him, William used terms of endearment toward her. William's presentation of an affectionate and therefore consensual sexual relationship with Rachel differentiated his actions from the brutality that early Americans would most easily recognize as rape.

Thus, the process of master–servant and master–slave sexual coercion was not exclusively tied to racial boundaries. Harriet Jacobs's and Rachel Davis's similarly recounted experiences suggest that their sexual interactions were more directly shaped by lines of status and dependency. These patterns would be repeated as masters and their servants or slaves struggled to control public perceptions of what had occurred.

CREATING MASTER NARRATIVES: THE PROCESS OF PUBLICITY

Given these different versions of events, how did families, other household members, and communities interpret evidence of a possibly coercive sexual interaction? How did assaulted women portray what had happened to them? Harriet Jacobs's and Rachel Davis's narratives show that the process of publicizing a master's sexual overtures was again structured by the woman's position as his personally dependent laborer. Words—the power to speak them and the power to construct their meaning—became the prize in a struggle among masters, mistresses, and the assaulted servant or slave.

After attempting sexual overtures toward their laborers, masters had to contend with the possibility that the women would tell others about their masters' behavior. Harriet Jacobs's and Rachel Davis's masters attempted to threaten their laborers into silence about their sexual interactions. Harriet wrote that her master "swore he would kill me, if I was not as silent as the grave."[11] Similarly, William told Rachel that if she told "any body, he wd be the death of me." When Rachel threatened to tell his wife what William had been doing, "he sd if I did, I shd repent." By demanding her silence, each master tried to dictate the parameters of his sexual interactions with his servant or slave without outside interference that might contradict his interpretation or stop his sexual pursuit.

But both women also believed that their masters were afraid of the damage that they could do by publicizing their sexual behavior. Besides his threats of physical violence, William promised Rachel a "gown if she would not tell" what he had done, and on another occasion, "begged [Rachel] not to tell" her new mistress because "it wd be the Ruin of him." Harriet similarly believed that her master "did not wish to have his villainy made public." Instead, he "deemed it prudent to keep up some outward show of decency." From each woman's vantage point, then, her master's concern about his public image again allowed her some room for negotiation: he needed his servant or slave to conceal their sexual interactions. But by not telling anyone about her master's sexual assaults, a woman increased the likelihood that their sexual relationship would not appear to be a rape. This double-edged sword made the servant or slave an unwilling accomplice in the masking of her own sexual coercion.[12]

If pressuring his servant or slave into silence through bribes or threats did not silence her, a master might try to control her description of their sexual interaction. William Cress enacted an elaborate punishment scene that forced Rachel Davis to claim responsibility for anything that may have passed between them. After Rachel's complaints to her mistress prompted Mary to confront her husband about Rachel's allegations, William immediately challenged Rachel. "Well Rachael," William accused, "what are this you have been scraping up about me?," denying even in his question the possibility of his own misdeeds. When Rachel could not present a satisfactory answer, William employed the power of physical correction allowed to him as her master to reform her story. According to Rachel, he "whipt me dreadfully & he said . . . that he never had such a name before. . . . I fell down—he damned me, & bad me beg his pardon. I said I did not know how—he bad me go on my knees . . . he bad me go to house & tell" his wife that she (Rachel) had lied. By whipping Rachel, William attempted to disprove her story of sexual assault: his wife had said that if Rachel's assertions of sexual relations between herself and William "was lies" as William claimed, "he ought to whip" Rachel for her dishonesty. This whipping was not just a punishment unfairly inflicted, it was a punishment that retroactively attempted to define the sexual interactions between a servant and a master. Once subjugated, Rachel was required to deny that William had forced her to have sex with him. Rachel's younger sister, also a servant to William, believed this new version of events: she admitted that "I do remember D[efendant] whipping my sister—it was for telling so many lies." William was using his position as master to rewrite the sexual act that had taken place between them.

Rachel ended her description of this incident by stating that after William had beaten her, "he went to church that day & I showed my back to [my] Sister." Those final words on her master's brutal punishment (a whipping that prevented Rachel from lying on her side for three weeks) revealed the irony of the situation: while William continued to appear as a publicly reverent and virtuous patriarch, Rachel secretly bore the signs of his sins, visible only to those most intimate with her. In the process of sexual coercion, force did not have

↳ If it was made an issue than it was rape

a solely physical purpose: masters also used force to create an image of consent.

Harriet Jacobs also noted the discrepancy between her master's public image and private behavior, telling her readers how he had preserved his image at her expense. When Harriet's mistress confronted Harriet with suspicions of her husband's sexual improprieties, Harriet swore on a Bible that she had not had a sexual relationship with her master. When Mary questioned her husband, however, James contradicted Harriet's statements. And just like Rachel's mistress, Harriet's mistress "would gladly have had me flogged for my supposed false oath." But unlike William Cress, James Norcum did not allow Harriet to be whipped because "the old sinner was politic. The application of the lash might have led to remarks that would have exposed him"·to his family and community.[13]

In Rachel's and Harriet's narratives, their mistresses—the wives of their abusers—played important roles in the categorization of the sexually abusive relationship. Each woman had to deal with a mistress who ultimately took her displeasure at her husband's sexual relationship out on her servant or slave. Each mistress also used her position of secondary mastery to create a temporary alliance with her servant or slave. Once this alliance outlived its usefulness, it became another tool with which the mistress could assist in redefining or denying the sexual relationship between the master and the slave or servant.

In both women's stories, the masters' wives did not immediately take their hostility at their sexually aggressive husbands out on the objects of their husbands' overtures. When Rachel and William came back from retrieving the "lost" sickle, his wife, Becky, asked "where he had been—he said, after the sickles, with nate (so they called me in family) she sd it was very extraordinary, no body else could go." Perhaps Becky suspected some sort of sexual liaison between her husband and their servant, and her pointed questions let her husband know of her suspicions. When Becky heard William trying to kiss Rachel in the cellar, she "said she had caught him & he wd deceive her no longer," but William denied any wrongdoing and Becky left in tears. These verbal confrontations apparently did not alter William's behavior; he continued to force himself sexually upon Rachel. Finally, Rachel's mistress "saw something was the matter with

me, & asked what it was. I told her." After questioning her husband had little visible effect, Becky turned to Rachel to find out about her husband's actions. This temporary alliance brought Rachel some protection from William's retribution, if not from his sexual overtures: when William heard that Rachel had told another relative some of what he had done to her, "he whipt me again, but not so bad—his wife wd not let him & said, he was in Fault."

Similarly, Harriet Jacobs believed that her mistress suspected James's illicit behavior: "She watched her husband with unceasing vigilance; but he was well practised in means to evade it." After Mary heard that her husband planned to have Harriet sleep in his room, she began questioning Harriet, who told her how James had been sexually harassing her. Harriet claimed that Mary, like most slave mistresses "had no compassion for the poor victim of her husband's perfidy. She pitied herself as a martyr." But Harriet also admitted that Mary "spoke kindly, and promised to protect me," ordering Harriet to sleep with her, rather than with James. This protective kindness also allowed Mary to try to obtain the "truth" of Harriet and James's relationship out of Harriet while Harriet slept: "she whispered in my ear, as though it was her husband who was speaking to me, and listened to hear what I would answer." When Harriet did not provide any self-incriminating information, Mary confronted her husband, but Mary's interventions did not end James's sexual overtures toward Harriet.[14]

If mistresses could not personally control their husbands' behavior, how could they stop the sexual relationship between master and laborer that was making a mockery of their marital vows? Theoretically, mistresses could turn to the legal system to petition for a divorce from their husbands. By the early nineteenth century, most states had divorce laws that allowed wives to apply for divorce on the grounds of their husbands' adultery, but women's petitions for divorce were more commonly based on charges of desertion.[15] Furthermore, proving adultery with a slave might be difficult without firsthand witnesses to the sexual interactions, since the slave was limited in her ability to testify against the white man. Married women also had a vested interest in their husbands' social and economic standing. Divorce or incarceration would most probably result in a woman's economic downturn from the loss of her husband's labor.

Ultimately, Rachel Davis's and Harriet Jacobs's mistresses concentrated their energies on removing their laborers from the household. Instead of bringing charges against her husband or applying for a divorce on the grounds of adultery, Becky Cress told Rachel Davis that she must "leave the house." Rachel recalled that "they then hired me out." Rachel's mistress may have ultimately recognized that her husband was (at best) complicit in his sexual relations with Rachel, but she also recognized that she, as his wife, was in a poor position to mandate a reform in his behavior. She could, however, as a mistress, remove the more disposable partner in the sexual relationship, and so she ordered Rachel to leave their home. Whether or not Becky believed Rachel's story of rape, she did not hold Rachel entirely innocent of wrongdoing. At the very least, she spread blame equally between her servant and her husband, with much of the resulting punishment falling on the more vulnerable of the two parties. As Rachel stated, "Before I was hired out, [my mistress] used me very bad & said she would knowck me down if I came to table to eat." Because William was a master—both of Rachel and of his household—his wife could enact only limited direct retribution against him. [She could watch his behavior, confront him, and let him know her displeasure, but ultimately, it was easier to remove the object of his overtures than publicly to accuse him of wrongdoing.] *All the wife could do*

Mary Norcum demanded that Harriet Jacobs leave the house once she learned that Harriet was pregnant, believing that conception was proof of their slave's sexual relationship with her husband. Harriet was not the only slave who was reputed to have been kicked out of her house because of a sexual relationship with the master. Recalling a story told to her by her grandmother about another slave, Harriet wrote that "her mistress had that day seen her baby for the first time, and in the lineaments of its fair face she saw a likeness to her husband. She turned the bondswoman and her child out of doors, and forbade her ever to return." In both of these examples, the mistress felt herself in sexual competition with the slave—even if the slave were not a willing competitor for the master's affections.[16]

Thus, while a wife's place in the household hierarchy may have proscribed her options, it did not leave her entirely at her husband's mercy. By forcing her husband to prove his marital loyalty by whipping the laborer for telling untruths about his sexual conduct, each mistress tried to create her own version of household sexual alliances. When mistresses could not force husbands to modify their behavior, these wives turned to regulating their servant's or slave's actions: first, by using them as the source of incriminating information, and later, as a problem that could be eliminated. Mistresses would not permanently join forces with slave or servant women to overthrow the household patriarch; they might want to change their husbands' behavior, but these wives did not wish publicly to condemn or disassociate themselves from their husbands through divorce or other legal action. *couldn't blame husband, have to blame slave*

The silencing of sexual coercion was more profound in Harriet Jacobs's autobiography than it was in Rachel Davis's court-ordered testimony specifically about rape. Harriet's representation of her conflict with her master centered on the power to create a singular version of reality through the privilege of public speech. Throughout her narrative, Harriet insisted that her master sexually assaulted her only with words, never with his body. She wrote that he "tried his utmost to corrupt the pure principles my grandmother had instilled. He peopled my mind with unclean images." Harriet silenced her own description of her master's actions by calling the sexual degradation of slavery "more than I can describe." Harriet's versions of her master's verbal actions may have stood in for the literally unspeakable physical sexual abuse she suffered at his hands. By describing only James's speech, Harriet turned his possibly physical assaults on her into verbal assaults that no reader could expect her to control.[17]

In a personal letter written a few years before the publication of *Incidents in the Life of a Slave Girl* in 1861, Harriet hinted that she had indeed concealed the extent of James's actions. While she had tried to give a "true and just" account of her life in slavery, she admitted that "there are somethings I might have made plainer I know—Woman can whisper—her cruel wrongs into the ear of a very dear friend—much easier than she can record them for the world to read." In this passage, Jacobs drew a distinction between the private version of her pain and the version she chose to present for

Didn't want to write about being abused → embarassment

public consumption. Victorian womanhood's emphasis on modesty and respectability as well as the established genre of sexual euphemism popularized in sentimental novels probably encouraged Harriet Jacobs to present a sanitized version of her master's assaults on her. But her decision may also have reflected a personal need to distance herself from painful events, and a difficulty in telling others about her suffering that was shared by other victims—black and white—of a master's sexual harassment.[18]

Both Harriet and Rachel first told those closest to them about their masters' unwelcome sexual overtures. Harriet originally hesitated to tell Molly Horniblow, her grandmother and closest living relative, how James was treating her. Harriet "would have given the world to have laid my head on my grandmother's faithful bosom, and told her all my troubles," but James's threats and her own fear of her grandmother's reaction made her stay silent. When Harriet eventually did talk to her grandmother, she told her only some of her difficulties: "I talked with my grandmother about it, and partly told her my fears. I did not dare to tell her the worst." Harriet also told her uncle about some of her suffering. He told another relative that "you don't know what a life they lead her. She has told me something about it, and I wish [her master] was dead, or a better man." Harriet's recollection of interactions with her grandmother and her uncle emphasized that neither relative knew the entire story of her master's abuses. Just as the reader was given a sanitized version in the public transcript of Harriet's life, her hesitancy to confess the full extent of sexual coercion was reiterated in Harriet's personal interactions. Her inability to confess "the worst" of her experiences may have maintained Harriet's image of sexual purity and self-identity, but it was at the cost of denying the full spectrum of her master's assaults on her.[19]

Similarly, Rachel eventually told people close to her—one of her sisters (a servant in another household), her aunt, and her new mistress—about what William was doing to her. She recounted that she was hesitant to tell the whole story even to them. Rachel told her new mistress "something of what passed in the meadow, but not the worst of it. I told my sister Becky . . . the whole of it." Like Harriet's claim that it was easier to tell a close friend than to proclaim one's victimization publicly, Rachel had an easier time confessing her problems to her sister than to her new mistress. When Rachel spoke with her aunt, Elizabeth

Ashton, she again refrained from disclosing the full extent of William's coercion. Elizabeth told the court that Rachel had explained how William had isolated her in the cellar, had told her to go to bed with him when his wife was away, had cornered her in the barn, and had forced her to go with him to retrieve the sickle in the meadow. But Rachel stopped short of telling her aunt that William had succeeded in raping her, that his manipulative maneuvers had led to forced sexual intercourse. Elizabeth specified under cross-examination that "*I did not understand from her that he had fully effected his purpose in the meadow.*"[20] By minimizing the extent of her master's abuse of her, Rachel created a public version of her master's actions that denied that she had been raped.

The victims of sexual coercion were not the only people who purposefully avoided discussions of sexual assaults. Elizabeth Ashton did not know that William had raped Rachel partly because, as she told the court, "I did not enquire whether he obtained his will in the meadow." When Rachel's sister told her own mistress that "Mr Cress wanted to be gret [great] with her sister Rachael," the mistress replied, "I wanted to hear no more." When this sister eventually told their father what had happened, Jacob Davis recalled that she "did not tell me directly, she did not tell me the worst—I did not think it was so bad." A voluntary conspiracy of silence—from the servant who had difficulty discussing what had happened, to the other women who wanted neither to hear nor tell the full extent of William's abuse of Rachel—worked to deny the sexual coercion that William committed on his servant.

Similarly, Harriet Jacobs's fellow slaves were hesitant to volunteer verbal or physical assistance. Harriet believed that while her friends and relatives knew that she was being sexually abused, they were unable to speak of it. Harriet recalled that "the other slaves in my master's house noticed" her changed behavior as a result of her master's treatment, but "none dared to ask the cause. . . . They knew too well the guilty practices under that roof; and they were aware that to speak of them was an offence that never went unpunished." Harriet's fellow slaves' silence, necessary for their own self-preservation, limited their ability to help Harriet resist their master's overtures. By controlling potential allies, a master enmeshed his original acts of sexual coercion in an ever-widening coercive web that structured his victim's possibilities for support or redress.[21]

By not telling others what had happened to her, Harriet was at the mercy of other people's versions of events. James's wife, Mary, went to the house of Harriet's free grandmother to tell her that Harriet was pregnant with James's baby. Molly Horniblow then turned on Harriet, apparently believing Mary's story that Harriet had consented to the relationship: "I had rather see you dead than to see you as you now are," she told her granddaughter. "You are a disgrace to your dead mother. . . . Go away . . . and never come to my house, again." Because Harriet had consistently denied or downplayed her master's sexual attempts on her, her grandmother believed Mary's story that Harriet had voluntarily had sexual relations with James. Later, Harriet's grandmother learned that Harriet had chosen to become pregnant with another man's baby to try to force her sexually abusive master to leave her alone or sell her. Once her grandmother understood "the real state of the case, and all I had been bearing for years. . . . She laid her old hand gently on my head, and murmured, 'Poor child! Poor child!'" Harriet's inability to speak about her master's sexual coercion temporarily isolated Harriet from the woman who was most able to support her. When Harriet ultimately received her grandmother's forgiveness, she also gained an ally in her fight against her master's sexual demands.[22]

Both Harriet and Rachel believed that an independently powerful figure outside of the household could counterbalance their masters' attempts at dominance. When Rachel's aunt questioned "why she did not go to a Squire to complain" about her master's sexual assaults, Rachel replied "she did not dare—she a bound girl & her father absent." After telling her sister what had happened, her sister "advised her to stay there & be a good girl. . . . I thought nothing could be done, as my father was away." Rachel herself told the court that "I did not know if I went to a Justice, he wd take notice of it. Enough people knew it, but waited till my Father came back." Without a patriarchal figure beside her, Rachel would not directly confront her master, and did not believe herself entitled to legal justice, a belief encouraged (or at least not contradicted) by the women in whom she confided. For Rachel, her father's support was crucial to her ability to receive public redress for her master's sexual assaults on her.

Enslaved women ordinarily did not have access to the protection offered by a patriarchal figure. Harriet Jacobs observed that enslaved men "strive to protect wives and daughters from the insults of their masters. . . . [but] Some poor creatures have been so brutalized by the lash that they will sneak out of the way to give their masters free access to their wives and daughters." Although Harriet Jacobs did not have a waiting patriarchal figure to whom she could turn for protection, supporters outside of the household were still crucial to her limited redress. Harriet repeatedly spoke of her free grandmother's respect in the community, of how James "dreaded" this woman's "scorching rebuke," so that "her presence in the neighborhood was some protection to me." Ultimately, her grandmother's home became a partial refuge from James's pursuit. Harriet also spoke of her white lover's assistance in combating her master's "persecutions" of her through his "wish to aid me." Harriet partly justified her decision to have sexual relations with this man (pseudonymously referred to as "Mr. Sands") because she was "sure my friend, Mr. Sands, would buy me . . . and I thought my freedom could be easily obtained from him." While Harriet could not hope for institutional retribution against her master, she could hope that her new lover would help provide freedom from her master.[23]

Both Harriet Jacobs and Rachel Davis fought similar battles against the veil of silence surrounding their masters' treatment of them. Both were confronted by relatives and neighbors who had limited authority over another household's problems. Both women turned to another powerful figure—father or free grandmother and elite white lover, respectively—to rescue them from their masters' sexual abuse. When Rachel finally told her father about her master's sexual assaults, Jacob Davis successfully encouraged the local legal system to begin a criminal prosecution. But neither Harriet Jacobs's ultimate confession to her grandmother nor her involvement with a white lover could lead to legal intervention. The legal system marked an irreversible disjuncture in the two women's experiences.

EPILOGUE: CREATING RAPE: THE LEGAL PROCESS

Following the process of sexual coercion has led us back to this essay's opening, as Harriet Jacobs's and Rachel Davis's parallel stories reach diametrically opposed conclusions: while Rachel's master was convicted of rape and served a substantial jail sentence, there is no evidence that Harriet's master was ever subject to legal repercussions for his behavior. When a master tried to define coercive sex as consensual sex, both servants and slaves could negotiate with his terms and battle against his actions. But when the legal system defined enslaved women outside the judicial parameters of rape, there was little room for negotiation. The parallels in Harriet Jacobs's and Rachel Davis's stories ended with the legal distinction of criminal behavior. Rachel Davis may not have had easy access to criminal justice—her master was convicted of rape several years after he had first assaulted her. Yet she ultimately received legal protections that were denied to Harriet Jacobs.

We need to understand not only the legal history of rape, but the social history of sexual coercion. By taking seriously the possibility that white and black women in early America could have some experiences in common, we can begin to reassemble the complicated interactions of race, gender, and social and economic status in American history. Certainly the comparative possibilities are not exhausted with these two stories. Historians could compare the sexual experiences of free and enslaved African American women or white and black free servants. Were similar strategies used outside of households, in any relationship between a powerful man and a less powerful woman? In all of these comparisons, we should think carefully about how sex was coerced and how the crime of rape was defined. If we frame our investigations using solely the legal judgment of rape, we not only miss much of the story, we again replace women's experiences—much as their coercers had tried to do—with external categorizations. Instead, by interrogating the multiple and contested meanings of sexual coercion, we can better understand the historical relationships of social and sexual power.

NOTES

1. "Commonwealth v. William Cress, Feb. 1808," Pennsylvania Court Papers, 1807–1809, Historical Society of Pennsylvania, Philadelphia, Pa. Unless otherwise noted, all quotations regarding Rachel Davis are from these documents. For the criminal prosecution of William Cress, see "Commonwealth v. William Cress, Philadelphia, Feb. 15, 1808," Pennsylvania Oyer and Terminer Docket, 1778–1827, 261, 262, 263, 265, Pennsylvania Historic and Museum Commission, Harrisburg, Pa.

2. Harriet Jacobs, *Incidents in the Life of a Slave Girl Written by Herself*, ed. Jean Fagan Yellin (1861; reprint, Cambridge, Mass.: Harvard University Press, 1987).

3. For examples of statutes specifying the crime of black-on-white rape, see John D. Cushing, ed., *The Earliest Printed Laws of Pennsylvania, 1681–1713* (Wilmington, Del.: Michael Glazier, 1978), 69; B. W. Leigh, ed., *The Revised Code of the Laws of Virginia* (n.p., 1819), 585–86. See also Peter Bardalgio, "Rape and the Law in the Old South: 'Calculated to Excite Indignation in Every Heart,'" *Journal of Southern History* 60 (1994): 756–58.

4. See Thomas D. Morris, "Slaves and the Rules of Evidence in Criminal Trials," *Chicago-Kent Law Review* 68 (1993): 1209–39.

5. For further discussion of the cultural definitions of rape in early America, see Sharon Block, *Rape and Sexual Power in Early America* (Chapel Hill: Omohundro Institute of Early American History and Culture with University of North Carolina Press, 2006).

6. Much of the following discussion about resistance's reformulation into consent was inspired by Ellen Rooney, "'A Little More than Persuading': Tess and the Subject of Sexual Violence," in *Rape and Representation*, eds. Lynn A. Higgins and Brenda R. Silver (New York: Columbia University Press, 1991), 87–114, and the fictional exploration of twentieth-century household sexual coercion in J. M. Redmann's three-book series culminating in *The Intersection of Law and Desire* (New York: W. W. Norton, 1995).

7. Jacobs, *Incidents*, 27, 28, 31–32. See also p. 41.

8. Ibid., 27, 28, 31, 32.

9. Ibid., 27, 35.

10. Italics added.

11. Jacobs, *Incidents*, 28. See also 32.

12. Ibid., 29.

13. Ibid., 34, 35.

14. Ibid., 31, 33, 34.

15. On divorce in the antebellum South, see Jane Turner Censer, "'Smiling Through Her Tears': Antebellum Southern Women and Divorce," *American Journal of Legal History* 25 (1981): 24–47; for Pennsylvania, see Merril D. Smith, *Breaking the Bonds: Marital Discord in Pennsylvania, 1730–1830* (New York: New York University Press, 1991); Thomas Meehan, "'Not Made out of Levity': Evolution of Divorce in Early Pennsylvania," *Pennsylvania Magazine of History and Biography* 92 (1968): 441–64.

16. Jacobs, Incidents, 59, 122.

17. Ibid., 27–28.

18. Harriet Jacobs to Amy Post, June 21, 1857, in Jacobs, *Incidents*, 242. For a discussion of African American women's psychological reactions to systemic sexual exploitation, see Darlene Clark Hine, "Rape and the Inner Lives of Black Women in the Middle West: Preliminary Thoughts on the Culture of Dissemblance," *Signs* 14 (1989), 265–277.

19. Jacobs, *Incidents*, 25, 28, 38.

20. Underlining in original.

21. Jacobs, *Incidents*, 28.

22. Ibid., 56, 57.

23. Ibid., 29, 54–55.

annotate

CARROLL SMITH-ROSENBERG
The Female World of Love and Ritual: Relations between Women in Nineteenth-Century America

arroll Smith-Rosenberg's close reading of middle-class girls' and women's diaries and letters to explore the nature of their intense friendships represented a radically new approach when it was published in 1975. It was pioneering in several areas of inquiry that have since become familiar—not just women's and gender history, but the histories of sexuality, family life, and emotions. Note that the essay was published in the pathbreaking, multidisciplinary, community-building women's studies journal *Signs*—and as the opening article in its first issue. As you read it, think about why the essay would have been disconcerting and challenging to many, if not most, members of the historical profession in the 1970s.

The author's work reflected the reinvigorated practices of women's history in the early 1970s, part of the transformation of scholarship and academia wrought by second-wave feminism. But new historical research on gender and sexuality took years to reach publication and constitute a critical mass. College teachers compiling syllabi for courses on women's history coped with a dramatic scarcity of secondary material that they could assign. Unlike the rich resources at our fingertips today, there were no women's history textbooks, syntheses, journals, or websites to consult.

Today, Smith-Rosenberg's nuanced analysis remains a touchstone for scholars' continuing investigation and vigorous debate on the historical existence and meanings of women's same-sex friendships, partnerships, and loves globally.*

The female friendship of the nineteenth century, the long-lived, intimate, loving friendship between two women, is an excellent example of the type of historical phenomena which most historians know something about, which few have thought much about, and which virtually no one has written about.[1] It is one aspect of the female experience which consciously or unconsciously we have chosen to ignore. Yet an abundance of manuscript evidence suggests that eighteenth- and nineteenth-century women routinely formed emotional ties with other women. Such deeply felt, same-sex friendships were casually accepted in American society. Indeed, from at least the late eighteenth through the mid-nineteenth century, a female world of varied and yet highly structured relationships appears to have been an essential aspect of American society. These relationships ranged from the supportive love of sisters, through the

---

*Leila Rupp, *Sapphistries: A Global History of Love between Women* (New York: New York University Press, 2009; Judith M. Bennett, "'Lesbian-like' and the Social History of Lesbianisms," *Journal of the History of Sexuality* 9 (2000): 1–24. For another pioneering integration of sexuality and social history, see Blanche Wiesen Cook, "Female Support Networks and Political Activism: Lillian Wald, Crystal Eastman, Emma Goldman," *Chrysalis* 3 (1977): 43–61.

enthusiasms of adolescent girls, to sensual avowals of love by mature women. It was a world in which men made but a shadowy appearance.[2] . . .

. . . Intimate friendships between men and men and women and women existed in a larger world of social relations and social values. To interpret such friendships more fully they must be related to the structure of the American family and to the nature of sex-role divisions and of male-female relations both within the family and in society generally. . . . The ties between mothers and daughters, sisters, female cousins and friends, at all stages of the female life cycle constitute the most suggestive framework for the historian to begin an analysis of intimacy and affection between women. Such an analysis would emphasize general cultural patterns rather than the internal dynamics of a particular family or childhood. . . .

This analysis . . . [is] based upon the correspondence and diaries of women and men in thirty-five families between the 1760s and the 1880s. These families, though limited in number, represented a broad range of the American middle class, from hard-pressed pioneer families and orphaned girls to daughters of the intellectual and social elite. It includes families from most geographic regions, rural and urban, and a spectrum of Protestant denominations ranging from Mormon to orthodox Quaker. Although scarcely a comprehensive sample of America's increasingly heterogeneous population, it does, I believe, reflect accurately the literate middle class to which the historian working with letters and diaries is necessarily bound. It has involved an analysis of many thousands of letters written to women friends, kin, husbands, brothers, and children at every period of life from adolescence to old age. Some collections encompass virtually entire life spans; one contains over 100,000 letters as well as diaries and account books. It is my contention that an analysis of women's private letters and diaries which were never intended to be published permits the historian to explore a very private world of emotional realities central both to women's lives and to the middle-class family in nineteenth-century America.[3]

The question of female friendships is peculiarly elusive; we know so little or perhaps have forgotten so much. . . . Before attempting to reconstruct their social setting, therefore, it might be best first to describe two not atypical

friendships. These two friendships, intense, loving, and openly avowed, began during the women's adolescence and, despite subsequent marriages and geographic separation, continued throughout their lives. For nearly half a century these women played a central emotional role in each other's lives, writing time and again of their love and of the pain of separation. Paradoxically to twentieth-century minds, their love appears to have been both sensual and platonic.

Sarah Butler Wister first met Jeannie Field Musgrove while vacationing with her family at Stockbridge, Massachusetts, in the summer of 1849. Jeannie was then sixteen, Sarah fourteen. During two subsequent years spent together in boarding school, they formed a deep and intimate friendship. Sarah began to keep a bouquet of flowers before Jeannie's portrait and wrote complaining of the intensity and anguish of her affection. Both young women assumed nom de plumes, Jeannie a female name, Sarah a male one; they would use these secret names into old age. They frequently commented on the nature of their affection: "If the day should come," Sarah wrote Jeannie in the spring of 1861, "when you failed me either through your fault or my own, I would forswear all human friendship, thenceforth." A few months later Jeannie commented: "Gratitude is a word I should never use toward you. It is perhaps a misfortune of such intimacy and love that it makes one regard all kindness as a matter of course, as one has always found it, as natural as the embrace in meeting."[4]

Sarah's marriage altered neither the frequency of their correspondence nor their desire to be together. In 1864, when twenty-nine, married, and a mother, Sarah wrote to Jeannie: "I shall be entirely alone [this coming week]. I can give you no idea how desperately I shall want you. . . ." After one such visit Jeannie, then a spinster in New York, echoed Sarah's longing: "Dear darling Sarah! How I love you & how happy I have been! You are the joy of my life. . . . I cannot tell you how much happiness you gave me, nor how constantly it is all in my thoughts. . . . My darling how I long for the time when I shall see you. . . ." After another visit Jeannie wrote: "I want you to tell me in your next letter, to assure me, that I am your dearest. . . . I do not doubt you, & I am not jealous but I long to hear you say it once more & it seems already a long time since your voice fell on my ear. So just fill a quarter page with caresses & expressions of endearment. Your silly Angelina." Jeannie ended one letter: "Goodbye my dearest, dearest lover—ever your own Angelina." And another, "I will go to bed . . . [though] I could write all night—A thousand kisses—I love you with my whole soul—your Angelina."

When Jeannie finally married in 1870 at the age of thirty-seven, Sarah underwent a period of extreme anxiety. Two days before Jeannie's marriage Sarah, then in London, wrote desperately: "Dearest darling—How incessantly have I thought of you these eight days—all today—the entire uncertainty, the distance, the long silence—are all new features in my separation from you, grevious to be borne. . . . Oh Jeannie. I have thought & thought & yearned over you these two days. Are you married I wonder? My dearest love to you wherever and whoever you are." Like many other women in this collection of thirty-five families, marriage brought Sarah and Jeannie physical separation; it did not cause emotional distance. Although at first they may have wondered how marriage would affect their relationship, their affection remained unabated throughout their lives, underscored by their loneliness and their desire to be together.[5]

During the same years that Jeannie and Sarah wrote of their love and need for each other, two slightly younger women began a similar odyssey of love, dependence and—ultimately—physical, though not emotional, separation. Molly and Helena met in 1868 while both attended the Cooper Institute School of Design for Women in New York City. For several years these young women studied and explored the city together, visited each other's families, and formed part of a social network of other artistic young women. Gradually, over the years, their initial friendship deepened into a close intimate bond which continued throughout their lives. The tone in the letters which Molly wrote to Helena changed over these years from "My dear Helena," and signed "your attached friend," to "My dearest Helena," "My Dearest," "My Beloved," and signed "Thine always" or "thine Molly."[6]

The letters they wrote to each other during these first five years permit us to reconstruct something of their relationship together. As Molly wrote in one early letter:

> I have not said to you in so many or so few words that I was happy with you during those few so incredibly short weeks but surely you do not need words to tell you what you must know. Those two or three days so dark without, so bright with firelight and contentment within I shall always remember as proof that, for a time, at least—I fancy for quite a long time—we might be sufficient for each other. We know that we can amuse each other for many idle hours together and now we know that we can also work together. And that means much, don't you think so?

She ended: "I shall return in a few days. Imagine yourself kissed many times by one who loved you so dearly."

The intensity and even physical nature of Molly's love was echoed in many of the letters she wrote during the next few years, as, for instance in this short thank-you note for a small present: "Imagine yourself kissed a dozen times my darling. Perhaps it is well for you that we are far apart. You might find my thanks so expressed rather overpowering. I have that delightful feeling that it doesn't matter much what I say or how I say it, since we shall meet so soon and forget in that moment that we were ever separated. . . . I shall see you soon and be content."[7]

At the end of the fifth year, however, several crises occurred. The relationship, at least in its intense form, ended, though Molly and Helena continued an intimate and complex relationship for the next half-century. The exact nature of these crises is not completely clear, but it seems to have involved Molly's decision not to live with Helena, as they had originally planned, but to remain at home because of parental insistence. Molly was now in her late twenties. Helena responded with anger and Molly became frantic at the thought that Helena would break off their relationship. Though she wrote distraught letters and made despairing attempts to see Helena, the relationship never regained its former ardor—possibly because Molly had a male suitor. Within six months Helena had decided to marry a man who was, coincidentally, Molly's friend and publisher. Two years later Molly herself finally married. The letters toward the end of this period discuss the transition both women made to having male lovers—Molly spending much time reassuring Helena, who seemed depressed about the end of their relationship and with her forthcoming marriage.[8]

It is clearly difficult from a distance of 100 years and from a post-Freudian cultural perspective to decipher the complexities of Molly and Helena's relationship. Certainly Molly and

Helena were lovers—emotionally if not physically. The emotional intensity and pathos of their love becomes apparent in several letters Molly wrote Helena during their crisis: "I wanted so to put my arms round my girl of all the girls in the world and tell her . . . I love her as wives do love their husbands, as *friends* who have taken each other for life—and believe in her, as I believe in my God. . . . If I didn't love you do you suppose I'd care about anything or have ridiculous notions and panics and behave like an old fool who ought to know better. I'm going to hang on to your skirts. . . . You can't get away from [my] love." Or as she wrote after Helena's decision to marry: "You know dear Helena, I really was in love with you. It was a passion such as I had never known until I saw you. I don't think it was the noblest way to love you." The theme of intense female love was one Molly again expressed in a letter she wrote to the man Helena was to marry: "Do you know sir, that until you came along I believe that she loved me almost as girls love their lovers. *I know I loved her so.* Don't you wonder that I can stand the sight of you." This was in a letter congratulating them on their forthcoming marriage.[9]

The essential question is not whether these women had genital contact and can therefore be defined as heterosexual or homosexual. The twentieth-century tendency to view human love and sexuality within a dichotomized universe of deviance and normality, genitality and platonic love, is alien to the emotions and attitudes of the nineteenth century and fundamentally distorts the nature of these women's emotional interaction. These letters are significant because they force us to place such female love in a particular historical context. There is every indication that these four women, their husbands and families—all eminently respectable and socially conservative—considered such love both socially acceptable and fully compatible with heterosexual marriage. Emotionally and cognitively, their heterosocial and their homosocial worlds were complementary.

One could argue, on the other hand, that these letters were but an example of the romantic rhetoric with which the nineteenth century surrounded the concept of friendship. Yet they possess an emotional intensity and a sensual and physical explicitness that is difficult to dismiss. Jeannie longed to hold Sarah in her arms; Molly mourned her physical isolation from Helena. Molly's love and devotion to Helena, the emotions that bound Jeannie and Sarah together, while perhaps a phenomenon of nineteenth-century society, were not the less real for their Victorian origins. A survey of the correspondence and diaries of eighteenth- and nineteenth-century women indicates that Molly, Jeannie, and Sarah represented one very real behavioral and emotional option socially available to nineteenth-century women.

This is not to argue that individual needs, personalities, and family dynamics did not have a significant role in determining the nature of particular relationships. But the scholar must ask if it is historically possible and, if possible, important, to study the intensely individual aspects of psychosexual dynamics. Is it not the historian's first task to explore the social structure and the worldview which made intense and sometimes sensual female love both a possible and an acceptable emotional option? From such a social perspective a new and quite different series of questions suggests itself. What emotional function did such female love serve? What was its place within the hetero- and homosocial worlds which women jointly inhabited? Did a spectrum of love-object choices exist in the nineteenth century across which some individuals, at least, were capable of moving? Without attempting to answer these questions it will be difficult to understand either nineteenth-century sexuality or the nineteenth-century family.

Several factors in American society between the mid-eighteenth and the mid-nineteenth centuries may well have permitted women to form a variety of close emotional relationships with other women. American society was characterized in large part by rigid gender-role differentiation within the family and within society as a whole, leading to the emotional segregation of women and men. The roles of daughter and mother shaded imperceptibly and ineluctably into each other, while the biological realities of frequent pregnancies, childbirth, nursing, and menopause bound women together in physical and emotional intimacy. It was within just such a social framework, I would argue, that a specifically female world did indeed develop, a world built around a generic and unself-conscious pattern of single-sex or homosocial networks. These supportive networks were institutionalized in social conventions or rituals which accompanied virtually every important event in a woman's life, from birth to death. Such female relationships were frequently supported and paralleled by severe social restrictions on intimacy between young men and women. Within such a world of emotional richness and complexity devotion to and love of other women became a plausible and socially accepted form of human interaction.

An abundance of printed and manuscript sources exists to support such a hypothesis. Etiquette books, advice books on child rearing, religious sermons, guides to young men and young women, medical texts, and school curricula all suggest that late eighteenth- and most nineteenth-century Americans assumed the existence of a world composed of distinctly male and female spheres, spheres determined by the immutable laws of God and nature.[10] The unpublished letters and diaries of Americans during this same period concur, detailing the existence of sexually segregated worlds inhabited by human beings with different values, expectations, and personalities. Contacts between men and women frequently partook of a formality and stiffness quite alien to twentieth-century America and which today we tend to define as "Victorian." Women, however, did not form an isolated and oppressed subcategory in male society. Their letters and diaries indicate that women's sphere had an essential integrity and dignity that grew out of women's shared experiences and mutual affection and that, despite the profound changes which affected American social structure and institutions between the 1760s and the 1870s, retained a constancy and predictability. The ways in which women thought of and interacted with each other remained unchanged. Continuity, not discontinuity, characterized this female world. Molly Hallock's and Jeannie Field's words, emotions, and experiences have direct parallels in the 1760s and the 1790s. There are indications in contemporary sociological and psychological literature that female closeness and support networks have continued into the twentieth century—not only among ethnic and working-class groups but even among the middle class.[11]

Most eighteenth- and nineteenth-century women lived within a world bounded by home, church, and the institution of visiting—that endless trooping of women to each other's homes for social purposes. It was a world inhabited by children and by other women. Women helped each other with domestic chores and in times of sickness, sorrow, or trouble. Entire days, even weeks, might be spent almost exclusively with other women. Urban and town women could devote virtually every day to visits, teas, or shopping trips with other women. Rural women developed a pattern of more extended visits that lasted weeks and sometimes months, at times even dislodging husbands from their beds and bedrooms so that dear friends might spend every hour of every day together. When husbands traveled, wives routinely moved in with other women, invited women friends to teas and suppers, sat together sharing and comparing the letters they had received from other close women friends. Secrets were exchanged and cherished, and the husband's return at times viewed with some ambivalence.[12]

Summer vacations were frequently organized to permit old friends to meet at water spas or share a country home. In 1848, for example, a young matron wrote cheerfully to her husband about the delightful time she was having with five close women friends whom she had invited to spend the summer with her; he remained at home alone to face the heat of Philadelphia and a cholera epidemic. Some ninety years earlier, two young Quaker girls commented upon the vacation their aunt had taken alone with another woman; their remarks were openly envious and tell us something of the emotional quality of these friendships: "I hear Aunt is gone with the Friend and wont be back for two weeks, fine times indeed I think the old friends had, taking their pleasure about the country . . . and have the advantage of that fine woman's conversation and instruction, while we poor young girls must spend all spring at home. . . . What a disappointment that we are not together. . . ."[13]

Friends did not form isolated dyads but were normally part of highly integrated networks. Knowing each other, perhaps related to each other, they played a central role in holding communities and kin systems together. Especially when families became geographically mobile women's long visits to each other and their frequent letters filled with discussions of marriages and births, illness and deaths, descriptions of growing children, and reminiscences of times and people past provided an important sense of continuity in a rapidly changing society.[14] Central to this female world was an inner core of kin. The ties between sisters, first cousins, aunts, and nieces provided the underlying structure upon which groups of friends and their network of female relatives clustered. Although most of the women within this sample would appear to be living within isolated nuclear families, the emotional ties between nonresidential kin were deep and binding and provided one of the fundamental existential realities of women's lives. Twenty years after Parke Lewis Butler moved with her husband to Louisiana, she sent her two daughters back to Virginia to attend school, live with their grandmother and aunt, and be integrated back into Virginia society. The constant letters between Maria Inskeep and Fanny Hampton, sisters separated in their early twenties when Maria moved with her husband from New Jersey to Louisiana, held their families together, making it possible for their daughters to feel a part of their cousins' network of friends and interests. The Ripley daughters, growing up in western Massachusetts in the early 1800s, spent months each year with their mother's sister and her family in distant Boston; these female cousins and their network of friends exchanged gossip-filled letters and gradually formed deeply loving and dependent ties.[15]

Women frequently spent their days within the social confines of such extended families. Sisters-in-law visited each other and, in some families, seemed to spend more time with each other than with their husbands. First cousins cared for each other's babies—for weeks or even months in times of sickness or childbirth. Sisters helped each other with housework, shopped and sewed for each other. Geographic separation was borne with difficulty. A sister's absence for even a week or two could cause loneliness and depression and would be bridged by frequent letters. Sibling rivalry was hardly unknown, but with separation or illness the theme of deep affection and dependency reemerged.[16]

Sisterly bonds continued across a lifetime. In her old age a rural Quaker matron, Martha Jefferis, wrote to her daughter Anne concerning her own half-sister, Phoebe: "In sister Phoebe I have a real friend—she studies my comfort and waits on me like a child. . . . She is exceedingly kind and this to all other homes (set aside yours) I would prefer—it is next to being with a daughter." Phoebe's own letters confirmed Martha's evaluation of her feelings. "Thou knowest my dear sister," Phoebe wrote, "there is no one . . . that exactly feels [for] thee as I do, for I think without boasting I can truly say that my desire is for thee."[17]

Such women, whether friends or relatives, assumed an emotional centrality in each other's lives. In their diaries and letters they wrote of the joy and contentment they felt in each other's company, their sense of isolation and despair when apart. The regularity of their correspondence underlies the sincerity of their words. Women named their daughters after one another and sought to integrate dear friends into their lives after marriage.[18] As one young bride wrote to an old friend shortly after her marriage: "I want to see you and talk with you and feel that we are united by the same bonds of sympathy and congeniality as ever." After years of friendship one aging woman wrote of another: "Time cannot destroy the fascination of her manner . . . her voice is music to the ear. . . ." Women made elaborate presents for each other, ranging from the Quakers' frugal pies and breads to painted velvet bags and phantom bouquets.[19] When a friend died, their grief was deeply felt. Martha Jefferis was unable to write to her daughter for three weeks because of the sorrow she felt at the death of a dear friend. Such distress was not unusual. A generation earlier a young Massachusetts farm woman filled pages of her diary with her grief at the death of her "dearest friend" and transcribed the letters of condolence other women sent her. She marked the anniversary of Rachel's death each year in her diary, contrasting her faithfulness with that of Rachel's husband who had soon remarried.[20]

These female friendships served a number of emotional functions. Within this secure and empathetic world women could share sorrows, anxieties, and joys, confident that other women had experienced similar emotions. One mid-nineteenth-century rural matron in a letter to her daughter discussed this particular aspect of women's friendships: "To have such a friend as thyself to look to and sympathize with her—and enter into all her little needs and in whose bosom she could with freedom pour forth her joys and sorrows—such a friend would very much relieve the tedium of many a wearisome hour. . . ." A generation later Molly more informally underscored the importance of this same function in a letter to Helena: "Suppose I come down . . . [and] spend Sunday with you quietly," she wrote Helena ". . . that means talking all the time until you are relieved of all your latest troubles, and I of mine. . . ." These were frequently troubles that apparently no man could understand. When Anne Jefferis Sheppard was

first married, she and her older sister Edith (who then lived with Anne) wrote in detail to their mother of the severe depression and anxiety which they experienced. Moses Sheppard, Anne's husband, added cheerful postscripts to the sisters' letters—which he had clearly not read—remarking on Anne's and Edith's contentment. Theirs was an emotional world to which he had little access.[21]

This was, as well, a female world in which hostility and criticism of other women were discouraged, and thus a milieu in which women could develop a sense of inner security and self-esteem. As one young woman wrote to her mother's longtime friend: "I cannot sufficiently thank you for the kind unvaried affection & indulgence you have ever shown and expressed both by words and actions for me. . . . Happy would it be did all the world view me as you do, through the medium of kindness and forbearance." They valued each other. Women, who had little status or power in the larger world of male concerns, possessed status and power in the lives and worlds of other women.[22]

An intimate mother-daughter relationship lay at the heart of this female world. The diaries and letters of both mothers and daughters attest to their closeness and mutual emotional dependency. Daughters routinely discussed their mother's health and activities with their own friends, expressed anxiety in cases of their mother's ill health and concern for her cares.[23] Expressions of hostility which we would today consider routine on the part of both mothers and daughters seem to have been uncommon indeed. On the contrary, this sample of families indicates that the normal relationship between mother and daughter was one of sympathy and understanding.[24] Only sickness or great geographic distance was allowed to cause extended separation. When marriage did result in such separation, both viewed the distance between them with distress.[25] Something of this sympathy and love between mothers and daughters is evident in a letter Sarah Alden Ripley, at age sixty-nine, wrote her youngest and recently married daughter: "You do not know how much I miss you, not only when I struggle in and out of my mortal envelop and pump my nightly potation and no longer pour into your sympathizing ear my senile gossip, but all the day I muse away, since the sound of your voice no longer rouses me to sympathy with your joys or sorrows. . . .

You cannot know how much I miss your affectionate demonstrations."[26] A dozen aging mothers in this sample of over thirty families echoed her sentiments.

Central to these mother-daughter relations is what might be described as an apprenticeship system. In those families where the daughter followed the mother into a life of traditional domesticity, mothers and other older women carefully trained daughters in the arts of housewifery and motherhood. Such training undoubtedly occurred throughout a girl's childhood but became more systematized, almost ritualistic, in the years following the end of her formal education and before her marriage. At this time a girl either returned home from boarding school or no longer divided her time between home and school. Rather, she devoted her energies on two tasks: mastering new domestic skills and participating in the visiting and social activities necessary to finding a husband. Under the careful supervision of their mothers and of older female relatives, such late-adolescent girls temporarily took over the household management from their mothers, tended their young nieces and nephews, and helped in childbirth, nursing, and weaning. Such experiences tied the generations together in shared skills and emotional interaction.[27]

Daughters were born into a female world. Their mother's life expectations and sympathetic network of friends and relations were among the first realities in the life of the developing child. As long as the mother's domestic role remained relatively stable and few viable alternatives competed with it, daughters tended to accept their mother's world and to turn automatically to other women for support and intimacy. It was within this closed and intimate female world that the young girl grew toward womanhood. . . .

At some point in adolescence, the young girl began to move outside the matrix of her mother's support group to develop a network of her own. Among the middle class, at least, this transition toward what was at the same time both a limited autonomy and a repetition of her mother's life seemed to have most frequently coincided with a girl's going to school. Indeed education appears to have played a crucial role in the lives of most of the families in this study. Attending school for a few months, for a year, or longer, was common even among daughters of relatively poor families, while middle-class girls routinely spent at least a year in boarding school. These school years ordinarily marked a girl's first separation from home. They served to wean the daughter from her home, to train her in the essential social graces, and, ultimately, to help introduce her into the marriage market. It was not infrequently a trying emotional experience for both mother and daughter.[28]

In this process of leaving one home and adjusting to another, the mother's friends and relatives played a key transitional role. Such older women routinely accepted the role of foster mother; they supervised the young girl's deportment, monitored her health and introduced her to their own network of female friends and kin. Not infrequently women, friends from their own school years, arranged to send their daughters to the same school so that the girls might form bonds paralleling those their mothers had made. For years Molly and Helena wrote of their daughters' meeting and worried over each other's children. When Molly finally brought her daughter east to school, their first act on reaching New York was to meet Helena and her daughters. Elizabeth Bordley Gibson virtually adopted the daughters of her school chum, Eleanor Custis Lewis. The Lewis daughters soon began to write Elizabeth Gibson letters with the salutation "Dearest Mama." . . .[29]

Even more important to this process of maturation than their mother's friends were the female friends young women made at school. Young girls helped each other overcome homesickness and endure the crises of adolescence. They gossiped about beaux, incorporated each other into their own kinship systems, and attended and gave teas and balls together. Older girls in boarding school "adopted" younger ones, who called them "Mother."[30] Dear friends might indeed continue this pattern of adoption and mothering throughout their lives; one woman might routinely assume the nurturing role of pseudomother, the other the dependency role of daughter. The pseudomother performed for the other woman all the services which we normally associate with mothers; she went to absurd lengths to purchase items her "daughter" could have obtained from other sources, gave advice and functioned as an idealized figure in her "daughter's" imagination. Helena played such a role for Molly, as did Sarah for Jeannie. Elizabeth Bordley Gibson bought almost all Eleanor Parke Custis Lewis's

necessities—from shoes and corset covers to bedding and harp strings—and sent them from Philadelphia to Virginia, a procedure that sometimes took months. Eleanor frequently asked Elizabeth to take back her purchases, have them redone, and argue with shopkeepers about prices. These were favors automatically asked and complied with. . . .[31]

A comparison of the references to men and women in these young women's letters is striking. Boys were obviously indispensable to the elaborate courtship ritual girls engaged in. In these teenage letters and diaries, however, boys appear distant and warded off—an effect produced both by the girl's sense of bonding and by a highly developed and deprecatory whimsy. Girls joked among themselves about the conceit, poor looks or affectations of suitors. Rarely, especially in the eighteenth and early nineteenth centuries, were favorable remarks exchanged. Indeed, while hostility and criticism of other women were so rare as to seem almost tabooed, young women permitted themselves to express a great deal of hostility toward peer-group men. . . .[32]

Even if young men were acceptable suitors, girls referred to them formally and obliquely: "The last week I received the unexpected intelligence of the arrival of a friend in Boston," Sarah Ripley wrote in her diary of the young man to whom she had been engaged for years and whom she would shortly marry. Harriet Manigault assiduously kept a lively and gossipy diary during the three years preceding her marriage, yet did not once comment upon her own engagement nor indeed make any personal references to her fiancé—who was never identified as such but always referred to as Mr. Wilcox.[33] The point is not that these young women were hostile to young men. Far from it; they sought marriage and domesticity. Yet in these letters and diaries men appear as an other or out group, segregated into different schools, supported by their own male network of friends and kin, socialized to different behavior, and coached to a proper formality in courtship behavior. As a consequence, relations between young women and men frequently lacked the spontaneity and emotional intimacy that characterized the young girls' ties to each other.

Indeed, in sharp contrast to their distant relations with boys, young women's relations with each other were close, often frolicsome, and surprisingly long lasting and devoted. They wrote secret missives to each other, spent long solitary days with each other, curled up together in bed at night to whisper fantasies and secrets. . . . Elizabeth Bordley and Nelly Parke Custis, teenagers in Philadelphia in the 1790s, routinely secreted themselves until late each night in Nelly's attic, where they each wrote a novel about the other.[34] Quite a few young women kept diaries, and it was a sign of special friendship to show their diaries to each other. The emotional quality of such exchanges emerges from the comments of one young girl who grew up along the Ohio frontier:

> Sisters CW and RT keep diaries & allow me the inestimable pleasure of reading them and in turn they see mine—but O shame covers my face when I think of it; theirs is so much better than mine, that every time. Then I think well now I *will* burn mine but upon second thought it would deprive me the pleasure of reading theirs, for I esteem it a very great privilege indeed, as well as very improving, as we lay our hearts open to each other, it heightens our love & helps to cherish & keep alive that sweet soothing friendship and endears us to each other by that soft attraction.

Girls routinely slept together, kissed and hugged each other. Indeed, while waltzing with young men scandalized the otherwise flighty and highly fashionable Harriet Manigault, she considered waltzing with other young women not only acceptable but pleasant.[35]

Marriage followed adolescence. With increasing frequency in the nineteenth century, marriage involved a girl's traumatic removal from her mother and her mother's network. It involved, as well, adjustment to a husband, who, because he was male came to marriage with both a different worldview and vastly different experiences. Not surprisingly, marriage was an event surrounded with supportive, almost ritualistic, practices. (Weddings are one of the last female rituals remaining in twentieth-century America.) Young women routinely spent the months preceding their marriage almost exclusively with other women—at neighborhood sewing bees and quilting parties or in a round of visits to geographically distant friends and relatives. Ostensibly they went to receive assistance in the practical preparations for their new home—sewing and quilting a trousseau and linen—but of equal importance, they appear to have gained emotional support and reassurance. Sarah Ripley spent over a month with friends and relatives in Boston and Hingham before her wedding; Parke Custis Lewis exchanged visits with her aunts and first cousins throughout Virginia. Anne Jefferis, who married with some hesitation, spent virtually half a year in endless visiting with cousins, aunts, and friends. Despite their reassurance and support, however, she would not marry Moses Sheppard until her sister Edith and her cousin Rebecca moved into the groom's home, met his friends, and explored his personality. The wedding did not take place until Edith wrote to Anne: "I can say in truth I am entirely willing thou shouldst follow him even away in the Jersey sands believing if thou are not happy in thy future home it will not be any fault on his part. . . ."[36]

Sisters, cousins, and friends frequently accompanied newlyweds on their wedding night and wedding trip, which often involved additional family visiting. Such extensive visits presumably served to wean the daughter from her family of origin. As such they often contained a note of ambivalence. Nelly Custis, for example, reported homesickness and loneliness on her wedding trip. "I left my Beloved and revered Grandmamma with sincere regret," she wrote Elizabeth Bordley. "It was sometime before I could feel reconciled to traveling without her." Perhaps they also functioned to reassure the young woman herself, and her friends and kin, that though marriage might alter it would not destroy old bonds of intimacy and familiarity.[37]

Married life, too, was structured about a host of female rituals. Childbirth, especially the birth of the first child, became virtually a *rite de passage*, with a lengthy seclusion of the woman before and after delivery, severe restrictions on her activities, and finally a dramatic reemergence. This seclusion was supervised by mothers, sisters, and loving friends. Nursing and weaning involved the advice and assistance of female friends and relatives. So did miscarriage.[38] Death, like birth, was structured around elaborate unisexed rituals. When Nelly Parke Custis Lewis rushed to nurse her daughter who was critically ill while away at school, Nelly received support, not from her husband, who remained on their plantation, but from her old school friend, Elizabeth Bordley. Elizabeth aided Nelly in caring for her dying daughter, cared for Nelly's other children, played a major role in the elaborate funeral arrangements (which the father did not attend), and frequently visited the girl's grave at the mother's request. For years Elizabeth continued to be the confidante of Nelly's anguished recollections of her lost daughter. These memories, Nelly's letters make clear, were for Elizabeth alone. "Mr. L. knows nothing of this," was a frequent comment.[39] Virtually every collection of letters and diaries in my sample contained evidence of women turning to each other for comfort when facing the frequent and unavoidable deaths of the eighteenth and nineteenth centuries. While mourning for her father's death, Sophie DuPont received elaborate letters and visits of condolence—all from women. No man wrote or visited Sophie to offer sympathy at her father's death. Among rural Pennsylvania Quakers, death and mourning rituals assumed an even more extreme same-sex form, with men or women largely barred from the deathbeds of the other sex. Women relatives and friends slept with the dying woman, nursed her, and prepared her body for burial.[40]

Eighteenth- and nineteenth-century women thus lived in emotional proximity to each other. Friendships and intimacies followed the biological ebb and flow of women's lives. Marriage and pregnancy, childbirth and weaning, sickness and death involved physical and psychic trauma which comfort and sympathy made easier to bear. Intense bonds of love and intimacy bound together those women who, offering each other aid and sympathy, shared such stressful moments.

These bonds were often physical as well as emotional. An undeniably romantic and even sensual note frequently marked female relationships. This theme, significant throughout the stages of a woman's life, surfaced first during adolescence. As one teenager from a struggling pioneer family in the Ohio Valley wrote in her diary in 1808: "I laid with my dear R[ebecca] and a glorious good talk we had until about 4[A.M.]—O how hard I do *love* her. . . ." Only a few years later Bostonian Eunice Callender carved her initials and Sarah Ripley's into a favorite tree, along with a pledge of eternal love, and then waited breathlessly for Sarah to discover and respond to her declaration of affection. The response appears to have been affirmative. A half-century later urbane and sophisticated Katherine Wharton commented upon meeting an old school chum: "She was a great pet of mine at school & I thought as I watched her light figure how often I had held her in my arms—how dear she had once been to me." Katie maintained a long intimate friendship with another girl. When a young man began to court this friend seriously, Katie commented in her diary that she had never realized "how deeply I loved Eng and how fully."

She wrote over and over again in that entry: "Indeed I love her!" and only with great reluctance left the city that summer since it meant also leaving Eng with Eng's new suitor.[41]

Peggy Emlen, a Quaker adolescent in Philadelphia in the 1760s, expressed similar feelings about her first cousin, Sally Logan. The girls sent love poems to each other . . . , took long solitary walks together, and even haunted the empty house of the other when one was out of town. Indeed Sally's absences from Philadelphia caused Peggy acute unhappiness. So strong were Peggy's feelings that her brothers began to tease about her affection for Sally and threatened to steal Sally's letters, much to both girls' alarm. In one letter that Peggy wrote the absent Sally she elaborately described the depth and nature of her feelings: "I have not words to express my impatience to see My Dear Cousin, what would I not give just now for an hours sweet conversation with her, it seems as if I had a thousand things to say to thee, yet when I see thee, everything will be forgot thro' joy. . . . I have a very great friendship for several Girls yet it dont give me so much uneasiness at being absent from them as from thee. . . . [Let us] go and spend a day down at our place together and there unmolested enjoy each others company."[42]

Sarah Alden Ripley, a young, highly educated woman, formed a similar intense relationship, in this instance with a woman somewhat older than herself. The immediate bond of friendship rested on their atypically intense scholarly interests, but it soon involved strong emotions, at least on Sarah's part. "Friendship," she wrote Mary Emerson, "is fast twining about her willing captive the silken hands of dependence, a dependence so sweet who would renounce it for the apathy of self-sufficiency?" Subsequent letters became far more emotional, almost conspiratorial. Mary visited Sarah secretly in her room, or the two women crept away from family and friends to meet in a nearby woods. Sarah became jealous of Mary's other young friends. Mary's trips away from Boston also thrust Sarah into periods of anguished depression. Interestingly, the letters detailing their love were not destroyed but were preserved and even reprinted in a eulogistic biography of Sarah Alden Ripley.[43]

Tender letters between adolescent women, confessions of loneliness and emotional dependency, were not peculiar to Sarah Alden, Peggy Emlen, or Katie Wharton. They are found throughout the letters of the thirty-five families studied. They have, of course, their parallel today in the musings of many female adolescents. Yet these eighteenth- and nineteenth-century friendships lasted with undiminished, indeed often increased, intensity throughout the women's lives. Sarah Alden Ripley's first child was named after Mary Emerson. . . . Eunice Callender remained enamored of her cousin Sarah Ripley for years and rejected as impossible the suggestion by another woman that their love might some day fade away. Sophie DuPont and her childhood friend, Clementina Smith, exchanged letters filled with love and dependency for forty years while another dear friend, Mary Black Couper, wrote of dreaming that she, Sophie, and her husband were all united in one marriage. Mary's letters to Sophie are filled with avowals of love and indications of ambivalence toward her own husband. Eliza Schlatter, another of Sophie's intimate friends, wrote to her at a time of crisis: "I wish I could be with you present in the body as well as the mind & heart—I would turn your *good husband out of bed*—and snuggle into you and we would have a long talk like old times in Pine St.—I want to tell you so many things that are not *writable*. . . ."[44]

Such mutual dependency and deep affection is a central existential reality coloring the world of supportive networks and rituals. In the case of Katie, Sophie, or Eunice—as with Molly, Jeannie, and Sarah—their need for closeness and support merged with more intense demands for a love which was at the same time both emotional and sensual. Perhaps the most explicit statement concerning women's lifelong friendships appeared in the letter abolitionist and reformer Mary Grew wrote about the same time, referring to her own love for her dear friend and lifelong companion, Margaret Burleigh. Grew wrote, in response to a letter of condolence from another woman on Burleigh's death: "Your words respecting my beloved friend touch me deeply. Evidently . . . you comprehend and appreciate, as few persons do . . . the nature of the relation which existed, which exists, between her and myself. Her only surviving niece . . . also does. To me it seems to have been a closer union than that of most marriages. We know there have been other such between two men and also between two women. And why should

there not be. Love is spiritual, only passion is sexual."[45]

How then can we ultimately interpret these long-lived intimate female relationships and integrate them into our understanding of Victorian sexuality? Their ambivalent and romantic rhetoric presents us with an ultimate puzzle: the relationship along the spectrum of human emotions between love, sensuality, and sexuality. . . .

It is possible to speculate that in the twentieth century a number of cultural taboos evolved to cut short the homosocial ties of girlhood and to impel the emerging women of thirteen or fourteen toward heterosexual relationships. In contrast, nineteenth-century American society did not taboo close female relationships but rather recognized them as a socially viable form of human contact—and, as normal such, acceptable throughout a woman's life. Indeed it was not these homosocial ties that were inhibited but rather heterosexual leanings. While closeness, freedom of emotional expression, and uninhibited physical contact characterized women's relationships with each other, the opposite was frequently true of male-female relationships. One could thus argue that within such a world of female support, intimacy, and ritual it was only to be expected that adult women would turn trustingly and lovingly to each other. It was a behavior they had observed and learned since childhood. A different type of emotional landscape existed in the nineteenth century, one in which Molly and Helena's love became a natural development.

Of perhaps equal significance are the implications we can garner from this framework for the understanding of heterosexual marriages in the nineteenth century. If men and women grew up as they did in relatively homogeneous and segregated sexual groups, then marriage represented a major problem in adjustment. From this perspective we could interpret much of the emotional stiffness and distance that we associate with Victorian marriage as a structural consequence of contemporary sex-role differentiation and gender-role socialization. With marriage both women and men had to adjust to life with a person who was, in essence, a member of an alien group. . . .

. . . Based on my research into this nineteenth-century world of female intimacy, I suggest that . . . we view sexual and emotional impulses as part of a continuum or spectrum of affect gradations strongly affected by cultural norms and arrangements, a continuum influenced in part by observed and thus learned behavior. At one end of the continuum lies committed heterosexuality, at the other uncompromising homosexuality; between, a wide latitude of emotions and sexual feelings. Certain cultures and environments permit individuals a great deal of freedom in moving across this spectrum. I would like to suggest that the nineteenth century was such a cultural environment. That is, the supposedly repressive and destructive Victorian sexual ethos may have been more flexible and responsive to the needs of particular individuals than those of mid-twentieth century.

NOTES

1. An exception to this rule is William R. Taylor and Christopher Lasch, "Two 'Kindred Spirits': Sorority and Family in New England, 1839–1846," *New England Quarterly* 36 (1963): 25–41. I do not accept the Taylor-Lasch thesis that female friendships developed in the mid-nineteenth century because of geographic mobility and the breakup of the colonial family. I have found these friendships as frequently in the eighteenth century as in the nineteenth and would hypothesize that the geographic mobility of the mid-nineteenth century eroded them as it did so many other traditional social institutions. . . .

2. I do not wish to deny the importance of women's relations with particular men. Obviously, women were close to brothers, husbands, fathers, and sons. However, there is evidence that despite such closeness relationships between men and women differed in both emotional texture and frequency from those between women. See my articles: "Puberty to Menopause: The Cycle of Femininity in Nineteenth-Century America," *Feminist Studies* 1 (1973):58–72, and, with Charles Rosenberg, "The Female Animal: Medical and Biological Views of Women in 19th Century America," *Journal of American History* 59 (1973):331–56.

3. See, e.g., the letters of Peggy Emlen to Sally Logan, 1768–72, Wells Morris Collection, Box 1, Historical Society of Pennsylvania, Philadelphia (hereafter, HSP); and the Eleanor Parke Custis Lewis Letters, HSP.

4. Sarah Butler Wister was the daughter of Fanny Kemble and Pierce Butler. In 1859 she married a Philadelphia physician, Owen Wister. (The novelist Owen Wister was her son.) Jeannie Field Musgrove was the half-orphaned daughter of constitutional lawyer and New York Republican politician David Dudley Field. Their correspondence (1855–98) is in the Sarah Butler Wister Papers, Wister Family Papers, HSP. Sarah Butler, Butler Place. S.C., to Jeannie Field, New York, Sept. 14, 1855; Sarah Butler Wister, Germantown, Pa., to Jeannie Field, New York, Sept. 25, 1862, Oct. 21, 1863; Jeannie Field. New York, to Sarah Butler Wister, Germantown, July 3, 1861, Jan. 23 and July 12, 1863; Sarah Butler Wister, Germantown,

to Jeannie Field, New York, June 5, 1861, Feb. 29, 1864; Jeannie Field to Sarah Butler Wister, Nov. 22, 1861, Jan. 4 and June 14, 1863.

5. Sarah Butler Wister, London, to Jeannie Field Musgrove, New York, June 18 and Aug. 3, 1870; for post-marriage, see two of Sarah's letters to Jeannie: Dec. 21, 1873, July 16, 1878.

6. This is the 1868–1920 correspondence between Mary Hallock Foote and Helena, a New York friend (the Mary Hallock Foote Papers are in the Manuscript Division, Stanford University). Like Molly and Helena, women frequently began letters to each other with salutations such as "Dearest," "My Most Beloved," "You Darling Girl," and signed them "tenderly" or "to my dear dear sweet friend, good-bye."

7. Mary Hallock [Foote] to Helena, n.d. [1869–70], n.d. [1871–72], Folder 1, Mary Hallock Foote Letters.

8. Mary Hallock [Foote] to Helena, Sept. 15 and 23, 1873, n.d. [Oct. 1873], Oct. 12, 1873; n.d. [Jan. 1874], n.d. [Spring 1874].

9. Mary Hallock [Foote] to Helena, Sept. 23, 1873; Mary Hallock [Foote] to Richard, Dec. 13, 1873. Molly's and Helena's relationship continued for the rest of their lives.

10. See Barbara Welter, "The Cult of True Womanhood: 1820–1860," *American Quarterly* 18 (Summer 1966):151–74; Anne Firor Scott, *The Southern Lady: From Pedestal to Politics, 1830–1930* (Chicago: University of Chicago Press, 1970), chaps. 1–2; Smith-Rosenberg and Rosenberg, "The Female Animal."

11. See, e.g., the letters of Peggy Emlen to Sally Logan, 1768–72. Elizabeth Botts, *Family and Social Network* (London: Tavistock Publications, 1957).

12. Harriet Manigault Wilcox Diary, June 28, 1814, and passim, HSP; Ann Sterling Biddle Family Papers, passim, Friends Historical Society, Swarthmore College; Phoebe Bradford Diary, Jan. 13, Nov. 16–19, 1832, Apr. 26 and May 7, 1833, HSP.

13. Lisa Mitchell Diary, 1860s, passim, Manuscript Division, Tulane University; Jeannie McCall, Cedar Park, to Peter McCall, Philadelphia, June 30, 1849, McCall Section, Cadwalader Collection, HSP; Peggy Emlen to Sally Logan, May 3, 1769.

14. For a prime example of this type of letter, see Eleanor Parke Custis Lewis to Elizabeth Bordley Gibson, passim.

15. Eleanor Parke Custis Lewis to Elizabeth Bordley Gibson, Apr. 20 and Sept. 25, 1848; Maria Inskeep to Fanny Hampton Correspondence, 1823–60, Inskeep Collection, Tulane University Library; Eunice Callender, Boston, to Sarah Ripley [Stearns], Sept. 24 and Oct. 29, 1803, Feb. 16, 1805, Apr. 29 and Oct. 9, 1806, May 26, 1810, Sarah Alden Ripley Correspondence, Schlesinger Library, Radcliffe College.

16. Sophie DuPont to her younger brother Henry, e.g., Dec. 13, 1827, Jan. 10 and Mar. 9, 1828, Feb. 4 and Mar. 10, 1832, Samuel Francis DuPont Papers, Eleutherian Mills Foundation, Wilmington, Del.; Mary B. Ashew Diary, July 11 and 13, Aug. 17, Summer and Oct. 1858.

17. Martha Jefferis to Anne Jefferis Sheppard, Jan. 12, 1845; Phoebe Middleton to Martha Jefferis, Feb. 22, 1848, Jefferis Family Correspondence, Chester County Historical Society, West Chester, Penna.

18. Rebecca Biddle to Martha Jefferis, 1838–49, passim; Martha Jefferis to Anne Jefferis Sheppard,

July 6, 1846; Anne Jefferis Sheppard to Rachael Jefferis, Jan. 16, 1865; Sarah Foulke Farquhar [Emlen] Diary, Sept. 22, 1813, Friends Historical Library, Swarthmore College.

19. Sarah Alden Ripley to Abba Allyn, n.d.; Phoebe Bradford Diary, July 13, 1832; Mary Hallock [Foote] to Helena, Dec. 23 [1868 or 1869]; Phoebe Bradford Diary, Dec. 8, 1832; Martha Jefferis and Anne Jefferis Sheppard letters, passim.

20. Martha Jefferis to Anne Jefferis Sheppard, Aug. 3, 1849; Sarah Ripley [Stearns] Diary, Nov. 12, 1808, Jan. 8, 1811.

21. Martha Jefferis to Edith Jefferis, Mar. 15, 1841; Mary Hallock Foote to Helena, n.d. [1874–75?]; Anne Jefferis Sheppard to Martha Jefferis, Sept. 29, 1841.

22. Frances Parke Lewis to Elizabeth Bordley Gibson, Apr. 29, 1821; Mary Jane Burleigh, Mount Pleasant, S.C., to Emily Howland, Sherwood N.Y., Mar. 27, 1872, Howland Family Papers.

23. See, e.g., Harriet Manigault Diary, Aug. 15, 21, and 23, 1814.

24. Mrs. S. S. Dalton, "Autobiography" (Circle Valley, Utah, 1876), pp. 21–22, Bancroft Library, University of California, Berkeley; Sarah Foulke Emlen Diary, Apr. 1809; Louisa G. Van Vleck, Appleton, Wis., to Charlena Van Vleck Anderson, Göttingen, n.d. [1875].

25. Abigail Brackett Lyman, Boston, to Mrs. Abigail Brackett (daughter to mother), n.d. [1797], June 3, 1800; Sarah Alden Ripley wrote weekly to her daughter, Sophy Ripley Fisher, after the latter's marriage (Sarah Alden Ripley Correspondence, passim). Daughters evidently frequently slept with their mothers—into adulthood (Harriet Manigault [Wilcox] Diary, Feb. 19, 1815; Eleanor Parke Custis Lewis to Elizabeth Bordley Gibson, Oct. 10, 1832). Daughters also frequently asked mothers to live with them and professed delight when they did so. . . . We did find a few exceptions to this mother-daughter felicity (M. B. Ashew Diary, Nov. 19, 1857, Apr. 10 and May 17, 1858). Sarah Foulke Emlen was at first very hostile to her step-mother (Sarah Foulke Emlen Diary, Aug. 9, 1807), but they later developed a warm supportive relationship.

26. Sarah Alden Ripley to Sophy Thayer, n.d. [1861].

27. See, e.g., Mary Hallock Foote to Helena [Winter 1873] (no. 52); Jossie, Stevens Point, Wis., to Charlena Van Vleck [Anderson], Appleton, Wis., Oct. 24, 1870, Anderson Family Papers, Manuscript Division, Stanford University; Pollie Chandler, Green Bay, Wis., to Charlena Van Vleck [Anderson], Appleton, n.d. [1870]; Eleuthera DuPont to Sophie DuPont, Sept. 5, 1829.

28. Sarah Foulke Emlen Journal, Sarah Ripley Stearns Diary, Mrs. S. S. Dalton, "Autobiography"; Maria Revere to her mother [Mrs. Paul Revere], June 13, 1801, Paul Revere Papers, Massachusetts Historical Society, Boston.

29. Frances Parke Lewis, Woodlawn, Va., to Elizabeth Bordley Gibson, Philadelphia, Apr. 11, 1821, Lewis Correspondence.

30. See, e.g., Sarah Ripley Stearns Diary, Mar. 9 and 25, 1810; Peggy Emlen to Sally Logan, Mar. and July 4, 1769; Deborah Cope, West Town School, to Rest Cope, Philadelphia, July 9, 1828, Chester County Historical Society, West Chester, Pa.

31. Anne Jefferis Sheppard to Martha Jefferis, Mar. 17, 1841.

32. See, e.g., Peggy Emlen to Sally Logan, Mar. 1769, Mount Vernon, Va. Sophie M. DuPont and Eleuthera DuPont, Brandywine, to Victorine DuPont Bauday, Philadelphia, Jan. 25, 1832.

33. Sarah Ripley [Stearns] Diary and Harriet Manigault Diary, passim.

34. Elizabeth Bordley Gibson, introductory statement to the Eleanor Parke Custis Lewis Letters [1850s], HSP. See also, e.g., Sophie Madeleine DuPont to Eleuthera DuPont, Dec. 1827; Clementina Beach Smith to Sophie Madeleine DuPont, Dec. 26, 1828; Sarah Faulke Emlen Diary, July 21, 1808, Mar. 30, 1809; Jeannie Field, New York, to Sarah Butler Wister, Germantown, Apr. 6, 1862.

35. Sarah Foulke [Emlen] Diary, Mar. 30, 1809; Harriet Manigault Diary, May 26, 1815.

36. Sarah Ripley [Stearns] Diary, May 17 and Oct. 2, 1812; Eleanor Parke Custis Lewis to Elizabeth Bordley Gibson, Apr. 23, 1826; Anne Jefferis to Martha Jefferis, Nov. 22 and 27, 1840, Jan. 13 and Mar. 17, 1841; Edith Jefferis, Greenwich, N.J., to Anne Jefferis, Philadelphia, Jan. 31, Feb. 6, and Feb. 1841.

37. Eleanor Parke Custis Lewis to Elizabeth Bordley, Nov. 4, 1799.

38. See, e.g., Mary Hallock to Helena DeKay Gilder [1876] (no. 81); n.d. (no. 83), Mar. 3, 1884; Mary Ashew Diary, vol. 2, Sept.–Jan. 1860; Fanny Ferris to Anne Biddle, Nov. 19, 1811; Eleanor Parke Custis Lewis to Elizabeth Bordley Gibson, Nov. 4, 1799, Apr. 27, 1827.

39. Eleanor Parke Custis Lewis to Elizabeth Bordley Gibson, Oct.–Nov. 1820, passim.

40. See, e.g., Emily Howland to Hannah, Sept. 30, 1866; Emily Howland Diary, Feb. 8, 11, and 27, 1880; Phoebe Bradford Diary, Apr. 12 and 13, and Aug. 4, 1833; Mary Black [Couper] to Sophie Madeleine DuPont, Feb. 1827 [Nov. 1, 1834], Nov. 12, 1834, two letters [late Nov. 1834]; Eliza Schlatter to Sophie Madeleine DuPont, Nov. 2, 1834; Martha Jefferis to Anne Jefferis Sheppard, Sept. 28, 1843, Aug. 21 and Sept. 25, 1844, Jan. 11, 1846, Summer 1848, passim.

41. Sarah Foulke [Emlen] Diary, Dec. 29, 1808; Eunice Callender, Boston, to Sarah Ripley [Stearns], Greenfield, Mass., May 24, 1803; Katherine Johnstone Brinley [Wharton] Journal, Apr. 26, May 30, and May 29, 1856, HSP.

42. A series of roughly fourteen letters written by Peggy Emlen to Sally Logan (1768–71) has been preserved in the Wells Morris Collection, Box 1, HSP (see esp. Jan. 8, 1768, May 3 and July 4, 1769).

43. The eulogistic biographical sketch appeared in Mrs. O. J. Wister and Miss Agnes Irwin, eds., Worthy Women of Our First Century (Philadelphia: J. B. Lippincott & Co., 1877).

44. See Sarah Alden Ripley to Mary Emerson, Nov. 19, 1823. Mary Black Couper to Sophie M. DuPont, Mar. 5, 1832. The Clementina Smith–Sophie DuPont correspondence is in the Sophie DuPont Correspondence. The quotation is from Eliza Schlatter, Mount Holly, N.J., to Sophie DuPont, Brandywine, Aug. 24, 1834.

45. Mary Grew, Providence, R.I., to Isabel Howland, Sherwood, N.Y., Apr. 27, 1892, Howland Correspondence, Sophia Smith Collection, Smith College.

JAMES C. MOHR
Abortion in America, 1800–1880

If we observe nineteenth-century society through women's eyes, surely no experience was as widely shared as the experience of childbirth. The biological act of
maternity created powerful bonds among women as they coped with the experience of childbirth. Until the twentieth century, most births took place at home,
where the birthing mother was likely to be surrounded by her mother, sisters, and
cousins, a midwife and other experienced women, and her woman friends. The
"female world of love and ritual" that Carroll Smith-Rosenberg describes "formed
across the childbirth bed," writes historian Judith Walzer Leavitt. "When women
had suffered the agonies of watching their friends die, when they had helped a
friend recover from a difficult delivery, or when they had participated in a successful birthing they developed a closeness that lasted a lifetime." Leavitt finds
that these circles of friendly support made significant choices. "The collectivity of
women gathered around the birthing bed made sure that birth attendants were
responsive to their wishes. They made decisions about when and if to call physicians to births that midwives were attending; they gave or withheld permission
for physicians' procedures; and they created the atmosphere of female support in
a room that might have contained both women and men." Leavitt argues that
when in the twentieth century birthing moved to hospitals, much of this support
evaporated; the reforms in hospital practices demanded by feminists since the
1970s have been an effort to reclaim what had been lost.*

During the centuries before reliable fertility control measures made it possible for women to set limits on reproduction, most married women and many unmarried women felt considerable physical and psychological burdens from
repeated pregnancies, childbirths, and postpartum recoveries. The cost in terms
of time, energy, dreams, and bodies was high. If we observe nineteenth-century
society through women's eyes, surely no statistic was as significant as the one that
marked the decline in the average number of children borne by each woman.
Childbirth was a time of terror.

It is therefore notable that in the early nineteenth century, a sharp decline took
place in the birth rates; the decline was particularly marked in urban areas. No innovations in birth control technology appeared in this period; the decline was the
result of choices—later age at marriage, abstinence from sexual intercourse—that

*Judith Walzer Leavitt, "Under the Shadow of Maternity: American Women's Responses to Death and De-
bility Fears in Nineteenth-Century Childbirth," *Feminist Studies* 12 (1986): 129–54. Maine midwife Martha
Ballard, who practiced up until her death in 1812 at age seventy-seven, left an extraordinary diary that reveals not only the community of women who gathered for births, but also Ballard's skill. She delivered
some 900 women without losing a mother in childbirth. See Laurel Thatcher Ulrich, *A Midwife's Tale: The
Life of Martha Ballard Based on Her Diary, 1785–1812* (New York: Alfred A. Knopf, 1990), esp. ch. 5; also the
90-minute film of the same name (produced by Laurie Kahn-Leavitt and directed by Richard P. Rogers for
PBS's *American Experience* series, 1997). The diary is reproduced in its entirety on www.dohistory.org, a
website with features that invite interactive analysis and exploration.

Excerpted from chs. 1 and 4 of *Abortion in America: The Origins and Evolution of National Policy* by James C. Mohr
(New York: Oxford University Press, 1978). Used by permission of the author and publisher. Notes have been
renumbered and edited.

functioned to limit the number of times women faced childbirth. In the mid-eighteenth century, the average rural woman of free status could expect to face childbirth eight or nine times; by the early nineteenth century, that number had dropped to six and in some urban areas to four. Except for occasional "baby booms," birth rates in the United States have fallen steadily and continue to stabilize in our own time.

When unsuccessful in avoiding pregnancies, many women attempted to abort them. The methods of the times were dangerous, but until the 1840s, the women were rarely censured by the community if fetal movement had not been felt (this was called quickening). It was not until the 1820s that states began to pass laws criminalizing certain methods of abortion performed after quickening; penalties fell on the medical practitioner not the pregnant woman. Legislators in this period were concerned that "rash" or "irregular" doctors were prescribing toxic potions or performing risky operations and thus endangering women's lives.* As these two sections from James Mohr's comprehensive study suggest, the vigorous attack on abortion after 1840 may well have been a response to the growing willingness of married women to attempt it.

What does the debate on abortion policy reveal about public attitudes toward women and their place in the family and in society?

ABORTION IN AMERICA, 1800–1825

In the absence of any legislation whatsoever on the subject of abortion in the United States in 1800, the legal status of the practice was governed by the traditional British common law as interpreted by the local courts of the new American states. For centuries prior to 1800 the key to the common law's attitude toward abortion had been a phenomenon associated with normal gestation known as quickening. Quickening was the first perception of fetal movement by the pregnant woman herself. Quickening generally occurred near the midpoint of gestation, late in the fourth or early in the fifth month, though it could and still does vary a good deal from one woman to another. The common law did not formally recognize the existence of a fetus in criminal cases until it had quickened. After quickening, the expulsion and destruction of a fetus without due cause was considered a crime, because the fetus itself had manifested some semblance of a separate existence: the ability to move. The crime was qualitatively different from the destruction of a human being, however, and punished less harshly. Before quickening, actions that had the effect of terminating what turned

out to have been an early pregnancy were not considered criminal under the common law in effect in England and the United States in 1800.[1]

Both practical and moral arguments lay behind the quickening distinction. Practically, because no reliable tests for pregnancy existed in the early nineteenth century, quickening alone could confirm with absolute certainty that a woman really was pregnant. Prior to quickening, each of the telltale signs of pregnancy could, at least in theory, be explained in alternative ways by physicians of the day. Hence, either a doctor or a woman herself could take actions designed to restore menstrual flow after one or more missed periods on the assumption that something might be unnaturally "blocking" or "obstructing" her normal cycles, and if left untreated the obstruction would wreak real harm upon the woman. Medically, the procedures for removing a blockage were the same as those for inducing an early abortion. Not until the obstruction moved could either a physician or a woman, regardless of their suspicions, be completely certain that it was a "natural" blockage—a pregnancy—rather than a potentially dangerous situation. Morally, the question of whether

---

*Chapters 2, 5, and 8 in Mohr, *Abortion in America*, address three distinct stages of legislation. For an examination of an abortion that led to a young women's death and a series of prosecutions in 1740s Connecticut, see Cornelia Hughes Dayton, "Taking the Trade: Abortion and Gender Relations in an Eighteenth-Century New England Village," *William and Mary Quarterly*, 3rd ser., 48 (Jan. 1991): 19–49.

or not a fetus was "alive" had been the subject of philosophical and religious debate among honest people for at least 5000 years. The quickening doctrine itself appears to have entered the British common law tradition by way of the tangled disputes of medieval theologians over whether or not an impregnated ovum possessed a soul.[2] The upshot was that American women in 1800 were legally free to attempt to terminate a condition that might turn out to have been a pregnancy until the existence of that pregnancy was incontrovertibly confirmed by the perception of fetal movement.

An ability to suspend one's modern preconceptions and to accept the early nineteenth century on its own terms regarding the distinction between quick and unquick is absolutely crucial to an understanding of the evolution of abortion policy in the United States. However doubtful the notion appears to modern readers, the distinction was virtually universal in America during the early decades of the nineteenth century and accepted in good faith. Perhaps the strongest evidence of the tenacity and universality of the doctrine in the United States was the fact that American courts pointedly sustained the most lenient implications of the quickening doctrine even after the British themselves had abandoned them. . . .

Because women believed themselves to be carrying inert non-beings prior to quickening, a potential for life rather than life itself, and because the common law permitted them to attempt to rid themselves of suspected and unwanted pregnancies up to the point when the potential for life gave a sure sign that it was developing into something actually alive, some American women did practice abortion in the early decades of the nineteenth century. One piece of evidence for this conclusion was the ready access American women had to abortifacient information from 1800 onward. A chief source of such information was the home medical literature of the era.

Home medical manuals characteristically contained abortifacient information in two different sections. One listed in explicit detail a number of procedures that might release "obstructed menses" and the other identified a number of specific things to be avoided in a suspected pregnancy because they were thought to bring on abortion. Americans probably consulted William Buchan's Domestic Medicine more frequently than any other home medical guide during the first decades of the nineteenth century.[3] Buchan suggested several courses of action designed to restore menstrual flow if a period was missed. These included bloodletting, bathing, iron and quinine concoctions, and if those failed, "a tea-spoonful of the tincture of black hellebore [a violent purgative] . . . twice a day in a cup of warm water." Four pages later he listed among "the common causes" of abortion "great evacuations [and] vomiting," exactly as would be produced by the treatment he urged for suppressed menses. Later in pregnancy a venturesome, or desperate, woman could try some of the other abortion inducers he ticked off: "violent exercise; raising great weights; reaching too high; jumping, or stepping from an eminence; strokes [strong blows] on the belly; [and] falls."[4] . . .

Like most early abortion material, Buchan's . . . advice harked back to almost primordial or instinctual methods of ending a pregnancy. Bloodletting, for example, was evidently thought to serve as a surrogate period; it was hoped that bleeding from any part of the body might have the same flushing effect upon the womb that menstrual bleeding was known to have. This primitive folk belief lingered long into the nineteenth century, well after bleeding was abandoned as medical therapy in other kinds of cases, and it was common for abortionists as late as the 1870s to pull a tooth as part of their routine.[5] . . .

In addition to home medical guides and health manuals addressed to women, abortions and abortifacient information were also available in the United States from midwives and midwifery texts.[6] . . .

Herbal healers, the so-called Indian doctors, and various other irregular practitioners also helped spread abortifacient information in the United States during the early decades of the nineteenth century. Their surviving pamphlets, of which Peter Smith's 1813 brochure entitled "The Indian Doctor's Dispensary" is an example, contained abortifacient recipes that typically combined the better-known cathartics with native North American ingredients thought to have emmenagogic properties. For "obstructed menses" Smith recommended a concoction he called "Dr. Reeder's chalybeate." The key ingredients were myrrh and aloes, combined with liquor, sugar, vinegar, iron dust, ivy, and Virginia or seneca snakeroot.[7]

A sweet-and-sour cocktail like that may or may not have induced abortion, but must certainly have jolted the system of any woman who tried one. . . .

Finally, and most importantly, America's regular physicians, those who had formal medical training either in the United States or in Great Britain or had been apprenticed under a regular doctor, clearly possessed the physiological knowledge and the surgical techniques necessary to terminate a pregnancy by mechanical means. They knew that dilation of the cervix at virtually any stage of gestation would generally bring on uterine contractions that would in turn lead to the expulsion of the contents of the uterus. They knew that any irritation introduced into the uterus would have the same effect. They knew that rupturing the amniotic sac, especially in the middle and later months of pregnancy, would usually also induce contractions and expulsion, regardless of whether the fetus was viable. Indeed, they were taught in their lecture courses and in their textbooks various procedures much more complex than a simple abortion, such as in utero decapitation and fetal pulverization, processes they were instructed to employ in lieu of the even more horribly dangerous Caesarean section. Like the general public, they knew the drugs and herbs most commonly used as abortifacients and emmenagogues, and also like the general public, they believed such preparations to have been frequently effective.[8] . . .

This placed great pressure on physicians to provide what amounted to abortion services early in pregnancy. An unmarried girl who feared herself pregnant, for example, could approach her family doctor and ask to be treated for menstrual blockage. If he hoped to retain the girl and her family as future patients, the physician would have little choice but to accept the girl's assessment of the situation, even if he suspected otherwise. He realized that every member of his profession would testify to the fact that he had no totally reliable means of distinguishing between an early pregnancy, on the one hand, and the amenorrhea that the girl claimed, on the other. Consequently, he treated for obstruction, which involved exactly the same procedures he would have used to induce an early abortion, and wittingly or unwittingly terminated the pregnancy. Regular physicians were also asked to bring to a safe conclusion abortions that irregulars or women themselves

had initiated. . . . And through all of this the physician might bear in mind that he could never be held legally guilty of wrongdoing. No statutes existed anywhere in the United States on the subject of abortion, and the common law . . . considered abortion actionable only after a pregnancy had quickened. No wonder then that Heber C. Kimball, recalling his courtship with a woman he married in 1822, claimed that she had been "taught . . . in our young days, when she got into the family way, to send for a doctor and get rid of the child"; a course that she followed.[9]

In summary, then, the practice of aborting unwanted pregnancies was, if not common, almost certainly not rare in the United States during the first decades of the nineteenth century. A knowledge of various drugs, potions, and techniques was available from home medical guides, from health books for women, from midwives and irregular practitioners, and from trained physicians. Substantial evidence suggests that many American women sought abortions, tried the standard techniques of the day, and no doubt succeeded some proportion of the time in terminating unwanted pregnancies. Moreover, this practice was neither morally nor legally wrong in the eyes of the vast majority of Americans, provided it was accomplished before quickening.

The actual number of abortions in the United States prior to the advent of any statutes regulating its practice simply cannot be known. But an equally significant piece of information about those abortions can be gleaned from the historical record. It concerns the women who were having them. Virtually every observer through the middle of the 1830s believed that an overwhelming percentage of the American women who sought and succeeded in having abortions did so because they feared the social consequences of an illegitimate pregnancy, not because they wanted to limit their fertility per se. The doctor who uncovered the use of snake root as an abortifacient, for example, related that in all of the many instances he heard about "it was taken by women who had indulged in illegitimate love. . . ."[10]

In short, abortion was not thought to be a means of family limitation in the United States, at least on any significant scale, through the first third of the nineteenth century. This was hardly surprising in a largely rural and essentially preindustrial society, whose birth-rates were exceeding any ever recorded in a European nation.[11] One could, along with medical student [Thomas] Massie, be less than enthusiastic about such an "unnatural" prac-tice as abortion, yet tolerate it as the "recourse ... of the victim of passion ... the child of nature" who was driven by "an unrelenting world" unable to forgive any "deviation from what they have termed virtue."[12] Conse-quently, Americans in the early nineteenth century could and did look the other way when they encountered abortion. Nothing in their medical knowledge or in the rulings of their courts compelled them to do otherwise, and, as Massie indicated, there was considera-ble compassion for the women involved. It would be nearly midcentury before the per-ception of who was having abortions for what reasons would begin to shift in the United States, and that shift would prove to be one of the critical developments in the evolution of American abortion policy.

A final point remains to be made about abortion in the United States during the first decades of the nineteenth century. Most ob-servers appeared to consider it relatively safe, at least by the medical standards of the day, rather than extremely dangerous. . . . This too must have reassured women who decided to risk an abortion before quickening. According to the lecture notes of one of his best students, Walter Channing told his Harvard classes that abortion could be troublesome when produced by external blows, because severe internal hemorrhage would be likely, but that generally considered, "abortion [was] not so dangerous as commonly supposed."[13]

The significance of these opinions lay less in whether or not they were accurate than in the fact that writers on abortion, including physicians, saw no reason to stress the dangers attendant to the process. Far from it. They were skeptical about poisons and purgatives, but appear to have assessed physically induced abortions as medically acceptable risks by the standards of the day, especially if brought on during the period of pregnancy when both popular belief and the public courts condoned them anyhow. Here again was a significant early perception that would later change. That change, like the shift in the perception of who was having abortions for what purposes, would also have an impact on the evolution of American abortion policy. . . .

THE SOCIAL CHARACTER OF ABORTION IN AMERICA, 1840–1880

Before 1840 abortion was perceived in the United States primarily as a recourse of the des-perate, especially of the young woman in trouble who feared the wrath of an overexacting society. After 1840, however, evidence began to accu-mulate that the social character of the practice had changed. A high proportion of the women whose abortions contributed to the soaring in-cidence of that practice in the United States be-tween 1840 and 1880 appeared to be married, native-born, Protestant women, frequently of middle- or upper-class status. The data came from disparate sources, some biased and some not, but in the end proved compelling.

Even before the availability of reliable evi-dence confirmed that the nation's birthrates were starting to plummet, observers noticed that abortion more and more frequently in-volved married women rather than single women in trouble. Professor Hugh L. Hodge of the University of Pennsylvania, one of the first physicians in the United States to speak out about abortion in anything approaching a public forum, lectured his introductory obstet-rics students in 1839 that abortion was fast be-coming a prominent feature of American life. Hodge still considered women trying "to de-stroy the fruit of illicit pleasure" to be the ones most often seeking abortions, but he alerted his students to the fact that "married women, also, from the fear of labor, from indisposition to have the care, the expense, or the trouble of children, or some other motive" were more and more frequently requesting "that the embryo be destroyed by their medical attendant." Hodge attributed a good deal of this activity to the quickening doctrine, which allowed "women whose moral character is, in other re-spects, without reproach; mothers who are de-voted, with an ardent and self-denying affection, to the children who already constitute[d] their family [to be] perfectly indifferent respecting the foetus in the utero."[14] . . .

Opinion was divided regarding the social status of the women who accounted for the great upsurge of abortion during the middle period of the nineteenth century. While most observers agreed "all classes of society, rich and poor" were involved to some extent, many thought that the middle and upper classes practiced abortion more extensively than the lower classes.[15] The Michigan State Medical So-ciety in 1859 declared that abortion "pervade[d] all ranks" in that state.[16] The Medical Society of Buffalo pointed out that same year "now we have ladies, yes, *educated and refined ladies*" involved as well.[17] On the other hand, court cases revealed at least a sprinkling of lower-class women, servant girls, and the like. . . .

Although the going price for an abortion varied tremendously according to place, time, practitioner, and patient, abortions appear to have been generally quite expensive. Regular physicians testified repeatedly throughout the period that the abortion business was enormously lucrative. Those doctors pledged not to perform abortions bitterly resented men like the Boston botanic indicted for manslaughter in an abortion case in 1851, who posted $8000 bond and returned to his offices, at a time when the average university professor in the United States earned under $2000 per year.[18] . . .

When women turned from regulars to the commercial abortionists, the prices were still not cheap. Itinerants and irregulars generally tried to charge whatever they judged the traffic would bear, which could vary anywhere from $5 to $500. During the 1840s, for example, Madame Restell charged $5 for an initial visit and diagnosis, then negotiated the price of the operation "according to the wealth and liberality of the parties." In a case for which she was indicted in 1846 she asked a young woman about "her beau's circumstances" before quoting a figure, and then tried to get $100 when she found out the man was a reasonably successful manufacturer's representative. The man thought that was too costly, and only after extensive haggling among go-betweens was a $75 fee agreed upon.[19] . . .

Despite the apparent gradual leveling of prices, however, the abortion business remained a profitable commercial venture well into the 1870s. Anthony Comstock, the single-minded leader of a massive anti-obscenity campaign launched in the United States during the 1870s, kept meticulous and extensive records of all of the people he helped arrest while operating as a special agent of the Post Office Department. Between 1872 and 1880 Comstock and his associates aided in the indictment of 55 persons whom Comstock identified as abortionists. The vast majority were very wealthy and posted large bonds with ease. . . .

. . . [A]bortion entered the mainstream of American life during the middle decades of the nineteenth century. While the unmarried and the socially desperate continued to have recourse to it as they had earlier in the century, abortion also became highly visible, much more frequently practiced, and quite common as a means of family limitation among white, Protestant, native-born wives of middle- and upper-class standing. These dramatic changes, in turn, evoked sharp comment from two ideologically opposed groups in American society, each of which either directly or indirectly blamed the other for the shift in abortion patterns. On one side of the debate were the antifeminists, led by regular physicians, and on the other side were the nation's feminists. Both groups agreed that abortion had become a large-scale and socially significant phenomenon in American life, but they disagreed over the reasons why.

Before examining the two chief explanations put forward by contemporaries for the striking shifts in the incidence and the character of abortion in the United States after 1840, two observations may be worth making. First, it is never easy to understand why people do what they do even in the most straightforward of situations; it is nearly impossible to know with certainty the different reasons, rational and irrational, why people in the past might have taken such a psychologically loaded action as the termination of a suspected pregnancy. Second, most participants on both sides of the contemporary debate over why so many American women began to practice abortion after 1840 actually devoted most of their attention to the question of why American women wanted to limit their fertility. This confirmed that abortion was important between 1840 and 1880 primarily as a means of family limitation, but such discussions offer only marginal help in understanding why so many American women turned to abortion itself as a means toward that end.

Cultural anthropologists argue that abortion has been practiced widely and frequently in preindustrial societies at least in part because "it is a woman's method [of limiting fertility] and can be practiced without the man's knowledge."[20] This implies a sort of women's conspiracy to limit population, which would be difficult to demonstrate in the context of nineteenth-century America. Nonetheless, there is some evidence, though it must be considered carefully, to suggest that an American variant of this proposition may have been at least one of the reasons why abortion became such a common form of family limitation in the United States during the period. A number of physicians, as will become evident, certainly believed that one of the keys to the upsurge of abortion was the fact that it was a uniquely female practice, which men could neither control nor prevent. . . .

Earlier in the century observers had alleged that the tract literature and lectures of the women's rights movement advocated family planning and disseminated abortifacient information.[21] In 1859 Harvard professor Walter Channing reported the opinion that "women for whom this office of foeticide, unborn-child-killing, is committed, are strong-minded," and no later writer ever accused them of being weak-minded.[22] . . .

The most common variant of the view that abortion was a manifestation of the women's rights movement hinged upon the word "fashion." Over and over men claimed that women who aborted did so because they cared more about scratching for a better perch in society than they did about raising children. They dared not waste time on the latter lest they fall behind in the former. Women, in short, were accused of being aggressively self-indulgent. Some women, for example, had "the effrontery to say boldly, that they have neither the time nor inclination to nurse babies"; others exhibited "self-indulgence in most disgusting forms"; and many of the women practicing abortion were described as more interested in "selfish and personal ends" or "fast living" than in the maternity for which God had supposedly created them.[23] . . . For this reason, some doctors urged that feticide be made a legal ground for divorce.[24] A substantial number of writers between 1840 and 1880, in other words, were willing to portray women who had abortions as domestic subversives. . . .

Notwithstanding the possibility that recourse to abortion sometimes reflected the rising consciousness of the women who had them, and notwithstanding the fact that some males, especially regular physicians, were distinctly uneasy about the practice because of what its ultimate effects upon the social position of women might be, the relationship between abortion and feminism in the nineteenth century nevertheless remained indirect and ironical. This becomes evident when the arguments of the feminists themselves are analyzed. One of the most forceful early statements of what subsequently became the feminist position on abortion was made in the 1850s in a

volume entitled _The Unwelcome Child._[25] The author, Henry C. Wright, asserted that women alone had the right to say when they would become pregnant and blamed the tremendous outburst of abortion in America on selfishly sensual husbands. Wright's volume was more interesting than other similar tracts, however, because he published a large number of letters from women detailing the circumstances under which they had sought abortions.

One of Wright's letters was from a woman who had her first abortion in 1841, because her one-year-old firstborn was sick and her husband was earning almost nothing. She "consulted a lady friend, and by her persuasion and assistance, killed" the fetus she was carrying. When she found herself pregnant again shortly thereafter she "consulted a physician. . . . He was ready with his logic, his medicines and instruments, and told me how to destroy it. After experimenting on myself three months, I was successful. I killed my child about five months after conception." She steeled herself to go full term with her next pregnancy and to "endure" an addition to her impoverished and unhappy household. When pregnant again she "employed a doctor, to kill my child, and in the destruction of it . . . ended my power to be a mother." The woman's point throughout, however, was that abortion "was most repulsive" to her and her recourse to it "rendered [her] an object of loathing to [her]self." Abortion was not a purposeful female conspiracy, but an undesirable necessity forced by thoughtless men. As this woman put it: "I was the veriest slave alive."[26] . . .

The attitudes expressed by Wright's correspondents in the 1840s and 1850s became the basis of the official position of American feminists toward abortion after the Civil War. As Elizabeth Cady Stanton phrased it, the practice was one more result of "the degradation of woman" in the nineteenth century, not of woman's rising consciousness or expanding opportunities outside the home.[27] . . . The remedy to the problem of abortion in the United States, in their view, was not legalized abortion open to all but "the education and enfranchisement of women" which would make abortion unnecessary in a future world of egalitarian respect and sexual discretion.[28] In short, most feminists, though they agreed completely with other observers that abortion was endemic in America by midcentury, did not blame the increase on the rising ambitions of women but asserted with Matilda E. J. Gage "that this crime of 'child murder,' 'abortion,' 'infanticide,' lies at the door of the male sex."[29] The *Woman's Advocate* of Dayton, Ohio, put it even more forcefully in 1869: "Till men learn to check their sensualism, and leave their wives free to choose their periods of maternity, let us hear no more invectives against women for the destruction of prospective unwelcome children, whose dispositions, made miserable by unhappy ante-natal conditions, would only make their lives a curse to themselves and others."[30] . . .

Despite the blame and recrimination evoked by the great upsurge of abortion in the United States in the nineteenth century, some of which was directed at women and some at men, it appears likely that most decisions to use abortion probably involved couples conferring together, not just men imposing their wills or women acting unilaterally, and that abortion was the result of diffuse pressures, not merely the rising consciousness of women or the tyrannical aggressions of men. American men and women wanted to express their sexuality and mutual affections, on the one hand, and to limit their fertility, on the other. Abortion was neither desirable nor undesirable in itself, but rather one of the few available means of reconciling and realizing those two higher priorities. And it seems likely that the man and woman agreed to both of those higher priorities in most instances, thus somewhat mooting in advance the question of which one was more responsible for the decisions that made abortion a common phenomenon in mid-nineteenth-century America.[31]

Court records provide one source of evidence for the mutuality of most abortion decisions. Almost every nineteenth-century abortion case that was written up, whether in the popular press, in medical journals, or in the official proceedings of state supreme courts, involved the agreement of both the man and the woman. There is no record of any man ever having sued any woman for aborting his child. . . .

Perhaps the best evidence for the likely mutuality of most abortion decisions is contained in the diary that Lester Frank Ward, who later became one of America's most famous sociologists, kept as a newlywed in the 1860s. Though Ward was unique in writing down the intimate decisions that he and his wife had to make, the couple seemed otherwise typical young Americans, almost

as Tocqueville might have described them, anxious for further education and ambitious to get ahead quickly. Both Ward and his wife understood that a child would overburden their limited resources and reduce the probability of ever realizing either their individual goals of self-improvement or their mutual goals as a couple. They avoided pregnancy in pre-marital intercourse, then continued to avoid it after their marriage in August 1862. Not until early in 1864 did Lizzie Ward become pregnant. In March, without consulting her husband, she obtained "an effective remedy" from a local woman, which made her very sick for two days but helped her to terminate her pregnancy. She probably took this action after missing three or four periods; it was still early enough in gestation that her husband did not realize she was pregnant but late enough that lactation had begun. Ward noted in his diary that "the proof" she had been pregnant was "the milk" that appeared after the abortion.[32]

Anti-feminists might have portrayed Lizzie Ward's action as diabolical, a betrayal of duty. Feminists might have viewed it as the only recourse open to a female who wanted both to further her own education and to remain on good terms with an ambitious spouse who would certainly have sacrificed his wife's goals to child-rearing, while he pursued his own. But the decision was really the result of a pre-existing consensus between the two of them. Though Ward had not been party to the process in a legal or direct sense, which may go some distance toward confirming the role of abortion as a more uniquely female method of family limitation than contraception, he was clearly delighted that his wife was "out of danger" and would not be having a child. After this brush with family responsibility, the Wards tried a number of new methods of contraception, which they presumably hoped would be more effective than whatever they had been using to avoid pregnancy before Lizzie had to resort to abortion. These included both "pills" and "instruments." Not until the summer of 1865, after Ward had obtained a decent job in Washington, did the couple have a baby.[33]

Abortion had been for the Wards what it apparently also was for many other American couples: an acceptable means toward a mutually desirable end, one of the only ways they had to allow themselves both to express their sexuality and affection toward each other with some degree of frequency and to postpone family responsibilities until they thought they were better prepared to raise children. The line of acceptability for most Americans trying to reconcile these twin priorities ran just about where Lizzie Ward had drawn it. Infanticide, the destruction of a baby after its birth, was clearly unacceptable, and so was abortion after quickening, though that was a much grayer area than infanticide. But abortion before quickening, like contraception itself, was an appropriate and legally permissible method of avoiding unwanted children. And it had one great advantage, as the Wards learned, over contraception: it worked. As more and more women began to practice abortion, however, and as the practice changed from being invisible to being visible, from being quantitatively insignificant to being a systematic practice that terminated a substantial number of pregnancies after 1840, and from being almost entirely a recourse of the desperate and the socially marginal to being a commonly employed procedure among the middle and upper classes of American society, state legislators decided to reassess their policies toward the practice. Between 1840 and 1860 law-makers in several states began to respond to the increase of abortion in American life.

NOTES

1. The quickening doctrine went back to the thirteenth century in England. . . . On quickening in the common law see Cyril C. Means, Jr., "The Law of New York concerning Abortion and the Status of the Foetus, 1664–1968: A Case of Cessation of Constitutionality," *New York Law Forum* XIV, no. 3 (Fall 1968): 419–26.
2. Ibid., pp. 411–19, and John T. Noonan, Jr., "An Almost Absolute Value in History," in John T. Noonan, Jr., ed., *The Morality of Abortion* (Cambridge, Mass., 1970), pp. 1–59. . . .
3. . . . Buchan's volume was published in Philadelphia as early as 1782, where it went through many editions. . . . This remarkably successful book continued to be reprinted in America through 1850.
4. Buchan, *Domestic Medicine*, pp. 400, 403–4.
5. See, for example, Frederick Hollick, *Diseases of Women, Their Causes and Cure Familiarly Explained: With Practical Hints for Their Prevention, and for the Preservation of Female Health: For Every Female's Private Use* (New York, 1849), p. 150. . . .
6. . . . [See] George Ellington, *The Women of New York, or the Under-World of the Great City* (New York, 1869), pp. 399–400.
7. Peter Smith, "The Indian Doctor's Dispensary, Being Father Peter Smith's Advice Respecting Diseases and Their Cure; Consisting of Prescriptions for Many Complaints: And a Description of Medicines, Simple and Compound, Showing Their Virtues and How to Apply Them," [1813] reproduced in

J. U. Lloyd, ed., *Bulletin of the Lloyd Library of Botany, Pharmacy and Materia Medica* (1901), Bull. #2, Reproduction Series #2, pp. 46–47.
8. John Burns, *Observations on Abortion: Containing an Account of the Manner in Which It Takes Place, the Causes Which Produce It, and the Method of Preventing or Treating It* (Troy, N.Y., 1808), pp. 73–81. . . .
9. Heber C. Kimball in the *Journal of Discourses,* 26 vols. (Liverpool, 1857), V:91–92.
10. Thomas Massie, "An Experimental Inquiry into the Properties of the Polygala Senega," in Charles Caldwell, ed., *Medical Theses,* . . . (Philadelphia, 1806), p. 203.
11. . . . William Petersen's widely used *Population* (New York, 3rd ed., 1975), p. 15, labels [the U.S. population from 1800 to 1830 as] the "underdeveloped" type and identifies its characteristics as a mixed economy, high fertility rates, falling mortality rates, and very high rates of population growth.
12. Massie, "Polygala Senega," p. 204.
13. John G. Metcalf, student notebooks written while attending Dr. Walter Channing's lectures of midwifery at Harvard Medical School, 1825–1826 (Countway Library, Harvard Medical School), entry for Dec. 27, 1825. . . .
14. Hugh L. Hodge in Francis Wharton and Moreton Stillé, *Treatise on Medical Jurisprudence* (Philadelphia, 1855), p. 270.
15. "Report on Criminal Abortion," *Transactions of the American Medical Association* XII (1859):75.
16. E. P. Christian, "Report to the State Medical Society on Criminal Abortions," *Peninsular & Independent Medical Journal* II:135.
17. "Criminal Abortions," *Buffalo Medical Journal and Monthly Review* XIV (1859):249.
18. *Boston Medical and Surgical Journal* XLIV, no. 14 (May 7, 1851):288. . . . Worthington Hooker, *Physician and Patient* . . . (New York, 1849), passim, and especially pp. 405–8. The estimate on income is from Colin B. Burke, "The Quiet Influence" (Ph.D. diss, Washington University of St. Louis, 1973):69, Table 2.19.
19. A Physician of New-York, *Trial of Madame Restell, For Producing Abortion on the Person of Maria Bodine,* . . . (New York, 1847), pp. 3–4, 10.
20. Kingsley Davis and Judith Blake, "Social Structure and Fertility: An Analytical Framework," *Economic Development and Cultural Change* IV, no. 3 (April 1956):230.
21. Hooker, *Physician and Patient,* p. 93; James Reed, *From Private Vice to Public Virtue: The Birth Control Movement and American Society since 1830* (New York, 1978), chaps. 1–5.
22. Walter Channing, "Effects of Criminal Abortion," *Boston Medical and Surgical Journal* LX (Mar. 17, 1859):135.
23. E. M. Buckingham, "Criminal Abortion," *Cincinnati Lancet & Observer* X (Mar. 1867):141; Channing, "Effects of Criminal Abortion," p. 135; J. C. Stone, "Report on the Subject of Criminal Abortion," *Transactions of the Iowa State Medical Society* I (1867):29; J. Miller, "Criminal Abortion," *The Kansas City Medical Record* I (Aug. 1884):296.
24. [See] H. Gibbons, Sr., "On Feticide," *Pacific Medical and Surgical Journal* (San Francisco) XXI, no. 3 (Aug. 1879):97–111; . . .

25. Henry C. Wright, *The Unwelcome Child; or, the Crime of an Undesigned and Undesired Maternity* (Boston, 1860). The volume was copyrighted in 1858.

26. Ibid., pp. 65–69.

27. E[lizabeth] C[ady] S[tanton], "Infanticide and Prostitution," *Revolution* I, no. 5 (Feb. 5, 1868):65.

28. Ibid. For the same point reiterated see "Child Murder," in ibid. I, no. 10 (Mar. 12, 1868): 146–47. . . .

29. Ibid. I, no. 14 (Apr. 9, 1868):215–16.

30. E. V. B., "Restellism, and the N.Y. Medical Gazette," *Woman's Advocate* (Dayton, Ohio) I, no. 20 (Apr. 8, 1869):16. . . .

31. Carl N. Degler is one of those who have argued persuasively that nineteenth-century American women were very much aware of their own sexuality and desirous, morality books notwithstanding, of expressing it: "What Ought To Be and What Was: Women's Sexuality in the Nineteenth Century," *American Historial Review* LXXIX, no. 5 (Dec. 1974):1467–90.

32. Lester Ward, *Young Ward's Diary*, Bernhard J. Stern, ed. (New York, 1935), p. 140.

33. Ibid., pp. 150, 152–53, 174.

Comstock Act, 1873

This "Act for the Suppression of Trade in, and Circulation of Obscene Literature and Articles of Immoral Use" was passed at the urging of Anthony Comstock, the head of the New York Society for the Suppression of Vice. The first section prohibited the sale of the described materials in the District of Columbia and the territories; subsequent sections prohibited the sending of these materials through the mails or their importation into the United States. Enforcement, as historian Helen Horowitz has explained, was placed in the hands of a newly created "special agent in the United States Post Office with power to confiscate immoral matter in the mails and arrest those sending it." In the 1870s, many states passed their own versions of the federal law.

The link of "obscene literature and articles of immoral use" reflected contemporary practice. Erotic literature and pornography were often sold in the same shops that sold condoms and other birth control devices; these devices, and substances offering to induce abortion, were often advertised in the pages of pornographic literature. Anthony Comstock included in this category writings on sexual reform and free love. The law reflected a belief that both contraception and abortion were acts of interference with the natural order and with God's intentions. No distinction was made between drugs used for abortion and materials used for contraception, or, indeed, pornographic pictures that encouraged masturbation; all were treated in the same terms. The law may have begun "as a measure to protect children against erotica," but it included "contraceptive information and materials and advertisements for abortion. . . . it was possible to construe this law as banning printed advocacy of free love."* Note the heavy penalties provided.

Be it enacted . . . That whoever, within the District of Columbia or any of the Territories of the United States . . . shall sell . . . or shall offer to sell, or to lend, or to give away, or in any manner to exhibit, or shall otherwise publish or offer to publish in any manner, or shall have in his possession, for any such purpose or purposes, any obscene book, pamphlet, paper, writing, advertisement, circular, print, picture, drawing or other representation, figure, or image on or of paper or other material, or any cast, instrument, or other article of an immoral nature, or any drug or medicine, or any article whatever, for the prevention of conception, or for causing unlawful abortion, or shall advertize the same for sale, or shall write or print, or cause to be written or printed, any card, circular, book, pamphlet, advertisement, or notice of any kind, stating when, where, how, or of whom, or by what means, any of the articles in this section . . . can be purchased or obtained, or shall manufacture, draw, or print, or in any wise make any of such articles, shall be deemed guilty of a misdemeanor, and on conviction thereof in any court of the United States . . . he shall be imprisoned at hard labor in the penitentiary for not less than six months nor more than five years for each offense, or fined not less than one hundred dollars nor more than two thousand dollars, with costs of court. . . .

*Helen Lefkowitz Horowitz, *Rereading Sex: Battles over Sexual Knowledge and Suppression in Nineteenth-Century America* (New York: Alfred A. Knopf, 2002), pp. 381, 385.

Public Laws of the United States of America, Passed at the Third Session of the Forty-Second Congress (Boston, 1873), p. 598.

REFORMING SOCIETY

SUSAN ZAESKE
Signatures of Citizenship: Debating Women's Antislavery Petitions

As women's activities during the Revolution demonstrate, women participated in politics and public life despite not having the vote. Petitioning legislatures, governors, and town governments had long been a strategy of women who wished to articulate a grievance or ask for relief, often on behalf not directly of themselves but of their family. In the decades before the Civil War, activist women working together presented the U.S. Congress with a radically innovative document: the large-scale collective petition.

The mass petition effort was motivated by the fervent desire some women felt to end slavery. In demanding that Congress hear their voices, abolitionist women had to have thick skins. Petitioning women often found other women hesitant and fearful, and found men scornful, even those political men who were supposed to take such good care of women's interests that they should be content not to have the vote.

The act of petitioning involved more than the silent scribbling of a signature, Susan Zaeske reports. To make a collective petition, someone had to carry it to potential signers and then convince a friend or neighbor or stranger to sign. The person who circulated the petition, who walked house to house in her neighborhood or brought it to church or market, had to be an articulate debater, prepared to meet contempt with patience and reason. As citizens who participate in political campaigns in our own time continually find, seeking political change is itself a politicizing experience.

What criticisms were leveled at women's efforts to petition for antislavery causes? Whose interests—besides those of slaveholders—were undermined by women's political participation? How did women—and their allies, like John Quincy Adams—defend their activities? How is it possible to have a political impact without the vote? (In our own time, young people involved in the environmental movement use some of the strategies that antislavery women devised.) What do you think is the relationship between the women's antislavery petition campaign and subsequent movements for women's rights and for the vote?

Early in February 1834 Louisa, Maria, Abigail, Rosey, and Caroline Dickinson signed their names to a petition addressed to the Senate and House of Representatives of the United States. They were joined by . . . scores of other Ohio women who together prayed Congress to abolish slavery in the District of Columbia. These westerners were among the first women

Excerpted from the introduction and chs. 5 and 6 of *Signatures of Citizenship: Petitioning, Antislavery, and Women's Political Identity* by Susan Zaeske (Chapel Hill: University of North Carolina Press, 2003). Reprinted by permission of the author and publisher. Notes have been edited and renumbered.

in the United States to collectively petition Congress on a political issue. In so doing they defied the long-standing custom of females limiting their petitioning of Congress to individual prayers regarding personal grievances. During the coming years hundreds of thousands of women from throughout the North would join the petition campaign and risk association with the unpopular cause of immediate abolitionism. Maria Weston Chapman, a leader of the petitioning effort, recalled that when antislavery women began to petition Congress, many Americans—male and female alike—were not "wont to witness the appeals kindly." Time and again female petitioners were assailed for leaving their "proper" sphere of the home and abandoning benevolent charitable causes to engage in petitioning and political action in the public arena. Yet antislavery women persevered, . . . seizing the radical potential of one of the few civil rights they were understood to possess—the right of petition—to assert substantial political authority.[1] . . . Large numbers of white and free black American women engaged in collective petitioning of Congress in an attempt to reshape public opinion and influence national policy. . . . [A]bsent the right of suffrage, petitioning provided a conduit for women to assert a modified form of citizenship. Although at the beginning of their involvement in the campaign in 1835 women tended to disavow the political nature of their petitioning, by the 1840s they routinely asserted the right of women to make political demands of their representatives. This change in the rhetoric of female antislavery petitions and appeals, from a tone of humility to a tone of insistence, reflected an ongoing transformation of the political identity of signers from that of subjects to that of citizens. Having encouraged women's involvement in national politics, women's antislavery petitioning created an appetite for further political participation and more rights. After female abolitionists established the right of women to petition Congress collectively on political issues, countless women employed that right to lobby their representatives and agitate public opinion to promote causes such as temperance, antilynching, and ultimately, woman suffrage.

From 1831 to 1863 women publicly expressed their opinion about slavery by affixing approximately 3 million signatures to petitions aimed at Congress. Women's efforts enabled abolitionists to send enough petitions to Congress to provoke debate over the question of slavery, a feat petitioning by men alone had failed to accomplish. . . . Deluged with petitions, in June 1836 the House of Representatives passed a rule immediately tabling all memorials on the subject of slavery. The [gag] rule proved a "godsend" to the struggling antislavery movement, for it linked the popular right of petition with the unpopular cause of immediate abolitionism. Petitioning was intended not only to pressure congressmen but also to rectify public opinion with regard to the sinfulness of slavery. By gathering signatures in family and female social networks as well as through soliciting door-to-door, women discussed the issue of slavery with people who would never go to hear an abolitionist lecturer and who could not read abolitionist tracts. . . .

Although women's petitioning soon became highly controversial, at the outset the philosophy of moral suasion and the tool of petitioning seemed to offer an especially suitable means for women to participate in the abolition movement. Women could use the right of petition—a right that, unlike the ballot, they were generally understood to possess—to apply the force of their supposedly superior morality to reform public opinion with regard to the sin of slavery. Although petitioning was less direct than voting, in the 1830s at least, it was not necessarily considered less powerful. Petitioning was seen as a pure expression of individual moral conscience, as opposed to the vote, which was viewed as tainted with personal interest and party spirit.

Central to comprehending the history of women's antislavery petitioning and its effect on women's political status is an understanding of the nature of the right of petition. At its core a petition is a request for redress of grievances sent from a subordinate (whether an individual or a group) to a superior (whether a ruler or a representative). As a genre of political communication, the petition is characterized by a humble tone and an acknowledgment of the superior status of the recipient.[2]

The supplicatory nature of the right of petition held radical potential for women, for natural law assumed that all subjects (and later all citizens) possessed the right of petition and that rulers (and later representatives) were obliged to receive and respond to petitions regardless of the subject of their prayer. Abolition women relied on the first assumption in order to claim and defend their right to petition amidst an environment in which their political status, like that of free blacks, was undergoing constant renegotiation. In fact, so labile was the political status of certain groups of inhabitants of the republic that state constitutional reform conventions of the 1820s and 1830s revoked free black men's voting rights, rights they had previously possessed and exercised. In 1837 the House of Representatives decided that slaves were not citizens and passed a resolution stating that they had no right of petition. For women, also a group whose political rights were vulnerable, petitioning amounted to an assertion that they possessed the right of petition and that they were citizens, though a type of citizen different from enfranchised men. By assuming the status of petitioners, women, though they lacked the vote, forced a hearing of their requests, for their representatives were obligated, in principle at least, to receive and respond to their grievances. Even when the House repeatedly passed gag rules that immediately tabled all antislavery petitions, through their continued petitioning, women kept alive the slavery question in public discourse. They added to congressional and general public debate, moreover, discussion of women's rights and the nature of female citizenship. . . .

. . . Sarah Grimké, an experienced signature gatherer, complained, "I have sometimes been astonished and grieved at the servitude of women, and at the little idea many of them have of their own moral existence and responsibilities. A woman who is asked to sign a petition for the abolition of slavery in the District of Columbia . . . not infrequently replies, 'My husband does not approve of it.'"[3] . . .

When women affixed their signatures to petitions, making a mark that authorized petitions as statements of their opinions, they threw off the cover of their husbands or fathers and asserted their existence as political individuals. For some women, lending their signature to a petition may have involved rejecting the notion that the signature of their husband, father, or brother adequately represented their opinion. For other women, signing a petition was an act of defiance against the wishes of male protectors, who might have opposed abolitionism or opposed women petitioning or both. It is worth noting, moreover, that throughout the campaign the vast majority of women eschewed the use of marital titles and signed petitions as, for example, Chloe F. Metcalf, Lydia W. Fairbanks, and even Philomela Johnson Jr. rather than Mrs. Metcalf, Mrs. Fairbanks, and Mrs. Johnson. Given that in 1890

Frances E. Willard was still urging women to write their names as individuals rather than as the wives of someone else, the petitioners' decision to drop "Mrs." during the 1830s appears to radically defy gendered signature norms.[4] . . .

Not only signing but also circulating petitions effected a transformation in women's political identities, for it provided practical experience in carrying out a campaign to influence public opinion. Female canvassers developed strategies specially suited to win women's signatures by incorporating women's daily routines and the spaces they inhabited into patterns of circulating petitions. Upper-class antislavery women, for instance, adapted the rituals associated with social visiting to the political activity of circulating antislavery petitions. . . . Middle-class women relied on family and religious networks in addition to other female associations, such as sewing circles, in order to circulate petitions. Hundreds of women of varying class and religious backgrounds went door-to-door seeking signatures from strangers.[5] . . .

Petition circulators also gained experience in practicing their skills of interpersonal persuasion, which involved internalizing arguments they read and heard as well as sharpening their skills of oral argumentation. Such skills are evident in a female signature gatherer's account of her interaction with an older woman who was reluctant to sign a petition. "My *darter* [daughter] says that you want the niggers and whites to marry together," the elder woman reportedly said. Yet when pressed by the petition circulator, the woman admitted that she did not understand abolitionists to condone amalgamation and asked if indeed they did. "Why, no—that's no business of ours," the abolitionist assured her. "We leave all to do as they please with regard to it." The canvasser then explained that the petition simply asked Congress to free slaves in the District of Columbia. After making clear the goal of the petition, the circulator stated, "I suppose you know that the colored people in the District are held as property, bought and sold like beasts, and treated very cruelly. Now what we ask is, that Congress, which 'possesses exclusive jurisdiction' there, should give all those slaves their freedom and place them under the protection of law." The older woman responded in agreement and lamented the fact that her daughter was so mistaken.[6]

Although signature gathering "engendered self-confidence and assertiveness" . . . the resistance they encountered understandably led female abolitionists to regard circulating petitions as an unpleasant duty.... Several members of the Providence Rhode Island Female Anti-Slavery Society reported that although they had won many signatures, they found petitioning to be a "self-denying, and unpleasant task."[7] ...

The burden of petitioning was worsened by denunciations from the press and the pulpit. Clergy and other traditionalists anxious about male political dominance were alarmed to see women encouraging one another to express publicly their opinions separate from those of their husbands. The *Boston Religious Magazine*, the *New York Commercial Advertiser*, and the *Providence Journal* all "sharpened their pens and brightened up their wits" to attack the idea of women circulating and signing petitions to Congress. These newspapers ... questioned whether women knew anything about slavery and despised the idea that women should meddle with politics. They scolded "female petitioners" for the "impertinence" of "undertaking to teach Congress their duty."[8]

As bad as the editorial condemnations were, they were nowhere near as punitive as those issued by clergymen such as Pastor Albert A. Folsom of the Universal Church in Hingham, Massachusetts.... Folsom spelled out the unfortunate consequences that would befall a woman who petitioned with the "clamorous" abolitionists. Such a woman, he said, would begin by seeking "relaxation too often from her domestic obligations." Then she would leave her children and become a slave to her "appetites and passions" while she interested herself "with wonderful zeal in the cause of the Southern negro." Besides suggesting that women petitioners were sexually involved with male slaves for whom they advocated, Folsom predicted that abolition petitioning would poison women's souls, embitter their affections, and exasperate their feelings. "She, who is naturally amiable and modest, ... is imperceptively transformed into a bigoted, rash, and morose being.... Self-sufficiency, arrogance and masculating boldness follow naturally in the train."[9] ...

Male editors and clergy were not alone in condemning the political activism of antislavery women generated by the petition campaign. Early in 1837 the well-known reformer and female educator Catharine E. Beecher launched her attack on abolitionists and female

activism through publication of *An Essay on Slavery and Abolitionism with Reference to the Duty of American Females*, which she wrote in response to Angelina Grimké's *Appeal to the Christian Women of the South*. In the process of encouraging women to petition and take action to abolish slavery, Grimké's *Appeal* advocated a radical expansion of women's role in reform work. Particularly alarming to Beecher was the fact that in carving out a role for women in the abolitionist movement, Grimké had described a model woman as deeply interested in political issues, critical of the clergy, resistant to social norms, confident of her authority to interpret the Bible, unwilling to subordinate herself to men, and defiant of the law. Beecher responded in her *Essay* that the plan of "arraying females" in the abolition movement was "unwise and inexpedient." Engaging in antislavery activity, she feared, would draw women "forth from their appropriate retirement" and thrust them into the "arena of political collision." Once woman entered the political sphere, Beecher predicted, she would be corrupted by power and would lose her "aegis of defence": her moral purity. Consequently she would forfeit "all the sacred protection of religion, all the generous promptings of chivalry, all the poetry of romantic gallantry." Rather than embracing Grimké's model of the active woman, Beecher pleaded with readers to preserve the status of woman by retaining "her place as dependent and defenceless, and making no claims, and maintaining no right but what are the gifts of honour, rectitude and love."[10]

Especially upsetting to Beecher were Grimké's entreaties for women to petition. "Petitions to congress, in reference to the official duties of legislators, seem, IN ALL CASES, to fall entirely without the sphere of female duty," Beecher retorted. The only proper persons to make appeals to rulers, she maintained, were those who appointed rulers: men. Women's role was not to petition legislators but to influence male friends and relatives to address legislators. "But if females cannot influence their nearest friends, to urge forward a public measure in this way, they surely are out of their place, in attempting to do it themselves...."[11]

On one hand, defenders of women's right of petition clung to the argument that female moral superiority rendered women uniquely suited to petition. On the other hand, advocates employed bolder arguments that women possessed a natural and constitutional right of petition and that they were endowed with equal responsibilities and therefore equal rights with man. Angelina Grimké went so far as to argue that the fact that women were denied the right to vote provided no reason to deny them the right of petition. Republican principles demanded that women be heard in some way, she maintained, or Congress would be guilty of taxation without representation. The same reasoning, she implied, also led to the conclusion that women possessed the right to vote. Grimké was not alone in defending women's right to petition and connecting it to the franchise. In the course of defending the right of women to petition against slavery, John Quincy Adams would question, on the floor of the U.S. House of Representatives, the practice of denying women the right to vote.

Although the flood of antislavery petitions that swept into Congress when it convened on December 7, 1837, was sandbagged by a gag [rule,] those pertaining to the annexation of Texas continued to seep onto the floor of the House of Representatives. On March 5, 1838, the House referred all memorials relating to the Texas question to the Committee on Foreign Affairs, which was charged with composing a report about the content of the petitions and the expediency of granting their requests. On June 14 the report was presented by the committee's chairman, Benjamin Howard of Maryland. Annoyed by the preponderance of petitions from females, Howard expressed his "regret" that so many of the memorials were signed by women. It was inappropriate for women to petition their legislators, he said, because females were afforded ample opportunity for the exercise of their influence by approaching their fathers, husbands, and children in the domestic circle and by "shedding over it the mild radiance of the social virtues, instead of rushing into the fierce struggles of political life." By leaving their proper sphere, Howard charged, women were "discreditable, not only to their own particular section of the country, but also to the national character."[12]

Although few northern representatives during the 1830s defended abolitionists' right of petition, especially that of abolitionist women, John Quincy Adams rose to the occasion. "Sir, was it from a son—was it from a father—was it from a husband, that I heard these words?" demanded the former president. "Does this gentleman consider that women, by petitioning this House in favor of suffering and distress, perform an office 'discreditable' to themselves, to the section of the country where they reside, and to the nation?" Adams offered Howard a chance to retract his assertion: "I have a right to make this call upon him. It is to the wives and to the daughters of my constituents that he applies this language." Howard stood his ground. Adams retorted with a four-day harangue defending the propriety of women involving themselves in political matters and of exercising their constitutional right of petition. . . .

. . . John Dickson of New York and Caleb Cushing and Levi Lincoln of Massachusetts, followed Adams's lead in answering attacks on female petitioners. . . . [P]resenting the petition from the 800 ladies of New York, Dickson emphasized the benevolent nature of women's memorializing. "In the Jewish, Greek, and Roman histories," he recalled, "female remonstrance" heard in public councils "were the cause of 'enlargement and deliverance,' of 'light, and gladness, and joy, and honor,' to a despised and an oppressed people." They were, he said, "all-powerful in expanding and extending the principles of charity, humanity, and benevolence, and in breaking the chains of oppression." . . . Dickson characterized female antislavery petitions as motivated not by political gain but by benevolence. "Surely," he hoped more than believed, "the chivalry of this House will never permit it to turn a deaf ear to the remonstrance of ladies, pleading, as they believe, for the wronged and oppressed."[13]

Given the obstreperous attacks southerners leveled against female petitioners, it was necessary for northern members to do much more than deny that antislavery women harbored political motivations. They had to defend the character of female petitioners. As Adams complained, the petitions had been treated with contempt, and "foul and infamous imputations" had been "poured upon a class of citizens as pure and virtuous as the inhabitants of any section of the Union": females. Likewise, Lincoln represented petitioners from his district as "pure, elevated, and [of as high] intellectual character as any in the world, men and women, kind and generous, and of tenderest sympathies, who would no sooner do an injury or an act of injustice to any human being than the most chivalrous or true-hearted of the sons or daughters of the South."[14]

Yet at issue in the arguments over the character of female antislavery petitioners was more than their reputations as women. At issue was their status as citizens. Adams readily apprehended that attacks on the character of female petitioners effectively denied women's right of petition, and he took [Benjamin] Howard to task for representing the exercise of the right of petition as disgraceful to women as well as to their section of the Union and the nation as a whole. "Now to say, respecting women, that any action of theirs was disgraceful, was more than merely contesting their legal right so to act," Adams averred; "it was contesting the right of the mind, of the soul, and the conscience." This was no "light question," no mere quarrel over the honor of a few women, he emphasized. It concerned "the very utmost depths of the Constitution of the country" and affected "the political rights of one half of the People of the nation."[15]

Throughout the debates . . . , Adams maintained vehemently that there was no legal or constitutional principle linking the right of petition with the character of petitioners. When Adams presented a petition purportedly signed by nine ladies of Fredericksburg, Virginia, Representative Patton, who had lived in that city, assailed Adams for bringing before the House a petition from "mulatto" women of "infamous character." . . . Patton's insinuation that the petition emanated from prostitutes, disclosed Adams, influenced him not a wit in deciding whether or not to present the paper. Rather than worrying over the character of the petitioners, Adams said that he "adhered to the right of petition."

> Where is your law which says that the mean, and the low, and the degraded, shall be deprived of the right of petition, if their moral characters is not good? Where, in the land of freemen, was the right of petition ever placed on the exclusive basis of morality and virtue? Petition is supplication— it is entreaty—it is prayer! And where is the degree of vice or immorality which shall deprive the citizen of the right to supplicate for a boon, or to pray for mercy?[16]

. . . Adams grasped the opportunity . . . to turn the table and question the character of opponents of women's petitions. When in the course of debate Patton disclaimed actually "knowing" the "bad" women who had signed the petition but stated that he "knew of them," Adams said he was glad to hear it, for otherwise he would ask "if they were infamous women, then who was it that had made them infamous?" Not their own color, he judged, but their masters. Adams said he was inclined to

believe this because "there existed great resemblances in the South between the progeny of the colored people and the white men who claimed the possession of them. Thus, perhaps, the charge of being infamous might be retorted upon those who made it, as originating from themselves."

Adams's comments threw the House into great agitation, for he had stabbed brutally at the honor of southern gentlemen. Despite the fact that in February 1837 he faced formal censure for casting character aspersions on southerners in return for the imputations against the Fredericksburg women, he persisted in the strategy of questioning the character of representatives who opposed female petitions. Adams shamed representatives who would turn a deaf ear to women's petitions, asking each member to suppose that his own mother was one of the petitioners: "Would you reject and turn the petition out of doors, and say that you would not even hear it read?" "Every member of the House has, or had, a mother," he observed, adding that "in the whole class of human affections, was there one sentiment more honorable, or more divested of earthly alloy, than that which every man must entertain for his mother.". . .[17]

. . . [I]n his 1838 speech Adams focused on extending the reach of women's duties to include political affairs. . . . In response to Howard's claim that women had no right to petition Congress on political subjects, Adams asked rhetorically, "What does the gentleman understand by 'political subjects'?" Adams answered that "every thing which relates to peace and relates to war, or to any other of the great interests of society, is a political subject. Are women to have no opinions or action on subjects relating to the general welfare?" Fellow Massachusetts representative Caleb Cushing bolstered Adams's statements, maintaining that "it seems to me a strange idea to uphold, in this enlightened age, that woman, refined and educated, intellectual woman, is to have no opinion, or no right to express that opinion." . . .[18]

Hoping to take advantage of patriotic sentiments, Adams also invoked heroines of the American Revolution. . . . He called up the example of Deborah [Sampson] Gannett, who had adorned herself in men's clothes, joined the patriot army, and fought for three years until she was wounded. Members of the House were aware of Gannett's feats because within recent memory they had voted to give her husband a military pension based on the services of his wife and had praised her on the grounds that she had "fought and bled for human liberty." After commending Gannett's actions, which involved rushing physically into "the vortex of politics," Adams asked how Howard could conceivably think it wrong for women to petition on a matter of politics. . . .[19]

Although Adams redefined politics to include all subjects relating to the general welfare and adduced numerous historical examples of women's involvement in politics, . . . he recommended a three-pronged test by which one could determine whether it was proper for women to deviate from the custom of remaining distant from politics. When presented with such a circumstance, prescribed Adams, one must inquire "into the motive which actuated them, the means they employ, and the end they have in view." Adams then applied this test to the case at hand, the petitions against annexation of Texas. As for the motive, he said, it was of the "highest order" of purity: "They petition under a conviction that the consequence of the annexation would be the advancement of that which is sin in the sight of God, viz: slavery." The means were appropriate, Adams said, because it was Congress who must decide the question, and it was Congress to whom the women must petition. Echoing a justification offered by the female petitioners themselves, he stated, "It is a petition—it is a prayer—a supplication—that which you address to the Almighty Being above you. And what can be more appropriate to their sex?" As for the end sought by female petitioners, it, too, was virtuous, pure, and of the most exalted character: "to prevent the perpetuation and spread of slavery through America." . . . Adams concluded, "the correct principle is, that women are not only justified, but exhibit the most exalted virtue when they do depart from the domestic circle, and enter on the concerns of their country, of humanity and of their God." Thus Adams repeated the argument employed in the women's appeals, addresses, circulars, and petitions that it was the moral duty of women to speak for those who could not speak for themselves and to help those who could not help themselves. In fact, Adams believed that benevolent activity was a particularly feminine trait: "I say that woman, by the discharge of her duties; has manifested a virtue which is even above the virtues of mankind, and approaches to a superior nature."[20] . . .

. . . Adams characterized Howard as denying women the right of petition because they had no right to vote. Then he asked, "Is it so clear that they have no such right as this last? And if not, who shall say that this argument of the gentleman's is not adding one injustice to another?" In a few short breaths Adams, son of the woman who in 1776 threatened that "the ladies . . . will not hold ourselves bound by any laws in which we have no voice, or representation," went so far as to suggest that women did, in fact, possess the right to vote and that it was an injustice that they were denied the practice of that right. In so doing he embraced a position more radical than that of many women's rights advocates of his time. On the floor of the House of Representatives he questioned the assumption that the Constitution denied women the right to vote. He suggested that the reason women did not vote was custom rather than lack of a right to the franchise. . . . It would be another eight years before the women of New York petitioned their legislature for the vote, a decade before the National Woman's Rights Convention would assert that women possessed the right of suffrage, and eight decades before an organized movement of women persuaded Congress and the public to adopt the position Adams began to articulate on Friday, June 29, 1838.[21]

Women who had signed petitions were particularly pleased to read Adams's defense of their actions and showered praises upon him. When he returned to Massachusetts after Congress had adjourned, Adams was greeted by expressions of approbation in the form of several celebratory events hosted by women in towns of his congressional district. On September 4, 1838, the ladies of Quincy hosted a formal picnic and ball to honor him for defending their rights. . . . When Adams addressed the group, he thanked the women for their kind celebration and acknowledged the large number of petitions he had received from females of the district. Reviewing scenes from the two most recent sessions of Congress, he recalled that Howard had committed a "violent outrage . . . upon the [female] petitioners, and [an] insult upon the sex." . . . Adams said that he believed questions about the duty of women to participate in public affairs should be left to women's own discretion, and he felt assured "there was not the least danger of their obtruding their wishes upon any of the ordinary subjects of legislation," such as banks, tariffs, and public lands, "all which so profoundly agitate the men of this country." Women, he trusted, were concerned with other kinds of matters. In fact, he believed that "far from being debarred by any rule of delicacy" from petitioning, by the "law of their nature," which rendered them kind, benevolent, and compassionate, women were "fitted above all others" for the exercise of this right.[22] Adams could not bring himself to endorse unlimited exercise by women of the absolute right of petition. Instead he trusted—or perhaps urged—that they would act only on public matters related to woman's moral duty and would take no interest in purely political matters such as banks and tariffs. In other words, Adams expected female moral duty to guide the exercise of women's natural rights.

. . . At the core of the southern case against receiving female petitions was the indictment that the petitions constituted not good works resulting from women's Christian duty but, rather, politically motivated machinations controlled by fanatical ministers and wholly improper actions for women. Conflating notions of female duty with political rights, southerners argued that the women's petitions should be ignored because, having transgressed beyond their proper duties, these women were not respectable, and the House was not obligated to accept petitions from people of questionable character.

Adams remained steadfast in his conviction that women possessed a natural right of petition and perhaps a natural right to vote, yet he linked the exercise of women's civil rights to their duties as women. . . . [He was not] willing to abandon the notion that men and women possessed different natures and therefore different duties. But Adams did attempt to use political philosophies associated with women's rights to expand significantly the entailments of women's duty into what many considered the male political realm. . . .

Notwithstanding the decline of organized abolition at the state and national levels in 1839, women continued to petition throughout the 1840s, 1850s, and 1860s, sending massive abolition petitions to Congress on the most pressing political issues of the day. . . . By the 1840s they had begun to mix their signatures with those of men; no longer did women accept the notion that men's names should be allowed to stand out because their opinions meant more to representatives. Moreover, the language of women's petitions during this later period dropped deferential overtures characteristic of the memorials of the 1830s and took on a bolder tone. By the 1850s female petitioning had grown so much

more acceptable and abolitionist sentiment so much more popular that even its most outspoken critic of the 1830s—Catharine E. Beecher—signed her name at the top of a petition. Acceptance of the propriety of women exercising their right to petition was crucial to the success of the petition campaign to win passage of the Thirteenth Amendment. Finally, after three decades of petitioning and due in large part to the ongoing efforts of women who signed and circulated petitions, abolitionists secured their ultimate goal of emancipating the slaves. In the process of petitioning to end slavery, many women transformed their political identity from humble subjects to national citizens.

NOTES

1. Maria Weston Chapman, *Right and Wrong in Massachusetts* (Boston: Henry L. Deveraux, 1840), pp. 11–13.

2. This definition of petitioning is drawn from the *Oxford English Dictionary*.

3. Sarah Grimké, *Letters on the Equality of the Sexes* (1837), in Larry Ceplair, ed., *The Public Years of Sarah and Angelina Grimké: Selected Writings* (New York: Columbia University Press, 1989), p. 239.

4. Frances E. Willard, "A White Life for Two" (1890), in Karlyn Kohrs Campbell, ed. *Man Cannot Speak for Her: Key Texts of the Early Feminists*, Vol. 2 (New York: Praeger, 1989), pp. 335–36.

5. Gerda Lerner, "The Political Activities of Antislavery Women," in *The Majority Finds Its Past: Placing Women in History* (New York: Oxford University Press, 1979), pp. 120–21.

6. *Liberator*, Aug. 4, 1837.

7. Lerner, "Political Activities of Antislavery Women," p. 125.

8. *Emancipator*, Aug. 17, 1837.

9. "A Lecture, Delivered Sunday Evening, by Albert A. Folsom, Pastor of the Universal Church, Hingham, Massachusetts," extracted in *Liberator*, Sept. 22, 1837.

10. Catharine E. Beecher, *An Essay on Slavery and Abolitionism, with Reference to the Duty of American Females* (Philadelphia: Henry Perkins, 1837), pp. 3–6, 97, 101.

11. Ibid., pp. 103–104.

12. John Quincy Adams, *Speech on the Right of the People, Men and Women, to Petition; on the Freedom of Speech and Debate in the House of Representatives of the United States; on the Resolutions of Seven State Legislatures and the Petitions of More than One Hundred Thousand Petitioners, Relating to the Annexation of Texas to this Union. Delivered in the House of Representatives of the United States, in fragments in the morning hour, from the 16th of June to the 7th of July, 1838, inclusive* (Washington, D.C.: Gales and Seaton, 1838), pp. 76–77.

13. *Gales and Seaton's Register of Debates in Congress*, 24th Cong., 1st sess., Feb. 2, 1835, pp. 1131–1132.

14. Ibid., 2d sess., Jan. 9 and Feb. 7, 1837, pp. 1315, 1624.

15. Adams, *Speech on the Right of the People to Petition*, pp. 74, 77–78.

16. *Gales and Seaton's Register of Debates*, 24th Cong., 2d sess., Feb. 6, 1837, pp. 1589, 1596.

17. Ibid., 2d sess., Feb. 9, 1837, p. 1675 and Jan. 9, 1837, p. 1315.

18. Adams, *Speech on the Right of the People to Petition*, pp. 65–66, 69; *Gales and Seaton's Register of Debates*, 24th Cong., 2d sess., Feb. 7, 1837, p. 1645.

19. Adams, *Speech on the Right of the People to Petition*, pp. 70–75.

20. Ibid., pp. 68, 81.

21. Ibid., pp. 65, 77. On the petitions for suffrage directed at the New York legislature, see Jacob Katz Cogan and Lori D. Ginzberg, "1846 Petition for Woman's Suffrage," *Signs* 22 (Winter 1997), pp. 427–439.

22. John Quincy Adams, *Memoirs of John Quincy Adams, Comprising Portions of his Diary from 1795 to 1848*, vol. 10, Charles Francis Adams, ed. (Philadelphia: J.B. Lippincott, 1874–77), pp. 35–37.

GERDA LERNER
The Meanings of Seneca Falls, 1848–1998

In the 1830s and 1840s, individual voices criticizing the way American law and custom defined gender relations began to be heard. The 1848 Declaration of Sentiments (see pp. 247–250) gathered these complaints into a manifesto and offered an agenda for change that would shape a women's rights movement deep into our own time. But the Declaration itself has its own history, emerging out of the specific social conditions in western New York State, out of political and religious arguments, and out of the personal experiences of the women and men who wrote its words and signed their names to it.

The meticulous research of Judith Wellman has enabled us to know the class position, religious affiliation, kin relations, and political sympathies of many of the signers at Seneca Falls. Two-thirds of the signers were women; the signers' ages stretched from fourteen-year-old Susan Quinn to sixty-eight-year-old George Pryor. Most came with another family member: wives with husbands, mothers with daughters, sisters with brothers. (Daniel Anthony was there, but his daughter Susan would not meet Stanton for another three years.) Seventy percent came from the immediate locality of Seneca Falls and neighboring Waterloo, an area that had seen substantial dislocation from a farm region to a manufacturing town, where a substantial group of men had broken with the Democratic and Whig parties to join the abolitionist Free Soilers, and where dissidents from the Quaker Genesee Yearly Meeting formed their own society of Friends devoted to egalitarian gender relations and abolition. Legislative battles over married women's property acts made women's rights especially visible in New York.*

The Declaration of Sentiments, Stanton's indictment of the relations between men and women in her own society, is still stunning in its energy, its precision, and its foresight. In the essay that follows, written for the quincentenary of the Seneca Falls convention, the distinguished historian Gerda Lerner reflects on the meaning of the Declaration for its time and for our own.

*Judith Wellman, "The Seneca Falls Woman's Rights Convention: A Study of Social Networks," *Journal of Women's History* 3 (1991): 9–37; and Wellman, *The Road To Seneca Falls: Elizabeth Cady Stanton and the First Woman's Rights Convention* (Urbana: University of Illinois Press, 2004).

Originally published in *Dissent* (Fall 1998): 35–41. Copyright © Gerda Lerner, 1998. All rights reserved. We mourn Gerda Lerner's death at age 92 on January 2, 2013. See the profile of her by historian Kathryn Kish Sklar at http://jwa.org/encyclopedia/article/lerner-gerda.

Elizabeth Cady Stanton at age 33.
In the most commonly-reproduced photographs of her, Elizabeth Cady Stanton comes to us as she appeared in her fifties and older—a plump, matronly woman with graying hair and a kindly face. But in 1848, when she wrote the great manifesto that set the agenda for the American women's movement for 150 years, she was thirty-three years old, and the one photograph we have of her from that time shows her to be slight and thin, her dark hair hanging in limp ringlets. She is pictured here with Daniel and Henry; the smallest, Gerrit, was a toddler. Did she look tired because she was the mother of three boys under six? Her future—and ours—lay before her. (Courtesy of Elizabeth Cady Stanton Trust/Coline Jenkins–Sahlin.)

In 1848, according to Karl Marx and Frederick Engels, "a specter [was] haunting Europe—the specter of communism." In that same year, the upstate New York village of Seneca Falls hosted a gathering of fewer than three hundred people, earnestly debating a Declaration of Sentiments to be spread by newsprint and oratory. The Seneca Falls Woman's Rights Convention marked the beginning of the woman's rights movement.

The specter that haunted Europe developed into a mighty movement, embracing the globe, causing revolutions, wars, tyrannies and counterrevolutions. Having gained state power in Russia, China and Eastern Europe, twentieth-century communism, in 1948, seemed more threatening a specter than ever before. Yet, after a bitter period of "cold war," which pitted nuclear nations against one another in a futile stalemate, it fell of its own weight in almost all its major centers.

The small spark figuratively ignited at Seneca Falls never produced revolutions, usurpation of power or wars. Yet it led to a transformation of consciousness and a movement of empowerment on behalf of half the human race, which hardly has its equal in human history.

Until very recently, the Seneca Falls convention of 1848 was not recognized as significant by historians, was not included in history textbooks, not celebrated as an important event in public schools, never mentioned in the media or the press. In the 1950s, the building where it was held, formerly the Wesleyan chapel, was used as a filling station. In the 1960s, it housed a laundromat. It was only due to the resurgence of modern feminism and the advances of the field of Women's History that the convention has entered the nation's consciousness. The establishment of Women's History Month as a national event during the Carter administration and its continuance through every administration since then has helped educate the nation to the significance of women's role in history. Still, it took decades of struggle by women's organizations, feminist historians and preservationists to rescue the building at Seneca Falls and finally to persuade the National Park Service to turn it into a historic site. . . . This history of "long forgetting and short remembering" has been an important aspect of women's historic past, the significance of which we only understood as we began to study women's history in depth.

Elizabeth Cady Stanton, the great communicator and propagandist of nineteenth-century feminism, has left a detailed account of the origins of the Seneca Falls convention both in her autobiography and in the monumental *History of Woman Suffrage*. The idea for such a meeting originated with her and with Lucretia Mott, when they both attended the 1840 World Antislavery Convention in London, at which representatives of female antislavery societies were denied seating and voting rights. Outraged by this humiliating experience, Stanton and Mott decided in London that they would convene a meeting of women in the United States to discuss their grievances as soon as possible. But her responsibilities as mother of a growing family intervened, and Stanton could not implement her plan until 1848, when Lucretia Mott visited her sister Martha Wright in Waterloo, a town near Seneca Falls. There, Stanton met with her, her hostess Jane Hunt and their friend Mary Ann McClintock. Stanton wrote: "I poured out that day the torrent of my long accumulating discontent with such vehemence and indignation that I stirred myself, as well as the rest of the party, to do or dare anything." The five drafted an announcement for a "Woman's Rights Convention" to be held at

Seneca Falls on the nineteenth and twentieth of July, and placed the notice in the local paper and the abolitionist press.

The five women who issued the call to the Seneca Falls convention were hardly as naive and inexperienced as later, somewhat mythical versions of the events would lead one to believe. Lucretia Mott was an experienced and highly acclaimed public speaker, a Quaker minister and longtime abolitionist. She had attended the founding meeting of the American Antislavery Society in 1833, which admitted women only as observers. She was a founder of the Philadelphia Female Anti-Slavery Society and its long-term president. The fact that she was announced as the principal speaker at the Seneca Falls convention was a distinct drawing card.

Elizabeth Cady Stanton's "long accumulating discontent" had to do with her struggle to raise her three children (she would later have four more) and run a large household in the frequent absences of her husband Henry, a budding lawyer and Free Soil politican. Still, she found time to be involved in the campaign for reform of women's property rights in New York state, where a reform bill was passed just prior to the convention, and she had spoken before the state legislature.

Martha Wright, Jane Hunt and Mary Ann McClintock were all separatist Quakers, long active in working to improve the position of women within their church. All of them were veterans of reform and women's organizations and had worked on antislavery fairs.

The [region] where they held their convention . . . had for more than two decades been the center of reform and utopian movements, largely due to the economic upheavals brought by the opening of the Erie Canal and the ensuing competition with western agriculture, which brought many farmers to bankruptcy. Economic uncertainty led many to embrace utopian schemes for salvation. The region was known as the "burned-over" district, because so many schemes for reforms had swept over it in rapid succession, from the evangelical revivalism of Charles Grandison Finney, to temperance, abolition, church reform, Mormonism and the chiliastic movement of William Miller, who predicted the second coming of Christ with precision for October 12, 1843 at three A.M. The nearly one million followers of Miller had survived the uneventful passing of that night and the similarly uneventful revised dates of March or October 1844, but their zeal for reform had not lessened.

The men and women who gathered in the Seneca Falls Wesleyan chapel were not a national audience; they all came from upstate New York and represented a relatively narrow spectrum of reform activists. Their local background predisposed them to accept radical pronouncements and challenging proposals. Most of them were abolitionists, the women having been active for nearly ten years in charitable, reform, and antislavery societies. They were experienced in running petition campaigns and many had organized antislavery fund-raising fairs. Historian[s] Nancy Isenberg [and Judith Wellman] who [have] analyzed the origins and affiliations of those attending the convention, showed that many were religious dissidents, Quakers, who just two months prior had separated from their more traditional church and would shortly form their own group, New York Congregationalist Friends. Another dissident group were Wesleyan Methodists who had been involved in a struggle within their church about the role of women and of the laity in church governance. Yet another group came from the ranks of the temperance movement. Among the men in attendance several were local lawyers with Liberty Party or Free Soil affiliations. Also present and taking a prominent part in the deliberations was Frederick Douglass, the former slave and celebrated abolitionist speaker, now editor of the *North Star*.

Far from representing a group of inexperienced housewives running their first public meeting, the majority of the convention participants were reformers with considerable organizational experience. For example, Amy Post and six other women from Rochester who came to Seneca Falls were able to organize a similar woman's rights convention in Rochester just two weeks later. One of the significant aspects of the Seneca Falls convention is that it was grounded in several organizational networks that had already existed for some time and could mobilize the energies of seasoned reform activists.

Most of the reformers attending had family, church and political affiliations in other areas of the North and Midwest. It was through them that the message of Seneca Falls spread quickly and led to the formation of a national movement. The first truly national convention on Woman's Rights was held in Worcester, Massachusetts in 1850. By 1860 ten national and many local woman's rights conventions had been organized.

THE DECLARATION OF SENTIMENTS

The first day of the Seneca Falls meeting was reserved to women, who occupied themselves with debating, paragraph by paragraph, the Declaration of Sentiments prepared by Elizabeth Cady Stanton. Resolutions were offered, debated and adopted. At the end of the second day, sixty-eight women and thirty-two men signed their names to a Declaration of Sentiments, which embodied the program of the nascent movement and provided a model for future woman's rights conventions. The number of signers represented only one third of those present, which probably was due to the radical nature of the statement. . . .

By selecting the Declaration of Independence for their formal model and following its preamble almost verbatim, except for the insertion of gender-neutral language, the organizers of the convention sought to base their main appeal on the democratic rights embodied in the nation's founding document. They also put the weight and symbolism of this revered text behind what was in their time a radical assertion: "We hold these truths to be self-evident: that all men and women are created equal."

The feminist appeal to natural rights and the social contract had long antecedents on the European continent, the most important advocate of it being Mary Wollstonecraft. Her work was well known in the United States, where the same argument had been well made by Judith Sargent Murray, Frances Wright, Emma Willard, Sarah Grimké and Margaret Fuller.

The second fundamental argument for the equality of woman was religious. As stated in the Declaration:

> Resolved, That woman is man's equal—was intended to be so by the Creator, and the highest good of the race demands that she should be recognized as such.

And one of the "grievances" is:

> He [man] has usurped the prerogative of Jehovah himself, claiming it as his right to assign to her a sphere of action, when that belongs to her conscience and her God.

The feminist argument based on biblical grounds can be traced back for seven hundred years prior to 1848, but the women assembled at Seneca Falls were unaware of that fact, because of the nonexistence of anything like Women's History. They did know the Quaker argument, especially as made in her public lectures by Lucretia Mott. They had read Sarah Grimke's *Letters on the Equality of the Sexes*, and several of the resolutions in fact followed her text. They knew the biblical argument by Ann Lee of the Shakers and they echoed the anti-slavery biblical argument, applying it to women.

The Declaration departed from precedent in its most radical statement:

> The history of mankind is a history of repeated injuries and usurpations on the part of man toward woman, having in direct object the establishment of an absolute tyranny over her.

The naming of "man" as the culprit, thereby identifying patriarchy as a system of "tyranny," was highly original, but it may have been dictated more by the rhetorical flourishes of the Declaration of Independence than by an actual analysis of woman's situation. When it came to the list of grievances, the authors departed from the text and became quite specific.

Woman had been denied "her inalienable right to the elective franchise"; she had no voice in the making of laws; she was deprived of other rights of citizenship; she was declared civilly dead upon marriage; deprived of her property and wages; discriminated against in case of divorce, and in payment for work. Women were denied equal access to education and were kept out of the professions, held in a subordinate position in Church and State and assigned by man to the domestic sphere. Man has endeavored to destroy woman's self-respect and keep her dependent.

They concluded that in view of the disfranchisement of one-half the people of this country

> . . . we insist that [women] have immediate admission to all the rights and privileges which belong to them as citizens of these United States.

It has been claimed by historians, and by herself, that Stanton's controversial resolution advocating voting rights for women—the only resolution not approved unanimously at the convention—was her most important original contribution. In fact, Sarah and Angelina Grimké had advocated woman's right to vote and hold office in 1838, and Frances Wright had done so in the 1830s. It was not so much the originality, as the inclusiveness of the listed grievances that was important.

The Declaration claimed universality, even though it never mentioned differences among women. Future woman's rights conferences before the Civil War would rectify this omission and pay particular attention to the needs of lower class and slave women.

While grievances pertaining to woman's sexual oppression were not explicitly included in the Declaration of Sentiments, they were very much alive in the consciousness of the leading participants. Elizabeth Cady Stanton had already in 1848 begun to include allusions to what we now call "marital rape" in her letters and soon after the Seneca Falls convention made such references explicit, calling on legislatures to forbid marriage to "drunkards." She soon became an open advocate of divorce and of the right of women to leave abusive marriages. Later woman's rights conventions would include some of these issues among their demands, although they used carefully guarded language and focused on abuses by "drunkards." This was a hidden feminist theme of the mainstream woman's temperance movement in the 1880s and caused many temperance women to embrace woman suffrage. What we now call "a woman's right to her body" was already on the agenda of the nineteenth-century woman's rights movement.

It was the confluence of a broad-ranging programmatic declaration with a format familiar and accessible to reformers that gave the event its historical significance. The Seneca Falls convention was the first forum in which women gathered together to publicly air their own grievances, not those of the needy, the enslaved, orphans or widows. The achievement of a public voice for women and the recognition that women could not win their rights unless they organized, made Seneca Falls a major event in history.

RIGHTS AND EMANCIPATION

. . . It is useful to think of women's demands as encompassing two sets of needs: women's rights and women's emancipation.

Women's rights essentially are civil rights—to vote, to hold office, to have access to education and to economic and political power at every level of society on an equal basis with men. . . . These rights are demanded on the basis of a claim to *equality:* as citizens, as members of society, women are by rights equal and must therefore be treated equally. All of the rights here listed are based on the acceptance of the status quo; . . . These are essentially reformist demands.

Women's emancipation is freedom from oppressive restrictions imposed by reason of sex; self-determination and autonomy. Oppressive restrictions are biological restrictions due to sex, as well as socially imposed ones. Thus, women's bearing and nursing children is a biological given, but the assignment to women of the major responsibility for the rearing of children and for housework is socially imposed.

Self-determination means being free to decide one's own destiny, to define one's own social role. Autonomy means earning one's status, not being born into it or marrying it. . . . It means freedom to define issues, roles, laws and cultural norms on an equality with men. The demands for emancipation are based on stressing women's difference from men, but also on stressing women's difference from other women. They are radical demands, which can only be achieved by transforming society for men and women, equalizing gender definitions for both sexes, assigning the reproductive work of raising the next generation to both men and women, and reorganizing social institutions so as to make such arrangements possible.

Women, just like men, are placed in society as individuals *and* as citizens. They are both equal *and* different. The demand for women's emancipation always includes the demand for women's rights, but the reverse is not true. Generally speaking, women's rights have been won or improved upon in many parts of the world in the past 150 years. Women's emancipation has not yet been won anywhere.

The movement started at Seneca Falls . . . from the start embraced both [concepts]—by demanding legal, property, civil rights; and by demanding changes in gender-role definition and in woman's rights to her own body. As the nineteenth-century movement matured, there developed some tension between advocates of these two different sets of demands, with the mainstream focusing more and more on legal and property rights, while radicals and outsiders, like sex reformers, birth control advocates, and socialist feminists, demanded more profound social changes.

. . . But the same distinctions and tensions . . . have appeared in . . . [the twentieth-century women's movement]. One wing focused mainly on women's rights—adoption of ERA, legal/political rights and representation and civil rights for women of different classes, races and sexual orientations. The other wing began as "radical women's liberation" and later branched off into many more specialized groups working on abortion rights; protection of women against violence and sexual harassment; the opening up to women of nontraditional occupations: self-empowerment and the creation of women cultural institutions, ranging from lesbian groupings to women's music festivals and pop culture. The two informally defined wings of the movement often overlapped, sometimes collaborated on specific narrow issues, and recently have worked more and more on bridge-building. The Women's Studies movement has struggled long and hard to bridge the two wings and encompass them educationally. Further, new forms of feminism by women of color or women who define themselves as "different" from the majority in various ways have sprung up and served their own constituencies. Their existence has not weakened the movement, as its critics like to claim, but has strengthened it immensely by grounding it more firmly in different constituencies.

Let us not forget, ever, that when we talk about women's rights we talk about the rights of half the human race. No one expects all men to have the same interests, issues or demands. We should therefore never expect women to have one agenda, one set of issues or demands.

The women's rights demands first raised at Seneca Falls have in the United States been generally achieved for middle-class white women. They have been partially achieved for working-class women and women of color, but progress has been very uneven. . . .

The feminization of poverty and the increasing income gap between the rich and the poor have turned many legal gains won by women into empty shells. An example is the way in which legal restrictions on women's right to choose abortion have fallen more heavily on poor women than on the well-to-do. The uneven availability of child care for working mothers is another example.

The cultural transformation on which demands for woman's emancipation build, has been enormous. Many demands that seemed outrageous 150 years ago are now commonly accepted, such as a woman's right to equal guardianship of her children, to divorce, to jury duty, to acceptance in nontraditional occupations. Female police and fire officers and female military personnel are accepted everywhere without question. Women's participation in competitive sports is another area in which progress has been great, though it is far from complete. Many other feminist demands that seemed outrageously radical thirty years ago have become commonplace today—the acceptance of lesbians as "normal" members of the community; single motherhood; the criminal character of sexual harassment and marital rape. The acceptance of such ideas is still uneven and different in different places, but generally, the feminist program has been accepted by millions of people who refuse to identify themselves as "feminists." What critics decry as the splintering and diffusion of the movement is actually its greatest strength today.

It should also be recognized that the aims of feminism are transformative, but its methods have been peaceful reform, persuasion and education. For 150 years feminists have organized, lobbied, marched, petitioned, put their bodies on the line in demonstrations, and have overcome ancient prejudices by heroic acts of self-help. Whatever gains were won, had to be won step by step, over and over again. Nothing "was given" to women; whatever gains we made we have had to earn. And perhaps the most precious "right" we have won in these two centuries, is the right to know our own history, to draw on the knowledge and experience of the women before us, to celebrate and emulate our heroines and finally to know that "greatness" is not a sexual attribute.

WHAT MEANING DOES SENECA FALLS HOLD TODAY?

* It shows that a small group of people, armed with a persuasive analysis of grievances and an argument based on generally held moral and religious beliefs, can, if they are willing and able to work hard at organizing, create a transformative mass movement. . . . The women who launched a small movement in 1848 had to . . . build, county by county, state by state, the largest grassroots movement of the nineteenth century and then build it again in the twentieth century to transform the right to vote into the right to equal representation. . . .

* Seneca Falls and the movement it spawned show that legal changes . . . can be reversed, unless social and cultural transformations sustain them. . . . Over the past 150 years all of the grievances listed at Seneca Falls have been resolved or at least dealt with, though new inequities and grievances arise in each generation. The "specter that haunted Europe" left some gains, but mostly bloodshed, terror and devastation in its wake, and most of the inequities it sought to adjust are still with us. Feminism has behind it a record of solid gains without the costs of bloody war and revolution.

Although the media and many politicians with monotonous frequency declare feminism to be dead, many of its goals have been accomplished and its momentum, worldwide, is steadily rising. [The worldwide movement of women for their emancipation is irreversible.] It will continue to live and grow, as long as women anywhere have "grievances" they can proclaim and as long as they are willing and able to organize to rectify them.

ROSE STREMLAU

"I Know What an Indian Woman Can Do": Sarah Winnemucca Writes about Rape on the Northern Paiute Frontier

The Comstock Lode—a rich vein of silver ore—was discovered by European Americans in the late 1850s in western Nevada, just east of Lake Tahoe and south of Pyramid Lake. Thousands of men trekked to the spot, coming westward over the Oregon Trail and eastward from California. As a consequence, the population of the nearest town, Virginia City, exploded, reaching 30,000 when extraction peaked in 1877. Anglos understood themselves to be seizing opportunity in the rugged wilderness. But far from being "virgin land," the forested mountains and river valleys of the surrounding landscape were the home territory of the Northern Paiutes. As had occurred in so many places in the Americas since 1492, a gender frontier—and a social flashpoint—was created as white settlers quickly outnumbered the locals who had different understandings of gender roles, manliness, and womanliness.

As Rose Stremlau's essay reveals, we know about the reactions of Northern Paiute women to the new dangers and survival challenges they faced because of the writings of one of them, Sarah Winnemucca (1844?–91). Active in lobbying military officers, territorial legislatures, the Interior Department in Washington, and President Hayes to improve conditions for her tribe and to compel governments to keep their promises, Winnemucca was an ardent reformer, a traveling lecturer, and an educator akin to the Grimké sisters. She befriended influential women in the East, securing their help in getting her autobiography published in Boston in 1883. Her biographer, Sally Zanjani, claims it to be "the first book written by an American Indian woman, the first by a Native American west of the Rockies, and the first to describe Paiute culture."* But Sarah Winnemucca died discouraged, with her people relegated to woefully inadequate reservation land, and the school she had established in her later years lacking sufficient external funding. If her vision of several such schools flourishing throughout the West had come to pass, the outcomes for many Indian children would have been very different (see Zitkala-Ša, pp. 345–349). Her statue now represents the state of Nevada in the U.S. Capitol Statuary Hall in Washington, D.C.

As you read the essay, ask yourself what skills and systems of knowledge Northern Paiute women needed for everyday living both before and after white settlers infiltrated their homelands. Compare to those of the white colonial goodwives described by Laurel Thatcher Ulrich (pp. 45–53). Given that Sarah Winnemucca's autobiography is 240 pages long, what insights do we gain by focusing on its stories of sexual violence and intimidation? Is Stremlau's evocation of a rape culture helpful in understanding other places and moments in U.S. history?

In April 1860, while Northern Paiute elders and leaders met in council at Pyramid Lake to determine how best to respond to the non-Indian invasion of their homeland and the destruction of their resource base, Northern Paiute families carried on their day-to-day subsistence work as best they could. Searching for one of their most important food sources, two young Northern Paiute women gathered roots near Williams's Station, a settlers' trading post. Several white men seized the girls, dragged them into a barn, and repeatedly gang raped them. The men . . . held the young women captive, and when the girls' families came searching for them, the men denied having seen them and threatened to shoot whoever continued to scout around their homestead for evidence of the girls. Their posturing was ineffective, however; the Northern Paiute men heard their women's screaming, and they would retaliate.[1]

*Online Nevada Encyclopedia, a project of Nevada Humanities, "Sarah Winnemucca," http://www.onlinenevada.org/sarah_winnemucca (accessed Mar. 20, 2009).

Excerpted from Rose Stremlau, "Rape Narratives on the Northern Paiute Frontier: Sarah Winnemucca, Sexual Sovereignty, and Economic Autonomy, 1844–1891," in *Portraits of Women in the American West*, ed. Dee Garceau-Hagen (New York: Routledge, 2005). Reprinted by permission of the author and publisher. Notes have been edited and renumbered.

In Sarah Winnemucca's autobiography, such stories of sexual victimization are as much a part of the Northern Paiute experience as their seasonal hunting and gathering cycle. In particular, Winnemucca described how sexual violence characterized many white men's relations with the Native American women and girls whom they considered racially and culturally inferior and economically marginal. But Winnemucca's life story should not be read as a police blotter detailing individual crimes. Her vivid descriptions of sexual violence suggest how Native people experienced and responded to interracial rape, and her stories of rape point to larger themes in Northern Paiute adaptation. Winnemucca posited that the Northern Paiutes' best chance at survival lay not in assimilation to white culture but in the restoration of their economic autonomy, symbolized by women's ability to work without fear of sexual assault.

Born in approximately 1844 near the Humboldt River in what is today western Nevada, Sarah Winnemucca grew to adulthood in a world turned upside down by rapid, unprecedented change. [Although] the Northern Paiutes had never met an American until the late 1840s, by 1859, non-Indians outnumbered her people in their own homeland. Winnemucca lived her life at an interchange of power relations that would confound even the brightest of us. As a young girl, she keenly perceived that gender roles functioned differently in white society than in her own. From her earliest contacts with Americans, she described a culture infused with masculinity and violence and in which the combination of the two equated to power. As an American Indian woman, Winnemucca had no claim to power in the rough West of non-Indian miners, soldiers, and settlers. But in her culture, she did have power, in part because Northern Paiutes valued the work that women did.

Prior to the non-Indian settlement of the Great Basin, the Northern Paiutes practiced an extremely flexible gendered division of labor that enabled them to adapt rapidly to changes in their environment. Their homeland covered over 70,000 square miles in present-day southeastern Oregon, southwestern Idaho, northwestern Nevada, and northeastern California. Microclimatic variation caused environmental diversity, and across the Great Basin, arid, desert landscapes blended into fertile, lush valleys and waterfronts. These Great Basin hunters and gatherers adapted to their environment by diversifying their sources of food and establishing extended kin relations, which enabled communication and cooperation among groups in times of abundance and need. While lean periods were common, starvation was not, because Native people utilized such a wide variety of natural resources.[2]

The Northern Paiutes migrated from food source to food source in small families and family groups or clusters. Depending on the availability of resources, a married couple or a set of married siblings and their children composed the core of groups that expanded to include a handful of families and then contracted back to the immediate family group. Households joined together for particular communal subsistence activities, especially the pine nut harvest and rabbit drives, or in particularly rich areas, such as near fisheries. Due to the limited food supplies throughout much of the Great Basin, however, the collective labor of larger groups usually proved a disadvantage over that of an individual or couple. Throughout most of the year, then, families functioned as self-contained units, and the gendered division of labor within families enabled the efficient exploitation of their environment.

Married couples comprised the basic unit of production and social reproduction. Among the Northern Paiutes, marriage was not a private concern between a man and a woman. Instead, married couples produced food and children, and the relationships between husbands and wives also bound kin groups together. Marriage among the Northern Paiutes was a mutually beneficial process rather than an event. When a man visited a woman's home at night and eventually moved his belongings into her home with her consent, the family recognized the couple as married and integrated them into the gendered, adult world of production and reproduction. Marriages ended as informally as they began when husbands moved out of, or were removed from, their wives' homes. . . . [W]hile Great Basin societies lacked the economic, social, political, or religious institutions that bound wives to husbands and ensured the permanence of marital unions, these societies valued the economic and social complementarity that husbands and wives provided each other.[3] . . .

. . . In her autobiography, Winnemucca emphasized the bonds of affection between husbands and wives; reciprocity, it seems, was emotional and physical as well as economic. Many relationships lasted for a lifetime. She explained, "They not only take care of their children together, but they do everything together; and when they grow blind, which I am sorry say is very common, for the smoke they live in destroys their eyes at last, they take sweet care of one another. Marriage is a sweet thing when people love each other."[4]

Married couples divided some tasks and shared others in order to maximize their utilization of local resources. Both spouses' labor was essential to a family's survival, and families formed self-sufficient economic units. Men usually hunted, trapped, and fished, but men also worked alongside their female relatives gathering when the needs of the family demanded it. Individually or in small groups, men stalked large game including deer, pronghorn, and bighorn sheep. Alternately, several hunters sometimes worked together to corral a herd of animals and to net rabbits and other small mammals and fish. Northern Paiute men developed a variety of ways to kill: they shot game with poisoned arrows; tracked them with dogs; prayed and sacrificed for them; ambushed them; enchanted them with spiritual power; netted them; snared them; charged at them in disguises; tricked them into entering traps with noises; and set out fishing lines with specified hooks. Winnemucca explained that because they avoided warfare, Northern Paiute conceptions of masculinity were bound up solely with the skills of hunting and fishing, which provided food for their families.

Women typically gathered plants, roots, and nuts, but they also hunted small animals and fished. Their selective utilization of natural resources and development of many specific subsistence technologies for procuring and processing food suggest that Northern Paiute women were skilled laborers. They developed, transmitted, and continuously perfected systems of knowledge that made edible and palatable piñon nuts, acorns, cattails, rice grass, many species of seeds, camas, swamp onion, biscuit roots, bitterroots, other types of roots, buckberries, wolfberries, other fruits and berries, leaves, stalks, and greens. Women also prepared meat and fish for consumption through a variety of techniques, including roasting and making pemmican. Northern Paiute women did not simply harvest the resources in their environment, however; they manipulated it to produce more abundant harvests in the future. They burned unwanted vegetation, pruned and plucked plants, and broadcast seeds. Just as importantly, they prayed and gave offerings to the spirits of the plants and animals that they consumed to ensure plentiful seasons in the future.[5]

Northern Paiute women may have provided . . . over half of their families' livelihood and perhaps the most important part. Plants provided a significant percentage of nutrients, and nuts provided valuable fat and protein in a diet otherwise prone to deficiencies. Women were accustomed to spending a significant amount of their time gathering away from men's supervision and protection. These women were independent workers unaccustomed to being sexually harassed.

Northern Paiute women's economic contributions accorded them high status as they wielded both spiritual and political power often seen as interrelated. Because of their ability to provide food, women had a political voice. Female and male leaders attained spiritual power in one of three ways: through dreams, through inheritance from a powerful, deceased relative, and through visiting foreign, unknown places. Male and female elders made decisions for family groups, and as Winnemucca explained, "The women know as much as the men do, and their advice is often asked. We have a republic as well as you. The council-tent is our Congress, and anybody can speak who has anything to say, women and all." . . . Notably, Winnemucca went on to explain that women and men sat in different circles in council, but she did not consider this a sign of inferiority. Rather, it was a sign of complementarily and social order.[6]

. . . [M]otherhood also accorded Northern Paiute women status. Whether from the earth or their bodies, women brought forth life, and they were valued for it. Beginning with their first menstruation, young Northern Paiute women underwent a period of seclusion involving fasting, laboring, and bathing in preparation for the roles of wife and mother. Once pregnant, both men and women followed specific taboos intended to insure the well-being of mothers and babies. For men, according to Winnemucca, this included assuming much of women's domestic labor. She wrote: "If he does not do his part in the care of the child, he is considered an outcast. . . . The young mothers often get together and exchange experiences about the attentions of their husbands; and inquire of each other if the fathers did their duty to their children, and were careful of their wives' health." . . . Such complementarity fostered a culture of respect between Northern Paiute men and women, one in which violence had no place.[7]

The sudden, unexpected influx of non-Indians into their homeland compromised the Northern Paiutes' natural resources and rendered their seasonal rounds impossible. While they had obtained horses and European goods by the mid to late eighteenth century, Northern Paiutes did not directly contact Europeans or non-Indian Americans until the early nineteenth century. They paid these trappers and traders little mind until the opening of the Oregon Trail and the discovery of gold in California during the 1840s brought thousands of migrants through the heart of their territory. . . . [I]n 1859, the discovery of gold and silver in Northern Paiute territory along the Virginia Range and the Owyhee Basin attracted thousands of settlers to the area. The Comstock Lode shifted the demographics of their territory within a few months as a minority population of a few hundred whites exploded into a majority of many thousands. As ethnohistorians Martha C. Knack and Omer C. Stewart explain, "Despite the initial trickle of transients, this onslaught of white domination was sudden, complete, and irreversible. The opportunity for natives to respond and resist was nearly gone before they could even comprehend the threat." Seeking rapid profits, these non-Indians destroyed Native hunting and gathering lands; miners cut down groves of piñon trees for shoring and building mine shafts and diverted streams for flumes; ranchers seized grasslands and water; and town dwellers seized timber and the choicest land.[8]

Women's contributions to the family pot may have taken on increasing importance as non-Indians consumed the natural resources most familiar to them, particularly game, and limited the Northern Paiutes' access to other resources, such as fisheries, by locating their settlements near the rivers and lakes. In response, women's skilled gathering of resources with which non-Indians were unfamiliar became vital to Northern Paiute survival. . . .

Northern Paiutes responded to the invasion by trying to maintain their seasonal hunting and gathering cycle, but they did so in different ways; some fled away from non-Indians and onto reservations where they tried to survive by supplementing their traditional food sources with rations and agriculture. Others relocated to the margins of non-Indian communities and combined the seasonal cycle with wage labor. Neither response enabled women to adequately gather, fish, or trap to feed their families. Regardless of their choices and however well they adapted to the new extractive, market-oriented economy of the Great Basin, many Northern Paiutes suffered from a new social ill—chronic starvation.

Most Northern Paiutes could not get far enough away from the newcomers. As early as the 1830s, the Northern Paiutes altered their hunting and gathering cycle by going to the mountains in the summer instead of the valleys where they usually gathered . . . In 1859, as miners flooded into the Great Basin, Northern Paiutes began relocating onto reservations. The Pyramid Lake reservation was established in 1859 and the Malheur in 1873, but poverty stalked the reservations, too. Even under the best of circumstances reservations wanted for funding and capable leadership. Sarah Winnemucca, like her father and many other Great Basin leaders, considered reservations no better than death camps. Unable to continue their seasonal hunting and gathering cycle with the necessary regularity, unprepared to farm, often swindled by the agents charged to care for them, and unsupplied with the rations promised in treaties, Great Basin Indians starved on reservations. Winnemucca wrote her autobiography as a condemnation of the corrupt reservation system, and she recalled a heated exchange between Chief Egan and Agent William Reinhart. Egan begged for the food locked in the agency storehouse: "My children are dying with hunger. I want what I and my people have worked for, that is, we want the wheat." Reinhart replied, "Nothing here is yours. It is all the government's." Like prison camps, reservations condemned Native people, even those who wanted to work to feed their families, to dependency on the government for food. According to Winnemucca, this dependency was emotionally, spiritually, physically, and mentally intolerable to men and women who had been self-sufficient adults just a few years earlier.[9]

Northern Paiutes who settled among non-Indians struggled, too. Forced to adapt and utilize non-Indians as another available resource, Northern Paiutes balanced their seasonal cycle with barter or wage labor in menial jobs. Men cut trees, hauled goods, and tended livestock. Because of the shortage of white women, Indian women easily found domestic work as housekeepers, seamstresses, and laundresses. . . . In the Indian shantytown that bordered Virginia City, Northern Paiute women with their gathering baskets rose early to pick rotting food from non-Indian trash piles. Others waited outside the mines for workers to empty the leftovers from their lunch pails into their baskets. Despite their meager resources. Northern Paiute women continued to provide a significant portion of their families' livelihoods through their adaptation of the subsistence round. Still, whether they lived on the reservations or in towns, Northern Paiute women were vulnerable to poverty and exploitation.[10]

Winnemucca exemplifies how Northern Paiute women put traditional skills to use at non-traditional work as they adapted to survive in the new Great Basin economy. During her early childhood, Winnemucca learned Northern Paiute women's customary domestic and subsistence tasks; she came to understand a woman's role by helping her mother care for her siblings and their household. For example, she prepared food like cattail pollen cakes and practiced crafts like weaving cattails and sagebrush into baskets for gathering and mats for clothing and shelter. As a teenager, her skill at handiwork enabled her to live by selling needlework door-to-door in Virginia City. In her early twenties, she worked as a laundress on the reservation. By her thirties, she had saved enough money to purchase a wagon and team, and when not working as a maid, she hired herself out as a teamster, not an unlikely job for a woman who grew up migrating and moving her home among campsites. In the 1870s, as the speaker of five languages; English, Paiute, Shoshone, Spanish, and Washoe; she translated and taught on the reservation. In the late 1870s, having gained familiarity with the territory through the seasonal round, she scouted for the United States Army. Beginning in the 1870s and through the rest of her life, Winnemucca, member of a chiefly family who had attained power in her own right, served as an ambassador and spokeswoman for her people: she wrote letters, visited American political leaders, gave lectures, and wrote her autobiography to obtain provisions and ensure safe communities for the Northern Paiutes. In the late 1880s, she established and ran a school that educated Northern Paiute children in their own and Anglo-American culture.[11] . . .

Poverty was not the only challenge that Northern Paiute women faced; their work as providers for their families also made them vulnerable to sexual assault. Hunting, gathering, and wage work took women beyond the protection of brothers, fathers, and husbands. In this new world following the non-Indian invasion, women's work became particularly unsafe. The influx of whites brought a disproportionate number of non-Indian men without families to Northern Paiute territory. The mining industry created several new types of communities: only corporations had the assets to transport the equipment necessary to procure minerals from bedrock, and these large mines sparked the establishment of towns, such as Virginia City. Other miners worked alone or in small groups and migrated from base camp to base camp. Mining also attracted supporting industries, such as trading and ranching. Bandits and outlaws roamed the basin looking for easy targets to plunder. Soldiers manned military posts established throughout the territory to protect mining interests and keep the peace between Indians and non-Indians. Many of these new non-Indian communities lacked permanent female residents. Northern Paiutes, who had no standing army or labor system that kept men away from women for long periods of time, noted the preponderance of men without women and families with disapproval.[12] . . .

Newcomers to the Great Basin did not appreciate the Northern Paiutes' egalitarian gender roles, and, often without women of their own, they considered Native women to be subject, sexual resources. While they had never seen a Northern Paiute woman before, many white male newcomers to the Great Basin believed that they were experts on the subject of Indian women. Since the colonial era, Anglo-American culture had adopted the image of the "Indian princess" to symbolize virtue, but Americans associated overt, primitive sexuality with her "darker twin," the "squaw." . . . According to the stereotype, Native women worked like slaves and had sex like animals. Moreover, like their European forebears, Americans claimed sexual access to women, along with other forms of property, as a right of conquest. These beliefs were not limited to men of low status. While recognizing that not all Indian women were "wanton,"

General Oliver O. Howard, under whom Winnemucca served as a scout and with whom she developed a mutually respectful friendship, commented that he understood why "squaw men" took Indian wives: allegedly the women were compliant and sexually eager.[13]

Some Northern Paiute women utilized their sexuality as another resource that enabled them to survive during this tumultuous period. Many Northern Paiute women, including Sarah Winnemucca and her sister, married white men, perhaps in an effort to broaden their resource base through extending kin ties as Northern Paiutes had always done. Others worked in a nontraditional industry—sex work. Indian women worked as prostitutes in frontier towns across the West during the Gold Rush. Regardless of whether or not particular Indian women actually were working as prostitutes, the predominance of stereotypes about Indian women's sexuality enabled whites to come to the conclusion that they were.[14] . . .

The discovery of Comstock Lode sparked a frenzied competition for resources in the Great Basin and created an environment particularly conducive to violence against American Indian women. Historians of rape have argued that sexual violence often occurs at societal flashpoints, places where diverging groups struggle over power and status. In particular, historians have suggested that men rape women whom they consider racially or culturally inferior and economically dependent. In the Humboldt Sink in the 1850s and 1860s, white men looked down on Northern Paiute women, and their economic vulnerability made them more readily accessible. Dismissed by the American legal system, Northern Paiute women were also not likely to bring charges against rapists.

. . . As whites became increasingly land-hungry, Native people became more defensive and vocal in demanding protection from the army and the federal government. Each resented the other's claim to the land and what grew on it or lay below the surface. Northern Paiute women could not gather roots in the same land that white men mined for silver. When they occupied the land and raped women who came near their camps and posts, these newcomers discouraged women from continuing their subsistence gathering cycle. White men did not simply rape to satisfy sexual urges; they raped Northern Paiute and other Great Basin Indian women to assert their dominance over them and the kinsmen unable to protect them. It worked. The Northern Paiutes were intimidated. Winnemucca explained, "My people have been so unhappy for a long time they now wish to disincrease, instead of multiply. The mothers are afraid to have more children, for fear they shall have daughters, who are not safe even in their mother's presence."[15]

It is historically and morally important to acknowledge that non-Indian men raped Indian women as part of the conquest of the American West. The Anglo-American West bred a *rape culture*, or a "complex of beliefs that encourages male sexual aggression and supports violence against women." Rape cultures equate domination and violence with sexuality, and in rape cultures women experience sexual violence along a continuum of behavior from economic marginalization to rape and murder. Perpetrators in a rape culture assume their behavior is a normal, inevitable aspect of life. While coined by activists working to end rape in contemporary culture, the term *rape culture* is useful to historians because it reminds us that sexual violence is culturally constructed: not all men across time and place have raped women, and when and where men have raped women, they have not committed rape for the same reasons. Likewise, while they may endure similar physical acts, women experience rape differently in cultures that provide for alternative frameworks for understanding rape other than victimization.[16] That we remember the role of rape in conquest is important, but it is just as important to understand the extent and meaning of Native women's resistance if we want to understand how Native people and their cultures adapted and survived. . . .

. . . While they adopted some aspects of American culture, Northern Paiutes rejected non-Indian redefinitions of sexually appropriate behavior, such as female economic dependence and male sexual aggression. They disapproved of sexually aggressive behavior and labeled men who raped as deviant. Northern Paiutes distinguished among non-Indians based, in part, on their treatment of Native women, and many white men behaved quite badly according to Northern Paiute conceptions of masculinity. Throughout her autobiography, Winnemucca alluded to the ever-present threat posed by "bad white men who might harm us" and noted that she and other Northern Paiute leaders complained about the frequency of sexual assaults to American leaders in the hopes that they would take steps to prevent them.

But Winnemucca and the Northern Paiutes did more than plead to outsiders for assistance; they adapted their own lifestyles to prevent sexual attacks on Northern Paiute women and girls. Because they often experienced sexual violence together as family groups, Northern Paiutes rearranged their domestic relationships to better ensure the safety of female family members. Winnemucca described in detail how her family prevented the gang rape of her sister. During her early childhood, her grandfather, Truckee, moved part of her family cluster to California where he and several of her brothers worked for a rancher. Several white ranch hands repeatedly tried to gang rape Winnemucca's older sister, a young teenager. Each night the family fled their camp as the men came for her sister. Fearing violent retaliation themselves, her kinsmen felt that they could not physically defend the girl. One evening, five men came into their camp, and two entered their darkened tent and closed off the exit behind them. Winnemucca's uncles and brothers attacked the men and scared them off, and the family then boarded with their employers away from the rest of the workers. Finally, after the men asked Truckee for the girl outright—a request he scornfully refused—the family decided the terrified girl would no longer work alongside her mother but would spend her days under the direct supervision of her grandmother in camp and away from the dangers women faced as they worked away from the safety of their base camp.... Northern Paiute families experienced sexual violence as a process and a persistent threat instead of as single events.

... Northern Paiute families looked to established and newly formed social networks for protection from violence. Above all, ... Northern Paiute women relied on kin for protection. In her autobiography, Winnemucca offered several examples of Northern Paiute men ensuring the safety of their female relatives.... But women also took care of each other. Winnemucca only left her sister-in-law, Mattie, at a military post because she knew her brother would arrive shortly....

Northern Paiutes also relied on some newcomers for protection from others. When traveling, Winnemucca took every opportunity to stay in homes occupied by white women, although this was not always possible because of the gender imbalance of the non-Indian community.... [she] also recognized that some white men posed no threat. When traveling, she commented, "No white women on all the places where we stopped—all men—yet we were treated kindly by all of them, so far."[17]

While fearing common soldiers, the Northern Paiutes sought protection from army officers against miners, settlers, and soldiers. Winnemucca and other Northern Paiute leaders developed close relationships with officers whom they identified as friendly and powerful allies. While scouting for them, Winnemucca accepted the escorts of officers who worried for her safety, but she was more proactive than that: she demanded protection when she felt vulnerable. Perhaps playing into her readers' expectations of feminine vulnerability, she recalled having once pleaded: "Colonel, I am all alone with so many men, I am afraid. I want your protection. I want you to protect me against your soldiers, and I want you to protect my people also."[18]

Unable to always prevent attacks, Northern Paiute women resisted sexual assaults the best they could with the options posed by their cultural worldview. Winnemucca's Anglo-American readers expected women to avoid rape by maintaining a virtuous appearance and reputation, a process that included keeping their bodies fully covered in clothing, appearing in public with appropriate male escorts, and not working outside their homes. While adapting some aspects of their dress, Northern Paiute women did not embrace constrictive gendered expectations of Anglo-American women concerning sexual violence. They continued to work alone or in small groups with other women and without male escort. They continued to gather outside their camps; they had to in order to eat. For Northern Paiute women, to do otherwise, such as send men to gather, made no sense.[19]

When threatened, Northern Paiute women attempted to outrun rapists. Winnemucca recalled an incident that occurred ... when [she was] traveling with her sister. [N]on-Indian men followed the women.... [They] resolved to go down fighting if overtaken:

> Away we went, and they after us like wild men. We rode on till our horses seemed to drop from under us. At last we stopped, and I told sister what to do if the whole three of them overtook us. We could not do very much, but we must die fighting. If there were only two we were all right,—we could kill them; if one we would see

what he would do. If he lassoed me she was to jump off her horse and cut the rope, and if he lassoed her I was to do the same. If he got off his horse and came at me she was to cut him, and I would do the same for her. Now we were ready for our work.[20]

In the end, Winnemucca and her sister escaped their would-be rapists. . . .

When unable to outrun perpetrators, . . . Northern Paiute women attacked them or outsmarted them, proving that successful resistance did not necessarily correspond with physical strength. Winnemucca suggested that Northern Paiute women verbally threatened would-be rapists with physical violence and implied that Northern Paiute women were often armed, and thus, that retaliation could hurt. Winnemucca bragged of breaking an offender's nose. The man, a fellow traveler bunked down near her, suggestively laid his hand on her in the middle of the night, and with one straight punch to his face, Winnemucca shunned his proposition. She bloodied his nose and sent him running for the door while she shouted, "Go away, or I will cut you to pieces, you mean man!" Winnemucca sliced another attempted rapist's face with a knife. On a March evening in 1875, Julius Argasse, a white man, either approached Winnemucca on the street or, according to another account, entered her home. Either way Winnemucca refused him with her knife. She was subsequently arrested, but the judge dismissed the charges against her.[21]

When other options for prevention and redress failed, Northern Paiutes and other Great Basin Natives killed rapists. Military doctor George M. Kober recalled a conversation he had with Winnemucca's father in which the chief blamed the ongoing violence on miners and Prospectors who "had no regard for the chastity of Indian women."[22] Winnemucca explained that the rapes of Native women and girls prompted the outbreak of the two Indian wars that she experienced. The Paiute War of 1860 began when the tribe retaliated against the men who kidnapped and raped the two young women who had been gathering roots. Outraged at the treatment of the young women and the men's initial denial of having seen them, the Northern Paiutes killed the four men. Some local whites considered the men upstanding citizens and led a campaign against the Northern Paiutes that resulted in their confinement at Pyramid Lake reservation by the end of the summer. Others, such as settler

Richard N. Allen, believed that the Northern Paiutes' retaliation was justified and clearly in response to a wrong committed by these brothers since nearby settlers were unharmed by the Northern Paiutes.[23] . . .

. . . [F]or many Northern Paiutes, distance from non-Indians provided the best protection from violence. The Northern Paiutes' rapid acceptance of reservations must be considered in this context. As Leggins and Egan, two chiefs, explained when the government threatened to open part of their reservation land to non-Indian settlement, "And another thing, we do not want to have white people near us. We know what they are, and what they do to our women and daughters."[24]

While accounts of and allusions to rape permeate her autobiography, Winnemucca revealed little information about the victims. The details she provided suggest that sexual violence threatened all Northern Paiute women. Victims were old and young. Some were women that she did not know while others were family. Winnemucca herself survived sexual violence. Notably, nearly all victims were working, somehow trying to provide food for their families, or in Winnemucca's case, for her people. While she appealed to her readers' belief in women's vulnerability, Winnemucca never questioned the chastity or moral character of victims, and she refused to engage in non-Indian culture's debate over Native sexuality or pander to their stereotypes of Native women. Winnemucca's accounts of rape suggest what experts on contemporary sexual violence confirm: rape is not an act of sexual pleasure reflective of the victim's sexual appeal according to societal standards of beauty; rather it is an act of power, domination, and conquest inseparable from its social, economic, racial, cultural, and gendered context. In other words, sexual violence was intertwined with racial and economic oppression. . . .

. . . While other members of her tribe took up arms against invaders, Winnemucca waged a war of words in defense of Northern Paiute lifeways. Beginning in 1870 with a letter that ended up in the hands of the commissioner of the Bureau of Indian Affairs, Winnemucca repeatedly brought the Northern Paiutes' suffering to the attention of outsiders and demanded redress. . . . At her people's request, Winnemuca wrote letters to influential military and civilian leaders, and then traveled to San Francisco to lecture and to Nevada to lobby politicians. She continued her letter and speaking campaigns following their removal to Malheur and subsequent removals and relocations. Always she pleaded with her readers and listeners for food and land for the Northern Paiutes. In 1880, Winnemucca led a Northern Paiute delegation to Washington, D.C. to meet with Secretary of the Interior Carl Schurz, who directed Indian affairs, in order to obtain the Northern Paiutes' release from their reservations and to secure the allotment of their land into 160-acre plots for each family. Once she returned west and was no longer the subject of stories in eastern newspapers, Schurz failed to deliver on his promises to her. So Winnemucca turned to western newspapers to attack the Bureau of Indian Affairs. In 1883, with the support of Protestant reformers, Winnemucca moved East where she lectured and wrote her autobiography.

Expecting to hear and read titillating accounts of indigenous cultural practices, audiences instead felt their heartstrings pulled by Winnemucca's account of the abuse of Northern Paiute women and girls. By recounting the Northern Paiutes' story, including stories about rape, she generated an enormous amount of sympathy for the Northern Paiutes and aroused anger against the Bureau. Instead of responding to her criticism, the Bureau of Indian Affairs countered with attacks on her character, particularly her chastity. Winnemucca responded by including character references in the conclusion of her autobiography.

Winnemucca's stories of rape did not just generate public sympathy for the Northern Paiutes; they posited solutions to the Northern Paiutes' problems. Historian Miranda Chaytor argues that women's accounts of rape reveal more than the details of their violation because in them, women name the violence, contain it, and identify the people and things that will enable their recovery. When describing rape in the Great Basin, Winnemucca emphasized the vulnerability of women at work. . . . For these women, labor ordered their lives and accorded them status by enabling them to sustain their families. Winnemucca's accounts of rape, therefore, point to what she felt her people had lost that made them so sexually vulnerable—their economic self-sufficiency and autonomy.[25]

. . . During the late nineteenth century, reformers endorsed allotment, or the subdivision of communal land and resources among individual male heads of households, as a means to rapidly assimilate Native Americans into Anglo-American culture. They . . . believed that private land ownership would destroy the extended families that characterized most Native cultures and replace them with patriarchal, nuclear families, complete with a husband in the fields and a wife in the home. . . . Winnemucca lobbied for allotments, . . . not to enable the Northern Paiutes to assimilate but to facilitate the restoration of their economic self-sufficiency. Though she recognized that their seasonal cycle was destroyed, Winnemucca did not believe that it was irreplaceable, and she looked to allotment to restore the economic autonomy of Northern Paiute families through ranching and farming. On allotments, Northern Paiute husbands and wives could work sometimes together and other times apart as they had always done in order to maintain their families in the Northern Paiute way.

Winnemucca spent her final years attempting to prove that Northern Paiute families could survive and even thrive on their own small farms. In 1885, her brother, Natches, purchased a 160-acre ranch, and while Natches farmed, Winnemucca established a school. She taught Northern Paiute children reading, writing, and arithmetic, and the children helped Natches with the farming, and domestic chores. Most importantly, she treated the children kindly according to Northern Paiute custom and schooled them in Northern Paiute culture. The Peabody Institute, named after an eastern donor, was enormously popular with Northern Paiute students and parents, who abhorred the militarized boarding schools that the government forced Indian children to attend. Natches and Winnemucca's ranch and school blossomed for several years until their financial burden and poor health forced them to close in the summer of 1889. Financially and emotionally exhausted, Winnemucca moved to her sister Elma's ranch where she died in 1891.

During her life and since her death, Winnemucca has been the subject of much controversy. Literary and academic audiences honor Winnemucca as the first Native American woman to write her autobiography, *Life among the Paiutes*, but many Native people criticize her for her more ambiguous accomplishments, such as scouting for the United States Army and endorsing assimilationist federal policies, particularly allotment. Some Northern Paiutes disown her for her inability to force the federal government to keep its promises to them, and pointing to her notoriety, they dismiss her as a self-serving opportunist. But other Northern Paiutes emphasize her devotion to their sovereignty and culture, generations before whites recognized the value of indigenous ways of life.

Perhaps Winnemucca remains so controversial because she was a leader ahead of her time. In the 1880s, she denounced the disproportionately high incidence of sexual violence against Native American women, and worked to ease their poverty and dramatize the relationship between sexual and economic oppression. Over a century later, the percentage of Native Americans living below the poverty line is over twice that of other Americans, and Native American women still experience sexual abuse in disproportionately high numbers— 3.5 times that of other American racial groups. Moreover, unlike other racial groups, someone of another race assaults 90 percent of American Indian rape victims.[26] But Winnemucca also remains controversial because she defied stereotypes of Native American women as sexually lax and available. She personified their power, rooted in cultures that have not totally adopted American culture's attitudes toward women and their sexuality. Through her autobiography, she made Northern Paiute women's power intelligible to white readers during an era when Anglo-Americans were struggling with the question of women's rights themselves; she provided them with an alternative model of gender relations other than male dominance. Winnemucca proclaimed: "I know what an Indian woman can do. . . . My dear reader, I have not lived in this world for over thirty or forty years for nothing, and I know what I am talking bout."[27]

NOTES

Hopkins was Winnemucca's married name; we've silently changed it to Winnemucca.

1. Richard N. Allen, *The Tennessee Letters: From Carson Valley, 1857–1869*, David Thompson, compiler (Reno: Grace Dangberg Foundation, 1983), 137–141, 157, 159–160; Myron Angel, *History of Nevada* (Oakland, CA: Thompson and West, 1881; New York: Arno Press, 1973), 150–158.

2. For a description of the Northern Paiute seasonal cycle, see Catherine S. Fowler and Sven Liljeblad, "Northern Paiute," in *The Handbook of North American Indians, Great Basin*, vol. 11, ed. Warren L. D'Azevedo (Washington, DC: Smithsonian Institution, 1986), 435–465; Martha C. Knack and Omer C. Stewart, *As Long as the River Shall Run: An Ethnohistory of the Pyramid Lake Indian Reservation* (Berkeley: University of California Press, 1984), chapter 1.

3. Judith Shapiro, "Kinship," in *The Handbook of North American Indians*, 620–629.

4. Sarah Winnemucca Hopkins, *Life Among the Piutes: Their Wrongs and Claims*, ed. Mrs. Horace Mann (New York: G. P. Putnam and Sons of New York, 1883; reprint, Reno: University of Nevada Press, 1994), 53 (hereafter cited as Winnemucca). Most scholars believe that Winnemucca wrote her autobiography with minimal editing by Mrs. Horace Mann. Sally Zanjani, *Sarah Winnemucca* (Lincoln: University of Nebraska Press, 2001).

5. Fowler, "Subsistence," in *The Handbook of North American Indians*, 64–97; Winnemucca, 50–51.

6 Fowler and Liljeblad, 450–452; Knack and Stewart, 230; and Winnemucca, 52–54.

7. Winnemucca, 45–51.

8. Fowler and Liljeblad; Knack and Stewart, chapter 2.

9. Winnemucca, chapters 5–8; Knack and Stewart, chapters 1–4.

10. Eugene M. Hattori, "'And Some of Them Swear Like Pirates': Acculturation of American Indian Women in Nineteenth Century Virginia City," in *Comstock Women: The Making of a Mining Community*, ed. Ronald M. James and C. Elizabeth Raymond (Reno: University of Nevada Press, 1998), 229–245; Knack and Stewart, chapter 2; Dorothy Nafus Morrison, *Chief Sarah: Sarah Winnemucca's Fight for Indian Rights* (New York: Atheneum, 1980), chapter 6.

11. For detailed accounts of all of Winnemucca's various jobs, see Winnemucca, Morrison, and Zanjani.

12. Winnemucca, 58–59, 231; Knack and Stewart, chapter 2.

13. Rayna Green, "The Pocahontas Perplex: The Images of Indian Women in American Culture," in *Unequal Sisters: A Multicultural Reader in U.S. Women's History*, ed. Ellen Carol DuBois (New York: Routledge, 1990), 15–21; Oliver O. Howard, *My Life and Experiences among Our Hostile Indians* (New York: Da Capo Press, 1972), 214, 222–223, 524–533.

14. Knack and Stewart, 47.

15. Winnemucca, 3–4; Knack and Stewart, chapters 2–8. For accounts of the rape of Indian women during the California Gold Rush, see Albert L. Hurtado, *Indian Survival on the California Frontier* (New Haven: Yale University Press, 1988), chapter 9.

16. Emilie Buchwald, Pamela Fletcher, and Martha Roth, preamble to *Transforming a Rape Culture* (Minneapolis, MN: Milkweed, 1993).

17. Winnemucca, 228.

18. Ibid., 100–104, 167, 178, 188, 231.

19. Hattori, 233–235; Knack and Stewart, chapters 4–5.

20. Winnemucca, 180–182, 228–230.

21. Winnemucca, 231; *Nevada State Journal*, 28 March 1875; *Silver State*, 27 March 1875; Zanjani, 126.

22. George M. Kober, *Reminiscences of George Martin Kober*, M.D., LL. D. (Washington, DC: Kober Foundation of Georgetown University, 1930), 280.

23. Fowler and Liljeblad, 457; Winnemucca, 70–73.

24. Winnemucca, 116.

25. "Husband(ry): Narratives of Rape in the Seventeenth Century," *Gender and History* 7 (1995): 378–407.

26. U.S. Department of Justice, Bureau of Justice Statistics, February 1999 for the period 1992–1996, http://www/vday.org/ie/index2cfm?articleID +864. U.S. Department of Commerce, *We the First Americans* (Washington, DC: Government Printing Office, 1993).

27. Winnemucca, 228.

The Grimké Sisters, Sarah and Angelina, Talk Truth to Power

Sarah and Angelina Grimké were the first, and it seems likely the only, women of a slaveholding family to speak and write publicly as abolitionists. They were the first women agents of the American Anti-Slavery Society to tour widely and to speak to audiences of men and women. They were the first women who, from within the abolitionist movement, defended their rights *as women* to free speech. They were sustained in their work by a deep religious devotion, and their writings are examples of the spirit in which many women's rights advocates developed a wide-ranging critique of the relationship between the state, churches, and families.

The Grimké sisters grew up in Charleston, South Carolina. Their father was a distinguished legislator and judge; although he gave his daughters a traditional female education (lacking Greek, Latin, and philosophy), when he trained his sons for the law he included his daughters in the exercises. Both young women were sensitive to the injustices of slavery; as a young woman Sarah broke the law against teaching slaves to read and Angelina held prayer meetings for the family's slaves. When she was twenty-four years old, Sarah accompanied her father to Philadelphia, where he sought medical treatment; after his death she returned there in 1821 to live among Quakers, who impressed her by their piety, simplicity, and refusal to hold slaves. In 1829 Angelina joined her; both became members of a Quaker meeting. Sarah committed herself to boycott products made in slavery; Angelina joined the Philadelphia Female Antislavery Society. When reformers faced violence from proslavery mobs in the summer of 1835, William Lloyd Garrison wrote strong editorials in the *Liberator* denouncing what he called a "reign of terror." Angelina Grimké responded with a letter complimenting him on his fortitude: "The ground on which you stand is holy ground," she wrote, "never—never surrender it."

Garrison surprised her by printing her letter; thus encouraged to write for a wide audience, Angelina went on to write *An Appeal to the Christian Women of the South*, part of which follows. The pamphlet sold widely in the North and made her reputation, but it was burned in Charleston.

When the American Anti-Slavery Society organized a group of "Agents" to travel and speak on slavery, Angelina and Sarah Grimké were among them. They began in late 1836, speaking to women in private parlors in New York City; by the turn of the year, no private room was big enough and they held their sessions in a Baptist church. They involved themselves in founding women's antislavery societies and organizing women's antislavery petitions to Congress; they published their speeches as pamphlets. In mid-1837 they moved on to Boston, where an intense debate among factions of abolitionists was already under way. Sarah wrote a series of essays that appeared first in newspapers and then as a pamphlet, *Letters on the Equality of the Sexes and the Condition of Women*. Here, we reprint excerpts from two of her letters.

In the summer of 1837, the Congregational ministers of Massachusetts published a "Pastoral Letter" attacking the Grimkés as unwomanly (partly reprinted here, with Sarah Grimké's response). In the past, the two reformers had offered their criticism of slavery in the context of religious faith; now they claimed that as moral individuals, women had as much right to take political positions as men. Though even some of their allies—including Theodore Dwight Weld, whom Angelina would soon marry—sought to dissuade them, they were forthright, as you can see, in their response to the clergymen. The term *feminist* had not yet been invented—it would be devised in the 1910s—but the ingredients of the concept were already present in the ideas of the Grimké sisters.*

ANGELINA GRIMKÉ, APPEAL TO THE CHRISTIAN WOMEN OF THE SOUTH (1836)

. . . Sisters in Christ I feel an interest in *you*, and often has the secret prayer arisen on your behalf, Lord "open thou their eyes that they may see wondrous things out of thy Law"—It is then, because I *do feel* and *do pray* for you, that I thus address you upon a subject about which of all others, perhaps you would rather not hear any thing; but, "would to God ye could bear with me a little in my folly, and indeed bear with me, for I am jealous over you with godly jealousy." Be not afraid then to read my appeal; it is *not* written in the heat of passion or prejudice, but in that solemn calmness which is the result of conviction and duty. It is true, I am going to tell you unwelcome truths, but I mean to speak those *truths in love*, and remember Solomon says, "faithful are the *wounds* of a friend." I do not believe the time has yet come when *Christian women* "will not endure sound doctrine," even on the subject of slavery, if it is spoken to them in tenderness and love, therefore I now address you. . . .

We must come back to the good old doctrine of our forefathers who declared to the world, "this self evident truth that *all* men are created equal, and that they have certain *inalienable* rights among which are life, *liberty*, and the pursuit of happiness." It is even a greater absurdity to suppose a man can be legally born a slave under *our free Republican* Government, than under the petty despotisms of barbarian Africa. If then, we have no right to enslave an African, surely we can have none to enslave an American; if it is a self evident truth that *all* men, every where and of every color are born equal, and have an *inalienable right to liberty*, then it is equally true that *no* man can be born a slave, and no man can ever *rightfully* be reduced to *involuntary* bondage and held as a slave, however fair may be the claim of his master or mistress through will and title-deeds. . . .

But perhaps you will be ready to query, why appeal to *women* on this subject? *We* do not make the laws which perpetuate slavery. No legislative power is vested in *us; We* can do nothing to overthrow the system, even if we wished to do so. To this I reply, I know you do not make the laws, but I also know that *you are the wives and mothers, the sisters and daughters of those who do*; and if you really suppose *you* can do nothing to overthrow slavery, you are greatly mistaken. You can do much in every way: four things I will name. 1st. You can read on this subject. 2d. You can pray over this subject. 3d. You can speak on this subject. 4th. You can *act* on this subject. I have not placed reading before praying because I regard it more important, but because, in order to pray aright, we must understand what we are praying for; it is only then we can "pray with the understanding and the spirit also."

1. Read then on the subject of slavery. Search the Scriptures daily, whether the things I have told you are true. Other books and papers might be a great help to you in this investigation, but they are not necessary. . . .

2. Pray over this subject. When you have entered into your closets, and shut to the doors,

*See Gerda Lerner, *The Grimké Sisters from South Carolina: Rebels Against Slavery* (Boston, 1967).

then pray to your father, who seeth in secret, that he would open your eyes to see whether slavery is *sinful*, and if it is, that he would enable you to bear a faithful, open and unshrinking testimony against it, and to do whatsoever your hands find to do . . .

3. Speak on this subject. It is through the tongue, the pen, and the press, that truth is principally propagated. Speak then to your relatives, your friends, your acquaintances on the subject of slavery; be not afraid if you are conscientiously convinced it is *sinful*, to say so openly, but calmly, and to let your sentiments be known. If you are served by the slaves of others, try to ameliorate their condition as much as possible; never aggravate their faults, and thus add fuel to the fire of anger already kindled in a master and mistress's bosom. . . .

4. Act on this subject. Some of you *own* slaves yourselves. If you believe slavery is *Sinful*, set them at liberty, "undo the heavy burdens and let the oppressed go free." If they wish to remain with you, pay them wages, if not let them leave you. Should they remain teach them, and have them taught the common branches of an English education; they have minds and those minds, *ought to be improved*. So precious a talent as intellect, never was given to be wrapt in a napkin and buried in the earth. It is the *duty* of all, as far as they can, to improve their own mental faculties, because we are commanded to love God with *all our minds*, as well as with all our hearts, and we commit a great sin, if we *forbid or prevent* that cultivation of the mind in others, which would enable them to perform this duty. Teach your servants then to read & c, and encourage them to believe it is their *duty* to learn, if it were only that they might read the Bible.

But some of you will say, we can neither free our slaves nor teach them to read, for the laws of our state forbid it. Be not surprised when I say such wicked laws *ought to be no barrier* in the way of your duty, and I appeal to the Bible to prove this position. What was the conduct of Shiphrah and Puah, when the king of Egypt issued his cruel mandate, with regard to the Hebrew children? *"They* feared *God*, and did *not* as the King of Egypt commanded them, but saved the men children alive." Did these *women* do right in disobeying that monarch? "*Therefore* (says the sacred text,) God *dealt well* with them, and made them houses."

SARAH M. GRIMKÉ, LETTERS ON THE EQUALITY OF THE SEXES AND THE CONDITION OF WOMEN (1837)

LETTER VIII: "ON THE CONDITION OF WOMEN IN THE UNITED STATES"

During the early part of my life, my lot was cast among the butterflies of the *fashionable* world; and of this class of women, I am constrained to say, both from experience and observation, that their education is miserably deficient; that they are taught to regard marriage as the one thing needful, the only avenue to distinction; hence to attract the notice and win the attentions of men, by their external charms, is the chief business of fashionable girls. They seldom think that men will be allured by intellectual acquirements, because they find, that where any mental superiority exists, a woman is generally shunned and regarded as stepping out of her "appropriate sphere," which, in their view, is to dress, to dance, to set out to the best possible advantage her person, to read the novels which inundate the press, and which do more to destroy her character as a rational creature, than any thing else. . . .

There is another and much more numerous class in this country, who are withdrawn by education or circumstances from the circle of fashionable amusements, but who are brought up with the dangerous and absurd idea, that *marriage* is a kind of preferment; and that to be able to keep their husband's house, and render his situation comfortable, is the end of her being. Much that she does and says and thinks is done in reference to this situation; and to be married is too often held up to the view of girls as the sine qua non of human happiness and human existence. . . . I do long to see the time, when it will no longer be necessary for women to expend so many precious hours in furnishing "a well spread table," but that their husbands will forego some of the accustomed indulgences in this way, and encourage their wives to devote some portion of their time to mental cultivation, even at the expense of having to dine sometimes on baked potatoes, or bread and butter. . . .

There is another way in which the general opinion, that women are inferior to men, is manifested, that bears with tremendous effect on the laboring class, and indeed on almost all who are obliged to earn a subsistence, whether it be by mental or physical exertion—I allude to the disproportionate value set on the time and labor of men and of women. A man who is engaged in teaching, can always, I believe, command a higher price for tuition than a woman—even when he teaches the same branches, and is not in any respect superior to the woman. This I know is the case in boarding and other schools with which I have been acquainted, and it is so in every occupation in which the sexes engaged indiscriminately. As for example, in tailoring, a man has twice, or three times as much for making a waistcoat or pantaloons as a woman, although the work done by each may be equally good. In those employments which are peculiar to women, their time is estimated at only half the value of that of men. A woman who goes out to wash, works as hard in proportion as a wood sawyer, or a coal heaver, but she is not generally able to make more than half as much by a day's work. . . .

There is another class of women in this country, to whom I cannot refer, without feelings of the deepest shame and sorrow. I allude to our female slaves. Our southern cities are whelmed beneath a tide of pollution; the virtue of female slaves is wholly at the mercy of irresponsible tyrants, and women are bought and sold in our slave markets, to gratify the brutal lust of those who bear the name of Christians. In our slave States, if amid all her degradation and ignorance, a women desires to preserve her virtue unsullied, she is either bribed or whipped into compliance, or if she dares resist her seducer, her life by the laws of some of the slave States may be, and has actually been sacrificed to the fury of disappointed passion. Where such laws do not exist, the power which is necessarily vested in the master over his property, leaves the defenceless slave entirely at his mercy, and the sufferings of some females on this account, both physical and mental, are intense.

Letter XV: Man Equally Guilty With Woman in the Fall

. . . In contemplating the great moral reformations of the day, and the part which they are bound to take in them, instead of puzzling themselves with the harassing, because unnecessary inquiry, how far they may go without overstepping the bounds of propriety, which separate male and female duties, they will only inquire, "Lord, what wilt thou have us do?" They will be enabled to see the simple truth, that God has made no distinction between men and women as moral beings; that the distinction now so much insisted upon between male and female virtues is as absurd as it is unscriptural, and has been the fruitful source of much mischief—granting to man a license for the exhibition of brute force and conflict on the battlefield; for sternness, selfishness, and the exercise of irresponsible power in the circle of home—and to woman a permit to rest on an arm of flesh, and to regard modesty and delicacy, and all the kindred virtues, as peculiarly appropriate to her. Now to me it is perfectly clear, that WHATSOEVER IT IS MORALLY RIGHT FOR A MAN TO DO, IT IS MORALLY RIGHT FOR A WOMAN TO DO; and that confusion must exist in the moral world, until woman takes her stand on the same platform with man, and feels that she is clothed by her Maker with the *same rights*, and, of course, that upon her devolve the *same duties*.

PASTORAL LETTER: THE GENERAL ASSOCIATION OF MASSACHUSETTS TO THE CHURCHES UNDER THEIR CARE

III.—We invite your attention to the dangers which at present seem to threaten the female character with wide spread and permanent injury.

The appropriate duties and influence of women are clearly stated in the New Testament. Those duties and that influence are unobtrusive and private, but the sources of mighty power. When the mild, dependant [sic], softening influence of woman upon the sternness of man's opinion is fully exercised, society feels the effects of it in a thousand forms. The power of woman is in her dependence, flowing from the consciousness of that weakness which God has given her for her protection, and which keeps her in those departments of life that form the character of individuals and of the nation. There are social influences which females use in promoting piety and the great objects of Christian benevolence which we cannot too highly commend. We appreciate the unostentatious prayers and efforts of woman in advancing the cause of religion at home and abroad; in Sabbath schools; in leading religious inquirers to the pastors for instruction; and in all such associated effort as becomes the modesty of her sex; and earnestly hope that she may abound more and more in these labors of piety and love.

But when she assumes the place and tone of man as a public reformer, our care and protection of her seem unnecessary; we put ourselves in self-defence against her; she yields the power which God has given her for protection, and her character becomes unnatural. If the vine, whose strength and beauty is to lean upon the trellis and half conceal its clusters, thinks to assume the independence and the overshading nature of the elm, it will not only cease to bear fruit, but fall in shame and dishonor into the dust. We cannot, therefore, but regret the mistaken conduct of those who encourage females to bear an obtrusive and ostentatious part in measures of reform, and countenance any of that sex who so far forget themselves as to itinerate in the character of public lecturers and teachers. We especially deplore the intimate acquaintance and promiscuous conversation of females with regard to things "which ought not to be named"; by which that modesty and delicacy which is the charm of domestic life, and which constitutes the true influence of woman in society is consumed, and the way opened, as we apprehend, for degeneracy and ruin. . . .

SARAH M. GRIMKÉ, RESPONSE TO "THE PASTORAL LETTER . . ."

The motto of woman, when she is engaged in the great work of public reformation should be,—"The Lord is my light and my salvation; whom shall I fear? The Lord is the strength of my life; of whom shall I be afraid?" She must feel, if she feels rightly, that she is fulfilling one of the important duties laid upon her as an accountable being, and that her character, instead of being "unnatural," is in exact accordance with the will of Him to whom, and to no other, she is responsible for the talents and the gifts confided to her. As to the pretty simile, introduced into the "Pastoral Letter," "If the vine whose strength and beauty is to lean upon the trellis work, and half conceal its clusters, thinks to assume the independence and the overshadowing nature of the elm," & c. I shall only remark that it might well suit the poet's fancy, who sings of sparkling eyes and coral lips, and knights in armor clad; but it seems to me utterly inconsistent with the dignity of a Christian body, to endeavor to draw such an anti-scriptural distinction between men and women. Ah! how many of my sex feel in the dominion, thus unrighteously exercised over them, under the gentle appellation of *protection*, that what they have leaned upon has proved a broken reed at best, and oft a spear.

Thine in the bonds of womanhood,

Sarah M. Grimké

Keziah Kendall Protests Coverture

W e know nothing more about "Keziah Kendall" than what she revealed in this letter, which historians Dianne Avery and Alfred S. Konefsky discovered among the papers of Simon Greenleaf, a prominent Harvard law professor. It has not been possible to locate the author in the usual places—tax lists, land records, church lists. Keziah and her sisters carry the names of Job's daughters; whether the names are real or fictional, the writer assumed that her readers would remember the biblical reference: ". . . in all the land there were no women so fair as Job's daughters; and their father gave them inheritance among their brothers."

Kendall had been dismayed by what she heard at a public lyceum lecture on women's rights given by Greenleaf in early 1839. At a time when the legal disabilities of inherited common law were increasingly being questioned—in Massachusetts, the abolitionists Sarah and Angelina Grimké had only recently delivered a

Letter from Keziah Kendall to Simon Greenleaf (undated), Box 3, Folder 10, Simon Greenleaf Papers, Harvard Law School Library. Excerpted from Diane Avery and Alfred S. Konefsky, "The Daughters of Job: Property Rights and Women's Lives in Mid-Nineteenth-Century Massachusetts," *Law and History Review* 10 (Fall 1992): 323–56. Notes have been renumbered and edited.

forthright series of lectures on the rights of women—Greenleaf devoted his lecture to the claim that American women were well protected by American law as it stood. He argued that excluding women from politics saved society from "uproar" and impropriety, and that constraints on married women's use of their property was merely a technicality because in a happy marriage all property became part of "a common fund . . . it can make but little difference . . . by whose name it is called." And he insisted that except for "restriction in *political matters*" there were no significant "distinctions between the legal rights of unmarried women, and of men."

Keziah Kendall was unpersuaded, and wrote to demand that Greenleaf offer another lecture, acknowledging the "legal wrongs" of women. What are Kendall's objections to the law as she experienced it? What connections does she draw between paying taxes, voting, and officeholding? Why does she blame Massachusetts property law for her fiancé's death? Why is she worried about her sister's forthcoming marriage?

Keziah Kendall to Simon Greenleaf [1839?] I take the liberty to write to you on the subject of the Lyceum lecture you delivered last Feb but as you are not acquainted with me I think I will introduce myself. My name is Keziah Kendall. I live not many miles from Cambridge, on a farm with two sisters, one older, one younger than myself. I am thirty two. Our parents and only brother are dead—we have a good estate—comfortable house—nice barn, garden, orchard & c and money in the bank besides. Jemima is a very good manager in the house, keeps everything comfortable—sees that the milk is nicely prepared for market—looks after everything herself, and rises before day, winter and summer,—but she never had any head for figures, and always expects me to keep all accounts, and attend to all business concerns. Keranhappuck, (who is called Kerry) is quite young, only nineteen, and as she was a little girl when mother died, we've always petted her, and let her do as she pleased, and now she's courted. Under these circumstances the whole responsibility of our property, not less than twenty five thousand dollars rests upon me. I am not over fond of money, but I have worked hard ever since I was a little girl, and tried to do all in my power to help earn, and help save, and it would be strange if I did not think more of it than those who never earned anything, and never saved anything they could get to spend, and you know Sir, there are many such girls nowadays. Well—our milkman brought word when he came from market that you were a going to lecture on the legal rights of women, and so I thought I would go and learn. Now I hope you wont think me bold when I say, I did not like that lecture much. I dont speak of the

manner, it was pretty spoken enough, but there was nothing in it but what every body knows. We all know about a widow's thirds,[1] and we all know that a man must maintain his wife, and we all know that he must pay her debts, if she has any—but I never heard of a yankee woman marrying in debt. What I wanted to know, was good reasons for some of those laws that I cant account for. I do hope if you are ever to lecture at the Lyceum again, that you will give us some. I must tell my story to make you understand what I mean. One Lyceum lecture that I heard in C. stated that the Americans went to war with the British, because they were taxed without being represented in Parliament. Now we are taxed every year to the full amount of every dollar we possess—town, county, state taxes—taxes for land, for movables, for money and all. Now I dont want to go representative or any thing else, any more than I do to be a "constable or a sheriff," but I have no voice about public improvements, and I dont see the justice of being taxed any more than the "revolutionary heroes" did. You mention that woman here, are not treated like heathen and Indian women—we know that—nor do I think we are treated as Christian women ought to be, according to the Bible rule of doing to others as you would others should do unto you. I am told (not by you) that if a woman dies a week after she's married that her husband takes all her personal property and the use of her real estate as long as he lives[2]—if a man dies his wife can have her thirds—this does not come up to the Gospel rule. Now the young fellow that is engaged to our Kerry, is a pleasant clever fellow, but he is not quite one and twenty, and I dont s'pouse he ever earned a coat in his life. Uncle told me there was a way for a woman to have her property trustee'd,[3] and I told it to Kerry—but she, poor girl has romantic notions owing to reading too many novels,[4] and when I told her of it, she would not hear of such a thing—"What take the law to keep my property away from James before I marry him—if it was a million of dollars he should have it all." So you see I think the law is in fault here—to tell you the truth I do not think young men are near so careful about getting in debt as girls, and I have known more than one that used their wife's money to pay off old scores. . . . I had rather go to my mantua maker[5] to borrow twenty dollars if I needed it, than to the richest married woman I know.

Another thing I have to tell you—when I was young I had a lover, Jos. Thompson, he went into business in a neighboring town, and after a year or two while I was getting the wedding things—Joe failed, he met with misfortunes that he did not expect,—he could have concealed it from me and married, but he did not—he was honorable, and so we delayed. He lived along here two or three years, and tried all he could to settle with his creditors, but some were stiff and held out, and thought by and by we would marry, and they should get my property. Uncle said he knew if we were married, there were those who would take my cattle and the improvement of my land. Joseph used to visit me often those years, but he lost his spirits and he could not get into business again, and he thought he must go to sea. I begged him not to, and told him we should be able to manage things in time, but he said no—he must try his luck, and at least get enough to settle off old scores, and then he would come here and live and we would make the best of what I had. We parted—but it pleased God he should be lost at sea. What I have suffered, I cannot tell you. Now Joe was no sailor when I engaged with him, and if it had been a thing known that I should always have a right to keep possession of my own, he need never have gone to sea, and we might have lived happily together, and in time with industry and economy, he might have paid off all. I am one that cant be convinced without better reasons than I have heard of, that woman are dealt with by the "gospel rule." There is more might than right in such laws as far as I can see—

if you see differently, do tell us next time you lecture. Another thing—you made some reflections upon women following the Anti's. . . . Women have joined the Antislavery societies, and why? Women are kept for slaves as well as men—it is a common cause, deny the justice of it, who can! To be sure I do not wish to go about lecturing like the Misses Grimkie, but I have not the knowledge they have, and I verily believe that if I had been brought up among slaves as they were, and knew all that they know, and felt a call from humanity to speak, I should run the venture of your displeasure, and that of a good many others like you.[6] I told Uncle that I thought your lecture was a one-sided thing—and he said, "why Keziah, Squire Greenleaf is an advocate, not a judge, you must get him to take t'other side next time." Now I have taken this opportunity to ask you to give us a remedy for the "legal wrongs" of women, whenever you have a chance. The fathers of the land should look to these things—who knows but your daughter may be placed in the sad situation I am in, or the dangerous one Kerry is in. I hear you are a good man, to make it certain—do all the good you can, and justify no wrong thing.

Yours with regard
Keziah Kendall

NOTES

1. She is, of course, referring to a widow's dower rights. (See pp. 85–86.)

2. "Kendall" was correct in her understanding of a husband's rights in his wife's personal property if she should die as early as "a week after she's married." But under the common law he would not inherit a life interest in her real estate unless they were parents of a child.

3. This is a reference to the equitable device of placing the woman's property in a trust before marriage for the purpose of avoiding the husband's common law rights in her property as well as protecting it from the husband's creditors. Under the trust agreement, the trustee would be obligated to manage the property for the benefit of the married woman.

4. "Kendall" shared a widely held distrust of romantic novels.

5. In the early republic, mantua makers [i.e., skilled dressmakers] were often economically independent women.

6. "Kendall" is probably referring here to the "Pastoral Letter" issued by the Congregationalist ministers in the summer of 1837 denouncing the public lecturing of the Grimké sisters. (see pp. 241–242).

Ellen F. Watkins Goes on the Lecture Circuit

At age twenty-nine, Frances Ellen Watkins (later Harper) set out to follow Sarah and Angelina Grimké's risk-strewn path, lecturing widely and publishing in protest of slavery and racial discrimination. In these decades, the vast majority of white Americans disdained and feared abolitionists as outrageous radicals. A prolific poet and essayist, and, later, novelist, Harper emerged over time as a revered literary figure. After the Civil War, she was an active reformer for decades on behalf of African American rights, temperance, peace, and women's rights; she died in 1911. Notably, she was one of a small number of black women to hold "positions of leadership in the national organizations controlled by white female reformers," such as the Women's Christian Temperance Union, the American Woman Suffrage Association, and the International Council of Women. Born in Baltimore in 1825, Harper was orphaned at age three when her mother, a free woman of color, died. She grew up in the household of her learned uncle, William J. Watkins, Sr., a United Methodist minister and founder of the Watkins Academy, which offered "one of the best educations" then available to African Americans and where his niece was a pupil. In the documents below, we hear her narrate her successes and troubles as a public activist early in her career, prior to her marriage in 1860 to Fenton Harper of Ohio.* Witness how her response to an urban streetcar operator marks her as an ally of Emma Coger, Ida B. Wells, Rosa Parks, and countless other women who refused to acquiesce to unequal treatment in public accommodations (see pp. 290–291, 323).

Chronicling her very first lecture in the summer of 1854 and on through the decade, Harper's letters serve as a journal of her travels and public lecturing as an employee of antislavery societies. Like other reformers on the lecture circuit, Harper's schedule could be grueling: for example, between September 5 and October 20, 1854, she spoke in twenty-one towns in Maine, and two to four times in some of them. When she was the featured speaker (not sharing the stage with another), she often spoke for an hour and a half. A former schoolteacher and seamstress, Harper (then Watkins) quickly acquired the reputation among abolitionists as being among the most effective female orators on circuit. Her friend, Philadelphia-based William Still, noted that "perhaps few speakers surpass her in using language and arguments, more potently, in impressing and charming her audiences." Fellow activist, African American newspaper editor Mary Ann Shadd Cary, wrote of a moment

---

*Bettye Collier-Thomas, "Frances Ellen Watkins Harper: Abolitionist and Feminist Reformer, 1825–1911," in *African American Women and the Vote, 1837–1965,* ed. Ann D. Gordon (Amherst: University of Massachusetts Press, 1997), 42, 44, 49. See also Frances Smith Foster, ed., *A Brighter Coming Day: A Frances Ellen Watkins Harper Reader* (New York: Feminist Press at the City University of New York, 1990), 3–47.

The following letters, except for the one dated April 1858, are excerpted from William Still, *The Underground Rail Road: A Record of Facts, Authentic Narratives, Letters, &c., Narrating the Hardships, Hair-breadth Escapes, and Death Struggles of the Slaves in their Efforts for Freedom, as Related by Themselves and Others, or Witnessed by the Author . . .* (Philadelphia: Porter and Coates, 1872), pp. 758–760. (Note: the book has been digitized by hathitrust.org.) The April 1858 letter from Watkins "to a friend" was published in William Lloyd Garrison's abolitionist newspaper, *The Liberator,* April 23, 1858, p. 3.

when they were both in Detroit: "why the whites & colored people here are just going crazy with excitement about her. She is the greatest female speaker ever was here, so wisdom obliges me to keep out of the way [e.g., not offer to lecture] as . . . there would just be no chance of favorable comparison."[†] In your experience, what qualities and strategies help a relatively young person be a successful public speaker—without amplification aids like a microphone?

Some of the most militant and determined abolitionists in Britain and the United States embraced the Free Produce movement, which Harper mentions approvingly. But committing oneself to purchase and use only commodities not produced by enslaved workers was logistically hard to pull off. The handful of Quaker shopkeepers in the nation who ran "free produce stores," such as Lydia White of Philadelphia, had difficulty keeping their shelves adequately stocked. Customers complained that the sugar they bought at these stores had "a very disagreeable taste and odor" and that the rice was "very poor, dark and dirty." One solution in terms of clothing was to avoid cotton altogether. Yet, ready-made "free labor" gowns often failed to sell, deemed either too ugly or not plain enough by abolitionist shoppers. While this early initiative to label ethical goods presaged many later episodes in what we now call consumer politics, by the 1850s most North American antislavery activists had given up on the exhausting and frustrating free produce endeavor, convinced that their energies were better channeled into direct political action.[**] One wonders how often the outspoken women reformers featured in this set of documents believed they were wearing free labor garments and at what point in their careers they decided other expressions of long-distance solidarity with oppressed workers were more effective.

Aug. 1854: Well, I am out lecturing. I have lectured every night this week; [and] besides [I] addressed a Sunday-school, and I shall speak, if nothing prevent it, to-night. My lectures have met with success. Last night I lectured in a white church in Providence. Mr. Gardener was present, and made the estimate of about six hundred persons. Never, perhaps, was a speaker, old or young favored with a more attentive audience. . . . My voice is not wanting in strength, as I am aware of, to reach pretty well over the house. . . . My maiden lecture was Monday night in New Bedford on the Elevation and Education of our People.

Sept. 28, 1854, from Buckstown Centre, Maine: I spoke in Boston on Monday night. . . . Well, I am but one, but can do something, and, God helping me, I will try. . . . [Since then,] the agent of the State Anti-Slavery Society of Maine travels with me, and she is a pleasant, dear, sweet lady.

I do like her so. We travel together, eat together, and sleep together. (She is a white woman.) In fact I have not been in one colored person's house since I left Massachusetts; but I have a pleasant time. . . . I have met with some of the kindest treatment up here that I have ever received. . . . I have lectured three times this week.

Thursday, Oct. 20, 1854, from Temple, Maine: [At the annual meeting of the Maine Anti-Slavery Society,] I spoke on Free Produce, and now by the way I believe in that kind of Abolition. Oh, it does seem to strike at one of the principal roots of the matter. I have commenced since I read Solomon Northrup. Oh, if Mrs. Stowe [Harriet Beecher Stowe, the novelist] has clothed American slavery in the graceful garb of fiction, Solomon Northrup comes up from the dark habitation of Southern cruelty where slavery fattens and feasts on human blood with such mournful revelations that one

[†] Still, *The Underground Rail Road*, 760; Still, in *Provincial Freeman* [Chatham, Ontario], March 7, 1857; Cary, quoted in Shirley J. Yee, *Black Women Abolitionists: A Study in Activism, 1828–1860* (Knoxville: University of Tennessee Press, 1992), 117.

[**] Lawrence B. Glickman, "'Buy for the Sake of the Slave': Abolitionism and the Origins of American Consumer Activism," *American Quarterly* 56 (Dec. 2004), 889–912, esp. 891 (quotation), 900.

might almost wish for the sake of humanity that the tales of horror which he reveals were not so.[††] Oh, how can we pamper our appetites upon luxuries [such as sugar] drawn from reluctant fingers? Oh, could slavery exist long if it did not sit on a commercial throne? . . . I have reason to be thankful that I am able to give [e.g., pay] a little more for a Free Labor dress, [even] if it is coarser. I can thank God that upon its warp and woof I see no stain of blood and tears [of enslaved cotton pickers]; that to procure a little finer muslin for my limbs no crushed and broken heart went out in sighs; and that from the field where it was raised went up no wild and startling cry unto the throne of God to witness there in language deep and strong, that in demanding that cotton I was nerving oppression's hand for deeds of guilt and crime. If the liberation of the slave demanded it, I could consent to part with a portion of the blood from my own veins if that would do him any good.

April 1858: Now let me tell you about Pennsylvania. I have been travelling nearly four years, and have been in every New England State, in New York, Canada and Ohio: but of all these places, this is about the meanest . . . as far as the treatment of colored people is concerned. I have been insulted in several railroad cars. The other day, in attempting to ride in one of the city cars, after I had entered, the conductor came to me, and wanted me to go out on the platform. Now, was not that brave and noble? As a matter of course, I did not. Some one interfered, and asked or requested that I might be permitted to sit in a corner. I did not move, but kept the same seat. When I was about to leave, he [the conductor] refused my money, and I threw it down on the car floor, and got out, after I had ridden as far as I wished. Such impudence!

On the Carlisle Road [west of Philadelphia and Lancaster], I was interrupted and insulted several times. Two men came after me in one day.

I have met, of course, with kindness among individuals and families; all is not dark in Pennsylvania; but the shadow of slavery, oh how drearily it hangs!

Declaration of Sentiments, 1848

The Declaration of Sentiments, Stanton's indictment of the relations between men and women in her own society, is still stunning in its energy, its precision, and its foresight. It challenged many elements of American law and social practice which—thanks to five generations of political activism—no longer exist.

But the Declaration was only the beginning. Out of their vision of a community of equals, out of their discomfort with a social environment that privileged men and undermined women, the men and women at Seneca Falls dedicated themselves to Herculean political work. In one seventeen-day period in 1855 they held sixteen political meetings in fourteen different counties in upstate New York. In 1864, when it seemed possible that an end to slavery might also mean universal equal citizenship, they sent petitions with 100,000 signatures to the Senate and dreamed of getting a million.

[††] Here, Harper refers to Harriet Beecher Stowe's best-selling novel, *Uncle Tom's Cabin; or, Life Among the Lowly*, published in March 1852, and to Northup's memoir, *Twelve Years a Slave: Narrative of Solomon Northup, a Citizen of New-York, Kidnapped in Washington City in 1841, and Rescued in 1853*, published in 1853. The latter was the basis of a 2013 feature film, *Twelve Years a Slave* (dir. Steve McQueen).

Declaration of Sentiments, in *History of Woman Suffrage*, vol. 1, ed. Elizabeth Cady Stanton, Susan B. Anthony, and Matilda Joslyn Gage (New York: Fowler & Wells, 1881), pp. 70–71. The Declaration and many related documents can be found at the website of the Papers of Elizabeth Cady Stanton and Susan B. Anthony, http://ecssba.rutgers.edu.

They denounced the exclusion of women from learned professions and "nearly all the profitable employments." Male teachers earned $700 a year; women teachers earned $250. Susan B. Anthony would soon be demanding "equal pay for equal work," but there would be no federal equal pay act until 1963.

If Stanton and her Seneca Falls colleagues were to reappear in our own time, what changes would please them? What elements of their agenda would they believe are still alive?

Seneca Falls, New York,
July 19–20, 1848

When, in the course of human events, it becomes necessary for one portion of the family of man to assume among the people of the earth a position different from that which they have hitherto occupied, but one to which the laws of nature and of nature's God entitle them, a decent respect to the opinions of mankind requires that they should declare the causes that impel them to such a course.

We hold these truths to be self-evident: that all men and women are created equal; that they are endowed by their Creator with certain inalienable rights; that among these are life, liberty, and the pursuit of happiness; that to secure these rights governments are instituted, deriving their just powers from the consent of the governed. Whenever any form of government becomes destructive of these ends, it is the right of those who suffer from it to refuse allegiance to it, and to insist upon the institution of a new government, laying its foundation on such principles, and organizing its powers in such form, as to them shall seem most likely to effect their safety and happiness. Prudence, indeed, will dictate that governments long established should not be changed for light and transient causes; and accordingly all experience hath shown that mankind are more disposed to suffer, while evils are sufferable, than to right themselves by abolishing the forms to which they were accustomed. But when a long train of abuses and usurpations, pursuing invariably the same object evinces a design to reduce them under absolute despotism, it is their duty to throw off such government, and to provide new guards for their future security. Such has been the patient sufferance of the women under this government, and such is now the necessity which constrains them to demand the equal station to which they are entitled.

The history of mankind is a history of repeated injuries and usurpations on the part of man toward woman, having in direct object the establishment of an absolute tyranny over her. To prove this, let facts be submitted to a candid world.

He has never permitted her to exercise her inalienable right to the elective franchise.

He has compelled her to submit to laws, in the formation of which she had no voice.

He has withheld from her rights which are given to the most ignorant and degraded men—both native and foreigners.

Having deprived her of this first right of a citizen, the elective franchise, thereby leaving her without representation in the halls of legislation, he has oppressed her on all sides.

He has made her, if married, in the eye of the law, civilly dead.

He has taken from her all right in property, even to the wages she earns.

He has made her, morally, an irresponsible being, as she can commit many crimes with impunity, provided they be done in the presence of her husband. In the covenant of marriage, she is compelled to promise obedience to her husband, he becoming, to all intents and purposes, her master—the law giving him power to deprive her of her liberty, and to administer chastisement.

He has so framed the laws of divorce, as to what shall be the proper causes, and in case of separation, to whom the guardianship of the children shall be given, as to be wholly regardless of the happiness of women—the law, in all cases, going upon a false supposition of the supremacy of man, and giving all power into his hands.

After depriving her of all rights as a married woman, if single, and the owner of property, he has taxed her to support a government which recognizes her only when her property can be made profitable to it.

He has monopolized nearly all the profitable employments, and from those she is permitted to follow, she receives but a scanty remuneration. He closes against her all the avenues to wealth and distinction which he considers most honorable to himself. As a teacher of theology, medicine, or law, she is not known.

He has denied her the facilities for obtaining a thorough education, all colleges being closed against her.

He allows her in Church, as well as State, but a subordinate position, claiming Apostolic authority for her exclusion from the ministry, and, with some exceptions, from any public participation in the affairs of the Church.

He has created a false public sentiment by giving to the world a different code of morals for men and women, by which moral delinquencies which exclude women from society, are not only tolerated, but deemed of little account in man.

He has usurped the prerogative of Jehovah himself, claiming it as his right to assign for her a sphere of action, when that belongs to her conscience and to her God.

He has endeavored, in every way that he could, to destroy her confidence in her own powers, to lessen her self-respect, and to make her willing to lead a dependent and abject life.

Now, in view of this entire disfranchisement of one-half the people of this country, their social and religious degradation—in view of the unjust laws above mentioned, and because women do feel themselves aggrieved, oppressed, and fraudulently deprived of their most sacred rights, we insist that they have immediate admission to all the rights and privileges which belong to them as citizens of the United States.

In entering upon the great work before us, we anticipate no small amount of misconception, misrepresentation, and ridicule; but we shall use every instrumentality within our power to effect our object. We shall employ agents, circulate tracts, petition the State and National legislatures, and endeavor to enlist the pulpit and the press in our behalf. We hope this Convention will be followed by a series of Conventions embracing every part of the country.

The following resolutions were discussed by Lucretia Mott, Thomas and Mary Ann McClintock, Amy Post, Catharine A. F. Stebbins, and others, and were adopted:

WHEREAS, The great precept of nature is conceded to be, that "man shall pursue his own true and substantial happiness." Blackstone in his Commentaries remarks, that this law of Nature being coeval with mankind, and dictated by God himself, is of course superior in obligation to any other. It is binding over all the globe, in all countries, and at all times; no human laws are of any validity if contrary to this, and such of them as are valid, derive all their force, and all their validity, and all their authority, mediately and immediately, from this original; therefore;

Resolved, That such laws as conflict, in any way, with the true and substantial happiness of woman, are contrary to the great precept of nature and of no validity, for this is "superior in obligation to any other."

Resolved, That all laws which prevent woman from occupying such a station in society as her conscience shall dictate, or which place her in a position inferior to that of man, are contrary to the great precept of nature, and therefore of no force or authority.

Resolved, That woman is man's equal—was intended to be so by the Creator, and the highest good of the race demands that she should be recognized as such.

Resolved, That the women of this country ought to be enlightened in regard to the laws under which they live, that they may no longer publish their degradation by declaring themselves satisfied with their present position, nor their ignorance by asserting that they have all the rights they want.

Resolved, That inasmuch as man, while claiming for himself intellectual superiority, does accord to woman moral superiority, it is preeminently his duty to encourage her to speak and teach, as she has an opportunity, in all religious assemblies.

Resolved, That the same amount of virtue, delicacy, and refinement of behavior that is required of woman in the social state, should also be required of man, and the same transgressions should be visited with equal severity on both man and woman.

Resolved, That the objection of indelicacy and impropriety, which is so often brought against woman when she addresses a public audience, comes with a very ill-grace from those who encourage, by their attendance, her appearance on the stage, in the concert, or in feats of the circus.

Resolved, That woman has too long rested satisfied in the circumscribed limits which corrupt customs and a perverted application of the Scriptures have marked out for her, and that it is time she should move in the enlarged sphere which her great Creator has assigned her.

Resolved, That it is the duty of the women of this country to secure to themselves their sacred right to the elective franchise.

Resolved, That the equality of human rights results necessarily from the fact of the identity of the race in capabilities and responsibilities.

Resolved, therefore, That, being invested by the Creator with the same capabilities, and the same consciousness of responsibility for their exercise, it is demonstrably the right and duty of woman, equally with man, to promote every righteous cause by every righteous means; and especially in regard to the great subjects of morals and religion, it is self-evidently her right to participate with her brother in teaching them, both in private and in public, by writing and by speaking, by any instrumentalities proper to be used, and in any assemblies proper to be held; and this being a self-evident

truth growing out of the divinely implanted principles of human nature, any custom or authority adverse to it, whether modern or wearing the hoary sanction of antiquity, is to be regarded as a self-evident falsehood, and at war with mankind.

At the last session Lucretia Mott offered and spoke to the following resolution:

Resolved, That the speedy success of our cause depends upon the zealous and untiring efforts of both men and women, for the overthrow of the monopoly of the pulpit, and for the securing to woman an equal participation with men in the various trades, professions, and commerce.

Married Women's Property Acts, New York State, 1848 and 1860

Ironically, the first married women's property acts, passed in Mississippi in 1839 and in New York in 1848, were supported by many male legislators out of a desire to preserve the estates of married daughters against spendthrift sons-in-law. Four out of the five sections of the Mississippi act broadened the rights of married women over their own slaves.

Note the limits of the 1848 New York law, and the ways in which women's rights were extended by the 1860 revision. This pattern—of an initial statute that offered married women very modest control over property, followed by subsequent revisions that slowly and very gradually extended their claims—was typical of virtually all states. Under coverture, husbands had property rights in their wives' services, and state legislatures were reluctant to erase these rights. These "services" included the right of "consortium"—understood as including not only housekeeping but also love, affection, companionship, and sexual relations. If a married woman were injured by the negligence of another person, her husband could sue for damages, which included a monetary estimate of the worth of his loss of consortium. A married woman had a right to financial support from her husband but no right to consortium, and if he were injured she had no claim for the loss of his companionship and sexual relations. This imbalance between the sexes in marriage was rarely tested, but when it was—in the case of major accidents—the impact was severe. Not until the early 1950s was a married woman successful in making such a claim (in Washington, D.C., in 1950; in Iowa in 1951) and the states were very slow to recognize it. Feminist lawyers, men and women, pressed the claim throughout the 1970s and 1980s, but not until the 1990s could it be said that all states recognized it.

Laws of the State of New-York, Passed at the Seventy-First Session of the Legislature . . . (Albany, 1848), pp. 307–8; *Laws of the State of New York, Passed at the Eighty-Third Session of the Legislature* . . . (Albany, 1860), pp. 157–59.

The nineteenth-century Married Women's Property Acts were narrowly interpreted. For example, although married women were authorized to "carry on
any trade or business, and perform any labor or services on her sole or separate
account," that authorization was regularly interpreted as applying only when
her work was not done on family property. When Mary Ann Brooks, a married
woman with a part-time job outside the home, was injured when hit by Adolphus
Schwerin's horse and wagon in the early 1870s, she brought suit in her own name
for damages. The New York court approved her suit to the limits of her lost
wages, but she did not have the right to sue for her inability to perform housework in her own home. For that, Mr. Brooks would have to sue. In some states,
when a woman purchased property with her own earnings, she would have to
register it in the county courthouse if she wished to assert control over it; if she
neglected to register, it could be seized for the payment of her husband's debts,
as one Mrs. Odell of Davenport, Iowa, discovered when the piano she had bought
with her own money and had shipped at great expense from Chicago was seized
when her husband's business went bankrupt.* A married woman could rarely
make claims for her earnings within the family; deep into the twentieth century,
farm women had no legal claim to the "butter and egg money" that custom encouraged them to talk about as theirs because they did the hard work of the barn
and the chicken coop.

1848
The real and personal property of any female
[now married and] who may hereafter marry,
and which she shall own at the time of marriage, and the rents issues and profits thereof
shall not be subject to the disposal of her husband, nor be liable for his debts, and shall continue her sole and separate property, as if she
were a single female. . . .

It shall be lawful for any married female
to receive, by gift, grant, devise or bequest,
from any person other than her husband and
hold to her sole and separate use, as if she
were a single female, real and personal property, and the rents, issues and profits thereof,
and the same shall not be subject to the disposal of her husband, nor be liable for his
debts. . . .

1860
[The provisions of the law of 1848 were retained, and others were added:]
A married woman may bargain, sell, assign,
and transfer her separate personal property,
and carry on any trade or business, and perform

any labor or services on her sole and separate
account, and the earnings of any married
woman from her trade . . . shall be her sole and
separate property, and may be used or invested
by her in her own name. . . .

Any married woman may, while married,
sue and be sued in all matters having relation to
her . . . sole and separate property . . . in the
same manner as if she were sole. And any married woman may bring and maintain an action
in her own name, for damages, against any
person or body corporate, for any injury to her
person or character, the same as if she were sole;
and the money received upon the settlement . . .
shall be her sole and separate property.

No bargain or contract made by any married woman, in respect to her sole and separate
property . . . shall be binding upon her husband, or render him or his property in any way
liable therefor.

Every married woman is hereby constituted and declared to be the joint guardian of
her children, with her husband, with equal
powers, rights, and duties in regard to them,
with the husband. . . .

*Brooks v. Schwerin, 54 N.Y. 343 (1873); Odell & Updegraff v. Lee & Kinnard et al., 14 Iowa 411 (1868).

Sojourner Truth's Visiting Card, 1864

Sojourner Truth (ca. 1797–1883) is better known in the twentieth century for words she did not utter—"ar'n't I a woman?"—than for her fierce and exemplary insistence on asserting her rights to express her religious convictions and to speak and act publicly. This portrait, made in a photographer's studio around 1864, depicts the reformer standing, with her hat, shawl, walking stick, and traveling bag, as if on the brink of departing for yet another speaking engagement. It is in the genre of *cartes de visite* (visiting cards), which were very popular in the mid-nineteenth century, both among middle-class women making social calls and as forms of publicity used by politicians, writers, and fund-raisers. As the card's inscription explains, Sojourner Truth sold copies of the card to support herself; her biographer Nell Irvin Painter reports that she charged the common market price of thirty-three cents per card.

I SELL THE SHADOW TO SUPPORT THE SUBSTANCE.

SOJOURNER TRUTH.

Entered according to Act of Congress, in the year 1864, by S. T. in the clerk's office of the U.S. District court, for Eastern District of Michigan. (Courtesy Sophia Smith Collection, Smith College, Northhampton, Mass.)

She was born into slavery as Isabella in the region north of New York City and south of Albany; her first language was Dutch, and in later life her fluent English would have a Dutch accent. As a child she had four different masters; when she married it was under an 1809 New York State law that recognized slave marriages and the legitimacy of children born to married couples, but Isabella's owner chose her husband for her. When Isabella achieved her freedom six months before New York's gradual emancipation law went into effect on July 4, 1827, she owed no further service, but her five children, born after 1799, remained bound—boys until they reached the age of twenty-eight, girls until they reached twenty-five. As indentured servants, her son would not be free until 1849, her daughters not until 1850 and 1851. Around the time Isabella became free, her owner sold her five-year-old son, Peter, to his brother, who resold the boy to another brother, who resold him yet again to a brother-in-law who took him to Alabama where slavery was permanent and legal. Newly freed, Isabella had the confidence to take the matter to court; with financial and legal support from prominent Quakers and Dutch men for whom she worked, she won her suit and his freedom. Her seven-year-old son returned covered with scars from violent whippings. His sisters remained bound to service.

In 1828 Isabella moved to New York City where she found work as a domestic servant. She joined an unorthodox Methodist church and then a radical religious commune; she made a reputation as a preacher at camp meetings. In 1843 divine inspiration directed her to take the name Sojourner Truth and become an itinerant preacher; she made her way up the Connecticut River Valley to Massachusetts, where she joined the Utopian Northampton Association, an abolitionist commune that had recently been founded by William Lloyd Garrison's sister and brother-in-law, Sarah and George Benson. Garrison himself was a frequent visitor; Frederick Douglass, a former slave and articulate abolitionist, was another. They drew her into abolitionist lecture tours and women's rights meetings. Indeed, she spoke at the first national women's rights convention, in Worcester, Massachusetts, held little more than a year after Seneca Falls and featuring some of the same leading participants, including Elizabeth Cady Stanton.

In 1850 Sojourner Truth dictated her life history to Olive Gilbert, a close friend of Sarah Benson; she paid for its publication and supported herself by selling copies of *The Narrative of Sojourner Truth* wherever she traveled, updating it throughout her long life.

Sojourner Truth spoke the words that would make her famous at a women's rights convention attended by hundreds of women and men in Akron, Ohio, in the summer of 1851. Contemporary newspapers reported various versions of what they agreed was powerful oratory: "I have heard much about the sexes being equal: I can carry as much as any man, and can eat as much too, if I can get it. . . . As for intellect, all I can say is, if a woman have a pint and a man a quart— why cant she have her little pint full? You need not be afraid to give us our rights for fear we will take too much,—for we cant take more than our pint'll hold. . . . I cant read, but I can hear. I have heard the bible and have learned that Eve caused man to sin. Well if woman upset the world, do give her a chance to set it right side up again."

But no contemporary witness noted her speaking the refrain "Ar'n't I a woman?" Historians agree that was added a dozen years later by Frances Dana Gage, a women's rights activist who had been at the Akron meeting, and who wrote a highly dramatized and elaborated version of the event, which underscored

Truth's strength and authority. Gage's version was reprinted by Elizabeth Cady Stanton and Susan B. Anthony in the first volume of *The History of Woman Suffrage* (1881) and from there found its way into widespread use.

Sojourner Truth would live until her mid-eighties. She embraced the Union cause during the Civil War, even before Lincoln embraced emancipation. She went door-to-door in Battle Creek, Michigan (where she had moved in the 1850s), to raise money to support the local African American regiment (in which her grandson was enlisted). She traveled from Michigan to Washington, D.C., making campaign speeches for Lincoln's reelection; she met Abraham Lincoln; she worked to help freedpeople find jobs, and she worked for projects to give former enslaved people free land in Kansas. With all this public activity, Sojourner Truth became famous—the "celebrated colored woman"—and visitors made their way to Battle Creek especially to meet her. Cared for by her children and grandchildren, who lived nearby, she died in Battle Creek in 1883.*

Consider how Sojourner Truth presents herself in the photograph here. What does she hope viewers—in her own time and in ours—will conclude about her?

*Nell Irvin Painter, *Sojourner Truth: A Life, A Symbol* (New York: W. W. Norton, 1996), chs. 18, 26; on speaking Dutch, see p. 7; on the *cartes de visite*, see ch. 20; on the ambivalence of the meeting with Lincoln, see ch. 21. See also Carlton Mabee, *Sojourner Truth: Slave, Prophet, Legend* (New York: New York University Press, 1993), and Margaret Washington, *Sojourner Truth's America* (Urbana: University of Illinois Press, 2009).

1. This English print, made between 1785 and 1805, was available for purchase. Anglo-Americans often displayed such prints as we would posters by preserving them in a scrapbook or affixing them to a wall. The multiple architectural features and banners of text were mnemonic (memory-aiding) devices, sending messages of caution and restraint. See how many you can identify! The central figure, whose upper-class status is given away by her fine apparel, is knotting or tatting even as she walks. In the upper left corner, a story unfolds about how indulging in a single vice (drinking) leads to other vices; where is the female protagonist in the final scene? What is the ultimate purpose of women, according to this item of prescriptive literature? (*Keep within Compass*, ca. 1785–1805. Courtesy of the Henry Francis du Pont Winterthur Museum.)

2. This engraving depicts George Washington with the First Regiment of the United States on his way to be inaugurated for his first term as president. Have the women, who fill the public space surrounding Washington and his aides, left the narrow bounds of the compass? They have brought their daughters with them; together they strew his path with flowers. Does the message on the banner acknowledge new political roles for women? (*George Washington on the Bridge at Trenton, New Jersey, 1789*. Courtesy of the Maine Historical Society.)

3. In the antebellum decades, many women embraced reform and benevolence activities, whether through their churches, all-female secular organizations, or ladies' auxiliaries of organizations run by men. They met on planning boards composed of women only, and when they spoke to large gatherings the audience was usually composed of women. By limiting their colleagues to women, they did not compete directly with men, and escaped some—but not all—severe criticism for stepping out of their appropriate sphere of activity. Only a minority of radical women, fiercely devoted to abolishing slavery, resolutely stepped outside the boundaries of the compass to agitate and speak in what critics derided as "promiscuous assemblies," meaning public gatherings that included women and men. (For women's antislavery petitions to Congress, see pp. 213–221.)

A year after its founding in 1837, the Pennsylvania Anti-Slavery Society opened its membership to women. Thereafter, women were integrated into the organization's leadership, as this image of the Executive Committee in 1850 or 1851 makes clear. Many on the committee, including the Motts and Sarah Pugh, were deeply involved in woman's suffrage, as well as belonging to multiple abolition groups. Those standing in the rear, from left to right, are Mary Grew, E. M. Davis, Haworth Wetherfield, Abby Kimber, J. Miller McKim, and Sarah Pugh; those seated, from left to right, are Oliver Johnson, Margaret Jones Burleigh, Benjamin C. Bacon, Robert Purvis, Lucretia Mott, and James Mott. (Phototype reproduction by Frederick F. Gutekunst, Jr. Courtesy of the Sophia Smith Collection, Smith College. For more on the image and its subjects, see "An Anti-Slavery Group of 1850," *Friends' Intelligencer*, Oct, 24, 1896, p. 732. We thank Sherrill Redmon of the Sophia Smith Collection and Christopher Densmore of the Friends Historical Library for their counsel and assistance in finding and identifying this image.)

WASHINGTON, D. C.—THE JUDICIARY COMMITTEE OF THE HOUSE OF REPRESENTATIVES RECEIVING A DEPUTATION OF FEMALE SUFFRAGISTS, JANUARY 11TH.—A LADY DELEGATE READING HER ARGUMENT IN FAVOR OF WOMAN'S VOTING, ON THE BASIS OF THE FOURTEENTH AND FIFTEENTH CONSTITUTIONAL AMENDMENTS.—SEE PAGE 267.

4. Printing technology improved markedly, and costs were lowered in the nineteenth century. Daily newspapers proliferated, as did magazines. Including illustrations became an important marketing strategy. Here, in the wake of the Civil War, a "female delegation" appears before the House Judiciary Committee to argue that the Fourteenth and Fifteenth amendments provided the constitutional basis for women to vote.

A few decades earlier, women's petitions to Congress were often tabled; women's bodies were allowed only in the spectator galleries. Women had to go to great lengths to have their voices reach male legislators. For example, in the 1850s, Susan B. Anthony repackaged an 1854 speech that Elizabeth Cady Stanton had given at the New York State Women's Rights Convention as a pamphlet retitled "Address . . . to the Legislature of New York." Copies were placed on the legislators' desks. But not until 1860 did Stanton actually speak in person to the legislature, and it was not until after the Civil War that a standing committee of the U.S. Congress took women's testimony.

This illustration shows Victoria Woodhull reading a statement on January 11, 1871, to members of the House Judiciary Committee. The room is filled by other women who spoke—Susan B. Anthony and Isabella Beecher Hooker (Harriet Beecher Stowe's sister)—and other women who had come to support them. Elizabeth Cady Stanton is sitting behind Woodhull's left elbow; would you recognize her from the photograph on page 222, taken more than twenty years before? The men in the room included some who supported woman suffrage, among them Albert Gallatin Riddle, a former congressman and leading Washington lawyer. The occasion was timed to coordinate with a national convention, which drew dozens of woman suffrage activists to Washington.

The journalist who reported the occasion used a patronizing tone typical of the era and a wide range of metaphors: "Miss Victoria C. Woodhull led her women-at-arms into the committee-room. . . . Among the warriors present were . . . Mrs. Stanton . . . [and] lesser lights. Shortly after ten o'clock Miss Victoria C. Woodhull opened the ball . . . Miss Woodhull . . .laid aside her alpine hat [and] pulled out a paper. . . . in which she took far higher ground than has usually been assumed by her coadjutors. Her sex's right of suffrage [already exists,] she claims, . . . without [the need for an additional] Amendment."

During the days that followed, women delegates to the convention lobbied members of Congress "with a ferocity never known before." They tallied their supporters carefully, counted approximately sixty votes on their side from the 243–member House of Representatives, and predicted victory in five years. ("The Feminine Invasion of the Capitol," *Frank Leslie's Illustrated Newspaper* 31, no. 801 (Feb. 4, 1871): 347, 349.)

5. Elizabeth Cady Stanton's daughter Harriot Stanton Blatch led New York City suffragists to adopt the tactic of annual parades as a way of making support for the vote visible. In 1910 some 400 women marched to Union Square, where 10,000 people gathered to hear the speakers; by 1912 it was estimated that there were 10,000 *marchers*. This was a time of transition for the movement from community organizing on a small scale to raising substantial amounts of money for more visible activities such as renting large halls for meetings, publishing and distributing newspapers, and hiring lobbyists and organizers who would make politics their profession. The ability to organize a major parade—which involved building speakers' platforms and hiring bands—was a mark of the maturity and newfound power of the movement. On October 23, 1915, a week before a state referendum on women's suffrage (and almost the 100th anniversary of Elizabeth Cady Stanton's birth), New York suffragists sponsored the parade shown in this dramatic photograph. Well over 25,000 women and 2,500 men marched; at least four times that many watched from sidewalks.

Women had won the right to serve as poll watchers for this special election, to guard against corruption by observing the counting of the ballots. The New York amendment was defeated by the relatively narrow margin of 250,000 votes. ("Suffrage Parade, New York City, October 23, 1915." Courtesy of George Grantham Bain Collection, LT 11052-4, Library of Congress, Prints and Photographs Division Washington, D.C.)

6. In his second successful campaign for the presidency, Woodrow Wilson promised—vaguely—to support woman suffrage. In January 1917, Alice Paul and the National Woman's Party undertook a permanent demonstration—a picket line—in front of the White House, near the gates, to hold the president to his promise. Their silent protest was modeled on the campaigns of British suffragists and may have been the first use of this political strategy in the United States. To provoke continued press attention and to represent the widespread support for the cause, Paul ingeniously arranged for themed days. First came State days—Maryland was first—in which the pickets came exclusively from the given state. On College Day, the one represented in this photograph, thirteen women wore sashes announcing their alma maters. On the afternoon of Wilson's second inaugural, March 4, 1,000 women, in a freezing rain, encircled the White house in one long, marching line, with the pictures and story generating unprecedented press coverage.

In April, with Congress about to declare war and the pickets' banners offering sharp political jibes, the strategy proved divisive among women's rights advocates. Some called the tactic indecorous, insulting to the president, and close to treasonous. Press commentary grew shrill, and the crowds gathered to heckle the "silent sentinels" grew violent; banners were torn to shreds. Arrests followed, in April and on into the fall—not of the attackers but of the pickets for "obstructing sidewalk traffic." These women accepted jail or workhouse terms rather than pay the $25 fine; and on release, they returned defiantly to the picket line.

The cycle of peaceful protest and violent response intensified in August, when the picketers provocatively carried banners mocking "Kaiser Wilson" and highlighting the contradiction between the U.S. policies of criticizing the kaiser for denying democracy in Germany and denying the vote to the half of the U.S. population. In the fall, jailed picketers, including Alice Paul, went on hunger strikes because they had asked for and been denied political prisoner status. Like British suffragists, they were force-fed—an intrusive act that was painful and medically dangerous. All were released in late November, when local officials anticipated (rightly) that the arrests and detentions would be ruled unconstitutional on appeal.

Meanwhile, the pickets of 1917, the private letters that Wilson received from feminists such as Jane Addams and Carrie Chapman Catt, and the exigencies of war led to a presidential change of mind: in early January 1918, Wilson announced his support for the federal woman suffrage amendment then making its way through Congress. In September, he went to the Senate to urge passage there, presenting the matter as critical to the war effort. However, it would take new elections and a newly constituted Senate for the bill to pass, and another year until ratification (see pp. 416–417). ("College Day in the Picket Line, Feb. 1917," National Women's Party Records, Library of Congress, Washington, D.C., LC-USZ62-31799. See Katherine H. Adams and Michael L. Keene, *Alice Paul and the American Suffrage Campaign* [Urbana: University of Illinois Press, 2007], and the documentary film by Ruth Pollak for the *American Experience* and WGBH, *One Woman, One Vote* [PBS Home Video, 1995; reissued on DVD, 2006], especially the closing episodes.)

7. Women used their vote for a wide range of political expression. The Ku Klux Klan began to recruit women in 1923, not long after the founding of the Klan itself. Many women found the Klan's claims of moral purity appealing; in some localities, Klansmen made themselves useful to white Protestant women by intimidating husbands who engaged in domestic violence. Klanswomen joined in opposing interracial marriage and in linking Catholics, Jews, and African Americans to degeneracy. Believing that immigrants were likely to undermine morality, they supported the exclusion of Asians and the restriction of immigration to Western Europeans. They energetically boycotted anti-Klan business owners and ran for positions on school boards, where they used their influence to fire Catholic and Jewish teachers and distribute Bibles in classes. Within a year of its founding, the Women's Ku Klux Klan claimed more than 250,000 members in each of the forty–eight states. Here they parade proudly down Pennsylvania Avenue in 1928; the U.S. Capitol looms in the background. (Courtesy of the Library of Congress, Prints and Photographs Division, Washington, D.C.)

8. In this photograph, taken sometime between 1935 and 1940, probably in New York City, laundry workers of the International Union, Local 135, strike for better working conditions. The scene reminds us that laundering and domestic service were often the only jobs open to African American women. Rain or no rain, the picture gives us a sense of workers' standards of how to dress when out in public. Look especially at their feet and heads. (Courtesy of the Library of Congress, Prints and Photographs Division, Washington, D.C.)

9. Young Elizabeth Eckford faces the gauntlet of racial heckling and hatred at the Court-ordered integration of schools in Little Rock, Arkansas, in 1957. When the Arkansas governor defied the Supreme Court order, President Dwight Eisenhower reluctantly sent in federal troops to enforce it. Even with military protection, the young people who actually integrated public schools had to put up with racist slurs, harassment, and intimidation that required of them daily displays of uncommon courage and self-possession. Summoning up such courage became commonplace for thousands of rank-and-file African Americans, many of them girls and women. Indeed, it was women who carried the civil rights struggle at the grassroots level, often at considerable risk to their physical safety and even their lives. As this picture makes clear, white women were prominent among the harassers. Other white women worked for integration in practice by keeping the schools open. (Photograph by Will Counts.)

10. This antidraft poster features singer and activist Joan Baez (*far left*) with her sisters, Pauline and Mimi. Proceeds from the poster sales went toward draft resistance for the Vietnam War. At a performance at Madison Square Garden in 1965, Baez told the crowd, "If you feel that to go to war is wrong, then you must say no to the draft. And if young ladies feel it's wrong to kill, then you can say yes to the young men that say no to the draft." In what senses do you think Baez meant women should say yes? Unidentified poster maker, "Girls Say Yes to Boys Who Say No," ca. 1968. Photomechanical lithograph, photograph by Larry Gates. Gift of William Mears. (Courtesy of the National Museum of American History, Smithsonian Institution.)

11. This famous photograph records the ceremonial last mile of the Torch Relay, a feat that ushered in the National Women's Conference in Houston in 1977. The United Nations had declared 1977 International Women's Year (later extending it to a decade), and President Ford had earlier signed legislation spearheaded by Congresswoman Bella Abzug authorizing the expenditure of $5 million to hold a national women's conference as part of the nation's bicentennial observance. Delegates were elected in all fifty states; three First Ladies attended (guess which three); and Maya Angelou read a poem composed for the occasion (one line reads: "We recognize . . . those unknown and unsung women whose strength gave birth to our strength"). The torch, which you see above runner Peggy Kokernot's head, had been carried by a sequence of over 2,000 women runners from Seneca Falls to Texas to symbolize the link between those early feminists who drafted the Declaration of Sentiments and their contemporary counterparts. The complex logistical work behind the relay was undertaken chiefly by the 13,000-member National Association of Girls and Women in Sports. All torchbearers wore bright blue T-shirts with the conference's logo and the relay-inspired slogan, Women on the Move.

The professional photographer who snapped the picture, Diana Mara Henry, recalls: "I was rushing backward as fast as I could in order to get the shot of these proud and happy women energetically marching" to the conference opening.* The mix of women in this front row—by age, ethnic heritage, and national/local prominence—sent a deliberate message about the appeal of feminist principles. Linked arm-in-arm from right to left are Billie Jean King, Susan B. Anthony II (namesake of her great aunt), and Bella Abzug. Next are Houston runners, Sylvia Ortiz, then a college senior, marathon runner Kokernot, and Mechele Cearcy, a high school track star. Next to Cearcy you may recognize Betty Friedan. Rather than an inclusive picture like Henry's, *TIME* chose for its cover a portrait of Peggy Kokernot applauding the proceedings. Why would the magazine editors choose that particular framing?

The Houston conference was a major milestone in feminist organizing and nationwide mobilization. The 20,000 persons at the gathering cheered or jeered the 2,000-plus delegates who, plank by plank, voted on a detailed plan of action geared toward achieving the elusive goal of gender equality. Twenty percent of delegates represented the conservative end of the political spectrum, and although they voted in favor of economic rights planks, they vigorously debated and mostly voted against planks on the equal rights amendment, lesbian rights, and abortion. A bipartisan effort mandated and funded by the U.S. Congress to address issues of concern to ordinary women, this sort of conference has never been repeated.

By the late 1970s, there were no longer strict dress codes for women in public; or, if some groups still believed in them, feminists deliberately flouted them. What range of choices in dress, accoutrements, and symbolic items were these women making? (Photograph copyright © 1978 by Diana Mara Henry.)

---

*Jewish Women's Archive, https://jwa.org/feminism/_html/JWA035.htm.

12. On November 12, 2002, a new woman-initiated grassroots group, CODEPINK, began a four-month vigil in front of the White House as a "pre-emptive strike for peace." Since the days of Alice Paul's radical, extended maneuver to post silent sentinels with banners at Woodrow Wilson's gates, protests at the White House fence had become a familiar part of the political scene. But in fall 1995, after the Oklahoma City bombing, this particular stretch—the block with the front of the White House on one side and Lafayette Park on the other—was closed to vehicular traffic as an antiterrorist precaution. Thus, White House picketers lost their ability to interact with the random public represented by drivers and riders in cars. The women who rotated on vigil duty in the winter before the official start of the war in Iraq chose to wear pink jackets and sport pink umbrellas. Ponder what messages they were sending in making that visually arresting choice, and what scenes in U.S. history they may have been conscious of echoing. The vigil culminated on March 8, 2003, International Women's Day, when over 10,000 activists marched in Washington, D.C., to protest U.S. militarism. In an echo of 1917, 25 women, including the feminist writers Alice Walker, Maxine Hong Kingston, and Susan Griffin, and CODEPINK cofounder Medea Benjamin, were arrested for protesting too close to the White House gates. Compare the details of CODEPINK's staged protest with that of the suffragists in the sixth image of this photo essay. ("Women for Peace." CODEPINK Demonstration at the White House, ca. 2002. Courtesy of CODEPINK.)

CIVIL WAR AND AFTERMATH

STEPHANIE MCCURRY
Women Numerous and Armed: Politics and Policy on the Confederate Home Front

The Civil War profoundly disrupted and reshaped American society; more people died in it than in all America's subsequent wars put together. It tested the stability of the Union and the meaning of democracy. Confederates insisted that their vision of a republic, which rested on racial hierarchy and the subordination of blacks, sustained the same claims to self-determination that had been central to the principles of the Revolution of 1776. The war would involve civilians in novel ways.

Because soldiers were recruited as companies from the same locality, it was not impossible for women to dress as men and enlist; buddies kept their secrets. A conservative estimate is that some 400 women joined in this way. A handful of women crossed military lines as spies, some disguising their race or their gender in the process. Thousands more women were recruited as hospital workers in both North and South; late in the war the Union recruited hundreds of freedwomen for this service. The bureaucracy of the federal government was vastly expanded during the war, and the personnel shortage was solved by hiring, for the first time in U.S. history, women to work in the same offices as men doing similar work.

Throughout the nation, familiar patterns of gender relations were disrupted as in the Revolutionary War, but on a far greater and more frightening scale. In the South, as Stephanie McCurry explains, the departure of white men for war meant that white women of all classes came into a more direct relationship with the government than ever before. Reading the letters and petitions that poured into the Confederate States of America (CSA) offices in Richmond, McCurry argues that a new political class, soldier's wives, suddenly became very visible.

Would you have joined the food riots described here? Create a historically based, imaginary biographical profile for yourself as food rioter and explain your motivations.

What types of southern, white women did not join these crowd actions? Does McCurry convince you that these women's actions changed Confederate policy in fundamental ways? What are examples from other wars around the globe where women's vigorous actions on the home front have had major political impacts?

Excerpted and slightly revised by the author from "Women Numerous and Armed: The Confederate Food Riots in Historical Perspective" by Stephanie McCurry, *OAH Magazine of History* 27, no. 2 (2009), 35–39, and *Confederate Reckoning: Power and Politics in the Civil War South* by Stephanie McCurry (Cambridge, Mass.: Harvard University Press, 2010), 154–55, 167, 192–96, 198–201, 209, 214–17.

The Confederate war ripped like an earthquake through the foundation of Southern life. Its impact registered in every domain from the high reaches of the central state to the intimate recesses of the household. Transformation is the essential characteristic of war because the calling in of obligations fundamentally changes the citizen's relationship to, and expectations of, the state. In the Confederate States of America, the government reached far past the ranks of those white men called upon to serve, to their dependents—the women, children, and slaves who made up the massive unfranchised Southern population. It is not too much to say that the war forged a new understanding of the relationship between citizens and their government, a renegotiation of the social contract. For white women who were not parties to the original contract—as citizens governed in the household state—the impositions and openings the war created were especially historic. When the conflict ended neither the idea of the people nor of the government was the same.

One consequence of war was the reconfiguration of Southern political life, particularly the way power on the home front shifted along gender lines, as white women emerged into authority and even leadership on a range of issues at the heart of popular politics in the Civil War South. The thousands of women's letters to government officials in archives testify to a fundamental shift in the very terms and practices of political representation in the war: the penetration of the state into their household business and also the rearrangement of household relations, local political networks, and modes of communication. Indeed, what these letters convey is the development of new, war-borne individual and collective political identities: chief among them, the "soldier's wife." There were new issues in Civil War politics, and there were also new players.

These developments are not easy to place historically. The key actors are Southern white women, most from yeoman, poor white, or urban laborer households. Their actions had nothing to do with feminism or the women's rights movement, and they were not part of an organized political movement in the institutional sense. They do not fit the usual interpretive categories of women's history or Civil War history, and they cannot be placed in the history of suffrage or Confederate nationalism. These women did not really speak a language of rights or of nationalism. But they made

themselves part of political life nonetheless, reshaping its organization, circuits of power and authority, and discourses of qualification and entitlement, thus redefining the relationship between the state in its various forms and the citizens and subjects it claimed to represent and rule. This was something new and, in the Confederacy at least, it made a difference.

If there had ever been a sense that women were outside politics that kind of thinking was obliterated by the shocking events of 1863. Then, in a wave of food riots, Confederate soldiers' wives impressed their politics on a shocked nation. The riots were spectacular and numerous: at least a dozen violent attacks (there are rumors of more) on stores, government warehouses, army convoys, salt works, railroad depots, and granaries by mobs of women, numbering between twelve and three hundred, armed with navy revolvers, pistols, repeaters, bowie knives, and hatchets. The attacks were carried out in broad daylight in the space of one month between the middle of March and the middle of April 1863: a Confederate spring of soldiers' wives' discontent.

The events were stunning: in their boldness, organization, violence, and in the shrewdness of the rioters' management of public opinion. For whatever mayors and editors said, the public simply assumed that the mobs were composed of soldiers' wives—as if prior developments had prepared them for the actions on the streets—as indeed they had. This was no simple expression of desperation. These were manifestly political events—a highly public expression of soldiers' wives' mass politics of subsistence—events in a women's political history we are just beginning to write.

The wave of riots in 1863 riveted public attention on soldiers' wives and their claims for justice for the Confederate poor, but the riots have a deep backstory, one not often told. It consists of a multitude of attempts by poor women to alert their leaders to the consequences of a conscription policy that eviscerated their livelihoods and violated the pledge made to soldiers that their families would be protected. The South was an agrarian society, whole regions of it populated by yeoman and poor white families. No one had ever imagined that women could make subsistence on those farms without the labor of men. And indeed they could not. By 1863, with husbands and sons in the service, the countryside was stripped of

SOWING AND REAPING.

[SOUTHERN WOMEN HOUNDING THEIR MEN ON TO REBELLION.   SOUTHERN WOMEN FEELING THE EFFECTS OF REBELLION, AND CREATING BREAD RIOTS.]

"Sowing and Reaping: Southern Women Hounding Their Men on to Rebellion . . . Southern Women Feeling the Effects of Rebellion, and Creating Bread Riots," engraving, 1863. Stephanie McCurry explains that "this illustration, published in Frank Leslie's Illustrated Newspaper *on May 23, 1863, depicts the emerging political power of women on the home front during the Civil War. The left half credits women with helping fill the ranks of the Confederate army, while the right half pictures the epitome of a politically empowered woman, standing defiantly in the midst of a bread riot with one hand clenched into a fist and the other holding a revolver." (Image courtesy of the Library of Congress, Prints and Photographs Division, Washington, D.C.)*

men and the food crisis in the Confederacy would reach starvation proportions.

1862 had seen a bad harvest, and in the following spring the prospect of another bore down on the Confederate States of America (C.S.A.), with public officials, journalists, and citizens alike warning that the situation was dire. In the Mississippi Valley, the drumbeat of battles was near. The Confederacy was still reeling from a series of military disasters in the winter and spring of 1862, the fall of Forts Donelson and Henry at the head of the Tennessee river system and the towns of Nashville, Corinth, and Memphis. Union armies marched steadily southward. As early as May 1862, the governor of Alabama, John Gill Shorter, had pleaded with the secretary of war to delay

conscription of yeoman soldiers in northern Alabama, concerned about the suffering of women and children if their men were taken before the grain and provision crops were harvested. Shorter was reacting to a series of letters he had received from soldiers, soldiers' wives, and military commanders describing dire conditions.[1]

Even in the east where General Robert E. Lee continued to hold off far larger Union armies, it is clear that 1863 was a moment in which most civilian and military men alike acknowledged that the war had entered a phase that tested the people and not just the armies. Few denied that home front and military conditions were inextricable. A debate about the equity of conscription had already erupted in the Confederate Congress in August 1862. But in that moment, with Union navies and armies penetrating by river into the very heart of the black belt South, concern for the Confederate poor was overridden by concern about how to maintain control of slaves. Congressmen, overwhelmingly slaveholders themselves, yielded to the demands of planters and the plaintive letters of planter women claiming protection and passed the notorious "twenty-negro law" [by which households owning twenty slaves or more could exempt one adult, white male from conscription]. Defended as a measure that would free up planters and their slaves to grow food for the armies and destitute civilians, the exemption was resisted from the outset as class legislation reflecting the government's blatant preference for the rich and its abandonment of the poor left to fight their wars. "Why not let the poor men stay at home to protect his own family against the slaves of the rich men," Mississippi senator James Phelan raged during the debate. "If we are to have class legislation . . . let's legislate in favor of the poor." But they did not. By December of 1862 public outrage over the law threatened to spill over into civil disobedience and mass desertion. The "twenty-negro law" spoke directly to the dilemma of the slave regime at war: how to protect the property of slaveholders without putting undue service burdens on backcountry yeomen—and on their women, left at home to shoulder the plow.[2]

As the food crisis mounted, yeoman and poor white women inundated politicians with petitions and letters, announcing in the process the formation of a new collective identity in Southern political life: soldiers' wives. "We soldier's wives as sign thare name," or more poignantly, as in another, "Mary Tisinger with 6 chilrin, soldier wife," "Mary Stilwell, soldiers widow 6 children," and so on down the list of signatures. Every woman who signed—there were twenty-three in this particular petition to the secretary of war—specified her identity in terms of the family relation to men in military service and the sacrifice made to the cause. For women identified as "soldier's wife," or sometimes just "sw," so obvious was the shorthand, sacrifice was grounds for entitlement, with the soldier's wife a critical new identity in relation to the state. At first, in 1862, the letters just begged for individual relief such as the release of a husband from the army. But by 1863 the correspondence had grown increasingly threatening, demanding a change

in government policies and justice for the Confederate poor. What emerges from the archives is a portrait of a political class coming into being.[3]

By 1863 soldiers' wives were legion in the Confederate states, as much a product of the draft as their soldier husbands. As a social group they were an index to the rapid process of state formation underway in the C.S.A. and to the problems faced by a slave regime at war. With 40 percent of its adult male population enslaved and unavailable for military service, the Davis administration had no choice but to dig ever deeper into the ranks of the male citizenry, mobilizing an estimated 75 to 85 percent of adult white men (in contrast to the Union's 50 percent).[4] In addition to conscription, the C.S.A. adopted a highly centralized taxation policy to feed and clothe the army. In April 1863 the Congress passed the infamous one-tenth tax or tithe, as it was called, which required citizens to surrender one-tenth of everything grown and raised on their farms and plantations beyond what was required for subsistence. The tax was to be paid in-kind, which required tax collectors, TIK men as they were called, to go into each household, farm, workshop, and plantation and remove part of everything produced there. It was not only onerous, it was highly intrusive, forcing ordinary men and, more often, women into regular confrontations with government agents. To poor soldiers' wives, the 10 percent tax was, quite literally, an impossible burden, the very difference between an eked-out subsistence and starvation. "They are gathering everything they can of the poor soldiers' wives and children," C. W. Walker protested to her governor about the TIK men in her community. "They are as grate enemys as the yankies."[5] Along with a stringent tax collection policy, conscription thickened the network of extraction and bureaucracy within which ordinary citizens, including women, became enmeshed. Tax and conscription agents were everywhere.

Left at home, women suffered under, and protested, the onslaught. The particular conditions were evident in the content of the politics they forged. The nexus of issues women agitated against—from the government's manpower policies, soldiers' wages, government prices for women's work, federal taxes, monetary policy, to inadequacy of relief—were as comprehensive as the struggle to sustain life itself. Together these issues constituted what we might call "a politics of subsistence." It took shape on the farms and in households of the rural and urban South, as poor white women struggled to scrape out subsistence absent the labor or wages of husbands and grown sons.

Up from the farmsteads, workshops, settlements, country towns, and cities came a tidal wave of protest and resistance, much of it from women in their newly useful identity as soldiers' wives. "As gustic [justice] belongs to the people," one woman memorably put it, "let us have it." Political danger loomed, not least in the easy way poor white women came to speak in the collective voice—for soldiers' wives, for nonslaveholders, or, more generally, for the poor. Clerks in government offices confronted with documents signed by large numbers of women must have wondered about the political backstory. How was the petition organized? Did someone carry it around the neighborhood? Was it written at a mass meeting? We do not know. We do know that there was no political institution or national or state organization behind them, and there were no preprinted forms as in Union women's antislavery petition drive. But in the winter and spring of 1863, as internal correspondence in the War Department confirmed the looming food crisis, the content of the mail bags made it clear that women were coming together to demand action.[6]

Nowhere was that more clear than in North Carolina, where the Gov. Zebulon Vance, was perceived as a sympathetic figure. He had already received threatening letters, including one that concluded a typical account of how women cannot "make support for ther familys" by warning that "the women talk of Making up Companys going to try to make peace." And then there was an anonymous letter that landed on Vance's desk exactly six weeks before the wave of food riots broke out in nearby Salisbury; the letter came from "a company" of women in Bladen County who called themselves "Reglators." The term was calculated to place the authors in the state's long (formerly male) tradition of rural justice and direct action. They would have corn at two dollars a bushel or they would seize it, the women informed Vance matter-of-factly in the opening line: "the time has come that we the comon people has to hav bread or blood and we are bound boath men and women to hav it or die in the attempt." The letter bore all the hallmarks of rural soldiers' wives' protests expressed in hundreds, maybe thousands, of other letters written in the Southern states by the end of the war. Even so, the cry of bread or blood—which would echo across the C.S.A. a few weeks later—was new. The Reglators laid out the crisis of subsistence that soldiers' wives faced: the erosion of household independence with the conscription of their men; the impossible equation between privates' pay and the prices planter speculators demanded for food; the need for the state to set prices in the interest of the poor. To that list the Reglators added a far more radical view of the war as a species of class warfare. This group was prepared to take matters into their own hands. "Sir," they told Vance, "we has sons, brothers an husbands now fighting for the big mans negro and we are determined to have bread out of their barns or we will slaughter as we go." Violence, or so they said, was part of the soldiers' wives' political repertoire.[7]

The food riots did not come out of nowhere. They were, rather, the most dramatic manifestation of poor white women's mass politics of subsistence. So while there is a long tradition of rough justice in which they might be seen, there is also a more immediate and local context: a mass movement of Confederate women, empowered as soldiers' wives, largely confined to nonviolent protest—and an emboldened minority who crossed the line from threats to violent direct action.

The food riot in Richmond was the biggest but not the first. The first was Atlanta, on March 16, 1863, then in Salisbury, North Carolina, then on the next day in Mobile, Alabama, and Petersburg, Virginia, and Richmond on April 2. "Bread or blood," the Richmond women notoriously shouted—a trademark cry already seen in Reglators' written threats and on the banners of Mobile's army of women (as one participant described them).[8]

Everything about the riots in Atlanta and elsewhere shows the connections between violent new developments and the local political culture of Confederate soldiers' wives. In Atlanta, the fifteen or twenty women who collected "in a body" and proceeded to sack provisions stores began and finished with speeches to the merchant and the public about the "impossibility of females in their condition" paying the asking price for the necessities of life. In Salisbury, the next day, when another mob of forty or fifty women mounted armed attacks on about seven merchant establishments, they justified their actions in the same language soldiers' wives used in their petitions. "We Governor are all soldiers' wives or mothers," Mary Moore, a member of the mob petitioned the governor for leniency, appealing "for protection and a remedy of these evils." Though criminal, the women's actions were effective. Moore admitted that they had stolen food and money at gun point—twenty-three barrels of flour, two sacks of salt, half a barrel of molasses, and twenty dollars in cash—but cast the riot as the seizure only of what was rightly owed to the people whose claims the women had decided to enforce. "Now Sir, this is all we have done" she finished. Moore's defense of the Salisbury women's mob action confidently tapped an idea about the social contract with soldiers and their wives that went deep in popular political culture and expressed a sense of entitlement that was clearly historic. What was owed to soldiers' wives? As in Salisbury, few argued with the women's view.[9]

After the actions in Atlanta and Salisbury came riots in Mobile, Petersburg, and Macon, Georgia—five or more in the space of two weeks. Then activity in Richmond and beyond. It was a strikingly coherent series of events, each organized and pulled off locally (as far as we know), yet so closely spaced, so similar in pattern that there was wild speculation about the connections. By the time the wave crested in Richmond, conspiracy theories abounded. "That they are the emissaries of the Federal Government it is . . . difficult to doubt" ventured the *Richmond Daily Examiner*. Such seemingly connected and highly organized events were far beyond the capacity of mere women. This had to be the work of professionals: Yankee operatives.[10]

In its respect for the level of organization achieved, the conspiracy theory, in fact, speaks powerfully to the political capacity of women. As the evidence accrued—a result of the Richmond city government's decision to pursue criminal charges—the Confederate public learned just how the riot was organized and pulled off. In other riots there are suggestions of prior organization—the way women (whether twelve or fifty) just materialized "in a body" at a particular, apparently predesignated time and place with banners, slogans, and speeches at the ready. In Richmond the sheer numbers— an estimated three hundred women followed by a crowd of about one thousand—confirm there was a plan.

Richmond puts to rest all questions about Confederate women's political ability. As shocking as it surely was to many, what came out in court testimony was indisputable evidence that the riot on April 2 was a highly organized event, planned for at least ten days and, despite widespread assertions that it was instigated by men, that it was, in fact, the work of Mary Jackson, soldier's mother, farm wife, and huckster in meat in Richmond's Second Market. Mary Jackson and about three hundred women planned and pulled off the biggest civilian riot in Confederate history.[11]

The Richmond riot offers a stunning portrait of poor white women's mass political mobilization. Recruiting apparently began around March 22, 1863, with Jackson organizing "a meeting of the women in relation to the high prices." Jackson's networks were rural as well as urban. Witnesses reported a stream of women coming in from the country the day before, joining women in the market where Jackson worked and at government clothing factories in town. More than three hundred women turned up for the planning in the Belvidere Baptist Church on Oregon Hill on April 1. "All were women there except two boys," one witness explained. By all accounts it was a rowdy meeting. Jackson was clearly in command. In a stunning assumption of male authority she "went up into the pulpit" to address the meeting and to issue instructions. "She didn't want the women to go along the streets like a parcel of heathens," one woman testified later, "but to go quietly to the stores and demand goods at government prices and if the merchants didn't grant their demand to break open the stores and take the goods." Jackson told the women to meet the next morning at nine a.m., to leave their children at home, and to come armed.[12]

As unusual and violent as the riot was, Jackson and the women who planned it were products of the same politics of subsistence as the mass of Confederate soldiers' wives. Jackson literally so. John Jones, a clerk in the War Department, knew her from her "frequent application at the war office for the discharge of her son." Before Jackson took to the streets, in other words, she had been one of the mass of ordinary petitioning Confederate women. Her strategy for the riot also suggests as much. In insisting that rioters first make an offer of government price for the goods they planned to seize and in first seeking an audience with the governor to air their grievances (an inspired bit of political choreography)—she showed the group's deep investment in the ideas and practices of white women's wartime political culture. The women had guns, but they also had a public relations strategy.[13]

Still, violence was planned for from the beginning. Jackson was seen with a bowie knife and six-barreled pistol as she left the market on the morning of the riot. When the mob surged out of Capitol Square, marching silently as Jackson had instructed, the women were heavily armed with domestic implements and the rejected contents of an old armory, as one witness described. For a good two hours they wreaked havoc on the streets of Richmond, targeting known speculators, smashing their way into stores with hatchets and axes, looting at gunpoint, and loading stolen goods onto wagons they impressed on the street. At least twelve stores were looted before the public guard was called out and, threatening to fire on the rioters, managed to quell the activity. Among those caught in the subsequent dragnet were otherwise unknown women such as Mary Duke, a soldiers' wife, left at home with four children and her husband in Robert E. Lee's army. The ringleaders, including Mary Jackson, were also caught; she was picked up around noon in a mob of women trying to break into a store, still unbowed, brandishing a bowie knife, saying "bread or blood."[14]

There would be more riots in 1863—six at least—and they also played out in violent form the politics of subsistence that soldiers' wives had forged. In all of them, women's anger was turned as much against government officials as against merchants and planters and had as much to do with the inadequacy of welfare as with speculation. That was one of the critical policy implications of the women's riots and is the chief measure of their efficacy in Confederate politics and policy. It was really only after—and in response to—the riots that local, state, and (to a lesser extent) federal officials undertook a systematic reform and extension of the traditional antebellum system of delivering relief.

In many places city officials promised aid even as rioters ran in the streets. In Atlanta, a group of gentlemen expressed a deep sympathy for the ladies by raising a fund for their relief. In Richmond, Governor John Letcher appeared in the midst of the action promising to distribute food. All of the city councils and Southern legislatures—even the Confederate Congress, which had long regarded social provision as the domain of the states—quickly took it up as a matter of public policy.[15]

The quantities of money involved varied from the local and small to the state and significant in terms of budget share. All the governments in the C.S.A. were highly strapped. Carving out significant chunks of money for welfare thus had to be a huge political priority. In the cities the aid poured in and took numerous forms. In Mobile the city council appropriated $15,000, created a Citizen Relief Committee to scour the countryside for food, and thereafter attended carefully to ensuring the provision of food at reasonable prices to the poor. In Richmond, the mayor formed a citywide committee to investigate the needs of soldiers' dependents. By April 13 the city council had written and passed new laws establishing a free market in food for the poor.[16]

On the level of the states, the response was also direct, nowhere with more urgency than in Georgia, where governor Joseph Brown jumped into action. Just nine days after the Atlanta food riot, he called the legislature back into session early and delivered the blunt message that in whole sections of the state where land was cultivated almost entirely by white labor, "the women and children are destitute of bread." Action was imperative: "the great question in this revolution is now a question of *bread*," he bellowed. Brown delivered property tax exemptions, free salt, free corn, and so much aid in money to the counties that, as a share of the state budget, it almost equaled that expended on wartime military costs. The legislature appropriated $2.5 million in 1863, $6 million in 1864, and $8 million in 1865 to "assist soldiers' families, the children and widows of deceased soldiers and disabled veterans," although it was never enough.[17]

In North Carolina a new law passed in 1863 was titled "Act for the Relief of the Wives and Families of Soldiers in the Army." The state funded that act to the tune of $1 million a year, although the treasurer often struggled to meet the fiscal obligations. At the local level, a considerable number of people and amounts of money passed through the system. In Orange County, 508 women and 735 children were on the rolls in late 1863; by 1865 more than 600 women and 800 children, 20 percent of the adult female population of the county and a whopping 35 percent of the white children. In

Duplin County even more white women met the official criterion of indigence, meaning "not enough food to sustain life." In the terrible year that spanned November 1863 to November 1864, agents in Randolph County collected and disbursed roughly $55,000, most of it distributed in small amounts. Local committeemen received detailed instructions: "the allowance for each *woman* shall not exceed three dollars per month, children under eight years of age, one dollar and fifty cents," one set read. "Needy fathers" and widows and children of deceased soldiers were to "receive the same as a lone woman." Indeed, as the court instructions assumed, women constituted the vast bulk of recipients of relief and received most of the welfare dollars. Clearly, the unprecedented expansion of state welfare was a political response to the mobilization of the yeoman and poor white women of the Confederacy. And that new welfare system was made in the image of the soldier's wife.[18]

Poor white Southern women kept themselves on the political agenda through local activism until the last days of the war, mobilizing to secure the entitlements already established. Whether they liked it or not—and most didn't—local officials were accountable to the women, forced to treat them as significant members of the political constituency they had been elected or appointed to serve. Poor white women, for their part, had learned how to hold the men accountable, how to make the system respond to their needs to some extent, to insist on a measure of self-representation. All of which is to say that they had entered fully into the practice of politics in the Civil War South.

In 1857 Supreme Court Justice Roger Taney had been able to define citizenship without any reference to women.[19] The architects of the Confederacy had been able to effect secession and declare war without their consent. But war had expanded the terms of consent and legitimacy, created new political identities, expanded the concept of the body politic, widened the conception of citizenship, rerouted the paths of power and patronage, and engendered new political subjects and constituencies. This war, the Confederate war, had its own unexpected developments, the significance of which intensifies in light of the original Confederate vision. Far from perfecting the republic of white men, fixing forever the exclusion of black and female dependents, the war had proved its undoing,

most unpredictably, perhaps, in the way it brought white women—especially poor white women—to a position of unquestionable salience in Confederate politics.

That much was strangely confirmed in 1866 when the North Carolina legislature (like a lot of other states) wiped the docket clean of all political crimes left over from the war by passing a blanket amnesty law that initially covered the political acts of soldiers. Three months later, with a docket still stacked with cases of women who had made "raids upon any county, state or Confederate States Commissaries or Quartermasters, or other person or persons," they extended the amnesty to include women, writing into law an explicit recognition of women's "crimes" as political acts. In doing so they offered an official acknowledgment of women as political subjects.[20]

It would be tempting to cast this history of Confederate women as an episode in the history of citizenship in the United States, to slot it into the dominant liberal framework of American political history by which disfranchised people progressively claimed citizenship and its attendant rights. But there is evidence supporting a less predictable interpretive approach. "Citizen" was a term rarely used by soldiers' wives. Unlike the masses of female petitioners who sought the abolition of slavery in the Union (see pp. 213–221, Zaeske's essay), Confederate soldiers' wives did not move to make their claims based on perceived rights as citizens of the nation. As an explicitly proslavery nation in conception and design, the C.S.A. had a deep investment in limiting democracy, and it was committed, as a matter of ideology, to the exclusion of free women and enslaved men and women from political life. White women occupied a peculiar position in that, unlike slaves, they did have civil standing as citizens. But not only did they lack the attendant political rights; most of the legal and civil rights of the married majority were vitiated by coverture. Fundamentally shaped by this state of affairs, Confederate soldiers' wives, in entering the political arena, did not—could not—advance a universal claim to the equal rights of citizens. That lay entirely outside the politics of the possible.[21]

But if Confederate soldiers' wives cannot simply be cast as a chapter in American political history as we usually tell it, they might prompt us to rethink the story outside national boundaries. For the mobilization of poor, mostly rural women in the Confederate South during the Civil War bears resemblance far more to the way politics was practiced by poor rural and urban people in the modern world: what one historian has called the politics of the governed. Indeed, in some respects Confederate women's behavior is so like that of the poor in twentieth-century India that it reminds us that the strategies of the governed (including violence) are needful and practiced—perhaps particularly by women—not just in non-Western, postcolonial societies but also in modern Western nation-states as well, long after the formal introduction of so-called universal suffrage, which meant, of course, suffrage only for men.[22]

Seen in this broad context, the situation as it unfolded in Confederate political life was strikingly like that in other modern, formally democratic societies in which the mass of people are "not proper members of civil society," have no right of representation or to hold office, but manage nonetheless to mobilize as particular communities to influence government policy in their favor. Unable to participate in political life as equal citizens, they instead take categories the state uses to govern the population—refugees, the poor, or "soldiers' wives"—and infuse them with moral content. In doing so, they effectively invest those categories with the imaginative possibilities of community and produce a new rhetoric of political claims. Although not advanced on the terrain of nation and citizenship, these claims are irreducibly political and constitute a separate and critical arena of political society.[23] It is hardly likely that Confederate state actors would have conceded that point of view, but it can hardly be denied that in their own creative, instrumental, if limited way one female part of the Confederate governed had managed to widen the field of popular democratic practice and had rendered suspect the practicality of the strictly delimited Confederate vision of the people.

NOTES

1. Armstead Robinson, *Bitter Fruits of Bondage: The Demise of Slavery and the Collapse of the Confederacy, 1861–1865* (Charlottesville, 2005), 118–31, 202–205, 215–216; John Gill Shorter to Randolph (Secretary of War), May 30, 1862, Letters Received by the Confederate Secretary of War, National Archives, Washington, D.C., roll 71.

2. Robinson, *Bitter Fruits of Bondage*, 184–187.

3. Mary C. Tisinger and others to Gov. Brown, Aug. 15, 1864, Upson County, Ga, Box 3, Executive

Department, Petitions, RG1–1, Georgia Department of Archives and History.

4. By 1864 military age was defined as ages 17–50. For the enlistment figures, see Gary Gallagher, *The Confederate War: How Popular Will, Nationalism, and Military Strategy Could Not Stave Off Defeat* (New York, 1997), 28–29, 16–18.

5. C. W. Walker to Gov. Vance, May 8, 1863, box 165, Zebulon B. Vance, Governors Papers, North Carolina Department of Archives and History (hereafter ZBV).

6. Sarah Halford and others to Governor Vance, Dec. 23, 1863, Rutherford County, NC, Box 172, ZBV.

7. Anonymous ["Reglators"] to Governor Vance, Feb. 18, 1863, Bladen County, NC, Box 162, ZBV.

8. Harriet E. Amos, "All Absorbing Topics: Food and Clothing in Confederate Mobile," *Atlanta Historical Journal*, 22 (Fall/Winter 1978), 23; *Richmond Daily Examiner*, April 4, April 24, 1863.

9. *Atlanta Intelligencer*, March 19, 20, 23, 1863. Mary C. Moore to Governor Vance, March 21, 1863, Salisbury, NC, Box 163, ZBV.

10. *Richmond Daily Examiner*, April 4, 1863.

11. Ibid.; Louis H. Manarin, ed., *Richmond at War: The Minutes of the City Council, 1861–1865* (Chapel Hill, 1966).

12. *Richmond Daily Examiner*, April 4, 24, 1863; Michael V. Chesson, "Harlots or Heroines? A New Look at the Richmond Bread Riot," *Virginia Magazine of History and Biography* 92, no.2 (Apr. 1984), 161.

13. Jones's testimony reported in *Richmond Daily Examiner*, April 6, 1863.

14. *Richmond Daily Examiner*, April 4, 6, 7, 8, 13, 24, Oct. 12, 1863. On Mary Duke, see Chesson, "Harlots or Heroines?" 165.

15. *Atlanta Intelligencer*, Mar. 19, 1863; Chesson, "Harlots or Heroines?" 149. On the upsurge of activity around welfare, see Drew Gilpin Faust, *The Creation of Confederate Nationalism: Ideology and Identity in the Civil War South* (Baton Rouge, 1988); Paul Escott, "The Moral Economy of the Crowd in Confederate North Carolina," *Maryland Historian* 13 (Spring/Summer, 1982), 1–18; and Robinson, *Bitter Fruits of Bondage*.

16. Amos, "All Absorbing Topics," 23–26; Manarin, *Richmond at War*, 312, 314–15, 317, 320; *Richmond Daily Examiner*, April 23, 1863.

17. Governor Joseph Brown, Message of March 25, 1863, in Allen Daniel Candler, ed., *Confederate Records of the State of Georgia*, 6 vols. (1909–1911; New York, 1972), 2:369–370; *Atlanta Intelligencer*, Mar. 24, 1863. See also Peter Wallenstein, *From Slave South to New South: Public Policy in Nineteenth-Century Georgia* (Chapel Hill, 1987), 105; and Paul Escott, "Joseph E. Brown, Jefferson Davis, and the Problem of Poverty in the Confederacy," *Georgia Historical Quarterly* 61 (Spring 1977), 65, 69.

18. *Public Laws of the State of North Carolina Passed by the General Assembly at Its Session of 1862–63* (Raleigh, 1863), 33–35. The evolution of welfare policy in Mississippi followed much the same pattern. For the Orange and Duplin County numbers (1863), see Paul Escott, "Poverty and Governmental Aid for the Poor in Confederate North Carolina," *North Carolina Historical Review* 61 (Oct. 1984), 477–480. For 1865: J. W. Norwood, Report of the County Corn Agent, Jan. 4, 1865, folder 3, Orange County, Misc. Records; Randolph County financing in Report

of the Committee on Finance, folder 3, Randolph County, Misc. Records (Civil War Records), both at the State Archives, Division of Archives and History, Raleigh, North Carolina. For the instructions to the agent, see Provisions for Families of Soldiers, folder 1, Orange County Court, Feb. term, Mar. 3, 1863 Orange County, Misc. Records, ibid.

19. Dred Scott v. Sandford, 60 U.S. (19 How.) 393 (1857). See Don E. Fehrenbacher, *The Dred Scott Case: Its Significance in American Law and Politics* (New York, 1978).

20. *Public Laws of the State of North Carolina Passed by the General Assembly at the Sessions of 1866–67* (Raleigh, 1867), 8–9.

21. Social citizenship is another rubric we might apply; see T. H. Marshall and Tom Bottomore, *Citizenship and Social Class* (London, 1992), 3–51; Judith N. Shklar, *American Citizenship: The Quest for Inclusion* (Cambridge, UK, 1991); and Rogers M. Smith, *Civic Ideals: Conflicting Visions of Citizenship in the United States* (New Haven, 1997). For antebellum women antislavery petitioners, see Susan Zaeske, *Signatures of Citizenship: Petitioning, Antislavery, and Women's Political Identity* (Chapel Hill, 2003).

22. Partha Chatterjee, *The Politics of the Governed: Reflections on Popular Politics in Most of the World* (New York, 2004); on gender, see 76. See also Ranajit Guha, *Elementary Aspects of Peasant Insurgency in Colonial India* (Durham, 1999), and a very moving short essay by Guha, "The Small Voice of History," in *Subaltern Studies IX*, ed. Shahid Amin and Dipesh Chakrabarty (Oxford, 1966), 1–12; James Scott, *Domination and the Arts of Resistance: Hidden Transcripts* (New Haven, 1990).

23. Chatterjee, *Politics of the Governed*, 47, 35, 59–60, 46, 69.

TERA W. HUNTER
Reconstruction and the Meanings of Freedom

When the Civil War was ended at Appomattox, a long and complex struggle over its meaning had just begun. The Thirteenth Amendment technically ended slavery, but it left much room for interpretation about the meaning of servitude. It said nothing about equality, leaving resentful southerners to conclude that the North would condone systems of racial hierarchy. Even after the 1868 passage of the Fourteenth Amendment, which provided that "[a]ll persons born or naturalized in the United States . . . are citizens of the United States and of the State wherein they reside," the meanings of "citizenship" remained to be defined.

The aftermath of defeat is an internationally shared phenomenon. How did white southerners understand their defeat? What tensions marked postwar society? What would it mean to "reconstruct" the former Confederacy? Tera Hunter examines the experiences of freedpeople in the city of Atlanta, Georgia—Roda Ann Childs lived not far away. She finds that the process of rebuilding their lives could be quite different for men than for women. What opportunities did African American men have that African American women did not? What strategies might freedwomen use to stabilize their lives? In what ways did freedwomen participate in political life?

The Union victory at Appomattox in the spring of 1865 marked the official end of the war and inspired somber reflection, foot-stomping church meetings, and joyous street parades among the newly free. African Americans eagerly rushed into Atlanta in even greater numbers than before. Between 1860 and 1870, blacks in Atlanta increased from a mere nineteen hundred to ten

Excerpted from "Reconstruction and the Meanings of Freedom," ch. 2 of *To 'Joy My Freedom: Black Women's Lives and Labors after the Civil War* by Tera W. Hunter (Cambridge, Mass.: Harvard University Press, 1997). Reprinted by permission of the author and publisher. Notes have been numbered and edited.

thousand, more than doubling their proportion in the city's population, from 20 to 46 percent. Women made up the majority of this burgeoning population.[1] . . .

Wherever they came from, virtually all black women were compelled to find jobs as household workers once they arrived in the city. Some had acquired experience in such jobs as house slaves; others had worked in the fields or combined field and domestic chores. Whether or not they were working as domestics for the first time, black women had to struggle to assert new terms for their labor. The Civil War had exposed the parallel contests occurring in white households as the conflict on the battlefield, in the marketplace, and in the political arena unfolded. The war continued on the home front during Reconstruction after the Confederacy's military defeat. . . .

Just as black women and men in Atlanta had to reconstitute their lives as free people and build from the ground up, the city was faced with similar challenges. The legacy of physical desecration left by Sherman's invasion was everywhere. Tons of debris, twisted rails, dislodged roofs, crumbled chimneys, discharged cannon balls, and charred frame dwellings cluttered the streets.[2] Visitors to the city swapped remarks on the distinctive spirit of industry exemplified in the repair and rebuilding. . . . Atlanta aspired to construct a city in the New South in the image of established cities above the Mason-Dixon line.[3]

The capitalist zeal that impressed outsiders offered few benefits to the average person, however. Overwhelmed contractors could not keep up with demands, which added to housing shortages that sent prices for rents soaring beyond the means of most residents.[4] . . . Some builders took advantage of the shortage to offer makeshift huts and shanties to freedpeople at exorbitant prices.[5] Ex-slaves in more dire straits assembled scanty lodging that consisted of tents, cabins, and shanties made of tin, line, and cloth on rented parcels of land.[6] . . . The cost of food and other consumer goods likewise followed the pattern of scarcity, poor quality, and deliberate price gouging.[7]

The abrupt population growth and the inability of private charities or public coffers to relieve the migrants of want exacerbated postwar privation. Almost everyone in the city, regardless of race, shared the status of newcomer. It was not just African Americans who were migrating to the city in large numbers; so did many whites. In 1860, there were 7,600 whites living in Atlanta, ten years later there were 11,900.[8] White yeoman farmers fled to the city to find wage labor in the wake of the elimination of their rural self-sufficiency. White Northern and foreign industrial workers followed the prosperity promised by the railroad and construction boom.

Women and children, black and white, were particularly noticeable among the destitute sprawled over the desolate urban landscape. The indigent included elderly, single women, widows of soldiers, and wives of unemployed or underemployed men. White women seamstresses who numbered in the thousands during the war were reduced to poverty with the collapse of military uniform manufacturers.[9] Labor agents egregiously contributed to the disproportionate sex ratio among urban blacks by taking away men to distant agricultural fields, leaving the women and children deserted.[10] Those abandoned wandered the streets and scavenged for food, often walking between ten and forty miles per day. "Sometimes I gits along tolerable," stated a widow washerwoman with six children. "Sometimes right slim; but dat's de way wid everybody—times is powerful hard right now."[11]

The municipal government showed neither the capability nor the ambition to meet the needs of the poor. It allocated few resources for basic human services. Yet the Freedmen's Bureau, which was established by the federal government in 1865 to distribute rations and relief to ex-slaves, to monitor the transition to a free labor system, and to protect black rights, proved inadequate also. The bureau was preoccupied with stemming migration, establishing order, and restoring the economy, which led it to force blacks into accepting contracts without sufficient regard for the fairness of the terms. The federals evicted ex-slaves from contraband camps or pushed them further from the center of town to the edges—out of sight and out of mind.[12] Bureau officials urged their agents: "You must not issue rations or afford shelter to any person who can, and will not labor for his or her own support."[13] . . .

Ex-slaves who were evicted from the camps by the end of 1865 were more fortunate than they could appreciate initially. They escaped a smallpox epidemic in the city that devastated the enclaves. One missionary reported a horrifying scene she witnessed in the camps: "Men, women, and children lying on the damp ground suffering in every degree from the mildest symptoms to the most violent. The tents crowded, no fire to make them comfortable, and worse all the poor creatures were almost destitute of wearing apparel."[14] The dead who lay around the sick and suffering were buried in the ground half-naked or without clothes at all. . . .

African-American women and men were willing to endure the adversities of food shortages, natural disasters, dilapidated housing, and inadequate clothing in postwar Atlanta because what they left behind in the countryside, by comparison, was much worse. In the city at least there were reasons to be optimistic that their strength in numbers and their collective strategies of empowerment could be effective. In rural areas, however, their dispersion and separation by miles of uninhabited backwoods left them more vulnerable to elements intent on depriving them of life, liberty, and happiness. Abram Colby, a Republican legislator from Greene County, summed up the motivations for migration by stating that blacks went to Atlanta "for protection." He explained further: "The military is here and nobody interferes with us here . . . we cannot stop anywhere else so safely."[15]

African Americans moved to the city not only in search of safety, but also in search of economic self-sufficiency. Though most ex-slaves held dreams of owning farm land, many preferred to set up households in a city with a more diverse urban economy. In Atlanta they encountered an economy that was quickly recovering from the war and continuing to grow in the direction propelled by military demands and the promise of modernization.[16] . . .

Though the kaleidoscope of industry appeared to offer vast possibilities for workers, African Americans were slotted into unskilled and service labor. Black men filled positions with the railroads; as day workers, they groomed roads, distributed ballast, and shoveled snow off the tracks. As brakemen, they coupled and uncoupled stationary cars and ran along the roof of moving trains to apply the brakes, risking life and limb. Many others worked in rolling and lumber mills, mostly in the lowest-paid positions as helpers to white men. Hotels employed black men as cooks, waiters, porters, bellhops, and barroom workers. A few ex-slaves worked in bakeries, small foundries, the paper mill, and candy factories. Slave artisans were high in number in the antebellum South, but in the postbellum era black men were rarely hired in skilled positions. They were able to benefit from the aggressive physical rebuilding of Atlanta, however, in the construction trades, as painters, carpenters, and brickmasons. Between 1870 and 1880, the proportion of black male shoemakers tripled to constitute the majority of the entire trade. A select few owned small businesses such as barber shops and grocery stores or worked in the professions as teachers and ministers.[17]

The range of job opportunities for black women was more narrow than for men. Black women were excluded from small manufacturing plants that hired white women, such as those that made candy, clothing, textiles, paper boxes, bookbinding, and straw goods. They were confined primarily to domestic labor in private homes as cooks, maids, and child-nurses. A few black women found related jobs in local hotels—a step above the same work performed in private households. Large numbers worked in their own homes in a relatively autonomous craft as laundresses, which had the advantage of accommodating family and community obligations. More desirable, yet less accessible, were skilled jobs outside domestic service as seamstresses or dressmakers. . . . Only a few black women were able to escape common labor and enter the professions as teachers.[18]

Reconstruction of the post-slavery South occurred on many levels. Just as the city's infrastructure had to be rebuilt for daily life to reach a new normalcy, so blacks had to rebuild their lives as free people by earning an independent living. Women's success or frustrations in influencing the character of domestic labor would define how meaningful freedom would be. Slave women had already demonstrated fundamental disagreements with masters over the principles and practices of free labor during the war. This conflict continued as workers and employers negotiated new terms. Even the most mundane and minute details of organizing a free labor system required rethinking assumptions about work that had previously relied on physical coercion. An employer acknowledged the trial-and-error nature of this process: "I had no idea what was considered a task in washing so I gave her all the small things belonging to the children taking out all the table cloths sheets counterpanes & c." The novice employer then decided in the same haphazard manner to pay the laundry worker 30 cents a day. But the laborer asserted her own understanding of fair work.

"She was through by dinner time [and] appeared to work steady. I gave her dinner and afterwards told her that I had a few more clothes I wished washed out," the employer explained. "Her reply was that she was tired." The worker and employer held different expectations about the length of the work day and the quantity of the output of labor.[19]

African Americans labored according to their own sense of equity, with the guiding assumption that wage labor should not emulate slavery—especially in the arbitrariness of time and tasks. The experience of an ex-slave named Nancy illustrates this point. As some ex-slaves departed from their former masters' households, the burden of the work shifted to those who remained. Consequently, when the regular cook departed, Nancy's employer added cooking and washing to her previous child-care job, without her consent. Nancy faked illness on ironing days and eventually quit in protest against the extra encumbrance.[20] If workers and employers disagreed on the assignment of specific tasks, they also disagreed on how to execute them. Workers held to their own methods and preferences; employers held to theirs. . . .

If [a worker's] frustrations reached an intolerable level, she could exercise a new privilege as a free worker to register the ultimate complaint: she could quit and seek better terms for her work. Ex-slaves committed themselves to this precept of free labor with a firmness that vexed employers. "We daily hear of people who are in want of servants, and who have had in their employ in the last three or four months, a dozen different ones," stated a familiar news report. "The common experience of all is that the servants of the 'African-persuasion' can't be retained," it continued. "They are fond of change and since it is their privilege to come and go at pleasure, they make full use of the large liberty they enjoy."[21] . . .

African-American women decided to quit work over such grievances as low wages, long hours, ill treatment, and unpleasant tasks. Quitting could not guarantee a higher standard of living or a more pleasant work environment for workers, but it was an effective strategy to deprive employers of complete power over their labor. . . .

Employers did not share the same interpretations of labor mobility, however. They blamed the subversive influence of Yankees and "pernicious" Negroes for inciting "bad" work habits, or they explained quitting as a scientifically proven racial deficiency.[22] Whereas recently freed slaves often worked as much as they needed to survive and no more, white Southerners believed that if they refused to work as hard as slaves driven by fear they were mendicants and vagrants. "When a wench gets very hungry and ragged, she is ready to do the cooking for any sized family," a news report exclaimed. "But after she gets her belly well filled with provender, she begins to don't see the use of working all day and every day, and goes out to enjoy her freedom."[23]

Although many white Southerners resented the presence of the Freedmen's Bureau as the Northern overseer of Reconstruction, they readily sought its assistance to stem the revolving door of domestic workers. "What are persons to do when a 'freedman' that you hire as a nurse goes out at any time & against your direct orders?" one former master queried the bureau. "What must be done when they are hired and do only just what they please? orders being disregarded in every instance," he asked further. A bureau agent responded with an answer to alleviate the employer's frustrations and to teach him a lesson about the precepts of free labor. "Discharge her and tell her she dont suit you," the agent stated simply. "If you have a written contract with them and they quit you without good and sufficient cause—I will use all my power to have them comply," he reassured. But if these words provided comfort, the bureau agent made clear that the operative words were "without good and sufficient cause." He reiterated the employers' obligations and responsibilities to respect the liberties of workers: "You are expected to deal with them as Freemen and Freewomen. Individual exceptions there may be but as a whole where they are well treated they are faithful and work well."[24]

The federal government refused to return to white employers unilateral power to prohibit the mobility of black workers, leading employers to elicit the support of local laws. Quitting work became defined as "idleness" and "vagrancy"—prosecutable offenses. Southern state legislatures began passing repressive Black Codes in 1865 to obstruct black laborers' full participation in the marketplace and political arena. In 1866, the Atlanta City Council responded in a similar vein to stop the movement of household workers: it passed a law requiring employers to solicit recommendations from previous jobs in order to distinguish "worthy" from "worthless" laborers and to make it more difficult for workers to change jobs. Complaints continued long after the law took effect, which suggests its ineffectiveness.[25] . . .

Black women used the marginal leverage they could exercise in the face of conflict between employers to enhance their wages and to improve the conditions of work. When Hannah, "a cook & washer of the first character," was approached by Virginia Shelton in search of domestic help, she bargained for an agreement to match her needs. Hannah wanted to bring along her husband, a general laborer, and expected good wages for both of them. Shelton made an initial offer of $5 per month to Hannah and $10 per month to her husband. But the couple demanded $8 and $15, to which Shelton acceded. Shelton realized that it was worth making compromises with a servant she had traveled a long distance to recruit.[26]

Not all negotiations ended so pleasantly or in the workers' favor, however. . . . Domestic workers often complained of physical abuse by employers following disputes about wages, hours of work, or other work-related matters. . . . Samuel Ellison explained the argument that led to the death of his wife, Eliza Jane. Mrs. Ellison had argued with her employer, Mrs. L. B. Walton, about washing clothes. According to Ellison's husband, "My wife asked Mrs. Walton who would pay her for her washing extra clothes and which she was not bound to do by her contract." Walton's husband intervened and "abused" the laundress for "insulting" his wife. He left the house, returned and began another argument, insisting to Ellison, "shut up you God damn bitch." The fight ended when Walton shot Eliza Jane Ellison to death.[27]

African-American women like Ellison undoubtedly paid a high price for the simple desire to be treated like human beings. Incidents like this one made it apparent that freedom could not be secured through wage labor alone. The material survival of African Americans was critical, but they also needed to exercise their political rights to safeguard it. The political system had to undergo dramatic transformation to advance their interests, but here too they faced many obstacles.

The Ku Klux Klan, an anti-black terrorist organization founded by former Confederate soldiers in 1866, mounted the most bitter opposition to black rights. The KKK quickly became dominated by Democratic Party officials bent on preempting black participation in the electoral arena. The Klan sought to wrest economic and political power from the governing Republicans in order to restore it to the antebellum planter elite and to the Democrats. KKK members victimized Republican politicians like Abram Colby, whom they stripped and beat for hours in the woods. They harassed registered voters and independent landholders, ransacked churches and schools, intimidated common laborers who refused to bow obsequiously to planters, and tormented white Republicans sympathetic to any or all of the foregoing.[28]

African Americans' recalcitrance in commonplace disagreements with employers routinely provoked the vigilantes. Alfred Richardson, a legislator from Clarke County, suggested how labor relations continued to have strong political ramifications. The KKK assisted employers in securing the upper hand in conflicts with wage household workers. "Many times, you know, a white lady has a colored lady for cook or waiting in the house, or something of that sort," Richardson explained. "They have some quarrel, and sometimes probably the colored woman gives the lady a little jaw. In a night or two a crowd will come in and take her out and whip her." The Klan stripped and beat African Americans with sticks, straps, or pistol barrels when all else failed to elicit their compliance.[29]

If the KKK was determined to halt the reconstruction of a free labor system, it was most insistent about eliminating black political power. Though women were denied the right to vote in the dominant political system, they actively engaged in a grass-roots political culture that valued the participation of the entire community. Black women and children attended parades, rallies, and conventions; they voiced their opinions and cast their votes on resolutions passed at mass meetings. In the 1860s and 1870s, women organized their own political organizations, such as the Rising Daughters of Liberty Society, and stood guard at political meetings organized by men to allow them to meet without fear of enemy raids. They boldly tacked buttons on the clothing they wore to work in support of favorite candidates. They took time off from work to attend to their political duties, such as traveling to the polls to make sure men cast the right ballots. White housekeepers were as troubled by the dramatic absences of domestic workers on election day or during political conventions as were the planters and urban employers of men.[30] During an election riot in nearby Macon, a newspaper reported: "The Negro women, if possible, were wilder than the men. They were seen everywhere, talking in an excited manner, and urging the men on. Some of them were almost furious, showing it to be part of their religion to keep their husbands and brothers straight in politics."[31]

Whether they gave political advice and support to the men in their families and communities or carried out more directly subversive activities, black women showed courage in the face of political violence. Hannah Flournoy, a cook and laundress, ran a boardinghouse in Columbus well known as a gathering place for Republicans. When George Ashburn, a white party leader stalked by the KKK, looked to her for shelter she complied, unlike his other supporters in the town. Flournoy promised him, "You are a republican, and I am willing to die for you. I am a republican, tooth and toe-nail."[32] But neither Flournoy nor Ashburn could stop the Klan in its determination to take the life of freedom fighters. After Klansmen killed Ashburn, Flournoy escaped to Atlanta, leaving behind valuable property.

Republican activists like Ashburn and Flournoy were not the only victims of KKK violence. The Klan also targeted bystanders who happened to witness their misdeeds. In White County, Joe Brown's entire family was subjected to sadistic and brutal harassment because Brown had observed a murder committed by the Klan. "They just stripped me stark naked, and fell to beating us," Brown reported later. "They got a great big trace-chain, swung me up from the ground, and swung [my wife] up until she fainted; and they beat us all over the yard with great big sticks." The Klan continued its torture against his mother-in-law and sister-in-law. "They made all the women show their nakedness; they made them lie down, and they jabbed them with sticks." Indiscriminate in violating adults and children, the KKK lined up Brown's young daughters and sons "and went to playing with their backsides with a piece of fishing-pole."[33] . . .

Migrating to Atlanta certainly improved the personal safety of ex-slaves escaping the KKK and sexual assaults, but it did not ensure foolproof protection against bodily harm. Black women risked sexual abuse no matter where they lived. Domestics in white homes were the most susceptible to attacks. A year after the war ended, Henry McNeal Turner and other black men mounted the podium and wrote petitions

to demand the cessation of sexual assaults upon black women. Freedom, they insisted, was meaningless without ownership and control over one's own body. Black men took great offense at the fact that while they were falsely accused of raping white women, white men granted themselves total immunity in the exploitation of black women. *"All we ask of the white man is to let our ladies alone,* and they need not fear us," Turner warned. "The difficulty has heretofore been *our ladies were not always at our disposal."*[34] In Savannah, black men mobilized the Sons of Benevolence "for the protection of female virtue" in 1865.[35] In Richmond, African Americans complained to military authorities that women were being "gobbled up" off the streets, thrown into the jail, and ravished by the guards. In Mobile, black men organized the National Lincoln Association and petitioned the Alabama State Constitutional Convention to enact laws to protect black women from assault by white civilians and the police.[36]

Most whites refused to acknowledge the culpability of white men in abusing black women. "Rape" and "black women" were words that were never uttered in the same breath by white Southerners. Any sexual relations that developed between black women and white men were considered consensual, even coerced by the seductions of black women's lascivious nature. Rape was a crime defined exclusively, in theory and in practice, as perceived or actual threats against white female virtue by black men, which resulted in lynchings and castrations of numbers of innocent black men. But Z. B. Hargrove, a white attorney, admitted with rare candor that the obsession with black men raping white women was misplaced. "It is all on the other foot," as he put it. The "colored women have a great deal more to fear from white men."[37]

Black Atlantans during Reconstruction were subjected to other kinds of physical violence, especially at the hands of white civilians and police. . . . When Mary Price objected to being called a "damned bitch" by a white neighbor, Mr. Hoyt, he brought police officer C. M. Barry to her door to reprimand her. Price's mother, Barbara, pregnant at the time, intervened and spoke to the police: "I replied that I would protect my daughter in my own house, whereupon he pulled me out of the house into the street. Here he called another man and the two jerked and pulled me along [the street] to the guard house and threw me in there." When a Freedmen's Bureau agent complained to the mayor and city council on the Prices' behalf, the complaint was rebuffed by a unanimous vote acquitting the policeman of all charges against him. Meanwhile, mother and daughter were arrested, convicted for using profane language, and forced to pay $350 each in fines and court costs. Only after it became clear that the Bureau would persist in its efforts to get justice for the Price women did the mayor have a change of heart and fine the offending policeman. Barry was one of the worst officers on the force, and the Freedmen's Bureau eventually forced the city council to fire him, though he was rehired a year later.[38]

African Americans not only had to ward off physical threats; they were also challenged by the existence of perfectly legal abuses that diminished the meaning of freedom. Ex-slaves defined the reconstruction of their families torn asunder by slavery and war as an important aspect of the realization of the full exercise of their civil rights. But former masters seized upon the misery of African Americans, with the assistance of the law, to prolong the conditions of slavery and deny them the prerogative of reuniting their families. The Georgia legislature passed an Apprentice Act in 1866, ostensibly to protect black orphans by providing them with guardianship and "good" homes until they reached the age of consent at twenty-one. Planters used the law to reinstate bondage through uncompensated child labor.[39] Aunts, uncles, parents, and grandparents inundated the Freedmen's Bureau with requests for assistance in rescuing their children, though this same agency also assisted in apprenticing black minors. Martin Lee, for example, a former slave living in Florence, Alabama, wrote to the chief of the Georgia bureau for help in releasing his nephew from bondage. He had successfully reunited part of his extended family, but could not gain the release of his nephew despite the fact that he and the child's mother, Lee's sister, were both willing and able to take custody.[40]

If admitted enemies of black freedom recklessly disregarded the unity of black families through apprenticeships, some of their friends operated just as wantonly. The American Missionary Association (AMA) sometimes impeded parents and relatives who wished to reclaim their children. In 1866, the AMA started an orphanage that operated out of a tent. Soon afterward they opened the Washburn Orphanage in a building to accommodate the large number of homeless black children

who were surviving on the streets on scant diets of saltpork and hardtack. But the asylum functioned as a temporary way station for children before apprenticing them out as domestic help to white sponsors. "I succeeded in getting a little girl from the orphans asylum by the name of Mary Jane Peirce," one eager patron of the orphanage exclaimed. "Her father and mother are both dead. She has a step mother and a little step brother." Peirce's new guardian minced no words in disclosing reckless disregard for the reunion of the child's family. "I am glad she will have no outside influence exherted upon her," the guardian admitted.[41] . . .

African Americans persisted in pursuing the reconstitution of family ties, despite the obstacles put in their way. [Rebeca] Craighead [the matron of the asylum,] recognized the persistence of these ex-slaves, yet she showed neither respect nor sensitivity toward the virtues of their ambition. "Somehow these black people have the faculty of finding out where their children are," she acknowledged.[42] Both the uncle, Martin Lee, who used official channels to retrieve his nephew, and the anonymous aunt, who relied on her own resources to "steal" her niece, displayed no small measure of resourcefulness in achieving their aims. Men no less than women, non-kin as well as kin, sought to recreate the family bonds that had been strained or severed by slavery and the Civil War.

Not all missionaries were as insensitive as Craighead; there were others, like Frederick Ayers, who fully appreciated the significance of family to ex-slaves. "The idea of 'freedom' of independence, of calling their wives and their children, and little hut their *own*, was a soul animating one, that buoyed up their spirits," he observed.[43] . . .

Broad understandings of kinship encouraged black women to assume responsibility for needy children other than their natural offspring. Silvey, for example, could hardly survive on the minimal subsistence she earned, yet she extended compassion to the youngsters lost or deserted by other ex-slaves. "She was hard put to it, to work for them all," observed her former owner, Emma Prescott. But "of course, as our means were all limited, we could not supply her enough to feed them. Her life, was anything but ease & it was a pitiful sight."[44] . . .

The most complicated family issues involved romantic relationships between women and men. For generations slaves had married one another and passed on the importance of conjugal obligations, despite the absence of legal protection. Marriages between slaves were long-term commitments, usually only disrupted by forcible separation or the death of a spouse. Emancipation offered new opportunities to reaffirm marital vows and to reunite couples who had previously lived "abroad" in the households of different masters. Even before the last shots of gunfire ending the Civil War, thousands of husbands and wives sought the help of Union officers and Northern missionaries to register their nuptials and to conduct wedding ceremonies.[45] The significance of formalizing these ties was articulated by a black soldier: "*I praise God for this day!* The Marriage Covenant is at the foundation of all our rights."[46] Putting marriages on a legal footing bolstered the ability of ex-slaves to keep their families together, to make decisions about labor and education, and to stay out of the unscrupulous grasp of erstwhile masters.

The hardships of slavery and war that disrupted families, however, meant that in the postwar period spouses were not always reunited without problems and tensions. Slaves traveled long distances to reunite with spouses from whom they had been separated for years. They wrote love letters and mailed them to churches and to the Freedmen's Bureau, and retraced the routes of labor agents who had taken their partners away.[47] Emotional bonds were sometimes so intense that spouses would choose to suffer indefinitely if they could not be reunited with their lost loved ones. But affections undernourished by hundreds of miles and many years might be supplanted by other relationships. Many ex-slaves faced awkward dilemmas when spouses presumed to be dead or long-lost suddenly reappeared. Ex-slaves created novel solutions for the vexing moral, legal, and practical concerns in resolving marital relations disrupted by forces beyond their control. One woman lived with each of her two husbands for a two-week trial before making a decision. Some men felt obligated to two wives and stayed married to one wife while providing support to the other. In one case, perhaps unique, a wife resumed her relationship with her first husband, while the second husband, a much older man, was brought into the family as a "poor relation."[48]

The presence of children complicated marriages even further. Some spouses registered their marriages with the Freedmen's Bureau or local courts even when their spouses were dead or missing, in order to give legal recognition to their children. When both parents were present and unable to reconcile their differences, child custody became a point of contention. Madison Day and Maria Richardson reached a mutual agreement to separate after emancipation. The love between husband and wife may have changed, but the love that each displayed for their children did not. The Richardsons put the Freedmen's Bureau agent in a quandary in determining who should receive custody. "Neither husband nor wife seem to be in a condition to provide for the children in a manner better than is usual with the freedpeople," the agent noted. "Still both appear to have an affectionate regard for the children and each loudly demands them."[49] . . .

Sheer survival and the reconstruction of family, despite all the difficulties, were the highest priorities of ex-slaves in the postwar period. But the desire for literacy and education was closely related to their strategies for achieving economic self-sufficiency, political autonomy, and personal enrichment. By 1860, 5 percent of the slave population had defied the laws and learned to read and write. Some were taught by their masters, but many learned to read in clandestine sessions taught by other blacks. African Americans all over the South organized secret schools long before the arrival of Northern missionaries. When a New England teacher arrived in Atlanta in 1865, he discovered an ex-slave already running a school in a church basement.[50]

African Americans welcomed the support of New England teachers and the federal government in their education movement. But centuries of slavery had stirred the longing for self-reliance in operating schools and filling teaching staffs, with assistance, but without white control. Ex-slaves enthusiastically raised funds and donated in-kind labor for building, repairing, and maintaining school houses. They opened their spartan quarters to house teachers and shared vegetables from their gardens to feed them. Ex-slaves in Georgia ranked highest in the South in the amount of financial assistance donated to their own education.[51]

The education movement among African Americans in Georgia went hand in hand with the demand for political rights. In January 1865, black ministers formed the Savannah Education Association, which operated schools staffed entirely with black teachers. Despite the efforts of General Davis Tillson, the conservative head of the Freedmen's Bureau, to keep politics out of the organization, African Americans and more

liberal white allies infused the group with political objectives. The name was changed to the
Georgia Equal Rights and Education Association, explicitly linking equal rights in the political arena with the pursuit of education. The
organization became an important training
ground for black politicians and laypersons at
the grass-roots level and functioned as the
state's predecessor to the Republican Party.[52] . . .

African Americans' advocacy of universal
public education did not fare well at the city
level, because the municipal government was
firmly controlled by Democrats and businessmen. William Finch, elected in 1870 as one of
Atlanta's first black city councilmen, made
universal education a hallmark of his election
campaign. Finch attempted, but failed, to galvanize the support of the white working class
on this issue. City Hall's cold reception shifted
the burden of basic education for blacks to private foundations. Finch did succeed in getting
the council to absorb two primary schools run
by the AMA. After his short term in office and
unsuccessful bid for reelection in December
1871, he continued to be a strong advocate of
public education and helped negotiate a deal
in 1872 whereby the city would pay nominal
costs for some blacks to receive secondary
training at Atlanta University. No publicly
funded high school for blacks would be created until a half-century later, however.[53]

Former slaves of all ages were undeterred
in their goals to achieve literacy, regardless of
the obstacles imposed by municipal and state
governments. "It is quite amusing to see little
girls eight or ten years old lead up full-grown
women, as well as children, to have their
names enrolled," remarked a missionary.
"Men, women, and children are daily inquir-
ing when the 'Free School' is to commence,
and whether all can come[.] There is a large
class of married women who wish to attend, if
the schools are not too crowded."[54] Household
workers figured prominently among this
group of older, eager scholars. Their eagerness
to learn was not diminished, although often
interrupted, by the pressing demands of gainful labor. In fact, these obstacles may have increased the value of education in the eyes of
the ex-slaves. Sabbath schools operated by
black churches and evening classes sponsored
by the Freedmen's Bureau and Northern missionaries afforded alternatives for those who
could not sacrifice time during the day. But
black women also inventively stole time away

from work by carrying their books along and
studying during spare moments—even fasten-
ing textbooks to backyard fences to glimpse
their lessons as they washed clothes.[55]

As parents, working-class adults were especially committed to the education of their
children. The story of Sarah J. Thomas, a young
woman from Macon, whose mother was a cook
and washerwoman, is a poignant illustration.
Thomas wrote Edmund Asa Ware, president of
Atlanta University, to gain his support in her
plans to enroll in the secondary school. "I expected to come to Atlanta to morrow but I am
dissapointed. The reason I can not come to
morrow is this. You know how mothers are! I
guess about their youngest children *girls* especially," she wrote. Mother Thomas was protective of her daughter and reluctant to send her
away alone. "In order that I may *come* Mr. Ware!
mother says can she get a place to work there in
the family?" she asked. The younger Thomas
boasted of her mother's fine skills and reputation and slipped in her salary history. She assured the president, surely swamped by
requests for financial aid, that her matricula-
tion depended upon parental supervision, not
the need for money. "Mother says she dont
mean not the least to work to pay for *my schooling?* father pays for that him self she dont have
any thing to do with it she only want to be
where she can see me."[56] The young scholar's
astute strategizing swayed both her mother
and the school's president; she entered Atlanta
University and achieved a successful teaching
career after graduation in 1875.

Clandestine antebellum activities and
values had bolstered the exemplary efforts of
African Americans to seek literacy and to
build and sustain educational institutions
after the war. Ex-slaves took mutual obligations seriously. Their belief in personal development was aided rather than hampered by
ideals that emphasized broad definitions of
kinship and community. Freedom meant the
reestablishment of lost family connections, the
achievement of literacy, the exercise of political
rights, and the security of a decent livelihood
without the sacrifice of human dignity or self-
determination. Ex-slave women migrated to
Atlanta, where they hoped they would have a
better chance of fulfilling these expectations.
They were faced with many challenges; uppermost among them were the white residents
who were resentful of the abolition of slavery
and persisted in thwarting the realization of

the true meaning of freedom. Black women continued to struggle, resilient and creative, in pursuing their goals for dignity and autonomy. The character of the contest had already been cast, but the many guises of domination and resistance had yet to be exhausted as life in the New South unfolded.

NOTES

1. . . . Franklin M. Garrett, *Yesterday's Atlanta* (Miami: E. A. Seeman, 1974), p. 38; Eric Foner, *Reconstruction: America's Unfinished Revolution, 1863–1877* (New York: Harper & Row, 1988), pp. 81–82; Leon F. Litwack, *Been in the Storm So Long: The Aftermath of Slavery* (New York: Knopf, 1979), pp. 310–316; U.S. Department of the Treasury, Register of Signatures of Depositors in the Branches of the Freedman's Savings and Trust Company, Atlanta Branch, 1870–1874 (Microfilm Publication, M-544), National Archives (hereafter cited as Freedman's Bank Records). Frederick Ayer to George Whipple, 15 February 1866 (Georgia microfilm reels), American Missionary Association Archives, Amistad Research Center, Tulane University (hereafter cited as AMA Papers).

2. John Richard Dennett, *The South As It Is: 1865–1866,* ed. Henry M. Christman (New York: Viking, 1965), pp. 267–271; Sidney Andrews, *The South Since the War: As Shown by Fourteen Weeks of Travel and Observation in Georgia and the Carolinas* (Boston, 1866; reprint ed., New York: Arno, 1970), pp. 339–340; Don H. Doyle, *New Men, New Cities, New South: Atlanta, Nashville, Charleston, Mobile, 1860–1910* (Chapel Hill: University of North Carolina Press, 1990), p. 31.

3. Rebecca Craighead to [Samuel] Grant, 15 January 1866, Georgia, AMA Papers; Andrews, *South Since the War,* p. 340; Whitelaw Reid, *After the War: A Tour of the Southern States, 1865–1866* (London, 1866; reprint ed., New York: Harper & Row, 1965), p. 355; Doyle, *New Men,* pp. 34–35; Howard N. Rabinowitz, *Race Relations in the Urban South 1865–1890* (New York: Oxford University Press, 1978), pp. 5–17.

4. See James Michael Russell, *Atlanta, 1847–1890: City Building in the Old South and the New* (Baton Rouge: Louisiana State University Press, 1988), pp. 117–128.

5. Frederick Ayers to Rev. George Whipple, 15 February 1866, Georgia, AMA Papers.

6. See Rebecca Craighead to Rev. Samuel Hunt, 30 April 1866, Georgia, AMA Papers; E. T. Ayer to Rev. Samuel Grant, 3 February 1866, Georgia, AMA Papers; Harriet M. Phillips to Rev. Samuel Grant, 15 January 1866, Georgia, AMA Papers; *American Missionary* 13 (January 1869): 4; John T. Trowbridge, *The South: A Tour of Its Battlefields and Ruined Cities* (Hartford, 1866; reprint ed., New York: Arno, 1969), p. 453.

7. Frederick Ayers to Rev. George Whipple, 15 February 1866, Georgia, AMA Papers.

8. *Ninth Census: Population* (1872), vol. 1, p. 102; *Tenth Census: Population* (1883), vol. 1, p. 417.

9. Gretchen Ehrmann Maclachlan, "Women's Work: Atlanta's Industrialization and Urbanization, 1879–1929" (Ph.D. diss., Emory University, 1992), p. 29.

10. H. A. Buck to General [Davis Tillson], 2 October 1865, Letters Recd., ser. 732, Atlanta, Ga. Subasst. Comr., Record Group 105: Bureau of Refugees, Freedmen, and Abandoned Lands (hereafter cited as BRFAL), National Archives (hereafter cited as NA), [FSSP A-5153]; Franklin Brown to Gen. Tillson, 30 July 1866, Unregistered Letters Recd., ser. 632, Ga. Asst. Comr., BRFAL, NA, [FSSP A-5327]; clipping from *Augusta Constitutionalist,* 16 February 1866, filed with Lt. Col. D. O. Poole to Brig. Gen. Davis Tillson, 19 February 1866, Unregistered Letters Recd., ser. 632, Ga. Asst. Comr., BRFAL, NA, [FSSP A-5447]. Citations for photocopied documents from the National Archives that were consulted at the Freedmen and Southern Society Project, University of Maryland, conclude with the designation "FSSP" and the project's document control number in square brackets: for example, [FSSP A-5447].

11. Quoted in Trowbridge, *South Tour,* pp. 453–454.

12. Jerry Thornbery, "The Development of Black Atlanta, 1865–1885" (Ph.D. diss., University of Maryland, 1977), pp. 48–53; Edmund L. Drago, *Black Politicians and Reconstruction in Georgia: A Splendid Failure* (Baton Rouge: Louisiana State University Press, 1982), pp. 113–116.

13. Brig. Genl. Davis Tillson to Captain George R. Walbridge, 12 March 1866, Letters Recd., ser. 732, Ga. Subasst. Comr., BRFAL, NA, [FSSP A-5153].

14. Rebecca Craighead to Rev. Samuel Hunt, 15 February 1866, Georgia, AMA Papers; see also F. Ayers to Rev. George Whipple, 15 February 1866, Georgia, AMA Papers.

15. Testimony of Abram Colby, 28 October 1871, in 42nd Congress, 2nd Session, House Report no. 22, pt. 6, *Testimony Taken by the Joint Select Committee to Inquire into the Condition of Affairs in the Late Insurrectionary States* (Washington, D.C., 1872), vol. 2, p. 700 (hereafter cited as KKK Hearings). See also testimony of Alfred Richardson, 7 July 1871, KKK Hearings, vol. 1, p. 12.

16. Doyle, *New Men,* pp. 38–48, 151; Jonathan W. McLeod, *Workers and Workplace Dynamics in Reconstruction Era Atlanta* (Los Angeles: Center for Afro-American Studies, University of California), pp. 10–16.

17. McLeod, *Workers and Workplace,* pp. 24–31, 45, 61, 75, 81, 91, 94.

18. Ibid., pp. 77–92, 100–103; Thornbery, "Black Atlanta," pp. 191–225.

19. Entry of 27 May 1865, Ella Gertrude Clanton Thomas Journal, William R. Perkins Library, Duke University (hereafter cited as DU).

20. See entries for May 1865, Thomas Journal, DU.

21. Atlanta *Daily Intelligencer,* 25 October 1865.

22. Emma J. S. Prescott, "Reminiscences of the War," typescript, pp. 49–50, 55, Atlanta History Center (hereafter cited as AHC).

23. Atlanta *Daily New Era,* 27 February 1868.

24. Mr. J. T. Ball to Maj. Knox, 19 March 1866, Unregistered Letters Recd., ser. 2250, Meridian, Miss. Subasst. Comr., BRFAL, NA, [FSSP A-9423].

25. Alexa Wynell Benson, "Race Relations in Atlanta, As Seen in a Critical Analysis of the City Council Proceedings and Other Related Works, 1865–1877" (M.A. thesis, Atlanta University, 1966), pp. 43–44; Foner, *Reconstruction,* pp. 199–202; Theodore Brantner Wilson, *The Black Codes of the South*

(University, Ala.: University of Alabama Press, 1965); Rabinowitz, *Race Relations,* pp. 34–35; Atlanta *Daily New Era,* 27 February 1868.

26. Virginia Shelton to William Shelton, 20 August 1866, Campbell Family Papers, DU. See also Ellen Chisholm to Laura Perry, 27 July 1867, Perry Family Papers, AHC.

27. Affidavit of Samuel Ellison, 16 Jan 1867 BRFAL, NA.

28. Foner, *Reconstruction,* pp. 425–444; see testimony of Abram Colby, 28 October 1871, KKK Hearings, vol. 2, pp. 699–702.

29. Testimony of Alfred Richardson, 7 July 1871, KKK Hearings, vol. 1, pp. 12, 18.

30. Foner, *Reconstruction,* pp. 87, 290–291; Elsa Barkley Brown, "Negotiating and Transforming the Public Sphere: African American Political Life in the Transition from Slavery to Freedom," *Public Culture* 7 (Fall 1994): 107–126; Thomas C. Holt, *Black Over White: Negro Political Leadership in South Carolina during Reconstruction* (Urbana: University of Illinois Press, 1977), pp. 34–35.

31. Macon *Georgia Weekly Telegraph,* 8 October 1872, as quoted in Edmund L. Drago, "Militancy and Black Women in Reconstruction Georgia," *Journal of American Culture* 1 (Winter 1978): 841.

32. Testimony of Hannah Flournoy, 24 October 1871, KKK Hearings, vol. 1, p. 533. On Ashburn's death see Drago, *Black Politicians,* pp. 145, 153.

33. Testimony of Joe Brown, 24 October 1871, KKK Hearings, vol. 1, p. 502.

34. Henry McNeal Turner's emancipation speech, 1 January 1866, Augusta, as quoted in Herbert G. Gutman, *The Black Family in Slavery and Freedom, 1750–1925* (New York: Pantheon Books, 1977), p. 388. See also Catherine Clinton, "Bloody Terrain: Freedwomen, Sexuality and Violence During Reconstruction," *Georgia Historical Quarterly* 76 (Summer 1992): 318; Atlanta *Weekly Defiance,* 24 February 1883.

35. Eliza Frances Andrews, *The War-Time Journal of a Georgia Girl, 1864–1865,* ed. Spencer Bidwell King, Jr. (Macon, Ga.: Arvidian Press, 1960), p. 349.

36. Gutman, *Black Family,* pp. 387–388.

37. Testimony of Z. B. Hargrove, 13 July 1871, KKK Hearings, vol. 1, p. 83. See also testimony of George B. Burnett, 2 November 1871, KKK Hearings, vol. 2, p. 949. See Jacquelyn Dowd Hall, *Revolt Against Chivalry: Jesse Daniel Ames and the Women's Campaign Against Lynching* (New York: Columbia University Press, 1974).

38. Affidavit of Barbara Price, 15 May 1867, Misc. Court Records, ser. 737, Atlanta, Ga. Subasst. Comr., BRFAL; Bvt. Maj. Fred. Mosebach to Mayor and City Council of Atlanta, 15 May 1867, and Bvt. Maj. Fred. Mosebach to Col. C. C. Sibley, 21 May 1867, vol. 99, pp. 49 and 53–54, Letters Sent, ser. 729, Atlanta, Ga. Subasst. Comr., BRFAL, NA, [FSSP A-5709]. See also James M. Russell and Jerry Thornbery, "William Finch of Atlanta: The Black Politician as Civic Leader," in Howard N. Rabinowitz, ed. *Southern Black Leaders of the Reconstruction Era* (Urbana: University of Illinois Press, 1982), pp. 317, 332.

39. The apprenticeship system was not entirely limited to the conscription of minors; young adults actively providing for themselves were also apprenticed. For example, a turpentine worker with a wife and child was defined as an orphan in North Carolina. See Foner, *Reconstruction,* p. 201.

40. Martin Lee to Mr. Tillson, 7 December 1866, in Ira Berlin et al., "Afro-American Families in the Transition from Slavery to Freedom," *Radical History Review* 42 (Fall 1988): 102–103.

41. Entry of 27 May 1865, Thomas Journal, DU. Evidence from ex-slave narratives suggests a pattern of exploitation of child laborers; they received little or no cash wages. See testimony of Nancy Smith, in George P. Rawick, ed., *The American Slave: A Composite Autobiography* (Westport, Conn.: Greenwood Press, 1941; 1972), *Georgia Narratives,* vol. 13, pt. 3, p. 302 (hereafter cited as WPA Ga. Narr.); testimony of Georgia Telfair, WPA Ga. Narr., vol. 13, pt. 4, p. 5.

42. Rebecca M. Craighead to Bvt. Brig. Gen. J. H. Lewis, 11 May 1866, Ga. Asst. Comr., C-69, 1867, Letters Recd., ser. 631, Ga. Asst. Comr., BRFAL, NA, [FSSP A-415].

43. F. Ayers to Rev. George Whipple, 15 February 1866, Georgia, AMA Papers.

44. Prescott, "Reminiscences of the War," p. 56, AHC. Prescott goes on to reveal that Silvey died penniless, without the help of former owners.

45. Gutman, *Black Family,* pp. 9–23; Berlin et al., "Afro-American Families," pp. 92–93.

46. Corporal Murray, as quoted in J. R. Johnson to Col. S. Lee, 1 June 1866, in Berlin et al., "Afro-American Families," p. 97.

47. For examples of these efforts see Wm. H. Sinclair to Freedmen's Bureau agent at Savannah, Ga., 12 September 1866, Unregistered Letters, ser. 1013, Savannah, Ga. Subasst. Comr., BRFAL, NA, [FSSP A-5762]; R. F. Patterson to Col. D. C. Poole, Letters Recd., ser. 732, Atlanta, Ga. Subasst. Comr., BRFAL, NA, [FSSP A-5704].

48. Gutman, *Black Family,* pp. 418–425.

49. 1st Lt. F. E. Grossmann to the Acting Assistant Adjutant General, 1 October 1866, in Berlin et al., "Afro-American Families," pp. 97–98. Gutman, *Black Family,* pp. 418–425.

50. James D. Anderson, *The Education of Blacks in the South, 1860–1935* (Chapel Hill: University of North Carolina Press, 1988), pp. 4–9, 16; Herbert G. Gutman, "Schools for Freedom: The Post-Emancipation Origins of Afro-American Education," in Herbert G. Gutman, *Power and Culture: Essays on the American Working-Class,* ed. Ira Berlin (New York: Pantheon, 1987), p. 294; Jacqueline Jones, *Soldiers of Light and Love: Northern Teachers and Georgia Blacks 1865–1873* (Chapel Hill: University of North Carolina Press, 1980), p. 59.

51. Gutman, "Schools for Freedom," pp. 286, 294; Jones, *Soldiers of Light and Love,* p. 62; Anderson, *Education of Blacks in the South,* pp. 4–32.

52. Drago, *Black Politicians,* pp. 27–28.

53. Russell and Thornbery, "William Finch of Atlanta," pp. 319, 322; Russell, *Atlanta,* p. 181.

54. Mrs. E. T. Ayers to Rev. Samuel Hunt, 1 September 1866, Georgia, AMA Papers.

55. Jennies Barium to Rev. Samuel Grant, 27 January 1866, Georgia, AMA Papers; Andrews, *South Since the War,* p. 338.

56. Sarah J. Thomas to Mr. [Edmund A.] Ware, 11 October 1869, Edmund A. Ware Papers, Robert W. Woodruff Library, Clarke Atlanta University.

A. S. Hitchcock, "Young women particularly flock back & forth . . ."

Early in the Civil War, before the Emancipation Proclamation, the Union Army occupied the Sea Islands off the coasts of South Carolina and Georgia; plantation owners fled and the army established base camps there. Although the Union forces expected former slaves to continue to work on their old plantations as contract laborers, freedpeople believed that the end of slavery should mean that they could travel freely and that they could choose other ways of supporting themselves.

How did Union officials interpret the movement of women around the islands (which included Beaufort and Hilton Head)? What limited types of work did they posit as appropriate for African American women and men? Note the ways in which black people's efforts at family reunion were criminalized.

A. S. HITCHCOCK, ACTING GENERAL
SUPERINTENDENT OF CONTRABANDS,
TO PROVOST MARSHAL GENERAL
OF THE DEPARTMENT OF THE SOUTH,
AUGUST 25, 1864

In accordance with a request made by you at this office . . . concerning measures to be instituted to lessen the number of idle & dissolute persons hanging about the central Posts of the Department & traveling to & from between them . . . I write this note. . . .

Had I the control of the negroes the first thing I would endeavor to do, & the thing I think of most importance to be done, is to Keep all the people possible on the farms or plantations at *honest steady* labor. As one great means to this end, I would make it as difficult as possible for them to get to the centres of population.—Young women particularly flock back & forth by scores to Hilton Head, to Beaufort, to the country simply to while away their time, or constantly to seek some new excitement, or what is worse to live by lasciviousness. . . . I would allow no peddling around camps whatsoever. . . . All rationing I would stop utterly, & introduce the poor house system, feeding none on any pretense who would not go to the place provided for all paupers to live. . . . All persons out of the poor house running from place to place to beg a living I would treat as vagabonds, & also all persons, whether in town or on plantations, white or black, who lived without occupation should either go to the poor house or be put in a place where they *must work*—a work house or chain gang, & if women where they could wash iron & scrub for the benefit of the public. . . .

SEPTEMBER 6, 1864
GENERAL ORDERS NO. 130

Hilton Head, S.C. . . . The practice of allowing negro women to wander about from one plantation to another, and from one Post or District to another, on Government transports, for no other purpose than to while away their time, or visit their husbands serving in the ranks of the Army, is not only objectionable in every point of view, both to the soldiers and to themselves, but is generally subversive of moral restraint, and must be discontinued at once. All negro women, in future found wandering in this manner, will be immediately arrested, and compelled to work at some steady employment on the Plantations.

Excerpted from *Freedom: A Documentary History of Emancipation, 1861–1867*, ser. 1, vol. 3, ed. Ira Berlin, Joseph P. Reidy, and Leslie S. Rowland, pp. 316–19. Reprinted with the permission of Cambridge University Press.

Roda Ann Childs, "I was more dead than alive"

In January 1865, before the Civil War was over, Congress and the states in the Union ratified the Thirteenth Amendment, putting an end to slavery and "involuntary servitude, except as punishment for crime whereof the party shall have been duly convicted." Once peace was established, it became clear that the states of the former Confederacy were quite creative in devising systems that maintained racial subordination (for example, broad definitions of what counted as "vagrancy" which, as crimes, could be punished by involuntary servitude). The Civil Rights Act of 1866 was designed to protect freedpeople; it promised "citizens of every race and color . . . full and equal benefit of all laws and proceedings for the security of person and property, as is enjoyed by white citizens. . . ." But the statute had been passed only over the veto of President Andrew Johnson, who denied that the states of the Confederacy had forfeited all civil rights and privileges by their rebellion. The Freedmen's Bureau was charged with protecting the rights of former slaves and assisting their transition to a market economy; it accomplished much, but it was always underfunded and understaffed, and many of its staff members were themselves deeply skeptical of freedpeople.

In a political climate marked by struggle between Congress and the President, the Ku Klux Klan and other vigilantes who wanted to intimidate freedpeople and take vengeance for their own defeat in war seized their opportunity. Not until 1871 did Congress pass the Ku Klux Klan Act, prescribing fines and imprisonment for those who went in disguise to terrorize others. The congressional committee that conducted a traveling inquiry into "the Condition of Affairs in the Late Insurrectionary States" filed a twelve-volume report. Its testimony of violence and intimidation, in excruciating detail, makes it clear that Roda Ann Childs's experience was replicated throughout the South.

Roda Ann Childs made her way to a Freedmen's Bureau agent in Griffin, Georgia, to swear this affidavit; she signed it with her mark. There is no evidence that her case was pursued. What clue does she offer for why she was a target for mob violence?

[*Griffin, GA*] Sept. 25, 1866 Roda Ann Childs came into this office and made the following statement:

Myself and husband were under contract with Mrs. Amelia Childs of Henry County, and worked from Jan. 1, 1866, until the crops were laid by, or in other words until the main work of the year was done, without difficulty. Then, (the fashion being prevalent among the planters) we were called upon one night, and my husband was demanded; I Said he was not there. They then asked where he was. I Said he was gone to the water mellon patch. They then Seized me and took me Some distance from the house, where they 'bucked' me down across a log, Stripped my clothes over my head, one of the men Standing astride my neck, and beat me across my posterior, two men holding my legs. In this manner I was beaten until they were tired. Then they turned me parallel with the log, laying my neck on a limb which projected from the log, and one man placing his foot upon my neck, beat me again on my hip and thigh. Then I was thrown upon the ground on my back, one

Excerpted from *Freedom: A Documentary History of Emancipation, 1861–1876,* ser. 2, ed. Ira Berlin, Joseph P. Reidy, and Leslie S. Rowland, p. 807. Reprinted with the permission of Cambridge University Press.

of the men Stood upon my breast, while two others took hold of my feet and stretched My limbs as far apart as they could, while the man Standing upon my breast applied the Strap to my private parts until fatigued into stopping, and I was more dead than alive. Then a man, Supposed to be an ex-confederate Soldier, as he was on crutches, fell upon me and ravished me. During the whipping one of the men ran his pistol into me, and Said he had a hell of a mind to pull the trigger, and Swore they ought to Shoot me, as my husband had been in the 'God damned Yankee Army,' and Swore they meant to kill every black Son-of-a-bitch they could find that had ever fought against them. They then went back to the house, Seized my two daughters and beat them, demanding their father's pistol, and upon failure to get that, they entered the house and took Such articles of clothing as Suited their fancy, and decamped. There were concerned in this affair eight men, none of which could be recognized for certain.

her
Roda Ann × Childs
mark

Reconstruction Amendments, 1868, 1870

Until 1868, the U.S. Constitution made no explicit distinctions on the basis of gender. Of qualifications for voters, it said only that "the electors in each State shall have the qualifications requisite for electors of the most numerous branch of the State legislature" (art. 1, sec. 2). Reformers merely needed to persuade each state legislature to change its own rules in order to enfranchise women in national elections.

The word *male* was introduced into the Constitution in section 2 of the Fourteenth Amendment, as part of a complex provision—never enforced—intended to constrain former Confederates from interfering with the civil rights of newly freed slaves. Suffragists were bitterly disappointed at the failure to include sex as a category in the Fifteenth Amendment. But until the test case of *Minor v. Happersett* (pp. 294–295), they clung to the hope that the first article of the Fourteenth Amendment would be interpreted broadly enough to admit women to the polls.

FOURTEENTH AMENDMENT, 1868

1. All persons born or naturalized in the United States, and subject to the jurisdiction thereof, are citizens of the United States and of the State wherein they reside. No State shall make or enforce any law which shall abridge the privileges or immunities of citizens of the United States; nor shall any State deprive any person of life, liberty, or property, without due process of law; nor deny to any person within its jurisdiction the equal protection of the laws.

2. Representatives shall be apportioned among the several States according to their respective numbers, counting the whole number of persons in each State, excluding Indians not taxed. But when the right to vote at any election for the choice of electors for President and Vice-President of the United States, Representatives in Congress, the executive and judicial officers of a State, or the members of the legislature thereof, is denied to any of the male inhabitants of such State, being twenty-one years of age and citizens of the United States, or in any way abridged, except for participation in rebellion, or other crime, the basis of representation therein shall be reduced in the proportion which the number of such male citizens shall bear to the whole number of male citizens twenty-one years of age in such State. . . .

FIFTEENTH AMENDMENT, 1870

The right of citizens of the United States to vote shall not be denied or abridged by the United States or by any State on account of race, color, or previous condition of servitude. . . .

Win Some, Lose Some: Women in Court: **Coger v. The North Western Union Packet Company,** *Supreme Court of Iowa, 1873;* **Bradwell v. Illinois,** *1873;* **Minor v. Happersett,** *1874*

COGER V. THE NORTH WESTERN UNION PACKET COMPANY, SUPREME COURT OF IOWA, 1873

A long-established rule of Anglo-American common law is that transportation services licensed by the state are "legally bound to carry all passengers or freight as long as there is enough space, the fee is paid, and no reasonable grounds to refuse to do so exist."* What counts as "reasonable grounds" is open to interpretation. One popular way to evade universal common carrier rules has been to charge different fees for first- and second-class accommodations—thus segregating by economic class—and make only second-class accommodations available to all people of color. The "ladies' car" in railroads or the "ladies' table" on steamships was a popular subterfuge for racial segregation. Throughout the post–Civil War years, African American women challenged their exclusion from ladies' accommodations—often at real physical risk to themselves. (Being thrown off a moving train was the worst of these risks.)

In 1873, Emma Coger, a schoolteacher of mixed race, tried to buy a first-class ticket on a steamboat that crossed the Mississippi from Keokuk, Iowa, to her hometown of Quincy, Illinois. She refused the clerk's offer of a ticket that did not entitle her to meals at the first-class table reserved for ladies traveling alone; she found another passenger, a white man, who purchased a first-class meal ticket on her behalf. When she took a seat at the ladies' table in the cabin, the guard told her to move to the deck or to the pantry, where people of color were to eat. She refused. The captain of the boat appeared, making the same demand; she again refused, and, as the subsequent court record describes it, "he proceeded by force to remove her from the table and the cabin of the boat."

The feisty Emma Coger did not go quietly. As one witness testified, "She swore and abused the captain, saying 'I told you I'd get even with you, you white-livered sons of bitches.' . . . Her conduct was very bad and her language worse. In the struggle, the covering of the table was torn off, dishes broke, and the officer received a slight injury."† Coger was defiant; she sued the steamship company for assault and battery.

Emma Coger hedged her bets. She claimed "she was as white as anybody." A jury trial was held in the Lee District Court. The judge instructed the jury that if Coger's "rights to first-class accommodations were denied her, simply because she has African or negro blood in her veins . . . then the court charges you that the plaintiff is entitled to recover" damages.

Coger won. The steamship company appealed to the Iowa Supreme Court, claiming that the well-known custom on all their boats was that "colored persons could not receive . . . first class privileges. . . . [Coger] purchased a ticket which entitled her to the rights of a colored person . . . and gave her no right to meals. . . .

---

*West Encyclopedia of American Law, 2008, http://legal-dictionary.thefreedictionary.com/Common+carrier.

†Record quoted in Barbara Young Welke, *Recasting American Liberty: Gender, Race, Law, and the Railroad Revolution, 1865–1920* (New York: Cambridge University Press, 2001), pp. 292–93.

Afterward, by fraud, she purchased such a ticket for meals as were sold to white persons. . . . [N]o greater force was used than was necessary to take her, against her resistance, from the table."

Earlier that year, dealing with Myra Bradwell's claim that the Fourteenth Amendment's promise of equal protection should sustain her right to practice law, the U.S. Supreme Court had interpreted the amendment very narrowly. But Iowa Chief Justice Joseph M. Beck had participated in the deliberations of his court when, only a few years before, it had ruled that racially segregated schools were a denial of equal protection of the laws—interpreting the Fourteenth Amendment broadly. Now he wrote the opinion for a unanimous court.

Iowa was unusual. Ten years later, in Tennessee, Ida B. Wells (see pp. 323–325) would have experiences similar to Emma Coger's, but with the opposite result. In 1883, Wells physically resisted her removal from a ladies' car, biting the conductor's hand as he forced her off the train. She sued the railroad company for discrimination; she won in the trial court but lost when the railroad appealed to the Tennessee Supreme Court. (The court offered the opinion that it was Wells who had, by her lawsuit, harassed the railroad.)

The lawsuits courageously brought by Emma Coger, Ida B. Wells, and dozens of other individual African American women in the years after the Civil War tested the claim that the common carriers (railroads, streetcars, steamboats) provided "separate but equal" accommodations to black and white people. Their lawsuits laid the ground for the famous test case challenging separate streetcars for whites and blacks, brought—at no physical risk to themselves—by Homer Plessy and a group of African American professional men in New Orleans at the end of the nineteenth century. In *Plessy v. Ferguson*, the U.S. Supreme Court ruled that laws requiring the separation of the races merely reflect social custom and do not label one race as inferior. *Plessy* would not be overturned until the Supreme Court's 1954 decision in *Brown v. Board of Education*.

How did the Iowa Supreme Court describe the issues on which it had to decide? On what grounds did they hold for Emma Coger? Contrast this interpretation of the meaning of the Fourteenth Amendment with the U.S. Supreme Court's decision in *Bradwell* and *Minor* rulings excerpted in this document cluster.

CHIEF JUSTICE JOSEPH BECK, FOR A UNANIMOUS COURT:

[I]n our opinion, the doctrines and authorities involved in the argument [that Coger is white] are obsolete, and have no longer existence and authority, anywhere within the jurisdiction of the federal constitution, and most certainly not in Iowa. The ground upon which we base this conclusion will be discovered, in the progress of this opinion, to be the absolute equality of all men. We will . . . accept the statement of fact as made by the counsel of [the steamship company], namely, that plaintiff is a woman of color.

In our opinion the plaintiff was entitled to the same rights and privileges while upon defendant's boat, notwithstanding the negro blood, be it more or less, admitted to flow in her veins, which were possessed and exercised by white passengers.

These rights and privileges rest upon the equality of all before the law, the very foundation principle of our government. If the negro must submit to different treatment, to accommodations inferior to those given to the white man, when transported by public carriers, he is deprived of the benefits of this very principle of equality. . . . It may be claimed that as he does not get accommodations equal to the white man he is not charged as great a price. But this does not modify the. . . absurdity and gross injustice of the rule—nay, its positive wickedness. . . .

Coger v. The North Western Packet Union Company, 37 Iowa 145 (1873).

The decision is planted on the broad and just ground of the equality of all men before the law, which is not limited by color, nationality, religion or condition in life. This principle of equality is announced and secured by the very first words of our State constitution which relate to the rights of the people, in language most comprehensive, and incapable of misconstruction, namely: "All men are, by nature, free and equal." . . . But the doctrine of equality and its application to the rights of [Emma Coger] . . . depend . . . not alone upon the constitution of this State [but also] . . . are recognized and secured by the recent constitutional amendments and legislation of the United States. . . . The persons contemplated by the [Fourteenth] amendment [see p. 309] are: 1. All persons born or naturalized in the United States. . . . These . . . are secured the right of citizenship of the United States, and protected against abridgment of their privileges and immunities. 2. All persons within the jurisdiction of the States . . . are protected and secured the equal protection of the laws. [Coger] belongs to both classes of persons, to whom rights are secured and protection extended. . . .

Her money would not purchase for her that which the same sum would entitle a white passenger to receive. . . . [S]he claimed no social privilege, but substantial privileges pertaining to her property and the protection of her person. It cannot be doubted that she was excluded from the table and cabin . . . because of prejudice entertained against her race, growing out of its former condition of servitude—a prejudice, be it proclaimed to the honor of our people, that is fast giving way to nobler sentiments, and, it is hoped, will soon be entombed with its parent, slavery. . . .

[A] common carrier cannot refuse to transport all persons without distinctions based upon color or nationality. . . . Her dinner ticket gave her a right to dine in the cabin on an equality with other passengers. . . .

BRADWELL V. ILLINOIS, 1873

Although she could not practice in the courts until the end of her career, Myra Bradwell was perhaps the most notable female lawyer of the nineteenth century. She read law in the office of her husband, a prominent Chicago attorney and county judge. In 1868 she began to publish the *Chicago Legal News,* a weekly newspaper covering developments in courts and legislatures throughout the country. Because she had received a special charter from the state legislature under which she was permitted to act without the usual legal disabilities of a married woman, she ran the *News* as her own business. She wrote vigorous editorials, evaluating legal opinions and new laws, assessing proposed state legislation, and supporting progressive developments like prison reform, the establishment of law schools, and women's rights. She drafted bills improving married women's rights to child custody and to property, including the Illinois Married Woman's Property Act of 1869. Thanks in part to her own lobbying efforts, Illinois permitted women to own property and to control their own earnings.

It was only logical that Myra Bradwell should seek admission to the bar. Although she passed the entrance tests in 1869, although the Illinois Married Woman's Property Act permitted her to own property, and although the law that gave the state supreme court the power to license attorneys did not explicitly exclude women, her application was rejected by the Illinois Supreme Court on the grounds that she was a married woman, and therefore not a truly free agent. Appealing to the United States Supreme Court, her attorney argued that among the "privileges and immunities" guaranteed to each citizen by the Fourteenth Amendment was the right to pursue any honorable profession. "Intelligence, integrity and honor are the only qualifications that can be prescribed . . . the broad shield of the Constitution is over all, and protects each in that measure of success which his or her individual merits may secure."

Bradwell v. Illinois, 83 U.S. 130 (1873).

The Court's decision came in two parts. Speaking for the majority and citing the most recent decision of the Supreme Court in the slaughterhouse cases, Justice Samuel F. Miller held that the right to practice law in the courts of any particular state was a right that had to be granted by the individual state; it was not one of the "privileges and immunities" of national citizenship. This judgment was supplemented by a concurring opinion, in which Justice Joseph P. Bradley offered an ideological justification for the Court's decision that was based on inherent differences between men and women and that was to be widely used thereafter to defend the exclusion of women from professional careers.

While her case was pending before the U.S. Supreme Court, Bradwell and Alta M. Hulett, another woman who had been refused admission to the bar even though she was otherwise qualified, successfully lobbied for a law that granted freedom of occupational choice to all Illinois citizens, both male and female. The bill was passed in 1872; a year later Alta Hulett was sworn in before the Illinois Bar. Bradwell did not think she should have to beg for admission, and she never formally applied for a license to practice law under the new statute. In the *Chicago Legal News* she observed that "having once complied with the rules and regulations of the court . . . [I] declined to . . . again ask for admission." In 1890, twenty years after her initial application, the Illinois Supreme Court admitted Bradwell to the bar. Two years before her death in 1894 she was admitted to practice before the U.S. Supreme Court, but she never did argue a case there.*

MR. JUSTICE JOSEPH P. BRADLEY:

The claim of the plaintiff, who is a married woman, to be admitted to practice as an attorney and counselor at law, is based upon the supposed right of every person, man or woman, to engage in any lawful employment for a livelihood. The supreme court of Illinois denied the application on the ground that, by the common law, which is the basis of the laws of Illinois, only men were admitted to the bar, and the legislature had not made any change in this respect. . . .

The claim that, under the 14th Amendment of the Constitution, which declares that no state shall make or enforce any law which shall abridge the privileges and immunities of citizens of the United States, and the statute law of Illinois, or the common law prevailing in that state, can no longer be set up as a barrier against the right of females to pursue any lawful employment . . . assumes that it is one of the privileges and immunities of women as citizens to engage in any and every profession, occupation or employment in civil life.

It certainly cannot be affirmed, as a historical fact, that this has ever been established as one of the fundamental privileges and immunities of the sex. On the contrary, the civil law, as well as nature herself, has always recognized a wide difference in the respective spheres and destinies of man and woman. Man is, or should be, woman's protector and defender. The natural and proper timidity and delicacy which belongs to the female sex evidently unfits it for many of the occupations of civil life. The constitution of the family organization, which is founded in the divine ordinance, as well as in the nature of things, indicates the domestic sphere as that which properly belongs to the domain and functions of womanhood. The harmony, not to say identity, of interests and views which belong or should belong to the family institution, is repugnant to the idea of a woman adopting a distinct and independent career from that of her husband. So firmly fixed was this sentiment in the founders of the common law that it became a maxim of that system of jurisprudence that a woman had no legal existence separate from her husband, who was regarded as her head and representative in the social state; and, notwithstanding some recent modifications of this civil status, many of the special rules of law flowing from and dependent

*See also Frances Olsen, "From False Paternalism to False Equality: Judicial Assaults on Feminist Community, Illinois, 1869–1895," *Michigan Law Review* 84 (1986): 1518–43.

upon this cardinal principle still exist in full force in most states. One of these is, that a married woman is incapable, without her husband's consent, of making contracts which shall be binding on her or him. This very incapacity was one circumstance which the supreme court of Illinois deemed important in rendering a married woman incompetent fully to perform the duties and trusts that belong to the office of an attorney and counselor.

It is true that many women are unmarried and not affected by any of the duties, complications, and incapacities arising out of the married state, but these are exceptions to the general rule. The paramount destiny and mission of woman are to fulfill the noble and benign offices of wife and mother. This is the law of the Creator. And the rules of civil society must be adapted to the general constitution of things, and cannot be based upon exceptional cases. . . .

MINOR V. HAPPERSETT, 1874

In 1872 suffragists in a number of places attempted to test the possibilities of the first section of the Fourteenth Amendment. "The power to regulate is one thing, the power to prevent is an entirely different thing," observed Virginia Minor, president of the Woman Suffrage Association of Missouri, and she presented herself at the polls in St. Louis in 1872. When the registrar refused to permit her to register to vote, she and her husband sued him for denying her one of the "privileges and immunities of citizenship"; when they lost the case they appealed to the Supreme Court.

In a unanimous opinion the justices held that if the authors of the Constitution had intended that women should vote, they would have said so explicitly. The decision of the Court meant that woman suffrage could not be developed by way of a quiet reinterpretation of the Constitution but would require an explicit amendment to the Constitution or a series of revisions in the laws of the states.

MR. CHIEF JUSTICE MORRISON R. WAITE DELIVERED THE OPINION OF THE COURT:

The question is presented in this case, whether, since the adoption of the fourteenth amendment, a woman, who is a citizen of the United States and of the State of Missouri, is a voter in that State, notwithstanding the provision of the constitution and laws of the State, which confine the right of suffrage to men alone. . . . The argument is, that as a woman, born or naturalized in the United States and subject to the jurisdiction thereof, is a citizen of the United States and of the State in which she resides, she has the right of suffrage as one of the privileges and immunities of her citizenship, which the State cannot by its laws or constitution abridge.

There is no doubt that women may be citizens. They are persons, and by the fourteenth amendment "all persons born or naturalized in the United States and subject to the jurisdiction thereof" are expressly declared to be "citizens of the United States and of the State wherein they reside." But, in our opinion, it did

not need this amendment to give them that position . . . sex has never been made one of the elements of citizenship in the United States. In this respect men have never had an advantage over women. The same laws precisely apply to both. The fourteenth amendment did not affect the citizenship of women any more than it did of men. . . . Mrs. Minor . . . has always been a citizen from her birth, and entitled to all the privileges and immunities of citizenship.

If the right of suffrage is one of the necessary privileges of a citizen of the United States, then the constitution and laws of Missouri confining it to men are in violation of the Constitution of the United States, as amended, and consequently void. The direct question is, therefore, presented whether all citizens are necessarily voters.

The Constitution does not define the privileges and immunities of citizens. For that definition we must look elsewhere. In this case we need not determine what they are, but only whether suffrage is necessarily one of them.

Minor v. Happersett, 88 U.S. 162 (1874).

It certainly is nowhere made so in express terms. The United States has no voters in the States of its own creation. The elective officers of the United States are all elected directly or indirectly by state voters ... it cannot for a moment be doubted that if it had been intended to make all citizens of the United States voters, the framers of the Constitution would not have left it to implication. ...

It is true that the United States guarantees to every State a republican form of government. ... No particular government is designated as republican, neither is the exact form to be guaranteed, in any manner especially designated. ... When the Constitution was adopted ... all the citizens of the States were not invested with the right of suffrage. In all, save perhaps New Jersey, this right was only bestowed upon men and not upon all of them. ... Under these circumstances it is certainly now too late to contend that a government is not republican, within the meaning of this guaranty in the Constitution, because women are not made voters. ... If suffrage was intended to be included within its obligations, language better adapted to express that intent would most certainly have been employed. ...

... For nearly ninety years the people have acted upon the idea that the Constitution, when it conferred citizenship, did not necessarily confer the right of suffrage. If uniform practice long continued can settle the construction of so important an instrument as the Constitution of the United States confessedly is, most certainly it has been done here. Our province is to decide what the law is, not to declare what it should be.

We have given this case the careful consideration its importance demands. If the law is wrong, it ought to be changed; but the power for that is not with us. ... No argument as to woman's need of suffrage can be considered. We can only act upon her rights as they exist. ...

The Women's Centennial Agenda, 1876

The capstone of the celebration of the Centennial was a public reading of the Declaration of Independence in Independence Square, Philadelphia, by a descendant of a signer, Richard Henry Lee. Elizabeth Cady Stanton, who was then president of the National Woman Suffrage Association, asked permission to silently present a women's protest and a written Declaration of Rights. The request was denied. "Tomorrow we propose to celebrate what we have done the last hundred years," replied the president of the official ceremonies, "not what we have failed to do."

Led by suffragist Susan B. Anthony, five women appeared at the official reading, distributing copies of their declaration. After this mildly disruptive gesture, they withdrew to the other side of Independence Hall, where they staged a counter-Centennial and Anthony read the following address. Compare it to the Declaration of Sentiments (pp. 247–250) of twenty-eight years before. Note the splendid oratorical flourish of the final paragraph.

July 4, 1876

While the nation is buoyant with patriotism, and all hearts are attuned to praise, it is with sorrow we come to strike the one discordant note, on this one-hundredth anniversary of our country's birth. When subjects of kings, emperors, and czars, from the old world join in our national jubilee, shall the women of the republic refuse to lay their hands with benedictions on the nation's head? Surveying America's exposition, surpassing in magnificence those of London, Paris, and Vienna, shall we not rejoice at the success of the youngest rival among the nations of the earth? May not our hearts, in

Excerpted from Susan B. Anthony, Declaration of Rights for Women by the National Woman Suffrage Association, in *History of Suffrage, vol. 3, ed.* Elizabeth Cady Stanton, Susan B. Anthony, and Matilda Joselyn Gage (Rochester, N.Y.: Susan B. Anthony, 1886), pp. 31–34.

unison with all, swell with pride at our great achievements as a people; our free speech, free press, free schools, free church, and the rapid progress we have made in material wealth, trade, commerce and the inventive arts? And we do rejoice in the success, thus far, of our experiment of self-government. Our faith is firm and unwavering in the broad principles of human rights proclaimed in 1776, not only as abstract truths, but as the corner stones of a republic. Yet we cannot forget, even in this glad hour, that while all men of every race, and clime, and condition, have been invested with the full rights of citizenship under our hospitable flag, all women still suffer the degradation of disfranchisement.

The history of our country the past hundred years has been a series of assumptions and usurpations of power over woman, in direct opposition to the principles of just government, acknowledged by the United States as its foundation. . . .

And for the violation of these fundamental principles of our government, we arraign our rulers on this Fourth day of July, 1876,—and these are our articles of impeachment:

Bills of attainder have been passed by the introduction of the word "male" into all the State constitutions, denying to women the right of suffrage, and thereby making sex a crime—an exercise of power clearly forbidden in article 1, sections 9, 10, of the United States constitution. . . .

The right of trial by a jury of one's peers was so jealously guarded that States refused to ratify the original constitution until it was guaranteed by the sixth amendment. And yet the women of this nation have never been allowed a jury of their peers—being tried in all cases by men, native, and foreign, educated and ignorant, virtuous and vicious. Young girls have been arraigned in our courts for the crime of infanticide; tried, convicted, hanged—victims, per chance, of judge, jurors, advocates—while no woman's voice could be heard in their defense. . . .

Taxation without representation, the immediate cause of the rebellion of the colonies against Great Britain, is one of the grievous wrongs the women of this country have suffered during the century. Deploring war, with all the demoralization that follows in its train, we have been taxed to support standing armies, with their waste of life and wealth. Believing in temperance, we have been taxed to support the vice, crime and pauperism of the liquor traffic. While we suffer its wrongs and abuses infinitely more than man, we have no power to protect our sons against this giant evil. . . .

Unequal codes for men and women. Held by law a perpetual minor, deemed incapable of self-protection, even in the industries of the world, woman is denied equality of rights. The fact of sex, not the quantity or quality of work, in most cases, decides the pay and position; and because of this injustice thousands of fatherless girls are compelled to choose between a life of shame and starvation. Laws catering to man's vices have created two codes of morals in which penalties are graded according to the political status of the offender. Under such laws, women are fined and imprisoned if found alone in the streets, or in public places of resort, at certain hours. Under the pretense of regulating public morals, police officers seizing the occupants of disreputable houses, march the women in platoons to prison, while the men, partners in their guilt, go free. . . .

Representation of woman has had no place in the nation's thought. Since the incorporation of the thirteen original States, twenty-four have been admitted to the Union, not one of which has recognized woman's right of self-government. On this birthday of our national liberties, July Fourth, 1876, Colorado, like all her elder sisters, comes into the Union with the invidious word "male" in her constitution. . . .

The judiciary above the nation has proved itself but the echo of the party in power, by upholding and enforcing laws that are opposed to the spirit and letter of the constitution. When the slave power was dominant, the Supreme Court decided that a black man was not a citizen, because he had not the right to vote; and when the constitution was so amended as to make all persons citizens, the same high tribunal decided that a woman, though a citizen, had not the right to vote. Such vacillating interpretations of constitutional law unsettle our faith in judicial authority, and undermine the liberties of the whole people.

These articles of impeachment against our rulers we now submit to the impartial judgment of the people. To all these wrongs and oppressions woman has not submitted in silence and resignation. From the beginning of the century, when Abigail Adams, the wife of one president and mother of another, said, "We will not hold ourselves bound to obey laws in which we have no voice or representation," until now, woman's discontent has been steadily increasing, culminating nearly thirty years ago in a simultaneous movement among the women of the nation, demanding the right of suffrage. In making our just demands, a higher motive than the pride of sex inspires us; we feel that national safety and stability depend on the complete recognition of the broad principles of our government. Woman's degraded, helpless position is the weak point in our institutions today; a disturbing force everywhere, severing family ties, filling our asylums with the deaf, the dumb, the blind; our prisons with criminals, our cities with drunkenness and prostitution; our homes with disease and death. It was the boast of the founders of the republic, that the rights for which they contended were the rights of human nature. If these rights are ignored in the case of one-half the people, the nation is surely preparing for its downfall. Governments try themselves. The recognition of a governing and a governed class is incompatible with the first principles of freedom. Woman has not been a heedless spectator of the events of this century, nor a dull listener to the grand arguments for the equal rights of humanity. From the earliest history of our country woman has shown equal devotion with man to the cause of freedom, and has stood firmly by his side in its defense. Together they have made this country what it is. Woman's wealth, thought and labor have cemented the stones of every monument man has reared to liberty.

And now, at the close of a hundred years, as the hour-hand of the great clock that marks the centuries points to 1876, we declare our faith in the principles of self-government; our full equality with man in natural rights; that woman was made first for her own happiness, with the absolute right to herself—to all the opportunities and advantages life affords for her complete development; and we deny that dogma of the centuries, incorporated in the codes of all nations—that woman was made for man—her best interests, in all cases, to be sacrificed to his will. We ask of our rulers, at this hour, no special privileges, no special legislation. We ask justice, we ask equality, we ask that all the civil and political rights that belong to citizens of the United States, be guaranteed to us and our daughters forever.

III

MODERN AMERICA EMERGES

1880–1920

GENDER AND THE
JIM CROW SOUTH

GLENDA GILMORE
Forging Interracial Links
in the Jim Crow South

Anna Julia Cooper—an extraordinary woman in her own right—wrote in 1892, "the colored woman of today . . . is confronted by a woman question and a race problem."* Equality of the sexes, Cooper insisted, would mean that black women should not be passive and subordinate in their relationships with black men; and black men should not criticize women's efforts to obtain equal rights. Equality of the sexes, Cooper continued, meant sharing the leadership burden in the struggle against racism. A remarkable group of African American women did just that.

Part of a small but growing black middle class in the South, they were prepared by education, professional training, and voluntary work to be the vanguard of their race. Following the disfranchisement of black men in the 1890s, they emerged not only as community activists but also as ambassadors to the white community and astute political strategists. Their political skills were put to the test when, during the most racist era in U.S. history, these black women attempted to forge links with elite white women in an interracial movement. At the forefront of the effort was a remarkable North Carolinian, Charlotte Hawkins Brown.

With sensitivity and insight, Glenda Gilmore illuminates Brown's search for fault lines in the system of white supremacy. She also demonstrates just how Brown manipulated class, gender, and even her own identity in the interests of racial justice. In the end, Brown's generation fell short of their goal of racial and sexual equality. The odds against them were overwhelming. In the process, however, they created and nourished a tradition of activism that would emerge with new force and greater success in the 1960s.

Consider Brown's strategy. What were her options? What were the personal costs? Do you agree with Gilmore's characterization of her as a "political genius"?

---

*Anna Julia Cooper, *A Voice from the South by a Black Woman of the South* (Xenia, Ohio: Aldine, 1892), p. 135.

Excerpted from "Forging Interracial Links," ch. 7 of *Gender and Jim Crow: Women and the Politics of White Supremacy in North Carolina, 1896–1920,* by Glenda Elizabeth Gilmore (Chapel Hill: University of North Carolina Press, 1996). Reprinted by permission of the author and publisher. The author has supplied new paragraphs, and renumbered and edited the notes.

In the segregated world of the Jim Crow South, laws told black and white people where to eat and where to sit. Undergirding those laws lay a complex web of custom. Its strands separated the races in places beyond the reach of legislation. Custom dictated, for example, which part of the sidewalk belonged to whites and which to blacks. When whites and blacks sometimes occupied the same space, custom demanded that African Americans behave in a subservient manner. Any breach of these codes by a black person could bring an instant response from a white person: a reprimand, a beating, a jail sentence, or even death at the end of a lyncher's rope.

Whites held two unshakable beliefs that gave them the courage and energy to structure such a complicated society, making good on its rules with violence and even murder. First, whites thought that they acted to protect white women from black men's sexual desires. Second, they firmly believed that African Americans should be excluded from the American democratic system. They spoke freely and acted openly against any extension of political rights to blacks. After the turn of the century, restrictive legislation prevented most southern black men from voting and segregation laws crowded the books. White men considered their work done. Henceforth, they thought, African Americans would be a permanent lower caste in southern society: physically separated and politically powerless.

But the white supremacists did not reckon with black women. From behind the borders of segregation and disfranchisement, African American women became diplomats to the white community. They built social service and civic structures that wrested some recognition and meager services from the expanding welfare state. Ironically, as black men were forced from the political sphere, the functions of government expanded, opening a new space for black women to approach officials as good citizens intent on civic betterment.

One of their political strategies was to build contacts with white women. Meager and unequal as they were, these interracial connections often provided black women access to resources for their families, students, and neighbors. Charlotte Hawkins Brown personified such black women across the South who forged invisible careers in interracial politics.

As president of the North Carolina Association of Colored Women's Clubs, Charlotte Hawkins Brown began to direct African American women's formal civic experiences in the state in 1912 and continued to do so for twenty-five years. . . . No black man could claim prominence to equal hers in . . . the state during the period. Brown's work and racialist ideologies illustrate that the decade before woman suffrage constituted a critical period in defining the boundaries of race relations that would remain in place until the post–World War II era.

Charlotte Hawkins Brown's life also provides a parable of the possibilities and the personal costs of interracial cooperation. Her story is so interwoven with myth—fiction that she fashioned to outmaneuver racism—that it is difficult to separate the reality of her experience from the result of her self-creation. The difference between her lived life and her public persona reveals a great deal about her perception of southern whites' racial ideologies and the points at which she saw possibility. Charlotte Hawkins Brown invented herself, repeatedly and with brilliance, but at great personal cost.[1]

According to her account, she was born in Henderson, North Carolina, in 1883 to Caroline Frances Hawkins, the daughter of Rebecca and Mingo Hawkins. Her father was Edmund H. Hight, from "whom fate separated me at birth" and who "belonged to a family that had grown up on the adjoining plantation."[2] Brown characterized her grandmother, Rebecca Hawkins, as a "fair" woman "with blue eyes," the African American sister of her white master, "a great railroad captain whose vision and foresight built up the great Southern Railroad." Brown cast the white master as the Hawkins family's "protector."[3] About the time of my birth, colored people in large numbers were leaving for parts north," she remembered. Charlotte moved with her mother and brother to Cambridge, Massachusetts, where her mother married and the family lived in a large, handsome house near Harvard University.[4] Caroline Hawkins managed a hand laundry in the basement, and Charlotte attended the public schools of Cambridge. Whisked away from the South at an early age, Charlotte was "not conscious of the difference in color and took part in all the activities of my class."[5] She acquired a New England accent, which she kept all of her life.

Charlotte Hawkins's family insisted that she get a practical education and sent her to

Massachusetts State Normal School in Salem. Alice Freeman Palmer, the wife of a Harvard professor and the first female president of Wellesley College, was a member of the state board of education that oversaw the school. One day a few months before she entered the normal school, as Charlotte Hawkins was pushing a baby carriage while reading a high school Latin textbook, she chanced to meet Palmer on the street. Hawkins was babysitting to raise money for a silk slip to wear under her new organdy graduation dress, but Palmer assumed that she was an impoverished student, overcoming all odds to get an education. Palmer mentioned Hawkins favorably to the principal of her high school when they next met, and the incident ended. Now, when Hawkins realized that Palmer was an overseer of her normal school, she wrote to her and reminded her of their chance meeting. Palmer responded by paying Hawkins's tuition.[6]

Several months before graduation, Charlotte Hawkins met a supervisor from the American Missionary Association (AMA) on a train. The AMA representative impressed upon Hawkins the needs of the South, and Hawkins left school to accept a position at a one-teacher school in Sedalia, North Carolina, near Greensboro in 1901.[7] The AMA funded the school for two years, then withdrew support. For a year, Hawkins drew no salary, and she and the students survived on what they grew, the produce their parents donated, and a $100 county appropriation. Charlotte Hawkins returned to Cambridge and approached Alice Freeman Palmer for financial help, which Palmer promised to consider when she returned from Europe some months later. Palmer died in Europe, however, and Hawkins decided to name the school in her memory. With continuing county support and private contributions, Palmer Memorial Institute taught practical vocational skills to its students, and Hawkins became active in the North Carolina Teachers Association and in women's club work. In 1911, Hawkins married Edward S. Brown. But the marriage lasted only a few months since Edward said he could not remain in Sedalia and be "Miss Hawkins's husband."[8]

In the South, Brown tells us, she demanded the respect of whites and received it from the "quality people." She insisted upon being addressed as "Miss," "Mrs.," or, after she gained honorary degrees, "Doctor."[9] She refused to be Jim Crowed and reported that

several times she was "put out of Pullman berths and seats during all hours of the night." . . . By 1920, with the support of prominent Greensboro whites, Brown built Palmer Memorial Institute into a sprawling complex. She was proud that the most powerful whites in Greensboro served on the Palmer board, including Lula McIver and Julius Cone, head of the huge Cone Mills.[10]

As Brown rendered it, the theme of her life story is challenge met through interracial cooperation. Brown shaped the narrative in two critical ways: she minimized the restrictions of race in her daily life and exaggerated whites' helpfulness at every critical juncture. She obscured the fact that she was illegitimate by making it seem as if her father, Edmund Hight, was separated from the family by slavery. Brown was born in 1883 and had an older brother, demonstrating that her mother had a long-term relationship with Hight. The Hight family continued to live near Henderson throughout the twentieth century. Brown's grandmother, Rebecca Hawkins, may have been the sister of railroad magnate Captain John Hawkins, Jr., but, far from acting as the family's protector, he retained no contact with his black relatives and was a Democrat of the white supremacist persuasion.[11]

Brown mythologized her birth to remind southern whites of slavery's legacy: their shared kinship with African Americans. At the same time, she drew whites as sympathetic figures, the "protectors" of their African American relatives. Such circumstances did exist in the South; they just did not happen to exist within Charlotte's immediate family. As whites created the fictional "good darky" who treasured the interpersonal relationships that sprang from the close association of whites and blacks during slavery, Brown created a fictional "good master" who realized the responsibilities of miscegenation and loved his family, white and black. She used this good master to assuage whites' guilt about slavery and to argue that even slaves and masters achieved interracial understanding. She did not have to fight whites who melded ancestral ties to romantic class mythologies; she could simply join them. She shared their aristocratic roots.

Brown had moved to Cambridge not "about the time of my birth" but at the age of six. Yet she claimed to have no memory of her early life in North Carolina, no first-hand recollection of discrimination against blacks in the South, indeed no racial consciousness while growing up, even though she spent a great deal of time in the South during her childhood, even entire summers. Brown remade herself as a New Englander. When asked how her name should appear on her high school diploma, she instantly dropped her North Carolina name—Lottie Hawkins— for the more genteel sounding "Charlotte Eugenia Hawkins," which she made up on the spot. She spoke in a manner that "combine[d] the mellow tones of the southern Negro and the quick clipped qualities of New England— people turn[ed] around to see who [was] speaking."[12]

By casting herself as a New Englander, Brown attempted to remain above the southern racial structure. In Greensboro, she occupied a place much like that of African diplomats to the United States—she was an exotic but North Carolina's own exotic. If whites accused her of being an outside agitator, Brown could fall back on her North Carolina roots. Then she presented herself as native stock, a female, black Ulysses who fought her way back to the South and to her own people, where she belonged.

The story of the AMA's dispatch of Charlotte Hawkins to the South to save her people competes with another, more complicated parable that Brown merely hinted at and may have consciously avoided dwelling upon. Rather than seeing herself as a New England missionary to a foreign place, Brown may have construed her return to North Carolina as coming to terms with the realities of race in her own life. One night at a Cambridge meeting, she watched magic lantern slides of the race work being done by African Americans in the South. She was particularly struck by two educators, Joseph Price, the founder of Livingstone College, and Lucy Laney, the founder of Haines Institute in Augusta, Georgia. She noted that both Price and Laney were, like herself, very dark skinned. Price and Laney were also brilliant, and their faces on the screen moved Brown to feel that there was a place where she might belong: the South.[13] Brown never acknowledged publicly that she had any personal reason for wanting to leave New England, choosing rather to emphasize the missionary aspect of her return.

As the years passed, accounts of the relationship between Alice Freeman Palmer and Brown made it seem as if Palmer had sent Brown to the South to found the school and that they had enjoyed a close friendship. . . . Contemporary newspaper accounts, which relied on Brown's own promotional material, reported that Palmer's "efforts" had made the school possible and "until her death she was an ardent supporter of her namesake."[14]

Although Brown did not actually lie about Palmer's interest in her and the school, she embroidered the truth. Brown and Palmer spent less than fifteen minutes together in their lifetimes, and Palmer never promised that she would personally contribute to the school. Instead, Palmer had told Brown upon their second meeting that she was too busy at the moment but that after her return from Europe she would contact friends in Boston to encourage them to support the school. Why, then, when Palmer never returned, did Brown name the school Palmer Memorial Institute? Actually, Brown originally named the school Alice Freeman Palmer Settlement in order to gain support from Palmer's friends in Boston.[15] Palmer, after a brilliant career, had died at a young age and was mourned by her friends, and a memorial to her could prompt contributions. . . .

Around 1910, Brown cannily began to play southern pride against northern dollars when she inspired white leaders in Greensboro to challenge their community to take over the financial support of Palmer.[16] In soliciting southern white support, Brown . . . most often called the school Sedalia rather than Palmer. For example, Brown named the group of students who sang African American spirituals the Sedalia Singers.[17] She understood the white southerners' sense of place, and since her school was the only thing in the crossroads of Sedalia, she did not encroach upon white territory in appropriating the name. The location of Palmer at Sedalia facilitated support from Greensboro whites. It was ten miles outside of the city, surrounded by sparsely populated farmland. Brown never permitted Palmer students to travel alone to Greensboro but instead brought them as a group, with the boys clad in coats and ties and the girls wearing hats and white gloves. Once in the city, they did not mingle with Greensboro's African Americans; rather, Brown negotiated special seating sections for her students at public events.[18]

Although Brown cloaked the curriculum at Palmer in vocational disguises and portrayed it to the press as an industrial school until the late 1930s, the institute offered mostly academic courses from its inception.[19] Booker T. Washington met Brown on a trip to Boston while she was still a student there and pronounced her "the only convert that he made in New England." If he believed her to be a convert, she outfoxed the Wizard himself.[20] . . . Brown never embraced Washington's vocational philosophy past the point of providing for the school's basic needs, but she portrayed the school as industrial, detailing "farm yields" in fund-raising letters.[21] An unidentified Palmer teacher explained the ruse this way: "[Brown] always had a college preparatory class . . . a cultural academic school. All the Negroes had to have that in order to get along in the South." Even though this teacher believed, along with Brown, that African Americans profited most from classical knowledge coupled with reinforcement of middle-class values, support for that sort of training did not exist. So Brown and her teachers positioned Palmer as a "vocational" school. Funding for industrial education "could always get through," the teacher recalled. Despite the vocational exterior, she continued, "you could teach anything you wanted when you got in your school. You came inside your class room and you taught them Latin and French and all the things you knew."[22] Although initially Brown's students were the poor children of the neighborhood, by 1920, Palmer functioned as an academic boarding school that drew students from counties across the state and included secondary grades.[23]

Notwithstanding her vocal cover, at times Brown argued that her approach to "cultural" instruction benefited whites as well as African Americans. She explained, "Recognizing the need of a cultural approach to life, believing absolutely in education through racial contacts, I have devoted my whole life to establish for Negro youth something superior to Jim Crowism." She tried to accomplish this "by bringing the two races together under the highest cultural environment that will increase race pride, mutual respect, confidence, sympathetic understanding, and interracial goodwill."[24]

Why did Brown repeatedly overdraw white understanding and support and minimize the restrictions that her color placed on her? Throughout her life, she operated by a simple rule: it is better to overestimate possibility than to underestimate it. Charlotte Hawkins Brown created a fictional mirror of civility in race relations and held it up to whites as a reflection of their better selves. From slavery, she drew compassion; from the loneliness of Cambridge, racial liberality among her schoolmates; from Alice Freeman Palmer's deferral, a legacy; and from frightened, pinched southern whites, chivalry of a sort. Brown was a political genius, especially suited for interracial work. Her renderings served her own purposes, but she did not . . . delude herself into thinking that they were true. Immune to her own romantic stories, Brown was the consummate pragmatist. So convinced was she of her mission and of her opponent's rigid character, that she could risk the heartbreak of gilding the lily. She expected nothing, received little, and turned that pittance into bounty.

But Charlotte Hawkins Brown was a double agent. When she refused to turn her head toward the "colored" waiting room, she must have felt the stares of its patrons burn into her consciousness. In the decade preceding 1920, Brown immersed herself in social welfare projects and political activity that she kept hidden from whites. After 1920, Brown acquired a national reputation for her interracial work and landed official positions in interracial organizations, success that brought her activities under public scrutiny. Until then, and thereafter when she could, Brown generally said one thing to whites and then did another if it suited her purposes.

Brown's double life left its mark on her. . . . Living her life as a diplomat to the white community, Brown could never be just Lottie Hawkins. African American women who chose to take up interracial work walked a tightrope that required them to be forever careful, tense, and calculating. One slip would end their careers; they worked without nets.

In Lula Martin McIver, Brown found an exception to her belief that the southern white woman stood at the center of the race "problem." Their first meeting represents a classic case of the Brown treatment. Constantly seeking funds for Palmer Memorial Institute, Brown decided in the spring of 1905 that she must approach prominent white men in Greensboro for support. In Greensboro, Brown had no magic key such as Alice Freeman Palmer's name. Sedalia was a crossroads, Palmer Institute tiny, and Brown unknown. She had no historic connections to white North Carolinians there, no reputation in the black community, no denominational bridge since she had converted to Congregationalism, a faith rare in the South among either African Americans or whites. She had only herself—the New England persona she so carefully cultivated—and courage.

In 1904, she had written a poignant letter to Charles McIver, president of the white women's normal college in Greensboro. It began, "This letter may come to you from a strange source, but it comes from one whose heart is in the educational and moral uplift of our people." It concluded by begging McIver to come to Palmer for a visit. A year later, Brown was still imploring him to the same end, touting the ease of the train ride and signing herself "Very Anxiously Yours."[25] Still McIver did not come. One morning Brown dressed carefully in her customary ankle-length dress, hat, and white gloves and set out to call on him in Greensboro. She had no appointment. Most often Brown did not write or telephone ahead and risk refusal from those she wished to meet but simply appeared on their doorstep. That morning she knocked on the front door of the president's residence and found that he was away. His wife, Lula Martin McIver, invited Brown in, an unusual act in itself. Lula McIver was stunned by Brown's appearance at the door. "Her daring, her enthusiasm, her faith intrigued me," McIver recalled. The two women talked for over an hour and warmed toward each other. Soon, McIver was advising Brown on "the best way to win friends" and on how to raise money among the Greensboro elite for the school.[26]

When Lula McIver opened the door, Brown chanced upon a valuable connection that would prove enduring. Brown sat in the parlor of the state's foremost white female educational advocate. Graduated from the Moravian academy in Salem, Lula Martin had longed to become a doctor like her father. After she learned that the profession was virtually closed to women, she became an outspoken feminist. As an adolescent, she abandoned the Moravians for the Methodists upon reading that the early Moravian settlers chose wives by lottery. In 1885, strong-willed Lula Martin met Charles Duncan McIver, a dedicated young teacher, who supported her feminist ideas and called her a "most sensible" woman. They married in a ceremony that omitted the word "obey," and Lula refused a wedding ring, which she regarded as a "badge of slavery."[27]

The McIvers worked to build North Carolina's white public educational system one school at a time. While Charles traveled throughout the state promoting grade school education, Lula served as his advance team, preceding him to scrub courthouse venues speckled with tobacco juice, to set up chairs, to post flyers, and to raise a crowd. She was delighted when Charles became first president of the state-supported normal school for white women since both felt that educating women would be the key to building an effective public school system. She helped to found the Woman's Association for the Betterment of Public School Houses, and after Charles's death, she accepted a paying position as its field secretary.[28]

The subtleties of Lula McIver's racial ideology are elusive, but at the center of her thinking about race lay the strongly held belief that African Americans deserved a good education. For nearly a half century after they met, McIver continually raised money for Palmer Memorial Institute. Lula McIver attended meetings of black women's clubs in Greensboro. After the early death of Charles McIver in 1909, and to the eternal perplexity of Greensboro whites, each semester Lula McIver invited a male African American student from nearby North Carolina Agricultural and Technical College to board in the president's residence where she lived until her death. There, surrounded by young white women students, Lula McIver offered an object lesson in race relations.[29]

Both Brown and McIver realized the restrictions on their relationship in the Jim Crow South. For starters, McIver was a woman and thus not powerful in her own right. Moreover, as the normal school's maternal figurehead, she had to act circumspectly since all of her actions reflected upon the school, which was still in the minds of some a dangerous experiment that wasted state money to educate women. Given these restrictions, McIver could do three concrete things for Brown: influence prominent white Greensboro men to support her, introduce leading club women to Palmer's mission, and raise money. She did another intangible and invaluable thing for Brown: Lula McIver publicly referred to Charlotte Hawkins Brown as her friend.[30]

It appears that Lula McIver realized that her husband's influence would be more valuable than her own, and she urged Charles to write an "open letter of endorsement" for Palmer Memorial Institute shortly after she met Brown. Since Charles McIver served on the Southern Education Board, his vote of confidence carried weight in the North as well as the South. The letter went out in June 1905, but Charles McIver admitted in it that he had never been to Palmer.[31] He died four years later. Long after that, Brown named Charles D. McIver as her "first friend" in North Carolina.[32] There is no record that McIver ever made the trip to Sedalia or that Brown ever met him. With Lula McIver's help, Brown appropriated the memory of Charles McIver as she had that of Alice Freeman Palmer.

Local support of Palmer flowered around 1914 when Lula McIver brought a delegation of white women from across the state to visit the school. A member of the delegation wrote an account of the visit that appeared in the *Greensboro Daily Record* and encouraged white women to take an interest in Brown's work. Brown struck just the right note in her solicitation letter: Palmer, she said, "has conducted its work for the past 13 years without seeking very much help from our southern friends." She claimed friendship and a debt come due in the same breath.[33] The 1914 campaign was the beginning of a steady stream of white visitors to the school and financial support from white North Carolinians.[34] In 1917, Lula McIver conducted some of Greensboro's leading white businessmen on a tour of the school. Many of the men who had ignored Brown's previous appeals converted after that visit. E. P. Wharton recalled that Charlotte Brown had called on him around 1903 to obtain support for Palmer and that he was "ashamed of [him]self for losing sight" of Brown's work. He subsequently served for decades as a Palmer trustee. By 1920, the board of Palmer Memorial Institute included a Greensboro attorney, a banker, and an industrial magnate.[35] McIver sought no publicity for a trip she made to Boston with Charlotte Hawkins Brown two years later. There McIver called upon prominent white women, vouched for Brown's success, and asked for contributions to Palmer. When northern white women visited Palmer, they would not spend the night at the black school but stayed instead with Lula McIver.[36]

In 1919, Charlotte Hawkins Brown, with the endorsement of Lula McIver, published a remarkable novel, *Mammy*. On its face, the appearance of *Mammy* places Brown squarely in the accommodationist camp of African Americans, currying favor from whites by invoking the ties of slavery. The story tells of a loving black woman who nurses a white family and raises its children. Then, when the woman becomes old and ill, the family provides no help beyond an occasional visit to her drafty log cabin. Ultimately, they stand by as Mammy goes to the county home. Brown dedicated the book to "my good friend, Mrs. Charles Duncan McIver." She continued, "It is with gratitude I acknowledge her personal interest in the colored members of her household."[37]

What could Brown have hoped to accomplish by the publication of *Mammy*? At the time, she served as president of the statewide Association of Colored Women's Clubs, refused Jim Crow seating, and was secretly organizing a campaign to interest the state's black women in woman suffrage. She had spent almost twenty years building her dignity in North Carolina. It was amazing that she would play the *Mammy* card now. A close reading of Brown's introduction and McIver's response to the dedication indicates that both saw *Mammy* as a tool to promote their agenda: interracial cooperation among women. Mammies represented the one point of contact between southern black and white women, and white women continually bragged about their love for their Mammies. But Brown's *Mammy* is not a tale of love rewarded; it is an indictment of white neglect of African Americans. Brown calls upon white women to remember their duty to black women and redefines that duty in new ways. It is no longer enough to be fond of ol' Mammy; white women must act on that affection.

McIver framed her endorsement of *Mammy* carefully. She said that today's white woman was not the person her mother was, for in her mother's day, there was "understanding and sympathy" between the races. The problem was the separation of the races since there could be no racial harmony without "knowledge of each other's problems and an active interest in solving them." McIver endorsed the concept of "racial integrity" but reminded white southerners that their "task [was the] training of the uncivilized African." Brown must have winced at that remark, but it preceded McIver's most important statement: "I verily believe that to the most intelligent southern white women we must look for leadership in keeping our 'ship of state' off the rocks of racial antagonism." She signed the piece, "Your friend, Lula Martin McIver."[38]

Interracial cooperation, association among black and white women to solve mutual problems, was the solution that *Mammy* endorsed. McIver did not propose that white women individually care for their mammies but that they enter the public sphere and provide leadership. Male sailors had steered the ship of state onto rocky racial shores. It was time for women to man the lifeboats and rescue government from the oppressive racial politics of the white supremacists. In the same month that *Mammy* appeared, the state's white and black women began to do just that by traveling to Memphis, Tennessee, for a formal interracial summit. The state associations of women's clubs and the YWCAs sent forth those first intrepid female navigators.

Most of the black women who traveled to the Memphis interracial summit learned leadership skills in the National Association of Colored Women, but their experience in working with white women had come from two other sources as well: heretofore racially segregated groups that came together on the homefront in World War I and the interracial work of the Young Women's Christian Association (YWCA). During World War I organizational lines between women's groups of both races blurred when the Council of National Defense chose white women from each southern state to head committees to coordinate work on the homefront. In North Carolina, white women set up integrated county councils that included African American and white women, carefully chosen to represent clubs, YWCAs, and denominational social service programs.[39]

The work of the black YWCA centered on another upheaval of the time: African American migration from farm to town. Southern black women believed strongly in the YWCA's ability to reach poor young women who had moved to the city to find work. The national YWCA board determined that any southern African American branch must be supervised by an existing "central" YWCA. "Central" meant white. Once founded, the black YWCA must be overseen by a management committee of three white women and two black women. The rules mandated interracial "cooperation" of a sort. Despite these humiliating restrictions, two southern black women, Mary McCrorey of Charlotte, North Carolina, and Lugenia Burns Hope of Atlanta, founded Ys in their cities.[40]

On the train to Memphis, a group of white men pulled Brown out of the Pullman car and marched her past "southern white women passing for Christians" who were on their way to the Memphis meeting. The white women sat silent as the men forced Brown to the Jim Crow car.[41] Brown probably recognized among the fellow Memphis delegates North Carolina white women whom she had come to know over the past decade. Among them was the wife of the governor, Fanny Bickett. . . .

When Brown rose to address the white women, the frustration of a decade of interracial work erupted, and she shared the humiliation of being ousted from the Pullman car two nights before. She exhorted white women to fight lynching, to recognize the dignity of the African American woman, and to help black women. Brown ended on an ominous note: "You are going to reach out for the same hand that I am reaching out for but I know that the dear Lord will not receive it if you are crushing me beneath your feet."[42] Most of the white women were profoundly moved.

As it happened, the women's Memphis interracial meeting foundered on the spot that Lula McIver had warned of in *Mammy*: the shoal of politics. Two months before the meeting, a federal amendment had mandated woman suffrage and a month after the meeting women would vote for the first time. Just before Brown left for Tennessee, she had been secretly organizing black women in North Carolina to register to vote. One faction of black women would not budge on the issue of suffrage at the Memphis meeting. A full year later, the white and black women still had not agreed on a statement of goals for an interracial movement. Brown, McCrorey, and Hope favored a version that included the controversial demand for protection of African American voting rights. Their language was blunt: "We believe that the ballot is the safe-guard of the Nation and that every citizen in the Nation should have the right to use it. We believe that if there is ever to be any justice before the law, the Negro must have the right to exercise the vote."[43] But the white women balked at the suffrage statement and the condemnation of lynching, both points "which the Negro women dared not leave out."[44] Whites suggested the wording, "We believe that the ballot is the safe-guard of the Nation, and that every *qualified* citizen in the Nation should have the right to use it."[45]

Interracial cooperation led straight into politics. As black and white women inched toward cooperation on a grass roots level, they came face-to-face with larger political forces. With a decade of women's interracial experience behind them, many African American women believed that the time had come to take a firm stand on suffrage. Black women looked to their white allies to support their right to vote, a gesture that underscores the success of interracial cooperation. Yet white women's confusion over black women's suffrage reveals the limits of voluntary interracial work. Upon the passage of woman suffrage, white women involved with interracial social service projects had to chose between gender and race. They could support black women's right to vote as women, or oppose their right to vote as *black* women. Charlotte Hawkins Brown called the question when she used the NACW to organize black women's voter registration drives in urban areas in the fall of 1920. Across the South, other black women did the same thing, reporting back to the National Association for the Advancement of Colored People (NAACP).

In Mobile, Alabama, registrars told black women that they must own property to vote, and when the black juvenile court officer challenged them, court officials fired her.[46] From Birmingham came the news that when a black teacher attempted to register, the registrar "called her an ugly name and ordered her out." Another teacher "answered every question asked her—ex post facto law, habeas corpus proceedings, etc." The frustrated registrar still would not yield and "tore up her card and threw it in her face."[47] Ultimately, in Birmingham, 225 black women succeeded in registering, although 4,500 made the attempt.[48]

It is impossible to judge Charlotte Hawkins Brown's success in the North Carolina registration campaign. Most registration books failed to survive, but those that exist show not only that black women succeeded in urban areas, but that voter registration increased for black men as well. Probably less than 1,000 black women registered in North Carolina that fall.[49] To judge the results of black women's drive for suffrage, however, one must look not just at the few thousand who managed to register in 1920, but at the heritage of interracial work upon which they built and at the example they set for those who followed. The number of black women who voted in 1920 may have

been small, but their significance in the South's racial politics was large. For the first time since the nineteenth century in the South, black voters approached the registrars en masse. They assembled as the result of a coordinated, subversive campaign that crossed over the boundaries of voluntary interracial work to reintroduce black civil rights in electoral politics. By their presence at the polls, black women dared whites to use violence and won the dare. In 1921, white supremacy still stood, but black women had found faultlines in its foundations.

NOTES

1. Ceci Jenkins, incomplete notes for "The Twig Bender of Sedalia" ([1946]), unpublished biography of Charlotte Hawkins Brown, reel 1, #12, Brown Collection, Manuscript Collection, Schlesinger Library (SL). See also Stephen Birmingham, *Certain People: America's Black Elite* (Boston: Little, Brown, 1977).

2. "A Biography," reel 1, and "Some Incidents in the Life and Career of Charlotte Hawkins Brown Growing out of Racial Situations, at the Request of Dr. Ralph Bunche," reel 1, #2, both in Brown Collection, SL.

3. "Some Incidents," 1–2, reel 1, #2, ibid.

4. "A Biography," reel 1, ibid. The language of "A Biography" is closely echoed in Sadie L. Daniel, *Women Builders* (Washington, D.C.: Associated Publishers, 1970), 133–63.

5. "A Biography," 13, reel 1, Brown Collection, SL.

6. On Palmer, see Ruth B. Bordin, *Alice Freeman Palmer: The Evolution of a New Woman* (Ann Arbor: University of Michigan Press, 1993). On the Brown/Palmer relationship, see "A Biography," 16–18, reel 1, and Jenkins, "Twig Bender of Sedalia," reel 1, #7, both in Brown Collection, SL.

7. Daniel, *Women Builders*, 139; "A Biography," 19, reel 1, Brown Collection, SL.

8. Charlotte E. Hawkins to Dr. Buttrick, 31 Aug. 1904, folder 1005, box 111, series 1, subseries 1, General Education Board Collection, RAC. Mary Grinnell to Charlotte Hawkins Brown, 4 Oct. 1910, 8 Feb. 1911; H. F. Kimball to Charlotte Hawkins Brown, 12 June 1911; and J. G. Bright to Charlotte Hawkins Brown, 1 Aug. 1911, all on reel 2, #33; Mary T. Grinnell to Charlotte Hawkins Brown, 6 Aug. 1912, 17 Feb. 1913, reel 2, #34; and Charlotte Hawkins Brown Ebony Questionnaire, 16, reel 1, #11, all in Brown Collection, SL.

9. Brown wrote that it was a "big surprise" that the white people in the South refused to "use the term 'Miss'" when they addressed black women. She continued, "Naturally I was constantly being insulting and insulted which merited for me the name 'Yankee Huzzy.'" See "Some Incidents," 5, reel 1, #2, Brown Collection, SL. Leading whites in Greensboro referred to her as "Dr. Brown" after she received honorary degrees from Wilberforce, Lincoln, and Howard universities. See Junius Scales to Glenda Gilmore, 4 Jan. 1990, in author's possession.

10. Letterhead, Palmer Memorial Institute, C. Hawkins Brown to W. E. B. Dubois [sic], to June 1930, W. E. B. Du Bois Papers, reel 33, University of Massachusetts, Amherst.

11. Ruth Anita Hawkins Hughes, *Contributions of Vance County People of Color* (Raleigh: Sparks Press, 1988).

12. Jenkins, "Twig Bender of Sedalia," 1, reel 1, #7, Brown Collection, SL.

13. Ibid., insert B; "Some Incidents," 9, reel 1, #2, Brown Collection, SL.

14. Eva M. Young, "Palmer Memorial Institute Unique," *Charlotte Observer*, 10 Mar. 1940, folder 51, box 94–3, ibid.

15. Jenkins, "Twig Bender of Sedalia," E.F. 16, reel 1, #7, Brown Collection, SL.

16. Ibid., E.F. 16, E.F. 17; "Some Incidents," reel 1, #2, Brown Collection, SL.

17. For an example of the conflation of Sedalia and Palmer Institute, see *Palmer Memorial Institute: The Mission and the Legacy* (Greensboro: Women of Greensboro, [1981]).

18. The description here is from interviews and conversations with Dawn Gilmore, Brooks Gilmore, and Lois MacKenzie, the author's aunt, uncle, and mother, respectively. The author's grandfather, Clyde Manly Gilmore, was Brown's physician, and the author's mother, MacKenzie, was her attorney's secretary in the 1950s.

19. Brown transformed the institute in the late 1930s into a preparatory school for upper-class African Americans. By 1940, the school letterhead read: "The Charm School Idea of the Palmer Memorial Institute, Charlotte Hawkins Brown, President and Promoter." See C. Hawkins Brown to My Dear Friend, 20 Mar. 1940, folder 124, box 112–4, Washington Conservatory of Music Records, Moorland-Spingarn Research Center, Howard University (MRSC).

20. Jenkins, "Twig Bender of Sedalia," insert G, reel 1, #7, Brown Collection, SL.

21. Charlotte Hawkins Brown to Wallace Buttrick, 19 Dec. 1912, folder 1005, box 111, series 1, subseries 1, General Education Board Collection, Rockefeller Archive Center (RAC).

22. "Charlotte Hawkins Brown," Dannett Collection, uncataloged, LC. See also Sylvia G. L. Dannett, *Profiles of Negro Womanhood* (New York: M. W. Lads, 1964–66), 59–63. The notes for Dannett's biographical sketches often do not identify the interviewee and are fragmentary.

23. Map, "Palmer Memorial Institute—Sedalia—Enrol[l]ment—1920–1921," folder 1006, box 111, series 1, subseries 1, General Education Board Collection, RAC.

24. "Some Incidents," reel 1, #2, Brown Collection, SL.

25. Board, 1904, Correspondence G-M, box 14, and C. E. Hawkins to Dr. McIver, 13 Apr. 1905, file Southern Education Board, 1905, Correspondence, E–L, box 15, both in Charles D. McIver Collection, University Archives, Walter Clinton Jackson Library, University of North Carolina, Greensboro (WCJL).

26. Mrs. Charles D. McIver to editor of *Greensboro Daily News*, [ca. 1940], reel 1, #13, and Jenkins, "Twig Bender of Sedalia," reel 1, #7, both in Brown Collection, SL.

27. Rose Howell Holder, *McIver of North Carolina* (Chapel Hill: University of North Carolina Press, 1917), 63–67. See also Virginia T. Lathrop, "Mrs. McIver Believes Greatness of the Past Holds State's Hope for Present and Future," *News and Observer*, 6 Oct. 1940, Clipping File, vol. 94, reel 24, 371–72, North Carolina Collection, University of North Carolina, Chapel Hill (NCC).

28. James Leloudis, "'A More Certain Means of Grace': Pedagogy, Self, and Society in North Carolina, 1880–1920" (Ph.D. diss., University of North Carolina at Chapel Hill, 1989), and Pamela Dean, "Covert Curriculum: Class and Gender in a New South Women's College" (Ph.D. diss., University of North Carolina at Chapel Hill, 1995). On the association, see James Leloudis, "School Reform in the New South: The Woman's Association for the Betterment of Public School Houses in North Carolina, 1902–1919," *Journal of American History* 69 (March 1983): 886–909. See also Lula Martin McIver to Charles L. Coon, 4 Feb. 1909, folder 28, box 2, and Lula Martin McIver to Charles L. Coon, 25 Jan. 1910, folder 29, box 2, both in Coon Papers, Southern Historical Collection, University of North Carolina, Chapel Hill (SHC).

29. Sallie Waugh McBryan to Mrs. McIver, 22 Nov. 1913, file Correspondence, 1909–44, box 141, Lula Martin McIver Collection, WCJL; "Famous Landmark at WCUNC Razed," *Durham Morning Herald*, 26 Oct. 1952, Clipping File, vol. 94, reel 24, 343–44, NCC.

30. Lula Martin McIver to Charlotte Hawkins Brown, 6 Apr. 1920, reel 2, #41, Brown Collection, SL.

31. Charles D. McIver letter, 5 June 1905, reel 2, #30, Correspondence, 1902–6, ibid.

32. "Award Will Go to Dr. Brown," *Greensboro Daily News*, 10 Apr. 1947, Clipping File, vol. 18, reel 5, 239, NCC.

33. C. Hawkins Brown to My dear Sir [Professor Julius I. Foust], 25 May 1914, file General Correspondence, 1913–15, box 57, Foust Collection, WCJL.

34. Jenkins, "Twig Bender of Sedalia," 77, reel 1, #12, Brown Collection, SL.

35. E. P. Wharton to Charlotte Hawkins Brown, 12 Jan. 1917, reel 2, #37, Jan.–Apr. 1917; Mrs. Charles D. McIver to editor of *Greensboro Daily News*, n.d., reel 1 #13; and Jenkins, "Twig Bender of Sedalia," 78, reel 1, #12, all in Brown Collection, SL.

36. H. F. Kimball to Charlotte Hawkins Brown, 6 Nov. 1916, reel 2, #36, 1916, and "Notes," copy of notebook maintained by Charlotte Hawkins Brown, reel 1, #8, both in Brown Collection, SL; Annie L. Vickery to My Dear Mrs. McIver, 7 Mar. 1917, file Correspondence, 1909–44, box 141, Lula Martin McIver Collection, WCJL.

37. Charlotte Hawkins Brown, *Mammy* (Boston: Pilgrim Press, 1919).

38. Lula Martin McIver to Charlotte Hawkins Brown, 6 Apr. 1920, reel 2, #41, Brown Collection, SL.

39. Laura Holmes Reilley to D. H. Hill, 18 Oct. 1917, file Women's Committee, box 30, North Carolina Council of Defense, World War I Papers, 1903–33, pt. 2, Military Collection, North Carolina Department of Archives and History.

40. Mary J. McCrorey to Mrs. Hope, 7 May 1920; "Mrs. Hope of the Cleveland Meeting, 1920," 29 May 1920; "What the Colored Women Are Asking of the

Y.W.C.A."; "To the National Board of the Young Women's Christian Association"; Minutes of the Cleveland Meeting, 1920; "Minutes of the meeting held in the offices of the South Atlantic Field Committee, Richmond, Virginia, 3 July 1920"; and Mary J. McCrorey to Mrs. Hope, 27 Jan. 1921, all in box 5, NU 14-C-5, Y.W.C.A., Neighborhood Union Papers, Special Collections, Robert Woodruff Library, Atlanta University, Atlanta, Georgia. Mary J. McCrorey to Charlotte Hawkins Brown, 2 Apr. 1920, reel 2, #41, Brown Collection, SL.

41. Jacquelyn Dowd Hall, *Revolt against Chivalry: Jessie Daniel Ames and the Women's Campaign against Lynching,* rev. ed. (New York: Columbia University Press, 1987), 93; "Some Incidents," reel 1, #2, Brown Collection, SL.

42. Brown address, folder 1, box 1, ibid.; Hall, *Revolt against Chivalry,* 93–94.

43. "First Draft," section 2, folder 1, box 1, ibid.

44. "Statement of Negro Women in Session, Mar. 26, 1921," folder 1, box 1.

45. Folder 1, box 1, ibid. (emphasis added).

46. W. E. Morton to NAACP, file Voting, 10–30 Nov. 1920, C284, National Association for the Advancement of Colored People Papers, Library of Congress.

47. H. M. Kingsley to NAACP, 9 Nov. 1920, file Voting, 1–9 Nov. 1920, C284, NAACP Papers.

48. Charles McPerson to NAACP, file Voting, 1–9 Nov. 1920, C284, NAACP Papers. For a summary of reports from across the South, see "Disfranchisement of Colored Americans in the Presidential Election of 1920" ([1920]), file Voting, Dec. 1920, C284, NAACP Papers.

49. Glenda E. Gilmore, *Gender and Jim Crow: Women and the Politics of White Supremacy in North Carolina, 1896–1920* (Chapel Hill: University of North Carolina Press, 1996), 219–224.

KIM E. NIELSEN
The Southern Identity of Helen Keller

Although Helen Keller is widely regarded as a "national icon representing the triumphs of the disabled," Kim E. Nielsen urges us to understand Keller in a more complex way by acknowledging that her regional background and racial identity shaped her life. In other words, Nielsen offers an intersectional analysis, analyzing how being white, southern, middle-class, and gendered female affected Keller's experience with disability. The author keeps in play many dimensions of Keller's life: her spirituality, her relationships with her parents, her activism (national and international), her geographic comings and goings, and her reading. Nielsen also helps us imagine what it might have been like for a displaced southerner like Keller to read *Gone with the Wind* the year it came out. Compare this with your own encounters with Margaret Mitchell's novel and the movie based on it.

Does Nielsen's portrayal of Keller change the ways you think about her? What do you see as the significance of her southern background? Why is Keller's whiteness important to understanding her identity?

Though Helen Keller left her parents' home in Tuscumbia, Alabama, at the young age of eight, the culture, people, and sensory adventures of her native state were essential to her outlook throughout her life. The deaf-blind activist, author, and world traveler, born in 1880, considered Ivy Green, her family's Tuscumbia home, as her own. Beginning in her lifetime and continuing today, Tuscumbia and Alabama have similarly regarded her as their own—even featuring her on the 2003 state quarter. Keller was also a child of the broader South. Though after her initial departure she always lived outside the region, her southern childhood and

Excerpted from "The Southern Ties of Helen Keller," *Journal of Southern History* 73:4 (November 2007): 783–806, by Kim E. Nielsen. Reprinted by permission of the author and publisher. Notes have been edited and renumbered.

family ties formed and constituted vital elements of her public and private identity. She claimed this identity fondly but frequently labeled as shameful the dominant southern racial ideologies and practices.

Paradoxically, it was perhaps Keller's disability that provided the opportunities that most frequently caused her to question southern gender and racial traditions. Her disability took her physically away from the South, as she and her family turned to northern educational institutions with historical ties to abolitionism. Her disability and her politics as an adult separated her from her family ideologically and geographically. Once she became world famous and increasingly active politically, those commenting upon or questioning her political ideas used her southern identity to either praise or deride her and her principles. As she traveled more, claiming global citizenship and analyzing national and world politics, she naturally did so from a base of knowledge and culture built on her southern background. Today, however, Keller is embraced as a national icon representing the triumphs of the disabled. Her image is now divorced from her southern identity. She is viewed as an American, devoid of regional affiliations or associations. In contrast, this essay positions Keller as a southerner of a Confederate family whose background and beliefs helped shape her worldview and her life as a white, southern woman with a disability.[1]

Keller and her family embraced an esteemed southern heritage, which they perhaps regarded as being more illustrious than it really had been. When Keller wrote her autobiography, *The Story of My Life,* in 1903, she described her lineage according to both geography and the Civil War. In this narrative the men served and the women sired. Helen's father, Arthur H. Keller, served as a captain and her maternal grandfather as a brigadier general for the Confederacy. Her paternal grandmother, she noted, was second cousin to Robert E. Lee. Captain Keller edited the Tuscumbia *North Alabamian* for many years and served in the mid-1880s as U.S. marshal for the northern district of Alabama. Through him, the young Helen claimed Alexander Spotswood, a lieutenant governor (and de facto governor) in early-eighteenth-century Virginia, as her great-great-grandfather.[2]

Captain Arthur Keller considered his family to be part of the deserving upper-class white elite. . . . Like many other southern landholding and formerly slaveholding whites, they had lost much of their wealth between 1860 and 1880. At the time of Helen Keller's birth, her family lived on the homestead her grandfather had built and named Ivy Green decades earlier due to the "beautiful English ivy" covering trees and fences. The Kellers were, however, no longer the wealthy family they once were. Moreover, the daily physical labor demanded to sustain the household, even with the aid of the formerly enslaved and their descendants, had surprised and exhausted Helen's young mother, Kate, after she became the second wife of the much older man whom all called Captain Keller.[3]

The young toddler Helen, Kate's first child, became blind and deaf due to an illness at the age of nineteen months. From Ivy Green, Arthur and Kate Keller sought assistance with the child whom they loved but, as she grew older, felt increasingly incapable of parenting. Family members encouraged placing the girl in an asylum or institution.

Talladega, only about 170 miles away from Tuscumbia, hosted both the Alabama School for the Deaf (founded in 1858) and the Alabama School for the Blind (founded in 1867). While technically separate, the schools had at one point shared a campus and were only blocks apart. Keller would not have been the first deaf-blind student, for another had enrolled as early as 1867. Neither school admitted African Americans.[4] Apparently neither Keller parent considered sending Helen to either of these schools, likely because both institutions had few resources and floundering reputations, having emerged from the Civil War damaged and inadequately funded.

Kate Keller initially refused to send her young child away from home. Like most Americans at that time, she doubted that a deaf-blind child could be educated. As a parent, however, she clearly had hopes for her daughter's life. In the mid-1880s the obviously literate Mrs. Keller read Charles Dickens's *American Notes* (1842) and in it his reference to Laura Bridgman and abolitionist Samuel Gridley Howe, the founder of Boston's Perkins Institution. Bridgman also had lost her sight and hearing at a fairly young age due to illness. Howe's successful effort to teach Bridgman to use the manual alphabet to communicate and perhaps his even greater success at publicizing her had made Howe, Perkins, and Bridgman nearly world famous.[5] Mrs. Keller reasoned that if Bridgman had learned such communication, so might Helen.

Kate Keller's first effort ended after she learned that Howe had died in 1876, but the mother of the young deaf-blind girl persisted. She and her husband tried again, contacting Baltimore oculist Dr. Julian Chisholm. He encouraged them to contact Alexander Graham Bell. . . . Captain Keller traveled by train first to Baltimore and then to Washington, D.C., with the six-year-old and apparently very unruly Helen in order to consult with both doctors personally. Bell recommended that the Kellers seek assistance for their daughter from the Perkins Institution, . . . [then directed by Howe's] son-in-law, Michael Anagnos. For Bell the school where the by-then-elderly Laura Bridgman still lived was the only logical place to seek an education for Helen.[6]

Southerners often looked at educational institutions for deaf and blind children with suspicion because of the linkage between educational reformers and abolitionism. Despite this source of doubt, Keller's parents were not alone as they turned to northern educational institutions. Southern whites with resources tended to send deaf or blind children to schools in the North. Northern educational institutions had stronger reputations, greater fiscal resources, enhanced international ties, and more highly educated teachers than did those in the South.[7]

In July 1886 Arthur Keller allowed his concern for his daughter to trump his hesitancy about northern educational institutions, and he wrote to Perkins's director. . . . Keller sought a skilled teacher willing to travel to Tuscumbia in order to care for young Helen. Anagnos said his thoughts "almost instinctively turned towards Miss Annie M. Sullivan," who was then summering in Brewster, Massachusetts. He recommended her "most highly and without any reservation." After exchanges of letters in numerous directions, Captain Keller agreed to Sullivan as an appropriate teacher and assured Anagnos that she would be treated "as one of our immediate family." He would pay her twenty-five dollars per month, a significant salary.[8]

The Keller family knew relatively little about Anne Sullivan. As the 1886 valedictorian of Perkins, she had given an address described . . . as "a beautiful original production, teeming with felicitous thoughts clothed in a graceful style."[10] Anagnos likely thought of her as a teaching candidate because of her intellectual skills, but he also considered her because she needed employment direly. Sullivan had arrived at Perkins via the almshouse. After the death of her mother and subsequently being deserted by her father, the blind, ten-year-old child of poor Irish immigrants had entered the almshouse of the Massachusetts State Infirmary at Tewksbury. Only by begging an education from touring philanthropists was the child able to enroll at Perkins. Numerous eye operations temporarily improved her eyesight; but her eyes frequently caused her pain, and her vision fluctuated. Despite graduating from Perkins, few respectable or viable employment opportunities existed for the twenty-year-old woman. . . .[9]

In March 1887 Anne Sullivan entered the gardens of Ivy Green with a northern viewpoint as firm as the Keller family's southern identity. . . . Sullivan grew up valorizing several sworn enemies of slavery and the Confederacy. Both Franklin B. Sanborn, who as general state inspector of charities in Massachusetts had enabled her escape from the Tewksbury almshouse, and Samuel Gridley Howe, founder of the Perkins Institution, had conspired as part of John Brown's so-called secret six [Bostonians who funded Brown's plan to start a slave insurrection in Virginia]. In the almshouse and at Perkins she had pored over the Boston *Pilot* (a weekly Irish American newspaper), particularly drawn to its coverage of abolitionist and orator Wendell Phillips. And to what must have been the horror of Captain Keller if he ever found out, Sullivan most favored Major General Benjamin Butler—the (in)famous Union "Beast" of New Orleans, supporter of black military regiments in the Civil War, female suffragist, punisher of the Confederacy, and Massachusetts advocate for the poor. As governor of Massachusetts from 1882 to 1886, he had rigorously investigated the ill treatment of residents at Tewksbury, and Sullivan adored him for it. Though many northerners increasingly "overlooked the history of American slavery" by the 1880s, Sullivan did not do so.[10] . . .

Sullivan purportedly hesitated to even accept employment in the Keller household for fear (correctly) that the family had once owned slaves. Friends warned her that she should "hold my peace while [in the] south, that any reference to conditions before or during the

Civil War would cause my instant dismissal." ... As Sullivan later put it, she "did not like the idea of going south to live in a family that had probably been slave-holders."[11]

The arrival at the segregated Tuscumbia train station of the twenty-one-year-old Boston girl with a lingering Irish accent was novel enough for it to be a community event. A crowd gathered alongside Kate Keller, eagerly awaiting a glimpse of "the Yankee girl who was going to teach the Keller child." And just as the Tuscumbia community had never before encountered anyone like Anne Sullivan, she in turn had never before been to a place like Tuscumbia.[12]

Sullivan's descriptions of her life in Tuscumbia focus almost exclusively either on Helen or on the characteristics that made the region both southern and disagreeable (in her opinion). Her criticisms ranged widely, including the "untidy, shiftless manner of keeping house," "the shabbiness of the grounds and out-houses," and the muddy state of country roads. "Finding it very difficult not to air my righteous indignation," she ignored the advice of her friends and argued the war vigorously with Keller family members, particularly Captain Keller's brother Frank. After one bitter argument with "Uncle Frank"—in which "all the torrents of my wrath broke restraint, and I opened fire, and I did not cease until I had my say out to the last bitter word"—she temporarily packed her carpetbag to leave.[13]

The household in which young Helen grew up and in which Sullivan struggled held a strong Confederate identity. By the time of Keller's birth in 1880, white Alabamians had brutally silenced the discussions of racial equality and freedom formulated during the Civil War. As Sullivan arrived in 1887, white Alabamians were building and observing Lost Cause mythology via memoirs, memorials, parades, the glorification of veterans such as Keller's father, and a widely celebrated statewide public tour by Jefferson Davis. In the words of historian David W. Blight, it was the "diehard era" of the Lost Cause, in which Civil War remembrance became "a lucrative industry."[14] ...

Keller thus grew up embedded in stories of the Old South and shared in the privileges of the Jim Crow "New" South. The household's daily schedule, labor divisions, and balances of power maintained the privileges of whiteness and patriarchy. Like other family members,

Helen Keller, young and disabled though she was, benefited from the system of racial inequalities.

Though deaf-blind and young, by 1887 the seven-year-old girl had already learned how to reinforce racial hierarchies. For example, the child Helen expected her nurse Viny and the household's cook, both African American servants, to serve her. This expectation is reflected unquestioningly in Keller's 1903 autobiography, *The Story of My Life*. Many of her childhood memories centered [on] Martha Washington, "a little coloured girl ... the child of our cook," who accompanied, entertained, and monitored the difficult child. ... As Keller put it unself-consciously, "I seldom had any difficulty in making her do just as I wished. It pleased me to domineer over her, and she generally submitted to my tyranny rather than risk a hand-to-hand encounter." In 1903 Keller attributed her successful dominance to the fact that she was "strong, active, indifferent to consequences," and willing "to fight tooth and nail"—not to her whiteness. Her biographers have generally attributed her violent behavior as a child to her frustration at being unable to communicate. Clearly, however, the young Keller directed her "tyranny" most often at Washington, for whom responding with physical violence held great consequence. Most likely Washington, two or three years older than Keller, respected the violence that the young white child could and did frequently accomplish. Yet Washington also undoubtedly knew that most African American boys and girls like herself were expected to serve white children. For whites, it was a way to care for their own children while indoctrinating black children in service and racial obsequiousness. Keller maintained her tyranny with the threat of personal violence, [an] ... aggression [that] was a part of and enabled by the much larger racial realities of post-Redemption Alabama.[15]

As Keller's knowledge of the world rapidly expanded after Sullivan arrived in 1887, the child also learned more about race and southern racial mores. Early in the educational process Sullivan explained to Keller, in a lesson the teacher considered to be about colors, that Keller was white and the servants black. Keller quickly "concluded that all who occupied a similar menial position were of the same hue." Race determined status. It humored Sullivan that Keller hesitantly replied "blue" when questioned about the "colour of some one whose occupation she did not know."[16]

The contradictory, changing, and sometimes uneasy nature of the lessons of race provided challenges to all involved. By Christmas 1892 the then-twelve-year-old had received substantial monetary gifts and publishing earnings from an article in the magazine *Youth's Companion*. She desired, at least according to Sullivan, to spend some of that money on Christmas presents for "two darkey namesakes." Her father prohibited it. Sullivan, apparently considering herself more racially enlightened (despite the "darkey" language she used), defied Mr. Keller and used her own funds to buy the presents. Sullivan proudly believed that "The servants, and indeed the Negroes generally, are devoted to Helen. Several of them have learned to talk to her and it is touching to see how patient and gentle she is with them always—ever ready with an excuse in explanation of their faults."[17] . . .

Keller's education included not only race but also the more formalized topics of literature, history, science, and religion. Everyone assumed that as a child Helen should learn of God in some way. . . . Sullivan, an alienated and angry Catholic, had little but scorn for religiosity during her early years with Helen in Tuscumbia, but Sullivan felt a . . . responsibility toward responding to Helen's questions truthfully.[18] . . . Keller's parents held other priorities.

Thus, though the daughter of a Presbyterian father and an Episcopalian mother, as a child Keller learned of religion primarily through Sullivan. The overwhelming cultural presence of religion and religiosity made it a topic impossible to avoid. In 1888 a group of Presbyterian clergy, meeting in Tuscumbia, encountered the increasingly famous child. When asked "What do ministers do?" Keller knew enough about organized religion to reply, "They read and talk loud for people to be good." Sullivan wrote privately of the ministers, presumably reflecting her larger attitudes and beliefs about religion, "And thirty such stupid and homely men I have never met before. If they had only been moderately good looking one might excuse the length, logic and nonsense of their fire and brimstone sermons. But being as ugly as it was possible for them to be one felt like saying very disagreeable things about them."[19]

The teacher did her best, but the literature and history she and Helen read, the discussions they had of creation and science, and the people around Keller prompted question after question from the inquisitive child. By early 1890 Sullivan found Keller's questions too much to handle and turned to the assistance of a major Bostonian religious figure, the Reverend Phillips Brooks, the rector of Trinity Church and an Episcopalian preacher at Harvard. . . . Keller and Brooks began a lengthy correspondence, and while in Boston she often met with him. Her parents left no record of their thoughts on their young child's religious inquiry, though it tied her to Boston and New England religiosity. Helen grew extremely fond and appreciative of Brooks. Her parents approved enough of the relationship to bend to eleven-year-old Helen's desire in 1891 to name her new baby brother Phillips Brooks Keller—likely one of the few white Alabamians of the late nineteenth century named after a Boston preacher.[20]

Within a year of her arrival in Tuscumbia, the forceful Sullivan persuaded Keller's reluctant parents to allow the pair to visit Boston and the Perkins Institution. She insisted to them that Keller needed to be removed from her overly protective family circle and that Perkins was the sensible educational choice. Privately she acknowledged her personal, almost desperate wish to return to Boston.[21] For the rest of the 1880s and 1890s Keller and Sullivan moved back and forth between Boston, Tuscumbia, and New York, though nearly always summering in Tuscumbia. After 1900, however, except for periods in the summers of 1916, 1919, and 1922, Keller spent little time in either Tuscumbia or the larger South. Anne Sullivan became the dominant and most consistent guide in her life. After her initial breakthrough in comprehending finger spelling, Keller also learned to write, to read lips by touch, and to speak. As an adolescent and adult, Keller reveled in the cultural and intellectual life of Boston—Harvard University and Radcliffe College specifically—and then New York.

Keller's conversion to the Christian faith tradition of Swedenborgianism further removed her from southern culture and society. . . . As a teenager, she had been unable to find all the answers she desired in the teachings and Christianity of Phillips Brooks. Guided by John Hitz, the secretary of Alexander Graham Bell who provided Emanuel Swedenborg's writings in Braille, she embraced Swedenborgianism in 1896 and followed it for the rest of her life. Many New England reformers, radicals, and spiritualists adopted the belief system, which was built on the eighteenth-century Christian mysticism of the Swedish Lutheran Swedenborg. He argued for the permeability of the veil between the physical and spiritual worlds. His writings taught Keller that her blindness and deafness mattered nil; her spiritual senses, her internal life, enabled her to access God. The faith also resonated with Keller's growing dedication toward action and service. Swedenborg equated love with service, but he believed that living a "life of the spirit" exemplified active service. Whatever form Keller's service took, again regardless of her disability, when done in a "life of the spirit" it qualified as vital and genuine Christian service.[22]

As an adult, Keller consistently sought a life of active public citizenship synonymous with her theological and political conceptualization of service. She first became familiar with radical and progressive analyses of hierarchy, oppression, and exploitation while a student at Boston's Radcliffe College (1900–1904), the prestigious female counterpart to Harvard. There she read, argued, listened, and was thrilled by the intellectual debates. Perhaps she attended services at the Swedenborgian congregation not far from Harvard Square. For the first time she testified before a state legislature. She began to realize that political efficacy was possible, even for a woman deaf, blind, and from Alabama.

Keller thus embraced a wide-ranging, enduring, and intensely active public life based on a commitment to compassion, justice, and equality. Like her mother, she embraced female suffrage (though Kate Keller likely did not endorse Alice Paul's National Woman's Party, as her daughter did). Helen went on to endorse birth control, the radical Industrial Workers of the World, racial equality, and the causes of striking workers, and she joined the Socialist Party of America in 1909. She advocated for people with disabilities but blamed the inequalities of capitalism for causing disability among a disproportionately high number of working-class people. She criticized World War I as a profit-making venture and later condemned the U.S. use of atomic weapons in World War II. For the American Foundation for the Blind she became an incredibly effective fund-raiser and lobbyist. International politics fascinated her, as did world travel and other cultures, and she became one of the nation's most successful unofficial ambassadors in the cold war era.[23]

Despite the intellectual life of her mother, as an adult Keller seems to have fallen prey to the stereotypical belief that all southern white women were apolitical and subservient. All evidence indicates that throughout her life she remained largely unaware of the various streams of reform and progressive activism percolating among some southern white women. Keller was simply one of a number of white women, liberals and radicals, who in varying ways sought to remake southern white womanhood throughout the decades of the twentieth century. . . . [Yet] throughout her lifetime Keller had very little contact with those engaged in similar efforts. Perhaps her disability, the viciousness of antiradical attacks on activists for racial equality, or simply her northern residency deterred this contact.[24]

Keller had become a displaced southerner. Her regional background, however, constituted a widely known part of her even more widely known personal story. She was a deaf-blind woman from a region frequently considered inferior: economically, socially, politically disabled. Northerners taught her oral language, while the South lacked the institutions and faculty to do so.[25] She became an uprooted southerner reconstructed by the North, but still always southern.

Throughout this transformation, what it meant to Keller and others for her to be southern was often unclear and contradictory. She left behind little reflective analysis of her southern identity, most likely because of her complicated uneasiness with that heritage. Some of her childhood memories brought her joy; southern racial inequalities made her "ashamed in my very soul." She knew that her own intellectual and personal renewal had come from northern reformers and their followers. She seemingly was unaware of homegrown efforts to refigure southern identity and cultural memories.[26] . . . Her most common acknowledgment of her southern identity was in superficial, and stereotypical, reflections on the beauty and sensuality of southern flowers and trees.

Keller's complicated relationship with her southern background often became entangled with another aspect of her identity—the essential question of her intellectual capacity and abilities, of her humanity. From childhood through old age, others frequently questioned whether she, as a person with a disability, had the capacity to genuinely know anything. As an adult attempting to shape an active political and intellectual life, she regularly encountered the belief that her disability disqualified her from such an undertaking. Because politics and political participation interested her intensely, this dismissal of her as unfit frustrated and enraged her.[27] Detractors made her battle for a public identity even more problematic when they voiced their criticisms in regional terms, as they frequently did.

For example, when as a young adult Keller expressed political opinions considered radical in the early 1900s, opponents from her home state of Alabama blamed it on the Yankee influence of her by-then-married teacher Anne Sullivan Macy and her husband John Macy. These criticisms became very explicit after Keller sent a hundred dollars and a statement of vigorous support—including an expression of shame in her southern heritage—to the National Association for the Advancement of Colored People (NAACP) in 1916. Her views became public after W. E. B. Du Bois printed the letter in the NAACP's newspaper, the Crisis. "I warmly endorse your efforts," she had written, "to bring before the country the facts about the unfair treatment of the colored people in some parts of the United States. What a comment upon our social justice is the need of an association like yours!" She felt that "It should bring the blush of shame to the face of every true American to know that ten millions of his countrymen are denied the equal protection of the laws." The Alabama daughter of a Confederate captain confessed, "Ashamed in my very soul I behold in my own beloved southland the tears of those who are oppressed, those who must bring up their sons and daughters in bondage, to be servants because others have their fields and vineyards, and on the side of the oppressor is power." She insisted, drawing on her own theological beliefs, that "The outrages against the colored people are a denial of Christ."[28]

Keller's sentiments did not go unnoticed. The Selma (Ala.) Journal reprinted the NAACP letter and accompanied it with an editorial that described the letter as "full of untruths, full of fawning and bootlicking phrases." Implying that Keller could not have generated such beliefs herself, the editorial blamed her teachers: "The people who did such wonderful work in training Miss Keller must have belonged to the old Abolition Gang for they seemed to have thoroughly poisoned her mind against her own people."[29] Her disability and resulting education supposedly left her politically pliable, especially vulnerable to northern educators and abolitionists, and incapable of intentional deliberation. It caused her to be a disloyal southerner.

Though her father was by then dead, Keller's family pressured her to retreat from her public stance in support of the NAACP. Her mother appealed for her to consider the reputations of extended family members living in Selma. Acquiescing, Keller wrote to the Selma Times, the competing newspaper of the Selma Journal, that the Journal had misinterpreted her letter to the NAACP. With unclear differentiation, she insisted that she had advocated "equality of all men before the law," rather than "the social equality of white people and Negroes."[30]

In early 1917 Keller's personal life fell into chaos that sent her southward into the fray. Perhaps this is one reason she resisted her family's pressure so halfheartedly. Anne Macy suffered ill health, tuberculosis, undoubtedly made worse by the deterioration of her marriage to John Macy and a relatively unsuccessful 1916 Chautauqua tour for the student and teacher duo. Doctors advised that Anne Macy have a rest, which she took, away from Keller, in Lake Placid and then Puerto Rico. Separated from her friend for one of the first times in decades, Keller planned to spend several months with her widowed mother in Alabama, perhaps smoothing over their relationship. Before leaving the North, however, she fell in love and made secret plans to marry a finger-spelling fellow socialist, Peter Fagan. The remaining members of Keller's nuclear family, already angry at Helen, drew the line. Purportedly sneaking her away on a forced midnight train trip and chasing Fagan away with a gun, they insisted to her that her disability rendered her ineligible for marriage and childbearing.[31]

Keller submitted and cut off contact with Fagan. . . . Presumably she grieved the close of her relationship with Fagan and the normality he represented in her life. She expressed constant concern to Anne Macy about the possibility of the war in Europe enveloping the United States. Keller complained that in Montgomery "[p]arties, dresses, babies, weddings—and obesity are the topics of conversation." In turn, Macy wrote with little cheer of her failed marriage to John and made preparations that assumed her death would come soon. She tried unconvincingly to reassure Helen. "Yes, it is true that most people you meet in Montgomery lack individuality," Macy wrote. "It is equally true of most places."[32]

As Keller understood and experienced her family relationships, both departure from the geographic South and her departure from the traditional gender and racial politics of the white South went hand in hand with emotional separation from her mother. Her fond but often uneasy adult relationship with her mother reflected these concerns. Contemplating their relationship eight years after her mother's death, she wrote in 1929, "My mother talked intelligently, brilliantly, about current events, and she had a Southerner's interest in politics. But after my mind took a radical turn she could never get over the feeling that we had drifted apart. It grieves me that I should have added to the sadness that weighed upon her."[33] To be a disloyal southerner, as her family understood it and as Keller often experienced it, meant geographical and familial exile.

Southerners sometimes questioned her southern identity, but people living in the North frequently defined Keller as inherently southern even though she lived most of her life in the northeastern United States. It was an identity she could not escape. In 1929 she spoke "as a representative of the South" at the monthly meeting of the group "Alabamians in New York." Along with a representative of the American Federation of Labor she there urged study of the working conditions of southern textile mill hands. . . . In 1938 publisher H. E. Maule approached her about writing a biography of Clara Barton. He picked her, he said, because "As a woman interested in social work and aid to the handicapped, and as a Southerner by birth, it occurred to me that you would be sympathetic to her great voice." [34] . . .

The 1937 publication of Margaret Mitchell's *Gone with the Wind* prompted Keller, like many other Americans, to reflect on the Old South, its meanings for United States race relations, and the implications for her personal identity. She read the twelve-volume Braille version . . . while sailing for Japan in April 1937. Anne Macy had died in October 1936. As an escape, and seeking new purpose, Keller seized the opportunity to advocate for blind people in other countries. Friends offered her the chance in Japan. She thus read the book while grieving the loss of Macy, pondering her past and better times, and attempting to determine the future course of her life.[35]

In many ways Mitchell's work enchanted Keller. "How charmingly the book opens," she wrote, "with a placid life on a Georgia plantation!" It was a sensual delight that drew to her memories of home. "It stirs in me a nostalgia for the drowsy, sweet spring and early summer days in Tuscumbia, the red earth, the huge old magnolia trees and live oaks. Again I smell Mother's royal wealth of roses, the masses of tangled honeysuckle and paulownia blossoms heavy in the afternoon heat. Again the air about me vibrates with excitement as the men fulminate against some political group or refight the Civil War." It caused her to remember, in terms and imagery paralleling Mitchell's images of slavery, "the Negroes" who gathered water at the spring. "Picturesque in bright-colored bandanas, barefooted, always singing or dancing or performing a cakewalk, they warm my heart, and I long for the joyous pickaninnies who so good-naturedly played with the insatiate tomboy I was."[36]

Mitchell's romanticization of white supremacy and her mythic Old South captivated Keller, just as it did many other readers. By the book's completion, Keller had even adopted Mitchell's historical analysis of Reconstruction. "For the first time," Keller proclaimed, "I am beginning to form a clear picture of the dreadful Reconstruction Period in the South. . . . The criminally stupid descent of the North upon prostrate states with a deluge of carpetbaggers and scalawags turns into a mockery the bloody Civil War fought to emancipate the slaves." Perhaps her embrace of Mitchell's version of history reflected her own yearnings for a happier time. *Gone with the Wind* offered examples of men and women struggling valiantly against economic depression, just as many Americans were doing in the late 1930s. It also offered solace in a false but idyllic past while Keller's own future grew increasingly uncertain. She yearned for Macy. As she wrote in March 1937, "from the moment I wake in the morning until I lie down at night there is an ache at my heart which never stops."[37] Mitchell's myth offered personal comfort and reflection that tomorrow would always come. It offered female models who survived. And . . . it "offered a nostalgic depiction of the Old South but did not advocate its return."[38]

Keller uncomfortably recognized the contradictions between her personal memories, the cultural memories reinforced by *Gone with the Wind*, and the personal knowledge she had garnered over the previous decades. She clearly enjoyed the book, but that pleasure discomforted her: she variably exclaimed passionate opinions about the actions and characters of Rhett, Scarlett, and Melanie and then disavowed her interest with calmer political analyses. The contradictions increased her discomfort and guilt. Despite her fervor for the book, she wrote that "time's disillusioning searchlight" forced her to realize that all may not have been happy in the Old South. "Sadly I recall the degrading poverty, the ignorance and superstition into which those little ones were born and the bitterness of the Negro problem through which many of them are still living."[39] . . . Luckily for her, perhaps, the intoxicating effects of *Gone with the Wind* did not last long. Confronting her personal shame and identity could be once more avoided. After her initial read in 1937, she never mentioned the book again.

U.S. politics, however, forced Keller to pay increasing attention to racial inequalities in both North and South as civil rights campaigns developed in the post–World War II period. . . . In 1946 she attended and spoke at a Danbury, Connecticut, rally "to urge justice to negroes of Connecticut." There she met black and white activists, including opera singer Marian Anderson.[40] Events such as these allowed her to acknowledge racial inequalities and her own shame about them, but in a context that spread responsibility for racial inequalities and shame over both the North and the South. . . . As she became more open with herself and others about racial inequalities, she also grew to realize those inequities went far beyond the geography of the American South.

After the Danbury rally, enthused and contemplative, Keller wrote to a friend that she felt "unquenchable shame" over the social, political, and economic conditions of African Americans. "This revolt has never slumbered within me since I began to notice for myself how they are degraded, and with what cold-blooded deliberation the keys of knowledge, self-reliance and well paid employment are taken from them, so that they may not enter the gate of social competence." She detailed a long list of incidents large and small that infuriated her. She remembered when a "colored

teacher of high culture and noble dignity" visited her and was forced to take the southern hotel's freight elevator. Continued lynching and violence "augur[ed] ill for America's future." The blinding of an African American veteran by a police officer who acted in supposed self-defense was "another abyss of evil . . . moral infection by traitors to Christianity and to the whole democratic spirit in the best traditions of America." She compared her "concentrated horror and fury" to that she had felt when reading Shakespeare's *King Lear* for the first time.[41]

Keller also began to draw connections between racism, the discrimination faced by people with disabilities, and the additive discrimination confronted by African Americans with disabilities. In her 1944 testimony to the House Labor Committee urging expansion of the Social Security Act, she highlighted the circumstances of "the colored blind" and "the deaf-blind." These were, she said, "the hardest pressed and least cared-for" among her "blind fellows." After the 1946 Danbury rally she continued: "It stabs me to the soul to recall my visits to schools for the colored blind which were shockingly backward, and what a hard struggle it was for them to obtain worth while instruction and profitable work because of race prejudice." . . . Her disability activism and the opportunities created by her fame as a person with a disability provided her with the tools necessary to begin to analyze southern racial mores. It did not, however, provide her with instant answers.[42]

A 1951 trip to South Africa pushed Keller to a deeper examination of racial inequalities globally and of the relationship between racism and discrimination against people with disabilities. The journey thrilled the seventy-one-year-old global adventurer. She traveled with the blessings and assistance of the U.S. State Department and the American Foundation for the Blind (an international educational, lobbying, and research group she had worked for since 1921). The State Department found her global travels extremely beneficial because of the positive press and goodwill she elicited. An invitation from the Reverend Arthur Blaxall, a white member of the South African National Council for the Blind and an acquaintance of hers since 1931, initiated the visit. Again her analyses began with memories of her childhood in Alabama. She wrote that she "was the more ready to accept Mr. Blaxall's invitation because I remembered the earliest years when little Afroamericans were my playmates."[43]

Keller's preparations for the trip pushed her further into national and international racial politics and into closer contact with African American and African activists. She read Alan Paton's *Cry the Beloved Country* and Mohandas Gandhi's *Autobiography* to learn more about South Africa's racial apartheid. She gleaned all she could about South African people, plants, and animals from an acquaintance. . . . In Harlem, perhaps for the first time, she attended a "colored debutantes' cotillion" as a guest of the Reverend Dr. Adam Clayton Powell Sr., famed race man and minister at Harlem's Abyssinian Baptist Church. There she met guest of honor Ralph Bunche, from whom she learned "the historic point of view." Only months previously, Bunche had been awarded the Nobel Peace Prize (for which Keller would later be nominated) for his powerful advocacy of civil rights and decolonization. The eloquence, charisma, and dynamism with which he critiqued South African racial injustices appealed to her sense of service. Energized, she committed herself to confronting South African racism.[44]

Keller sought to do so directly but proceeded cautiously. She knew that disregard and lack of social support made the lives of many blind people across the world difficult, but racism compounded the problem for "the colored blind" in South Africa. Her goal, as she described it to her host Arthur Blaxall before departure, was to use "skill and tact as well as enthusiasm to obtain the right help for the colored blind, who, owing to their handicap are more subject to the arbitrary will of white society than their seeing fellows."[45] . . .

Once in South Africa, Keller found the country's beauty contrasted sharply with its brutality and racial inequality. She could not deny her enjoyment at being covered with the spray of Victoria Falls or the awesomeness of Kruger National Park. Once, looking for hippopotami, she stood alone: "the tall grasses rustled against me, and I drank in the sweet, clean air and the sense of four hundred miles where wild animals were free to roam." And, as wherever she went when she traveled, she attracted immense attention. As her host described it, "for two months she was the center of interests, and a subject of conversation, eclipsing even the parliamentary news of the day."[46]

In spite of the warm welcome she and her companion Polly Thomson received at the twenty-eight schools and institutions she visited and the forty-eight meetings and receptions she addressed, "the bitter sense of racial discrimination and injustice" soured her visit. Racism even compounded her schedule, as the laws and attitudes of apartheid required separate assemblies for "the whites, the colored people, the natives and the Indians."[47]

Despite efforts to "keep watch over our mutinous lips" around powerful and wealthy donors, Keller did criticize apartheid publicly. She acknowledged, however, that it took "all the courage and fortitude Polly and I could command" to do so. Her insistence on addressing and visiting assemblies of nonwhites forced acknowledgment of their existence and needs. On at least one occasion her address to a white audience included "concern about the thousands of natives who were as yet untaught and unbefriended." She wrote to one dear friend, "Many times my heart sank as I observed how apathetic many of the public had been toward those unfortunates ["the natives blind or deaf"], and occasionally in my dreams I banged my head against an impenetrable wall trying to discover a break-through." . . . Nothing, she wrote privately, "made me more ashamed of my own race" than the ideology of "Afrikaaners."[48] Just as in the United States, racism compounded the discrimination and limited options of people of African descent who had disabilities.

In the years following Keller's return from South Africa, . . . the United States civil rights movement grew in activism and success. Evidence indicates that she followed and approved of its course, but she was never actively involved (perhaps partly due to her age). In response to Emmett Till's death in 1955 she sought to give financial assistance to the NAACP.[49] No evidence remains of ties to other white female dissidents [and advocates of racial equality] from the South, like Anne Braden or Katharine Lumpkin. . . .

Examining Keller's southern identity reveals the important role of region in forming personal identity. Keller never questioned the region's uniqueness and its influence on her. Though geographically separated from the South and often in conflict with her family (which to her sometimes seems to have become synonymous with the region) because of her politics, she retained a personal identification as a southerner. Her southern roots also shaped how others defined her. For some, it caused pride, for others derision, and it led many to expect or demand political stances from her that reflected dominant southern hierarchies of race, gender, and class.

Keller both savored and resented this southern identification. At times it gave her pleasure, at other times discomfort. In either case, however, she could not shed the collective cultural memories and regional identity integral to forming her personal outlook. As an adult, she struggled to separate regional identity from acceptance of Lost Cause mythology.

Examining Keller as a southerner provides an example of the historical and personal evolution of white shame, the term she frequently used in the latter half of her life. As Tara McPherson has written, "guilt emerges as a central aspect of twentieth-century southern feeling, and a variety of approaches to managing guilt are tracked across the southern landscape."[50] Racial politics remained central to a southern white identity in the late-nineteenth- and twentieth-century United States, even for one who had moved far away from her Alabama childhood. Race and the South's regionally focused politics based on maintaining the color line lingered omnipresent in her analyses, her sense of home, and her exploration of world politics. While claiming her southern ties fondly, Keller tended to do so only by linking them with accompanying statements of shame and disavowal.

As an adult Keller increasingly drew connections between racism, the discrimination faced by people with disabilities, and the additive discrimination confronted by African Americans with disabilities. Examining her as a southerner provides clues as to how, unaided by other intellectual theorists, she grew to comprehend that systems of hierarchy—whether based upon race, class, gender, or the abilities of one's body—were inherently linked and intertwined. Like others, she struggled to clarify and articulate the connections between efforts to end discrimination and stereotyping. Keller did not, however, connect with the organizations and people of the rapidly growing disability rights movement, just as she failed to do so during her earlier years.[51] Even today, activists in the racial freedom movements, the disability rights movement, and the feminist movement seek to fully theorize these connections.

Finally, examining Helen Keller as a southerner expands the realization that southern womanhood is not monolithic. . . . Keller's experience of southern white womanhood—and her attempts to reformulate it—was influenced equally by factors as disparate as family tales of the glory days of the Old South, her disability, and her northern education. While Keller studied at Radcliffe and walked the streets of Cambridge, Massachusetts, between 1900 and 1904, she wrote, "Never have I found in the greenhouses of the North such heart-satisfying roses as the climbing roses of my southern home. They used to hang in long festoons from our porch, filling the whole air with their fragrance, untainted by any earthly smell; and in the early morning, washed in the dew, they felt so soft, so pure, I could not help wondering if they did not resemble the asphodels of God's garden."[52] To her, though she never again lived for a long period in the South, the region always remained an idyllic and sensual geography. The physicality of place became the easiest way, or perhaps simply the least complicated way, for her to feel southern.

NOTES

1. For more on Helen Keller see Kim E. Nielsen, "Was Helen Keller Deaf? Blindness, Deafness, and Multiple Identities," in Brenda Jo Brueggemann and Susan Burch, eds., *Women and Deafness: Double Visions* (Washington, D.C., 2006); Kim E. Nielsen, ed., *Helen Keller: Selected Writings* (New York, 2005); Kim E. Nielsen, *The Radical Lives of Helen Keller* (New York, 2004); Joseph P. Lash, *Helen and Teacher: The Story of Helen Keller and Anne Sullivan Macy* (New York, 1980); and Dorothy Herrmann, *Helen Keller: A Life* (New York, 1998).

2. Helen Keller, *The Story of My Life: With Supplementary Accounts by Anne Sullivan and John Albert Macy,* edited by Roger Shattuck and Dorothy Herrmann (1903; new ed., New York, 2003), 12–13; Herrmann, *Helen Keller,* 8.

3. Keller, *Story of My Life,* 14.

4. In 1892 educators founded the Alabama School for the Negro Deaf and Blind, also in Talladega. See the website of the Alabama Institute for Deaf and Blind at http://www.aidb.org/aidb-story-overview/.

5. See Ernest Freeberg, *The Education of Laura Bridgman: First Deaf and Blind Person to Learn Language* (Cambridge, Mass., 2001); and Elisabeth Gitter, *The Imprisoned Guest: Samuel Howe and Laura Bridgman, the Original Deaf-Blind Girl* (New York, 2001).

6. Keller described this trip in *Story of My Life,* 23–24.

7. See Hannah Joyner, "'This Unnatural and Fratricidal Strife': A Family's Negotiation of the Civil War, Deafness, and Independence," in Paul K. Longmore and Lauri Umansky, eds., *The New Disability*

History: American Perspectives (New York, 2001), 83–106; Hannah Joyner, *From Pity to Pride: Growing Up Deaf in the Old South* (Washington, D.C., 2004); and Steven Noll, *Feeble-Minded in Our Midst: Institutions for the Mentally Retarded in the South, 1900–1940* (Chapel Hill, 1995).

8. *Fifty-Sixth Annual Report of the Trustees of the Perkins Institution*, 79, 81; Arthur Keller to Michael Anagnos, January 28, 1887 (Samuel P. Hayes Research Library, Perkins School for the Blind, Watertown, Mass.).

9. *Fifty-Sixth Annual Report of the Trustees of the Perkins Institution*, 79; Herrmann, *Helen Keller,* chap. 3.

10. "Teacher's Life, Tewksbury," undated and unnumbered notes by Anne Sullivan Macy, Notes of Nella Braddy Henney, Nella Braddy Henney Collection (Hayes Research Library, Perkins School for the Blind); Nella Braddy Henney, *Anne Sullivan Macy: The Story Behind Helen Keller* (Garden City, N.Y., 1933), 34; Nina Silber, *The Romance of Reunion: Northerners and the South, 1865–1900* (Chapel Hill, 1993), 124.

11. "The South," undated and unnumbered notes by Anne Sullivan Macy, Notes of Nella Braddy Henney, Henney Collection.

12. "Going to Tuscumbia," undated and unnumbered notes by Anne Sullivan Macy, ibid.

13. "The South," undated and unnumbered notes by Anne Sullivan Macy, ibid.

14. David W. Blight, *Race and Reunion: The Civil War in American Memory* (Cambridge, Mass., 2001), 171, 260. See also Gaines M. Foster, *Ghosts of the Confederacy: Defeat, the Lost Cause, and the Emergence of the New South, 1865 to 1913* (New York, 1987).

15. Keller, *Story of My Life*, 18, 163–64. The enslaved girl's name, Martha Washington, clearly begs for analysis. Whether the name Keller used in her autobiography was indeed the girl's name—or a pseudonym—is unclear.

16. Ibid., 174.

17. Anne Sullivan to Michael Anagnos, January 23, 1893, Annie Sullivan Letters (Manuscript Department, American Antiquarian Society, Worcester, Mass.).

18. Nielsen, *Radical Lives*, 20.

19. Ibid., 182; Anne Sullivan to Michael Anagnos, April 20, 1888, Sullivan Letters.

20. Anne Sullivan to Michael Anagnos, July 7, 1890, Sullivan Letters; Lash, *Helen and Teacher*, 780.

21. For example, see Annie M. Sullivan to Michael Anagnos, April 22, 1888, Sullivan Letters.

22. Helen Keller, "A Vision of Service," quoted in Keller, *Light in My Darkness*, edited by Ray Silverman (1994; 2nd ed., New York, 2000), 107. Keller's most lengthy explanation of her faith is in Keller, *My Religion* (New York, 1927).

23. Nielsen, *Radical Lives*.

24. On southern women's activism, see, for example, Elna C. Green, *Southern Strategies: Southern Women and the Woman Suffrage Question* (Chapel Hill, 1997); Anastatia Sims, *The Power of Femininity in the New South: Women's Organizations and Politics in North Carolina, 1880–1930* (Columbia, S.C., 1997); Elizabeth Hayes Turner, *Women, Culture, and Community: Religion and Reform in Galveston, 1880–1920* (New York, 1997); Jane Turner Censer, *The Reconstruction of White Southern Womanhood, 1865–1895* (Baton Rouge, 2003); Jacquelyn Dowd Hall, "Open

Secrets: Memory, Imagination, and the Refashioning of Southern Identity," *American Quarterly*, 50 (March 1998), 109–24; Catherine Fosl, *Subversive Southerner: Anne Braden and the Struggle for Racial Justice in the Cold War South* (New York, 2002); and Jacquelyn Dowd Hall, "Women Writers, the 'Southern Front,' and the Dialectical Imagination," *Journal of Southern History*, 69 (February 2003), 3–38.

25. Educators generally considered northern educational institutions for deaf people superior because of their post–Civil War switch to oralism rather than sign language. Southern institutions remained signing institutions largely because of funding shortages that made hiring and training new oralist teachers difficult. See Douglas C. Baynton, *Forbidden Signs: American Culture and the Campaign against Sign Language* (Chicago, 1996).

26. Nielsen, *Radical Lives*, 38–39 (quotation on p. 38), 42. After 1924 Keller primarily expressed her interest in radical politics privately, but her interest remained.

27. Kim Nielsen, "Helen Keller and the Politics of Civic Fitness," in Longmore and Umansky, eds., *New Disability History*, 268–90.

28. New York *Crisis*, April 1916, pp. 305–6; Nielsen, *Radical Lives*, 38–39, 42; Lash, *Helen and Teacher*, 454–56; Herrmann, *Helen Keller*, 204.

29. Lash, *Helen and Teacher*, 454; Herrmann, *Helen Keller*, 205.

30. Herrmann, *Helen Keller*, 205; Lash, *Helen and Teacher*, 454–55.

31. Nielsen, *Radical Lives*, 40–41. Keller's mother, Kate Keller, was particularly opposed to a possible marriage and any form of a sexual life for her daughter. Not only did Keller's family and Anne Sullivan Macy hold eugenic fears about Helen's possible reproduction and sexuality, but also many state laws prohibited women with disabilities from marriage and children. For information on eugenics and disability see Wendy Kline, *Building a Better Race: Gender, Sexuality, and Eugenics from the Turn of the Century to the Baby Boom* (Berkeley, 2001); Martin S. Pernick, *The Black Stork: Eugenics and the Death of "Defective" Babies in American Medicine and Motion Pictures Since 1915* (New York, 1996); and Steven Selden, "Eugenics and the Social Construction of Merit, Race and Disability," *Journal of Curriculum Studies*, 32 (March 2000), 235–52.

32. Lash, *Helen and Teacher*, 452; Anne Sullivan Macy to Helen Keller, undated letter from 1917, Folder 5, Box 69, Helen Keller Archives (American Foundation for the Blind, New York).

33. Helen Keller, *Midstream: My Later Life* (1929; reprint, New York, 1968), 220.

34. "Sees Much Poverty in Trade Centres," *New York Times*, November 13, 1929, p. 46; H. E. Maule to Helen Keller, June 16, 1938 (copy to Nella Braddy Henney), Henney Collection.

35. For more on Keller's travels to Japan, see Nielsen, *Radical Lives*, chaps. 3 and 4.

36. Helen Keller, *Helen Keller's Journal, 1936–1937* (Garden City, N.Y., 1938), 281, 298.

37. Ibid., 305; Keller, *Helen Keller's Journal*, 231.

38. However, the female models who survived [in the book] were white women whose survival became racially defined. On this point, see Tara

McPherson, *Reconstructing Dixie: Race, Gender, and Nostalgia in the Imagined South* (Durham, N.C., 2003), 47–64. Nostalgic depiction: Sarah E. Gardner, *Blood and Irony: Southern White Women's Narratives of the Civil War, 1861–1937* (Chapel Hill, 2004), 239. See also Marian J. Morton, "'My Dear, I Don't Give A Damn': Scarlett O'Hara and the Great Depression," *Frontiers* 5 (Autmun 1980), 52–56; Drew Gilpin Faust, "Clutching the Chains that Bind: Margaret Mitchell and *Gone with the Wind*," *Southern Cultures* 5 (Spring 1999), 6–20; Elizabeth Fox-Genovese, "Scarlett O'Hara: The Southern Lady as New Woman," *American Quarterly* 33 (Autumn 1981), 391–41.

39. Keller, *Helen Keller's Journal*, 298–99.

40. Helen Keller to Nella Braddy Henney, September 22, 1946, Henney Collection.

41. Ibid.

42. Helen Keller's speech before the House Labor Committee Investigating Aid to the Handicapped. October 3, 1944. Legislation-Federal Folder, Social Security Act—Title X, Folder 4, Box 36, Helen Keller Archives. See also "Helen Keller Urges More Help to Blind," *New York Times,* October 4, 1944, p. 25. Helen Keller to Nella Braddy Henney, September 22, 1946, Henney Collection.

43. Arthur William Blaxall, *Helen Keller Under the Southern Cross* (Cape Town, 1952), 32. For more on Keller's travels to South Africa see Nielsen, *Radical Lives,* 102–5.

44. Blaxall, *Helen Keller Under the Southern Cross,* 32; Nielsen, *Radical Lives,* 102–5; Helen Keller to Jo Davidson, January 24, 1951, Jo Davidson File, Folder 9, Box 52, Helen Keller Archives (quotations).

45. Lash, *Helen and Teacher,* 724.

46. Helen Keller to Jo Davidson, August 1, 1951, Box 11, Papers of Jo Davidson (Manuscript Division, Library of Congress, Washington, D.C.). Blaxall, *Helen Keller Under the Southern Cross,* 25.

47. Helen Keller to Jo Davidson, August 1, 1951, Box 11, Papers of Jo Davidson.

48. Undated newspaper clipping from 1951, Nella Braddy Henney Journal, Henney Collection; Blaxall, *Helen Keller Under the Southern Cross,* 36; Helen Keller to Jo Davidson, August 1, 1951, Box 11, Papers of Jo Davidson.

49. Nella Braddy Henney to Polly Thomson, October 23, 1955, Nella Braddy Henney File, Folder 7, Box 58, Helen Keller Archives.

50. McPherson, *Reconstructing Dixie,* 6.

51. For further information on the disability rights movement, see Joseph P. Shapiro, *No Pity: People with Disabilities Forging a New Civil Rights Movement* (New York, 1993); Paul K. Longmore and David Goldberger, "The League of the Physically Handicapped and the Great Depression: A Case Study in the New Disability History," *Journal of American History* 87 (December 2000), 888–922; and Doris Zames Fleischer and Frieda Zames, *The Disability Rights Movement: From Charity to Confrontation* (Philadelphia, 2001). For more on Keller's relationship with the disability rights movement, see Nielsen, *Radical Lives,* chap. 5.

52. Keller, *Story of My Life,* 14–15.

Ida B. Wells, *Southern Horrors* (with an introduction by Patricia A. Schechter)

Ida B. Wells's 1892 pamphlet *Southern Horrors: Lynch Law in All Its Phases* launched a critical phase of the African American struggle for civil rights. Its statistical refutation of the rape charge against black men that was used to justify lynching is a sociological breakthrough that has stood the test of time and study. Wells also demonstrates how the concepts of "race" and "rape" were tied to power relations in the administration of justice, in the media, and in everyday life. Finally, Wells expounds the racial and class dimensions of the sexual double standard in ways that connect to contemporary feminist concerns with violence against all women, communities of color, and the poor in the United States and globally.

The insights expressed in *Southern Horrors* reflect Wells's personal and community survival strategy in the New South. Her situation was shaped by both new opportunities and new oppressions facing the first generation of free African Americans who came of age after the Civil War. Wells's parents, who had been slaves in Mississippi, bequeathed to their children a legacy of strong religious faith, pride in wage-earning, and a commitment to education that echoes through the many projects their daughter undertook over her lifetime. Wells's father, James Wells, was a skilled carpenter and a member of the Masons who, after the war, served on the board of Holly Springs local American Missionary Association school, Rust College, which his daughter attended. Wells's mother, "Lizzie" Warrenton Wells, worked as a cook and was a devout Methodist who made sure her children attended church, where she herself learned to read the Bible. After James and Lizzie's untimely deaths in 1878 from a yellow fever epidemic that swept the Delta, sixteen-year-old Ida B. Wells was left to care for her five siblings, earning money by teaching school.

The prospect of better wages and the presence of extended family soon drew Wells to Memphis, Tennessee. There, her intellectual, social, and political horizons expanded in a burgeoning black community notable for its highly accomplished middle-class and elite members. Aspirations for equality nourished community institutions like schools, newspapers, social clubs, literary lyceums, and churches, especially the Baptist and African Methodist Episcopal denominations. In Memphis, Wells found encouragement to turn her intellectual talents into leadership by teaching Sunday school and by pursuing literary activities, especially journalism. Her first newspaper article appeared in 1883 in a Baptist weekly. It explained how Wells had been unfairly ejected from a first-class "ladies" railroad coach and how she fought racial discrimination by taking her case to court. While tens of thousands of educated women joined the paid labor force as

This introduction was written by the author expressly for *Women's America*. © by Patricia A. Schechter, published by permission of the author.

school "ma'ams," religious educators, and journalists in the late nineteenth century, these social roles had particular significance for African American women, whose personal, family, and community well-being was intimately bound up with their wage-earning, educational activities, and community-betterment work.

As *Southern Horrors* emphatically argues, a white racist backlash followed closely upon the achievements of African Americans after Reconstruction. The result of this backlash was "Jim Crow" segregation, a set of laws designed for the economic deprivation, social marginalization, and political disfranchisement of black people. Jim Crow was established and enforced through systematic violence and terror. Ida B. Wells's eight pamphlets, written between 1892 and 1920, painstakingly document the ways in which African Americans were deprived of their rights through mob and police violence, through negative propaganda campaigns in the media, and through the elimination of economic opportunity and political rights.* Few aspects of Jim Crow escaped Wells's sharp scrutiny in the press and eventually, while in Memphis, she caught the negative attention of critics. As the following excerpt explains, she was forced to leave the South as a kind of political exile, first traveling to New York, then to Great Britain, and finally settling in Chicago in 1895. There, she married lawyer and fellow activist Ferdinand L. Barnett (hyphenating her name to Wells-Barnett) and raised a family of four children.

Post-exile, Wells-Barnett's writing and activism were sustained through African American community networks and by organizations shared by black and white women reformers, such as the Woman's Christian Temperance Union. Her work with black women's church and club networks nurtured her into a powerful public speaker and political organizer. Between 1892 and 1895, Wells-Barnett organized scores of antilynching committees and women's clubs all over the United States and abroad, and helped inaugurate the National Association of Colored Women (NACW), a group that functioned as the preeminent civil rights organization up to World War I. In 1909, Wells-Barnett cofounded the National Association for the Advancement of Colored People (NAACP), which, in 1917, assumed principal leadership of the antilynching fight in the United States.

The trajectory of Wells-Barnett's civil rights agitation was neither simple nor smooth. Controversy followed her and her work, especially during its first decade. White supremacists in the North and South vilified her in the press, slandering her morals and threatening her with violence for speaking out against lynching. While most African American communities embraced Wells-Barnett as a heroine, there was little consensus about how, exactly, to end lynching or resist Jim Crow. Black leaders were a diverse group ideologically and generationally; regional considerations also came into play as black southerners found themselves more circumscribed than their northern peers. Women's roles were also fundamental to the building of black communities and to resistance work. Though black women's families and communities were dependent upon their contributions, any move on their part into official political and intellectual leadership—especially where interactions with whites were concerned—usually sparked controversy. Whether in

*Besides *Southern Horrors*, the pamphlets were *The Reason Why the Colored American Is Not in the World's Columbian Exposition: The Afro-American's Contribution to Columbian Literature* (Chicago: Ida B. Wells, 1893); *United States Atrocities: Lynch Law* (London: Lux Publishing, 1894); *A Red Record: Tabulated Statistics and Alleged Causes of Lynchings in the United States, 1892–1893–1894* (Chicago: Donahue & Henneberry, 1895); *Lynch Law in Georgia* (Chicago: Ida B. Wells-Barnett, 1899); *Mob Rule in New Orleans: Robert Charles and His Fight to the Death* (Chicago: Ida B. Wells-Barnett, 1900); *The East St. Louis Massacre: The Greatest Outrage of the Century* (Chicago: The Negro Fellowship Herald Press, 1917); *The Arkansas Race Riot* (Chicago: Ida B. Wells-Barnett, 1920).

journalism, public speaking, or institutional leadership—as with her Chicago social settlement, the Negro Fellowship League (1909–1919)—Wells-Barnett's initiatives were always double-edged, affording new spaces for community defense and activism while potentially exposing black men as somehow deficient in their protective or leadership roles. For every celebration of her hard work and successes, there were always powerful voices affirming the propriety of male ministers, business leaders, and elected officials leading the civil rights agenda for African Americans. Wells-Barnett remained staunchly committed to equality for black women, however, fighting hard for suffrage rights in Illinois and nationally. After the passage of the Nineteenth Amendment, she eventually ran for public office herself, in 1930.

Wells-Barnett's steadfast commitment to full equality not just for lynching victims but for "every citizen" rings through *Southern Horrors*, lending the text its prophetic, visionary quality; hers is a plea, to quote further from the pamphlet's preface, that "justice be done though the heavens fall." *Southern Horrors* draws on a number of powerful currents in American thought and style to make its case. As a graphic exposé, *Southern Horrors* shares kinship with muckraking journalism, a hallmark of the U.S. press at the turn of the century. Its empirical bent draws on statistical work to be found in the nascent academic field of sociology. *Southern Horrors* also stands in a tradition of radical pamphleteering in U.S. history that includes Tom Paine's *Common Sense* (1776) and David Walker's *Appeal to the Colored People of the Americas* (1829). Like these texts, *Southern Horrors* is peppered with wilting sarcasm and theatrical asides designed to provoke, starting with its title, a mocking send up of "southern honor." Instead of the neat closure of genteel fiction, *Southern Horrors* is full of questions and commands in a kind of call-and-response engagement with the reader, a pattern of expression at the heart of black worship traditions and one designed to work a deep transformation in participants. Finally, *Southern Horrors* ends with a practical list of strategies for "self-help," including education, boycotts, migration, agitation for protective legislation, suing through the courts, and even armed self-defense, to be "used to give that protection which the law refuses to give." Nearly five thousand Americans, almost three-fourths of them black, were lynched in Wells-Barnett's lifetime. Repeated efforts of African American activists to pass federal legislation making lynching a crime were defeated in Congress in 1922, 1937, and 1940.

What are the different kinds of violence or threats of violence that Wells documents in *Southern Horrors*? How is violence linked to issues of sexual, racial, and class privilege? How does Wells compare the social and sexual experiences of black and white women under Jim Crow? In what ways does class shape the social behavior and political strategies of the historical actors Wells describes?

CHAPTER I: THE OFFENSE

Wednesday evening May 24th, 1892, the city of Memphis was filled with excitement. Editorials in the daily papers of that date caused a meeting to be held in the Cotton Exchange Building; a committee was sent for the editors of the *Free Speech*, an Afro-American journal published in that city, and the only reason the open threats of lynching that were made were not carried out was because they could not be found. The cause of all this commotion was the following editorial published in the *Free Speech* May 21st, 1892, the Saturday previous.

> Eight negroes lynched since last issue of the *Free Speech*, one at Little Rock, Ark., last Saturday morning where the citizens broke (?) into the

Excerpted from Ida B. Wells, *Southern Horrors: Lynch Law in All Its Phases* (New York: New York Age, 1892).

penitentiary and got their man; three near Anniston, Ala., one near New Orleans; and three at Clarksville, Ga., the last three for killing a white man, and five on the same old racket—the new alarm about raping white women. The same programme of hanging, then shooting bullets into the lifeless bodies was carried out to the letter.

Nobody in this section of the country believes the old threadbare lie that Negro men rape white women. If Southern white men are not careful, they will over-reach themselves and public sentiment will have a reaction; a conclusion will then be reached which will be very damaging to the moral reputation of their women.

The Daily Commercial of Wednesday following, May 25th, contained the following leader:

Those negroes who are attempting to make the lynching of individuals of their race a means for arousing the worst passions of their kind are playing with a dangerous sentiment. The negroes may as well understand that there is no mercy for the negro rapist and little patience with his defenders. A negro organ printed in this city, in a recent issue publishes the following atrocious paragraph: "Nobody in this section of the country believes the old thread-bare lie that negro men rape white women. If Southern white men are not careful they will over-reach themselves, and public sentiment will have a reaction; and a conclusion will be reached which will be very damaging to the moral reputation of their women."

The fact that a black scoundrel is allowed to live and utter such loathsome and repulsive calumnies is a volume of evidence as to the wonderful patience of Southern whites. But we have had enough of it.

There are some things that the Southern white man will not tolerate, and the obscene intimations of the foregoing have brought the writer to the very outermost limit of public patience. We hope we have said enough.

The *Evening Scimitar* of same date, copied the *Commercial's* editorial with these words of comment: "Patience under such circumstances is not a virtue. If the negroes themselves do not apply the remedy without delay it will be the duty of those whom he has attacked to tie the wretch who utters these calumnies to a stake at the intersection of Main and Madison Sts., brand him in the forehead with a hot iron and perform upon him a surgical operation with a pair of tailor's shears."

Acting upon this advice, the leading citizens met in the Cotton Exchange Building the same evening, and threats of lynching were freely indulged, not by the lawless element upon which the deviltry of the South is usually saddled—but by the leading business men, in their leading business centre. Mr. Fleming, the business manager and owning a half interest the *Free Speech*, had to leave town to escape the mob, and was afterwards ordered not to return; letters and telegrams sent me in New York where I was spending my vacation advised me that bodily harm awaited my return. Creditors took possession of the office and sold the outfit, and the *Free Speech* was as if it had never been.

The editorial in question was prompted by the many inhuman and fiendish lynchings of Afro-Americans which have recently taken place and was meant as a warning. Eight lynched in one week and five of them charged with rape! The thinking public will not easily believe freedom and education more brutalizing than slavery, and the world knows that the crime of rape was unknown during four years of civil war, when the white women of the South were at the mercy of the race which is all at once charged with being a bestial one.

Since my business has been destroyed and I am an exile from home because of that editorial, the issue has been forced, and as the writer of it I feel that the race and the public generally should have a statement of the facts as they exist. They will serve at the same time as a defense for the Afro-American Sampsons who suffer themselves to be betrayed by white Delilahs.

The whites of Montgomery, Ala., knew J. C. Duke sounded the keynote of the situation—which they would gladly hide from the world, when he said in his paper, *The Herald*, five years ago: "Why is it that white women attract negro men now more than in former days? There was a time when such a thing was unheard of. There is a secret to this thing, and we greatly suspect it is the growing appreciation of white Juliets for colored Romeos." Mr. Duke, like the *Free Speech* proprietors, was forced to leave the city for reflecting on the "honah" of white women and his paper suppressed; but the truth remains that Afro-American men do not always rape (?) white women without their consent.

Mr. Duke, before leaving Montgomery, signed a card disclaiming any intention of slandering Southern white women. The editor of the *Free Speech* has no disclaimer to enter, but asserts instead that there are many white women in the South who would marry colored men if such an act would not place them at once beyond the pale of society and within the clutches of the law. The miscegnation laws of the South only operate against the legitimate union of the races; they leave the white man free to seduce all the colored girls he can, but it is death to the colored man who yields to the force and advances of a similar attraction in white women. White men lynch the offending Afro-American, not because he is a de-spoiler of virtue, but because he succumbs to the smiles of white women.

CHAPTER II: THE BLACK AND WHITE OF IT

The *Cleveland Gazette* of January 16, 1892, publishes a case in point. *Mrs. J. S. Underwood*, the wife of a minister of Elyria, Ohio, accused an Afro-American of rape. She told her husband that during his absence in 1888, stumping the State for the Prohibition Party, the man came to the kitchen door, forced his way in the house and insulted her. She tried to drive him out with a heavy poker, but he overpowered and chloroformed her, and when she revived her clothing was torn and she was in a horrible condition. She did not know the man but could identify him. She pointed out William Offett, a married man, who was arrested and, being in Ohio, was granted a trial.

The prisoner vehemently denied the charge of rape, but confessed he went to Mrs. Underwood's residence at her invitation and was criminally intimate with her at her request. This availed him nothing against the sworn testimony of a minister's wife, a lady of the highest respectability. He was found guilty, and entered the penitentiary, December 14, 1888, for fifteen years. Some time afterwards the woman's remorse led her to confess to her husband that the man was innocent.

These are her words: "I met Offett at the Post Office. It was raining. He was polite to me, and as I had several bundles in my arms he offered to carry them home for me, which he did. He had a strange fascination for me, and I invited him to call on me. He called, bringing chestnuts and candy for the children. By this means we got them to leave us alone in the room. Then I sat on his lap. He made a proposal to me and I readily consented. Why I did so, I do not know, but that I did is true. He visited me several times after that and each time I was indiscreet. I did not care after the first

time. In fact I could not have resisted, and had no desire to resist."

When asked by her husband why she told him she had been outraged, she said: "I had several reasons for telling you. One was the neighbors saw the fellow here, another was, I was afraid I had contracted a loathsome disease, and still another was that I feared I might give birth to a Negro baby. I hoped to save my reputation by telling you a deliberate lie." Her husband horrified by the confession had Offett, who had already served four years, released and secured a divorce.

There are thousands of such cases throughout the South, with the difference that the Southern white men in insatiate fury wreak their vengeance without intervention of law upon the Afro-Americans who consort with their women. A few instances to substantiate the assertion that some white women love the company of the Afro-American will not be out of place. Most of these cases were reported by the daily papers of the South.

In the winter of 1885–6 the wife of a practicing physician in Memphis, in good social standing whose name has escaped me, left home, husband and children, and ran away with her black coachman. She was with him a month before her husband found and brought her home. The coachman could not be found. The doctor moved his family away from Memphis, and is living in another city under an assumed name. . . .

Sarah Clark of Memphis loved a black man and lived openly with him. When she was indicted last spring for miscegenation, she swore in court that she was *not* a white woman. This she did to escape the penitentiary and continued her illicit relation undisturbed. That she is of the lower class of whites, does not disturb the fact that she is a white woman. "The leading citizens" of Memphis are defending the "honor" of *all* white women, *demi-monde* included.

Since the manager of the *Free Speech* has been run away from Memphis by the guardians of the honor of Southern white women, a young girl living on Poplar St., who was discovered in intimate relations with a handsome mulatto young colored man, Will Morgan by name, stole her father's money to send the young fellow away from that father's wrath. She has since joined him in Chicago. . . .

The very week the "leading citizens" of Memphis were making a spectacle of themselves in defense of all white women of every kind, an Afro-American, M. Stricklin, was found in a white woman's room in that city. Although she made no outcry of rape, he was jailed and would have been lynched, but the woman stated she bought curtains of him (he was a furniture dealer) and his business in her room that night was to put them up. A white woman's word was taken as absolutely in this case as when the cry of rape is made, and he was freed.

What is true of Memphis is true of the entire South. . . . Frank Weems of Chattanooga who was not lynched in May only because the prominent citizens became his body guard until the doors of the penitentiary closed on him, had letters in his pocket from the white woman in the case, making the appointment with him. Edward Coy who was burned alive in Texarkana, January 1, 1892, died protesting his innocence. Investigation since as given by the Bystander in the *Chicago Inter-Ocean*, October 1, proves: . . . The woman who was paraded as a victim of violence was of bad character; her husband was a drunkard and a gambler. . . . She was compelled by threats, if not by violence, to make the charge against the victim. . . . When she came to apply the match Coy asked her if she would burn him after they had "been sweethearting" so long. . . .

Hundreds of such cases might be cited, but enough have been given to prove the assertion that there are white women in the South who love the Afro-American's company even as there are white men notorious for their preference for Afro-American women.

There is hardly a town in the South which has not an instance of the kind which is well-known, and hence the assertion is reiterated that "nobody in the South believes the old thread-bare lie that negro men rape white women." Hence there is a growing demand among Afro-Americans that the guilt or innocence of parties accused of rape be fully established. They know the men of the section of the country who refuse this are not so desirous of punishing rapists as they pretend. The utterances of the leading white men show that with them it is not the crime but the *class*, Bishop Fitzgerald has become apologist for lynchers of the rapists of *white* women only. . . . But when the victim is a colored woman it is different.

Last winter in Baltimore, Md., three white ruffians assaulted a Miss Camphor, a young Afro-American girl, while out walking with a young man of her own race. They held her escort and outraged the girl. It was a deed dastardly enough to arouse Southern blood, which gives its horror of rape as excuse for lawlessness, but she was an Afro-American. The case went to the courts, an Afro-American lawyer defended the men and they were acquitted.

In Nashville, Tenn., there is a white man, Pat Hanifan, who outraged a little Afro-American girl, and, from the physical injuries received, she has been ruined for life. He was jailed for six months, discharged, and is now a detective in that city. . . . Only two weeks before Eph. Grizzard, who had only been *charged* with rape upon a white woman, had been taken from the jail, with Governor Buchanan and the police and militia standing by, dragged through the streets in broad daylight, knives plunged into him at every step, and with every fiendish cruelty a frenzied mob could devise, he was at last swung out on the bridge with hands cut to pieces as he tried to climb up the stanchions. . . .

At the very moment these civilized whites were announcing their determination "to protect their wives and daughters," by murdering Grizzard, a white man was in the same jail for raping eight-year-old Maggie Reese, an Afro-American girl. He was not harmed. The "honor" of grown women who were glad enough to be supported by the Grizzard boys and Ed Coy, as long as the liasion was not known, needed protection; they were white. The outrage upon helpless childhood needed no avenging in this case; she was black. . . .

CHAPTER III: THE NEW CRY

. . . Thoughtful Afro-Americans with the strong arm of the government withdrawn and with the hope to stop such wholesale massacres urged the race to sacrifice its political rights for the sake of peace. They honestly believed the race should fit itself for government, and when that should be done, the objection to race participation in politics would be removed.

But the sacrifice did not remove the trouble, nor move the South to justice. One by one the Southern States have legally (?) disfranchised the Afro-American, and since the repeal of the Civil Rights Bill nearly every Southern State has passed separate car laws with a penalty against their infringement. The race regardless of advancement is penned into filthy, stifling partitions cut off from smoking cars. . . . The dark and bloody record of the

South shows 728 Afro-Americans lynched during the past eight years; ... and not less than 150 have been known to have met violent death at the hands of cruel bloodthirsty mobs during the past nine months.

To palliate this record (which grows worse as the Afro-American becomes intelligent) and excuse some of the most heinous crimes that ever stained the history of a country, the South is shielding itself behind the plausible screen of defending the honor of its women. This, too, in the face of the fact that only *one-third* of the 728 victims to mobs have been *charged* with rape, to say nothing of those of that one-third who were innocent of the charge. . . .

Even to the better class of Afro-Americans the crime of rape is so revolting they have too often taken the white man's word and given lynch law neither the investigation nor condemnation it deserved.

They forget that a concession of the right to lynch a man for a certain crime, not only concedes the right to lynch any person for any crime, but (so frequently is the cry of rape now raised) it is in a fair way to stamp us a race of rapists and desperadoes. They have gone on hoping and believing that general education and financial strength would solve the difficulty, and are devoting their energies to the accumulation of both. . . .

Mary McLeod Bethune,
"How the Bethune-Cookman College Campus Started"

Mary McLeod Bethune was one of the most distinguished educators of her generation. The daughter of slaves, she received her early education from missionary teachers. Like others of her race who saw education as a key to racial advancement at a time when the white South was indifferent if not hostile to the aspirations of African-Americans, Bethune faced extraordinary obstacles. When she began a little school at Daytona Beach, Florida, in 1904, America was entering an era of reform. Yet even most northern progressives—with the notable exception of women such as Mary White Ovington, one of the founders of the NAACP—shared the racist assumptions of that era, believing that the future of black women, like immigrant women, lay in domestic service. Bethune had larger dreams. Because of her courage, energy, and vision, she was able to keep her school afloat with her intrepid fund-raising, guiding its growth from grammar school to high school and to what finally became an accredited four-year college. President of the institution from its founding until her resignation in 1942, she remained a trustee of Bethune-Cookman College until her death in 1955. She was an activist and held many important posts within the black community, founding such organizations as the National Association of Colored Women's Clubs and the National Council of Negro Women. A national figure as well, she served in the Roosevelt administration during the 1930s, advising the president on minority affairs. She was also involved in early efforts on behalf of the United Nations. Her many offices and honors, however, never diverted her from her primary purpose—the pursuit of full citizenship rights for all black Americans.*

*See Joyce A. Hanson, *Mary McLeod Bethune and Black Women's Political Activism* (Columbia: University of Missouri Press, 2003).

Excerpted from "Faith That Moved a Dump Heap" by Mary McLeod Bethune, in *Who, The Magazine about People* 1, no. 3 (June 1941): 31–35, 54.

Soon after opening the Daytona Educational and Industrial Institute for Negro Girls, its founder, Mary McLeod Bethune, posed with pupils lining the road leading to its first Daytona Beach build-ing—a four-room cottage. One of the fields nearby, nicknamed Hell's Hole, would soon be pur-chased by Bethune as the foundation of a genuine campus. At the time, Florida's handful of state-supported public "high" schools for blacks operated only five months a year, in contrast to nine for whites' schools. Bethune, a tireless fundraiser, chose Daytona Beach, despite the fact that it was home to a Ku Klux Klan chapter, because of two primary factors: it had a fast-growing black population attracted by relatively good jobs, and its wealthy whites, both year-round and summer residents, included some who supported her efforts. (Courtesy of the State Archives of Florida.)

On October 3, 1904, I opened the doors of my school, with an enrollment of five little girls, aged from eight to twelve, whose parents paid me fifty cents' weekly tuition. My own child was the only boy in the school. Though I hadn't a penny left, I considered cash money as the smallest part of my resources. I had faith in a living God, faith in myself, and a desire to serve. . . .

We burned logs and used the charred splinters as pencils, and mashed elderberries for ink. I begged strangers for a broom, a lamp, a bit of cretonne to put around the packing case which served as my desk. I haunted the city dump and the trash piles behind hotels, retriev-ing discarded linen and kitchenware, cracked dishes, broken chairs, pieces of old lumber. Eve-rything was scoured and mended. This was part of the training to salvage, to reconstruct, to

make bricks without straw. As parents began gradually to leave their children overnight, I had to provide sleeping accommodations. I took corn sacks for mattresses. Then I picked Spanish moss from trees, dried and cured it, and used it as a substitute for mattress hair.

The school expanded fast. In less than two years I had 250 pupils. In desperation I hired a large hall next to my original little cottage, and used it as a combined dormitory and class-room. I concentrated more and more on girls, as I felt they especially were hampered by lack of educational opportunities. . . .

I had many volunteer workers and a few regular teachers, who were paid from fifteen to twenty-five dollars a month and board. I was supposed to keep the balance of the funds for my own pocket, but there was never any bal-ance—only a yawning hole. I wore old clothes sent me by mission boards, recut and redesigned for me in our dress-making classes. At last I saw that our only solution was to stop renting space, and to buy and build our own college.

Near by was a field, popularly called Hell's Hole, which was used as a dumping ground. I approached the owner, determined to buy it. The price was $250. In a daze, he finally agreed to take five dollars down, and the balance in two years. I promised to be back in a few days with the initial payment. He never knew it, but I didn't have five dollars. I raised this sum selling ice cream and sweet-potato pies to the workmen on construction jobs, and I took the owner his money in small change wrapped in my handkerchief.

That's how the Bethune-Cookman college campus started. . . .

As the school expanded, whenever I saw a need for some training or service we did not supply, I schemed to add it to our curriculum. Sometimes that took years. When I came to Florida, there were no hospitals where a Negro could go. A student became critically ill with appendicitis, so I went to a local hospital and begged a white physician to take her in and operate. My pleas were so desperate he finally agreed. A few days after the operation, I visited my pupil.

When I appeared at the front door of the hospital, the nurse ordered me around to the back way. I thrust her aside—and found my little girl segregated in a corner of the porch behind the kitchen. Even my toes clenched with rage.

That decided me. I called on three of my faithful friends, asking them to buy a little cottage behind our school as a hospital. They agreed, and we started with two beds.

From this humble start grew a fully equipped twenty-bed hospital—our college infirmary and a refuge for the needy throughout the state. It was staffed by white and black physicians and by our own student nurses. We ran this hospital for twenty years as part of our contribution to community life; but a short time ago, to ease our financial burden, the city took it over.

Gradually, as educational facilities expanded and there were other places where small children could go, we put the emphasis on high-school and junior-college training. In 1922, Cookman College, a men's school, the first in the state for the higher education of Negroes, amalgamated with us. The combined coeducational college, now run under the auspices of the Methodist Episcopal Church, is called Bethune-Cookman College. We have fourteen modern buildings, a beautiful campus of thirty-two acres, an enrollment in regular and summer sessions of 600 students, a faculty and staff of thirty-two, and 1,800 graduates. The college property, now valued at more than $800,000, is entirely unencumbered.

When I walk through the campus, with its stately palms and well-kept lawns, and think back to the dump-heap foundation, I rub my eyes and pinch myself. And I remember my childish visions in the cotton fields.

But values cannot be calculated in ledger figures and property. More than all else the college has fulfilled my ideals of distinctive training and service. Extending far beyond the immediate sphere of its graduates and students, it has already enriched the lives of 100,000 Negroes.

In 1934, President Franklin D. Roosevelt appointed me director of the division of Negro affairs of the National Youth Administration. My main task now is to supervise the training provided for 600,000 Negro children, and I have to run the college by remote control. Every few weeks, however, I snatch a day or so and return to my beloved home.

This is a strenuous program. The doctor shakes his head and says, "Mrs. Bethune, slow down a little. Relax! Take it just a little easier." I promise to reform, but in an hour the promise is forgotten.

For I am my mother's daughter, and the drums of Africa still beat in my heart. They will not let me rest while there is a single Negro boy or girl without a chance to prove his worth.

WOMEN IN THE WEST

PEGGY PASCOE
Ophelia Paquet, a Tillamook of Oregon, Challenges Miscegenation Laws

When Ophelia Paquet's husband died in 1919, the county court recognized her as his widow—the Paquets had been married for thirty years—and appointed Ophelia to administer his estate. As there were no children, Ophelia stood to inherit her late husband's property. It was a just arrangement inasmuch as it was her money that had been used to purchase the land and pay taxes on it. John Paquet, Fred's disreputable brother, thought otherwise. Ultimately the court awarded the estate to him, leaving the sixty-five-year-old widow destitute.

Ophelia's story is a complicated one. It illuminates many issues: the purpose of miscegenation laws, the role of marriage in the transmission of property, the "invisibility" of married women's economic contributions, and the way race can compound gender disadvantage.

In what respects does John Paquet's victory illuminate the convergence of race and class? What parallels does Pascoe draw between the Paquet case and contemporary debates over same-sex marriage? How is the failure to count Ophelia's economic contribution to the marriage related to the "pastoralization" of housework that Jeanne Boydston discusses on pages 128–139?

Although miscegenation laws are usually remembered (when they are remembered at all) as a Southern development aimed at African Americans, they were actually a much broader phenomenon. Adopted in both the North and the South in the colonial period and extended to western states in the nineteenth century, miscegenation laws grew up with slavery but became even more significant after the Civil War, for it was then that they came to form the crucial "bottom line" of the system of white supremacy embodied in segregation.

The earliest miscegenation laws, passed in the South, forbade whites to marry African Americans, but the list of groups prohibited from marrying whites was gradually expanded, especially in western states, by adding first American Indians, then Chinese and Japanese (both often referred to by the catchall term "Mongolians"), and then Malays (or Filipinos). And even this didn't exhaust the list. Oregon prohibited whites from marrying "Kanakas" (or native Hawaiians); South Dakota proscribed "Coreans"; Arizona singled out Hindus; and

From "On the Significance of Miscegenation Law in United State History," in *New Viewpoints in Women's History: Working Papers from the Schlesinger Library 50th Anniversary Conference, March 4–5, 1994,* ed. Susan Ware (Cambridge, Mass.: Arthur and Elizabeth Schlesinger Library on the History of Women in America, Radcliffe College, [1994]). Condensed and reprinted by permission of the author. Notes have been renumbered and edited. We mourn Peggy Pascoe's death on July 23, 2010. For Estelle Freedman's remembrance, see http://www.historians.org/publications-and-directories/perspectives-on-history/november-2010/in-memoriam-peggy-pascoe.

Georgia prohibited whites from marrying "West" and "Asiatic" Indians.

Many states packed their miscegenation laws with multiple categories and quasi-mathematical definitions of "race." Oregon, for example, declared that "it shall not be lawful within this state for any white person, male or female, to intermarry with any negro, Chinese, or any person having one fourth or more negro, Chinese, or Kanaka blood, or any person having more than one half Indian blood." Altogether, miscegenation laws covered forty-one states and colonies. They spanned three centuries of American history: the first ones were enacted in the 1660s, and the last ones were not declared unconstitutional until 1967.

Although it is their sexual taboos that have attracted most recent attention, the structure and function of miscegenation laws were . . . more fundamentally related to the institution of marriage than to sexual behavior itself. In sheer numbers, many more laws prohibited interracial marriage than interracial sex. And in an even deeper sense, all miscegenation laws were designed to privilege marriage as a social and economic unit. Couples who challenged the laws knew that the right to marry translated into social respectability and economic benefits, including inheritance rights and legitimacy for children, that were denied to sexual liaisons outside marriage. Miscegenation laws were designed to patrol this border by making so-called "miscegenous marriage" a legal impossibility. Thus criminal courts treated offenders as if they had never been married at all; that is, prosecutors charged interracial couples with the moral offense of fornication or other illicit sex crimes, then denied them the use of marriage as a defense.

Civil courts guarded the junction between marriage and economic privilege. From Reconstruction to the 1930s, most miscegenation cases heard in civil courts were ex post facto attempts to invalidate relationships that had already lasted for a long time. They were brought by relatives or, sometimes, by the state, after the death of one partner, almost always a white man. Many of them were specifically designed to take property or inheritances away from the surviving partner, almost always an African American or American Indian woman. By looking at civil law suits like these (which were, at least in appeals court records, more common than criminal cases), we can begin to trace the links between white

patriarchal privilege and property that sustained miscegenation laws.

Let me illustrate the point by describing [a] sample case, *In re Paquet's Estate*, decided by the Oregon Supreme Court in 1921.[1] The Paquet case, like most of the civil miscegenation cases of this period, was fought over the estate of a white man. The man in question, Fred Paquet, died in 1919, survived by his 63-year-old Tillamook Indian wife, named Ophelia. The Paquet estate included 22 acres of land, some farm animals, tools, and a buggy, altogether worth perhaps $2500.[2] Fred and Ophelia's relationship had a long history. In the 1880s, Fred had already begun to visit Ophelia frequently and openly enough that he had become one of many targets of a local grand jury which periodically threatened to indict white men who lived with Indian women.[3] Seeking to formalize the relationship—and, presumably, end this harrassment—Fred consulted a lawyer, who advised him to make sure to hold a ceremony which would meet the legal requirements for an "Indian custom" marriage. Accordingly, in 1889, Fred not only reached the customary agreement with Ophelia's Tillamook relatives, paying them $50 in gifts, but also sought the formal sanction of Tillamook tribal chief Betsy Fuller (who was herself married to a white man); Fuller arranged for a tribal council to consider and confirm the marriage.[4] Afterwards Fred and Ophelia lived together until his death, for more than thirty years. Fred clearly considered Ophelia his wife, and his neighbors, too, recognized their relationship, but because Fred died without leaving a formal will, administration of the estate was subject to state laws which provided for the distribution of property to surviving family members.

When Fred Paquet died, the county court recognized Ophelia as his widow and promptly appointed her administrator of the estate. Because the couple had no children, all the property, including the land, which Ophelia lived on and the Paquets had owned for more than two decades, would ordinarily have gone to her. Two days later, though, Fred's brother John came forward to contest Ophelia for control over the property.[5] John Paquet had little to recommend him to the court. Some of his neighbors accused him of raping native women, and he had such an unsavory reputation in the community that at one point the county judge declared him "a man of immoral habits ... incompetent to transact ordinary business affairs and generally untrustworthy."[6] He was, however, a "white" man, and under Oregon's miscegenation law, that was enough to ensure that he won his case against Ophelia, an Indian woman.

The case eventually ended up in the Oregon Supreme Court. In making its decision, the key issue for the court was whether or not to recognize Fred and Ophelia's marriage, which violated Oregon's miscegenation law.[7] The Court listened to—and then dismissed—Ophelia's argument that the marriage met the requirements for an Indian custom marriage and so should have been recognized as valid out of routine courtesy to the authority of another jurisdiction (that of the Tillamook tribe).[8] The Court also heard and dismissed Ophelia's claim that Oregon's miscegenation law discriminated against Indians and was therefore an unconstitutional denial of the Fourteenth Amendment guarantee of equal protection. The Court ingenuously explained its reasoning; it held that the Oregon miscegenation law did not discriminate because it "applied alike to all persons, either white, negroes, Chinese, Kanaka, or Indians."[9] Following this logic, the Court declared Fred and Ophelia's marriage void because it violated Oregon's miscegenation law; it ordered that the estate and all its property be transferred to "the only relative in the state," John Paquet, to be distributed among him, his siblings and their heirs.[10]

As the Paquet case demonstrates, miscegenation law did not always prevent the formation of interracial relationships, sexual or otherwise. Fred and Ophelia had, after all, lived together for more than thirty years and had apparently won recognition as a couple from many of those around them; their perseverance had even allowed them to elude grand jury crackdowns. They did not, however, manage to escape the really crucial power of miscegenation law: the role it played in connecting white supremacy to the transmission of property. In American law, marriage provided the glue which allowed for the transmission of property from husbands to wives and their children; miscegenation law kept property within racial boundaries by invalidating marriages between white men and women of color whenever ancillary white relatives like John Paquet contested them.[11] ... Property, so often described in legal sources as simple economic assets (like land and capital) was

actually a much more expansive phenomenon, one which took various forms and structured crucial relationships. ... Race is in and of itself a kind of property.[12] As [legal scholar] Derrick Bell ... explains, most whites did—and still do—"expect the society to recognize an unspoken but no less vested property right in their 'whiteness.'" "This right," Bell maintains, "is recognized and upheld by courts and the society like all property rights under a government created and sustained primarily for that purpose."[13]

As applied to the Paquet case, this theme is easy to trace, for, in a sense, the victorious John Paquet had turned his "whiteness" (the best—and perhaps the only—asset he had) into property, and did so at Ophelia's expense. This transformation happened not once but repeatedly. One instance occurred shortly after the county judge had branded John Paquet immoral and unreliable. Dismissing these charges as the opinions of "a few scalawags and Garibaldi Indians," John Paquet's lawyers rallied enough white witnesses who would speak in his defense to mount an appeal which convinced a circuit court judge to declare Paquet competent to administer the estate.[14] Another example of the transformation of "whiteness" into property came when the Oregon Supreme Court ruled that Ophelia Paquet's "Indianness" disqualified her from legal marriage to a white man; with Ophelia thus out of the way, John and his siblings won the right to inherit the property.

The second property relationship [is] illuminated by the etymological connection between the words "property" and "propriety." Miscegenation law played on this connection by drawing a sharp line between "legitimate marriage" on the one hand and "illicit sex" on the other, then defining all interracial relationships as illicit sex. The distinction was a crucial one, for husbands were legally obligated to provide for legitimate wives and children, but men owed nothing to "mere" sexual partners: neither inheritance rights nor the legitimacy of children accompanied illicit relationships.

By defining all interracial relationships as illicit, miscegenation law did not so much prohibit or punish illicit sex as it did create and reproduce it. Conditioned by stereotypes which associated women of color with hypersexuality, judges routinely branded long-term settled relationships as "mere" sex rather than marriage. Lawyers played to these assumptions by reducing interracial relationships to interracial sex, then distinguishing interracial sex from marriage by associating it with prostitution. Describing the relationship between Fred and Ophelia Paquet, for example, John Paquet's lawyers claimed that "the alleged 'marriage' was a mere commercial affair" that did not deserve legal recognition because "the relations were entirely meretricious from their inception."[15]

It was all but impossible for women of color to escape the legacy of these associations. Ophelia Paquet's lawyers tried to find a way out by changing the subject. Rather than refuting the association between women of color and illicit sexuality, they highlighted its flip side, the supposed connection between white women and legitimate marriage. Ophelia Paquet, they told the judge, "had been to the man as good a wife as any white woman could have been."[16] In its final decision, the Oregon Supreme Court came as close as any court of that time did to accepting this line of argument. Taking the unusual step of admitting that "the record is conclusive that [Ophelia] lived with [Fred] as a good and faithful wife for more than 30 years," the judges admitted that they felt some sympathy for Ophelia, enough to recommend—but not require—that John Paquet offer her what they called "a fair and reasonable settlement."[17] But in the Paquet case, as in other miscegenation cases, sexual morality, important as it was, was nonetheless still subordinate to channelling the transmission of property along racial . . . lines. Ophelia got a judicial pat on the head for good behavior, but John and his siblings got the property.

Which brings me to the third form of property relationship structured by miscegenation laws—and, for that matter, marriage laws in general—and that is women's economic dependence on men. Here the problems started long before the final decision gave John Paquet control of the Paquet estate. One of the most intriguing facts about the Paquet case is that everyone acted as if the estate in question belonged solely to Fred Paquet. In fact, however, throughout the Paquet marriage, Fred had whiled away most of his time; it was Ophelia's basket-making, fruit-picking, milk-selling, and wage work that had provided the income they needed to sustain themselves. And although the deed to their land was made out in Fred Paquet's name, the couple had used Ophelia's earnings, combined with her proceeds from

government payments to Tillamook tribal members, both to purchase the property and to pay the yearly taxes on it. It is significant . . . that, although lawyers on both sides of the case knew this, neither they nor the Oregon Supreme Court judges considered it a key issue at the trial in which Ophelia lost all legal right to what the courts considered "Fred's" estate.

Indeed, Ophelia's economic contribution might never have been taken into account if it were not for the fact that in the wake of the Oregon Supreme Court decision, United States Indian officials found themselves responsible for the care of the now impoverished Ophelia. Apparently hoping both to defend Ophelia and to relieve themselves of the burden of her support, they sued John Paquet on Ophelia's behalf. Working through the federal courts that covered Indian relations and equity claims, rather than the state courts that enforced miscegenation laws, they eventually won a partial settlement. Yet their argument, too, reflected the assumption that men were better suited than women to the ownership of what the legal system referred to as "real" property. Although their brief claimed that "Fred Paquet had practically no income aside from the income he received through the labor and efforts of the said Ophelia Paquet," they asked the Court to grant Ophelia the right to only half of the Paquet land.[18] In the end, the Court ordered that Ophelia should receive a cash settlement (the amount was figured at half the value of the land), but only if she agreed to make her award contingent on its sale.[19] To get any settlement at all, Ophelia Paquet had to relinquish all claims to actual ownership of the land, although such a claim might have given her legal grounds to prevent its sale and so allow her to spend her final years on the property.

It is not even clear that she received any payment on the settlement ordered by the court. As late as 1928, John Paquet's major creditor complained to a judge that Paquet had repeatedly turned down acceptable offers to sell the land; perhaps he had chosen to live on it himself.[20]

Like any single example, the Paquet case captures miscegenation law as it stood at one moment, and a very particular moment at that, one that might be considered the high water mark of American courts' determination to structure both family formation and property transmission along racial dividing lines.

Today, most Americans have trouble remembering that miscegenation laws ever existed . . . [and] are incredulous at the injustice and the arbitrariness of the racial classifications that stand out in [such] . . . cases. [Yet] few . . . notice that one of the themes raised in the Paquet case—the significance of marriage in structuring property transmission—not only remains alive and well, but has, in fact, outlived both the erosion of traditional patriarchy and the rise and fall of racial classifications in marriage law.

More than a generation after the demise of miscegenation laws . . . the drawing of exclusionary lines around marriage [continues]. . . . The most prominent—though hardly the only—victims are lesbian and gay couples, who point out that the sex classifications currently embedded in marriage law operate in much the same way that the race classifications embedded in miscegenation laws once did: that is, they allow courts to categorize same-sex relationships as illicit sex rather than legitimate marriage and they allow courts to exclude same-sex couples from the property benefits of marriage, which now include everything from tax advantages to medical insurance coverage.

Both these modern legal battles and the earlier ones fought by couples like Fred and Ophelia Paquet suggest . . . that focusing on the connections between property and the political economy of marriage . . . offer a revealing vantage point from which to study both the form and power of analogies between race and sex classifications in American law and the relationships between race and gender hierarchies in American history.

NOTES

1. The Paquet case can be followed not only by reading the text of the appeals court decision, In re Paquet's Estate, 200 P 911 (Oregon 1921), but also in the following archival case files: *Paquet v. Paquet,* file No. 4268, Oregon Supreme Court, 1920; *Paquet v. Henkle,* file No. 4267, Oregon Supreme Court, 1920; and Tillamook County Probate file #605, all in the Oregon State Archives; and in *U.S. v. John B. Paquet,* Judgment Roll 11409, Register No. 8-8665, March 1925, National Archives and Records Administration, Pacific Northwest Branch.

2. Initial estimates of the value of the estate were much higher, ranging from $4500 to $12,500. I have relied on the figure of $2528.50 provided by court-appointed assessors. See Tillamook Country Probate file #605, Inventory and Appraisement, June 15, 1920.

3. *Paquet v. Paquet,* Respondent's brief, November 1, 1920, pp. 2–5.

4. Tillamook County Probate file #605, Judge A.M. Hare, Findings of Facts and Conclusions of Law, February 3, 1920; *Paquet v. Paquet,* Appellants Abstract of Record, September 3, 1920, pp. 10–16.

5. *Paquet v. Paquet,* Appellants Abstract of Record, September 3, 1920, p. 3.

6. Tillamook County Probate file #605, Judge A. M. Hare, Findings of Fact and Conclusions of Law, February 3, 1920.

7. Court records identify Fred Paquet as being of French Canadian origin. Both sides agreed that Fred was a "pure" or "full-blooded" "white" man and Ophelia was a "pure" or "full-blooded" "Indian" woman. *Paquet* v. *Paquet,* Appellant's First Brief, October 8, 1920, p. 1; *Paquet v. Paquet;* Respondent's brief, November 1, 1920, p. 2.

8. The question of legal jurisdiction over Indian tribes was—and is—a very thorny issue. Relations with Indians were generally a responsibility of the U.S. federal government, which, although it advocated assimilating Indian families into white middle-class molds, had little practical choice but to grant general recognition to tribally-determined marriages performed according to Indian custom. In the U.S. legal system, however, jurisdiction over marriage rested with the states rather than the federal government. States could, therefore, use their control over marriage as a wedge to exert some power over Indians by claiming that Indian-white marriages, especially those performed outside recognized reservations, were subject to state jurisdiction. In the Paquet case, for example, the court insisted that, because the Tillamook had never been assigned to a reservation and because Fred and Ophelia lived in a mixed settlement, Ophelia could not be considered part of a recognized tribe nor a "ward" of the federal government. As events would later show, both contentions were inaccurate: Ophelia was an enrolled member of the Tillamook tribe, which was under the supervision of the Siletz Indian Agency; the federal government claimed her as "a ward of the United States." See *U.S. v. John B. Paquet,* Bill of Complaint in Equity, September 21, 1923, p. 3.

9. In re Paquet's Estate, 200 P 911 at 913 (Oregon 1921).

10. In re Paquet's Estate, 200 P 911 at 914 (Oregon 1921).

11. Although the issue did not come up in the Paquet case, . . . in miscegenation cases, not only the wife but also the children might lose their legal standing, for one effect of invalidating an interracial marriage was to make the children technically illegitimate. According to the law of most states, illegitimate children automatically inherited from their mothers, but they could inherit from their fathers only if their father had taken legal steps to formally recognize or adopt them. Since plaintiffs could rarely convince judges that fathers had done so, the children of interracial marriages were often disinherited along with their mothers.

12. Derrick Bell, "Remembrances of Racism Past," in Hill and Jones, *Race in America: The Struggle for Equality* (Madison: University of Wisconsin Press, 1992), 78. See also Bell, "White Superiority in America: Its Legal Legacy, Its Economic Costs," *Villanova Law Review* 33 (1988), 767–779.

13. *Paquet v. Henkle,* Respondent's brief, March 14, 1920, p. 6; *Paquet v. Henkle,* Index to Transcript, August 25, 1920, p. 3.

14. *Paquet v. Paquet,* Respondent's brief, November 1, 1920, p. 7. Using typical imagery, they added that the Paquet relationship was "a case where a white man and a full blooded Indian woman have chosen to cohabit together illictly [sic], to agree to a relation of concubinage, which is not only a violation of the law of Oregon, but a transgression against the law of morality and the law of nature" (p. 16).

15. *Paquet v. Paquet,* Appellant's First Brief, October 8, 1920, p. 2.

16. In re Paquet's Estate, 200 P 911 at 914 (Oregon 1921).

17. *U.S. v. John B. Paquet,* Bill of Complaint in Equity, September 21, 1923, pp. 4, 6–7.

18. *U.S. v. John B. Paquet,* Stipulation, June 2, 1924; *U.S. v. John B. Paquet,* Decree, June 2, 1924.

19. Tillamook County Probate file #605, J. S. Cole, Petition, June 7, 1928. Cole was president of the Tillamook-Lincoln County Credit Association.

20. For a particularly insightful analysis of the historical connections between concepts of "race" and "family," see Liu, "Teaching the Differences among Women in a Historical Perspective," *Women's Studies International Forum* 14 (1991): 265–276.

JUDY YUNG

Unbound Feet: From China to San Francisco's Chinatown

The imbalance of men and women in the largest Chinese community on the West Coast was a source of immense frustration, especially after the Immigration Act of 1924 effectively barred Chinese wives, even those married to U.S. citizens, from entering the country. Pany Lowe, an American-born Chinese man, expressed the feelings of men: "I think most Chinese in this country like have their son go to China get married. Under this new law . . . can't do this. No allowed marry white girl. Not enough American-born Chinese to go around. China only place to get wife. Not allowed to bring them back. For Chinaman, very unjust."* Although the act was amended in 1930 to allow the entry of women who had been married to U.S. citizens prior to May 26, 1924, the process of gaining entrance was lengthy, costly, and humiliating for most Chinese women. Many men, like Pany Lowe, chose to visit their wives in China rather than subject them to the ordeal of immigration.

Judy Yung's essay traces the experiences of three women from Guangdong Province who arrived in San Francisco in 1922. Two, Wong Ah So and Law Shee Low, came from impoverished villages to join their husbands in arranged marriages. Wong Ah So was in for a major surprise when she discovered her "marriage" was part of a system of enslaving women in forced prostitution to fill what was perceived to be a pressing need in a Chinese bachelor society. The third woman came from a different background with different expectations. Jane Kwong Lee was an urbanized, unmarried "new woman" who came to the

*Quoted in Judy Yung, *Unbound Feet: A Social History of Chinese Women in San Francisco* (Berkeley: University of California Press, 1995), p. 58.

United States to further her education. While she would endure many of the same gender and racial restrictions as the other two women, differences in her class and education made her experience—and the opportunities available to her—significantly different from that of other immigrant Chinese women in the 1920s.

Women's emancipation was heralded in San Francisco's Chinatown on the afternoon of November 2, 1902, when Sieh King King, an eighteen-year-old student from China and an ardent reformer, stood before a theater full of men and women and, according to newspaper accounts, "boldly condemned the slave girl system, raged at the horrors of foot-binding and, with all the vehemence of aroused youth, declared that men and women were equal and should enjoy the privileges of equals."[1] Her talk and her views on women's rights were inextricably linked with Chinese nationalism and the 1898 Reform Movement, which advocated that China emulate the West and modernize in order to throw off the yoke of foreign domination. Elevating the status of women to the extent that they could become "new women"—educated mothers and productive citizens—was part of this nationalist effort to strengthen and defend China against further encroachment.

What Sieh King King advocated on behalf of Chinese women—unbound feet, education, equal rights, and public participation—remained at the heart of social change for Chinese women for the next three decades. This was due largely to the continuous influence of nationalism and women's emancipation in China, the reform work of Protestant missionary women in Chinatown, and Chinese women's entry into the urban economy. By 1929, immigrant women had made considerable progress toward freeing themselves of social restrictions and moving into the public arena. Footbinding was no longer practiced, prostitution had been eradicated, and a substantial number of women were working outside the home, educating themselves and their daughters, and playing a more visible role in community affairs. This discussion of the lives of Chinese immigrant women from 1902, when Sieh King King introduced her feminist views in San Francisco, to 1929, the beginnings of the Great Depression, will illustrate how socioeconomic developments in China and the United States

facilitated the unbinding of their feet and of their lives.

JOURNEY TO GOLD MOUNTAIN

At the time of Sieh King King's speech, China was still suffering under the stranglehold of Western imperialism and the inept rule of the Manchus. Life for the ordinary Chinese remained disrupted; survival was precarious. Consequently, many able-bodied peasants in Southeast China continued to emigrate overseas where kinfolk had already settled. Despite the Chinese Exclusion Acts and anti-Chinese hostilities, a good number went to California, the Gold Mountain. As increased numbers of Chinese sojourners became settlers, some found the economic means by which to get married or send for their wives and children from China. American immigration laws and the process of chain migration determined that most Chinese women would continue to come from the rural villages of Guangdong Province, where traditional gender roles still prevailed. Among these women were Wong Ah So and Law Shee Low, who both emigrated as obedient daughters in 1922 to escape poverty at home. Jane Kwong Lee, who also came the same year, was among the small number of urbanized "new women" who emigrated on their own for educational reasons. Together, these three women's stories provide insights into the gender roles and immigration experiences of Chinese women in the early twentieth century.

"I was born in Guangdong Province," begins Wong Ah So's story. "My father was sometimes a sailor and sometimes he worked on the docks, for we were very poor."[2] Patriarchal cultural values often put the daughter at risk when poverty strikes: From among the five children in the family, her mother chose to betroth her, the eldest daughter, to a Gold Mountain man in exchange for a bride price of 450 Mexican dollars.

> I was 19 when this man came to my mother and said that in America there was a great deal of gold. Even if I just peeled potatoes there, he told my

mother I would earn seven or eight dollars a day, and if I was willing to do any work at all I would earn lots of money. He was a laundryman, but said he earned plenty of money. He was very nice to me, and my mother liked him, so my mother was glad to have me go with him as his wife.

Out of filial duty and economic necessity, Ah So agreed to sail to the United States with this laundryman, Huey Yow. He had a marriage certificate prepared and told her to claim him as her husband to the immigration officials in San Francisco, although as she admitted later, "I claimed to be the wife of Huey Yow, but in truth had not at any time lived with him as his wife."

In Law Shee Low's case, her family succumbed to poverty after repeated raids by roving bandits in the Chungshan District of Guangdong Province. Conditions became so bad that the family had to sell their land and give up their three servants; all four daughters had to quit school and help at home. Speaking of her arranged marriage to a Gold Mountain man, she said, "I had no choice; we were so poor. We had no food to go with rice, not even soy sauce or black bean paste. Some of our neighbors even had to go begging or sell their daughters, times were so bad. So my parents thought I would have a better future in Gold Mountain."[3] Her fiancé said he was a clothing salesman in San Francisco and a Christian. He had a minister from Canton preside over the first "modern" wedding in his village. Law was eighteen and her husband, thirty-four. Nine months after the wedding, they sailed for America.

Born in 1902 to wealthy parents of the Toishan District, Guangdong Province (her family owned land and her father and uncle were successful businessmen in Australia), Jane Kwong Lee was able to acquire a Western education in the treaty port of Canton. There she was first exposed to American ideas of democracy and women's emancipation. During her last year in school, she was swept up by the May Fourth Movement, in which students agitated for political and cultural reforms in response to continuing foreign domination. At the time of her graduation from middle school, she observed that classmates were either entering technical institutions or getting married. "I thought otherwise," she said. "I enjoyed studying and I wanted to be economically independent. In that sense, it was clear in my mind that I had to have as much formal education as possible."[4]

Although she wanted to become a doctor, medical school was out of the question, as her father's remittances from Australia could no longer support both her and her younger brother's education. Arguing that graduates trained in American colleges and universities were drawing higher salaries in China than local graduates, Jane convinced her mother to sell some of their land in order to pay her passage to the United States. She then obtained a student's visa and sailed for America, planning to earn a doctorate and return home to a prestigious academic post. Jane Kwong Lee's class background, education, and early exposure to Western ideas would lead her to a different life experience in America than Law Shee Low and Wong Ah So, who came as obedient wives from sheltered and impoverished families.

The San Francisco Chinatown that the three women came to call home was different from the slum of "filth and depravity" of bygone days. After the 1906 earthquake and fire destroyed Chinatown, Chinese community leaders seized the opportunity to create a new "Oriental City" on the original site. The new Chinatown, in stark contrast to the old, was by appearance cleaner, healthier, and more modern with its wider paved streets, brick buildings, glass-plated storefronts, and pseudo-Chinese architecture. In an effort to establish order in the community, nurture business, and protect the growing numbers of families, the merchant elite and middle-class bourgeoisie established new institutions: Chinese schools, churches, a hospital, newspapers, and a flurry of civic and political organizations. Soon after the 1911 Revolution in China, queues and footbinding were eliminated, tong wars and prostitution reduced, and more of Chinatown's residents were dressing in Western clothing and adopting democratic ideas. Arriving in San Francisco's Chinatown at this juncture in time gave immigrant women such as Wong Ah So, Law Shee Low, and Jane Kwong Lee unprecedented opportunities to become "new women" in the modern era of Chinatown.

ESCAPING "A FATE WORSE THAN DEATH"

Upon landing in America, Wong Ah So's dreams of wealth and happiness vanished when she found out that her husband, Huey

Yow, had in fact been paid $500 by a madam to procure her as a slave.

> When we first landed in San Francisco we lived in a hotel in Chinatown, a nice place, but one day, after I had been there for about two weeks, a woman came to see me. She was young, very pretty, and all dressed in silk. She told me that I was not really Huey Yow's wife, but that she had asked him to buy her a slave, that I belonged to her, and must go with her, but she would treat me well, and I could buy back my freedom, if I was willing to please, and be agreeable, and she would let me off in two years, instead of four if I did not make a fuss.

For the next year, Wong Ah So worked as a prostitute for the madam in various small towns. She was also forced to borrow $1,000 to pay off Huey Yow, who was harassing her and threatening her life. Soon after, she was sold to another madam in Fresno for $2,500. Meanwhile, her family in China continued to write her, asking for money. Even as her debts piled up and she became ill, she fulfilled her filial obligation by sending $300 home to her mother, enclosed with a letter that read in part:

> Every day I have to be treated by the doctor. My private parts pain me so that I cannot have intercourse with men. It is very hard. . . . Next year I certainly will be able to pay off all the debts. Your daughter is even more anxious than her mother to do this. Your daughter will do her part so that the world will not look down upon us.

Then one evening at a tong banquet where she was working, Wong Ah So was recognized by a friend of her father's, who sought help from the Presbyterian Mission Home on her behalf. Ten days later, she was rescued and placed in the care of Donaldina Cameron, the director of the home. As she wrote, "I don't know just how it happened because it was all very sudden. I just know that it happened. I am learning English and to weave, and I am going to send money to my mother when I can. I can't help but cry, but it is going to be better. I will do what Miss Cameron says." A year later, after learning how to read Chinese and speak English and becoming a Christian, Ah So agreed to marry Louie Kwong, a merchant in Boise, Idaho.

Wong Ah So's story harks back to the plight of the many Chinese women who were brought to the United States as prostitutes to fill a specific need in the Chinese bachelor society. By the 1920s, however, the traffic had gone underground and was on the decline due to the Chinese exclusion laws, anti-prostitution legislation, and the efforts of Protestant missionaries. In 1870, the peak year of prostitution, 1,426 or 71 percent of Chinese women in San Francisco were listed as prostitutes. By 1900 the number had dropped to 339 or 16 percent; and by 1910, 92 or 7 percent. No prostitutes could be found in the 1920 census, although English- and Chinese-language newspaper accounts and the records of the Presbyterian Mission Home indicate that organized prostitution continued through the 1920s.[5]

Most well known for her rescue work in Chinatown, Donaldina Cameron was a product of the Social Gospel and Progressive movements, which sought to uplift the "uncivilized" throughout the world and eradicate political corruption and social vices in the nation's cities. Unable to work effectively among Chinatown bachelors and spurned by white prostitutes, Cameron found her calling among Chinese prostitutes and slave girls. In turn, some Chinese prostitutes, calculating their chances in an oppressive environment with few options for improvement, saw the Mission Home as a way out of their problems. Cameron made it her crusade to free them from "a fate worse than death" by first rescuing them, and then inculcating them with Christian moral values. Numerous accounts in newspapers and religious publications describe in vivid detail the dangerous raids led by Cameron, who was credited with rescuing hundreds of Chinese slave girls during her forty years of service at the Presbyterian Mission Home.[6]

Once rescued, the young women were brought back to the Mission Home to be educated, trained in the domestic arts and industrial skills, and, most importantly, indoctrinated with Victorian moral values. The goal was to regroom them to enter society as Christian women. While some women chose to return to China under Christian escort, others opted to enter companionate marriages, pursue higher education, or become missionary workers. Wong Ah So—a direct beneficiary of the efforts of Protestant missionary women—was among the last to be rescued, Christianized, and married to a Chinese Christian.

Newly-arrived Chinese women and children awaiting interrogation at the Immigration Station on Angel Island, near San Francisco, sometime after 1910. (Courtesy of California Historical Society, FN-18240.)

IMMIGRANT WIVES AS INDISPENSABLE PARTNERS

Immigrant wives like Law Shee Low also found their lives transformed by the socioeconomic conditions in Chinatown. They did not find streets paved with gold, but practically speaking, they at least had food on the table and hope that through their hard work conditions might improve for themselves and their families. Although women were confined to the domestic sphere within the borders of Chinatown, their contributions as homemakers, wage earners, and culture bearers made them indispensable partners to their husbands in their struggle for economic survival. Their indispensability, combined with changing social attitudes toward women in Chinatown, gave some women leverage to shape gender arrangements within their homes and in the community.

Upon arrival in San Francisco, Law Shee Low moved into a one-room tenement apartment in Chinatown with her husband, where she lived, worked, and gave birth to eleven children, eight of whom survived. While her husband worked in a restaurant that catered to

black customers on the outskirts of Chinatown, Law stayed home and took in sewing. Like other immigrant women who followed traditional gender roles, Law believed that the proper place for a woman was at home. As she recalls those days,

> There was no time to feel imprisoned; there was so much to do. We had to cook, wash the clothes and diapers by hand, the floors, and sew whenever we had a chance to sit still. It was the same for all my neighbors. We were all good, obedient, and diligent wives. All sewed; all had six or seven children. Who had time to go out?

Fortunately for Law Shee Low, her husband turned out to be cooperative, supportive, and devoted. Until he developed a heart condition in the 1950s, he remained the chief breadwinner, first cooking at a restaurant, then picking fruit in Suisun [California], sewing at home during the depression, and finally working in the shipyards during World War II. Although he refused to help with housecleaning or childcare, he did all the shopping, cooked the rice, and hung out the wash. In his own way, he showed concern for his wife. "When he was afraid I wasn't eating, he would tell me to eat more. Even though it was an arranged marriage, we got along well. I didn't complain that he went out every day. We hardly talked. Good or bad, we just struggled along as we had work to do."

As far as children were concerned Law Shee Low, like her neighbors, had not known how to interfere with nature. "We didn't know about birth control. We would become pregnant every year without realizing it. Even if we didn't want it, we didn't have the money to go see the doctor." All of Law's children were born at home, with the help of neighbors or the local midwife. Fortunately, her husband wanted children and was more than willing to provide for them all regardless of sex. "Other men would scold their children and beat them. One woman who had four children told me her husband would drag her out of bed and beat her because she didn't want to have any more children. We heard all kinds of sad stories like that, but my husband never picked on me like that."

It was not until her children were older that Law Shee Low went out to work in the sewing factories and to the Chinese movies on Saturdays, but she still did not leave the confines of Chinatown. Prior to that, she went out so seldom that one pair of shoes lasted her ten years. Since their first responsibility was to their families, many immigrant wives like Law found themselves housebound, with no time to learn English or to participate in social activities outside the home. Their husbands continued to be the chief breadwinner, to hold the purse strings, and to be their liaison to the outside world. But in the absence of the mother-in-law, immigrant wives usually ruled the household and assumed the responsibility of disciplinarian, culture-bearer, and of maintaining the integrity of their families. With few exceptions, they were hardworking, frugal, and tolerant, faithful and respectful to their husbands, and self-sacrificing toward their children. As such, they were indispensable partners to their husbands in their efforts to establish and sustain family life in America. And although they presented a submissive image in public, many immigrant women were known to "wear the pants" at home.

Overall, as compared to their predecessors, immigrant women in the early twentieth century were less tolerant of abuses to their persons and more resourceful in upgrading their status, thanks to the influence of the press,

the support of Protestant organizations in the community, and a legal system that was sympathetic toward abused women. Although most immigrant wives like Law Shee Low could not read the Chinese newspapers, they were affected by public opinion as filtered through their husbands, neighbors, and social reformers looking after their interests. Law noted that after the 1911 Revolution it was no longer considered "fashionable" to have bound feet, concubines, or slave girls. And as housebound as Law was, she was aware of the mission homes that rescued prostitutes, helped abused women, and provided education for children and immigrant women.

CHINESE WOMEN IN THE LABOR MARKET

Compared to Wong Ah So and Law Shee Low, Jane Kwong Lee had an easier time acclimating to life in America. Not only was she educated, Westernized, English-speaking, and unencumbered by family responsibilities, but she also had the help of affluent relatives who provided her with room and board, financial support, and important contacts that enabled her eventually to strike out on her own.

Arriving in the middle of a school semester and therefore unable to enroll in a college, she decided to look for a job. In spite of her educational background and qualifications, she found that only menial jobs and domestic service were opened to her. "At heart I was sorry for myself; I wished I were a boy," she wrote in her autobiography. "If I were a boy, I could have gone out into the community, finding a job somewhere as many newcomers from China had done." But as a Chinese woman, she had to bide her time and look for work appropriate for her race and gender. Thus, until she could be admitted to college, and during the summers after she enrolled at Mills College, Jane took whatever jobs were open to Chinese women. She tried embroidery work at a Chinatown factory, sorting vegetables in the wholesale district, working as a live-in domestic for a white family, peeling shrimp, sorting fruit at a local cannery, and sewing flannel nightgowns at home.

As was true for European immigrant women, the patterns of work for Chinese women were shaped by the intersection of the local economy, ethnic traditions, language and job skills, and family and child-care needs, but in addition, race was an influential factor. At the time of Jane's arrival, San Francisco was experiencing a period of growth and prosperity. Ranked the eighth largest city in the country, it was the major port of trade for the Pacific Coast and touted as the financial and corporate capital of the West. Jobs were plentiful in the city's three largest economic sectors—domestic and personal service, trade and transportation, and manufacturing and mechanical industries—but they were filled according to a labor market stratified by race and gender, with Chinese men occupying the lowest tier as laborers, servants, factory workers, laundrymen, and small merchants, while Chinese women, handicapped further by gender, worked primarily in garment and food-processing factories for low piece-rate wages. With inadequate child-care services in the community, most seamstresses worked with their children close by or had their babies strapped to their backs.

For Jane Kwong Lee, being Chinese and a woman was a liability in the job market, but because she spoke English, was educated, and had good contacts among Chinese Christians, she was better off than most other immigrant women. She eventually got a scholarship at Mills College and part-time work teaching Chinese school and tutoring Chinese adults in English at the Chinese Episcopal Church in Oakland. After earning her bachelor's degree in sociology, she married, had two children, and returned to Mills College, where she received a master's degree in sociology and economics in 1933. She then dedicated herself to community service, working many years as coordinator of the Chinese YWCA and as a journalist and translator for a number of Chinatown newspapers.

For most immigrant women, joining the labor market proved to be a double-edged sword: On the one hand, their earnings helped to support their families and elevate their socioeconomic status; on the other hand, they became exploited laborers in the factory system, adding work and stress to their already burdensome lives. On the positive side, however, working outside the home offered women social rewards—a new sense of freedom, accomplishment, and camaraderie. They were no longer confined to the home, they were earning money for themselves or the family, and they were making new acquaintances and becoming exposed to new ideas. As Jane Kwong Lee observed, having money to spend made the women feel more liberated in America than in China: "They can buy things for themselves, go out to department stores to choose their own clothes instead of sewing them."

FIRST STEPS TOWARD SOCIAL ACTIVISM

For working-class women like Law Shee Low, family and work responsibilities consumed all their time and energy, leaving little left over for self-improvement or leisure activities, and even less for community involvement. This was not the case for a growing group of educated and professional women like Jane Kwong Lee, who, inspired by Christianity, Chinese nationalism, and Progressivism, took the first steps toward social activism. Prior to the 1911 Revolution in their homeland, Chinese women in America followed the tradition of remaining publicly invisible. They seldom ventured out of their homes except perhaps to shop or go to the Chinese opera, where they sat in a segregated section apart from the men.

The Protestant churches and Chinese YWCA were the first to encourage Chinese women's participation in organized activities outside the home, as evidenced by the small but visible number of them at Sunday services, English classes, meetings, outings, and other church-sponsored programs. Some of the churches also helped organize Chinese women's societies to encourage involvement in Christian activities. Members of these groups met regularly to have lunch or socialize, and paid dues to help support the work of Bible women in their home villages in China.[7]

Aside from Christianity, the intense nationalistic spirit that took hold in the early twentieth century also affected Chinese women in far-reaching ways. Not only did the call for modernization include the need to improve conditions for Chinese women, but reformers also solicited women's active participation in national salvation work. Fundraising for disaster relief and the revolution in China opened up opportunities for women to become involved in the community, develop leadership abilities, and move into the male-dominated public sphere. The Tongmenghui, the revolutionary party founded by Dr. Sun Yat-sen to overthrow the Qing dynasty and establish a republic in China, was the earliest organization to accept women into its ranks. While women in China participated in benefit performances, enlisted in the army, and engaged in dangerous undercover work, women in San Francisco also did their share for the revolutionary effort—making patriotic speeches, donating money and jewelry for the cause, and helping with Red Cross work—sometimes under the auspices of Protestant churches, other times under the banner of the Women's Young China Society.

Although the success of the revolution and the establishment of a republic in China failed to bring peace and prosperity to the country, it did have a lasting impact on the lives of Chinese American women. As Jane Kwong Lee observed, "After the establishment of the Republic of China, Chinese women in this country picked up the forward-looking trend for equality with men. They could go to school, speak in public places, have their feet free from binding, and go out to work in stores and small factories if they needed to work."[8]

Arriving as a liberated woman at the time when she did, Jane did not hesitate to join other women in becoming socially active in the Chinatown community. In her capacity as a community worker at the Chinese YWCA, she made house visits, wrote articles that were published in the local newspapers, and implemented programs that benefited Chinese women in the community. She was particularly known for her loud and forceful speeches that she delivered in Chinese at churches and street corners in support of Christianity and nationalist causes, and before Chinatown organizations on behalf of the Chinese YWCA. Jane also made presentations in English to groups interested in learning more about Chinese culture, and traveled as a Chinese delegate to YWCA functions outside of Chinatown. On one of these occasions, she was so moved by a discussion on racial discrimination that she surprised herself and African Americans at a YWCA meeting by speaking up for them. "I said, you are all equal; nobody is inferior to another."[9]

CONCLUSION

As Sieh King King had advocated in 1902, Chinese women unbound their feet and began to unbind their lives in America during the first three decades of the twentieth century. Most, like Law Shee Low and Wong Ah So, had immigrated for a better livelihood but found themselves exploited as prostitutes or working wives at the bottom of a labor market stratified by race and gender. Some, like Jane Kwong Lee, had come from a privileged background yet still encountered discrimination in the workplace and in the larger American society. But like many other immigrant women before them, they not only persevered and survived, but took advantage of new circumstances to improve their lives and contribute to the well-being of their families and community. Even as immigrant women began to enjoy their new roles as emancipated women, economic depression set in and war loomed large in their homeland. The challenges of the 1930s and 1940s—economic survival and the war effort on two fronts—would lead to even greater dramatic changes in their lives, allowing them to take the first steps toward fuller participation in American society.

NOTES

1. *San Francisco Chronicle,* November 3, 1902, p. 7.

2. Wong Ah So's story is taken from "Story of Wong Ah So—Experiences as a Prostitute," *Orientals and Their Cultural Adjustment,* Social Science Source Documents, no. 4 (Nashville: Social Science Institute, Fisk University, 1946), pp. 31–35; and Donaldina Cameron, "The Story of Wong So," *Women and Missions* 2, no. 5 (August 1925):169–72.

3. Law Shee Low's story is based on her interview with Sandy Lee, May 2, 1982; and interview with author, October 20, 1988.

4. Jane Kwong Lee's story is based on her unpublished autobiography, "A Chinese American," in the possession of her daughter Priscilla Holmes.

5. See Lucie Cheng Hirata, "Free, Indentured, Enslaved: Chinese Prostitutes in Nineteenth-Century California," *Signs: Journal of Women in Culture and Society* 5, no. 1 (autumn 1979):3–29. The figures for 1900, 1910, and 1920 are based on my computations from the U.S. National Archives, Record Group 29, "Census of U.S. Population" (manuscript), San Francisco, California.

6. See Peggy Pascoe, *Relations of Rescue: The Search for Female Moral Authority in the American West, 1874–1939* (New York: Oxford University Press, 1990).

7. See Wesley Woo, "Protestant Work among the Chinese in the San Francisco Bay Area, 1850–1920," Ph.D. dissertation, University of California, Berkeley, 1983.

8. Jane Kwong Lee, "Chinese Women in San Francisco," *Chinese Digest* (June 1938):8.

9. Jane Kwong Lee, interview with author, November 2, 1988.

Zitkala-Ša (Gertrude Simmons Bonnin), ". . . this semblance of civilization . . ."

Zitkala-Ša (1876–1938), whose mother was Sioux and father was Anglo-American, sought throughout her life to bridge the cultures of Native Americans and the United States. She was one of the first American Indian women who built an independent career as a writer; her voice, as the following selection from her early writing shows, could be simultaneously eloquent, sentimental, and bitter. Zitkala-Ša was eight years old when she left her home on the Yankton Sioux Agency in South Dakota for White's Indiana Manual Labor Institute in Wabash, Indiana, a training school funded by Quakers. She continued her education first at a teacher training school close to her home, then at Earlham College, and finally at the New England Conservatory of Music in Boston where she studied the violin.

After her marriage in 1901, Zitkala-Ša worked with her husband, Raymond Bonnin, who was an employee of the Bureau of Indian Affairs (BIA), advocating citizenship for Indians, exposing corruption in the BIA, and insisting on the dignity of Indian religions. In this stage of her life, she used her anglicized married name, Gertrude Simmons Bonnin. Bonnin lobbied for the Indian Citizenship Act of 1924; she founded the National Council of American Indians; and she sought to shape the Indian policy of the New Deal years.

When she wrote this memoir of her childhood in 1900 at age twenty-four, Zitkala-Ša had not yet taught at the Carlisle Indian School in Pennsylvania. The experience would strengthen her criticism of the practice of removing native children from their homes. It would also lead her to expose the corruption she found among the school's directors, who received federal money for each child they boarded and whose promotion of "Americanization" could be harsh and cruel. To what extent did her mother anticipate that the experience at the mission school would be difficult? What advantage did the educators think would result from cutting girls' hair? What evidence is there to suggest that she herself was involved in the process of acculturation? Compare Bonnin's education and geographic mobility to that of Sarah Winemucca (see Rose Stremlau's essay, pp. 227–237) and Wilma Mankiller (pp. 785–790).

The first turning away from the easy, natural flow of my life occurred in an early spring. It was in my eighth year; in the month of March, I afterward learned. At this age I knew but one language, and that was my mother's native tongue.

From some of my playmates I heard that two paleface missionaries were in our village. They were from that class of white men who wore big hats and carried large hearts, they said. Running direct to my mother, I began to question her why these two

Excerpted from "Impressions of an Indian Childhood," "The School Days of an Indian Girl," and "An Indian Teacher among Indians," by Zitkala-Ša, *Atlantic Monthly* 85 (January, February, March 1900): 45–47, 186–87, 386.

Zitkala-Ša, ca. 1898, posed in traditional dress.
This photograph is one in a series taken by the professional photographer Gertrude Käsebier, who had a studio on Fifth Avenue in New York City. In other images taken at the same sitting, Zitkala-Ša is in western dress (a white gown), and in some she holds in her lap a book, her violin, or an Indian basket. For interpretations of Käsebier's portraits of Zitkala-Ša and other Indians, see Laura Wexler, Tender Violence: Domestic Visions in an Age of U.S. Imperialism *(Chapel Hill: University of North Carolina Press, 2000), pp. 115–124, 177–208; and Elizabeth Hutchinson, "When the 'Sioux Chief's Party Calls': Käsebier's Indian Portraits and the Gendering of the Artist's Studio,"* American Art *16 (Summer 2002), 40-65. (Courtesy of the Smithsonian Institution.)*

strangers were among us. She told me, after I had teased much, that they had come to take away Indian boys and girls to the East. My mother did not seem to want me to talk about them. But in a day or two, I gleaned many wonderful stories from my playfellows concerning the strangers.

"Mother, my friend Judéwin is going home with the missionaries. She is going to a more beautiful country than ours; the palefaces told her so!" I said wistfully, wishing in my heart that I too might go.

Mother sat in a chair, and I was hanging on her knee. Within the last two seasons my big brother Dawée had returned from a three years' education in the East, and his coming back influenced my mother to take a farther step from her native way of living. First it was a change from the buffalo skin to the white man's canvas that covered our wigwam. Now she had given up her wigwam of slender poles, to live, a foreigner, in a home of clumsy logs.

Judéwin had told me of the great tree where grew red, red apples; and how we could reach out our hands and pick all the red apples we could eat. I had never seen apple trees. I had never tasted more than a dozen red apples in my life; and when I heard of the orchards of the East, I was eager to roam among them. The missionaries smiled into my eyes, and patted my head. I wondered how mother could say such hard words against them.

"Mother, ask them if little girls may have all the red apples they want, when they go East," I whispered aloud, in my excitement.

The interpreter heard me, and answered: "Yes, little girl, the nice red apples are for those who pick them; and you will have a ride on the iron horse if you go with these good people."

I had never seen a train, and he knew it.

"Mother, I'm going East! I like big red apples, and I want to ride on the iron horse! Mother, say yes!" I pleaded.

My mother said nothing. The missionaries waited in silence; and my eyes began to blur with tears, though I struggled to choke them back. The corners of my mouth twitched, and my mother saw me.

"I am not ready to give you any word," she said to them. "Tomorrow I shall send you my answer by my son."

With this they left us. Alone with my mother, I yielded to my tears, and cried aloud, shaking my head so as not to hear what she was saying to me. This was the first time I had

ever been so unwilling to give up my own desire that I refused to harken to my mother's voice.

There was a solemn silence in our home that night. Before I went to bed I begged the Great Spirit to make my mother willing I should go with the missionaries.

The next morning came, and my mother called me to her side. "My daughter, do you still persist in wishing to leave your mother?" she asked.

"Oh, mother, it is not that I wish to leave you, but I want to see the wonderful Eastern land," I answered. . . .

. . . My brother Dawée came for mother's decision. I dropped my play, and crept close to my aunt.

"Yes, Dawée, my daughter, though she does not understand what it all means, is anxious to go. She will need an education when she is grown, for then there will be fewer real Dakotas, and many more palefaces. This tearing her away, so young, from her mother is necessary, if I would have her an educated woman. The palefaces, who owe us a large debt for stolen lands, have begun to pay a tardy justice in offering some education to our children. But I know my daughter must suffer keenly in this experiment. For her sake, I dread to tell you my reply to the missionaries. Go, tell them that they may take my little daughter, and that the Great Spirit shall not fail to reward them according to their hearts."

Wrapped in my heavy blanket, I walked with my mother to the carriage that was soon to take us to the iron horse. I was happy. I met my playmates, who were also wearing their best thick blankets. We showed one another our new beaded moccasins, and the width of the belts that girdled our new dresses. Soon we were being drawn rapidly away by the white man's horses. When I saw the lonely figure of my mother vanish in the distance, a sense of regret settled heavily upon me. I felt suddenly weak, as if I might fall limp to the ground. I was in the hands of strangers whom my mother did not fully trust. I no longer felt free to be myself, or to voice my own feelings. The tears trickled down my cheeks, and I buried my face in the folds of my blanket. Now the first step, parting me from my mother, was taken, and all my belated tears availed nothing.

Having driven thirty miles to the ferryboat, we crossed the Missouri in the evening.

Then riding again a few miles eastward, we stopped before a massive brick building. I looked at it in amazement, and with a vague misgiving, for in our village I had never seen so large a house. Trembling with fear and distrust of the palefaces, my teeth chattering from the chilly ride, I crept noiselessly in my soft moccasins along the narrow hall, keeping very close to the bare wall. I was as frightened and bewildered as the captured young of a wild creature.

The first day in the land of apples was a bitter-cold one; for the snow still covered the ground, and the trees were bare. A large bell rang for breakfast, its loud metallic voice crashing through the belfry overhead and into our sensitive ears. The annoying clatter of shoes on bare floors gave us no peace. The constant clash of harsh noises, with an undercurrent of many voices murmuring an unknown tongue, made a bedlam within which I was securely tied. And though my spirit tore itself in struggling for its lost freedom, all was useless.

A paleface woman, with white hair, came up after us. We were placed in a line of girls who were marching into the dining room. These were Indian girls, in stiff shoes and closely clinging dresses. The small girls wore sleeved aprons and shingled hair. As I walked noiselessly in my soft moccasins, I felt like sinking to the floor, for my blanket had been stripped from my shoulders. I looked hard at the Indian girls, who seemed not to care that they were even more immodestly dressed than I, in their tightly fitting clothes. While we marched in, the boys entered at an opposite door. I watched for the three young braves who came in our party. I spied them in the rear ranks, looking as uncomfortable as I felt. . . .

. . . Late in the morning, my friend Judéwin gave me a terrible warning. Judéwin knew a few words of English; and she had overheard the paleface woman talk about cutting our long, heavy hair. Our mothers had taught us that only unskilled warriors who were captured had their hair shingled by the enemy. Among our people, short hair was worn by mourners, and shingled hair by cowards!

We discussed our fate some moments, and when Judéwin said, "We have to submit, because they are strong," I rebelled.

"No, I will not submit! I will struggle first!" I answered.

I watched my chance, and when no one noticed I disappeared. I crept up the stairs as quietly as I could in my squeaking shoes—my moccasins had been exchanged for shoes. Along the hall I passed, without knowing whither I was going. Turning aside to an open door, I found a large room with three white beds in it. The windows were covered with dark green curtains, which made the room very dim. Thankful that no one was there, I directed my steps toward the corner farthest from the door. On my hands and knees I crawled under the bed, and cuddled myself in the dark corner.

From my hiding place I peered out, shuddering with fear whenever I heard footsteps near by. Though in the hall loud voices were calling my name, and I knew that even Judéwin was searching for me, I did not open my mouth to answer. Then the steps were quickened and the voices became excited. The sounds came nearer and nearer. Women and girls entered the room. I held my breath, and watched them open closet doors and peep behind large trunks. Some one threw up the curtains, and the room was filled with sudden light. What caused them to stoop and look under the bed I do not know. I remember being dragged out, though I resisted by kicking and scratching wildly. In spite of myself, I was carried downstairs and tied fast in a chair.

I cried aloud, shaking my head all the while until I felt the cold blades of the scissors against my neck, and heard them gnaw off one of my thick braids. Then I lost my spirit. Since the day I was taken from my mother I had suffered extreme indignities. People had stared at me. I had been tossed about in the air like a wooden puppet. And now my long hair was shingled like a coward's! In my anguish I moaned for my mother, but no one came to comfort me. Not a soul reasoned quietly with me, as my own mother used to do; for now I was only one of many little animals driven by a herder. . . .

. . . Now, as I look back upon the recent past, I see it from a distance, as a whole. I remember how, from morning till evening, many specimens of civilized peoples visited the Indian school. The city folks with canes and eyeglasses, the countrymen with sunburnt cheeks and clumsy feet, forgot their relative social ranks in an ignorant curiosity. Both sorts of these Christian palefaces were alike astounded at seeing the children of savage warriors so docile and industrious.

As answers to their shallow inquiries they received the students' sample work to look upon. Examining the neatly figured pages, and gazing upon the Indian girls and boys bending over their books, the white visitors walked out of the schoolhouse well satisfied: They were educating the children of the red man! They were paying a liberal fee to the government employees in whose able hands lay the small forest of Indian timber.

In this fashion many have passed idly through the Indian schools during the last decade, afterward to boast of their charity to the North American Indian. But few there are who have paused to question whether real life or long-lasting death lies beneath this semblance of civilization.

CHANGE AGENTS

KATHRYN KISH SKLAR
Florence Kelley and Women's Activism in the Progressive Era

Florence Kelley was a remarkable woman who lived in a period when attempts to address the problems created by industrialization and urbanization generated both the early social sciences and the foundation of the welfare state. Kathryn Sklar, Kelley's biographer, provides in this authoritative and highly informative essay an account of a single individual that also illuminates the pursuit of social justice in which many progressive women of Kelley's generation were involved. Sklar reveals the factors that made it possible for these women to influence public policy even before they were allowed to vote. She also describes the changing political context that limited their influence following the Red Scare at the end of World War I.

What were the influences, personal and intellectual, that shaped Kelley's vision of social reform? What strategies did she employ in pursuit of that vision? What does Sklar mean when she says that Kelley used gender-specific legislation as a surrogate for class legislation? Precisely how did the Red Scare affect the political agenda of women's organizations? In what respects were at least three of the four significant features of women's power in the Progressive era that Sklar identified highly gendered? As we move into reading about the 1930s and beyond, think about which of the features persist and which do not.

One of the most powerful women in American history deserves to be better known today. Florence Kelley (1859–1932) was well known to her contemporaries as a leading champion of social justice legislation. For most of the 1890s she lived in the nation's leading reform institution, Hull House, a social settlement founded in Chicago by Jane Addams in 1889. Between 1899 and 1932 she served as head of the National Consumers' League in New York City.

Living collectively with other women reformers in Chicago and New York, Florence Kelley was able to make the most of her talents; for four decades she occupied the vanguard of social reform. Her forceful personality flourished in the combative atmosphere generated by her struggles for social justice. Jane Addams's nephew, who resided with Kelley at Hull House, was awed by the way she "hurled the spears of her thought with such apparent carelessness of what breasts they pierced." He thought her "the toughest customer in the reform riot, the finest rough-and-tumble fighter for the good life for others, that Hull House ever knew: Any weapon was a good weapon in her hand—evidence, argument, irony or invective." Nevertheless, he said, those who were close to her knew she was "full of love."[1]

Kelley's career, like that of many of her reform contemporaries, was responding to

Written expressly for *Women's America*. A revised version of this essay appears in Rima Lunin Schultz and Adele Hast, eds., *Women Building Chicago, 1790–1990: A Biographical Dictionary* (Bloomington: Indiana University Press, 2001.) Copyright © by Kathryn Kish Sklar.

profound changes in American social and economic life. Rapid industrialization was recasting the economy, massive immigration was reconstituting the working class, and sustained urbanization was making cities the focus of social change.[2] In this context, college-educated women reformers often achieved what men and male-dominated organizations could not.

Florence Kelley's life helps us understand how women reformers accomplished their goals. Her reform career exemplified four significant features of women's power in the Progressive era: their access to higher education; their prominence in early social science; the political autonomy of their separate institutions; and their ability to challenge American traditions of limited government. Having experienced these ingredients of women's power in her own life before 1899, thereafter, as the General Secretary of the National Consumers' League, she integrated them into her strategies for pursuing social justice.[3]

WOMEN'S ACCESS
TO HIGHER EDUCATION

When she graduated from Cornell University in 1882, Florence Kelley joined thousands of other young women in her generation who received college educations. Two changes in the 1860s and 1870s enabled white, middle-class women to attend college in sufficient numbers to become a sociological phenomenon. Elite women's colleges, such as Vassar, Smith, and Wellesley, began accepting students between 1865 and 1875, providing equivalents to elite men's colleges such as Harvard, Yale, and Princeton. And state universities, established through the allocation of public lands in the Morrill Act of 1862 and required to be "open for all," gradually made college educations accessible for the first time to large numbers of women in the nation's central and western states. By 1880 women, numbering forty thousand, constituted 33 percent of all enrolled students in higher education.[4] Though a small percentage of all women, they exercised an influence disproportionate to their numbers.

To Cornell Kelley brought a social conscience shaped by her family. Born into an elite Philadelphia family with Quaker and Unitarian political traditions, she grew up against the background of the Civil War and Reconstruction—dramas in which her father and her mother's aunt played major roles. Her father,

William Durrah Kelley, one of the founders of the Republican Party, was reelected to fifteen consecutive terms in the U.S. Congress between 1860 and 1890. As a Radical Republican, he advanced the cause of black suffrage and tried to forge a biracial Republican Party in the South. Her mother's aunt, Sarah Pugh, served as president of the Philadelphia Female Anti-Slavery Society almost every year between 1838 and 1870. In the 1860s and 1870s, Pugh accompanied her close friend, Lucretia Mott, to early woman suffrage conventions. To young "Florrie," Sarah Pugh was conscience incarnate, a full-time reformer who lived her beliefs, never wearing slave-made cotton or eating slave-produced sugar.[5]

During six mostly schoolless years before she entered Cornell, Florence systematically read through her father's library, imbibing the fiction of Dickens and Thackeray, Louisa May Alcott and Horatio Alger; the poetry of Shakespeare, Milton, Byron, and Goldsmith; the writings of James Madison; histories by Bancroft, Prescott, and Parkman; and the moral and political philosophy of Emerson, Channing, Burke, Carlyle, Godwin, and Spencer. These readings helped her reach out to her moody and distant father. For that purpose she also began reading government reports at the age of ten and, on trips to Washington, began using the Library of Congress by the time she was twelve.

A darker side of Kelley's childhood was shaped by her mother's permanent depression—caused by the death of five of her eight children before they had reached the age of six. Caroline Bonsall Kelley was a descendant of John Bartram, the Quaker botanist. Orphaned at the age of nine, she was raised in the Pugh family. With the death of her infants, Caroline developed a "settled, gentle melancholy" that threatened to envelop her daughter as long as she lived at home.[6] Florence grew up with two brothers, but no sisters survived. Keenly aware of the high social cost of infant mortality to nineteenth-century families, she developed a rage against human suffering that formed her lifelong career as a reformer.

WOMEN'S PROMINENCE
IN EARLY SOCIAL SCIENCE

Like higher education, the newly emerging field of social science served as a critical vehicle by which middle-class women expanded the space they occupied within American civic life between 1860 and 1890. Social science leveled the playing field on which women interacted with men in public life. It offered tools of analysis that enhanced women's ability to investigate economic and social change, speak for the welfare of the whole society, devise policy initiatives, and oversee their implementation. Yet at the same time, social science also deepened women's gender identity in public life and attached their civic activism even more securely to gender-specific issues.[7]

Kelley's early commitment to social science as a tool for social reform built on a generation of women's presence in American social science. Women came with the civic territory that social science embraced. Caroline Dall had been a cofounder of the association in 1865, and other women were especially active in the American Social Science Association's (ASSA) department of education, public health, and social economy, which gave them clear but limited mandates for leadership.

The question of "After college, what?" was as pertinent to Florence Kelley as it was to other women graduates.[8] Barred from admission to graduate study at the University of Pennsylvania because she was a woman, she faced a very limited set of opportunities. First she threw her energies into the New Century Working Women's Guild, an organization that fostered middle-class aid for self-supporting women. She helped found the Guild, taught classes in history, and assembled the group's library. Then, remaining a dutiful daughter, in 1882 she accompanied her brother when his doctor prescribed a winter of European travel to cure temporary blindness. In Europe she encountered M. Carey Thomas, a Cornell acquaintance, who had just completed a Ph.D. at the University of Zurich, the only European university that granted degrees to women. Thomas recommended that Kelley go to Zurich for graduate study.

Initially accompanied by her mother and younger brother, Kelley studied government and law at Zurich between 1883 and 1886. There she promptly befriended exiled socialist students from Russia and Germany. To the shocked amazement of her family and friends, in 1885 she married Lazare Wischnewetzky, a Russian, Jewish, socialist, medical student. She then gave birth to three children in three years.

Cloaked with her new personal identity as a European married woman, she stopped communicating with her family and began to forge a new political identity. Rejecting American public culture because it limited her opportunities for social service and because her father's career revealed so starkly that culture's tolerance of social injustice, she underwent a dramatic conversion to socialism, joined the German Social Democratic Party (SPD), and began to translate the writings of Friedrich Engels and Karl Marx. Outlawed in Germany, the SPD maintained its European headquarters in Zurich, where Kelley met many of its leaders. Since the death of Marx in 1885, Engels had become the chief theoretician of German socialism. Kelley's translation of his 1845 book, *The Condition of the Working Class in England*, is still the preferred scholarly version of that now-classic social science study. This project launched a close but troubled relationship with Engels that persisted until his death in 1895.[9]

When Kelley returned to the United States in 1886 with her small family, she searched without success for a political context capable of sustaining her newfound radicalism. Settling in New York City, within a year she was expelled from the Socialist Labor Party, predominantly a German-speaking immigrant group, for "incessant slander" against party leaders, whom she denounced for failing to recognize the importance of the writings of Marx and Engels.[10] Having reached a political dead-end, Kelley reoriented her use of social science as a vehicle for her activism. She resumed contact with her Philadelphia family and became a self-taught authority on child labor in the United States, as well as a sharp critic of state bureaus of labor, the agencies responsible for monitoring child labor. Writing articles on child labor that deployed both statistical and rhetorical power, she discovered that her most responsive publisher was the Woman's Temperance Publication Association, which printed her lengthy, hard-hitting pamphlet, *Our Toiling Children,* in 1889.

Lazare Wischnewetzky, meanwhile, never having managed to establish a medical practice, began battering her. After enduring this for more than a year, she borrowed money from a friend and fled with her children to Chicago. There she headed for the Woman's Temple, a twelve-story office building and hotel constructed by the Woman's Christian Temperance Union, where she was directed to an even more congenial place—Hull House, the nation's preeminent social settlement founded by Jane Addams and Ellen Gates Starr in 1889.

THE POLITICAL AUTONOMY OF WOMEN'S SEPARATE INSTITUTIONS

"We were welcomed as though we had been invited," Kelley later wrote about her arrival at Hull House. "We stayed."[11] Addams arranged for Kelley's children, Nicholas, Margaret, and John, age seven, six, and five, to live with the family of Henry Demarest Lloyd and his wife, Jessie Bross Lloyd. That winter Kelley cast her lot with Addams and Hull House, remaining until May 1, 1899, when she returned to New York as a figure who had achieved national renown as a reformer of working conditions for women and children.

Chicago and the remarkable political culture of the city's women opened opportunities to Kelley that she had sought in vain in Philadelphia, Germany, and New York. Exploiting those opportunities to the fullest, she drew on the strength of three overlapping circles of politically active women. The core of her support lay with the community of women at Hull House. This remarkable group helped her reconstruct her political identity within women's class-bridging activism, and provided her with an economic and emotional alternative to married family life. Partly overlapping with this nucleus were women trade unionists. By drawing women and men trade unionists into the settlement community, she achieved the passage of pathbreaking legislation. Toward the end of her years in Chicago, she worked with the circle of middle-class and upper-middle-class women who supported Hull House and labor reform.

Florence Kelley's life in Chicago began with her relationship with Jane Addams. Julia Lathrop, another Hull House resident, reported that Kelley and Addams "understood each other's powers" instantly and worked together in a "wonderfully effective way."[12] Addams, the philosopher with a deep appreciation of the unity of life, was better able to construct a vehicle for expressing that unity in day-to-day living than she was capable of devising a diagram for charting the future. And Kelley, the politician with a thorough understanding of what the future should look like, was better able to invoke that future than to express it in her day-to-day existence. Addams

taught Kelley how to live and have faith in an imperfect world, and Kelley taught Addams how to make demands on the future.

At Hull House Kelley joined a community of college-educated women reformers who, like Addams and herself, sought work commensurate with their talents. Julia Lathrop, almost twenty years later the first director of the U.S. Children's Bureau, had joined the settlement before Kelley. Alice Hamilton, who arrived in 1897, developed the field of industrial medicine. These four, with Mary Rozet Smith, Jane Addams's life partner, became the settlement's main leaders. In addition to these women, Kelley forged close ties with Mary Kenney, a trade union organizer affiliated with the settlement, who lived nearby with her mother.

Since her father had lost most of his money before his death in 1890, Kelley had to support herself and her children. She first did so by working for the Illinois Bureau of Labor Statistics and the U.S. Department of Labor, collecting data for governmental studies of working conditions. A good example of the empowerment of her Hull House residence lay in her use of data collected for the U.S. Department of Labor, which in 1895 formed the basis of the maps published in *Hull House Maps and Papers*. She and four government "schedule men" collected responses to sixty-four questions on printed schedules from "each house, tenement, and room" in the ward surrounding Hull House.[13] From this data Carroll Wright, head of the Department of Labor, constructed scores of tables. But Kelley and Hull House associates, using only data about nationalities and wages in conjunction with residential information, created color-coded maps that displayed geographic patterns that told more than Wright's charts. Because the maps defined spatial relationships among human groups, they vividly depicted social and economic relationships: the concentration of certain ethnic groups in certain blocks; the relationship between poverty and race; the distances between the isolated brothel district and the rest of the ward; the very poor who lived in crowded, airless rooms in the rear of tenements and those with more resources in the front; and the omniscient observer and the observed. Expressing the democratic relationship among Hull House residents, *Hull House Maps and Papers* listed only "Residents of Hull House" as the volume's editors.

Kelley described the transformative effect of the Hull House community on her personal life in a letter to her mother a few weeks after her arrival. "In the few weeks of my stay here I have won for the children and myself many and dear friends whose generous hospitality astonishes me. It is understood that I am to resume the maiden name and that the children are to have it."[14] By joining a community of women, she had achieved a new degree of personal autonomy.

CHALLENGING TRADITIONS OF LIMITED GOVERNMENT

In the spring of 1892, Kelley used Hull House as a base to exert leadership within an anti-sweatshop campaign that had been launched in 1888 by the Illinois Woman's Alliance, a class-bridging coalition of women's organizations. At mass meetings that attacked the sweatshop system, Kelley shared the podium with Mary Kenney, Henry Demarest Lloyd, and other Chicago notables such as Reverend Jenkin Lloyd Jones, minister at All Souls' Unitarian Church, the most liberal pulpit in Chicago, and with young trade union organizers in the clothing industry such as Abraham Bisno.

Campaigns against sweatshops were widespread in American cities in the 1890s. These efforts targeted "predatory management" and "parasitic manufacturers" who paid such low wages to their workers as to require them to seek support from relief or charity, thereby indirectly providing employers with subsidies that enabled them to lower wages further.[15] Supported by trade unions, these campaigns used a variety of strategies to shift work from tenement sweatshops to factories. In factories, union organizing could more easily succeed in improving working conditions and raising wages to levels necessary to sustain life.

Outcries raised by anti-sweatshop campaigns prompted government inquiries, and in 1893, after intense lobbying in Springfield by Hull House residents and other well-known Chicago women, the passage of pathbreaking legislation drafted by Florence Kelley. That year Governor John Peter Altgeld appointed Kelley to a position the new statute created: Chief Factory Inspector of Illinois. Nowhere else in the Western world was a woman trusted to enforce the labor legislation of a city, let alone of a large industrial region the size of Illinois. With eleven deputies, five of whom were required to be women, and a budget of $28,000, for the next three years Kelley enforced the act's chief clauses. The act banned the labor of children under fourteen years of age; it regulated the labor of children age fourteen to sixteen; it outlawed the production of garments in tenements; it prohibited the employment of women and minors for more than eight hours a day; and it created a state office of factory inspection.

The statute's eight-hour clause made it the most advanced in the United States, equaled only by an eight-hour law for all workers in Australia. The limitation of hours, whether through statutes or union negotiations with employers, was the second most important goal of the labor movement between 1870 and 1910, the first being the recognition of the right of workers to form unions. Skilled workers had acquired the eight-hour day for themselves in many trades by the 1890s, but since women were not admitted to most skilled occupations, their hours remained long, often extending to twelve or even fourteen hours a day. In the late 1880s more than 85 percent of female wage earners were between the ages of fourteen and twenty-five and only about 5 percent were married.[16] Excluded from access to skilled jobs and presumed to leave the paid labor force upon marriage, they were crowded into a few unskilled occupations, where they were easily replaced, and employers exploited them by requiring long hours and paying low wages. Statutes that limited women's hours limited this exploitation. How to achieve such reduction of hours without reducing wages was a challenge that Kelley's office met by promoting the formation of unions among affected women workers, thereby helping them negotiate better wages for the hours they worked.

But the reduction of women's hours by statute had other beneficial effects: in many occupations it also reduced the hours of unskilled men, as was the case in garment-making sweatshops. In this and many other occupations, it proved impossible to keep men working longer than the legal limit of the working day for women. Therefore, hours statutes drove sweatshops out of business, since their profits could only be achieved through long hours. In the United States more than in other industrializing nations, the union movement consisted with few exceptions (miners being the chief exception) of skilled workers who shunned responsibility for the welfare of unskilled workers. Therefore, in the United States more than in elsewhere, gender-specific reforms like Kelley's 1893 legislation—undertaken by women for women—also had the effect of aiding all unskilled workers, men as well as women and children. In the United States, where labor movements were not as strong as they were elsewhere, gender-specific reforms accomplished goals that elsewhere were achieved under the auspices of class-specific efforts.[17]

In an era when courts nullified legislative attempts to intervene in the laissez-faire relationship between capital and labor, Kelley's enforcement of this new eight-hour law was inevitably challenged in the courts. In 1895 the Illinois Supreme Court found the eight-hour clause of the 1893 law unconstitutional because it violated women's right to contract their labor on any terms set by their employer. This setback made Kelley determined to change the power of state courts to overturn hours laws for women.

The high tide of Kelley's achievements between 1893 and 1896 ebbed quickly when Altgeld lost the election of 1896. His successor replaced her with a person who did not challenge the economic status quo, and she was unable to find work commensurate with her talents. German admirers came to her rescue. For fifty dollars a month she provided a leading German reform periodical with assessments of recent American social legislation. She also worked in the Crerar Library, a reference library specializing in economic, scientific, and medical topics.

Needing to reach beyond the limits of Hull House activities, Kelley began to work more closely with Ellen Henrotin. Wife of a leading Chicago banker, Henrotin had supported Kelley's legislation in 1892, and spoke vigorously at a rally to defend the law in 1894, urging those in attendance to "agitate for shorter hours for women because it means in the end shorter hours for all workers, men and women."[18] Henrotin's organization in 1893 of thirty women's congresses at the Chicago World's Fair catapulted her into the presidency of the General Federation of Women's Clubs (GFWC; founded 1890) from 1894 to 1898. By 1897 the GFWC served as an umbrella organization for more than five hundred women's clubs, including the powerful Chicago Women's Club. Fostering the creation of over twenty state federations to coordinate those clubs, Henrotin moved the GFWC in progressive directions by establishing national committees on industrial working conditions and national health. In this way she directed the path of what was to become one of the largest grass-roots organizations of American women beyond the minimal goals of good government and civil service reform to the more challenging issues of social inequalities and social justice.

Reflecting her growing awareness of the potential power of women's organizations as a vehicle for her social justice agenda, in 1897 Kelley began to work closely with Henrotin in organizing an Illinois Consumers' League. They built on the example of the New York Consumers' League, which had been founded in 1891 to channel consumers' consciousness toward political action on behalf of workers who made the goods that consumers purchased.

THE NATIONAL CONSUMERS' LEAGUE AND NEW STRATEGIES FOR SOCIAL JUSTICE

Kelley's work with Henrotin helped her make the biggest career step of her life when, in 1899, she agreed to serve as Secretary of the newly formed National Consumers' League, a position she held until her death in 1932. With a salary of $1,500 plus traveling and other expenses, the job offered financial stability and a chance to develop a more radical and more focused women's organization than the GFWC.

When she carried her formidable talents into the National Consumers' League in 1899, women's political culture gained a warrior with formidable rhetorical and organizational skills. She quickly made the National Consumers' League (NCL) into the nation's leading promoter of protective labor legislation for women and children. Between 1900 and 1904 she built sixty-four local consumer leagues—one in nearly every large city outside the South. Through a demanding travel schedule, which required her to spend one day on the road for every day she worked at her desk, Kelley maintained close contact with local leagues, urging them to implement the national organization's agenda and inspiring them to greater action within their states and municipalities. At the age of forty she had finally found a platform that matched her talents and goals.

In New York she lived until 1926 at Lillian Wald's nurses' settlement on Henry Street on Manhattan's Lower East Side. Her children moved east with her. Supported by aid from Jane Addams's life partner, Mary Rozet Smith, Nicholas Kelley graduated from Harvard in 1905 and then from Harvard Law School. Living in Manhattan, he became his mother's closest advisor. In a blow that caused Kelley to spend the rest of that year in retirement in Maine, her daughter Margaret died of heart failure during her first week at Smith College in 1905. After this bereavement Kelley maintained a summer home on Penobscot Bay, Maine, where she retreated for periods of intense work with a secretary each summer. John Kelley never found a professional niche, but remained close to his mother and joined her in Maine each summer.

THE WHITE LABEL CAMPAIGN: NEW WAYS OF EDUCATING MIDDLE-CLASS WOMEN ABOUT INDUSTRIAL WORKING CONDITIONS

The national branch of the Consumers' League was formed in 1898 to coordinate the efforts of previously existing leagues in New York, Brooklyn, Philadelphia, Boston, and Chicago, all of which had conducted campaigns against sweatshops. At a convention of the local leagues called to coordinate their anti-sweatshop efforts, Kelley proposed the creation of a consumers' label as a way of identifying goods made under fair conditions. Her proposal galvanized the convention into creating a national organization "for the express purpose of offering a Consumers' League Label" nationally, recognizing that local efforts against sweatshops could never succeed until all producers were "compelled to compete on a higher level," and agreeing that the label could be a means of achieving that goal.[19] The NCL awarded its label to manufacturers who obeyed state factory laws, produced goods only on their own premises, did not require employees to work overtime, and did not employ children under sixteen years of age. To enforce the label, however, factories had to be inspected. Local leagues had employed their own factory inspectors; Kelley became the league's national inspector.

In determining whether local factories qualified for the label, local league members had to educate themselves about local working conditions. They had to pose and answer questions new to middle-class women, though painfully familiar to union organizers: Did the manufacturer subcontract to home workers in tenements? Were children employed? Were state factory laws violated? Could workers live on their wages, or were they forced to augment their pay with relief or charitable donations? How far below the standard set by the consumers' label were their own state laws? Even more technical questions arose when leagues came into contact with factory inspectors, bureaus of labor statistics, state legislatures, and courts. Should the state issue licenses for home workers? What was the relationship between illiteracy in child workers and the enforcement of effective child labor laws? Was their own state high or low on the NCL's ranked list showing the number of illiterate child workers in each? Should laws prohibit the labor of children at age fourteen or sixteen? Should exceptions be made for the children of widows? How energetically were state factory laws enforced? How could local factory standards be improved? These questions, recently quite alien to middle-class women, now held the interest of thousands of the most politically active among them. This was no small accomplishment. State leagues differed in the degree to which they worked with state officials, but wherever they existed they created new civic space in which women used their new knowledge and power to expand state responsibility for the welfare of women and children workers.

On the road steadily between 1900 and 1907, Kelley inspected workshops, awarded the label to qualified manufacturers, and strengthened local leagues. Her efforts were rewarded by the spectacular growth of NCL locals, both in number and location. The NCL's 1901 report mentioned thirty leagues in eleven states; by 1906 they numbered sixty-three in twenty states.

Flourishing local leagues sustained the national's existence, channeling money, ideas, and the support of other local groups into the national office. At the same time, locals implemented the national's agenda at the state level. Most league members were white, urban, northern, middle-class Protestants, but Jewish women held important positions of leadership. Catholic women became more visible after Cardinal James Gibbons of Baltimore consented to serve as vice president of a Maryland league and Bishop J. Regis Canevin of Pittsburgh encouraged members of that city's Ladies Catholic Benevolent Association to join. Two important reasons for the absence of black women from the NCL's membership and agenda were the league's focus on Northern urban manufacturing, and the residence of 90 percent of the nation's black population in the South, employed primarily in agriculture, in 1900.

10-HOUR LAWS FOR WOMEN: NEW USES OF SOCIAL SCIENCE

The work of educating her constituency being achieved by 1907, Kelley implemented a second stage of league work. With the use of social science data, the NCL overcame legal obstacles to the passage of state laws limiting women's hours. The overturning of Illinois's 1893 law by Illinois's Supreme Court in 1895 made Kelley determined to defend such laws before the U.S. Supreme Court. When an Oregon ten-hour law came before the court in 1907, she threw the resources of the NCL into its defense. This case, *Muller v. Oregon,* pitted the NCL and its Oregon branch against a laundry owner who disputed the state's ability to regulate working hours in non-hazardous occupations. For what became known as the "Brandeis Brief," Kelley's Research Director, Josephine Goldmark, gathered printed evidence from medical and other authorities (most of whom were British or European) to demonstrate that workdays longer than ten hours were hazardous to the health of women. Goldmark obtained the services of her brother-in-law, Louis D. Brandeis, a leading Boston attorney, who successfully argued the case on sociological rather than legal grounds, using the evidence that Goldmark had compiled. Thus at the same time that this case cleared the way for state hours laws for women, it also established the court's recognition of sociological evidence, a strategy that sustained the court's ruling against segregated schools in *Brown v. Board of Education* in 1954.

In the years immediately following the *Muller* decision, inspired by Kelley's leadership, and supported by other groups, local consumer leagues gained the passage in twenty states of the first laws limiting women's working hours. Also responding to the decision, nineteen other states revised and expanded their laws governing women's working hours.

The Supreme Court's 1908 opinion tried to block the possibility of extending such protections to men by emphasizing women's special legal status (they did not possess the same contractual rights as men) and their physiological difference from men (their health affected the health of their future children). Nevertheless, in 1917 Kelley and the NCL again cooperated successfully with the Oregon league in arguing another case on sociological grounds before the U.S. Supreme Court, *Bunting v. Oregon,* in which the Court upheld the constitutionality of hours laws for men in non-hazardous occupations. Viewing laws for women as an entering wedge for improving conditions for all working people, Kelley achieved that goal in the progression from *Muller* to *Bunting.* In this as in other aspects of her work with the League, though nominally focused on gender, her reforms had class-wide effects.

THE MINIMUM WAGE CAMPAIGN: NEW USES OF THE POWER OF WOMEN'S ORGANIZATIONS

As early as 1899, Florence Kelley had hoped "to include a requirement as to minimal wages" in the NCL's White Label. Australia and New Zealand had already organized wage boards as part of compulsory arbitration, but the path to an American equivalent did not seem clear until she and other Consumers' League members in 1908 attended the First International Conference of Consumers' Leagues, in Geneva, where they learned about the proposed British wage law of 1909, which that year implemented minimum wages for all workers in certain poorly paid occupations.

Almost immediately on her return, Kelley established her leadership in what became an enormously successful campaign for minimum wage laws for women in the United States. In her campaign she denounced the large profits made in three industries: retail stores, sweatshop garment making, and textile manufacturers. "Low wages produce more poverty than all other causes together," she insisted, urging that "goods and profits are not ends in themselves to which human welfare may continue to be sacrificed."[20]

Kelley argued that minimum wages would raise the standards in women's employment by recognizing their need to support themselves. "So long as women's wages rest upon the assumption that every woman has a husband, father, brother, or lover contributing to her support, so long these sinister incidents of women's industrial employment (tuberculosis, insanity, vice) are inevitable." She urged that "society itself must build the floor beneath their feet."[21]

Minimum wage legislation was much more difficult to achieve than maximum hours laws because, as one of Kelley's allies put it, wage legislation "pierces to the heart the classic claim that industry is a purely private affair."[22] For this reason, Kelley and the NCL were unaided in their efforts by their male-dominated equivalent, the American Association for Labor Legislation (AALL). When Kelley appealed in 1910 to their executive director, John Andrews, he loftily replied: "I question very seriously the wisdom of injecting the minimum wage proposal into the legislative campaign of this year, because I do not believe our courts would at the present time uphold such legislation, and I am afraid it would seriously jeopardize the splendid progress now being made to establish maximum working hours."[23] Two years later the AALL still opposed wage legislation as premature.

Kelley and the NCL were able to move ahead with this pathbreaking legislation because they could mobilize grass-roots support for it at local and state levels. The AALL had no local branches; instead, their power flowed from a network of male academic experts who advised politicians about legislation. If politicians were not ready to move, neither was the AALL. The NCL, by contrast, had in its sixty-four local branches enough political muscle to take the initiative and lead politicians where they otherwise wouldn't have gone.

In 1912 Massachusetts passed the first minimum wage law for women, followed in 1913 by eight additional states: California, Colorado, Minnesota, Nebraska, Oregon, Utah, Washington, and Wisconsin. By 1919 fourteen states and the District of Columbia and Puerto Rico had enacted minimum wage statutes for women. The success of these laws influenced the inclusion of a minimum wage for men *and* women in the Fair Labor Standards Act (FLSA) of 1938. In 1942, when the U.S. Supreme Court approved the constitutionality of the FLSA, the eight-hour day and the minimum wage became part of the social contract for most American workers. The class-bridging activism of middle-class women

in the NCL forged the way with these fundamental reforms.

GAINS AND SETBACKS IN THE 1920S

At Henry Street, Kelley continued to benefit from the same consolidation of female reform talents that had sustained her efforts at Hull House in Chicago. The creation of the U.S. Children's Bureau in 1911 sprang from her discussions with Lillian Wald. The Children's Bureau was the only governmental agency in any industrial society that was headed and run by women. Kelley thought that her most important contribution to social change was the passage in 1921 of the Sheppard-Towner Maternity and Infancy Protection Act, which first allocated federal funds to health care. She was instrumental in the creation of the coalition that backed the act's passage, the Women's Joint Congressional Committee, and in the coalition's successful campaign for the bill in Congress. Although limited to a program administered by the Children's Bureau to combat infant and maternal mortality, Kelley thought the Sheppard-Towner Act marked the beginning of a national health care program.[24]

After this high point in 1921, however, the decade brought a series of reversals that threatened to undo most of her achievements. In 1923 the U.S. Supreme Court in *Adkins* v. *Children's Hospital* found Washington, D.C.'s wage law for women unconstitutional. Many state wage boards continued to function during the 1920s and 1930s, however, providing ample evidence of the benefits of the law, but no new wage laws were passed. In 1926, Congress refused to allocate new funds for Sheppard-Towner programs, and responsibility for maternal and infant health returned to state and county levels.[25]

Just as important, by 1922 Kelley's strategy of using gender-specific legislation as a surrogate for class legislation had generated opposition from a new quarter—women who did not themselves benefit from gendered laws. The National Woman's Party (NWP), formed in 1916 by the charismatic leadership of Alice Paul and funded almost entirely by Alva Belmont, created a small coalition consisting primarily of professional women with some wage-earning women who worked in male-dominated occupations. Despite Kelley's strong objections over the damage they would do to gender-specific legislation, including the Sheppard-Towner Act, in 1921 the NWP proposed an Equal Rights Amendment to the U.S. Constitution (ERA). Although mainstream organizations such as the General Federation of Women's Clubs and the League of Women Voters continued to support gender-specific legislation, the NWP's proposed amendment undercut the momentum of such gendered strategies. In the 1920s most wage-earning women opposed the ERA because they stood to lose rather than benefit from it. By the 1970s changes in working conditions and protective labor laws meant that most wage-earning women stood to benefit from the amendment, and many more supported it.[26]

Even more damaging than these reversals, however, were the right-wing attacks launched by hyperpatriots against Kelley and other women reformers during the "red scare" of the 1920s. *The Woman Patriot* exemplified these attacks. Launched in 1916 and published twice a month, before the enactment of the woman suffrage amendment this newsletter was subtitled *Dedicated to the Defense of Womanhood, Motherhood, the Family and the State AGAINST Suffragism, Feminism and Socialism.* After 1920 the newsletter dropped its reference to suffrage, but continued its virulent attacks on the social agenda of women reformers. "SHALL BOLSHEVIST-FEMINISTS SECRETLY GOVERN AMERICA?" their headlines screamed, referring to the Sheppard-Towner Act. When *The Woman Patriot* referred to Kelley as "Mrs. Wischnewtzky" and called her "Moscow's chief conspirator," Kelley urged Addams to join her in a libel suit against them. Addams gently persuaded her to ignore the attacks. Kelley then wrote an impassioned series of autobiographical articles that established her lineage as an inheritor of American ideals and a dedicated promoter of American values.[27]

Attacks on women reformers in the 1920s were in part generated by supporters of American military expansion in the aftermath of World War I, when Kelley and many other women reformers were actively promoting peace and disarmament. For example, *The Woman Patriot* characterized the support that women reformers were giving to disarmament as "an organized internationalist Bolshevist-Feminist plot to embarrass the Limitation of Armaments Conference." Government employees joined the attack in 1924, when Lucia Maxwell of the Chemical

Warfare Department of the Department of War issued a "Spider Web Chart" entitled "The Socialist-Pacifist Movement in America Is an Absolutely Fundamental and Integral Part of International Socialism." Depicting the connections between women's organizations and Congressional lobbying for social legislation and for disarmament, the chart sought to characterize as "pacifist-socialist" most women's organizations in the United States, including the National Consumers' League, the National League of Women Voters, the General Federation of Women's Clubs, the Woman's Christian Temperance Union, the National Congress of Mothers and Parent-Teachers Association, the National Women's Trade Union League, the American Home Economics Association, the American Association of University Women, the National Council of Jewish Women, the Girls' Friendly Society, the Young Women's Christian Association, and the National Federation of Business and Professional Women.[28]

Historians have not measured the effect of these attacks on the political agendas of women's organizations, but after these attacks the agendas of many women's organizations, for example that of the League for Women Voters, shifted from social justice to good government projects, from support for a Child Labor Amendment to the U.S. Constitution to advocacy for a city manager form of governance.[29] Such a shift was in keeping with the demise of the Progressive movement after World War I. But that demise was hastened by the rise of "red scare" tactics in American political culture.

Florence Kelley did not live to see many of her initiatives incorporated into federal legislation in the 1930s. Faced with the collapse of the American economy in the Great Depression of 1929–1939, policymakers drew heavily on the legacy of Progressive reforms initiated between 1890 and 1920. Florence Kelley's legacies, including the minimum wage and maximum hours legislation incorporated in the Fair Labor Standards Act of 1938, were strong enough to survive the reversals of the 1920s. In 1933, with the inauguration of Franklin Delano Roosevelt, Kelley's protégée Frances Perkins became the first woman to serve as a cabinet member. Reflecting the power of women's organizations in shaping a new social contract for American working people, Perkins was appointed Secretary of Labor.[30]

But Kelley's legacy reaches beyond any specific policies. U.S. Supreme Court Justice Felix Frankfurter said in 1953 that the nation owed Kelley an "enduring debt for the continuing process she so largely helped to initiate, by which social legislation is promoted and eventually gets on the statute books."[31] As Kelley shaped it during her long reform career between 1890 and 1930, that process relied heavily on women's organizations and their ability to act independently of the political status quo.

NOTES

1. James Weber Linn, *Jane Addams: A Biography* (New York, 1938), 138.

2. For an overview of social change in the Progressive era, see Steven J. Diner, *A Very Different Age: Americans of the Progressive Era* (New York, 1998).

3. For more on Kelley before 1900, see Kathryn Kish Sklar, *Florence Kelley and the Nation's Work: The Rise of Women's Political Culture, 1830–1900* (New Haven, 1995). Specific page references are provided for quotations used below.

4. Mabel Newcomer, *A Century of Higher Education for American Women* (New York, 1959), 37, 46. See also Barbara Miller Solomon, *"In the Company of Educated Women": A History of Women and Higher Education in America* (New Haven, 1985), 62–77.

5. For Kelley's childhood, see Kathryn Kish Sklar, ed., *The Autobiography of Florence Kelley: Notes of Sixty Years* (Chicago, 1986).

6. Sklar, *Autobiography of Florence Kelley*, 30.

7. Kathryn Kish Sklar, "Hull House Maps and Papers: Social Science as Women's Work in the 1890s," in Helene Silverberg, ed., *Gender and American Social Science: The Formative Years* (Princeton, 1998).

8. See Joyce Antler, "After College, What?: New Graduates and the Family Claim," *American Quarterly* 32 (Fall 1980):409–34.

9. See Dorothy Rose Blumberg, "'Dear Mr. Engels': Unpublished Letters, 1884–1894, of Florence Kelley (Wischnewetzky) to Friedrich Engels," *Labor History* 5 (Spring 1964), 103–33.

10. Sklar, *Florence Kelley*, 129.

11. Sklar, *Autobiography of Florence Kelley*, 77.

12. Jane Addams, *My Friend Julia Lathrop* (New York, 1935), 77.

13. Residents of Hull House, *Hull House Maps and Papers* (New York, 1895).

14. FK to Caroline B. Kelley, Chicago, Feb. 24, 1892, Nicholas Kelley Papers, New York Public Library.

15. Kathryn Kish Sklar, "Two Political Cultures in the Progressive Era: The National Consumers' League and the American Association for Labor Legislation," in Linda K. Kerber, Alice Kessler-Harris and Kathryn Kish Sklar, eds., *U.S. History as Women's History: New Feminist Essays* (Chapel Hill, N.C., 1995), 58.

16. U.S. Commissioner of Labor, *Fourth Annual Report, Working Women in Large Cities* (Washington, D.C., 1889), 62–64.

17. For a full argument of this point, see Kathryn Kish Sklar, "The Historical Foundations of Women's Power in the Creation of the American Welfare State, 1830–1930," in Seth Koven and Sonya Michel, eds., *Mothers of a New World: Maternalist Politics and the Origins of Welfare States* (New York, 1993).

18. "Hit at Sweat Shops," *Chicago Tribune*, April 23, 1894; Sklar, *Florence Kelley*, 261.

19. Sklar, *Florence Kelley*, 309.

20. Florence Kelley, "Minimum Wage Boards," *American Journal of Sociology* 17 (Nov. 1911), 303–14.

21. Florence Kelley, "Ten Years from Now," *Survey*, March 26, 1910, 978–81.

22. Sklar, "Two Political Cultures," 60.

23. See, for example, John B. Andrews to Erich Stern, New York, Dec. 14, 1910, American Association for Labor Legislation Papers, Cornell University.

24. See Molly Ladd-Taylor, *Mother-Work: Women, Child Welfare, and the State, 1890–1930* (Urbana, Ill., 1994), 167–96.

25. See J. Stanley Lemons, *The Woman Citizen: Social Feminism in the 1920s* (Urbana, Ill., 1973), 169–76.

26. For the opposition of the progressive mainstream of the women's movement, see Kathryn Kish Sklar, "Why Did Most Politically Active Women Oppose the ERA in the 1920s?" in Joan Hoff-Wilson, ed., *Rights of Passage: the Past and Future of the ERA* (Bloomington, Ind., 1986).

27. *The Woman Patriot*, Vol. 5, no. 29, Nov. 1, 1921, 1. For the complete documents of this correspondence between Kelley and Addams, see Anissa Harper, "Pacifism vs. Patriotism in Women's Organizations in the 1920s: How Was the Debate Shaped by the Expansion of the American Military," in *Women and Social Movements in the United States, 1830–1930*, an Internet website edited by Kathryn Kish Sklar and Thomas Dublin, http://womhist .binghamton.edu. See also Nancy F. Cott, *The Grounding of Modern Feminism* (New Haven, 1987), 243–67.

28. The Spider Web Chart is reproduced in Helen Baker, "How Did the Women's International League for Peace and Freedom Respond to Right Wing Attacks in the 1920s?" in *Women and Social Movements* at http://womhist.binghamton.edu.

29. For example, see the furor aroused within the League of Women Voters over the proposed Child Labor Amendment to the U.S. Constitution in 1924, in Louise M. Young, *In the Public Interest: The League of Women Voters, 1920–1970* (New York, 1989), 97–98.

30. For Perkins see Susan Ware, *Beyond Suffrage: Women in the New Deal* (Cambridge, Mass., 1981), *passim*.

31. Felix Frankfurter, "Foreword," in Josephine Goldmark, *Impatient Crusader: Florence Kelley's Life Story* (Urbana, Ill., 1953), v.

ANNELISE ORLECK
From the Russian Pale to Labor Organizing in New York City

The pale of Jewish settlement was a territory within Russia to which Jews were restricted during the eighteenth and nineteenth centuries and where they were frequently subjected to ferocious outbursts of anti-Semitic violence. Crossing from the pale to the teeming streets of Manhattan's Lower East Side was a frontier crossing of major proportions. Yet two million European Jews who came to the United States between 1880 and 1924 made it across, among them the remarkable young women who are the subjects of Annelise Orleck's lively and informative essay.

Like so many of their fellow immigrants, Rose Schneiderman, Fannia Cohn, Clara Lemlich, and Pauline Newman gravitated to one of the earliest industries to employ women—the garment industry. Based in New York City, the industry had long provided countless married women with piecework to take back to dimly lit tenements, where they often enlisted the help of grandmothers and children. By the turn of the century, much of the work had been transferred to sweatshops and factories that were notorious for their low wages and squalid working conditions. Because so many of the female employees were young single women who presumably regarded their work as a temporary necessity until rescued by marriage, labor leaders usually assumed that the women were virtually unorganizable. Yet between 1909 and 1915, women garment workers in New York as well as in other cities exploded in labor militancy. By 1919, half of all women garment workers belonged to trade unions and many had joined the suffrage struggle as well. The role these four young women played in this process is the focus of Orleck's essay.

What experiences shaped their political consciousness and propelled their activism? As young girls forced to work and forego school and college, how did they educate themselves and for what purpose? Who were their allies and why were these alliances so necessary, yet so unstable? How was the balancing act required of the four with respect to male trade unionists and elite female reformers similar to that required of Charlotte Hawkins Brown, albeit in a different context (see Glenda Gilmore's essay, pp. 300–310)? What attracted these young working women to suffrage? What is meant by the term "industrial feminists"? You will find Pauline Newman's reminiscence of garment work in the documents that accompany this cluster of essays.

During the summer of 1907, when New York City was gripped by a severe economic depression, a group of young women workers who had been laid off and were facing eviction took tents and sleeping rolls to the verdant Palisades overlooking the Hudson River. While rising rents and unemployment spread panic among the poor immigrants of Manhattan's Lower East Side, these teenagers lived in a makeshift summer camp, getting work where they could

Excerpted from the prologue, and chs. 1 and 2 of *Common Sense and a Little Fire: Women and Working-Class Politics in the United States, 1900–1965*, by Annelise Orleck (Chapel Hill: University of North Carolina Press, 1995). Used by permission of the author and publisher. Notes have been edited and renumbered.

find it, sharing whatever food and drink they could afford, reading, hiking, and gathering around a campfire at night to sing Russian and Yiddish songs. "Thus we avoided paying rent or, worse still, being evicted," Pauline Newman later recalled. "Besides which, we liked living in the open—plenty of fresh air, sunshine and the lovely Hudson for which there was no charge."[1]

Away from the clatter of the shops and the filth of Lower East Side streets, the young women talked into the night, refreshed by what Newman called "the cool of the evening, glorious sunsets, the moon and stars." They shared personal concerns as well as shop-floor gripes—worries about love, about the future, and about the pressing problems of housing and food.

Their cliffside village meant more to Newman and her friends than a summer escape. They had created a vibrant alternative to the tenement life they found so oppressive, and their experience of it had set them to wondering. Perhaps the same sense of joy and comradeship could help workers transcend the drudgery of the garment shops and form the basis for effective organizing.[2]

At season's end, they emerged with strengthened bonds and renewed resolve to organize their communities around issues that the recent depression had brought into sharp relief: the need for stabilized rent and food prices, improved working conditions, and housing for the poor.[3]

The spirit of intimacy and solidarity that pervaded the summer of 1907 would inspire much of Pauline Newman's later organizing. Indeed, it became a model for the vision of change that Newman shared with her fellow Jewish immigrant radicals Fannia Cohn, Rose Schneiderman and Clara Lemlich. The four women moved to political struggle not simply by the need for better wages, hours and working conditions but also, in Newman's words, by a need to ensure that "poverty did not deprive us from finding joy and satisfaction in things of the spirit."[4] This essay examines the early careers of these four remarkable organizers and the role they played in building a militant working women's movement during the first decades of the twentieth century.

For even as girls, these marginally educated immigrants wanted to be more than ... shop-floor drudges. They wanted lives filled with beauty—with friendships, books, art,

music, dance, fresh air, and clean water. "A working girl is a human being," Newman would later tell a legislative committee investigating factory conditions, "with a heart, with desires, with aspirations, with ideas and ideals." That image nourished Newman, Schneiderman, Lemlich, and Cohn throughout their long careers. And it focused them on a single goal: to reshape U.S. society so that "working girls" like themselves could fulfill some of their dreams.[5]

The four women moved through strikingly different cultural milieus over the course of long careers that would carry them in different directions. Still, they each bore the imprint of the shared culture in which they were raised, first in Eastern Europe and then in New York City. That common experience gave them a particular understanding of gender, class, and ethnicity that shaped their later activism and political thought.

All four were born in the Russian-dominated pale of Jewish settlement during the last two decades of the nineteenth century. Rose Schneiderman was born in the Polish village of Saven in 1882; Fannia Cohn was born in Kletsk, Poland, in 1885; Clara Lemlich was born in the Ukrainian village of Gorodok in 1886; and Pauline Newman was born in Kovno, Lithuania, around 1890.[6]

They were ushered into a world swept by a firestorm of new ideas, where the contrasting but equally messianic visions of orthodox Judaism and revolutionary Socialism competed for young minds. The excitement of living in a revolutionary era imbued these young women with a faith in progress and a belief that political commitment gave life meaning. It also taught them, at an early age, that gender, class, and ethnicity were fundamental social categories and essential building blocks for political change. Being born into turbulence does not in itself make a child into a political activist. But the changes sweeping the Russian Empire toward the end of the nineteenth century shaped the consciousness of a generation of Eastern European Jews who contributed, in wildly disproportionate numbers, to revolutionary movements in Russia and to the labor and radical movements in the United States.[7]

The four were exposed to Marxist ideas at a tender age. As Eastern Europe shifted uneasily from feudalism to capitalism in the latter part of the nineteenth century, class analysis became part of the common parlance of young people in Jewish towns and villages. "Behind every other volume of Talmud in those years, there was a volume of Marx," one union organizer recalled of his small Polish town. Clara Lemlich grew up on revolutionary tracts and songs; Fannia Cohn considered herself a committed Socialist by the age of sixteen.[8]

Their awareness of ethnicity was even more keen. As Jews in Eastern Europe, the four learned young that ethnic identity was a double-edged sword. It was a source of strength and solace in their bitterly poor communities, but it also enabled Tsarist authorities to single Jews out and sow seeds of suspicion among their peasant neighbors. Jews living under Russian rule were made painfully aware of their status as permanent "others" in the land where they had lived for centuries. Clara Lemlich's family lived not far from Kishinev, where in 1903 the Tsar's government openly and unabashedly directed an orgy of anti-Jewish violence that shocked the world. In cosmopolitan Minsk, where she had gone to study, Fannia Cohn watched with dismay as the revolutionary populist organization she had joined began mouthing the same anti-Semitic conspiracy theories spewed by the government they despised. Frustration turned to fear when her brother was almost killed in yet another pogrom.[9]

Sex was just as distinct a dividing line as class and ethnicity. Eastern European Jews had observed a strict sexual division of labor for more than a thousand years. But by the late nineteenth century, as political and economic upheaval jolted long-accepted ways of thinking, sex roles too were being questioned. And so the four girls' understandings of gender were informed both by traditional Jewish conceptions of womanhood and by the challenges issued by new political movements.

In traditional Jewish society, mothers were also entrepreneurs. Clara Lemlich, Pauline Newman, and Rose Schneiderman were all raised by mothers who were skilled businesswomen. Jewish mothers' success in this role grew out of and reinforced a belief that women were innately suited to competition in the economic sphere. In contrast to the image of the sheltered middle-class housewife then dominant in the United States, Eastern European Jewish religious tradition glorified strong, economically sophisticated wives and mothers.

But as much as women's entrepreneurship was respected, a far higher premium was placed on study and prayer. And that, religious tradition dictated, could be performed only by men. A woman was expected to be pious, to read the vernacular Yiddish—rather than ancient Hebrew—translation of the Bible, and perhaps to attend women's services at the synagogue. But her primary religious role was as keeper of the home. Formal religious education was offered only to males.[10] Because Eastern European Jewish women had to fight for every scrap of education they received, many began to see education as the key to independence from all masters. This view would strongly influence their political organizing once in the United States.

The four emigrated as part of the mass movement that brought two million Jews from Eastern Europe to the United States between 1881 and 1924. Schneiderman came in 1890, Newman in 1901, Lemlich in 1903, and Cohn in 1904. Like most of their compatriots, they arrived in New York Harbor and settled on Manhattan's Lower East Side, the largest settlement of Eastern European Jews in the United States.[11] The newcomers were tantalized by the exciting diversions that New York life promised: libraries, theater, music, department stores, and amusement parks. But they had neither time nor money to indulge in such pleasures, for all of them soon found themselves laboring long hours to support their families.

At an age when most girls in the United States were still in grade school, immigrant working girls like Newman spent twelve- to fourteen-hour days in the harshest of atmospheres. Their bodies and minds reeled from the shock of the shops: the deafening noise, the brutal pace, and the rebukes of foremen. Some children were able to slough off the hardship with jokes and games. Others, realizing that they were destined to spend their youth in dank factories rather than in classrooms or schoolyards, grew sullen and withdrawn.

Clara Lemlich, like so many others, was quickly disillusioned by her first job in a New York garment shop: "I went to work two weeks after landing in this country. We worked from sunrise to set seven days a week. . . . Those who worked on machines had to carry the machines on their back both to and from work. . . . The shop we worked in had no central heating, no electric power. . . . The hissing of the machines, the yelling of the foreman, made life unbearable."[12]

Newly arrived European women undergoing medical examinations at Ellis Island, ca. 1900.
"The day of the emigrant's arrival in New York was the nearest earthly likeness to the final day of Judgement, when we have to prove our fitness to enter Heaven." The words are those of a sympathetic journalist who shared the anxiety-ridden experience awaiting the immigrants at the port of entry. Failing the medical test could mean deportation. (Courtesy of Brown Brothers, Sterling, Pennsylvania.)

Anger drove young women workers like Lemlich and Newman to band together. Untrained and largely unschooled, these young women were drawn to Socialism and trade unionism not because they felt an ideological affinity but because they had a desperate need to improve their working conditions. "I knew very little about Socialism," Lemlich recalled. "[But] the girls, whether Socialist or not, had many stoppages and strikes." Newman too found that for most young women workers, political understanding followed action rather than precipitating it: "We of the 1909 vintage knew nothing about the economics of . . . industry or for that matter about economics in general. All we knew was the bitter fact that, after working seventy and eighty hours in a seven day week, we did not earn enough to keep body and soul together." These assertions reveal much about the political development of the tens of thousands of women

garment workers who would soon amaze New York and the nation with their militancy.[13]

Shop-floor culture fed the young women's emerging sense of political identity. Working alongside older men and women who discussed Socialism daily, they began to feel a sense of belonging to a distinct class of people in the world: workers. This allegiance would soon become as important to them as their Judaism. The shops also provided an opportunity for bonding with other women. Slowly, out of their workplace experiences, they began to develop a complex political identity in which class, gender and ethnicity overlapped. Young women workers were moved by the idea of sisterhood. It captured their own experiences in the sex-segregated shops where they worked. The majority of New York's garment workers were little more than girls, and the relationships they forged with factory friends were similar to those of schoolgirls—intense, melodramatic, and deeply loyal. They were teenage confidantes as well as fellow workers, and they relied on shop-floor rapport to soften the harshness of factory life.[14] For young immigrant women trying to build lives in a new land, such bonds were powerful and lasting. From these shop-floor friendships would soon evolve the ties of union sisterhood.[15]

Pauline Newman and her co-workers at the Triangle Shirtwaist Factory literally grew up together. Only twelve when she first came to Triangle, Newman was assigned to a corner known as "the kindergarten," where workers as young as eight, nine, or ten years old trimmed threads from finished garments. They labored, Newman later recalled, "from 7:30 A.M. to 6:30 at night when it wasn't busy. When the season was on we worked till 9 o'clock. No overtime pay." Their only taste of a normal childhood came through the songs and games they invented to help pass the time, the stories they told and the secrets they shared.[16]

By the early twentieth century, New York State had passed laws prohibiting night work for children. But little attempt was made to enforce them. On the rare occasions when an inspector showed up at her factory, Newman remembered, "the employers were always tipped off. . . . 'Quick,' they'd say, 'Into the boxes!' And we children would climb into the big box the finished shirts were stored in. Then some shirts were piled on top of us and when the inspector came—No children." In a way it was fun, Newman remembered. They thought they were playing a game like hide and seek.[17]

But it wasn't really a game. Children who had to help support their parents grew up quickly. Rose Schneiderman was thirteen when her mother begged United Hebrew Charities, an organization run by middle-class German Jews, to find her daughter a "respectable job" at a department store. Retail jobs were deemed more respectable than factory work because the environment was more pleasant and sexual harassment was thought to be less common. Deborah Schneiderman worried that factory work would sully Rose's reputation and make her less marriageable. A job as a fashionable salesgirl, she hoped, would usher Rose into the middle class. The single mother who had fed her children on charity food baskets and had been forced to place them in orphanages was grimly determined to help them escape poverty.

But then as now, pink-collar jobs paid significantly less than industrial work. Anxious to free her mother from the rigors of maintaining their tenement building, Schneiderman left her job in Ridley's department store for the harsher and more morally suspect conditions of an industrial shop. Making linings for caps and hats, she immediately raised her weekly income from $2.75 to $6. As the sole supporter of her family, the sixteen-year-old hoped to work her way up quickly to a skilled job in the cap trade.[18]

Clara Lemlich's family also relied on her wages, particularly because her father was unemployed. She aspired to the skilled position of draper, one of the highest-paid positions a woman could attain in the dressmaking trade. Despite terrible working conditions, many ambitious young women chose garment work over other jobs because it seemed to offer their greatest chance to acquire skills and command high wages. When these hopes were dashed, some young workers grew angry. That anger was fanned and channeled by older women in the shops who were itching to challenge the authority of the bosses.[19]

That is what happened to Rose Schneiderman, who, like many skilled women garment workers, was blocked from advancement by the unofficial gender hierarchy at her factory. Finding that all the highest-paid jobs in her capmaking shop were reserved for men, Schneiderman asked around about ways to break through those barriers. When she approached fellow worker Bessie Braut with her concerns, Schneiderman was initiated simultaneously into trade unionism, Socialism, and feminism. Schneiderman recalled, "Bessie was an unusual person. Her beautiful eyes shone out of a badly pockmarked face and the effect was startling. An outspoken anarchist, she made a strong impression on us. She wasted no time in giving us the facts of life—that the men in our trade belonged to a union and were, therefore, able to better their conditions. She added pointedly that it would be a good thing for the lining-makers to join a union along with the trimmers, who were all women."[20]

Schneiderman, Braut, and several other workers called on the secretary-treasurer of the United Cloth Hat and Cap Makers to request union recognition for their fledgling local of trimmers and lining makers. Within a few days they had enough signatures to win a charter for their local, and Schneiderman was elected secretary.[21]

Surprising even herself, the once-shy redhead soon found she could be an eloquent and fierce advocate for her fellow workers. In recognition of her growing reputation, the capmakers elected her to the Central Labor Union of New York. Deborah Schneiderman was disturbed by the turn Rose's life was taking. She warned Rose that if she pursued a public life she would never find a husband. No man wants a woman with a big mouth, her mother said.[22]

In the flush of excitement at the praise and warmth suddenly coming her way, young Rose did not stop to worry. In organizing, she had found both a calling and a world of friends. She had no intention of turning back. "It was such an exciting time," she wrote later. "A new life opened up for me. All of a sudden I was not lonely anymore. . . . It was the beginning of a period that molded all my subsequent life."[23]

Fannia Cohn, too, chose garment work as her path to a career. And like Schneiderman, Lemlich, and Newman, she found a community there. Unlike the others, however, she did not enter a garment factory looking for work that paid well. She was a comfortable middle-class woman in search of a trade ripe for unionizing.

Cohn arrived in New York in 1904 and moved in with her affluent cousins. There was little about her early days in the United States that was comparable to the hard-pressed scrambling for a living that the Schneidermans, Lemlichs, and Newmans experienced. "My family suggested that I complete my studies and then join the labor movement but I rejected this as I did not want to come into it from 'without' but from 'within.' I realized then that if I wanted to really understand the mind, the aspirations of the workers, I should experience the life of the worker in a shop."[24] In 1905, Fannia Cohn became a sleevemaker. For a year she moved from shop to shop until, in the "white goods" trade, she found the organizing challenge she was looking for.

Shops that manufactured white goods—underwear, kimonos, and robes—were considered particularly hard to organize. Production took place in tiny sweatshops, not large factories, and the manufacturing process had been broken down into small tasks that required little skill. The majority of white goods workers were immigrant girls under the age of fifteen. And because they came from a wide range of backgrounds—Jewish, Italian, Syrian, Turkish, and Greek—it was difficult for them to communicate with each other, let alone organize. As a result, these workers were among the lowest paid in the garment trades.

At twenty, Cohn was an elder in the trade. With her high school education and fluency in three languages, she was seen as a mother figure by many of the adolescents in the shops. She and a handful of older women workers began to operate as mentors, meeting with the girls in each shop and identifying potential leaders. Cohn taught her co-workers to read, write, and speak in public, hoping they would channel those skills into the union struggle. Cohn had already created the role that she would play throughout her career: an educator of younger workers.[25]

Education was a primary driving force in the metamorphosis of all four young women from shop workers to union organizers. From the isolated towns and restive cities of Eastern Europe, where gender, class, and ethnicity stymied Jewish girls' hopes for education, the lure of free public schooling in the United States beckoned powerfully. Having to drop out of school to work was more than a disappointment for many Jewish immigrant girls; it was their first great disillusionment with the dream of America. And they did not give that dream up easily.

"When I went to work," Rose Schneiderman remembered, "I was determined to continue my studies." Her only option was to attend one of the many night schools then open to immigrant workers in New York. Having carried with her from Poland the ideal of education as an exalted, liberating process, she was disgusted by the mediocre instruction she encountered and felt betrayed by teachers who seemed to be patronizing her. "I enrolled and went faithfully every evening for about four weeks. But I found that . . . the instructor seemed more interested in getting one-hundred-percent attendance than in giving one-hundred-percent instruction. He would joke and tell silly stories. . . . I soon realized I was wasting my time." Schneiderman left the evening school but did not stop studying. She asked older co-workers if she could borrow books that she had discussed with them in the shop. In the evenings, she read with her mother at home. Serializations of Emile Zola's *J'Accuse* and other contemporary writings in the Yiddish evening paper *Abendblatt* gave Rose a taste for literature. "I devoured everything I could get my hands on."[26]

Clara Lemlich was an equally avid reader. At the end of each twelve-hour day stitching shirtwaists, she would walk from her factory to the East Broadway branch of the New York Public Library. There she read the library's entire collection of Russian classics. "I was so eager to learn things," she later recalled. When she tired of solitary study, Lemlich joined a free night school on Grand Street. She returned home late each night, ate the dinner her mother had kept warm for her, then slept for just a few hours before rising again for work.[27]

Not surprisingly, young women like Schneiderman, Newman, and Lemlich turned to radical politics to fulfill their desire for a life of the mind. If no other school was available, then what Pauline Newman called "the school of solidarity" would have to do. Membership in the Socialist Party and in unions, tenant organizations, and benevolent societies provided immigrant women with an opportunity to learn and study that most would never have gotten otherwise. And as Newman put it, "Because they were hitherto deprived of any tutorship, they at once became ardent students."[28]

Pauline Newman was just fifteen when she first knocked on the doors of the Socialist Literary Society. Although women were not yet allowed to join, she was permitted to attend classes. The Literary Society was a revelation to the young worker. There she was introduced to the writings of Shakespeare, George Eliot, and Thomas Hardy and personally met writers like Jack London and Charlotte Perkins Gilman, who came to speak there. Gratitude, however, didn't stop her from joining a successful petition drive to admit women to the society.

For Newman—as for Clara Lemlich, who attended Marxist theory classes at the Socialist Party's Rand School—studying was more than a distraction from work. The "desire to get out of the shop," Newman wrote later, "to learn, to understand, became the dominant force in my life." But unlike many immigrants, who saw schooling as a ladder out of the working class, both she and Lemlich were committed to helping others rise with them. So Newman and Lemlich formed study groups that met during lunch hours and after work to share what they were learning with their friends.[29]

"We tried to educate ourselves," Newman remembered of her co-workers at the Triangle Shirtwaist Factory. "I would invite the girls to my room and we took turns reading poetry in English to improve our understanding of the language." Because they had to steal the time to study, the young women approached everything they read with a heightened sensitivity. And when something they were reading struck a chord of recognition, seemed to reflect on their own lives, the catharsis was not only emotional; it was political.[30]

The evolution of Lemlich's study group illustrates how study often led to union activity. Older workers, who were teaching Lemlich the craft of draping, invited her to join their lunchtime discussion groups to learn more about trade unionism. Soon Lemlich and a group of young women waistmakers formed their own study group. Discussion quickly escalated to action, and they decided to form a union.[31]

Skilled male workers in the shirtwaist trade had been trying to establish a union since 1900. But after five years the union had managed to attract only ten members. The problem, Lemlich told her male colleagues, was that women workers had to be approached by an organizer who understood their particular needs as women. They bristled at the suggestion that this young girl might know more about their business than they did. But years later, one conceded that the failure of the first waistmakers' union was due at least in part to their ham-fisted tactics: "We would issue a circular reading somewhat as follows: 'Murder the exploiters, the blood-suckers, the manufacturers. . . . Pay your dues. . . . Down with the Capitalists!'" Few women or men showed up at their meetings.[32]

During the spring of 1905 the union disbanded and reorganized as Local 25 of the ILGWU, with Clara Lemlich and a group of six young women from her waistmaking shop on the executive board. Taking their cue from Lemlich, the new union used women organizers to attract women workers. Lemlich addressed street-corner meetings in English and Yiddish and found Italian women to address the Italian workers. Soon, like Schneiderman, Newman, and Cohn, she realized that she had found a calling.[33]

In the progressive atmosphere of early-twentieth-century New York City, influential people quickly noticed the militant young working women. Older Socialists, trade unionists, and middle-class reformers offered their assistance. These benefactors helped the young organizers sharpen their arguments, provided

Rose Schneiderman addresses a street rally in New York City, probably 1910s. (Courtesy of Brown Brothers, Sterling, Pennsylvania.)

financial assistance, and introduced them to politicians and public officials. The protégés recognized the importance of this informal mentoring and would later work to recreate such networks in the unions, schools, and training programs they built for young women workers. Schneiderman, Newman, Lemlich, and Cohn were keenly aware that young working women needed help from more experienced and more powerful allies. But they also worried that the voices of women workers might be outshouted in the clamorous process of building alliances. From these early days, they battled to preserve the integrity of their vision.

Pauline Newman found her first mentors in the Socialist Party, which she joined in 1906 at the age of fifteen. Older women, including former garment worker Theresa Serber Malkiel, took her on as a protégé. Newman quickly blossomed under their tutelage. Before long she was running street-corner meetings. Armed with a sonorous voice and the certitude of youth, she would take "an American flag and a soapbox and go from corner to corner," exhorting the gospel of Socialism in Yiddish

and English. "I, like many of my friends and comrades, thought that socialism and socialism alone could and would someday fill the gap between rich and poor," Newman recalled. In a neighborhood crowded with sidewalk proselytizers, this child evangelist became one of the party's most popular street-corner attractions.[34]

In 1908, nine years before New York State gave women the vote, seventeen-year-old Newman was nominated by the Socialist Party to run for New York's Secretary of State. Newman used her campaign as a platform for suffrage. Her speeches were heckled by some Socialist men, and her candidacy provoked amused commentaries in New York City newspapers; some writers snickered at the prospect of a "skirted Secretary of State." It was a largely symbolic crusade, but Newman felt that she got people talking about the idea of women in government. The highlight of the campaign was her whistlestop tour with presidential candidate and Socialist leader Eugene V. Debs on his "Red Special" train.

The Socialist Party opened up a new world to Newman, who, after all, had never graduated from elementary school. Along with Debs, she met future Congressmen Meyer Berger and Morris Hillquit and leading Socialist intellectuals. Newman later wrote about the excitement of discussions that carried over from meetings and went into the night as she and her friends walked through Central Park, arguing till the sun came up. Those nights made her feel part of a historic moment.[35]

While Newman was being nurtured by the Socialist Party, Rose Schneiderman found her mentors in the United Cloth Hat and Cap Makers. At the union's 1904 convention she was elected to the General Executive Board; she was the first woman to win such a high-level post in the American labor movement. During the winter of 1904–5, Schneiderman's leadership skills were tested when owners tried to open up union shops to nonunion workers. The largely immigrant capmaker's union called for a general strike. The 1905 strike was a watershed event in Schneiderman's emerging career. Her role as the only woman leader in the union won attention from the press and lasting respect from male capmakers, including the future president of the union, Max Zaritsky, who became a lifelong friend and admirer.[36]

It also brought her to the attention of the newly formed Women's Trade Union League (WTUL), an organization of progressive middle- and upper-class women reformers founded in 1903 to help working women organize. Schneiderman had misgivings about the group because she "could not believe that men and women who were not wage earners themselves understood the problems that workers faced." But she trusted the League's best-known working-class member, Irish shirtmaker Leonora O'Reilly. And she could not ignore the favorable publicity that the WTUL won for the strikers. By March 1905, Schneiderman had been elected to the executive board of the New York WTUL. In 1906, the group elected her vice president.[37]

Schneiderman's entrance into the New York WTUL was an important turning point for both her and the organization. Three years after its founding, the WTUL remained dominated by affluent reformers who had dubbed themselves "allies" of the working class. Despite their genuine commitment to trade unionism, League leaders had credibility problems among women workers. Schneiderman had joined the League recognizing that working women lacked the education, the

money, and the political clout to organize effectively without powerful allies. Still, she remained ambivalent for a variety of reasons.[38]

The progressive reformers who dominated the League tried to steer workers away from radical influences, particularly the Socialist Party. Yet Schneiderman and O'Reilly, the League's leading working-class organizers, were Socialist Party members and saw unionism as a potentially revolutionary tool. As a result, the pair often felt torn by competing loyalties. Socialists distrusted their work with upper-crust women reformers. Union men were either indifferent or openly hostile to working women's attempts to become leaders in the labor movement. And the League women often seemed to Schneiderman and O'Reilly to act out of a patronizing benevolence that had little to do with real coalition building. The two grew angry at what they saw as attempts by wealthy allies to manipulate them. In January 1906, Leonora O'Reilly announced the first of her many resignations from the League, claiming "an overdose of allies."[39]

There were a few deep friendships between affluent WTUL leaders and working women like Schneiderman, O'Reilly, and Pauline Newman, who joined the League in 1909. Such bonds created hope that intimacy was possible between women of different classes; but cross-class friendships were the exception rather than the rule. Working women like Newman never lost sight of the ways their class background separated them from wealthy reformers. Sisterhood was exhilarating, but outside the WTUL, their lives and political agendas diverged sharply.[40]

Consequently, these women's relations with most wealthy League supporters were marked by deep ambivalence inasmuch as WTUL backers wanted to distance the League from radical working-class activism and to stake out a decidedly middle ground in the struggle for women's rights that was then gathering steam.

Schneiderman tried to counterbalance such influences by encouraging male union leaders to play a more active role in the League, but she had little success. She told them that the WTUL could help the labor movement by successfully organizing women workers, whose low wages might otherwise exert a downward pressure on unionized male wages. A *women's* trade union league was needed, she insisted, because women workers responded to different arguments than did men workers. The League could focus on the particular concerns of women, such as the double shift—having to perform household chores after coming home from long days in the factory. Her suggestions were greeted with indifference.

Addressing the First Convention of American Women Trade Unionists, held in New York on July 14, 1907, Schneiderman reported that she "was very much surprised and not a little disappointed that the attention of men unionists was so small." The truth is, she told her audience, working women needed more than unions. They needed political power. "The time has come," she said firmly, "when working women of the State of New York must be enfranchised and so secure political power to shape their own labor conditions." The convention passed a suffrage resolution, one of the first prosuffrage statements by any organization representing American working-class women.[41]

Schneiderman confronted middle- and upper-class allies with equal frankness. She told the NYWTUL executive board that they were having little success organizing women workers because they approached their task like scholars, not trade unionists. They surveyed conditions in the women's trades, noting which had the lowest salaries, the longest hours, and the worst hygienic conditions. Then they established committees to study the possibilities for unionizing each trade. Finally they went into the shops to explain their findings to the working women. Schneiderman suggested a simpler alternative: take their lead from women workers and respond to requests for aid from women workers who were already trying to organize. It was something they had never thought to do.[42]

Before long, requests for help were pouring in, mostly from immigrant Jewish women. In the dress trade, where Clara Lemlich was working, and in the white goods trade, where Fannia Cohn was organizing, women workers had launched a series of wildcat strikes. "It was not unusual for unorganized workers to walk out without having any direct union affiliation," Schneiderman later recalled.[43]

By 1907, long-simmering anger over speedups, wage cuts, and the requirement that employees pay for their own thread reached a boiling point. Foreshadowing its role in the decades to come, the Women's Trade Union League decided to champion women workers ignored by the male unions. The strike fever soon engulfed Brooklyn, where for two years Fannia Cohn had been struggling against male union leaders' indifference to organize white goods workers. So when three hundred workers in one shop decided to strike in 1908, they bypassed the UGW and called for help from Schneiderman and the WTUL.

Since the ethnic makeup of the Brooklyn white goods trade was far more diverse than any other in the garment industry, this strike raised a new challenge for Schneiderman: how to forge a sense of solidarity between working-class women of many religions and nationalities. Schneiderman decided that the best way to reach immigrant workers was through organizers who literally spoke their language.[44]

She decided to focus first on Italian workers because, after Jews, they comprised the single largest ethnic group in the garment trades. Recognizing the cultural as well as linguistic differences that separated her from Italian immigrant women, Schneiderman tried a strategy she would employ many times over the years to come: to identify and cultivate a leader from within the ranks of the workers. She began working with a Brooklyn priest on ways to approach young Italian women. She also got the League to hire an Italian-speaking organizer who assembled a committee of progressive New York Italians—including prominent women professionals and the editor of a popular evening paper *Bolatino de la Sera*— to popularize trade unionism among Italian women workers.[45]

The strategy proved successful. By 1909 enough workers had enlisted that the ILGWU finally recognized the Brooklyn white goods workers' union. The vast majority of its members were teenage girls; these young women elected their mentor, Fannia Cohn, then twenty-four, to the union's first executive board. Cohn, who stepped off the shop floor to a policy-making position, would remain a paid union official for the rest of her life.[46]

In 1909, Clara Lemlich—then in her twenties and on the executive board of ILGWU Local 25—enlisted Schneiderman's aid in her drive to organize shirt-waist makers. For the past three years, Lemlich had been zigzagging between small shops, stirring up trouble. Her first full-scale strike was at Weisen and Goldstein's Manhattan factory. Like the Triangle Shirtwaist Factory, where Newman worked, Weisen and Goldstein's was considered a model shop. The workrooms were modern and airy—a pleasant contrast to the dark basement rooms where most white goods workers labored. However, the advantages of working in a clean, new factory were offset by the strains of mechanization. In 1907 the workers at Weisen and Goldstein's went on strike to protest speedups.

Older male strikers proved critical to Lemlich's political education. Confused by an argument between workers at a strike meeting, Lemlich asked one to explain the difference between Socialist unionism and the "pure and simple trade unionism" of the American Federation of Labor (AFL). When the meeting ended, the man took Lemlich for a long walk. He explained Socialism in terms she could use with her fellow workers. "He started with a bottle of milk—how it was made, who made the money from it through every stage of its production. Not only did the boss take the profits, he said, but not a drop of that milk did you drink unless he allowed you to. It was funny, you know, because I'd been saying things like that to the girls before. But now I understood it better and I began to use it more often—only with shirtwaists."[47]

Lemlich returned to the picket line with a more sophisticated view of organizing. She became a regular at Socialist Party meetings and began attending classes at the Rand School. Through the Socialist Party she became friends with Rose Schneiderman, Pauline Newman, and other young women organizers. Both individually and in tandem, this group of radical young women organized strikes across the Lower East Side.

In 1909, after being fired from two more shops for leading strikes, Lemlich began working at the Leiserson shop. Brazenly, she marched uninvited into a strike meeting that had been called by the shop's older male elite— the skilled cutters and drapers. Warning them that they would lose if they attempted to strike without organizing the shop's unskilled women, Lemlich demanded their help in organizing women workers. They bridled at her nerve, but ultimately they helped her unionize the women.[48]

Lemlich's reputation as a leader grew rapidly during the fall of 1909 as stories of her bravery spread. During the Leiserson strike, which began that September, she was arrested seventeen times and had six ribs broken by club-wielding police and company guards. Without complaint, she tended to her bruises and returned to the line. By November 1909, when she stepped onto the stage in Cooper Union's Great Hall of the People to deliver the speech that would spark the largest women's strike the nation had yet seen, Lemlich was not the anonymous "wisp of a girl" that news accounts described. She was a battle-scarred veteran of the labor movement, well known among her fellow workers.[49]

Still, it is worth remembering that in this period, the four women activists were just barely adults. Newman, Schneiderman, and Lemlich still lived with their parents. During the Leiserson strike, Lemlich was so fearful that her parents would try to keep her home if they knew about her injuries that she hid her escapades and bruises from them. Later she explained the events to her grandson: "Like rain the blows fell on me. The gangsters hit me. . . . The boys and girls invented themselves how to give back what they got from the scabs, with stones and whatnot, with sticks. . . . Sometimes when I came home I wouldn't tell because if I would tell they wouldn't want me to go anymore. Yes, my boy, it's not easy. Unions aren't built easy."[50]

On November 23, 1909, New York City awoke to a general strike of shirtwaist makers, the largest strike by women workers the United States had ever seen. Overnight, between 20,000 and 40,000 workers—most of them teenage girls—silenced their sewing machines to protest the low wages, long hours, and dangerous working conditions. Though the magnitude of the strike amazed nearly everyone, including Schneiderman, Newman, Cohn, and Lemlich, the four knew that this was no spontaneous uprising: they had been organizing feverishly for almost three years and had noted a transformation in the working women they talked to, a growing sense of collective identity matched by an increasing militancy. They had laid the groundwork through a series of smaller strikes and had trained fellow workers to expect and respond to the violent and divisive tactics used by bosses to break the strike.

Despite their effectiveness, the strike was threatened by the escalation of police violence against the young women picketers. Two weeks after the strike call, Schneiderman and Dreier led ten thousand young waistmakers on a march to city hall to demand that Mayor

George McClellan rein in the police. He promised an investigation but did little. One month into the strike, there had been 771 arrests, many made with undue force.[51]

WTUL leaders decided to try a different tack. They called a mass meeting of all the young women who had been attacked by police. The press and wealthy supporters were invited. One after another, adolescent girls rose to the stage to tell their stories. Mollie Weingast told a cheering crowd that when an officer tried to arrest her, she informed him that she had a constitutional right to picket. Minnie Margolis demanded that a policeman protect her from physical attack by her boss. When he refused, she took down his badge and precinct numbers. It was, she told the audience, an officer's job to protect her right to protest peacefully. Celie Newman, sixteen, said that police had manhandled her and dragged her into court, where her boss told a judge that she was an anarchist and should be deported. At another meeting earlier that week, seventeen-year-old Etta Ruth said that police had taunted her with lewd suggestions.[52]

Implying that picketers were little better than streetwalkers, employers often resorted to sexual innuendos to discredit the strikers. The workers clearly resented the manner in which middle-class standards of acceptable feminine behavior were used to manipulate them even though they enjoyed none of the advantages of middle-class birth. Then as now, society offered a limited range of cultural images of working-class women. They were either "good" girls who listened docilely to fathers, employers, and policemen, or "bad" women whose aggressive behavior made them akin to prostitutes. By walking on picket lines and going public with their demands, they'd forfeited their claims to femininity and respectability—and thus to protection.[53]

Such women were shown little deference by police and company thugs, who attacked them with iron bars, sticks, and billy clubs. And they received little sympathy in court when they attempted to press charges. One young woman appeared in court with a broken nose, a bruised face, and a head swathed in bandages. Yet the judge dropped her assault charge against police. "You are on strike against God and nature," one magistrate told a worker. Only the League's decision to invite college students and wealthy women onto the picket lines ended the violence. Alva Belmont and Anne Morgan led a contingent of New York's wealthiest women in what newspapers dubbed "mink brigades," which patrolled the dirty sidewalks of the Lower East Side. Fearful of clubbing someone on the Social Register, police grew more restrained.[54]

The socialites' presence generated both money and press for the strikers. The move proved politically wise for the suffrage cause as well, because the constant proselytizing of suffrage zealot Alva Belmont, who often bailed strikers out of jail, got young workers talking about the vote. But rubbing elbows with the mink brigade did not blind workers to the class-determined limits of sisterhood. How far they were from the protected status of more affluent women was made abundantly clear by the violence they encountered at the hands of police and company guards and by the fact that the mink brigades were able to end police brutality simply by joining the picket lines.

Encounters in court and with feminist allies speeded the growth of group consciousness. Telling their stories in court, to reporters, and to sympathetic audiences of college and society women, the strikers grew more confident of their speaking abilities and of their capacity to interpret their world. They became more aware of the distribution of power in the United States. And finally, the violence directed against them intensified their bonds with one another.

For Schneiderman, Newman, and Lemlich, the 1909 shirtwaist uprising sped their maturation as organizers and political leaders. The strike breathed new life into a struggling immigrant labor movement and transformed the tiny ILGWU into a union of national significance. Still, it ended with mixed success for workers. Many won pay increases and union recognition; others did not. And the contracts hammered out by ILGWU negotiators left a devastating legacy, for without consulting the strikers, male union negotiators decided that safety conditions were less important than other issues. Their concessions would come back to haunt the entire labor movement two years later, when the Triangle Shirtwaist Factory burned.[55]

Flames from the volcanic 1909 uprising licked industrial cities from New York to Michigan. Within a matter of weeks, 15,000 women waistmakers in Philadelphia walked off their jobs. The spirit of militancy soon touched the Midwest. In 1910, Chicago women led a strike of 41,000 men's clothing makers. The following year, women workers and the wives of male workers played key roles in a bitter cloakmakers' strike in Cleveland. Meanwhile, in Muscatine, Iowa, young women button makers waged and won a long battle for union recognition. In 1912, corset makers in Kalamazoo, Michigan, launched a campaign for better working conditions that polarized their city and won national press attention. In 1913, a strike of underwear and kimono makers swept up 35,000 young Brooklyn girls and women. Finally, in 1915, Chicago dressmakers capped this period of women's labor militancy by winning recognition of their local union after years of struggle. They elected their organizer, Fannia Cohn, as the first woman vice president of a major American labor union.[56]

Cohn, Rose Schneiderman, Pauline Newman, and Clara Lemlich were at the center of a storm that by 1919 had brought half of all women garment workers into trade unions. Individually and in tandem, the four women participated in all of the major women's strikes between 1909 and 1915, arguably the most intense period of women's labor militancy in U.S. history. This wave of "uprisings" seemed to herald the birth of a working women's movement on a scale never before seen. And it catapulted the four young women into positions of leadership, forcing them, in conjunction with colleagues, to articulate a clearly defined set of goals for the new movement.[57] In the passion and excitement of the years that followed, Schneiderman, Newman, Lemlich, and Cohn would begin to mature as political leaders and to forge a vision of political change that originated in their years on the shop floor. Pauline Newman would later describe this new brand of activism as politics of the 1909 vintage, fermented during a brief era of young women's mass protest. That description expresses the importance of the 1909 strike as both symbol and catalyst for a new working women's politics.

"Industrial feminism," the phrase coined in 1915 by scholar Mildred Moore to describe working women's militancy over the previous six years, evokes the same spirit but focuses more broadly. It simultaneously captures the interaction between women workers and feminist activists and recognizes the profound influence that the shop floor had on shaping working women's political consciousness. Industrial feminism accurately depicts the contours of an emerging political movement that by decade's end would propel the problems and concerns of industrial working women to the center of U.S. political discourse and make them players in the Socialist Party, the suffrage movement, and the politics of progressive reform.[58]

Industrial feminism was not a carefully delineated code of political thought. It was a vision of change forged in an atmosphere of crisis and awakening, as women workers in one city after another "laid down their scissors, shook the threads off their clothes and calmly left the place that stood between them and starvation." These were the words of former cloakmaker, journalist, and Socialist Party activist Theresa Malkiel, a partisan chronicler of women's labor militancy. Once an organizer, later a mentor for Newman, Lemlich, and Schneiderman, Malkiel told readers of the *New York Call* that they should not be surprised by the seemingly sudden explosion of young women workers' discontent. As hard as they might find it to take seriously the notion of a "girl's strike," she warned them, this was no outburst of female hysteria. "It was not . . . a woman's fancy that drove them to it," she wrote, "but an eruption of a long smoldering volcano, an overflow of suffering, abuse and exhaustion."[59]

Common sense, Pauline Newman would later say, dictated the most immediate goals of industrial feminists in the era of women's strikes. Given the dire realities of garment workers' lives, the first order of business had to be to improve their wages, hours, and working conditions. Toward that end the "girl strikers" of 1909–15 followed the most basic tenets of unionism. They organized, struck, and negotiated through their labor unions. But the "long-smoldering volcano" that Malkiel cautioned her readers to heed had been stirred to life by more than dissatisfaction over low wages and poor conditions.

The nascent political philosophy that began to take shape after the 1909 strike was more complex than the bread-and-butter unionism of AFL president Samuel Gompers. Why, young working women reasoned, should unions only negotiate hours and wages? They wanted to build unions that would also offer workers educational and cultural activities, health care, and maybe even a chance to leave the city and enjoy the open countryside.

Such ambitious goals derived largely from the personal experiences of industrial feminist leaders like Cohn, Schneiderman, Lemlich, and Newman. Political activism had enriched the four young women's lives, exposing them to more interesting people than they would have met had they stayed on the shop floor: writers, artists, professors, people with ideas. Through politics they had found their voices and a forum in which to raise them. The personal excitement and satisfaction they found in activism in turn shaped the evolution of their political vision: they wanted to create institutions that would provide some of the same satisfactions to any working woman who joined.

But alone, working women had none of the political or economic clout needed to open up such doors of opportunity. To build a successful movement, the four knew that they would have to win the support of more powerful allies. So they learned to build coalitions. From the time they left the shop floor until the end of their careers, they operated within a tense nexus of union men, progressive middle- and upper-class women, and the working women they sought to organize. These alliances shifted continuously, requiring the four women to perform a draining and politically hazardous balancing act. But each core group contributed an important dimension to the political education of the four organizers.

With their male counterparts and older women in the labor movement, they shared a class solidarity that would always remain at the heart of their politics. Traveling around the country, they met coal miners, loggers, and railroad workers who shared both their experiences of exploitation as laborers and their exhilaration in the economic and political strength that trade unions gave them.

From the middle- and upper-class women who joined them on the picket lines and lent them both financial and strategic support, they learned that trade union activism was not the only way to fight for improved work conditions. These allies would expose Newman, Cohn, Schneiderman, and Lemlich to a world of power and political influence, encouraging them to believe that through suffrage and lobbying, government could be put to work for their benefit.

Finally, as they began to think in terms of forging a national movement, they were forced to develop new techniques to reach women workers of different races, religions, and ethnicities. They learned from the women they sought to organize that just as women workers were best reached by women organizers, so Italian, Polish, and Hispanic immigrants and native-born black and white Protestant women were better reached by one of their own than by Jewish women steeped in the political culture of Eastern Europe and the Lower East Side. Though each of the four women had some success in bridging racial and ethnic divisions, they were forced to acknowledge their limitations. They could not do it all themselves; they had to nurture women shop-floor leaders from different backgrounds.

The work required to remain politically effective in this nexus of often-conflicting relationships yielded some real rewards, both strategically and personally. But sometimes the constant struggling wore on them. Conflicts and tensions were brought into sharp relief as the four exhausted themselves making speeches and giving pep talks to weary workers, when they themselves needed reassurance: although they had achieved recognition by the end of the 1909 strike, Schneiderman, Cohn, Newman, and Lemlich were still poor, uneducated, and young. Newman was only eighteen years old when the strike began, and Lemlich twenty-three. Even the elders in the circle, Cohn and Schneiderman, were only twenty-five and twenty-eight, respectively.

Letters between Newman and Schneiderman from that era reveal their vulnerability to slights and criticisms by male union leaders and female reformers. Life on "the battlefield," as Newman referred to it, was lonely. At an age when other women were contemplating marriage and family, they spent their nights in smoky union halls or the cheap, dingy hotel rooms that unions rented for their organizers. They sometimes questioned their life choices, for the reality of union work was far less glamorous than it had seemed in their shop-floor days. Indeed, Newman would quit several times before decade's end. Ultimately, though, their disillusionment did not drive the four women from the union movement. Instead, it fueled their desire to broaden the vision of U.S. trade unionism. When Schneiderman said "The working woman needs bread, but she needs roses, too," she was speaking from personal experience.[60]

NOTES

1. Pauline Newman, "Letters to Hugh and Michael" (1951–69), Box 1, Folder 3, Pauline M. Newman Papers, Schlesinger Library, Radcliffe College, Cambridge, Mass. (hereafter cited as Newman Papers).

2. Ibid.

3. Ibid.; *New York Times,* November 2, 25, December 3, 26, 1907.

4. Newman, "Letters to Hugh and Michael."

5. "The Testimony of Miss Pauline M. Newman," in *Hearings of the New York State Factory Investigating Commission* (Albany: J. B. Lyons Printers, 1915), 2868–71.

6. My estimate of Newman's age is based on evidence suggesting that she was around eighteen years old at the time of the 1909 shirtwaist strike. Newman, like many Jews of her generation, never knew for sure how old she was. Her birthdate was recorded only on the flyleaf of the family Bible. After the Bible was lost in transit, she could only guess at her age.

7. For analyses of the position of Jews in Russian society at the turn of the century, see S. Ettinger, "The Jews at the Outbreak of the Revolution," in *The Jews in Soviet Russia since 1917,* ed. Lionel Kochan, 3d ed. (Oxford: Oxford University Press, 1978), 15–30; see also Salo Baron, *The Russian Jew under Tsars and Soviets* (New York: Macmillan, 1976).

8. Sidney Jonas, interview by author, Brooklyn, N.Y., August 10, 1980; Paula Scheier, "Clara Lemlich Shavelson: Fifty Years in Labor's Front Line," *Jewish Life,* November 1954; Ricki Carole Myers Cohen, "Fannia Cohn and the International Ladies' Garment Workers' Union" (Ph.D. diss., University of Southern California, 1976), 5.

9. Newman, "Letters to Hugh and Michael"; Cohen, "Fannia Cohn," chap. 1; Scheier, "Clara Lemlich Shavelson"; Fannia M. Cohn to "Dear Emma," May 15, 1953, Fannia M. Cohn Papers, Astor, Lenox, and Tilden Foundations, Rare Books and Manuscripts Division, New York Public Library (hereafter cited as Cohn Papers).

In March 1903, gangs organized by Russian police rampaged through the Ukrainian town of Kishinev, killing 51 Jewish men, women, and children, and wounding at least 495 others. Edward H. Judge, *Eastern Kishinev: Anatomy of a Pogrom* (New York: New York University Press, 1992).

10. See Charlotte Baum, Paula Hyman, and Sonya Michel, *The Jewish Woman in America* (New York: NAL/Dutton, 1977), 55–91; Mark Zborowski and Elizabeth Herzog, *Life Is with People* (New York: Schocken, 1962); Jack Kugelmass and Jonathan Bayarin, *From a Ruined Garden: The Memorial Books of Polish Jewry* (New York: Schocken Books, 1985).

11. The Lower East Side continued to receive Jewish immigrants from Eastern Europe into the 1920s. See Ettinger, "Jews at the Outbreak of the Revolution," 19–22; Celia Heller, *On the Edge of Destruction* (New York: Schocken, 1980), 45–55; and Irving Howe, *World of Our Fathers* (New York: Harcourt Brace & Jovanovich, 1976), xix.

12. Clara Lemlich Shavelson to Morris Schappes, March 15, 1965, published in *Jewish Currents* 36, no. 10 (November 1982): 9–11.

13. Clara Lemlich, "Remembering the Waistmakers' General Strike, 1909," *Jewish Currents,* November 1982; Newman, "Letters to Hugh and Michael."

14. Much has been written about the importance of women's colleges to the various social reform movements of the Progressive Era. Stephen Norwood makes a similar argument for high schools. Norwood, *Labor's Flaming Youth: Telephone Workers and Labor Militancy, 1878–1923* (Urbana: University of Illinois Press, 1990).

15. Newman, "Letters to Hugh and Michael"; Pauline Newman, interview by Barbara Wertheimer, New York, N.Y., November 1976; Pauline Newman résumé, n.d., Newman Papers.

16. Pauline Newman, interview by author, New York, N.Y., February 9, 1984; Newman, interview by Wertheimer.

17. Joan Morrison and Charlotte Fox Zabusky, eds., *American Mosaic* (New York: E. P. Dutton, 1980).

18. See Rose Schneiderman, *All for One* (New York: Paul S. Eriksson, 1967), 35–42, and Susan Porter Benson, "The Customers Ain't God: The Work Culture of Department Store Saleswomen, 1890–1940," in *Working Class America,* ed. Michael Frisch and Daniel J. Walkowitz (Urbana: University of Illinois Press, 1983), 185–212.

19. Scheier, "Clara Lemlich Shavelson." See also Susan Glenn, *Daughters of the Shtetl: Work, Unionism and the Immigrant Generation* (Ithaca: Cornell University Press, 1990), 122–31.

20. Schneiderman, *All for One,* 48.

21. Ibid., 48–50.

22. Ibid.

23. Ibid.

24. FMC to Selig Perlman, December 26, 1951, Box 5, Cohn Papers.

25. Information on the problems of organizing the white goods trade is located in Minutes of the Executive Board of the NYWTUL, February 28, August 22, and November 26, 27, 1907, Reel 1, Papers of the New York Women's Trade Union League, Tamiment Institute Library, New York University (hereafter cited as NYWTUL Papers); information on Cohn comes from Cohen, "Fannia Cohn," 11–21.

26. Schneiderman, *All for One,* 39–40.

27. Scheier, "Clara Lemlich Shavelson."

28. Pauline Newman, "The White Goods Workers' Strike," *Ladies' Garment Worker* 4, no. 3 (March 1913): 1–4.

29. Scheier, "Clara Lemlich Shavelson"; Pauline Newman, Fragments 1958–61, Box 1, Newman Papers.

30. Newman, interview by Wertheimer; Newman, interview in Morrison and Zabusky, *American Mosaic.*

31. Scheier, "Clara Lemlich Shavelson."

32. Louis Levine [Lewis Lorwin], *The Women's Garment Workers: A History of the International Ladies' Garment Workers' Union* (New York: B. W. Huebsch, 1924), 148–49.

33. This information is pieced together from Scheier, "Clara Lemlich Shavelson"; Dora Smorodin, interview by author, Maplewood, N.J., March 12, 1991; and Levine, *Women's Garment Workers,* 148–49.

34. Newman, interview by Wertheimer; Newman, "Letters to Hugh and Michael."

35. Ibid.

36. Schneiderman, *All for One,* 58–60.

37. Ibid., 73–77; Minutes of the NYWTUL Executive Board, February 24, March 24, 1905. Reel 1, NYWTUL Papers.

38. Nancy Schrom Dye, *As Equals and as Sisters: Feminism, Unionism and the Women's Trade Union League of New York* (Columbia: University of Missouri Press, 1980), 110–22.

39. Ibid.; Minutes of the NYWTUL Executive Board, January 25, 1906, Reel 1, NYWTUL Papers.

40. Newman, interview by Wertheimer; Newman, interview by author, February 9, 1984, New York.

41. See also Alice Kessler-Harris, "Rose Schneiderman," in *American Labor Leaders*, ed. Warren Van Tine and Melvyn Dubofsky (Urbana: University of Illinois Press, 1987), 160–84.

42. Minutes of the NYWTUL Executive Board, February 24, 1905-February 1, 1909, Reel 1, NYWTUL Papers.

43. Schneiderman, *All for One*, 84.

44. Minutes of the NYWTUL Executive Board, February 28, August 22, November 26, 27, 1907, Reel 1, NYWTUL, Papers; Levine, *Women's Garment Workers*, 220.

45. Minutes of the NYWTUL Executive Committee, November 26, 27, 1907, Reel 1, NYWTUL Papers.

46. Levine, *Women's Garment Workers*, 220; Cohen, "Fannia Cohn," 36–43.

47. Scheier, "Clara Lemlich Shavelson."

48. Martha Schaffer, telephone interview by author, March 11, 1989; Joel Schaffer, Evelyn Velson, and Julia Velson, interview by author, Oakland, Calif., September 9, 1992.

49. Scheier, "Clara Lemlich Shavelson."

50. Clara Lemlich Shavelson, interview by Martha and Joel Schaffer, Los Angeles, Calif., February 2, 1974.

51. *New York Call*, November 30, December 4, 5, 6, 7, 8, 29, 1909.

52. *New York Call*, December 5, 7, 8, 1909.

53. *New York Call*, December 29, 1909. For complete coverage of day-to-day events on the picket line, see the *New York Times*, November 5, 6, and 14, 1909, and almost daily from November 23, 1909, through January 28, 1910.

54. Minutes of the New York Women's Trade Union League Membership Meeting, April 20, June 15, 1910, Reel 1, NYWTUL Papers.

55. See Meredith Tax, *The Rising of the Women: Feminist Solidarity and Class Conflict, 1880–1917* (New York: Monthly Review Press, 1980), pp. 230–240. Tax discusses the hierarchical union structure and the ways that union-appointed arbitrators undermined the women workers' control of the strike.

56. For information on the many women's strikes of the period, read the WTUL publication *Life and Labor*, which covered them all in some detail. The progressive magazine *The Survey* (1909–1914) also has good coverage of most of the strikes. See too, Pauline Newman, "The White Goods Workers' Strike," *Ladies' Garment Worker* 4, number 3 (March 1913): 1–4; on the Chicago strike see Mari Jo Buhle, *Women and American Socialism, 1870–1920* (Urbana: University of Illinois Press, 1981), 194–198. On the Kalamazoo strike see Karen Mason, "Feeling the Pinch: The Kalamazoo Corset Makers' Strike of 1912," in *To Toil the Livelong Day: America's Women at Work*, ed. Carol Groneman and Mary Beth Norton (Ithaca: Cornell University Press, 1987), 141–60. On the 1915 strike see *Chicago Day Book* cited in Winifred Carsel, *A History of the Chicago Ladies' Garment Workers' Union* (Chicago: Normandie House, 1940).

57. Gladys Boone, *The Women's Trade Union Leagues* (New York: Columbia University Press, 1942), 112–14.

58. Mildred Moore, "A History of the Women's Trade Union League of Chicago" (M.A. thesis, University of Chicago, 1915), cited in Diane Kirkby, "The Wage-Earning Woman and the State: The National Women's Trade Union League and Protective Labor Legislation, 1903–1923," *Labor History* 28, no. 1 (Winter 1987): 58–74.

59. Theresa Malkiel, "The Uprising of the 40,000," *New York Call*, December 29, 1909.

60. Pauline Newman, "From the Battlefield—Some Phases of the Cloakmakers' Strike in Cleveland," *Life and Labor*, October 1911.

Pauline Newman, "We fought and we bled and we died . . ."

One of the four young garment industry workers whose organizing activities emerged so vividly from the pages of Annelise Orleck's account, Pauline Newman had started out at the Triangle Shirtwaist Factory, which became the scene of one of the great industrial tragedies in New York City's history. Although the factory contained several elevators and two staircases, the eight-story wooden building had no sprinkler system; the doors to the fire escapes were locked to prevent outdoor relaxation. When fire broke out in 1911, 500 employees—many of them young Jewish and Italian women—were trapped behind locked doors. Some on the upper floors jumped to their deaths; others burned or asphyxiated while trapped inside. Altogether, the fire claimed the lives of 146 women. Viewing their charred bodies on the street, one reporter recalled that some of these same women had gone on strike only the year before to demand decent wages, more sanitary working conditions, and safety precautions.

The young women who died at the Triangle fire were buried together under a single monument. Hundreds of thousands of New Yorkers walked in the funeral procession in a driving rain. Not until 2011, a hundred years later, were they identified. The last living survivor of the fire, Rose Freedman, died in 2001 at the age of 107. She had saved herself by asking: what are the executives doing? She headed for their offices on the tenth floor, and then to the roof by way of the freight elevator, from which firefighters pulled them to safety. She never forgave the executives for saving themselves but leaving the doors locked, or, later, attempting to bribe her to testify that the doors were unlocked.

Unsafe buildings, blocked exits, and inadequate sprinkler systems threaten garment workers again today. The mass-market clothes that American women wear are often made in substandard conditions—in the United States when minimum wage, maximum hour, and occupational health and safety laws are unenforced, and abroad, in places where such standards barely exist. In an eerie reprise of the Triangle Fire, almost exactly 102 years later, in April 2013, the Rana Plaza factory in Dhaka, Bangladesh, collapsed, killing 1,129 workers, mostly women, who made cheap clothes for Western markets. (The United States suspended trade preferences for Bangladesh in recognition of labor rights violations and the persistence of safety problems, but unsafe factories continue to be used in that country and elsewhere.)*

---

*"100 Years Later, the Roll of the Dead in a Factory Fire is Complete," *New York Times*, Feb. 20, 2011; "Rose Freedman, Last Survivor of Triangle Fire, Dies at 107," ibid., Feb. 17, 2001; "Manufacturers in Bangladesh Resist Closing Garment Factories," ibid., June 26, 2014, pp. B1, B7.

Adapted from "Pauline Newman," in *American Mosaic: The Immigrant Experience in the Words of Those Who Lived It*, ed. Joan Morrison and Charlotte Fox Zabusky (New York: E. P. Dutton, 1980), pp. 9–14. Copyright © 1980 by Joan Morrison and Charlotte Fox Zabusky. Reprinted by permission of the publisher.

Educational director for the International Ladies' Garment Workers' Union until her death in 1986, Newman conveys in her own words what it was like to be a garment worker in the early twentieth century. What does she feel has been gained by organized labor? What does she feel has been lost over the years?

A cousin of mine worked for the Triangle Shirtwaist Company and she got me on there in October of 1901. It was probably the largest shirtwaist factory in the city of New York then. They had more than two hundred operators, cutters, examiners, finishers. Altogether more than four hundred people on two floors. The fire took place on one floor, the floor where we worked. You've probably heard about that. But that was years later.

We started work at seven-thirty in the morning, and during the busy season we worked until nine in the evening. They didn't pay you any overtime and they didn't give you anything for supper money. Sometimes they'd give you a little apple pie if you had to work very late. That was all. Very generous.

What I had to do was not really very difficult. It was just monotonous. When the shirtwaists were finished at the machine there were some threads that were left, and all the youngsters—we had a corner on the floor that resembled a kindergarten—we were given little scissors to cut the threads off. It wasn't heavy work, but it was monotonous, because you did the same thing from seven-thirty in the morning till nine at night.

Well, of course, there were [child labor] laws on the books, but no one bothered to enforce them. The employers were always tipped off if there was going to be an inspection. "Quick," they'd say, "into the boxes!" And we children would climb into the big boxes the finished shirts were stored in. Then some shirts were piled on top of us, and when the inspector came—no children. The factory always got an okay from the inspector, and I suppose someone at City Hall got a little something, too.

The employers didn't recognize anyone working for them as a human being. You were not allowed to sing. Operators would have liked to have sung, because they, too, had the same thing to do and weren't allowed to sing. We weren't allowed to talk to each other. Oh, no, they would sneak up behind if you were found talking to your next colleague. You were admonished: "If you keep on you'll be fired." If

you went to the toilet and you were there longer than the floor lady thought you should be, you would be laid off for half a day and sent home. And, of course, that meant no pay. You were not allowed to have your lunch on the fire escape in the summertime. The door was locked to keep us in. That's why so many people were trapped when the fire broke out.

My pay was $1.50 a week no matter how many hours I worked. My sisters made $6.00 a week; and the cutters, they were skilled workers, they might get as much as $12.00. The employers had a sign in the elevator that said: "If you don't come in on Sunday, don't come in on Monday." You were expected to work every day if they needed you and the pay was the same whether you worked extra or not. You had to be there at seven-thirty, so you got up at five-thirty, took the horse car, then the electric trolley to Greene Street, to be there on time. . . .

I stopped working at the Triangle Factory during the strike in 1909 and I didn't go back. The union sent me out to raise money for the strikers. I apparently was able to articulate my feelings and opinions about the criminal conditions, and they didn't have anyone else who could do better, so they assigned me. And I was successful getting money. After my first speech before the Central Trade and Labor Council I got front-page publicity, including my picture. I was only about fifteen then. Everybody saw it. Wealthy women were curious and they asked me if I would speak to them in their homes. I said I would if they would contribute to the strike, and they agreed. So I spent my time from November to the end of March upstate in New York, speaking to the ladies of the Four Hundred [the elite of New York's society] and sending money back. . . .

We didn't gain very much at the end of the strike. I think the hours were reduced to fifty-six a week or something like that. We got a 10 percent increase in wages. I think that the best thing that the strike did was to lay a foundation on which to build a union. There was so much feeling against unions then. The judge, when one of our girls came before him,

There was no morgue in New York City large enough to hold the bodies of the young women who had jumped from the burning buildings of the Triangle Shirtwaist Company in 1911. They were laid out on a pier for families to identify. Six of the victims were so badly burned that even relatives could not recognize them. (Courtesy of UNITE Archives, Kheel Center for Labor-Management Documentation and Archives, School of Industrial and Labor Relations, Cornell University, Ithaca, New York.)

said to her: "You're not striking against your employer, you know, young lady. You're striking against God," and sentenced her to two weeks on Blackwell's Island, which is now Welfare Island. And a lot of them got a taste of the club. . . .

After the 1909 strike I worked with the union, organizing in Philadelphia and Cleveland and other places, so I wasn't at the Triangle Shirtwaist Factory when the fire broke out, but a lot of my friends were. I was in Philadelphia for the union and, of course, someone from here called me immediately and I came back. It's very difficult to describe the feeling because I knew the place and I knew so many of the girls. The thing that bothered me was the employers got a lawyer. How anyone could have *defended* them!—because I'm quite sure that the fire was planned for insurance purposes. And no one is going to convince me

otherwise. And when they testified that the door to the fire escape was open, it was a lie! It was never open. Locked all the time. One hundred and forty-six people were sacrificed, and the judge fined Blank and Harris seventy-five dollars!

Conditions were dreadful in those days. But there was something that is lacking today and I think it was the devotion and the belief. We *believed* in what we were doing. We fought and we bled and we died. Today they don't have to.

You sit down at the table, you negotiate with the employers, you ask for 20 percent, they say 15, but the girls are working. People are working. They're not disturbed, and when the negotiations are over they get the increases. They don't really have to fight. Of course, they'll belong to the union and they'll go on strike if you tell them to, but it's the inner faith that people had in those days that I don't see today. It was a terrible time, but it was interesting. I'm glad I lived then.

Even when things were terrible, I always had that faith. . . . Only now, I'm a little discouraged sometimes when I see the workers spending their free hours watching television—trash. We fought so hard for those hours and they waste them. We used to read Tolstoy, Dickens, Shelley, by candlelight, and they watch the *Hollywood Squares*. Well, they're free to do what they want. That's what we fought for.

Crystal Eastman, Now We Can Begin

Crystal Eastman charts an agenda for feminists after the achievement of suffrage. For all humankind, what should we think of as being embraced by her observation that "freedom is a large word"? Most of her short essay focuses on how to achieve "woman's freedom" as she saw it through her particular early twentieth-century feminist frame. Do you agree that the issues she identifies needed to be prioritized in the 1920s? Are these issues still relevant today?

We invite you to do background research on Crystal Eastman and *The Liberator*, a magazine published in New York City starting in 1918 and named for William Lloyd Garrison's legendary abolitionist newspaper of the early nineteenth century. What things do you find most striking about Eastman's life? Who published *The Liberator* and for how long? Take a moment to open up the link to the digitized December 1920 issue so that you can see her short essay alongside other essays, artwork, and advertisements, imagining yourself as someone who moved in Eastman's circles in the 1920s.

Most women will agree that August 23, the day when the Tennessee legislature finally enacted the Federal suffrage amendment, is a day to begin with, not a day to end with. Men are saying perhaps "Thank God, this everlasting woman's fight is over!" But women, if I know them, are saying, "Now at last we can begin." In fighting for the right to vote most women have tried to be either non-committal or thoroughly respectable on every other subject. Now they can say what they are really after; and what they are after, in common with all the rest of the struggling world, is *freedom*.

Freedom is a large word.

Many feminists are socialists, many are communists, not a few are active leaders in these movements. But the true feminist, no matter how far to the left she may be in the revolutionary movement, sees the woman's battle as distinct in its objects and different in its methods from the workers' battle for industrial freedom. She knows, of course, that the vast majority of women as well as men are without property, and are of necessity bread and butter slaves under a system of society which allows the very sources of life to be privately owned by a few, and she counts herself a loyal soldier in the working-class army that is marching to overthrow that system. But as a feminist she also knows that the whole of woman's slavery is not summed up in the profit system, nor her complete emancipation assured by the downfall of capitalism.

Woman's freedom, in the feminist sense, can be fought for and conceivably won before the gates open into industrial democracy. On

Crystal Eastman, "Now We Can Begin," *The Liberator*, 3, no. 12 (December 1920), 23–4. For an open-access, digitized copy of the magazine issue, go to http://www.marxists.org/history/usa/culture/pubs/liberator/1920/12/v3n12-w33-dec-1920-liberator.pdf.

the other hand, woman's freedom, in the feminist sense, is not inherent in the communist ideal. All feminists are familiar with the revolutionary leader who "can't see" the woman's movement. "What's the matter with the women? My wife's all right," he says. And his wife, one usually finds, is raising his children in a Bronx flat or a dreary suburb, to which he returns occasionally for food and sleep when all possible excitement and stimulus have been wrung from the fight. If we should graduate into communism tomorrow this man's attitude to his wife would not be changed. The proletarian dictatorship may or may not free women. We must begin now to enlighten the future dictators.

What, then, is "the matter with women"? What is the problem of women's freedom? It seems to me to be this: how to arrange the world so that women can be human beings, with a chance to exercise their infinitely varied gifts in infinitely varied ways, instead of being destined by the accident of their sex to one field of activity—housework and child-raising. And second, if and when they choose housework and child-raising, to have that occupation recognized by the world as work, requiring a definite economic reward and not merely entitling the performer to be dependent on some man.

This is not the whole of feminism, of course, but it is enough to begin with. "Oh, don't begin with economics," my friends often protest, "Woman does not live by bread alone. What she needs first of all is a free soul." And I can agree that women will never be great until they achieve a certain emotional freedom, a strong healthy egotism, and some unpersonal sources of joy—that in this inner sense we cannot make woman free by changing her economic status. What we can do, however, is to create conditions of outward freedom in which a free woman's soul can be born and grow. It is these outward conditions with which an organized feminist movement must concern itself.

Freedom of choice in occupation and individual economic independence for women: How shall we approach this next feminist objective? First, by breaking down all remaining barriers, actual as well as legal, which make it difficult for women to enter or succeed in the various professions, to go into and get on in business, to learn trades and practice them, to join trades unions. Chief among these remaining barriers is inequality in pay. Here the ground is already broken. This is the easiest part of our program.

Second, we must institute a revolution in the early training and education of both boys and girls. It must be womanly as well as manly to earn your own living, to stand on your own feet. And it must be manly as well as womanly to know how to cook and sew and clean and take care of yourself in the ordinary exigencies of life. I need not add that the second part of this revolution will be more passionately resisted than the first. Men will not give up their privilege of helplessness without a struggle. The average man has a carefully cultivated ignorance about household matters—from what to do with the crumbs to the grocer's telephone number—a sort of cheerful inefficiency which protects him better than the reputation for having a violent temper. It was his mother's fault in the beginning, but even as a boy he was quick to see how a general reputation for being "no good around the house" would serve him throughout life, and half-consciously he began to cultivate that helplessness until today it is the despair of feminist wives.

A growing number of men admire the woman who has a job, and, especially since the cost of living doubled, rather like the idea of their own wives contributing to the family income by outside work. And of course for generations there have been whole towns full of wives who are forced by the bitterest necessity to spend the same hours at the factory that their husbands spend. But these breadwinning wives have not yet developed homemaking husbands. When the two come home from the factory the man sits down while his wife gets supper, and he does so with exactly the same sense of fore-ordained right as if he were "supporting her." Higher up in the economic scale the same thing is true. The business or professional woman who is married, perhaps engages a cook, but the responsibility is not shifted, it is still hers. She "hires and fires," she orders meals, she does the buying, she meets and resolves all domestic crises, she takes charge of moving, furnishing, settling. She may be, like her husband, a busy executive at her office all day, but unlike him, she is also an executive in a small way every night and morning at home. Her noon hour is spent in planning, and too often her Sundays and holidays are spent in "catching up."

Two business women can "make a home" together without either one being over-burdened or over-bored. It is because they both know how and both feel responsible. But it is a rare man who can marry one of them and continue the homemaking partnership. Yet if there are no children, there is nothing essentially different in the combination. Two self-supporting adults decide to make a home together: if both are women it is a pleasant partnership, more fun than work; if one is a man, it is almost never a partnership—the woman simply adds running the home to her regular outside job. Unless she is very strong, it is too much for her, she gets tired and bitter over it, and finally perhaps gives up her outside work and condemns herself to the tiresome half-job of housekeeping for two.

Cooperative schemes and electrical devices will simplify the business of homemaking, but they will not get rid of it entirely. As far as we can see ahead people will always want homes, and a happy home cannot be had without a certain amount of rather monotonous work and responsibility. How can we change the nature of man so that he will honorably share that work and responsibility and thus make the home-making enterprise a song instead of a burden? Most assuredly not by laws or revolutionary decrees. Perhaps we must cultivate or simulate a little of that highly prized helplessness ourselves. But fundamentally it is a problem of education, of early training—we must bring up feminist sons.

Sons? Daughters? They are born of women—how can women be free to choose their occupation, at all times cherishing their economic independence, unless they stop having children? This is a further question for feminism. If the feminist program goes to pieces on the arrival of the first baby, it is false and useless. For ninety-nine out of every hundred women want children, and seventy-five out of every hundred want to take care of their own children, or at any rate so closely superintend their care as to make any other full-time occupation impossible for at least ten or fifteen years. Is there any such thing then as freedom of choice in occupation for women? And is not the family the inevitable economic unit and woman's individual economic independence, at least during that period, out of the question?

The feminist must have an answer to these questions, and she has. The immediate feminist program must include voluntary motherhood. Freedom of any kind for women is hardly worth considering unless it is assumed that they will know how to control the size of their families. "Birth control" is just as elementary an essential in our propaganda as "equal pay." Women are to have children when they want them, that's the first thing. That ensures some freedom of occupational choice; those who do not wish to be mothers will not have an undesired occupation thrust upon them by accident, and those who do wish to be mothers may choose in a general way how many years of their lives they will devote to the occupation of child-raising.

But is there any way of insuring a woman's economic independence while child-raising is her chosen occupation? Or must she sink into that dependent state from which, as we all know, it is so hard to rise again? That brings us to the fourth feature of our program—motherhood endowment. It seems that the only way we can keep mothers free, at least in a capitalist society, is by the establishment of a principle that the occupation of raising children is peculiarly and directly a service to society, and that the mother upon whom the necessity and privilege of performing this service naturally falls is entitled to an adequate economic reward from the political government. It is idle to talk of real economic independence for women unless this principle is accepted. But with a generous endowment of motherhood provided by legislation, with all laws against voluntary motherhood and education in its methods repealed, with the feminist ideal of education accepted in home and school, and with all special barriers removed in every field of human activity, there is no reason why woman should not become almost a human thing.

It will be time enough then to consider whether she has a soul.

EMPIRE AND INTERNATIONALISM

LAURA WEXLER
A Lady Photojournalist Goes to the 1904
St. Louis World's Fair

How might *you* stage a world's fair, organizing the grounds, pavilions, and interior displays? With numerous nations and peoples showcased, there is inevitably a politics to how the various groups are represented. Laura Wexler's essay explores the gender, racial, and imperial politics of the 1904 World's Fair in St. Louis. Let's note two things about the timing of this fair.

First, many white Americans felt they were at a crossroads. At the previous world's fair, held in 1893 in Chicago, historian Frederick Jackson Turner had given a speech that quickly became famous, entitled "The Significance of the Frontier for American History."* He argued that the existence of a frontier, "a meeting place between savagery and civilization," and the availability of "free land" had been the crucial elements in shaping American society. The frontier experience of free land shaped the American people, particularly Euro-American men, fostering democratic and independent values. As much as his talk celebrated Anglo-American westward expansion, it also mourned what he understood to be the end of the frontier, as the 1890 census reported that pockets of settlement interrupted what had once been clear lines of division between Anglo-American and aboriginal settlement. Without the frontier, what would happen to democracy in the United States?

Second, during the last decade of the nineteenth century, the U.S. government engaged in a series of economic, political, and military endeavors to extend the American frontier beyond the continent. During this decade, the United States fought the Spanish-American War, thereby acquiring control over islands in the Caribbean. It also incorporated islands in the Pacific Ocean—Hawaii, Guam, Samoa, and the Philippines—that could serve as stepping stones or way stations for commercial and military endeavors. Nationalists in the Philippines, a colony of Spain, had supported the United States during the war, anticipating their own independence. However, once Spain was vanquished, the United States occupied and controlled the islands, refusing to recognize Filipino demands for independence. Filipino nationalists resisted; the United States responded with force. The three-year

---

*Frederick Jackson Turner, "The Significance of the Frontier in American History," Paper presented at the American Historical Association, Chicago, 1893; excerpts are available at http://nationalhumanitiescenter.org/pds/gilded/empire/text1/turner.pdf.

Excerpted from the introduction and ch. 7 of *Tender Violence: Domestic Visions in an Age of U.S. Imperialism* by Laura Wexler (Chapel Hill: University of North Carolina Press, 2000). Reprinted by permission of the author and publisher. Notes have been edited and renumbered.

guerrilla war that ensued resulted in the death of hundreds of thousands of Filipinos (some 20 percent of the population) and 4,000 Americans.[†]

The 1904 World's Fair in St. Louis provided an opportunity for the United States to display its new imperial possessions. Wexler's essay focuses on one of the white, middle-class female photographers who frequented and worked at the fair, Jessie Tarbox Beals. Becoming a lady photographer allowed a woman to travel and document (and hence interpret) the world around her. Wexler complicates this narrative of gender liberation, however, by emphasizing the racial impact of privileged white women's photography, especially given its embeddedness in an "Age of Imperialism" for the United States.

The first cohort of American women photographers to achieve serious public careers as photojournalists at the turn of the century often used the "innocent eye" attributed to them by white domestic sentiment to construct images of war as peace, images that were, in turn, a constitutive element of the social relations of United States imperialism during the era's annexation and consolidation of colonies. My term, "the innocent eye," designates a deeply problematic practice of representation that developed within the private domain of family photography at midcentury in the United States. At that time, white middle-class women, in both the North and the South, were regularly portrayed in family photographs as if looking out from within, without seeing the race and class dynamics of the household. [The "innocent eye"] . . . of domestic sentiment functioned to normalize . . . raced and classed relations of dominance during slavery and to reinscribe them after its legal end. As a representational practice, this private gaze took on a new national significance when in the late 1890s and early 1900s a certain group of American "New Women" photographers—among them Frances Benjamin Johnston; Gertrude Käsebier; Alice Austen; the Gerhard sisters, Emme and Mamie; and Jessie Tarbox Beals . . . —learned to turn it to their professional advantage by ensuring that from the panorama of foreign wars fought by white American men, white American women would construct visions of domestic peace.

When the World's Fair opened in St. Louis, Missouri, in 1904, thirty-four-year-old photojournalist Jessie Tarbox Beals was there— along with many other white, middle-class, American women photographers. The spectacle of the nineteenth century's great fairs and expositions held strong attractions for them,

and they often went to great lengths to photograph them. For the World's Columbian Exposition of 1893, for instance, Jessie (then Tarbox), a single, twenty-three-year-old, Canadian-born schoolteacher, had taken the train to Chicago from her home in Greenfield, Massachusetts. She stayed for twenty-five days in the women's dormitory, shooting photographs with her new little Kodak (she could not get a permit for a larger view camera with tripod) and developing her own film in the public darkroom facilities that the Exposition's photography department provided. After Chicago, no longer would her own life look the same to her.

She returned to small-town existence in western Massachusetts and to schoolteaching, writes her biographer Alexander Alland, "consumed with the desire to visit the foreign places whose makeshift villages she had seen and photographed at the exposition."[1] When she then discovered that she could make more money in one summer of selling freelance pictures than she could in a year of teaching school, she was spoiled for "protected" feminine domestic gentility for ever. Within seven years, Jessie Tarbox had married Alfred Beals, an Amherst College graduate who was working as a machinist in Greenfield, quit schoolteaching, and persuaded Alfred to give up his job, become her darkroom assistant, and set off to see what possibilities there were in earning their living as itinerant photographers. They started in Vermont, traveled for a year through Florida, and regrouped to upstate New York. Alfred, it turned out, had married a "lady" photographer. At the time, neither he nor she quite knew what that was going to mean. . . .

To the photographing woman, the fairs and expositions offered congenial stimulation and a way to gain recognition and make some money selling photographs. Simultaneously,

---

[†]This war was an early occasion in which U.S. military forces used waterboarding; see Paul Kramer, "The Water Cure: Debating Torture and Counterinsurgency—A Century Ago," *The New Yorker*, February 25, 2008.

they offered a way to construct a larger identity as a "lady photographer." If, as many scholars have proposed, the fairs performed the public function of remaking a national self-definition for a United States reunited a generation after the Civil War and newly emerging as an industrial world power, they also served the private purpose of self-making for white women photographers of the era. The fairs encouraged them to emerge from domestic confinement and to test just how far the designation "lady with a camera" would go.

St. Louis was very much a southern city at the start of the nineteenth century. From the time of the Missouri Compromise in 1820, through the 1857 *Dred Scott v. Sanford* decision, which ruled that a slave who lived in a free state or territory was still a slave, debates over slavery and abolition gave a veneer of political debate to St. Louis; meanwhile, slave auctions took place on the steps of the very courthouse where these decisions were handed down. The citizens of St. Louis defiantly elected a Secessionist governor before the Civil War, although the state of Missouri stayed in the Union. Because of strong economic ties to the north, St. Louis eventually became a center of Union support and a staging ground for Union troops, but many there never altered their allegiance to the South.

And now, at the turn of the century, the St. Louis World's Fair of 1904 invited the city and the world to contemplate the triumph of yet another new formulation of United States power. America's recent victory in the war with Spain highlighted the global ambitions of the new American state. More than 1,270 acres of Forest Park had been given over to display the nationalist fervor of a new imperial order. The fair transformed both the resistant sectionalism of the Old South and the resilient commercialism of the New beyond all possibilities of imagining earlier in the century.

Not that the voices of the Old South were stilled, by any means. Widespread Democratic anti-imperialist agitation built heavily upon the racist presumptions of men like Thomas Nelson Page, author of *Red Rock* (1898), and Thomas Dixon, author of *The Leopard's Spots* (1902), *The Clansman* (1905), and *The Traitor* (1907). Both these men argued against annexation of the Philippines on the grounds that imperial acquisition was unconstitutional and anti-republican and that Filipino self government was the only way to avoid burdening the United States with what Mrs. Jefferson Davis

called "fresh millions of foreign negroes, even more ignorant and more degraded . . . than those at home."[2]

However, the thrust of the times was against them. Pro-annexation arguments were neither more egalitarian nor necessarily less racist. They simply alleged that in the Philippines "Caucasians were ushering in a new era in human history," an era in which "human culture is become unified, not only through diffusion but through the extinction of lower grades."[3] The cotton plantations of the Old South were a model for prospective fruit, sugar, and hemp plantations in Hawaii and the Philippines. Nineteen hundred four was one of the peak years of immigration to the United States by whites from western and eastern Europe, most of them poorly educated peasants looking for ways to better themselves and escape from lives of unremitting manual labor. Many blacks were also arriving from the West Indies, not all of whom were fully indoctrinated into the culture of American race relations. Nativist sentiment had not yet pushed Congress toward immigration restriction and overall quotas—that would take another twenty years—but its organization was growing. . . .

Above all else, then, the St. Louis World's Fair was advancing an argument for the vigor of the Caucasian culture of the Unites States and its capacity to incorporate the labor of such immigrants, since it had been able so successfully to discipline and assimilate its former slaves and aboriginal Others into a seemingly credible domestic "peace." In exemplifying how the United States had already dealt with similar tasks, the St. Louis World's Fair was addressing the greatest anxieties of its day, to indicate where and how white Americans could and would prevail. Industrial leaders believed that "the burden of humanity is already in large measure the White Man's burden—for, viewing the human world as it is, white and strong are synonymous terms."[4] They looked forward to shouldering America's load.

These particular views on race and national destiny were, in fact, the sentiments of Mr. W. J. McGee, one of the chief officers of the St. Louis Fair. McGee, the head of the Anthropology Department of the fair, reasoned that it was precisely the new global industrial opportunities that rationalized the horrific cost of the Civil War and the preservation of the Union. In the south, Reconstruction was over; its demise left a growing ambition to explore these new opportunities. McGee portrayed the field for action as nearly limitless: "It is the duty of the strong man to subjugate lower nature, to extirpate the bad and cultivate the good among living things, to delve in earth below and cleave the air above in search of fresh resources, to transform the seas into paths for ships and pastures for food-fishes, . . . and in all ways to enslave the world for the support of humanity and the increase of human intelligence."[5]

McGee and the rest of the team designed the St. Louis World's Fair to make the perspective of scientific racism and the imperative of United States imperialism seem equally valid and inevitable. . . . The St. Louis World's Fair was also the Louisiana Purchase Centenary Celebration. It commemorated the treaty which in 1803 had more than doubled the geographical size of the United States and simultaneously transformed the old Creole town of St. Louis into a booming American city, "the gateway to the West." It also celebrated a potent analogy constructed between pacification of "domestic" tribes of Native Americans and "foreign" tribes of Filipinos. As one of the official publications of the Exposition explained, "The time is coming when the purchase and retention of the Philippine Islands will seem as wise to our descendants as does the Louisiana Purchase seem to us who live today."[6]

In the brief nine months that it was open, St. Louis World's Fair of 1904 formulated for almost 19 million people who participated in its construction or visited its grounds a vision not only of the fruits of the past hundred years of expansion and conquest but also of the promising connection between that past and future acquisitions. The intertwined notions of imperialism and progress that the fair projected captured the spirit of the twentieth century as "The American Century," at its very moment of inception. . . .

Beals and her husband Alfred traveled to St. Louis from Albany, New York, where Jessie had been working as the "first official woman" staff photographer for the *Buffalo Courier*, with Alfred as her darkroom assistant. Beals regularly photographed suicides, murder trials, and fires for the paper when she could. When times were slow, she showed up where work crews met, or lingered at factory doors, or rode door-to-door on her bicycle, balancing twenty- to thirty-odd pounds of camera equipment and soliciting the chance to take portraits. Business was good. Her photographer's diary from the time is peppered with phrases such as "got a fine list of orders" and "Work has been booming–16 to 30 pictures taken daily. Poor Beals is kept busy developing and printing." When they left Albany on April 4, 1904, her departure was mourned in the Buffalo newspapers as the loss not simply of a newspaper photographer but of a *woman* newspaper photographer: "Buffalo lost one of its best professional women today when Mrs. Jessie Tarbox Beals, staff camera artist, departed on an early morning train for St. Louis." At the farewell party they hosted for her, . . . "the staffs of the two dailies Jessie worked for presented her with a parting gift—a gold enameled pin studied with pearls."[7] It was a gift particularly appropriate for the "woman" part of the equation, and it must have encouraged Beals about the viability of her plans to go to St. Louis as a "professional woman." . . .

"Lady" photographers had a larger official role at St. Louis . . . than at any other fair. . . . But what the presence of these [other] women meant in practice for Jessie Tarbox Beals was that when she arrived at St. Louis, at first all the doors were closed to her: "She had hoped her reputation in Buffalo would warrant an official press card. But officials at the exposition said that the Buffalo newspapers were regional and of no value to the national promotion of the fair. She applied to the St. Louis newspapers; they were fully staffed. She kept overhearing remarks that working on the crowded fairgrounds was too much for a woman to tackle."[8] This was the problem of tokenism. . . .

Beals solved this problem in a characteristic way. She transformed the fair officials' anxiety that a woman was of "no value to the national promotion of the fair" into evidence that the "nation" could be promoted by a women. First, she wrangled a "Pre-Exhibition Permit," which allowed her into the fair but limited her to making photographs "prior to the opening of the fair" and prevented her from selling any of the images or using them "in any other way except as ordinary illustrations . . . every negative made under the permit and not accepted as an illustration is to be destroyed."[9] The fair's officials were so eager to marshal all the images of the fair into the

Jessie Tarbox Beals taking pictures from a ladder at the St. Louis World's Fair, 1904, photographer unknown. The ladder is supported by her assistant, "Pumpkin." (Courtesy of the Schlesinger Library, Radcliffe Institute, Harvard University.)

grand educational (and commercial) scheme that Beals worked on pain of expulsion from the fairgrounds if she was found to violate these conditions.

If they were used to controlling the access of women photographers, the officials apparently didn't figure on Beals's next step: "Undaunted by the rules, Jessie roamed the fairgrounds as she saw fit, photographing what interested her. Most of the other photographers there concentrated on the sumptuous exhibits of the industrial nations; Jessie was drawn instead to the scenes of the daily lives of exotic, little-known peoples in their native habitats. She took pictures of the Igorots, the Bogobos, the Zulus, the Hottentots, the Eskimos, the Filipinos and other defenseless recipients of missionary barrels," writes Alland. Her multicultural pictures of domesticity read much like a precursor to [photographer Edward] Steichen's famous *Family of Man* exhibit.[10]

And then came some good luck. Regular hard work photographing the daily lives of

"exotic, little-known peoples" happened to put Beals at the scene when some "Patagonian Giants" of South America arrived at the "village" next door to the "Ainus of Japan." At first, she was the only photographer there. By the time the other photographers arrived, Beals had already made her interpretation of the event. As Alland reports, "An old Patagonian woman issued an edict that no black boxes were to be pointed at her people and she chased the camera men over a barbed wire fence. But Jessie had already made her images, and they were exclusives."[11]

What Beals had done was to show "Patagonian Giants" next to "pygmies," in a comparison by size that imaged the anthropometric premise of the fair—the belief that the essential information about where a group of people fell on the evolutionary ladder could be gleaned from their physical characteristics. Her pictures sold all over the country—providing the "national exposure" the Fair's officials craved—not only because they were positioned as "exclusive images" but [also] because they were images of

"Pygmy and Patagonian Giant," Jessie Tarbox Beals, photographer. (Courtesy of St. Louis Public Library.)

an "exclusive" position that white Americans were constructing for themselves—as the physical golden mean and the evolutionary model.

Beals was rewarded for this work of making material the abstract racial premise of the anthropological "display." The next day's headlines trumpeted the news: "Woman Gets Permit to Take Pictures at the Fair." The story read, "The first permit to be issued to a woman authorizing the taking of photographs in the World's Fair Grounds has been given to Mrs. T. Beals. Mrs. Beals secured notice through her work in obtaining photographs of the double suicide of Mr. and Mrs. Pennell of Buffalo, who rode their automobile over a cliff into a quarry." The pygmy/Patagonian comparison showed the fair officials that Beals's eye was . . . good. . . . With it, Beals had become the "First Pictorial Journalist of Her Sex," even though she was not, as we have seen, the first woman licensed to take photographs in the "World's Fair Grounds."[12]

What really made Beals "first" . . . was that she had understood . . . that in St. Louis, juxtaposition was the clearest signifier of American size and strength. The St. Louis World's Fair was the largest international exposition ever yet presented. Its total exhibition space exceeded that of the Chicago Exposition of 1893

by more than one-third. The fair cost $15 million to produce, the same amount of money originally paid for the entire Louisiana Territory. The fair was so big that medical advisers warned "neurasthenic" patients to avoid the fair entirely, for fear of mental collapse, and "brain-fagged businessmen" and "men of affairs" were encouraged to spend "at least several weeks or months in order to avoid the almost certain breakdown that would result from a hurried visit."[13] It took a week merely to view the agricultural display. However, the real core . . . was the Department of Anthropology, . . . and the "exposition within an exposition," the U.S. government's Philippine Reservation. Other world's fairs, notably the one in Chicago, had featured anthropological divisions, but St. Louis's was by far the largest and the most central.

On the Anthropology Department's grounds and at the Philippine Reservation were displayed "specimens" of the peoples that American civilization had conquered and was now in the process of "educating," "disciplining," and "converting." The Philippine Reservation consisted of almost twelve hundred Filipinos living in villages on a 47-acre site that was deliberately called a "reservation" to make plain the parallel between the subjugation of the Native Americans and the domestication of the Philippines. The grounds were carefully laid out to represent "a sequential synopsis of the developments that have marked man's progress." In an essay entitled "The Trend of Human Progress," McGee explained that process as . . . "a trend of vital development from low toward the high, from dullness toward brightness, from idleness groveling toward intellectual uprightness. . . . It is a matter of common observation that the white man can do more and better than the yellow, the yellow man more and better than the red or black. . . . Classed in terms of blood, the peoples of the world may be grouped in several races; classed in terms of what they do rather than what they merely are, they are conveniently grouped in the four culture grades of savagery, barbarism, civilization, and enlightenment." McGee believed that at the turn of the century "perfected man is over-spreading the world." "Perfected man," in McGee's terms, meant "the two higher culture-grades—especially the Caucasian race, and (during recent decades) the budded enlightenment of Britain and full-blown enlightenment of America."[14]

To illustrate these "common observations," the Anthropology Department portrayed a "logical arrangement" of ethnological displays of "villages" of "non-white types" and "culture grades." Besides the twelve hundred Filipinos, these "types" included pygmies from the Congo, Japanese Ainu, Patagonian "giants," Kwakiutl Indians from Vancouver Island, and several groupings of Native Americans. Also on exhibit were the Apache leader Geronimo (under armed guard as a military prisoner), Chief Joseph of the Nez Percé, and Quanah Parker of the Comanche. The Indian School Building and the Philippine Reservation were carefully placed to make the instrumental relation between the two as plain as possible. Calling the Indian School building "designed not merely as a consummation, but as a prophecy," McGee explained the rationale behind its inclusion at the Fair: "now that other primitive peoples are passing under the beneficent influence and protection of the Stars and Stripes, it is needful to take stock of past progress as a guide to the future."[15] . . .

Beals played the woman's angle for all it was worth, which was considerable. She made many sets of "sympathetic" pictures of domestic life in the anthropology exhibits. Seen as "ethnological studies," they were eagerly bought by Harvard and Yale Universities and by natural history museums all over the country. Perhaps her most famous set of pictures was *Mother and Babe at the Exhibition*; but Beals made other sets of photographs as well, such as the *The Children of the Fair, Musical Instruments, Native Habitations, Strange Wedding Ceremonies, Head Dress, Dances of All Nations, Cooking Methods,* and *The Mutilation Practices.* In fact, Beals's work at St. Louis was taken as so good a model for ethnographic photography that in 1906 she was invited to exhibit some of it at a "women photographers" exhibition (the first ever in New England) at the Camera Club of Hartford, Connecticut, where confused critics singled out her work as "one of the best exhibits," crediting her with having "furnished several scenes in Japan (taken at the St. Louis World's Fair)."[16] . . .

As if all this were not recognition enough, Beal's photographs of the Philippine reservation were met with such consummate delight by the organizers of that exhibit that they brought them to the notice of Secretary of War William Howard Taft, previously governor-general of the Philippines. Much impressed, Taft offered Beals "a passport and a free round-trip to the islands . . . to bring back, as a contribution to science, pictorial records of the daily life of the little-known wild tribes."[17] Beals was elated, but unfortunately Alfred didn't want to go, quite possibly because he was aware that the fighting still continued in the Philippines.

Beals also exploited her angle of vision in a literal way, by choosing dramatic vantage points from which to photograph and allowing herself to be photographed and written about "as a woman" while in such stances. For instance, she climbed a twenty-foot ladder to photograph a parade. And just before the beginning of the International Balloon Race she climbed into one of the [balloon] baskets with her camera. One newspaper years later memorialized the event this way: "Just as one of the balloons was being set free, the huge crowd was thunderstruck to see a woman, a camera slung over her shoulder, grip the top of a basket and pull herself aboard. The balloon was off, and with it the intrepid woman photographer." Dr. David Francis, president of the Exposition, published the resulting panoramas of the fairgrounds, which Beals made from 900 feet aloft, in the official *Louisiana Purchase Exposition Bulletin.* Her bird's-eye view photographs were, he

"As the Lady Managers wanted to have them" –Pierre Chouteau.

"As the Lady Managers wanted to have them—Prime Christians," Jessie Tarbox Beals's satiric photograph of Filipinos (mis)representing their customary dress and lifeways, on the Philippine Reservation at the St. Louis World's Fair, 1904. (Courtesy of Missouri History Museum.)

wrote, "a view which I wish to remember."[18] This is perhaps not surprising, since, like the eye of the American eagle, they dominated what they surveyed.

But what exactly *was* the point of view of the "intrepid woman photographer"? The people in Beals's photographs were neither given derogatory names nor photographed as fetishes for the contemplation of nude bodily display. Her images are therefore less overtly racist than the productions of [other women's photographers such as] the Gerhard Sisters [Emme and Mamie]. Indeed, Beals made a photograph that explicitly mocked the sanctimonious (and highly publicized) efforts of the Board of Lady Managers to make the Igorots wear full sets of clothes rather than the loincloths that were their accustomed dress because it seemed to them that the male nudity was drawing

prurient looks, especially from "lady" visitors. In her hilarious but sharply pointed image, the Filipinos cooperate with Beals in performing a satiric pantomime of "'As the Lady Managers wanted to have them'—Prime Christians," which is how she captioned the photograph. Fully and awkwardly covered in heavy robes, coats, and wearing hats, but still barefoot, five Philippine Reservation inhabitants walk in a line, evidently performing one of their ceremonial dances the "Prime Christian" way.

Nor do Beals's images reproduce the sensational stereotypes of turn-of-the-century primitivism's imaginary [created by other women photographers at the fair] . . . . On the contrary, Beals felt that she had made "many new friends" among the "foreign" people she photographed and "would treasure their many parting gifts, particularly the pina fiber dress presented by the Filipino villagers and the exquisite bolt of Chinese silk given to her by Prince Pu Lun of China."[19] Given the American occupation of the Philippines, such "friend-ships" must have had a considerable compo-nent of fantasy.

Nonetheless, Beals seems to have been personally affected by the racial vision of the fair. The photographs she made are com-plexly complicit in keeping offstage any vision of the violence of the pacification of a people. While she was still at the fair, Beals made a collage of her photographs from the anthropological villages. The pictures are uniformly gracious and dignified domestic scenes, with their grass-rooted huts, their pastoral waterways, their smiling children, and their graceful young mothers. . . . [T]hey argue for the unharmed humanity of those they picture but without challenging the vio-lent framework in which that humanity was concurrently differentiated, primitivized, and separated from the "higher" domestic forms of the "white race."

Thus, Beals's pictures extended sympa-thy, but they also fully eradicated any traces of the military surveillance that had accompa-nied the Filipinos to St. Louis. That is to say, first, they normalized the presence among the fair's Filipino delegation of several hundred members of the Philippine constabulary, a paramilitary force of Philippine collaborators set in place by the American occupation; one of them, photographed with an "innocent eye" by Beals, was included in the upper right-hand corner of her collage. Second, they re-mained oblivious to the fact that the Philippine villages were surrounded by high board fences and their inhabitants monitored by curfews, in a direct quotation of the so-called "reloca-tion camps" in which thousands of their countrymen were being interned back in the Philippines at that very moment. And third, they avoided any view of the outer perimeter of the Philippine "reservation" itself, which was designed as a model of the old Spanish defense of the city of Manila. When walking through it to the ethnic villages, every visitor–and every Filipino inhabitant–re-created the heroic story of [Commodore George] Dewey's conquest and penetration of the city [in 1898] to gain access to the nation of "primitives" that supposedly lay beyond.[20] Even though during the whole time the fair was open in

St. Louis, Filipino insurgents were continuing to battle the United States occupation, and the United States was continuing to execute Filipino patriots as "outlaws," there is no sign of this activity in Beals's images. Her collage of domestic life in the Anthropological De-partment so completely illustrates the present success and bright future of the American rule of peace that it is no wonder that Taft himself, the author of the concept of "benevo-lent assimilation," longed to send her to the Philippines. . . .

Beals photographed the virtual geography of the fair by moving freely between the obvi-ously "fake" Manila and the "obviously" real St. Louis, but it is difficult to distinguish the two in her photographs. This was, of course, the desired effect. The fact that Harvard and Yale Universities bought Beals's exposition images as ethnographic studies is one result of this confusion. . . . But the most significant re-ality effect of this simulacrum was that in con-struing the Philippine present as coterminous with the Southern past, the fair was portraying that past as the progressive and inevitable future of the American empire. Conversely, it was erasing actual Philippine history in order to rescript it as naturally consonant with the context of the American South.

In an essay entitled "The Sign as a Site of Class Struggle," Jo Spence identifies the ideo-logical work of photographs as the production of an "imaginary coherence," one in which "images from . . . photography . . . are immedi-ate yet appear to be retrospective," and in which "their presence confirms the absence of what appears to have been previously pre-sent."[21] This elegant formulation exactly de-scribes what Beals's photographs accomplished. Their normalization of [the ethnic villages of the] St. Louis [Fair] as the Philippine future confirms the influence of the Southern past as constitutive of the Philippine's immediate real-ity. Never mind that it was a coherence that was patently corrupt; the conjuncture was made potent by Jim Crow—and rendered in-visible by Jessie Beals.

However, the experience of working at the fair, with its emphasis on racial "diversity" and racial "progress," not only translated into pho-tographs that configured the way that viewers were to see the coming American Century; it also prophesied a new Beals. After her work in St. Louis, Beals evolved into an even more ambitious photographer and an even less conventional woman. Beals was aware of its importance to herself. Some years after returning from St. Louis, Beals made another photographic collage, this time a narrative of her own life. The two panels document changes in a small-town girl's experience as she discovers photography. The world in the pictures steadily expands. In them, Beals and her camera conquer obstacles, travel, go to parties, and meet interesting and famous people. There are more photographs of Beals at the fair than at any other period of her life. In the photographs of St. Louis we see Beals in the balloon, Beals on the twenty-foot ladder, Beals working at the fair with her camera assistant named "Pumpkin," and Beals's hard-won press pass and photo ID card. Functioning as the fulcrum of Beals's autobiography, the fair separates her own experience into a "before," and "after." The collage demonstrates that as a sentimental indoctrination, the fair had apparently fulfilled an inner, as well as an ideological mission.

Indeed, life "before" was one thing, but life "after" was something else again. For a long time after St. Louis, nothing measured up for Jessie to the intensity of the nine months she had spent photographing the fair. Perhaps it was that Alfred Beals had dragged his feet about the trip to the Philippines and prevented her accepting the assignment from Taft. Perhaps it was that Jessie Beals was nearing forty and after many years of marriage she and Alfred still had no children. Her only infant, a girl born in 1901, had died only a few hours after birth. Perhaps it was simply that Beals had grown weary of the concept of "woman photographer" that juxtaposed her solely to Alfred or to other photographing women, when she had seemed in St. Louis to have the whole world as her counterpart.

NOTES

1. Alexander Alland, Sr., *Jessie Tarbox Beals: First Woman News Photographer* (New York: Camera/Graphic Press, 1978), 22. Other published sources of information on Beals include Jane Cutler, *Song of the Molimo* (New York: Farrar Straus Giroux, 1998).

2. Mrs. Jefferson Davis is quoted in Walter Benn Michaels, "Anti-Imperial Americanism," in *Cultures of U.S. Imperialism*, ed. Amy Kaplan and Donald Pease (Durham, N.C.: Duke University Press, 1993), 387 n. 1.

3. Robert W. Rydell, *All the World's a Fair: Visions of American Empire at American International Expositions, 1876–1916* (Chicago: University of Chicago Press, 1987), 161.

4. W. J. McGee, "Trend of Human Progress," quoted in Rydell, *All the World's a Fair*, 161.

5. W. J. McGee, "National Growth and National Character," quoted in ibid., 161.

6. W. J. McGee, quoted in ibid., 167.

7. Alland, *Beals*, 26, 40-41.

8. Ibid., 43.

9. Ibid.

10. Ibid. [In 1955 Steichen, as the director of photography at the Museum of Modern Art in New York, organized a monumental show of 503 photographs taken by 273 artists from 68 nations. The exhibit aimed to show life experiences and emotions shared across cultures. It went on a worldwide tour and became a best-selling book.]

11. Ibid.

12. Ibid., 43, 45.

13. Rydell, *All the World's a Fair*, 157.

14. McGee quoted in Ibid., 160, 161.

15. Ibid., 167.

16. Camera Club of Hartford, Conn., April 1906, quoted in Alland, *Beals*, 62.

17. Ibid., 52.

18. *Philadelphia Public Ledger,* January 26, 1921, and David Francis, both quoted in Alland, *Beals*, 48.

19. Ibid.

20. Beverly K. Grindstaff, "Creating Identity: Exhibiting the Philippines at the 1904 Louisiana Purchase Exhibition," in Donald Preziosi and Claire J. Farago, eds., *Grasping the World: The Idea of the Museum* (Aldershot, UK: Ashgate, 2003), 298–320.

21. Jo Spence, "The Sign as a Site of Class Struggle," in *Photography/Politics: Two*, ed. Patricia Holland, Jo Spence, and S. Watney (London: Commedia, 1986), 176.

LEILA J. RUPP
Sexuality and Politics in the Early Twentieth–Century International Women's Movement

We often imagine that in U.S. history "the sexual revolution" took place in the 1960s. Historians, however, perceive what they sometimes call a first sexual revolution, occurring early in the twentieth century (although this ignores changing ideas about sexual expression and gender roles in the 1700s and 1800s*). Two broad shifts were at work in mainstream American culture after the turn of the twentieth century, most notably in the 1920s. The first concerned homosociality, or the extent to which persons of one perceived sex spend most of their time with members of the same sex. For decades prior to 1920, women and men were expected largely to occupy different social realms. Around the period of the "roaring twenties," some Europeans and Americans began to pursue and celebrate heterosocial patterns of engagement, both in informal social activities and the organizations they joined. At the same time, heterosexual experimentation prior to and outside of marriage became more acceptable in some circles. One consequence of these shifts was that same-sex emotional and physical intimacy became increasingly stigmatized and labeled (pejoratively) as homosexuality.

Leila J. Rupp's essay tells us about the political alliances forged across national borders by women in Europe and the Americas, with the sexual revolution of the early twentieth century as a backdrop. These activists could afford to travel overseas and to devote themselves full-time to volunteer or paid work on the behalf of organizations such as the International Council of Women. They were often fluent in several languages. Some lived openly as same-sex couples. Others gloried in their heterosexual marriages or did not do much to hide their many affairs with men. Rupp reads personal correspondence and organizational records to find out how much sexual (or "affectional," as in where you place your most important affections) life choices factored in the political differences among the activists—such as over the issue of woman-only gatherings. She finds that national, class, and generational differences were just as important.

How do you think her insights about sexuality and politics might apply to activists today? Rupp's study focuses on transnational connections among women in the West. How might issues relating to sexual politics be similar or different if we examined transnational women's activism today between the global North and global South?

---

*For arguments about major shifts prior to 1830, see Richard Godbeer, *Sexual Revolution in Early America* (Baltimore: Johns Hopkins University Press, 2002); and Clare A. Lyons, *Sex Among the Rabble: An Intimate History of Gender and Power in the Age of Revolution, Philadelphia, 1730-1830* (Chapel Hill: University of North Carolina Press, 2006).

Excerpted from "Sexuality and Politics in the Early Twentieth Century: The Case of the International Women's Movement," by Leila J. Rupp, in *Feminist Studies* 23, no. 3 (Fall 1997): 577–605. Reprinted by permission of the author and publisher. Notes have been renumbered and edited.

In her autobiography, Lena Madesin Phillips, U.S. founder of the International Federation of Business and Professional Women, who lived for thirty-three years with a woman to whom she "lost her heart," reported that an Austrian colleague had once asked her about the large number of unmarried women in the organization. "You women seem quite content to have meetings without men present; to be happy though unmarried. . . . American women told us they had a splendid banquet where women had a fine meal, some speeches, and no men," the Austrian woman remarked with evident astonishment. Within the same international women's movement circles, Brazilian International Alliance of Women member Bertha Lutz expressed her disgust at the lobbying tactics of Inter-American Commission of Women head Doris Stevens, an American "emancipated woman" who worked for an international equal rights treaty by seeking the support of male government representatives to the Pan American Union. Lutz called Stevens a "nymphomaniac" and accused her of "paying the mexican delegates in kisses . . . [and] luring the haitians with a french secretary she has."[1]

These contrasting observations—about a surprisingly happy female world and a disturbingly (hetero)sexual one—alert us to some of the tensions that simmered beneath the seemingly placid surface of early-twentieth-century international women's organizations. In the industrialized societies of the Euroamerican arena, the first decades of the century marked a critical transition, sometimes graced with the label of "sexual revolution," from a world of privatized to a world of more public and commercialized sexuality. As the barriers between women's and men's public worlds began to break down in the decades on either side of 1900 and young women in Chicago and Harlem, London, and Copenhagen, laid assertive new claims to their own sexuality, increasingly rigid definitions of heterosexuality and homosexuality cast more and more suspicion on a whole range of women's relationships and forms of organizing.[2] Women might step over the line of respectable heterosexuality by cavorting with men outside of marriage, but women without men—whether "spinsters" or women in same-sex couples—came more frequently to earn the label "deviant." And, as I argue here, these moves had consequences for the politics of women's single-sex organizing.

Sexual respectability was not a new concern in the women's movement of the early twentieth century—one has only to think of the scandals that surrounded Mary Wollstonecraft or Victoria Woodhull [for Woodhull, see pp. 258–259]. But heightened attention to the deviant lesbian subject did transform the context in which women gathered in single-sex organizations. Before the categorization of the "female invert" or "lesbian" at the end of the nineteenth century, women in the women's movement could more easily form intense and passionate relationships as "romantic friends" or choose to live out their lives as single women without a diagnosis of abnormality.[3] Scholarship has long emphasized the importance of supportive relationships among women for the strength of the women's movement.[4] Although recent work has opened our eyes to the ease with which romantic friends in the nineteenth century and earlier could transgress what the counsel for the defense in a famous [Scottish] case called "ordinary female friendship," there is no question that coupled women had to trod ever more carefully as time wore on.[5]

The organizations making up the international women's movement provide a particularly interesting case study of such tensions, because these bodies came to life as shifts in the conceptualization of women's relationships proceeded. They also brought together women from a variety of cultures, if primarily middle-and upper-class women of European origin from the countries of Western Europe and North America. As we shall see, not only affectional but generational, class, and national differences—and their complex interplay in the lives of women—shaped responses to the practice of single-sex organizing.

My research concentrates on the three major transnational women's groups—the International Council of Women, the International Alliance of Women, and the Women's International League for Peace and Freedom—and the more narrowly focused bodies with which they interacted on a regular basis in the years between the emergence of international organizing in the 1880s and the conclusion of the Second World War, which marked the end of the first wave of the international women's movement (and the lull before the swell of the second). In this period all three organizations remained heavily elite and Euroamerican in composition and leadership. Not only did Europe and what have been called the "neo-Europes" contribute

Farewell banquet, International Council of Women, Quinquennial Congress at the Mayflower Hotel, May 13, 1925.
Reproduced from the Report on the Quinquennial Meeting, *Washington, D.C., 1925. (Image courtesy of Leila Rupp.)*

all but one of the national sections until 1923 but women from the United States, Great Britain, and Western and Northern Europe also served as the founders and leaders. This pattern perpetuated itself through the choice of official languages—English, French, and German—and the location of congresses primarily in Europe, with a few excursions to North America. Although women from Latin America, the Middle East, Asia, and Africa increasingly found their voices within the international organizations after the First World War undermined European dominance of the world system, their relative silence in the recorded debate about sexuality is testimony to their marginality in the organizational friendship circles.[6]

The International Council of Women (ICW), the most vaguely defined group, came together in 1888 and welcomed all women's organizations with whatever purposes, bringing in a huge number of members but forestalling commitment to controversial goals. The International Woman Suffrage Alliance (IWSA), later known as the International Alliance of Women (IAW), split off from the ICW in 1904 in order to take a position in favor of suffrage and remained a strongly feminist-identified

body, even after the increasing extension of the vote to women in the years after the First World War undermined the group's original rationale. The Women's International League for Peace and Freedom (WILPF), founded in 1915 by IWSA members who insisted on meeting despite wartime hostilities, consistently took quite radical positions on a range of issues.[7] These three groups, in conjunction with a wide array of bodies organized on a regional basis, or comprised of particular constituencies of women, or devoted to single issues, formed coalitions in the years between the wars to coordinate international collective action, especially lobbying at the League of Nations.

The transnational women's groups focused on issues of women's rights, peace, and women's work, paying minimal attention to questions of sexuality, with the exception of what they called "the traffic in women." The dialogue about sexuality and politics, then, must be ferreted out of the sources, read from assumptions and associations. As I explored discussions of difference between women and men, arguments about the appropriateness of single-sex organizing, and correspondence about personal relationships, I began to perceive tensions within the international organizations and patterns linking women's personal lives and cultural contexts to their political choices.

SAME-SEX LOVE, HOMOSOCIALITY, AND SEPARATISM

Within the international women's organizations, some women coupled with women in what seem to have been "lesbian" relationships or as "romantic friends," sometimes in relationships in which one woman served as a kind of caretaker for the other. Some women never formed intimate relationships with either women or men. None of these women can be easily categorized, but in one way or another all made their lives with other women.

We have no direct evidence that any of the women involved in the international women's movement identified as lesbians, but the concept of lesbianism was not unknown in their intellectual world. As early as 1904, in a speech to the Scientific Humanitarian Committee, the pioneering German homosexual rights group, Anna Ruhling associated lesbians ("Uranian women" in the terminology of the time) with the international women's movement, asserting that

> the homosexual woman is particularly capable of playing a leading role in the international women's rights movement for equality. And indeed, from the beginning of the women's movement until the present day, a significant number of homosexual women assumed the leadership in the numerous struggles and, through their energy, awakened the naturally indifferent and submissive average women to an awareness of their human dignity and rights.[8]

. . . That women in the international women's movement had some familiarity with the discourse of "homosexuality" as it emerged in the late nineteenth century is clear. . . . Discussion within international women's movement circles of "fairies," use of the terms "queer" and "perverse from a sexual point of view," [and] references to "Manly-Looking" women and women who "went about together at the Hague, hair cropped short and rather mannish in dress," . . . suggest that at least the European women had some familiarity with the work of the sexologists [such as Havelock Ellis].[9]

Despite such derogatory usages, women within the movement accepted women's couple relationships, conceptualizing them as romantic friendships or "Boston marriages" rather than lesbian love affairs. Anita Augspurg and Lida Gustava Heymann formed one such couple within the circle of internationally organized women. Augspurg, leading member of the radical wing of the German women's movement and the country's first woman lawyer, met Heymann, who had freed herself from the life of a daughter of a rich Hamburg merchant to become a social worker and trade union organizer, at an 1896 international women's conference in Berlin. In their memoirs, Heymann described her first vision of the woman she came to live with for over forty years. Arrested by Augspurg's powerful voice, she saw her at the lectern, dressed in a brown velvet dress. "Already graying short hair framed a high forehead, under which two clearsighted eyes sparkled. A sharp profile contrasted markedly but not unharmoniously with a delightful small mouth, chin, and small ears."[10] Obviously it was a momentous meeting, and the physical description smacks of a "love at first sight" genre.

Although early on the two women decided not to live together, they happily broke that promise. "Every year brought us closer," Heymann wrote, "deepened our friendship, let us know that not only in questions of Weltanschauung [worldview] . . . but also in all the events of daily life . . . we stood in exquisite harmony." They moved to the country where they launched a series of ambitious, and successful, agricultural enterprises, a quite unusual undertaking for two women. As a result, they reported that their Upper Bavarian peasant neighbors viewed them with some suspicion. In the section of their memoirs entitled "Private Life," Heymann recounted that "it excited the envy and anger of the farmers that two 'vagabonds in petticoats' were successful, creative, and happy to organize their lives according to their own desires and inclinations." One day a cattle dealer came to call with proposals of marriage for both women, explaining that the farm was splendid and lacked only a man. "It took all our effort to remain serious and make clear to the man the hopelessness of his desire. As he left, we shook with laughter," Heymann commented.[11]

As such descriptions make clear, Heymann and Augspurg presented themselves in public, in their daily lives, and unselfconsciously as a couple, and that is certainly how they were treated within the international women's movement. Correspondents regularly sent messages to and received them from both women. Heymann sent "Heartfelt greetings from us both" to Rosika Schwimmer in 1919. . . . Augspurg and Heymann stayed in double rooms when they attended congresses, entertained movement friends at their home, and described a happy family life: "I had a very good journey home and found Anita and our dog in good health," Heymann wrote [to the French WILPF leader] on her return from a trip to Paris. When Heymann planned to travel to Geneva for a meeting in 1930, a WILPF staff member reported that "she is coming without Dr. Augspurg which is scarcely believable!"[12]

Heymann and Augspurg were enjoying a Mediterranean vacation in March of 1933 when Hitler came to power in Germany. As pacifists and feminists they had made themselves enemies of the Nazis, so they never returned to the land of their birth. Although in this way they stayed out of the Nazis' clutches, the regime seized all their property, including their books and personal papers, prompting WILPF friends to try to help them. Swiss WILPF cochair Clara Ragaz, hoping to arrange hospitality at headquarters in Geneva, commented about Augspurg, who suffered from heart disease, that "it is a very hard time for her friend—and of course for herself." When Heymann died in June of 1943, American Emily Greene Balch worked to raise money to support Heymann's "life-long friend and co-worker . . . , for whom she had cared so devotedly." But as it turned out, Augspurg did not survive long. "Did you notice that Lida Gustava Heymann and Dr. Anita Augspurg died within a few short weeks of each other?" Rosika Schwimmer asked a friend.[13]

Augspurg and Heymann made the acquaintance of another well-known couple, Hull House founder and WILPF president Jane Addams and Mary Rozet Smith, in the course of their work in the international women's movement. The German women enjoyed the hospitality of Addams and Smith when they came to the United States for the WILPF congress in 1924. . . . Like the German couple, Addams and Smith sent and received messages for one another, made arrangements for double-bedded rooms when they traveled, and took care of each other, although that responsibility fell more heavily on [the younger] Smith. . . .[14]

. . . Such relationships between older and younger, or more and less powerful, women [like Smith's devoted service to her more prominent partner] seemed to obscure the bond of love from the vision of outsiders. The relationship between Anna Howard Shaw, American minister, charismatic orator, and international leader, and Lucy Anthony, a niece of . . . Susan B. Anthony, falls into this category. Shaw had a reputation within suffrage circles for her "strong and passionate attachments to other women," some of which "have broken up in some such tempestuous fashion." Shaw described her "abiding love for home and home life" at her country house, Moylan, which she shared with Anthony. When Shaw fell and broke her foot and Anthony, at the same time, fractured her elbow, Shaw ruefully labeled them "rather a broken up couple." Yet Aletta Jacobs [Dutch IWSA leader and WILPF founder] saw Anthony as Shaw's "secretary, friend, and housekeeper," since Shaw paid her a salary. Anthony herself called Shaw, after her death, "my Precious Love," "the joy of my life."[15]

The same confusion greeted the relationship of International Woman Suffrage Alliance president Carrie Chapman Catt and New York suffrage leader Mary Garrett Hay. Catt's reserve and distaste for emotional display—one intimate friend likened her to "cold boiled halibut"—may have obscured the reality of her relationships, or the fact that Catt married twice may have led observers—as it has scholars—to undervalue her ties to women.[16] But Catt did not even live full time with her husband when he was alive, and when he died she and Hay set up housekeeping together. . . . Apparently rather authoritarian, Hay was not popular in international circles. Shaw, who detested her, ... did "not think there is any hope of breaking that affair off." . . . [W]hen Catt died in 1947, she was buried, at her request, not with either of her two husbands but next to her "unforgettable friend and comrade" Hay.[17]

More ambivalent, but following a similar pattern, was the relationship of Emily Greene Balch, Wellesley professor, WILPF leader, and winner of the Nobel Peace Prize, and her childhood friend Helen Cheever. Balch, like Catt, was a reserved woman; she described her Yankee background as one that valued "restraint not only of expression of emotion but of emotion itself." Cheever was a wealthy woman who financially supported Balch and wanted to live with her on a permanent basis. But Balch, who admitted that she both loved and was irritated by Cheever, balked. Perhaps, she wrote her sister, it was a result of Cheever's "giving me more love than I can quite digest." Yet when Balch was in Geneva as international secretary of WILPF, her coworkers eagerly anticipated, on Balch's behalf, a visit from Cheever. "I think she is homesick and it would be very good if her friend from America came soon to keep her company and also attend a bit to her physical health," Heymann confided to Jane Addams. Three years later Cheever wanted to resign her offices in the U.S. section of WILPF in order to go to Geneva where "my usefulness to the W.I.L. will be confined to being with Miss Balch." . . . [In the end] Balch resisted becoming part of a female couple and identified [instead] as an unmarried woman. . . . Unmarried women [found it] strange, [she later explained to Jane Addams, that] . . . "everything that is not concerned with the play of desire between men and women [is seen] as without adventure."[18]

The public defensiveness of single women may have originated in the awakened suspicion that women living without men might have perverse desires or it might simply have been provoked by popular assumptions that such women had no intimate ties. In a 1931 German anthology on the modern single career woman, Elisabeth Busse explained that such women were not "amazonian," "inverts," or "homosexuals," although "they lived in women's unions." So it is not surprising that ICW secretary Alice Salomon, a German Jewish pioneer in the world of social work who never married, apologized in her autobiography that "this book may sometimes seem as much a book about women as though I had lived in a harem." Actually, she assured her readers, "I always had men and women, old and young, rich and poor, and sometimes whole families as my friends." But, in fact, Salomon made her life in the female world of social reform and the women's movement. She apparently felt compelled to discuss why she never married, explaining that her work . . . "made me reluctant to form a union which could not combine love with common interests and convictions."[19]

In the ICW *Bulletin* of October 1932, Salomon published a defense of unmarried women, the first generation of independent women who pursued careers. She recognized that the

discipline of psychology had changed attitudes toward single women—that they were reputed to be warped by celibacy—but quoted a woman of "international fame" to the effect that "they are alive, active, and they fully participate in present-day life by means of a thousand interests." Similarly, Lena Madesin Phillips recognized: "To live an old maid was . . . considered something to be greatly deplored"; but she insisted that she had "no complaints, no regrets, no fears" about her own unmarried, but woman-coupled life. Helen Archdale, a British equal rights advocate active in the international arena, reacted testily to a paean to marriage penned [by a friend] . . . . "What you say about the beneficial effects of marriage on one's life rather puzzles me. Why should 'spinsterhood' be gray?" Archdale shared a London flat and country home with Lady Margaret Rhondda, another international activist, in the 1920s, after which they "personally drifted very far apart."[20] Such defensiveness and defiance about living apart from men reflects the power of the intensified vision of married life as the only healthy alternative for women.

In the first decades of the twentieth century, then, overlapping frames of lesbianism, romantic friendship, devoted service, and singleness existed for women's choices in their personal lives. Women-only organizations offered an appealing haven for those who made their lives with other women, whatever the nature of their ties. But in a context in which homosociality often cast a pall of deviance, the desire to work apart from men grew more complex.

Almost all participants in the major international women's organizations accepted—or did not raise public objections to—an ideology of fundamental difference between women and men. The notion of difference underlay . . . "maternalist politics"—the construction of public positions on the foundation of women's biological and social roles as mothers.[21] But among women not involved in intimate relationships with men, belief in female values—read superior values—also led in a different direction: to the regular expression of anti-male sentiments in both private and public life. Heymann and Augspurg tried as far as possible to hire only women to manage their farm, and Heymann contrasted their satisfaction with their women employees to their displeasure with a male manager: "Vanity, thy name is man!" she proclaimed. "The customary judgment maintains, of course, that the female sex is the one enslaved by vanity, but this customary assertion is only a diversion and contradicts the law of nature among humans and animals."[22]

Similarly, Anna Howard Shaw had little use for men in her private life. When Lucy Anthony's broken arm failed to heal properly, Shaw announced that if a woman physician had treated Anthony everything would have been all right. During the First World War, Shaw complained about "male experts" wasting "millions of dollars on smoke and drink" while advising housewives to tighten their belts. "Men, I am convinced, never grow up and of all the animal creation are the least capable of reason."[23]

Such views spilled over into work in the international women's movement, merging especially with the common association of men with war and women with peace. The outbreak of the First World War unleashed a veritable barrage of anti-male proclamations. Shaw found men's "war madness and barbarism" "unthinkable" and claimed, despite her already low opinion of men, that "I have not half the respect for man's judgment or common sense that I used to have, that they are such fools as to go out and kill and be killed without knowing why." Heymann condemned men's "lies and hatred and violence" at the WILPF congress in 1919, proclaiming that the war would "never have come to pass had we women, the mothers of the world, been given the opportunity of helping to govern the people and join in the social life of nations." At the 1934 WILPF congress, Augspurg denounced the "world of men" as "built up on profit and power, on gaining material wealth and oppressing other people." Women "would be able to build a new world which would produce enough for all." According to Carrie Chapman Catt, "All wars are men's wars. Peace has been made by women but war never."[24]

Advocacy of separatist organizing logically flowed from such assumptions about women's moral superiority and potential efficacy in creating a peaceful world. It is not that women who built lives apart from men never associated or worked with them—both Heymann and Addams, for example, participated in political parties—but that they seemed particularly to value the women's world of the women's movement. Yet few women in the international women's movement explicitly defended the practice

of separatism. Emily Greene Balch seemed to prefer work with women but to feel that WILPF had to consider admitting men. In the first year after the [1915] Hague congress, she wrote that "my interest and belief in our woman's organization is as strong as ever." WILPF debated its commitment to separatism in the early 1920s but decided to remain a woman-only organization on the international level, in the process putting out a pamphlet that explained the reasons for keeping out men, one of the only public documents to defend the practice of separatism. . . .[25]

Given the persistence of all-female groups, the lack of vigorous defense of the principle of separatism is curious. Yet such silence speaks. It is possible that the need never occurred to those long committed to organizing in woman-only groups. But because the question of admitting men did arise, perhaps the silence was a sign of uneasiness over the old-fashioned associations of single-sex organizing in an increasingly heterosocial world. That separatist inclinations remained strong is clear from the apology of Eva Fichet, member of the mixed-gender Tunis section of WILPF, who planned to bring her member husband to the 1934 international congress. Noting that "his presence will offend some of our collaborators," she promised that "he will only make an appearance at public meetings, if there are any." Still, the comments of British suffragist and WILPF member Catherine E. Marshall, who never married, stand out in the records of the international women's movement: "It is always a pleasure to meet Women fellow workers. . . . I do like women best! Who was it said: The more I see of men the better I think of women!"[26] Such sentiments expressed the conviction that women had more in common with one another than with men and underlay the inclination to make both a personal and work life with other women.

HETEROSEXUALITY AND WORK WITH MEN

Some women within the international women's movement lived traditional married lives, while others engaged in more unconventional forms of heterosexual relationships. The model of the woman leader married to a supportive husband received a great deal of praise, but unorthodox heterosexuality crossed the line of respectability in a way that women's same-sex relationships did not and as a result met with disapproval. This difference probably reflects the generational divide that separated the predominantly older women of the international women's movement from younger cohorts more blasé about heterosexual expressiveness and more attuned to the sexual possibilities between women.

Lady and Lord Aberdeen, Scottish aristocrats, were without doubt the most lauded couple in international women's movement circles. The ICW regularly held them up as an exemplar of a couple committed to the same work, even though Lord Aberdeen in fact played no role in the organization. . . . Lady Aberdeen's devoted friend Alice Salomon described the Aberdeen marriage as modern and ideal and insisted that the ICW was as much a matter of concern to Lord Aberdeen as to Lady Aberdeen. The ICW president herself appreciated her husband's "never wavering support and . . . belief in the I.C.W." that had made possible everything she had accomplished. Emma Ender, the president of the German section of the ICW, responded that she knew from her own experience "what it means, to live at the side of a man who totally understands and supports the life work that we have taken on." Even after Lord Aberdeen's death, Lady Aberdeen referred to "the inestimable blessing of husbands who wish us to enter into all the fullness of life in service and responsibility."[27]

Aletta Jacobs, the first woman physician in the Netherlands and an international leader, and her husband, Carel Victor Gerritsen, also attracted favorable attention as a model couple within the international women's movement. Jacobs entered into [the] marriage, despite her perception of the institution's injustice, in deference to her husband's political career and their mutual desire to have a child. She described Gerritsen as "a feminist from the start," and when they married she kept her own name and they maintained separate quarters within the house they shared. Gerritsen actually took up Jacobs's cause by not only supporting her but by also speaking himself in favor of women's suffrage.[28] . . .

[Some] married women leaders [spoke] out on behalf of cooperation across the lines of gender. In her 1899 presidential address, Lady Aberdeen referred to separate women's organizations as a "temporary expedient to meet a temporary need" and hoped that they would not be allowed "to crystallise into a permanent element in social life." Her successor as [ICW] president, American May Wright Sewall, also a married woman, agreed: "the Council idea does not stand for the separation of women from men, but rather for the reunion of women with men in the consideration of great general principles and large public interests." In a 1976 interview, Margery Corbett Ashby [president of the IWSA/IAW from 1923 to 1946] explained that the goal of women's organizations was to eliminate the need for women's organizations, although she admitted that it could be difficult for devoted members to accept this.[29]

. . . [Tension arose in the case of] women perceived as too involved—or in improper relationships-with men attracted harsh criticism. Martina Kramers, who maintained a long-term but unconventional liaison with a man, faced the censure of Carrie Chapman Catt in 1913. Bobbie, whom Kramers called her "left-handed husband," was a socialist and married man whose wife refused to divorce him. As president of the IWSA, Catt wrote to Kramers to recommend that she resign as editor of the organization's journal, *Jus Suffragii*, because her "moral transgressions" had provoked "horror and repugnance" among U.S. IWSA members. Kramers reacted with incredulity and defiance, refusing to give up either her man or her work and insisting to Catt that she was not a "propagandist of free love." She also implicitly equated the unconventionality but acceptability of her relationship with same-sex sexuality by comparing her situation to "the cases of Anita Augspurg [and] Kathe Schirmacher . . . accused by many gossipers of homosexual intercourse." . . . But to no avail. Catt managed, as Kramers put it, "to throw me out of the whole movement" by moving the office of *Jus Suffragii* to London and appointing a new editor. . . .[30]

[Controversy also swirled around Doris Stevens's work at] the Inter-American Commission of Women, as seen [in this essay's opening paragraph]. Stevens struck Bertha Lutz, a single woman who called herself Catt's "daughter," . . . as a "sex-mad psychopath" and a "mentally deranged woman." In fact, Stevens did engage in heterosexual activities outside of marriage, and in her work for the Inter-American Commission of Women she pursued flirtatious relationships with several Latin American diplomats. Far from [being] ashamed of such interactions, she remarked that women and men active in politics together were likely to find that the "deep personal

bond takes the form of heterosexual love." . . .
[But heterosexually active women like Stevens
drew from some female comrades] strong criticism of [not only their allegedly] disreputable
behavior but also [their] political [alliances]
with men.[31] . . .

I do not mean to imply that the lines on the
question of separatism ran strictly in accordance with sexuality or that no other factors
shaped the political practices of separatist
organizing. As the evidence presented here
makes clear, women within the international
women's movement in the first half of the twentieth century formed a variety of relationships,
with both women and men, and cannot easily
be categorized as "homosexual" and "heterosexual" in any case. There were married women
such as Carrie Chapman Catt who lived with
and loved women, and single women such as
Alice Salomon who lavished devoted admiration on Lord and Lady Aberdeen. Coupled
women's relationships might be characterized
as lesbian partnerships, romantic friendships,
loving caretaking, or some combination. In
fact, given the variety of bonds, we might
wonder whether internationally organized
women managed to cross the boundaries of
sexuality more easily than those of class, religion, and nationality.[32] Certainly the conflicts
over sexuality within the movement tended to
pit "respectable" against unconventional behavior rather than same-sex against heterosexual relationships.

And even if we could divide women into
neat categories, the association would not be
perfect. Rosika Schwimmer, who was married
briefly in her youth but lived most of her life
in close association with women, grew disgusted with separatist organizing in the
1930s. Mildred Scott Olmstead, a U.S. WILPF
leader who maintained an intimate relationship with a woman throughout her married
life, proposed in 1934 that the international
organization admit men.[33] And the married
women leaders and heterosexual renegades
all continued to commit themselves to all-female groups, whatever their ideas about the
proper way to organize.

Furthermore, affectional choices alone did
not fashion the politics of separatism. National
and generational differences, which helped to
construct interpretations of sexuality, are particularly striking. European women seemed
both more open to sexual expression and less

interested in single-sex organizing than their
Anglo-American colleagues. . . . [European
women tended to associate separatism, like
sexual prudery,] with the "New World."
Danish women responded to the announcement of the Woman's Peace Party in the United
States and a call for the formation of similar
groups in other countries by asserting that "we
preferred to work together, men and women,
in the same organisation." At the 1915 Hague
congress, Dutch women called for the concentration of all forces, female and male, working
for peace. They noted that "a special women's
movement is not necessary and therefore undesired. The force of a movement where two
sexes cooperate will come to better results
than an organisation of one sex only." Women
trade unionists from Germany and Austria refused to send representatives to the second
congress of the International Federation of
Working Women in 1921, because they were
"opposed to taking part in a separate women's
trade union organisation" in the American
fashion. . . .[34]

Similarly, women struggling side by side
with men of their class or national group for
justice or independence had reason to look
critically at separatist organizing. . . . In 1935,
Margery Corbett Ashby reported that the enormous difficulties facing the nationalist struggle
in Egypt "bring the men and women nearer
together" and found the leading Egyptian nationalist movement, the Wafd, "quite progressive as regards women's position." A Syrian
woman, speaking at the Istanbul congress of
the IAW in the same year, asserted her belief in
the necessity of working shoulder to shoulder
with men in her country for prosperity and
freedom. "The economic and political situation of my country is so desperate that it is
extremely difficult for us women to give our
wholehearted energies to the cause of feminism alone."[35]

Generational differences on the question
of separatism are also striking. Young women
experiencing firsthand the breakdown between female and male social spheres in the
twentieth-century world challenged women-
only groups more readily than their older colleagues who clung to separatist organizing. . . .
In 1931, Canadian Dorothy Heneker pointed
out that young European women thought that
women should work with men, and the IAW
Youth Committee reported in 1938 that the
general feeling favored a mixed organization

of young women and men.[36] Generational, like national, differences on the question of separatism grew from distinctive patterns of homosocial versus heterosocial interaction, and so resistance to all-female groups came from both traditional and progressive sources.

The case of the international women's movement in this period illuminates the paradoxes of a women's world in an era undergoing profound change in the relations between the sexes. Internationally organized women, or at least some of them, knew about lesbianism but chose to view the same-sex relationships of their coworkers in an older frame, [not as pathologized]. Single women alternated between defiance and defensiveness, suggesting that the declining social segregation of the sexes in the industrialized Western world and the more insistent labeling of women without men as lesbians or old maids made a woman's choice of a female—or no—partner more suspicious and thus the women's world of separatist organizations more precarious. The ... reservation of the strongest condemnation for women who challenged respectability through their sexual liaisons with men hints at the unease that spilled over from the transformation of social and sexual relations to the process of political organizing.

The story of the international women's movement also reveals how important it is to attend to the interaction of sexuality and politics. Conflict over sexuality and separatism added to the national, class, and generational tensions already bubbling within the international organizations and foreshadowed some of the contemporary critiques of lesbian separatism in the United States by working-class women and women of color.[37] At the same time, the silencing of the defenders of separatist organizing may have helped to undermine the potential power of a global women's movement in these years by questioning the validity of gathering apart from men in an increasingly heterosocial world. Whatever the case, the dynamics within the first wave of international organizing among women make clear that our contemporary struggles over sexuality and politics have a longer and more complex history than we sometimes think.

NOTES

1. Marjory Lacey-Baker, "Chronological Record of Events and Activities for the Biography of Lena Madesin Phillips, 1881–1955"; Lena Madesin Phillips,

"Unfinished History of the International Federation of Business and Professional Women," Phillips Papers, cartons 7 and 9, Schlesinger Library, Radcliffe College, Cambridge, Mass.; Lutz to Carrie Chapman Catt, 12 Feb. 1934, 7 July 1936, National American Woman Suffrage Association (NAWSA) Papers, reel 12, Library of Congress, Washington, D.C.

2. See Joanne J. Meyerowitz, *Women Adrift: Independent Wage Earners in Chicago, 1880–1930* (Chicago: University of Chicago Press, 1988); Kathy Peiss, *Cheap Amusements: Working Women and Leisure in Turn-of-the-Century New York* (Philadelphia: Temple University Press, 1986); Hazel V. Carby, "'It Jus Be's Dat Way Sometime': The Sexual Politics of Women's Blues," in *Unequal Sisters: A Multicultural Reader in U.S. Women's History*, ed. Ellen Carol DuBois and Vicki L. Ruiz (New York: Routledge, 1990), 238–49; Judith R. Walkowitz, *City of Dreadful Delight: Narratives of Sexual Danger in Late-Victorian London* (Chicago: University of Chicago Press, 1992); Birgitte Søland, *Becoming Modern: Young Women and the Reconstruction of Womanhood in the 1920s* (Princeton, N.J.: Princeton University Press, 2000).

3. On the emergence of the category and identity "lesbian" at the turn of the century, see George Chauncey Jr., "From Inversion to Homosexuality: Medicine and the Changing Conceptualization of Female Deviance," *Salmagundi*, nos. 58–59 (Fall 1982–Winter 1983): 114–46; and Lisa Duggan, "The Trials of Alice Mitchell: Sensationalism, Sexology, and the Lesbian Subject in Turn-of-the-Century America," *Signs* 18 (Summer 1993): 791–814.

4. See, for example, Mineke Bosch with Annemarie Kloosterman, *Politics and Friendship: Letters from the International Woman Suffrage Alliance, 1902–1942* (Columbus: Ohio State University Press, 1990); Ian Tyrrell, *Woman's World, Woman's Empire: The Woman's Christian Temperance Union in International Perspective, 1880–1930* (Chapel Hill: University of North Carolina Press, 1991), which discusses couples within the World Woman's Christian Temperance Union; and Johanna Alberti, *Beyond Suffrage: Feminists in War and Peace, 1914–1928* (London: Macmillan, 1989), which describes women's love for other women within the British women's movement; and Leila J. Rupp and Verta Taylor, *Survival in the Doldrums: The American Women's Rights Movement, 1945 to the 1960s* (New York: Oxford University Press, 1987), which emphasizes the centrality of coupled women in the U.S. women's rights movement.

5. In this early-nineteenth-century case, a well-connected girl accused her two schoolmistresses of engaging in sexual behavior, causing the ruin of the school; see Lillian Faderman, *Scotch Verdict* (New York: William Morrow, 1983). For more on the acceptability issue, see Martha Vicinus, "'They Wonder to Which Sex I Belong': The Historical Roots of the Modern Lesbian Identity," *Feminist Studies* 18 (Fall 1992): 467–97; Lisa Moore, "'Something More Tender Still than Friendship': Romantic Friendship in Early-Nineteenth-Century England," ibid., 499–520; and Marylynne Diggs, "Romantic Friends or a 'Different Race of Creatures'? The Representation of Lesbian Pathology in Nineteenth-Century America," *Feminist Studies* 21 (Summer 1995): 317–40.

6. The neo-Europes included Australia, New Zealand, the United States, and Canada. See Leila J.

Rupp, "Constructing Internationalism: The Case of Transnational Women's Organizations, 1888–1945," *American Historical Review* 99 (Dec. 1994): 1571–1600, and Rupp, "Challenging Imperialism in International Women's Organizations," *NWSA Journal* 8 (Spring 1996): 8–27.

7. *Women in a Changing World: The Dynamic Story of the International Council of Women since 1888* (London: Routledge and Kegan Paul, 1966); Arnold Whittick, *Woman into Citizen* (London: Athenaeum with Frederick Muller, 1976), on the International Alliance of Women; and Bosch, *Politics and Friendship*. On WILPF, see, for example, Gertrude Bussey and Margaret Tims, *Women's International League for Peace and Freedom, 1915–1965* (London: George Allen and Unwin, 1965); Lela B. Costin, "Feminism, Pacifism, Internationalism, and the 1915 International Congress of Women," *Women's Studies International Forum* 5, no. 3/4 (1982): 301–15; Catherine Foster, *Women for All Seasons: The Story of the Women's International League for Peace and Freedom* (Athens: University of Georgia Press, 1989).

8. Anna Ruhling, "Welches Interesse hat die Frauenbewegung an der Losing des homosexuellen problems?" [What interest does the women's movement have in the homosexual question?], in *Lesbian-Feminism in Turn-of-the-Century Germany*, ed. and trans. Lillian Faderman and Brigitte Eriksson ([Weatherby Lake, Mo.]: Naiad Press, 1980), 81–91 (quotation on 88).

9. Rosika Schwimmer to Wilhelmina van Wulfften Palthe, 29 July 1917, Schwimmer-Lloyd Collection, box A-90, Rare Books and Manuscripts Division, New York Public Library, Astor, Lenox, and Tilden Foundations; Marguerite Gobat to Vilma Glucklich [French], 27 Oct. 1924, Women's International League for Peace and Freedom Papers, reel 1; Aletta Jacobs to Rosika Schwimmer, 3 May 1909, Schwimmer-Lloyd Collection, box A-20; Helen Archdale to Anna Nilsson, 17 May 1933, Equal Rights International Papers, box 331, Fawcett Library, London Guildhall University.

10. Lida Gustava Heymann with Anita Augspurg, *Erlebtes-Erschautes: Deutsche Frauen kampfen fur Freiheit, Recht und Frieden 1850–1940*, ed. Margrit Twellman (Meisenheim am Glan: Anton Hain, 1972), 62. See also Regina Braker, "Bertha von Suttner's Spiritual Daughters: The Feminist Pacifism of Anita Augspurg, Lida Gustava Heymann, and Helene Stocker at the International Congress of Women at The Hague, 1915," *Women's Studies International Forum* 18, no. 2 (1995): 103–11.

11. Heymann with Augspurg, *Erlebtes-Erschautes*, 64, 74, 76.

12. Heymann to Schwimmer [in German], 3 Oct. 1919, Schwimmer-Lloyd Collection, box A-119; Emily Balch to Aletta Jacobs, 15 Nov. 1916, Jacobs Papers, box 2, Internationaal Informatiecentrum en Archief voor de Vrouwenbeweging, Amsterdam (hereafter, IIAV); Emily Hobhouse to Aletta Jacobs, 24 Apr. 1920, ibid., box 1; "List of individuals expected in Innsbruck" [German], [1925], WILPF Papers, reel 2; Heymann to Gabrielle Duchene, 17 Feb. 1926, Dossiers Gabrielle Duchene, Fol Res. 206, Bibliotheque de Documentation Internationale Contemporaine, University of Paris, Nanterre; Anne Zueblin to Jane Addams, 17 Jan. 1930,

Addams Papers, reel 21 (University Microfilms International).

13. Clara Ragaz to K.E. Innes and Gertrud Baer, 18 Apr. 1940, WILPF Papers, reel 4; Rosika Schwimmer to Alice Park, 7 Jan. 1944, Alice Park Papers, box 1, Hoover Institution, Stanford, California.

14. Heymann to Mary Rozet Smith [in German and English], 5 June 1924, Addams Papers, reel 16; Anne Zueblin to M. Illova, 10 June 1929, WILPF Papers, reel 19. On Addams and Smith, see Blanche W. Cook, "Female Support Networks and Political Activism: Lillian Wald, Crystal Eastman, Emma Goldman," *Chrysalis* 3 (Autumn 1977): 43–61. Addams described Smith as her "most intimate friend"; Addams to Heymann, 23 Feb. 1924, Addams Papers, reel 16.

15. For the theme of devoted service in these relationships, see Karin Lutzen, *Was das Herz begehrt: Liebe und Freundschaft zwischen Frauen*, translated from Danish by Gabriele Haefs (Hamburg: Ernst Kabel Verlag, 1990), 110–38. Shaw: Rachel Foster Avery to Aletta Jacobs, 14 July 1910, Jacobs Papers; Biography of Anna Howard Shaw, Dillon Collection, box 18, Schlesinger Library; Anna Howard Shaw to Aletta Jacobs, 19 Mar. 1914, Jacobs Papers; Aletta H. Jacobs, *Uithet leven van merkwaardige vrouwen* (Amsterdam: F. van Rossen, 1905), 37, quoted in Bosch, *Politics and Friendship*, 25; Barbara R. Finn, "Anna Howard Shaw and Women's Work," *Frontiers* 4 (Fall 1979): 21–25, quoted in ibid., 26.

16. Mary G. Peck to Carrie Chapman Catt, 6 Feb. 1929, quoted in Robert Booth Fowler, *Carrie Catt: Feminist Politician* (Boston: Northeastern University Press, 1986), 42. Catt also carried on a romantic relationship with Peck, who herself lived with another woman; see Catt to Frances Squire Potter, n.d., quoted in Bosch, *Politics and Friendship*, 38.

17. Anna Howard Shaw to Aletta Jacobs, 8 Feb. 1909, 7 Apr. 1911, and 14 Dec. 1908, Jacobs Papers, box 2; Rachel Foster Avery to Aletta Jacobs, 14 July 1910, ibid.; Anna Manus-Jacobi, tribute to Carrie Chapman Catt [in German], 11 Mar. 1947, Manus Papers, IIAV.

18. Quoted in Mercedes Randall, *Improper Bostonian: Emily Greene Balch* (New York: Twayne Publishers, 1964), 397, 299; Heymann to Addams [in German], 16 Sept. 1919, and Helen Cheever to Jane Addams, 13 Sept. 1922, both in Addams Papers, reel 12 and 15; Jane Addams, *Second Twenty Years at Hull House*, 197–98, quoted in Randall, *Improper Bostonian*, 399.

19. Elisabeth Busse, "Das moralische Dilemma in der modernen Madchenerziehung," in Ada Schmidt-Beil, *Die Kultur der Frau* (Berlin: Verlag fur Kultur und Wissenschaft, 1931), 594; Alice Salomon, "Character Is Destiny," 218 and 39–42, Alice Salomon Papers, Memoir Collection, Leo Baeck Institute, New York.

20. Alice Salomon, "The Unmarried Woman of Yesterday and Today," ICW *Bulletin* 11 (October 1932); Lena Madesin Phillips to Carrie Probst, 28 May 1935, Phillips Papers, carton 4, Schlesinger Library (on Phillips's relationship, see Rupp and Taylor, *Survival in the Doldrums*, 121–24); Archdale to Doris Stevens, 14 Feb. 1936, and Lady Rhondda to Doris Stevens [May 1928], both in Stevens Papers, cartons 4 and 5, Schlesinger Library. On Lady

Rhondda's relationships with women, see Shirley M. Eoff, *Viscountess Rhondda: Equalitarian Feminist* (Columbus: Ohio State University Press, 1991), 107–16.

21. See Rupp, "Constructing Internationalism." On maternalist politics, see the various contributions to Lynn Y. Weiner et al., "Maternalism as a Paradigm," *Journal of Women's History* 5 (fall 1993): 95–131; Seth Koven and Sonya Michel, "Womanly Duties: Maternalist Politics and the Origins of the Welfare States in France, Germany, Great Britain, and the United States, 1880–1920," *American Historical Review* 95 (October 1990): 1076–1108; and Karen Offen, "Defining Feminism: A Comparative Historical Approach," *Signs* 14 (Autumn 1988): 119–57.

22. Heymann with Augspurg, *Erlebtes-Erschautes*, 70.

23. Lucy Anthony to Aletta Jacobs, 10 Jan. 1915, and Anna Howard Shaw to Aletta Jacobs, 30 Aug. 1917, both in Jacobs Papers, box 2.

24. Anna Howard Shaw to Aletta Jacobs, 22 Aug. 1915 and 18 Apr. 1916, Jacobs Papers, box 2; speech of Lida Gustava Heymann, WILPF Zurich Congress, [1919], WILPF Papers, reel 17; Minutes, WILPF International Congress, 3–8 Sept. 1934, WILPF Papers, reel 20; "Man Made Wars," *Pax* 6 (May 1931).

25. Emily Greene Balch to Aletta Jacobs, 15 Nov. 1916, Jacobs Papers, reel 9.

26. Eva Fichet to Emily Balch [French], 19 Aug. 1934, WILPF Papers, reel 20; Catherine E. Marshall to Vilma Glucklich, 14 May [1923], Addams Papers, reel 15. On Marshall, see Jo Vellacott, *From Liberal to Labour with Women's Suffrage: The Story of Catherine Marshall* (Buffalo, N.Y.: McGill-Queen's University Press, 1993).

27. Alice Salomon, "To Lord and Lady Aberdeen on the Occasion of Their Golden Wedding, November 7th, 1927," ICW *Bulletin* 6 (November 1927); Lady Aberdeen to Emma Ender [in German], 31 Jan. 1928, Helene-Lange-Archiv, 78–315 (1), Landesarchiv Berlin; Emma Ender to Lady Aberdeen [German], 13 Feb. 1928, Helene-Lange-Archiv, 85–333 (2), Landesarchiv Berlin; "Lady Aberdeen's Response to Toast Proposed by Baroness Boel . . .," 13 July 1938, ICW, *President's Memorandum Regarding the Council Meeting of the ICW held at Edinburgh, (Scotland), July 11th to 21st 1938*, 15–17.

28. Aletta Jacobs to Rosika Schwimmer [in German], 18 Nov. 1903, Schwimmer-Lloyd Collection, box A-4; see Bosch, *Politics and Friendship*, 9–12, 53–55. Jacobs's reminiscences have been translated and published as *Memories: My Life as an International Leader in Health, Suffrage, and Peace*, ed. Harriet Feinberg, trans. Annie Wright (New York: Feminist Press, 1996).

29. Lady Aberdeen, "Presidential Address," ICW, *Report of Transactions of Second Quinquennial Meeting Held in London July 1899*, ed. Countess of Aberdeen (London: T. Fisher Unwin, 1900), v. 1, 49;

ICW, *Report of Transactions*, 1899, v. 1, 56; Margery Corbett Ashby interview, 21 Sept. 1976, conducted by Brian Harrison, Corbett Ashby Papers, cassette #6, Fawcett Library, London.

30. Catt to Kramers, 21 May 1913, box A-33; Kramers to Schwimmer [in German], 27 May 1913 and 2 June 1913, box A-32 and box A-33; Kramers to Schwimmer [in German], 31 May 1907 and 7 Oct. 1908, box A-12 and box A-17, all in Schwimmer-Lloyd Collection.

31. Lutz to Carrie Chapman Catt, 7 July 1936, 12 Feb. 1934, 15 July 1936, NAWSA Papers, reel 12; Doris Stevens, transcription of taped reminiscences, Stevens Papers, carton 3, Schlesinger Library. See Leila J. Rupp, "Feminism and the Sexual Revolution in the Early Twentieth Century: The Case of Doris Stevens," *Feminist Studies* 15 (Summer 1989): 289–309.

32. I am indebted to Susan Hartmann for this insight.

33. Rosika Schwimmer to Gabrielle Duchene, [1934], WILPF Papers, reel 20; Minutes, Eighth International Congress, Zurich, 3–8 Sept. 1934, WILPF Papers, reel 20. On Mildred Scott Olmstead's complex personal life, see Margaret Hope Bacon, *One Woman's Passion for Peace and Freedom: The Life of Mildred Scott Olmstead* (Syracuse: Syracuse University Press, 1993).

34. Elizabeth Baelde, "Impressions of the Visit of the I.C.W. to Canada," in *Our Lady of the Sunshine*, ed. Countess of Aberdeen (London: Constable, 1909), 310–34; Eline Hansen to Rosika Schwimmer, 12 Mar. 1915, and Edna Munch to Schwimmer, 18 Mar. 1915, both in Schwimmer-Lloyd Collection, box A-55 and A-57; "Report of Business Sessions," 29 Apr. and 1 May [1915], *International Committee of Women for Permanent Peace, International Congress of Women, The Hague—April 28th to May 1st 1915: Report*, 111–17, 162–63; "Stenographic Report of Second Congress," 17 Oct. 1921, International Federation of Working Women Papers, Schlesinger Library.

35. Margery Corbett Ashby to Josephine Schain, 5 Feb. 1935, Schain Papers, box 4 [Mrs. Bader Dimeschquie], "Delegates and Friends," 1935, International Alliance of Women Papers, box 1, both in Sophia Smith Collection, Smith College, Northampton, Mass.

36. Idola Saint-Jean to Helen Archdale, 15 Sept. 1931, Equal Rights International Papers, box 334; Minutes, Meeting of the International Alliance of Women for Suffrage and Equal Citizenship Board, Paris, 6–9 Dec. 1938, International Alliance of Women Papers, both at Fawcett Library.

37. For more on the national, ethnic, class, and generational tensions within the international women's movement, see Leila J. Rupp, *Worlds of Women: The Making of an International Women's Movement* (Princeton, N.J.: Princeton University Press, 1997).

SUFFRAGE AND CITIZENSHIP

ELLEN CAROL DUBOIS

The Next Generation of Suffragists: Harriot Stanton Blatch and Grassroots Politics

Campaigns to expand suffrage require that voters who are reasonably content with the status quo be persuaded to welcome new and unpredictable constituencies into the political arena. It is perhaps no surprise that the expansion of suffrage met severe resistance, in the North where there were considerable doubts about the immigrant vote and especially in the South where the franchise had been restricted (through literacy tests and poll taxes) to exclude African Americans and, in the process, many poor whites.

The campaign for woman suffrage presented a formidable challenge to established political theory that held a married woman's political interests were represented by her husband. It proceeded with a successful national mass mobilization at a time when even presidential campaigns hardly met that criteria. And it required brilliant street theater on a massive scale and, simultaneously, clever and delicate political maneuvering for which women were not noted. Although the accomplishment of woman suffrage in 1920 is well known, the complexity of the work that was required and the high level of political skill that women had to acquire is less appreciated than it deserves to be.

Harriot Blatch, the daughter of Elizabeth Cady Stanton, led the efforts of the Women's Political Union (WPU) to win suffrage for the women of New York State. From 1910 to 1915, the WPU lobbied state legislators to support the suffrage bill. They also targeted public support with parades, suffrage shops, and films. (See Photo Essay: "Women in Public," pp. 255–266.)

Ironically, many suffrages who demanded the vote were deeply skeptical about politics. Believing that women were more pure than men and that politics were corrupt, they insisted that if women had the vote, they would put an end to partisanship. In fact, their views were not so far apart from antisuffragists who resisted the vote precisely because they felt partisan politics would corrupt American womanhood. To their credit, Harriot Blatch and her colleagues understood that acquiring political skills and understanding partisanship were essential to acquiring the vote and, once acquired, using it effectively.

The battle for women's rights had begun in the state of New York, the birthplace of Elizabeth Cady Stanton and the longtime home of Susan B. Anthony. In Seneca Falls, New York, the Declaration of Rights and Sentiments had been rousingly proclaimed in 1848. In Albany, both Stanton and Anthony testified in the 1850s before the New York Senate's Judiciary Committee. There they argued, with some success, for changes in state law to establish women's guardianship rights over their children, grant property and earnings rights to married women, and deliver woman suffrage. In 1915, nearly seventy years later, the struggle, now led by a new generation, had come to focus on woman suffrage. Fittingly, Harriot Stanton Blatch, Elizabeth Cady Stanton's daughter, led this major effort to win woman suffrage in its home state. But even in the early twentieth century, success was uncertain.

Harriot Stanton, the second daughter and sixth child of Elizabeth Cady and Henry Brewster Stanton, inherited her role as defender of her sex from her mother. She was born in Seneca Falls in 1856, during a period when Elizabeth Cady Stanton was immersed in women's issues and the development of a convention movement to publicize concerns as revolutionary as liberalizing divorce. . . . While other Victorian girls followed their mothers into quiet lives based on family service, Harriot was taught to be assertive and independent. . . . Her mother prepared her daughters to go out into the world not only to make their individual marks on it but also to embody her convictions about women's untapped capacities. . . .

. . . In 1874, [Harriot] enrolled at Vassar, the first all-female college established in the United States. There, she elected an unconventional course of study focused on science, politics, and history. Upon graduation, she became a member of the first generation of women college graduates, one of only a few thousand women in the United States who held a bachelor's degree. . . .

[In 1882,] she met William Blatch, the handsome, accommodating son of a wealthy brewer from Basingstoke, Hampshire, England. Harriot and William married in 1882, and the couple's first child Nora (named after the heroine of Ibsen's *A Doll's House*) was born in England the next year. A second child, Helen, born in 1892, died of whooping cough in 1896. Like her mother but with fewer children, more money,

and a compliant husband, Harriot Blatch managed to combine marriage and motherhood with an energetic commitment to reform activities. She joined with veteran British women activists to revive the British suffrage movement. . . . In 1890, she joined the socialist Fabian Society, where she fought for, but failed to win, strong support for women's rights. For two decades as an [expatriate] in Edwardian England, she honed her political skills and updated her mother's feminist convictions, speaking at meetings, writing for suffrage journals, and becoming involved in local politics as a member of the Women's Local Government Society.

In 1902, with her daughter Nora grown and studying engineering at Cornell, and her husband Henry able to retire, Harriot Blatch moved permanently to New York to take up the task she had inherited—leadership of the American suffrage movement. She joined the Women's Trade Union League, a pioneering effort of elite settlement house women and female wage earners joined together to empower, not patronize, working women. There she came to see that to be modern and effective the suffrage movement in the United States must unite women across the classes in a militant effort. She also saw, as other women activists did not, that women's growing interest in electoral politics was crucial to the reinvigoration of the suffrage movement. Like the English suffragist Emmeline Pankhurst, she was committed to forcing the political parties to address the suffrage issue and winning from them the political support necessary to gain victory. . . .

To enact her vision of a militant, democratic suffrage organization based on a coalition of working-class and middle-class working women, Harriot Blatch organized the Equality League of Self-Supporting Women in 1907, renamed the Women's Political Union (WPU) in 1910. Although it gradually moved away from reliance on wage-earning women for its most active participants, the WPU went on to spearhead a political effort to force the New York legislature to pass a bill authorizing a referendum to amend the state constitution to grant women suffrage.

The WPU suffrage campaign, which ran from 1910 to 1915, involved an exhausting and elaborate two-pronged effort: First, both houses of the state legislature had to pass a bill authorizing a referendum on woman suffrage, and then the state's all-male electorate had to approve the referendum.... [S]uffragists in New York took hope from a narrowly won suffrage victory in California in October 1911.... By 1912, California was the sixth state in which women were voting in the presidential election. Blatch and her followers were determined that New York women would do the same in the next presidential election....

Harriot Blatch had a talent and taste for partisan politics that was unusual in the movement. Although many of the new generation of suffragists were college-trained professionals, Mary Beard, the historian and a close friend, wrote of Blatch that more than others, "she worked steadfastly to root the suffrage movement in politics, where alone it could reach its goal."[1] She certainly had the lineage. Her mother and Susan B. Anthony had immersed themselves in party politics. From them, from her father, and from her years in England, Harriot had come to see that if suffragists were ever to win, they would have to go behind the scenes and engage in precisely the political maneuvering and lobbying that women had traditionally repudiated as the unhappy consequence of the male monopoly of public life. While such openly political methods distressed many older women reformers, they invigorated Harriot.

In one episode, which became a staple of suffrage legend, Harriot and other WPU leaders tracked down a particularly elusive senator. By this time, opposition to suffrage had moved from ridicule to avoidance. "The chase led up and down elevators in and out of the Senate chamber and committee rooms." Finally, they ferreted out his hiding place and cornered him; he could no longer avoid the issue. The WPU account reversed the standard metaphors of gender to emphasize the senator's humiliation at the hands of women. "Of slight build," he was literally overpowered by the suffragists. "With Mrs. Blatch walking on one side with her hand resting ever so slightly on his sleeve [sic]," the women led him into the committee room and got his vote. "I'll never forgive this," he told Blatch. "Oh yes, you will," she responded, "some day you will be declaring with pride how your vote advanced the suffrage resolution."[2]

The WPU won a similar battle with Robert Wagner, the new Democratic majority leader of the state Senate and one of the most determined opponents of suffrage in the New York legislature. To prevent Wagner from once again employing the delaying legislative tactics of moving to table or returning the referendum resolution to committee for another year, Harriot arranged for three hundred New York City suffragists to go to Albany to pressure him to set a date for a vote. Some fifty or sixty women crowded into the committee room, with the rest gathered in the corridor outside. When Wagner moved to take his place in the chair at the front of the room, the aisle filled with suffragists. "There were no antisuffragists to rescue him," wrote Harriot later. "There were only all about him, the convinced and ruthless members of the Women's Political Union." He grudgingly agreed to set a date for the state Senate to vote on the suffrage resolution.[3]

In both episodes, the WPU's power rested not only in numbers but also in its willingness to exploit the gendered meanings of power. Wagner yielded because he could not afford to let it be known that he had been physically and politically outmaneuvered by women. The newspapers predictably reported what the women requested, and Wagner graciously granted a date for the Senate vote. But at a time in which accounts of British militant suffragists smashing windows were prominently featured in American papers, the sense of sexual warfare, of women besting men, was close to the surface and hard to overlook.

The Senate debate and vote took place on the date Wagner had guaranteed. Harriot and her followers watched from the gallery. Like good politicians, they had carefully counted their supporters, knew that they had just the right number of votes with not one to spare, and "were full of confidence" that the referendum would carry.[4] Across the hall, the lower house was giving them an unanticipated victory. It looked like the legislative battle might actually be won. But at the last moment a perfidious senator abandoned the public pledge he had given the WPU, shifted his vote, and denied them their victory.

With this undeserved defeat uppermost in her mind, Blatch went to the people. The WPU had organized parades twice before, but the 1912 New York City parade was by far the most carefully organized street demonstration in U.S. suffrage history. The WPU spared no effort at recruiting and educating a large number of marchers and alerting the public to the meaning and significance of the parade. Pledge cards were circulated, committing marchers to take to the streets. Newspapers eagerly covered the clever "stunts" that suffragists devised to advertise the parade: suffragists at the circus, "suffragette hats" for sale at department stores, recruitment booths behind the Public Library.

Harriot was determined that the parade give evidence of a massive, disciplined army of women with which politicians would have to come to terms. She paid great attention to the details of the march, the numbers of marching columns, and the spacing of the lines of marchers. Women were instructed to dress simply, walk erectly, and keep their eyes forward. The spectacle was to be an emotional and sensual evocation of women's power. Opponents, according to Blatch, should be converted through their eyes. "The enemy must see women, marching in increasing numbers year by year out on the public avenues, holding high their banner, Votes For Women." On the appointed day, more than ten thousand took to the streets: women college graduates in their academic gowns, working women by trades and industries, prominent wealthy women, even some men. The president of the national suffrage society marched with a banner that read "Catching Up with China"—a reference to reports that insurgent nationalists in one of China's provincial legislatures had declared women enfranchised. Public demonstrations of this sort were new and a bit daunting to many women. "I marched the whole length," one demonstrator proudly reported to a friend.[5]

In 1912, the emergence of a third national political party, the Progressives, affected the task of getting a suffrage referendum. While Progressive leaders begged women for their support, Blatch was disappointed with the tepid role the party had played in a woman suffrage referendum in Ohio earlier in that year. And former president Theodore Roosevelt, the party's candidate for president in 1912, repeatedly embarrassed himself and his party by sexist declarations that suffragists were "indirectly encouraging immorality."[6] Still, the Progressive Party's support was crucial for the WPU's plans in New York because of the leverage it gave in prying support out of the Republicans, who were struggling to keep voters from bolting to the new party. First the Progressives and then the Republicans endorsed the submission of the suffrage referendum to New York voters at their state conventions. . . .

[T]he Democrats followed the other two parties in urging submission of the referendum. Victory, at least in the legislature, was assured. The election of 1912 swept the Democrats . . . into power in the state, and, under the leadership of Woodrow Wilson, into the presidency as well.

There was a last-minute complication when the Republicans added a clause to the referendum subjecting immigrant women, who were citizens by marriage, to special requirements for voting, and the Democrats objected. The issue was a difficult one for Blatch. On the one hand, she had lost her American citizenship by virtue of her marriage to an Englishman and was sympathetic to women whose citizenship was altered by marriage. On the other hand, like her mother decades before, she had her own nativist prejudices, as did many of her middle-class followers. In the end, she decided the issue politically: Keeping the clause would gain the referendum more upstate Republican votes than it would lose downstate Democrats.

Party leaders followed her lead, and in January 1913, both houses passed legislation proposing an amendment to the state constitution striking out the word male and enfranchising citizens over twenty-one "provided that a citizen by marriage should have been an inhabitant of the United States for five years."[7] Blatch had worked three years for this moment, a long time for a single bill. And even with this victory, the most difficult task lay ahead—the winning of the referendum itself. Now the suffrage leaders would have to convince a majority of New York men to vote for woman suffrage.

Harriot Blatch and the leaders of the WPU had no illusions about how difficult this might be. "The task we must accomplish between now and election day 1915 [when the referendum would appear on the ballot] is a Herculean one, compared to that we have just completed," the Executive Committee of the Women's Political Union declared. Harriot had her misgivings about immigrant voters, with their "Germanic and Hebraic attitude toward women," but she counted on the democratic logic of the situation, believing that men who were being allowed to exercise the franchise could be convinced to vote in favor of women's demand to share it. [But a great deal was riding on the New York referendum. "If we win the Empire State all the states will come tumbling down like a deck of cards," she promised.[8]]

To cultivate the voters, the WPU played on its strengths. It based its suffrage advocacy on the proliferating devices of modern mass culture—forms of commercial recreation, methods of advertising, and the pleasures of consumerism. Californians had used billboards, automobile caravans, and suffrage postcards to bring their cause before the electorate in their successful campaign of 1911. New York women had to do the same. ["If we are to reap a victory in 1915, we must cultivate every inch of soil and sow our suffrage seed broadcast in the Empire state," Harriot declared.[9]]

Such an approach conformed to Harriot's view of democracy which, she believed, should be based on the heart rather than the head. Emotions were the key to popular democracy, not reason. "We learned . . . as we toiled in our campaign," she later wrote, "that sermons and logic would never convince. . . . Human beings move because they feel, not because they think."[10] This was not an expression of any special contempt for either women or working-class voters; on the contrary, she considered men (especially politicians) more irrational than women and the rich more prejudiced and conservative than the poor. She believed particularly that changes in women's status and in power relations between the sexes could never be reduced to rational arguments and dispassionate appeals, even to venerable principles of American democracy such as equality and civic virtue.

"Democracy was the keynote" of the grand suffrage ball that the WPU sponsored in January 1913 to inaugurate the referendum campaign. Extensively advertised, it took place in New York City's Seventy-First Street Armory, which was barely large enough for the eight thousand men and women who attended. Rich and poor, working-class and society women alike paid fifty cents to dance the turkey trot and other popular new dances. The event proved, as the WPU put it, "that love of liberty and democracy did not belong to one class or one sex but is deeply rooted in human nature itself."[11] . . .

Given Harriot's appreciation for the role of emotions in mass politics, she was especially intrigued by new technologies of mass communication. "I stand for the achievements of the twentieth century," she declared. "I will make use of . . . anything which civilization places at my command."[12] Lee de Forest, her

former son-in-law (Nora's brief marriage to him had ended after a year), was one of the pioneers of modern radio broadcasting. . . . At his invitation, she delivered a radio talk on woman suffrage from the newly opened broadcasting station in downtown Manhattan.

Moving pictures represented another new technology with political possibilities. The WPU arranged for a commercial movie company to produce *The Suffragette and the Man*, a romantic comedy in which the beautiful young heroine, forced to choose between her suffrage principles and her fiancé, first picks principles and then overcomes an anti-suffrage competitor and wins back her lover.

In 1913, the WPU collaborated on a second movie entitled *What 8,000,000 Women Want*. This time the romantic triangle did not involve good and bad men fighting for a heroine's heart but good and bad politics fighting for the hero's soul. Newsreel footage of actual suffrage parades was interspersed with the dramatic action. Harriot played herself and brought to the screen her self-confident authority and her genuine pleasure at conducting the struggle. . . .

[In 1913, as in previous years, the most spectacular suffrage event was the parade organized by the WPU. Each year, the parades had become more stunning affairs, symbolically conveying both the diversity and the unity of modern women.] The 1913 parade was one of the high points of Harriot's suffrage leadership. "We will muster an army fifty thousand strong this year," she predicted. The marchers were arranged by divisions. At the head were two dozen female marshals mounted on horseback and dressed in stylish adaptations of men's evening wear, black cutaways and silk hats with streamers of green, purple, and white, the WPU's colors and those of the movement in England. Leading them, dressed in white and astride a white horse, was Inez Millholland, "the official beauty of the parade." The intention was to provide unforgettable visual images of all kinds of women marching shoulder to shoulder together. "In these times of class wars," Harriot observed, could men really afford "to shut out from public affairs that fine spirit of fellowship" that suffragism represented?[13]

The effectiveness of the parade as political propaganda infuriated antisuffragists, for whom the spectacular aspect of the movement was proof positive of the social and cultural upheaval that votes for women threatened. The antisuffragists charged that the bold stance of the marchers smacked of the deliberate exploitation of "sex appeal." . . . Harriot Blatch found the charges amusing. "Funny idea of sex appeal. Twenty thousand women turn out on a hot day. 87 degrees and march up Fifth Avenue to the blaring music of thirty-five bands; eyes straight to the front; faces red with the hot sun. . . . If it had been mellow moonlight. . . . But a sex appeal set to brass bands! That certainly is a new one."[14] The WPU was determined to finesse the conventional notions of female beauty that had so long restrained women's public activities. . . .

During the legislative lobbying years from 1910 to 1913, Harriot and the WPU had not faced much organizational opposition within the New York suffrage movement. The state suffrage organization was small and ineffective. But once the referendum campaigning began in earnest, the Woman's Political Union, led by the blunt, sometimes undiplomatic Blatch, came into direct conflict with the other great figure of New York suffragism, the moderate, circumspect Carrie Chapman Catt. Within the women's movement, Catt embodied the progressive faith in organizational structure and administrative centralization. In contrast, Harriot celebrated individual initiative, modern invention, and personal freedom. Notwithstanding lofty suffrage rhetoric about the unity of all womanhood and the solidarity of the sex, these two were bound to clash. . . . Catt was always more concerned to unify and reconcile all existing suffragists than to reach out and create new ones. While some activists believed that Blatch was autocratic and highhanded, the ever-diplomatic Catt prized harmony within the movement above all things. Catt's efforts went to creating internal order rather than tackling external obstacles. Unlike Blatch, Catt had little skill or interest in the intricacies of partisan politics and legislative maneuvers.

Catt's plan was to bring all the suffrage societies in New York . . . under one wing, but the Women's Political Union [crucial to her efforts and the richest organization in the state] refused to subsume itself under Catt's leadership. . . . By 1914, it was clear that two parallel suffrage campaigns would be conducted in New York, one by Catt's Empire State Campaign Committee and the other by Harriot Blatch's Women's Political Union. Both raised money for the referendum effort; both sent paid agents around the state; both set up separate offices, sometimes generating considerable conflict among activists in smaller communities in upstate New York. The suffrage movement had survived previous internal divisions and would face others in the future. . . .

In the last six months of the campaign, the WPU flooded the state with publicity-generating gimmicks and stunts. Suffragists played both ends of the gender divide to demonstrate that they could join in traditional male activities as good fellows and at the same time retain their female virtue. On Suffrage Day at the Polo Grounds, New York suffrage organizations competed with each other to sell tickets to a benefit baseball game between the New York Giants and the Chicago Cubs. . . . To counter the anti-suffrage claims that they were bitter women who wanted the ballot as compensation for their inability to find husbands, they even held a series of "married couple days," in which husbands and wives declared their mutual happiness and support of votes for women. . . .

Ten weeks before the end of the campaign, Harriot's single-minded attention to the cause was shattered by the sudden death of her husband, William Blatch, who was accidentally electrocuted. . . . Before leaving [for England to tend to her husband's estate], she took advantage of one benefit of widowhood and resumed her U.S. citizenship. Harriot's decision to leave the country so close to the end of the 1915 campaign is something of a puzzle. She could have postponed the trip a few months. Moreover, England was already at war with Germany, and the transatlantic trip was dangerous. Perhaps she was growing weary of the unrelenting labor of trying to convert New York voters, or perhaps she sensed that she was losing her position as New York's foremost suffragist to Carrie Chapman Catt. . . . By the time she returned in mid-October, the Empire State Campaign Committee . . . had taken over organization of the final suffrage parade. . . .

November 2, 1915, the day toward which Harriot Blatch, Carrie Catt, and thousands of other New York women had been working for years, was the kind of warm, sunny day for which hard-working campaigners pray. When the polls opened at 6 A.M., several thousand suffrage activists were in their places as pollwatchers, guarding against any effort to cheat them of their victory. . . .

By midnight, it was clear that the woman suffrage amendment had been defeated. Out of 1,200,000 votes cast across the state, woman suffrage had been defeated by 190,000 votes, about 16 percent of the total. All the boroughs of New York City voted against woman suffrage as well as fifty-six of the state's sixty-one counties.

Most New York suffragists kept the bitter disappointment they felt to themselves and declared the referendum a moral triumph. "On the whole we have achieved a wonderful victory," Carrie Chapman Catt proclaimed. "It was short of our hopes but the most contemptuous opponents speak with newly acquired respect for our movement."[15] Catt's wing of the campaign announced the day after the election that a second referendum campaign would begin as soon as state law permitted. . . .

Harriot Blatch was one of the few suffrage leaders who dared to react with open anger. She was "disgusted at the conditions which had forced women to campaign in the streets" and humiliated at having to appeal to immigrant men to gain her native-born rights as an American citizen.[16] She vowed she would never make another street-corner speech. Her retreat into this outraged elitism recalled her mother's reaction to her own crushing disappointment at the failure of the Reconstruction constitutional amendments to include women. Blatch also blamed the suffrage forces themselves for the defeat, at least the Catt wing of the movement, which she thought had neglected upstate New York. She believed a second referendum would be a mistake because the antisuffragists would be even better organized for the next round.

In this she was wrong. In 1917, a second voters' referendum was victorious in New York, thus winning an incalculably important political prize in the battle that was intensifying nationwide. Yet Harriot was correct in a larger way. The era of state suffrage referenda was over; with the exception of New York, no other state was won by this method after 1915. From this point on, attention, energy, and political initiative shifted to the federal arena, to the constitutional amendment Elizabeth Cady Stanton and Susan B. Anthony had first introduced and

which had been stalled in congressional committee for almost fifty years. In less than five years, the amendment was moved onto the floor, secured a two-thirds vote in the House and three years later in the Senate, and was ratified by three-quarters of the state legislatures to become the law of the land. . . .

NOTES

1. "Foreword" by Mary Beard, in Harriot Stanton Blatch and Alma Lutz, *Challenging Years: The Memoirs of Harriot Stanton Blatch* (New York: G. P. Putnam's Sons, 1940), p. vii.

2. Nora de Forest, "Political History of Women's Political Union," reel 1, Harriot Stanton Blatch Papers, Library of Congress, pp. 13–14; *Challenging Years*, pp. 162–63.

3. *Challenging Years*, pp. 163–64.

4. Ibid., pp. 169–70; Women's Political Union 1912–1913 Annual Report, pp. 7–8.

5. *Challenging Years*, p. 180; "Chinese Women Parade for Suffrage," *New York Times*, April 14, 1912, pt. 7, p. 5; Katherine Devereux Blake to Alice Park, n.d., Susan B. Anthony Memorial Collection, Huntington Library, San Marino, CA.

6. "Roosevelt Is for Woman Suffrage," *New York Times*, February 3, 1912, p. 7.

7. "Official Copy of Proposed Amendment," November 2, 1915, Blatch Papers, Library of Congress.

8. "The Referendum Policy of the Women's Political Union," p. 19, reel 1, Blatch Papers, Library of Congress. "Mrs. Blatch Plans Hot Fight to Win New York to Suffrage," *Chicago Tribune*, March 16, 1913. Blatch to Alice Paul, August 26, 1913, reel 4, National Woman's Party Papers: Suffrage Years.

9. Blatch, "Seed Time and Harvest," *Women's Political World*, June 16, 1913, p. 2.

10. *Challenging Years*, p. 192.

11. "Suffragists Tour City to Boom Ball," *New York Daily Mail*, January 11, 1913; "Charity Versus Votes," *Women's Political World*, January 15, 1913, p. 7.

12. "Barnard Girls Test Wireless Phones," *New York Times*, February 26, 1909, p. 7.

13. ". . . with Suffrage Workers," *New York Post*, March 7, 1913; "Eyes to the Front," *New York Tribune*, May 3, 1913; Blatch, "A Reviewing Stand," *Women's Political World*, May 15, 1913, p. 1.

14. "Answers Anti Attack," *New York Times*, May 13, 1913, p. 3.

15. Catt to Mary Grey Peck, December 12, 1912, Catt Papers, Library of Congress.

16. "Mrs. Blatch Pours Out Wrath . . . ," *New York Times*, November 4, 1915, p. 3.

Chinese Exclusion: The Page Act and Its Aftermath

Named for the California congressman Horace F. Page, who was its most ardent supporter, the Page Act of 1875 was the nation's first federal exclusion of certain kinds of immigrants. Public and congressional debate on expanding the statute continued, and within seven years, the much more expansive Chinese Exclusion Act of 1882 barred virtually all but elite Chinese from entering the United States and reiterated the exclusion of women. "The Exclusion Act is clearly the pivot on which all American immigration policy turned," writes historian Roger Daniels, "the hinge on which Emma Lazarus's 'Golden Door' began to swing toward a closed position. It initiated an era of steadily increasing restrictions on immigration of all kinds that lasted until 1943."* Not until our alliance with China in World War II was the Chinese exclusion law repealed.

The Page Act, like the more capacious legislation that followed, was fueled by a mixture of policies: racist hostility to Asians; hostility to unscrupulous entrepreneurs who recruited unskilled workers, pressured them into multiyear contracts, brought them to the United States, and then undercut established wages; and authentic fears of prostitution rings. Knowledge that Chinese families practiced polygamy and foot-binding fueled generalizations about immorality and sexual exploitation. One San Francisco politician conceded that "as a class Chinese are intelligent," but insisted that among "the multitudes of Chinese women in our state there is not a wife or virtuous female in their number."†

The Page Act gestured in the direction of outlawing contract labor but actually focused on trafficking in women. It made the American consular officers in Chinese ports responsible for interrogating all prospective immigrants; in practice, any woman who wished to travel to the United States had first to persuade the consul that she was not a prostitute. Memories of this humiliating experience have been passed down over many generations in some Chinese-American families.

The impact of the law was quickly felt. In the two years between 1880 and 1882, some 50,000 Chinese men entered the United States, but only 220 Chinese women did so. In 1910 the gender ratio among Chinese in the United States was 14:1. The principle that prospective immigrant women had the additional burden of proving their morality persisted. The 1891 Immigration Act required all incoming pregnant women to prove that they were married. It also provided for the

---

*Roger Daniels, *Guarding the Golden Door: American Immigration Policy and Immigrants since 1882* (New York: Hill and Wang, 2004), p. 19.
†For a helpful overview, see Martha Gardner, *The Qualities of a Citizen: Women, Immigration, and Citizenship, 1870–1965* (Princeton, N.J.: Princeton University Press, 2005).

Page Act of 1875, 43rd Cong., 2nd sess., ch. 141.

expulsion of immigrants who became a public charge within a year of entry. That time limit was gradually expanded—to two years, then three, then five. In 1910, a new statute provided that alien women who turned to sex work could be deported at any time. In the debates over immigration policy in the early twenty-first century, shrill accusations against pregnant women seeking entry are again heard. Why do you think immigration officials and the American public are so concerned about female sexuality and reproductive capabilities?

The second gatekeeping mechanism in the Page Act (see the final paragraph) took on renewed vigor in later acts and with the construction of immigrant receiving stations—Ellis Island in New York Harbor in 1892 and Angel Island in San Francisco Bay in 1910. At the latter, Asian immigrant women tended to be detained longer than men, as well as grilled about their sexual character, plans to marry (if single), and ability to support themselves in the United States. See photograph on p. 341.

Be it enacted . . . that in determining whether the immigration of any subject of China, Japan, or any Oriental country, to the United States, is free and voluntary . . . it shall be the duty of the . . . consul of the United States residing at the port from which it is proposed to convey such subjects, in any vessels enrolled or licensed in the United States . . . to ascertain whether such immigrant has entered into a contract or agreement for a term of service within the United States, for lewd and immoral purposes; and if there be such contract or agreement, the said . . . consul shall not deliver the required permit or certificate . . .

. . . That the importation into the United States of women for the purposes of prostitution is hereby forbidden; and all contracts and agreements in relation thereto, made in advance or in pursuance of such illegal importation and purposes, are hereby declared void; and whoever shall knowingly and willfully import, or cause any importation of, women into the United States for the purposes of prostitution, or shall knowingly or willfully hold, or attempt to hold, any woman to such purposes, in pursuance of such illegal importation and contract or agreement, shall be deemed guilty of a felony, and, on conviction thereof, shall be imprisoned not exceeding five years and pay a fine not exceeding five thousand dollars . . .

. . . That it shall be unlawful for aliens of the following [two] classes to immigrate into the United States, namely, persons who are undergoing a sentence for conviction in their own country of felonious crimes other than political . . . and women "imported for the purposes of prostitution." Every vessel arriving in the United States may be inspected under the direction of the collector of the port at which it arrives, if he shall have reason to believe that any such obnoxious persons are on board. . . .

Mackenzie v. Hare, 1915

The persistent expansion of married women's property acts and the increasing popularity of woman suffrage make it tempting to conclude that the practice of coverture—women's legal and civic subordination to men—steadily dissolved over the course of the nineteenth and early twentieth centuries. But although it is true that some aspects of coverture eroded, others were sustained and even strengthened.

Mackenzie v. Hare, 239 U.S. 299 (1915).

Although Chief Justice Morrison R. Waite had been right when he observed in *Minor v. Happersett* (1874) (pp. 294–295) that "[t]here is no doubt that women may be citizens," he was wrong when he went on to claim that "sex has never been made one of the elements of citizenship. . . . [M]en have never had an advantage over women." According to the common law and early American practice, white women, like men, became citizens either by birth or by their own choice to be naturalized. But in 1855, following practices established in France by the conservative Code Napoleon (1804) and in Britain in 1844, the U.S. Congress extended the principle of marital unity to provide that "any woman who might lawfully be naturalized under the existing laws, married, or shall be married to a citizen of the United States shall be deemed and taken to be a citizen." That is, foreign women who married male citizens did not need to go through a naturalization process or even take an oath of allegiance. The law did not explain what should happen when a woman with U.S. citizenship married a noncitizen man. For the next fifty years, there was little consistency in how courts dealt with related cases that came before them. Often the principle of "marital unity" prevailed, meaning that women who were American citizens lost their citizenship by marrying a foreign national. In 1907, Congress passed a statute explicitly providing that women take the nationality of their husbands when they marry.

Expatriation—the loss of citizenship—traditionally has been a very severe punishment, usually reserved for cases of treason. If a married woman had to assume the nationality of her husband, she might become the subject of a king or czar in a political system that offered her even less protection than did the United States. She might even become stateless. If Americans claimed to base their political system on the "consent of the governed," could women's "consent" be arbitrarily denied? In time of war, the American woman who married, say, a German national could change her status overnight from a citizen to an alien enemy. President Ulysses S. Grant's daughter lost her citizenship when she married an Englishman in 1874; it required a special act of Congress to reinstate her citizenship when she returned from England as a widow in 1898.

Ethel Mackenzie, who had been born in California, married Gordon Mackenzie, a British subject, in 1909—two years after the passage of the Citizenship Act of 1907. She was active in the woman suffrage movement in California, and when it was successful in 1911 she worked in the San Francisco voter registration drive. It is not surprising that she herself should try to register to vote. When the Board of Election Commissioners denied her application, holding that upon her marriage to a British subject she had "ceased to be a citizen of the United States," she refused to let her husband apply for citizenship and instead challenged the law, claiming that Congress had exceeded its authority. She could not believe that Congress had actually *intended* to deprive her of the citizenship she understood to be her birthright. Why did the Supreme Court deny her claim? What "ancient principle of jurisprudence" did they rely on? Why did the Court think that the marriage of an American woman to a foreign man should be treated differently from the marriage of an American man to a foreign woman?

MR. JUSTICE MCKENNA:

. . . The question . . . is, Did [Ethel Mackenzie] cease to be a citizen by her marriage? . . . [Mackenzie contends] that it was not the intention [of Congress] to deprive an American-born woman, remaining within the jurisdiction of the United States, of her citizenship by reason of her marriage to a resident foreigner. . . . [She is trying to persuade the Court that the citizenship statute was] beyond the authority of

Congress.... [She offered the] earnest argument ... that ... under the Constitution and laws of the United States, [citizenship] became a right, privilege and immunity which could not be taken away from her except as a punishment for crime or by her voluntary expatriation....

[But the Court concludes:] ... The identity of husband and wife is an ancient principle of our jurisprudence. It was neither accidental nor arbitrary and worked in many instances for her protection. There has been, it is true, much relaxation of it but in its retention as in its origin it is determined by their intimate relation and unity of interests, and this relation and unity may make it of public concern in many instances to merge their identity, and give dominance to the husband. It has purpose, if not necessity, in purely domestic policy; it has greater purpose and, it may be, necessity, in international policy.... Having this purpose, has it not the sanction of power?

... The law in controversy deals with a condition voluntarily entered into.... The marriage of an American woman with a foreigner has consequences ... [similar to] her physical expatriation.... Therefore, as long as the relation lasts it is made tantamount to expatriation. This is no arbitrary exercise of government.... It is the conception of the legislation under review that such an act [marriage to a foreign man] may bring the Government into embarrassments and, it may be, into controversies.... [Marriage to a foreign man] is as voluntary and distinctive as expatriation and its consequence must be considered as elected.

The decision in *Mackenzie* angered suffragists and energized them; American women needed suffrage to protect themselves against involuntary expatriation and statelessness. The repeal of the Citizenship Act of 1907 was high on the suffragists' agenda, and they returned to it as soon as suffrage was accomplished (see Equal Suffrage [Nineteenth] Amendment). The Cable Act of 1922 provided that "the right of a person to become a naturalized citizen shall not be denied to a person on account of sex or because she is a married woman," but it permitted American women who married foreigners to retain their citizenship only if they married men from countries whose subjects were eligible for U.S. citizenship— that is, not from China or Japan. American-born women who married aliens from China or Japan still lost their citizenship. American-born women who married aliens not from China or Japan were treated as naturalized citizens who would lose their citizenship should they reside abroad for two years.

The Cable Act was extended by amendments well into the 1930s, but some exclusions remained, and the improvements were generally not retroactive. Thus, as late as the 1950s, some American-born women were denied passports because they had married foreign men before 1922. In 1998, 2001, and again in 2011, the U.S. Supreme Court upheld a practice of different rules for non-marital children born abroad. The child born to an unmarried citizen mother and a noncitizen man is a citizen at birth (so long as the mother has lived in the United States for at least one year). The child born to an unmarried citizen father and a noncitizen woman can be a citizen only if the father has met a number of requirements. Among them are that he must have lived in the United States for a specified number of years after he reached the age of fourteen. (The number of years changed when Congress revised the statute: until 1986 it was five years; then it was reduced to two years.) The father must also formally legitimize and financially support the child before the child reaches the age of eighteen.*

---

*Miller v. Albright , 523 U.S. 420 (1998); Nguyen v. Immigration and Naturalization Service, 533 U.S. 53 (2001); Flores-Villar v. United States, 131 S. Ct 2312 (2011). This note draws on Candice Lewis Bredbenner, *A Nationality of Her Own: Women, Marriage and the Law of Citizenship* (Berkeley: University of California Press, 1998).

In sustaining different rules for mothers and fathers, the Supreme Court majority emphasized the possibility of fraudulent claims of citizenship by unmarried noncitizen mothers and their children; the dissenting minority emphasized the ease with which men could avoid responsibility for the nonmarital children they had fathered.

Equal Suffrage (Nineteenth) Amendment, 1920

When the Fourteenth and Fifteenth Amendments (see p. 289) failed to provide for universal suffrage, a federal amendment was introduced into the Senate by S. C. Pomeroy of Kansas in 1868 and into the House by George W. Julian of Indiana in March 1869. Historian Ellen DuBois has observed, "Previously the case for suffrage had consistently been put in terms of the individual rights of all persons, regardless of their sex and race. Angered by their exclusion from the Fifteenth Amendment, women's rights advocates began to develop fundamentally different arguments for their cause. They claimed their right to the ballot not as individuals but as a sex. . . . The reason women should vote was not that they were the same as men but that they were different. That made for a rather thorough reversal of classic women's rights premises."*

Arguing for the vote on the basis of women's *difference* from men could be effective in strengthening women's sense of group consciousness, but it also was compatible with racist and nativist arguments that white women needed the vote to counteract the suffrage of black and immigrant men. The old alliance of woman suffrage and abolitionist activism eroded, even though voting rights for black men were under siege after Reconstruction. The suffrage efforts of 1870 to 1920 continued to display arguments on the basis of equality, but younger generations of activists were increasingly likely to emphasize difference—what one activist called "the mother instinct for government."

Woman suffrage was not accomplished easily. One scholar has counted 480 suffrage campaigns waged at the state level between 1870 and 1910, but in the end only seventeen referenda were held, with only two successes (in Colorado and Idaho).** Stanton died in 1902; Anthony in 1906. But a new, younger generation adopted new strategies. Americans were inspired by the militancy of the British suffrage movement. In 1902 Carrie Chapman Catt was simultaneously president of the International Woman Suffrage Alliance and the National American Woman Suffrage Association (NAWSA). By 1910 it was clear that a reinvigorated movement was under way, using door-to-door campaigns, street-corner speakers, and poll watchers on Election Day. For the first time, cross-class suffrage organizations, like New York's Equality League of Independent Women, were mobilizing

---

*Ellen Carol DuBois, "Outgrowing the Compact of the Fathers: Equal Rights, Woman Suffrage, and the United States Constitution, 1820–1878," *Journal of American History* 74 (December 1987): 848.

**Eleanor Flexner, *Century of Struggle* (Cambridge, Mass.: Belknap Press of Harvard University Press, 1959), 13; Rebecca Edwards, "Pioneers at the Polls: Woman Suffrage in the West," in *Votes for Women: The Struggle for Suffrage Revisited*, ed. Jean H. Baker (New York: Oxford University Press, 2002), pp. 90–101.

support for suffrage. Suffragists staged public parades that attracted tens of thousands of supporters.

Although many suffragists had claimed that when women got the vote, there would be no more American endorsements of war, Catt swung NAWSA behind Woodrow Wilson, American support for the allies, and, eventually, the nation's entry into World War I in April 1917. The more radical National Women's Party (NWP), under the leadership of Alice Paul, staked out a very public position protesting Wilson's failure to explicitly endorse a federal guarantee for women's suffrage. (For an image and more on the story of the NWP's picketing of the White House in 1917, see p. 261) Putting aside his states' rights approach, the president publicly endorsed a constitutional amendment in early 1918. One day later, the House of Representatives passed the suffrage amendment, barely achieving the required two-thirds majority. But despite a personal appearance from Wilson, it failed by only two votes to carry the Senate.

As state after state enacted woman suffrage for statewide elections, the number of members of Congress dependent on women's votes increased. With the federal suffrage amendment slated to come before Congress again and again, these men were likely to believe that they had no choice but to support it. In the fall 1918 elections, NAWSA targeted four senators for defeat; two of them failed to be reelected. Moreover, energetic campaigns in the states to elect prosuffrage candidates to Congress worked. When the amendment came up in the new Congress, according to Anne F. Scott and Andrew Scott, "224 of those voting yes came from suffrage states, and eighty from nonsuffrage states."[†] It squeaked by in the Senate. It was ratified by thirty-five states by August 1920; the final state was Tennessee, where, after a bitter struggle, it was ratified by a single vote, just in time to permit women to vote in the elections of 1920.

When Puerto Rican women attempted to register to vote in 1920, however, the U.S. Bureau of Insular Affairs decided that the Nineteenth Amendment did not automatically apply to U.S. territories. Suffragist groups mobilized in Puerto Rico, lobbying throughout the next decade both on the island and in Washington, D.C., with support from the NWP. In 1929 the territorial legislature granted suffrage to women restricted by a literacy requirement; not until 1935 was universal suffrage established in Puerto Rico.

Many southern states had excluded African American men from voting by using literacy tests, poll taxes, and intimidation; in those states black women could vote no more easily than black men, and suffrage was an empty victory. The state of Georgia effectively discouraged white women from voting as well by providing that any woman who did not choose to register to vote did not have to pay the poll tax. This law, which encouraged women—and their husbands—to see voting as an expensive extravagance, was upheld by the U.S. Supreme Court in 1937 (*Breedlove v. Suttles*, 302 U.S. 277).

Section 1. The right of the citizens of the United States to vote shall not be denied or abridged by the United States or by any State on account of sex.

Section 2. Congress shall have power to enforce this article by appropriate legislation.

[†]Anne F. Scott and Andrew MacKay Scott, *One Half the People: The Fight for Woman Suffrage* (Urbana: University of Illinois Press, 1982; orig. publ. Philadelphia: Lippincott, 1975), p. 45.

IV

STORMS ON MANY FRONTS

1920–1945

SEXUALITY AND THE BODY

JOAN JACOBS BRUMBERG
Fasting Girls: The Emerging Ideal of Slenderness in American Culture

Although anorexia nervosa is generally considered a modern disease, appetite control has long been an important dimension of female experience. Joan Jacobs Brumberg's pioneering study of anorexia nervosa traces changing cultural pressure on women to control their appetite. Exploring the links between food and femininity in the nineteenth century, Brumberg found that by 1890 thinness had become a way in which young privileged women could distance themselves from their working-class counterparts. More important, food preferences and thin bodies also sent moral and aesthetic messages. The young woman whose frail, delicate frame demonstrated her rejection of all carnal appetites more closely approached the Victorian ideal of femininity than did her more robust counterpart whose heavier physique signaled sexual craving. The twentieth century brought additional pressures to control body weight, according to Brumberg, with the development of scientific nutrition and the standard sizing of clothes. By 1920, fat had become a moral issue. Combined with social changes having to do with food and sexuality occurring in the 1960s, the stage was set for the epidemic of eating disorders evident in the 1980s and 1990s. What evidence is there of the persistence of these disorders in the twenty-first century? What is it that we expect our bodies to convey?

Within the first two decades of the twentieth century, even before the advent of the flapper, the voice of American women revealed that the female struggle with weight was under way and was becoming intensely personal. As early as 1907 an *Atlantic Monthly* article described the reaction of a woman trying on a dress she had not worn for over a year: "The gown was neither more [n]or less than anticipated. But I ... *the fault was on me* ... I was more! Gasping I hooked it together. The gown was hopeless, and I ... I am fat."[1] ... By the twentieth century ... overweight in women was not only a physical liability, it was a character flaw and a social impediment.

Early in the century elite American women began to take body weight seriously as fat became an aesthetic liability for those who followed the world of haute couture. Since the mid-nineteenth century wealthy Americans—the wives of J. P. Morgan, Cornelius Vanderbilt, and Harry Harkness Flagler, for instance—had traveled to Paris to purchase the latest creations from couturier collections such as those on view at Maison Worth on the famed rue de la Paix. The couturier was not just a dressmaker who made clothes for an individual woman; rather, the couturier fashioned "a look" or a collection of dresses for an abstraction—the stylish woman. In order to be stylish and wear couturier clothes, a woman's body had to conform to the dress rather than the dress to the body, as had been the case when the traditional dressmaker fitted each garment.[2] . . .

In 1908 the world of women's fashion was revolutionized by Paul Poiret, whose new silhouette was slim and straight. . . . Almost immediately women of style began to purchase new kinds of undergarments that would make Poiret's look possible; for example, the traditional hourglass corset was cast aside for a rubber girdle to retract the hips.

After World War I the French continued to set the fashion standard for style-conscious American women. In 1922 Jeanne Lanvin's chemise, a straight frock with a simple bateau neckline, was transformed by Gabrielle Chanel into the uniform of the flapper. Chanel dropped the waistline to the hips and began to expose more of the leg: in 1922 she moved her hemlines to midcalf, and in 1926–27 the ideal hem was raised to just below the knee. In order to look good in Chanel's fashionable little dress, its wearer had to think not only about the appearance of her legs but about the smoothness of her form.[3] Women who wore the flapper uniform turned to flattening brassieres constructed of shoulder straps and a single band of material that encased the body from chest to waist. In 1914 a French physician commented on the revised dimensions of women's bodies: "Nowadays it is not the fashion to be corpulent; the proper thing is to have a slight, graceful figure far removed from embonpoint, and *a fortiori* from obesity. For once, the physician is called upon to interest himself in the question of feminine aesthetics."[4]

The slenderized fashion image of the French was picked up and promoted by America's burgeoning ready-to-wear garment industry.[5] Stimulated by the popularity of the Gibson girl and the shirtwaist craze of the 1890s, ready-to-wear production in the United States accelerated in the first two decades of the twentieth century. Chanel's chemise dress was a further boon to the garment industry. Because of its simple cut, the chemise was easy to copy and produce, realities that explain its quick adoption as the uniform of the 1920s. According to a 1923 *Vogue*, the American ready-to-wear industry successfully democratized French fashion: "Today, the mode which originates in Paris is a factor in the lives of women of every rank, from the highest to the lowest."[6]

In order to market ready-to-wear clothing, the industry turned in the 1920s to standard sizing, an innovation that put increased emphasis on personal body size and gave legitimacy to the idea of a normative size range. For women, shopping for ready-to-wear clothes in the bustling department stores of the early twentieth century fostered heightened concern about body size.[7] With a dressmaker, every style was theoretically available to every body; with standard sizing, items of clothing could be identified as desirable, only to be rejected on the grounds of fit. (For women the cost of altering a ready-made garment was an "add-on"; for men it was not.) Female figure flaws became a source of frustration and embarrassment, not easily hidden from those who accompanied the shopper or from salesclerks. Experiences in department-store dressing rooms created a host of new anxieties for women and girls who could not fit into stylish clothing. . . .

Ironically, standard sizing created an unexpected experience of frustration in a marketplace that otherwise was offering a continually expansive opportunity for gratification via purchasable goods. Because many manufacturers of stylish women's garments did not make clothing in large sizes, heavy women were at the greatest disadvantage. In addition to the moral [disgrace] of overweight, the standardization of garment production precluded fat women's participation in the mainstream of fashion. This situation became worse as the century progressed. Fashion photography was professionalized, a development that paralleled the growth of modern advertising, and models became slimmer both to compensate for the distortions of the camera and to accommodate the new merchandising canon—modern fashion was best displayed on a lean body.[8]

The appearance in 1918 of America's first best-selling weight-control book confirmed that weight was a source of anxiety among women and that fat was out of fashion. *Diet and Health with a Key to the Calories* by Lulu Hunt Peters was directed at a female audience and based on the assumption that most readers wanted to lose rather than gain weight. . . . "You should know and also use the word calorie as frequently, or more frequently, than you use the words foot, yard, quart, gallon and so forth. . . . Hereafter you are going to eat calories of food. Instead of saying one slice of bread, or a piece of pie, you will say 100 calories of bread, 350 calories of pie."[9]

Peters' book was popular because it was personal and timely. Her 1918 appeal was related to food shortages caused by the exigencies of the war in Europe. Peters told her readers that it was "more important than ever to reduce" and recommended the formation of local Watch Your Weight Anti-Kaiser Classes. "There are hundreds of thousands of individuals all over America who are hoarding food," she wrote. "They have vast amounts of this valuable commodity stored away in their own anatomy." In good-humored fashion Peters portrayed her own calories counting as both an act of patriotism and humanitarianism:

> I am reducing and the money that I can save will help keep a child from starving . . . [I am explaining to my friends] that for every pang of hunger we feel we can have a double joy, that of knowing we are saving worse pangs in some little children, and that of knowing that for every pang we feel we lose a pound. A pang's a pound the world around we'll say.[10]

But Peters showed herself to be more than simply an informative and patriotic physician. Confessing that she once weighed as much as 200 pounds, the author also understood that heavy women were ashamed of their bulk and unlikely to reveal their actual weight. Peters observed that it was not a happy situation for fat women. "You are viewed with distrust, suspicion, and even aversion," she told her overweight readers. . . .

Peters' book was among the first to articulate the new secular credo of physical denial: modern women suffered to be beautiful (thin) rather than pious. Peters' language and thinking reverberated with references to religious ideas of temptation and sin. For the modern female dieter, sweets, particularly chocolate, were the ultimate temptation. Eating chocolate violated the morality of the dieter and her dedication to her ideal, a slim body. Peters joked about her cravings ("My idea of heaven is a place with me and mine on a cloud of whipped cream") but she was adamant about the fact that indulgence must ultimately be paid for. "If you think you will die unless you have some chocolate creams [go on a] *debauch*," she advised. "'Eat 10 or so' but then *repent* with a 50-calorie dinner of bouillon and crackers." (Italics added.)[11]

Although the damage done by chocolate creams could be mediated by either fasting or more rigid dieting, Peters explained that there

was a psychological cost in yielding to the temptation of candy or rich desserts. Like so many modern dieters, Peters wrote about the issue of guilt followed by redemption through parsimonious eating: "Every supposed pleasure in sin [eating] will furnish more than its equivalent of pain [dieting]." But appetite control was not only a question of learning to delay gratification, it was also an issue of self-esteem. "You will be tempted quite frequently, and you will have to choose whether you will enjoy yourself hugely in the twenty minutes or so that you will be consuming the excess calories, or whether you will dislike yourself cordially for the two or three days you lose by your lack of will power." For Peters dieting had as much to do with the mind as with the body. "There is a great deal of psychology to reducing," she wrote astutely.[12] In fact, with the popularization of the concept of calorie counting, physical features once regarded as natural—such as appetite and body weight—were designated as objects of conscious control. The notion of weight control through restriction of calories implied that . . . overweight resulted solely from lack of control; to be a fat woman constituted a failure of personal morality.

The tendency to talk about female dieting as a moral issue was particularly strong among the popular beauty experts, that is, those in the fashion and cosmetics industry who sold scientific advice on how to become and stay beautiful. Many early-twentieth-century beauty culturists, including Grace Peckham Murray, Helena Rubenstein, and Hazel Bishop, studied chemistry and medical specialties such as dermatology. The creams and lotions they created, as well as the electrical gadgets they promoted, were intended to bring the findings of modern chemistry and physiology to the problem of female beauty. Nevertheless, women could not rely entirely on scientifically achieved results. The beauty experts also preached the credo of self-denial: to be beautiful, most women must suffer.

Because they regarded fat women as an affront to their faith, some were willing to criminalize as well as medicalize obesity. In 1902 *Vogue* speculated, "To judge by the efforts of the majority of women to attain slender and sylphlike proportions, one would fancy it a crime to be fat." By 1918 the message was more distinct: "There is one crime against the modern ethics of beauty which is unpardonable; far better it is to commit any number of petty crimes than to be guilty of the sin of growing fat." By 1930 there was no turning back. Helena Rubenstein, a high priestess of the faith, articulated in *The Art of Feminine Beauty* the moral and aesthetic dictum that would govern the lives of subsequent generations of women: "An abundance of fat is something repulsive and not in accord with the principles that rule our conception of the beautiful.[13] . . .

In adolescence fat was considered a particular liability because of the social strains associated with that stage of life. In the 1940s articles with titles such as "What to Do about the Fat Child at Puberty," "Reducing the Adolescent," and "Should the Teens Diet?" captured the rising interest in adolescent weight control.[14] Women's magazines, reflecting the concerns of mothers anxious to save their daughters from social ostracism, for the first time promoted diets for young girls. According to the *Ladies' Home Journal:* "Appearance plays too important a part in a girl's life not to have her grow up to be beauty-conscious. Girls should be encouraged to take an interest in their appearance when they are very young."[15] . . . Adolescent weight control was also promoted by popular magazines hoping to sell products to young women. . . . *Seventeen's* adoption of the cause of weight control confirmed that slimness was a critical dimension of adolescent beauty and that a new constituency, high school girls, was learning how to diet. From 1944 [when it was founded] to 1948, *Seventeen* had published a full complement of articles on nutrition but almost nothing on weight control. Following the mode of earlier home economists and scientific nutritionists, the magazine had presented basic information about food groups and the importance of each in the daily diet; balance but not calories had been the initial focus. In 1948, however, *Seventeen* proclaimed overweight a medical problem and began educating its young readers about calories and the psychology of eating. Adolescent girls were warned against using eating as a form of emotional expression (do not "pamper your blues" with food) and were given practical tips on how to avoid food bingeing. No mention was made of the new "diet pills" (amphetamines) introduced in the 1930s for clinical treatment of obesity. Instead, teenagers were encouraged to go on "sensible" and "well-rounded" diets of between 1,200 and 1,800 calories. By the 1950s advertisements for "diet foods" such as Ry-Krisp were offering assistance as they told the readership "Nobody Loves a Fat Girl."[16] Girls,

much as adult women, were expected to tame the natural appetite.

Although adolescent girls were consistently warned against weight reduction without medical supervision, dieting was always cast as a worthwhile endeavor with transforming powers. "Diets can do wonderful things. When dispensed or approved by your physician . . . all you have to do is follow whither the chart leads."[17] The process of metamorphosis from fat to thin always provided a narrative of uplift and interest. "The Fattest Girl in the Class" was the autobiographical account of Jane, an obese girl who, after suffering the social stigma associated with teenage overweight, went on a diet and found happiness.[18] Being thin was tied to attractiveness, popularity with the opposite sex, and self-esteem—all primary ingredients in adolescent culture. Nonfiction accounts of "make-overs" became a popular formula in all the beauty magazines of the postwar period and provided a tantalizing fantasy of psychological and spiritual transformation for mature and adolescent women alike.[19]

The popularization of adolescent female weight control in the postwar era is a prime component of the modern dieting story and a critical factor in explaining anorexia nervosa as we know it today. . . . Since the 1960s the dieting imperative has intensified in two noticeable and important ways. . . . First, the ideal female body size has become considerably slimmer. After a brief flirtation with full-breasted, curvaceous female figures in the politically conservative postwar recovery of the 1950s, our collective taste returned to an ideal of extreme thinness and an androgynous, if not childlike, figure.[20] A series of well-known studies point to the declining weight since the 1950s of fashion models, Miss America contestants, and *Playboy* centerfolds.[21] Neither bosoms, hips, nor buttocks are currently in fashion as young and old alike attempt to meet the new aesthetic standard. A Bloomingdale's ad posits, "Bean lean, slender as the night, narrow as an arrow, pencil thin, get the point?"[22] It is appropriate to recall Annette Kellerman who, at 5 feet 3¾ inches and 137 pounds, epitomized the body beautiful of 1918. Obviously, our cultural tolerance for body fat has diminished over the intervening years.

Second, notably since the middle to late 1970s, a new emphasis on physical fitness and athleticism has intensified cultural pressures on the individual for control and mastery of the body. For women this means that fitness has been added to slimness as a criterion of perfection.[23] Experts on the subject, such as Jane Fonda, encourage women to strive for a lean body with musculature. The incredible popularity among women of aerobics, conditioning programs, and jogging does testify to the satisfactions that come with gaining physical strength through self-discipline, but it also expresses our current urgency about the physical body. Many who are caught up in the exercise cult equate physical fitness and slimness with a higher moral state. . . . Compulsive exercising and chronic dieting have [thus] been joined as twin obsessions. . . . [In the] 1980s clinical reports and autobiographical statements show a clear-cut pattern of anorexic patients who exercise with ritualistic intensity. How much one runs and how little one eats is the prevailing moral calculus in present-day anorexia nervosa. . . .

The proliferation of diet and exercise regimens in the past decade, although an important context for understanding the increase in anorexia nervosa, is not the whole story. For a more complete explanation we must turn to some other recent social changes, keeping in mind that no one factor has caused the contemporary problem. Rather, it is the nature of our economic and cultural environment, interacting with individual and family characteristics, which exacerbates the social and emotional insecurities that put today's young women at increasing risk for anorexia nervosa. Two very basic social transformations are relevant to the problem: one has to do with food; the other, with new expectations between the sexes.

Since World War II, and especially in the last two decades, middle-class Americans have experienced a veritable revolution in terms of how and what we eat, as well as how we think about eating.[24] The imperatives of an expanding capitalist society have generated extraordinary technological and marketing innovations, which in turn have transformed food itself, expanded our repertoire of foods, and affected the ways in which we consume them. Even though much contemporary food is characterized by elaborate processing and conservation techniques that actually reduce and flatten distinctive textures and flavors, the current array of food choices seems to constitute an endless smorgasbord of new and different tastes. [Since] the 1980s an individual in an urban center looking for a quick lunch [has been] able to choose from tacos with guacamole and salsa, hummus and falafel in pita, sushi, tortellini, quiche, and pad thai—along with more traditional "American" fare such as hamburgers. Thirty years ago this diversified international menu was as unknown to most Americans as were many of the food products used to create it. . . . As a consequence of [the expansion of our food repertoire], we are faced with an abundance of food which, in our obesophobic society, necessitates ever greater self-control. . . . It is no wonder, then, that we talk so incessantly about food and dieting.

The food revolution is a matter of ideas and manners as much as technology and markets. . . . In our society food is chosen and eaten not merely on the basis of hunger. It is a commonplace to observe that contemporary advertising connects food to sociability, status, and sexuality. In an affluent society, in particular, where eating appears to involve considerable individual choice, food is regarded as an important analogue of the self.

In the 1960s, for example, many young people in the counterculture gave up goods associated with their bourgeois upbringing and turned instead to a diet of whole grains, unprocessed foods, and no meat. This new diet made a statement about personal and political values and became a way of separating one generation from another. . . . In the 1980s, the extent to which the choice of cuisine dominates and defines the sophisticated life-style [among well-to-do urbanites] is reflected in a recent *New Yorker* cartoon, which shows a young professional couple after a dinner party given by friends. In complete seriousness they say to each other, "We could get close with David and Elizabeth if they didn't put béarnaise sauce on everything."[25] The anorectic is obviously not alone in her use of food and eating as a means of self-definition. There are many others who internalize the dictum "You are what you eat"— or, for that matter, what you don't eat.[26]

Along with the expansion of our food repertoire and our extraordinary attention to food selection, the eating context has changed. Eating is being desocialized. In American society today, more and more food is being consumed away from the family table or any other fixed center of sociability. This process began in the postwar period with the introduction of convenience foods and drive-in restaurants, precursors of the fast-food chains that now constitute a $45-billion-a-year industry.... Americans [now] eat everywhere—in the classroom; in theaters, libraries, and museums; on the street; at their desks; on the phone; in hot tubs; in cars while driving.... Signs saying "no food and drink," infrequent in other parts of the world, adorn our public buildings, a clear sign of our pattern of vagabond eating.[27]

On college and university campuses, where eating disorders are rampant, the situation is exaggerated. By the early 1970s most undergraduate students were no longer required to take any sit-down meals at fixed times in college dormitories.... Typically, students frequent a series of university cafeterias or commercial off-campus restaurants where they can obtain breakfast, lunch, or dinner at any time of the day. Some campus food plans allow unlimited amounts, a policy that fuels the behavior of the bulimic: "I used to go to Contract, eat a whole bunch of stuff, go to the bathroom, throw it up, come back, eat again, throw it up, eat again."[28] In addition, the availability of nearly any kind of food at any time contributes to a pattern of indiscriminate eating. Traditions of food appropriateness—that is, that certain foods are eaten at particular times of the day or in a certain sequence—disappear in this unstructured climate. Thus, an ice-cream cone, a carbonated soft drink, and a bagel constitute an easy popular "meal" that may be eaten at any time of day. Most colleges and the surrounding communities have made provisions to gratify student appetites no matter what the hour. Snack bars and vending machines adorn nearly every free alcove in classroom buildings and residence halls; pizza and Chinese food are delivered hot in the middle of the night.

In a setting where eating is so promiscuous, it is no wonder that food habits become problematic. This is not to say that our universities, on their own, generate eating-disordered students. They do, however, provide fertile ground for those who carry the seeds of disorder with them from home. In the permissive and highly individualized food environment of the post-1970 college or university, overeating and undereating become distinct possibilities.[29]

For those young women with either incipient or pronounced anorexia nervosa, the unstructured college life ... often accentuates the anorectic's physical and emotional problems. [As one young anorectic explained]:

I don't know any limits here at all. At home, I have my mom dishing out my food ... But when

I'm here it's a totally different story—I can't tell portion size at all. I always get so afraid afterwards, after eating. Oh my God did I eat that much or this much? So I just pass things up altogether and don't eat.[30]

The anorectic's preoccupation with appetite control is fueled by incessant talk about dieting and weight even among friends and associates who eat regularly. Diet-conscious female students report that fasting, weight control, and binge eating are a normal part of life on American college campuses.[31] ... In our obesophobic society women struggle with food because, among other things, food represents fat and loss of control. For a contemporary woman to eat heartily, energetically, and happily is usually problematic (and, at best, occasional). As a result, some come to fear and hate their own appetite; eating becomes a shameful and disgusting act, and denial of hunger becomes a central facet of identity and personality....

Among adolescents concerned with the transition to adulthood, an intense concern with appetite control and the body [also] operates in tandem with increasing anxiety over sexuality and the implications of changing sex roles. For sex is the second important arena of social change that may contribute to the rising number of anorectics. There are, in fact, some justifiable social reasons why contemporary young women fear adult womanhood. The "anorexic generations," particularly those born since 1960, have been subject to a set of insecurities that make heterosexuality an anxious rather than a pleasant prospect. Family insecurity, reflected in the frequency of divorce, and changing sex and gender roles became facts of life for this group in their childhood.... Although there is no positive correlation between divorced families and anorexia nervosa, family disruption is part of the world view of the anorexic generations. Its members understand implicitly that not all heterosexual relationships have happy endings.

As a consequence of these social changes, some young women are ambivalent about commitments to men and have adopted an ideal of womanhood that reflects the impact of post-1960 feminism. Although they generally draw back from an explicitly feminist vocabulary, most undergraduate women today desire professional careers of their own without forsaking the idea of marriage and a family. A 1985 study of college women by sociologist Mirra Komarovsky reveals that finding one's place in the world of work has become essential for personal dignity in this generation—yet a career without marriage was the choice of only 2 percent of the sample.[32] Convinced that individuality can be accommodated in marriage, these young women are interested in heterosexuality, but admit that "relationships with guys" are difficult even in college. Komarovsky describes conflict over dating rituals (who takes the initiative and who pays), decision making as a couple, intellectual rivalries, and competition for entrance into graduate school. Unlike Mother, who followed Dad to graduate school and supported him along the way, today's undergraduate—whether she is a declared feminist or not—wants her own professional career both as a ticket to the good life and as a protection for herself in case of divorce.

Sexual activity also requires an extraordinary degree of self-protection in the modern world of AIDS. While premarital sex is acceptable (if not desirable), it is an understandable source of worry among female undergraduates. An advertisement in a 1986 issue of *Ms.*, aimed at selling condoms to young women, captured the current ambivalence about the physical side of heterosexuality: "Let's face it, sex these days can be risky business, and you need all the protection you can get. Between the fear of unplanned pregnancy, sexually transmitted diseases, and the potential side effects of many forms of contraception, it may seem like sex is hardly worth the risk anymore."[33] For some students the unprecedented privacy and freedom of modern university life generates as much fear as pleasure. It bears repeating that clinical materials suggest an *absence* [emphasis is the editors'] of sexual activity on the part of anorectics.

Even though feminine dependency is no longer in fashion, these same young women combine traditional expectations with a quest for equity and power. To be brainy and beautiful; to have an exciting $75,000-a-year job; to nurture two wonderful children in consort with a supportive but equally high-powered husband—these are the personal ambitions of many in the present college generation. In order to achieve this level of personal and social perfection, young women must be extremely demanding of themselves: there can be no distracting personal or avocational detours— they must be unrelenting in the pursuit of goals. The kind of personal control required to become the new Superwoman (a term popularized by

columnist Ellen Goodman)[34] parallels the single-mindedness that characterizes the anorectic. In sum, the golden ideal of this generation of privileged young women and their most distinctive pathology appear to be flip sides of the same record.

My assertion that the post-1960 epidemic of anorexia nervosa can be related to recent social change in the realm of sexuality [and gender roles] is not an argument for turning back the clock. . . . [H]istorical investigation demonstrates that anorexia nervosa was latent in the economic and emotional milieu of the bourgeois family as early as the 1950s. It makes little sense to think a cure will be achieved by putting women back in the kitchen, reinstituting sit-down meals on the nation's campuses, or limiting personal and professional choices to what they were in the Victorian era. On the basis of the best current research on anorexia nervosa, we must conclude that the disease develops as a result of the intersection of external and internal forces in the life of an individual. External forces such as those described here do not, by themselves, generate psychopathologies, but they do give them shape and influence their frequency.

In the confusion of this transitional moment, when a new future is being tentatively charted for women but gender roles and sexuality are still constrained by tradition, young women on the brink of adulthood are feeling the pain of social change most acutely.[35] They look about for direction, but find little in the way of useful experiential guides. What parts of women's tradition do they want to carry into the future? What parts should be left behind? These are difficult personal and political decisions, and most young women are being asked to make them without benefit of substantive education in the history and experience of their sex. In effect, our young women are being challenged and their expectations raised without a simultaneous level of support for either their specific aspirations or for female creativity in general.

Sadly, the cult of diet and exercise is the closest thing our secular society offers women in terms of a coherent philosophy of the self.[36] This being the case, anorexia nervosa is not a quirk and the symptom choice is not surprising. When personal and social difficulties arise, a substantial number of our young women become preoccupied with their bodies and control of appetite. Of all the messages they hear, the imperative to be beautiful and good, by being thin, is still the strongest and most familiar. Moreover, they are caught, often at a very early age, in a deceptive cognitive trap that has them believing that body weight is entirely subject to their conscious control. Despite feminist influences on the career aspirations of the present college-age generation, little has transpired to dilute the basic strength of this powerful cultural prescription that plays on both individualism and conformity. The unfortunate truth is that even when she wants more than beauty and understands its limitations as a life goal, the bourgeois woman still expends an enormous amount of psychic energy on appetite control as well as on other aspects of presentation of the physical self.

And what of the future? . . .

We can expect to see eating disorders continue, if not increase, among young women in those postindustrial societies where adolescents tend to be under stress. For both young men and young women, vast technological and cultural changes have made the transition to adulthood particularly difficult by transforming the nature of the family and community and rendering the future unpredictable. According to psychologist Urie Bronfenbrenner and others, American adolescents are in the worst trouble: we have the highest incidence of alcohol and drug abuse among adolescents of any country in the world; we also have the highest rate of teenage pregnancy of any industrialized nation; and we appear to have the most anorexia nervosa.[37]

Although the sexually active adolescent mother and the sexually inactive adolescent anorectic may seem to be light-years apart, they are linked by a common, though unarticulated, understanding. For adolescent women the body is still the most powerful paradigm regardless of social class. Unfortunately, a sizable number of our young women—poor and privileged alike—regard their body as the best vehicle for making a statement about their identity and personal dreams. This is what unprotected sexual intercourse and prolonged starvation have in common. Taken together, our unenviable preeminence in these two domains suggests the enormous difficulty involved in making the transition to adult womanhood in a society where women are still evaluated primarily in terms of the body rather than the mind.

NOTES

1. "On Growing Fat," *Atlantic Monthly* (Mar. 1907):430–31.

2. Jo Ann Olian, *The House of Worth: The Gilded Age, 1860–1918* (New York: Museum of the City of New York, 1982); Jane Beth Abrams, "The Thinning of America: The Emergence of the Ideal of Slenderness in American Popular Culture, 1870–1930" (B.A. thesis, Harvard University, 1983), chap. 2.

3. Michael Batterberry and Ariane Batterberry, *Mirror Mirror: A Social History of Fashion* (New York: Holt, Rinehart and Winston, 1977), pp. 289–97; Diane DeMarly, *The History of Haute Couture, 1850–1950* (New York: Holmes & Meier, 1980), pp. 81–83.

4. P. Rostaine, "How to Get Thin," *Medical Press and Circular* 149 (Dec. 23, 1914):643–44.

5. Stuart Ewen and Elizabeth Ewen, *Channels of Desire: Mass Images and the Shaping of American Consciousness* (New York: McGraw-Hill, 1982), pt. 4; Claudia Kidwell and Margaret C. Christman, *Suiting Everyone: The Democratization of Clothing in America* (Washington, D.C.: Smithsonian Institution Press, 1974).

6. *Vogue* (Jan. 1, 1923):63.

7. Lois W. Banner, *American Beauty* (New York: Random House, 1983), p. 262; Ewen and Ewen, *Channels of Desire*, pp. 193–98.

8. Banner, *American Beauty*, p. 287; Anne Hollander, *Seeing through Clothes* (New York: Viking Press, 1975).

9. Lulu Hunt Peters, *Diet and Health with a Key to the Calories* (Chicago: The Reilly & Britton Company, 1918), pp. 24, 39.

10. Ibid., pp. 12, 104, 110.

11. Ibid., pp. 85, 94.

12. Ibid., pp. 85, 93, 94.

13. "On Her Dressing Table," *Vogue* (Apr. 24, 1902):413; ibid. (July 1, 1918):78.

14. Mildred H. Bryan, "Don't Let Your Child Get Fat!" *Hygeia* 15 (1937):801–3; G. D. Schultz, "Forget That Clean-Plate Bogey!" *Better Homes and Gardens* 21 (Sept. 1942):24.

15. Louise Paine Benjamin, "I Have Three Daughters," *Ladies Homes Journal* 57 (June 1940):74.

16. "You'll Eat It Up at Noon," *Seventeen* (Sept. 1946):21–22; Irma M. Phorylles, "The Lost Waistline," ibid. (Mar. 1948):124; "Overweight?" ibid. (Aug. 1948):184.

17. Ibid.

18. "Fattest Girl in the Class," ibid. (Jan. 1948): 21–22.

19. "Psychology of Dieting," *Ladies' Home Journal* (Jan. 1965):66.

20. Banner, *American Beauty*, pp. 283–85.

21. David M. Garner et al., "Cultural Expectations of Thinness in Women," *Psychology Reports* 47 (1980):483–91.

22. Rita Freedman, *Beauty Bound* (Lexington: Lexington Books, 1986), p. 150.

23. "Coming on Strong: The New Ideal of Beauty," *Time* (Aug. 30, 1983):71–77.

24. William Chafe, *The Unfinished Journey: America since World War II* (New York: Oxford University Press, 1986).

25. *New Yorker* (July 21, 1986):71.

26. "What's Your Food Status Because the Way You Live Has a Lot to Do with the Way You Eat," *Mademoiselle* (Sept. 1985):224–26; "Food as Well as

Clothes, Today, Make the Man—As a Matter of Life and Style," *Vogue* (June 1985):271–73.

27. "Severe Growing Pains for Fast Food," *Business Week* (Mar. 22, 1985):225.

28. Greg Foster and Susan Howerin, "The Quest for Perfection: An Interview with a Former Bulimic," *Iris: A Journal about Women* [Charlottesville, Va.] (1986):21.

29. Before they even arrive on campus, during their senior year in high school and the summer before entering college, many girls began to talk about the "freshmen 10 or 15." This is the weight gain predicted as a result of eating starchy institutional food and participating in late-night food forays with friends.

30. Elizabeth Greene, "Support Groups Forming for Students with Eating Disorders," *Chronicle of Higher Education* (Mar. 5, 1986):1, 30.

31. K. A. Halmi, J. R. Falk, and E. Schwartz, "Binge-Eating and Vomiting: A Survey of a College Population," *Psychological Medicine* 11 (1981): 697–706; R. L. Pyle et al., "The Incident of Bulimia in Freshman College Students," *International Journal of Eating Disorders* 2, 3 (1983):75–86.

32. Mirra Komarovsky, *Women in College: Shaping the New Feminine Identities* (New York: Basic Books, 1985), pp. 89–92, 225–300.

33. *Ms.* (Sept. 1986):n.p. The condom is called Mentor.

34. Ellen Goodman, *Close to Home* (New York: Fawcett Crest, 1979).

35. In *Theories of Adolescence* (New York: Random House, 1962), R. E. Muuss wrote: "Societies in a period of rapid transition create a particular adolescent period; the adolescent has not only the society's problem to adjust to but his [or her] own as well" (p. 164).

36. My view of this issue complements ideas presented in Robert Bellah et al., *Habits of the Heart: Individualism and Commitment in American Life* (New York: Harper & Row, 1986).

37. These data are synthesized in Urie Bronfenbrenner, "Alienation and the Four Worlds of Childhood," *Phi Delta Kappan* (Feb. 1986):434.

VICKI L. RUIZ

The Flapper and the Chaperone: Mexican American Teenagers in the Southwest

Over one million Mexicans immigrated to the United States between 1900 and 1930, forming new communities or settling alongside families whose descendants had migrated north decades and centuries before. This essay plunges us into the decisions to be made about dating, dancing, and dressing up by young women growing up Mexican American in western cities and farm towns from the 1920s to the 1940s. Focusing on first-generation teenagers, Vicki L. Ruiz insists that we see them not as caught between the mores of their Mexican-born Catholic parents and the freedoms of modern America, but rather as navigating "across multiple terrains" simultaneously. Home for most if not all of these young women was located in the *barrios*, dense neighborhoods where Mexican and Mexican American families, businesses, and parishes were clustered.

Ruiz's goal is to uncover the dreams and strategies of young women rather than those of *pachucos*, or zoot-suiters, the youthful male subculture that has drawn scholarly attention. What range of sources and methods does she employ? If you were conducting such a study of teenage girls in the 1970s, or during the past decade, what research techniques and documents would be available to you?

Excerpted from "The Flapper and the Chaperone," ch. 3 of *From Out of the Shadows: Mexican Women in Twentieth-Century America* by Vicki L. Ruiz (New York: Oxford University Press, 1998). Reprinted by permission of the author and publisher. Notes have been edited and renumbered.

In the interwar years, a central figure in cross-sex socializing was the chaperone—*la dueña*. Why do you think adult women and not men were called on to fill the role in Mexican American culture? What cultural messages would be sent if chaperones dogged youthful men's activities, not young women's? Ruiz finds that second-generation women, once married with their own children, tended not to continue the chaperoning tradition. In the 1960s, activist women of Mexican descent embraced the identity of Chicana and, as Ruiz indicates at the close of her essay, issued new challenges to conventional expectations shaped by popular culture, family oligarchy, and men's demands. (See Jennie V. Chávez's 1972 activist statement, pp. 733–735.)

Imagine a gathering in a barrio hall, a group of young people dressed "to the nines" trying their best to replicate the dance steps of Fred Astaire and Ginger Rogers. This convivial heterosocial scene was a typical one in the lives of teenagers during the interwar period. But along the walls, a sharp difference was apparent in the barrios. Mothers, fathers, and older relatives chatted with one another as they kept one eye trained on the dance floor. They were the chaperones—the ubiquitous companions of unmarried Mexican-American women. Chaperonage was a traditional instrument of social control. Indeed, the presence of *la dueña* was the prerequisite for attendance at a dance, a movie, or even church-related events. "When we would go to town, I would want to say something to a guy. I couldn't because my mother was always there," remembered Maria Ybarra. "She would always stick to us girls like glue. . . . She never let us out of her sight."[1]

An examination of events like this one reveals the ways in which young Mexican women in the United States between the wars rationalized, resisted, and evaded parental supervision. It offers a glimpse into generational conflict that goes beyond the more general differences in acculturation between immigrants and their children. Chaperonage existed for centuries on both sides of the political border separating Mexico and the United States. While conjuring images of patriarchal domination, chaperonage is best understood as a manifestation of familial oligarchy whereby elders attempted to dictate the activities of youth for the sake of family honor. A family's standing in the community depended, in part, on women's purity. Loss of virginity not only tainted the reputation of an individual, but of her kin as well. For Mexicano immigrants living in a new, bewildering environment filled with temptations, the enforcement of chaperonage assumed a particular urgency.[2] . . .

Confronting "America" began at an early age. Throughout the Southwest, Spanish-speaking children had to sink or swim in an English-only environment. Even on the playground, students were punished for conversing in Spanish. Admonishments, such as "Don't speak that ugly language, you are an American now," not only reflected a strong belief in Anglo conformity but denigrated the self-esteem of Mexican-American children. As Mary Luna stated: "It was rough because I didn't know English. The teacher wouldn't let us talk Spanish. How can you talk to anybody? If you can't talk Spanish and you can't talk English. . . . It wasn't until maybe the fourth or fifth grade that I started catching up. And all that time I just felt I was stupid." Yet Luna credited her love of reading to a Euro-American educator who had converted a small barrio house into a makeshift community center and library. Her words underscore the dual thrust of Americanization—education and consumerism. "To this day I just love going into libraries . . . there are two places that I can go in and get a real warm, happy feeling; that is, the library and Bullock's in the perfume and make-up department."[3] . . .

For Mexican Americans, second-generation women as teenagers have received scant scholarly attention. Among Chicano historians and writers, there appears a fascination with the sons of immigrants, especially as *pachucos*.[4] Young women, however, may have experienced deeper generational tensions as they blended elements of Americanization with Mexican expectations and values. . . .

. . . The recollections of seventeen women serve as the basis for my reconstruction of adolescent aspirations and experiences (or dreams and routines). The women themselves, . . . with two [major] exceptions, . . . are U.S. citizens by birth and attended southwestern schools. All the interviewees were born between 1908 and 1926. Although three came from families once considered middle class in Mexico, most can be considered working class in the United States. Their fathers' typical occupations included farm worker, miner, day laborer, and railroad hand. These women usually characterized their mothers as homemakers, although several remembered that their mothers took seasonal jobs in area factories and fields. The most economically privileged woman in the sample, Ruby Estrada, helped out in her family-owned hardware and furniture store. She is also the only interviewee who attended college. It should be noted that seven of the seventeen narrators married Euro-Americans. Although intermarriage was uncommon, these oral histories give us insight into the lives of those who negotiated across cultures in a deeply personal way and who felt the impact of acculturation most keenly. Rich in emotion and detail, these interviews reveal women's conscious decision-making in the production of culture. In creating their own cultural spaces, the interwar generation challenged the trappings of familial oligarchy.[5]

... Within families, young women, perhaps more than their brothers, were expected to uphold certain standards. Parents, therefore, often assumed what they perceived as their unquestionable prerogative to regulate the actions and attitudes of their adolescent daughters. Teenagers, on the other hand, did not always acquiesce in the boundaries set down for them by their elders. Intergenerational tension flared along several fronts.

Like U.S. teenagers, in general, the first area of disagreement between an adolescent and her family would be over her personal appearance.... [T]he length of a young woman's tresses was a hot issue spanning class, region, and ethnic lines. During the 1920s, a woman's decision "to bob or not bob" her hair assumed classic proportions within Mexican families. After considerable pleading, Belen Martinez Mason was permitted to cut her hair, though she soon regretted the decision. "Oh, I cried for a month." Differing opinions over fashions often caused ill feelings. One Mexican American woman recalled that as a young girl, her mother dressed her "like a nun" and she could wear "no make-up, no cream, no nothing" on her face. Swimwear, bloomers, and short skirts also became sources of controversy. Some teenagers left home in one outfit and changed into another at school. Once María Fierro arrived home in her bloomers. Her father inquired, "Where have you been dressed like that, like a clown?" "I told him the truth," Fierro explained

"He whipped me anyway.... So from then on whenever I went to the track meet, I used to change my bloomers so that he wouldn't see that I had gone again."[6] ... [A] popular ballad chastised Mexican women for applying makeup so heavily as to resemble a piñata.[7]

The use of cosmetics, however, cannot be blamed entirely on Madison Avenue ad campaigns. The innumerable barrio beauty pageants, sponsored by *mutualistas*, patriotic societies, churches, the Mexican Chamber of Commerce, newspapers, and even progressive labor unions, encouraged young women to accentuate their physical attributes. Carefully chaperoned, many teenagers did participate in community contests from La Reina de Cinco de Mayo to Orange Queen. They modeled evening gowns, rode on parade floats, and sold raffle tickets.[8] ...

The commercialization of personal grooming made additional inroads into the Mexican community with the appearance of barrio beauty parlors. Working as a beautician conferred a certain degree of status—"a nice, clean job"—in comparison to factory or domestic work. As one woman related:

> I always wanted to be a beauty operator. I loved makeup; I loved to dress up and fix up. I used to set my sisters' hair. So I had that in the back of my mind for a long time, and my mom pushed the fact that she wanted me to have a profession—seeing that I wasn't thinking of getting married.[9]

While further research is needed, one can speculate that neighborhood beauty shops reinforced women's networks and became places where they could relax, exchange *chisme* (gossip), and enjoy the company of other women.

During the 1920s, the ethic of consumption became inextricably linked to making it in America. The message of affluence attainable through hard work and a bit of luck was reinforced in English and Spanish-language publications. Mexican barrios were not immune from the burgeoning consumer culture. The society pages of the influential Los Angeles-based *La Opinion*, for example, featured advice columns, horoscopes, and celebrity gossip. Advertisements for makeup, clothing, even feminine hygiene products reminded teenagers of an awaiting world of consumption.[10] ...

Advertisements aimed at women promised status and affection if the proper bleaching cream, hair coloring, and cosmetics were purchased. Or, as one company boldly claimed, "Those with lighter, more healthy skin tones will become much more successful in business, love, and society." A print ad [in English] for Camay Soap carried by *Hispano America* in 1932 reminded women readers that "Life Is a Beauty Contest." Flapper fashions and celebrity testimonials further fused the connections between gendered identity and consumer culture. Another promotion encouraged readers to "SIGA LAS ESTRELLAS" (FOLLOW THE STARS) and use Max Factor cosmetics.[11] . . .

. . . Mexican women interpreted these visual representations in a myriad of ways. Some ignored them, some redefined their messages, and other internalized them. The popularity of bleaching creams offers a poignant testament to color consciousness in Mexican communities, a historical consciousness accentuated by Americanization through education and popular culture.

Reflecting the coalescence of Mexican and U.S. cultures, Spanish-language publications promoted pride in Latino theater and music while at the same time celebrated the icons of Americanization and consumption. Because of its proximity to Hollywood, *La Opinion* ran contests in which the lucky winner would receive a screen test. On the one hand, *La Opinion* nurtured the dreams of "success" through entertainment and consumption while, on the other, the newspaper railed against the deportations and repatriations of the 1930s. Sparked by manufactured fantasies and clinging to youthful hopes, many Mexican women teenagers avidly read celebrity gossip columns, attended Saturday matinees, cruised Hollywood and Vine, and nurtured their visions of stardom. A handful of Latina actresses, especially Dolores del Rio and Lupe Velez, whetted these aspirations and served as public role models of the "American dream." As a *La Opinion* article on Lupe Velez idealistically claimed, "Art has neither nationalities nor borders".[12]

. . . Mexican-American women teenagers . . . positioned themselves within the cultural messages they gleaned from English and Spanish-language publications, afternoon matinees, and popular radio programs. Their shifting conceptions of acceptable heterosocial behavior, including their desire "to date," heightened existing generational tensions between parents and daughters.

Obviously, the most serious point of contention between an adolescent daughter and her Mexican parents regarded her behavior toward young men. In both cities and rural towns, close chaperonage was a way of life.

Recalling the supervisory role played by her "old maid" aunt, María Fierro laughingly explained, "She'd check up on us all the time. I used to get so mad at her." Ruby Estrada recalled that in her small southern Arizona community, "all the mothers" escorted their daughters to the local dances. Estrada's mother was no exception when it came to chaperoning her daughters. "She went especially for us. She'd just sit there and take care of our coats and watch us." Even talking to male peers in broad daylight could be grounds for discipline. Adele Hernández Milligan, a resident of Los Angeles for over fifty years, elaborated: "I remember the first time that I walked home with a boy from school. Anyway, my mother saw me and she was mad. I must have been sixteen or seventeen. She slapped my face because I was walking home with a boy"[13] . . .

Faced with this type of situation, young women had three options: they could accept the rules set down for them; they could rebel; or they could find ways to compromise or circumvent traditional standards. "I was *never* allowed to go out by myself in the evening; it just was not done," related Carmen Bernal Escobar. In rural communities, where restrictions were perhaps even more stringent, "nice" teenagers could not even swim with male peers. According to Ruby Estrada, "We were ladies and wouldn't go swimming out there with a bunch of boys." Yet many seemed to accept these limits with equanimity. Remembering her mother as her chaperone, Lucy Acosta insisted, "I could care less as long as I danced." "It wasn't devastating at all," echoed Ruby Estrada. "We took it in stride. We never thought of it as cruel or mean. . . . It was taken for granted that that's the way it was."[14] . . .

Women in cities had a distinct advantage over their rural peers in that they could venture miles from their neighborhood into the anonymity of dance halls, amusement parks, and other forms of commercialized leisure. With carnival rides and the Cinderella Ballroom, the Nu-Pike amusement park of Long Beach proved a popular hangout for Mexican youth in Los Angeles. It was more difficult to abide by traditional norms when excitement loomed just on the other side of the streetcar line.

Some women openly rebelled. They moved out of their family homes and into apartments. Considering themselves freewheeling single women, they could go out with men unsupervised as was the practice among their Anglo peers. Others challenged parental and cultural standards even further by living with their boy-friends. In his field notes, University of California economist Paul Taylor recorded an incident in which a young woman had moved in with her Anglo boyfriend after he had convinced her that such arrangements were common among Americans. "This terrible freedom in the United States," one Mexicana lamented. "I do not have to worry because I have no daughters, but the poor *señoras* with many girls, they worry".[15]

Those teenagers who did not wish to defy their parents openly would "sneak out" of the house to meet their dates or attend dances with female friends. Whether meeting some-one at a drugstore, roller rink, or theater, this practice involved the invention of elaborate stories to mask traditionally inappropriate be-havior. In other words, they lied.[16] . . .

. . . [W]hat other tactics did teenagers devise? . . . Alicia Mendeola Shelit recalled that one of her older brothers would accompany her to dances ostensibly as a chaperone. "But then my oldest brother would always have a blind date for me." Carmen Bernal Escobar was per-mitted to entertain her boyfriends at home, but only under the supervision of her brother or mother. The practice of "going out with the girls," though not [generally] accepted until the 1940s, was fairly common. Several Mexican-American women, often related, would escort one another to an event (such as a dance), so-cialize with the men in attendance, and then walk home together. In the sample of seven-teen interviews, daughters negotiated their ac-tivities with their parents. Older siblings and extended kin appeared in the background as either chaperones or accomplices. . . .

. . . [M]any teenage women knew little about sex other than what they picked up from friends, romance magazines, and the local theater. As Mary Luna remembered, "I thought that if somebody kissed you, you could get pregnant." In *Singing for My Echo*, New Mexico native Gregorita Rodríguez confided that on her wedding night, she knelt down and said her rosary until her husband gently asked, "Gregorita, *mi esposa*, are you afraid of me?" At times this naiveté persisted beyond the wed-ding. "It took four days for my husband to touch me," one woman revealed. "I slept with dress and all. We were both greenhorns, I guess."[17] . . .

Chaperonage . . . exacerbated conflict not only between generations but within individu-als as well. In gaily recounting tales of ditching the *dueña* or sneaking down the stairwell, the laughter of the interviewees fails to hide the painful memories of breaking away from fa-milial expectations. Their words resonate with the dilemma of reconciling their search for au-tonomy with their desire for parental affirma-tion. . . . [E]very informant who challenged or circumvented chaperonage held a fulltime job, as either a factory or service worker. In contrast, most women who accepted constant supervi-sion did not work for wages. Perhaps because they labored for long hours, for little pay, and frequently under hazardous conditions, factory and service workers were determined to exer-cise some control over their leisure time.[18] . . .

It may also be significant that none of the employed teenagers had attended high school. They entered the labor market directly after or even before the completion of the eighth grade. Like many female factory workers in the United States, most Mexican operatives were young, unmarried daughters whose wage labor was essential to the economic survival of their fami-lies. As members of a "family wage economy," they relinquished all or part of their wages to their elders. According to a 1933 University of California study, of the Mexican families sur-veyed with working children, the children's monetary contributions constituted 35 percent of total household income. Cognizant of their earning power, they resented the lack of per-sonal autonomy.[19]

Delicate negotiations ensued as both par-ents and daughters struggled over questions of leisure activities and discretionary income. Could a young woman retain a portion of her wages for her own use? If elders demanded every penny, daughters might be more in-clined to splurge on a new outfit or other per-sonal item on their way home from work or, even more extreme, they might choose to move out, taking their paychecks with them. Recog-nizing their dependence on their children's income, some parents compromised. Their concessions, however, generally took the form of allocating spending money rather than re-laxing traditional supervision. Still, women's earning power could be an important bargain-ing chip. . . .

To complete the picture, we also have to consider the perspective of Mexican immigrant parents who encountered a youth culture very different from that of their generation. For them, courtship had occurred in the plaza; young women and men promenaded under the watch-ful eyes of town elders, an atmosphere in which an exchange of meaningful glances could well portend engagement. One can understand their consternation as they watched their daughters apply cosmetics and adopt the apparel advertised in fashion magazines. In other words, "If she dresses like a flapper, will she then act like one?" Seeds of suspicion reaffirmed the penchant for traditional supervision. . . .

. . . [P]arents in the barrios of major cities fought a losing battle against urban anonymity and commercialized leisure. The Catholic Church was quick to point out the "dangerous amusement" inherent in dancing, theater-going, dressing fashionably, and reading pulp fiction. Under the section, "The Enemy in the Ballroom," a Catholic advice book warned of the hidden temptations of dance. "I know that some persons can indulge in it without harm; but sometimes even the coldest temperaments are heated by it." Therefore, the author offered the following rules:

(1) If you know nothing at all . . . about dancing do not trouble yourself to learn (2) Be watchful. . . . and see that your pleasure in dancing does not grow into a passion. . . . (3) Never frequent fairs, picnics, carnivals, or public dancing halls where Heaven only knows what sorts of people congregate. (4) Dance only at private parties where your father or mother is present.

Pious pronouncements such as these had little impact on those adolescents who cherished the opportunity to look and act like vamps and flappers.[20]

Attempting to regulate the social life of young parishioners, barrio priests organized gender-segregated teen groups. In Los Angeles, Juventud Católica Feminina Mexicana (JCFM) had over fifty chapters. In her autobiography *Hoyt Street*, Mary Helen Ponce remembered the group as one organized for "nice" girls with the navy blue uniform as its most appealing feature. . . .

Ponce enjoyed going to "*las vistas*," usually singing cowboy movies shown in the church hall after Sunday evening rosary. . . . The cut-rate features . . . raised money for local activities. . . . In an era of segregated theaters, church halls tendered an environment where Mexicanos and their children could enjoy inexpensive entertainment and sit wherever they pleased.[21] . . .

[P]opular culture offered an alternative vision to parental and church expectations complete with its own aura of legitimacy. . . . Even the Spanish-language press fanned youthful passions. On May 9, 1927, *La Opinion*

ran an article entitled; "How do you kiss?" Informing readers that "el beso no es un arte sino una ciencia" [kissing is not an art but rather a science], this short piece outlined the three components of a kiss: quality, quantity, and topography. The modern kiss, furthermore, should last three minutes.[22] Though certainly shocking older Mexicanos, such titillating fare catered to a youth market. . . .

Mexican-American women were not caught between two worlds. They navigated across multiple terrains at home, at work, and at play. They engaged in cultural coalescence. The Mexican-American generation selected, retained, borrowed, and created their own cultural forms. Or as one woman informed anthropologist Ruth Tuck, "Fusion is what we want—the best of both ways."[23] These children of immigrants may have been captivated by consumerism, but few would attain its promises of affluence. Race and gender prejudice as well as socioeconomic segmentation constrained the possibilities of choice. . . .

. . . [W]hat seems most striking is that the struggle over chaperonage occurred against a background of persistent discrimination. During the early 1930s, Mexicans were routinely rounded up and deported and even when deportations diminished, segregation remained. Historian Albert Camarillo has demonstrated that in Los Angeles restrictive real estate covenants and segregated schools increased dramatically between 1920 and 1950. The proportion of Los Angeles area municipalities with covenants prohibiting Mexicans and other people of color from purchasing residences in certain neighborhoods climbed from 20 percent in 1920 to 80 percent in 1946. Many restaurants, theaters, and public swimming pools discriminated against their Spanish-surnamed clientele. In southern California, for example, Mexicans could swim at the public plunges only one day out of the week (just before they drained the pool). Small-town merchants frequently refused to admit Spanish-speaking people into their places of business. "White Trade Only" signs served as bitter reminders of their second-class citizenship.[24]

Individual acts of discrimination could also blunt youthful aspirations. Erminia Ruiz recalled that from the ages of thirteen to fifteen, she worked full-time to support her sisters and widowed mother as a doughnut maker. "They could get me for lower wages." When health officials would stop in to check the premises, the underage employee would hide in the flour bins. At the age of sixteen, she became the proud recipient of a Social Security card and was thrilled to become the first Mexican hired by a downtown Denver cafeteria. Her delight as a "salad girl" proved short-lived. A co-worker reported that $200 had been stolen from her purse. In Erminia's words:

> Immediately they wanted to know what I did with the $200.00. I didn't know what they were talking about so they got . . . a policewoman and they took me in the restroom and undressed me. [Later they would discover that the co-worker's friend had taken the money.] I felt awful. I didn't go back to work.

Though deeply humiliated, Erminia scanned the classified ads the next day and soon combined work with night classes at a storefront business college.[25]. . .

    Mexican-American adolescents felt the lure of Hollywood and the threat of deportation, the barbs of discrimination, and the reins of constant supervision. In dealing with all the contradictions in their lives, many young women focused their attention on chaperonage, an area where they could make decisions. The inner conflicts expressed in the oral histories reveal that such decisions were not made impetuously. Hard as it was for young heterosexual women to carve out their own sexual boundaries, imagine the greater difficulty for lesbians coming of age in the Southwest barrios. . . .

    . . . Although still practiced in some areas, chaperonage appeared less frequently after World War II. By the 1950s, chaperonage had become more of a generational marker. Typically only the daughters of recent immigrants had to contend with constant supervision. Mexican Americans relegated chaperonage to their own past, a custom that, as parents, they chose not to inflict on their children. Family honor also became less intertwined with female virginity; but the preservation of one's "reputation" was still a major concern.[26] In the poem "Pueblo, 1950," Bernice Zamora captures the consequences of a kiss:

> I remember you, Fred Montoya
> You were the first *vato* to ever kiss me
> I was twelve years old.
> My mother said shame on you,
>
> my teacher said shame on you, and
> I said shame on me, and nobody
> said a word to you.[27]. . .

In challenging chaperonage, Mexican-American teenagers did not attack the foundation of familial oligarchy—only its more obvious manifestation. It would take later generations of Chicana feminists to take on this task.

NOTES

1. Interview with Maria Ybarra, December 1, 1990, conducted by David Pérez.

2. For colonial New Mexico, Ramón Gutiérrez convincingly demonstrates how family honor was tied, in part, to women's *vergüenza* (literally, shame or virginity). See Ramón Gutiérrez, "Honor, Ideology, and Class Gender Domination in New Mexico, 1690–1846," *Latin American Perspectives* 12 (Winter 1985): 81–104.

3. Ruth D. Tuck, *Not with the Fist: Mexican-Americans in a Southwest City* (New York: Harcourt, Brace and Co., 1946; rpt. Arno Press, 1974), 185–88; Vicki L. Ruiz, "Oral History and La Mujer: The Rosa Guerrero Story," *in Women on the U.S.-Mexico Border: Responses to Change* (Boston: Allen and Unwin, 1987), 226–27; *interview* with Mary Luna, Volume 20 of *Rosie the Riveter Revisited: Women and the World War I Work Experience,* ed. Sherna Berger Gluck (Long Beach: CSULB Foundation, 1983), 9–10. Bullock's was a major department store in the West. During the 1940s, bilingual education appeared as an exciting experiment in curriculum reform.

4. Mauricio Mazón's *The Zoot Suit Riots* (Austin: University of Texas Press, 1984) and the Luis Valdez play and feature film, *Zoot Suit,* provide examples of the literature on *pachucos.*

5. María Fierro, Rose Escheverria Mulligan, Adele Hernández Milligan, Beatrice Morales Clifton, Mary Luna, Alicia Mendeola Shelit, Carmen Bernal Escobar, Belen Martínez Mason, and Julia Luna Mount grew up in Los Angeles. Lucy Acosta and Alma Araiza García came of age in El Paso and Erminia Ruiz in Denver. Representing the rural experience are María Arredondo and Jesusita Torres (California), María Ybarra (Texas), and Ruby Estrada (Arizona). As a teenager, Eusebia Buriel moved with her family from Silvis, Illinois, to Riverside, California. Nine of these women were born between 1908 and 1919, and eight between 1920 and 1926. This sample includes some who were chaperoned during the 1920s and others who were chaperoned during the thirties and forties. Nine interviews are housed in university archives, seven are part of the *Rosie the Riveter* collection at California State University, Long Beach, California.

6. F. Scott Fitzgerald, "Bernice Bobs Her Hair," *Flappers and Philosophers* (London: W. Collins Sons and Co., Ltd., 1922), 209–46; Martínez Mason interview, 44; interview with Alicia Mendeola Shelit, Volume 37 of *Rosie the Riveter,* 18; Paul S. Taylor, *Mexican Labor in the United States, Volume II* (Berkeley: University of California Press, 1932), 199–200; interview with María Fierro, Volume 12 of *Rosie the Riveter,* 10. [Vicki Ruiz Writes:] Changing clothes at school is not peculiar to our mothers and grandmothers. As a high school student in the early 1970s, I was not allowed to wear the fashionable micromini skirts. But I bought one anyway. I left home in a full dirndl skirt with a flowing peasant blouse, but once I arrived at school, I would untie the skirt

(which I would then dump in my locker) to reveal the mini-skirt I had worn underneath.

7. Taylor, *Mexican Labor, Vol. II*, vi–vii.

8. Rodolfo F. Acuña, *Community Under Siege: A Chronicle of Chicanos East of the Los Angeles River, 1945–1975* (Los Angeles: UCLA Chicano Studies Publications, 1984), 278, 407–408, 413–414, 418, 422.

9. Sherna B. Gluck, *Rosie the Riveter Revisited: Women, The War and Social Change* (Boston: Twayne Publishers, 1987), 81, 85.

10. For examples, *see La Opinion*, September 26, 1926; May 14, 1927; June 5, 1927; September 9, 1929; January 15, 1933; January 29, 1938.

11. *La Opinion*, September 29, 1929; *Hispano-America*, July 2, 1932.

12. For examples, *sec La Opinion*, September 23, 24, 27, and 30, 1926; March 2, 1927.

13. Interview with Adele Hernández Milligan, Volume 26 of *Rosie the Riveter*, 17.

14. Escobar interview, 1986; Estrada interview, 11, 13; interview no. 653 with Lucy Acosta conducted by Mario T. García, October 28, 1982 (on file at the Institute of Oral History, University of Texas, El Paso), 17.

15. Paul S. Taylor, "Women in Industry," field notes for his book, *Mexican Labor in the United States, 1927–1930*, Bancroft Library, University of California, 1 box; Richard G. Thurston, "Urbanization and Sociocultural Change in a Mexican-American Enclave" (Ph.D. dissertation, University of California, Los Angeles, 1957).

16. Martínez Mason interview, 30; Ruiz interviews (1990, 1993); Thomas Sheridan, *Los Tucsonenses* (Tucson: University of Arizona Press, 1986), 131–32.

17. Interview with Julia Luna Mount, November 17, 1983, by the author; Fierro interview, 18; Luna interview, 29; Ruiz interview (1993); Gregorita Rodríguez, *Singing for My Echo* (Santa Fe: Cota Editions, 1987), 52; Martínez Mason interview, 62.

18. See Douglas Monroy, "An Essay on Understanding the Work Experiences of Mexicans in Southern California, 1900–1939," *Aztlán* 12 (Spring 1981): 70. Feminist historians have also documented this push for autonomy among the daughters of European immigrants.

19. Heller Committee for Research in Social Economics of the University of California and Constantine Panuzio, *How Mexicans Earn and Live*, University of California Publications in Economics, XIII, No. 1, Cost of Living Studies V (Berkeley: University of California, 1933), 11, 14, 17; Taylor notes; Luna Mount interview; Ruiz interviews (1990, 1993); Shelit interview, 9.

20. Rev. F. X. Lasance, *The Catholic Girl's Guide and Sunday Missal* (New York: Benziger Brothers, 1905), 249–75. I have a 1946 reprint edition passed down to me by my older sister who had received it from our mother.

21. George J. Sanchez, *Becoming Mexican American: Ethnicity, Culture, and Identity in Chicano Los Angeles, 1900–1945* (New York: Oxford University Press, 1993), 167; Mary Helen Ponce, *Hoyt Street* (Albuquerque: University of New Mexico Press, 1993), 258, 266–71.

22. *La Opinion*, May 9, 1927.

23. Tuck, *Not with the Fist*, 134.

24. Rodolfo Acuña, *Occupied America: A History of Chicanos*, 2nd ed. (New York: Harper & Row, 1981), 310, 318, 323, 330–31; Shelit interview, 15; Paul S. Taylor, *Mexican Labor in the United States*, Vol. I (Berkeley: University of California Press, 1930; rpt. Arno Press, 1970), 221–24; Arredondo interview; Ruiz interviews (1990, 1993).

25. Ruiz interview (1993).

26. Acosta interview: Tuck, *Not with the Fist*, 126–27; Thurston, "Urbanization," 109, 117–119; Ruiz interviews (1990, 1993).

27. Bernice Zamora, "Pueblo, 1950," in *Infinite Divisions: An Anthology of Chicana Literature*, eds. Tey Diana Rebolledo and Eliana Rivero (Tucson: University of Arizona Press, 1993), 315.

CHERYL D. HICKS

Mabel Hampton in Harlem: Regulating Black Women's Sexuality in the 1920s

It can be very difficult for historians to unearth how people in the past experienced sexuality. Not only might sexuality be a taboo topic, but some women resist telling the truth about their experiences, fantasies, and desires as a form of self-protection. Darlene Clark Hine calls this practice among black women "a culture

Excerpted from ch. 7 of *Talk with You Like a Woman: African American Women, Justice, and Reform in New York, 1890–1935* by Cheryl D. Hicks (Chapel Hill: University of North Carolina Press, 2010). Reprinted by permission of the author and publisher. Notes have been edited and renumbered.

of dissemblance." Because black women have been stereotyped as hypersexual, some shield their sexual lives from public scrutiny.

Cheryl D. Hicks takes us behind this veil of silence to explore the sexual lives of some working-class residents of Harlem, New York, in the 1920s. The black population of the neighborhood was growing by leaps and bounds. In what is called the Great Migration, approximately one million African Americans in the South relocated to the North during World War I, seeking jobs in the wartime economy and fleeing the Jim Crow (segregated) South. They came mostly to the largest cities, where, to their disappointment, they met with racial discrimination in workplaces and in the housing market. Many who came to New York ended up living in a 48-block area centered on West 134th Street in Manhattan. Nonresidents often referred to this part of Harlem as a "slum," given its dilapidated and crowded housing. Yet Harlem had also become a commercial and tourist destination associated with jazz and sex. White New Yorkers, as well as visitors from around the world, went to Harlem to sample the nightlife—to go "slumming."

Hicks shows us that sexual repression and policy were very much present during this supposed era of sexual liberation. After arrest and conviction on charges like vagrancy and soliciting sex, Hicks's subjects found themselves detained in the New York State Reformatory for Women in rural Bedford, about 50 miles north of the city. The admission interview, Hicks argues, was one of the few times in their lives some girls and women spoke about their sexual desires, practices, and histories (including sexual abuse). What emerges in these accounts of "sex and the city"? Why do you think surveillance goes hand in hand with liberation?

Mabel Hampton's experiences in Harlem never quite measured up to the popular image of the black neighborhood. Visitors from other parts of the city would go to "the night-clubs . . . and dance to such jazz music as can be heard nowhere else." Elite and middle-class white voyeurs, finding confirmation for their own ideas about the authenticity of primitive black culture, enjoyed Harlem's "'hot' and 'barbaric' jazz, the risqué lyrics and the 'junglelike' dancing of its cabaret floor shows, and all its other 'wicked' delights." As the black writer and activist James Weldon Johnson put it, after "a visit to Harlem at night," partygoers who practiced slumming believed that the town "never sleeps and that the inhabitants . . . jazz through existence."[1] Hampton's everyday life was strikingly different from the romanticized image of Harlem. In 1924, the twenty-one-year-old southern migrant was doing domestic work by day and occasionally dancing in a chorus line at night. She learned to navigate Harlem's social and cultural complexities as she encountered its opportunities and hardships and faced its pleasures and dangers. The fact that she was sexually attracted to women, rather than to men, intensified the paradox: Harlem offered her real freedoms, but also significant constraints.

At the same historical moment when Harlem was touted by white New Yorkers as one of the most sexually liberated spaces in the city, women experienced critical surveillance and their romantic attachments came under intense scrutiny. With the growing popularity of movies, dance halls, and amusement parks, families and community members became more and more concerned about how and with whom young women were spending their leisure time. Reformers and the police attempted to regulate working-class women's social lives, especially their sexuality. During World War I, the federal government showed particular concern because of the fear that women would spread venereal disease to soldiers, weakening the armed forces and endangering the war effort. Anxieties about working-class women's sexual behavior influenced the passing of numerous state laws that were proposed by reformers, approved by legislatures, and enforced by police officers. During the period that scholars have noted as the early-twentieth-century sexual revolution, the active pursuit of romance and sex by young working-class women caused their elders unease, in part because these women failed to conform to traditional courtship practices. . . . [2]

Race and ethnicity influenced reformers' and criminal justice administrators' interactions with their charges. Reformers and the police targeted white immigrant and native-born working-class women for questionable moral behavior, but they generally believed these women could be reformed. Black women, whom whites characterized as innately promiscuous because of their African ancestry and the legacy of American enslavement, were seen as less amenable to rehabilitation. The fact that many African American women lived in Harlem, which was seen as a center of social and sexual abandon, reinforced their libidinous image and inflected police officers' and criminal justice administrators' assessments of their culpability in sexual offenses.

Young black women, incarcerated primarily for sex-related offenses on charges that included vagrancy, disorderly conduct, and prostitution, usually rejected reformers' concerns and believed they were unfairly targeted. Mabel Hampton contended that her imprisonment at the New York State Reformatory for Women at Bedford for solicitation stemmed from a false arrest. Other inmates recounted their problems with law enforcement and disagreed with the verdict that their behavior was criminal. For the years between 1917 and 1928, one hundred black women appear in Bedford's case files. Fifty-one were New York natives, immigrants, or migrants from New England or the Midwest. Forty-nine were southern migrants who embraced a social and political freedom that had been unavailable in the South but found themselves on the wrong side of the law. During this time period, many young working-class women grappled with the relentless surveillance of concerned relatives, community members, police officers, and urban reformers as they pursued personal autonomy and sexual expression.

During admission interviews and throughout their association with Bedford, black women revealed personal experiences that were far more complex than public perceptions of their sexual behavior suggested. Most importantly, their varying responses provide a lens through which we can understand how working-class black women dealt with sex in the city. Like their white counterparts, they experimented with courting, treating, and the sex trade, but what Evelyn Brooks Higginbotham calls the "metalanguage of race," especially "racial constructions of sexuality,"

influenced the distinct reactions of authority figures. Racial stereotypes led the police and Bedford administrators to view black women's "sexual delinquency" as natural, rather than judging the conduct of individuals.[3] Essentialized renderings of black women's sexuality, coupled with black reformers' concerted efforts to counter these negative images by repressing discussions of sexual desire, have obscured ordinary black women's decisions and dilemmas regarding sex. While black women enjoyed a greater range of choices regarding the conduct of their social lives, they faced more restrictive treatment by public officials and higher expectations from their community. The stories of black women offer a window into how they remembered and decided to describe past sexual encounters. This [essay] focuses on the ways in which working-class black women constructed their own narratives and the kinds of details they chose to reveal about their sexual experiences. In early-twentieth-century New York, a moral panic about working-class female sexuality shaped the agenda of urban reformers and the criminal justice system. Local and state officials' racialized conceptions of women's sexual behavior influenced the dynamics of reform in black communities as well as the tenor of Bedford's institutional policies.

Incarcerated women offer a perspective that places black working-class women's own ideas about and experiences with sexuality at the center of the discussion. While historians have explored the sexuality of white working-class women, the sexual experiences of black working-class and poor women have rarely been examined. Female offenders' viewpoints vividly underscore the complexity of the black working class. Black women understood, experienced, and expressed heterosexual and same-sex desire at the same time that they had to deal with others' perceptions of and attempts to regulate their sexuality.[4] Looking at this dynamic from the perspective of a specific group of working-class women responds to Evelynn Hammonds's call to consider "how differently located black women engaged in reclaiming the body and expressing desire." Scholarship on black women's sexuality at the turn of the twentieth century has emphasized that black women refrained from discussing sexual desire and advocated behavior that rejected stereotypes that defined them as sexually promiscuous or deviant. Black female activists promoted what Evelyn Brooks Higginbotham calls the "politics of respectability"; decorous behavior was a defensive response to gendered images of black immorality as well as to civil and political inequalities.[5] Black women enacted what Darlene Clark Hine calls a "culture of dissemblance," creating "the appearance of openness and disclosure but actually" fashioning a silence about their personal and sexual lives that protected them "from their oppressors." Hammonds argues that the "politics of silence" worked so successfully that black women eventually "lost the ability to articulate any conception of their sexuality." The most significant exception was the blues singer, who expressed sexual desire through explicit lyrics and performance.[6]

Black women confined at Bedford include both those who practiced a "politics of silence" and those who openly expressed an identity as sexual beings. Answering the explicit questions that Bedford administrators asked all women during the admissions process, black domestics, laundresses, factory workers, and children's nurses between the ages of sixteen and twenty-eight revealed a range of sexual experiences that occurred as a result of desire, ignorance, or abuse. In some cases, administrators became frustrated when black women acknowledged their involvement in the sex trade but were reticent about conveying further details. For example, a twenty-year-old Virginia native was characterized as "pleasant" and "truthful" but provided officials with "little information about herself."[7] White female administrators (and one white male superintendent) documented black inmates' sense of propriety when they refused to talk about their sexual experiences or said they complied with moral proscriptions by rejecting premarital sex.

Female offenders' responses to prison administrators might be seen as evidence of the state's intrusion into black women's lives and an attempt to construct and reinforce derogatory racialized images. Yet black women understood administrators' skepticism when what they recounted did not coincide with long-standing stereotypes. Consider, for instance, the sexual history of one inmate who revealed that she had been raped and had prostituted herself twice but adamantly denied that she was promiscuous. The administrator seemed to dismiss the woman's difficult circumstances by focusing solely on her demeanor,

noting that the woman's "better education" had given her a "superior manner" and her "distant and haughty" attitude kept her from having an "attractive personality." Indeed, what administrators thought, as well as what they observed and chose to hear from black women, shaped the information recorded in all the case files.[8] But these partial transcripts also show how inmates challenged the public discourse that characterized all black women as pathologically promiscuous. These women's responses were particularly influenced by their attempts to negotiate Bedford's indeterminate sentencing; depending on how an administrator assessed an inmate's behavioral improvement, she could be given a minimum sentence of several months or a maximum sentence of three years.

... [B]lack women who felt compelled to silence outside the prison walls may have seen the admission interview as an opportunity to articulate their desires as well as to reveal sexual abuse. Some women described experiences that ranged from romance to participation in the sex trade. Others revealed the dangers encountered by young women alone in a large city. Understanding that white society believed that black women were complicit in their rapes, these inmates may have viewed administrators' direct question about whether their first "sexual offense" was consensual or rape as a chance to address their abuse in ways that may not have been possible with friends, family members, community leaders, or the police. Administrators' decision to label young women's first sexual encounters as criminal offenses reminds us of their moral position on premarital sex and makes clear their preconceived notions about working-class women.

Officials also observed and documented what they called "harmful intimacy": interracial relationships among the women incarcerated at Bedford. In 1917, "the disciplinary records of 175 women were studied for information as to the amount of harmful intimacy reported of officers ... and it was found that these inmates were frequently punished for such offenses." While acknowledging the prevalence of same-sex desire among white inmates, administrators were most concerned with attachments between black and white women. Records of conduct violations in white women's files, described variously as "fond of colored girls" or "seen passing notes to black inmates," provide evidence of these relationships.[9] Black women also received conduct violations, which indicates that they actively participated in inter-racial liaisons. Administrators, however, por-trayed "harmful intimacy" as white women's heterosexual attraction to black women whose dark skin color represented masculine virility rather than same-sex desire.[10] Officials attempted to ignore black women's participation in roman-tic relationships with other black women.

Prison officials overlooked their own evi-dence of black women's varied sexual experi-ences and instead based many of their evaluations on powerful racial stereotypes. Centuries-old preconceptions that defined black women as immoral and pathological deeply influenced their perceptions. As histori-ans Deborah Gray White and Jennifer Morgan have shown, seventeenth-century male Euro-peans depicted African women's bodies as savage, lewd, and unfeminine, and unleashed Christian condemnations of "uncivil" cultural practices, such as semi-nudity, polygamy, and dancing, that eventually justified the slave trade. (See Morgan's essay, pp. 24–33.) The as-sociation of lasciviousness with Africans shaped the development of slavery, [with] . . . Europeans view[ing] black men and women's bodies as "icon[s] for deviant sexuality." South-ern slaveholders accepted the notion that en-slaved women were sexually insatiable and depicted white men as victims of dark tempt-resses. The direct connections that southerners made between black women, immorality, and promiscuity remained vivid in popular culture long after slavery's demise. In 1904, when one southern white woman commented that she could not "imagine such a creation as a virtuous black woman," she articulated the sentiments of many late-nineteenth- and early-twentieth-century white Americans.[11]

When black women were imprisoned for sex-related and other minor offenses, prevail-ing stereotypes influenced Bedford prison of-ficials' assessment of their culpability. . . . Such written comments as "true African type . . . inclined to be somewhat vicious looking" and "a typical African cunning calculating eyes" indicate the depth of their prejudices in evalu-ating individual women. Observations were always qualified by race, ranging from "re-fined looking pretty colored girl" to "very infe-rior looking colored girl."[12] More positive appraisals, such as "appears intelligent for one of her race and station" and "has little moral sense but appears more decent than the aver-age colored girl," reveal officials' belief in black

inferiority. Regional biases are also apparent in initial interviews. Administrators observed the marks of southern origins—"peculiar way of speaking, a drawl and a typically Southern way of pronouncing words"—and questioned migrants' level of intelligence, fitness for urban life, and predisposition to criminality based on their diction.[13]

In 1924, Mabel Hampton, described by Bedford superintendent Amos Baker as a "small, rather bright and good looking colored girl," complicated Bedford officials' assump-tions. Administrators never questioned the va-lidity of her arrest, despite her fervent denials of solicitation. Yet they acknowledged that Hampton seemed unique. . . . They found her "alert" and "composed," with a "pleasant voice and manner of speaking." In another interview, they noted that Hampton's "attitude and manner seem truthful" and that she talked "freely and frankly conceal[ing] nothing." Al-though administrators found Hampton per-sonable and honest, they still imprisoned her. Ignoring their own observations regarding her credibility, officials judged Hampton based on their preconception that, even when black women had not violated the law, their sexual misconduct could be attributed to their innate susceptibility to "bad company." Hampton ex-plained her altercation with the police quite dif-ferently, calling her arrest a "put up job."[14]

The "ill-feeling" that Hampton expressed "toward her accuser" mirrored the sentiments of many black women and community mem-bers who contended that police corruption rather than women's behavior accounted for high numbers of prostitution arrests. Caught in a house raid when her employer of two years took an extended European trip, Hampton was most likely arrested because she was "between jobs." The fact that Hampton had access to her employer's home shows that she was trusted, but Hampton had no one to vouch for her repu-tation in court.[15] Her arrest resulted from the fact that the legislature and the courts had ex-panded the legal definition of vagrancy, which had applied only to public drunkards and per-sons "with no visible means of support," to in-clude anyone who "in any way, aids and abets or participates" in the sex trade. A plainclothes detective charged Hampton with being an ac-cessory to a sex crime by alleging that she per-mitted a female friend to use her employer's apartment for the "purposes of prostitution." According to Hampton, on the night of the arrest, she and a friend were waiting for their dates, "who promised to take them to a cabaret." Shortly after the men arrived, the police raided her employer's home and arrested both women. Hampton denied ever prostituting herself, contending that she had been seeing her date for a month and he "wanted to marry her." Hampton's perception of her boyfriend changed when she surmised that her date worked as a stool pigeon or police accomplice and arranged for her arrest. Hampton's evening excursion led to her imprisonment because in court, the police officer's word was deemed more legitimate than a young black domestic's.[16]

Young black working women who sought entertainment and companionship found themselves exposed to myriad danger. Not only could they be harassed by men at cabarets and dance halls, but they also could be arrested in a police set-up. In 1923, Harriet Holmes, a laundress making $15 a week, argued that she was falsely arrested when leaving a popular dance hall. It is not clear whether she arrived at the function with friends, but when she left at half past one o'clock in the morning she was alone. The twenty-three-year-old said that when she was walking to her apartment on West 133rd Street, a car stopped at the curb and four men claiming to be police officers pulled her into the car "without any reason . . . [and] declared that she was guilty of prostitution."[41] In a similar case, a twenty-two-year-old left a cabaret alone at half past one o'clock in the morning but followed her sister's advice to "always take a taxi" home after dark. When she got in the cab, "two men stepped in with her." She fought them, thinking they were robbers. Instead, they were policemen, who took her to the police station and arrested her for prostitution.[17]

Young black women found that the cheap and pleasurable practice of visiting friends' homes could also be a dangerous form of leisure. A number of women were arrested for solicitation while enjoying the company of friends in their tenement or boardinghouse rooms. Twenty-four-year-old Millie Hodges, for example, had separated from her husband of nine years and decided to leave Chicago and come to New York. She was visiting her friend's boardinghouse on 132nd Street when it was raided and its occupants were charged with "being disorderly."[18] Her denial that she had been soliciting and her assertion that she had

never been arrested did nothing to change her fate; she was convicted and sent to Bedford simply for visiting her friend's home at the wrong time. Young black women in Harlem enjoyed the freedom to partake of commercial and informal amusements, but the stigmas attached to working-class and black communities meant that their behavior was regulated on a discriminatory basis. . . .

Twenty-two-year-old Wanda Harding, a native of the British West Indies, acknowledged her misconduct in terms drawn from her Pentecostal background, recognizing her "great weakness and craving for the attractions of this world" and remarking that "everybody . . . is a born a sinner." Harding was acutely aware of her mistakes and struggled to face their consequences. Stating that "her father and mother were devout Christians" and concerned about her moral quandary, Harding's minister concluded that "through bad company she went astray [and] through good company she will be brought back again to the narrow way."[19] Relatives and black community members believed that young women should socialize only with respectable people and under appropriate circumstances.

While black people were aware of rampant police corruption, they expressed serious concerns about young women's naive or wayward behavior. Even though they sympathized with those who had been falsely arrested for prostitution, they also questioned these young women's decisions to attend unsupervised dances, associate with unsavory people, or walk unaccompanied late at night. The families of young women were especially anxious. The mother of an eighteen-year-old Long Island native declared: "Her going to the bad was going to dances and then being led by others older than herself." This mother protested that she worked diligently to safeguard her children: "I have tried to bring my children up in a [C]hristian way [and] have done the best I knew of, but you know the world has to[o] many charms for young people of today." Working-class parents shared reformers' belief that "silk and electric lights" and other "evil influences" such as dance halls and saloons caused young women to go astray.[20]

Although they were acutely aware of black people's second-class citizenship and of racial discrimination, many young women simply wanted to enjoy Harlem's social life. While they understood their relatives' anxieties about its temptations, they sought diversion after they had worked all day. Many had been employed since they were twelve or thirteen years old. As a nineteen-year-old domestic from Washington, DC, asked: "Why shouldn't I go out some times if I worked?" These women hoped that the easy pleasure of commercial leisure would temporarily transport them from their everyday drudgery and the constant struggle to make ends meet. When they had extra money or they had a date, they spent their time in dance halls, gyrating enthusiastically to popular tunes. To the horror of most of their parents and community members, young women quickly learned popular dances, such as the "turkey trot" in the early 1910s and the "black bottom," the "mess around," and the "Charleston" in the 1920s. In 1914, Rev. Adam Clayton Powell noted that young blacks' fascination with music and dancing was evident "not only in their conversations but in the movement of their bodies about the home and on the street." This anxiety about the unrestrained black female body epitomized the black community's concerns about individual women's welfare, in addition to their belief that respectability was essential for a stable family life and a viable strategy for racial advancement.[21] Attending dances, cabarets, and movie theaters was not the most pressing problem or seductive inducement, however. Socializing within smaller, unsupervised, mixed-sex groups and the concomitant romantic and sexual interests alarmed adults and excited young women. Young women in prison disclosed the reasons why they rejected or became involved in premarital sexual relationships. Some were seduced by the promise of marriage, were led astray by curiosity, were too ignorant to understand the situation, or were willing to barter sex for nice things; others were subject to coercion.

Relatives constantly sought to prevent young women from acting independently and hoped to guide their moral lives. They chaperoned their young women, set up strict curfews, and encouraged them to devote their leisure time to church activities. In some instances, their efforts were successful, as a number of women prisoners adamantly denied ever having premarital intercourse. Relatives dealt directly with the consequences of young women's disobedient behavior. A twenty-three-year-old Cuban immigrant, for example, explained that after she became pregnant at the age of

fifteen, her aunt forced her to marry the baby's father.[22]

Miranda Edmonds's experience illustrates the tensions within families over leisure activities and sexuality. When recalling her first sexual encounter, the seventeen-year-old North Carolina migrant said that she was "partly forced" to have intercourse with her boyfriend. While she blamed the troubling experience on her "ignorance," she was "clear in opinion" that her parents were also at fault because the incident "would not have happened if she had had sex instruction." Edmonds raises a critical point that suggests how the "politics of silence" could injure young women even though their relatives believed that they were protecting their kin. Moreover, many working-class black parents agreed with the tenets of racial uplift's concern about sexual purity and reproduction but, in certain instances, chose not to be as open or explicit about "sex instruction" as the etiquette, sex, and home manuals that black leaders provided for black community members. Edmonds's position also highlights the complex consequences of her inexperience and her disregard for family rules regarding respectability: she was sent to Bedford by her mother as an incorrigible case because she stayed away from home for two consecutive days with her boyfriend.[23] Edmonds suffered from the gap between the adult behavior young women thought they exhibited when they dated and became sexually active and the maturity they actually needed to live as independent adults.

Many black women acknowledged that ignorance and curiosity fueled their sexual encounters. One twenty-five-year-old divulged that she had sex at fifteen but still "had no idea why." A twenty-year-old noted that her first encounter occurred because "she was [simply] foolish." A number of women admitted that they had intercourse because they "saw other girls do it" or that they were "curious to know what sex experience was." In another case, a nineteen-year-old revealed that she consented to sex with a boy because he was someone "she had known for some time," suggesting a degree of trust. These accounts convey these women's youthful lack of forethought about the physical and moral dangers of sexual relationships.[24]

The promise of marriage prompted a number of single women to engage in premarital sex. As romantic relationships transitioned into more intimate contact, young men, whether they were sincere or not, negotiated with girlfriends about the meaning of sex in relation to the couple's courtship and future commitment. For example, a nineteen-year-old baby nurse explained that she consented to sex because she "liked the man" and he "promised to marry her." In another case, a twenty-one-year-old unmarried waitress noted that she had her first sexual relationship at eighteen because she was "engaged." These women's expectation that marriage would follow their decision to have premarital sex was quite conventional. A boyfriend's refusal to marry a young woman in the wake of an unplanned pregnancy challenged her beliefs about courtship. . . . [25]

In the early twentieth century, young women's sexual activity was becoming more than a precursor to marriage. Some working women engaged in consensual and noncommercial sexual relationships outside of serious courtships. Scholars have highlighted the phenomenon known as "treating," in which women bartered sex or sexual favors for goods or commercial amusements rather than accepting money for intercourse. A nineteen-year-old black domestic, for example, emphasized that she took "presents from the men she went with but . . . never accepted money." Evelyn Pitts, who was also nineteen, claimed that she never prostituted herself but did have sex "off and on with two or three different men since she was 17." Like many other young women, she stressed that she "never [took] . . . money for it." The terms some women used to refer to their sexual partners, such as friend, sweetheart, or lover, suggest these women's distinct perceptions of acceptable heterosexual relationships. . . . [26]

. . . Relatives, reformers, and prison administrators viewed these women's situations quite differently; for them, treating represented a new form of female sexual delinquency. Young women's frequent admissions to being "immoral" suggest how they responded to administrators' specific questions about their premarital sexual practices. Like the twenty-three-year-old who disclosed that she had been "immoral" but denied that she had "ever practiced prostitution," these working women insisted that they had made an independent choice to engage in sex solely for the enjoyment it provided, not for income.[27]

Not all black women's sexual relationships were consensual, however. Young women recounted experiences of sexual harassment, rape, and abuse by employers as well as within their families. Mabel Hampton, for example, recalled that when she was eight years old her uncle had raped her; and when she was working as a domestic, men in the household "would try to touch" her inappropriately.[28] Like most women, Hampton understood that in any disclosure of sexual harassment, her credibility, not her assailant's would be questioned.

Some black women were abused by men they knew. A twenty-one-year-old told how she was raped by "the husband of her foster parent," and a twenty-four-year-old disclosed that she was raped by a "friend who was visiting her sister's house." Even seemingly innocent interactions between young women and men could lead to horrific consequences. A twenty-three-year-old domestic recalled that she was forced into intercourse at fifteen when she and a boy "were playing school" and then a game called "Mama and Papa," which she "did not understand" until it was too late.[29]

Even as they were indicted for sexual offenses themselves, these women disclosed that rape committed by a family member, friend, or neighbor had made a huge impact on their lives. In this forum with prison administrators, where they knew their stories would be recorded, black women revealed their harrowing experiences. They understood that administrators would not take legal action against their abusers, but they believed that speaking of their trauma was important enough to provide details about it. Some may have sought to mitigate administrators' negative view of them as well. Twenty-three-year-old domestic and Colorado native Sally Bruce seems to have blamed herself for her abuse when she explained how she dealt with her rape. She revealed that her "first time was at 20 years [old] without her consent" but decided to continue with the relationship, rationalizing that "she was a woman, no longer a child and intended to marry" her abuser. Indeed, Bruce's belief that she had no other options highlights the difficult choices working women made when negotiating their sexuality in light of the longstanding pernicious belief that black women could not be raped.[30]

Black women's decision to enter the sex trade represented a difficult choice for those who did so to supplement their paltry salaries as personal-service laborers. Highlighting the contrast between the inadequate wages paid for menial labor work and the higher earnings brought by solicitation, Heather Hayes, a twenty-six-year-old New York native who toiled as a cook and chambermaid, acknowledged that she had "practiced prostitution off and on since she was seventeen" to supplement her income. This sort of testimony was corroborated by a 1914 Women's Court investigation that concluded that black women's "meager salaries and uncongenial surroundings tend to produce a state of dissatisfaction which sometimes leads . . . to prostitution." Unlike the twenty-two-year-old laundress who admitted to being a "habitual prostitute," many black women claimed that they solicited only infrequently. For instance, a twenty-three-year-old acknowledged that she "prostituted with 2 men in 3 years" but, while conceding that she had been "immoral," denied "being promiscuous."[31]

Black women's behavior after arrest suggests that they struggled with the psychological consequences of their decision to solicit. The 1914 Women's Court study indicated that when questioned during admission interviews, twenty-four out of fifty-six women stated that they were single and alone in the city "without near relatives." At least eight of these women "admitted having mothers" in New York but refused to provide their addresses to court administrators because they did not want their relatives "to know where they were." The investigation concluded that most of the women came from "poor but respectable homes" but eventually buckled under the pressures of inadequate wages and bad company. . . . [32]

The lure of easy money led some young women to enter the sex trade full time. A seventeen-year-old domestic earning $7 a month claimed she was able to make "about $10 a week" as a prostitute. A few women needed money to support their drug habit. And a small group of women claimed that they solicited because they enjoyed sex and needed money for material possessions. The same year that one sixteen-year-old domestic consented to have sex with her "boy-sweetheart," she also began prostituting herself for "money and pleasure." Another woman entered the sex trade because "she saw other girls with nice things and wanted them too." . . . [33]

Poor black women who made a difficult but definite choice to work in legitimate jobs understood the impact of prostitution on their lives all too well. Often living in the same neighborhoods where the trade thrived, they negotiated their moral stance against the sex trade on a daily basis and contended with the

generally accepted notion that black women were its natural participants. Although most black reformers expressed their frustration with prostitution in a public forum and incorporated their concerns in their work, like-minded working women must have also talked with one another and their families about their anxieties. One twenty-four-year-old domestic told prison administrators that "prostitution is . . . the worst crime anybody can . . . commit because you have to do things that take away your self-respect." Women like her made a conscious choice not to prostitute and were frustrated that they were consistently mistaken for and often arrested as sex workers. Relatedly, they made specific distinctions between immorality and promiscuity. During the period of what scholars have defined as the early-twentieth-century sexual revolution, where working-class women "self-consciously rejected Victorian mores," they understood their elders' condemnation of premarital sex and would agree that having sex before marriage and with men they did not intend to marry was immoral.[34] Their making a choice to engage in premarital intercourse, whether they considered themselves promiscuous or not, was quite different than their being innately drawn to sex because of their racial and socioeconomic status. Indeed, black working women were in a tenuous position as they negotiated their perceived as well as actual sexual identities. These women's concerns about prostitution reflected the negative consequences they feared and experienced when they exposed their sexual desires within their community.

During the 1920s, Harlem was the site not only of a renaissance in black cultural production but also for the open expression of various forms of sexuality. Many black residents and community leaders expressed grave concerns about the confluence of popular entertainment and nonmarital sex. They were particularly concerned about the growing visibility of same-sex relationships. Many were aware of the lesbian references in songs like Gertrude Ma Rainey's "Prove It on Me Blues" and the popular, sexually explicit parties held in Harlem.[35] Within many working-class communities, however, the public expression of sexual desire—of heterosexual desire, not to mention same-sex desire—was discouraged. With relatively few exceptions, black churches enunciated and attempted to enforce conservative gender and sexual norms.[36]

Ironically, some black ministers were discovering, or rather exposing, their own gay congregants during this time. Denunciation of these relationships conflated two distinct issues: same-sex desire and ministers who preyed on young male congregants. Rev. Adam Clayton Powell of the Abyssinian Baptist Church lamented that young women were increasingly involved in same-sex relationships, although he did not distinguish consensual from predatory relationships. "Homosexuality and sex-perversion among women," he thundered, "has grown into one of the most horrible debasing, alarming and damning vices of present day civilization." According to Powell, homosexuality was "prevalent to an unbelievable degree" and "increasing day by day." Powell's conflation of same-sex desire with the sexual abuse of children gained strong support from his colleagues as well as his congregation, whose responses on the day of his sermon indicated that his "opinions were endorsed and approved without limitations."[37] Mabel Hampton would have understood the minister's sentiments as representing the views of most Harlem residents, since she hid her sexual orientation in her neighborhood but participated in private rent parties. Many Harlemites gladly paid to enjoy a night of food, bootleg liquor, music, and dancing while helping a neighbor pay the rent. According to Hampton, partygoers might eat "chicken and potato salad," "pig feet, chittlins," and black-eyed peas and "dance and have fun" until the wee hours. But Hampton partied exclusively with other women, which some black Harlemites would not have accepted. Explaining her predicament in retrospect, Hampton revealed that as a young woman in Harlem she experienced a "free life" where she "could do anything she wanted," but publicly expressing her desire for women was out of the question. "When I was coming along everything was hush-hush," she recalled. She and women like her felt safer meeting at house parties, "private things where you'd go with" a woman without fear of reprisals.[38]

Hampton's recollections indicate that black women who desired women usually disguised their feelings in public, in order to avoid both the police and other black Harlemites. When women attended all-female parties, "very seldom did any of them [wear] . . . slacks . . . because they had to come through the streets." Instead, they played it safe and dressed in women's suits. "You couldn't go out there with too many pants on because the men was ready to see . . . and that was no good," Hampton stated. "You had to protect yourself and protect the woman that you was with." . . . Hampton's case . . . suggests that lesbians were less accepted in black neighborhoods than gay men, regardless of the residents' socioeconomic status.[39]

Hampton did not reveal whether she had experienced repercussions from exposing her attraction to women, but her fear prompted her to take precautions. She managed by limiting her contact with people who were not "in the life." Much later, she told a friend that even during the height of the Harlem Renaissance "you had to be very careful," which meant that Hampton and her friends "had fun behind closed doors."[40] Going out to bars was too much of a hassle because, as she recalled, "too many men was [tangled] up with it; . . . they didn't know you was a lesbian . . . [and] they didn't care. . . . You was a woman . . . [so] you had the public [and] you had the men to tolerate." Although she met a number of girlfriends when she was working as a dancer in Harlem cabarets such as the Garden of Joy, she eventually stopped dancing because, in her experience, it required exchanges with men. "I gave up the stage," she explained, "because unless you go with men you don't eat." As a gay rights activist later in life, Hampton spoke about herself as having embraced lesbianism directly and publicly as a young adult, yet when she was arrested for prostitution in 1924 she was not forthcoming about her sexual orientation. . . . [41]

Hampton's same-sex inclinations were shared by other women, black and white, but urban reformers and criminal justice administrators focused on regulating the behavior of heterosexual working-class women. During World War I, the federal government attempted to prevent the spread of venereal disease, not only by distributing condoms to the troops, but also by appropriating funds for at least forty-three reformatories and houses of detention that confined and treated "women and girls who, as actual and potential carriers of venereal diseases, were a menace to the health of the Military Establishment of the United States."[42] . . .

Bedford's goal was to reform young women by instilling morality and restraining sexual conduct. The institution opened in 1901, just when perceptions of aberrant female behavior were changing from the nineteenth-century idea of the "fallen woman" to the twentieth-century notion of the sexual delinquent. During the 1870s, reformers concerned about the growing number of young women in custodial prisons pushed for segregating women under thirty from older women because they believed that young first offenders had the capacity to be reformed. During Bedford's initial years, administrators believed that working-class women's delinquent behavior could be addressed and even eliminated through proper training. Bedford's first superintendent, Katharine Bement Davis, stated that the women who entered the institution were "capable of . . . education and industrial training" that "would restore them to society, self-respecting and self-supporting."[43] City magistrates and some state legislators, however, found the reformatory's operation too expensive, and it was consistently underfunded. Reformers argued that expenses related to rehabilitation far outweighed the consequences of being apathetic about urban crime. Bedford officials agreed. "The cost to the State of allowing [young women] to lead dishonorable, and perhaps criminal lives, . . . [perpetuating] their kind in succeeding generations in an ever-increasing propensity to evil," they declared, "is so very great [that] reformation . . . is the cheapest means of securing the public welfare."[44]

Reformers advocated practical programs of reform with varying degrees of success. Over the years, the institution ensured that inmates were constantly occupied, through industrial classes, religious services, or extracurricular activities. Instead of prison cells, women resided in individual cottages with matrons who encouraged family-style relationships. Some inmates seemed to enjoy this arrangement, as a number of paroled women wrote Bedford for permission to return to visit their friends. Inmates were separated by age in 1901. By 1924, when Ruby Brooks and Mabel Hampton were admitted, Bedford was segregated according to inmates' psychological diagnosis and race, with cottages designated for a range of inmates from "feeble-minded" white girls to newly admitted black girls.[45] . . .

Administrators agreed that the advent of probation, in which a woman was supervised in her community rather than being imprisoned, changed the type of inmate they received. Introduced in 1901, probation slowly parceled out the most redeemable female offenders and left the institution populated with probation violators, recidivists, and uncontrollable women. Katharine Bement Davis identified these inmates as the major impediment to Bedford's rehabilitation process. In 1906, Davis argued that if Bedford was to "receive so large a proportion of 'difficult' young women, whom probation and private institutions . . . have failed to help, the public must recognize the task" Bedford had before it. Since black women had more difficulty obtaining probation, their disproportionate representation in the institution's population increased as its reputation as a model reformatory declined. Black women who were first-time offenders, like Brooks and Hampton, were admitted along with white women whose behavior failed to warrant probation or who had violated probation. More young women were also being committed to Bedford, which led to overcrowding.[46]

Bedford's problems led to a 1914 State Commission of Prisons inspection and a scathing report, followed by public hearings a year later. While inspector Rudolph Diedling's report noted myriad problems with Bedford, ranging from its rural location to the fact that it could be more self-sustaining because it held "several hundred able-bodied young women delinquents whose labors should suffice for their maintenance," the report focused on the institution's inability to maintain discipline. During the public hearings, investigators noted that the most troubling issue involved same-sex romances between black and white inmates. Bedford's administrators publicly disclosed that the institution's primary disciplinary quandary stemmed from "harmful intimacy," or, rather, interracial sex.[47]

When the State Board of Charities' special investigative committee addressed Bedford's "harmful intimacy," it focused on the fact that, unlike most women's prisons in the North or the South, Bedford was racially integrated. When questioned about this policy, former superintendent Katharine Davis explained that she did "not believe in segregation by color in principle and [had] not found it to work well in practice." The committee strongly recommended segregation. With Davis no longer the superintendent, Bedford's Board of Managers agreed with the committee's final recommendations, which pronounced segregation to be the most viable solution to inappropriate interracial relationships. Denying any accusation of racism, the board declared that "most undesirable sex relations grow out of . . . mingling of the two races." The board defended its right to segregate inmates against the protests of those who argued that racial segregation was "contrary to the equal rights of all citizens under the Constitution." Explaining the discretionary power given to them by the State Charities Law, the Board of Managers argued that "individual rights are not disturbed by the separation of delinquents into groups when such segregation is likely to promote reformation and prevent undesirable relations."[48] In 1917, Bedford institutionalized racial segregation with two cottages "set apart" for black women. Superintendent Helen Cobb explained that, in addition to disciplinary concerns, the separate cottages were established as a result of written requests by black inmates. . . . Ironically, even after racial segregation was established, administrators failed to acknowledge publicly that "harmful intimacy" persisted as inmates continued to pursue relationships across the color line.[49]

The actions of Bedford administrators and state officials coincided with the views of psychiatrists and prison reformers. Generally, psychiatrists and prison reformers addressed the issue of female homosexuality by emphasizing, to the virtual exclusion of other romantic or sexual attachments, the problem of developing relationships between white and black inmates. They portrayed white women's participation in same-sex, interracial relationships within the confines of the prison as a longing for masculinity. The psychologist Margaret Otis voiced the opinions of many scientific observers when she argued in the *Journal of Abnormal Psychology* in 1913 that whether viewed as "an affair simply for fun and . . . lack of anything more interesting to take up their attention" or as a relationship of "serious fascination and . . . [an] intensely sexual nature," this kind of association had a racial and gendered character. "The difference in color," she added, "takes the place of difference in sex." Much like Cesare Lombroso's 1895 linkage of black women's color and physical features with masculinity and criminality, Otis's explanation of same-sex desire equated black women's darker skin color with virility. Moreover, these relationships could be described as an example of what Regina Kunzel calls "racialized gender inversion." For example, a white woman to whom Otis referred in her article "admitted that the colored girl she loved seemed the man." In 1921, a Bedford official explained that black women's "abandon and virility . . . offered" white women "the nearest

substitute" for the opposite sex. According to her, black women functioned as masculine substitutes who fulfilled white women's heterosexual desire. Psychologists and prison administrators characterized white inmates' attraction to one another as nothing more than crushes. In their courtships, according to one report, women "vow that they will be friends forever, dream and plan together, confide their deepest secrets," and there is no serious connection to homosexuality. White inmates, whether or not they were aggressors in these affairs, maintained a normative heterosexual status. In this sense, administrators failed to address same-sex desire directly, but rather constructed their explanations so that, as Kunzel remarks, "homosexuality was heterosexuality; the unnatural was natural." In contrast to white inmates, black women at Bedford were rarely portrayed as initiating relationships, although they may have done so. Administrators did not characterize black women as responding in like manner to the attentions of white women, or as experiencing crushes among themselves. By and large, black women's romantic attachments, whether heterosexual or homosexual, were ignored.[50] . . .

The attraction that white inmates expressed for black women . . . was usually diagnosed by administrators as mental deficiency, which they described variously in terms that ranged from feeblemindedness to psychopathology. When defending Bedford from charges that the institution fomented interracial, same-sex relationships, the president of the Board of Managers, James Woods, conflated women's working-class status with deviant sexual behavior, arguing that women initiated these kinds of associations before they entered the reformatory. Addressing the problem without direct reference to black women, Woods remarked that this behavior was "not uncommon among the people of this class and character in the outside world, and when inmates addicted to these practices come into the institution it is practically impossible to prevent them finding an opportunity in some way or other to continue them." Woods's assessment shows how administrators attempted to deflect responsibility for an escalating disciplinary problem by suggesting that these relationships should not be solely defined as "situational homosexuality," that is, the consequence of incarceration among women. Indeed, Woods's perspective highlighted what administrators had already discovered: that homoerotic relationships were also emerging in the larger society, both black and white.[51] . . .

[Lynette] Moore's case illustrates the fluid nature of sexuality: some women desired men as well as women. . . . Moore married and became pregnant after being discharged, but she stayed in contact with Connie Carlson, the white inmate with whom she developed an "undesirable friendship" in Bedford. After Moore became estranged from her husband, the two women began living together. At some point, an anonymous letter was sent to a charitable agency informing it that Moore had become a beggar and Carlson was "usually with her." In contrast to Mabel Hampton, who attempted to keep her romantic relationships private, Moore did not conceal her romance—and suffered the consequences. Five years later, Moore was arrested for gun possession and again sent to Bedford. Bedford officials refused to keep her, but they did interview her. Moore explained that while working as a nightclub hostess she had continued to experience relationship problems, as she wanted to marry her boyfriend but had not divorced her first husband. Her second case file documents her continuing tie to Carlson. Although neither woman could support the other or Moore's infant and they stopped living together, Moore acknowledged her continued connection with Carlson.[52] Moore's reference to Carlson as a friend indicates that she boldly defied Bedford's continual attempts to keep the women apart. Yet the institution was simply another conduit for enforcing a respectable domesticity and de facto racial segregation. Both women were married with children; Moore lived in Manhattan while Carlson resided in Long Island. Moore's simple but bold actions provide us with a hint of the struggle that she and Carlson faced as they attempted to maintain a connection with one another.

Mabel Hampton's experience complicates prison officials' essentialized portraits of homoerotic relationships. The story of her lesbianism, which was never directly mentioned in her case file but revealed through her subsequent social activism, challenges Bedford administrators' premise about "harmful intimacy" and highlights many of the institution's evaluative discrepancies. In Hampton's brief account of her Bedford experience, she openly acknowledged the prevalence of same-sex relationships and affirmed her participation in them, though she did not indicate whether they were interracial or intraracial. She remembered these relationships as comforting. After she and another prisoner revealed their attraction to one another, Hampton recalled, the woman "took me in her bed and held me in her arms and I went to sleep." Although Hampton was attracted to women and dated men before her imprisonment, her Bedford experience may have provided her with an opportunity to embrace her same-sex desire more fully. . . . Hampton's case [also] suggests the extent of administrators' indifference to black women's sexuality within the prison. Yet Hampton's post-Bedford life as a lesbian was in some ways an open secret: she and her black partner, Lillian Foster, who met in 1932 and remained together until Foster's death in 1978, "negotiated the public world as 'sisters.'" . . . Referring to themselves as sisters protected them from unwanted attention and allowed "expressions of affection" that "demanded a recognition of their intimacy."[53]

Mabel Hampton's experiences in Harlem and at Bedford as recorded by prison administrators and her subsequent reflections upon her life provide a unique lens through which we can view black women's sexuality. She was neither a reformer advocating the "politics of respectability" nor a blues singer expressing sexual desire through performance. Rather, her life shows the complex ways that young women acknowledged the importance of decorum at the same time that they participated in consumer culture and popular amusements. Women faced enormous challenges as they sought to establish their independence in a society that simultaneously offered uninhibited opportunities for pleasure and was threatened by working-class women's sexual behavior. Relatives, community members, and the police monitored young women's sexual expression and generally supported the rehabilitative objectives of state institutions like Bedford.

The case files of black women at Bedford give us a sense of the language that ordinary black women used to describe their sexual experiences. Although the information found in prisoners' case files has been mediated through prison administrators' biases, we can discern the stories that black women chose to impart behind officials' responses to those narratives. The sexual experiences that are documented in Bedford's records range from premarital heterosexual intercourse and same-sex desire to rape and prostitution. The concerns of black women's relatives and community members often conflicted with what black women wanted for themselves. In their interactions with the community residents black women acted as cautiously as they did around representatives of the state. Mabel Hampton's reflections about Harlem highlight how she dissembled in her neighborhood. Black women who were attracted to women "had to be careful" and "had fun behind closed doors."[54]

Although Hampton seems to have hidden her relationships with women when she was incarcerated, other women, black and white, flaunted their attachments. Bedford claimed that the majority of their disciplinary problems stemmed not simply from same-sex relationships but from "harmful intimacy," that is, intimacy that crossed the color line. Prison administrators' anxieties about interracial relationships mirrored the national preoccupation with interracial social and sexual relationships. Instituting racial segregation did more to assuage their racial anxieties than to address the issue of "harmful intimacy." When some officials acknowledged that young women brought same-sex romance into the institution and that same-sex relationships might not be a consequence of imprisonment, they illuminated the fact that sexual expression took many forms both within and outside Bedford. . . .

Notes

1. James Weldon Johnson, *Black Manhattan* (New York: Da Capo Press, 1991; orig. publ., New York, 1930), 160–61; Jervis Anderson, *This Was Harlem: A Cultural Portrait, 1900-1950* (New York: Farrar, Straus, and Giroux, 1982), 139. Regarding the practice of slumming, see Kevin J. Mumford, *Interzones: Black/White Districts in Chicago in the Early Twentieth Century* (New York: Columbia University Press, 1997), 133-56; and Chad Heap, *Slumming: Sexual and Racial Encounters in American Nightlife, 1885–1940* (Chicago: University of Chicago Press, 2009).

2. Allan M. Brandt, *No Magic Bullet: A Social History of Venereal Disease in the United States since 1880* (New York: Oxford University Press, 1985); Elizabeth Alice Clement, *Love for Sale: Courting, Treating, and Prostitution in New York City, 1900–1945* (New York: Basic Books, 1994), esp. chs. 4 and 7; Estelle Freedman, *Their Sisters's Keepers: Women's Prison Reform in America, 1830–1930* (Ann Arbor: University of Michigan Press, 1981), 109–142; Mary Odem, *Delinquent Daughters: Protecting and Policing Adolescent Female Sexuality in the United States, 1885–1920* (Chapel Hill: University of North Carolina Press, 1985), 1–7, 95–127; Ruth Alexander, *The "Girls' Problem": Female Sexual Delinquency in New York, 1890–1930* (Ithaca, N.Y.: Cornell University Press,

1995), 1–7, 33–66; Joanne Meyerowitz, "Sexual Geography and Gender Economy: The Furnished-Room Districts of Chicago, 1890–1930," in *Unequal Sisters: A Multi-Cultural Reader in U.S. Women's History*, 3rd ed., ed. Vicki L. Ruiz and Ellen Carol DuBois (New York: Routledge, 2000), 307–23.

3. Evelyn Brooks Higginbotham, "African-American Women's History and the Metalanguage of Race," *Signs* 17 (Winter 1992), 262.

4. My thinking about working-class women's sexuality has been influenced by Kathy Peiss, "'Charity Girls' and City Pleasures: Historical Notes on Working-Class Sexuality, 1880–1920," in *Passion and Power: Sexuality in History*, ed. Kathy Peiss and Christina Simmons with Robert A. Padgug (Philadelphia: Temple University Press, 1989), 57–69; Peiss, *Cheap Amusements: Working Women and Leisure in Turn-of-the-Century New York* (Philadelphia: Temple University Press, 1986); and Christine Stansell, *City of Women: Sex and Class in New York, 1789–1860* (Urbana: University of Illinois Press, 1987). Examples of black women expressing same-sex desire are found Hansen, "'No Kisses Like Youres': An Erotic Friendship between Two African-American Women during the Mid-Nineteenth Century," *Gender & History* 7 (August 1995), 153–82; Farah Jasmine Griffin, ed., *Beloved Sisters and Loving Friends: Letters from Rebecca Primus of Royal Oak, Maryland, and Addie Brown of Hartford, Connecticut, 1854–1868* (New York: Knopf, 1999); and Elizabeth Lapovsky Kennedy and Madeline D. Davis, *Boots of Leather, Slippers of Gold: The History of a Lesbian Community* (New York: Routledge, 1993).

5. Evelynn M. Hammonds, "Black (W)holes and the Geometry of Black Female Sexuality," *differences: A Journal of Feminist Cultural Studies* 6, nos. 2–3 (Summer 1994), 138; Higginbotham, *Righteous Discontent, The Women's Movement in the Black Baptist Church, 1880–1920* (Cambridge, MA: Harvard University Press, 1993), 185–229. Elsa Barkley Brown has pointed out that "the struggle to present Black women and the Black community as 'respectable' eventually led to repression within the community"; "Imaging Lynching: African American Women, Communist Struggle, and Collective Memory," in *African American Women Speak Out on Anita Hill-Clarence Thomas*, ed. Geneva Smitherman (Detroit: Wayne State University Press, 1995), 108.

6. On black women's sexuality in relation to the blues, see Hazel V. Carby, "'It Jus Be's Dat Way Sometime': The Sexual Politics of Black Women's Blues," in *Unequal Sisters*, 330–41. See also Angela Davis, *Blues Legacies and Black Feminism: Gertrude "Ma" Rainey, Bessie Smith and Billie Holiday* (New York: Vintage Books, 1998), 40; Ann Ducille, "Blue Notes on Black Sexuality: Sex and the Texts of Jessie Fauset and Nella Larsen," *Journal of the History of Sexuality* 3, no. 3 (1993), 418–44; Hortense J. Spillers, "Interstices: A Small Drama of Words," in *Pleasure and Danger: Exploring Female Sexuality*, edited by Carole S. Vance (Boston: Routledge and Kegan Paul, 1984), 74.

7. All women who entered Bedford were asked who told them about sex, when and at what age they had their first sexual encounter, and whether that encounter was consensual. Finally, they were asked whether they practiced prostitution and, if they did,

at what age they entered the trade as well as how much money they earned; Inmate #3724, Admission Record, August 1924; and Recommendation for Parole, March 10, 1925, Bedford Hills Correctional Facility, 14610–77B Inmate Case Files, ca. 1915–30, 1955–65, Records of the Dept. of Correctional Services, New York State Archives, State Education Dept., Albany, NY (hereafter, BH). [I have used a pseudonym for inmates' names but have retained original case numbers.]

8. Inmate #3706, History Blank, July 8, 1924, BH. For some issues of interpretation, see Regina Kunzel, "Pulp Fictions and Problem Girls: Reading and Rewriting Single Pregnancy in the Postwar United States," *American Historical Review* 100 (Dec. 1995), 1468–69, and Timothy Gilfoyle, "Prostitutes in History: From Parables of Pornography to Metaphors of Modernity," *American Historical Review* 104 (Feb. 1999), 139–40.

9. State of New York, State Board of Charities, *Report of the Special Committee*, 7; Inmate #2475, Conduct Record, Oct.–Dec. 1918; and Inmate #4044, Conduct Record, June 13, 1926, BH.

10. Margaret Otis, "A Perversion Not Commonly Noted," *Journal of Abnormal Psychology* 3, no. 2 (June–July 1913), 113.

11. Jennifer L. Morgan, "'Some Could Suckle over Their Shoulder': Male Travelers, Female Bodies, and the Gendering of Racial Ideology, 1500–1770," *William and Mary Quarterly*, 3rd ser., 54 (Jan. 1997) 167–92; Deborah Gray White, *Ar'n't I a Woman? Female Slaves in the Plantation South*, rev. ed. (New York: W.W. Norton, 1999), 29–34; Sander L. Gilman, "Black Bodies, White Bodies: Toward and Iconography of Female Sexuality in Late Nineteenth-Century Art, Medicine, and Literature," *Critical Inquiry* 12, no. 1 (Autumn 1985), 209 (quotation); "Experiences of the Race Problem: By a Southern White Woman," *Independent* 56 (Mar. 17, 1904): 46 (quotation).

12. Inmate #3533, History Blank, Oct. 24, 1923; Inmate #3521, History Blank, Sept. 20, 1923; Inmate #3333, History Blank, Dec. 26, 1922; Inmate #3728, Admission Record, Aug. 19, 1924, BH.

13. Inmate #3699, Admission Record, July 10, 1924; Inmate #3502, History Blank, Aug. 22, 1923; Inmate #4477, Escape Description Record, July 19, 1928, BH.

14. Inmate #3696, History Blank, July 10, 1924; Recommendation for Parole, Jan. 1925; and History blank, July 10, 1924, BH. I have revealed this inmate's name and case file in accordance with the Freedom of Information Act of 1966, 5 USC Sec. 552, Part I, Subchapter II.

15. After returning from Europe, Hampton's employer was apparently so "indignant at the idea of her apartment having been used for purposes of prostitution that she refused to appear" in court to vouch for Hampton's character, although Hampton had been in "faithful service" for at least two years. See Inmate #3696, letter from Amy M. Prevost to Dr. Amos T. Baker, Nov. 13, 1924, BH.

16. Arthur B. Springarn, *Laws Relating to Sex Morality in New York City* (New York: Century Co., 1915 (revised by W. Bruce Cobb in 1926), 32–33; Joan Nestle, "'I Lift My Eyes to the Hill': The Life of Mabel Hampton as Told by a White Woman," in Nestle, *A Fragile Union: New and Selected Writings*

(San Francisco: Cleis Press, 1998), 34; Inmate #3696, Recommendation for Parole, Jan. 13, 1925, BH.

17. Inmate, 3474, History Blank, July 1923; Inmate #3489, History Blank, Aug. 1, 1923; and Preliminary Investigation, ca. June 1923, BH.

18. Inmate #3535, History Blank, Oct. 18, 1923, BH. On visiting, see William Fielding Ogburn, "The Richmond Negro in New York City: His Social Mind as Seen in His Pleasures" (Master's thesis, Columbia University, 1909), 60–61.

19. Inmate #3377, History Blank, Feb. 16, 1923 and letter from Minister to Bedford Reformatory, Aug. 13, 1923, BH.

20. Inmate #4058, letter of Inmate's Mother to Superintendent Baker, April 26, 1926, BH; "Silk and Lights Blamed for Harlem Girls' Delinquency," *Baltimore Afro-American*, May 19, 1928, Reel 31, Tuskegee Institute Clippings File (hereafter, TNCF).

21. Inmate #2505, Mental Examination, Attitude Toward Offense, Sept. 18, 1917, BH; "Race is Dancing Itself to Death," *New York Age*, Jan. 8, 1914. See Higginbotham, *Righteous Discontent*, 194–204; Kevin K. Gaines, *Uplifting the Race: Uplifting the Race: Black Leadership, Politics, and Culture in the Twentieth Century* (Chapel Hill: University of North Carolina Press, 1996), 152–78; and Michele Mitchell, *Righteous Propagation: African Americans and the Politics of Racial Destiny after Reconstruction*, 76–140.

22. Inmates #3696, 3389, 4058, 2796; Cuban immigrant: Inmate #3501, History Blank, Aug. 21, 1923, BH.

23. Inmate #4028, History Blank, ca. Feb, 1926, BH. On manuals, see Mitchell, *Righteous Propagation*, chs. 3 and 4.

24. Inmate #3722, History Blank, Aug. 26, 1924; Inmate #3721, History Blank, Oct. 10, 1924; Inmate #2760, History Blank, ca. Dec. 7, 1925; Inmate #3699, History Blank, July 19, 1924; Inmate #2504, Statement of Girl, Aug. 8, 1917, BH.

25. Inmate #3705, History Blank, July 18, 1924; and Inmate #4498, History Blank, ca. Mar. 30, 1926, BH; see Clement, *Love for Sale*, 18–25.

26. Inmate #2505, Statement of Girl, Aug. 2, 1917; Inmate #2504, Statement of Girl, Aug. 8, 1917; Inmates #3367, 3386, 2505, BH. On treating, see Peiss, *Cheap Amusements*, 108–14; and Clement, *Love for Sale*, 45–75.

27. Inmate #3718; also see Inmates #3533, 3474, 4498, BH.

28. Rape: Nestle, "Excerpts from the Oral History of Mabel Hampton," 930; see also Nestle, *Fragile Union*, 32. Touching: excerpt from tape-recorded oral history interviews with Mabel Hampton, by Joan Nestle, MH-2 Box 3, Mabel Hampton Special Collection, Lesbian Herstory Archives, Brooklyn, NY (hereafter, MHSC).

29. Inmate #4501, Summary Report on Application for Parole, ca. 1928; Inmate #2480, Statement of Girl, June 23, 1917; Inmate #4078, History Blank, ca. May 1, 1926, BH.

30. Inmate #3706, History Blank, July 18, 1924, BH; see Melton A. McLaurin, *Celia, A Slave* (New York: Bard, 1991).

31. Inmate #3494, Recommendation for Parole, ca. 1924, BH; Carietta V. Owens, "Investigation of Colored Women at Night Court. From June 8th to August 8th 1914," Folder-Women's Court-Negro Cases, Box 63, p. 7, Committee of Fourteen Collection,

New York Public Library, Rare Books and Manuscripts Division, Astor, Lenox, and Tilden Foundations, New York, NY (hereafter, COF); Inmate #3497, History Blank, Aug. 13, 1923; Inmate #3706, History Blank, July 18, 1924, BH.

32. Owens, "Investigation of Colored Women at Night Court," p. 7. For background on reformers' argument about the relationship between women's low wages and prostitution, see Freedman, *Their Sisters' Keepers*, 114, 123–24.

33. Inmate #2497, Verified History, July 26, 1917; Inmate #3365, History Blank, Feb. 8, 1923; Inmate #4063, History Blank, ca. April 23, 1926, BH.

34. Inmate #2480, Information Concerning the Patient, June 23, 1917, BH. See Meyerowitz, "Sexual Geography," 307.

35. Kevin J. Mumford, "Homosex Changes: Race, Cultural Geography, and the Emergence of the Gay," *American Quarterly* 48 (Sept. 1996): 400, 402–405; Angela Davis, *Blues Legacies and Black Feminism: Gertrude "Ma" Rainey, Bessie Smith and Billie Holiday* (New York: Vintage Books, 1998), 39–40; and Carby, "'It Jus Be's Dat Way Sometime,'" 337.

36. Evelyn Brooks Higginbotham, "Rethinking Vernacular Culture: Black Religion and Race Records in the 1920s and 1930s," in *The House That Race Built: Black Americans, U.S. Terrain*, ed. Wahneema Lubiano (New York: Pantheon Books, 1997), 157–77. In his discussion of Chicago minister Clarence Cobbs, Wallace D. Best argues that the black working class seemed more accepting of gay black men than the black middle class; see Best, *Passionately Human, No Less Divine: Religion and Culture in Black Chicago* (Princeton, N.J.: Princeton University Press, 2005), 188–89.

37. Eric Garber, "A Spectacle in Color: The Lesbian and Gay Subculture of Jazz Age Harlem," in *Hidden from History: Reclaiming the Gay and Lesbian Past*, ed. Martin Baumal Duberman, Martha Vicinus, and George Chauncey, Jr. (New York: New American Library, 1989), 318–31. See also, "Dr. A. C. Powell Scores Pulpit Evils," *New York Age*, Nov. 16, 1929, p. 1; "Dr. Powell's Crusade against Abnormal Vice Is Approved," ibid., Nov. 23, 1929; and "Corruption in the Pulpit," *New York Amsterdam News*, Dec. 11, 1929, p. 20. George Chauncey, Jr., discusses this issue in *Gay New York: Gender, Urban Culture, and the Making of the Gay Male World, 1890–1940* (New York: Basic Books, 1994), 254–57.

38. Mabel Hampton interview by Joan Nestle, May 21, 1981, Hampton tape, 10, 11, MHSC.

39. Mabel Hampton interview by Joan Nestle, *LFL Coming Out Stories*, June 21, 1981, 8, Box 3, MHSC. Another version is in Nestle, *Fragile Union*, 36.

40. Hampton interview by Nestle, May 21, 1981, Hampton tape, 9, MHSC. The statements quoted in the text came in response to Nestle's question: "How would you describe the twenties? Was it a good period to be gay?"

41. Hampton interview by Nestle, *LFL Coming Out Stories*, June 21, 1981, 9, Box 3, MHSC.

42. Mary Macey Dietzler, *Detention Houses and Reformatories as Protective Social Agencies in the Campaign of the United States against Venereal Diseases* (Washington, D.C.: U.S. Government Printing Office, 1922), 27. See also Allan M. Brandt, *No Magic Bullet: A Social History of Venereal Disease in the United States since 1880* (New York: Oxford University Press), 52–121; and Clement, *Love for Sale*, 114–43.

43. Katharine Bement Davis, "A Plan for the Conversion of the Laboratory of Social Hygiene at Bedford Hills to a State Clearing House . . . ," Bureau of Social Hygiene General Material 1911-16, Box 6, Record Group 2, Rockefeller Boards, Rockefeller Archive Center, Tarrytown, NY.

44. New York State Reformatory for Women at Bedford Hills, *Annual Report of the New York State Reformatory for Women at Bedford for the Year Ending September 30, 1901* (Albany, N.Y.: J. B. Lyon, 1902), 7, New York State Library, Cultural Education Center, Albany, NY (hereafter, NYSL). For the trajectory of women's prison reform from private benevolence to state control, see Gunja Sen-Gupta, *From Slavery to Poverty: The Racial Origins of Welfare in New York, 1840–1918* (New York: New York University Press, 2009).

45. See, for example, Inmate #2507, letter from Inmate to Superintendent Cobb, March 1, 1920, BH. New York State Reformatory for Women at Bedford, *Annual Report . . . for the Year Ending September 30, 1901*, 17–18. Expectant mothers and inmates who had children no older than two years were also housed in a separate cottage.

46. Freedman, *Their Sisters' Keepers*, 138–39; Charles L. Chute, "Probation and Suspended Sentence," *Journal of Criminal Law and Criminology* 12 (Feb. 1922), 559; State of New York, *New York State Reformatory for Women at Bedford, Sixth Annual Report . . .* (Albany: J. B. Lyon, 1906), 17, NYSL. According to Davis, administrators noticed the change in the type of inmate committed to Bedford in 1905.

47. State of New York, State Commission of Prisons, *Twentieth Annual Report of the State Commission of Prisons* (Albany, N.Y.: The Commission, 1914), 116–19, NYSL; State of New York, State Board of Charities, *Report of the Special Committee, Consisting of Commissioner Kevin, Smith, and Mulry, Appointed to Investigate Charges Made against the New York State Reformatory for Women at Bedford Hills* (Albany, N.Y.: J. B. Lyon, 1915), 3–29 ("harmful intimacy," 7).

48. "Miss Davis Stands by Bedford Home," *New York Herald*, Dec. 24, 1914, p. 8; State of New York, State Board of Charities, *Report of the Special Committee*, 26–27; State of New York, State Board of Charities, *Annual Report for the Year* (Albany, N.Y.: J. B. Lyon, 1915), 96, NYSL.

49. State of New York, New York State Reformatory for Women at Bedford, *Seventeenth Annual Report . . .* (Albany, N.Y.: J. B. Lyon, 1918,) 8, 16, NYSL; Inmate #4044, Conduct Record, June 13, 1926, BH.

50. Otis, "A Perversion Not Commonly Noted," 114; Estelle Freedman, "The Prison Lesbian: Race, Class, and the Construction of the Aggressive Female Homosexual, 1915–1965," *Feminist Studies* 22 (Summer 1996): 400–401; Regina G. Kunzel, "Situating Sex: Prison Sexual Culture in the Mid-Twentieth-Century United States," *GLQ: Journal of Lesbian and Gay Studies* 8 (May 2002): 262; Moreno, *Who Shall Survive?*, 229, 230. See also Anne Meis Knupfer, "'To Become Good, Self-Supporting Women': The State Industrial School for Delinquent Girls at Geneva, Illinois, 1900–1935," *Journal of the History of Sexuality* 9 (Oct. 2000): 437–41.

51. State of New York, State Board of Charities, *Report of the Special Committee*, 8. See also Sarah

Potter, "'Undesirable Relations': Same-Sex Relationships and the Meaning of Sexual Desire at a Women's Reformatory during the Progressive Era," *Feminist Studies* 30 (Summer 2004): 400; Kunzel, "Situating Sex," 253–70, esp. 256–56.

52. Inmate #2503, letter from Church Mission of Help to Bedford, June 9, 1921, and letter from Church Mission of Help to Superintendent Baker, ca. June 1921, BH; Inmate #4092, Family History, ca. 1926, BH.

53. Joan Nestle, "Lesbians and Prostitutes: An Historical Sisterhood," in Nestle, *A Restricted Country* (New York: Firebrand Books, 1987), 169; Nestle, *Fragile Union*, 34–35, 40–41, 43. Billie Holiday noted the prevalence of same-sex relations when she was an inmate in the Federal Women's Reformatory at Alderson, Virginia; see Holiday, with William Duffy, *Lady Sings the Blues* (New York: Lancer Books, 1969), 132.

54. Mabel Hampton interview by Joan Nestle, May 21, 1981, Hampton tape, 9, MHSC.

LESLIE J. REAGAN
When Abortion Was a Crime: Reproduction and the Economy in the Great Depression

The frequency with which women—especially those who were married, native-born Protestant, and middle- or upper-middle-class—resorted to abortion fueled a movement to criminalize the practice, as James Mohr discussed in Part II. Motivated by a variety of factors that had little to do with the protection of women's health, which was the primary reason advanced by the physicians who led the movement, antiabortionists succeeded in making the practice illegal in the post–Civil War era. Some states did allow physicians to perform therapeutic abortions if the woman's life was threatened by carrying the pregnancy to term. In many states, however, the requirements for getting clearance to perform a therapeutic abortion in a hospital setting made this loophole virtually meaningless, especially when a vigilant district attorney was prepared to pit his interpretation against the physician's.

Leslie Reagan's prizewinning study of the practice and policing of abortion during the century it was criminalized (1867–1973) reveals that, despite the law, millions of abortions were performed during those years—and by no means all by "back-alley" butchers.

"My husband has been out of work for over six months and no help is in sight," wrote one mother to Margaret Sanger and the American Birth Control League; "I can't afford more children." Every year she performed two abortions upon herself, and she reported, "I have just now gotten up from an abortion and I don't want to repeat it again."[1] The disaster of the Great Depression touched all aspects of women's lives, including the most intimate ones, and brought about a new high in the incidence of abortion. As jobs evaporated and wages fell, families found themselves living on insecure and scanty funds. Many working people lost their homes; tenants had their belongings put out on the street. Married couples gave up children to orphanages because they could not support them.

As women pressured doctors for help, the medical practice of abortion, legal and illegal, expanded during the 1930s. Physicians granted, for the first time, that social conditions were an essential component of medical judgment in therapeutic abortion cases. Medical recognition of social indications reveals the ways in which political and social forces shaped medical thinking and practice. A handful of radical physicians, who looked to Europe as a model, raised the possibility of liberalizing the abortion law. . . .

If we move away from the dramatic narratives about abortion produced at inquests or in newspapers, which tell of the deaths and dangers of abortion, and step into the offices of physician-abortionists, a different story can be discerned. Abortion was not extraordinary, but ordinary. The proverbial "back-alley butcher" story of abortion overemphasizes fatalities and limits our understanding of the history of illegal abortion. Case studies of the "professional abortionists" and their practices in the 1930s provide a unique opportunity to analyze the experiences of the tens of thousands of women who went to physician-abortionists. Many women had abortions in a setting nearly identical to the doctors' offices where they received other medical care. These doctors specialized in a single procedure, abortion. They used standard medical procedures to perform safe abortions routinely and ran what may be called abortion clinics. Furthermore, abortion specialists were an integral part of regular medicine, as the network of physicians who referred patients to these physician-abortionists demonstrates. . . .

The Depression years make vivid the relationship between economics and reproduction. Women had abortions on a massive scale. Married women with children found it impossible to bear the expense of another, and unmarried women could not afford to marry. As young working-class women and men put off marriage during the Depression to support their families or to save money for a wedding, marriage rates fell drastically. Yet while they waited to wed, couples engaged in sexual relations, and women became pregnant. Many had abortions.[2]

During the Depression, married women were routinely fired on the assumption that jobs belonged to men and that women had husbands who supported them. Discrimination against married women forced single women to delay marriage and have abortions in order to keep their jobs. One such woman was a young teacher whose fiancé was unemployed. As her daughter recalled fifty years later, "She got pregnant. What were her choices? Marry, lose her job, and bring a child into a family with no means of support? Not marry, lose her job and reputation, and put the baby up for adoption or keep it?" As this scenario makes clear, she had no "choice." Furthermore, it points to the limitations of the rhetoric of "choice" in reproduction: Social forces condition women's reproductive options.[3] . . .

Medical studies and sex surveys demonstrated that women of every social strata turned to abortion in greater numbers during the Depression. Comparative studies by class and race appeared for the first time in the 1930s. Induced abortion rates among white, middle- and upper-class married women rose during the Depression years. The Kinsey Institute for Sex Research, led by Paul H. Gebhard, analyzed data from over five thousand married, white, mostly highly educated, urban women. The researchers found that "the depression of the 1930's resulted in a larger proportion of pregnancies that were artificially aborted." For every age group of women, born between 1890 and 1919, the highest induced abortion rate occurred during "the depth of the depression." White, married women were determined to avoid bearing children during the Depression: They reduced their rate of conception as well.[4] . . . The findings of Kinsey researchers suggest that aborting first pregnancies early in marriage might have been a growing trend, particularly among more educated, urban white women.[5]

Married black women, like their white counterparts, used abortion more during the Depression. . . . Dr. Charles H. Garvin, an esteemed black surgeon from Cleveland, commented in 1932 "that there has been a very definite increase in the numbers of abortions, criminally performed, among the married."[6] . . . In 1935, Harlem Hospital, which cared for mostly poor black patients, opened a separate ward, "The Abortion Service," to treat the women who came for emergency care following illegal abortions. . . .

A study of reproductive histories collected from forty-five hundred women at a New York clinic between 1930 and 1938 suggested that when class was controlled, working-class women, black and white alike, induced abortions at the same rate.[7] . . .

The key difference between black and white women was in their response to pregnancy outside of marriage, not their use of abortion. Unmarried white women who became pregnant were more likely to abort their pregnancies than were African American women in the same situation. Instead, more black women bore children out of wedlock and did so without being ostracized by their families and community. . . .

The tolerance of illegitimacy among African Americans was tempered by class. As African Americans advanced economically, they held their unwed daughters and sons to more rigid standards of chastity. Similarly, by the time the Kinsey Institute interviewed black women in the 1950s, there were clear class differences in the use of abortion by unmarried black women: Those with more education (and presumably more affluence) aborted at a higher rate than those with less education.[8]

. . . A study of working-class women in New York in the 1930s found almost identical abortion rates among Catholic, Jewish, and Protestant women.[9] However, researchers found striking differences in the reproductive patterns followed by women of different religious groups, a finding that seems to reflect class differences. Catholic and Jewish women tended to have their children earlier in their lives and began aborting unwanted pregnancies as they got older; Protestant women tended to abort earlier pregnancies and bear children later.[10] The Kinsey Report found for both married and unmarried white women, the more devout the woman, the less likely she was to have an abortion; the more religiously "inactive" a woman, the more likely she was to have an abortion.[11]

Access to physician-induced abortions and reliance upon self-induced methods varied greatly by class and race. Most affluent white women went to physicians for abortions, while poor women and black women self-induced them. Physicians performed 84 percent of the abortions reported by the white, urban women to Kinsey researchers. Fewer than 10 percent of the affluent white women self-induced their abortions, though black women and poor white women, because of poverty or discrimination in access to medical care, often did so. According to the Kinsey study on abortion, 30 percent of the lower-income and black women reported self-inducing their abortions.[12] . . .

Low-income women's and black women's greater reliance upon self-induced methods of abortion meant that the safety of illegal abortion varied by race and class. . . .

Since poor women and black women were more likely to try to self-induce abortions and less likely to go to doctors or midwives, they suffered more complications. . . . Women reported having no complications after their abortions in 91 percent of the abortions performed by doctors and 86 percent of those performed by midwives. In contrast, only 24 percent of the self-induced abortions were without complications.[13] . . .

As more women had abortions during the Depression, and perhaps more turned to self-induced measures because of their new poverty, growing numbers of women entered the nation's hospitals for care following their illegal abortions. The Depression deepened an earlier trend toward the hospitalization of women who had abortion-related complications in public hospitals. As childbirth gradually moved into the hospital, so too did abortion. . . . One intern at Cook County Hospital recalled that in 1928 she saw at least thirty or forty abortion cases in the month and a half she worked there; or, one woman a day and several hundred women a year entered the hospital because of postabortion complications. In 1934, the County Hospital admitted 1,159 abortion cases, and reported twenty-two abortion-related deaths that year.[14] . . .

Doctors and public health reformers began to realize the importance of illegal abortion as a contributor to maternal mortality. . . . [Obstetrician Frederick J.] Taussig estimated that approximately fifteen thousand women died every year in the United States because of abortion.[15] . . . In hospital wards, doctors saw women with septic infections, perforations of the uterus, hemorrhages, and mutilation of intestines and other organs caused by self-induced abortions or ineptly performed operations.

The hospital atmosphere . . . helped forge a liberal consensus within a section of the medical profession about the horrors of self-induced and poorly performed criminal abortions, together with an acceptance of performing abortions for needy patients or referring them to abortionists. . . .

Most cities had several physicians who "specialized" in abortion, and many small towns had at least one physician-abortionist. . . .

In the mid-1930s one businessman set up a chain of abortion clinics in cities on the West Coast. Doctors Gabler, Keemer, and Timanus, of Chicago, Detroit, and Baltimore respectively, were physician-abortionists who performed abortions for tens of thousands of women during the 1930s. The decades-long existence of these specialty practices points to the tolerance and accessibility of abortion during these years.

Physician-abortionists practiced in a legally and medically gray area. It was not always clear whether they performed illegal abortions or legal, therapeutic abortions. As physicians, the law allowed them to perform therapeutic abortions in order to preserve a woman's life, but abortion was illegal and frowned upon by the profession. What made physician-abortionists different from other doctors was the volume of abortions performed, often to the exclusion of other medical practice. As long as these physicians received referrals from other physicians, practiced safely, and avoided police interference, they might consider the abortions to be therapeutic. Yet any physician who regularly performed abortions also knew that the procedure was criminal and that he or she practiced on a fine line. . . .

It is difficult for the historian to gain access to patient records, and this is particularly true for an illegal procedure. Yet I have uncovered records of abortion patients and have reconstructed, for the first time, the daily practice of an underground abortion clinic and the characteristics of its clientele. Seventy patient records of women who had abortions at a Chicago clinic owned by Dr. Josephine Gabler have been preserved in legal documents. . . . The Gabler clinic (later run by Ada Martin) serves as a case study of a specialty practice and reveals the abortion experiences of many women who found physician-abortionists.[16]

Dr. Josephine Gabler was a major source of abortions for Chicago women and other Midwesterners in the 1930s. She graduated from an Illinois medical school in 1905 and received her Illinois medical license that year. She established herself as a specialist in abortion by the late 1920s, perhaps earlier. Over eighteen thousand abortions were performed at her State Street office between 1932 and 1941.[17] In other words, the clinic provided approximately two thousand abortions a year—about five a day, if it operated seven days a week. Dr. Gabler, and other doctors who worked at the State Street office, provided needed abortion services to women from the entire region, including patients from Illinois, Indiana, Michigan, and Wisconsin. . . .

The Gabler-Martin clinic demonstrates that doctors have been more responsive to the demands of their female patients—even demands for an illegal procedure—than previously suspected. Over two hundred doctors, including some of Chicago's most prominent physicians and AMA members, referred patients to Gabler and Martin for abortions.[18] . . .

When Mrs. Helen B. learned of her pregnancy in 1940, she wanted an abortion. She "finally persuaded" her doctor that she needed an abortion and was given Dr. Josephine Gabler's business card.[19] The use of business cards itself emphasizes the openness of abortion practice in this period. . . .

Gabler and Martin showed their appreciation for referrals—and encouraged their colleagues and allies to keep referring—by paying commissions to those who sent patients. Investigators reported that the payments were usually fifteen dollars each, which was about a quarter of the average fee for abortion. . . .

The other major path to an abortionist's office was through women's personal networks. An abortionist's name and address were critical information, which women shared with each other. In this sample, of the cases where the source of the referral is identifiable, almost a third of the patients found their way to the clinic through friends. . . . Every woman who went to 190 North State Street for an abortion became a potential source of information for others in the same predicament. . . .

In many ways, the experience of getting an abortion at the State Street clinic was like going into any other doctor's office for medical care. Referrals from physicians, note taking by a receptionist, women dressed in white uniforms, instruments and delivery tables, and the instructions for after-care were all typical in a doctor's office—and familiar to women who had previously delivered babies in hospitals. The women received anesthesia and, apparently, a dilation and curettage of the uterus—the same procedure they would have had if they had a legal, therapeutic abortion in the hospital.

Nonetheless, the criminality of abortion made its practice clandestine. Two safeguards designed to shield the people performing abortions made the procedures in Martin's office different from legal, hospital procedures: covering the eyes of patients in order to make identifying the physician-abortionist impossible and warning women not to go to anyone else if they experienced complications. The clinic did not abandon its clients if problems developed following the abortion, but they did not want them going to physicians or local hospitals who might alert authorities.

The majority of women in the State Street patient records were married when they had their abortions. . . . Over half of the married women (thirty-two women, or 57 percent) had children. Over a third of these women had children under two years old. Mothers seemed strongly motivated to avoid having two babies in diapers at once. . . .

A second, and large, group of the married women (twenty-four, or 43 percent) had no children at all. This is not what we would expect; we have learned that married women used birth control and abortion after they had children, not before. . . .

Could they represent a significant number of married couples who intended to have no children at all? Since the records do not say how long they had been married, it is possible that these were abortions of prebridal pregnancies. Perhaps some worried about extramarital affairs. Some may have been college students or married to students. Perhaps they needed an abortion because they could not risk losing their jobs. Probably most who had abortions in the early years of their marriages had children later. Class could shape reproduction in complicated ways. Working women and more affluent college women found it necessary to delay childbearing for different reasons and at different times.

The age range of the State Street patients reflected the diversity of women's reproductive patterns and needs. The ages of the women having abortions in this sample ranged from eighteen to forty-eight years. . . . Their average age was twenty-seven years, but over half were under twenty-five. In 1992, for comparison, most of the women who had abortions were unmarried and under twenty-five years old.[20] . . . The difference is that most of the women in the Martin case records ended their pregnancies within the context of marriage: 80 percent of the Gabler-Martin clinic patients were married; now, 80 percent are unmarried. Today, most of the women who have abortions do so when they are single and finishing high school or college and expect to bear children later.[21] . . .

It is difficult to determine the class of . . . the patients at 190 North State Street, but it seems to have been a mixed group. The records of this office show we cannot assume that working-class women were never able to get safe abortions from physicians. . . . Information about income or the occupation of the woman's husband, if married, was not included in the patient records, but the records show that at least a third of the women worked for wages. . . .

The racial composition of the women who relied upon the abortion services of Dr. Gabler is even more obscure. There is no racial information in the patient records. . . .

Gabler and Martin could provide illegal abortions openly because they paid for protection from the law. Bribery of police and prosecutors underpinned the abortion practice. We only know of the corruption of legal authorities in Chicago because police officer Daniel Moriarity tried to kill Martin in order to silence her.[22] . . .

The office at 190 North State Street where thousands of women obtained abortions from a skilled practitioner was not a rarity.[23] . . .

In Detroit, African American physicians might refer patients to Dr. Edgar Bass Keemer Jr. . . . Throughout his career as an abortionist, which lasted into the 1970s, Keemer served primarily poor women and black women. In thirty-five years, he performed over thirty thousand abortions.[24] . . .

In Baltimore, reputable physicians referred their patients to Dr. George Loutrell Timanus, one of two well-known physician-abortionists in [the city]. Dr. Timanus had a close relationship to Baltimore's white medical elite at Johns Hopkins University, where the faculty taught Timanus's techniques to their students and called him a friend. . . .

Doctors Gabler, Keemer, and Timanus represent a larger pattern of medical involvement in illegal abortion and an expansion of the medical provision of abortions during the 1930s. . . . [Their practices were not temporary, but established; they were not located in back alleys, but on main streets. Dr. Gabler had a business card; Dr. Timanus was listed in the phone book and his office had a sign in front.]

Thousands of women obtained abortions from physicians in conventional medical settings and suffered no complications afterwards. . . . A mixed group of patients—working-class and middle-class women, white and black—reached these trusted physicians. . . .

NOTES

1. "Unemployment," *Birth Control Review (BCR)* 5 (May 1931):131.

2. Lois Rita Helmbold, "Beyond the Family Economy: Black and White Working-Class Women

During the Great Depression," *Feminist Studies* 13 (Fall 1987):640–641; A. J. Rongy, *Abortion: Legal or Illegal?* (New York: Vanguard Press, 1933), p. 111.

3. Alice Kessler-Harris, *Out to Work: A History of Wage-Earning Women in the United States* (Oxford: Oxford University Press, 1982), pp. 256–257; quotations from typed letter from Charleston, IL 61920, April 20, 1985, "Silent No More" Campaign, National Abortion Rights Action League (NARAL), Chicago.

4. Paul H. Gebhard et al., *Pregnancy, Birth and Abortion* (New York: Harper and Brothers and Paul B. Hoeber Medical Books, 1958), pp. 113–114, 140, table 55. Since much of the data comes from the earlier Kinsey studies on sexuality and this report came out of his institute, hereafter I refer to this book in the text as the Kinsey report or study on abortion.

5. The percentage of first pregnancies aborted in this young generation was no more than 10 percent, but it was more than double the rate of earlier generations of women.

6. Charles H. Garvin, "The Negro Doctor's Task," *BCR* 16 (November 1932):270.

7. Endre K. Brunner and Louis Newton, "Abortions in Relation to Viable Births in 10,609 Pregnancies: A Study Based on 4,500 Clinic Histories," *American Journal of Obstetrics and Gynecology* 38 (July 1939):82–83, 88.

8. Gebhard et al., *Pregnancy, Birth and Abortion*, p. 162. Regina G. Kunzel also finds class difference among African-Americans in their use of maternity homes; Kunzel, *Fallen Women, Problem Girls: Unmarried Mothers and the Professionalization of Social Work, 1890–1945* (New Haven: Yale University Press, 1993), p. 73.

9. Brunner and Newton, "Abortions in Relation to Viable Births," pp. 85, 90.

10. Ibid., p. 87, fig. 4.

11. Gebhard et al., *Pregnancy, Birth and Abortion*, pp. 64–65, 114–118.

12. Ibid., pp. 194–195, 198.

13. Regine K. Stix, "A Study of Pregnancy Wastage," *Milbank Memorial Fund Quarterly* 13 (October 1935):362–363.

14. Dr. Gertrude Engbring in Transcript of *People v. Heissler*, 338 Ill. 596 (1930), Case Files, vault no. 44783, Supreme Court of Illinois, Record Series 901, Illinois State Archives, Springfield; Augusta Weber, "Confidential Material Compiled for Joint Commission on Accreditation, June 1964," box 5, "Obstetrics Department—Accreditation 1964," Office of the Administrator, Cook County Hospital Archives. An "Abortion Service" was opened at Harlem Hospital in 1935. Peter Marshall Murray

and L. B. Winkelstein, "Incomplete Abortion: An Evaluation of Diagnosis and Treatment of 727 Consecutive Cases of Incomplete Abortions," *Harlem Hospital Bulletin* 3 (June 1950):31.

15. Fred J. Taussig, "Abortion in Relation to Fetal and Maternal Welfare," *American Journal of Obstetrics and Gynecology*, p. 872.

16. This case study is based on patient records and other legal documents discovered in the Transcript of *People v. Martin*, 382 Ill. 192 (1943), Case Files, vault no. 51699, Supreme Court of Illinois, Record Series 901.

17. Supplemental Report, Statement of Gordon B. Nash, Assistant State's Attorney, April 23, 1942, in Transcript of *People v. Martin*.

18. Of the eighteen doctors named in the patient records, eleven could be identified. (Sometimes only a last name was included on the record.) All eleven were AMA members and eight were specialists of various types.

19. Mrs. Helen B. in transcript of *People v. Martin*.

20. "Abortion Surveillance: Preliminary Data— United States, 1992," *Morbidity and Mortality Weekly Report: CDC Surveillance Summaries* 43 (December 23, 1994):930, 932, table I.

21. Recent abortion data show the trend to delaying childbearing. Teenagers make up a smaller proportion of the women having abortions than in the past: in 1972, 33 percent of the women who had abortions were nineteen years old or less; in 1992, teenagers were only 20 percent of the women having abortions, and women twenty-five or older made up 45 percent of the women having abortions. "Abortion Surveillance," p. 932, table I.

22. As a police officer, Moriarity received a little less than $2,500 per year. Quotations in George Wright, "Tells Bribe Behind Killing," *Chicago Daily Tribune,* May 2, 1941, p. 1.

23. Other doctors who appear to have specialized in abortion in Chicago include Dr. William E. Shelton, who may have been involved with Martin ("Dr. William Eugene Shelton," *Daily Tribune,* September 27, 1928; "Loop Physician Held in Abortion Conspiracy Case," *Daily Tribune,* November 21, 1940); Dr. Joseph A. Khamis ("Doctor Accused Second Time as an Abortionist," *Daily Tribune,* August 18, 1942); Dr. Justin L. Mitchell (*People v. Mitchell,* 368 Ill. 399); and Dr. Edward Peyser (*People v. Peyser,* 380 Ill. 404). All newspaper clippings in Abortionists Files, Historical Health Fraud Collection, American Medical Association, Chicago.

24. Ed Keemer, *Confessions of a Pro-Life Abortionist* (Detroit: Vinco Press, 1980), pp. 13, 18, 27, 29, 89–93.

D O C U M E N T

Margaret Sanger, "I resolved that women should have knowledge of contraception. . ."

The contrast between the high fertility of newly arriving immigrants and the low birth rate among old-stock Americans around the turn of the century prompted such leaders as Theodore Roosevelt to lament "race suicide" and to exhort women of the "proper sort" to perform their maternal functions in the selfless fashion dictated by time and tradition. Viewed through women's eyes, however, these population trends looked different, as this selection on the beginnings of the birth control movement dramatically illustrates. Although a few radicals such as Emma Goldman saw contraception as a means of liberating women by restoring to them control over their own bodies and thereby lessening their economic dependence on men, it was Margaret Higgins Sanger whose name would become most closely linked with the crusade for birth control.

The factors that propelled Sanger—a complex personality—to leadership were many. One of eleven children, she helped bury her mother, who died of tuberculosis. Young Margaret, however, was convinced that the sexual demands of her father (who lived to be eighty) were the real cause of her mother's death. A nursing career also shaped Sanger's thinking, as the following account suggests. Arrested under the Comstock Act (pp. 207–212) for publication of a newspaper advocating contraception, she fled in 1914 to England with her husband and three children. There she met the famous British psychologist and sex expert, Havelock Ellis, who further convinced her that sexual experience should be separated from reproduction, enabling couples to enhance the quality of their sexual relationship. Returning to New York, the Sangers continued their activities on behalf of birth control. The opening of the Brownsville clinic in 1916, recounted here, resulted in still further confrontation with authorities, including arrests. The hunger strike of Sanger's sister, Ethel Byrne, a nurse at the clinic, was followed by Sanger's own trial. Convicted of "maintaining a public nuisance," she was sentenced to thirty days in prison. When her lawyer asked for a suspended sentence in exchange for her promise not to break the law again, she announced, "I cannot promise to obey a law I do not respect." Ever the iconoclast and rebel, she gave talks to other inmates on sex hygiene when the prison guards were out of sight. Even after she was released, her attorney pursued an appeal. In January 1918, the New York Court of Appeals upheld her conviction, but interpreted the law in question broadly, allowing physicians to provide contraceptives to *married* women "to cure or prevent [venereal] disease." Sanger appealed unsuccessfully for the right of *nurses* to also provide contraceptives. Still, establishing the right of physicians to deliver birth control was a key breakthrough; it was the foundation of the birth control movement in the twentieth century, and would be a central element in the decision in *Roe v. Wade* (see pp. 658–661).

Excerpted from "Awakening and Revolt," "A 'Public Nuisance,'" and "Hunger Strike," chs. 3, 12, and 13 of *My Fight for Birth Control* by Margaret Sanger (New York: Farrar & Reinhart, 1931). Copyright © 1931 by Margaret Sanger. Reprinted by permission of Grant Sanger.

Margaret Sanger, following her conviction by the New York Court of Appeals in 1918.
She and her supporters treated the outcome as a victory because the court allowed physicians
to provide contraceptives to married women "to cure or prevent [venereal] disease." (Photograph
reprinted by permission of Planned Parenthood Federation of America.)

Divorcing William Sanger in 1920, Sanger founded the American Birth Control League in 1921 (in 1942 it was transformed into the Planned Parenthood Federation of America). She soon married William Slee, a wealthy oil man whose
resources would be a key source of support for her causes. These included the first
doctor-staffed birth control clinic in the United States, a model for hundreds of
clinics throughout the nation. Long before medical schools routinely taught the
fitting of diaphragms, these clinics, staffed by physicians, made reliable contraceptive services widely available. In 1936 Sanger and her colleagues forced the
courts to revisit the Comstock Act: a woman physician in New York ordered a
package of diaphragms (also known as pessaries) from Japan; the Customs Bureau
seized them as obscene articles. But the U.S. Court of Appeals for the Second Circuit ruled that objects ordered by physicians in good faith were exempted from
the punishments of the law (*U.S v. One Package*, 86 F.2d 737).

Important financial aid would come in later years from the wealthy feminist
Katherine McCormick, who shared Sanger's commitment to research in contraception. In the early 1950s, McCormick provided funds for experiments in endo-
crinology that led to the development of the birth control pill. At a time when few
scientists thought an oral contraceptive was possible, the insistence of Sanger and
McCormick that every woman had the right to control her own body helped bring
about a major breakthrough in medical technology. In 1960, the year of Sanger's
death, "the pill" became available to the public. The timing was propitious, for it

coincided with a period of sexual liberation that, while proving in some respects to be a mixed blessing for women, also coincided with new recognition of the intensity of their sexual drive and capacity for sexual pleasure. (See Beth Bailey's essay, pp. 629–637.)

Although Sanger saw the development of an oral contraceptive as another victory in a long and difficult struggle for reproductive freedom, others viewed the birth control movement differently. Arguments that limiting family size could not only free women's energies for social reform but prevent the world's poor from producing children they were unable to care for met with opposition from some women in the early years of Sanger's crusade. Some feared that birth control would contribute to promiscuity; others feared it would deny women the dignity that was theirs by virtue of motherhood. The Roman Catholic Church was unrelenting in its opposition, maintaining that the use of contraceptives is a sin. Sanger is still being angrily attacked; her contribution to the lives of modern American women remains a matter of political debate. Birth control is not only a technical way of spacing and limiting children so as to benefit both mother and child but is part of a larger debate about the extent to which women should be able to control their own reproductive lives.

AWAKENING AND REVOLT

Early in the year 1912 I came to a sudden realization that my work as a nurse and my activities in social service were entirely palliative and consequently futile and useless to relieve the misery I saw all about me. . . .

It is among the mothers here that the most difficult problems arise—the outcasts of society with theft, filth, perjury, cruelty, brutality oozing from beneath.

Ignorance and neglect go on day by day; children born to breathe but a few hours and pass out of life; pregnant women toiling early and late to give food to four or five children, always hungry; boarders taken into homes where there is not sufficient room for the family; little girls eight and ten years of age sleeping in the same room with dirty, foul smelling, loathsome men; women whose weary, pregnant, shapeless bodies refuse to accommodate themselves to the husbands' desires find husbands looking with lustful eyes upon other women, sometimes upon their own little daughters, six and seven years of age.

In this atmosphere abortions and birth become the main theme of conversation. On Saturday nights I have seen groups of fifty to one hundred women going into questionable offices well known in the community for cheap abortions. I asked several women what took place there, and they all gave the same reply: a quick examination, a probe inserted into the uterus and turned a few times to disturb the fertilized ovum, and then the woman was sent home. Usually the flow began the next day and often continued four or five weeks. Sometimes an ambulance carried the victim to the hospital for a curetage, and if she returned home at all she was looked upon as a lucky woman.

This state of things became a nightmare with me. There seemed no sense to it all, no reason for such waste of mother life, no right to exhaust women's vitality and to throw them on the scrap-heap before the age of thirty-five.

Everywhere I looked, misery and fear stalked—men fearful of losing their jobs, women fearful that even worse conditions might come upon them. The menace of another pregnancy hung like a sword over the head of every poor woman I came in contact with that year. The question which met me was always the same: What can I do to keep from it? or, What can I do to get out of this? Sometimes they talked among themselves bitterly.

"It's the rich that know the tricks," they'd say, "while we have all the kids." Then, if the women were Roman Catholics, they talked about "Yankee tricks," and asked me if I knew what the Protestants did to keep their families down. When I said that I didn't believe that the rich knew much more than they did I was laughed at and suspected of holding back information for money. They would nudge each other and say something about paying me before I left the case if I would reveal the "secret." . . .

I heard over and over again of their desperate efforts at bringing themselves "around"—drinking various herb-teas, taking drops of turpentine on sugar, steaming over a chamber of boiling coffee or of turpentine water, rolling down stairs, and finally inserting slippery-elm sticks, or knitting needles, or shoe hooks into the uterus. I used to shudder with horror as I heard the details and, worse yet, learned of the conditions *behind the reason* for such desperate actions.

. . . Each time I returned it was to hear that Mrs. Cohen had been carried to a hospital but had never come back, that Mrs. Kelly had sent the children to a neighbor's and had put her head into the gas oven to end her misery. Many of the women had consulted midwives, social workers and doctors at the dispensary and asked a way to limit their families, but they were denied this help, sometimes indignantly or gruffly, sometimes jokingly; but always knowledge was denied them. Life for them had but one choice: either to abandon themselves to incessant childbearing, or to terminate their pregnancies through abortions. Is it any wonder they resigned themselves hopelessly, as the Jewish and Italian mothers, or fell into drunkenness, as the Irish and Scotch? The latter were often beaten by husbands, as well as by their sons and daughters. They were driven and cowed, and only as beasts of burden were allowed to exist. . . .

They claimed my thoughts night and day. One by one these women, with their worried, sad, pensive and aging faces would marshal themselves before me in my dreams, sometimes appealingly, sometimes accusingly. I could not escape from the facts of their misery, neither was I able to see the way out of their problems and their troubles. . . .

Finally the thing began to shape itself, to become accumulative during the three weeks I spent in the home of a desperately sick woman living on Grand Street, a lower section of New York's East Side.

Mrs. Sacks was only twenty-eight years old; her husband, an unskilled worker, thirty-two. Three children, aged five, three and one, were none too strong nor sturdy, and it took all the earnings of the father and the ingenuity of the mother to keep them clean, provide them with air and proper food, and give them a chance to grow into decent manhood and womanhood.

Both parents were devoted to these children and to each other. The woman had become

pregnant and had taken various drugs and purgatives, as advised by her neighbors. Then, in desperation, she had used some instrument lent to her by a friend. She was found prostrate on the floor amidst the crying children when her husband returned from work. Neighbors advised against the ambulance, and a friendly doctor was called. The husband would not hear of her going to a hospital, and as a little money had been saved in the bank a nurse was called and the battle for that precious life began.

. . . The three-room apartment was turned into a hospital for the dying patient. Never had I worked so fast, so concentratedly as I did to keep alive that little mother. . . .

. . . July's sultry days and nights were melted into a torpid inferno. Day after day, night after night, I slept only in brief snatches, ever too anxious about the condition of that feeble heart bravely carrying on, to stay long from the bedside of the patient. With but one toilet for the building and that on the floor below, everything had to be carried down for disposal, while ice, food and other necessities had to be carried three flights up. It was one of those old airshaft buildings of which there were several thousands then standing in New York City.

At the end of two weeks recovery was in sight, and at the end of three weeks I was preparing to leave the fragile patient to take up the ordinary duties of her life, including those of wifehood and motherhood. . . .

But as the hour for my departure came nearer, her anxiety increased, and finally with trembling voice she said: "Another baby will finish me, I suppose."

"It's too early to talk about that," I said, and resolved that I would turn the question over to the doctor for his advice. When he came I said: "Mrs. Sacks is worried about having another baby."

"She well might be," replied the doctor, and then he stood before her and said: "Any more such capers, young woman, and there will be no need to call me."

"Yes, yes—I know, Doctor," said the patient with trembling voice, "but," and she hesitated as if it took all of her courage to say it, "what can I do to prevent getting that way again?"

"Oh ho!" laughed the doctor good naturedly, "You want your cake while you eat it too, do you? Well, it can't be done." Then, familiarly slapping her on the back and picking up his hat and bag to depart, he said: "I'll tell you the only sure thing to do. Tell Jake to sleep on the roof!"

With those words he closed the door and went down the stairs, leaving us both petrified and stunned.

Tears sprang to my eyes, and a lump came in my throat as I looked at that face before me. It was stamped with sheer horror. I thought for a moment she might have gone insane, but she conquered her feelings, whatever they may have been, and turning to me in desperation said: "He can't understand, can he?—he's a man after all—but you do, don't you? You're a woman and you'll tell me the secret and I'll never tell it to a soul."

She clasped her hands as if in prayer, she leaned over and looked straight into my eyes and beseechingly implored me to tell her something—something *I really did not know*. . . .

I had to turn away from that imploring face. I could not answer her then. I quieted her as best I could. She saw that I was moved by the tears in my eyes. I promised that I would come back in a few days and tell her what she wanted to know. The few simple means of limiting the family like *coitus interruptus* or the condom were laughed at by the neighboring women when told these were the means used by men in the well-to-do families. That was not believed, and I knew such an answer would be swept aside as useless were I to tell her this at such a time. . . .

The intelligent reasoning of the young mother—how to prevent getting that way again—how sensible, how just she had been— yes, I promised myself I'd go back and have a long talk with her and tell her more, and perhaps she would not laugh but would believe that those methods were all that were really known.

But time flew past, and weeks rolled into months. . . . I was about to retire one night three months later when the telephone rang and an agitated man's voice begged me to come at once to help his wife who was sick again. It was the husband of Mrs. Sacks, and I intuitively knew before I left the telephone that it was almost useless to go.

. . . I arrived a few minutes after the doctor, the same one who had given her such noble advice. The woman was dying. She was unconscious. She died within ten minutes after my arrival. It was the same result, the same story told a thousand times before—death from abortion. She had become pregnant, had

used drugs, had then consulted a five-dollar professional abortionist, and death followed.

The doctor shook his head as he rose from listening for the heart beat. . . . The gentle woman, the devoted mother, the loving wife had passed on leaving behind her a frantic husband, helpless in his loneliness, bewildered in his helplessness as he paced up and down the room, hands clenching his head, moaning "My God! My God! My God!"

The Revolution came—but not as it has been pictured nor as history relates that revolutions have come. . . .

After I left that desolate house I walked and walked and walked; for hours and hours I kept on, bag in hand, thinking, regretting, dreading to stop; fearful of my conscience, dreading to face my own accusing soul. At three in the morning I arrived home still clutching a heavy load the weight of which I was quite unconscious.

. . . As I stood at the window and looked out, the miseries and problems of that sleeping city arose before me in a clear vision like a panorama: crowded homes, too many children; babies dying in infancy; mothers overworked; baby nurseries; children neglected and hungry—mothers so nervously wrought they could not give the little things the comfort nor care they needed; mothers half sick most of their lives—"always ailing, never failing"; women made into drudges; children working in cellars; children aged six and seven pushed into the labor market to help earn a living; another baby on the way; still another; yet another; a baby born dead—great relief; an older child dies—sorrow, but nevertheless relief— insurance helps; a mother's death—children scattered into institutions; the father, desperate, drunken; he slinks away to become an outcast in a society which has trapped him.

. . . There was only one thing to be done: call out, start the alarm, set the heather on fire! Awaken the womanhood of America to free the motherhood of the world! I released from my almost paralyzed hand the nursing bag which unconsciously I had clutched, threw it across the room, tore the uniform from my body, flung it into a corner, and renounced all palliative work forever.

I would never go back again to nurse women's ailing bodies while their miseries were as vast as the stars. I was now finished with superficial cures, with doctors and nurses and social workers who were brought face to face with this overwhelming truth of women's needs and yet turned to pass on the other side. They must be made to see these facts. I resolved that women should have knowledge of contraception. They have every right to know about their own bodies. I would strike out—I would scream from the housetops. I would tell the world what was going on in the lives of these poor women. *I would* be heard. No matter what it should cost. *I would be heard.* . . .

I announced to my family the following day that I had finished nursing, that I would never go on another case—and I never have.

I asked doctors what one could do and was told I'd better keep off that subject or Anthony Comstock would get me. I was told that there were laws against that sort of thing. This was the reply from every medical man and woman I approached. . . .

A "PUBLIC NUISANCE"

The selection of a place for the first birth control clinic was of the greatest importance. No one could actually tell how it would be received in any neighborhood. I thought of all the possible difficulties: The indifference of women's organizations, the ignorance of the workers themselves, the resentment of social agencies, the opposition of the medical profession. Then there was the law—the law of New York State.

Section 1142 was definite. It stated that *no one* could give information to prevent conception to *anyone* for any reason. There was, however, Section 1145, which distinctly stated that physicians (*only*) could give advice to prevent conception for the cure or prevention of disease. I inquired about the section, and was told by two attorneys and several physicians that this clause was an exception to 1142 referring only to venereal disease. But anyway, as I was not a physician, it could not protect me. Dared I risk it?

I began to think of the doctors I knew. Several who had previously promised now refused. I wrote, telephoned, asked friends to ask other friends to help me find a woman doctor to help me demonstrate the need of a birth control clinic in New York. None could be found. No one wanted to go to jail. No one cared to test out the law. Perhaps it would have to be done without a doctor. But it had to be done; that I knew.

Fania Mindell, an enthusiastic young worker in the cause, had come on from Chicago to help me. Together we tramped the streets on that dreary day in early October, through a driving rainstorm, to find the best location at the cheapest terms possible . . .

Finally at 46 Amboy Street, in the Brownsville Section of Brooklyn, we found a friendly landlord with a good place vacant at fifty dollars a month rental; and Brownsville was settled on. It was one of the most thickly populated sections. It had a large population of working class Jews, always interested in health measures, always tolerant of new ideas, willing to listen and to accept advice whenever the health of mother or children was involved. I knew that here there would at least be no breaking of windows, no hurling of insults into our teeth; but I was scarcely prepared for the popular support, the sympathy and friendly help given us in that neighborhood from that day to this. . . .

With a small bundle of handbills and a large amount of zeal, we fared forth each morning in a house-to-house canvass of the district in which the clinic was located. Every family in that great district received a "dodger" printed in English, Yiddish and Italian. . . .

Women of every race and creed flocked to the clinic with the determination not to have any more children than their health could stand or their husbands could support. Jews and Christians, Protestants and Roman Catholics alike made their confessions to us, whatever they may have professed at home or in the church. Some did not dare talk this over with their husbands; and some came urged on by their husbands. Men themselves came after work; and some brought timid, embarrassed wives, apologetically dragging a string of little children. . . .

When I asked a bright little Roman Catholic woman what she would say to the priest when he learned that she had been to the Clinic, she answered indignantly: "It's none of his business. My husband has a weak heart and works only four days a week. He gets twelve dollars, and we can barely live on it now. We have enough children."

Her friend, sitting by, nodded a vigorous approval. "When I was married," she broke in, "the priest told us to have lots of children, and we listened to him. I had fifteen. Six are living. Nine baby funerals in our house. I am thirty-six years old now. Look at me! I look sixty."

As I walked home that night, I made a mental calculation of fifteen baptismal fees, nine funeral expenses, masses and candles for the repose of nine little souls, the physical suffering of the mother, and the emotional suffering of both parents; and I asked myself, "Was it fair? Is this the price of Christianity?" . . .

Ethel Byrne, who is my sister and a trained nurse, assisted me in advising, explaining, and demonstrating to the women how to prevent conception. As all of our 488 records were confiscated by the detectives who later arrested us for violation of the New York State law, it is difficult to tell exactly how many more women came in those days to seek advice; but we estimate that it was far more than five hundred. As in any new enterprise, false reports were maliciously spread about the clinic; weird stories without the slightest foundation of truth. We talked plain talk and gave plain facts to the women who came there. We kept a record of every applicant. All were mothers; most of them had large families.

It was whispered about that the police were to raid the place for abortions. We had no fear of that accusation. We were trying to spare mothers the necessity of that ordeal by giving them proper contraceptive information. . . .

The arrest and raid on the Brooklyn clinic was spectacular. There was no need of a large force of plain clothes men to drag off a trio of decent, serious women who were testing out a law on a fundamental principle. My federal arrest, on the contrary, had been assigned to intelligent men. One had to respect the dignity of their mission; but the New York city officials seem to use tactics suitable only for crooks, bandits and burglars. We were not surprised at being arrested, but the shock and horror of it was that a *woman,* with a squad of five plain clothes men, conducted the raid and made the arrest. A woman—the irony of it!

I refused to close down the clinic, hoping that a court decision would allow us to continue such necessary work. I was to be disappointed. Pressure was brought upon the landlord, and we were dispossessed by the law as a "public nuisance." In Holland the clinics were called "public utilities."

When the policewoman entered the clinic with her squad of plain clothes men and announced the arrest of Miss Mindell and myself (Mrs. Byrne was not present at the time and her arrest followed later), the room was crowded to suffocation with women waiting in the outer room. The police began bullying these mothers, asking them questions, writing down their names in order to subpoena them to testify against us at the trial. These women, always afraid of trouble which the very presence of a policeman signifies, screamed and cried aloud. The children on their laps screamed, too. It was like a panic for a few minutes until I walked into the room where they were stampeding and begged them to be quiet and not to get excited. I assured them that nothing could happen to them, that I was under arrest but they would be allowed to return home in a few minutes. That quieted them. The men were blocking the door to prevent anyone from leaving, but I finally persuaded them to allow these women to return to their homes, unmolested though terribly frightened by it all.

. . . The patrol wagon came rattling through the streets to our door, and at length Miss Mindell and I took our seats within and were taken to the police station. . . .

HUNGER STRIKE

Out of that spectacular raid, which resulted in an avalanche of nation-wide publicity in the daily press, four separate and distinct cases resulted:

Mrs. Ethel Byrne, my sister, was charged with violating Section 1142 of the Penal Code, designed to prevent dissemination of birth control information.

Miss Fania Mindell was charged with having sold an allegedly indecent book entitled "What Every Girl Should Know" written by Margaret Sanger.

I was charged with having conducted a clinic at 46 Amboy Street, Brooklyn, in violation of the same section of the Penal Code.

Having re-opened the clinic, I was arrested on a charge of "maintaining a public nuisance," in violation of Section 1530 of the Penal Code.

The three of us were held for trial in the Court of Special Sessions, with bail fixed at $500 each. This meant that our cases would be decided by three judges appointed by the Mayor and not by a jury. . . .

My sister was found guilty, and on January 22 she was sentenced to thirty days in the Workhouse. A writ of habeas corpus as a means of suspending sentence during appeal was refused by Supreme Court Justice Callahan. She spent the night in jail.

Ethel Byrne promptly declared a hunger strike. I knew that she would not flinch. Quiet, taciturn, with a will of steel hidden by a diffident air, schooled by her long training as a professional nurse, she announced briefly that she would neither eat, drink, nor work until her release. Commissioner of Correction Burdette G. Lewis promptly announced that she would be permitted to see no one but her attorney.

While the newspapers were reporting—always on the front page—the condition of the hunger striker, plans were hastened for a monster mass meeting of protest, to be held in Carnegie Hall. Helen Todd acted as chairman, and Dr. Mary Halton was an additional speaker. The hall was crowded by a huge audience of all classes. The women patients of the Brownsville clinic were given places of honor on the platform. The salvos of applause which greeted me showed that intelligent opinion was strongly behind us, and did much to give me the courage to fight with renewed strength for the immediate release of Ethel Byrne.

This meeting was acclaimed by the press as a "triumph of women, for women, by women." The meeting was said to have struck the right note—that of being instructive and persuasive, instead of agitational.

In the meantime, Ethel Byrne's refusal to eat and drink was crowding all other news off the front pages of the New York papers. Her defiance was sharpening the issue between self-respecting citizens and the existing law, which was denounced on every street corner as hypocritical. In the subway crowds, on street-corners, everywhere people gathered, the case was discussed. "They are imprisoning a woman for teaching physiological facts!" I heard one man exclaim. . . .

"It makes little difference whether I starve or not," she replied, through her attorney, "so long as this outrageous arrest calls attention to the archaic laws which would prevent our telling the truth about the facts of life. With eight thousand deaths a year in New York State from illegal operations on women, one more death won't make much difference."

All this served to convince the now panic-stricken Mr. Lewis [Commissioner of Correction in charge of Blackwell's Island] that Mrs. Byrne was different, after all, from the alcoholics and drug addicts who had given him his previous experience, and with whom he had gallantly compared her. When she had gone 103 hours without food, he established a precedent in American prison annals. He ordered her forcibly fed. She was the first woman so treated in this country. . . .

The truth was that Mrs. Byrne was in a critical condition after being rolled in a blanket and having milk, eggs and a stimulant forced into her stomach through a rubber tube. I realized this as soon as I heard that she was "passive under the feeding." Nothing but loss of strength could have lessened the power of her resistance to such authority. Nothing but brutality could have reduced her fiery spirit to acquiescence. I was desperate; torn between admiration for what she was doing and misery over what I feared might be the result.

On January 31st, a committee headed by Mrs. Amos Pinchot, Jessie Ashley and myself went to Albany for the purpose of asking Governor Whitman to appoint a commission to investigate birth control and make a report to the state legislature. Governor Whitman, a wise, fair, intelligent executive and statesman, received us, and listened to our exposition of the economic and moral necessity for birth control; the medical theory behind its justification. He promised to consider appointing the commission. During the interview Miss Jessie Ashley introduced the subject of Mrs. Byrne's treatment on Blackwell's Island and the anxiety we felt about her condition. We tried to make him see the outrage committed by the state in making anyone suffer for so just a cause. The Governor offered Mrs. Byrne a pardon on condition that she would not continue to disseminate birth control information. . . .

When we left Albany that day, I had the promise of a provisional pardon for Mrs. Byrne, but best of all I had in my purse a letter from the Governor to the authorities at Blackwell's Island authorizing me to see her. I was shocked and horrified when, in the late afternoon of February 1st, I saw my sister. She was lying semi-conscious on a cot in a dark corner of the prison cell. . . .

There was not time to inform her of the conditions of her pardon, and moreover she was too ill to face the question. I still believe that I was right in accepting the conditions which the Governor imposed. There was no other course. I saw that she was dangerously ill, that nothing further was to be gained by her keeping on, and that her death would have been a terrible calamity. Her life was what mattered to me, regardless of her future activities. . . .

At any rate, by the time she was released the subject was a burning issue. Newspapers which previously had ignored the case, had to mention a matter important enough to bring the Governor of the State from Albany to New York.

How women manage their physical appearance is only in part a response to the aesthetics of changing fashions. What women wear and the spirit in which they wear it can code a range of changing judgments about their social role, their political views, and their understanding of their bodies. (Why men's fashion has shifted far more slowly is a question worth pondering.)

As you examine the images that follow, consider the extent to which women's clothing has linked them to the issues that are discussed in the documents and essays. What do you understand to be the relationships between women's bodies and their clothing in different periods of time? In different regions of the country? Among different classes of people?

What personal and political meaning do you find in your own clothing and the clothing that you see around you?

1. Long dresses dragged in muddy ground, signaling that the wearer was not expected to exert herself. By the mid-nineteenth century, as these dresses show, fashionable ball gowns featured wide, heavy skirts over petticoats and impossibly narrow waists. Wearing dresses like these required wearing corsets, often of whalebone, to hold the body rigid and constrict the breathing. ("Fashions for June," *Harper's New Monthly Magazine* 7, no. 37 [June 1853]: 143–44.)

2. Amelia Bloomer did not invent the short skirt and trousers that came to bear her name; known as the "Turkish style," it appeared here and there in the 1840s. Elizabeth Cady Stanton's cousin Elizabeth Miller wore it when she visited Seneca Falls. Stanton envied her ease of movement and began to wear it. Bloomer was the editor of a women's rights journal, the *Lily*, which supported the principle of dress reform. "It seemed proper that I should practise [*sic*] as I preached," she would write years later. "At the outset, I had no idea of fully adopting the style . . . no thought that my action would create an excitement . . . and give to the style my name and the credit due Mrs. Miller. This was all the work of the press. I stood amazed at the furor." Bloomer would wear the costume on her lecture tours throughout the country for the next six years or so; "I found the dress comfortable, light, easy and convenient, and well adapted to the needs of my busy life," she insisted. But Stanton gave up the dress within three years because she found that ridicule deflected attention from her serious arguments about women's right to education, the ballot, and a wide range of work and better pay.*

This was not the first time, nor would it be the last, that critics of women's political positions attacked women's dress rather than debate women's ideas directly. Can you think of occasions in recent years when criticism of women's fashion was also a criticism of women's behavior? (Amelia Bloomer in the "short dress," ca. 1852–1853. Courtesy of the Seneca Falls Historical Society, #1425; see http://cr.nps .gov/history/online_books/wori/shs4.htm)

---

*Dexter Bloomer, *The Life and Writings of Amelia Bloomer* (Boston: Arena, 1985), pp. 67–70.

WOMAN'S EMANCIPATION.
(BEING A LETTER ADDRESSED TO MR. PUNCH, WITH A DRAWING, BY A STRONG-MINDED AMERICAN WOMAN.)

3. Women who adopted the Bloomer costume quickly were subjected to withering scorn, as in this cartoon from *Harper's*, a widely circulated magazine whose editors were certain they had the correct position on what women ought to wear. (See "Fashions for June," p. 465.) What message about women does the cartoon convey? ("Women's Emancipation," *Harper's New Monthly Magazine* 3, no. 15 [Aug. 1851]: 424.)

4. By 1874 dress reform had more modest goals. At this meeting at the Freeman Place Chapel in Boston, Massachusetts, the speakers do not display the traditional Bloomer costume. Instead of short skirts and trousers, they emphasize the absence of whalebone stays on their undergarments, and hidden bloomers instead of petticoats. Note the dress and headwear of the attentive women in the pews.

Frank Leslie's Illustrated Newspaper was notably friendly to women's reform causes (see its coverage of suffragists before a congressional committee, pp. 258–259). When Frank Leslie died in 1881, his wife and collaborator, Miriam Squier Leslie, had her own name legally changed to Frank Leslie and continued his publishing enterprises for the rest of her life. When she died in 1914, she left her considerable fortune to Carrie Chapman Catt for use in the final stages of the suffrage campaign. (Sketched by E. R. Morse, "The Dress Reform Meeting in Boston," *Frank Leslie's Illustrated Newspaper* 38, no. 77 [June 20, 1874]: 209, 229. For more on the publishers, see Madeleine Stern, *Purple Passage: The Life of Mrs. Frank Leslie* [Norman: University of Oklahoma Press, 1953], and Lynne Vincent Cheney, "Mrs. Frank Leslie's Illustrated Newspaper," *American Heritage* 26, no. 6 [Oct. 1975].)

FRANK LESLIE'S ILLUSTRATED NEWSPAPER

NEW YORK, JUNE 20, 1874.

GETTING ON BROADWAY CAR

5. Street railways and long-distance railroads were among the benefits of the Industrial Revolution, but, as historian Barbara Welke writes, "[T]he physical act of jumping or stepping from train or streetcar to the ground was qualitatively different for women than the same act undertaken by able-bodied men. Women . . . [were] often burdened by children or by pregnancy." From the years in which the railroad was first invented until the 1920s, fashion details may have changed, but "women's long skirts swept across road and farmyard." Whether hoop skirt, bustle, or Gibson girl look, women's clothing was "long, dark, and cumbersome." At a time when men took pride in jumping on and off railroads and streetcars as they started to move or came to a stop, railroad and streetcar accident reports were "filled with stories of women falling because their skirts caught on a projection or were stepped on by another passenger as they alighted."* What dangers does this woman face? (Photograph courtesy of the Library of Congress, George Grantham Bain Collection, LC-USZ62-91532.)

---

*Barbara Young Welke, *Recasting American Liberty: Gender, Race, Law, and the Railroad Revolution, 1865–1920* (New York: Cambridge University Press, 2001), pp. 55–56. This photograph appears on page 58.

6. The woman on the left, a *mexicana* who perhaps belonged to a family that had settled in New Mexico almost three centuries earlier, is clearly skilled at carrying an *olla* full of water on her head. Photographed in Santa Fe in the mid- or late nineteenth century, she wears the looser, layered clothing long utilized by European women of the laboring classes. The image on the right, taken in a Tucson, Arizona, photography studio probably at the turn of the 1800s, is of a member of a prominent local Mexican American family. The young woman had the privilege of wearing at her wedding the elaborately tailored gown with train, feathered hat, and white gloves that were the height of fashion for elites in the dominant Anglo society.

The twinned practice of wearing an elegant white wedding gown, and staging an elaborate formal wedding was initially restricted to elite Britons and Americans (emulating Queen Victoria's 1840 wedding). By the early twentieth century, urban middle-class couples adopted the "white wedding." It became a widespread practice, supported by burgeoning commercial bridal and related enterprises, only after World War II.* (*Image on left*: Courtesy of the Palace of the Governors / New Mexico History Museum, division of New Mexico Department of Cultural Affairs, negative 3150. *Image on right*: Courtesy of the Arizona Historical Society, Tucson; image #73800, item in the Mexican Heritage Project, donation of Maria Urquides. We are grateful to Elizabeth "Betita" Martínez for identifying and pairing these images in her book, *500 Years of Chicana Women's History/ Años de la Mujer Chicana* [New Brunswick, N.J.: Rutgers University Press, 2008], p. 43.)

---

*Katherine Jellison, introduction to *It's Our Day: America's Love Affair with the White Wedding, 1945–2005* (Lawrence: University Press of Kansas, 2008).

7. The bicycle offered women the opportunity to travel cheaply and independently in public space; it undermined long-standing assumptions about proper feminine behavior.* Note this woman's clothing and the camera she carries. Almost as soon as the bicycle with two wheels of the same size was invented, women embraced it enthusiastically. Susan B. Anthony observed that "the bicycle had done more to emancipate women than anything else in the world." The bicyclist chose where she would go at the rate she wished to go. On the bicycle, the corset had to be abandoned; shorter skirts, even divided skirts and long bloomers suddenly became a matter of necessity. "If women ride," wrote the reformer Frances E. Willard in 1895, "they must, when riding, dress more rationally than they have been wont to do. If they do this many prejudices as to what they may be allowed to wear will melt away. . . . [T]he comfortable, sensible and artistic wardrobe of the rider will make the conventional style of woman's dress absurd to the eye and unendurable to the understanding." How accurate was Willard's prediction? ("Woman on Bicycle," ca. 1917. Harris & Ewing, photographer. Courtesy of the Library of Congress, Prints and Photographs Division, Washington, D.C.)

---

*Frances E. Willard, *A Wheel Within a Wheel: How I Learned to Ride the Bicycle* (Chicago: Women's Temperance Union Publishing House, 1895), p. 39.

8. Congressman T. S. McMillan of Charleston, South Carolina, poses with Miss Ruth Bennett and Miss Sylvia Clavins, who are doing the Charleston on a railing; the U.S. Capitol looms behind them. The short skirts, short hair, and brash behavior marked the women as "flappers." Note the contrast between their clothes and those worn by suffragists demonstrating in front of the White House less than ten years before (see Photo Essay: "Women in Public," p. 261). What difference do you think this change of style made in the lives of women who adopted it? ("Charleston at the Capitol," ca. 1920s. Photo-print by National Photo Company. Courtesy of the Library of Congress, Prints and Photographs Division, Washington D.C.)

9. Women traditionally devised shampoos and cosmetics for themselves, in their own homes. In the early twentieth century, a number of women entrepreneurs, among them Elizabeth Arden, Helena Rubenstein, and Madam C. J. Walker, invented the concept of the commercial beauty product, made in factories and mass marketed. Walker, who was the daughter of former slaves, was born in 1867; she was probably the first woman self-made millionaire in the nation. In 1905 she developed a scalp-conditioning formula for African Americans. At its peak in the second decade of the century, her business employed some 3,000 people—in a factory in Indianapolis, in hair and manicure salons across the country, and as door-to-door saleswomen. Walker took pride in offering women well-paid alternatives to domestic labor, and in her support for African American philanthropies, especially the antilynching efforts of the NAACP and Bethune-Cookman College (for Bethune-Cookman, see pp. 329–331). She died in 1919. This photograph by the distinguished photographer James VanDerZee was taken in her New York salon and offices in 1929, a decade after Walker's death. How would you describe the hairstyles of these Harlemites, who sported the sophisticated urban look that Madam Walker's products and styling supported? (Courtesy of the Metropolitan Museum of Art, New York © Donna Mussenden VanDerZee.)

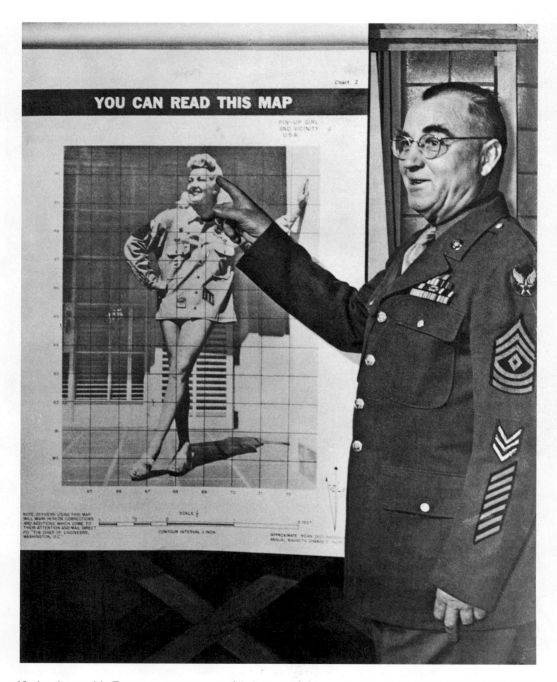

10. An Army Air Forces sergeant uses this image of the movie star Betty Grable (1916–73) to instruct military recruits in the skills of map reading during World War II. The original caption included this line: "The picture of the girl is divided into sections with lines, each of which is numbered, and by checking the lines on it, as on a real map, soldiers can locate any given spot—knowledge which in actual combat can mean the difference between life and death." What messages about women's bodies does this use of her photo—in this pose—convey? (Courtesy of Corbis). (For a subtle cultural analysis of the pinup, see Robert B. Westbrook, "'I Want a Girl Just Like the Girl Who Married Harry James': Women and the Problem of Political Obligation in World War II," *American Quarterly* 42 [Dec. 1990]: 587–614.) We are grateful to Robert Westbrook for identifying this photograph.

11. Barbie debuted in 1959 after much persistence and research by her creator, Ruth Handler. In the mid-1940s, Handler had founded a small company called Mattel, together with her husband and a partner who soon sold the Handlers his share. Initially housed in their southern California garage, Mattel produced picture frames but soon began to specialize in dollhouse furniture and toys. In 1955 and 1956, Handler had little success in convincing the company's male employees that there was a waiting market for adult-looking dolls aimed at prepubescent girls. She had noticed that her daughter Barbara, having outgrown baby dolls, enjoyed cutting out clothes and accessories from magazines to create adult paper dolls and assign them imaginary grown-up roles and professions. Handler was convinced that a three-dimensional adult doll would help girls become acquainted with the bodily changes they would experience during puberty. On a European family vacation, Handler came upon Lilli, a German-manufactured doll representing a buxom, blond young woman (Lilli had originated in a satirical, adult-oriented newspaper comic strip). The doll could be bought in various outfits, but the clothes were not sold separately. Mattel acquired the patent and rights for the doll, worked with Japanese

manufacturers to perfect the vinyl molding phase of production, and hired designers (including women) who embraced Handler's vision of a set of dolls for whom a wide wardrobe and accessories could be purchased.

The first Barbie measured 11.5 inches and was marketed as a "teen-age fashion model" and "a new kind of doll from real life." The purchaser chose between the blond and the brunette versions. *Barbie* (always written in a distinctive script) came in an attractive oblong box illustrated with alluring wardrobe possibilities; inside was a miniature catalog with more details. She cost three dollars. Note the designers' genius: whereas Lilli's earrings and shoes were molded and painted on, Barbie had bare feet and pierced ears, allowing for endless accessorizing options. The small-waisted, ever-smiling, preternaturally young doll soon made its way into the hands of millions of young girls, who were drawn to her long, malleable hair, her ever-expanding wardrobe, her supernatural womanly figure, and her "boyfriend" Ken and their coterie.*

During the 1970s, feminists began to ask challenging questions about the relationship between toys such as Barbie, body image, sexism, consumerism, and racial stereotypes. Many of these questions remain unresolved. To what extent do Barbie dolls teach young women to become consumers? Is it sufficient for Mattel simply to change the shade of Barbie's skin to appeal to children of various races and ethnicities? College health and wellness programs often use Barbie as a hook on their websites, pointing out, for example, that a real-life Barbie would be unable to walk given her top-heavy frame. What connections do you think exist between Barbie and eating disorders among adolescents? Between Barbie and the popularity of plastic surgery and tanning salons? If you played with Barbie dolls as a child, what types of scenes did you enact? How did you imagine adulthood through the lens of Barbie? (Photo by Joan Ashabraner. We are grateful to Joan Ashabraner for this image. For a provocative assessment of Barbie threaded with an interview with Ruth Handler, see Susan Stern's 1998 documentary, *Barbie Nation: An Unauthorized Tour* [videorecording, New Day Films].)

---

*Marco Tosca, *Barbie: Four Decades of Fashion, Fantasy, and Fun,* trans. Linda M. Eklund (New York: Harry N. Abrams, 1998), pp. 24–33.

12. From the 1600s onward, African American women felt pressure to adopt beauty regimens that made them appear "whiter." Light-skinned people, who often had straighter hair than dark-skinned African Americans, were granted more privileges on plantations during slavery. Throughout the nineteenth and twentieth centuries, many African Americans straightened their hair in order to appear respectable as they sought economic and social rights. By the 1960s, with the civil rights movement ever more visible and the black power movement on the rise, the emphasis on a look that bespoke respectability and conformity began to crumble. Many activist African Americans forged connections with their African past, adopting African styles of dress and hairstyles. Noted civil rights activist Angela Davis popularized the Afro hairstyle when she spoke across the United States. Here, Davis speaks at a street rally in Raleigh, North Carolina, on July 4, 1974. The Afro not only required a fraction of the care of previously popular hairstyles, but it also embodied the recognition that "black is beautiful." Some older African Americans, including religious people and civil rights activists, criticized the Afro as confrontational, fearing that it would limit African Americans' upward social mobility in white-controlled environments. Instead, the model spread to other ethnic groups, helping to make a wider range of hairstyles fashionable. However, as many recent memoirs and blogs by African-descended women have recounted, the "hair wars" in the black family and community have not ended; see the wry commentary of A'Lelia Bundles, who is a great-great granddaughter of Madam C. J. Walker. ("Hair Peace: A 5-Part Manifesto," *The Root*, Mar. 26, 2009, http://www.theroot.com/ views/ hair-peace-5-part-manifesto?). (Courtesy of Corbis.)

13. Dolores Huerta, a cofounder of the United Farm Workers of America, articulated the grievances of thousands of exploited Mexican and Mexican American farm laborers who toiled in
California fields. In this 1973 photograph, Huerta is shown using not only her voice to denounce
harsh living conditions and inadequate pay, but also powerful imagery on her T-shirt. Consider
how clothing can serve both as a political signal and as a historical artifact. What information
does Huerta's T-shirt convey? How might you use this photograph as a historical source?
("There's blood on those grapes!" Photograph by Chris Sanchez, likely taken during the Gallo
strike, Livingston, California, 1973. Courtesy of the United Farm Workers Collection #273, Walter
P. Reuther Library, Wayne State University.)

14. Ever since patriot women boycotted elaborate and expensive British imports during the Revolutionary era as a way of expressing their political principles, resistance to fashion trends has been a recurring theme in women's clothing choices. Challenging the fashion industry, women's liberation activists rebelled against uncomfortable and binding clothing. If you view all the photos in this book depicting pre-1970s events (despite Amelia Bloomer and dress reformers), you will see that this rebellion was a very radical gesture. At mid-century, respectable professional dress required nylon stockings held up by girdles or garter belts, making breathing uncomfortable; narrow skirts that prevented running away from danger; and high heels that over the long run shortened muscles and created corns and bunions in the name of looking sexy. (Fifteen times as many women as men develop bunions requiring surgery.) Women who adopted looser, more comfortable clothing risked scorn and even the loss of their jobs. Until Title VII, it was not illegal to treat the display of beauty as a reasonable professional qualification for many lines of work, including flight attendants and executive secretaries. (See the concept of the Bona Fide Occupational Qualification [BFOQ] in the Civil Rights Act 1964, pp. 745–746.) It took two decades, from the mid-1970s to the mid-1990s, before flight attendants—who, it is estimated, walk as much as 225 miles up and down airplane aisles each year—were able to force most airlines to relax rules requiring them to wear shoes with 2 or 2 1/2-inch heels. (Male attendants could always wear loafers.)*

The "Stamp Out High Heels" poster was a grassroots expression of rebellion, addressing issues of health, safety, and cultural conformity. It augured a dramatic shift in sartorial choices. For example, the pants suit may seem dated now, but in the 1970s it was an important wedge for working women, especially in white-collar jobs. Over the past thirty years, the clothes acceptable for women to wear to work and in public have become very diverse—in style, color, fabric, and so on. This diversity, plus the informal, athletic look so prevalent in women's clothes and shoes, owes much to 1970s feminist activism. How many of the claims and slogans featured in the poster do you agree with? ("American Foot Binding: Stamp Out High Heels," poster, Houston, n.d. Courtesy Duke University Library Special Collections, ALFA Collection, Box 12. We are grateful to Rosalyn Baxandall and Linda Gordon, *Dear Sisters: Dispatches from the Women's Liberation Movement* [New York: Basic Books, 2000], p. 40, for identifying this image.)

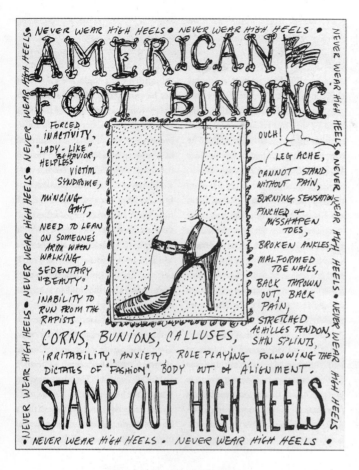

*See Marc Linder, "Smart Women, Stupid Shoes, and Cynical Employers: The Unlawfulness and Adverse Health Consequences of Sexually Discriminatory Workplace Footwear Requirements for Female Employees," *Journal of Corporation Law* 22 (1996–97): 296–97, 308–12.

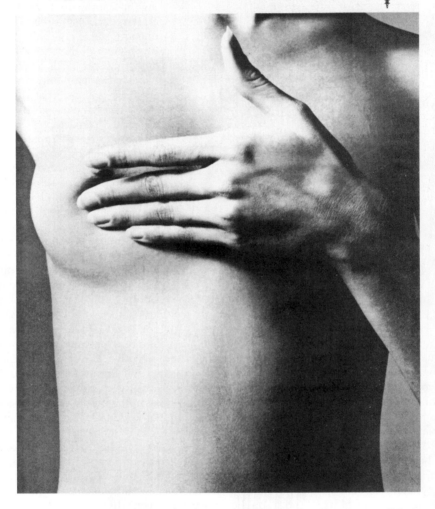

Cancer.
Sometimes you can put your finger on it.

One of the seven warning signals of cancer is a thickening or lump in the breast or elsewhere.

There are six more that you should be aware of. Indigestion or difficulty in swallowing. An obvious change in a wart or mole. A nagging cough or hoarseness. A change in bowel or bladder habits. A sore that does not heal. Unusual bleeding or discharge.

If you notice any one of these warning signals, there's only one thing to do. See your doctor.

We want to wipe out cancer in your lifetime.
Give to the American Cancer Society.

15. Second-wave feminists urged women to take responsibility for their own well-being. As more was understood about breast cancer, it became clear that annual examinations by physicians were not enough to track its appearance; in the 1970s, as today, women are urged to examine their own bodies regularly. Over the years, unclothed women in art and advertising have presented their bodies to the male gaze; in a sharp departure from tradition, the model here is concerned with herself and her own health, encouraging women viewers to knowingly touch their own bodies as an act of self-preservation and self-empowerment. The advertisement appeared in the first issue of *Ms.* magazine. (Photo reprinted by the permission of The American Cancer Society, Inc. for historical purposes only. All rights reserved. See *Ms.* 1, no.1 [July 1972]: 35.)

16. Graduation ceremony at a large public university, May 2009. What meanings are conveyed by the footwear of these two women? (Photo by Tom Langdon.)

LABOR AND ACTIVISM

JACQUELYN DOWD HALL
Disorderly Women: Gender and Labor Militancy in the Appalachian South

By the 1920s, unionization had not taken hold in the former states of the Confederacy as it had in heavily industrialized areas of the Northeast and Midwest (see Annelise Orleck's essay, pp. 361–376). Moreover, working conditions had worsened as factory owners introduced new innovations designed to improve productivity. Southern textile mills, as employers of large numbers of poorly paid white women, were especially vulnerable to strikes. And indeed, this work force was white. Nearly all mill and factory work in the South was closed to African Americans until the 1960s.*

Jacquelyn Dowd Hall focuses on one of the many strikes exploding across the South in that tumultuous decade, exploring female activism in an essay that calls into question old stereotypes about southern workers as individualistic, docile, and "hard to organize." In this important study, Hall illuminates the distinctive style of collective action that the women of Elizabethton, Tennessee, employed and the self-concepts and family networks on which that style relied.

In what respects did working conditions resemble those confronting the young immigrant women in New York's garment district about whom Orleck wrote? What were the critical differences? Were the factors that inspired and sustained resistance similar? How does Hall view the actions of Trixie Perry and Texas Bill?

The rising sun "made a sort of halo around the crown of Cross Mountain" as Flossie Cole climbed into a neighbor's Model T and headed west down the gravel road to Elizabethton, bound for work in a rayon plant. Emerging from Stoney Creek hollow, the car joined a caravan of buses and self-styled "taxis" brimming with young people from dozens of tiny communities strung along the creek branches and nestled in the coves of the Blue Ridge Mountains of East Tennessee. The caravan picked up speed as it hit paved roads and crossed the Watauga River bridge, passing beneath a sign advertising the county seat's new-found identity as a "City of Power." By the time Cole reached the factory gate, it was 7:00 A.M., time to begin another ten-hour day as a reeler at the American Glanzstoff plant.[1]

The machines whirred, and work began as usual. But the reeling room stirred with anticipation. The day before, March 12, 1929, all but seventeen of the 360 women in the inspection room next door had walked off their jobs. Now they were gathered at the factory gate,

---

*Timothy Minchin, *Hiring the Black Worker: The Racial Integration of the Southern Textile Industry, 1960–1980* (Chapel Hill: University of North Carolina Press, 1999).

refusing to work but ready to negotiate. When 9:00 A.M., approached and the plant manager failed to appear, they broke past the guards and rushed through the plant, urging their co-workers out on strike. By 1:40 P.M. the machines were idle and the plant was closed.

The Elizabethton conflict rocked Carter County and made national headlines. Before March ended, the spirit of protest had jumped the Blue Ridge and spread through the Piedmont. Gastonia, Marion, and Danville saw the most bitter conflicts, but dozens of towns were shocked by an unexpected workers' revolt.[2]

The textile industry has always been a stronghold of women's labor, and women were central to these events. They were noted by contemporaries, sometimes as leaders, more often as pathetic mill girls or as "Amazons" providing comic relief.[3] In historical renditions they have dropped out of sight. The result has been thin description: a one-dimensional view of labor conflict that fails to take culture and community into account.

Elizabethton, of course, is not unusual in this regard. Until recently, historians of trade unionism, like trade unionists themselves, neglected women, while historians of women concentrated on the Northeast and the middle class. There were few scholarly challenges to the assumption that women workers in general and southern women in particular were "hard to organize" and that women as family members exercised a conservative pull against class cohesion. Instances of female militancy were seen and not seen.[4] Because they contradicted conventional wisdom, they were easily dismissed.

Recent scholarship has revised that formulation by unearthing an impressive record of female activism. But our task is not only to describe and celebrate but also to contextualize, and thus to understand. In Elizabethton the preindustrial background, the structure of the work force and the industry, the global forces that impinged on local events—these particularities of time and place conditioned women's choices and shaped their identities. Equally important was a private world traditionally pushed to the margins of labor history. Female friendships and sexuality, cross-generational and cross-class alliances, the incorporation of new consumer desires into a dynamic regional culture—these too energized women's participation. Women in turn were historical subjects, helping to create the circumstances from

which the strike arose and guiding by their actions the course the conflict took.

With gender at the center of analysis, unexpected dimensions come into view. Chief among them is the strike's erotic undercurrent, its sexual theme. The activists of Elizabethton belonged to a venerable tradition of "disorderly women," women who, in times of political upheaval, embody tensions that are half-conscious or only dimly understood.[5] Beneath the surface of a conflict that pitted workers and farmers against a new middle class in the town lay an inner world of fantasy, gender ideology, and sexual style.

The melding of narrative and analysis that follows has two major goals. The first is a fresh reading of an important episode in southern labor history, employing a female angle of vision to reveal aspects of the conflict that have been overlooked or misunderstood. The second is a close look at women's distinctive forms of collective action, using language and gesture as points of entry to a culture.

The Elizabethton story may also help to make a more general point. Based as it is on what Michel Foucault has termed "local" or "subjugated" knowledge, that is, perceptions that seem idiosyncratic, naive, and irrelevant to historical explanation, this study highlights the limitations of conventional categories.[6] The women of Elizabethton were neither traditionalists acting on family values nor market-oriented individualists, neither peculiar mountaineers nor familiar modern women. Their irreverence and inventiveness shatter stereotypes and illuminate the intricacies of working-class women's lives.

In 1925 the J. P. Bemberg Company of Barmen, Germany, manufacturer of high-quality rayon yarn by an exclusive stretch spinning process, began pouring the thick concrete floors of its first United States subsidiary. Three years later Germany's leading producer of viscose yarn, the Vereinigte Glanzstoff Fabriken, A.G., of Elberfeld opened a jointly managed branch nearby. A post-World War I fashion revolution, combined with protective tariffs, had spurred the American rayon industry's spectacular growth. As one industry publicist put it, "With long skirts, cotton stockings were quite in order; but with short skirts, nothing would do except sheer, smooth stockings. . . . It was on the trim legs of post-war flappers, it has been said, that rayon first stepped out into big business."

Dominated by a handful of European giants, the rayon industry clustered along the Appalachian mountain chain. By World War II, over 70 percent of American rayon production took place in the southern states, with 50 percent of the national total in Virginia and Tennessee alone.[7]

When the Bemberg and Glanzstoff companies chose East Tennessee as a site for overseas expansion, they came to a region that has occupied a peculiar place in the American economy and imagination. Since its "discovery" by local-color writers in the 1870s, southern Appalachia has been seen as a land "where time stood still." Mountain people have been romanticized as "our contemporary ancestors" or maligned as "latter-day white barbarians." Central to both images is the notion of a people untouched by modernity. In fact, as a generation of regional scholars has now made clear, the key to modern Appalachian history lies not in the region's isolation but in its role as a source of raw materials and an outlet for investment in a capitalist world economy.[8]

Frontier families had settled the fertile Watauga River Valley around Elizabethton before the Revolution. Later arrivals pushed farther up the mountains into the hollows carved by fast-falling creeks. Stoney Creek is the oldest and largest of those creek-bed communities. Here descendants of the original settlers cultivated their own small plots, grazed livestock in woods that custom held open to all, hunted and fished in an ancient hardwood forest, mined iron ore, made whiskey, spun cloth, and bartered with local merchants for what they could not produce at home.

In the 1880s East Tennessee's timber and mineral resources attracted the attention of capitalists in the United States and abroad, and an era of land speculation and railroad building began. The railroads opened the way to timber barons, who stripped away the forests, leaving hillsides stark and vulnerable to erosion. Farmers abandoned their fields to follow the march of the logging camps. Left behind, women and children did their best to pick up the slack.[9] But by the time Carter County was "timbered out" in the 1920s, farm families had crept upward to the barren ridge lands or grown dependent on "steady work and cash wages." Meanwhile, in Elizabethton, the county seat, an aggressive new class of bankers, lawyers, and businessmen served as brokers for outside developers, speculated in land, invested in homegrown factories, and looked

beyond the hills for their standards of "push, progress and prosperity."[10]

Carter County, however, lacked Appalachia's grand prize: The rush for coal that devastated other parts of the mountains had bypassed that part of East Tennessee. Nor had county farmers been absorbed into the cotton kingdom, with its exploitative credit system and spreading tenancy. To be sure, they were increasingly hard pressed. As arable land disappeared, farms were divided and redivided. In 1880 the average rural family had supported itself on 140 acres of land; by 1920 it was making do on slightly more than 52 acres. Yet however diminished their circumstances, 84.5 percent still owned their own land.[11] The economic base that sustained traditional expectations of independence, production for use, and neighborly reciprocity tottered but did not give way.

The coming of the rayon plants represented a coup for Elizabethton's aspiring businessmen, who wooed investors with promises of free land, tax exemptions, and cheap labor. But at first the whole county seemed to share the boomtown spirit. Men from Stoney Creek, Gap Creek, and other mountain hamlets built the cavernous mills, then stayed on to learn the chemical processes that transformed the cellulose from wood pulp and cotton linters (the short fibers that remain on cotton seeds after longer, spinnable fibers are removed) into "artificial silk." Women vied for jobs in the textile division where they wound, reeled, twisted, and inspected the rayon yarn. Yet for all the excitement it engendered, industrialization in Carter County retained a distinctly rural cast. Although Elizabethton's population tripled (from 2,749 in 1920 to 8,093 in 1930), the rayon workers confounded predictions of spectacular urban growth, for most remained in the countryside, riding to work on chartered buses and trains or in taxis driven by neighbors and friends.

Women made up approximately 37 percent of the 3,213 workers in the mills. Most were under twenty-one, but many were as young as twelve, or more commonly, fourteen. By contrast, the work force contained a large proportion of older, married men. Those men, together with a smaller number of teenage boys, dominated the chemical division, while young women processed the finished yarn.[12]

Whether married or single, town- or country-bred, the men who labored in the rayon plants followed in the footsteps of fathers, and sometimes grandfathers, who had combined farming with a variety of wage-earning occupations. To a greater extent than we might expect, young women who had grown up in Elizabethton could also look to earlier models of gainful labor. A search of the 1910 manuscript census found 20 percent (97/507) of women aged fourteen and over in paid occupations. The largest proportion (29.6 percent) were cooks and servants. But close behind were women in what mountain people called "public work": wage-earning labor performed outside a household setting. For rayon workers from the countryside it was a different story. Only 5.2 percent of adult women on Stoney Creek were gainfully employed (33/638). Nineteen of these were farmers. The rest—except for one music teacher—were servants or washerwomen.[13]

These contrasts are telling, and from them we can surmise two things. The first is that industrialization did not burst upon a static, conflict-free "traditional" world. The women who beat a path to the rayon plants came from families that had already been drawn into an economy where money was a key to survival. The second is that the timber industry, which attracted Carter County's men, undermined its agricultural base, and destroyed its natural resources, created few opportunities for rural women. No wonder that farm daughters in the mills counted their blessings and looked on themselves as pioneers.

Whether they sought work out of family need or for more individualistic reasons, these "factory girls" saw their jobs as a hopeful gamble rather than a desperate last resort, and they remembered the moment with astounding precision. "I'll never forget the day they hired me at Bemberg," said Flossie Cole. "We went down right in front of it. They'd come out and they'd say, 'You and you and you,' and they'd hire so many. And that day I was standing there and he picked out two or three more and he looked at me and he said, 'You.' It thrilled me to death." She worked 56 hours that week and took home $8.16.[14]

Such pay scales were low even for the southern textile industry, and workers quickly found their income eaten away by the cost of commuting or of boarding in town. When the strike came it focused on the issue of Glanzstoff women's wages, which lagged behind those at the older Bemberg plant. But workers had other grievances as well. Caustic chemicals were used to turn cellulose into a viscous fluid that was then forced through spinnerets, thimble-shaped nozzles pierced with tiny holes. The fine, individual streams coagulated into rayon filaments in an acid bath. In the chemical division men waded through water and acid, exposed all day to a lethal spray. Women labored under less dangerous conditions, but for longer hours and less pay. Paid by the piece, they complained of rising production quotas and what everyone referred to as "hard rules."[15]

Women in particular were singled out for petty regulations, aimed not just at extracting labor but at shaping deportment as well. They were forbidden to wear makeup; in some departments they were required to purchase uniforms. Most galling of all was company surveillance of the washroom. According to Bessie Edens, who was promoted to "forelady" in the twisting room, "men could do what they wanted to in their own department," but women had to get a pass to leave the shop floor. "If we went to the bathroom, they'd follow us," Flossie Cole confirmed, "'fraid we'd stay a minute too long." If they did, their pay was docked; one too many trips and they lost their jobs.[16]

Complaints about the washroom may have had other meanings as well. When asked how she heard that a strike was brewing, Nettie Reece cited "bathroom gossip."[17] As the company well knew, the women's washroom, where only a forelady, not a male supervisor, could go, might serve as a communications center, a hub of gossip where complaints were aired and plans were formulated.

The German origins of the plant managers contributed to the tension. Once the strike began, union organizers were quick to play on images of an "imported Prussian autocracy." The frontier republicanism of the mountains shaded easily into post–World War I Americanism as strikers demanded their rights as "natural-born American citizens" oppressed by a "latter day industrialism." In that they had much in common with other twentieth-century workers, for whom the democratic values articulated during the war became a rallying cry for social justice at home. The nationality of the managers helped throw those values into sharp relief.[18]

The strike came on March 12, 1929, led by women in Glanzstoff inspection department, by what one observer called "girls in their teens [who] decided not to put up with the present conditions any longer." The county court immediately issued injunctions forbidding all demonstrations against the company. When strikers ignored the injunctions, the governor sent in the National Guard. The strikers secured a charter from the American Federation of Labor's United Textile Workers union (UTW). Meeting in a place called the Tabernacle, built for religious revivals, they listened to a Baptist preacher from Stoney Creek warn: "The hand of oppression is growing on our people. . . . You women work for practically nothing. You must come together and say that such things must cease to be." Each night more workers "came forward" to take the union oath.[19]

Meanwhile, UTW and Federal Conciliation Service officials arrived on the scene. On March 22 they reached a "gentlemen's agreement" by which the company promised a new wage scale for "good girl help" and agreed not to discriminate against union members. The strikers returned to work, but the conflict was far from over. Higher paychecks never materialized; union members began losing their jobs. On April 4 local businessmen kidnapped two union organizers and ran them out of town. Eleven days later the workers responded with what most observers agreed was a "spontaneous and complete walkout."[20]

This time the conflict quickly escalated. More troops arrived, and the plants became fortresses, with machine guns on the rooftops and armed guardsmen on the ground. The company sent buses manned by soldiers farther up the hollows to recruit new workers and escort them back to town. Pickets blocked narrow mountain roads. Houses were blown up; the town water main was dynamited. An estimated 1,250 individuals were arrested in confrontations with the National Guard.[21]

As far as can be determined, no women were involved in barn burnings and dynamitings—what Bessie Edens referred to as "the rough . . . stuff" that accompanied the second strike. Men "went places that we didn't go," explained Christine Galliher. "They had big dark secrets . . . the men did." But when it came to public demonstrations women held center stage. At the outset "hundreds of girls" had ridden down main street "in buses and taxis, shouting and laughing at people who watched them from windows and doorsteps." Now they blocked the road at Gap Creek and refused soldiers' orders that they walk twelve miles to jail in town. "And there was one girl that was awful tough in the bunch. . . . She

said, 'No, by God. We didn't walk out here, and we're not walking back!' And she sat her hind end down in the middle of the road, and we all sat down with her. And the law used tear gas on us! . . . And it nearly put our eyes out, but we still wouldn't walk back to town." In Elizabethton after picket duty, women marched down the "Bemberg Highway . . . draped in the American flag and carrying the colors"— thereby forcing the guardsmen to present arms each time they passed. Inventive, playful, and shrewd, the women's tactics encouraged a holiday spirit. They may also have deflected violence and garnered community support.[22]

Laughter was among the women's most effective weapons. But beneath high spirits the terms of battle had begun to change. Local organizers were hobbled by a national union that lacked the resources and commitment to sustain the strike. Instead of translating workers' grievances into a compelling challenge, the UTW pared their demands down to the bone. On May 26, six weeks after the strike began, the union agreed to a settlement that made no mention of wages, hours, working conditions, or union recognition. The company's only concession was a promise not to discriminate against union members. The workers were less than enthusiastic. According to one reporter, "It took nine speeches and a lot of question answering lasting two and a half hours to get the strikers to accept the terms."[23]

The press, for the most part, greeted the settlement as a workers' victory, or at least a satisfactory resolution of the conflict. Anna Weinstock, the first woman to serve as a federal conciliator, was credited with bringing the company to the bargaining table and was pictured as the heroine of the event. "SETTLED BY A WOMAN!" headlined one journal. "This is the fact that astounds American newspaper editors." "Five feet five inches and 120 pounds of femininity; clean cut, even features"— and so on, in great detail. Little was made of Weinstock's own working-class origins. She was simply a "new woman," come to the rescue of a backward mountain folk. The strikers themselves dropped quickly from view.[24]

From the outside, the conflict at Elizabethton looked like a straightforward case of labor-management strife. But it appeared quite different from within. Everyone interviewed put the blame for low wages on an alliance between the German managers and the "leading citizens" of the town. Preserved in the oral tradition is the story of how the "town fathers" promised the company a supply of cheap and unorganized labor. Bessie Edens put it this way: They told the company that "women wasn't used to working, and they'd work for almost nothing, and the men would work for low wages. That's the way they got the plant here." In this version of events the strike was part of a long-term struggle, with development-minded townspeople on one side and workers, farmers, and country merchants on the other.[25]

Workers' roots in the countryside encouraged resistance and helped them to mobilize support once the strike began. "These workers have come so recently from the farms and mountains ... and are of such independent spirit," Alfred Hoffman observed, "that they 'Don't care if they do lose their jobs' and cannot be scared." Asked by reporters what would happen if strike activity cost them their jobs, one woman remarked, "I haven't forgotten how to use a hoe," while another said, "We'll go back to the farm."[26] Such threats were not just bravado. High levels of farm ownership sustained cultural independence. Within the internal economy of families, individual fortunes were cushioned by reciprocity; an orientation toward subsistence survived side by side with the desire for cash and store-bought goods.

Stoney Creek farmers were solidly behind the sons and daughters they sent to the factories, as were the small shopkeepers who relied on farmers for their trade. In county politics Stoney Creekers had historically marshaled a block vote against the town. In 1929 Stoney Creek's own J. M. Moreland was county sheriff, and he openly took the strikers' side. A strike leader in the twisting room ran a country store and drove his working neighbors into town. "That's why he was pretty well accepted as their leader," said a fellow worker. "Some of them were cousins and other relations. Some of them traded at his store. Some of them rode in his taxi. All intertwined."[27]

The National Guard had divided loyalties. Parading past the plants, the strikers "waved to and called the first names of the guardsmen, for most of the young men in uniforms [were friends of] the men and girls on strike." Even when the local unit was fortified by outside recruits, fraternizing continued. Nettie Reece, like a number of her girlfriends, met her future husband that way; she saw him on the street and "knew that was mine right there." Some guardsmen went further and simply refused to serve. "The use of the National Guard here was the dirtiest deal ever pulled," one protested. "I turned in my equipment when I was ordered to go out and patrol the road. I was dropped from the payroll two weeks later."[28]

In this context of family- and community-based resistance, women had important roles to play. Farm mothers nurtured the strikers' independence simply by cleaving to the land, passing on to their children a heritage at odds with the values of the new order and maintaining family production as a hedge against the uncertainties of a market economy. But the situation of farm mothers had other effects as well, and it would be a mistake to push the argument for continuity too far. As their husbands ranged widely in search of wage labor, women's work intensified while their status— now tied to earning power—declined. The female strikers of Elizabethton saw their mothers as resourceful and strong but also as increasingly isolated and hard pressed. Most important, they no longer looked to their mothers' lives as patterns for their own.[29]

The summer after the strike, Bessie Edens attended the Southern Summer School for Women Workers, a workers' education project in North Carolina, where she set the group on its ear with an impassioned defense of women's rights:

> It is nothing new for married women to work. They have always worked.... Women have always worked harder than men and always had to look up to the man and feel that they were weaker and inferior.... If we women would not be so submissive and take every thing for granted, if we would awake and stand up for our rights, this world would be a better place to live in, at least it would be better for the women.
>
> Some girls think that as long as mother takes in washings, keeps ten or twelve boarders or perhaps takes in sewing, she isn't working. But I say that either one of the three is as hard work as women could do. So if they do that at home and don't get any wages for it, why would it not be all right for them to go to a factory and receive pay for what they do?

Edens had been the oldest of ten children. She had dreamed of going to nursing school, but her poverty-stricken parents had opposed her plan. At fifteen, she had gone to work as a servant. "Then I'd come back when Momma had a baby and wait on her, and help if she needed me in any way." Asked fifty years later about a daughter's place on a hardscrabble farm, Edens replied: "The girls were supposed to do housework and work in the fields. They were supposed to be slaves."[30]

Bessie Edens was unusual in her articulation of a working-class feminism. But scattered through the life histories written by other students are echoes of her general themes. Read in the context of farm daughters' lives—their first-hand exposure to rural poverty, their yearnings for a more expansive world—these stories reflect the "structure of feeling" women brought to the rayon plants and then to the picket line and union hall.[31] Women such as Edens, it seems, sensed the devaluation of women's handicraft labor in the face of cheap consumer goods. They feared the long arm of their mothers' fate, resented their fathers' distant authority, and envied their brothers' exploits away from home. By opting for work in the rayon plants, they struck out for their own place in a changing world. When low wages, high costs, and autocratic managers affronted their dignity and dashed their hopes, they were the first to revolt.

The Elizabethton story thus presents another pattern in the female protest tradition. In coal-mining communities a rigid division of labor and women's hardships in company towns have resulted, paradoxically, in the notable militancy of miners' wives. By contrast, tobacco factories have tended to employ married women, whose job commitments and associational lives enable them to assume leadership roles in sustained organizing drives. In yet other circumstances, such as the early New England textile mills or the union insurgency of the 1920s and 1930s, single women initiated independent strikes or provided strong support for male-led, mixed-sex campaigns. Where, as in Elizabethton, people were mobilized as family and community members rather than as individual workers, non-wage-earning women could provide essential support. Once in motion, their daughters might outdo men in militancy, perhaps because they had fewer dependents than their male co-workers and could fall back more easily on parental resources, perhaps because the peer culture and increased independence encouraged by factory labor stirred boldness and inspired experimentation.[32]

The fact of women's initiative and participation in collective action is instructive. Even more intriguing is the gender-based symbolism of their protest style. Through dress, language,

and gesture, female strikers expressed a complex cultural identity and turned it to their own rebellious purposes.

Consider, for instance, Trixie Perry and a woman who called herself "Texas Bill." Twenty-eight-year-old Trixie Perry was a reeler in the Glanzstoff plant. She had apparently become pregnant ten years before, had married briefly and then divorced, giving her son her maiden name. Her father was a butcher and a farmer, and she lived near her family on the edge of town. Trixie later moved into Elizabethton. She never remarried but went on to have several more children by other men. Texas Bill's background is more elusive. All we know is that she came from out of state, lived in a boardinghouse, and claimed to have been married twice before she arrived in town. These two friends were ringleaders on the picket line. Both were charged with violating the injunction, and both were brought to trial.[33]

Trixie Perry took the stand in a dress sewn from red, white, and blue bunting and a cap made of a small American flag. The prosecuting attorney began his cross-examination:

> "You have a United States flag as a cap on your head?"
> "Yes."
> "Wear it all the time?"
> "Whenever I take a notion."
> "You are dressed in a United States flag, and the colors?"
> "I guess so, I was born under it, guess I have a right to."

The main charge was that Perry and her friend had drawn a line across the road at Gap Creek and dared the soldiers to cross it. Above all they were accused of taunting the National Guard. The defense attorney, a fiery local lawyer playing to a sympathetic crowd, did not deny the charges. Instead, he used the women to mock the government's case. Had Trixie Perry threatened a lieutenant? "He rammed a gun in my face and I told him to take it out or I would knock it out." Had she blocked the road? "A little thing like me block a big road?" What had she said to the threat of a tear gas bomb? "That little old fire cracker of a thing, it won't go off."[34]

Texas Bill was an even bigger hit with the crowd. The defense attorney called her the "Wild Man from Borneo." A guard said she was "the wildest human being I've ever seen." Texas Bill both affirmed and subverted her reputation. Her nickname came from her habit of wearing "cowboy" clothes. But when it was her turn to testify, she "strutted on the stand" in a fashionable black picture hat and a black coat. Besides her other transgressions, she was accused of grabbing a soldier's gun and aiming it at him. What was she doing on the road so early in the morning? "I take a walk every morning before breakfast for my health," Texas replied with what a reporter described as "an assumed ladylike dignity."[35]

Witnesses for the prosecution took pains to contradict Texas Bill's "assumed ladylike dignity." A guardsman complained that she called him a "'God damned yellow son-of-a-bitch,' and then branched out from that." Texas offered no defense: "When that soldier stuck his gun in my face, that did make me mad and I did cuss a little bit and don't deny it." Far from discrediting the strikers, the soldiers' testimony added to their own embarrassment and the audience's delight. In tune with the crowd, the defense attorney "enjoyed making the guards admit they had been 'assaulted' . . . by 16- and 18-year-old girls."[36]

Mock gentility, transgressive laughter, male egos on the line—the mix made for wonderful theater, and proved effective in court as well. The judge reserved maximum sentences for three especially aggressive men; all the women and most of the men were found not guilty or were lightly fined. In the end even those convictions were overturned by the state court of appeals.[37]

Trixie Perry and Texas Bill certainly donned the role of "disorderly woman." Since, presumably, only extraordinary circumstances call forth feminine aggression, women's assaults against persons and property constitute a powerful witness against injustice. At the same time, since women are considered less rational and taken less seriously than men, they may meet less resistance and be punished less severely for their crimes.[38]

But Trixie Perry and Texas Bill were not just out of line in their public acts; they also led unconventional private lives. It was this erotic subtext that most horrified officialdom and amused the courtroom crowd. The only extended discussion of the strike that appears in the city council minutes resulted in a resolution that read in part:

> WHEREAS, it has come to [our] attention . . . that the moral tone of this community has been lowered by reason of men and women congregating in various houses and meeting-places in Elizabethton and there practicing lewdness all hours of the night, in defiance of morality, law and order. . . .
>
> NOW, THEREFORE, BE IT RESOLVED, that the police force of the City arrest and place in the City Jail those who are violating the laws by practicing lewdness within the City of Elizabethton. . . .[39]

Union representatives apparently shared, indeed anticipated, the councilmen's concern. Worried by rumors that unemployed women were resorting to prostitution, they had already announced to the press that 25 percent of the strikers had been sent back to their hillside homes, "chiefly young single girls whom we want to keep off the streets." The townsmen and the trade unionists were thus united in drawing a line between good women and bad, with respectability being measured not only by chastity but by nuances of style and language as well.[40] In the heat of the trial, the question of whether or not women—as workers—had violated the injunction took second place to questions about their status *as women*, as members of their sex. Had they cursed? Had they been on the road at odd hours of the day or night? Was Texas Bill a lady or a "wild man from Borneo"? Fearing that "lewd women" might discredit the organizing drive, the organizers tried to send them home. To protect the community's "moral tone," the city council threatened to lock them up.

There is nothing extraordinary about this association between sexual misbehavior and women's labor militancy. Since strikers are often young single women who violate gender conventions by invading public space customarily reserved for men (and sometimes frequented by prostitutes)—and since female aggressiveness stirs up fears of women's sexual power—opponents have often undercut union organizing drives by insinuations of prostitution or promiscuity. Fearing guilt by association, "respectable" women stay away.[41]

What is impressive here is how Trixie Perry and Texas Bill handled the dichotomy between ladyhood and lewdness, good girls and bad. Using words that, for women in particular, were ordinarily taboo, they refused deference and signaled disrespect. Making no secret of their sexual experience, they combined flirtation with fierceness on the picket line and adopted a provocative courtroom style. And yet, with the language of dress—a cap made of an American flag, an elegant wide-brimmed hat—they claimed their rights as citizens and their place in the female community.

Moreover, that community upheld their claims. The defense attorney chose unruly women as his star witnesses, and the courtroom spectators enthusiastically cheered them on. The prosecuting attorney recommended dismissal of the charges against all the women on trial except Trixie Perry, Texas Bill, and a "hoodlum" named Lucille Ratliffe, on the grounds that the rest came from "good families." Yet in the court transcripts, few differences can be discerned in the behavior of good girls and bad. The other female defendants may have been less flamboyant, but they were no less sharp-tongued. Was Vivian King a member of the UTW? "Yes, and proud of it." Had she been picketing? "Yes, proud of that." What was a young married woman named Dorothy Oxindine doing on Gap Creek at five o'clock in the morning? "Out airing." Did Lena May Jones "holler out 'scab'"? "No, I think the statement made was 'I wouldn't be a scab' and 'Why don't you come and join our organization.'" Did she laugh at a soldier and tell him his gun wouldn't shoot? "I didn't tell him it wouldn't shoot, but I laughed at him . . . and told him he was too much of a man to shoot a lady."[42]

Interviewed over fifty years later, strike participants still refused to make invidious distinctions between themselves and women like Trixie Perry and Texas Bill. Bessie Edens was a settled, self-educated, married woman. But she was also a self-described "daredevil on the picket line," secure in the knowledge that she had a knife hidden in her drawstring underwear. To Edens, who came from a mountain hamlet called Hampton, the chief distinction did not lie between herself and rougher women. It lay between herself and merchants' wives who blamed the trouble on "those hussies from Hampton." When asked what she thought of Trixie Perry and Texas Bill, she answered simply, "There were some girls like that involved. But I didn't care. They did their part."[43]

Nettie Reece, who lived at home with parents who were "pretty particular with [their] daughters," shared Bessie Edens's attitude. After passing along the town gossip about Trixie Perry, she was anxious to make sure her meaning was not misconstrued. "Trixie was not a woman who sold her body," she emphasized. "She just had a big desire for sex. . . . And when she had a cause to fight for, she'd

fight." Reece then went on to establish Perry's claim to a certain kind of respectability. After the strike Perry became a hard-working restaurant cook. She was a good neighbor: "If anybody got sick, she was there to wait on them." The children she bore out of wedlock did well in life, and they "never throwed [their mother] aside."[44]

Industrialization, as we know, changed the nature of work, the meaning of time. In Carter County it entailed a shift of economic and political power from the countryside to the town. At issue too were more intimate matters of fantasy, culture, and style.

Implicit in the conflict were two different sexual systems. One, subscribed to by union officials and the local middle class, mandated chastity before marriage, men as breadwinners, and women as housewives in the home. The other, rooted in a rural past and adapted to working-class life, recognized liaisons established without the benefit of clergy or license fees and allowed legitimacy to be broadly construed. It was unfamiliar with—or pragmatic about—prostitution. It circumscribed women's roles without investing in abstract standards of femininity. It was, in short, a society that might produce a Trixie Perry or defend "hussies from Hampton" against the snubs of merchants' wives.

This is not to say that the women of Elizabethton were simply acting on tradition. On the contrary, the strikers dressed the persona of the disorderly woman in unmistakably modern garb. Women's behavior on the witness stand presupposed a certain sophistication: A passing familiarity allowed them to parody ladyhood and to thumb a nose at the genteel standards of the town. Combining garments from the local past with fragments of an expansive consumer culture, the women of Elizabethton assembled their own version of a brash, irreverent Jazz Age style.

By the early 1920s radios and Model Ts had joined railroads and mail-order catalogs as conduits to the larger world. Record companies had discovered hill-country music and East Tennessee's first country-music stars were recording hits that transformed ballad singing, fiddle playing, and banjo picking into one of America's great popular-music sounds. The banjo itself was an Afro-American instrument that had come to the mountains with the railroad gangs. Such cultural interchanges multiplied during the 1920s as rural traditions met the upheavals of industrial life. The result was an explosion of musical creativity—in the hills of Tennessee no less than in New York City and other cosmopolitan centers.[45] Arriving for work in the rayon plants, young people brought with them the useable past of the countryside, but they quickly assimilated the speeded-up rhythms of a changing world.

Work-related peer groups formed a bridge between traditional loyalties and a novel youth culture. Whether married or single, living with parents or on their own, women participated in the strike in same-sex groups. Sisters boarded, worked, and demonstrated together. Girlfriends teamed up in groups or pairs. Trixie Perry and Texas Bill were a case in point. But there were others as well. Nettie Reece joined the union with her parents' approval but also with her whole school girl gang in tow. Ethel and M. C. Ashworth, ages eighteen and seventeen, respectively, came from Virginia to work in the plants. "Hollering and singing [in a] Ford touring car," they were arrested in a demonstration at Watauga Point. Ida and Evelyn Heaton boarded together on Donna Avenue. Evelyn Heaton was hit by a car on the picket line, swore out a warrant, and had the commander of the National Guard placed under arrest. After the strike she was blacklisted, and Ida attended the Southern Summer School.[46]

The sudden gathering of young people in the town nourished new patterns of heterosociability, and the strike's erotic undercurrent surfaced not only in Trixie Perry's "big desire for sex" but also in the behavior of her more conventional peers. The loyalties of the national guardsmen were divided, but their sympathy was obvious, as was their interest in the female strikers. Most of the Elizabethton women were in their teens or early twenties, the usual age of marriage in the region, and the strike provided unaccustomed opportunities for courtship. Rather than choosing a neighbor they had known all their lives, under watchful parental eyes, women flirted on the picket lines or the shop floor. Romance and politics commingled in the excitement of the moment, flowering in a spectrum of behavior—from the outrageousness of Trixie Perry to a spate of marriages among other girls.

What needs emphasis here is the dynamic quality of working-class women's culture—a quality that is sometimes lost in static oppositions between modernism and traditionalism, individualism and family values, consumer and producer mentalities. This is especially important where regional history has been so thoroughly mythologized. Appalachian culture, like all living cultures, embraced continuity and discontinuity, indigenous and borrowed elements.[47] As surely as Anna Weinstock—or Alabama's Zelda Fitzgerald—or any city flapper, the Elizabethton strikers were "new women," making their way in a world their mothers could not have known but carrying with them values handed down through the female line.

Two vignettes may serve to illustrate that process of grounded change.

Flossie Cole's mother, known by everyone on Stoney Creek as "Aunt Tid," was Sheriff Moreland's sister, but that didn't keep her from harboring cardplayers, buckdancers, and whiskey drinkers in her home. Aunt Tid was also a seamstress who "could look at a picture in a catalog and cut a pattern and make a dress just like it." But like most of her friends, Cole jumped at the chance for store-bought clothes: "That first paycheck, that was it . . . I think I bought me some new clothes with the first check I got. I bought me a new pair of shoes and a dress and a hat. Can you imagine someone going to a plant with a hat on? I had a blue dress and black shoes—patent leather, honey, with real high heels—and a blue hat." Nevertheless, before Cole left home in the morning for her job in the rayon plant, Aunt Tid made sure that around her neck—beneath the new blue dress—she wore a bag of asafetida, a strong-smelling resin, a folk remedy to protect her from diseases that might be circulating in the town.[48]

Second, there is visual evidence: a set of sixteen-millimeter films made by the company in order to identify—and to blacklist—workers who participated in the union. In those films groups of smiling women traipse along the picket line dressed in up-to-date clothes.[49] Yet federal conciliator Anna Weinstock, speaking to an interviewer forty years later, pictured them in sunbonnets, and barefooted. "They were," she explained, "what we would normally call hillbillies": women who "never get away from their shacks."[50] This could be seen as the treachery of memory, a problem of retrospection. But it is also an illustration of the power of stereotypes, of how cultural difference is registered as backwardness, of how images of poverty and backwardness hide the realities of working-class women's lives.

The strike, as we know, was defeated. Participants were blacklisted. The Great Depression settled over the mountains, rekindling reliance on older ways of making do. Flossie Cole, for instance, had been new to factory labor, but she was no stranger to women's work. While her brothers had followed their father's lead to the coal mines, she had pursued the two most common occupations of the poorest mountain girls: agricultural labor and domestic service. "We would hire out and stay with people until they got through with us and then go back home. And when we got back home, it was workin' in the corn or wash for people." When Cole lost her job after the strike she went back to domestic service, "back to the drudge house," as she put it.[51]

Young women had poured eagerly into the rayon mills, drawn at least in part by the promise of independence, romance and adventure. As hard times deepened, such motives paled beside stark necessity. Two statistics make the point: The percentage of Carter County women who were gainfully employed held steady through the thirties. But by the end of the period a larger proportion than before worked as servants in other people's homes. When Flossie Cole went "back to the drudge house," she had plenty of company.[52]

Still, despite subsequent hardships, the spirit of the 1920s flickered on. Setting out to explore the strike through oral-history interviews, we expected to find disclaimers or silences. Instead, we heard unfaded memories and no regrets. "I knew I wasn't going to get to go back, and I didn't care," said Bessie Edens. "I wrote them a letter and told them I didn't care whether they took me back or not. I didn't! If I'd starved I wouldn't of cared, because I knew what I was a'doing when I helped to pull it. And I've never regretted it in any way. . . . And it did help the people, and it's helped the town and the country."[53] For those, like Edens, who went on to the Southern Summer School or remained active in the union, the strike was a pivot around which the political convictions and personal aspirations of a lifetime turned. For them, there were intangible rewards: a subtle deepening of individual power, a belief that they had made history and that later generations benefited from what they had done.

The strike, of course, made a fainter impression on other lives. Women's rebelliousness neither redefined gender roles nor overcame economic dependency. Their desire for the trappings of modernity could blur into a self-limiting consumerism. An ideology of romance could end in sexual danger or a married woman's burdensome double day. Still, the women of Elizabethton left a legacy. A norm of female public work, a new style of sexual expressiveness, the entry of women into public space and political struggles previously monopolized by men—all these pushed against traditional constraints even as they created new vulnerabilities. The farm daughters who left home for the rayon plants pioneered a new pattern of female experience, and they created for their post–World War II daughters an environment far different from the one they, in their youth, had known. It would be up to later generations to wrestle with the costs of commercialization and to elaborate a vision that embraced economic justice and community solidarity as well as women's liberation.

NOTES

This study began as a collaborative endeavor with Sara Evans of the University of Minnesota, who helped to gather many of the interviews on which I have relied. Rosemarie Hester and Jennifer Dowd also joined me on trips to the mountains, and I benefited from their companionship, ideas, and research. I owe a special debt to Christopher Daly, Lu Ann Jones, Robert Korstad, James Leloudis, and Mary Murphy, with whom I have co-written *Like a Family: The Making of a Southern Cotton Mill World* (Chapel Hill, 1987).

   1. Dan Crowe, *Old Town and the Covered Bridge* (Johnson City, Tenn., 1977), pp. 32, 71; Florence (Cole) Grindstaff interview by Jacquelyn Hall, July 10, 1981 (in Hall's possession).

   2. For this strike wave, see Tom Tippett, *When Southern Labor Stirs* (New York, 1931); James A. Hodges, "Challenge to the New South: The Great Textile Strike in Elizabethton, Tennessee, 1929," *Tennessee Historical Quarterly* 23 (Dec. 1964):343–57; . . .

   3. Contemporary observations include, *Knoxville News Sentinel,* May 17, 1929; Florence Kelley, "Our Newest South," *Survey,* June 15, 1929, pp. 342–44; . . .

   4. Anne Firor Scott, "On Seeing and Not Seeing: A Case of Historical Invisibility," *Journal of American History* 71 (June 1984):7–8.

   5. Natalie Zemon Davis, *Society and Culture in Early Modern France* (Stanford, 1975), pp. 124–51. . . .

   6. Michel Foucault, *Power/Knowledge: Selected Interviews and Other Writings, 1972–1977,* trans. and ed. Colin Gordon (New York, 1980), p. 81.

   7. Joseph Leeming, *Rayon: The First Man-Made Fiber* (Brooklyn, 1950), pp. 1–82; Jesse W. Markham, *Competition in the Rayon Industry* (Cambridge, Mass., 1952), pp. 1–38, 97, 186, 193, 209.

   8. Bruce Roberts and Nancy Roberts, *Where Time Stood Still: A Portrait of Appalachia* (New York, 1970); William Goodell Frost, "Our Contemporary

Ancestors in the Southern Mountains," *Atlantic Monthly* 83 (March 1899):311; Arnold J. Toynbee, *A Study of History*, 2 vols. (New York, 1947), II: 312; . . .

9. For this preindustrial economy, and its transformation, see Eller, *Miners, Millhands, and Mountaineers*, pp. 3–38, 86–127. . . .

10. *Mountaineer*, Dec. 28, Dec. 31, 1887.

11. U.S. Department of the Interior, Census Office, *Report on the Productions of Agriculture as Returned at the Tenth Census* (June 1, 1880) (Washington, 1883), pp. 84–85, 132, 169; U.S. Department of Commerce, Bureau of the Census, *Fourteenth Census of the United States Taken in the Year 1920: Agriculture*, vol. VI, pt. 2 (Washington, [D.C.,] 1922), pp. 446–47.

12. Holly, "Elizabethton, Tennessee," pp. 123, 133–38, 156, 198; U.S. Congress, Senate, Committee on Manufactures, *Working Conditions of the Textile Industry in North Carolina, South Carolina, and Tennessee*, 71 Cong., 1 sess., May 8, 9, and 20, 1929, p. 95; Henry Schuettler interview by Hall, n.d. [1981] (in Hall's possession).

13. Thirteenth Census of the United States, 1910, Manuscript Population Schedule, Carter County, Tenn., district 7; ibid., district 15; ibid., district 10; ibid., district 12.

14. Grindstaff interview.

15. *Scraps of Work and Play*, Southern Summer School for Women Workers in Industry, Burnsville, N.C., July 11–Aug. 23, 1929, typescript, pp. 21–22, 24, box 111, American Labor Education Service Records (Martin P. Catherwood Library, New York State School of Industrial and Labor Relations, Cornell University, Ithaca, N.Y.); Bessie Edens interview by Mary Frederickson, Aug. 14, 1975, pp. 1–2, 31–32, Southern Oral History Program Collection, Southern Historical Collection (Wilson Library, University of North Carolina at Chapel Hill) [hereafter SOHP].

16. Edens interview, Aug. 14, 1975, p. 32; Grindstaff interview.

17. Nettie Reece [pseud.] interview by Hall, May 18 and 19, 1983 (in Hall's possession).

18. *Knoxville News Sentinel*, May 13, 1929; *American Bemberg Corporation* v. *George Miller, et al.*, East Tennessee District Supreme Court, Jan. 29, 1930, record of evidence, typescript, box 660 (Tennessee State Library and Archives, Nashville) [hereafter Record of Evidence]. . . .

19. *Knoxville News Sentinel*, Mar. 14, 1929; Christine (Hinkle) Galliher and Dave Galliher interview by Hall, Aug. 8, 1979, pp. 8–9, SOHP; Tom Tippett, "Southern Situation," speech typescript, meeting held at the National Board, May 15, 1929, p. 3, box 25, Young Women's Christian Association Papers, Sophia Smith Collection (Smith College, Northampton, Mass.); Tom Tippett, "Impressions of Situation at Elizabethton, Tenn., May 10, 11, 1929," typescript, p. 1, ibid.

20. *Knoxville News Sentinel*, Mar. 20, Mar. 29, 1929; "Instructions for Adjustment of Wage Scale for Girl Help," Mar. 15, 1929, Records of the Conciliation Service, RG 280 (National Archives); Committee of Striking Workers[,] Members of United Textile Workers of America to the Honorable Herbert Hoover, Apr. 16, 1929, ibid; "Preliminary Report of Commissioner of Conciliation," Apr. 16, 1929, ibid.

21. Dr. J. A. Hardin to Hon. H. H. Horton, May 16, 1929, box 12, Governor Henry H. Horton Papers (Tennessee State Library and Archives); *Knoxville News Sentinel*, May 6, May 10, May 12, May 14, May 19, May 24, 1929.

22. Edens interview, Aug. 14, 1975, pp. 40, 49; Galliher interview, 33; *Knoxville News Sentinel*, Mar. 15, May 16, 1929.

23. *Knoxville News Sentinel*, May 27, 1929; Ina Nell (Hinkle) Harrison interview by Hall, Aug. 8, 1979, p. 2, SOHP; Mary Heaton Vorse, "Rayon Strikers Reluctantly Accept Settlement," press release, May 27, 1929, box 156, Mary Heaton Vorse Papers, Archives of Labor and Urban Affairs (Walter P. Reuther Library, Wayne State University, Detroit, Mich.).

24. "Rays of Sunshine in the Rayon War," *Literary Digest*, June 8, 1929, p. 12; *Charlotte Observer*, June 2, 1929; *Raleigh News and Observer*, May 24, 1929.

25. Edens interview, Aug. 14, 1975, pp. 43–44; Myrtle Simmerly interview by Hall, May 18, 1983 (in Hall's possession); Ollie Hardin interview by Hall and Sara Evans, Aug. 9, 1979 (in Hall's possession); Effie (Hardin) Carson interview by Hall and Evans, Aug. 6, 1979, p. 41, SOHP; Holly, "Elizabethton, Tennessee," 306–7.

26. James Myers, "Field Notes: Textile Strikes in the South," box 374, Archive Union Files (Martin P. Catherwood Library); *Raleigh News and Observer*, Mar. 15, 1929.

27. Hoffmann, "Mountaineer in Industry," 2–5; Robert (Bob) Moreland and Barbara Moreland interview by Hall, July 11, 1981 (in Hall's possession); *Knoxville News Sentinel*, Mar. 15, 1929; Honard Ward interview by Hall, n.d. [1981] (in Hall's possession).

28. *Knoxville News Sentinel*, May 15, 1929; Reece interview; . . .

29. For the argument that precisely because they are "left behind" by the economic developments that pull men into wage labor, woman-centered families may harbor alternative or oppositional values, see Mina Davis Caulfield, "Imperialism, the Family, and Cultures of Resistance," *Socialist Revolution* 4 (Oct. 1974):67–85; . . .

30. Bessie Edens, "Why a Married Woman Should Work," in *Scraps of Work and Play*, pp. 30–31; Edens interview, Aug. 14. 1975, pp. 14, 21, 34–35; Bessie Edens interview by Hall, Aug. 5, 1979 (in Hall's possession); Millie Sample, "Impressions," Aug. 1931, box 9, American Labor Education Service Records.

31. Mirion Bonner, "Behind the Southern Textile Strikes," *Nation*, Oct. 2, 1929, pp. 351–52; "Scraps From Our Lives," in *Scraps of Work and Play*, pp. 5–11; . . .

32. Corbin, *Life, Work, and Rebellion*, pp. 92–93; Louise A. Tilly, "Paths of Proletarianization: Organization of Production, Sexual Division of Labor, and Women's Collective Action," *Signs* 7 (Winter 1981): 400–17; . . .

33. *Elizabethton Star*, Nov. 14, 1953, Jan. 31, 1986; Reece interview; Carson interview, 25; Nellie Bowers interview by Hall, May 15, 1983 (in Hall's possession); *Knoxville News Sentinel*, May 17, May 18, 1929.

34. Record of Evidence.

35. *Knoxville News Sentinel*, May 17, 1929.

36. Ibid.; Record of Evidence.

37. *American Bemberg Corporation* v. *George Miller, et al.*, minute books "Q" and "R," Chancery Court minutes, Carter County, Tenn., July 22, 1929

(Carter County Courthouse, Elizabethton, Tenn.);
American Bemberg Corporation v. *George Miller, et al.,*
Court of Appeals, #1, Sept. 5, 1930 (Supreme Court
and Courts of Appeal, State of Tennessee,
Knoxville).

38. Davis, *Society and Culture in Early Modern
France*, pp. 124–51; Laurel Thatcher Ulrich, *Good
Wives* (New York, 1982), pp. 191–97.

39. Elizabethton City Council, Minutes, May
23, 1929, Minute Book, vol. 5, pp. 356–57 (City Hall,
Elizabethton, Tenn.).

40. *Knoxville News Sentinel,* May 5, 1929; Myers,
"Field Notes." . . .

41. See, for instance, Alice Kessler-Harris, "The
Autobiography of Ann Washington Craton," *Signs* 1
(Summer 1976):1019–37.

42. *Knoxville News Sentinel,* May 18, 1929; Record
of Evidence.

43. Edens interview, Aug. 5, 1979.

44. Reece interview, May 19, 1983.

45. Charles K. Wolfe, *Tennessee Strings: The
Story of Country Music in Tennessee* (Knoxville, 1977),
pp. 22–90; Barry O'Connell, "Dick Boggs, Musician
and Coal Miner," *Appalachian Journal* 11 (Autumn-
Winter 1983–84):48.

46. *Miller's Elizabethton, Tenn., City Directory,*
1930; Reece interview; Record of Evidence; *Knoxville
News Sentinel,* May 16, May 17, 1929; . . .

47. David E. Whisnant, *All That Is Native and
Fine: The Politics of Culture in an American Region*
(Chapel Hill, 1983), p. 48.

48. Grindstaff interview; Moreland interview.

49. *Knoxville Journal,* Apr. 22, 1929; sixteen-
millimeter film (1 reel), ca. 1929, Helen Raulston Collection, Archives of Appalachia (East Tennessee
State University, Johnson City); sixteen-millimeter
film (20 reels), ca. 1927–1928, Bemberg Industry Records (Tennessee State Library and Archives). . . .

50. Anna Weinstock Schneider interview by
Julia Blodgett Curtis, 1969, pp. 161, 166, 172–3, 177,
Anna Weinstock Schneider Papers, box 1 (Martin P.
Catherwood Library).

51. Grindstaff interview.

52. Bureau of the Census, *Fifteenth Census of
the United States: 1930. Population,* vol. III, pt. 2
(Washington, [D.C.], 1932), p. 909; U.S. Department
of Commerce, Bureau of the Census, *Sixteenth
Census of the United States: 1940. Population,* vol. II, pt.
6 (Washington, [D.C.], 1943), p. 616.

53. Edens interview, Aug. 14, 1975, p. 50. . . .

DEVRA ANNE WEBER
Mexican Women on Strike in 1933: The Structure of Memory

Did you ever wish you could travel back in time and ask someone directly about a historical event? Historians can't time travel, but they can interview people. When interviews are conducted in order to archive and make them acces-sible, this methodology is called oral history. What do you think are the strengths and weaknesses of using oral history? Whose history can we access if we incorpo-rate oral history rather than primarily using written documents? How do we ac-count for selective or faulty memory?

Devra Anne Weber's article analyzes why oral history is such a powerful methodology and how even mis-rememberings or inaccurate accounts of the past can still tell us quite a bit. She analyzes oral history accounts of Mexican Ameri-can women who engaged in a cotton strike in California in the 1930s. As you read this article, think about how the oral history accounts give us different insights into the past.

Excerpted from "Mexican Women on Strike: Memory, History and Oral Narratives" by Devra Anne Weber
in *Between Borders: Essay on Mexicana/Chicana History*, ed. Adelaida R. Del Castillo (Encino, Calif.: Floricanto
Press, 1990), pp. 175–200. Reprinted by permission of the author and publisher. Notes have been edited and
renumbered.

Oral histories, more than any other historical source, pivot around the central if complex relationship between memory and history. Flowing from this relationship is the source of the richness, immediacy, and unique value of oral histories. But it is just this relation to memory which can be both frustrating and challenging to historians and readers of history.

Oral histories are shaped by two simultaneous dialogues. One occurs between the individual and his or her own memory. The other occurs with the interviewer. The relationship with the interviewer determines how much will be shared or what will be shared or, perhaps, altered or fabricated. This is shaped by the questions asked, the class, ethnicity, and gender of the two people, and the subjective elements of sensitivity and compatibility which may bridge or accentuate differences between them. The individual's dialogue with his or her own memory determines the internal structuring of the individual consciousness and the oral history created by this. Yet memory, reflecting the complexity of human beings, can be contradictory and contentious, as well as reflective, insightful, articulate, and perceptive. Most importantly, memory is ultimately faithful only to an internal logic of consciousness.

Oral histories are a crucial source for exploring the history of Mexican women. Oral histories provide some answers to fundamental questions about life and work, culture and cultural change, women's perceptions, values and consciousness which are unavailable from more traditional sources. Yet there are problems with oral sources. One is the problem of memory: a frequent lament is that oral histories are factually inaccurate and thus a poor historical source. Another problem arises from how oral sources are used. In our enthusiasm over these sources which carry us out of dusty archives and into the world, oral histories are often used without critical analysis. They are often used in historical reassessments which aim, in part, to reconnect people with their own history. Yet we all act within a framework of institutional relations, struggles and divisions, change and process. As a result, using oral histories uncritically and without reevaluating the overall historical framework may ultimately reinforce what we are trying to change—peoples' alienation from their own past—by including them in a written history only to relegate them to anecdotal and colorful bystanders watching the traditionally conceived parade of historical process march by in front of them.[1]

This [essay] will explore how oral histories can be used, with their strengths and their weaknesses. This will touch upon the obvious—of how oral narratives can yield information about daily life and work. It will also address how oral histories can help in understanding the consciousness of these women and how, in this case, factual inaccuracies, frustrating as they are, follow an inherent logic which can be revealing of the internal meaning of these narratives and lead us to a greater understanding of peoples' interpretation of these events. [My research] draws on a series of oral histories with Mexican women who were cotton pickers in California's San Joaquin Valley during the 1930s and participated in the 1933 cotton strike by over 18,000 workers. [Here I] focus on the oral narrative of Rosaura Valdez.[2]

Mrs. Valdez, born near Torreon, Mexico, was not atypical of women who were in the strike. She came from Mexico, where her father had been a *sembrador,* a small farmer or sharecropper, eking out a livable but bleak existence. She had barely reached adolescence when the Mexican revolution broke out in 1910. With the exception of a rebellious sister-in-law, neither she nor her immediate family participated in the revolution.[3] As with many noncombatants, her memories of the revolution were not of the opposing ideologies nor issues, but of hunger, fear and death. Fleeing the revolution, the family crossed the border into Texas and three years later settled in the Los Angeles *colonia* of Maravilla. By 1933, she was 24, married, with two children and lived in a small San Joaquin Valley town.[4]

The agricultural industry in which she worked was, by 1933, California's major industry and cotton the most rapidly expanding crop in the states cornucopia. Cotton depended on Mexican labor, and highly capitalized, large cotton ranches of over 300 acres dominated the industry and hired the largest number of agricultural workers in the state. Approximately 20,000 workers picked the 208,000 acres of San Joaquin Valley cotton. Social relations were shaped by the size and the managerial structure on the ranches. Mexican workers migrated annually to the San Joaquin Valley to live on private labor camps which were rural versions of company towns. Here they lived in company owned housing, bought from company stores to which many remained in perpetual debt, and on the larger ranches sent their children to company schools. Their work and daily lives were supervised by a racially structured hierarchy dominated by Anglo managers and foremen: below them were Mexican contractors who recruited the workers, supervised work, and acted as the intermediary between workers and their English speaking employers.[5]

With the onslaught of the depression, agricultural prices fell and growers slashed wages. Workers, who had received $1.25 per a hundred pounds of cotton in 1926, were now receiving only 60 cents for the same amount in 1933. In response—and despite the threat of deportation—Mexican farm workers went on strike in crop after crop in California, convulsing the agricultural industry and sending tremors through the San Joaquin Valley. Encouraged by the erroneous belief that they were included in section 7A of the National Recovery Act of the New Deal which guaranteed the right of workers to bargain collectively, they shut down the agricultural heartland of the biggest industry of California. The wave of strikes began in May in southern California, around Los Angeles, and by August spread north into the San Joaquin Valley. While under the banner of the Cannery and Agricultural Workers Industrial Union (CAWIU), the strikes were conducted largely by Mexican workers and Mexican organizers. Extensive familial and social networks among the workers acted as conduits in spreading the strike and galvanizing workers to walk out. Thus the spread and success of the strikes depended as much, if not more, on the family and social networks of the Mexican workers as it did on the small but effective and ambitious union.

In October the strike wave crested in the cotton fields of the San Joaquin Valley when 18,000 cotton pickers went on strike. The strike brought picking to a standstill over one hundred miles of the California cotton belt. Growers evicted strikers from their ranch homes and the evicted strikers formed ad hoc camps on empty land. The largest camp was near the town of Corcoran where 3,500 strikers congregated. Strikers formed mobile picket lines which paraded in front of selected ranches where some workers still picked. Growers, panicked by the realization that anticipated new workers would not be forthcoming to pick their crop, retaliated by organizing groups of armed vigilantes who worked with local law enforcement to stop picketing and intimidate strikers.

Workers were beaten and within two weeks growers had shot and killed three strikers.

As the intensity of the conflict escalated, the strike became the unintentional testing ground for the New Deal's as yet unclear agricultural policy. The federal government sent in food to starving strikers. George Creel, an arbitrator with the National Recovery Administration, was sent in to settle the strike. But the strikers held out for over a month before a negotiated settlement between growers, and the California, United States, and Mexican governments reached a compromised wage of 75 cents per one hundred pounds.[6]

Mexicanas were a vital part of the strike, and about half of the strikers at Corcoran were women. They ran the camp kitchen, cared for the children, and marched on picket lines. They distributed food and clothing. Some attended strike meetings and a few spoke at the meetings. And it was the women who confronted Mexican strikebreakers. In short, women were an essential element to this strike but have been basically obscured from its history. Mrs. Valdez went on strike and was on the picket lines. She was not a leader, but one of the many women who made the strike possible.

Before launching into the content of the oral histories, a word is in order about the voice, the tone of oral histories. How information is conveyed is often as important as what is said, and can emphasize or contradict the verbal message. Conversation and social interaction are a major part of women's lives and gesture and voice are crucial to these communications. The verbal message, the "song" of a story, is especially important for people with a strong oral tradition. . . . Oral traditions are often also an art form, drama and literature. Oral histories are often dramatic and move with a grace and continuity which embodies analytical reflections to communicate an understanding of social relations and the complexities of human existence.

Mrs. Valdez structured her oral history in the form of stories or vignettes. Most sections had distinct beginnings and endings, interrupted only if I interjected a question. She developed characters, villains and heroes, hardship and tragedy (but little comedy). How this story was constructed and its characters developed embodied her assessment of the conflict.

As she told her story, the characters developed voices of their own, each with separate and distinct tones and cadence which reflected, perhaps to some extent, their personalities but moreover her assessment of them and their role in the drama. Strike breakers, for example, spoke in high-pitched and pleading voices: the listener understood immediately that they were measly cowards. The strikers voices were a clear contrast, as they spoke in sonorous, deep, and steady tones: they had the voice of authority, seemed to represent a communal voice, and verbalized what Mrs. Valdez considered community values.

Mrs. Valdez's sense of collective values, later expressed in the collective action, either by strikers as a whole or by women, was expressed in a collective voice. At times individuals spoke in her stories: the grower, Mr. Peterson; her contractor, "Chicho" Vidaurri; and the woman leader "la Lourdes." But more often people spoke in one collective voice which transcended the individual. This sense of community as told through the voices became a central feature of her narrative and permeated everything she said about the strike. Thus, in effect, a sense of unanimity permeated her story: an analysis of solidarity and clear cut division. In short, how she told the story underlined, accentuated and modified the meaning of the story itself.[7]

The "story" she told conveyed not only the "facts" as she remembered them but also conveyed nonverbal analysis. Mrs. Valdez's voice, gestures, and inflections conveyed both implications and meanings. She gestured with her arms and hands—a flat palm hard down on the table to make a point, both hands held up as she began again. Her "stories" had clear beginnings and often ended with verbal punctuations such as "and that's the way it was." She switched tenses around as in the heat of the story the past became the present and then receded again into the past. Vocal inflections carried a tonal counterpoint to her words as they jumped, vibrated, climbed, and then descended on the tone of her voice.

Mrs. Valdez's memories of the 1933 strike focused on two major concerns: providing and caring for her family and her role as a striker. How she structured these memories reveals something about her perceptions and her consciousness as a woman, a Mexican, and a worker. Her memories of the strike focused on the collectivity of Mexicans and, within this, the collectivity of Mexican women.

Mrs. Valdez's narrative suggests a sense of national identity which is an important underpinning to her narrative and reflects the importance of national cohesion against an historic background of Anglo-Mexican hostility. Mrs. Valdez vividly recounted the story of the United States' appropriation of Mexican land in 1848 and the Treaty of Guadalupe Hidalgo which ceded the area to the United States. She drew from stories of Mexican rebellion against U.S. rule in California and the nineteenth-century California guerrillas, Tiburcio Vasquez and Joaquin Murietta: the knowledge that Mexicans were working on the land which once belonged to Mexico increased her antagonism towards Anglo bosses. Mrs. Valdez may well have felt like Mrs. Martinez who, upon arriving at the valley, pointed out to her son and told him "Mira lo que nos arrebataron los bárbaros."[8]

The Mexican revolution of 1910 to 1920 influenced strikers in several ways. Only a few years away from the revolution, most Mexicans on strike had lived through the revolution and, some, the reverberations and conflicts which rocked Mexico in its wake. For many, such as Mrs. Valdez, their memories of the revolution were of hunger, death, and disruption. Yet the legacy of the revolution was important in several respects. The military experience was crucial in protecting the camp: often led by ex-military officers, Mexican veterans at the Corcoran camp formed a formidable armed security system which even the gun-happy growers shrank from attacking, and organized groups patrolled the roads to deter potential strikebreakers. Yet Mrs. Valdez remembers that the strike encouraged the recounting of stories of the revolution which were told, retold, and debated in the camp, punctuated by arguments between various factions of the revolution. The extent to which Mexicans employed the images and slogans of the revolution helped solidify a sense of community. Workers named the rough roads in the camp after revolutionary heroes and Mexican towns which suggested their common roots. Even Mrs. Valdez, whose individual memories of the revolution were primarily of the terror it held for her, shared in a collective memory of a national struggle and its symbols: Mrs. Valdez disdainfully compared the strikebreakers with the traitors who had "sold the head of Pancho Villa."

. . . Mrs. Valdez expressed a sense of collectivity among Mexicans. It needs to be pointed out that there were, in fact, many divisions among Mexicans: between different workers; between strikers and strikebreakers; between contractors and workers; between people from different areas of Mexico; and between people who had fought with different factions of the revolution or the Cristero movement in the 1920s. Yet working for Anglo bosses and the conflict of the strike emphasized an identification as Mexicans which overshadowed other divisions. This no doubt contributed to the recollection of many interviewed of an overall collectivity of Mexican strikers.

Mrs. Valdez's memories of the beginnings of the strike and the ensuing conflict with the grower suggest a sense of a collectivity as workers. On the Peterson ranch where Mrs. Valdez worked with her husband, the grower refused to meet strikers' demands for $1 for picking 100 pounds of cotton and workers walked out. The 150 workers who left the fields confronted their labor contractor ["Chicho"] Narciso Vidaurri. Mrs. Valdez recounted the confrontation between the interests of the workers, the grower and the contractor. All are represented with one voice.

> Chicho said, "You'd better go and work because if you don't go they're going to throw you out of the camp!"
> "So they throw us out! We're not afraid. But we won't pick any more unless they pay us to pick."
> Then he said, "He's (the grower, Peterson) not going to pay more and he wants the cabins vacated immediately in order to house other people who will pick."
> [Mrs. Valdez leaned forward and interjected her own comment into the dialogue:]
> But you think they could have gotten other people?! . . . When *everybody* was on strike? . . . Who would have picked?
> Then Chicho said, "Do what you think . . . If you want to work it's up to you. If you don't want to work, its up to you. The point is that those who won't work will be thrown out . . ."
> And the people said, "NONE OF US WILL WORK!!" Yes, that is what they said, "NONE OF US!!"
> Then old man Peterson asked him. "What did they say?" And he [Chicho] said, "They said no. That if one goes, they all go. That if one stays, they all stay. But they want more pay." . . . Peterson said, "No. No. They aren't going to be paid more."[9]

Within minutes, Peterson's men loaded the strikers' belongings onto trucks and dumped them onto the highway adjoining the ranch. The evicted strikers joined those evicted from other ranches on a plot of land on the outskirts of town. Within a week 3,500 strikers were camped at what became known as the Corcoran camp. The camp resembled a small town, larger than the adjacent town of Corcoran itself. Rows of cars attached to lean-tos formed rough roads in the camp, each corresponding to workers from a particular ranch. Workers formed a camp security force. The Circo Azteca, a small traveling circus unexpectedly stranded on the land, stayed through the strike and provided nightly entertainment and diversion. The camp became the hub of strike activity, the center for the CAWIU office on the west side of the San Joaquin Valley, the base for picket lines, a meeting place for daily strike meetings, and a visiting point, later, for government officials and the press.

Mrs. Valdez also remembered a collectivity of Mexican women. By 1933, Mexican women worked alongside men in the fields. They, as the men, were paid piece rates, 60 cents for each one hundred pounds of cotton picked. It required skill and experience to choose which bolls to pick and which to leave, to adroitly pick the bolls while avoiding twigs and dirt, and to pick rapidly enough to make money. Women picked, on the average, two hundred pounds per ten-hour day. Picking in the mile-long rows of cotton required strength, skill, and stamina:

> But let me describe to you what we had to go through. I'd have a twelve foot sack, about this wide. I'd tie the sack around my waist and the sack would go between my legs and I'd go on the cotton row, picking cotton and just putting it in there . . . So when we finally got it filled real good then we would pick up the [hundred pound] sack, toss [sic] it up on our shoulders, and then I would walk, put it up there on the scale and have it weighed, put it back on my shoulder, climb up a ladder up on a wagon and empty that sack in.[10]

Mrs. Valdez recounted the hardships which women faced in caring for their families: the houses without heat which contributed to disease; preparing food for her family without stoves, and cooking over fires in oil barrels. The issue of food played a central role in her memory. Getting enough food to eat could be a problem when wages were low, and the depression forced some women to forage for berries to eat. Others subsisted at times on flour and water. Food was an issue of survival. As in almost all societies, women were in charge of preparing the food and Mrs. Valdez's concern about food was repeated in oral histories with other women. While men recounted the depression and strike in terms of wages and conditions in general, women remembered these events in terms of food. This is not to say that men were oblivious or unconcerned. Rather it suggests that the woman's role in preparing food made this a central aspect of their consciousness and affected the way they perceived, remembered, and articulated the events of the strike.

Who Mrs. Valdez remembered as leaders is reflective of this sense of a community of women. When initially asked about leaders, Mrs. Valdez replied there were none. Later she named two, her labor contractor Chicho Vidaurri and Lourdes Castillo. Chicho she considered a leader, in the sense of someone you go to resolve problems, get help from, and use as a resource. This indeed fits, in many respects, the role that contractors played on the camps. But within the strike, Chicho was replaced in her memory by Lourdes Castillo. Lourdes is an interesting choice for several reasons.

Most obviously, Lourdes was a woman. But beyond that, Lourdes represented the transition which many Mexican women were undergoing during the process of the revolution, migration, and change in work. The Mexican revolution had convulsed Mexican families and, with it, the role of women. Women left alone to fend for themselves took care of farming [and] the family; [they] often migrated; and women sometimes fought on their own. The "soldaderas" were camp followers who went with men of all factions into battle. Most cooked, nursed, and provided sexual and emotional comfort. But some fought and were even executed in the course of battle. This image of "la soldadera," the woman fighting on behalf of the Mexican community as a whole, was praised as a national symbol of strength and resistance. Yet it was an ambivalent precedent. For while soldaderas may have fought in the revolution, in so doing they broke with traditional values. Thus while people praised the *image* of the *soldadera* within the context of an often mythified revolution, they were critical of the relative sexual freedom and independence which accompanied it. The term "soldadera" became double edged and, when used against individual women, was at times synonymous with "whore."

Ambivalence about independent women followed Mexicanas to the United States. The gender mores of the United States differed in some respects from rural Mexico. Some of these changes were cosmetic. Women bobbed their hair, adopted new dress, wore make up. But such changes reflected a changing gender division of labor. In the United States women began to work for wages. Often these were the younger, unmarried women who worked in canneries or garment factories unobserved by watchful male relatives.[11]

Some moved out of their family houses. And some women became financially independent, running bars and *cantinas,* often to support their children. Financial independence and a changing gender division of labor outside the house altered expectations of women's responsibilities and obligations. Women who adopted these new ways, either in appearance or through financial or social independence still risked ... [disapproval from] segments of the community, male and female.

Lourdes Castillo was an attractive, single woman who lived in the town of Corcoran. She wore make up, bobbed her hair, and wore stylish dresses. Financially independent, she owned and ran the local bar. Lourdes became involved with the strike when union organizers asked her to store food for the camp in her cantina. Mrs. Valdez remembers that Lourdes was in charge of keeping a log of who entered and left the camp and spoke at meetings. She was also in charge of distributing food.[12] Thus Lourdes reflects women's concern about food. At the same time she epitomized the cultural transition of Mexican women and the changing gender roles from pre-revolutionary Mexico to the more fluid wage society of California. Within the context of the strike, it was precisely her financial independence which enabled her to perform this function of storing and distributing the food. Mrs. Valdez's enthusiastic memories of Lourdes perhaps suggest Mrs. Valdez's changing values for women, even if not directly expressed in her own life.

While Mrs. Valdez described the abysmal conditions under which women labored, the women were active, not passive, participants in the strike. Women joined the daily picket lines which paraded in front of the cotton fields where strikebreakers picked. Older women still sporting the long hair and rebozos of rural Mexico, younger women who had adapted the flapper styles of the United States, and young girls barely into their teens rode together in trucks to the picket lines where they badgered strikebreakers into leaving the fields. Their activities on the picket line led women to set up make shift child care centers to care for children, and they established a camp kitchen which fed men without families.

As the weeks wore on women expanded their role. When, after three weeks growers still refused to settle, the women organized and led confrontations with Mexican strikebreakers which resulted in pitched battles. Mrs. Valdez remembers that the women decided that they, not the men, would enter the fields to confront strikebreakers. They reasoned that strikebreakers would be less likely to physically hurt the women.[13]

In organized groups, the women entered the field to talk to strikebreakers. The women appealed to strikebreakers on the grounds of the community good to leave the fields and join the strike. They appealed on class and national grounds—as "poor people" and "Mexicanos" to join the strike. Those from the same regions or villages in Mexico sought out compatriots to appeal to them on the basis of more localized, and usually stronger, loyalties. Those who refused to join the strike were denounced as a disgrace. . . .

Few strikebreakers left the fields, and exhortations turned to threats. A strikebreaker who had the audacity to work after being fed by the striking women in the camp was threatened with a painful poisoning if he tried to touch the food again. Talking turned to armed conflict. Women who had come armed with lead pipes and knives, in expectation of using these more persuasive methods if verbal appeals were unheeded, went after the strikebreakers. One ripped a cotton sack with a knife, emptying its contents onto the ground. Others began to hit the strikebreakers with the pipes, their fists, or whatever was handy.

Although strikers had felt that the women would not be hurt, the male strikebreakers retaliated, and at least one woman was brutally beaten.

> The same women who were in the trucks, who were in the . . . picket line . . . these women went in and beat up all those that were inside (the fields) picking cotton . . . They tore their clothes. They ripped their hats and the [picking] sacks . . . And bad. Ohhh! It was ugly! It was an ugly sight. I was just looking and said "No. No." I watched the blood flowing from them.
> [She imitated the strikebreakers' voice in a high-pitched, pleading tone.] "Don't hit us. Leave them [other strikebreakers] alone. Don't hit them."
> [Her voice drops as the collective voice of the strikers speak.] "Let them be set upon," she says.

> "If we are going cold and hungry then you should too," she says. "They're cowards . . . sell outs. Scum," she said.
> [Her voice rises as the strikebreakers continue their plea.] "Because we live far away, we come from Los Angeles . . . We need to have money to leave . . . "
> "Yes," she says [her voice lowers and slows as it again becomes the voice of the strikers] "We also have to eat and we also have family," she says. "But we are not sell outs!"

Several points in this passage underline the importance of the collectivity of women in Mrs. Valdez's memory. Mrs. Valdez's statement that the women went in because, at least in this instance, it was more women's business, suggests a sense that women were acting on behalf of the community. For Mrs. Valdez, it also carried a suggestion that it was the role of women to do this and that the men had little to do with the decision or even opposed it. "Because women take more chances. The men always hold back because they are men and all. But the women, no. The men couldn't make us do anything. They couldn't make us do anything (to prevent us from going) and so we all went off in a flash." She also focuses, again, on food: the confrontation between the women and strikebreakers focused on feeding their families. At this juncture, the two strands of her narration come together. Her memories of the need for strikers to stay together collectiv[ely are] presented in relationship to the availability of food. Of course this underlines a harsh reality: strikebreakers chose to continue to work in order to feed their families in the face of the depression; and without food, strikers would eventually be forced back to work. In any case, her recollection suggests not only the reality of this confrontation, but what Mrs. Valdez understood as the central strike issues and the strength of her support of the strike. . . . Discussions about staying on strike, discussions about negotiations were all couched in relation to food or the lack of food. Thus her concerns as a woman are underscored by her concerns in the strike. Her interests as a Mexican worker were considered, weighed, and expressed within the context of her interest as a woman, mother, and wife.

For Mrs. Valdez, food remained central in her memory of the strike. As the strike wore on, conditions grew harsher in the Corcoran camp. Growers lobbed incendiaries over the fence at night. Food became hard to get and at least one child died of malnutrition. About two weeks into the strike, partially in response to growing public concern about the killing of several strikers, California Governor Rolph overrode NRA regulations which stipulated that relief was not to be given to strikers not under arbitration, and, over the protestations of local boards of supervisors, sent in trucks of milk and other food to the embattled camp. Mrs. Valdez remembers nothing about the role of federal, state, or local relief agencies, but she remembered the foods brought in: "rice, beans, milk. . . . " At a meeting where Lourdes was talking to strikers, the issue of food, or the lack of food, was juxtaposed against their stance in the strike.

> She [Lourdes] was telling them that they might have to go hungry for awhile.
> "But look," she said, " . . . they are bringing us food. We'll each get just a little, but we're not going to starve," she says. "But don't leave. But don't ANYBODY go to work. Even if a rancher comes and tells you 'come on, let's go,' don't anybody go," she says. "Look, even if it's a little bit, we're eating. But we aren't starving. They're bringing us food."
> [Mrs. Valdez interjected.] They brought us milk and everything. Yes everybody that was working [in the strikers camp] were told not to go with any rancher. They were told not to believe any rancher. But everyone had to stand together as one. Everyone had an equal vote [in what was decided] . . . equal.

The themes of unity and the importance of women were carried over into her recollection of the final negotiations.

> The Portuguese [a growers' representative] told [the strikers' representative] that the ranchers . . . were going to have a meeting at [the strikers' camp] with "la Lourdes."
> "Yes," he says, . . . "We're going to pay you so much. All of us are going to sign so that then all of you can return to your camps to work."
> "Yes," said [the strikers' representative.] "But not a cent less. No. We won't go until we have a set wage. Then all of us go. But if there is something more [if there is more trouble] NONE of us go. Not even ONE of us leave the camp."
> [Mrs. Valdez leaned back and summed it up] And all that . . . And that's the way it was. That's the way it was.

The strike was settled, the ranchers had been beaten, and wages went up. Mrs. Valdez continued:

> They paid $2.50 per hundred pounds . . . Yes. Yes . . . Look, they were paid well. They were paid well for the hundred pounds. Forty cents wasn't

money. Forty cents for the hundred pounds wasn't money. But $2.50, I believe that is . . . And then the following year, three dollars, and then after three and a half. And then four.

Mrs. Valdez's account of the strike and the role of women in it was revealing. What she remembered, how she structured her memories, and the meaning she gave to them, in short, her consciousness and perception of events, tell us more about why Mexicanas supported the strike than interviews with leaders might have. Without the perceptions of women such as Mrs. Valdez it would be more difficult to understand the dynamics of the strike and why people supported it for over a month. [What] Rosaura Valdez remembered [about] her life as a farmworker, life in the Corcoran, daily activities on the picket lines, and strike leaders [is] unrecorded in written accounts.

Even more to the point, she remembers (or recounts) a collectivity of spirit and action among the Mexican striking community. In her telling of the story workers speak in a collective voice and act as a united group. She remembers little or no dissent. In her account, *all* the workers on the Peterson ranch walked out together to join the strike, *all* the women were on the picket lines, and *all* the strikers voted unanimously to stay on strike. Growers were also a united group, spoke with one voice, and were presented as a collective opposition. The lines between worker and grower were clearly drawn. Mrs. Valdez credits the solidarity of the strikers for the strike's success. . . .

Mrs. Valdez also focused on a largely female collectivity. She remembered the hardships of Mexican women. For Mrs. Valdez, as other women, getting enough food for her family was a constant theme. Perhaps this is why, in part, Lourdes stands out so clearly in her memories. . . . Women also stand out most vividly in her memories of the strike and picket lines. In her description of the women's decision to enter the fields she also implies a judgment about men and women, and she praised the women's cohesion as a group.

Women's participation in the strike also changed their self perception and aspects of their relations with their husbands and the community. A large part of this was implicit. Mrs. Valdez praised women for their role in the confrontation and described them as "brave," "tough," and "mean." Even some men admiringly remembered women who were brave and, in a denial that this was a female role at all, who "could fight like a man." Yet this admiration was evidently short lived or at best ambivalent. All of the women interviewed admiringly described the actions of *other* women, but denied that they had taken part in the beatings. This included one woman who, according to all other informants, had beaten strikebreakers with a lead pipe.

For Mrs. Valdez, her active participation in the strike provided some compensation for the hurts of a philandering and abusive husband. She was contemptuous of her husband who, while a striker, did not go on picket lines and thus was not, by her estimation, a "real striker." By implication it was the people on the picket line, picket lines composed largely of women, who were the real strikers. She also remembered the strikebreakers as being males. Thus the confrontations between strikebreakers and strikers was, in her memory, also a confrontation between men and women. In her memory, she pictures these conflicts as between authoritative and strong women representing the community, and simpering, pleading men who were betraying the women and the community as a whole.[14] Mrs. Valdez stated flatly that the women were braver than the men and men played little part in her narrative. She remembered female leadership, female participation, female concerns, and a largely female victory. While other interviews and sources may disagree, her narrative suggests something about Mrs. Valdez's reality of the strike of 1933.

What Mrs. Valdez didn't say was both revealing and suggestive of the limitations of oral narratives in writing history. Mrs. Valdez either did not know about or did not recount several crucial factors in the strike. Mrs. Valdez, as many other strikers interviewed, knew nothing of the CAWIU per se, despite daily strike meetings and the small CAWIU office, marked by a handwritten sign in Spanish hung loosely over a wooden table in the middle of the camp.[15] This was not confined to the women, as several men also knew nothing of the union. Perhaps the union didn't reach the strikers, or seemed irrelevant. Understandably, she also didn't recognize the names of Anglo strike leaders mentioned in accounts.

The role of the New Deal and the negotiations of the governments—Mexican, United States, and Californian—play no part in her narrative. She didn't know about or didn't remember that the Mexican consul, Enrique Bravo, visited the camp and talked to an assembly of strikers. She didn't recount visits by government officials nor threats to deport strikers. And she recounted nothing about the negotiations which led to the eventual settlement of the strike. Her memory of the strike was, in looking at the entire history, thus limited. Her memory of the strike settlement was also factually inaccurate. The wage at the beginning of the season had been set at 60 cents per one hundred pounds. The final settlement of the strike resulted in a compromise wage of 75 cents per hundred pounds. Yet Mrs. Valdez remembers the original pay as 40 cents and the settlement wage as $2.50.

Thus her narrative could be criticized as both incomplete and inaccurate. Yet her narrative has an underlying logic which is faithful to the overall structure of her memory, of her reality. Why is her memory inaccurate? In part she may have simply not known of some of the events, an interesting point in itself. But, as in the case of the wages, there are points she would have known but which she remembers, or recounts, inaccurately. Perhaps she confuses the 1933 wage increase with the wage increases of the 1940s. Perhaps it was a lapse of memory and a confusion with other events which we don't have sufficient information to fully understand. Or perhaps she wanted to make it clear how successful the strike had been. This would have been in keeping with other parts of her interview. A main theme throughout the narrative, for instance, is her emphasis on the complete unity of the Mexican workers. Yet there is clear evidence of tension and discord: the confrontations with the strikebreakers, the initial dispute with her contractor, [and] her own marital battles with her husband. Yet although Mrs. Valdez may even remember this discord, what she either remembered or at least told me—as the history of the strike—was an overwhelming unity. Her narration of the high wages makes the same point: that the strike was successful. It was her *interpretation* of the strike which ultimately structured how she remembered the strike, organized her facts, and recounted the outcome to me. Her factual inaccuracies may say as much if not more about what the strike *meant* to her than a careful rendition of the facts.

Mrs. Valdez's memories of the strike were similar to those of other women I spoke with. Like her, the women did not know about or recall the union, conventional strike leadership, or the role of the governments in ending the strike. Yet they expressed similar assumptions about the collective nature of the strike. . . .

Oral narratives thus reflect peoples' memory of the past: they can be inaccurate, contradictory, and show the influence of the passage of time and the effects of alienation. As people become more alienated from the meaning of their history, they tend to individualize their lives and experiences. For example, Michael Frisch points out that in Studs Terkel's book *Hard Times*, many of the people interviewed perceived the devastating effects of the [Great D]epression not as evidence of systemic collapse but as a manifestation of personal failure.[16] Certainly there are exceptions, people who have developed an historical perspective on their own lives, work, and society.

We confront the same problem of alienation when using oral narratives. How oral narratives are understood reflects the consciousness of the reader. Used uncritically, they are open to misinterpretation and may reinforce rather than alleviate the separation from a meaningful past. This is especially true of people who have been ignored by written history. Readers may have no concept of the history of Mexican working women, for example, and lack an historical framework within which to situate and understand their narratives. The filters of cultural and class differences and chauvinism may also be obstacles. And some may embrace these narratives as colorful and emotional personal statements while ignoring Mexican women as reflective and conscious participants in history.

As valuable as oral testimonies are, they are not a complete history nor can they, by themselves, address the problems of historical amnesia. To do this, oral narratives need to be interpreted and placed within an historical framework encompassing institutional and social relations, struggle, and change. Yet within this they provide a unique and invaluable historical source. Used critically, oral narratives can reveal the transformations in consciousness and culture over time. They can be used to place self conscious and reflective people in the front of the parade of the historical process. And, perhaps, they can help return to us all a greater understanding of our lives by reuniting us with the meaning of our past.

NOTES

1. For intriguing discussions of these questions see: Michael Frisch, "The Memory of History,"

Radical History Review 25 (October 1981); Michael Frisch, "Oral History and *Hard Times*: A Review Essay," *Red Buffalo*, vols. 1 and 2, n.d.; Ronald J. Grele, *Envelopes of Sound: The Art of Oral History*, 2nd ed. (Chicago: Precedent, 1981).

2. All of the names used are pseudonyms. Interview by author with Rosaura Valdez, Hanford, California, January 1982. All but one of the women I spoke with had been born and partially raised in Mexico. Although all have lived in the United States over fifty years, all but one identified themselves as Mexicanas by birth, culture and ethnicity. The one woman born and raised in the United States referred to herself interchangeably as Mexicana and Chicana.

3. The sister-in-law is an interesting, if fragmentary, part of Mrs. Valdez's memory. From Mrs. Valdez's account, the sister-in law left her husband (Mrs. Valdez's brother) to join a group of revolutionaries, as a *compañera* of one of them. When she returned to see her children, she threatened to have the entire family killed by her new lover. It was in the wake of this threat that the family fled to the United States.

4. She and her husband migrated every year to pick grapes with their labor contractor, Narciso "Chicho" Vidaurri, and then returned to the town of Corcoran where they lived and worked on the Peterson ranch for around six months of every year. Their limited migration pattern was not atypical, but they were slightly more stable than many of the workers who migrated from southern California and worked in more crops.

5. In California, any piece of cultivated land over a few acres is consistently called a ranch. By 1933, the overwhelming majority of Mexican workers in cotton did not migrate annually from Mexico. Most had settled in neighborhoods in the Los Angeles area or in the Imperial Valley, adjacent to the Mexican border. Others migrated from Texas. Some of the younger pickers were citizens.

6. Paul S. Taylor and Clark Kerr, "Documentary History of the Cotton Strike," in U.S. Congress, Senate, Subcommittee of the Committee on Education and Labor, *Hearings on S. Res. 266. Violations of Free Speech and the Rights of Labor*, Report no. 1150, 77th Cong., 2nd Sess. (Washington, D.C.: Government Printing Office, 1942) pt. 4. See also Cletus Daniel, *Bitter Harvest: A History of California Farmworkers, 1870–1941* (Ithaca: Cornell University Press, 1981).

7. For those of you who are pausing to question her analysis, I want to emphasize that this is her analysis. I would disagree with her analysis of solidarity, and the disputes among strikers would I think bear this out. Nevertheless, the point here is that even if her historical analysis is questionable, it tells us a great deal about her conception of the strike and perhaps her conception of what I should be told about it.

8. "Look at what the barbarians have stolen from us." Interview by author with Guillermo Martinez, Los Angeles, April 1982.

9. The original Spanish for all translations in this essay is available in the endnotes of the essay as originally published.

10. Interview by author with Lydia Ramos, Fresno, California, June 1981.

11. Mrs. Valdez, in describing her brother who kept an eye on her during a dance in Maravilla, near Los Angeles, said that he watched her "in the style of those on the other side." In other words, she was aware that this "watchful" behavior had its roots in the other side, in Mexico, and was different from the mores in the United States.

12. It is unclear whether Lourdes did keep the log. In a brief interview, Lourdes confirmed that she spoke at meetings and distributed food.

13. It is unclear exactly who made this decision. Roberto Castro, a member of the central strike committee, said the strike committee made the decision that women should enter the fields to confront strikebreakers because the women would be less likely to be hurt. The women remembered no such decision and said that the women made the decision. It is hard to ferret out the origins of the idea.

Even if the strike committee made the decision, the action was in keeping with spontaneous decisions by women which both antedated and followed this strike. Mexican women in Mexico City and other parts of the republic had taken part in bread riots in the colonial period. They had fought in the revolution. And in California, later strikes, both in the 1930s, but also as recently as the 1980s, were punctuated by groups of Mexican women invading the fields to confront strikebreakers both verbally and physically.

14. It is not clear if this was correct or not. Given the tensions of the strike, it is possible that only the men went out to pick [as strikebreakers].

15. This may have been due to several factors. The union was small and had few organizers in the Valley. These were English speaking and relied on Mexicans, some of whom did join the union, to contact workers. This should not discount the role of the CAWIU, however. The union was crucial as a rallying point, and linked the disparate groups together, helped organize picket lines, wrote leaflets and played a role in publicizing the strike and in the final negotiations.

16. Michael Frisch, "Oral History and *Hard Times,*" p. 231.

GENDERING THE NATION-STATE

NANCY F. COTT

Equal Rights and Economic Roles: The Conflict over the Equal Rights Amendment in the 1920s

The vote achieved, former suffragists turned their attention to sex-based discrimination in the law. To some, the proper strategy, as in suffrage, seemed to be a constitutional amendment affirming equal rights; men and women would have to be treated under the law as equals and as individuals. In contrast, suffragists who had struggled to pass legislation shortening hours and improving working conditions for women in industry had achieved that goal only because the Supreme Court was prepared to regard women as a special class of workers in need of governmental protection because of their childbearing role. (See the discussion of *Muller v. Oregon* in Sklar's essay, p. 357.) An equal rights amendment (ERA) would invalidate sex-based labor laws, they feared, since comparable protection would not be extended to men. The ensuing debate was a critical one creating deep and lasting divisions. Unable to agree on a unified agenda for four decades, veterans of the first women's movement expended energy in internal conflict, thereby diluting their political effectiveness. Not surprisingly women's issues made little headway until the 1960s.

The debate over the ERA was critical not only because of its long-term consequences, but because it highlighted differing views within feminism of the social significance of gender and the meaning of equality. Does equality require that men and women have the "same" rights and be subject to the "same" treatment, or does equality require "different" treatment? How should the law treat the difference created by women's unique reproductive system? With these questions in mind, Nancy F. Cott carefully assesses the initial debate over the ERA, making clear the assumptions and limitations inherent in the arguments of each side.

Campaigning for ratification of the Equal Rights Amendment during the 1970s, feminists who found it painful to be opposed by other groups of women were often unaware that the first proposal of that amendment in the 1920s had likewise caused a bitter split between women's groups claiming, on both sides, to represent women's interests. The 1920s conflict itself echoed some earlier ideological and tactical controversies. One central strategic question for the women's rights movement in the late nineteenth century had concerned alliances: should proponents of "the cause of woman" ally with advocates for the rights for

Nancy F. Cott, "Historical Perspectives: The Equal Rights Amendment in the 1920s," in *Conflicts in Feminism*, ed. Marianne Hirsch and Evelyn Fox Keller (London and New York: Routledge, Chapman, and Hall, part of the Taylor & Francis Group, 1990), pp. 44–59. Reprinted by permission of the author and publisher. Notes have been edited.

freed slaves, with temperance workers, or labor reformers, or a political party, or none of them? At various times different women leaders felt passionately for and against such alliances, not agreeing on what they meant for the breadth of the women's movement and for the priority assigned to women's issues.[1] The 1920s contest over the equal rights amendment reiterated that debate insofar as the National Woman's Party, which proposed the ERA, took a "single-issue" approach, and the opposing women's organizations were committed to maintaining multiple alliances. But in even more striking ways than it recapitulated nineteenth-century struggles the 1920s equal rights conflict also predicted lines of fracture of the later twentieth-century women's movement. The advantages or compromises involved in "multi-issue" organizing are matters of contemporary concern, of course. Perhaps more important, the 1920s debate brought into sharp focus (and left for us generations later to resolve) the question whether "equal rights"—a concept adopted, after all, from the male political tradition—matched women's needs. The initial conflict between women over the ERA set the goal of enabling women to have the same opportunities and situations as men against the goal of enabling women freely to be different from men without adverse consequences. As never before in nineteenth-century controversies, these two were seen as competing, even mutually exclusive, alternatives.

The equal rights amendment was proposed as a legal or civic innovation but the intrafeminist controversy it caused focused on the economic arena. Indeed, the connection between economic and political subordination in women's relation to men has been central in women's rights advocacy since the latter part of the nineteenth century. In the Western political tradition, women were historically excluded from political initiatives because they were defined as dependent—like children and slaves—and their dependence was read as fundamentally economic. Nineteenth-century advocates, along with the vote, claimed women's "right to labor," by which they meant the right for women to have their labor recognized, and diversified. They emphasized that women, as human individuals no less than men, had the right and need to use their talents to serve society and themselves and to gain fair compensation. Influential voices such as Charlotte Perkins Gilman's at the turn of the

century stressed not only women's service but the necessity and warrant for women's economic independence. Gilman argued simultaneously that social evolution made women's move "from fireside to factory" inevitable, and also that the move ought to be spurred by conscious renovation of outworn tradition.

By the 1910s suffragists linked political and economic rights, and connected the vote with economic leverage, whether appealing to industrial workers, career women or housewives. They insisted on women's economic independence in principle and defense of wage-earning women in fact. Since the vast majority of wage-earning women were paid too little to become economically independent, however, the two commitments were not identical and might in practice be entirely at odds.[2] The purpose to validate women's existing economic roles might openly conflict with the purpose to throw open economic horizons for women to declare their own self-definition. These tensions introduced by the feminist and suffrage agitation of the 1910s flashed into controversy over the equal rights amendment in the 1920s.

The ERA was the baby of the National Woman's Party, yet not its brainchild alone. As early as 1914, a short-lived New York City group called the Feminist Alliance had suggested a constitutional amendment barring sex discrimination of all sorts. Like the later NWP, the Feminist Alliance was dominated by highly educated and ambitious women in the arts and professions, women who believed that "equal rights" were their due while they also aimed to rejuvenate and reorient thinking about "rights" around female rather than only male definition. Some members of the Feminist Alliance surely joined the NWP, which emerged as the agent of militant and political action during the final decade of the suffrage campaign.[3]

A small group (engaging perhaps 5 percent of all suffragists), the NWP grew from the Congressional Union founded by Alice Paul and Lucy Burns in 1913 to work on the federal rather than the state-by-state route to woman suffrage. Through the 'teens it came to stand for partisan tactics (opposing all Democrats because the Democratic administration had not passed woman suffrage) and for flamboyant, symbolic, publicity-generating actions—large parades, pickets in front of the White House, placards in the Congress, hunger-striking in jail, and more. It gained much of its energy from leftwing radical women who were attracted to its wholesale condemnation of gender inequality and to its tactical adaptations from the labor movement; at the same time, its imperious tendency to work from the top down attracted crucial financial and moral support from some very rich women. When the much larger group, the National American Woman Suffrage Association, moved its focus to a constitutional amendment in 1916, that was due in no little part (although certainly not solely), to the impact of the NWP. Yet while imitating its aim, NAWSA's leaders always hated and resented the NWP, for the way it had horned in on the same pro-suffrage turf while scorning the NAWSA's traditional nonpartisan, educative strategy. These resentments festered into deep and long-lasting personal conflicts between leaders of the two groups.

Just after the 19th Amendment was ratified in August of 1920, the NWP began planning a large convention at which its members would decide whether to continue as a group and, if so, what to work for. The convention, held six months later and tightly orchestrated by chairman Alice Paul, brushed aside all other suggestions and endorsed an ongoing program to "remove all remaining forms of the subjection of women," by means of the elimination of sex discrimination in law.[4] At the outset, NWP leaders seemed unaware that this program of "equal rights" would be much thornier to define and implement than "equal suffrage" had been. They began surveying state legal codes, conferring with lawyers, and drafting numerous versions of equal rights legislation and amendments at the state and federal levels.

Yet the "clean sweep" of such an approach immediately raised a problem: would it invalidate sex-based labor legislation—the laws regulating women's hours, wages, and conditions of work, that women trade unionists and reformers had worked to establish over the past thirty years? The doctrine of "liberty of contract" between employer and employed had ruled court interpretations of labor legislation in the early twentieth century, stymying state regulation of the wages and hours of male workers. State regulation for women workers, espoused and furthered by many women in the NWP, had been made possible only by differentiating female from male wage-earners on the basis of physiology and reproductive functions. Now members of the NWP had to grapple with the question whether such legislation was sex "discrimination," hampering women

workers in the labor market. Initially, there was a great deal of sentiment within the NWP, even voiced by Alice Paul herself, that efforts at equal rights legislation should not impair existing sex-based protective labor legislation. However, there was also contrary opinion, which Paul increasingly heeded; by late November 1921 she had come to believe firmly that "enacting labor laws along sex lines is erecting another handicap for women in the economic struggle." Some NWP affiliates were still trying to draft an amendment that would preserve special labor legislation, nonetheless, and continued to introduce equal rights bills with "safeguards" in some states through the following spring.[5]

Meanwhile women leaders in other organizations were becoming nervous and distrustful of the NWP's intentions. Led by the League of Women Voters (successor to the NAWSA), major women's organizations in 1920 formed a national lobbying group called the Women's Joint Congressional Committee. The LWV was interested in eliminating sex discrimination in the law, but more immediately concerned with the extension of sex-based labor legislation. Moreover, the LWV had inherited NAWSA's hostility to Alice Paul. The first president of the LWV, Maud Wood Park, still smarted from the discomfiture that NWP picketing tactics had caused her when she headed the NAWSA's Congressional Committee from 1916 to 1920.[6] Other leading groups in the Women's Joint Congressional Committee were no less suspicious of the NWP. The National Women's Trade Union League since the mid-1910s had concentrated its efforts on labor legislation to protect women workers. Florence Kelley, director of the National Consumers' League, had been part of the inner circle of the NWP during the suffrage campaign, but on the question of protective labor laws her priorities diverged. She had spent three decades trying to get state regulation of workers' hours and conditions, and was not about to abandon the gains achieved for women.[7]

In December 1921, at Kelley's behest, Paul and three other NWP members met for discussion with her and leaders of the League of Women Voters, the National Women's Trade Union League, the Woman's Christian Temperance Union, and the General Federation of Women's Clubs. All the latter objected to the new constitutional amendment now formulated by the NWP: "No political, civil or legal disabilities or inequalities on account of sex, or on account of marriage unless applying alike to both sexes, shall exist within the United States or any place subject to their jurisdiction." Paul gave away no ground, and all left feeling that compromise was unlikely. Each side already thought the other intransigent, though in fact debate was still going on within the NWP.[8]

By mid-1922 the National Consumers' League, the LWV, and the Women's Trade Union League went on record opposing "blanket" equal rights bills, as the NWP formulations at both state and federal levels were called. About the same time, the tide turned in the NWP. The top leadership accepted as definitive the views of Gail Laughlin, a lawyer from Maine, who contended that sex-based labor legislation was not a lamented loss but a positive harm. "If women can be segregated as a class for special legislation," she warned, "the same classification can be used for special restrictions along any other line which may, at any time, appeal to the caprice or prejudice of our legislatures." In her opinion, if "protective" laws affecting women were not abolished and prohibited, "the advancement of women in business and industry will be stopped and women relegated to the lowest, worst paid labor."[9] Since NWP lobbyists working at the state level were making little headway, a federal constitutional amendment appeared all the more appealing. In November 1923, at a grand conference staged in Seneca Falls, New York, commemorating the seventy-fifth anniversary of Elizabeth Cady Stanton's Declaration of Sentiments, the NWP announced new language: "Men and women shall have equal rights throughout the United States and every place subject to its jurisdiction." The constitutional amendment was introduced into Congress on December 10, 1923.[10]

In the NWP view, this was the logical sequel to the 19th Amendment. There were so many different sex discriminations in state codes and legal practices—in family law, labor law, jury privileges, contract rights—that only a constitutional amendment seemed effective to remove them. The NWP took the language of liberal individualism, enshrined in the catchphrase of "equal rights," to express its feminism. As Alice Paul saw it, what women as a gender group shared was their subordination and inequality to men as a whole; the legal structure most clearly expressed this subordination and inequality, and therefore was the

logical point of attack. The NWP construed this agenda as "purely feminist," that is, appealing to women as women, uniting women around a concern common to them regardless of the other ways in which they might differ. Indeed, at its founding postsuffrage convention the NWP leadership purposely bypassed issues it saw as less "pure," including birth control, the defense of black women's voting rights in the South, and pacifism, which were predictably controversial among women themselves.

The NWP posited that women could and would perceive self-interest in "purely" gender terms. Faced by female opponents, its leaders imagined a fictive or abstract unity among women rather than attempting to encompass women's real diversity. They separated the proposal of equal rights from other social and political issues and effects. Although the campaign for equal rights was initiated in a vision of inclusiveness—envisioned as a stand that all women could take—it devolved into a practice of exclusiveness. The NWP's "appeal for conscious sex loyalty" (as a member once put it) went out to members of the sex who could subordinate identifications and loyalties of class, ethnicity, race, religion, politics, or whatever else to a "pure" sense of themselves as women differentiated from men. That meant principally women privileged by the dominant culture in every way except that they were female.[11]

In tandem with its lobbying for an equal rights amendment, the NWP presented its opposition to sex-based labor legislation as a positive program of "industrial equality." It championed women wage-earners who complained of "protective" legislation as restrictive, such as printers, railroad conductors, or waitresses hampered by hours limitation, or cleaning women fired and replaced by men after the passage of minimum-wage laws. Only a handful of working-class women rose to support for the ERA, however.[12] Mary Anderson, former factory worker herself and since 1919 the director of the U.S. Women's Bureau, which was founded to guide and assist women workers, threw her weight into the fight against the amendment. Male trade unionists—namely leaders of the American Federation of Labor—also voiced immediate opposition to the NWP aims, appearing at the very first U.S. Senate subcommittee hearings on the equal rights amendment. Male unionists or class-conscious workers in this period put their faith in collective bargaining and did not seek labor legislation for themselves, but endorsed it for women and child workers. This differentiation derived partly from male workers' belief in women's physical weakness and veneration of women's "place" in the home, partly from presumptions about women workers being difficult to organize, and also from the aim to keep women from competing for men's jobs. Male unionists tended to view wage-earning women first as women—potential or actual wives and mothers—and only secondarily as workers. For differing reasons women and men in the labor movement converged in their support of sex-based legislation: women because they saw special protection necessary to defend their stake in industry and in union organizations, limited as it was; men to hold at bay women's demands for equal entry into male-controlled union jobs and organizations.[13]

The arguments against the equal rights amendment offered by trade unionists and by such women's organizations as the League of Women Voters overlapped. They assumed that an equal rights amendment would invalidate sex-based labor laws or, at least, destine them for protracted argument in the courts, where judges had shown hostility to any state regulation of employer prerogatives. They insisted that the greatest good for the greatest number was served by protective labor laws. If sex-based legislation hampered some—as the NWP claimed, and could be shown true, for instance, in the case of women linotypists, who needed to work at night—then the proper tactic was to exempt some occupations, not to eliminate protective laws whole. They feared that state welfare legislation in place, such as widows' pensions, would also be at risk. They contended that a constitutional amendment was too undiscriminating an instrument: objectionable sex discriminations such as those concerning jury duty, inheritance rights, nationality, or child custody would be more efficiently and accurately eliminated by specific bills for specific instances. Sometimes, opponents claimed that the ERA took an unnecessarily federal approach, overriding states' rights, although here they were hardly consistent for many of them were at the same time advocating a constitutional amendment to prohibit child labor.

Against the ERA, spokeswomen cited evidence that wage-earning women wanted and valued labor legislation and that male workers, too, benefitted from limits on women's hours

in factories where men and women worked at interdependent tasks. Before hours were legally limited, "we were 'free' and 'equal' to work long hours for starvation wages, or free to leave the job and starve!" WTUL leader Pauline Newman bitterly recalled. Dr. Alice Hamilton, pioneer of industrial medicine, saw the NWP as maintaining "a purely negative program, . . . holding down in their present condition of industrial slavery hundreds of thousands of women without doing anything to alleviate their lot."[14] Trade-unionist and Women's Bureau colleagues attacked the NWP's vision as callously class-biased, the thoughtless outlook of rich women, at best relevant to the experience of exceptional skilled workers or professionals. They regularly accused the NWP of being the unwitting tool (at best) or the paid servant of rapacious employers, although no proof of the latter was ever brought forward. They heard in the NWP program the voice of the ruling class and denounced the equal rights amendment as "class" legislation, by and for the bourgeoisie.[15]

Indeed, at the Women's Bureau Conference on Women in Industry in 1926, the NWP's opposition to sex-based labor legislation was echoed by the president of the National Association of Manufacturers, who declared that the "handful" of women in industry could take care of themselves and were not served by legislative "poultices." In this controversy, the positions also lent themselves to, and inevitably were colored by, male "allies" whose principal concerns dealt less with women's economic or legal protection or advancement than political priorities of their own. At the same conference the U.S. Secretary of Labor appointed by President Coolidge took the side of sex-based protective legislation, proclaiming that "The place fixed for women by God and Nature is a great place," and "wherever we see women at work we must see them in terms of motherhood." What he saw as the great danger of the age was the "increasing loss of the distinction between manliness and true femininity."[16]

Often, ERA opponents who supported sex-based labor legislation—including civic-minded middle-class women, social welfare reformers, government officials, and trade union men—appeared more concerned with workingwomen's motherhood than with economic justice. "Women who are wage earners, with one job in the factory and another in the home have little time and energy left to carry on the fight to better their economic status. They need the help of other women and they need labor laws," announced Mary Anderson. Dr. Hamilton declared that "the great inarticulate body of working women . . . are largely helpless, . . . [and] have very special needs which unaided they cannot attain. . . ."[17] Where NWP advocates had before their eyes women who were eager and robust, supporters of protective legislation saw women overburdened and vulnerable. The former claimed that protective laws penalized the strong; the latter claimed that the ERA would sacrifice the weak. The NWP looked at women as individuals and wanted to dislodge gender differentiation from the labor market. Their opponents looked at women as members of families—daughters, wives, mothers, and widows with family responsibilities—and believed that the promise of "mere equality" did not sufficiently take those relationships into account. The one side tacitly positing the independent professional woman as the paradigm, the other presuming the doubly burdened mother in industry or service, neither side distinguished nor addressed directly the situation of the fastest-growing sector of employed women, in white-collar jobs. At least half of the female labor force—those in manufacturing and in domestic and personal service—worked in taxing, menial jobs with long hours, unpleasant and often unhealthy conditions, very low pay, and rare opportunities for advancement. But in overall pattern women's employment was leaving these sectors and swelling in clerical, managerial, sales, and professional areas. White-collar workers were fewer than 18 percent of all women employed in 1900, but the proportion more than doubled by 1920 and by 1930 was 44 percent.[18]

The relation of sex-based legislation to women workers' welfare was more ambiguous and complicated than either side acknowledged. Such laws immediately benefitted far larger numbers of employed women than they hindered, but the laws also had a negative impact on women's overall economic opportunities, both immediately and in the long term. Sex segregation of the labor market was a very significant factor. In industries monopolizing women workers, where wages, conditions, and hours were more likely to be substandard, protective legislation helped to bring things up to standard. It was in more desirable crafts and trades more unusual for women workers, where

skill levels and pay were likely to be higher—that is, where women needed to enter in order to improve their earnings and economic advancement—that sex-based protective legislation held women back. There, as a contemporary inquiry into the issue said, "the practice of enacting laws covering women alone appears to discourage their employment, and thereby fosters the prejudice against them." The segregation of women into low-paid, dead-end jobs that made protective laws for women workers necessary, was thus abetted by the legislation itself.[19]

By 1925, all but four states limited workingwomen's hours; eighteen states prescribed rest periods and meal hours; sixteen states prohibited night work in certain occupations; and thirteen had minimum wage regulations. Such regulation was passed not only because it served women workers, but also because employers, especially large corporate employers, began to see benefits in its stabilization of the labor market and control of unscrupulous competition. Although the National Association of Manufacturers, fixed on "liberty of contract," remained opposed, large employers of women accepted sex-based labor legislation on reasoning about "protection of the race," or could see advantages for themselves in it, or both. A vice-president of Filene's, a large department store in Boston, for instance, approved laws regulating the hours, wages, and conditions of women employees because "economies have been effected by the reduction of labor turnover; by reduction of the number of days lost through illness and accidents; and by increase in the efficiency of the working force as well as in the efficiency of management." He appreciated the legislation's maintaining standards as to hours, wages, and working conditions "throughout industry as a *whole,* thus preventing selfish interests from indulging in unfair competition by the exploitation of women. . . ."[20]

While the anti-ERA side was right in the utilitarian contention that protective laws meant the greatest good to the greatest number of women workers (at least in the short run), the pro-ERA side was also right that such laws hampered women's scope in the labor market and sustained the assumption that employment advantage was not of primary concern to women. Those who advocated sex-based laws were looking at the labor market as it was, trying to protect women in it, but thereby contributing to the perpetuation of existing inequalities. They envisaged wage-earning women as veritable beasts of burden. That group portrait supplanted the prior feminist image of wage-earning women as a vanguard of independent female personalities, as equal producers of the world's wealth. Its advocates did not see that their conception of women's needs helped to confirm women's second-class position in the economy. On the other hand, the ERA advocates who opposed sex-based "protections" were envisioning the labor market as it might be, trying to ensure women the widest opportunities in that imagined arena, and thereby blinking at existing exploitation. They did not admit to the vulnerabilities that sex-based legislation addressed, while they overestimated what legal equality might do to unchain women from the economic stranglehold of the domestic stereotype.

Women on both sides of the controversy, however, saw themselves as legatees of suffragism and feminism, intending to defend the value of women's economic roles, to prevent economic exploitation of women and to open the doors to economic opportunity. A struggle over the very word feminism, which the NWP had embraced, became part of the controversy. For "us even to use the word feminist," contended Women's Trade Union League leader Ethel Smith, "is to invite from the extremists a challenge to our authenticity." Detractors in the WTUL and Women's Bureau called the NWP "ultra" or "extreme" feminists. Mary Anderson considered herself "a good feminist" but objected that "over-articulate theorists were attempting to solve the working women's problems on a purely feministic basis with the working women's own voice far less adequately heard." Her own type of feminist was moderate and practical, Anderson declared; the others, putting the "woman question" above all other questions, were extreme and abstract. The bitterness was compounded by a conflict of personalities and tactics dragged on from the suffrage years. Opponents of the ERA, deeply resenting having to oppose something called equal rights, maligned the NWP as "pernicious," women who "discard[ed] all ethics and fair play," an "insane crowd" who espoused "a kind of hysterical feminism with a slogan for a program."[21] Their critiques fostered public perception of feminism as a sectarian and impracticable doctrine unrelated to real life and blind to injustices besides sex inequality. By the end of the 1920s women outside the NWP rarely made efforts to reclaim the term feminist for themselves, and the meaning of the term was depleted.

Forced into theorizing by this controversy, not prepared as philosophers or legal theorists, spokeswomen on either side in the 1920s were grappling with definitions of women's rights as compared to men's that neither the legal nor economic system was designed to accommodate. The question whether equality required women to have the same rights as men, or different rights, could not be answered without delving into definitions. Did "equality" pertain to opportunity, treatment, or outcome?[22] Should "difference" be construed to mean separation, discrimination, protection, privilege— or assault on the very standard that the male was the human norm?[23]

Opponents of the ERA believed that sex-based legislation was necessary because of women's biological and social roles as mothers. They claimed that "The inherent differences are permanent. Women will always need many laws different from those needed by men"; "Women as such, whether or not they are mothers present or prospective, will always need protective legislation"; "The working mother is handicapped by her own nature."[24] Their approach stressed maternal nature and inclination as well as conditioning, and implied that the sexual division of labor was eternal.

The NWP's approach, on the other hand, presupposed that women's differentiation from men in the law and the labor market was a particular, social-historical, and not necessary or inevitable construction. The sexual division of labor arose from archaic custom, enshrined in employer and employee attitudes and written in the law. The NWP approach assumed that wives and mothers as well as unencumbered women would want and should have open access to jobs and professions. NWP proponents imagined that the sexual division of labor (in the family and the marketplace) would change if women would secure the same rights as men and have free access to wage-earning. Their view made a fragile potential into a necessary fact. They assumed that women's wage-earning would, by its very existence, challenge the sexual division of labor, and that it would provide the means for women's economic independence—although neither of these tenets was necessarily being realized.

Wage-earning women's experience in the 1910s and 1920s, as documented by the Women's

STORMS ON MANY FRONTS 1920–1945

Bureau, showed that the sexual division of labor was budged only very selectively and marginally by women's gainful employment. Most women's wages did not bring them economic independence; women earned as part of a plan for family support (as men did, though that was rarely stressed). Contrary to the NWP's feminist visions, in those places in the nation where the highest proportions of wives and mothers worked for pay, the sexual division of labor was most oppressively in place. To every child growing up in the region of Southern textile and tobacco mills, where wives and mothers worked more "jobs" at home and in the factory than any other age or status group—and earned less—the sexual division of labor appeared no less prescriptive and burdensome than it had before women earned wages.[25]

Critiques of the NWP and its ERA as "abstract" or "extreme" or "fanatical" represented the gap between feminist tenets and harsh social reality as an oversight of the NWP, a failure to adjust their sights. Even more sympathetic critics, such as one Southern academic, asked rhetorically, "Do the feminists see in the tired and haggard faces of young waitresses, who spend seventy hours a week of hard work in exchange for a few dollars to pay for food and clothing, a deceptive mask of the noble spirit within?" She answered herself, "Surely it is not an increasing army of jaded girls and spent women that pours every day from factory and shop that the leaders of the feminist movement seek. But the call for women to make all labor their province can mean nothing more. They would free women from the rule of men only to make them greater slaves to the machines of industry."[26] Indeed, the exploitation of female service and industrial workers at "cheap" wages cruelly parodied the feminist notion that gainful employment represented an assertion of independence (just as the wifely duties required of a secretary parodied the feminist expectation that wage-earning would challenge the sexual division of labor and reopen definitions of feminity). What such critics were observing was the distance between the potential for women's wage-earning to challenge the sexual division of labor, and the social facts of gender and class hierarchy that clamped down on that challenge.

Defenders of sex-based protective legislation, trying to acknowledge women's unique reproductive endowments and social obligations, were grappling with problems so difficult they would still be present more than half a century later. Their immediate resolution was to portray women's "difference" in merely customary terms. "Average American women prefer to make a home for husbands and children to anything else," Mary Anderson asserted in defense of her position. "They would rather fulfill this normal function than go into the business world."[27] Keeping alive a critique of the class division of wealth, protective legislation advocates lost sight of the need to challenge the very sexual division of labor that was the root of women's "handicap" or "helplessness." As compared to the NWP's emphasis on the historical and social construction of gender roles, advocates of sex-based protective legislation echoed customary public opinion in proposing that motherhood and wage-earning should be mutually exclusive. They easily found allies among such social conservatives as the National Council of Catholic Women, whose representatives testified against the ERA because it "seriously menaced . . . the unity of the home and family life" and contravened the "essential differences in rights and duties" of the two sexes which were the "result of natural law." Edging into plain disapproval of mothers of young children who earned, protective legislation supporters became more prescriptive, less flexible, than wage-earning mothers themselves, for whom cash recognition of their labor was very welcome. "Why should not a married woman work [for pay], if a single one does?" demanded a mill worker who came to the Southern Summer School for Women Workers. "What would men think if they were told that a married man should not work? If we women would not be so submissive and take everything for granted, if we would awake and stand up for our rights, this world would be a better place to live in, at least it would be better for the women. . . . "[28]

The onset of the Depression in many ways worsened the ERA controversy, for the one side thought protective legislation all the more crucial when need drove women to take any jobs available, and the other side argued that protective legislation prevented women from competing for what jobs there were. In the 1930s it became clear that the labor movement's and League of Women Voters' opposition to the equal rights amendment ran deeper than concern for sex-based legislation as an "entering wedge." The Fair Labor Standards Act of 1938 mandated wages and hours regulation for all workers, and the U.S. Supreme Court upheld it in 1941; but the labor movement and the LWV still opposed the ERA. Other major women's organizations, however—most importantly the National Federation of Business and Professional Women's Clubs and the General Federation of Women's Clubs—and the national platforms of both the Republican [Party] and the Democratic Party endorsed the ERA by 1944.[29]

We generally learn "winners'" history—not the history of lost causes. If the ERA passed by Congress in 1972 had achieved ratification by 1982, perhaps historians of women would read the trajectory of the women's movement from 1923 to the present as a steady upward curve, and award the NWP unqualified original insight. The failure of the ERA this time around (on new, but not unrelated, grounds) compels us to see the longer history of equal rights in its true complexity.[30] The ERA battle of the 1920s seared into memory the fact of warring outlooks among women while it illustrated the inevitable intermeshing of women's legal and political rights with their economic situations. If the controversy testified to the difficulty of protecting women in the economic arena while opening opportunities to them, even more fundamentally the debate brought into question the NWP's premise that the articulation of sex discrimination—or the call for equal rights—would arouse all women to mobilize as a group. What kind of a group were women when their occupational and social and other loyalties were varied, when not all women viewed "women's" interests, or what constituted sex "discrimination," the same way? The ideological dimensions of that problem cross-cut both class consciousness and gender identity. The debate's intensity, both then and now, measured how fundamental was the revision needed if policies and practices of economic and civic life deriving from a male norm were to give full scope to women—and to women of all sorts.

Notes

1. An essential text on the mid-nineteenth-century split is Ellen Carol DuBois, *Feminism and Suffrage: The Emergence of an Independent Women's Movement, 1848–1869* (Ithaca, N.Y., 1978).

2. See Leslie Woodcock Tentler, *Wage-Earning Women: Industrial Work and Family Life in the U.S., 1900–1930* (New York, 1979), chap. 1, on industrially employed women's wages, keyed below subsistence.

3. On feminists in the final decade of the suffrage campaign, see Nancy F. Cott, *The Grounding of Modern Feminism* (New Haven, Conn., 1987), pp. 23–66.

4. For more detailed discussion of the February 1921 convention, see Nancy F. Cott, "Feminist Politics in the 1920s: The National Woman's Party," *Journal of American History* 71 (June 1984).

5. Paul to Jane Norman Smith, Nov. 29, 1921, folder 110, J. N. Smith Collection, Schlesinger Library (hereafter SL). See NWP correspondence of Feb.–Mar. 1921 in the microfilm collection "The National Woman's Party, 1913–1974" (Microfilm Corp. of America), reels #5–7 (hereafter NWP.), and Cott, *Grounding*, pp. 66–74, 120–25.

In Wisconsin, prominent NWP suffragist Mabel Raef Putnam put together a coalition which successfully lobbied through the first state equal rights bill early in 1921. This legislation granted women the same rights and privileges as men *except for* "the special protection and privileges which they now enjoy for the general welfare."

6. Maud Wood Park, *Front Door Lobby,* ed. Edna Stantial (Boston, 1960), p. 23.

7. Historians' treatments of women's organizations' differing views on the ERA in the 1920s include J. Stanley Lemons, *The Woman Citizen: Social Feminism in the 1920s* (Urbana, Ill., 1973), pp. 184–99; William Chafe, *The American Woman: Her Changing Social, Economic and Political Roles* (New York, 1972), pp. 112–32; Susan Becker, *Origins of the Equal Rights Amendment: American Feminism between the Wars* (Westport, Conn, 1981), pp. 121–51; and Alice Kessler-Harris, *Out to Work: A History of Wage-Earning Women in the U.S.* (New York, 1982), pp. 194–95, 205–12. Fuller documentation of my reading of both sides can be found in Cott, *Grounding*, pp. 122–29.

8. "Conference on So-Called 'Equal Rights' Amendment Proposed by the National Woman's Party Dec. 4, 1921," ts. NWTUL Papers, microfilm reel 2.

9. NWP National Council minutes, Dec. 17, 1921, Feb. 14, 1922, Apr. 11, 1922, NWP #114. To the NWP inner circle Laughlin's point was borne out by a 1923 ruling in Wisconsin, where, despite the Equal Rights Bill, the attorney general declined to strike down a 1905 law which prohibited women from being employed in the state legislature. He likened the prohibition to an hours-limitation law, because legislative service required "very long and often unreasonable hours."

10. National Council Minutes, June 19, 1923, NWP #114. Before 1923, the ERA went through scores of drafts. Not until 1943 was the amendment introduced into Congress in the form "Equality of rights under the law shall not be denied or abridged by the United States or by any state on account of sex," modeled on the Nineteenth Amendment, which in turn was modeled on the Fifteenth Amendment.

11. Quotation from Edith Houghton Hooker, Editor's Note, *Equal Rights* (the NWP monthly publication), Dec. 22, 1928, p. 365. See Cott, *Grounding*, pp. 75–82.

12. The two most seen on NWP platforms were Josephine Casey, a former ILGWU organizer, suffrage activist, later a bookbinder, and Mary Murray, a Brooklyn Railway employee who had resigned from her union in 1920 to protest its acceptance of laws prohibiting night work for women.

13. Kessler-Harris, *Out to Work,* 200–5.

14. More extensive documentation of the debate can be found in the notes in Cott, *Grounding,* pp. 325–26.

15. Kessler-Harris, *Out to Work*, pp. 189–94, reveals ambivalent assessments of labor legislation by ordinary wage-earning women.

16. Printed release from the National Association of Manufacturers, "Defend American Womanhood by Protecting Their Homes, Edgerton Tells Women in Industry," Jan. 19, 1926, in folder 1118, and ts. speech by James Davis, U.S. Secretary of Labor, Jan. 18, 1926, in folder 1117, Box 71, Mary Van Kleeck Collection, Sophia Smith Collection, Smith College.

17. Mary Anderson, "Should There Be Labor Laws for Women? Yes," *Good Housekeeping*, Sept. 1925.

18. See Valerie K. Oppenheimer, *The Female Labor Force in the U.S.* (Westport, Conn., 1976), pp. 3, 149; Winifred Wandersee, *Women's Work and Family Values 1920–1940* (Cambridge Mass., 1981), pp. 85, 89.

19. Elizabeth F. Baker, "At the Crossroads in the Legal Protection of Women in Industry," *Annals of the American Academy of Political and Social Science* 143 (May 1929):277.

20. T. K. Cory to Mary Wiggins, Nov. 10, 1922, folder 378, Consumers' League of Mass. Coll., SL.

21. Ethel M. Smith, "What Is Sex Equality and What Are the Feminists Trying to Accomplish?" *Century Monthly Magazine* 118 (May 1929):96. . . . Mary Anderson, *Woman at Work: The Autobiography of Mary Anderson as Told to Mary N. Winslow* (Minneapolis, 1951), p. 168.

22. See Jean Bethke Elshtain, "The Feminist Movement and the Question of Equality," *Polity* 7 (Summer 1975):452–77.

23. This is the set of issues that preoccupied feminist lawyers in the 1980s. For a sense of the debate, see, e.g., Wendy Williams, "The Equality Crisis: Some Reflections on Culture, Courts, and Feminism," *Women's Rights Law Reporter* 7 (Spring 1982):175–200; and Joan Williams, "Deconstructing Gender," *Michigan Law Review* 87 (Feb. 1989):797–845.

24. Florence Kelley, "Shall Women Be Equal before the Law?" (debate with Elsie Hill), *Nation* 114 (Apr. 12, 1922):421.

25. Dolores Janiewski, *Sisterhood Denied: Race, Gender and Class in a New South Community* (Philadelphia: Temple University Press, 1985), pp. 30–32, 127–50.

26. Guion G. Johnson, "Feminism and the Economic Independence of Woman," *Journal of Social Forces* 3 (May 4, 1925):615.

27. Mary Anderson quoted in unidentified newspaper clipping, Nov. 25, 1925, in folder 349, Bureau of Vocational Information Collection, SL. Cf. Ethel Smith's objection that the NWP's feminism required that "men and women must have exactly the same things, and be treated in all respects as if they were alike," as distinguished from her own view that "men and women must each have the things best suited to their respective needs, which are not all the time, nor in all things, alike." Smith, "What Is Sex Equality?", p. 96.

28. National Council of Catholic Women testimony at U.S. Congress (House of Representatives) subcommittee of Committee on the Judiciary, hearings, 1925, quoted in Robin Whittemore, "Equality vs. Protection: Debate on the Equal Rights Amendment, 1923–1937" (M.A. thesis, Boston University, 1981), p. 19; mill worker quoted in Mary Frederickson, "The Southern Summer School for Women Workers," *Southern Exposure* 4 (Winter 1977):73. See also Maurine Greenwald, "Working-Class Feminism and the Family Wage Ideal: The Seattle Debate on Married Women's Right to Work, 1914–1920," *Journal of American History* 76 (June 1989):118–49.

29. For the history of the NWP in the 1930s and 1940s see Becker, *Origins of the Equal Rights Amendment.*

30. Jane L. Mansbridge's astute analysis, *Why We Lost the ERA* (Chicago, 1986), is essential reading on the failed 1970s campaign for ratification.

ALICE KESSLER-HARRIS
Designing Women and Old Fools: Writing Gender into Social Security Law

One historian has called the Social Security Act of 1935 "the most important single piece of social legislation in all American history . . . in terms of historical decisiveness and direct influence upon the lives of individual Americans."* It continues to sustain the modern welfare state, providing the basic foundation for old-age pensions and for unemployment insurance. Its conceptualization of how needy mothers and children could claim government assistance was not replaced for sixty years, and continues to haunt debates over welfare. (President Franklin Delano Roosevelt also hoped to include a national system of health care but could not find congressional support.)

The drive to design the legislation and shepherd it through Congress was led by Frances Perkins, secretary of labor and the first woman cabinet member. It was not easy; anything resembling charity was widely resented. Many compromises were made in order to get enough votes in Congress. Perhaps the most significant was the decision not to conceptualize benefits as entitlement to all citizens. Instead, benefits were linked to payroll taxes paid by employers and employees, who could conclude that they were getting back only what they had put in. The strategy left nearly half the working population—including those who were seasonally or marginally employed—not covered. In the short run, there was a deflationary effect, as money paid into the Social Security Administration was pulled out of circulation. By 1937, efforts to amend the law were under way.

Politicians, economists, and other experts struggled to reform the law. They worked, for the most part, in good faith; they understood themselves to be seeking fairness and equity. They spoke of "the people" or "the worker"; their words were general and generic. But, as historian Alice Kessler-Harris read the minutes of meetings and considered the conversations and arguments, she found that the words they chose inadvertently revealed that the reformers' ideas of fairness rested on their own assumptions about work, family, citizenship, gender, and race. Behind what they would have called "the common sense of the matter" lurked unspoken beliefs that women are not serious or long-term workers and that African Americans were doomed to marginal employment.

→ women weren't serious workers

---

*Kenneth S. Davis, *FDR, the New Deal Years, 1933–1937: A History* (New York: Random House, 1986), p. 437; see also David M. Kennedy, *Freedom from Fear: The American People in Depression and War, 1929–1945* (New York: Oxford University Press, 1999), pp. 257–73.

Excerpted from "Maintaining Self Respect" and "Questions of Equity," chs. 2 and 3 of *In Pursuit of Equity: Women, Men, and the Quest for Economic Citizenship in 20th-Century America* by Alice Kessler-Harris (New York: Oxford University Press, 2001). Reprinted by permission of the author and publisher. Notes have been edited and renumbered.

What were the bureaucrats and legislators trying to accomplish by reforming the social security law? What were they trying to avoid? How did the law reflect their understandings of fairness? How did the new law reflect their view of the appropriate relationship between men and women? Between husbands and wives? Between blacks and whites? between the citizen and the state? Why were concepts that had lasted since the 1930s attacked at the beginning of the 1970s?

[In the 1930s,] Americans moved from staunch opposition to federal government intervention in the lives of most men (but not women) to eager experiments with government mediation of every kind. Newly adopted social policies had many goals, but among the most dramatic were those connected with earning wages and keeping jobs. . . .

Achieving consensus on issues of who deserved employment and who could languish in uncompensated unemployment required some hard decisions, especially around questions of inclusion and exclusion. For the government to regulate working conditions and monitor benefits for those without jobs, legislators would have to agree on, and administrators determine, eligibility. Someone would have to decide who could be described as a "worker" and who didn't fit the picture; what jobs counted as work and what didn't; how many hours constituted full-time work and how few precluded the activity from being called "work" at all. Innovative programs and policies demanded clarifications and classifications, precisely placing individuals in their relationships to paid and unpaid activities of different sorts. Each categorization opened or closed a door to the status, social rights, and economic security that measured progress toward economic citizenship for someone. Not only did benefits and entitlements rest on symbols of belonging, but so, ultimately, did the identities of workers, as well as their self-respect, political participation, and a newly differentiated set of meanings for crucial concepts like breadwinning, manhood, and citizenship.

The social constraints that guided these decisions had many roots, including most crucially ideologies of race and of American freedom and liberty. Historians are only now beginning to understand the degree to which they reflected a fundamental consensus around issues of race. But the new policies were also deeply embedded in a widespread and widely shared set of assumptions about gender. The

Social Security Act of 1935 provides a case in point.

The pressing need of old people in the 1930s was for assistance or relief, not insurance. Advocates ranging from Abraham Epstein, whose American Association for Old Age Security proposed federal grants to the states, to Francis Townsend, whose plan to give everyone over sixty-five two hundred dollars a month to spend at will exceeded all others in popularity, stimulated the public to believe that the federal government could and should help the states solve this problem. Over this, there was little controversy. The very first title of the Social Security Act, Title I, provided states with matching grants to give relief to the needy aged and to care for unemployable old people. It replaced the mostly inadequate state-based programs with uniform federal standards and more generous grants than all but a handful of states had been able to provide. But Old Age Assistance came at a price: it subjected recipients to the indignities of means testing, fostering an unmanly spirit of dependency. . . .

Social insurance advocates sought to circumvent this anxiety with insurance rather than relief: They sought to prevent destitution and "obviate the necessity of public charity" by protecting family breadwinners against the potential hazards of industrial life. . . .

In the United States, the idea of government-subsidized insurance ran counter to the American grain, which reified independence and self-reliance. If there were to be any old age insurance program at all, its designers faced a formidable challenge: to remove aging workers from the labor force (which required that they be adequately supported) while affirming the dignity of pension recipients (which required that the program be self-supporting). To solve the labor force problem, policy makers imagined a program tied to work rather than to citizenship. Deciding which workers would be covered, however, created two classes of citizens: those who participated regularly in the kind of wage work where resolving unemployment seemed most important, and those who did not. In 1930, men made up the vast majority of gainfully employed persons (75 percent of the total); about 12 percent of this number were classified by the census as "Negro." But most African American men did not work in the core industrial sectors, where issues of unemployment and labor force stability mattered most. And while women made up a quarter of all wage earners, their tenuous rights to work led many to assume they had little commitment to wage labor. . . . Despite women's own efforts to seek jobs during the depression, public opinion resolutely condemned wage work for those with husbands and fathers who could support them. Through the depression years, less than 15 percent of married women earned wages. Consciously or not, policy makers imagined a program available to most white wage-earning men that would omit "as a matter of course" most African Americans, by virtue of their positions in the labor market, and most women, whose positions appeared derivative of their marital partners.

Efforts to preserve the dignity of beneficiaries participated in the same gendered imagination. In the battle over unemployment compensation, men fought to maintain a sense of themselves as self-sufficient, independent, free, and capable of providing for their families and especially for the dependent women within them. In the struggle for Old Age Insurance (which we now call Social Security), participants deployed gender in more subtle but equally aggressive ways, not only to promote a conception of fairness that relied on the language of male dignity and female dependence but to ensure adequate support for all the aged. Gendered constructs helped to soothe a public increasingly enamored of government-funded assistance (which seemed to some policy makers an appropriate and to others a short-sighted and short-term solution). And they provided the language of family normalcy that convinced reluctant policy makers who remained skeptical of the capacity of an insurance program to solve employment problems without depending on general taxation. Ultimately, gendered conceptions provided the keystone that maintained public confidence in the core old age program and justified its redistributive goals. By providing economic security

in particular ways and to particular people, old age insurance defined a new category of economic citizenship; at the same time . . . it fueled the desires of the excluded for fuller participation. . . .

No sooner had the Social Security Act been signed into law on August 14, 1935, than issues of adequacy began to surface. The bill provided for a 1 percent payroll tax, payable by employers, to be instituted in 1936 and matched by an equivalent contribution from every employee; benefits would not be payable until January 1942. The lag produced a surplus that, in a depression economy, threatened to exercise a deflationary effect. Most important, the exclusions written into the old age insurance provisions of the Social Security Act exempted nearly half the working population, evoking questions about its fairness as well as about its capacity to provide for the aged.[1] Because the program did not provide benefits to those who worked intermittently or for only a few years even when they worked in covered occupations, more than three-fifths of fully employed African Americans were denied coverage. Sixty percent of the excluded workers were female. . . . Probably as many as 85 percent of wage-earning black women were deprived of participation and benefits.[2]

At the same time, powerful popular support continued to build for the state-run, noncontributory old age assistance pensions that provided more generous benefits to the needy aged than those envisioned under Social Security for most contributors. . . . [These fueled] a sense of entitlement to old age pensions as a matter of justice. . . . Everyone knew that even when the insurance program started paying benefits in 1942, they would go at first to only three hundred thousand people, compared to the estimated two million needy elderly who would then be receiving noncontributory assistance.

. . . What was to be done? The solution seemed to be to spend the surplus. But how? And on whom? Despite the sharp and purposeful distinctions between adequacy and equity, the principle was violated by the very first set of amendments, which added old age insurance benefits for wives and widows who had not paid for them. No charitable impulse toward women motivated this act; no concern for their poverty inspired it. Rather, Congress added dependent wives and aged widows in order to shore up the legitimacy of a system in trouble. It did this by enhancing the benefits of already covered (mostly white) males to ensure extra income to those who had aged wives to support and extra insurance to those with young children who survived them. These amendments, adopted in 1939, reinforced the prerogatives, self-images, and citizenship rights of some males while reaffirming racialized conceptions of gender. They redefined equity to incorporate more adequate and appropriate provision for some men, infusing the American system of entitlements with the peculiar imbalance from which it has struggled to release itself since the early 1970s.

In the spring of 1937, the Senate Finance Committee pressured the Social Security Board into creating a federal Advisory Council to suggest remedies. In May, when the new Advisory Council, which J. Douglas Brown agreed to chair, was announced, it consisted of twenty-four members. Six represented employers; six came from the labor movement; and twelve were designated as "public" participants, most of them academics and businessmen. [The public members included three women.][3] . . .

Together with the Social Security Board and several congressional committees, the Advisory Council worked through the following year and a half to recommend basic changes. Their charge from Congress was clear: They had to recommend a permanent way of dealing with ballooning reserves. They were to do this by beginning old age insurance benefits earlier than the originally mandated January 1942 start-up date and by making them larger. They were to explore the possibility of extending benefits to the disabled, to survivors, and to excluded groups. In the end, the council sidestepped the challenge of significantly extending insurance to most of the excluded groups, including the disabled, domestic servants, and agricultural workers and chose to rely instead on a new and expensive package of benefits for aged wives and survivors to reduce the surplus.[4]

The discussions over these alternatives tell us something about how invisible assumptions about men and women informed an entire network of social policy. For when the council moved toward emphasizing expanding benefits to those already covered, it utilized gender to mediate the conflict between adequacy and equity—a conflict in which women played little role but issues of manliness and

womanliness assumed paramount importance. . . . The council, as its chairman, Douglas Brown, put it, had adopted "the principle of family protection."

The conversations within the Advisory Council and in Congress clarify the meaning of that principle. The council quickly agreed on pensions for fatherless children—an idea that already had popular support.[5] The Advisory Council adopted the notion rapidly because it promised to significantly reduce the numbers receiving means-tested assistance under both Title I (Old Age Assistance) and Title IV (Aid to Dependent Children) and strengthen the entire Social Security program by providing the illusion that their support was a product of insurance, the provenance of thoughtful and thrifty fathers. . . .

The Advisory Council relied on the same ideas of fairness to provide benefits for the widowed mothers of young children. These widows were to have benefits only as long as their children were young. The sums granted, and the restrictions on them, suggest that insurance for widowed mothers was conceived of as a matter of peace of mind for the husband. The widowed mother was to get three fourths of what her husband's pension would have been. The pension was granted as a matter of need, to enable "the widow to remain at home and care for the children."[6] It was to be reduced or eliminated if her earnings exceeded fifteen dollars a month (a tiny sum, even in 1939), thus encouraging her not to try to earn wages. In the likely event a widow's children reached eighteen before she reached sixty-five, the council recommended that all support end, to be resumed again when she became sixty-five, if in the meantime she had not remarried.[7] A young widow without children lacked any "rights" in her husband's contribution and got no benefits until and unless she grew old without remarrying.

Tying the dignity of men (defined by their capacity to provide) to the virtue of women (their willingness to remain dependent on men and to rear children) proved to be a continuing problem for young and old widows alike. The Social Security Board was fully cognizant of what it called the "widow's gap," noting at congressional hearings that "middle aged widows find it more difficult to become self-supporting." Still, . . . it deferred the annuity of an under-sixty-five widow until she reached that age, on the grounds that "there is some likelihood that the widow may reenter covered employment."[8] Its sympathies for widows whose children were grown could not overcome internalized portraits of the family that fully rationalized its position: "They are likely to have more savings than younger widows and many of them have children who are grown and able to help them until they reach 65 years of age."[9]

The conversations within the council and the provisions finally adopted suggest that old age insurance was never imagined in terms of fair treatment to women—a product of the joint efforts of a marriage partnership. Consistent with the notion of sustaining male provision for the family, and over the objections of some members of the Social Security Board, the council voted to eliminate any annuity to a widow who remarried lest it construct a system that, in the words of one member, constituted widows "a prize for the fellow that has looked for it."[10] It recommended a plan that gave a wife no rights at all in the husband's insurance in consequence of his contributions to it, though demanding that she forfeit everything if she remarried clearly violated the equity principle that promised a return for what had been put in. . . .

. . . Once a woman was no longer dependent on the earnings of a particular male (dead or alive), the council contended, his support for her should cease, "rendering the woman ineligible whether she is the widow of an annuitant or the widow of a worker who dies before 65."[11] As long as she remained dependent on him, the level of the surviving widow's benefits . . . would be tied to the earnings of the deceased male, feeding the illusion that families deprived of a father or husband would nevertheless conceive him in the abstract as a continuing provider. . . .

We have no need to guess at the gendered images that sustained these seemingly arbitrary decisions. They pop up everywhere. For example, halfway through its eighteen months of deliberations, the Advisory Council confronted the question of what allowance to provide to aged widows. Should it be half of what their provider-husbands would have received? Two thirds? Three quarters? After several hours of debate over what proportion of a husband's benefit might appropriately descend to his widow, one member thought to ask a question that had escaped scrutiny: "Why should you pay the widow less than the individual

himself gets if unmarried?" "She can look after herself better than he can," shot back the group's actuary.[12] But the question would not die. Two months later the Advisory Council returned to the issue. This time the chairman, prodded by one of its three female members, took up the defense. "A single woman" he suggested, can "adjust herself to a lower budget on account of the fact that she is used to doing her own housework whereas the single man has to go out to a restaurant."[13] By now, though, others had joined the fray. When the argument resumed at the next meeting, Douglas Brown tried to end it by painting a portrait everyone could accept. Lower rates for women made sense, he argued, his patience clearly worn thin,

> on the principle that it is more costly for the single man to live than for the single woman if she is able to avail herself of the home of the child. A woman is able to fit herself into the economy of the home of the child much better than the single man, that is, the grandmother helps in the raising of the children and helps in home affairs, whereas the aged grandfather is the man who sits out on the front porch and can't help much in the home.[14]

Such homely images shaped decisions that influenced the lives of almost everyone. They appeared at sporadic moments of unguarded conversation. Imagining women as irresponsible, the council voted to remove the original act's lump-sum death benefit to widows. "Such settlements," its minutes recorded, "are likely to be used for many other purposes long before her old age." Women could also be greedy and unprincipled. To avoid what it referred to as "deathbed marriages," the council adopted a clause requiring a pair to have been married and living together for at least a year before the husband died or reached sixty for his widow to be eligible for benefits on his account.[15] No benefits accrued to the woman who married a man over the age of sixty, unless she had lived with him for at least a year before he died.

The imagery became more complicated around the question of whether to increase benefits by providing more to every contributor or by enhancing the benefits of married men. Here the council clearly had in mind the normative 1930s household in which wives earned little or nothing, and it wanted to protect the economic well-being of the husbands who supported them. No one noted that its image failed to account for the more than 15 percent of white and at least 33 percent of African American households in which women earned regular wages. Rather, members noted that even the original bill had been criticized by social insurance advocates like Abraham Epstein for its failure to include additional benefits for men with aged wives.... Advisory Council staff members, including Wilbur Cohen and Isadore Falk, ... claimed that old age insurance would be perceived as more fair if it treated married men with greater generosity....

[After considering a number of suggestions for an aged wives' allowance, the Advisory Council] explicitly proposed "that the enhancement of early old-age benefits under the system be attained, not by increasing the amount of benefit now payable to an individual, but by the method of paying to a married annuitant on behalf of an aged wife a supplementary allowance equivalent to fifty percent of the husband's own benefit."[16] ...

None of the three women on the Advisory Council (Theresa McMahon, Elizabeth Wisner, and Josephine Roche, who seems to have been there only rarely) raised a question about gender equity or the rights of women. Neither did political activist and reformer, Mary Dewson, who attended council meetings as a member of the Social Security Board....

We can speculate that under the historical circumstances the proposals of the Advisory Council offered far more security to the families of covered workers than most women could expect to provide through earnings.... [I]nfluential women social reformers had long since accepted that providing security for the family was the most likely way to safeguard women.... With the exception of McMahon, the women engaged in the Advisory Council's deliberations had been involved in some part of the effort to develop state-run welfare systems, and all were more or less hostile to the efforts of more radical feminists to fight for women's individual rights.... In addition, at least some members of the women's reform network (including perhaps Dewson herself) had become convinced of the need to abandon an earlier strategy of seeking benefits for women only and to focus instead on an integrated system of security. Family benefits would encourage this direction.

If the suggestion to provide dependents' allowances for aging wives appealed to some because it recognized the family responsibilities of men, it appealed to others because it retained equity among covered men by maintaining a relationship between contributions and benefits. This strategy was essential to garnering the votes of southern racists....

[As one council member argued,] "It is impractical to have a level benefit in this country because of the differences between the colored workers of the south and the skilled workers of the north. A single flat figure for everybody would not work."[17] ... [It was important to the council that it not transgress the] relative expectations of income based on occupation or race....

In adopting the program, Congress accepted, with little debate, the relatively rigid definition of the family it demanded. For covered workers, the 1939 amendments provided benefits, without means tests, to fatherless children, widowed mothers of small children, and aged wives and widows. It did not extend benefits to the surviving children of covered women or to aged husbands, aged widowers, or widowed fathers of small children. Thus fatherless children might learn the sweet lesson of continuing parental support beyond the grave, and aging wives would continue to be dependent, though on phantom earnings. But motherless children and aged husbands without resources received quite another lesson in citizenship rights.[18] ...

Three million domestic workers (including two and a quarter million in private households) counted themselves among the women who learned bitter lessons. Like three and a half million agricultural workers, mostly male, they found themselves among the still "uncovered" workers when the 1939 amendments emerged from Congress.[19] In fact, as a group, they had received a slap in the face. Following the Advisory Council's recommendations, Congress incorporated more than a million seamen and bank employees into the old age insurance program. At the same time, it excluded an equal number of mostly female and largely African American workers by eliminating even the few who had crept under the wire. Three hundred thousand domestic workers in clubs, fraternities, and large households and about seven hundred thousand food-processing workers lost their coverage....

When Congress agreed to save the old age insurance system by changing its financing and using the funds generated annually to provide family protection, legislators altered expectations of the Social Security program and provoked a set of new, vaguely antici-pated pressures toward universal coverage. Abandoning the idea that each generation of recipients would build a reserve fund that would support its own retirement in favor of a pay-as-you-go system required each generation of working people to subsidize the retirements of its predecessors. The shift turned a program that had originally been perceived primarily as a labor regulation device meant to preserve the dignity of workers who made way for the next generation into something more clearly approx-imating a promise of economic security freed of its rigid requirement for an equitable return on individual contributions. Adequate insurance for families displaced individual equity as the primary measure of fairness.

The inexorable logic of a system tilted toward adequacy fueled the hopes of policy makers and the excluded that old age insurance could more quickly include everyone and effec-tively replace the costly and demeaning charity offered by old age assistance. Advisory Council member Paul Douglas warned his colleagues that the changes made there raised the question of why the council could not recommend an "all-inclusive universal system": "If everybody is in from the standpoint of benefits, then every-body is in from the standpoint of contributions, and if there is to be a government subsidy . . . for only the industrial part of the population, it is going to be difficult to have the entire popula-tion pay taxes for benefits designed for only half of the population."[20] As Douglas noticed, by enhancing the value of social insurance for some groups of relatively privileged wage earn-ers without extending coverage to significant numbers of additional workers, the program, which was now called Old-Age and Survivors Insurance (OASI), created two classes of citi-zens. For one of these, the "right to work" had become a more valuable commodity, carrying with it significant economic benefits and social rights for which the other half was indirectly paying. A large proportion of this other half consisted of self-supporting women (black and white) and African Americans of both sexes.

Afterward, the implications of these dis-tinctions became clear. For one thing, some sur-vivors benefited more than others. The family benefits offered under contributory social in-surance slowly removed most widows and their children from the public assistance rolls.[21] By 1960, OASDI (disability insurance was added in 1941) covered 93 percent of widows with children. Most of these were the dependents of men who had held covered jobs, leaving only a tiny number of children and their wid-owed mothers to rely on relief, or what quickly became known as welfare. The result was to produce an invidious distinction between those said to have earned benefits as of right and those for whom benefits remained a matter of public charity. Both systems exer-cised some controls over the behavior of mothers caring for children, restricting the amount of income a mother could earn before benefits were lost and removing benefits on remarriage, but charitable provision subjected women to stringent moral and supervisory controls as well.[22] At the same time, the prom-ise of more immediate and more reasonable provenance for the aged, anchored in their own virtue and thrift, successfully under-mined public support for noncontributory old age assistance schemes, which soon suffered from derogatory labels. Because so many of the poorest and least stable workers could not collect Social Security benefits, these changes also made racial exclusion more visible.

For another, women quickly learned the costs of a gender-segregated labor market, and black women learned the bitterest lessons of all.[23] The poorest-paid workers, invariably women and people of color, appeared to have been multiply disadvantaged. As workers, they would see their intermittent contributions cap-tured by an insurance program that excluded them, to be used to subsidize more stable work-ers. As consumers, they would pay higher prices as employers factored their share of taxes into the prices of goods and services. As citizens, they were not only deprived of the dignity at-tached to a contributory program, but they were compelled to support a dual system of noncon-tributory and contributory relief, producing the apparent injustice of some receiving a demean-ing "free" benefit while others received a due return on their investment. . . .

The system's planners had anticipated that some part of the contributions of intermit-tent workers would be captured and returned to beneficiaries. In their imagination, these workers were single women who would soon marry or married women who, though they worked intermittently, would ultimately reap enhanced benefits earned by their husbands. Policy makers frequently articulated these as-sumptions. With congressional concurrence, the council agreed on the irrelevance of most women's wage work with respect to this new citizenship right. "A married woman whether she works or no," it decided, "will receive an allowance because of her husband's earning." Its intent could not have been plainer. While "a single woman earns her own benefit rights," it concluded that "a married woman who works will not get advantage . . . of her own earnings, as in any case she will receive the 50% allowance for her husband."[24]

The actual situation was even worse. The council fully expected that married women would work occasionally and that their contributions, as well as the early contributions of single women who then married, would be absorbed by the system and help to sustain its financial health without necessarily yielding any direct benefit to the female contributor. There is no question that this was intentional, done, as Douglas Brown told the House Ways and Means Committee that affirmed the council's recommendations, "in order to control the cost of the system."[25] . . .

While some members of the council deplored its failure to provide equitable treatment to wives who earned wages, suggesting, for example, that "women who work all their lives should have a larger return than those who don't," most symbolically shrugged their shoulders along with Paul Douglas, who declared: "Of course, wives work too." Congress apparently concurred that wives who worked would simply have to sacrifice because, as one put it, "most wives in the long run will build up wage credits on their own account."[26] . . .

The 1939 council that designed this trade-off also aimed to discourage family members from taking advantage of the insurance program. Fearing inflated claims to benefits by women who falsely maintained they had worked for their husbands, Congress excluded "service performed by an individual in the employ of his spouse." . . . The issue of "forfeited" contributions had lasting resonance, for wives were not the only ones who forfeited their contributions. "Scrubwomen on their knees" fell victim, too, as well as all those who earned less than two hundred dollars a year from a single employer.[27] This hit African Americans particularly hard, as a special 1941 Senate report lamented when it deplored the unfairness to "contributors who fail to qualify because of insufficient employment or low wages. . . . Money thus forfeited by the dispossessed of the act will flow into the insurance

fund and from there it will be distributed to workers everywhere."[28]

The architects of the 1939 amendments surely never intended to harm poor women, but the particular ways in which their gendered imagination infused the legislation nevertheless produced negative consequences. In 1940, the male-breadwinner family remained the modal family. Only 15 percent of wives with husbands present earned wages. If countless numbers of others hid the incomes they earned by taking in sewing, laundry, and boarders, still, most white women and men gratefully accepted the derivative benefits offered to wives and widows. Not so for African American women. As the depression deepened throughout the 1930s, racial segregation made wage work an absolute necessity for many black women, regardless of their marital status. At the same time, gender segregation confined more and more women of color to domestic service jobs, most often in private households. Of the two and a quarter million private household workers in the United States in 1940, about 90 percent were women.[29] A little less than half were African Americans. In contrast, men made up 94 percent of agricultural workers. Yet viewed from the perspective of the prospective worker, the figures take on a different cast. Nearly a third of all black workers (1.6 million men and women) and two-thirds of black working women (compared to less than 18 percent of white women workers) were in domestic service.[30] Of the five and a half million African Americans in the labor force in 1935, fully two-thirds were excluded from old age insurance because they belonged to noncovered occupations. No constitutional impediments stood in the way of including them, especially after the Supreme Court sustained the Social Security Act on the grounds of the welfare clause. In contrast to agricultural workers, whom farm interests desperately wanted excluded, and unlike some other groups, such as nonprofits, retail clerks, and the self-employed, no large interest group lobbied to keep domestic workers out of the old age insurance provisions of the new law. Race alone united them.[31] . . .

. . . [The Committee on Economic Security] sent its proposal to Congress with domestic and agricultural workers included. They were eliminated again by the House Ways and Means Committee on the probably specious grounds that their contributions could not buy sufficient benefits and that in any event collecting their taxes and administering benefits would be costly.[32] Agitation to include both groups continued even as the Social Security Act made its way through Congress. Mary Anderson wrote hopefully that she expected, regardless of what happened to the unemployment provisions, that "all workers regardless of occupation will be eligible to share in the old age benefits of the Economic Security Bill."[33]

Her hopes, of course, did not materialize. . . . A racialized conception of gender created the double jeopardy of black women. The policy committees publicly cited putative administrative difficulties that stood in the way of enrolling workers employed in single-person workplaces; in private they admitted the difficulties of offending southern sensibilities. In public, legislators repeatedly sought to protect white housewives, whose ability to handle the paperwork they denigrated; at the same time, they labeled household workers as "girls" and fostered disrespect for the occupation. Over more than a decade, they deployed race to exaggerate the differences between household workers and their employers while seeking to attach to each the special attributes of gender. . . .

Providing benefits for domestics would offer tangible benefits to poorly paid workers, enhance the appearance of fairness, and solve some of the program's financial problems as well. Yet, for many years, pleas to extend coverage to domestic workers, including the recommendation of the Social Security Board, fell on deaf ears. What had made it possible to ignore domestics, argued a piece in the AFL's journal, *American Federationist*, in the fall of 1939, is that they were thought of as different. Ninety percent female, 45 percent African American, with greater proportions married, widowed, deserted, or divorced, and still working in their older years, they simply did not fit the profile of the stable industrial worker for whom social legislation was constructed.[34] Nor did they conform to the restricted images of womanhood within which the 1939 Advisory Council constructed its system of benefits. So they had been left out partly because they were different and mostly because "we have gotten into the habit of excluding them." . . .

Still, for most purposes, most members of Congress and officials of the Social Security Administration continued to support programs that radically distinguished between men and women as contributors. From the perspective of contributors, women's taxes continued to buy far less insurance protection than those of men. . . . From that of beneficiaries, men lacked the protections that their wives had. In 1961, Congress changed the law so that a wife's contributions covered aged husbands and widowers as well. Once again Congress insisted that they demonstrate financial dependency.

. . . The debate rendered voiceless a significant minority of women who believed that if they contributed at the same level as men, their contributions ought to buy their spouses and their children the same protection.

In the 1970s, these women found their voices. The rapidly rising numbers of wage-earning women and of women who did not marry, and the emergence of a dynamic and angry women's movement, soon rendered the discrepancies questionable and led some men and women to wonder if they were discriminatory. "The income security programs of this nation were designed for a land of male and female stereotypes," wrote Representative Martha Griffiths in 1973.[35] A series of court decisions confronted the issue, peaking on March 19, 1975, in the landmark decision of *Weinberger v. Wiesenfeld*. Eight justices of the U.S. Supreme Court (the ninth abstaining) agreed that Stephen Wiesenfeld, a widower and lone parent of an infant child, was entitled to Social Security benefits. Wiesenfeld claimed the benefits on the basis of contributions made by his wife, Paula, who had been a schoolteacher before she died in childbirth. But the Social Security Administration had turned him down: widows' benefits were available only to women. Now the Supreme Court demurred. "A father no less than a mother," said the Court, "has a constitutionally protected right to the companionship, care, custody, and management of children he has sired and raised."[36] On this basis, the Court struck down forty years of "archaic and overbroad generalizations," accepting the argument put forth in Wiesenfeld's defense that such generalizations unfairly discriminated against women because their contributions to Social Security did not buy as much as the contributions of men. Wisenfeld's lawyer, Ruth Bader Ginsburg, had done her part to draw a new image of gender to the Court's attention.

The Court's majority decision, written by Justice William J. Brennan, explicitly challenged assumptions about men's and women's wage-earning that underlay the Social Security

Act and anchored its old age insurance provisions. As late as 1971, an Advisory Council on Social Security had insisted that men rarely became homemakers after the death of a spouse and that, given their attachment to the workforce, widowed fathers did not require benefits to enable them to provide a home for their children. Acknowledging the truth of the generalization that men had been, and were more likely to be, the principal supporters of their families, Brennan nevertheless argued that this assumption did not "suffice to justify the denigration of efforts of women who do work and whose earnings contribute significantly to families' support." Dismissing the government's claim that benefits were unrelated to contributions, the Court held that statutory rights to benefits were directly "related to years worked and amount earned by a covered employee, and not to the need of the beneficiaries directly." Benefits had to be related to some reasonable classification; they could not be based solely on sex. Wiesenfeld's wife had not only been deprived of the security "a similarly situated male" would have received, she had been "deprived of a portion of her own earnings in order to contribute to the fund out of which benefits would be paid to others." As Justice Lewis Powell put it in a concurring opinion, the statute "discriminates against one particular category of family—that in which the female spouse is a wage-earner covered by social security."[37]

The decision in *Wiesenfeld* was followed by others. An aged widower was entitled to benefits on his wife's earnings whether or not he had been dependent on her, just as a widow was entitled to benefits earned by her husband, the Court declared two years later.[38] . . . With the Department of Health, Education, and Welfare and the Social Security Administration fighting every step, the Court methodically overturned a carefully structured set of images about women's roles in the family. Henceforth, the Court concluded, classifications by gender "must serve important governmental objectives."[39] Imaging women as nonworkers no longer met that test.

NOTES

1. Paul H. Douglas, *Social Security in the United States: An Analysis and Appraisal of the Federal Social Security Act* (New York: McGraw-Hill, 1936), estimates that 47 percent of those working would not come under the old age insurance features and thus would require old age assistance.

2. The most careful analysis of the data concludes that 86.69 percent of black female workers and 53.6 percent of black male workers were excluded; F. Davis, "The Effects of the Social Security Act upon the Status of the Negro," Ph.D. diss., University of Iowa, 1939, p. 99, n. 211, and 102, tables 21, 23.

3. "Social Security Advisory Council Is Appointed," typescript of press release, May 10, 1937, File 025: Advisory Council 1937, Box 10, Chairman's Files, RG47, NA2.

4. Typescript, I. S. Falk to the Advisory Council, November 5, 1937, "Benefits for Disabled Persons and Survivors, and Supplemental Allowances for Dependents," ibid., passim.

5. See, for example, Abraham Epstein, *Insecurity: A Challenge to America, a Study of Social Insurance in the United States and Abroad* (New York: Random House, 1938 [1933]), part 9.

6. Advisory Council on Social Security, *Final Report*, Senate Document no. 4, 76th Cong., 1st sess., December 10, 1938 (Washington, D.C.: GPO, 1939), p. 18; hereafter, Advisory Council, *Final Report*.

7. Advisory Council Minutes, April 29, 1938, morning session, pp. 8–10 and ff.

8. Advisory Council, *Final Report*, p. 17.

9. House, *Hearings on Social Security Act Amendments of 1939*, p. 6.

10. Advisory Council Minutes, April 29, 1938, second half of morning session, p. 9, A. L. Mowbray of the University of California, Berkeley, speaking.

11. Ibid., pp. 3, 40.

12. Ibid., February 19, 1938, afternoon session, p. 18. The actuary was William Williamson.

13. Ibid., April 29, 1938, first half of morning session, p. 41.

14. Ibid., April 29, 1938, second half of morning session, pp. 5–6.

15. Ibid., first half of morning session, pp. 37–38.

16. Typescript headed "Strictly Confidential," October 22, 1938, File 025, Box 138, Executive Director's Files, Advisory Council on Social Security, RG47, NARA.

17. Jill Quadagno, *The Transformation of Old Age Security: Class and Politics in the American Welfare State* (Chicago: University of Chicago Press, 1988), p. 39, and see ch. 6 on the influence of southern politicians on the old age assistance portion of the Social Security Act.

18. These amendments also included altering the fiscal plan to a pay-as-you-go system, paying benefits on the basis of a wage-averaging device rather than on the basis of accumulated benefits, and expanding the categories of agricultural and domestic workers excluded from coverage. See Edward D. Berkowitz, "The First Social Security Crisis," *Prologue* 15, no. 3 (1983):133–49, for a summary of their full contents.

19. These figures come from the testimony of Sumner Slichter, *Hearings on the Social Security Act Amendments of 1939*, p. 1512. Slichter estimated that eleven million self-employed farmers and others, and about a million employees of nonprofit corporations, also remained uncovered.

20. Advisory Council Minutes, February 19, 1938, afternoon session, p. 20.

21. Gwendolyn Mink, *The Wages of Motherhood: Inequality in the Welfare State, 1917–1942* (Ithaca: Cornell University Press, 1995), p. 175.

22. The best discussion of this issue is in ibid., chs. 6–7.

23. Edward J. McCaffery, *Taxing Women* (Chicago: University of Chicago Press, 1997), ch. 4.

24. Brown, Advisory Council Minutes, February 18, 1938, morning session, p. 14.

25. House, *Hearings on the Social Security Act Amendments of 1939*, p. 1218.

26. Testimony of Sen. Sheridan Downey of California, *Congressional Record—Senate*, July 13, 1939, p. 9012.

27. Downey, *Congressional Record—Senate*, July 13, 1939, p. 9012.

28. *Senate Resolution Preliminary Report, 1941*, p. 8.

29. Thus, though African Americans made up about 10 percent of the labor force, they constituted nearly half of the women in domestic service. Cf. Testimony of Margaret Plunkett, chief, Division of Legislation, Women's Bureau, Department of Labor, U.S. Congress, House, *Hearings before the Committee on Ways and Means, House of Representatives on Social Security Legislation, Amendments to the Social Security Act of 1946*, 79th Cong., 2nd sess. (Washington, D.C.: GPO, 1946), p. 542; hereafter, House, *Hearings on Amendments to the Social Security Act of 1946*. Plunkett also says that 6 percent of agricultural workers were women (p. 545).

30. Figures from Albion Hartwell, "The Need of Social and Unemployment Insurance for Negroes," *Journal of Negro Education* 5 (January 1936), pp. 79–87.

31. This argument appears in the testimony of Edgar G. Brown, director, National Negro Council, Washington, D.C., at U.S. Congress, House, *Hearings on Social Security Act Amendments of 1949*, p. 1878.

32. See the account of this incident in Edwin E. Witte, *The Development of the Social Security Act: A Memorandum on the History of the Committee on Economic Security and Drafting and Legislative History of the Social Security Act* (Madison: University of Wisconsin Press, 1962), pp. 152–53.

33. Mary Anderson, "The Plight of Negro Domestic Labor," *Journal of Negro Education* 5 (January 1936), p. 71.

34. Rae Needleman, "Are Domestic Workers Coming of Age," *American Federationist* 46 (October 1939), pp. 1070–75.

35. Martha W. Griffiths, "Sex Discrimination in Income Security Programs," *Notre Dame Lawyer* 49 (February 1974), p. 534.

36. *Weinberger v. Wiesenfeld*, 420 U.S. 636 (1975), p. 652.

37. Ibid., pp. 645, 647.

38. *Califano v. Goldfarb*, 97 S.Ct. 1021 (1977), p. 1023. Justice William J. Brennan for the Court.

39. *Califano v. Goldfarb*, p. 1028.

BLANCHE WIESEN COOK
Storms on Every Front: Eleanor Roosevelt and Human Rights at Home and in Europe

A woman of limitless energy, compassion, and humanitarian zeal, Eleanor Roosevelt was the most active and controversial First Lady in the nation's history. A fascinating figure, her ability to grow in understanding never ended. She began her adult life as a shy, insecure woman who had imbibed the racism and anti-Semitism of the privileged world to which she was born. She ended her life a feminist and a political champion of civil rights, civil liberties, social justice, and world peace—a woman whose activism was played out on a world stage.

The transformation was well under way by the 1920s. Indeed, it was accelerated when Franklin Delano Roosevelt was paralyzed by polio in 1921 and Eleanor began serving as his representative in the political arena. Long a political activist, she became a shrewd analyst of the political scene. When FDR became president, ER found herself in an increasingly complex political context. She could try to persuade the president in private conversation; she could also use public pulpits of her own. She was the only First Lady ever to write a long-running daily syndicated newspaper column, "My Day." She could choose (or refuse) speaking

Excerpted and revised by the author from ch. 27 of *Eleanor Roosevelt: The Defining Years, 1933–1938,* by Blanche Wiesen Cook (New York: Viking/Penguin, 1999). Published by permission of the author and publisher. Readers will find ch. 16, "A Silence Beyond Repair," a critical framework for this selection.

invitations, and use her opportunities to speak about issues that mattered to her. As the Nazi threat grew, ER found that the State Department insisted on her silence; she would have to find other ways of expressing her commitment to human rights.

Between 9 and 15 November [1938], Jewish homes, schools, hospitals, synagogues, businesses, and cemeteries were invaded, plundered, burned. Kristallnacht, the night of broken glass, was a week of contempt, abuse, destruction.

If anybody doubted the intent of Hitler's words, so clearly revealed in his writings, speeches, and previous outrages, those November days in Germany, Austria, and the Sudetenland shattered any illusion. The violence coincided with Armistice Day, 11 November, when the Allies ended World War I. The defeat of that war was for Hitler to be avenged with new blood, and unlimited terror.

The violence began on 28 October, when Germany expelled thousands of Polish Jews who had lived for decades within the historically changing borders of Germany. Nazis rounded up children and old people on the streets, emptied houses and apartment buildings, allowed people to take nothing with them except 10 marks ($4) and the clothes they wore, shoved them into waiting trucks and trains, and dumped them across the border onto the desolate flats of Poland's borderlands. More than ten thousand Jews were deported in this manner.

Among the deportees was the family of Zindel Grynszpan, whose seventeen-year-old son, Heschel, had previously fled the family home in Hanover to Paris. When he received a letter from his father recounting his family's ordeal, Heschel Grynszpan bought a gun and on 7 November walked to the German embassy in Paris to assassinate the ambassador. Ironically, he was detained by a minor official, Ernst vom Rath, who was himself under investigation by the Gestapo for his opposition to the increasing anti-Semitic violence, and shot him. This murder was the immediate excuse used to launch the well-orchestrated burnings, lootings, and round-ups known as Kristallnacht.

Then on 12 November, German Jews were fined a billion marks—$400 million—as penalty for the murder. This "money atonement" was astronomical and rendered it virtually impossible for most Jews to retain sufficient savings to emigrate. Yet another decree ordered the victims to pay for the repair and restoration of their former shops, buildings, and homes— from which they were permanently banished.

These fines had another, more sinister purpose. Hitler had announced: "If there is any country that believes it has not enough Jews, I shall gladly turn over to it all our Jews." Now, if they left, they left penniless. Moreover, most countries had closed their doors, and those who would accept Jews would not accept paupers.

It was a major challenge for FDR, whose policy was to do nothing to involve the United States in European affairs, but who wanted to respond somehow to the thousands of refugees who stood for hours before the U.S. embassy seeking asylum, only to be routinely turned away.

Within days, Jews were stripped of their remaining human rights. They were no longer permitted to drive cars, travel on public transportation, walk in parks, go to museums, attend theaters or concerts. Passports and visas were canceled. They were stateless and impoverished. Charged for the violence and fined for the damage, the Jewish community now owed the Reich, collectively, one billion Reichsmarks. For a time, they were not molested in their homes. But there was nothing to do, no work to be had; no place to pray; no recourse from agony. Many committed suicide; most tried to leave.

For all moral and political purposes, Kristallnacht was the terminal event. Civility in the heart of western Europe lay in ruins, surrounded by broken glass, bloodied streets, desecrated temples, burned Torahs, ripped books of prayer to the one shared God. Hitler's intentions were flagrant, and the whole world was invited to witness. Twenty thousand Jews were removed to concentration camps, which the Anglo-American press named: Dachau near Munich, Oranienburg-Sachsenhausen north of Berlin, Buchenwald near Weimar. . . .

ER's formerly private protests against bigotry were increasingly for public attribution. Although she had resigned in silence from the Colony Club for its discrimination against Elinor Morgenthau, she now canceled a speaking engagement at a country club in Lancaster, Pennsylvania, with a statement of distress that it excluded Jews.

While she counseled complete assimilation and urged Jews to "wipe out in their own consciousness any feeling of difference by joining in all that is being done by Americans" for justice and democracy, she also spoke on behalf of support for refugees in Palestine. . . . On 6 December 1938, ER appealed to fifteen hundred people assembled at the Hotel Astor under the auspices of a national committee for refugees chaired by William Green, president of the American Federation of Labor, to help promote the Léon Blum colony in Palestine for the settlement of one thousand Jewish refugee families. . . .

While ER called for demonstrations of "thought and example," little was done, or said, by FDR's administration to indicate official outrage at Hitler's violence. No message of protest warning of boycott or economic reprisal was sent. Yet history abounds in such protests on behalf of victimized peoples. In 1903 and 1906, Theodore Roosevelt protested against Jewish pogroms in Russia, after Jacob Schiff lobbied for an official U.S. condemnation of the massacre of Jews in Odessa. . . .

FDR sent no similar message to Germany.

FDR did respond to the pitiless carnage and massacre in China. In December 1937, Japan destroyed Nanking in a vicious episode of rape, horror, and death. Half the population, an estimated 300,000 people, were tortured and killed. Whether the details were immediately known to FDR, even of Japan's 12 December sinking of the U.S. gunboat *Panay,* remains controversial. But on 11 January 1938, FDR sent a memo to Cordell Hull and Admiral Cary T. Grayson, head of the American Red Cross. He called for additional relief funds for the "destitute Chinese civilians" and for medical aid. "I think we could raise $1,000,000 without any trouble at all." On 17 January, the U.S. Red Cross launched an appeal for aid to the Chinese people, initiated by FDR's formal request for such a drive.[1]

No similar appeal was made by FDR to the Red Cross on behalf of Europe's Jews.*

Since he was considered by many the best friend American Jews ever had, FDR's reactions to the European events of 1938 are unexplainable. . . . Except for Father Charles E. Coughlin, who hailed the violence against "Jewish-sponsored Communism," the press was unanimous in its condemnation. . . .

. . . FDR agreed to allow all German aliens on visitor visas to remain in the United States

for six months "and for other like periods so long as necessary." At the time there were between twelve thousand and fifteen thousand political refugees covered by his order, and "not all Jews, by any means," the president assured the press. "All shades of liberal political thought and many religions are represented."[2]

Anti-Semitism in FDR's State Department increased after Hitler's November atrocities. Breckenridge Long now dedicated himself to keeping refugees out of America. Curiously, FDR continually promoted Breckenridge Long, who had life-and-death control over visas and passports. Nevertheless, in 1938, for the first time, the United States filled its refugee quota.

ER and her asylum-seeking circle faced the urgent refugee crisis in a lonely political environment. Thousands of the earliest refugees who left in 1933 were still wandering Europe seeking safety and political asylum. After 31 January 1933, over 30 percent of Germany's 500,000 Jews had become refugees. After the March 1938 Anschluss, Germany's annexation of Austria, when the Nazis began to expel Austria's 190,000 Jews, the situation became critical. The flight of Czech Jews compounded the problem, and Kristallnacht ignited refugee panic.

FDR expanded his search for underpopulated and suitable lands upon which to place the world's unwanted Jews . . . but told his press conference that he had no intention of asking Congress to alter existing immigration quotas. . . .

During her own press conference, ER called for temporary emergency measures to do whatever was possible "to deal with the refugee problem, and at home, for renewed devotion to . . . the American way of life." Wary of her husband's strategies, she [rarely criticized] him directly. . . . "For ourselves, "[she said]," I hope we will do, as individuals, all we can to preserve what is a traditional right in this country—freedom for different races and different religions." . . .

[From 1938 to 1940, a committee of geographers, scholars, and members of the State Department explored the possibilities of sanctuary for Jews outside the United States, without success. ER was staggered by the contempt for human suffering expressed by the failure of

---

*During the 1940s, the International Red Cross deflected complaints about its neglect of Jewish needs, given the magnitude of the mounting tragedy, with the explanation that the Red Cross "could not interfere in the internal affairs of a belligerent nation." Blood plasma for U.S. troops was segregated into "white" and "colored," "Christian" and "Hebrew." It was not desegregated until 1954.

other nations to welcome refugees.] In the bitter time before the burning time there was hope for rescue country by country. But there was no official objection to Hitler's intention to remove Jews from Germany and all his new territories. ER increasingly bypassed State Department restrictions; she worked, often covertly, with private groups and individuals. She campaigned for a less restrictive refugee policy, pursued visas for individuals, and answered and passed on to government officials every appeal sent to her.

Revolted by world events, ER called for entirely new levels of action. Her speeches became more pointed and vigorous, and she spent more time in the company of radical activists, especially members of the American Youth Congress whose ardent views now coincided most completely with her own.

For ER, AYC leaders represented hope for the best of liberal America. Christian theology students, Jewish children of immigrants, black and white activists from the rural South and urban North imagined a nation united for progressive antifascist action.

A week after Kristallnacht, ER ... defended the AYC at the annual luncheon of New York's branch of the American Association of University Women and spoke of the need for courage and fearlessness in perilous times. ... ER's speech was bold: She rejected the current Red Scare tactics which branded the AYC communist and her a dupe or fool: Such name-calling had destroyed democracy in Europe, and she wanted democracy to survive here.

"People whose opinions I respect" had warned her not to attend the AYC convention.

> [But] I didn't think that those youngsters could turn me into a Communist, so I went just the same. ...
>
> I listened to speeches which you and I could easily have torn to shreds. The Chinese listened while the Japanese spoke; the boy from India spoke with the British delegates. ... Nobody hissed or left the room. I have been in lots of gatherings of adults who did not show that kind of respect. ...

She spoke with many delegates, asked what they thought of the Soviet Union; she left convinced that there was interest in communism, but not domination by communists: "We who have training, and have minds that we know how to use must not be swept away" by fear and propaganda. The urgent problems before the United States and the world required scrutiny, debate, honest disagreement, democratic participation, not a wild and fearful flight from controversy. ...

On 22 November 1938, ER embarked on a dangerous mission when she keynoted the radical biracial Southern Conference on Human Welfare, in Birmingham, Alabama. For the first time since the Civil War, Southern liberals were determined to face the race issue embedded within the region's struggling economy. Since 1890 there had been talk of a "New South," but always before, racial cruelties at the heart of peonage and poverty had been ignored in the interest of white supremacy. ...

In the aftermath of Kristallnacht, there was a new level of commitment and urgency at the Birmingham meeting. Regional race and antiunion violence was behind the call for the SCHW, first conceived as a civil liberties conference by [pioneering progressive activists] Joseph Gelders and Lucy Randolph Mason. According to Virginia Durr, they wanted to deal with the "terrible things happening" to CIO organizers in Mississippi. Many people were beaten [and run out of town,] crosses were burned. ...

While the South "led the world" in cotton, tobacco, paper, and other products, it was a disaster area. The average per capita income was half the nation's; the poll tax limited voting rights to 12 percent of the population in eight Southern states, including Virginia; the region's children were being undereducated. The South was hampered by backward and colonial customs; and its entrenched leaders wanted no changes.

The Southern Conference on Human Welfare determined to change the South and challenge segregation. Fifteen hundred delegates, black and white, sat anywhere they wanted Sunday night, 21 November 1938, in the city auditorium of downtown Birmingham. According to Virginia Durr: "Oh, it was a love feast. ... Southern meetings always include a lot of preaching and praying and hymn singing. ... The whole meeting was just full of love and hope. It was thrilling. ... The whole South was coming together to make a new day."[3]

Somebody reported the integrated seating at the opening-night gala, and the next morning the auditorium was surrounded. ... Every police van in the city and county was there. Policemen were everywhere, inside and out.

And there was Eugene "Bull" Connor "saying anybody who broke the segregation law of Alabama would be arrested." Tensions escalated; violence was in the air. The delegates complied and arranged themselves into separate sections.

ER, Mary McLeod Bethune, and Aubrey Williams arrived late that day, out of breath. ER "was ushered in with great applause," looked at the segregated audience—and took her seat on the black side. One of Bull Connor's police officers tapped ER on the shoulder and told her to move. . . .

As if to announce fascism would not triumph here, ER refused to "give in" and placed her chair between the white and black sections. Pauli Murray recalled that ER's demonstration of defiance and courage meant everything to the young people of the South, who now knew they were not alone. Although the national press did not report ER's brave action, the weekly *Afro-American* editorialized: "If the people of the South do not grasp this gesture, we must. Sometimes actions speak louder than words."[4]

ER was given a little folding chair and sat in the middle of whatever meeting hall or church she attended for the rest of the four-day meeting. She said she refused to be segregated, and carried the folding chair with her wherever she went. According to Durr: "Policemen followed us everywhere to make sure the segregation laws were observed, but they didn't arrest Mrs. Roosevelt."

ER's address to the SCHW stirred the packed auditorium:

We are the leading democracy of the world and as such must prove to the world that democracy is possible and capable of living up to the principles upon which it was founded. The eyes of the world are upon us, and often we find they are not too friendly eyes.

ER emphasized "universal education" in which "every one of our citizens, regardless of nationality, or race," might be allowed to flourish.[5] . . .

The 1938 SCHW adopted thirty-six resolutions, all of which involved the plight of African Americans, and eight of which directly concerned racial issues, including freedom for the four Scottsboro boys who remained in prison; availability of medical services by African American physicians in all public health facilities; more funding for public housing and recreation facilities for African Americans; equal funding for graduate education in state-supported colleges; and—inspired by ER's demonstration—a resolution to support fully integrated SCHW meetings.

Perceived as "one of the gravest sins that a white southerner could commit," that direct assault against tradition created a furor. The antisegregation resolution divided the delegates, some of whom withdrew, and was branded communist, subversive, and un-American. On the other hand, it transformed national assumptions about the unspeakable: White supremacy, and its primary bulwark, segregation, were forevermore on the nation's agenda—put there by an integrated conference, led by Southern New Dealers.[6]

Traditional "race etiquette" was also challenged when Louise Charlton called on Mary McLeod Bethune to speak. (See Bethune, pp. 329–331.) According to Virginia Durr:

She said, "Mary, do you wish to come to the platform?" Mrs. Bethune rose. She looked like an African queen. . . . "My name is Mrs. Bethune." So Louise had to say, "Mrs. Bethune, will you come to the platform?" That sounds like a small thing now, but that was a big dividing line. A Negro woman in Birmingham, Alabama, was called Mrs. at a public meeting. . . .

Virginia Durr, wife of Clifford Durr, the assistant general counsel of the Reconstruction Finance Corporation, and sister-in-law of Justice Hugo Black, addressed the meeting to denounce the South's refusal to educate its people and the prevailing ignorance so general throughout the country. The reasons for an uninformed public, she declared, were propaganda and a controlled press dominated by Wall Street. She accused the National Manufacturers Association of being a "huge propaganda machine" intent on the "liquidation of organized labor." . . .

[A week after the SCHW], the Nazi press announced that Germany had embarked upon "the final and unalterably uncompromising solution" to the Jewish question. In the Gestapo's official paper, *Das Schwarze Korps*, on 24 November, the front-page feature announced that it should have been done immediately, brutally, and completely in 1933. But "it had to remain theory" for lack of the "military power we possess today."

Because it is necessary, because we no longer hear the world's screeching and because, after all, no power on earth can hinder us, we will now bring the Jewish question to its totalitarian solution.[7]

Two weeks after Kristallnacht, accepted without notable "screeching" from any government, Hitler felt sufficiently unrestrained to publish his intentions for all Jews caught in his widening web. First would come pauperization, isolation, ghettoization. They would all be marked for positive identification. Nobody would escape. Then, the starving, bedraggled remnant would become a scrounging, begging scourge. They would be forced to crime, would be an "underworld" of "politico-criminal subhumans," breeders of Bolshevism. At that stage "we should therefore face the hard necessity of exterminating the Jewish underworld. . . . The result will be the actual and definite end of Jewry . . . and its complete extermination."

While the announcement was made two years and eight months before it was actually implemented, the time to protest and resist was at hand. After it was reprinted in the U.S. and European press, many understood the implications of such crude words given the reality of the cruelties under way in Germany, Austria, and Czechoslovakia. Since Kristallnacht, race hatred had triumphed completely and Jews had been removed from all German institutions, doomed to a pariah existence in complete segregation. Jews could no longer dine with Gentiles—not in restaurants, not anywhere; nor could they buy food in the same stores. Nazis established separate stores where Jews were restricted in the purchase of life's staples—milk, bread.

Such laws cast a torchlight on American traditions. ER made the connections: brown shirts, white sheets; the twisted cross, the burning cross. Yet the internal affairs of a nation were deemed sacrosanct, nobody else's business. ER and other citizens no longer agreed with that diplomatic principle.

FDR remained virtually silent about human rights abuses, and did not end trade with Germany, but he began a vigorous rearmament program, emphasizing military planes and naval construction. Immediately after Kristallnacht, on 14 November, he reported to Josephus Daniels, his Wilson-era boss, that he was working on "national defense—especially mass production of planes." By December, he ordered the navy yards to run full-time, "two shifts or even three" wherever possible. It "is time to get action."

While ER approved of all defense programs, she also called for a worldwide educational crusade to address prejudice. . . . After the SCHW meetings, ER wrote her first articles specifically about Jews and race hatred. One, initially called "Tolerance," was for the *Virginia Quarterly* and attacked the kind of anticommunist hysteria that had resulted in fascist triumph and appeasement throughout so much of Europe. The other, which addressed the mounting hatred against Jews, was dated 25 November 1938. . . .

Untitled, ER's "Jewish article" called for a campaign of understanding to confront "the present catastrophe for Jew and Gentile alike. . . . In books . . . schools, newspapers, plays, assemblies we want incessant truth telling about these old legends that divide and antagonize and waste us."

As she struggled to understand "the kind of racial and religious intolerance which is sweeping the world today," ER rejected her former emphasis on assimilation. . . . Now ER assessed the historic hatred of Jews, their isolation, and forced ghettoization in the Middle Ages, and the ongoing contempt for Jews. . . . ER now pointed out that even when Jews attempted to assimilate they were condemned for "being too ostentatiously patriotic and of pushing themselves forward as nationals," as in Austria and Germany.

ER was also sensitive to the difficulties assimilated Jews faced among their coreligionists, who resented those who strayed from tradition. Never quite accepted into the majority culture, they were everywhere marginalized. . . . ER rejected ghettoization and deplored signs that appeared in many American neighborhoods that read "No Dogs or Jews Allowed."

Written from within the veil of her own stereotypes, ER concluded that the future was not up to the Jews.

> The Jew is almost powerless today. It depends almost entirely on the course of the Gentiles what the future holds. . . . If they perish, we perish sooner or later. . . .

She recalled that as a child her uncle Theodore Roosevelt once said "that when you are afraid to do a thing, that was the time to go and do it. Every time we shirk making up our minds or standing up for a cause in which we believe, we weaken our character and our ability to be fearless." . . .

ER challenged Americans to think and act politically, to engage in activist citizenship, to become their best selves. A sense of personal unimportance was encouraged by dictators. Democracy depended on "freedom from prejudice, and public awareness." It required education, economic security, and personal devotion, "a real devotion to freedom. . . . Freedom is something to guard jealously," but it can never be "freedom for me and not for you."

The bolder ER became, the tougher and more adamant her statements, the higher her public approval rating soared. On 16 January 1939, the *New York Times* published a poll taken by George Gallup regarding America's feelings about ER during 1938. The results were astounding. Two voters in every three voted in her favor (67 percent approved of her conduct, 33 percent disapproved). . . . According to the poll she had a greater approval rating than FDR. . . . Given the nature of the controversies ER engaged in and her challenge to work for the transformation of customs and traditions that subjected so many to poverty and powerlessness, America's response indicated a commitment to the very democracy she spoke about so earnestly. ER touched a nerve center in America, and the country would never be the same.

On 10 February 1938, ER [had] commemorated the seventy-fifth anniversary of the Emancipation Proclamation by asserting that while Abraham Lincoln took the "first step toward the abolition of slavery . . . we still do tolerate slavery in several ways." Her words, addressed to nine thousand people at a meeting sponsored by the National Negro Congress, were electrifying:

There are still slaves of many different kinds, and today we are facing another era in which we have to make certain things become facts rather than beliefs.

As Europe fell to fascism, ER and her new network of youth and race radicals heralded the greatest changes in America since the betrayal of Reconstruction.

In her 8 December 1938 column, ER criticized liberals, smug partisans, and patriots for celebrating incomplete victories. . . .

As I listened [to speeches to promote the Leon Blum colony for refugees in Palestine] . . . I could not help thinking how much all human beings like to fool themselves. . . . [They] made us feel that . . . we were more virtuous and fortunate than any other people in the world. Of course, I concede this, and I feel for me it is true, for I have been free and fortunate all my life. While I listened, however, I could not help thinking of some of the letters which pass through my hands.

Are you free if you cannot vote, if you cannot be sure that the same justice will be meted out to you as to your neighbor, . . . if you are barred from certain places and from certain opportunities? . . .

Are you free when you can't earn enough, no matter how hard you work, to feed and clothe and house your children properly? Are you free when your employer can turn you out of a company house and deny you work because you belong to a union?

Her thoughts turned to refugees in this country, "of the little girl who wrote me not long ago: 'Why do other children call me names and laugh at my talk? I just don't live in this country very long yet.'" ER concluded:

There are lots and lots of things which make me wonder whether we ever look ourselves straight in the face and really mean what we say when we are busy patting ourselves on the back.

With grit, determination, and a very high heart, ER helped launch America's crusade for freedom in the fascist era. She was fortified every day by her new allies, her abiding partnership with FDR, love for the people in her life, and love of the world.

NOTES

1. FDR to Cordell Hull, Jan. 11, 1938, in *FDR: His Personal Letters, 1928–1945*, Elliott Roosevelt and Joseph P. Lash, eds. (Millwood, N.Y.: Kraus Reprint, 1970), IV, pp. 744–45; see also Iris Chang, *The Rape of Nanking: The Forgotten Holocaust of World War II* (New York: Penguin, 1997).

2. *New York Times,* Nov. 19, 1938.

3. Linda Reed, *Simple Decency and Common Sense: The Southern Conference Movement, 1938–1945* (Bloomington: Indiana University Press, 1991), pp. 15–16 and passim; Virginia Durr, *Outside the Magic Circle: The Autobiography of Virginia Durr* (Tuscaloosa: Univ. of Alabama Press, 1985).

4. Pauli Murray, *Song in a Weary Throat: An American Pilgrimage* (New York: Harper & Row, 1987), p. 113.

5. For ER's Nov. 22, 1938 speech at the SCHW, see Allida Black, ed., *Courage in a Dangerous World: The Political Writings of Eleanor Roosevelt* (New York: Columbia University Press, 1999).

6. Reed, pp. 46–48.

7. *New York Times,* Nov. 24, 1938; Arthur D. Morse, *While Six Million Died: A Chronicle of American Apathy* (New York: Random House, 1968); Michael Berenbaum, *The World Must Know* (Boston: Little Brown, 1993), p. 35.

WOMEN AND WAR

VALERIE MATSUMOTO

Japanese American Women During World War II

On no group of U.S. citizens did the war have greater impact than upon Japanese Americans. Fearful of a Japanese fifth column on American shores, military and civilian leaders urged Franklin Roosevelt to issue an executive order removing Americans of Japanese descent on the West Coast to relocation camps inland. Despite the fact that a vast majority of the nearly 120,000 Japanese Americans in the United States were citizens with the same rights and obligations as any other citizen, the president succumbed to pressure and issued Executive Order 9066 in February 1942, which ultimately resulted in the establishment of ten concentration camps, most of which were in remote areas of the West. Forced to leave their homes and businesses at great financial cost, both Japanese-born parents, the Issei, and their American-born children, the Nisei, faced the trauma of removal and the shame of implied disloyalty. Not until 1990 would the nation acknowledge the magnitude of its offense and begin providing financial redress for survivors of the camps.

The following essay explores what life in the camps was like for women and the efforts of younger ones to reconstruct a life after internment.

The life here cannot be expressed. Sometimes, we are resigned to it, but when we see the barbed wire fences and the sentry tower with floodlights, it gives us a feeling of being prisoners in a "concentration camp." We try to be happy and yet oftentimes a gloominess does creep in. When I see the "I'm an American" editorial and write-ups, the "equality of race etc."—it seems to be mocking us in our faces. I just wonder if all the sacrifices and hard labor on [the] part of our parents has gone up to leave nothing to show for it?

Letter from Shizuko Horiuchi,
Pomona Assembly Center, May 24, 1942

Overlying the mixed feelings of anxiety, anger, shame, and confusion [of the Japanese Americans who were forced to relocate] was resignation. As a relatively small minority caught in a storm of turbulent events that destroyed their individual and community security, there was little the Japanese Americans could do but shrug and say, "*Shikata ga nai,*" or "It can't be helped," the implication being that the situation must be endured. The phrase lingered on many lips when the Issei, Nisei [second generation], and the young Sansei [third generation] children prepared for the move—which was completed by November 1942—to the ten permanent relocation camps organized by the War Relocation Authority: Topaz, Utah; Poston and Gila River, Arizona; Amache, Colorado; Manzanar and Tule Lake, California; Heart Mountain, Wyoming; Minidoka, Idaho; Denson and Rohwer, Arkansas.[1] Denson and Rohwer were located in the swampy lowlands of Arkansas;

Pledge of Allegiance, 1942.
Dorothea Lange had a keen eye for irony, as in this photograph of Japanese American girls in California a few weeks before they were deported to relocation camps. (Photograph courtesy of the National Archives.)

the other camps were in desolate desert or semi-desert areas subject to dust storms and extreme temperatures reflected in the nicknames given to the three sections of the Poston Camp: Toaston, Roaston, and Duston.

The conditions of camp life profoundly altered family relations and affected women of all ages and backgrounds. Family unity deteriorated in the crude communal facilities and cramped barracks. The unceasing battle with the elements, the poor food, the shortages of toilet tissue and milk, coupled with wartime profiteering and mismanagement, and the sense of injustice and frustration took their toll on a people uprooted, far from home.

The standard housing in the camps was a spartan barracks, about twenty feet by one

hundred feet, divided into four to six rooms furnished with steel army cots. Initially each single room or "apartment" housed an average of eight persons; individuals without kin nearby were often moved in with smaller families. Because the partitions between apartments did not reach the ceiling, even the smallest noises traveled freely from one end of the building to the other. There were usually fourteen barracks in each block, and each block had its own mess hall, laundry, latrine, shower facilities, and recreation room. . . . The even greater lack of privacy in the latrine and shower facilities necessitated adjustments in former notions of modesty. There were no partitions in the shower room, and the latrine consisted of two rows of partitioned toilets "with nothing in front of you, just on the sides."[2] . . . A married woman with a family wrote from Heart Mountain:

> Last weekend, we had an awful cold wave and it was about 20° to 30° below zero. In such a weather, it's terrible to try going even to the bath and latrine house. . . . It really aggravates me to hear some politicians say we Japanese are being coddled, for *it isn't so!!* We're on ration as much as outsiders are. I'd say welcome to anyone to try living behind barbed wire and be cooped in a 20 ft. by 20 ft. room. . . . We do our sleeping, dressing, ironing, hanging up our clothes in this one room.[3]

After the first numbness of disorientation, the evacuees set about making their situation bearable, creating as much order in their lives as possible. With blankets they partitioned their apartments into tiny rooms and created benches, tables, and shelves as piles of scrap lumber left over from barracks construction vanished; victory gardens and flower patches appeared. . . .

Despite the best efforts of the evacuees to restore order to their disrupted world, camp conditions prevented replication of their prewar lives. Women's work experiences, for example, changed in complex ways during the years of internment. Each camp offered a wide range of jobs, resulting from the organization of the camps as model cities administered through a series of departments headed by European American administrators. The departments handled everything from accounting, agriculture, education, and medical care to mess hall service and the weekly newspaper. The scramble for jobs began early in the assembly centers and camps, and all able-bodied persons were expected to work.

Even before the war many family members had worked, but now children and parents, men and women all received the same low wages. In the relocation camps, doctors, teachers, and other professionals were at the top of the pay scale, earning $19 per month. The majority of workers received $16, and apprentices earned $12. The new equity in pay and the variety of available jobs gave many women unprecedented opportunities for experimentation, as illustrated by one woman's account of her family's work in Poston:

> First I wanted to find art work, but I didn't last too long because it wasn't very interesting . . . so I worked in the mess hall, but that wasn't for me, so I went to the accounting department—timekeeping—and I enjoyed that, so I stayed there. . . . My dad . . . went to a shoe shop . . . and then he

was block gardener. . . . He got $16. . . . [My sister] was secretary for the block manager; then she went to the optometry department. She was assistant optometrist; she fixed all the glasses and fitted them. . . . That was $16.[4]

As early as 1942, the War Relocation Authority began to release evacuees temporarily from the centers and camps to do voluntary seasonal farm work in neighboring areas hard hit by the wartime labor shortage. The work was arduous, as one young woman discovered when she left Topaz to take a job plucking turkeys:

> The smell is terrific until you get used to it. . . . We all wore gunny sacks around our waist, had a small knife and plucked off the fine feathers.
>
> This is about the hardest work that many of us have done—but without a murmur of complaint we worked 8 hours through the first day without a pause.
>
> We were all so tired that we didn't even feel like eating. . . . Our fingers and wrists were just aching, and I just dreamt of turkeys and more turkeys.[5]

Work conditions varied from situation to situation, and some exploitative farmers refused to pay the Japanese Americans after they had finished beet topping or fruit picking. One worker noted that the degree of friendliness on the employer's part decreased as the harvest neared completion. Nonetheless, many workers, like the turkey plucker, concluded that "even if the work is hard, it is worth the freedom we are allowed." . . .

Like their noninterned contemporaries, most young Nisei women envisioned a future of marriage and children. They—and their parents—anticipated that they would marry other Japanese Americans, but these young women also expected to choose their own husbands and to marry "for love." This mainstream American ideal of marriage differed greatly from the Issei's view of love as a bond that might evolve over the course of an arranged marriage that was firmly rooted in less romantic notions of compatibility and responsibility. The discrepancy between Issei and Nisei conceptions of love and marriage had sturdy prewar roots; internment fostered further divergence from the old customs of arranged marriage. In the artificial hothouse of camp, Nisei romances often bloomed quickly. As Nisei men left to prove their loyalty to the United States in the 442nd Combat Team and the 100th Battalion, young Japanese Americans strove to grasp what happiness and security they could, given the uncertainties of the future. Lily Shoji, in her "Fem-a-lites" newspaper column, commented upon the "changing world" and advised Nisei women: "This is the day of sudden dates, of blind dates on the up-and-up, so let the flash of a uniform be a signal to you to be ready for any emergency. . . . Romance is blossoming with the emotion and urgency of war."[6]

In keeping with this atmosphere, camp newspaper columns like Shoji's in *The Mercedian*, *The Daily Tulean Dispatch's* "Strictly Feminine," and the *Poston Chronicle's* "Fashionotes" gave their Nisei readers countless suggestions on how to impress boys, care for their complexions, and choose the latest fashions. These evacuee-authored columns thus mirrored the mainstream girls' periodicals of the time. Such fashion news may seem incongruous in the context of an internment camp whose inmates had little choice in clothing beyond what they could find in the Montgomery Ward or Sears and Roebuck mail-order catalogues. These columns, however, reflect women's efforts to remain in touch with the world outside the barbed wire fence; they reflect as well women's attempt to maintain morale in a drab, depressing environment. "There's something about color in clothes," speculated Tule Lake columnist "Yuri"; "Singing colors have a heart-building effect. . . . Color is a stimulant we need—both for its effect on ourselves and on others."[7] . . .

RESETTLEMENT: COLLEGE AND WORK

Relocation began slowly in 1942. Among the first to venture out of the camps were college students, assisted by the National Japanese American Student Relocation Council, a non-governmental agency that provided invaluable placement aid to 4,084 Nisei in the years 1942–46.[8] Founded in 1942 by concerned educators, this organization persuaded institutions outside the restricted Western Defense zone to accept Nisei students and facilitated their admissions and leave clearances. A study of the first 400 students to leave camp showed that a third of them were women.[9] Because of the cumbersome screening process, few other evacuees departed on indefinite leave before 1943. In that year, the War Relocation Authority tried to expedite the clearance procedure by broadening an army registration program aimed at Nisei males to include all adults. With this policy

change, the migration from the camps steadily increased.[10]

Many Nisei, among them a large number of women, were anxious to leave the limbo of camp and return "to normal life again."[11] . . . An aspiring teacher wrote: "Mother and father do not want me to go out. However, I want to go so very much that sometimes I feel that I'd go even if they disowned me. What shall I do? I realize the hard living conditions outside but I think I can take it."[12] Women's developing sense of independence in the camp environment and their growing awareness of their abilities as workers contributed to their self-confidence and hence their desire to leave. Significantly, Issei parents, despite initial reluctance, were gradually beginning to sanction their daughters' departures for education and employment in the Midwest and East. One Nisei noted: "[Father] became more broad-minded in the relocation center. . . . At first he didn't want me to relocate, but he gave in. . . . He didn't say I could go . . . but he helped me pack, so I thought, 'Well, he didn't say no.'"[13]

The decision to relocate was a difficult one. . . . Many internees worried about their acceptance in the outside world. The Nisei considered themselves American citizens, and they had an allegiance to the land of their birth. . . . But evacuation had taught the Japanese Americans that in the eyes of many of their fellow Americans, theirs was the face of the enemy. Many Nisei were torn by mixed feelings of shame, frustration, and bitterness at the denial of their civil rights. . . . "A feeling of uncertainty hung over the camp; we were worried about the future. Plans were made and remade, as we tried to decide what to do. Some were ready to risk anything to get away. Others feared to leave the protection of the camp."[14]

Thus, those first college students were the scouts whose letters back to camp marked pathways for others to follow. May Yoshino sent a favorable report to her family in Topaz from the nearby University of Utah, indicating that there were "plenty of schoolgirl jobs for those who want to study at the University."[15] Correspondence from other Nisei students shows that although they succeeded at making the dual transition from high school to college and from camp to the outside world, they were not without anxieties as to whether they could handle the study load and the reactions of the European Americans around them. One student at Drake University in Iowa wrote to her interned sister about a professor's reaction to her autobiographical essay, "Evacuation": "Today Mr.—, the English teacher that scares me, told me that the theme that I wrote the other day was very interesting. . . . You could just imagine how wonderful and happy I was to know that he liked it a little bit. . . . I've been awfully busy trying to catch up on work and the work is so different from high school. I think that little by little I'm beginning to adjust myself to college life."[16] . . . Lillian . . . Ota, a Wellesley student, reassured [her interned friends contemplating college:] "During the first few days you'll be invited by the college to teas and receptions. Before long you'll lose the awkwardness you might feel at such doings after the months of abnormal life at evacuation centers."[17] Although Ota had not noticed "that my being a 'Jap' has made much difference on the campus itself," she offered cautionary and pragmatic advice to the Nisei, suggesting the burden of responsibility these relocated students felt, as well as the problem of communicating their experiences and emotions to European Americans.

> It is scarcely necessary to point out that those who have probably never seen a nisei before will get their impression of the nisei as a whole from the relocated students. It won't do you or your family and friends much good to dwell on what you consider injustices when you are questioned about evacuation. Rather, stress the contributions of [our] people to the nation's war effort.[18] . . .

Armed with [such] advice and drawn by encouraging reports, increasing numbers of women students left camp.[19] . . . The trickle of migration from the camps grew into a steady stream by 1943, as the War Relocation Authority developed its resettlement program to aid evacuees in finding housing and employment in the East and Midwest. . . . [But] leaving camp meant [more changes.] Even someone as confident as Marii Kyogoku . . . found that reentry into the European American–dominated world beyond the barbed wire fence was not a simple matter of stepping back into old shoes. Leaving the camps—like entering them—meant major changes in psychological perspective and self-image.

> I had thought that because before evacuation I had adjusted myself rather well in a Caucasian society, I would go right back into my former frame of mind. I have found, however, that though the center became unreal and was as if it had never existed as soon as I got on the train at Delta, I was never so self-conscious in all my life.

Kyogoku was amazed to see so many men and women in uniform and, despite her "proper" dining preparation, felt strange sitting at a table set with clean linen and a full set of silverware.

> I felt a diffidence at facing all these people and things, which was most unusual. Slowly things have come to seem natural, though I am still excited by the sounds of the busy city and thrilled every time I see a street lined with trees, I no longer feel that I am the cynosure of all eyes.[20] . . .

Many relocating Japanese Americans received moral and material assistance from a number of service organizations and religious groups, particularly the Presbyterians, the Methodists, the Society of Friends, and the Young Women's Christian Association. One such Nisei, Dorcas Asano, enthusiastically described to a Quaker sponsor her activities in the big city:

> Since receiving your application for hostel accommodation, I have decided to come to New York and I am really glad for the opportunity to be able to resume the normal civilized life after a year's confinement in camp. New York is really a city of dreams and we are enjoying every minute working in offices, rushing back and forth to work in the ever-speeding subway trains, counting our ration points, buying war bonds, going to church, seeing the latest shows, plays, operas, making many new friends and living like our neighbors in the war time. I only wish more of my friends who are behind the fence will take advantage of the many helpful hands offered to them.[21]

The Nisei also derived support and strength from networks—formed before and during internment—of friends and relatives. The homes of those who relocated first became way stations for others as they made the transition into new communities and jobs. In 1944, soon after she obtained a place to stay in New York City, Miné Okubo found that "many of the other evacuees relocating in New York came ringing my doorbell. They were sleeping all over the floor!"[22] Single women often accompanied or joined sisters, brothers, and friends as many interconnecting grapevines carried news of likely jobs, housing, and friendly communities. . . .

For Nisei women, like their non-Japanese sisters, the wartime labor shortage opened the door into industrial, clerical, and managerial occupations. Prior to the war, racism had excluded the Japanese Americans from most white-collar clerical and sales positions, and, according to sociologist Evelyn Nakano Glenn, "the most common form of nonagricultural employment for the immigrant women (Issei) and their American-born daughters (Nisei) was domestic service."[23] The highest percentage of job offers for both men and women continued to be requests for domestic workers. In July 1943, the Kansas City branch of the War Relocation Authority noted that 45 percent of requests for workers were for domestics, and the Milwaukee office cited 61 percent.[24] However, Nisei women also found jobs as secretaries, typists, file clerks, beauticians, and factory workers. By 1950, 47 percent of employed Japanese American women were clerical and sales workers and operatives; only 10 percent were in domestic service.[25] The World War II decade, then, marked a turning point for Japanese American women in the labor force. . . .

[Improved opportunities could not compensate for the] uprooting [of] communities and [the] severe psychological and emotional damage [inflicted upon Japanese Americans by internment.] The vast majority returned to the West Coast at the end of the war in 1945—a move that, like the initial evacuation, was a grueling test of flexibility and fortitude. Even with the assistance of old friends and service organizations, the transition was taxing and painful; the end of the war meant not only long-awaited freedom but more battles to be fought in social, academic, and economic arenas. The Japanese Americans faced hostility, crude living conditions, and a struggle for jobs. Few evacuees received any compensation for their financial losses, estimated conservatively at $400 million, because Congress decided to appropriate only $38 million for the settlement of claims.[26] It is even harder to place a figure on the toll taken in emotional shock, self-blame, broken dreams, and insecurity. One Japanese American woman still sees in her nightmares the watchtower searchlights that troubled her sleep forty years ago.

The war altered Japanese American women's lives in complicated ways. In general, internment and resettlement accelerated earlier trends that differentiated the Nisei from their parents. Although most young women, like their mothers and non-Japanese peers, anticipated a future centered on a husband and children, they had already felt the influence of mainstream middle-class values of love and marriage and quickly moved away from the pattern of arranged marriage in the camps. There, increased peer group activities and the relaxation of parental authority gave them more independence. The Nisei women's expectations of marriage became more akin to the companionate ideals of their peers than to those of the Issei.

As before the war, many Nisei women worked . . . , but the new parity in wages they received altered family dynamics. And though they expected to contribute to the family economy, a large number did so in settings far from the family, availing themselves of opportunities provided by the student and worker relocation programs. In meeting the challenges facing them, Nisei women drew not only upon the disciplined strength inculcated by their Issei parents but also upon firmly rooted support networks and the greater measure of self-reliance and independence that they developed during the crucible of the war years.

NOTES

1. Many of the Japanese community leaders arrested by the FBI before the evacuation were interned in special all-male camps in North Dakota, Louisiana, and New Mexico. Some Japanese Americans living outside the perimeter of the Western defense zone in Arizona, Utah, etc., were not interned.

2. Chieko Kimura, personal interview, Apr. 9, 1978, Glendale, Arizona.

3. Shizuko Horiuchi to Henriette Von Blon, Jan. 24, 1943, Henriette Von Blon Collection, Hoover Institution Archives ([hereafter] HIA).

4. Ayako Kanemura, personal interview, Mar. 10, 1978, Glendale, Arizona.

5. Anonymous, *Topaz Times*, Oct. 24, 1942, p. 3.

6. Lily Shoji, "Fem-a-lites," *The Mercedian*, Aug. 7, 1942, p. 4.

7. "Yuri," "Strictly Feminine," *The Daily Tulean Dispatch*, Sept. 29, 1942, p. 2.

8. From 1942 to the end of 1945 the Council allocated about $240,000 in scholarships, most of which were provided through the donations of the church and the World Student Service Fund. The average grant for student for was $156.73, which in that area was a major contribution towards the cost of higher education. Source: National Japanese American Student Relocation Council, Minutes of the Executive Committee Meeting, Philadelphia, Pennsylvania, Dec. 19, 1945.

9. Robert O'Brien, *The College Nisei* (Palo Alto: Pacific Books, 1949), pp. 73–74.

10. The disastrous consequences of the poorly conceived clearance procedure had been examined by Robert Wilson and Bill Hosokawa, *East to America: A History of the Japanese in the United States* (New York: Morrow, 1980), pp. 226–27, and Audrie Girdner and Anne Loftis, *The Great Betrayal: The Evacuation of the*

Japanese-Americans during World War II (New York: Macmillan, 1969), pp. 342–43.

11. May Nakamoto to Mrs. Jack Shoup, Nov. 20, 1943, Mrs. Jack Shoup Collection, HIA.

12. Toshiko Imada to Margaret Cosgrave Sowers, Jan. 16, 1943, Margaret Cosgrave Sowers Collection, HIA.

13. Ayako Kanemura, personal interview, Mar. 24, 1978, Glendale, Arizona.

14. Miné Okubo, *Citizen 13660* (New York: Columbia University Press, 1946), p. 66.

15. *Topaz Times*, Oct. 24, 2942, p. 3.

16. Masako Ono to Atsuko Ono, Sept. 28, 1942, Margaret Cosgrave Sowers Collection, HIA. Prior to the war, few Nisei had college experience: the 1940 census lists 674 second-generation women and 1,507 men who had attended or who were attending college.

17. Lillian Ota, "Campus Report," Trek (Feb. 1943), p. 33.

18. Ota, pp. 33–34.

19. O'Brien, p. 84.

20. Marii Kyogoku, *Resettlement Bulletin* (July 1943), p. 5.

21. Dorcas Asano to Josephine Duveneck, Jan. 22, 1944, Conard-Duveneck Collection, HIA.

22. Miné Okubo, *Miné Okubo: An American Experience*, exhibition catalogue (Oakland: Oakland Museum, 1972), p. 84.

23. Evelyn Nakano Glenn, "The Dialectics of Wage Work: Japanese American Women and Domestic Servants, 1905–1940," *Feminist Studies* 6, no. 3 (Fall 1980):412.

24. Advisory Committee of Evacuees, *Resettlement Bulletin* (July 1943), p. 4.

25. 1950 United States Census, Special Report.

26. Susan M. Hartmann, *The Home Front and Beyond, American Women in the 1940s* (Boston: Twayne Publishers, 1982), p. 126. There is some debate regarding the origins of the assessment of evacuee losses at $400 million. However, a recent study by the Commission on Wartime Relocation and Internment of Civilians has estimated that the Japanese Americans lost between $149 million and $370 million in 1945 dollars, and between $810 million and $2 billion in 1983 dollars. See the *San Francisco Chronicle*, June 16, 1983, p. 12.

RUTH MILKMAN
Gender at Work: The Sexual Division of Labor During World War II

As the nation, struggling with economic depression, began to fight its second world war in a single generation, unemployment lines quickly vanished. Manpower shortages meant that women would once again move into jobs in industry. They would experience new vocational opportunities; a lessening of discrimination based on marital status, age, and race; and public praise for their wartime contributions as workers. Using the techniques of advertising, the federal government publicized women's industrial work as patriotic support for the war by personifying the worker as "Rosie the Riveter." In short order, a catchy song circulated, written by Redd Evans and John Jacob Loeb:

All the day long, / Whether rain or shine, / She's a part of the assembly line.
She's making history, / Working for victory, / Rosie the Riveter

A witty Norman Rockwell painting for the cover of the popular magazine the *Saturday Evening Post* made it easy to visualize such a woman.*

*The cover appeared on May 29, 1943, several months after the song was published. A prizewinning documentary by Connie Field, *The Life and Times of Rosie the Riveter*, was made in 1980.

Excerpted from "Redefining 'Women's Work'" and "Demobilization and the Reconstruction of 'Woman's Place' in Industry," chs. 4 and 7 of *Gender at Work: The Dynamics of Job Segregation by Sex During World War II* by Ruth Milkman (Urbana: University of Illinois Press, 1987). Reprinted by permission of the author and the publisher. Notes have been renumbered and edited and figures omitted.

The potential provided by the war for refashioning gender roles was enormous, but the results were disappointing. The expectation was that once the men came home, women would happily exchange industrial tools for the broom and mop or new vacuum cleaner and the baby bottle. Polls showed that up to 85 percent of these women needed to continue working and expected that job seniority would entitle them to return after veterans had been absorbed in the work force.

The redefining of "men's jobs" and "women's jobs" precipitated by wartime mobilization and the rapid return to the prewar sexual division of labor is the subject of Ruth Milkman's study. Focusing especially on the auto and electronics industry, she provides unmistakable evidence of the persistence of occupational segregation at a time when the very survival of democracy was at stake. Note how job segregation demonstrates the double meaning of Milkman's title *Gender at Work*. What was the rationale for segregating jobs by sex? What evidence does Milkman provide to suggest that the designation of jobs as "male" or "female" was often arbitrary? Given management's assessment of women's job performance during the war, how does she explain the reversion to old patterns? What factors were involved? What explanation is offered for the fact that black men were able to hold on to wartime gains in industry whereas white and black women were not?

If it is true that occupational sex typing becomes even more important when women's labor force participation increases, what trends do you foresee for the postwar decades given the changes in the pattern of women's labor force participation noted by Milkman for the 1940s? How does job segregation help to explain the fact that women have yet to close the earnings gap with men when both are full-time workers (see this volume's introduction, p. 6)?

Conversion to war production involved redefinition of the entire employment structure. Some civilian automobile production jobs were also necessary for the production of tanks, aircraft, engines and ordnance; other war jobs were completely new. The changeover to war production in electrical manufacturing was less dramatic, but also involved shifts in the character and distribution of jobs. Thus, many of the war jobs that had to be filled (in both industries) were not clearly labeled as "women's" or "men's" work, at least at first. . . .

While the government had actively pressured some firms to hire women, it made no effort whatsoever to influence their placement within industry once management complied. The U.S. Employment Service routinely filled employer job openings that called for specific numbers of women and men. Although ceilings were imposed on the number of men who could be allocated to each plant, employers had a free hand in placing women and men in particular jobs within this constraint.[1] Although the unions sometimes contested the sexual division of labor after the fact, the initial job assignments were left entirely to management.

Women were not evenly distributed through the various jobs available in the war plants, but were hired into specific classifications that management deemed "suitable" for women and were excluded from other jobs. Some employers conducted special surveys to determine the sexual division of labor in a plant; probably more often such decisions were made informally by individual supervisors.[2] Although data on the distribution of women through job classifications in the wartime auto and electrical industries are sketchy, there is no mistaking the persistence of segregation by sex. A 1943 survey of the auto industry's Detroit plants, for example, found more than one-half of the women workers clustered in only five of seventy-two job classifications. Only 11 percent of the men were employed in these five occupations.[3]

Jobs were also highly segregated in the electrical industry during the war. A 1942 study of electrical appliance plants (most of which had already been converted to military

Frances Green, Peg Kirchner, Ann Waldner, and Blanche Osborne emerging from their four-engine, B-17 Flying Fortress.

See the painted lettering on the plane's nose for the name given it by these pilots, following a long-standing military tradition. They were among the 1,074 Women's Airforce Service Pilots (WASPs) who flew noncombat missions during World War II. Although 38 died in the line of duty, WASPs were not eligible for military insurance or GI benefits. At the end of the war, the WASPs were disbanded. Not until 1978 were the survivors offered veteran's status. In 2009, when barely 300 of the original 1,000 WASPs were still alive, the WASPs were awarded a Congressional Gold Medal. (Courtesy of the U.S. Army Museum.)

production when surveyed) found women, who were 30 percent of the workers, in only twenty-one job classifications, whereas men were spread across seventy-two of them. Nearly half of the women (47 percent) were employed in a single job category, and 68 percent were clustered in four occupations. Only 16 percent of the men were in these four job classifications.[4] . . .

Job segregation by sex was explicitly acknowledged in many war plants: Jobs were formally labeled "male" and "female." The two largest electrical firms, GE and Westinghouse, continued this practice until the end of the war. And in 45 percent of the auto plants with sexually mixed work forces responding to a survey conducted in mid-1944 by the UAW Women's Bureau, jobs were formally categorized as "male" or "female."[5] Available records suggest that sex segregation also existed elsewhere, even if it was not formally acknowledged. . . .

Segregation appears to be a constant across both industries during the war years.

However, in both industries there was considerable plant-to-plant variation in patterns of employment by sex. In the Detroit area, for example, there was a wide range in the proportion of women employed, even among plants manufacturing the same products. In April 1943, women were 29 percent of the workers at the GM Cadillac plant, which was producing engine parts, but women made up 59 percent of the work force at the Excello Corporation's Detroit plant, which made the same product. Similarly, although women were only 2 percent of the workers at Continental Motors, they were 27 percent of those at the Jefferson Avenue plant of the Hudson Motor Car Company. Both plants made aircraft motors.[6] In the electrical industry, too, there was considerable variation of this sort, even among plants owned by the same company and producing similar goods. . . .

Whatever the sexual division of labor happened to be at a given point in time, management always seemed to insist that there was no alternative. When a War Department representative visited an airplane plant where large numbers of women were employed, he was told that the best welder in the plant was a woman. "Their supervisors told me that their work is fine, even better than that of the men who were formerly on those jobs," he reported. "In another plant in the same area, I remarked on the absence of women and was told that women just can't do those jobs—the very same jobs. It is true, they can't do that type of work—as long as the employer refuses to hire and train them."[7]

Although the specifics varied, everywhere management was quick to offer a rationale for the concentration of women in some jobs and their exclusion from others. . . . "Womanpower differs from manpower as oil fuel differs from coal," proclaimed the trade journal *Automotive War Production* in October 1943, "and an understanding of the characteristics of the energy involved was needed for obtaining best results." Although it was now applied to a larger and quite different set of jobs, the basic characterization of women's abilities and limitations was familiar. As *Automotive War Production* put it:

On certain kinds of operations—the very ones requiring high manipulative skill—women were found to be a whole lot quicker and more efficient than men. Engineering womanpower means realizing fully that women are not only different from men in such things as lifting power and arm reach—but in many other ways that pertain to their physiological and their social functions. To understand these things does not mean to exclude women from *the jobs for which they are peculiarly adapted,* and where they can help to win this war. It merely means using them as women, and not as men.[8]

The idiom of women's war work in the electrical industry closely paralleled that in auto. "Nearly every Westinghouse plant employs women, especially for jobs that require dexterity with tiny parts," reported an article in *Factory Management and Maintenance* in March 1942. "At the East Pittsburgh plant, for instance, women tape coils. The thickness of each coil must be identical to within close limits, so the job requires feminine patience and deft fingers. Another job that calls for unlimited patience is the inspection of moving parts of electric instruments. . . . " Repeatedly stressed, especially in auto, was the lesser physical strength of the average woman worker. "Woman isn't just a 'smaller man,'" *Automotive War Production* pointed out. "Compensations in production processes must be made to allow for the fact that the average woman is only 35 percent muscle in comparison to the average man's 41 percent. Moreover, industrial studies have shown that only 54 percent of woman's weight is strength, as against man's 87 percent, and that the hand squeeze of the average woman exerts only 48 pounds of pressure, against man's 81 pounds."[9]

Accompanying the characterization of women's work as "light" was an emphasis on cleanliness. "Women can satisfactorily fill all or most jobs performed by men, subject only to the limitations of strength and physical requirements," a meeting of the National Association of Manufacturers concluded in March 1942. "However . . . jobs of a particularly 'dirty' character, jobs that subject women to heat process or are of a 'wet' nature should not be filled by women . . . despite the fact that women could, if required, perform them."[10]

The emphasis in the idiom of sex-typing on the physical limitations of women workers had a dual character. It not only justified the sexual divison of labor, but it also served as the basis for increased mechanization and work simplification. "To adjust women's jobs to such [physical] differences, automotive plants have added more mechanical aids such as conveyors, chain hoists, and load lifters," reported *Automotive War Production*. A study by Constance

Green found job dilution of this sort widespread in electrical firms and other war industries in the Connecticut Valley as well. "Where ten men had done ten complete jobs, now . . . eight women and two, three, or possibly four men together would do the ten split-up jobs," she noted. "Most often men set up machines, ground or adjusted tools, and generally 'serviced' the women who acted exclusively as machine operators."[11]

Although production technology was already quite advanced in both auto and electrical manufacturing, the pace of development accelerated during the war period. Management attributed this to its desire to make jobs easier for women, but the labor shortage and the opportunity to introduce new technology at government expense under war contracts were at least as important. However, the idiom that constructed women as "delicate" and, although poorly suited to "heavy" work, amenable to monotonous jobs, was now marshaled to justify the use of new technology and work "simplification." At Vultee Aircraft, for example, a manager explained:

> It definitely was in Vultee's favor that the hiring of women was started when production jobs were being simplified to meet the needs of fast, quantity production. . . . Special jigs were added to hold small tools, such as drills, so that women could concentrate on employing more effectively their proven capacity for repetitive operations requiring high digital dexterity.
>
> Unlike the man whom she replaced, she as a woman, had the capacity to withstand the monotony of even more simplified repetitive operations. To have suspended the air wrench from a counterbalanced support for him would have served merely to heighten his boredom with the job. As for the woman who replaced him, she now handles two such counterbalanced, air-driven wrenches, one in each hand.[12] . . .

There was a contradiction in the management literature on women's war work. It simultaneously stressed the fact that "women are being trained in skills that were considered exclusively in man's domain" and their special suitability for "delicate war jobs."[13] These two seemingly conflicting kinds of statements were reconciled through analogies between "women's work" at home and in the war plants. "Note the similarity between squeezing orange juice and the operation of a small drill press," the Sperry Gyroscope Company urged in a recruitment pamphlet. "Anyone can peel potatoes," it

went on. "Burring and filing are almost as easy." An automotive industry publication praised women workers at the Ford Motor Company's Willow Run bomber plant in similar terms. "The ladies have shown they can operate drill presses as well as egg beaters," it proclaimed. "Why should men, who from childhood on never so much as sewed on buttons," inquired one' manager, "be expected to handle delicate instruments better than women who have plied embroidery needles, knitting needles and darning needles all their lives?"[14] The newsreel *Glamour Girls of '43* pursued the same theme: "Instead of cutting the lines of a dress, this woman cuts the pattern of aircraft parts. Instead of baking cake, this woman is cooking gears to reduce the tension in the gears after use. . . . "[15] In this manner, virtually any job could be labeled "women's work."

Glamour was a related theme in the idiom through which women's war work was demarcated as female. As if calculated to assure women—and men—that war work need not involve a loss of femininity, depictions of women's new work roles were overlaid with allusions to their stylish dress and attractive appearance. "A pretty young inspector in blue slacks pushes a gauge—a cylindrical plug with a diamond-pointed push-button on its side—through the shaft's hollow chamber," was a typical rendition.[16] Such statements, like the housework analogies, effectively reconciled woman's position in what were previously "men's jobs" with traditional images of femininity.

Ultimately, what lay behind the mixed message that war jobs were at once "men's" and "women's" jobs was an unambiguous point: Women *could* do "men's work," but they were only expected to do it temporarily. The ideological definition of women's war work explicitly included the provision that they would gracefully withdraw from their "men's jobs" when the war ended and the rightful owners returned. Women, as everyone knew, were in heavy industry "for the duration." This theme would become much more prominent after the war, but it was a constant undercurrent from the outset.

Before the war, too, women had been stereotyped as temporary workers, and occupational sex-typing had helped to ensure that employed women would continue to view themselves as women first, workers second. Now this took on new importance, because the reserves of "womanpower" war industries drew on included married women, even mothers of young children, in unprecedented numbers. A study by the Automotive Council for War Production noted that of twelve thousand women employed during the war by one large automotive firm in Detroit, 68 percent were married, and 40 percent had children. And a 1943 WPB study found that 40 percent of one hundred fifty thousand women war workers employed in Detroit were mothers. "With the existing prejudice against employing women over forty, the overwhelming majority of these women workers are young mothers with children under 16."[17]

This was the group of women least likely to have been employed in the prewar years. "In this time of pressure for added labor supply," the U.S. Women's Bureau reported, "the married women for the first time in this country's history exceeded single women in the employed group."[18] . . .

Some firms made deliberate efforts to recruit the wives and daughters of men whom they had employed before the war. A 1942 study by Princeton University's Industrial Relations Section reported on the reasons given by employers for this policy: "(1) It increases the local labor supply without affecting housing requirements; (2) it brings in new employees who are already acquainted with the company and who are likely to be as satisfactory employees as their male relatives; and (3) it may help to minimize postwar readjustment since wives of employed men are not looking for permanent employment."[19] Similarly, the Detroit Vickers aircraft plant had a policy of hiring "members of men's families who have gone to forces so that when these men come back there will be less of a problem in getting the women out of the jobs to give them back to the men."[20]

The dramatic rise in married women's employment during the war raised the longstanding tension between women's commitment to marriage and family and their status as individual members of the paid work force to a qualitatively different level. Before the war, the bulk of the female labor force was comprised of unmarried women; young wives with no children; and self-supporting widowed, divorced, and separated women. When married women and mothers went to work during the war, the occupational sex-typing that linked women's roles in the family and in paid work, far from disintegrating, was infused with new energy. . . .

DEMOBILIZATION AND THE RECONSTRUCTION OF "WOMAN'S PLACE" IN INDUSTRY

The war's end generated renewed upheaval in the sexual division of labor. As reconversion brought massive layoffs and then new hiring, the issue of women's position in industry came to the fore. . . . Would there be a return to the "traditional," prewar sexual division of labor as the mobilization-era ideology of "woman's place" in the war effort had promised? Or would the successful wartime deployment of women in "men's jobs" lead to a permanent shift in the boundaries between women's and men's jobs? Or—a third alternative—would completely new, postwar exigencies reshape, or even eliminate, the sexual division of labor?

Reversion to prewar patterns, which ultimately did occur, might appear to have been the only real possibility. Had not the nation been repeatedly assured that women's entrance into industry was a temporary adaptation to the extraordinary needs of war? . . . Such a view is consistent with the prevailing ideology of the demobilization period, but it obscures the significance of the war years themselves. Wartime conditions were indeed transitory, yet the extraordinary period between Pearl Harbor and V-J Day left American society permanently transformed. One legacy of the war years, from which no retreat would be possible, was the increase in female labor force participation. On an individual basis, to be sure, many women faced conflicting pressures after the war—to continue working for pay on the one hand, and to go back to the home on the other. Yet a permanent shift had occurred for women as a social group. Despite the postwar resurgence of the ideology of domesticity, by the early 1950s the number of gainfully employed women exceeded the highest wartime level. And as early as 1948, the labor force participation rate of married women was higher than in 1944, the peak of the war boom. The rise in female employment, especially for married women, would continue throughout the postwar period, and at a far more rapid rate than in the first half of the century. In this respect, far from being a temporary deviation, the war was a watershed period that left women's relationship to work permanently changed.[21]

The crucial issue, then, was not whether women would remain in the work force, but rather which women would do so and on what terms. What would the postwar sexual division of paid labor look like? Would women retain their wartime foothold in basic industries like auto and electrical manufacturing? To what extent would they be able to find work in fields that had been predominantly male before the war? For women who worked for pay, whether by choice or necessity, exclusion from "men's jobs" did not mean the housewifery first celebrated and later decried as the "feminine mystique." Instead, it meant employment in low-wage "female" jobs, especially clerical, sales, and service work—all of which expanded enormously in the postwar decades.

That the war brought a permanent increase in female employment made the demobilization transition particularly consequential. The opportunity was there for incorporating the dramatic wartime changes in women's position in industry into the fabric of a postwar order in which paid work would become increasingly central to women's lives. In the absence of any events affecting the labor market as fundamentally and cataclysmically as the war, there has been no comparable occasion for a wholesale restructuring of the sexual division of labor since the 1940s. The fact that the opportunity the wartime upheaval presented was lost had enormous implications for the entire postwar era.

Why, then, was the potential for an enduring transformation in the sexual division of labor not fulfilled in the 1940s? There are two standard explanations. One focuses on the postwar resurgence of domesticity, both as a practice and as an ideology, and suggests that women war workers themselves relinquished the "men's jobs" they held during the war—either because of the genuine appeal of traditional family commitments or because they were ideologically manipulated. The second explanation, in contrast, suggests that the key problem was the operation of union-instituted seniority systems, and their manipulation by male unionists, to exclude women and to favor returning male veterans in postwar employment.

. . . [B]oth these accounts of the postwar transition, while partially correct, are inadequate. . . . A large body of evidence demonstrates that management took the lead both in purging women from "men's jobs" after the war and in refusing to rehire them (except in traditionally "female" jobs) as postwar production resumed. Management chose this course despite the fact that most women war workers wanted to keep doing "men's work," and despite the fact that refusing to rehire women often violated seniority provisions in union contracts. . . .

I will offer a two-part explanation for management's postwar policy. First, in both auto and electrical manufacturing, the "traditional" sexual division of labor had a historical logic embodied in the structure of each industry, which remained compelling in the demobilization period. At one level, indeed, reconstructing the prewar sexual division of labor was a foregone conclusion from management's perspective. Wartime female substitution was an experiment that employers had undertaken unwillingly and only because there was no alternative. Despite the success with which women were integrated into "men's jobs," the war's end meant an end to the experiment, and management breathed a collective sigh of relief.

But that is only half of the story. The postwar purge of women from men's jobs also reflected management's assessment of labor's position on the issue. For one thing, the CIO's wartime struggles for equal pay for women workers, which narrowed sex differentials in wages considerably, made permanent female substitution less appealing than it might otherwise have been. Moreover, in the reconversion period, male workers displayed a great deal of ambivalence about the postwar employment rights of women war workers, even those with seniority standing. The CIO's official policy was to defend women's job rights in line with the seniority principle, but in practice there was substantial opposition to retaining women in "men's jobs." This, I will suggest, effectively reinforced management's determination to reconstruct the prewar sexual division of labor. . . .

MANAGERIAL POLICY TOWARD WOMEN WORKERS DURING THE WAR—AND AFTER

. . . Why was management so determined to oust women from the positions that they had occupied during the war? Women war workers wanted to keep their jobs, and union seniority policies did not stand in the way of hiring women, yet they were purged. The problem is all the more puzzling in light of contemporary evidence that management was highly satisfied with women war workers' abilities and performance. While initially employers had strenuously resisted replacing men with women in war industries, once having reconciled themselves to the inevitable, they seemed very pleased with the results. Moreover, because sex differentials in wages, although smaller than before, persisted during the war, one might expect management to have seriously considered the possibility of permanent female substitution on economic grounds.

There is no doubt that women's wartime performance proved satisfactory to management. Under the impact of the "manpower" crunch in the seven months following Pearl Harbor, the proportion of jobs for which the nation's employers were willing to consider women rose from 29 to 55 percent. And management praised women's industrial performance extravagantly during the mobilization period. "Women keep piling up evidence that they *can do*, and *do well*, a multitude of jobs," proclaimed the American Management Association in a 1943 report. "The distribution of basic aptitudes between the two sexes does not differ to any appreciable extent. . . . What is needed is *training*—training to develop latent aptitudes, to increase mechanical knowledge and skill, and to overcome any fear of the machine."[22] . . .

. . . In a 1943 National Industrial Conference Board survey of 146 executives, nearly 60 percent stated without qualification that women's production was equal to or greater than that of men on similar work. Similarly, a study by the Bureau of Employment Security of several California war plants found an increase in production per hour of workers of both sexes, and a lowering of costs per hour when women were employed, in every plant studied. The BES study also found that women were easier to supervise, and that labor turnover and accident rates decreased with the introduction of women.[23]

Many traditional management policies toward women workers were revised or eliminated with their successful incorporation into war industry. For example, physical segregation of the sexes was no longer deemed necessary; the belief "that men and women could work satisfactorily side by side" was held by the majority of executives questioned by the magazine *Modern Industry* as early as mid-1942. There were also many efforts to promote women to supervisory posts, especially at the lower levels, although women were almost never given authority over male workers, and there was a lingering conviction that women workers themselves preferred male bosses.[24]

Women workers' wartime performance, then, stood as evidence that they could be successfully incorporated into the industrial labor force. In addition, wage differentials between the sexes persisted during the war years—a consideration that one might expect to have enhanced management's interest in retaining women permanently in the postwar era. The unions, to be sure, had successfully contested sex discrimination in wages in many "equal pay for equal work" cases before the War Labor Board. But although sex differentials were narrowed as a result of these struggles, they were not eliminated. The Conference Board's composite earnings index for twenty-five manufacturing industries registered only a modest increase in the ratio of female to male average hourly earnings, from 61.5 percent in 1941 to 66.4 percent in 1945.[25] . . .

Still, because men and women rarely did "equal work" even during the war, the outcome of successful WLB equal pay cases was to narrow sex differentials in wages, not to eliminate them. And the Board's equal pay policy was not fully enforced, so that even when jobs were identical, or nearly so, women were often paid less than men. The Conference Board found differentials in starting rates paid to men and to "women hired for men's jobs" in nearly half the 148 plants that it surveyed in 1943, well after equal pay "for comparable quality and quantity of work" had become official WLB policy. Of the ninety-two plants in the survey that had systems of automatic progression in wage rates, twenty-five had sex differentials built into the progression systems despite the fact that the WLB had declared this practice improper.[26]

Similarly, a study of women's wages by the New York State Department of Labor found that 40 percent of the 143 plants surveyed had different starting rates for men and women on "men's jobs." When the state's investigators asked employers to account for such differences, most simply referred to "tradition," standard practice, prevailing wage rates, and custom. "It's also cheaper," said one manager.[27] . . .

There were some extra costs associated with the employment of women, to be sure, particularly in previously all-male plants. Women's absenteeism was generally higher than men's, especially if they were married and had domestic responsibilities, although employers succeeded in narrowing or even eliminating the gap in some plants.[28] UAW

President R. J. Thomas, summarizing the reasons auto industry employers were reluctant to hire women for postwar jobs, noted other costs associated with expanding or introducing female employment in a plant. "First is that as you know on most jobs equal rates are paid for equal jobs today," he pointed out. "Management doesn't want to pay women equal rates with men. Not only that but in many of these plants additional facilities have to be put in, such as toilet facilities to take care of women. More space has to be taken to give an opportunity of changing clothes and more safety measures have to be instituted. I think it is pretty well recognized that it is an additional expense to a management to have women."[29]

This is an accurate rendition of the reasons auto industry managers themselves adduced for their reluctance to employ women. Yet it is an inadequate explanation for managerial hostility toward female employment. The costs of maintaining special "facilities" for women were largely absorbed by the government during the war, and could hardly have been a major financial consideration in any event. Surely the savings associated with sex differentials in pay would outweigh any expense firms would incur in continuing to maintain such facilities. Indeed, if only the direct economic costs and benefits of female employment are taken into account, one would expect management to have consistently discriminated *in favor of* women and against men in postwar layoffs and rehiring. Particularly in view of the vigorous efforts of employers to increase labor productivity in the reconversion period, management should have preferred to retain women permanently in the "men's jobs" they had just demonstrated their ability to perform.[30]

Industrial employers chose the opposite course, however, defying not only the apparent imperatives of economic rationality, but also the stated preference of women war workers to keep their war jobs and the unions' official policy that layoffs and rehiring be done strictly by seniority. Rather than institutionalizing the wartime incorporation of women into male jobs, management returned to its prewar practices. . . .

THE ROOTS OF MANAGEMENT'S POSTWAR POLICY

In retrospect, then, management's determination to restore the status quo ante seems altogether irrational. Yet from the perspective of employers themselves at the time, it was a foregone conclusion. Management viewed the successful performance of women war workers as, at best, the fortunate outcome of an experiment in which it had participated with great trepidation and only because there was no alternative. To be sure, women had proved better workers than anyone had expected during the war. But now men's jobs were men's jobs once more. The ideology of sex-typing emerged triumphant again, defining the postwar order along prewar lines in both auto and electrical manufacturing.

In part, the explanation for management's postwar policy involves the logic of the sexual division of labor as it had first developed within the auto and electrical industries a half-century earlier. Not only did the traditions of sex-typing established then have a continuing influence in the post–World War II period, but the factors that had originally shaped those traditions remained salient. In auto, wage levels were still high relative to other industries and would continue to increase in the postwar decades. As in the prewar years, automotive management's efforts to boost productivity focused on tightening control over labor, not on reducing pay levels.[31] Under these conditions, female substitution had little to recommend it, and employers continued to indulge the conviction . . . that women simply were not suitable for employment in automotive production jobs.

In electrical manufacturing, too, prewar traditions of sex-typing persisted in the postwar [era]. But in this industry, the prewar sexual division of labor was historically rooted in a logic of feminization linked to labor-intensity and piecework systems. So why should the further extension of feminization during the war have been rolled back? Even in the case of the automobile industry, why was there a permanent departure from prewar tradition in regard to black employment while the sexual division of jobs persisted virtually unaltered? The historical, industry-specific logic of sex-typing seems to constitute only a partial explanation for management's postwar determination to reconstruct the prewar order.

It is tempting to look outside of the industrial setting to the arena of family and social reproduction in seeking a better solution to the conundrum of management's postwar policies. The interest of capital in reconstructing a family structure in which women are responsible for the generational and daily reproduction of the working class, one might argue, ruled out the permanent employment of women in the well-paid manufacturing jobs that they had during the war. In this view, if women—and more significantly, married women—were to be employed outside the home in ever-increasing numbers in the postwar era, it was crucial that they be confined to poorly paid, secondary jobs that would not jeopardize their primary allegiance to family.

The difficulty with this line of argument is in specifying how the presumed interest of collective capital in reconstituting traditional family forms was translated into the actual employer policies with respect to women workers that emerged in this period. The historical record offers no evidence that such familial considerations played a role in shaping managerial policy in the postwar transition.[32] Although the idea that "woman's place is in the home" was pervasive in the postwar period, it was seldom invoked by employers as a justification for restoring the prewar sexual division of jobs. Instead, management tended to define the issue in economic terms and, above all, by reference to women's physical characteristics and supposed inability to perform "men's jobs."

Although it would be extremely difficult to demonstrate that management policy was rooted in conscious concern over social reproduction, there is evidence for a different kind of explanation: that the postwar purge of women from "men's jobs" involved employers' assessment of the implications of their policies toward women for labor relations. The wartime struggles over equal pay indicated that the unions were committed to resisting any effort to substitute women for men in order to take advantage of their historically lower wages. If wage savings could not be garnered from substitution, or if they could only be garnered at substantial political cost, then why attempt to preserve the wartime sexual division of jobs after the war? In addition, given the widespread fear of postwar unemployment, management might reasonably have anticipated that unemployed male workers would be a source of potential political instability, given the working-class cultural ideal of the "family wage" and the obvious ambivalence of male unionists about women's postwar employment rights.

In short, management had good reason to believe that a wholesale postwar reorganization of the sexual division of labor, in defiance of the wartime assurances that women were in "men's jobs" only for the duration, could precipitate widespread resistance from labor. The unions were at the peak of their strength at this time, and at the war's end they were no longer constrained by the no-strike pledge. As one contemporary analyst noted, consideration of labor's reaction figured prominently in employers' postwar policies:

> Employers in plants where women had long been assigned to some jobs were disposed favorably to widening the fields of work open to women, unless the job dilutions had proved complicated and costly. In fact, union men declared that some companies, unless prevented by organized labor, would try to continue to use women on men's work because they could be hired at lower initial base pay, be upgraded more slowly, and would be throughout more docile. With the installation of mechanical aids, which using women had necessitated, already paid for out of war profits, management had frequently no particular reason to oppose keeping women on. . . . Yet most companies frankly admitted that, given full freedom of choice after the war, if only out of deference to prevailing male opinion in the shops, management would revert to giving men's jobs, so called, only to men. *And employers generally assumed that labor would permit no choice.*[33]

Understanding management's postwar policy in these terms helps explain why, in the auto case, women and blacks were treated differently. Despite their common history of exclusion from most auto jobs in the prewar era, the two groups stood in very different positions at the war's end. Organized feminism was at its nadir in the 1940s, and the labor movement's commitment to sexual equality was limited, so that management had little reason to fear that purging women from the industry would meet with substantial political opposition. In contrast, at least in the North, there was a large and vital black civil rights movement, which enjoyed substantial UAW support and from which management could expect vigorous protests if it pursued racially discriminatory employment policies.[34]

Only a few years earlier, when blacks were first hired in large numbers in Detroit's auto factories during the war mobilization, white workers had been vocal in their opposition, most notably in the numerous hate strikes which erupted in the plants and in the race riot of the summer of 1943.[35] But during the war, Detroit became a stronghold of the civil rights movement. The Motor City had the largest branch of the National Association for the Advancement of Colored People (NAACP) of any city in the nation, with a membership of twenty thousand by 1943, and the UAW had become a strong ally of the NAACP and other civil rights groups. While racial discrimination persisted in the auto industry in regard to promotion to the elite skilled trades, no one contested blacks' claims to semi-skilled jobs in the aftermath of the war.[36]

The sharp regional variation in racial patterns of hiring within the auto industry suggests the critical importance of the political dimension in shaping management's employment policies. Although the proportion of blacks in Detroit's auto plants rose dramatically in the 1940s and 1950s, reaching well over 25 percent of the production work force by 1960, in the nation as a whole the percentage of nonwhite auto workers grew much more modestly, from 4 percent in 1940 to only 9 percent in 1960. The national figures reflect the continuing practice of excluding blacks from employment in southern plants. As a manager at a GM plant in Atlanta told the *Wall Street Journal* in 1957, "When we moved into the South, we agreed to abide by local custom and not hire Negroes for production work. This is no time for social reforming and we're not about to try it."[37]

The situation of women auto workers was entirely different from that of northern blacks. Although the incorporation of women into the industry during the war had not provoked riots or hate strikes, this was primarily because female employment was explicitly understood to be a temporary expedient, "for the duration" only. After the war, women were expected to go "back to the home." There was no parallel expectation regarding black men. And while women war workers wanted to remain in the auto industry, as we have seen, their preferences (unlike blacks') lacked legitimacy. While black workers had the civil rights movement behind them, there was no mass feminist movement or even popular consciousness of women's job rights at this critical juncture, when the sexual division of labor that would characterize the postwar period was crystallizing. . . .

NOTES

1. U.S. Senate Hearings, *Manpower Problems in Detroit*, 79th Cong. 1st sess., pp. 9–13 (Mar. 1945), pp. 13534, 13638; interview with Edward Cushman.

2. Reference to such a survey made "to determine those operations which were suitable for female operators" is made on pp. 2–3 of the Summary Brief Submitted by Buick Motor Division, Melrose Park, General Motors Corporation, "In the Matter of GMC–Buick, Melrose Park, Ill., and UAW-CIO," 14 June 1943, Walter Reuther Collection, WSU Archives, box 20, folder: "WLB, GM Women's Rates." A survey of this type was also conducted at the Ford Willow Run plant; see the section on "Training of Women" in *Willow Run Bomber Plant, Record of War Effort* (notebook), vol. 2, pt. 2, Jan.–Dec. 1942, p. 30, La Croix Collection, Accession 435, Ford Archives, Dearborn, Michigan, box 15.

3. Computed from data in U.S. Department of Labor, Bureau of Labor Statistics, Division of Wage Analysis, Regional Office no. 8-A, Detroit, Michigan, Dec. 3, 1943, serial no. 8-A-16 (mimeo), "Metalworking Establishments, Detroit, Michigan, Labor Market Area, Straight-Time Average Hourly Earnings, Selected Occupations, July, 1943." UAW Research Department Collection, WSU Archives, box 28, folder: "Wage Rates (Detroit) Bureau of Labor Statistics, 1943–45." . . .

4. Computed from data in "Earnings in Manufacture of Electrical Appliances, 1942," p. 532.

5. Regarding GE and Westinghouse, see U.S. National War Labor Board, *War Labor Reports*, vol. 28, pp. 677–78. . . .

6. See "Summary Employment Status Report for Michigan," Apr. 30, 1943, Records of the U.S. Employment Service, National Archives, Record Group 183, box 181, folder: "Michigan Statewide."

7. Press release of Office of Production Management, Labor Division, Dec. 5, 1941, UAW Research Department Collection, WSU Archives, box 32, folder: "Women Employment 1941."

8. "Engineers of Womanpower," *Automotive War Production* 2 (Oct. 1943):4–5 (emphasis added). . . .

9. "What Women Are Doing in Industry," *Factory Management and Maintenance* 100 (March 1942):63; "Provisions in Plants for Physical Differences Enable Women to Handle Variety of War Jobs," *Automotive War Production* 2 (Sept. 1943):7.

10. "Report of Two Special Meetings on Employing and Training Women for War Jobs," attended by executives from 85 N.A.M. companies from the East and Midwest, Mar. 27 and 30, 1942, in Records of the Automotive Council for War Production, Detroit Public Library, folder: "Manpower: Source Material: New Workers," p. 1.

11. "Provisions in Plants"; Constance Green, "The Role of Women as Production Workers in War Plants in the Connecticut Valley," *Smith College Studies in History* 28 (1946):32. . . .

12. W. Gerald Tuttle, "Women War Workers at Vultee Aircraft," *Personnel Journal* 21 (Sept. 1942):8–9.

13. "Women Work for Victory," *Automotive War Production* 1 (Nov. 1942):4; "Engineers of Womanpower," p. 4.

14. "There's a Job for You at Sperry . . . Today" (pamphlet), Records of UE District 4, UE Archives, University of Pittsburgh folder 877; "Hiring and Training Women for War Work," *Factory Management and Maintenance* 100 (Aug. 1942):73; "Engineers of Womanpower," p. 4.

15. The transcript of this newsreel was made available to me by the Rosie the Riveter Film Project, Emeryville, California.

16. "Engineers of Womanpower," p. 4.

17. "New Workers," *Manpower Reports* 10 (published by the Manpower Division of the Automotive Council for War Production), p. 4; Anne Gould, "Problems of Woman War Workers in Detroit," Aug. 20, 1943, Records of the War Production Board, National Archives, RG 179, box 203, folder: "035.606 Service Trades Divisions, WPB Functions," p. 2.

18. U.S. Department of Labor, Women's Bureau, Special Bulletin no. 20, *Changes in Women's Employment During the War* (1944), p. 18.

19. Helen Baker, *Women in War Industries* (Princeton: Princeton University Press, 1942), p. 15.

20. "Report of Mrs. Betty Sturges Finan on Cleveland Detroit Trip, Feb. 9–17 [1943] inclusive," pp. 3–4, Records of the War Manpower Commission, National Archives, Record Group 211, Series 137, box 977, folder. "Consultants—Betty Sturges Finan." See also "Report of Two Special Meetings," p. 6.

21. See U.S. Bureau of the Census, *Historical Statistics of the U.S.: Colonial Times to 1970* (1975), pp. 131, 133. This claim is considerably more modest than William Chafe's controversial thesis that the wartime changes in female labor force participation make the 1940s a key "turning point in the history of American women." See William H. Chafe, *The American Woman: Her Changing Social, Economic, and Political Role, 1920–1970* (New York: Oxford University Press, 1972), p. 195. . . .

22. Chafe, *The American Woman*, p. 137; American Management Association, Special Research Report no. 2, *Supervision of Women on Production Jobs: A Study of Management's Problems and Practices in Handling Female Personnel* (1943), pp. 8–10 (emphasis in the original).

23. National Industrial Conference Board, "Wartime Pay of Women in Industry," *Studies in Personnel Policy*, no. 58 (1943):27; "Woman's Place," *Business Week* (May 16, 1942):20–22. . . .

24. *Modern Industry*, July 15, 1942, summarized in *Management Review* 31 (Sept. 1942):303–4. Regarding the use of women as supervisors, see *Supervision of Women on Production Jobs*, pp. 24–27. . . .

25. Computed from data in *The Management Almanac 1946* (New York: National Industrial Conference Board, 1946), p. 77.

26. "Wartime Pay of Women in Industry," pp. 18–19. . . .

27. New York State Department of Labor, Division of Women in Industry, *Women's Wages on Men's Jobs* (1944), p. 26.

28. See New York State Department of Labor, Division of Women in Industry, *Absenteeism in New York State War Production Plants* (1943); National Industrial Conference Board, "The Problem of Absenteeism," *Studies in Personnel Policy*, no. 53 (1943); "Women Workers on War Production," *UAW Research Report* 3 (Mar. 1943):3. . . .

29. *Manpower Problems in Detroit*, pp. 13112–13.

30. See Howell John Harris, *The Right to Manage: Industrial Relations Policies of American Business in the 1940s* (Madison: University of Wisconsin Press, 1982), pp. 66–67, 91–93.

31. Ibid. This is Harris's main thesis.

32. Denise Riley, "The Free Mothers': Pronatalism and Working Women in Industry at the End of the Last War in Britain," *History Workshop* II (Spring 1981):59–118, presents the most convincing case for this argument in regard to the postwar transition for the British case, but she relies on evidence about state policy with virtually none directly from employers.

33. Green, "Role of Women as Production Workers," pp. 64–65 (emphasis added).

34. August Meier and Elliot Rudwick, *Black Detroit and the Rise of the U.A.W.* (New York: Oxford University Press, 1979).

35. Ibid.; Robert C. Weaver, *Negro Labor: A National Problem* (New York: Harcourt, Brace, and World, 1946).

36. Meier and Rudwick, *Black Detroit*, p. 113. See also Karen Anderson, "Last Hired, First Fired: Black Women Workers during World War II," *Journal of American History* 69 (June 1982), especially pp. 86–87, where white male workers' attitudes toward women and blacks are compared.

37. Both the employment figures and the quote are cited in Herbert R. Northrup, Richard L. Rowan, et al., *Negro Employment in Basic Industry*, Industrial Research Unit, Wharton School of Finance and Commerce, University of Pennsylvania (1970), pp. 65–75. The national employment figures are from the U.S. Census, and because (unlike the figures for Detroit) they include both production and nonproduction workers, they overstate the difference between Detroit and the nation as a whole, for the vast majority of nonproduction workers were white in this period. The quote is from the *Wall Street Journal*, Oct. 24, 1957.

V

A TRANSFORMING WORLD

1945–2014

COLD WAR HETERONORMATIVITY

SUSAN K. CAHN
"Mannishness," Lesbianism, and Homophobia in U.S. Women's Sports

In the 1950s some women who identified as lesbians organized to gain constitutional protection, but their efforts were blocked, especially in New York City, where the local chapter of the Daughters of Bilitis was discovered to have subsequently been infiltrated with informants who were supplying names to the FBI and CIA. (The group was founded in San Francisco in the mid-1950s to work for social and civil rights for lesbians.) In an era when sexual conformity was seen as essential to national security, it is hardly surprising that *all* women who engaged in any same-sex activity were suspect. (See Margot Canaday's essay in this volume on the impact of sexuality investigations on women's military careers in the 1950s, pp. 678–689). Women athletes were particularly vulnerable.

In the following essay, Susan K. Cahn explores the suspicions and the reality behind those suspicions in women's athletics. Note the persistence of concerns about feminine sexuality, whether heterosexual or homosexual, throughout the history of women's sports. What measures did colleges and universities take to protect women's sports from charges of lesbianism? What was the price of such actions? Since those athletes who were lesbian could not afford to proclaim their sexual identity publicly, why does Cahn argue that athletics nonetheless afforded them social and psychic space to affirm their identity and find community? Do you agree?

In 1934, *Literary Digest* subtitled an article on women's sports, "Will the Playing Fields One Day Be Ruled by Amazons?" The author, Fred Wittner, answered the question affirmatively and concluded that as an "inevitable consequence" of sport's masculinizing effect, "girls trained in physical education to-day may find it more difficult to attract the most worthy fathers for their children."[1] The image of women athletes as mannish, failed heterosexuals represents a thinly veiled reference to lesbianism in sport. At times, the homosexual allusion has been indisputable, as in a journalist's description of the great athlete Babe Didrikson as a "Sapphic, Brobdingnagian woman" or in television comedian Arsenio Hall's more recent witticism, "If we can put a man on the moon, why can't we get one on Martina Navratilova?"[2] More frequently, however, popular commentary on lesbians in sport has taken the form of indirect references, surfacing through denials and refutations rather than open acknowledgment. When in 1955 an *Ebony* magazine article on African American track stars insisted that "off track, girls are entirely feminine. Most of them like boys, dances, club affairs," the reporter answered the implicit but unspoken charge that athletes, especially Black

Excerpted from "From the 'Muscle Moll' to the 'Butch' Ballplayer: Mannishness, Lesbianism, and Homophobia in U.S. Women's Sports" by Susan K. Cahn, in *Feminist Studies* 19, no. 2 (Summer 1993): 343–68. Reprinted by permission of the author and publisher. Notes have been edited and renumbered.

women in a "manly" sport, were masculine manhaters, or lesbians.[3]

The figure of the mannish lesbian athlete has acted as a powerful but unarticulated "bogey woman" of sport, forming a silent foil for more positive, corrective images that attempt to rehabilitate the image of women athletes and resolve the cultural contradiction between athletic prowess and femininity. As a stereotyped figure in U.S. society, the lesbian athlete forms part of everyday cultural knowledge. Yet historians have paid scant attention to the connection between female sexuality and sport.[4] This essay explores the historical relationship between lesbianism and sport by tracing the development of the stereotyped "mannish lesbian athlete" and examining its relation to the lived experience of mid-twentieth-century lesbian athletes.

I argue that fears of mannish female sexuality in sport initially centered on the prospect of unbridled heterosexual desire. By the 1930s, however, female athletic mannishness began to connote heterosexual failure, usually couched in terms of unattractiveness to men, but also suggesting the possible absence of heterosexual interest. In the years following World War II, the stereotype of the lesbian athlete emerged full blown. The extreme homophobia and the gender conservatism of the postwar era created a context in which longstanding linkages among mannishness, female homosexuality, and athletics cohered around the figure of the mannish lesbian athlete. Paradoxically, the association between masculinity, lesbianism, and sport had a positive outcome for some women. The very cultural matrix that produced the pejorative image also created possibilities for lesbian affirmation. Sport provided social and psychic space for some lesbians to validate themselves and to build a collective culture. Thus, the lesbian athlete was not only a figure of discourse but a living product of women's sexual struggle and cultural innovation.

The athletic woman sparked interest and controversy in the early decades of the twentieth century. In the United States and other Western societies, sport functioned as a male preserve, an all-male domain in which men not only played games together but also demonstrated and affirmed their manhood.[5] The "maleness" of sport derived from a gender ideology which labeled aggression, physicality,

competitive spirit, and athletic skill as masculine attributes necessary for achieving true manliness. This notion found unquestioned support in the dualistic, polarized concepts of gender which prevailed in Victorian America. However, by the turn of the century, women had begun to challenge Victorian gender arrangements, breaking down barriers to female participation in previously male arenas of public work, politics, and urban nightlife. Some of these "New Women" sought entry into the world of athletics as well. On college campuses students enjoyed a wide range of intramural sports through newly formed Women's Athletic Associations. Off-campus women took up games like golf, tennis, basketball, swimming, and occasionally even wrestling, car racing, or boxing. As challengers to one of the defining arenas of manhood, skilled female athletes became symbols of the broader march of womanhood out of the Victorian domestic sphere into once prohibited male realms.

The woman athlete represented both the appealing and threatening aspects of modern womanhood. In a positive light, she captured the exuberant spirit, physical vigor, and brazenness of the New Woman. The University of Minnesota student newspaper proclaimed in 1904 that the athletic girl was the "truest type of All-American coed."[6] Several years later, *Harper's Bazaar* labeled the unsportive girl as "not strictly up to date," and *Good Housekeeping* noted that the "tomboy" had come to symbolize "a new type of American girl, new not only physically, but mentally and morally."[7]

Yet, women athletes invoked condemnation as often as praise. Critics ranged from physicians and physical educators to sportswriters, male athletic officials, and casual observers. In their view, strenuous athletic pursuits endangered women and threatened the stability of society. They maintained that women athletes would become manlike, adopting masculine dress, talk, and mannerisms. In addition, they contended, too much exercise would damage female reproductive capacity [interfering with menstruation and causing reproductive organs to harden or atrophy]. And worse yet, the excitement of sport would cause women to lose [sexual] control, . . . unleash[ing] nonprocreative, erotic desires identified with male sexuality and unrespectable women. . . . These fears collapsed into an all-encompassing concept of "mannishness," a term signifying female masculinity . . .

The public debate over the merits of women's athletic participation remained lively throughout the 1910s and 1920s. On all sides of the issue, however, the controversy about sports and female sexuality presumed heterosexuality. Neither critics nor supporters suggested that "masculine" athleticism might indicate or induce same-sex love. And when experts warned of the "amazonian" athlete's possible sexual transgressions, they linked the physical release of sport with a loss of hetero-sexual *control,* not of *inclination.*

In the 1930s, however, the heterosexual understanding of the mannish "amazon" began to give way to a new interpretation which educators and promoters could not long ignore. To the familiar charge that female athletes resembled men, critics added the newer accusation that sport-induced mannishness disqualified them as candidates for heterosexual romance. In 1930, an *American Mercury* medical reporter decried the decline of romantic love, pinning the blame on women who entered sport, business, and politics. He claimed that such women "act like men, talk like men, and think like men." The author explained that "women have come closer and closer to men's level," and, consequently, "the purple allure of distance has vamoosed."[8] . . . Although the charges didn't exclusively focus on athletes, they implied that female athleticism was contrary to heterosexual appeal, which appeared to rest on women's difference from and deference to men.

The concern with heterosexual appeal reflected broader sexual transformations in U.S. society. Historians of sexuality have examined the multiple forces which reshaped gender and sexual relations in the first few decades of the twentieth century. Victorian sexual codes crumbled under pressure from an assertive, boldly sexual working-class youth culture, a women's movement which defied prohibitions against public female activism, and the growth of a new pleasure-oriented consumer economy. In the wake of these changes, modern ideals of womanhood embraced an overtly erotic heterosexual sensibility. At the same time, medical fascination with sexual "deviance" created a growing awareness of lesbianism, now understood as a form of congenital or psychological pathology. The medicalization of homosexuality in combination with an antifeminist backlash in the 1920s against female autonomy and power contributed to a more fully articulated

taboo against lesbianism. The modern heterosexual woman stood in stark opposition to her threatening sexual counterpart, the "mannish" lesbian.[9]

By the late 1920s and early 1930s, with a modern lesbian taboo and an eroticized definition of heterosexual femininity in place, the assertive, muscular female competitor roused increasing suspicion. It was at this moment that both subtle and direct references to the lesbian athlete emerged in physical education and popular sport. Uncensored discussions of intimate female companionship and harmless athletic "crushes" disappear from the record, pushed underground by the increasingly hostile tone of public discourse about female sexuality and athleticism. Fueled by the gender antagonisms and anxieties of the Depression, the public began scrutinizing women athletes—known for their appropriation of masculine games and styles—for signs of deviance.

Where earlier references to "amazons" had signaled heterosexual ardor, journalists now used the term to mean unattractive, failed heterosexuals. Occasionally, the media made direct mention of athletes' presumed lesbian tendencies. A 1933 *Redbook* article, for example, casually mentioned that track and golf star Babe Didrikson liked men just to horse around with her and not "make love," adding that Babe's fondness for her best girlfriends far surpassed her affection for any man.[10] The direct reference was unusual; the lesbian connotation of mannishness was forged primarily through indirect links of association. . . .

Tentatively voiced in the 1930s, these accusations became harsher and more explicit under the impact of wartime changes in gender and sexuality and the subsequent panic over the "homosexual menace." In a post–World War II climate markedly hostile to nontraditional women and lesbians, women in physical education and in working-class popular sports became convenient targets of homophobic indictment.

World War II opened up significant economic and social possibilities for gay men and women. Embryonic prewar homosexual subcultures blossomed during the war and spread across the midcentury urban landscape. Bars, nightclubs, public cruising spots, and informal social networks facilitated the development of gay and lesbian enclaves. But the permissive atmosphere did not survive the war's end. Waving the banner of Cold War political and social conservatism, government leaders acted at the federal, state, and local levels to purge gays and lesbians from government and military posts, to initiate legal investigations and prosecutions of gay individuals and institutions, and to encourage local police crackdowns on gay bars and street life. The perceived need to safeguard national security and to reestablish social order in the wake of wartime disruption sparked a "homosexual panic" which promoted the fear, loathing, and persecution of homosexuals.[11]

Lesbians suffered condemnation for their violation of gender as well as sexual codes. The tremendous emphasis on family, domesticity, and "traditional" femininity in the late 1940s and 1950s reflected postwar anxieties about the reconsolidation of a gender order shaken by two decades of depression and war. As symbols of women's refusal to conform, lesbians endured intense scrutiny by experts who regularly focused on their subjects' presumed masculinity. Sexologists attributed lesbianism to masculine tendencies and freedoms encouraged by the war, linking it to a general collapsing of gender distinctions which, in their view, destabilized marital and family relations.[12]

Lesbians remained shadowy figures to most Americans, but women athletes—noted for their masculine bodies, interests, and attributes—were visible representatives of the gender inversion often associated with homosexuality. Physical education majors, formerly accused of being unappealing to men, were increasingly charged with being uninterested in them as well. The 1952 University of Minnesota yearbook snidely reported: "Believe it or not, members of the Women's Athletic Association are normal" and found conclusive evidence in the fact that "at least one . . . of WAA's 300 members is engaged."[13]

The lesbian stigma began to plague popular athletics too. . . . The career of Babe Didrikson, which spanned the 1920s to the 1950s, illustrates the shift. In the early 1930s the press had ridiculed the tomboyish track star for her "hatchet face," "door-stop jaw," and "button-breasted" chest. After quitting track, Didrikson dropped out of the national limelight, married professional wrestler George Zaharias in 1938, and then staged a spectacular athletic comeback as a golfer in the late 1940s and 1950s. Fascinated by her personal transformation and then, in the 1950s, moved by her battle with cancer, journalists gave Didrikson's comeback

extensive coverage and helped make her a much-loved popular figure. In reflecting on her success, however, sportswriters spent at least as much time on Didrikson's love life as her golf stroke. Headlines blared, "Babe Is a Lady Now: The World's Most Amazing Athlete Has Learned to Wear Nylons and Cook for Her Huge Husband," and reporters gleefully described how "along came a great big he-man wrestler and the Babe forgot all her man-hating chatter."[14] . . . The challenge for women athletes was not to conquer new athletic feats, which would only further reduce their sexual appeal, but to regain their womanhood through sexual surrender to men.

Media coverage in national magazines and metropolitan newspapers typically focused on the sexual accomplishments of white female athletes, but postwar observers and promoters of African American women's sport also confronted the issue of sexual normalcy. In earlier decades, strong local support for women's sport within Black communities and the racist gender ideologies that prevailed outside Black communities may have weakened the association between African American women athletes and "mannish" lesbianism. Historically, European American racial thought characterized African American women as aggressive, coarse, passionate, and physical—the same qualities assigned to manliness and sport.[15] Excluded from dominant ideals of womanhood, Black women's success in sport could therefore be interpreted not as an unnatural sexual deviation but, rather, as the natural result of their reputed closeness to nature, animals, and masculinity.[16] . . . Moreover, stereotypes of Black females as highly sexual, promiscuous, and unrestrained in their heterosexual passions further discouraged the linkage between mannishness and lesbianism. . . .

Although Black athletes may initially have encountered few lesbian stereotypes . . . circumstances in the broader society eventually pressed African American sport promoters and journalists to address the issue of mannish sexuality. The strong postwar association of sports with lesbianism developed at the same time as Black athletes became a dominant presence in American sport culture. . . . Therefore, while there was no particular correlation between Black women and lesbianism, the association of each with mannishness and sexual aggression potentially linked the two. . . . In the late 1950s, Black sport promoters and journalists joined others in taking up the question of sexual "normalcy." One Black newspaper in 1957 described tennis star Althea Gibson as a childhood "tomboy" who "in later life . . . finds herself victimized by complexes."[17] The article did not elaborate on the nature of Gibson's "complex," but lesbianism is inferred in the linkage between "tomboys" and psychological illness. This connotation becomes clearer by looking at the defense of Black women's sport. Echoing *Ebony's* avowal that "entirely feminine" Black female track stars "like boys, dances, club affairs," in 1962 Tennessee State University track coach Ed Temple asserted, "None of my girls have any trouble getting boy friends. . . . We don't want amazons."[18]

Constant attempts to shore up the heterosexual reputation of athletes can be read as evidence that the longstanding reputation of female athletes as mannish women had become a covert reference to lesbianism. By midcentury, a fundamental reorientation of sexual meanings fused notions of femininity, female eroticism, and heterosexual attractiveness into a single ideal. Mannishness, once primarily a sign of gender crossing, assumed a specifically lesbian-sexual connotation. In the wake of this change, the strong cultural association between sport and masculinity made women's athletics ripe for emerging lesbian stereotypes. This meaning of athletic mannishness raises further questions. What impact did the stereotype have on women's sport? And was the image merely an erroneous stereotype, or did lesbians in fact form a significant presence in sport? . . .

The image of the mannish lesbian athlete had a direct effect on women competitors, on strategies of athletic organizations, and on the overall popularity of women's sport. The lesbian stereotype exerted pressure on athletes to demonstrate their femininity and heterosexuality, viewed as one and the same. Many women adopted an apologetic stance toward their athletic skill. Even as they competed to win, they made sure to display outward signs of femininity in dress and demeanor. They took special care in contact with the media to reveal "feminine" hobbies like cooking and sewing, to mention current boyfriends, and to discuss future marriage plans.[19]

Leaders of women's sport took the same approach at the institutional level. In answer to portrayals of physical education majors and teachers as social rejects and prudes, physical educators revised their philosophy to place heterosexuality at the center of professional objectives. . . . Curricular changes implemented between the mid-1930s and mid-1950s institutionalized the new philosophy. In a paper on postwar objectives, Mildred A. Schaeffer explained that physical education classes should help women "develop an interest in school dances and mixers and a desire to voluntarily attend them."[20] To this end, administrators revised coursework to emphasize beauty and social charm over rigorous exercise and health. They exchanged old rationales of fitness and fun for promises of trimmer waistlines, slimmer hips, and prettier complexions. . . . Some departments also added co-educational classes to foster "broader, keener, more sympathetic understanding of the opposite sex."[21] Department heads cracked down on "mannish" students and faculty, issuing warnings against "casual styles" which might "lead us back into some dangerous channels."[22] They implemented dress codes which forbade slacks and men's shirts or socks, adding as well a ban on "boyish hair cuts" and unshaven legs.[23]

Popular sport promoters adopted similar tactics. Martialing sexual data like they were athletic statistics, a 1954 AAU poll sought to sway a skeptical public with numerical proof of heterosexuality—the fact that 91 percent of former female athletes surveyed had married.[24] Publicity for the midwestern All-American Girls Baseball League included statistics on the number of married players. . . . Behind the scenes, teams passed dress and conduct codes. For example, the All-American Girls Baseball League prohibited players from wearing men's clothing or getting "severe" haircuts.[25] That this was an attempt to secure the heterosexual image of athletes was made even clearer when league officials announced that AAGBL policy prohibited the recruitment of "freaks" and "Amazons."[26]

In the end, the strategic emphasis on heterosexuality and the suppression of "mannishness" did little to alter the image of women in sport. The stereotype of the mannish lesbian athlete grew out of the persistent commonsense equation of sport with masculinity. Opponents of women's sport reinforced this belief when they denigrated women's athletic efforts and ridiculed skilled athletes as "grotesque," "mannish," or "unnatural." Leaders of women's sport unwittingly contributed to the same set of ideas when they began to orient their programs around the new feminine heterosexual idea. As physical education policies and media campaigns worked to suppress lesbianism and marginalize athletes who did not conform to dominant standards of femininity, sport officials embedded heterosexism into the institutional and ideological framework of sport. The effect extended beyond sport to the wider culture, where the figure of the mannish lesbian athlete announced that competitiveness, strength, independence, aggression, and physical intimacy among women fell outside the bounds of womanhood. As a symbol of female deviance, she served as a powerful reminder to all women to toe the line of heterosexuality and femininity or risk falling into a despised category of mannish (non-women) women. . . .

[But] was the mannish lesbian athlete merely a figure of homophobic imagination, or was there in fact a strong lesbian presence in sport? When the All-American Girls Baseball League adamantly specified, *"Always appear in feminine attire* . . . MASCULINE HAIR STYLING? SHOES? COATS? SHIRTS? SOCKS, T-SHIRTS ARE BARRED AT ALL TIMES,"* and when physical education departments threatened to expel students for overly masculine appearance, were administrators merely responding to external pressure?[27] Or were they cracking down on women who may have indeed enjoyed the feel and look of a tough swagger, a short haircut, and men's clothing? And if so, did mannishness among athletes correspond to lesbianism, as the stereotype suggested? In spite of the public stigmatization, [is it probable that] some women may have found the activities, attributes, and emotions of sport conducive to lesbian self-expression and community formation?

As part of a larger investigation of women's athletic experience, I conducted oral histories with women who played competitive amateur, semiprofessional, and professional sports between 1930 and 1970. The interviews included only six openly lesbian narrators and thirty-six other women who either declared their heterosexuality or left their identity unstated.[28] Although the sample is too small to stand as a representative study, the interviews . . . and scattered other sources indicate that sport, particularly softball, provided an important site for the development of lesbian subculture

and identity in the United States.[29] Gay and straight informants alike confirmed the lesbian presence in popular sport and physical education. Their testimony suggests that from at least the 1940s on, sport provided space for lesbian activity and social networks and served as a path into lesbian culture for young lesbians coming out and searching for companions and community.

Lesbian athletes explained that sport had been integral to their search for sexual identity and lesbian companionship. Ann Maguire, a softball player, physical education major, and top amateur bowler from New England, recalled that as a teenager in the late 1950s,

> I had been trying to figure out who I was and couldn't put a name to it. I mean it was very— no gay groups, no literature, no characters on *Dynasty*—I mean there was just nothing at that time. And trying to put a name to it. . . . I went to a bowling tournament, met two women there [and] for some reason something clicked and it clicked in a way that I was not totally aware of.

She introduced herself to the women, who later invited her to a gay bar. Maguire described her experience at age seventeen:

> I was being served and I was totally fascinated by the fact that, oh god, here I am being served and I'm not twenty-one. And it didn't occur to me until after a while when I relaxed and started realizing that I was at a gay bar. I just became fascinated. . . . And I was back there the next night. . . . I really felt a sense of knowing who I was and feeling very happy. Very happy that I had been able to through some miracle put this into place.[30] . . .

For women like Maguire, sport provided a point of entry into lesbian culture.

The question arises of whether lesbians simply congregated in athletic settings or whether a sports environment could actually "create" or "produce" lesbians. Some women fit the first scenario, describing how, in their struggle to accept and make sense out of lesbian desire, sport offered a kind of home that put feelings and identities into place. For other women, it appears that the lesbian presence in sport encouraged them to explore or act on feelings that they might not have had or responded to in other settings. Midwestern baseball player Nora Cross remembered that "it was my first exposure to gay people. . . . I was pursued by the one I was rooming with, that's how I found out." She got involved with her roommate and lived "a gay lifestyle" as long as she stayed in sport. Dorothy Ferguson Key also noticed that sport changed some women, recalling that "there were girls that came in the league like this . . . yeah, gay," but that at other times "a girl came in, and I mean they just change. . . . When they've been in a year they're completely changed. . . . They lived together."[31]

The athletic setting provided public space for lesbian sociability without naming it as such or excluding women who were not lesbians. This environment could facilitate the coming-out process, allowing women who were unsure about or just beginning to explore their sexual identity to socialize with gay and straight women without having to make immediate decisions or declarations. Gradually and primarily through unspoken communication, lesbians in sport recognized each other and created social networks. Gloria Wilson, who played softball in a mid-sized midwestern city, described her entry into lesbian social circles as a gradual process in which older lesbians slowly opened up their world to her and she grew more sure of her own identity and place in the group.

> A lot was assumed. And I don't think they felt comfortable with me talking until they knew me better. Then I think more was revealed. And we had little beer gatherings after a game at somebody's house. So then it was even more clear who was doing what when. And then I felt more comfortable too, fitting in, talking about my relationship too—and exploring more of the lesbian lifestyle, I guess.[32]

In an era when women did not dare announce their lesbianism in public, the social world of popular sport allowed women to find each other as teammates, friends, and lovers. But if athletics provided a public arena and social activity in which lesbians could recognize and affirm each other, what exactly was it that they recognized? This is where the issue of mannishness arises. Women athletes consistently explained the lesbian reputation of sport by reference to the mannishness of some athletes. . . . Suspected lesbians were said to "act like a man, you know, the way they walked, the way they talked, the things they did."

Such comments could merely indicate the pervasiveness of the masculine reputation of athletes and lesbians. However, lesbian narrators also suggested connections, although more complicated and nuanced, between athletics, lesbianism, and the "mannish" or "butchy" style which some lesbians manifested. None reported any doubt about their own gender identification as girls and women, but they indicated that they had often felt uncomfortable with the activities and attributes associated with the female gender. They preferred boyish clothes and activities to the conventional styles and manners of femininity.

Several spoke of . . . their relief upon finding athletic comrades who shared this sensibility. Josephine D'Angelo recalled that as a lesbian participating in sport, "you brought your culture with you. You brought your arm swinging . . . , the swagger, the way you tilted or cocked your head or whatever. You brought that with you." She explained that this style was acceptable in sports: "First thing you did was to kind of imitate the boys because you know, you're not supposed to throw like a girl." Although her rejection of femininity made her conspicuous in other settings, D'Angelo found that in sport "it was overlooked, see. You weren't different than the other kids. . . . Same likeness, people of a kind."[33]

These athletes were clearly women playing women's sports. But in the gender system of U.S. society, the skills, movements, clothing, and competition of sport were laden with impressions of masculinity. Lesbianism too crossed over the bounds of acceptable femininity. Consequently, sport could relocate girls or women with lesbian identities or feelings in an alternative nexus of gender meanings, allowing them to "be themselves"—or to express their gender and sexuality in an unconventional way. This applied to heterosexual women as well, many of whom also described themselves as "tomboys" attracted to boyish games and styles. As an activity that incorporated prescribed "masculine" physical activity into a way of being in the female body, athletics provided a social space and practice for reorganizing conventional meanings of embodied masculinity and femininity. *All* women in sport gained access to activities and expressive styles labeled masculine by the dominant culture. However, because lesbians were excluded from a concept of "real womanhood" defined around heterosexual appeal and desire, sport formed a milieu in which they could redefine womanhood on their own terms. . . .

However, the connections among lesbianism, masculinity, and sport require qualification.

Many lesbians in and out of sport did not adopt "masculine" markers. And even among those who did, narrators indicated that butch styles did not occlude more traditionally "feminine" qualities of affection and tenderness valued by women athletes. Sport allowed women to combine activities and attributes perceived as masculine with more conventionally feminine qualities of friendship, cooperation, nurturance, and affection. Lesbians particularly benefited from this gender configuration, finding that in the athletic setting, qualities otherwise viewed as manifestations of homosexual deviance were understood as inherent, positive aspects of sport.[34] Aggressiveness, toughness, passionate intensity, expanded use of motion and space, strength, and competitiveness contributed to athletic excellence. With such qualities defined as athletic attributes rather than psychological abnormalities, the culture of sport permitted lesbians to express the full range of their gendered sensibilities while sidestepping the stigma of psychological deviance. For these reasons, athletics, in the words of Josephine D'Angelo, formed a "comforting" and "comfortable" place.[35]

Yet lesbians found sport hospitable only under certain conditions. Societal hostility toward homosexuality made lesbianism unspeakable in any realm of culture, but the sexual suspicions that surrounded sport made athletics an especially dangerous place in which to speak out. Physical educators and sport officials vigilantly guarded against signs of "mannishness," and teams occasionally expelled women who wore their hair in a "boyish bob" or engaged in obvious lesbian relationships. Consequently, gay athletes avoided naming or verbally acknowledging their sexuality. Loraine Sumner explained that "you never talked about it. . . . You never saw anything in public amongst the group of us. But you knew right darn well that this one was going with that one. But yet it just wasn't a topic of conversation. Never."[36] Instead, lesbian athletes signaled their identity through dress, posture, and look, reserving spoken communication for private gatherings among women who were acknowledged and accepted members of concealed communities.

Although in hindsight the underground nature of midcentury lesbian communities may seem extremely repressive, it may also have had a positive side. Unlike the bars where women's very presence declared their status as sexual outlaws, in sport athletes could enjoy the public company of lesbians while retaining their membership in local communities where neighbors, kin, and coworkers respected and sometimes even celebrated their athletic abilities. The unacknowledged, indefinite presence of lesbians in sport may have allowed for a wider range of lesbian experience and identity than is currently acknowledged in most scholarship. For instance, among women who did not identify as lesbian but were sexually drawn to other women, sport provided a venue in which they could express their desires without necessarily having articulated their feelings as a distinct sexual identity. The culture of sport provided space for some women to create clearly delineated lesbian identities and communities, at the same time allowing other women to move along the fringes of this world, operating across sexual and community lines without a firmly differentiated lesbian identity.

Women in sport experienced a contradictory array of heterosexual imperatives and homosexual possibilities. The fact that women athletes disrupted a critical domain of male power and privilege made sport a strategic site for shoring up existing gender and sexual hierarchies. The image of the mannish lesbian confirmed both the masculinity of sport and its association with female deviance. Lesbian athletes could not publicly claim their identity without risking expulsion, ostracism, and loss of athletic activities and social networks that had become crucial to their lives. Effectively silenced, their image was conveyed to the dominant culture primarily as a negative stereotype in which the mannish lesbian athlete represented the unfeminine "other," the line beyond which "normal" women must not cross.

The paradox of women's sport history is that the mannish athlete was not only a figure of homophobic discourse but also a human actor engaged in sexual innovation and struggle. Lesbian athletes used the social and psychic space of sport to create a collective culture and affirmative identity. The pride, pleasure, companionship, and dignity lesbians found in the athletic world helped them survive in a hostile society. The challenge posed by their collective existence and their creative reconstruction of womanhood formed a precondition for more overt, political challenges to lesbian oppression which have occurred largely outside the realm of sport.

NOTES

1. Fred Wittner, "Shall the Ladies Join Us?" *Literary Digest* 117 (19 May 1934): 43.

2. Jim Murray, *Austin American Statesman* (n.d.), Zaharias scrapbook, Barker Texas History Center ([hereafter] BTHC), University of Texas, Austin; Arsenio Hall Show, 1988.

3. "Fastest Women in the World," *Ebony* 10 (June 1955): 28.

4. Helen Lenskyj, *Out of Bounds: Women, Sport, and Sexuality* (Toronto: Women's Press, 1986); Yvonne Zipter, *Diamonds Are a Dyke's Best Friend: Reflections, Reminiscences, and Reports from the Field on the Lesbian National Pastime* (Ithaca: Firebrand Books, 1988).

5. J. A. Mangan and Roberta J. Park, eds., *"Fair Sex" to Feminism: Sport and the Socialization of Women in the Industrial and Post-Industrial Era* (London: Frank Cays, 1987).

6. 1904–5 Scrapbooks of Anne Maude Butner, Butner Papers, University of Minnesota Archives, Minneapolis (UMA).

7. Violet W. Mange, "Field Hockey for Women," *Harper's Bazaar* 44 (Apr. 1910): 246; Anna de Koven, "The Athletic Woman," *Good Housekeeping* 55 (Aug. 1912): 150.

8. George Nathan, "Once There Was a Princess," *American Mercury* 19 (Feb. 1930):242.

9. This is an extremely brief and simplified summary of an extensive literature. For a good synthesis, see Estelle Freedman and John D'Emilio, *Intimate Matters: A History of Sexuality in America* (New York: Harper & Row, 1988), chaps. 8–10.

10. William Marston, "How Can a Woman Do It?" *Redbook* (Sept. 1933):60.

11. John D'Emilio, *Sexual Politics, Sexual Communities: The Making of a Homosexual Minority in the United States, 1940–1970* (Chicago: University of Chicago Press, 1983), pp. 9–53; Alan Berube, *Coming Out Under Fire: The History of Gay Men and Women in World War Two* (New York: Free Press, 1990).

12. Donna Penn, "The Meanings of Lesbianism in Post-War America," *Gender and History* 3 (Summer 1991):190–203; Wini Breines, "The 1950s: Gender and Some Social Science," *Sociological Inquiry* 56 (Winter 1986): 69–92.

13. Gopher Yearbook (1952), p. 257, UMA.

14. Paul Gallico, *Houston Post*, 22 Mar. 1960; Pete Martin, "Babe Didrikson Takes Off Her Mask," *Saturday Evening Post* 20 (Sept. 1947): 26–27.

15. Paula Giddings, *When and Where I Enter: The Impact of Black Women on Race and Sex in America* (New York: William Morrow, 1984), chaps. 1, 2, 4; Patricia Hill Collins, *Black Feminist Thought: Knowledge, Consciousness, and the Politics of Empowerment* (Boston: Unwin Hyman, 1990), chaps. 4, 8.

16. Elizabeth Lunbeck, "'A New Generation of Women': Progressive Psychiatrists and the Hypersexual Female," *Feminist Studies* 13 (Fall 1987): 513–43.

17. *Baltimore Afro-American*, 29 June 1957.

18. "Fastest Women in the World," pp. 28, 32; *Detroit News* 31 (July 1962): 1.

19. Patricia Del Rey, "The Apologetic and Women in Sport," in Carole Oglesby, ed., *Women and Sport* (Philadelphia: Lea & Febiger, 1978), pp. 107–11.

20. Mildred A. Schaeffer, "Desirable Objectives in Post-war Physical Education," *Journal of Health and Physical Education* 16 (Oct. 1945): 44–47.

21. "Coeducational Classes," *Journal of Health, Physical Education, and Recreation* 26 (Feb. 1955):18. For curricular changes, I examined physical education records at the universities of Wisconsin, Texas, and Minnesota, Radcliffe College, Smith College, Tennessee State University, and Hampton University.

22. Dudley Ashton, "Recruiting Future Teachers," *Journal of Health, Physical Education, and Recreation* 28 (Oct. 1957): 49.

23. The 1949–50 Physical Training Staff Handbook at the University of Texas stated, "Legs should be kept shaved" (p. 16). Box 3R213 of Department of Physical Training for Women Records, BTHC.

24. Roxy Andersen, "Statistical Survey of Former Women Athletes," *Amateur Athlete* (Sept. 1954):10–11.

25. All-American Girls Baseball League (AAGBL) 1951 Constitution, AAGBL Records.

26. Morris Markey, "Hey Ma, You're Out!" (n.d.), 1951 Records of the AAGBL; and "Feminine Sluggers," *People and Places* 8 (1952), AAGBL Records.

27. AAGBL 1951 Constitution, AAGBL Records.

28. The sample included forty-two women, ranging in age from their forties to their seventies, who had played a variety of sports in a range of athletic settings in the West, Midwest, Southeast, and Northeast. The majority were white women from urban working-class and rural backgrounds.

29. Zipter, *Diamonds Are a Dyke's Best Friend*; Lillian Faderman, *Odd Girls and Twilight Lovers: A History of Lesbian Life in Twentieth-Century America* (New York: Columbia University Press, 1991), pp. 154, 161–62.

30. Ann Maguire, interview with the author, Boston, 18 Feb. 1988.

31. Nora Cross (pseudonym), interview with the author, 20 May 1988; Dorothy Ferguson Key, interview with the author, Rockford, Ill., 19 Dec. 1988.

32. Gloria Wilson (pseudonym), interview with the author, 11 May 1988.

33. Josephine D'Angelo, interview with the author, Chicago, 21 Dec. 1988.

34. Joseph P. Goodwin, *More Man Than You'll Ever Be! Gay Folklore and Acculturation in Middle America* (Bloomington: Indiana University Press, 1989), p. 62.

35. D'Angelo interview.

36. Loraine Sumner, interview with the author, West Roxbury, Mass., 18 Feb. 1988.

JOYCE ANTLER
Imagining Jewish Mothers in the 1950s

The wartime alliance between the United States and the USSR melted quickly as the defeat of Germany was followed by a ruthless Soviet occupation of Eastern Europe. The use of the atomic bomb at Hiroshima and Nagasaki in the summer of 1945 was both indication of and cause for heightened mistrust, and failure to develop international control of atomic energy made it worse. By 1948 the former allies had become antagonists. The United States and major Western European nations joined in a mutual defense agreement that anticipated the North Atlantic Treaty Organization (NATO); the USSR and pro-Soviet regimes in Eastern Europe shaped what would eventually become the Warsaw Pact.

As historian William Chafe has observed, in this climate "legitimate concerns could easily spill into paranoia."* President Harry S Truman created a Federal Employee Loyalty Program, appointing a panel authorized to screen for sympathy toward "totalitarian, fascist or subversive" organizations. What counted as sympathy and what counted as subversive were left vague. The House Committee on Un-American Activities (HUAC) was uncompromising—investigating many who had only the vaguest connection with Communist organizations and demanding that witnesses not only account for their own activities but also name others with whom they had associated. If they refused to name others, they were held in contempt of Congress. The only alternative to naming friends and associates was to refuse to answer at all, citing the Fifth Amendment's protection against self-incrimination. When HUAC investigated Communist influence on the entertainment industry, even actors whose programs had no political content could be swept up, as Gertrude Berg would find.

When the Soviet Union tested its first atomic bomb in 1949, the American public was shaken. Early the following year, Klaus Fuchs, a British physicist, was convicted of spying for the Soviet Union. The FBI search for his American collaborators soon found Harry Gold, a Philadelphia chemist, who confessed to his own complicity, and David Greenglass, a machinist, who confessed and also implicated his brother-in-law, Julius Rosenberg. Shortly afterword, Julius's wife, Ethel, was also arrested on suspicion of conspiracy to commit espionage by passing atomic secrets to the Soviets. The evidence against them was fragile, drawn from alleged conversations for which there were no third-party witnesses. But the Rosenbergs' Communist sympathies were invoked at every turn in the trial; they were blamed for the vulnerability of the United States and for making feasible the Communist aggression in Korea. Both Rosenbergs protested their innocence; both were sentenced to death.

*William Chafe, *The Unfinished Journey: America Since World War II* (New York: Oxford University Press, 1986), p. 98.

An extended series of unsuccessful legal appeals followed; the Rosenberg case became an international cause. The famous Spanish artist Pablo Picasso offered lithograph portraits of the couple as fund-raisers for the costs of their defense; there were mass rallies on their behalf in European and American cities. In June 1953, President Eisenhower refused a last plea for clemency; he explained his decision in a letter to his son John:

> I must say that it goes against the grain to avoid interfering in the case where a woman is to receive capital punishment. . . . [But] in this instance it is the woman who is the strong and recalcitrant character. The man is the weak one. . . . [I]f there would be any commuting of the woman's sentence without the man's then from here on the Soviets would simply recruit their spies from among women.[†]

Julius and Ethel Rosenberg were executed at Sing Sing prison, New York, on June 19, 1953. Nearly 50 years later, Ethel's brother, who had given damning testimony that she had typed spy notes, admitted to a reporter that he had lied on the witness stand to avoid implicating his own wife.[**]

Popular cultural ideas, including images of good mothers, seeped into the ways in which Ethel Rosenberg was judged by the media and the general public. Political anxieties about international relations made radio and television celebrities like Gertrude Berg cautious about the message they sent. And even after the entire European Jewish population had barely survived the Holocaust, Berg and Rosenberg's Jewishness made both vulnerable.

For most Americans, and not least for American Jews, the postwar period represented a paradoxical time in political as well as popular culture. Recovering from the Depression and World War II, Jews continued their move into the mainstream of American life, enjoying unprecedented economic prosperity and a great increase in opportunities for education, the professions, and business.

Yet troubling signs rippled the smooth surface of Jewish acculturation. Despite its decline, anti-Semitism remained a significant factor in American life, with almost sixty known anti-Semitic organizations operating in 1950. Also ominous was the association of American Jews in the public mind with the menace of communism, an association fostered by the trial and conviction of Ethel and Julius Rosenberg. Although the trial did not trigger the kind of virulent anti-Semitic tirades that many Jewish leaders had feared, the anxiety it caused among Jews suggested that they were perhaps not as at home in America as they had believed.

The polar experiences of American Jews in the 1950s—their spectacular arrival in the American mainstream coupled with lingering fears of anti-Semitism and doubts about Jewish acculturation—are represented by two famous Jewish women of the time: the cherubic, smiling Molly Goldberg, the radio and TV sitcom heroine of the long-running series "The Goldbergs," and the taut, drawn, unsmiling Ethel Greenglass Rosenberg herself.

Although a fictional character, Molly Goldberg was played with such verisimilitude by Gertrude Berg—in fact an American-born, middle-class Jew—that the public easily confused the mythical Molly with her real-life impersonator. Berg, who created the character, lived a very different life from that of Molly Goldberg. Yet Molly/Gertrude was powerful in popular culture precisely because she ostensibly represented reality. Molly's character, tied

---

**Robert D. McFadden, "David Greenglass, Who Helped Seal the Rosenbergs' Doom, Dies at 92," *New York Times*, Oct. 15, 2014, p. A1 (New York edition).

†John Lewis Gaddis, *Strategies of Containment: A Critical Appraisal of Postwar American National Security Policy* (New York: Oxford University Press, 1982), p. 138, n. 31.

to Gertrude Berg, not only mobilized the cultural power of a "real" person but, in some sense, became a real person. In much the same way that Molly Goldberg enjoyed a reality independent of Gertrude Berg, so did the media representations of Ethel Greenglass Rosenberg come to dominate public perceptions of the real Ethel. Yet the flesh-and-blood Rosenberg differed as much from the media's Ethel as Gertrude did from Molly.[1]

Second-generation daughters of East European immigrant families, Gertrude Berg and Ethel Rosenberg exemplify the changing aspirations, and the changing representations, of Jewish women in the 1950s. Both women defied convention: Gertrude, by building a media career and directing and producing a long-running hit series, all the while managing her own household and family life; Ethel, by combining a staunch commitment to radical ideology with a conscientious, even obsessive, motherhood. For a generation or more, however, the cultural construction of "Molly" and "Ethel" has left little room for imagining the full historical matrix in which Gertrude and Ethel lived their lives. The potent alliance between media and politics that characterized the Red Scare years obliterated all but the masks of Molly and Ethel.[2]

Molly and Ethel were not the only representations of Jewish women in the politicized culture of the 1950s. Another archetypal middle-class Jewish woman of the decade was "Shirley," a type made famous by Herman Wouk in his 1955 novel, *Marjorie Morningstar*. Selling millions of copies and made into a successful movie starring the popular actress Natalie Wood, the book depicted the transformation of a young, ambitious, "emancipated" Jewish girl into a conventional suburban matron, a Shirley. Rebellious as a youth Marjorie/Shirley matured into "the respectable girl, the mother of the next generation, all tricked out to appear gay and girlish and carefree but with a terrible threatening dullness jutting through"; later Marjorie/Shirley became a regular synagogue goer, active in the Jewish organizations of the town," a model, in fact, of the many thousands of Jewish women who belonged to temple sisterhoods, Hadassah, the National Council of Jewish Women, and similar organizations. While Wouk treats Shirley sympathetically, Mrs. Patimkin, the Shirley-like Jewish mother in Philip Roth's 1959 novella, *Good-bye Columbus*, is portrayed as vain, empty-headed, materialistic. Her daughter,

Brenda, demonstrating the worst qualities of 1950s suburban Jewish affluence, joined Marjorie Morningstar as one in a series of indelible images of a new kind of Jewish heroine—assimilated, smoothly confident, flirtatious, beautiful, spoiled. Together with Ethel and Molly, these fictional representations would provide enduring images of Jewish American womanhood—mothers and daughters, protectors and princesses—that would wield more power and influence than their creators could ever have expected.[3]

Yet these images do not do justice to the varied experiences of Jewish women in postwar America. The activism demonstrated by such groups as the National Council of Jewish Women and the Emma Lazarus Federation of Jewish Women's Clubs (a left-wing group created after the Holocaust by a group of largely Yiddish-speaking women of the immigrant generation) belies the homogeneity of the period and demonstrates that "Molly," "Ethel," and "Shirley" were cultural constructs after all.

... "The Rise of the Goldbergs" was one of the most popular serials in radio's golden era, running from 1929 through 1946, and ... 1949 to 1950. After 1931, the show aired nightly, for some years carried by both the CBS and NBC networks. In 1946, the show (known as "The Goldbergs") made the transition to television, running through 1955. It was revived in the early 1960s as "Mrs. G," a new series about Molly at college. Along the way there were also a comic strip, a syndicated column ("Mamatalks"), a published version of the show's early scripts, a cookbook, a hit Broadway play (*Me and Molly*), two films, and Berg's autobiography, *Molly and Me*. So identified was Gertrude Berg with Molly Goldberg that she signed autographs in the character's name. Yet it was Berg, the consummate professional, who wrote as well as starred in the show's five thousand-plus radio scripts as well as the later television programs.

During the second quarter of the twentieth century, Molly Goldberg became the quintessential representation of the American Jewish mother in popular culture. "Kind-hearted," "humane," "gentle," "gracious," "sympathetic," and "tender"—these were the words typically used in advertisements for the show—Molly Goldberg, like her creator Gertrude Berg, was nonetheless a woman of force and dominance. [Her] genius was to wed the iron qualities of traditional East European Jewish women with a charm and humor that counteracted the threat of their power. During the Depression, when a negative stereotype of the Jewish mother as materialistic and pushy began to appear in the works of Clifford Odets and other Jewish male writers, Berg's Molly had a more positive appeal.[4]

Molly's compassion and the comic elements in her character diverted attention from other, potentially troublesome traits. At best meddlesome and at worst nagging and controlling, Molly got her way in almost every show, but always for the purpose of helping others. Molly's speech, full of malapropisms, reflected her status as an immigrant whose eagerness to adopt American usages was greater than her knowledge: "Come sit on the table, dinner is ready . . . You'll swallow a cup, darling? . . . Throw an eye into the ice-box and give me an accounting. . . . "[5] Molly's generosity and the quaintness of her language—including the famous opening line of the show, "Yoo hoo Mrs. Bloom," which she yelled out the window to her tenement neighbor—endeared her to audiences.

No matter how exaggerated, caricatured, or sentimental the show's characters, to audiences they seemed believable and realistic. Writing in 1951, novelist Charles Angoff praised the show for its realistic representation of "virtually the whole panorama of middle-class Jewish-American life":

> There are the neighbors who borrow from and lend to one another, and who offer advice, whether asked or not . . . there are the sisters and cousins and aunts, with all their jealousies and bickerings and generosities and meddlings . . . the young folk who sometimes think they have "outgrown" their parents but who find that for comfort and counsel there are no substitutes . . . and there is Molly herself, whose heart bleeds for every unmarried girl and starving butcher and lonely grocer, and who is as quick as the proverbial lightning in concocting ideas to get the "right" girl and the "right" man together, to straighten out family squabbles, to help out a reformed thief, to get her own son to invite her to a college affair—in short, Molly the Mixer and the Fixer.

Together these characters presented "neurotic tensions, despair, ecstasy, conniving, kindliness, back-biting . . . the normal life of Bronx and Brooklyn and Manhattan and Chicago and Boston and Philadelphia and San Francisco Jews." Angoff concluded: "I have never heard anyone who knows Jewish life say that 'The Goldbergs' are not true to life. Molly Goldberg, indeed, is so basically true a character that I sometimes think she may become an enduring name in the national literature. She is the prototype of the Jewish mother during the past twenty-five years."[6]

A good part of the praise for "The Goldbergs" was due to its uplifting message about American family life and moral values. Berg once described the show to a reporter, using Molly's lines: "Jake wants the children to have everything money can buy, and I want them to have everything money can't buy." This philosophical difference formed the core of the show's dramatic conflict, and despite the Goldbergs' upward mobility, it was always resolved in Molly's favor. Listeners found the message of "The Goldbergs" inspirational: ministers composed sermons around the program, and at least one Orthodox rabbi instructed congregants not to turn their radios off on Friday afternoon, so that they could listen to Molly on Shabbos evening "without breaking the law." During wartime, especially, the show received accolades as "a force for decency and the democratic way of life."[7]

Three points stand out regarding the Molly Goldberg character. First, Molly as a Jewish mother was an odd but lovable, generous woman who solved all the problems of her family, neighborhood, and community through her skillful "mixing-in." She was a voluble, talkative busybody, a *balaboste*, but one with a loving heart who could always be trusted to do the right thing.

The second point is that in spite of her ethnicity, which was always prominent (even when the use of dialect subsided), Molly and her children espoused assimilationist values. Over the decades, the audience saw the family leave their Bronx neighborhood, move to the suburbs, and send the children off to college. In this respect, "The Goldbergs" was an accurate representation of the Jewish middle-class's entry into the American mainstream. Despite the family's economic transformation, Molly herself changed very little. Even in the mid-1950s, she looked and sounded like a newly arrived immigrant; in this respect, Molly remained in a television time warp.[8]

The third point is that as the Goldbergs became America's surrogate family, Molly became everybody's mother, a woman who, *because* of her ethnicity (that is, her difference), represented the American ideal of brotherly love and interreligious cooperation. This point was borne out in the huge amount of fan mail Berg received and in the accolades from non-Jewish as well as Jewish organizations.

In order to achieve such wide acceptance in both mainstream and Jewish audiences, Berg made a conscious decision, as she told one reporter, not to bring in

> anything that will bother people . . . unions, politics, fundraising, Zionism, socialism, intergroup relations, I don't stress them. After all, aren't such things second to daily living? The Goldbergs are not defensive about their Jewishness, or especially aware of it. I keep things average. I don't want to lose friends.[9]

Like other situation comedies of the 1950s, "The Goldbergs" portrayed the family as a sea of domestic tranquillity—a "suburban middle landscape," according to one critic—isolated from problems in the larger society. Sitcoms were "Cold War comedies of reassurance," in which politics, "by its telling absence . . . was a contaminating force to be kept beyond the threshold of the private household." In shows like "Leave It to Beaver," "Father Knows Best," "The Adventures of Ozzie and Harriet," "The Donna Reed Show," "I Remember Mama," and "Make Room for Daddy/The Danny Thomas Show," television reinforced values of family togetherness—responsibility, maturity, adjustment, and "enlightened permissiveness."[10] In most of these comedies, it was not the maternal figure but the benevolent patriarch who navigated his family through the shoals of neighborhood life. Yet Molly Goldberg's affable, homespun wisdom, like that of the Norwegian mother in "I Remember Mama" (played by Peggy Wood), was no less authoritative than that of her male counterparts. As women in command of a vast repository of folk wisdom, Berg and Wood steered their families through the special challenges of modern American life, while demonstrating for the television audience that conflict could be easily managed and contained if "normal" family values were upheld.

But this is not the whole story. Gertrude Berg could eliminate controversy from her show, but not from her life. Philip Loeb, who played Molly's husband, Jake, on radio in the late 1940s and took the character to TV in 1949 was a victim of the blacklist in 1950. After a debate with her sponsors (who eventually pulled out), Gertrude Berg succumbed and fired Loeb in 1952; he committed suicide three years

later. Comedian Milton Berle reveals in his memoirs that in 1950, when Berg was "fighting the witch-hunters" who had "enough juice to hurt [her] in every way," his sponsors and NBC would not permit Berg to appear on his show, even though she had her own. . . . It is possible that Berg, a member of an actors' group that included many well-known left-wing artists such as Paul Robeson, was herself the target of a blacklist.[11]

The portrait of Molly Goldberg as the ideal Jewish mother of the 1950s may thus have clashed with the reality of Gertrude Berg's own politics; it certainly contrasted with the fact of her career. Married and the mother of two children, Berg had grown up writing skits to amuse the guests at her parents' summer hotel in the Catskills. Even after marriage and motherhood, she was determined to pursue her career as a writer, but the short stories she submitted to popular magazines all came back with rejection slips. Then came her breakthrough in a trial run of "Goldberg" scripts, written for radio. Almost immediately, Berg became a highly successful media entrepreneur. She was no Molly Goldberg, stay-at-home housewife, though she prided herself on her "normal" family life.

Berg's decision to eschew politics and what she described as "defensive" Jewishness reflected a common strategy of leading Jewish organizations of the period. In the late 1940s and the 1950s, these groups embarked on new ventures designed to counteract the forces of bigotry and enhance interreligious and interethnic harmony. Rather than responding exclusively to direct threats to American Jewry, they took action on a panoply of social and cultural concerns, including opposition to McCarthyism and the promotion of civil rights and the ideals of the welfare state. "The Goldbergs," with its exhortation to celebrate human brotherhood and its conscious disregard of difference, mirrored these objectives.

The example of compassionate concern that Molly Goldberg demonstrated to her Christian friends and neighbors was embodied in the postwar program of the National Council of Jewish Women. In 1947, the NCJW introduced a new initiative on "intercultural relations." The initiative, entitled "cultural democracy," exposed the flaws in the idea of the melting pot and championed the free expression of cultural differences. "Something good is lost when people are melted down to a uniform consistency," the NCJW asserted; it was the "diversity of [many] cultures which make the American society strong." According to the NCJW, the prophetic imperative to brotherhood and other Judaic teachings made "the universal concern for all people" a guide for American Jews. But the Council insisted that it was an American as well as a Jewish obligation to eradicate intolerance. . . .

Recognizing prejudice was . . . not sufficient to eradicate it. Council leaders argued that it was crucial to be "'good neighbors,' understanding and respecting our fellow citizens of different racial and religious backgrounds." For this purpose, chapters were instructed to work with other local groups on such issues as eliminating stereotypes and stimulating public interest in building better intercultural understanding. But it was equally important to develop a positive program of action, seeking "economic and social justice" for all people regardless of their race, religion, or national origin.[12] For this reason, the NCJW extended the project on interfaith harmony beyond such local issues as schools, housing, and citizenship to include broad questions of public policy, social legislation, and even international affairs, all of which it considered integral to intercultural work. During the 1950s, the NCJW promoted these objectives through public education and lobbying on behalf of such causes as immigration reform and civil rights.[13]

In 1952, the NCJW launched a related project, the Freedom Campaign, designed to educate the public to the importance of civil liberties and to encourage people in "speaking up for what they believe is right" while "respecting the beliefs of others." Declaring its staunch opposition to communism, the NCJW also declared war on Senator McCarthy and the House Un-American Activities Committee's "campaign of vilification" against "everyone who has ever held an original idea or participated in the activities of a minority group." . . . The Council formed a special alliance with the Young Women's Christian Association (YWCA) in this campaign.[14]

The common ground of racial and religious tolerance that guided NCJW's postwar intercultural effort was specifically acknowledged in 1961, when the council and the YWCA came together again to commemorate the fiftieth anniversary of both organizations' initial commitment to seek public policy protection for working women and children. . . . [They]

issued a ten-point "Code of Personal Commitment," stressing opposition to prejudice, protection of individual liberties, and efforts toward world peace. "I will cultivate objectivity of thought / And will consider new and different points of view," the statement read. "I will recognize my common kinship with all / and remember that whatever happens to anyone happens to me."[15]

Despite the NCJW's freedom campaign and its dedication to protecting the rights of political dissidents and racial, religious, and ethnic minorities, the Council, like Gertrude Berg herself, had little to say about the Rosenberg case or Ethel Rosenberg as a Jewish woman.

Like Gertrude Berg, Ethel Rosenberg aspired to an artistic career, although it was as a singer and actress, rather than a writer, that she hoped to make her mark. An excellent student at Seward Park High School on Manhattan's Lower East Side, Ethel planned to attend college and took college preparatory courses. Graduating in 1931 at the height of the Depression, however, she felt lucky to obtain a clerical job with the National New York Shipping and Packing Company. The Clark House Players, an amateur theater group sponsored by a settlement house around the corner from her home, was the object of most of her enthusiasm over the next few years; she also took acting classes at the Henry Street Settlement and attended lectures by members of several experimental theater companies. At nineteen, Ethel was accepted into the prestigious Schola Cantorum, becoming the choir's youngest member; the group occasionally sang at the Metropolitan Opera House. The following year, singing an operatic solo at a benefit for the International Seamen's Union, Ethel met Julius Rosenberg, who claimed she had the most beautiful voice he had ever heard. They were married three years later.[16]

Ethel pursued her singing and acting interests only sporadically after her marriage. Her independent involvement in political action also declined. Before meeting Julius, she had helped to organize the Ladies Apparel Shipping Clerks Union at her company, serving as the only woman on a four-person strike committee that called a citywide action in which over 10,000 workers participated. Fired for her role in this strike, Ethel brought a complaint before the newly formed National Labor Relations Board; the case was later decided in her favor. By this time, she had found employment as a stenographer with Bell Textile Company. She left this job after Julius found work with the United States Signal Corps, turning her attention to volunteer activities. Among the groups she joined were the women's auxiliary of her husband's union—the Federation of Architects, Engineers, Chemists and Technicians (FAECT)—and, after the start of World War II, the Lower East Side Defense Council.

After the births of her sons—Michael in 1943 and Robert four years later—Rosenberg became increasingly absorbed in family matters. According to one neighbor, she was "literally a mother 24 hours out of 24."[17] But motherhood did not come as easily to Ethel as it did to Molly Goldberg and Gertrude Berg. Beset by physical ailments resulting from chronic scoliosis and the emotional strain of dealing with young children, she grew increasingly concerned about her parenting skills. Setting limits for her children—responding to them with both the generosity and the authority that she felt good parenting entailed—was especially problematic; the importance of these qualities was continually being emphasized in the pages of *Parents Magazine*, which Rosenberg read religiously, and in the vastly popular performances of Gertrude Berg. Seeking guidance, Rosenberg took a course on child psychology at the New School for Social Research and enlisted the help of a social worker at the Jewish Board of Guardians; soon afterward, she began to see a private psychiatrist. Though she deeply loved and respected Julius, he could not alleviate her anxieties about raising their sons. Despite their political radicalism, both accepted the gender role division that allotted breadwinning responsibilities to the husband and child rearing to the wife. "The good mother is the key to proper child rearing," Rosenberg wrote to her lawyer, Manny Bloch, after she had been arrested and imprisoned along with Julius on charges of conspiracy to commit espionage.[18]

In view of Rosenberg's faith in communism, her resorting to psychoanalysis and social work may seem surprising. But Rosenberg's worries as a mother apparently overshadowed any doubts she may have had about succumbing to such capitalist opiates. In the emphasis she placed on child rearing, Rosenberg was in fact not far removed from Molly Goldberg. Whether she read Gertrude Berg's advice column in the 1930s, or listened to any of the Goldberg shows on radio or TV, is unknown, but her idea of what characterized the "good" mother certainly overlapped with Berg's portrayal of Molly as understanding, tolerant, generous—everything Rosenberg's own mother, Tessie Greenglass, was not.

Tessie Greenglass was an unhappy, troubled woman, disappointed in her husband's lack of ambition and inability to move the family out of poverty. Unlike the Goldbergs or the Bergs, the Greenglasses never realized their dream of American success; Tessie's frustrations with this failure were apparently visited on her only daughter. Favoring her three sons, especially the youngest, David, she treated Ethel with disrespect bordering on cruelty; certainly Ethel was abused emotionally (and sometimes physically, since Tessie used corporal punishment on all the children). Despite (or because of) Ethel's excellence at school and her good-girl demeanor at home, she was also the butt of her brothers' jealousy; she was very much the scapegoat of the entire family.[19]

When, years later, David Greenglass accused Ethel and Julius of masterminding the spy ring in which he was allegedly involved at Los Alamos, Rosenberg was not surprised that her mother accepted her brother's story rather than her own. But the extent of her mother's lack of support for her, and for her children, hurt Ethel Rosenberg enormously. When Tessie first visited Rosenberg in prison it was only to scream at her for harming David and to call her a "dirty Communist." After Rosenberg was transferred to solitary confinement at Sing Sing, Tessie did not visit her at all for two years; when she finally did it was only to urge her daughter to confess. Ethel Rosenberg responded angrily, but admitted to her lawyer that she would "still give anything in the world for one kind word from her." Tessie returned two months before Rosenberg's execution to insist again that she affirm her brother's account and admit her guilt. According to the prison official who was present, Rosenberg, enraged, called her mother a "witch" and "yelled and raved to such an extent that she was cautioned by the guard that the interview would be terminated unless she quieted down." That was the last time Rosenberg saw Tessie.[20]

No doubt Ethel Rosenberg's troubled relationship with her mother accounted in good part for her concerns about her own parenting. But her anxieties about her performance as a mother and her children's emotional well-being were also the product of cultural messages that she, like others with her background and aspirations, absorbed from the surrounding culture. Under the growing influence of child guidance specialists and behavioral psychologists, parenting in the late 1940s and early 1950s became more than ever a matter of expert counseling and knowledge rather than innate capability. During these years, the notion of motherhood as "pathology" was a staple in both the popular and scientific press, with all manner of experts holding mothers accountable for withdrawn, destructive, disturbed, and "deviant" children.[21] If Ethel Rosenberg blamed herself for child-rearing problems—however normal—she was merely reflecting the accepted wisdom. Rosenberg's faith in professional child guidance in fact illuminates why Molly Goldberg was so popular a figure in the postwar period. In representing an earlier time, when parents dominated their children's lives and truly "knew best," sitcoms like "The Goldbergs" provided nostalgic reassurance to a generation increasingly troubled about the viability of a harmonious family life in the context of a pluralistic society. Rosenberg's concern about her own family, and her employment of therapy for herself and counseling for the children, suggests how deeply a part of her generation she was.

In spite of her intense concerns about her children, Ethel Rosenberg's behavior during her trial convinced the jurors and the American public that she was guilty—not because of the evidence, but because she lacked "maternal feeling." That Rosenberg was arrested and tried as a "lever" to force her husband to talk is now well documented. Based wholly on the testimony of her brother David and his wife, Ruth, the case was "not too strong against Mrs. Rosenberg," as one prosecutor acknowledged privately. Such doubts continued after Ethel's conviction and remain today, even though Julius's guilt now appears certain. "Was your wife cognizant of your activities?" prosecutors asked Julius Rosenberg in a questionnaire submitted to him at the Sing-Sing Death House.[22] Given the paucity of evidence regarding her participation in the conspiracy, Ethel Rosenberg's appearance at the trial became all-important.

To the public Ethel Rosenberg's failure to break down under the pressure of her arrest and trial appeared to confirm that she cared more about ideology than about her offspring,

and was therefore guilty. Her denial of guilt, along with her repeated reliance on the Fifth Amendment, created the impression, according to one legal scholar, of a "cold, well-composed woman lacking 'normal' feminine characteristics." Because of her failure to lose her composure on the witness stand (both her husband [and] his co-defendant, Morton Sobell, appeared much more uneasy), Rosenberg seemed enigmatic, "unnatural." To the jury foreman she was a "steely, stoney, tight-lipped woman. She was the mastermind. Julius would have spoken if she would have permitted him. He was more human. She was more disciplined." According to another juror, she was certainly guilty—of being a bad mother: "I had two daughters at the time, and it bothered me how they would subject their children to such a thing. I just couldn't understand it."[23]

After the Rosenbergs were convicted and sentenced to death, the image of Ethel as an "unnatural" woman and mother blocked appeals for clemency. FBI director J. Edgar Hoover used the fact of Rosenberg's failure to talk with her own mother for two years as evidence of her evil nature; when Douglas Dillon, then ambassador to France, protested the severity of her sentence compared to those of convicted British spies Klaus Fuchs and Allan Nunn May, Hoover reported that when Tessie Greenglass urged Rosenberg to confess to spare her children, Rosenberg had rebuked her with the words, "Don't mention the children. Children are born every day of the week." Although he had previously opposed the execution of Ethel as well as Julius on the grounds that it would leave two young children orphaned, Hoover changed his mind after receiving the FBI's report that "Ethel was not a good mother after all." President Eisenhower used similar gender-based reasoning in his denial of clemency: "In this instance, it is the woman who is the strong and recalcitrant character, the man who is the weak one." He believed that as the unquestioned "leader in the spy ring," Ethel Rosenberg had renounced all rights to special treatment as a woman and mother of two young children.[24] She was the first American woman to be executed for the crime of conspiracy to commit espionage.

No greater contrast could exist than that between the Molly Goldberg ideal of the 1950s—friendly, garrulous, kindhearted, family-oriented, non-controversial, and nonpolitical—and the public image of Ethel Rosenberg: silent and mysterious, conspiratorial and political, dominating and evil. Blindly loyal to her husband at the cost of abandoning her own children, she seemed, above all—and perhaps most dangerously—a neglectful, uncaring mother. Many Americans who loved Molly Goldberg were deeply shocked by Ethel Rosenberg.

This portrait of Ethel Rosenberg, elaborated in the media, was especially troubling to Jews.[25] In contrast to the Goldbergs, with their seamless adjustment to American society, the Rosenbergs appeared as an alien couple linked to a foreign power; their rejection of mainstream American values, such as those espoused by the Goldbergs and other TV sitcom families, spoke to the dark underside of the American dream and enhanced the presumption of guilt. Moreover, in contrast to the wholesome Goldberg family ("Allow me to ask whether in Jewish families nothing ever goes wrong," one viewer wrote to ask. "Is it always 'Papa darling' and 'Mama darling'? . . . no wrangling, no quibbling?") the Rosenberg family was fatally divided between brothers and sister, mother and daughter.[26] In the early 1950s, when such a family was not yet labeled "dysfunctional," the Rosenbergs seemed not only abnormal but un-American. . . .

That the Molly Goldberg ideal coincided with the aspirations of the real Ethel Rosenberg was no more ironic than the fact that Ethel—a woman excessively concerned about mothering—was portrayed by government officials and the media as a cold, uncaring "monster" of a mother. Ethel's convincing stoicism in the face of her most enormous loss—that of her children—may have been her finest performance.

NOTES

1. For an extended discussion of Molly Goldberg in relation to Ethel Rosenberg, see my "A Bond of Sisterhood: Ethel Rosenberg, Molly Goldberg, and Radical Jewish Women of the 1950s," in Marjorie Garber and Rebecca L. Walkowitz, eds. Secret Agents: The Rosenberg Case, McCarthyism, and Fifties America (New York: Routledge, 1995): 197–214.
2. On the politicization of culture during the 1950s, see Stephen J. Whitfield, The Culture of the Cold War (Baltimore: Johns Hopkins University Press, 1991). On women's roles, see Elaine Tyler May, Homeward Bound: American Families in the Cold War Era (New York: Basic Books, 1988); Wini Breines, Young, White, and Miserable: Growing Up Female in the Fifties (Boston: Beacon, 1992); and Joanne Meyerowitz, ed. Not June Cleaver: Women and Gender in Postwar America, 1945–1960 (Philadelphia: Temple University Press, 1994).

3. Herman Wouk, Marjorie Morningstar (Boston: Little Brown, 1955/1983), 172, 562; Philip Roth, Goodbye Columbus and Five Short Stories (Boston: Houghton Mifflin, 1959/1989).
4. B. G. Bienstock, "The Changing Image of the American Jewish Mother," in Virginia Tufte and Barbara Myerhoff, eds. Changing Images of the Family (New Haven: Yale University Press, 1979).
5. Charles Angoff, "'The Goldbergs' and Jewish Humor," Congress Weekly 18 (March 5, 1951): 13; "The Goldbergs March On," Life (April 25, 1949): 59; "The Goldbergs," script, Oct. 3, 1949, Gertrude Berg Papers, Special Collections, Syracuse University, Syracuse, N.Y.
6. Angoff, "The Goldbergs," 12–13. Gertrude Berg cited in Jack Long, "Her Family Is Her Fortune," American, n.d., Ill, Gertrude Berg Papers.
7. Joan Jacobs Brumberg, "Gertrude Berg," in Barbara Sicherman and Carol Hurd Green, eds., Notable American Women—The Modern Period: A Biographical Dictionary (Cambridge: Belknap Press of Harvard University Press, 1980), 73–74; Sulamith Ish-Kishor, "Interesting People: Gertrude Berg," Jewish Tribune (Oct. 10, 1930), 7.
8. Morris Freedman, "The Real Molly Goldberg," Commentary 21 (April 1954), 364; also see Donald Weber, Haunted in the World: Jewish American Culture from Cahan to "The Goldbergs" (Bloomington: Indiana University Press, 2005); and Glenn D. Smith, Something on My Own: Gertrude Berg and American Broadcasting, 1929–1956 (Syracuse: Syracuse University Press, 2007).
9. Freedman, "The Real Molly Goldberg," 360.
10. Hal Himmelstein, Television Myth and the American Mind (New York: Praeger, 1984), 84–97; David Marc, Comic Visions: Television Comedy and American Culture (Boston: Unwin Hyman, 1989), 65; Darrell Y. Hamamoto, Nervous Laughter : Television Situation Comedy and Liberal Democratic Ideology (New York: Praeger, 1989), 24–25.
11. Milton Berle, Milton Berle: An Autobiography (New York: Delacorte Press, 1974), 293–94.
12. National Council of Jewish Women, "Cultural Democracy—Pattern for America" (mimeograph, Sept. 1947): 5, 4, 11, 9–10, 19, NCJW Papers, Library of Congress, Washington, D.C.
13. National Council of Jewish Women, Committee on Education and Social Action, Spotlight, Vols. 5–9, [1949–53], NCJW Papers.
14. Spotlight, Vols. 8–9.
15. National Council of Jewish Women and YWCA, Joint Statement, Dec. 6, 1961, NCJW Papers.
16. See Ilene Philipson, Ethel Rosenberg: Beyond the Myths (New Brunswick, N.J.: Rutgers University Press, 1988) and Carol Hurd Green, "Ethel Rosenberg," in Sicherman and Green, Notable American Women, 601–4.
17. Sheila M. Brennan, "Popular Images of American Women in the 1950s and Their Impact on Ethel Rosenberg's Trial and Conviction," Women's Rights Law Reporter 14, No. 1 (Winter 1992): 47.
18. Ethel Rosenberg to Emanuel Bloch, August 31, 1951–Sept. 6, 1951, in Robert Meeropol and Michael Meeropol, We Are Your Sons: The Legacy of Ethel and Julius Rosenberg (Boston: Houghton Mifflin, 1975), 101.
19. Philipson, Ethel Rosenberg, 28. The testimony of David Greenglass and especially his wife, Ruth

Greenglass, played a major role in convicting Ethel. In recent years, David admitted that he made up the story; see Sam Roberts, *Brother: The Untold Story of the Rosenberg Case* (New York: Random House, 2003). Filmmaker Ivy Meeropol, the granddaughter of Ethel and Julius, explores the Greenglass' involvement, and reflects on Ethel's family roles, in her moving documentary, *Heir to an Execution* (2004).

20. Philipson, 345.

21. See, for example, Barbara Ehrenreich and Deirdre English, *For Her Own Good: 150 Years of the Experts' Advice to Women* (New York: Doubleday, 1978), ch. 7.

22. Ronald Radosh and Joyce Milton, *The Rosenberg File: A Search for the Truth* (New York: Holt, Rinehart and Winston, 1973), 417.

23. Brennan, "Popular Images of American Women," 56–59.

24. Fuchs and May received fourteen- and ten-year terms, respectively. Brennan, "Popular Images," 60.

25. See Deborah Dash Moore, "Reconsidering the Rosenbergs: Symbol and Substance in Second Generation American Jewish Consciousness," *Journal of American Ethnic History* 8, No. 1 (Fall 1988): 21–37.

26. Cited by Donald Weber, "Situating Gertrude Berg: *The Goldbergs* and the Construction of Jewish American Identity, 1930–50," in Joyce Antler, ed., *Talking Back: Images of Jewish Women in American Popular Culture* (Hanover, N.H.: University Press of New England, 1998).

WOMEN'S COLD WAR ACTIVISM

DANIEL HOROWITZ
Betty Friedan and the Origins of Feminism in Cold War America

The years immediately after World War II were marked by a resurgent domesticity. The average age at marriage of women dropped sharply—by the end of the 1950s it was 20. Women's age at the birth of their first child also decreased precipitously; the number of children per family increased sharply. The proportion of women in college fell in comparison to men; many others dropped out of college to marry or because they saw no advantage in increased education.

In 1963 Betty Friedan published *The Feminine Mystique,* a searing indictment of the triviality and frustrations of postwar domesticity (pp. 606–610). She wrote in the voice of an author who located herself in the middle-class suburbs and whose ethnicity was unmarked. But as Daniel Horowitz explains in the essay that follows, Friedan's analysis emerged not only from her experience of suburban life, but also from her experience in left-wing politics and in the labor movement—experiences she did not mention in *The Feminine Mystique.* The execution of Ethel and Julius Rosenberg for spying in 1952 frightened many progressive Jewish organizations lest they be tainted as communist sympathizers; they would subsequently be inhospitable to reformers from the left. (For more about Ethel Rosenberg, see the essay by Joyce Antler on pp. 559–568.) Many elements of Cold War politics and culture may have contributed to the choices Friedan made as she developed her voice.

In 1951, a labor journalist with a decade's experience in protest movements described a trade union meeting where rank-and-file women talked and men listened. Out of these conversations, she reported, emerged the realization that the women were "fighters—that they refuse any longer to be paid or treated as some inferior species by their bosses, or by any male workers who have swallowed the bosses' thinking."[1] The union was the UE, the United Electrical, Radio and Machine Workers of America, the most radical American union in the postwar period and in the 1940s what historian Ronald Schatz ... has called "the largest communist-led institution of any kind in the United States."[2] In 1952 that same journalist wrote a pamphlet, *UE Fights for Women Workers,* that the historian Lisa Kannenberg, unaware of the identity of its author, has called "a remarkable manual for fighting wage discrimination that is, ironically, as relevant today as it was in 1952." At the time, the pamphlet helped raise the consciousness of Eleanor Flexner, who in 1959 would publish *Century of Struggle,* the

Excerpted from Daniel Horowitz, "Rethinking Betty Friedan and *The Feminine Mystique*: Labor Union Radicalism and Feminism in Cold War America," *American Quarterly* 48 (March 1996): 1–42. Copyright © The American Studies Association. Reprinted with permission of the author and Johns Hopkins University Press. Notes have been renumbered and edited.

first scholarly history of American women. In 1953–54, Flexner relied extensively on the pamphlet when she taught a course at the Jefferson School of Social Science in New York on "The Woman Question." Flexner's participation in courses at the school, she later said, "marked the beginning of my real involvement in the issues of women's rights, my realization that leftist organizations—parties, unions—were also riddled with male supremacist prejudice and discrimination."[3] The labor journalist and pamphlet writer was Betty Friedan.

In 1973 Friedan remarked that until she started writing *The Feminine Mystique* (1963), "I wasn't even conscious of the woman problem." In 1976 she commented that in the early 1950s she was "still in the embrace of the feminine mystique."[4] Although in 1974 she revealed some potentially controversial elements of her past, even then she left the impression that her landmark book emerged only from her own captivity by the very forces she described. Friedan's portrayal of herself as so totally trapped by the feminine mystique was part of a reinvention of herself as she wrote and promoted *The Feminine Mystique*. Her story made it possible for readers to identify with its author and its author to enhance the book's appeal. However, it hid from view the connection between the union activity in which Friedan participated in the 1940s and early 1950s and the feminism she inspired in the 1960s. In the short term, her misery in the suburbs may have prompted her to write *The Feminine Mystique*; a longer term perspective makes clear that the book's origins lie much earlier—in her college education and in her experiences with labor unions in the 1940s and early 1950s.[5] . . . Friedan's life provides evidence of . . . continuity . . . between the struggle for justice for working women in the 1940s and the feminism of the 1960s. This connection gives feminism and Friedan, both long under attack for a lack of interest in working class and African American women, a past of which they should be proud. . . . Moreover, a new reading of *The Feminine Mystique* sheds light on the remaking of progressive forces in America, the process by which a focus on women and the professional middle and upper middle classes supplemented, in some ways replaced a focus on unions. Finally, an examination of *The Feminine Mystique* reminds us of important shifts in the ideology of the left: from an earlier economic analysis based on Marxism to one

developed in the 1950s that also rested on humanistic psychology, and from a focus on the impact of conditions of production on the working class to an emphasis on the effect of consumption on the middle class.

In print and in interviews, Friedan has offered a narrative of her life that she popularized after she became famous in 1963.[6] A full biography might begin in Peoria, where Bettye Naomi Goldstein was born February 4, 1921 and grew up with her siblings and their parents: a father who owned a jewelry store and a mother who had given up her position as a society editor of the local paper to raise a family.[7] My analysis of Friedan's political journey starts with her years at Smith College, although it is important to recognize Friedan's earlier sense of herself as someone whose identity as a Jew, a reader, and a brainy girl made her feel freakish and lonely.[8]

As an undergraduate, she has suggested, her lonely life took a turn for the better. "For the first time," she later remarked of her years in college, "I wasn't a freak for having brains." Friedan has acknowledged that she flourished at Smith, with her editorship of the student newspaper, her election to Phi Beta Kappa in her junior year, and her graduation *summa cum laude* among her most prominent achievements. She has told the story of how Gestalt psychology and Kurt Koffka (one of its three founders) were critical in her intellectual development.[9]

Friedan has described the years between her graduation from Smith in 1942 and the publication of her book twenty-one years later as a time when the feminine mystique increasingly trapped her. In her book and in dozens of speeches, articles, and interviews beginning in 1963, she mentioned a pivotal moment in her life, one that she felt marked the beginning of the process by which she succumbed. She told how, while in graduate school at Berkeley in the year after her graduation from college, the university's offer of a prestigious fellowship forced her to make a painful choice. Her first serious boyfriend, a graduate student who had not earned a similarly generous award, threatened to break off the relationship unless she turned down her fellowship. "I never could explain, hardly knew myself, why" she turned away from a career in psychology, she wrote in 1963. She decided to reject the fellowship because she saw herself ending up as an "old maid college teacher" in part because at Smith, she said, there were so few female professors who had husbands and children.[10] The feminine mystique, she insisted, had claimed one of its first victims.[11]

After leaving Berkeley, the copy on the dust jacket of *The Feminine Mystique* noted, Friedan did some "applied social-science research" and freelance writing for magazines. Friedan's biography in a standard reference book quotes her as saying that in the 1940s, "for conscious or unconscious reasons," she worked at "the usual kinds of boring jobs that lead nowhere."[12] This story continues in 1947 with her marriage to Carl Friedan, a returning vet who would eventually switch careers from theater to advertising and public relations. She has told of how she gave birth to three children between 1948 and 1956 and the family moved to the suburbs, with these experiences making her feel trapped. Friedan's picture of her years in the suburbs is not one of contentment and conformity.[13] Though she acknowledged her role in creating and directing a program that brought together teenagers and adult professionals, Friedan portrayed herself as someone who felt "freakish having a career, worried that she was neglecting her children."[14] In an oft-repeated story whose punch line varied, Friedan recounted her response to the census form. In the space where it asked for her occupation, she put down "housewife" but remained guilty, hesitant, and conflicted about such a designation, sometimes pausing and then adding "writer."[15]

Friedan laced *The Feminine Mystique* with suggestions of how much she shared with her suburban sisters. In the opening paragraph, she said that she realized something was wrong in women's lives when she "sensed it first as a question mark in my own life, as a wife and mother of three small children, half-guiltily, and therefore half-heartedly, almost in spite of myself, using my abilities and education in work that took me away from home." Toward the end of the paragraph, when she referred to "a strange discrepancy between the reality of our lives as women and the image to which we were trying to conform," she suggested that she experienced the feminine mystique as keenly and in the same way as her readers. Using the second person plural, she wrote that "all of us went back into the warm brightness of home" and "lowered our eyes from the horizon, and steadily contemplated our own navels." Her work on newspapers, she wrote in *The Feminine Mystique*, proceeded "with

no particular plan." Indeed, she claimed that she had participated as a writer in the creation of the image of the happy housewife.[16]

Friedan asserted she embarked on a path that would lead to *The Feminine Mystique* only when, as she read over the responses of her college classmates to a questionnaire in anticipation of their fifteenth reunion in 1957, she discovered what she called "The Problem That Has No Name," the dissatisfaction her suburban peers felt but could not fully articulate. When she submitted articles to women's magazines, Friedan said, editors changed the meaning of what she had written or rejected outright her suggestions for pieces on controversial subjects. Then at a meeting of the Society of Magazine Writers, she heard Vance Packard recount how he had written *The Hidden Persuaders* (1957) after *Reader's Digest* turned down an article critical of advertising. Friedan decided to write her book.[17]

In *"It Changed My Life": Writings on the Women's Movement* (1976), a book that included a 1974 autobiographical article, Friedan suggested some of what she had omitted from earlier versions of her life.[18] Perhaps responding to attacks on her for not being sufficiently radical, she acknowledged that before her marriage and for several years after she participated in radical activities and worked for union publications.[19] She and the friends with whom she lived before marrying considered themselves in "the vanguard of the working-class revolution," participating in "Marxist discussion groups," going to political rallies, and having "only contempt for dreary bourgeois capitalists like our fathers." Without getting much more specific, Friedan noted that right after the war she was "very involved, consciously radical. Not about women, for heaven's sake!" but about African Americans, workers, the threat of war, anti-communism, and "communist splits and schisms." This was a time, Friedan reported briefly, when, working as a labor journalist, she discovered "the grubby economic underside of American reality."[20]

"I was certainly not a feminist then—none of us," she remarked in the mid-1970s, "were a bit interested in women's rights." She remembered one incident, whose implications she said she only understood much later. Covering a strike, she could not interest anyone in the fact that the company and the union discriminated against women. In 1952, she later claimed, pregnant with her second child, she was fired from her job on a union publication and told that her second pregnancy was her fault. The Newspaper Guild, she asserted, was unwilling to honor its commitment to grant pregnancy leaves. This was, Friedan later remembered, as she mentioned her efforts to call a meeting in protest, "the first personal stirring of my own feminism, I guess. But the other women were just embarrassed, and the men uncomprehending. It was my own fault, getting pregnant again, a *personal* matter, not something you should take to the union. There was no word in 1949 for 'sex discrimination.'"[21]

Though in the 1970s Friedan suggested this more interesting version of her life in the 1940s and 1950s, she distracted the reader from what she had said. She began and ended the 1974 piece with images of domestic life. Even as she mentioned participation in Marxist discussion groups, she talked of how she and her friends read fashion magazines and spent much of their earnings on elegant clothes. Describing what she offered as a major turning point in her life, she told of how, after campaigning for Henry Wallace in 1948, all of a sudden she lost interest in political activity. The 1940s and 1950s were a period, she later asserted, when she was fully exposed to what she would label the feminine mystique as she learned that motherhood took the place of career and politics. She gave the impression of herself in the late 1940s as a woman who embraced domesticity, motherhood, and housework, even as she admitted that not everything at the time resulted from the feminine mystique.[22]

In her 1974 article Friedan filled her descriptions of the late 1940s and 1950s with a sense of the conflicts she felt over her new roles, as she surrendered to the feminine mystique with mixed emotions. She reported how wonderful was the time in Parkway Village, Queens, a period when she experienced the pleasure of a spacious apartment, edited the community newspaper, and enjoyed the camaraderie of young marrieds. Yet, having read Benjamin Spock's *Child and Baby Care,* she felt guilty when she returned to work after a maternity leave. With her move to a traditional suburb, she said, the conflicts intensified. She spoke of driving her children to school and lessons, participating in the PTA, and then, when neighbors came by, hiding "like secret drinking in the morning" the book she was working on.[23]

Accomplishing practical, specific tasks around the house and in local politics was "somehow more real and secure than the schizophrenic and even dangerous politics of the world revolution whose vanguard we used to fancy ourselves." Friedan remarked that by 1949 she realized that the revolution was not going to happen in the United States as she anticipated, in part because workers, like others, wanted kitchen gadgets. She reported that she found herself disillusioned with what was happening in unions, in Czechoslovakia, and in the Soviet Union, despite the fact that cries about the spread of Communism merely provided the pretext for attacks on suspected subversives. In those days, she continued, "McCarthyism, the danger of war against Russia and of fascism in America, and the reality of U.S. imperial, corporate wealth and power" combined to make those who once dreamed of "making the whole world over uncomfortable with the Old Left rhetoric of revolution." Using the first person plural as she referred to Margaret Mead's picture in *Male and Female* (1949) of women fulfilled through motherhood and domesticity, Friedan wrote, "we were suckers for that apple." It hardly occurred to any of those in her circle, who themselves now wanted new gadgets, that large corporations profited from marketing household appliances by "overselling us on the bliss of domesticity."[24]

The new information Friedan offered in 1974 did not dislodge the accepted understanding of how she became a feminist . . . [Yet] what the written record reveals of Friedan's life from her arrival at Smith in the fall of 1938 until the publication of *The Feminine Mystique* makes possible a story different from the one she has told. To begin with, usually missing from her narrative is full and specific information about how at college she first developed a sense of herself as a radical.[25] Courses she took, friendships she established with peers and professors, events in the United States and abroad, and her campus leadership all turned Friedan from a provincial outsider into a determined advocate of trade unions as the herald of progressive social change, a healthy skeptic about the authority and rhetorical claims of those in power, a staunch opponent of fascism, a defender of free speech, and a fierce questioner of social privilege expressed by the conspicuous consumption of some of her peers.[26]

What and with whom she studied points well beyond Gestalt psychology and Koffka.[27]

Though Friedan acknowledged the importance of James Gibson, she did not mention his activity as an advocate of trade unions.[28] Moreover, her statement that at Smith there were few role models is hard to reconcile with the fact that the college had a number of them; indeed she took courses from both James Gibson and Eleanor Gibson, husband and wife and parents of two children, the first of them born in 1940.[29] As a women's college, and especially one with an adversarial tradition, Smith may well have fostered in Friedan a feminism that was at least implicit—by enabling her to assume leadership positions and by encouraging her to take herself seriously as a writer and thinker.

In the fall of her junior year, Friedan took an economics course taught by Dorothy W. Douglas, Theories and Movements for Social Reconstruction. Douglas was well known at the time for her radicalism.[30] In what she wrote for Douglas, and with youthful enthusiasm characteristic of many members of her generation, Friedan sympathetically responded to the Marxist critique of capitalism as a cultural, economic, and political force.[31]

Friedan also gained an education as a radical in the summer of 1941 when, following Douglas's suggestion, she participated in a writers' workshop at the Highlander Folk School in Tennessee, an institution active in helping the CIO organize in the South. The school offered a series of summer institutes for fledgling journalists which, for 1939 and 1940 (but not 1941), the communist-led League of American Writers helped sponsor. For three years beginning in the fall of 1939, opponents of Highlander had sustained a vicious redbaiting attack, but a FBI investigator found no evidence of subversive activity.[32] In good Popular Front language, Friedan praised Highlander as a truly American institution that was attempting to help America to fulfill its democratic ideals. She explored the contradictions of her social position as a Jewish girl from a well-to-do family who had grown up in a class-divided Peoria, gave evidence of her hostility to the way her parents fought over issues of debt and extravagance, and described the baneful influence of the mass media on American life. Though she also acknowledged that her Smith education did "not lead to much action," she portrayed herself as someone whose radical consciousness relied on the American labor movement as the bulwark against fascism.[33]

At Smith Friedan linked her journalism to political activism. She served as editor-in-chief of the campus newspaper for a year beginning in the spring of 1941. The campaigns she undertook and the editorials she wrote reveal a good deal of her politics. Under Friedan's leadership, the newspaper's reputation for protest was so strong that in a skit a fellow student portrayed an editor, perhaps Friedan herself, as "a strident voice haranguing from a perpetual soap-box."[34] While at Smith, a Peoria paper reported in 1943, Friedan helped organize college building and grounds workers into a union.[35] Under her leadership, the student paper took on the student government for holding closed meetings, fought successfully to challenge the administration's right to control what the newspaper printed, campaigned for the relaxation of restrictions on student social life, censured social clubs for their secrecy, and published critiques of professors' teaching.[36] In response to an article in a campus humor magazine that belittled female employees who cleaned the students' rooms and served them food, an editorial supported the administration's censorship of the publication on the grounds that such action upheld "the liberal democratic tradition of the college."[37]

The editorials written on her watch reveal a young woman who believed that what was involved with almost every issue—at Smith, in the United States and abroad—was the struggle for democracy, freedom, and social justice. Under Friedan's leadership the editors supported American workers and their labor unions in their struggles to organize and improve their conditions. . . . The inequality of power in America, the editorial argued in good social democratic terms, "has to be admitted and dealt with if democracy is to have meaning for 95% of the citizens of this country."[38]

Above all, what haunted the editorials was the spread of fascism and questions about America's involvement in a world war. In April of 1941, the editors made it clear that the defeat of fascism was their primary goal and one that determined their position on questions of war or peace. In the fall of 1941, after the German invasion of the Soviet Union during the preceding summer, the editors increasingly accepted the inevitability of war even as they made it clear that they believed "fighting fascists is only one part of fighting fascism."[39] Some Smith students responded with redbaiting to the newspaper's anti-fascism and reluctance to support intervention wholeheartedly, accusing the editorial board of being dominated by communists, at a time when the Party reached its greatest membership in the years after Pearl Harbor while the United States and the Soviet Union were allies. Though one editor denied the charge of communist influence, like many newspapers at American colleges in these years, on the paper's staff were students attracted to the political analysis offered by radical groups. In the fall of 1940 one columnist argued against lumping communists and Nazis together, remarking that communism was not a "dark terror" but "a precarious scheme worked out by millions of civilized men and women."[40]

When America entered the war in December of 1941, the editors accepted the nation's new role loyally, albeit soberly. The central issue for them was how American students, especially female ones, could "contribute actively to the American cause." . . .

Friedan's experiences at Smith cast a different light on her decision to leave Berkeley after a year of graduate school. The editorials she and her peers had written immediately after Pearl Harbor revealed an impatience to be near the action. A 1943 article in the Peoria paper reported that Friedan turned down the fellowship because "she decided she wanted to work in the labor movement—on the labor press."[41] . . . Off and on from October 1943 until July 1946 she was a staff writer for the Federated Press, a left-wing news service that provided stories for newspapers, especially union ones, across the nation.[42] Here Friedan wrote articles that supported the aspirations of African Americans and union members. She also criticized reactionary forces that, she believed, were working secretly to undermine progressive social advances.[43] As early as 1943, she pictured efforts by businesses, coordinated by the National Association of Manufacturers (NAM), to develop plans that would enhance profits, diminish the power of unions, reverse the New Deal, and allow businesses to operate as they pleased.[44]

At Federated Press, Friedan also paid attention to women's problems. Right after she began to work there, she interviewed UE official Ruth Young, one of the clearest voices in the labor movement articulating women's issues. In the resulting article, Friedan noted that the government could not solve the problem of turnover "merely by pinning up thousands of glamorous posters designed to lure

more women into industry." Neither women, unions, nor management, she quoted Young as saying, could solve problems of escalating prices or inadequate child care that were made even more difficult by the fact that "women still have two jobs to do." Action of the federal government, Friedan reported, was needed to solve the problems working women faced.[45]

She paid special attention to stories about protecting the jobs and improving the situation of working women, including married ones with children.

For about six years beginning in July, 1946, precisely at the moment when the wartime Popular Front came under intense attack, Friedan was a reporter for the union's paper UE News.[46] At least as early as 1943, when she quoted Young, Friedan was well aware of the UE's commitments to equity for women.[47]

. . . In 1949–50, union activists who followed the recommendations of the Communist Party . . . advocated the automatic granting of several years of seniority to all African Americans as compensation for their years of exclusion from the electrical industry. If the UE pioneered in articulating what we might call affirmative action for African Americans, then before and during World War II it advocated what a later generation would label comparable worth. Against considerable resistance from within its ranks, the UE also worked to improve the conditions of working-class women in part by countering a seniority system which gave advantage to men.[48] After 1949, with the UE out of the CIO and many of the more conservative union members out of the UE, women's issues and women's leadership resumed the importance they had in the UE during World War II, when it had developed, Ruth Milkman has written, a "strong ideological commitment to gender equality."[49]

Beginning in 1946, Friedan [also] witnessed the efforts by federal agencies, congressional committees, major corporations, the Roman Catholic Church, and the CIO to break the hold of what they saw as the domination of the UE by communists. The inclusion of a clause in the Taft-Hartley Act of 1947, requiring union officers to sign an anticommunist affidavit if they wished to do business with the National Labor Relations Board, helped encourage other unions to challenge the UE, whose leaders refused to sign.[50] Internecine fights took place within the UE, part of a longer term fight between radicals and anticommunists in its ranks. . . . Before long, . . . the UE was greatly weakened: in 1949, its connection with the CIO was severed and the newly-formed and CIO-backed IUE recruited many of its members. Membership in UE, numbering more than 600,000 in 1946, fell to 203,000 in 1953 and to 71,000 four years later.[51]

At *UE News,* from her position as a middle-class woman interested in the lives of the working class, Friedan continued to articulate a progressive position on a wide range of issues. She again pointed to concerted efforts, led by big corporations under the leadership of the NAM, to increase profits, exploit labor, and break labor unions.[52] In 1951, she contrasted the extravagant expenditures of the wealthy with the family of a worker who could afford neither fresh vegetables nor new clothes.[53] Friedan also told the story of how valiant union members helped build political coalitions to fight Congressional and corporate efforts to roll back gains workers made during the New Deal and World War II.[54] She drew parallels between the United States in the 1940s and Nazi Germany in the 1930s as she exposed the way HUAC [the House Committee on Un-American Activities, U.S. Congress] and big business were using every tactic they could to destroy the UE. Friedan hailed the launching of the Progressive Party in 1948.[55] She exposed the existence of racism and discrimination, even when they appeared among union officials and especially when directed against Jews and African Americans. Praising heroic workers who struggled against great odds as they fought monopolies, Friedan, probably expressing her hopes for herself, extolled the skills of a writer "who is able to describe with sincerity and passion the hopes, the struggle and the romance of the working people who make up most of America."[56]

Throughout her years at *UE News,* Friedan participated in discussions on women's issues, including the issue of corporations' systematic discrimination against women. Going to factories to interview those whose stories she was covering, she also wrote about working women, including African Americans and Latinas.[57] In the worlds Friedan inhabited in the decade beginning in 1943, as the historian Kathleen Weigand has shown, people often discussed the cultural and economic sources of women's oppression, the nature of discrimination based on sex, the special difficulties African American women faced, and the dynamics

of discrimination against women in a variety of institutions, including the family.[58] Moreover, for the people around Friedan and doubtlessly for Friedan herself, the fight for justice for women was inseparable from the more general struggle to secure rights for African Americans and workers.[59] As she had done at the Federated Press, at *UE News* in the late 1940s and early 1950s she reported on how working women struggled as producers and consumers to make sure their families had enough to live on.[60]

Friedan's focus on working women's issues resulted in her writing the pamphlet, *UE Fights for Women Workers,* published by the UE in June of 1952.[61] She began by suggesting the contradiction in industry's treatment of women as consumers and as producers. "In advertisements across the land," Friedan remarked, "industry glorifies the American woman—in her gleaming GE kitchen, at her Westinghouse laundromat, before her Sylvania television set. Nothing," she announced as she insightfully explored a central contradiction women faced in the postwar world, "is too good for her—unless" she worked for corporations, including GE, or Westinghouse, or Sylvania.[62]

The central theme of the piece was how, in an effort to improve the pay and conditions of working women, the UE fought valiantly against greedy corporations that sought to increase their profits by exploiting women. Friedan discussed a landmark 1945 National War Labor Board decision on sex-based wage discrimination in favor of the UE. Remarking that *"fighting the exploitation of women is men's business too,"* she emphasized how discriminatory practices corporations used against women hurt men as well by exerting downward pressure on wages of all workers. To back up the call for equal pay for equal work and to fight against segregation and discrimination of women, she countered stereotypes justifying lower pay for women: they were physically weaker, entered the work force only temporarily, had no families to support, and worked only for pin money. She highlighted the "even more shocking" situation African American women faced, having to deal as they did with the "double bars" of being female and African American.[63] Friedan set forth a program that was, Lisa Kannenberg has noted, "a prescription for a gender-blind workplace."[64]

The conditions under which she left Federated Press and *UE News* are not entirely clear.

In May of 1946, during her second stint at Federated Press, she filed a grievance with the Newspaper Guild, saying she had lost her job in June of 1945 to a man she had replaced during the war. Later she claimed she was "bumped" from her position "by a returning veteran." There is evidence, however, that Friedan had to give up her position to a man who returned to the paper after two years in prison because he refused to serve in the military during what he considered a capitalists' war.[65] Friedan later claimed that she lost her job at the UE during her second pregnancy because the labor movement failed to honor its commitment to maternity leaves. Yet a knowledgeable observer has written that when the union had to cut the staff because of the dramatic drop in its membership, something that resulted from McCarthyite attacks, Friedan "offered to quit so another reporter," a man with more seniority, could remain at *UE News*.[66] Although her experience with unions may have provided a negative spur to her feminism, it also served as a positive inspiration. Friedan was indebted to the UE for major elements of her education about gender equity, sex discrimination, and women's issues.

The reason Friedan left out these years in her life story is now clear. Her stint at the *UE News* took place at the height of the anti-communist crusade, which she experienced at close quarters. When she emerged into the limelight in 1963, the issue of affiliation with communists was wracking SANE, SDS, and the civil rights movement. In the same years, HUAC was still holding hearings, the United States was pursuing an anti-communist war in Vietnam, and J. Edgar Hoover's FBI was wire-tapping Martin Luther King, Jr., ostensibly to protect the nation against communist influence. Had Friedan revealed all in the mid-1960s, she would have undercut her book's impact, subjected herself to palpable dangers, and jeopardized the feminist movement, including the National Organization for Women (NOW), an institution she was instrumental in launching. Perhaps instead of emphasizing continuities in her life, she told the story of her conversion in order to heighten the impact of her book and appeal to white middle-class women. Or . . . Friedan may have come to believe a narrative that outlived the needs it originally fulfilled.

Until 1952, almost everything Friedan published as a labor journalist appeared under the name Betty Goldstein, though she had married in 1947. When she emerged as a writer for women's magazines in 1955, it was as Betty Friedan. Aside from indicating her marital status, the change in name was significant. It signaled a shift from an employee for a union paper who wrote highly political articles on the working class to a free-lance writer for mass circulation magazines who concentrated on the suburban middle class in more muted tones [and in the 1950s became a suburbanite herself. In 1957, the Friedans moved into an] eleven-room Victorian house, which they bought with the help of the GI Bill and some money Friedan inherited from her father.[67]

What Friedan wrote for mass circulation women's magazines [during those years] belies her claim that she had contributed to what she later attacked in *The Feminine Mystique.*

Sylvie Murray has demonstrated that Friedan drafted, but was unable to get into print, articles that fully celebrated women's political activism, expressed skepticism about male expertise, and described blue collar and lower middle-class families, not generic middle-class ones. Yet Friedan was able to sell articles that went against the grain of the Cold War celebration by criticizing middle-class conformity. . . . Friedan critiqued suburban life by drawing a dismal picture of those who conformed, by offering alternatives to conventional choices, and by exploring the strength of cooperative communities.[68] She drew portraits of American women that opposed the picture of the happy, suburban housewife who turned her back on a career in order to find satisfaction at home.[69] Friedan also portrayed women accomplishing important tasks as they took on traditionally feminine civic roles, thus implicitly undercutting the ideal of the apolitical suburban housewife and mother.[70]

In one particularly revealing piece, Friedan prefigured some of the issues she later claimed she only began to discover when she started to work on *The Feminine Mystique*. In "I Went Back to Work," published in *Charm* in April 1955, she wrote that initially she did not think highly of housework or of housewives and was guilty about what she was doing. Eventually she decided that her commitment to being a good mother was not "going to interfere with what I regarded as my 'real' life." Finding it necessary to be away from home for nine hours a day in order to work, she solved the problem of child care by hiring "a really good mother-substitute—a housekeeper-nurse." In the end, Friedan had no regrets about her decision or apparently about her privileged position. She believed her work outside the home improved her family's situation and acknowledged that her "whole life had always been geared around creative, intellectual work" and "a professional career."[71]

In what ways, then, was Friedan a captive of the feminine mystique? There is no question but that she was miserable in the suburbs. Her emphasis on her captivity may have expressed one part of her ambivalence. Yet, though she claimed that she shared so much with her suburban, white, middle-class sisters in the postwar world, during much of the two decades beginning in 1943 Friedan was participating in left-wing union activity, writing articles that went against the grain of Cold War ideology, and living in a cosmopolitan, racially integrated community. During most of the time between her marriage in 1947 and the publication of The Feminine Mystique, Friedan combined career and family life. As a woman who worked with her at Federated Press later noted, at the time Friedan and her female colleagues expected to have professional careers.[72] Caution about the predominantly suburban origins of her book is also in order because Friedan's move to suburban Rockland County in 1956 preceded by only a few months her initial work on the survey for her reunion that was so critical to The Feminine Mystique.[73]

To be sure, in the postwar world Friedan experienced at first hand the trials of a woman who fought against considerable odds to combine marriage, motherhood, and a career.[74] Yet in critical ways her difficulties did not stem from the dilemmas she described in her book: lack of career and ambition, a securely affluent household, and absence of a political sensibility. Friedan experienced psychological conflicts over issues of creativity in writing and motherhood.[75] Researching and writing her free-lance articles was a laborious process.[76] She had three young children, hardly felt comfortable in the suburbs, had no local institutions to provide a supportive environment for an aspiring writer, and continually faced financial difficulties. Her income from writing articles was unpredictable, a situation exacerbated by the pressure she was under to help support the household and justify the expenses for child care. Tension persisted between the Friedans over a wide range of issues, including

who was responsible for earning and spending the family's income. Moreover, she was in a marriage apparently marked by violence.[77]

Friedan was largely right when she said "all the pieces of my own life came together for the first time in the writing" of The Feminine Mystique. The skills as a journalist she had developed beginning as a teenager stood her in good stead as she worked to make what she had to say accessible to a wide audience. Her identity as a Jew and an outsider gave her a distinctive perspective on American and suburban life. Her years at Smith boosted her confidence and enhanced her political education. Her life as a wife and mother sensitized her to the conflicts millions of others experienced but could not articulate. Her education as a psychologist led her to understand the gestalt, the wholeness of a situation, and to advocate self-fulfillment based on humanistic psychology. Above all, her work as a labor journalist and activist provided her with the intellectual depth, ideological commitments, and practical experiences crucial to her emergence as a leading feminist in the 1960s.

Why did a woman who had spent so much energy advocating political solutions focus in The Feminine Mystique largely on adult education and self-realization and turn social problems into psychological ones? How did a woman who had fought to improve the lives of African Americans, Latinas, and working-class women end up writing a book that saw the problems of America in terms of the lives of affluent, suburban white women?[78]

Even at the time, at least one observer, Gerda Lerner, raised questions about what Friedan emphasized and neglected. Active in the trade union movement in the 1940s, present at the founding meeting of NOW, and after the mid-1960s one of the nation's leading historians of women, in February 1963 Lerner wrote Friedan. "I have just finished reading your splendid book and want to tell you how excited and delighted I am with it. . . . You have done for women," she remarked as she referred to the author who had warned about the destruction of the environment, "what Rachel Carson did for birds and trees." Yet, Lerner continued:

> I have one reservation about your treatment of your subject: you address yourself solely to the problems of middle class, college-educated women. This approach was one of the shortcomings of the suffrage movement for many years

and has, I believe, retarded the general advance of women. Working women, especially Negro women, labor not only under the disadvantages imposed by the feminine mystique, but under the more pressing disadvantages of economic discrimination. To leave them out of consideration of the problem or to ignore the contributions they can make toward its solution, is something we simply cannot afford to do. By their desperate need, by their numbers, by their organizational experience (if trade union members), working women are most important in reaching *institutional* solutions to the problems of women.[79]

The dynamics of Friedan's shifts in attention from working-class to middle-class women are not entirely clear. At some point after May 1953, when she followed the proceedings at the UE conference on the problems of women workers, Friedan turned away from working-class and African American women, something that undercut the power of *The Feminine Mystique*. An important question is whether the shift from her UE radicalism and focus on working-class women was a rhetorical strategy designed for the specific situation of *The Feminine Mystique* or part of a longer-term deradicalization. Until her personal papers are fully open and extensive interviewing is carried out, and perhaps not even then, we may not know the dynamics of this change.

Notes

1. Betty Goldstein, "UE Drive on Wage, Job Discrimination Wins Cheers from Women Members," *UE News*, 16 Apr. 1951, 6. My interview of Friedan in 1987 first brought to my attention the possibility of this alternative story, as did the research my colleague, Helen L. Horowitz, carried out in the late 1980s. The appearance of the article by Joanne Meyerowitz in 1993, cited below, added an important piece of evidence. Because Friedan has denied me permission to quote from her unpublished papers and has not responded to my request that she grant me an opportunity to interview her or to have her respond to my questions, I have not been able to present as full and perhaps as accurate a story as I wished to do.

2. Ronald W. Schatz, *The Electrical Workers: A History of Labor at General Electric and Westinghouse, 1923–60* (Urbana, Ill., 1983), xiii.

3. Lisa Kannenberg, "The Impact of the Cold War on Women's Trade Union Activism: The UE Experience," *Labor History* 34 (spring-summer 1993): 318; Jacqueline Van Voris, interview with Eleanor Flexner, Northampton, Mass., 16 Oct. 1982, 70–71, Eleanor Flexner Papers, Schlesinger Library, Radcliffe College, Cambridge, Mass.

4. Betty Friedan, "Up From the Kitchen Floor," *New York Times Magazine*, 4 Mar. 1973, 8; Betty Friedan,

"*It Changed My Life": Writings on the Women's Movement* (New York, 1976), 304.

5. For evidence of the continuing importance of Friedan and her book, see, for example, Elaine T. May, *Homeward Bound: American Families in the Cold War Era* (New York, 1988), 209–17, 219.

6. For biographical information, in addition to what Friedan has said in print, I am relying on, among others, Kathleen Wilson, "Betty (Naomi) Friedan," *Contemporary Authors*, New Revision Series (New York, 1995) 45: 133–36; David Halberstam, *The Fifties* (New York, 1993), 592–98; Marilyn French, "The Emancipation of Betty Friedan," *Esquire* 100 (Dec. 1983): 510, 512, 514, 516, 517; Daniel Horowitz, interview of Betty Friedan, Santa Monica, Calif., 18 Mar. 1987. As late as 6 Nov. 1995, the date she sent me a letter denying me permission to quote from her unpublished papers, Friedan reiterated key elements of her story: I am grateful to Rachel Ledford for reporting to me on Friedan's 6 Nov. 1995 talk at the Smithsonian Institution, Washington, D.C. Ironically, two biographies aimed at children provide fuller stories than do other treatments (for instance, they are the only published sources I have been able to locate that make clear that Friedan worked for the UE): Sondra Henry and Emily Taitz, *Betty Friedan: Fighter for Women's Rights* (Hillside, N.J., 1990) and Milton Meltzer, *Betty Friedan: A Voice for Women's Rights* (New York, 1985).

7. This article is based on considerable but hardly exhaustive examination of the available written record. When other researchers examine the Friedan papers (including those to which access is restricted) and are able to carry out extensive interviews, they will be able to offer a fuller exploration of several issues, especially the shifts in Friedan's commitments as a radical at a time of great factionalism, when and how the feminine mystique did or did not trap her, how she interpreted the research on which *The Feminine Mystique* relied, and the pressures Friedan faced from her publisher to shape her 1963 book in certain ways.

8. An examination of what Friedan wrote for her high school paper reveals someone less lonely than she has often portrayed herself: see articles by Friedan in *Peoria Opinion* from the fall of 1936 until the spring of 1938.

9. Friedan, quoted in Wilkes, "Mother Superior," 140; Betty Friedan, *The Feminine Mystique* (New York, 1963), 12.

10. Friedan, *Feminine Mystique*, 70. On the paucity of role models at Smith, see Van Voris, Friedan interview.

11. Horowitz, interview.

12. Dust jacket of 1963 copy of *The Feminine Mystique*, author's possession.

13. Friedan, quoted in "Betty Friedan," *Current Biography Yearbook 1970*, ed. Charles Moritz (New York, 1971), 146; Betty Friedan, "New York Women: Beyond the Feminine Mystique," *New York Herald Tribune*, 21 Feb. 1965, 7–15, women's liberation, biographics, individuals, box 4, folder 31, clippings on Betty Friedan, Sophia Smith Collection, Smith College.

14. Tornabene, "Liberation," 138. See Betty Friedan, "The Intellectual Pied Pipers of Rockland County," unpublished paper, written in 1960–61, FP-SLRC, carton 9, folder 347, Friedan Collection,

Schlesinger Library, Radcliffe College, Cambridge, Mass. [hereinafter cited as BF-SLRC; unless otherwise noted, the references are to collection 71–62 . . . 81-M23].

15. Rollene W. Saal, "Author of the Month," *Saturday Review,* 21 Mar. 1964, women's liberation, biographies, individuals, box 4, folder 31, SSC-SC.

16. Friedan, *Feminine Mystique,* 9, 20, 66, 70, 186–87.

17. Horowitz, interview: Betty Friedan, "Introduction to the Tenth Anniversary Edition" of *Feminine Mystique* (New York, 1974), 1–5.

18. The 1974 article, which in the book was called "The Way We Were—1949," was originally published with some relatively unimportant differences, but with a more revealing title, as Betty Friedan, "In France, de Beauvoir Had Just Published 'The Second Sex,'" *New York* 8 (30 Dec. 1974–6 Jan. 1975): 52–55. In Horowitz, interview, which covered mainly the years up to 1963, Friedan discussed her move to a radical politics even as she emphasized captivity by the feminine mystique beginning in the Berkeley years. Though Friedan has revealed a good deal about her life, to the best of my knowledge she has not acknowledged in print the full range of reasons she left Berkeley, that she worked for the UE, her authorship of the 1952 pamphlet, and her leadership of the rent strike. Moreover, she has insisted that in the late 1940s and early 1950s, she had interest neither in a career nor in women's problems.

19. I am grateful to Judith Smith for helping me to think through this and other issues.

20. Friedan, *Changed My Life,* 6, 8–9.

21. Friedan, *Changed My Life,* 6, 9, 16; Halberstam, *Fifties,* 593; French, "Emancipation," 510. Horowitz, interview, dates the firing in 1952. In the immediate postwar years, the term "feminist" often referred to women who were Republicans, independent businesswomen, and professionals.

22. Friedan, *Changed My Life,* 5, 6–7, 8–9, 15, 16.

23. Friedan, *Changed My Life,* 14–16.

24. Friedan, *Changed My Life,* 12, 16.

25. Cohen, *Sisterhood,* 63 and Wilkes, "Mother Superior," 140 briefly draw a picture of Friedan as a college rebel but to the best of my knowledge, the politics of that rebellion have remained largely unknown.

26. This summary relies on unsigned editorials that appeared under Friedan's editorship, which can be found in SCAN [*Smith College Associated News*] from 14 Mar. 1941 to 10 Mar. 1942, p. 2. Although members of the editorial board held a wide range of opinions, I am assuming that as editor-in-chief Friedan had a significant role in shaping editorials.

27. For the article she published on the basis on her honors thesis, see H. Israel and B. Goldstein, "Operationism in Psychology," *Psychological Review* 51 (May 1944): 177–88.

28. See James J. Gibson, "Why a Union For Teachers?" *Focus* 2 (Nov. 1939): 3–7.

29. I am grateful to Margery Sly, Archivist of Smith College, for providing this information. She has also pointed out that teaching at Smith in Friedan's years were several married, female faculty members who had children and that Harold Israel and Elsa Siipola, two of Friedan's mentors, were married but without children.

30. In 1955 Douglas took the Fifth Amendment before HUAC as she was redbaited, accused of having been a member of a communist teachers union in the late 1930s. I am grateful to Margery Sly and Jacquelyn D. Hall for providing this information on Douglas. For Friedan's continued use of Marxist analysis, see Friedan, *It Changed My Life,* 110.

31. Bettye Goldstein, "Discussion of Reading Period Material," paper for Economics 319, 18 Jan. 1941, carton 1, folder 257, BF-SLRC, 1, 2, 4, 8.

32. John M. Glen, *Highlander: No Ordinary School, 1932–1962* (Lexington, Ky., 1988), 47–69.

33. Bettye Goldstein, "Highlander Folk School—American Future," unpublished paper, 1941, carton 6, folder 274, BF-SLRC; Goldstein, "Learning the Score," 22–24.

34. "Epilogue of Failure," *SCAN,* 10 Mar. 1942, 2.

35. "Betty Goldstein, Local Girl, Makes Good in New York," clipping from Peoria newspaper, probably 10 Dec. 1943 issue of *Labor Temple News,* carton 1, folder 86, BF-SLRC.

36. "Behind a Closed Door," *SCAN,* 3 Oct. 1941, 2; "Declaration of Student Independence," *SCAN,* 5 Dec. 1941, 1–2; "SCAN Protests Against Censorship," *SCAN,* 5 Dec. 1941, 1; "A Few Hours More," *SCAN,* 10 Oct. 1941, 2; "Review of Philosophy Courses," *SCAN,* 10 Mar. 1942, 2.

37. "The Tatler Suspension," *SCAN,* 7 Nov. 1941, 2; for the article in question see "Maids We Have Known and Loved," *Tatler,* Oct. 1941, 9, 21.

38. "Education in Emergency," *SCAN,* 15 Apr. 1941, 2; "The Right to Organize," *SCAN,* 21 Oct. 1941, 2; "Comment," *SCAN,* 14 Nov. 1941, 2; Filene's advertisement, *SCAN,* 21 Oct. 1941, 2.

39. "They Choose Peace," *SCAN,* 22 Apr. 1941, 2; for the minority opinion, see "The Case for Intervention," *SCAN,* 2 May 1941, 2; "War Against Fascism," *SCAN,* 24 Oct. 1941, 2. Placing the editorials written on Friedan's watch in the national context of student politics makes clear that after the Nazi-Soviet pact the student movement was more active and radical at Smith than elsewhere. On the national context see Robert Cohen, *When the Old Left Was Young: Student Radicals and America's First Mass Student Movement, 1929–1941* (New York, 1993), especially 315–37.

40. J. N., "The Red Menace," *SCAN,* 14 Oct. 1941, 2; Neal Gilkyson, "The Gallery," *SCAN,* 21 Oct. 1941, 2.

41. "Betty Goldstein, Local Girl," Meltzer, *Friedan,* 21 provides explanations for Friedan's decision that do not rely on the standard story.

42. For information on the Federated Press, see Doug Reynolds, "Federated Press," *Encyclopedia of the American Left,* ed. Mari Jo Buhle, Paul Buhle, and Dan Georgakas (New York, 1990), 225–27.

43. Editorials in clippings: carton 8, folder 328, BF-SLRC.

44. Betty Goldstein, "Big Business Getting Desperate, Promising Postwar Jobs," Federated Press, 19 Nov. 1943, carton 8, folder 328, BF-SLRC; Betty Goldstein, "NAM Convention Pro-War—For War on Labor, New Deal, Roosevelt," Federated Press, 14 Dec. 1943, carton 8, folder 328, BF-SLRC; Betty Goldstein, "Details of Big Business Anti-Labor Conspiracy Uncovered," Federated Press, 11 Feb. 1946, carton 8, folder 328, BF-SLRC.

45. Betty Goldstein, "Pretty Posters Won't Stop Turnover of Women in Industry," Federated Press,

26 Oct. 1943, and Ruth Young quoted in same, carton 8, folder 328, BF-SLRC.

46. Job application, 1951.

47. For information on women in the UE see Schatz, *Electrical Workers*; Ruth Milkman, *Gender at Work: The Dynamics of Job Segregation by Sex During World War II* (Urbana, 1987); Kannenberg, "Impact."

48. Schatz, *Electrical Workers*, 30, 89, 116–27, 129–30.

49. Milkman, *Gender at Work*, 77–78.

50. Zieger, *CIO*, 251.

51. This summary relies on Schatz, *Electrical Workers*, 167–240 (quotation, 181).

52. Betty Goldstein, "NAM Does Gleeful War Dance to Profits, Wage Cuts, Taft Law," *UE News*, 13 Dec. 1947, 4. What follows relies on the more than three dozen articles signed by Betty Goldstein in the *UE News* from the fall of 1946 until early 1952.

53. Betty Goldstein, "A Tale of 'Sacrifice': A Story of Equality in the United States, 1951," *March of Labor*, May 1951, 16–18, carton 8, folder 334, BF-SLRC.

54. Betty Goldstein, columns in *UE News*, 7 Dec. 1946, 9; 31 May 1947, 5, 8; 23 Aug. 1947, 4.

55. Betty Goldstein, columns in *UE News*, 12 May 1947, 5; 8 Nov. 1947, 6–7; 4 Sept. 1948, 6–7; 22 Aug. 1949, 4; 9 Jan. 1950, 5; 31 July 1948, 6–7.

56. B. G., review of Sinclair Lewis, *Kingsblood Royal*, *UE News*, 6 Sept. 1947, 7; B. G., review of the movie "Gentleman's Agreement," *UE News*, 22 Nov. 1947, 11; B. G., review of movie "Crossfire," *UE News*, 9 Aug. 1947, 8–9; Betty Goldstein, "CIO Sold Out Fight for FEPC, T-H Repeal, Rep. Powell Reveals," *UE News*, 17 Apr. 1950, 4; B. G., review of Fielding Burke, *Sons of the Stranger*, *UE News*, 24 Jan. 1948, 7.

57. These two sentences rely on James Lerner, interview. For treatments of the relationship between communism and women's issues, see Ellen K. Trimberger, "Women in the Old and New Left: The Evolution of a Politics of Personal Life," *Feminist Studies* 5 (fall 1979): 432–61.

58. Though she does not discuss Friedan's situation, the best treatment of the prominent role of women's issues in radical circles in the 1940s and 1950s is Weigand, "Vanguards."

59. Chinoy, interview.

60. Betty Goldstein, "Price Cuts Promised in Press Invisible to GE Housewives," *UE News*, 1 Feb. 1947, 7; Betty Goldstein, "Union Members Want to Know—WHO Has Too Much Money to Spend," *UE News*, 26 Mar. 1951, 8.

61. [Betty Goldstein], *UE Fights for Women Workers*, UE Publication no. 232, June 1952 (New York, 1952). To authenticate her authorship, I am relying on the following: Horowitz, interview; James Lerner, interview; Betty Friedan, postcard to author, late August, 1995; Meltzer, *Friedan*, 25.

62. [Goldstein], *UE Fights*, 5.

63. [Goldstein], *UE Fights*, 9–18, 26–27, 38.

64. Kannenberg, "Impact," 318.

65. Friedan, *Changed My Life*, 9; Mim Kelber, phone conversation with Daniel Horowitz, 16 Sept. 1995, identified the man as James Peck; obituary for James Peck, *New York Times* 13 July 1993, B7.

66. Meltzer, *Friedan*, 29.

67. To date these moves, I am relying on a number of sources, including Betty Friedan to Mrs. Clifford P. Cowen, 5 Aug. 1957, carton 7, folder, 313, BF-SLRC; Friedan, "New York Women"; "About the Author," in "New York Women"; "Friedan," *Current Biography*, 146; *Smith College Bulletin*.

68. Betty Friedan, "Two Are an Island," *Mademoiselle* 41 (July 1955): 88–89, 100–101; Betty Friedan, "Teenage Girl in Trouble," *Coronet* 43 (Mar. 1958): 163–68; Betty Friedan. "The Happy Families of Hickory Hill," *Redbook*, Feb. 1956, 39, 87–90; Sylvie Murray's "Suburban Citizens: Domesticity and Community Politics in Queens, New York, 1945–1960," Ph.D. diss., Yale University, 1994 ably contrasts the adversarial politics of Friedan's unpublished pieces with the milder tone of her published ones; on the difficulty of getting into print articles on women who were not middle-class, I am relying on Sylvie Murray, phone conversation with Daniel Horowitz, 9 Oct. 1995.

69. An influential book on the origins of 1960s feminism begins with a discussion of Friedan's magazine articles without seeing how they might connect parts of her career: Sara Evans, *Personal Politics: The Roots of Women's Liberation in the Civil Rights Movement and the New Left* (New York, 1979), 3.

70. Betty Friedan, "Now They're Proud of Peoria," *Reader's Digest* 67 (Aug. 1955): 93–97.

71. Betty Friedan, "I Went Back to Work," *Charm*, Apr. 1955, 145, 200.

72. Kelber, conversation.

73. Parkway Village had some suburban characteristics and was marketed on the basis of its suburban qualities: Murray, conversation. Yet Friedan has made it clear that she was happy there: Friedan, *Changed My Life*, 14.

74. Especially crucial but nonetheless elusive is the period from May 1953, when she appears to have ended her union work, and 1955, when her first article appeared in a woman's magazine.

75. Friedan, "How to Find and Develop Article Ideas," 12–15 has some discussion of these conflicts.

76. This becomes clear through an examination of her files on her free-lance work, especially when compared with the files of Vance Packard in the same years.

77. Wilkes, "Mother Superior," 141. On violence in the marriage, see also Tornabene, "Liberation," 138; Cohen, *Sisterhood*, 17–18; Meyer, "Friedan," 608.

79. Gerda Lerner to Betty Friedan, 6 Feb. 1963, box 20a, folder 715, BF-SLRC; quoted with permission of Gerda Lerner. For information on Lerner's participation in the labor movement, the Congress of American Women, and at the founding meeting of NOW, I am relying on Daniel Horowitz, phone conversation with Gerda Lerner, 18 Oct. 1995; Amy Swerdlow, "The Congress of American Women: Left-Feminist Peace Politics in the Cold War," in *U.S. History as Women's History: New Feminist Essays*, ed. Linda K. Kerber, Alice Kessler-Harris, and Kathryn Kish Sklar (Chapel Hill, 1995), 306.

MICHELLE M. NICKERSON
Politically Desperate Housewives in Southern California

Betty Friedan became a feminist in reaction to her life as a middle-class housewife who sought to be a journalist in 1950s America. Other housewives experienced a different sort of political awakening and emerged as energetic foot soldiers (or, shall we say mothers?) of conservatism.

Michelle Nickerson examines greater Los Angeles, with its spreading freeway system and booming economy, to ask what features of the Cold War era motivated middle-class white women to become energetic political actors, whether in women's clubs of the Republican Party or in homegrown groups, such as the Tuesday Morning Study Club and the Minute Women of the U.S.A. Publishing newsletters, attending lectures, gathering in reading groups, mobilizing voters, and protesting curriculum in the public schools they saw as dangerous, these women embraced the domestic as well as the political, and they poured their talents and skill into their volunteerism. A sense of divine mission, and a conviction that they "spoke the truth" to combat communism and other ills, united Catholic and Protestant women. "All politics is local" is a slogan that these historical subjects would heartily endorse. These activists saw their distinctive insights and effectiveness as stemming from their community watchfulness, common sense, and antielitism. And they would have agreed they were the "conservative sex" because the men in their lives, with salaried jobs, had far less time for political work.

How do you think the geographical location of these female activists shaped their politics? How do they compare to Betty Friedan or to Betty Jean Owens (in Danielle McGuire's essay that follows this one) or Phyllis Schlafly (pp. 610–614)? Be sure to check out the author's concluding question: is there such a thing as a "conservative feminist identity"?

Weary of war and relieved to be free of the Great Depression, Americans embraced family life with zeal in the 1950s. Women occupied a revered place in this revived domesticity that valorized homemaking and motherhood through television programming, film, and advertisements for appliances. Although the iconic 1950s housewife offers an abundance of insight into the ideals of the postwar generation, she obscures the countless ways that actual women attempted to live out those ideals. Operating among the legions of self-identified housewives who did not stay home in those years [was] a grassroots subculture of women that emerged mostly behind the scenes of the nascent conservative movement. These female activists on the right made the domestic ideology guiding their family, social, and civic lives into political careers by translating widespread cultural assumptions about female intuition into a basis for asserting authority in local affairs. . . . [This was an] animated, combative, and perfumed world of metropolitan politics. . . .

Important origins of the postwar right took root in such settings, where women shaped the conservative ascendancy with concerns, ideas, and issues that were drawn from

Excerpted, and slightly revised, from introduction, ch. 2, and conclusion of *Mothers of Conservatism: Women and the Postwar Right* by Michelle M. Nickerson (Princeton, N.J.: Princeton University Press, 2012). Reprinted by permission of the author and publisher. Notes have been edited and renumbered.

the fabric of their everyday lives. Capitalizing upon cultural assumptions about women and motherhood, they put themselves forward as representatives of local interests who battled bureaucrats for the sake of family, community, and God. Armed with a strong collective sense of where they and their local crusades fit into the global struggles against communism, they successfully overpowered school administrators, boards of education, and teachers in the name of local control and protection of parental authority. Female activists forced their priorities onto the larger agenda of the movement by anointing themselves spokespeople for parents, children, and local communities against the predatory interventionist state. . . .

[The back story lies in] the Great Depression. . . . The severe economic crisis invigorated the nation's appreciation for no-nonsense women with the wits to carry their families through the hard times. The new political woman of the 1930s was not the "angel of her home" housewife who volunteered to Americanize immigrants, rescue prostitutes, or save the nation from demon alcohol. She was an everywoman housewife, [often working-class,] who worked to keep her family and neighborhood intact— to maintain as much normalcy and security as possible. . . . Historian Temma Kaplan . . . sees "female consciousness," which relies upon assumptions about the "maternal duty to preserve life," as distinct from "feminist consciousness," which demands that women be given rights based on basic principles of equality.[1] . . .

. . . As the Depression wore on and World War II engulfed Europe and threatened to involve the United States, rage against Wall Street and landlords turned toward Washington as if financial and government leaders operated as one, centralized cabal. Indignation against economic elites shaded into anticommunist and anti-Semitic protest, attributing the nation's woes to New Deal bureaucrats as well as international Jewish bankers, eventually inflecting protests against U.S. entry into World War II with isolationist overtones. Feminine ideals contributed to a conservative political consciousness in formation. To be a "moral guardian" of society, in the minds of many women, meant to protect the nation from aliens, internationalism, and power-hungry bureaucrats in Washington. . . . Isolationist women found common cause in shared feelings of marginality, along with a sense of duty to family and community. Postwar women then updated its

political styles and culture for the conservatism of a new era.

Not until the early 1960s did American conservatism become a recognizable and self-conscious "movement," though its major ideological components, institutions, and political actors had been aligning since the end of World War II. While the Cold War and red scare of the 1950s revived anticommunism, critics of the New Deal welfare state . . . articulated economic arguments against centralized government. As the word "liberal," once associated with laissez-faire economic principles and small government as the means of realizing American egalitarianism, became linked during the Depression to federal growth and intervention on behalf of economic equality, proponents of small government formerly known as liberals claimed the designation "libertarian." . . . [Others] argued for a revival of faith and moral absolutes as the necessary antidotes for confronting recent scourges on the Western world, like genocide and totalitarianism. Anticommunism . . . gave conservatism the characteristics of a crusade around which adherents who disagreed about some things could rally. Conservatives gradually seized control of the GOP through important state battles, nominated conservative Barry Goldwater for president in 1964, and launched the political career of Ronald Reagan, who would complete the conservative revolution as president in the 1980s.[2] . . .

This study of women and conservatism examines how the anticommunist protest that scorched Southern California politics in the 1950s fueled a local conservative movement with broad national importance. [While] Orange County tends to win recognition as the epicenter of California conservatism, ... [I focus on the] more politically, racially, ethnically, and economically, diverse Los Angeles County, [which] figured centrally in this movement. . . . The growth of the defense industries, influx of migrants, rapidly changing demographics, expanded highway system, proliferation of suburbs, industrialization of those suburbs, and court rulings that chipped away at segregation fueled the metropolitan-based conservative movement. The sense of political community that made conservatism feel like a crusade in Southern California enveloped activists across greater Los Angeles. Southland activists built a movement that took advantage of their multinodal cityscape. Housewives who lived in

Pasadena drove cars over the hills to meetings in Encino and speaking engagements downtown. While living rooms in the newer suburbs proved comfortable for study groups, old Los Angeles venues like the First Congregational Church and Ambassador Hotel provided room, grandeur, and centralized locations appropriate for prominent lecturers. The new freeways made it easy for activists to attend each other's events and haul the cartons of the mimeographed literature they printed in their garages. The thirty-six different right-wing bookstores that opened across Southern California in the 1960s assisted each other like branches of the same regional bank, rather than competitors.[3] . . .

. . . [In] Southern California, community battles against school integration actually preceded the *Brown v. Board of Education* decision that mandated desegregation nationwide in 1954. California had been experimenting with integration and parents had been expressing their defiance of it for several years before the Warren Court handed down *Brown.* After the U.S. Court of Appeals for the Ninth Circuit in California upheld the *Mendez v. Westminster* ruling of 1946 that "segregation of Mexican youngsters found no justification in the laws of California," the [legislature] repealed segregationist statutes. School administrators then slowly crafted policies to bring their districts in line with the new mandates. . . . Conservative activists in greater Los Angeles worked in concert with activists all over the country, mainly in the South, to protect segregation in the public education system, an institution they recognized for its importance in maintaining racial order, [and] to forge a common anticommunist discourse of protest against the civil rights movement.[4]

Conservative women fought desegregation with the belief that their communities were under siege by political elites inciting turmoil that they, as women, needed to repel as housewives—the humblest, most self-sacrificial, and least pretentious members of American society. Women activists thus cultivated a gender consciousness, already in formation on the right, that valorized the local community as the fountainhead of American democracy. The links they made between feminine powerlessness and community powerlessness in the age of federal welfare and intervention isolated an amorphously defined centralized state as the most dangerous threat to freedom. Convinced

that progressive educators, civil rights activists, UNESCO [United Nations Educational, Scientific, and Cultural Organization], and the Supreme Court constituted a unified assault on community sovereignty . . . , they conflated problems of racial and bureaucratic outsiders.

Claiming a stake in these battles as representatives of the family—mothers and housewives protecting children, home life, and neighborhoods—women drew power from their class position and from [anticommunist] anxiety. . . . These female activists, in dialectic with conservative men, also cultivated an essentialist interpretation of women's political talents and duties, asserting that housewives and mothers were better suited than men to the work of anticommunist vigilance. Emphasizing that their flexible schedules gave them time to study communism, they argued that women were more politically aware than men, since husbands necessarily focused on the economic well-being of the family. [Indeed,] the economic status of female activists [was] vitally important, since a higher family income translated into political connections, an automobile, and funds for events, travel, or child care.

Los Angeles established a new paradigm of urban growth in the post–World War II era that facilitated transmission of conservative thought and activist culture. The region thrived over the 1950s from the billions of dollars of Pentagon defense contracts, which employed hundreds of thousands of workers in aircraft or missile manufacturing. Northrup, Lockheed, Douglas, and other companies . . . dispers[ed] their plants within and outside Los Angeles city limits. Manufacturers also built acres of single-family home communities for workers close to facilities. Long Beach to the south, Lakewood to the west, and the San Fernando Valley to the north bled urban and industrial sectors of the city into each other, creating new metropolitan economic and community relationships. Migrants, meanwhile, streamed in to fill jobs. Japanese and Mexican Americans arrived, but southerners represented the largest percentage of newcomers. . . . Millions of African Americans [went] to Los Angeles from the South during and after World War II. . . . [Another] exodus of white workers mainly from Texas, Arkansas, and Oklahoma start[ed] in the 1940s [and] infused the region with its own brand of religious culture and conservative politics.[5]

Map of Los Angeles County, 1963.

Mid-century Los Angeles also became a thought center for a Christian-inflected form of libertarianism. At the heart of these developments stood Spiritual Mobilization (SM), a nonprofit religious organization that endeavored to rescue God's relationship with the individual. SM intercepted ideas and money streaming between East Coast and West Coast libertarians. Launched by a cadre of economic thinkers in Europe and the United States, libertarianism advocated minimal or no government intervention in economic affairs.... A spate of books published between 1943 and 1944 revived conservatives ... with fresh inspiration. *The Road to Serfdom* by London School of Economics professor Friedrich Hayek, [a powerfully articulated polemic against governmental planning,] became the signature tome of the libertarian revival.... More popular than Hayek, however, Russian Jewish immigrant Ayn Rand published her ground-breaking utopian capitalist novel, *The Fountainhead,* in 1943.[6]...

... [By the 1950s] in the greater Los Angeles area, the political "right" [was] becoming a vast subculture with its own literature, radio broadcasts, workshops, home-based study groups, speaking circuits, and, by 1961, bookstores.

Anybody with enough time and money could rent a P.O. box, publish a newsletter, and circulate self-made leaflets, thus disseminating whatever literature they wished. A mother with two school-age children could do this as easily as a dentist or a clothing salesman, as long as she had the means. A mishmash discourse combining anticommunist, libertarian, and Christian ideas erupted on the local political scene.... Wealthy backers assisted with the proliferation of the materials, and not uncommon were partnerships between corporate leaders—men with money—and housewives—middle-class women with the time....

... As conservative magazines, books, and speaking events proliferated in the mid-1950s, the ranks of conservative female activists grew. While ink dried on the first issues of the *National Review,* mimeograph machines across Los Angeles County spat out newsletters, many of them composed and printed by teams of housewives. When not clipping newspapers or poring over the political literature stacked on their credenzas, women attended lectures or gave their own prepared talks to audiences. They squeezed meetings, study, writing, and printing into daytime and nighttime hours between trips to the grocery store, meal preparation, and help with homework. Conservative women approached political work like other forms of civic work—as an extension of their household duties that fulfilled feminine responsibilities to the family and community.

Many activists developed their earliest feelings of political community and identity in Republican women's clubs. Since the 1920s, the GOP had been recruiting female voters by appealing to popular beliefs about the inherent differences between men and women. . . . [In earlier decades party leaders had fashioned] an "outsider" political style that emphasized women's moral superiority.[7] Officers framed involvement with the Republican Party in moralistic terms and conducted party work in settings familiar to women—homes, churches, and libraries. GOP women's clubs thus functioned as a feminine outlet to the traditionally masculine world of partisan politics. Democratic women's clubs offered the same menu of activities and relied on the similar politics of difference, but did not adhere to sex-segregated institutions in the party nearly as long, . . . pushing . . . for integration into the party's male-dominated power structure. . . . [In] the post–World War II era, Republican women's club literature emphasize[d] women's influence in the community, [and] stressed the importance of the warmth, sparkling personality, and overall positive attitude that it believed women could contribute to politics.

Reflecting the broader culture's celebration of domesticity, Republican club-women discourse of the 1950s and early 1960s also celebrated the American housewife. Literature, rituals, and speeches exhibited an optimistic view of how the nation's wives and mothers could harness their compassion, warmth, and femininity for the good of the party. The so-called "natural" political virtues of women, like moral superiority and mothering instincts, still found their way into the rhetoric of Republican leaders, yet its emphasis shifted to other attributes, namely feminine cheeriness and hospitality. "Organize your enthusiasm," commanded the president of the National Federation of Republican Women, "if you want to elect the nominee of the Republican national convention. . . . " Catherine Gibson assumed the office in the late fifties, stressing "neighbor-to-neighbor contacts."[8] Club leaders added new symbols to their campaign slogans, like the Republican "saleswomen," which invoked both the growing importance of women to the retail industry as well as traits assumed to be intrinsically feminine, namely good manners and friendliness. Events designed for fun and sociability—teas, bridge games, fashion shows, and garden parties—became especially popular in this period. Club leaders extolled graciousness and affability as natural female qualities that could be marshaled for the benefit of the party.[9]

Though the ideal American housewife . . . ventured forth as a social and charitable community-builder, she also remained symbolically and spatially linked to the home. Activists opted increasingly to utilize their Formica kitchen tables, polyester living-room sectionals, and outdoor patio furniture for organizing-entertaining. These domestic settings provided a warm and nonintimidating atmosphere meant to promote the overlapping goals of political discussion and sociability. The National Federation of Republican Women encouraged women to use their homes through a variety of campaigns, including "Operation Coffee Cup." Launched during the 1956 Presidential campaign, the television broadcast presented Eisenhower and Nixon in conversation with different women's groups. The NFRW encouraged club leaders to watch alongside women guests to initiate discussion.[10] Indeed, study groups thrived in the home-centered atmosphere of postwar Republican women's clubs, especially as leaders took greater interest in promoting community relations skills among volunteers. One Republican women's study group met near the San Fernando Valley house of Jean Ward Fuller, who became president of the California Federation of Republican Women. . . . Her spacious abode, with housekeeper, in Encino helped to accommodate the sizeable number of clubwomen who hauled their bridge tables over to do mailings for political candidates. Her group, Fuller claimed, could turn out 60,000 pieces of mail within three days. "Everybody would bring their sandwiches," she recalled later, "and I'd have coffee for them and everybody would just work like beavers."[11]

Southern California became a hub of Republican clubwomen activism in the 1950s. Indeed, GOP women's clubs in California experienced their highest rate of growth in these years. In 1949, at 12,000, the California Federation of Republican Women became the sixth largest state federation in the nation, and by 1957 its ranks had swelled to 50,000 women. The Southern Division, always the strongest, included 123 clubs. . . . The San Fernando Valley, Glendale, San Marino, and Long Beach clubs represented its largest units. And in 1958 the National Federation of Republican Women boasted half a million members, while the Democratic National Committee counted only 100,000 women in female clubs.[12]

While the Republican women's clubs that met throughout Southern California's valleys politicized women, the Freedom Club, located in downtown Los Angeles, further encouraged militancy on the right. James Fifield's Freedom Club became a gathering place for conservatives, where like-minded suburbanites connected with each other as they eagerly imbibed the orations of speakers they admired. Established in 1950, the monthly series offered dinner, lectures, and discussion. With their hands busy with plates of jellied cranberry salad or turkey with gravy, participants listened and chatted about the evils of the income tax or mental health legislation. While Fifield's Spiritual Mobilization politicized clergymen, his Freedom Club politicized activists, especially female activists. Fifield attracted women to his ministry by appealing to both their sense of patriotism and their piety. Reared in a preacher's family, he acted on his familiarity with the ways that churches had historically relied on women to show spiritual devotion, inculcate religious values in children, and arrange church functions. Forceful women speakers like activist Phyllis Schlafly and foreign correspondent Freda Utley inspired housewives in the audience to shake off their timidity and push the boundaries of politeness on behalf of their families and the nation.[13]

A female right became visible and militant starting in 1950, as conservative women discovered and connected with each other in Republican women's clubs, the Freedom Club, and school board meetings. Indeed, debates about public education especially animated mothers after conservative parents successfully pressured school board members to fire the superintendent in one of the nation's finest school districts, Pasadena. Anticommunist attacks against the progressive education agenda of Superintendent Willard Goslin caused many mothers to look with new skepticism at the pedagogy employed by schoolteachers, making them wonder if leftist educators were trying to indoctrinate their children. A concerted campaign against UNESCO fueled such concerns, as

critics of "internationalism" fought to ban educational materials published by the agency from Los Angeles schools.[14] The controversies surrounding Pasadena's superintendent and UNESCO inspired the formation of numerous organizations by women who came to see communist subversion as a grave problem and themselves and values they associated with femininity—vigilance, selflessness, carefulness, patience, and spirituality—as the solution. American Public Relations Forum, Pro-America, the Tuesday Morning Study Club, and Minute Women of the U.S.A., Incorporated, became the most active groups in the region.

"Politically desperate" to have their voices heard, they were by no means hysterical or pathological but rather approached their activist work with fervor and urgency. American Public Relations Forum, Pro-America, the Tuesday Morning Supper Club, and Minute Women of the U.S.A., Incorporated, became the most active groups in the region.

A housewife in Burbank by the name of Stephanie Williams founded American Public Relations Forum. Williams, a devout and fervent Catholic, joined a swelling number of parishioners who expanded the Los Angeles Catholic community after World War II with scores of churches that added hundreds of thousands of new members. As the church prospered and grew, the archdiocese exerted a conservative force on the political landscape mainly through Archbishop James McIntyre and its newspaper organ, *The Tidings*. Ordained the first Catholic cardinal from the American West in 1953, McIntyre sent priests to attend conservative political meetings, barred the sisters of the Immaculate Heart from teaching in the archdiocese after they stopped wearing the habit, and reformed other rules of discipline.[15] . . .

With the blessing of McIntyre, Williams formed the American Public Relations Forum, which gathered monthly in a few different locations. Forum meetings opened with a prayer, often featured a guest lecturer, and followed with a discussion. The organization coordinated correspondence campaigns by mailing its members bulletins regarding bills before Congress and by making cards available at gatherings so those present could write to their representatives together.[16] . . .

Minute Women of the U.S.A., which also operated from the San Fernando Valley, represented another popular choice for women who felt somewhat shy but wanted to do something about communism. The Southern

California unit worked in concert with the national organization, founded in 1949. . . . Minute Women were white, middle- and upper-class, between the ages of thirty and sixty, with school-age or grown children. In 1952 the organization boasted 50,000 members in forty-seven states. . . . Southern California claimed some of the strongest units, though the Minute Women's secrecy policy has kept their exact numbers unknown. . . . Newsletters represented the organization's lifeblood. Members rarely met but received mailings from the California chapter chairman and from the national leadership. . . . [17]

The Minute Women's anonymity might also have provided members with a sense of security or power at a time when secrecy yielded rewards. This was [after all] the McCarthy era; your cat could have been spying on you. Government officials, including J. Edgar Hoover, . . . encouraged women to look hard for communists in their midst . . . [because] the government was ill equipped to do so. Without enough agents in the FBI to find and thwart the red menace, Hoover asserted, private citizens needed to be eternally watchful. . . . Female activists took it upon themselves to adopt vigilance as their job, one they could do better than anyone else.

[At the same time] they knew that leftist opponents were infiltrating their ranks. The Community Relations Committee (CRC), a moderate civil rights organization affiliated with the Jewish National Committee, spied on conservatives. . . . Concerned about the threat posed by groups on the right like the Forum, the CRC regularly monitored their meetings and labeled typed manuscripts of minutes . . . "spy reports." . . . The culture of fear, mistrust, and secrecy touched activists across the political spectrum.[19]

The Tuesday Morning Study Club (TMSC) was formed a few years after the Forum and Minute Women in the rolling Linda Vista neighborhood of Pasadena. . . . Some Pasadena mothers, not content to play bridge, gathered instead in a backyard recreational space behind the lovely home of activist Marjorie Jensen. One Tuesday a month, in the Jensen "playhouse," as they called the small, simply crafted structure, TMSC meetings started with a guest speaker and ended with discussion. Early on, the gatherings tended to be small, sometimes including only seven women, but at the height of TMSC popularity in the late 1950s, attendance regularly reached 50 women or more. When 130 people arrived one day, filling the playhouse, yard, and back room of Jensen's house, the club began renting larger spaces. On those occasions when the TMSC invited prominent speakers to Pasadena, they reserved a conference room at the Huntington Hotel, where they could accommodate larger mixed-sex crowds for evening events. Almost all of the Tuesday Morning Study Club programs focused on education. Topics ranged from UNESCO to "State Curriculum and the 'New' Education," from "Civic Groups, Educating Toward World Citizenship," to "Indoctrination Through Literature."[20]

A mix of international, national, and local affairs filled the meeting agendas of the different conservative women's organizations. It was never necessary for any of these groups to announce that they were for women; the format, presentations, and rituals made that announcement. Men, in fact, attended meetings sometimes—they were generally welcome—but only rarely. . . . The ways in which group members talked about God [also] made these organizations female. . . . Most conservative women were Christian, though organizations did not tend to identify with particular churches or intensity of religious devotion. In Los Angeles, Catholic and Protestant women mixed quite comfortably in the conservative movement while antagonism characterized relations between the groups in the rest of the country.[21] . . . In Southern California, Catholic and Protestant women . . . cultivated political camaraderie not only from the fight against atheistic communism, but also from their common need to develop spiritual interpretations of the changing world around them. Activists from both faiths lamented the secularization of American society as well as numerous social problems that they attributed to that trend, from rising crime rates to juvenile delinquency to loosening sexual norms.

Conservative women contributed to the developing unity between Catholics and Protestants, not only by making all Christian women welcome in their meetings, but by cultivating a cross-denominational political style and culture. The American Public Relations Forum officially started its institutional life as a Catholic women's organization, but by the late 1950s the group listed two officers who were Protestant. . . . The Minute Women's membership policy welcomed women of all "faiths." The language of its literature suggests, though, that non-Christian women need not apply. From the rhetoric and practices of both groups emerged pan-Christian ideals of political femininity.

The American Public Relations Forum and Minute Women of the U.S.A. especially promulgated the idea that women had a divinely mandated role to fulfill in the defense of freedom. The Forum encouraged its members, first and foremost, to think about God with every political action they undertook, whether it involved the stroke of a pen or an uncomfortable confrontation with local school administrators. For God you could and should act unladylike. Though it was "nonsectarian" and included non-Catholic members, the group operated under the auspices of the Catholic Church.... Forum president Stephanie Williams reminded her members that while they toiled at their political tasks they must submit to God and pray. "We must place God as the senior of the family." ... [22]

... The Forum and Minute Women fixat[ed] on a scripturally-defined understanding of the truth. "[S]peak the truth and shame the devil," declared the Minute Woman national president.[23] Her organization recognized, as one of its duties, protection of God's pronouncements—as well as those made by founding fathers—from the treachery of artful wordsmiths. Subversion, in their minds, stood for cunning.... Clipping newspapers and writing letters did not win glory, but did rescue facts from the chicanery of subversives....

In oral history interviews with five women [active in the 1950s in the greater Los Angeles area], a common theme ... was the [political] awakening. The activists tend[ed] to emphasize distinct moments when someone or a series of events made them alert, as they often put it, to how communism menaced their freedom. The process of becoming aware, in recollections, frequently followed a something-not-feeling-right period. Awakenings discourse thus presupposed that the political subjects lived for some time in the dark, and that most other Americans at the time continued to be oblivious.... Activists equated the acquisition of *vision* with political transformation. Indeed, this power of *sight*—to conquer one's enemy by shining light on his or her activities—became a powerful way for women to understand their unique political effectiveness. What others would describe as red-baiting, they interpreted as exposure of the truth.[24] ...

The emphasis on awakenings resonated with the ways in which women talked about the political work that came to fill their days.

Never referring to conservatism as a "movement," activists instead remembered "patriotic" Americans rousing each other from a stupor and devoting themselves to saving the country. Subjects describe their involvement as if they had no serious interest in politics until the light had been turned on for them.... Although activists betrayed a shared love for the movement's labor in their oral histories, they almost never said outright that they joined organizations for any fulfillment of a personal need.... [They] instead privileged the gravity of dangers that created the political work for them. Activists, in other words, liked to talk about work—hard work—without calling it "work." ... [T]he vigor of the conservative movement owes much to this labor of middle- and upper-class women who might have enjoyed professional "careers" given their backgrounds, but would not likely legitimize professional "career" employment as a choice for women....

In their relentless defense of community-level decision making, [conservative] women [of the Cold War era] stoked populist outrage.... In campaigns against progressive educators, programs, and federal funding, they denounced administrators as elitist outsiders who aimed to use children for social experiments designed at far-away Ivy League institutions. To stem the problems they associated with social decline in the United States, they advocated for stronger parental and clerical influence in the lives of children. Although many of the women involved in these battles were born, raised, and college-educated in other parts of the country, [in Southern California] they developed an insider-outsider dichotomy—a sharp community boundary line between them on the inside and their opponents on the outside. This housewife populism contributed to the conservative movement's identification with the everyman, real people, and middle America. Women on the right also spoke out as taxpayers, linking the interests of property holders and families in an alliance against state intervention.

Among the most important lessons to be drawn from this history of conservative women concerns their ability to manage ideological ambiguity. [We find such ambiguity in many social and political movements. For example, women's] right to vote was won in the 1910s with a careful balance between seemingly contradictory arguments for sameness and difference. Women demanded the ballot on the basis of universal, democratic, egalitarian ideals stemming from the Enlightenment—on the principle that they should have the same rights as men. Yet they also argued that womanly virtues made them worthy of the vote, that their feminine instincts for morality, spirituality, and purity would uplift the corrupt world of politics. . . . [In the 1970s] Equal Rights Amendment opponents . . . valorized full-time motherhood, yet worked as full-time activists. [A third example are] religious conservatives who decry every form of state intervention except those that serve to enforce their Christian ideals. [All] exhibit what [some] . . . describe as "cognitive dissonance." [The most interesting question to ask of conservative Southern California women activists, as of other political actors, is:] How did [they] resolve and deploy such dissonance for their own political purposes?

The endurance of housewife populism stands as a testament to the power of this ambiguity. A distinguishing characteristic of the post-1970 "new right" was the vehemence of its attacks against "women libbers." Make no mistake: this "backlash" was real. . . . Like the feminists they attacked, conservative women participated in an organic process of reviving, reformulating, and building upon traditions started by political foremothers. The "pro-family" agenda of the late twentieth century included familiar advocacy on behalf of parental authority over the state. Bridging multiple generations of women, housewife populism coursed through the defensive, maternal, communitarian rhetoric of these new-right women. In campaigns against abortion and the Equal Rights Amendment, activists represented themselves as champions of real, ordinary people battling a rarified class of secular elites so entombed in the trappings of their privilege that they lost touch with the most basic principles of morality. They also introduced stronger Christian elements into the feminine political styles of earlier generations.

A driving theme of the anti-ERA campaign . . . was the danger of "losing of one's children" to educators and government officials who meddled in the relationships between parents, sons, and daughters. Critiques of "forced equality" adapted female traditions of antistatist protest for the new battles, equating the ERA with other unwanted state interventions into the family, including government-sponsored desegregation. One

woman accused ERA ratificationists of trying to "desexegrate" society. . . . Phyllis Schlafly, whose *Eagle Forum* established a long and continuing pattern of attacking the United Nations, World Health Organization, and other international organizations for threatening U.S. sovereignty, now targets "globalism," described by Schlafly as socialism enforced through global regulatory structures like the World Trade Organization. Housewife populism marshals women against globalism today much as it did to mobilize them against communism in the 1950s and 1960s.[25]

Opposition to the Equal Rights Amendment also assumed the populist inflections that Cold War conservatives added to political discourse. Antiratificationists represented themselves as "the people in arms." . . . [26] The fearsome and deeply entrenched antielitism in conservative political culture of the Cold War era endured, fueling the popular notion that feminist demands for "rights" and "equality" would improve the lives of privileged women only. Regular wives and mothers, on the other hand, needed the armor of patriarchy and sex-based protectionist legislation that, opponents believed, the Equal Rights Amendment would undo. . . .

After Barack Obama won election in 2008, [conservative] populist style carried over into the Tea Party movement, an alliance of organizations and bloggers that emerged in opposition to government-sponsored economic stimulus, health-care reform, and numerous other grievances. . . . The movement has served as a conduit for [new versions of] housewife populist outrage. . . . [In 2010] polls indicated that women represented 45 to 55 percent of the membership and an even greater share of the leadership positions. Six of the eight Tea Party Patriots board members who also serve as national coordinators for the movement [were] women; [and so were] fifteen of the twenty-five state coordinators. At a summer 2010 gathering of the abortion-opposing organization Susan B. Anthony List, [Sarah] Palin identified the women's empowerment trend on the right as a "conservative feminist identity."[27]

Conservative feminists? . . . As oxymoronic as the expression . . . appears, its logic lies in the tribute that conservative women should properly pay [to a wide variety of self-identified feminists, such as Alice Paul, bell hooks, and Kate Millett.] Conservative women have been able to hold public office because of feminist pressure for antidiscrimination legislation that opened doors for women in education, the professions, the business world, and politics— legislation that antifeminist women opposed vigorously. The Susan B. Anthony List illustrates how the process of creating a conservative feminist consciousness is, indeed, a project of cognitive dissonance, selective memory, and mythmaking.

NOTES

1. Temma Kaplan, "Female Consciousness and Collective Action: the Case of Barcelona, 1910–1918," *Signs* 7, no. 3 (Spring 1982), 545–66.

2. On the evolution of conservatism in the 1950s and 1960s, see, for example, Donald Critchlow, *Phyllis Schlafly and Grassroots Conservatism: A Woman's Crusade* (Princeton, N.J.: Princeton University Press, 2005), 5–7; George H. Nash, *The Conservative Intellectual Movement in America Since 1945* (reprint, Wilmington, Del.: Intercollegiate Studies Institute, 1996; orig. pub. 1975); and Elizabeth Tandy Shermer, "Origins of the Conservative Ascendancy: Barry Goldwater's Early Senate Career and the De-legitimatization of Organized Labor," *Journal of American History* 95 (Dec. 2008), 678–709.

3. On women and postwar conservatism, see Lisa McGirr, *Suburban Warriors: The Origins of the New American Right* (Princeton, N.J.: Princeton University Press, 2001); Mary Brennan, *Wives, Mothers, and the Red Menace: Conservative Women and the Crusade Against Communism* (Boulder: University of Colorado Press, 2008). On California, see Kurt Schuparra, *Triumph of the Right: The Rise of the California Conservative Movement, 1945–1966* (Armonk, N.Y.: M. E. Sharpe, 1998).

4. Vicki Ruiz, "Nuestra América: Latino History as American History," *Journal of American History* 93 (Dec. 2006), 670; *Mendez et al. v. Westminster School District of Orange County*, 64 F. Supp. 544 (C.D. Cal. 1946).

5. Greg Hise, *Magnetic Los Angeles: Planning the Twentieth-Century Metropolis* (Baltimore: Johns Hopkins University Press, 1997); Josh Sides, *L.A. City Limits: African American Los Angeles from the Great Depression to the Present* (Berkeley: University of California Press, 2003); and Darren Dochuk, *From Bible Belt to Sunbelt: Plain-Folk Religion, Grassroots Politics, and the Rise of Evangelical Conservatism* (New York: Norton, 2010), esp. xv–xx.

6. F. A. Hayek, *The Road to Serfdom* (Chicago: University of Chicago Press, 1944); Jennifer Burns, *Goddess of the Market: Ayn Rand and the American Right* (New York: Oxford University Press, 2009); Nash, *Conservative Intellectual Movement*, 3.

7. Michael McGerr, "Political Style and Women's Power, 1830–1930," *Journal of American History* 77 (Dec. 1990), 864–85; Catherine Rymph, *Republican Women: Feminism and Conservatism from Suffrage through the Rise of the New Right* (Chapel Hill: University of North Carolina Press, 2006), 5–6.

8. Jean Ward, "Organize Your Enthusiasm . . . ," *Los Angeles Examiner*, Nov. 14, 1959, Regional History Collection, University of Southern California.

9. Mrs. Vernon W. Janney, Report of the Los Angeles County Federation of Republican Women's Clubs: Annual Convention (Jan. 25, 1956), National Federation of Republican Women records (hereafter, NFRW), Dwight D. Eisenhower Library, Abilene, KS, 1; "New GOP Fashion Set by Women," *Los Angeles Times*, Mar. 5, 1956, p. 2; "Fashion Lunch Planned by GOP in Long Beach," ibid., Mar. 6, 1956, p. B3; Letter to Mrs. Peter Gibson, Sep. 16, 1957, NFRW.

10. Rymph, *Republican Women*, 138–39.

11. Jean Ward Fuller, "Organizing Women: Careers in Volunteer Politics and Government Administration," an oral history conducted Oct. 1977 by Miriam Stein, Regional Oral History Office, Bancroft Library, University of California, Berkeley, 35–37.

12. Jacqueline R. Braitman, "Legislated Parity: Mandating Integration of Women into California Political Parties, 1930s–1950s," in *We Have Come to Stay: American Women and Political Parties, 1880–1960*, ed. Melanie Gustafson, Kristie Miller, and Elisabeth Israels Perry (Albuquerque: University of New Mexico Press, 1999), 180; Mrs. Robert W. Malcauley to Mrs. Paul Jasper, 1949, NFRW; Program, California Federation of Republican Women, *Tenth Biennial Convention* (Santa Barbara, Calif., 1957); California Federation of Republican Women, *The Federation*, Sept. 1954, *Scrapbook*; Fuller, "Organizing Women," 101–102; Jo Freeman, *A Room at a Time: How Women Entered Party Politics* (Lanham, Md.: Rowman and Littlefield, 2000), 158.

13. *Freedom Club Bulletin* (Nov. 20, 1856), and ibid., 8, no. 5 (April 1, 1958), both in Marie Koenig Personal Collection; ibid., 18, no. 2 (Nov. 7, 1967), 1, Social Protest Collection, Bancroft Library; Community Relations Committee, "Report on Reverend Fifield Dinner Meeting—Freedom Clubs—First Congregational Church, April 15, 1952," Community Relations Committee Collection (hereafter, CRC), Urban Archives Center, California State University, Northridge.

14. Glen Warren Adams, "The UNESCO Controversy in Los Angeles, 1951–1953: A Case Study of the Influence of Right-Wing Groups on Urban Affairs" (Ph.D. diss., University of Southern California, 1970); David Hulburd, *This Happened in Pasadena* (New York: MacMillan, 1951).

15. McGirr, *Suburban Warriors*, 107; "Religion: The Immaculate Heart Rebels," *Time*, Feb. 16, 1970.

16. Community Relations Committee, American Public Relations Forum Meeting ["spy report"], May 2, 1952, CRC.

17. "Minute Women Band to Fight Reds and Pink," *Chicago Daily Tribune*, May 6, 1950, p. 4F. Personal Collection of Marie Koenig; Don Carlton, *Red Scare!: Right-wing Hysteria, Fifties Fascism and Their Legacy in Texas* (Austin: Texas Monthly Press, 1985), 111–34; Timothy G. Turner, "Minute Women Leader Begins L.A. Campaign," *Los Angeles Times*, Feb. 7, 1952, CRC. One chapter in Texas had its own male auxiliary, but those were few.

18. J. Edgar Hoover, *Masters of Deceit: The Story of Communism in American and How to Fight It* (New York: Henry Holt and Co., 1958), 310.

19. See the voluminous "spy reports" of the Community Relations Committee, CRC.

20. Marjorie Jensen, taped interview with author, Pasadena, Calif., July 15, 2002, 6–7; Tuesday Morning Study Club, *Program and Directory*, 4–5.

21. Robert Wuthnow, *The Restructuring of American Religion: Society and Faith Since World War II* (Princeton, N.J.: Princeton University Press, 1988), 72–75, 93.

22. Community Relations Committee, "American Public Relations Forum, Inc." [report of Aug. 15, 1952 meeting], 1, CRC.

23. Minute Women of the U.S.A., Inc., newsletter, Apr. 1954, 1, Marie Koenig Personal Collection.

24. Jensen, interview; Jane Crosby, taped interview with author, San Juan Capistrano, Calif., Feb. 26, 2001; Marie Koenig, taped interview with author, Pasadena, Calif., Apr. 5, 2001; Florence Ranuzzi and Mary Cunningham, taped interview with author, Tehachapi, Calif., Feb. 11, 2001; Marion Miller, *I Was a Spy: The Story of a Brave Housewife* (New York: Bobbs-Merrill Co., 1960).

25. Donald G. Mathews and Jane Sherron DeHart, *Sex, Gender, and the Politics of the ERA: A State and the Nation* (New York: Oxford University Press, 1990), 156–57, 172; "Globalism: Enemy of the Middle Class," *The Phyllis Schlafly Report* (Feb. 2007), http://www.eagleforum.org/psr/2007/feb07/psrfeb07.html (last accessed Mar. 25, 2011).

26. Mathews and DeHart, *Sex, Gender, and the Politics of the ERA*, 173.

27. Hanna Rosin, "Is the Tea Party a Feminist Movement?" *Slate*, May 12, 2010; Amy Gardner, "Palin Pushes Abortion Foes to Form 'Conservative Feminist Identity,'" *Washington Post*, May 15, 2010, http://www.washingtonpost.com/wp-dyn/content/article/2010/05/15/AR2010051500002.html (last accessed July 15, 2010).

DANIELLE L. McGUIRE

Sexual Violence and the Long Civil Rights Movement

What role did African American women play in the civil rights movement? Our understanding of the civil rights movement, like other historical events, has changed over time. A previous focus on charismatic leaders, like Martin Luther King, Jr., has expanded to include female organizers—Rosa Parks, Fannie Lou Hamer, Ella Baker, and Diane Nash—as well as the rank and file, many of whom were women.

In addition, scholars now call for a "long civil rights" perspective that expands the chronology beyond the 1954–1965 period, bookended by the 1954 *Brown v. Board of Education* desegregation decision and the 1965 Voting Rights Act. The black freedom struggle can be dated at least back to the interracial labor movements of the 1930s or even to the resistance movements against slavery. It can go forward in time to encompass the black power movement and beyond.

Danielle L. McGuire argues powerfully that sexual violence against black women has inspired much civil rights campaigning. In addition to political equality, desegregation, and access to jobs, civil rights activists demanded respect and bodily autonomy for black women. She insists that it is important, though painful, to face—to see—the violence directed toward black women, because only then can we understand the individual and collective grounding of resistance. The story she tells here centers on college students: Betty Jean Owens and her friends returning from a dance, and the student body of Florida A&M, a historically black university. Would the students' rallying cry, "It Was Like All of Us Had Been Raped," be an effective organizing tool on campuses today? *

\

*Jacquelyn Dowd Hall, "The Long Civil Rights Movement and the Political Uses of History," *Journal of American History* 91 (March 2005): 1233–63. For more on the contemporary vexation over sexual assault on or near college campuses, see pp. 750–751.

Excerpted from " 'It Was Like All of Us Had Been Raped:' Sexual Violence, Community Mobilization, and the African American Freedom Struggle" by Danielle L. McGuire, *Journal of American History* 91 (Dec. 2004): 906–31. Reprinted with permission of the author and publisher. Notes have been edited and renumbered.

On Saturday, May 2, 1959, four white men in Tallahassee, Florida, made a pact, one of their friends testified in court later, to "go out and get a nigger girl" and have an "all night party." That evening, they armed themselves with shotguns and switchblades and crept up behind a car parked alongside a quiet road near Jake Gaither Park. At about 1:00 A.M. on May 3, Patrick Scarborough pressed a sixteen-gauge shotgun against the driver's nose and ordered Richard Brown and his companions out of the car. Dressed in formal gowns and tuxedoes, the four African Americans—all students at Florida A&M University who had spent the evening dancing at the Green and Orange Ball—reluctantly stepped out of the car. Scarborough forced the two black men to kneel, while his friend David Beagles held the two black women at knifepoint. When Betty Jean Owens began to cry, Beagles slapped her and told her to "shut up" or she "would never get back home." Waving his gun, Scarborough ordered Richard Brown and his friend Thomas Butterfield back in the car and told them to leave. As Brown and Butterfield began to move toward the car and then slowly drove away, Edna Richardson broke free and ran to the nearby park, leaving Betty Jean Owens alone with their attackers. Beagles pressed the switchblade to Owens's throat and growled, "We'll let you go if you do what we want," then forced her to her knees, slapped her as she sobbed, and pushed her into the backseat of their blue Chevrolet; the four men drove her to the edge of town, where they raped her seven times.[1]

Analyses of rape play little or no role in most histories of the civil rights movement, even as stories of violence against black and white men—from Emmett Till to Andrew Goodman, Michael Schwerner, and James Chaney—provide gripping examples of racist brutality.[2] Despite a growing body of literature that focuses on the roles of black and white women and the operation of gender in the movement, sexualized violence—both as a tool of oppression and as a political spur for the movement—has yet to find its place in the story of the African American freedom struggle.[3] Rape, like lynching and murder, served as a tool of psychological and physical intimidation that expressed white male domination and buttressed white supremacy. During the Jim Crow

era, women's bodies served as signposts of the social order, and white men used rape and rumors of rape not only to justify violence against black men but to remind black women that their bodies were not their own.

African American women frequently retaliated by testifying about their brutal experiences. I argue that, from Harriet Jacobs to Ida B. Wells to the women of the present, the refusal of black women to remain silent about sexualized violence was part of a long-standing tradition. Black women described and denounced their sexual misuse, deploying their voices as weapons in the wars against white supremacy. Indeed, their public protests often galvanized local, national, and even international outrage and sparked campaigns for racial justice and human dignity. When Betty Jean Owens spoke out against her assailants, and when the local black community mobilized in defense of her womanhood in 1959, they joined in this tradition of testimony and protest.

The arrest, trial, and conviction of Owens's white rapists by an all-white jury marked a dramatic change in the relations between this tradition of testimony and a tradition of silence that Darlene Clark Hine has termed the "culture of dissemblance."[4] The verdict not only broke with southern tradition but fractured the philosophical and political foundations of white supremacy by challenging the relationship between sexual domination and racial inequality. For perhaps the first time since Reconstruction, southern black communities could imagine state power being deployed in defense of their respectability as men and women. As a result, the 1959 Tallahassee rape case was a watershed event that remains as revealing now as it was important then.

The sexual exploitation of black women had its roots in slavery. Slave owners, overseers, and drivers took advantage of their positions of power and authority to rape slave women, sometimes in the presence of their husbands or families. White slave owners' stolen access to black women's bodies strengthened their political, social, and economic power, partly because colonial laws made the offspring of slave women the property of their masters. After the fall of slavery, when African Americans asserted their freedom during the interracial experiment in democracy that briefly characterized Reconstruction, former slaveholders and their sympathizers used violence and terror to reassert control over the social, political, and economic agency of freedpeople. At the heart of this violence, according to Gerda Lerner, rape became a "weapon of terror" to dominate the bodies and minds of African American men and women.[5]

"Freedom," as Tera Hunter notes, "was meaningless without ownership and control over one's own body." During Reconstruction and Jim Crow, sexualized violence served as a "ritualistic reenactment of the daily pattern of social dominance," and interracial rape became the battleground upon which black men and women fought for ownership of their own bodies. Many African American women who were raped or assaulted by white men fought back by speaking out. Frances Thompson told a congressional committee investigating the 1866 Memphis race riot that seven armed white men broke into her house on a Tuesday afternoon, "drew their pistols and said they would shoot us and fire the house if we did not let them have their way with us." Four of the men raped Frances, while the other three choked and raped sixteen-year-old Lucy Smith and left her close to death. In 1871, Harriet Simril testified in front of a congressional committee investigating Ku Klux Klan terror during Reconstruction that she was beaten and "ravished" by eight men in South Carolina who broke into her house to force her husband to "join the democratic ticket." Essic Harris, appearing before the same committee, reported that "the rape of black women was so frequent" in the postbellum South that it had become "an old saying by now." Ferdie Walker, who grew up during the height of segregation in the 1930s and 1940s in Fort Worth, Texas, remembered being "scared to death" by a white police officer who often exposed himself to her while she waited at the bus stop when she was only eleven years old. The sexual abuse of black women, she recalled, was an everyday occurrence. "That was really bad and it was bad for *all black girls*," she recalled.[6]

John H. McCray, editor of the South Carolina *Lighthouse and Informer*, reported that it was "a commonplace experience for many of our women in southern towns . . . to be propositioned openly by white men." He said, "You can pick up accounts of these at a dime a dozen in almost any community." African American women that I interviewed in Birmingham, Alabama, in March 2003 echoed Ferdie Walker's and McCray's comments. Nearly all of them testified about being sexually abused or intimidated by white men—particularly bus drivers, police officers, and employers.[7]

The acclaimed freedom fighter Fannie Lou Hamer knew that rape and sexual violence was a common occurrence in the segregated South. . . . Hamer's grandmother, Liza Bramlett, spoke often of the "horrors of slavery," including stories about "how the white folks would do her." . . . Twenty of the twenty-three children Bramlett gave birth to were products of rape. Hamer grew up with the clear understanding that a "black woman's body was never hers alone." If she was at all unclear about this lesson, the forced hysterectomy she received in 1961 and the brutal beating she received in the Winona, Mississippi, jail in 1963 left little room for confusion. After being arrested with other Student Nonviolent Coordinating Committee (SNCC) activists for desegregating a restaurant, Hamer received a savage and sexually abusive beating by the Winona police. "You bitch," one officer yelled, "we going to make you wish you was dead." He ordered two black inmates to beat Hamer with "a long wide blackjack," while other patrolmen battered "her head and other parts of her body." As they assaulted her, Hamer felt them repeatedly "pull my dress over my head and try to feel under my clothes." She attempted to pull her dress down during the brutal attack in order to "preserve some respectability through the horror and disgrace." Hamer told this story on national television at the Democratic National Convention in 1964 and continued to tell it "until the day she died," offering her testimony of the sexual and racial injustice of segregation.[8]

By speaking out, whether it was in the church, the courtroom, or a congressional hearing, black women used their own public voices to reject the stereotypes used by white supremacists to justify economic and sexual exploitation, and they reaffirmed their own humanity. Additionally, African American women's refusal to remain silent offered African American men an opportunity to assert themselves as *men* by rallying around the protection of black womanhood. Many other men, however, remained silent since speaking out was often dangerous, if not deadly. Most important, women's testimonies were a political act that exposed the bitter ironies of segregation and white supremacy, helped to reverse the shame and humiliation rape inflicts, and served as catalysts in mobilizing mass movements.[9]

Only after local and national groups were organized, black women's testimony began to spark public campaigns for equal justice and protection of black womanhood. In this respect, World War II served as a watershed for African Americans—especially in the South. Black women's testimony and the willingness of black leaders to protect black womanhood must be viewed as part of these resistance movements. For example, in Montgomery, Alabama, the organizational infrastructure that made the Montgomery bus boycott possible in 1955 stemmed in part from decades of black women's activism and a history of gendered political appeals to protect black women from sexual assault. The majority of leaders active in the Montgomery Improvement Association in 1955 cut their political teeth demanding justice for black women who were raped in the 1940s and early 1950s.[10]

In 1944, the kidnapping and gang rape of Mrs. Recy Taylor by six white men in Abbeville, Alabama, sparked what the *Chicago Defender* called "the strongest campaign for equal justice to Negroes to be seen in a decade." Taylor, a twenty-four-year-old African American woman, was walking home from the Rock Hill Holiness Church near Abbeville on September 3 when a carload of six white men pulled alongside her, pointed a gun at her head, and ordered her to get into the car. They drove her to a vacant patch of land where Herbert Lovett pointed his rifle at Taylor and . . . held her at gunpoint while each of the white men took turns "ravishing" her. After the men raped her, Lovett blindfolded her, pushed her into the car, and dropped her off in the middle of town. That night, Recy Taylor told her father, her husband, and Deputy Sheriff Lewey Corbitt the details of her harrowing assault.[11]

Within a few weeks, the Committee for Equal Justice for Mrs. Recy Taylor formed and was led on a local level by Rosa Parks, E. D. Nixon, Rufus A. Lewis, and E. G. Jackson (editor of the *Alabama Tribune*), all of whom later became pivotal figures in the Montgomery bus boycott. By utilizing the political infrastructure designed to defend the Scottsboro boys a decade earlier and employing the rhetoric of democracy sparked by World War II, Parks, Nixon, and their allies secured the support of national labor unions, African American organizations, women's groups, and thousands of individuals who demanded that Gov.

Chauncey Sparks order an immediate investigation and trial. "The raping of Mrs. Recy Taylor was a fascist-like, brutal violation of her personal rights as a woman and as a citizen of democracy," Eugene Gordon, a reporter for the *New York Daily Worker*, wrote in a pamphlet about the case; "Mrs. Taylor was not the first Negro woman to be outraged," he argued, "but it is our intention to make her the last. White-supremacy imitators of Hitler's storm troopers [will] shrink under the glare of the nation's spotlight." Gordon closed by universalizing the rape: "The attack on Mrs. Taylor was an attack on all women. Mrs. Taylor is a Negro . . . but no woman is safe or free until all women are free."[12] Few African Americans were surprised when the Henry County Grand Jury twice failed to indict the white men—despite the governor's belief that they were, in fact, guilty. Still, Recy Taylor's testimony launched a national and international campaign for equal justice that must not be ignored.[13]

Five years later, African Americans in Montgomery, Alabama, rallied to the defense of a twenty-five-year-old black woman named Gertrude Perkins. On March 27, 1949, Perkins was walking home when she was arrested for public drunkenness and attacked by two white police officers in uniform. After forcing her into their squad car, they drove her to the edge of town and raped her repeatedly at gunpoint. Afterwards, they threw her out of their car and sped away. Somehow, she found the strength to stagger into town, where she went directly to Rev. Solomon Seay Sr.'s house. Awaking him, she told him the details of her brutal assault through sobs and tears. "We didn't go to bed that morning," remembered Seay; "I kept her at my house, carefully wrote down what she said, and later had it notarized." Seay sent Perkins's horror story to the syndicated columnist Drew Pearson, who let the whole country know what happened in his daily radio address before Montgomery's white leaders knew what hit them.[14]

The leaders of the local Interdenominational Ministerial Alliance, the Negro Improvement League, and the National Association for the Advancement of Colored People (NAACP), led by E. D. Nixon and the Reverend Mr. Seay, joined together to form the Citizens Committee for Gertrude Perkins. Mary Fair Burks and her newly formed Women's Political Council may have been involved since one of their early goals was to "aid victims of rape." Although the community mobilized on behalf of Perkins, a grand jury failed to indict the assailants a few weeks later, despite running the full process of "the Anglo-Saxon system of justice." Still, Joe Azbell, editor of the *Montgomery Advertiser,* thought Gertrude Perkins, who bravely spoke out against the men who raped her, "had as much to do with the bus boycott and its creation as anyone on earth." The Perkins protest did not occur in isolation. In February 1951, Rufus A. Lewis . . . led a boycott of a grocery store owned by Sam E. Green, a white man, who was accused of raping his black teenage babysitter while driving her home. Lewis, a World War II veteran and football coach at Alabama State University, organized other veterans and members of the Citizens' Coordinating Committee in the successful campaign to close the store and bring Green to trial.[15]

The 1955 Montgomery bus boycott itself can be viewed as the most obvious example of the African American community coming to the rescue of a black woman, Rosa Parks, though not because of rape. When Parks sat down in a bus's "no-man's land" and was arrested for refusing to give up her seat to a white man, Montgomery blacks found the *perfect* woman to rally around. "Humble enough to be claimed by the common folk," Taylor Branch notes, Rosa Parks was "dignified enough in manner, speech, and dress to command the respect of the leading classes." Rosa Parks fit the middle-class ideals of "chastity, Godliness, family responsibility, and proper womanly conduct and demeanor" and was the kind of woman around which all the African Americans in Montgomery could rally. It is clear that her symbolic role as icon of virtuous black womanhood was decisive in Montgomery. Rev. Martin Luther King Jr.'s first speech at Holt Street Baptist Church stressed this point. "And since it had to happen," the young preacher told the crowd, "I'm happy it happened to a person like Mrs. Parks. Nobody can doubt the height of her character; nobody can doubt the depth of her Christian commitment."[16]

By selecting Rosa Parks as the symbol of segregation instead of other, less exemplary black women who had been arrested on buses earlier in 1955, black leaders in Montgomery embraced the "politics of respectability" . . . as a matter of political necessity amidst the burning white backlash that the 1954 Supreme

Court decision in *Brown v. Board of Education* sparked. The White Citizens' Councils, a kind of uptown Ku Klux Klan, led the movement for massive resistance to school integration by relying heavily on sexual scare tactics and white fears of racial amalgamation.[17] . . .

. . . [The strategies of emphasizing] respectability and . . . [maintaining] silence [about] black sexuality, [has meant that] . . . violence toward black women has not been as "vividly and importantly retained in our collective memory" . . . as the lynching of and violence against black men. . . . Over the past two decades, historians have sharpened their focus on the gendered meanings of respectability, but they have lost sight of the role rape and the threat of sexual violence played in the daily lives of African American women as well as within the larger black freedom struggle.[18] Yet throughout the Jim Crow South African American women such as Recy Taylor in 1944, Gertrude Perkins in 1949, and Betty Jean Owens in 1959 refused to shield their pain in secrecy, thereby challenging the pervasiveness of the politics of respectability. Following in the footsteps of their Reconstruction-era counterparts, they testified about their assaults, leaving behind critical evidence that historians must find the courage to analyze. . . .

When the four armed white men in Tallahassee forced Thomas Butterfield and Richard Brown to get into their car and drive away, leaving Betty Jean Owens and Edna Richardson at the mercy of their assailants, the two black men did not abandon them but drove around the corner and waited. As the blue Chevrolet disappeared down the street, Brown and Butterfield hurried back to the scene. Edna Richardson, the black woman who was able to get away, saw her friends from her hiding spot, called out to them, and then ran to the car. Hoping to save Owens, the Florida A&M students rushed to the local police station to report the crime.[19]

Similar situations in other southern towns had typically left African Americans without police aid. The officer on duty that night in Tallahassee was Joe Cooke Jr., a nineteen-year-old intern from the all-white Florida State University. Much to the surprise of the three black students, he agreed to look for Owens and her assailants. After a lengthy search, one of the students finally spotted the blue Chevrolet and shouted, "That's it!" It was just after 4:00 A.M.

Deputy Cooke turned on his flashers and drove alongside the car. Attempting to escape, the kidnappers led Cooke "twisting and turning through the dark streets of Tallahassee at speeds up to 100 miles per hour." . . . Finally, [the driver, William] Collinsworth pulled the car to the curb, grabbed his shotgun, and got out of the car. Deputy Cooke drew his pistol and ordered all four to line up against the car or, he threatened, "I will shoot to kill."[20]

As they waited for assistance from Cooke's supervisor, they heard muffled screams coming from the car. Richard Brown and Deputy Cooke peered through the rear window and saw Betty Jean Owens, bound and gagged, lying on the backseat floorboards. Brown tried to help her out of the car, but, as her feet touched the ground, she collapsed. Cooke drove Betty Jean Owens and her friends to the local colored hospital at Florida A&M while Deputy Sheriff W. W. Slappey arrested the four white men and drove them to the jailhouse.[21]

Laughing and joking on the way to the police station, the four white men apparently did not take their arrest seriously, nor did they think they had done anything wrong. Collinsworth, for example, worried less about the charges against him than about the safety of his car. Deputy Sheriff Slappey revealed his disgust when he handed the men over to Sheriff Raymond Hamlin Jr. "They all admitted it," Slappey said; "they didn't say why they did it and that's all I'm going to say about this dirty business." William Collinsworth, David Beagles, Ollie Stoutamire, and Patrick Scarborough confessed in writing to abducting Betty Jean Owens at gunpoint and having "sexual relations" with her. When Sheriff Hamlin asked the men to look over their statements and make any necessary corrections, David Beagles, smiling, bent over the table and made one minor adjustment before he and his friends were hustled off to jail.[22]

If the four white men did not take their arrests seriously, students at Florida A&M University flew into a rage. Many of them were veterans of the Tallahassee bus boycott in 1957, a Montgomery-inspired campaign that highlighted the trend in students' preference for direct action rather than the more respectable and slower litigation favored by the NAACP throughout the 1940s and 1950s. When the students heard news of the attack on Owens and the subsequent arrest of four white men, a small group planned an armed march to city hall to let city officials know that they were willing to protect black womanhood the same way whites "protected" white womanhood—with violence or at least a show of force. Mainstream student leaders persuaded them that an armed march was "the wrong thing to do" and patched together a "Unity" demonstration on Sunday, May 3, only twelve hours after Betty Jean Owens was admitted to the hospital and the four white men were taken to jail.[23]

Fifteen hundred students filled Lee Auditorium, where Clifford Taylor, president of the Student Government Association, said he "would not sit idly by and see our sisters, wives, and mothers desecrated." Using language white men in power could understand, student leaders professed their "belief in the dignity, respect, and protection of womanhood" and announced that they would petition the governor and other authorities for a "speedy and impartial trial."[24]

Early the next day, a thousand students gathered in the university's grassy quadrangle with signs, hymns, and prayers aimed at the national news media, which sent out stories of the attack across the country. The students planned to show Tallahassee and the rest of the nation that white men could no longer attack black women without consequence. Student protesters held signs calling for "Justice"; other posters declared, "It could have been YOUR sister, wife, or mother." Some students linked the attack in Tallahassee to larger issues related to the black freedom struggle: two students held up a poster depicting scenes from Little Rock, Arkansas, which read, "My God How Much More of This Can We Take."[25]

It was the deeply personal violation that rape inflicts, however, that gave the students their focus. Patricia Stephens Due remembered feeling helpless and unsafe. She recalled, "we all felt violated, male and female. It was like all of us had been raped." The student leader Buford Gibson, speaking to a crowd, universalized the attack when he said, "You must remember it wasn't just one Negro girl that was raped—it was all of Negro womanhood in the South."[26] By using Betty Jean Owens as a black Everywoman, Gibson challenged male students to rise up in protest and then placed the protection of black womanhood in their hands. Gibson's exhortation inspired students at Florida A&M to maintain their nonviolent demonstration, unlike white men who historically used the protection of white womanhood to inspire mob violence against black men. . . .

Accelerating media coverage, student-led protests, and a threat to boycott classes at Florida A&M forced Judge W. May Walker to call members of the grand jury into special session in Tallahassee on May 6, 1959. Over two hundred black spectators, mostly students, squeezed into the segregated balcony at the Leon County Courthouse to catch a glimpse of Betty Jean Owens and her attackers before they retreated into the secret hearing. Still undergoing hospital treatment for injuries inflicted during the attack and for "severe depression," Owens was accompanied to the court-house by a nurse, the hospital administrator, and her mother.[27]

Gasps and moans emanated from the balcony when, after two hours behind closed doors, William Collinsworth, David Beagles, Patrick Scarborough, and Ollie Stoutamire emerged, calmly faced the judge, and pleaded innocent to the charge of rape, making a jury trial mandatory. African Americans in the balcony roared with disapproval. Dr. M. C. Williams, a local black leader, shouted, "four colored men would be dead if the situation had been reversed. It looks like an open and shut case." Defense attorneys for Collinsworth and Scarborough argued for a delay, insisting that public excitement threatened a fair trial, but Judge Walker ignored their objections. For the first time in Florida history, a judge sent the white defendants charged with raping an African American woman back to jail to await their trial. . . . [28]

Justice was the last thing the black community expected. In the thirty-four years since Florida began sending convicted rapists to the electric chair instead of the gallows, the state had electrocuted thirty-seven African Americans charged with raping white women. Before this, Florida led the country in per capita lynchings, even surpassing such notoriously violent states as Mississippi, Georgia, and Louisiana. From 1900 to 1930, white Floridians lynched 281 people, 256 of whom were African American. Throughout its history, Florida never executed or lynched a white man for raping a black woman. . . . [29]

News that four white men would actually face prosecution for raping a black woman plunged both whites and blacks into largely unfamiliar territory. . . . According to the *Pittsburgh Courier*, the arraignment made the "arguments for white supremacy, racial discrimination, and segregation fall by the wayside" and the arguments against school desegregation

seem "childishly futile." "Time and again," another newspaper editor argued, "Southern spokesmen have protested that they oppose integration in the schools only because it foreshadows a total 'mingling of the races.' The implication is that Negroes are hell-bent for intimacy, while whites shrink back in horror." "Perhaps," the writer argued, "as Lillian Smith and other maverick Southerners have suggested, it is not quite that simple."[30]

While prominent members of the white community expressed their shock and horror at the rape, they continued to stumble into old narratives about race and sex. The indictment helped incite age-old fears of miscegenation and stereotypes of the so-called black beast rapist. . . . White women around Tallahassee began to speak openly about their "fear of retaliation," while young white couples avoided parking "in the country moonlight lest some Negroes should be out hunting in a retaliatory mood." Reflecting this fear as well as the larger concern with social equality, Florida legislators, like other lawmakers throughout the South, passed a series of racist bills designed to segregate children in schools by sex in order to circumvent the *Brown v. Board of Education* decision and "reduce the chances of interracial marriage."[31] The extent to which the myth of the black beast rapist was a projection of white fears was never clearer than when the gang rape of a black woman conjured up terror of *black-on-white* rape. The fact that the black community rallied around Betty Jean Owens and her womanhood threatened white male power—making the myth of the black savage a timely political tool. . . .

Ella Baker, director of the Southern Christian Leadership Conference (SCLC), felt that the evidence in the Tallahassee case was so strong that "not even an all white Florida jury could fail to convict." Reminding whites of their tendency to mete out unequal justice toward black men, she warned, "with memories of Negroes who have been lynched and executed on far less evidence, Negro leaders from all over the South will certainly examine every development in this case. . . . What will Florida's answer be?" The *New York Amsterdam News* called for equal justice, noting that the "law which calls for the death sentence does not say that Negro rapists should be punished by death and white rapists should be allowed to live." . . . [32]

Martin Luther King Jr., at the annual SCLC meeting in Tallahassee a few days after the indictment, praised the student protesters for giving "hope to all of us who struggle for human dignity and equal justice." But he tempered his optimism with political savvy, calling on the federal government to force the country to practice what it preached in its Cold War rivalry with the Soviet Union. "Violence in the South can not be deplored or ignored," King declared, directing his criticism at President Dwight D. Eisenhower; "without effective action, the situation will worsen." King exploited a political context in which America's racial problems were increasingly an international issue. The British Broadcasting Corporation (BBC) broadcast segments of the Florida A&M University student speeches condemning the rape and racial injustice, while newspapers throughout Europe closely watched the case unfold. "It is ironical that these un-American outrages occur as our representatives confer in Geneva to expand democratic principles . . . it might well be necessary and expedient," King threatened, "to appeal to the conscience of the world through the Commission on Human Rights of the United Nations." This international angle was a strategy shared by mainstream integrationists, leftist radicals, and black nationalists alike. Audley "Queen Mother" Moore, leader of the Universal Association of Ethiopian Women, Inc., petitioned the United Nations Human Rights Commission in person to end the "planned lynch terror and willful destruction of our people." She tied issues of race, gender, sex, and citizenship together by demanding Justice Department assistance for Betty Jean Owens's rape case, an FBI investigation of a [recent lynching in Mississippi], and basic voting rights.[33]

On June 11, 1959, at least four hundred people witnessed Betty Jean Owens face her attackers and testify on her own behalf. Owens approached the witness box with her head bowed. She wore a white embroidered blouse and a black-and-salmon checked skirt with gold earrings. The African American press had cast her in the role of respectable womanhood by characterizing her as a God-fearing, middle-class college co-ed "raised in a hardworking Christian household" with parents devoted to the "simple verities of life that make up the backbone of our democracy." Unlike white women, who were often able to play the role of "fair maiden" before a lynch mob worked its will on their alleged attackers, Betty

Jean Owens had to tell her story knowing that the four white men who raped her might go unpunished. Worse, Owens had to describe the attack in front of hundreds of white people in a segregated institution that inherently denied her humanity.[34] Though it may seem unnecessary, even lurid, to bear witness to the details of her testimony today, it is crucial that we hear the same testimony that the jurors heard. Owens's willingness to identify those who attacked her and to testify against them in public broke the institutional silence surrounding the centuries-long history of white men's sexual violation of black women, made a white southern judge and jury recognize her womanhood and dignity, and countered efforts to shame or stereotype her as sexually unchaste. As a result, her testimony alone is a momentous event.

Owens remained strong as state prosecutor William Hopkins asked her to detail the attack from the moment she and her friends left the Florida A&M dance. This she did powerfully and emotionally. "We were only parked near Jake Gaither Park for fifteen minutes," she said, when "four white men pulled up in a 1959 blue Chevrolet." She identified Patrick Scarborough as the man who pressed the shotgun into her date's nose and yelled, "Get out and get out now." When Owens began to cry, David Beagles pressed a "wicked looking foot long knife" to her throat and forced her down to the ground. . . . Owens testified that Beagles pushed her into the car and then "pushed my head down in his lap and yelled at me to be quiet or I would never get home." "I knew I couldn't get away," she stated; "I thought they would kill me if I didn't do what they wanted me to do."[35]

She continued with the horrid details. . . . Owens testified that the men eagerly watched one another have intercourse with her the first time around but lost interest during the second round. "Two of them were working on taking the car's license plate off," she said, "while the oldest one" offered her some whiskey. "I never had a chance to get away," she said quietly; "I was on the ground for two or three hours before the one with the knife pushed me back into the car." After the men had collectively raped her seven times, Ollie Stoutamire and Beagles blindfolded her with a baby diaper and pushed her onto the floorboards of the car, and they all drove away. When she heard the police sirens and felt the car stop, she pulled the blindfold down and began yelling for help.

After police ordered the men out of the car, Owens recalled, "I was so scared and weak and nervous that I just fell on the ground and that is the last thing I remember."[36]

Betty Jean Owens then described the physical injuries she sustained from the attack. "One arm and one leg," she said, "were practically useless" to her for several days while she was at the hospital. A nurse had to accompany her to the grand jury hearing a few days after the attack, and she needed medication for severe depression. She also had a large bruise on her breast where the bodice stay from her dress dug into her skin as the four men pressed their bodies into hers. Asking her to identify some of the exhibits, Hopkins flipped open the switchblade used the night of the attack, startling some of the jurors. Immediately the four defense attorneys jumped up and vehemently called for a mistrial, arguing that "by flashing the knife Mr. Hopkins tried to inflame the jury and this prejudiced their clients' constitutional rights to a fair trial." Judge Walker denied their motion, signaling Hopkins to continue. When asked whether she consented, Owens clearly told Hopkins and the jury, "No sir, I did not."[37]

Defense attorneys grilled Owens for more than an hour, trying to prove that she consented because she never struggled to get away and that she actually enjoyed the sexual encounter. "Didn't you derive any pleasure from that? Didn't you?" the attorney Howard Williams yelled repeatedly. He kept pressing her, "Why didn't you yell or scream out?" "I was afraid they would kill me," Owens said quietly. She showed signs of anger when Williams repeatedly asked if she was a virgin in an attempt to characterize her as a stereotypical black jezebel. Owens retained her composure, refused to answer questions about her chastity, and resisted efforts to shame her. The defense made a last-ditch effort to discredit Owens by arguing that, if the young men had actually raped her and threatened her life, she would have sustained more severe injuries.[38]

Proceeding with the state's case, William Hopkins called the doctors, both black and white, who examined Owens after the attack. They told the jury that they found her in a terrible condition and that she "definitely had sexual relations" that caused the injuries that required a five-day hospital stay. Richard Brown, Thomas Butterfield, and Edna Richardson took the stand next. They all corroborated Owens's testimony. . . . When the prosecution finally rested its case at 8:30 P.M. on June 11, defense attorneys moved for a directed verdict of acquittal, claiming the state failed to prove anything except sexual intercourse. Judge Walker vigorously denied the motion and insisted the defense return the next day to present their defense.

Amid a sea of people in the tiny courtroom, David Beagles, an eighteen-year-old high school student, sat rigidly on the stand, pushing a ring back and forth on his finger as he answered questions from his attorney. His mother buried her head in her arms as she listened to her son tell the jury his side of the story. Beagles testified that he had a knife and William Collinsworth had a shotgun. The four of them were out "looking around for Negroes who had been parking near Collinsworth's neighborhood and bothering them." When they came upon the Florida A&M students, Beagles admitted holding the switchblade but then said he put it away when he saw they were dressed in formal wear. He admitted that they ordered Brown and Butterfield to drive away but insisted that he *asked* the girls to get into the car." He denied the rape, arguing that Owens consented and even asked them to take her "back to school to change her dress." Under cross-examination, Beagles admitted that he "pushed her, just once . . . not hard," into the car, that he said, "If you do what we want you to, we'll let you go," and that he blindfolded her with a diaper after the attack. Defense attorney Howard Williams then asked Judge Walker to remove the jury as Beagles detailed the confession he made the night of the crime. Williams argued that when police officers arrested the young men, they "were still groggy from a night of drinking," making their confessions inadmissible. Under Hopkins's cross-examination, however, Beagles admitted that he was not pressured to say anything, that his confession was voluntary, and that he actually looked over the written statement and made an adjustment.[39]

Patrick Scarborough, who admitted that he was married to a woman in Texas, testified that he had intercourse with Owens twice but emphatically denied using force. When Hopkins questioned him, Scarborough admitted that Owens pleaded, "please don't hurt me," but he insisted that she offered "no resistance." He denied kissing her at first and then said he kissed her on the neck while he had sex with her.[40]

Defense attorneys [tried a series of contradictory approaches to win over the jury. First, they] focused on discrediting Owens instead of defending their clients because the prosecution repeatedly drew self-incriminating information from them. . . . [Then they] tried to use each man's ignorance to prove his innocence, highlighting their low IQ's and poor educations. When that failed, they detailed the dysfunctional histories of each defendant, as though to diminish the viciousness of the crime by offering a rationale for the men's depravity. Character witnesses for William Collinsworth, for example, described his sordid home life and drinking problem. Nearly every member of Collinsworth's family took the stand, spilling sorrowful stories about their poverty and dysfunction. . . . His wife, Pearlie, told the jury through sobs and tears that he was "not himself when he was drunk," but when he was sober "you couldn't ask for a better husband." On the stand, she failed to mention what her letter to the judge had made explicit: that her husband regularly beat her.[41] . . .

Finally, the defense appealed to the jury's prejudices. Collinsworth blamed his actions on the "Indian blood" pulsing through his veins; the Pensacola psychiatrist Dr. W. M. C. Wilhoit backed him up when he argued, "It is a known fact that individuals of the Indian race react violently and primitively when psychotic or intoxicated." When Collinsworth added alcohol to his "Indian blood," Wilhoit argued, "he was unable to discern the nature and quality of the crime in question." The attorney for Ollie Stoutamire, city judge John Rudd, blamed "outside agitators." The defendants are "being publicized and ridiculed to satisfy sadists and people in other places," Rudd yelled during closing arguments. "Look at that little skinny, long legged sixteen-year-old boy. Does he look like a mad rapist who should die . . . should we kill or incarcerate that little boy because he happened to be in the wrong place at the wrong time?"[42]

In their summations to the jury, defense attorneys S. Gunter Toney and Harry Michaels followed Rudd's lead. Michaels insisted that "the crime here is insignificant . . . the pressure, clamor, and furor are completely out of proportion." Pointing to Scarborough, Michaels told the jury, "his motives, intentions, and designs that night were wholesome, innocent and decent." The fact that Owens could "have easily walked ten feet into the woods where nobody

could find her," Michaels said, proved she consented. Waving her gold and white gown in front of the jury, he pointed out that it was "not soiled or torn," which he said proved no brutality was involved. Finally, he called for an acquittal, arguing that the jury could not possibly convict on the basis of "only one witness—the victim, and confessions that admitted only one fact—sexual intercourse." Sitting in the segregated balcony, Charles U. Smith, a sociologist at Florida A&M University, said he gasped when he heard Howard Williams yell, "Are you going to believe this nigger wench over these four boys?"[43]

In his summation, prosecuting attorney William Hopkins jumped up, grabbed the shotgun and Betty Jean Owens's prom dress, and appealed to the jury for a conviction.

> Suppose two colored boys and their moron friends attacked Mrs. Beagles' daughter . . . had taken her at gunpoint from a car and forced her into a secluded place and regardless of whether they secured her consent or not, had intercourse with her seven times, leaving her in such a condition that she collapsed and had to be hospitalized?

Betty Jean Owens, he said, "didn't have a chance in the world with four big boys, a loaded gun and a knife. She was within an inch of losing her life . . . she was gang-raped SEVEN times." "When you get to the question of mercy," he told the jury, "consider that they wouldn't even let that little girl whimper."[44]

Restless spectators, squeezed into every corner of the segregated courthouse, piled back into their seats when jurors emerged after three hours of deliberation with a decision. An additional three hundred African Americans held a silent vigil outside. A. H. King, the jury foreman and a local plantation owner, slowly read aloud the jury's decision for all four defendants: "guilty with a recommendation for mercy." The recommendation for mercy saved the four men from the electric chair and, according to the *Baltimore Afro-American*, "made it inescapably clear that the death penalty for rape is only for colored men accused by white women. . . ." Judge Walker deferred sentencing for fifteen days, cleared the courtroom, and sent the four white men to Raiford prison.[45]

African Americans who attended the trial quietly made their way home after the bittersweet verdict. Betty Jean Owens's mother told reporters that she was "just happy that the jury upheld my daughter's womanhood."

Rev. A. J. Reddick, former head of the Florida NAACP, snapped, "If it had been Negroes, they would have gotten the death penalty." "Florida," he said, "has maintained an excellent record of not veering from its pattern of never executing a white man for the rape of a Negro," but he acknowledged that the conviction was "a step forward." Betty Jean Owens showed a similar ambivalence in an interview by the *New York Amsterdam News*. "It is something," she said; "I'm grateful that twelve white men believed the truth, but I still wonder what they would have done if one of our boys raped a white girl."[46]

Florida A&M students, who had criticized Butterfield and Brown for failing to protect black womanhood a week earlier, were visibly upset after the trial. In fact, letters to the editors of many African American newspapers condemned the two men and all black men for failing to protect "their" women. Mrs. C. A. C. in New York City felt that all Negro men were "mice" and not worthy of respect because "they stand by and let the white men do anything they want to our women." She then warned all black men that they "would never have freedom until [they] learn to stand up and fight." In a letter to the *Baltimore Afro-American*, a black man accepted her challenge: "unless we decide to protect our own women," he argued, "none of them will be safe." Some African American women felt they should protect themselves. A white woman sent her black maid home one day after she came to work with a knife, "in case any white man came after her," reported the *Tallahassee Democrat*. Still, many felt that "someone should have burned."[47]

Despite their anger at the unequal justice meted out, some African Americans in the community considered the guilty verdict a victory. The Reverend C. K. Steele Jr., head of the Tallahassee chapter of the SCLC, said it showed progress, reminding others that four white men "wouldn't have even been arrested twenty years ago." The Reverend Leon A. Lowery, state president of the Florida NAACP, saw a strategy in the mercy recommendation. He thought that it could help "Negroes more in the long run" by setting a precedent for equal justice in future rape cases. After Judge Walker handed down life sentences to the four white men, some African Americans in Tallahassee applauded what they felt was a significant step in the right direction; many others, however, exhibited outrage. Roy Wilkins openly praised

the verdict as a move toward equal justice but acknowledged in a private letter the "glaring contrast that was furnished by the Tallahassee verdict." . . . Editors of the *Louisiana Weekly* called the trial a "figment and a farce" and insisted that anyone who praised the verdict "confesses that he sees nothing wrong with exacting one punishment for white offenders and another, more severe for others."[48]

Any conviction was too much for some whites who felt that sending four white men to jail for raping a black woman upset the entire foundation of white supremacy. Many believed the guilty verdict was the result of a Communist-inspired NAACP conspiracy, which would ultimately lead to miscegenation. Letters to Judge Walker featured a host of common fears and racist stereotypes of black men and women. Fred G. Millette reminded the judge that a conviction "would play into the hands of the Warren Court, the NAACP, and all other radical enemies of the South . . . even though the nigger wench probably had been with a dozen men before." Mrs. Laura Cox wrote to Judge Walker that she feared this case would strengthen desegregation efforts, posing a direct threat to white children who might attend integrated schools. "If the South is integrated," she argued, "white children will be in danger because the Negroes carry knives, razors, ice picks, and guns practically all the time." Petitioning Judge Walker for leniency, Mrs. Bill Aren reminded him to remember that "Negro women like to be raped by the white men" and that "something like this will help the Supreme Court force this low bred race ahead, making whites live and eat with him and allow his children to associate with the little apes, grow up and marry them."[49] . . .

While the verdict was likely the confluence of localized issues—a politically mobilized middle-class African American community, the lower-class status of the defendants (who were politically expendable), Florida's status as a "moderate" southern state dependent on northern tourism, and media pressure—it had far-reaching consequences.[50] The Tallahassee case focused national attention on the sexual exploitation of black women at the hands of white men, leading to convictions elsewhere that summer. In Montgomery, Alabama, Grady F. Smith, a retired air force colonel, was sentenced to fourteen months of hard labor for raping a seventeen-year-old African American girl. In Raleigh, North Carolina, Ralph Lee Betts, a thirty-six-year-old white man, was sentenced to life imprisonment for kidnapping and molesting an eleven-year-old African American girl. And in Burton, South Carolina, an all-white jury sent a white marine named Fred Davis to the electric chair—a first in the history of the South—for raping a forty-seven-year-old African American woman. In each case, white supremacy faltered in the face of the courageous black women who testified on their own behalf.[51]

Betty Jean Owens's grandmother recognized the historic and political significance of the verdicts. "I've lived to see the day," she said, "where white men would really be brought to trial for what they did." [Newspaper editor] John McCray . . . realized the importance of guilty verdicts. "This forced intimacy," he argued, "goes back to the days of slavery when our women were the chattel property of white men." For McCray, the life sentences indicated a new day: "Are we now witnessing the arrival of our women? Are they at long last gaining the emancipation they've needed?"[52]

McCray's connection between the conviction of white men for raping black women and black women's emancipation raises important questions that historians are just beginning to ponder. How did the daily struggle to gain self-respect and dignity, rooted in ideas of what it meant to be men and women, play out in the black freedom struggle? It is not just a coincidence that black college students, struggling for their own identity and independence, sparked the sit-in movement soon after Betty Jean Owens was brutally raped. In Tallahassee, Patricia Stephens Due, who felt that the rape symbolized an attack on the dignity and humanity of all African Americans, organized the city's first Congress of Racial Equality (CORE) chapter just six weeks after Owens's trial. Florida A&M CORE members launched an uneventful sit-in campaign that fall, but, like other black students throughout the South, successfully desegregated local lunch counters, theaters, and department stores in the spring of 1960. The students later led the "jail, no bail" tactic popularized by SCLC and SNCC.[53] While the rape alone may not have been the galvanizing force that turned students into soldiers for freedom, the sexual and racial dynamics inherent in this case speak to larger themes in the African American freedom struggle.

The politics of respectability—Betty Jean Owens's middle-class background, her college education, and her chastity—may have enabled

African Americans on the local and national level to break through the "culture of dissemblance" and speak out against her rape. But it was the convergence of the politics of respectability, Owens's testimony, and African Americans' growing political influence on the national and international stage in the late 1950s that made the legal victory possible. Still, the long tradition of black women's testimony, stretching back to slavery and Reconstruction, makes it clear that some elements of the Tallahassee case were not aberrations. The testimonies and trials of Betty Jean Owens, Gertrude Perkins, and Recy Taylor, to name just a few, bear witness to these issues, forcing historians to reconsider the individual threads that make up the fabric of African American politics. Black women not only dissembled where it was necessary but testified where it was possible. Not only silence but often protest surrounded the sexualized violence against African American women. If we are fully to understand the role of gender and sexuality in larger struggles for freedom and equality, we must explore these battles over manhood and womanhood, frequently set in the context of sexualized violence, that remain at the volatile core of the modern civil rights movement.

NOTES

1. *New York Amsterdam News,* June 20, 1959, p. 37. Trezzvant W. Anderson, "Rapists Missed Out on First Selection," *Pittsburgh Courier,* June 20, 1959, p. 3; "Four Convicted in Rape Case," *Tallahassee Democrat,* June 14, 1959, p. 7. "I Was Scared," *Pittsburgh Courier,* June 20, 1959, p. 1. "Four Begin Defense in Trial on Rape," *New York Times,* June 13, 1959, p. A13. See also criminal case file #3445, *State of Florida v. Patrick Gene Scarborough, David Ervin Beagles, Ollie Odell Stoutamire, and William Ted Collinsworth,* 1959 (Leon County Courthouse, Tallahassee, Fla.) (copy in author's possession). Thanks to the Leon County Courthouse for sending me the file. Because the original trial transcript is no longer available, I have had to rely on newspaper reports, particularly those in African American newspapers: the *Baltimore Afro-American,* the *Louisiana Weekly,* the *New York Amsterdam News,* the *Pittsburgh Courier,* and the South Carolina *Lighthouse and Informer.*

2. The murders of Emmett Till in 1955 and Andrew Goodman, Michael Schwerner, and James Chaney in 1963 are considered pivotal moments in the civil rights movement. Their stories are given prominent attention in the PBS *Eyes on the Prize* series and Hollywood films such as the 1988 thriller *Mississippi Burning.* For monographs on these murders, see, for example, Nicolaus Mills, *Like a Holy Crusade: Mississippi 1964—The Turning Point of the Civil Rights Movement in America* (Chicago, 1992); and

Stephen J. Whitfield, *A Death in the Delta: The Story of Emmett Till* (Baltimore, 1991).

3. Historians have only recently begun to explore how gender and sexuality affected the civil rights movement. On the ways women changed the civil rights movement and how it changed their lives as well, see, for example, Vicki L. Crawford, Jacqueline Anne Rouse, and Barbara Woods, eds., *Women in the Civil Rights Movement: Trailblazers and Torchbearers, 1941–1965* (New York, 1990); and Belinda Robnett, *How Long? How Long? African-American Women in the Struggle for Civil Rights* (New York, 1997). Recent works place black and white women and their long-standing traditions of community organizing and resistance in the forefront of the movement; see, for example, Charles M. Payne, *I've Got the Light of Freedom: The Organizing Tradition and the Mississippi Freedom Struggle* (Berkeley, 1995); and Barbara Ransby, *Ella Baker and the Black Freedom Movement: A Radical Democratic Vision* (Chapel Hill, 2003).

4. Darlene Clark Hine, "Rape and the Inner Lives of Black Women in the Middle West: Preliminary Thoughts on a Culture of Dissemblance," *Signs*, 14 (Summer 1989), 912–20.

5. Gerda Lerner, ed., *Black Women in White America: A Documentary History* (New York, 1972), 172.

6. Tera W. Hunter, *To 'Joy My Freedom: Southern Black Women's Lives and Labors after the Civil War* (Cambridge, Mass., 1997), 34. Winthrop Jordan, *White over Black: American Attitudes toward the Negro, 1550–1812* (Chapel Hill, 1968), 141. Frances Thompson quoted in Lerner, ed., *Black Women in White America*, 174–75; Harriet Simril quoted ibid., 183–85. Essic Harris quoted in Elsa Barkley Brown, "Negotiating and Transforming the Public Sphere: African American Political Life in the Transition from Slavery to Freedom," *Public Culture*, 7 (1994), 112n8; Ferdie Walker quoted in William Chafe, Raymond Gavins, and Robert Korstad, eds., *Remembering Jim Crow: African Americans Tell about Life in the Segregated South* (New York, 2001), 9–10.

7. John H. McCray, "South's Courts Show New Day of Justice," *Baltimore Afro-American*, July 11, 1959. Theralene Beachem interview by McGuire, March 19, 2003, audiotape (in McGuire's possession); Gloria Dennard interview by McGuire, March 19, 2003, audiotape, ibid.; Linda S. Hunt interview by McGuire, March 19, 2003, audiotape, ibid.; Mrs. Lucille M. Johnson interview by McGuire, March 16, 2003, audiotape, ibid.

8. Chana Kai Lee, *For Freedom's Sake: The Life of Fannie Lou Hamer* (Urbana, 1999), 9, 10, 78–81. Though over a half century old, two of the best articulations of the sexual subtext of segregation that exist are John Dollard, *Caste and Class in a Southern Town* (Madison, 1937); and Lillian Smith, *Killers of the Dream* (New York, 1949). See also Kay Mills, *This Little Light of Mine: The Life of Fannie Lou Hamer* (New York, 1993).

9. See Deborah Gray White, *Too Heavy a Load: Black Women in Defense of Themselves, 1894–1994* (New York, 1999), 60–66. John Lewis Adams, "Arkansas Needs Leadership': Daisy Bates, Black Arkansas, and the National Association for the Advancement of Colored People" (M.A. thesis, University of Wisconsin, Madison, 2003). Thanks to John Adams for sharing his research with me. On "reversing the shame," see

Temma Kaplan, "Reversing the Shame and Gendering the Memory," *Signs*, 28 (Autumn 2002), 179–99. Jo Ann Robinson, *The Montgomery Bus Boycott and the Women Who Started It: The Memoir of Jo Ann Gibson Robinson*, ed. David J. Garrow (Knoxville, 1987), 37.

10. On the impact of World War II, see, for example, Timothy B. Tyson, "Wars for Democracy: African American Militancy and Interracial Violence in North Carolina during World War II," in *Democracy Betrayed: The Wilmington Race Riot of 1898 and Its Legacy*, ed. David Cecelski and Timothy B. Tyson (Chapel Hill, 1998), 254–75; and Harvard Sitkoff, "Racial Militancy and Interracial Violence in the Second World War," *Journal of American History*, 58 (Dec. 1971), 661–81. My research indicates that African Americans throughout the South used World War II as a wedge to publicize southern injustice, especially sexual violence by white men. Between 1942 and 1950, African American women accused white men of rape, testified about their assaults, and sparked community mobilization efforts in a number of southern towns, often securing convictions, mostly on minor charges with small fines assessed.

11. Fred Atwater, "$600 to Rape Wife? Alabama Whites Make Offer to Recy Taylor Mate," *Chicago Defender*, n.d., clipping, Recy Taylor case, folder 2, Administrative Files, Gov. Chauncey Sparks Papers, 1943–1947 (Alabama Department of Archives and History, Montgomery); N. W. Kimbrough and J. V. Kitchens, "Report to Governor Chauncey Sparks," Dec. 14, 1944, ibid.; John O. Harris, N. W. Kimbrough, and J. V. Kitchens to Gov. Chauncey Sparks, "Supplemental Report, December 27, 1944," ibid. See also "Grand Jury Refuses to Indict Attackers," *Pittsburgh Courier*, Feb. 24, 1945, folder 3, ibid.; "This Evening," *Birmingham News*, Feb. 21, 1945, ibid.; and "Second Grand Jury Finds No Bill in Negro's Charges," *Dothan Eagle*, Feb. 15, 1945, ibid.

12. On Scottsboro's political infrastructure, see Dan T. Carter, *Scottsboro: A Tragedy of the American South* (New York, 1971); and James Goodman, *Stories of Scottsboro* (New York, 1994). Over thirty national labor unions and many more locals supported Recy Taylor. See "Press release," Feb. 3, 1945, folder 4, box 430, Earl Conrad Collection (Cayuga Community College Library, Auburn, N.Y.). Other organizations that played an active role in Recy Taylor's defense include the Southern Conference for Human Welfare, the National Council of Negro Women, the Southern Negro Youth Congress, the National Negro Congress, the International Labor Defense, and the Birmingham and Montgomery branches of the NAACP: "Partial Sponsor List," Dec. 28, 1944, ibid.; Earl Conrad, Eugene Gordon, and Henrietta Buckmaster, "Equal Justice under Law," pamphlet draft, ibid.

13. See Kimbrough and Kitchens, "Report to Governor Chauncey Sparks"; Harris, Kimbrough, and Kitchens to Sparks, "Supplemental Report." See also "Grand Jury Refuses to Indict Attackers," *Pittsburgh Courier*, Feb. 24, 1945; "Dixie Sex Crimes against Negro Women Widespread," *Chicago Defender*, n.d., Scrapbook Collection, Conrad Collection; "Alabama Rapists Came from Church to Join White Gang in Sex Crime," *Chicago Defender*, March 24, 1945, ibid.; and "Alabama Has No Race Problem, Claims Official," *Chicago Defender*, n.d., ibid.

14. See *Montgomery Advertiser*, April 5, 1949, p. 8A; April 6, 1949, p. 1B; April 7, 1949, p. 2A; S. S. Seay, *I Was There by the Grace of God* (Montgomery, 1990), 130–31. "Drew Pearson Changes Mind; Criticizes City," *Montgomery Advertiser*, May 3, 1949, p. 1A; ibid., May 21, 1949, p. 1A; "Anglo-Saxon System of Justice," ibid., May 22, 1949, p. 2B.

15. "Rape Cry against Dixie Cops Fall on Deaf Ears," *Baltimore Afro-American*, April 9, 1949, p. 1; Stewart Burns, ed., *Daybreak of Freedom: The Montgomery Bus Boycott* (Chapel Hill, 1997), 7; Joe Azbell quoted in "Cradle of the Confederacy," transcript, *Will the Circle Be Unbroken*, Southern Regional Council Web site (March 1997; not currently available; printout in McGuire's possession). Rufus A. Lewis story in Townsend Davis, *Weary Feet, Rested Souls: A Guided History of the Civil Rights Movement* (New York, 1998), 34.

16. Taylor Branch, *Parting the Waters: America in the King Years, 1954–1963* (New York, 1988), 130 (first and last quotations). Marissa Chappell, Jenny Hutchinson, and Brian Ward, "'Dress modestly, neatly . . . as if you were going to church'; Respectability, Class, and Gender in the Montgomery Bus Boycott and the Early Civil Rights Movement," in *Gender in the Civil Rights Movement*, ed. Peter J. Ling and Sharon Monteith (New York, 1999), 87.

17. Black leaders in Montgomery decided against using the arrests of Claudette Colvin, an unwed pregnant teenager, and Mary Louise Smith, the daughter of a local drunk, as test cases for desegregating the buses; see Branch, *Parting the Waters*, 123–28; Lynn Olson, *Freedom's Daughters: The Unsung Heroes of the Civil Rights Movement from 1830–1970* (New York, 2001), 94–95. Neil R. McMillen, *The Citizens' Council: Organized Resistance to the Second Reconstruction, 1954–1964* (Urbana, 1994), 184, 186.

18. Brown, "Negotiating and Transforming the Public Sphere," 146. Historians of the modern day civil rights movement are beginning to build upon work that chronicled the ways respectability, dignity, and manhood and womanhood shaped the strategies and goals of the middle- and working-class black activists during Reconstruction and the Progressive Era; see, for example, Glenda Gilmore, *Gender and Jim Crow: Women and the Politics of White Supremacy in North Carolina, 1896–1920* (Chapel Hill, 1999); and Evelyn Brooks Higginbotham, *Righteous Discontent. The Women's Movement in the Black Baptist Church, 1880–1920* (Cambridge, Mass., 1993).

19. "Deputy Tells of Confessions," *Tallahassee Democrat*, June 12, 1959.

20. Saunders, "Report on Tallahassee Incident."

21. "Deputy Tells of Confessions," *Tallahassee Democrat*, June 12, 1959. Original reports stated that Owens was "bound and gagged," but she later testified that she was only blindfolded; after she pulled the blindfold down, she appeared to have been gagged.

22. "Four Whites Seized in Rape of Negro," *New York Times*, May 3, 1959, p. A45.

23. On the Tallahassee bus boycott, see Glenda Alice Rabby, *The Pain and the Promise: The Struggle for Civil Rights in Tallahassee, Florida* (Athens, Ga., 1999), 9–46. Robert M. White, "The Tallahassee Sit-ins and CORE: A Nonviolent Revolutionary Sub-movement" (Ph.D. diss., Florida State University, 1964), 65.

24. White, "Tallahassee Sit-ins and CORE," 65.

25. "Rapists Face Trial," *Famuan*, 27 (May 1959), 1, 3; "Negroes Ask Justice for Co-ed Rapists," *Atlanta Constitution*, May 4, 1959, p. 2; "Four Whites Seized in Rape of Negro," *New York Times*, May 3, 1959, p. A45; ibid., May 5, 1959, p. A23; "Mass Rape of Co-ed Outrages Students," *Louisiana Weekly*, May 9, 1959, p. 1; *L'Osservatore Romano*, June 12, 1959; *Herald Tribune–London*, June 13, 1959; "Jury to Take Up Rape of Negro Co-ed," *Atlanta Constitution*, May 5, 1959, p. 5.

26. Patricia Stephens Due telephone interview by McGuire, March 4, 1999 (notes in McGuire's possession).

27. "4 Indicted in Rape of Negro Co-ed," *New York Herald Tribune*, May 7, 1959, p. 5; Moses Newson, "Leaves Hospital to Give Testimony," *Pittsburgh Courier*, May 16, 1959, pp. 1–2.

28. M. C. Williams quoted in "Packed Court Hears Not Guilty," *Pittsburgh Courier*, May 16, 1959, pp. 1–2; "Judge Instructs July Here," *Tallahassee Democrat*, May 6, 1959, p. 1; "Sobbing Co-ed Bares Ordeal," *Baltimore Afro-American*, May 16, 1959, p. 1; "Indictment for Rape," criminal case file #3445, *Florida v. Scarborough, Beagles, Stoutamire, and Collinsworth*; "Four Plead Not Guilty to Rape," *Tallahassee Democrat*, n.d., clipping, folder 4, box 912, W. May Walker Papers (Special Collections, Robert Manning Strozier Library, Florida State University, Tallahassee).

29. Statistics are from David R. Colburn and Richard K. Scher, *Florida's Gubernatorial Politics in the Twentieth Century* (Gainesville, 1995), 13.

30. "Another Dixiecrat Headache," *Pittsburgh Courier*, June 20, 1959; "The Other Story," n.d., clipping, folder 1, box 912, Walker Papers.

31. William H. Chafe, "Epilogue from Greensboro, North Carolina," in *Democracy Betrayed*, ed. Cecelski and Tyson, 281–82. "Senate to Get Racial Measures," *Tallahassee Democrat*, June 14, 1959, p. 1; "Pent Up Critique on the Rape Case," ibid., May 14, 1959.

32. Ella Baker quoted in *Pittsburgh Courier*, May 30, 1959, p. 3; see also Ransby, *Ella Baker and the Black Freedom Movement*, 210. "Enforce the Law," *New York Amsterdam News*, May 9, 1959.

33. "King Asks Ike to Go to Mississippi," *Baltimore Afro-American*, May 23, 1959. "Report from Europe," *Baltimore Afro-American*, May 23, 1959. For the impact of the Cold War on civil rights, see, for example, Mary L. Dudziak, *Cold War Civil Rights: Race and the Image of American Democracy* (Princeton, 2000); and Thomas Borstelmann, *The Cold War and the Color Line: American Race Relations in the Global Arena* (Cambridge, Mass., 2001). "Appeal to U.N. to Stop Race Violence," *Louisiana Weekly*, May 9, 1959, p. 1.

34. *Tallahassee Democrat*, May 4, 1959. On the "fair Maiden," see Jacquelyn Dowd Hall, "'Not That Sort of Woman': Race, Gender, and Sexual Violence during the Memphis Riot of 1866," in *Sex, Love, Race: Crossing Boundaries in North American History*, ed. Martha Hodes (New York, 1999), 267–93.

35. "I Was Scared," *Pittsburgh Courier*, June 20, 1959; see also "Did Not Consent," *Tallahassee Democrat*, June 11, 1959; "Rape Co-eds Own Story," *New York Amsterdam News*, June 20, 1959, p. 1; *Atlanta Constitution*, June 12, 1959; "Negro Girl Tells Jury of Rape by Four," *New York Times*, June 12, 1959, p. A16. Coverage of Owens's testimony was nearly identical in newspapers cited.

36. "Did Not Consent," *Tallahassee Democrat*, June 11, 1959; ibid.; ibid.; "I Was Scared," *Pittsburgh Courier*, June 20, 1959, p. 1; "Did Not Consent," *Tallahassee Democrat*, June 11, 1959; ibid.; see also *Charlotte Observer*, June 12, 1959, p. 1A.

37. "Did Not Consent," *Tallahassee Democrat*, June 11, 1959; "I Was Scared," *Pittsburgh Courier*, June 20, 1959; "State's exhibits" (knife) in criminal case file #3445, *Florida v. Scarborough, Beagles, Stoutamire, and Collinsworth*, 1959.

38. "Rape Co-eds Own Story," *New York Amsterdam News*, June 20, 1959, p. 1; "I Was Scared," *Pittsburgh Courier*, June 20, 1959, p. 1; see also "Four Begin Defense in Trial on Rape," *New York Times*, June 13, 1959, p. A13.

39. Anderson, "Rapists Missed Out on First Selection," *Pittsburgh Courier*, June 20, 1959, p. 3; "Four Begin Defense in Trial on Rape," *New York Times*, June 13, 1959, p. A13; Howard Williams quoted in "Rape Defendants Claim Consent," *Tallahassee Democrat*, June 13, 1959.

40. "Negro Co-ed Gave Consent, Rape Defendants Tell Jury" *Atlanta Constitution*, June 13, 1959.

41. William Hopkins quoted in "Four Convicted in Rape Case; Escape Chair; 2 hr 45 min Verdict Calmly Received in Court," *Tallahassee Democrat*, June 14, 1959, p. 1; Pearlie Collinsworth and friends quoted in "Rape Defendants Claim Consent," ibid., June 13, 1959; Maudine Reeve's history of Ted Collinsworth, "State's exhibit #15," criminal case file #3445, *Florida v. Scarborough, Beagles, Stoutamire, and Collinsworth*, 1959; letter from Mrs. W. T. Collinsworth, "State's exhibit #16," ibid.

42. W. M. C. Wilhoit's testimony in "Motion for Leave to File Notice of Defense of Insanity," May 28, 1959, criminal case file #3445, *Florida v. Scarborough, Beagles, Stoutamire, and Collinsworth*, 1959. "Four Begin Defense in Trial on Rape," *New York Times*, June 13, 1959, p. A13; John Rudd quoted in "Four Guilty of Raping Negro; Florida Jury Votes Mercy," ibid., June 14, 1959, p. A1.

43. "Four Guilty of Raping Negro; Florida Jury Votes Mercy," *New York Times*, June 14, 1959, p. A1. Charles U. Smith interview by Jackson Lee Ice, 1978, in Jackson Lee Ice Interviews, Florida Governors Manuscript Collection (Special Collections, Strozier Library); verified in Charles U. Smith telephone interview by McGuire, March 9, 1999 (notes in McGuire's possession).

44. "Precedent Seen in Rape Trial," *Tampa Tribune*, June 15, 1959; *Tallahassee Democrat*, June 14, 1959, p. 1.

45. "Verdict," June 14, 1959, criminal case file #3445, *Florida v. Scarborough, Beagles, Stoutamire, and Collinsworth*, 1959. "Guilty as Charged," *Baltimore Afro-American*, June 20, 1959.

46. Sitton, "Negroes See Gain in Conviction of Four for Rape of Co-ed," *New York Times*, June 15, 1959, p. A1; "I'm Leaving Dixie," *New York Amsterdam News*, June 20, 1959.

47. Apparently students at Florida A&M ostracized Thomas Butterfield and Richard Brown for failing to protect Betty Jean Owens and Edna Richardson; students thought they ought to have shown some "physical resistance" rather than run away from the "point of a knife and gun": "I'm Leaving Dixie," *New York Amsterdam News*, June 20, 1959. "Hits Negro Men," ibid., June 6, 1959, p. 8. "Williams Was Right," *Baltimore Afro-American*, June 27, 1959; "Four Convicted in Rape Case," *Tallahassee Democrat*, June 14, 1959, p. 7; "I'm Leaving Dixie," *New York Amsterdam News*, June 20, 1959.

48. Sitton, "Negroes See Gain in Conviction of Four for Rape of Co-ed," *New York Times*, June 15, 1959, p. A1. "Negroes Say They Will Use Tallahassee Case as Precedent in Rape Trials," *Tampa Tribune*, June 15, 1959; "This Is Not Equal Justice," *Louisiana Weekly*, July 4, 1959.

49. Fred G. Millette to Judge W. May Walker, June 15, 1959, box 912, folder 1, Walker Papers; Mrs. Laura Cox to Judge Walker, June 15, 1959, ibid.; Mrs. Bill Aren to Judge Walker, June 15, 1959, ibid.

50. See Tom Wagy, *Governor LeRoy Collins of Florida: Spokesman of the New South* (University, Ala., 1985); and Steven F. Lawson, "From Sit-in to Race Riot: Businessmen, Blacks, and the Pursuit of Moderation in Tampa, 1960–1967," in *Southern Businessmen and Desegregation*, ed. Elizabeth Jacoway and David R. Colburn (Baton Rouge, 1982), 257–81.

51. Cases cited in Kimberly R. Woodard, "The Summer of African-American Discontent," unpublished paper, Duke University, 1992 (in McGuire's possession). See also "Death to Be Demanded in Rape Case," *Baltimore Afro-American*, July 4, 1959; John H. McCray, "Marine Doomed to Electric Chair in S.C. Rape Case," ibid., July 11, 1959, p. 1; Clarence Mitchell, "Separate but Equal Justice," ibid.; "Girlfriend Turns in Rape Suspect," ibid., Aug. 1, 1959; Trezzvant Anderson, "Negroes Weep as Georgia White Is Acquitted," *Pittsburgh Courier*, Sept. 2, 1959.

52. "The Tallahassee Case: A Turning Point in South," *New York Amsterdam News*, July 18, 1959; John H. McCray, "South's Courts Show New Day of Justice," *Baltimore Afro-American*, June 11, 1959.

53. Richard Haley, "Report on Events in Tallahassee, October 1959–June 1960," folder 7, box 10, series 5, Congress of Racial Equality Papers (Wisconsin Historical Society, Madison).

Betty Friedan, "The problem that has no name"

In the late 1950s, Elvis Presley monopolized the top of the rock and roll charts. The Beatles would not arrive until 1964. But by 1960 African American girl groups, led by the Shirelles and the Supremes, were elbowing for the top place, and in December 1960, the top song was the Shirelles hit, "Will You Love Me Tomorrow?" As their most astute analyst, Susan Douglas, has written, they had emerged from the black gospel tradition; they were not voices of social complacency or homogenized commercialism (such as Doris Day's hit "How Much is that Doggie in the Window?"). Their music was "revolutionary . . . [It] conveyed both a moral authority and a spirited hope for the future." They questioned men's reliability:

Tonight you're mine completely
You give your love so sweetly
Tonight the light of love is in your eyes
But will you love me tomorrow?

Is this a lasting treasure
Or just a moment's pleasure?
Can I believe the magic of your sighs . . .

As their songs "gave voice to girls' changing attitudes toward sex," and claimed the power to make their own choices, girl groups of the period sang "that they, as a generation, would not be trapped."*

Mothers who worried about their daughters had their own set of frustrations. They were not much better than their daughters at articulating their discomfort and malaise. It was 1963 when Betty Friedan, identifying herself as a suburban housewife, did the job for them, exposing the triviality and frustrations of a resurgent domesticity.

Friedan's indictment, a brief portion of which appears here, was the subject of much controversy. Women who found the gratification associated with child care and housework vastly overemphasized applauded Friedan's forceful articulation of their own dissatisfactions. Other women objected vehemently, insisting that, as wives and mothers and perhaps community activists, they enjoyed a lifestyle that not only benefited both their families and communities but also provided them personally with freedom, pleasure, and a sense of self-worth. (Among Friedan's critics was Phyllis Schlafly, whose criticism of the women's liberation movement appears in the next selection.)

Among the thousands of letters that Friedan received was one from Gerda Lerner, then a 43-year-old mother and graduate student studying history at Columbia University. (Lerner's essay on the continuing relevance of the 1848 Seneca

Falls Declaration of Sentiments appears on pp. 221–227). "I have just finished reading your splendid book," Lerner wrote; "and want to tell you how excited and delighted I am . . . I am sure it will unsettle a great many smug certainties, cause a lot of healthy doubts, and, I hope, will stir up controversy. . . . The more controversy, the better, for the sooner people will begin to think of new solutions. You have done for women what Rachel Carson has done for birds and trees."**

But Lerner was not uncritical. Her life as a Jewish refugee from Nazis (she had been briefly imprisoned in Vienna) had sensitized her to the marginalized, and she had found friends and colleagues among black women ever since arriving in the United States. Now she wrote:

> I have one reservation . . . you address yourself solely to the problems of middle-class, college-educated women. . . . Working women, especially Negro women, labor not only under the disadvantages imposed by the feminine mystique, but under the more pressing disadvantages of economic discrimination. To leave them out of consideration of the problem or to ignore the contributions they can make toward its solution, is something we simply cannot afford to do. . . . It is my belief, that one of the most insidious results of the feminine mystique is that it led women to believe that their problems could be solved on the basis of the individual family. This is, in fact, a serious retrogression, for American women learned before the turn of the century that community solutions to their problems were more . . . far-reaching than the best individual solutions. I have in mind . . . a system of social reforms (daycare centers, maternity benefits . . .), which would bring our social services up to a standard already taken for granted in many European and Scandinavian countries.

How are we to explain such different responses to Friedan's book—in some cases instant agreement, in others instant rejection, and then the complex response articulated by Lerner? Is "the problem" that Friedan identifies a universal one?

The problem lay buried, unspoken, for many years in the minds of American women. It was a strange stirring, a sense of dissatisfaction, a yearning that women suffered in the middle of the twentieth century in the United States. Each suburban wife struggled with it alone. As she made the beds, shopped for groceries, matched slipcover material, ate peanut butter sandwiches with her children, chauffeured Cub Scouts and Brownies, lay beside her husband at night, she was afraid to ask even of herself the silent question—"Is this all?"

For over fifteen years there was no word of this yearning in the millions of words written about women, for women, in all the columns, books and articles by experts telling women their role was to seek fulfillment as wives and mothers. Over and over women heard in voices of tradition and of Freudian sophistication that they could desire no greater destiny than to glory in their own femininity. Experts told them how to catch a man and keep him, how to breast-feed children and handle their toilet training, how to cope with sibling rivalry and adolescent rebellion; how to buy a dishwasher, bake bread, cook gourmet snails, and build a swimming pool with their own hands; how to dress, look, and act more feminine and make marriage more exciting; how to keep their husbands from dying young and their sons from growing into delinquents. They were taught to pity the neurotic, unfeminine, unhappy women who wanted to be poets or physicists or presidents. They learned that truly feminine women do not want careers, higher education, political rights—the independence and the

---

*This interpretation is offered in Susan Douglas, *Where the Girls Are: Growing Up Female with the Mass Media* (New York: Times Books, 1994), ch. 4.

**Gerda Lerner to Betty Friedan, Feb. 6, 1963, in Folder 715, Box 57, Betty Friedan Papers, MC 575, Schlesinger Library, Radcliffe Institute, Harvard University. Reprinted by permission of Stephanie Lerner Lapidus. For digital images of the two-page, typed letter, see http://schlesingerlibrary.omeka.net/items/show/55. Biologist Rachel Carson's *Silent Spring*, an indictment of the human illness and environmental damages caused by pesticides, was published in Sept. 1962, but initially was serialized in *The New Yorker* in the previous months. It garnered much attention and enormous sales.

opportunities that the old-fashioned feminists fought for. Some women, in their forties and fifties, still remembered painfully giving up those dreams, but most of the younger women no longer even thought about them. A thousand expert voices applauded their femininity, their adjustment, their new maturity. All they had to do was devote their lives from earliest girlhood to finding a husband and bearing children.

By the end of the 1950s, the average marriage age of women in America dropped to 20, and was still dropping, into the teens. Fourteen million girls were engaged by 17. The proportion of women attending college in comparison with men dropped from 47 percent in 1920 to 35 percent in 1958. A century earlier, women had fought for higher education; now girls went to college to get a husband. By the mid-fifties, 60 percent dropped out of college to marry, or because they were afraid too much education would be a marriage bar. Colleges built dormitories for "married students," but the students were almost always the husbands. A new degree was instituted for the wives—"Ph.T." (Putting Husband Through).

Then American girls began getting married in high school. And the women's magazines, deploring the unhappy statistics about these young marriages, urged that courses on marriage, and marriage counselors, be installed in the high schools. Girls started going steady at twelve and thirteen, in junior high. Manufacturers put out brassieres with false bosoms of foam rubber for little girls of ten. And an advertisement for a child's dress, size 3–6x, in the *New York Times* in the fall of 1960, said: "She Too Can Join the Man-Trap Set."

By the end of the fifties, the United States birthrate was overtaking India's. The birth-control movement, renamed Planned Parenthood, was asked to find a method whereby women who had been advised that a third or fourth baby would be born dead or defective might have it anyhow. Statisticians were especially astounded at the fantastic increase in the number of babies among college women. Where once they had two children, now they had four, five, six. Women who had once wanted careers were now making careers out of having babies. So rejoiced *Life* magazine in a 1956 paean to the movement of American women back to the home.

In a New York hospital, a woman had a nervous breakdown when she found she could not breast-feed her baby. In other hospitals, women dying of cancer refused a drug which research had proved might save their lives: Its side effects were said to be unfeminine. "If I have only one life, let me live it as a blonde," a larger-than-life-sized picture of a pretty, vacuous woman proclaimed from newspaper, magazine, and drugstore ads. And across America, three out of every ten women dyed their hair blonde. They ate a chalk called Metrecal, instead of food, to shrink to the size of the thin young models. Department-store buyers reported that American women, since 1939, had become three and four sizes smaller. "Women are out to fit the clothes, instead of vice-versa," one buyer said.

Interior decorators were designing kitchens with mosaic murals and original paintings, for kitchens were once again the center of women's lives. Home sewing became a million-dollar industry. Many women no longer left their homes, except to shop, chauffeur their children, or attend a social engagement with their husbands. Girls were growing up in America without ever having jobs outside the home. In the late fifties, a sociological phenomenon was suddenly remarked: A third of American women now worked, but most were no longer young and very few were pursuing careers. They were married women who held part-time jobs, selling or secretarial, to put their husbands through school, their sons through college, or to help pay the mortgage. Or they were widows supporting families. Fewer and fewer women were entering professional work. The shortages in the nursing, social work, and teaching professions caused crises in almost every American city. Concerned over the Soviet Union's lead in the space race, scientists noted that America's greatest source of unused brainpower was women. But girls would not study physics: It was "unfeminine." A girl refused a science fellowship at Johns Hopkins to take a job in a real-estate office. All she wanted, she said, was what every other American girl wanted—to get married, have four children, and live in a nice house in a nice suburb.

The suburban housewife—she was the dream image of the young American women and the envy, it was said, of women all over the world. The American housewife—freed by science and labor-saving appliances from the drudgery, the dangers of childbirth, and the illnesses of her grandmother. She was healthy, beautiful, educated, concerned only about her husband, her children, her home.

She had found true feminine fulfillment. As a housewife and mother, she was respected as a full and equal partner to man in his world. She was free to choose automobiles, clothes, appliances, supermarkets; she had everything that women ever dreamed of.

In the fifteen years after World War II, this mystique of feminine fulfillment became the cherished and self-perpetuating core of contemporary American culture. Millions of women lived their lives in the image of those pretty pictures of the American suburban housewife, kissing their husbands good-bye in front of the picture window, depositing their station wagons full of children at school, and smiling as they ran the new electric waxer over the spotless kitchen floor. They baked their own bread, sewed their own and their children's clothes, kept their new washing machines and dryers running all day. They changed the sheets on the beds twice a week instead of once, took the rug-hooking class in adult education, and pitied their poor frustrated mothers, who had dreamed of having a career. Their only dream was to be perfect wives and mothers; their highest ambition to have five children and a beautiful house, their only fight to get and keep their husbands. They had no thought for the unfeminine problems of the world outside the home; they wanted the men to make the major decisions. They gloried in their role as women, and wrote proudly on the census blank: "Occupation: housewife."

For over fifteen years, the words written for women, and the words women used when they talked to each other, while their husbands sat on the other side of the room and talked shop or politics or septic tanks, were about problems with their children, or how to keep their husbands happy, or improve their children's school, or cook chicken or make slipcovers. Nobody argued whether women were inferior or superior to men; they were simply different. Words like "emancipation" and "career" sounded strange and embarrassing; no one had used them for years. When a Frenchwoman named Simone de Beauvoir wrote a book called *The Second Sex,* an American critic commented that she obviously "didn't know what life was all about," and besides, she was talking about French women. The "woman problem" in America no longer existed.

If a woman had a problem in the 1950s and 1960s she knew that something must be wrong with her marriage, or with herself.

Other women were satisfied with their lives, she thought. What kind of a woman was she if she did not feel this mysterious fulfillment waxing the kitchen floor? She was so ashamed to admit her dissatisfaction that she never knew how many other women shared it. If she tried to tell her husband, he didn't understand what she was talking about. She did not really understand it herself. For over fifteen years women in America found it harder to talk about this problem than about sex. Even the psychoanalysts had no name for it. When a woman went to a psychiatrist for help, as many women did, she would say, "I'm so ashamed," or "I must be hopelessly neurotic." "I don't know what's wrong with women today," a suburban psychiatrist said uneasily. "I only know something is wrong because most of my patients happen to be women. And their problem isn't sexual." Most women with this problem did not go to see a psychoanalyst, however. "There's nothing wrong really," they kept telling themselves. "There isn't any problem."

But on an April morning in 1959, I heard a mother of four, having coffee with four other mothers in a suburban development fifteen miles from New York, say in a tone of quiet desperation, "the problem." And the others knew, without words, that she was not talking about a problem with her husband, or her children, or her home. Suddenly they realized they all shared the same problem, the problem that has no name. They began, hesitantly, to talk about it. Later, after they had picked up their children at nursery school and taken them home to nap, two of the women cried, in sheer relief, just to know they were not alone.

Gradually I came to realize that the problem that has no name was shared by countless women in America. As a magazine writer I often interviewed women about problems with their children, or their marriages, or their houses, or their communities. But after a while I began to recognize the telltale signs of this other problem. I saw the same signs in suburban ranch houses and split-levels on Long Island and in New Jersey and Westchester County; in colonial houses in a small Massachusetts town; on patios in Memphis; in suburban and city apartments; in living rooms in the Midwest. Sometimes I sensed the problem, not as a reporter, but as a suburban housewife, for during this time I was also bringing up my own three children in Rockland County, New York. I heard echoes of the problem in college dormitories and semi-private maternity wards, at PTA meetings and luncheons of the League of Women Voters, at suburban cocktail parties, in station wagons waiting for trains, and in snatches of conversation overheard at Schrafft's. The groping words I heard from other women, on quiet afternoons when children were at school or on quiet evenings when husbands worked late, I think I understood first as a woman long before I understood their larger social and psychological implications.

Phyllis Schlafly, "The thoughts of one who loves life as a woman . . ."

Not all well-educated, white middle-class family women with energy and ability to spare reacted to the resurgent domesticity of the Cold War years as did Betty Goldstein Friedan. Phyllis Stewart Schlafly is a case in point. The two women had much in common. Separated in age by only three years, both were the first child born to their respective families, the Goldsteins, who were Jewish, and the Stewarts, who were Roman Catholic. Both grew up during the Depression years in Illinois and were valedictorians of their high school classes. Both attended women's colleges, Goldstein choosing prestigious Smith College in Massachusetts and Stewart attending College of the Sacred Heart in Maryville, Illinois, before transferring to Washington University in St. Louis. Excelling in college, both entered graduate school, Goldstein studying for an M.A. in psychology at the University of California, Berkeley, Stewart earning an M.A. in political science at Radcliffe College and Harvard University. (She would later return to Washington University for a law degree.)

Both went on to interesting jobs, Stewart as a congressional researcher in Washington, Goldstein as a journalist in New York City. Both subsequently married, Stewart choosing John Fred Schlafly, Jr., a lawyer and fellow conservative, and Goldstein choosing Carl Friedan, a theatrical producer and later an advertising executive. Both women had children, Schlafly six and Friedan three, whom they reared in suburbia along with the millions of other middle-class families caught up in the resurgent domesticity of the postwar years.

Energetic and intelligent, neither found domesticity sufficient. Friedan continued to write, as did Schlafly, who also became a community volunteer, Republican Party activist, and, in 1952, a congressional candidate, winning her primary but losing in the general election. In the early 1960s, both published first books that became best-sellers—Friedan *The Feminine Mystique* and Schlafly *A Choice Not an Echo*, a political endorsement of conservative Arizona senator Barry Goldwater, the Republican presidential candidate in 1964.

Yet despite these similarities, the personal became political for these two women in ways that would lead them in sharply divergent directions in the years ahead. Friedan's name would become synonymous with a resurgent feminism, Schlafly's with antifeminism. Friedan, as a founder and the first president of the National Organization for Women (NOW), would champion equal rights for women. (For more about the shaping of Friedan's career, see the essay by Daniel Horowitz, pp. 569–580.) Schlafly, creator and author of the *Phyllis Schlafly Report*, would devote her extraordinary energy as well as formidable organizational and speaking skills to defeat of the Equal Rights Amendment (ERA) (see p. 746–747). Equality between the sexes, she insisted, would harm rather than help women.

While Schlafly's states' rights stance partially explains her opposition to using the federal government on behalf of sexual equality, more is involved, as is evident in the following document.

The cry of "women's liberation" leaps out from the "lifestyle" sections of newspapers and the pages of slick magazines, from radio speakers and television screens. Cut loose from past patterns of behavior and expectations, women of all ages are searching for their identity—the college woman who has new alternatives thrust upon her via "women's studies" courses, the young woman whose routine is shattered by a chance encounter with a "consciousness-raising session," the woman in her middle years who suddenly finds herself in the "empty-nest syndrome," the woman of any age whose lover or lifetime partner departs for greener pastures (and a younger crop).

All of these women, thanks to the women's liberation movement, no longer see their predicament in terms of personal problems to be confronted and solved. They see their own difficulties as a little cog in the big machine of establishment restraints and stereotypical injustice in which they have lost their own equilibrium. Who am I? Why am I here? Why am I just another faceless victim of society's oppression, a nameless prisoner behind walls too high for me to climb alone? . . .

For a woman to find her identity in the modern world, the path should be sought from the Positive Women who have found the road and possess the map, rather than from those who have not. In this spirit, I share with you the thoughts of one who loves life as a woman and lives love as a woman, whose credentials are from the school of practical experience, and who has learned that fulfillment as a woman is a journey, not a destination.

Like every human being born into this world, the Positive Woman has her share of sorrows and sufferings, of unfulfilled desires and bitter defeats. But she will never be crushed by life's disappointments, because her positive mental attitude has built her an inner security that the actions of other people can never fracture. To the Positive Woman, her

particular set of problems is not a conspiracy against her, but a challenge to her character and her capabilities.

The first requirement for the acquisition of power by the Positive Woman is to understand the differences between men and women. Your outlook on life, your faith, your behavior, your potential for fulfillment, all are determined by the parameters of your original premise. The Positive Woman starts with the assumption that the world is her oyster. She rejoices in the creative capability within her body and the power potential of her mind and spirit. She understands that men and women are different, and that those very differences provide the key to her success as a person and fulfillment as a woman.

The women's liberationist, on the other hand, is imprisoned by her own negative view of herself and of her place in the world around her. . . . Someone—it is not clear who, perhaps God, perhaps the "Establishment," perhaps a conspiracy of male chauvinist pigs—dealt women a foul blow by making them female. It becomes necessary, therefore, for women to agitate and demonstrate and hurl demands on society in order to wrest from an oppressive male-dominated social structure the status that has been wrongfully denied to women through the centuries. . . . Confrontation replaces cooperation as the watchword of all relationships. Women and men become adversaries instead of partners. . . . Within the confines of the women's liberationist ideology, therefore, the abolition of this overriding inequality of women becomes the primary goal.

This goal must be achieved at any and all costs—to the woman herself, to the baby, to the family, and to society. Women must be made equal to men in their ability *not* to become pregnant and *not* to be expected to care for babies they may bring into the world. This is why women's liberationists are compulsively involved in the drive to make abortion and

Phyllis Schlafly demonstrated the domestic ideal by posing cooking her husband's breakfast the morning after her victory in the 1952 Republican congressional primary. She would lose her bid for a congressional seat but continue to be active as a party volunteer. In 1964, she was a strong supporter of Republican presidential candidate Barry Goldwater, and the author of one of the most effective pieces of his campaign literature, A Choice Not an Echo. *The first printing sold more than 600,000 copies and made her national reputation; there were two more printings before Election Day. In 1967, she lost her bid for the presidency of the National Federation of Republican Women (NFRW). In the early 1970s, the NFRW endorsed the ERA. Independently, Schlafly mobilized women behind conservative issues like free enterprise and support for nuclear weapons development. When she began to publicize her opposition to the ERA, the circulation of* The Phyllis Schlafly Report *bounced quickly from 3,000 to 35,000 and continued to grow. Her organization, the Eagle Forum, took the lead in developing opposition to the ERA and to feminism generally. (St. Louis Globe-Democrat photo. Courtesy of the Collections of the St. Louis Mercantile Library at the University of Missouri–St. Louis. Caption courtesy of Catherine Rymph.)*

child-care centers for all women, regardless of religion or income, both socially acceptable and government-financed. . . .

If man is targeted as the enemy, and the ultimate goal of women's liberation is independence from men and the avoidance of pregnancy and its consequences, then lesbianism is logically the highest form in the ritual of women's liberation. . . .

The Positive Woman will never travel that dead-end road. It is self-evident to the Positive Woman that the female body with its baby-producing organs was not designed by a conspiracy of men but by the Divine Architect of the human race. Those who think it is unfair that women have babies, whereas men cannot, will have to take up their complaint with God because no other power is capable of changing that fundamental fact. . . . The Positive Woman looks upon her femaleness and her fertility as part of her purpose, her potential, and her power. She rejoices that she has a capability for creativity that men can never have.

The third basic dogma of the women's liberation movement is that there is no difference between male and female except the sex organs, and that all those physical, cognitive, and emotional differences you *think* are there, are merely the result of centuries of restraints imposed by a male-dominated society and sex-stereotyped schooling. The role imposed on women is, by definition, inferior, according to the women's liberationists. . . .

There are countless physical differences between men and women. The female body is 50 to 60 percent water, the male 60 to 70 percent water, which explains why males can dilute alcohol better than women and delay its effect. The average woman is about 25 percent fatty tissue, while the male is 15 percent, making women more buoyant in water and able to swim with less effort. Males have a tendency to color blindness. Only 5 percent of persons who get gout are female. Boys are born bigger. Women live longer in most countries of the world, not only in the United States where we have a hard-driving competitive pace. Women excel in manual dexterity, verbal skills, and memory recall. . . .

Does the physical advantage of men doom women to a life of servility and subservience? The Positive Woman knows that she has a complementary advantage which is at least as great—and, in the hands of a skillful woman, far greater. The Divine Architect who gave men a superior strength to lift weights also gave women a different kind of superior strength. . . . A Positive Woman cannot defeat a man in a wrestling or boxing match, but she can motivate him, inspire him, encourage him, teach him, restrain him, reward him, and have power over him that he can never achieve over her with all his muscle. How or whether a Positive Woman uses her power is determined solely by the way she alone defines her goals and develops her skills.

The differences between men and women are also emotional and psychological. Without woman's innate maternal instinct, the human race would have died out centuries ago. . . . The overriding psychological need of a woman is to love something alive. A baby fulfills this need in the lives of most women. If a baby is not available to fill that need, women search for a baby-substitute. This is the reason why women have traditionally gone into teaching and nursing careers. They are doing what comes naturally to the female psyche. The schoolchild or the patient of any age provides an outlet for a woman to express her natural maternal need. . . . The Positive Woman finds somebody on whom she can lavish her maternal love so that it doesn't well up inside her and cause psychological frustrations. Surely no woman is so isolated by geography or insulated by spirit that she cannot find someone worthy of her maternal love. . . .

One of the strangest quirks of women's liberationists is their complaint that societal restraints prevent men from crying in public or showing their emotions, but permit women to do so, and that therefore we should "liberate" men to enable them, too, to cry in public. The public display of fear, sorrow, anger, and irritation reveals a lack of self-discipline that should be avoided by the Positive Woman just as much as by the Positive Man. Maternal love, however, is not a weakness but a manifestation of strength and service, and it should be nurtured by the Positive Woman. . . .

Another silliness of the women's liberationists is their frenetic desire to force all women to accept the title *Ms* in place of *Miss* or *Mrs*. If Gloria Steinem and Betty Friedan want to call themselves *Ms* in order to conceal their marital status, their wishes should be respected. But most married women feel they worked hard for the *r* in their names; and they don't care to be gratuitously deprived of it. . . .

Finally, women are different from men in dealing with the fundamentals of life itself. Men are philosophers, women are practical, and 'twas ever thus. Men may philosophize about how life began and where we are heading; women are concerned about feeding the kids today. No woman would ever, as Karl Marx did, spend years reading political philosophy in the British Museum while her child starved to death. Women don't take naturally to a search for the intangible and the abstract. . . . Where man is discursive, logical, abstract, or philosophical, woman tends to be emotional, personal, practical, or mystical. Each set of qualities is vital and complements the other. Among the many differences explained in [Amaury] de Riencourt's book, [*Sex and Power in History*], are the following:

> Women tend more toward conformity than men—which is why they often excel in such disciplines as spelling and punctuation where there

is only one correct answer, determined by social authority. Higher intellectual activities, however, require a mental independence and power of abstraction that they usually lack, not to mention a certain form of aggressive boldness of the imagination which can only exist in a sex that is basically aggressive for biological reasons.

To sum up: The masculine proclivity in problem solving is analytical and categorical; the feminine, synthetic and contextual. . . . Deep down, man tends to focus on the object, on external results and achievements; woman focuses on subjective motives and feelings. If life can be compared to a play, man focuses on the theme and structure of the play, woman on the innermost feelings displayed by the actors.

De Riencourt provides impressive refutation of two of the basic errors of the women's liberation movement: (1) that there are no emotional or cognitive differences between the sexes, and (2) that women should strive to be like men. . . . An effort to eliminate the differences by social engineering or legislative or constitutional tinkering cannot succeed, which is fortunate, but social relationships and spiritual values can be ruptured in the attempt. . . .

RETHINKING FAMILY AND SEX

JOANNE MEYEROWITZ
Christine Jorgensen and the Story of How Sex Changed

In 1952, Christine Jorgensen made the front-page of newspapers around the world. Jorgensen, an Army veteran, underwent medical procedures to transform from being a man to a woman. Examining the publicity about Jorgensen, and tracing the media attention to transsexuals back to the 1930s, Joanne Meyerowitz argues that a modern transsexual identity was created partly through the media. Some readers identified with and sought the advice of those who had sex changes. Before the mid-twentieth century, these surgical procedures had taken place only in Europe.

Why did Jorgensen become a celebrity in the 1950s? How does her treatment in the media mirror and differ from other press interest in transsexuals? How does transsexuality raise questions about what it means to be a woman? What characteristics makes one a woman? What does it mean to identify as a woman?

On December 1, 1952, the *New York Daily News* announced the "sex change" surgery of Christine Jorgensen. The front-page headline read: "Ex-GI Becomes Blonde Beauty: Operations Transform Bronx Youth," and the story told how Jorgensen had traveled to Denmark for "a rare and complicated treatment." For years, Jorgensen, born and reared as a boy, had struggled with what she later described as an ineffable, inexorable, and increasingly unbearable yearning to live her life as a woman. In 1950 she sailed to Europe in search of a doctor who would alter her bodily sex. Within months she found an endocrinologist who agreed to administer hormones if she would in return cooperate with his research. Over the next two years she took massive doses of estrogen and underwent two major surgeries to transform her genitals. At the end of 1952 the *New York Daily News* transformed her obscure personal triumph into mass media sensation.

The initial scoop immediately escalated to a frenzy. In the first two weeks of coverage, according to *Newsweek*, the three major wire services sent out 50,000 words on the Christine Jorgensen story. Reporters cast Jorgensen, who was young and conventionally beautiful, as the personification of glamour, akin to a Hollywood starlet on the rise. They followed her every move in Copenhagen and hounded her parents at their home in the Bronx. In the winter of 1953 Jorgensen returned to the United States and surrendered to her celebrity. In the summer she launched a successful nightclub act that kept her name on marquees and her body in spotlights for the rest of the decade.[1]

Jorgensen was more than a media sensation, a stage act, or a cult figure. Her story opened debate on the visibility and mutability of sex. It raised questions that resonated with force in the 1950s and engage us still today. How do we determine who is male and who is female,

Excerpted and slightly revised by the author from *How Sex Changed: A History of Transsexuality in the United States* by Joanne Meyerowitz (Cambridge, Mass.: Harvard University Press, 2002), 1–5, 95–97, 286; and "Sex Change and the Popular Press: Historical Notes on Transsexuality in the United States, 1930–1955," by Joanne Meyerowitz, in *GLQ: A Journal of Lesbian and Gay Studies* 4, no. 2 (1998): 159–187. Reprinted by permission of the author and publishers. Notes have been edited and renumbered.

HERE IS A CLOSEUP of blue-eyed, blonde Christine as she meets the barrage of questions hurled at her by reporters on her flying arrival from Denmark, via Scandinavian Airlines.

Christine Jorgensen is met by the press on the day she returns to New York, after surgery in Denmark. New York Daily Mirror, *Feb. 13, 1953. (Image courtesy of the Kinsey Institute for Research in Sex, Gender, and Reproduction.)*

and why do we care? Can humans actually change sex? Is sex less apparent than it seems? As a narrative of boundary transgression, the Jorgensen story fascinated readers and elicited their surprise, and as an unusual variant on a familiar tale of striving and success, it inspired them. It opened possibilities for those who questioned their own sex and offered an exoticized travelogue for armchair tourists who had never imagined that one could take a journey across the sex divide. In the post–World War II era, with heightened concerns about science and sex, the Jorgensen story compelled some readers to spell out their own versions of the boundaries of sex, and it convinced others to reconsider the categories they thought they already knew. In response, American doctors and scientists began to explore the process of defining sex.

In the mid-twentieth century, sex was already high on the American cultural agenda. For decades Americans of all sorts had found themselves inundated with news, research, stories, opinions, and imperatives about the multiple meanings of "sex." The study of sex hormones and sex chromosomes had removed the biology of sex from the visible realm of genitals to the microscopic gaze, and the uncertainty of it all eventually set the International Olympic Committee, among others, on an elusive quest to decide who counts as a woman and who counts as a man. The growing numbers of women in the labor force and the early twentieth-century women's movement had put issues of sex equality and sex difference at the forefront of political life, and the emergence of gay and lesbian subcultures had created visible spots of sexual variation within the urban landscape. Meanwhile the mass media had made sex a mainstay of the visual culture, and popular versions of Freud and other sexologists had given sex a recognized role in the modern discourse of psychology. The new ideal of "consenting adults" had positioned sex as a key component of liberal freedom, while older ideals still made moving targets of anyone who strayed from expectations that sex belonged in marriage. In broad outline and narrow, American society had "sexualized" in the first half of the century.[2]

And the vocabulary of sex had begun to change. At the dawn of the century the word *sex* covered a range of phenomena. In popular and scientific formulations, sex signified not only female and male but also traits, attitudes, and behaviors associated with women and men and with erotic acts. In various attempts to delineate the components of sex, some observers tried to sort the sex "characteristics." They separated "primary sexual features," found in the genitals and gonads, from "secondary" features, seen in breasts, beards, and other physical differences that usually appeared after puberty, from "tertiary" features, as evidenced in erotic drives, from "fourth-order" features, manifest in traits, mannerisms, and even occupations and clothes. Or they distinguished "anatomical" sex, the sex of the body, from "functional" sex, the ways men and women thought and behaved.[3] Despite a few dissenters, most observers adhered to a biological determinism. The desires and practices known as masculine and feminine seemed to spring from the same biological processes that divided female and male. All came bundled together within the broad-ranging concept of "sex."

By midcentury this concept had begun to break down. Various experts used different terms to distinguish one meaning of sex from another. Anthropologist Margaret Mead chose *sex roles* to describe the culturally constructed behaviors expected of women and men. Sex researcher Alfred C. Kinsey adopted the term *sexual behavior* to outline a range of erotic practices. And the "sex" of the body no longer provided adequate explanation of either "sex roles" or "sexual behavior." By the end of the century the earlier understanding of sex had given way to three categories of inquiry and analysis: "biological sex" referred to chromosomes, genes, genitals, hormones, and other physical markers, some of which could be modified and some of which could not; "gender" represented masculinity, femininity, and the behaviors commonly associated with them; and "sexuality" connoted the erotic, now sorted into a range of urges, fantasies, and behaviors. Once seen as outgrowths of a primary sex division, "gender" and "sexuality" no longer seemed to spring directly from the biological categories of female and male. In fact some scholars envisioned sex, gender, and

sexuality as constructed categories constantly defined and redefined in social, cultural, and intellectual processes and performances.[4] They thus directly rejected the older belief in a universal, unchanging biological sex that dictated both the behavior of women and men and their sexual desires.

Jorgensen's story and the history of transsexuality are central parts of this reconceptualization of sex in the twentieth century. The notion that biological sex is mutable, that we define and redefine it, that we can divide it into constituent parts, such as chromosomes, hormones, and genitals, and modify some of those parts, that male and female are not opposites, that masculinity and femininity do not spring automatically from biological sex, that neither biological sex nor gender determines the contours of sexual desire—these were significant shifts in American social and scientific thought. . . . [These shifts] occurred piecemeal through vociferous conflict and debate, and because not everyone accepted them, they laid the groundwork for ongoing contests over the meanings of biological sex, the sources of gender, and the categories of sexuality. . . .

Jorgensen was not the first transsexual, nor was the publicity accorded her the first media coverage of sex-change surgery. Cross-gender identification, the sense of being the other sex, and the desire to live as the other sex all existed in various forms in earlier centuries and other cultures. The historical record includes countless examples of males who dressed or lived as women and females who dressed or lived as men.[5] Transsexuality, the quest to transform the bodily characteristics of sex via hormones and surgery, originated in the early twentieth century. By the 1910s European scientists had begun to publicize their attempts to transform the sex of animals, and by the 1920s a few doctors, mostly in Germany, had agreed to alter the bodies of a few patients who longed to change their sex.

In Europe, the medical practice of sex change arose less as a result of new technology than as a result of new understandings of sex. . . . [T]he scientists and doctors who endorsed sex-change surgery posited a universal mixed-sex condition, in which all males had female features and all females male features. This theory of universal bisexuality directly challenged a[n earlier] . . . vision of binary sex that saw female and male as distinct, immutable, and opposite. With this novel conception of sex, a few doctors began to use hormones and surgery to enable a few people who pleaded for bodily change to move toward the female or male ends of a perceived continuum.

In the United States the public discourse on transsexuals came first through popular culture, then through science and medicine, and eventually through the courts. It also came from the people who hoped to change their sex. They were a diverse group with a wide array of political views. They were [neither] "dupes of gender," who tampered with their bodies in the name of gender ideology, [n]or conscious radicals, who purposefully [wished to] ... destabilize traditional norms.[6] Many ... expressed the desire to live as men or women, and not as something other or in between ... Like everyone else, they articulated their sense of self with the language and cultural forms available to them. They were neither symbols ... nor heroes or villains engaged in mythic battles to further or stifle progress. They were instead ordinary and extraordinary human beings who searched for workable solutions to pressing personal problems. In so doing they investigated, debated, promoted, and accelerated new definitions of sex, gender, and sexuality.[7]

B.C. (BEFORE CHRISTINE)

... Surgical attempts at changing sex first won publicity in the early 1910s when Eugen Steinach, a physiologist in Vienna, attracted international acclaim for his "transplantation" experiments on rats and guinea pigs. In 1912, Steinach published "Arbitrary Transformation of Male Mammals into Animals with Pronounced Female Sex Characteristics and Feminine Psyche," followed in 1913 by "Feminization of Males and Masculization of Females." The articles, soon scientific classics, demonstrated that castrated infant male guinea pigs implanted with ovaries developed certain characteristics associated with females and that castrated infant female guinea pigs implanted with testes developed characteristics of males. Steinach claimed to have found the specific impacts of "male" and "female" hormones, thus placing his research in the larger turn-of-the-century scientific project that attempted to locate a biological sexual essence in gonadal secretions. His research also suggested the possibility of medically transforming sex. As he put it, "The implantation of the gonad of the opposite sex transforms the original sex of an animal." His work directly influenced Magnus Hirschfeld, Harry Benjamin, and other sexological scientists.[8]

... A few records of surgery for humans [exist in this period for the United States. They involved] removal of body parts such as testicles, uteri, and breasts, [thus] a form of intervention that did not require advanced medical technology. Alberta Lucille Hart, a [young] physician in Oregon, pursued surgery as a means of changing sex. As a child, Hart, reared as a girl, considered himself a boy, and as an adult he wore masculine collars, ties, hats, and shoes along with the requisite skirts. In 1917, at the age of twenty-six, Hart persuaded psychiatrist J. Allen Gilbert to recommend hysterectomy. The surgery required medical justification, in this case the relief of painful menstruation. In the quest for surgery, Hart also employed a form of eugenic reasoning, advising "sterilization" for "any individual" with "abnormal inversion." ... After surgery, haircut, and change of attire, Hart "started as a male with a new hold on life," and as Alan Lucill Hart he had successful careers as a radiologist and a novelist.[9]

Although we have isolated examples of early surgery in the United States, the quest for sex change seems to have been more widely acknowledged in Europe. ... By the 1920s, Germany stood at the forefront of the human sex change experiments, with Magnus Hirschfeld's Institute for Sexual Science in Berlin at center stage. Hirschfeld encountered female-to-male "transvestites" who requested mastectomy and preparations for beard growth and males-to-females who sought castration, elimination of facial hair, and "apparatus for making the breasts bigger." For Hirschfeld, hermaphrodites, androgynes, homosexuals, and transvestites constituted distinct types of sexual "intermediates," natural variations that all likely had inborn, organic bases. He considered transvestism "a harmless inclination" and advocated the social acceptance of transvestites. He listened seriously to the desire to change sex expressed by some of the subjects he studied, and he began to recommend surgery. In 1931, German physician Felix Abraham, who worked at the Institute, published the first scientific report on modern transsexual surgery, an article on the male-to-female genital transformation (*Genitalumwandlung*) of two "homosexual transvestites." The illustrated account of surgery included castration, amputation of the penis, and creation of an artificial vagina. Abraham believed that countless other patients wanted similar operations.[10]

Word of the sex change experiments in Germany reached a wider public in the early

1930s when the press reported on Danish artist Einar Wegener, who became Lili Elbe. The operations began with castration in Berlin, following psychological tests conducted by Hirschfeld at the Institute for Sexual Science. Later, in Dresden, doctors removed the penis and allegedly also transplanted human ovaries. Elbe died from heart failure in 1931 after a final operation, an attempt to create a "natural outlet from the womb." Before her death, the story broke in Danish and German newspapers and soon thereafter appeared in book form in both Danish and German.[11] . . .

At least one American, Florence Winter (a pseudonym), born around 1900, investigated the medical possibilities for female-to-male sex change in Europe. She went to Germany, probably in the 1920s, "to find solutions to her problems of homosexuality and transvestism." In Chicago, she had felt "isolated from her kind," but in Berlin she found others like her through association with Hirschfeld's Institute. She underwent "years of analysis before she could overthrow her guilt feelings about herself." Hirschfeld himself agreed to arrange her sex change surgery. "However, when he warned her that after the operations she would not be either a man or a woman, she backed out." Perhaps Hirschfeld meant that Winter would not have reproductive capacities, or perhaps be referred to the crude technology of phalloplasty that could not create a functioning penis. In any case, after living for "a long time" as a man, Winter left Europe at the outbreak of World War II and returned to Chicago, where she lived again as a lesbian.[12]

While few Americans, it seems, traveled to Europe for sex changes, more began to learn through the mass media of new possibilities for medical intervention. . . . In 1933, Dutton published the first English translation of the Lili Elbe story, *Man into Woman: An Authentic Record of a Change of Sex.* The book presented its subject as an occasional cross-dresser whose female personality had come to predominate. More dubiously, it also depicted her as a hermaphrodite with "stunted and withered ovaries" as well as testicles. The book included an introduction by British sexologist Norman Haire, who informed readers of Steinach's transplantation experiments on animals but considered it "unwise to carry out, even at the patient's own request, such operations" as those performed on Elbe.[13] . . .

These and other stories of sex changes attempted to lure American readers with shocking accounts of unusual behavior, rare biological problems, and astonishing surgical solutions. Such stories often appeared on the margins of the mainstream press, in sensational magazines, tabloid newspapers, or publications like *Sexology* that presented the science of sex to a popular audience. They covered cases of cross-gender behavior, intersexuality, homosexuality, and transvestism, sometimes without distinguishing among them, and frequently depicted them all as interrelated pathologies in need of medical cure. They occasionally mentioned "sex reversals" of the "purely psychical" kind but presented them as homosexuality that did not qualify for surgery. Sometimes they reported metamorphoses wherein a woman or man, perhaps with a glandular disturbance, underwent spontaneous changes in bodily sex and gendered behavior during late adolescence or adulthood. (A typical headline read, "Boy Prisoner Slowly Changing into a Girl.") More generally, though, the articles mentioned surgery but failed to specify what it entailed. They depicted sex change surgery as unveiling a true but hidden physiological sex and thus tied the change to a biological mooring that justified surgical intervention. These stories often reinforced stereotypes of gender and sexuality by locating the sources of gendered and erotic behavior in the sex of the physical body. In this binarist vision of sex, science could and should correct nature's tragic "rare blunders," creating an unambiguous male or female sex from a condition of ambiguity.[14]

In the second half of the 1930s, these features appeared in widely reported accounts of European women athletes who became men. In 1935, twenty-three-year-old Belgian cycling champion Elvira de Bruyne changed sex and began to live as Willy. About a year later, British shot-put and javelin champion Mary Edith Louise Weston underwent two operations and adopted the name Mark, and Czechoslovakian runner Zdenka Koubkova became Zdenek Koubkov through what one report termed "a delicate surgical operation." Because he came to New York in 1936, the American press covered Koubkov's case extensively. Considered female at his birth in 1913, Koubkov grew up as "an utterly masculine youth" who resisted feminine clothes and domestic training. As he aged, "the feeling of masculinity began to assert itself," and he longed for women sexually, "his imagination inflamed by reading French novels." He competed as a woman in the 1932 Olympics, setting a world record in the 800-meter event, but in his early twenties "a great light dawned," and he realized he was a man. Four months after a procedure described only as a "flick of a surgeon's scalpel," Koubkov came to New York to perform in a *tableau vivant* in the French Casino, a Broadway club. He ran on a treadmill, chasing a woman, foreshadowing Christine Jorgensen's later staged performances of gender.[15] In part, the press attention reflected discomfort with women athletes and confirmed popular opinions that athletic women were, if not actually men, at least suspiciously mannish. But the stories also provided further publicity for the possibility of changing sex.[16] . . .

[Some physicians] tried to dissuade readers [from imagining that] "we are on the threshold of new discoveries which will enable any individual to be changed to the sex he or she prefers."[17] . . . Despite the warning, . . . the publicity accorded to sex change surgery caught the attention of individuals who identified possibilities in it for themselves. *Sexology* published several letters from readers in search of information. In 1934, one letter writer explained: "I have a peculiar complex—I believe it is called 'Eonism.' That is, I desire to dress as a woman. . . . The fact is I have an even stronger desire, and that is—I wish I were a woman. . . . I am interested in the Steinach operation in regard to change of sex. I would like more information." In 1937, a "Miss E. T." from Nebraska asked: "Is it possible through a surgical operation, or several operations, to change a female into a male? I have read something—not very informative—about such things having been done. . . . Could you give me any idea of the method, and also of the cost?" In "They Want to Change Sexes" (1937), *Sexology* acknowledged that press reports on European athletes had "stirred" some of its readers, who now asked "whether it is possible, and if so, how and where." The magazine summarized a handful of letters (both male-to-female and female-to-male). The fragmentary presentation of the letters makes it impossible to know to what extent readers used the popular narratives to plot stories about themselves, but one letter suggests some readers might have fitted the stories of intersexuality to their own wants. A woman who described herself as "nothing feminine" but "apparently of [the female] sex" asked: "If it were true that I have both male and female organs of reproduction, would it not be advisable to undergo what operations are necessary to become the male I wish to be? Can you refer me to a competent surgeon who would be interested in my case?"[18]

The magazine did not offer the information that letter writers sought and tried instead to discourage them. In response to one male-to-female inquiry, the editor acknowledged that the letter writer could have "the operation of complete castration" and thereafter live as a woman but warned that surgery would create a "completely sexless creature." The editor stated bluntly to a female-to-male correspondent, "There is no operation whereby a *normal female* can be changed to a normal male, or a normal male into normal female. The operations you have read of were performed on 'hermaphrodites.'" Through the 1940s, *Sexology* continued to advise such readers, whom it sometimes called "inverts" or "homosexuals," that doctors performed such surgery for cases of intersexuality only. Nevertheless, it continued to run stories about men who became women and women who became men, and letter writers continued to ask for sex change operations.[19]

Dr. David O. Cauldwell, *Sexology*'s question-and-answer department editor, coined the English-language term transsexual. In a 1949 article, he chose the phrase "psychopathia transexualis" . . . to describe the case of "Earl," who asked Cauldwell "to find a surgeon" who would remove breasts and ovaries, "close the vagina," and construct "an artificial penis." Cauldwell acknowledged that a surgeon could perform such operations, but he refused to endorse them, stating that the artificial penis would have "no material use" and "no more sexual feeling than a fingernail." Furthermore, he considered it "criminal" for a doctor to remove healthy glands and tissues.[20]

What distinguished this article from earlier ones was the definition of "psychopathia transexualis" as an independent sexological category. Cauldwell dissociated this request for surgery from cases of intersexuality and glandular disorder. To Cauldwell, a psychiatrist, transsexuals were "products, largely of unfavorable childhood environment." And although Earl was sexually drawn to women, the article also distinguished transsexuals from homosexuals. The caption to an accompanying surreal illustration (of a double-headed man/woman binding his/her breasts) read, "Many individuals have an irresistible desire to have their sex changed surgically. . . . These persons are not necessarily homosexuals." Cauldwell elaborated in a 1950 pamphlet, *Questions and Answers on the Sex Life and Sexual Problems of Trans-Sexuals*. The pamphlet's subheading summarized the key points: "Trans-sexuals are individuals who

Sept.   *1937*

SEXOLOGY

THE MAGAZINE OF
SEX SCIENCE
ILLUSTRATED

CONTENTS

TRUTHFUL AND EDUCATIONAL

5      $3.
                                                      A YEAR

KNOWLEDGE OF SELF
THE DOORWAY TO

As Joanne Meyerowitz explains, "from the 1930s on, the popular magazine Sexology *carried articles on sex changes, including the article 'They Want to Change Sexes' in this September 1937 issue." (Image Courtesy of the Kinsey Institute for Research in Sex, Gender, and Reproduction.)*

are physically of one sex and apparently psychologically of the opposite sex. Trans-sexuals include heterosexuals, homosexuals, bisexuals and others. A large element of transvestites have trans-sexual leanings."[21] In this way, Cauldwell separated gender, described as psychological sex, from biological sex and sexuality. Cross-gender identification and the request for surgery were not necessarily linked either to intersexed conditions or to same-sex desire.

In constructing his definition, Cauldwell relied on the letters of those he now called "trans-sexuals." He had a voluminous correspondence—in part as a *Sexology* editor but even more as the author of numerous pamphlets on sex published in the popular Blue Book series of Haldeman-Julius Publications, a counter-cultural "freethinking" press.[22] In the pamphlet on transsexuals, Cauldwell quoted extensively from letters he had received. Some letter writers already expressed a sense of the surgical possibilities, and sometimes they explained their knowledge with direct reference to what they had read in magazines, newspapers, and sexological writings. A thirty-three-year-old male-to-female cross-dresser who had lived as a woman for fourteen years wrote: "Everything leads to the fact that I have developed a burning desire to be made into a woman. I've read of a number of such instances. The reports were in the daily press and must have been true." Cauldwell expressed annoyance with the persistent requests for surgery. He blamed medicine for creating "fantastic hopes" and popular magazines for publishing "tales of magic cures and magical accomplishments of surgeons."[23]

Indeed, by midcentury, some popular American magazines, especially of the sensational bent, no longer insisted that sex change surgery was for intersexed conditions only. One article stated: "With hormones plus surgery, there's little doubt that, in the not far future . . . doctors can take a full grown normal adult and—if he or she desires it—completely reverse his or her sex." Another granted: "The fact that sex is mutable has been illustrated in definite instances of men who have been physiologically turned to women and women to men."[24] Doctors could, as the magazines claimed, alter the bodily sex characteristics of nonintersexed patients, but in the United States they still generally refused to do so. While the popular literature increasingly broached the possibility of surgically altering sex, even a sympathetic doctor could not arrange the operations.

Endocrinologist Harry Benjamin—born, reared, and trained in Germany—came to the United States in 1913 and established himself as an expert on aging and prostitution. . . . Benjamin saw himself as "a maverick or an outsider," an advocate for sexual freedom who did not have the same hesitancy to intervene on behalf of transgendered patients that American-born doctors often exhibited. As an endocrinologist, he placed greater faith in hormone treatments and glandular surgery than in attempts at psychotherapeutic cures. A friend and follower of both Steinach and Hirschfeld, he assumed that cross-gender identification had some physiological cause and saw transsexuals as desperate patients in need of his medical help.[25]

In 1949 Benjamin met a patient, referred [to him] by Kinsey, who was desperate to change sex. Val Barry (a pseudonym), who already lived as a woman, had spent most of her childhood as a girl. In 1948, at the age of twenty-two, she entered a hospital in her home state of Wisconsin for psychiatric examination. Like many other transgendered individuals, she had read a variety of works on sex and sexology, including *Man into Woman*, and she now expressed the "desire to be changed surgically." She "refused to consider any other alternative," including any "brain surgery" that might eliminate her "desire to remain a female mentally." More than thirty hospital staff members met to discuss her case and recommended castration and plastic surgery, but the state attorney general's office "ruled against the operations as constituting mayhem," a strange interpretation of statutes descended from British common law forbidding the maiming of potential soldiers.[26]

In May 1949, Barry wrote to Benjamin for help. After reading her medical history, Benjamin promised to write to Germany to find out what the law stipulated there. In the meantime, he advised female hormones and also raised the possibility of "x-ray castration" as well as "x-ray treatment of your face to remove the hair growth." In the summer of 1949, at his office in San Francisco, he began to administer hormones to Barry and to search for surgeons in the United States. He contacted district attorney (later governor) Edmund G. Brown about the legality of castration in California. Initially, Brown did not envision any legal obstacles to sex-change surgery, but after consulting another lawyer he sent Benjamin a discouraging memorandum. . . . Soon after, psychiatrists at the Langley Porter Clinic in San Francisco refused to endorse the surgery, and a surgeon in Chicago, initially sympathetic, also failed to help.[27] It was not until 1953, after the publicity about Jorgensen, that Barry finally had her surgery in Sweden.

A.D. (AFTER DENMARK)

In 1952 and 1953, the coverage of Christine Jorgensen far exceeded any previous reporting on sex changes. Jorgensen rose to the rank of celebrity in the mainstream press as well as in tabloid, pulp, and countercultural publications. Aside from their more extensive dissemination, though, the initial stories on Jorgensen generally replicated the key features found in earlier accounts of sex change. They announced a startling bodily change, referred to surgery but usually failed to specify what it encompassed, and attempted to tie the change of sex to an intersexed condition. Reporters consulted American doctors, most of whom assumed that Jorgensen was a pseudohermaphrodite with internal female gonads but external male characteristics. For one Associated Press story, "Thousands Do Not Know True Sex," a reporter went to the American Medical Association convention and interviewed doctors, who immediately associated sex change surgery with such intersexed conditions. In other reports, journalists found doctors who reported cases of pseudohermaphroditism that they considered similar to Jorgensen's. Urologist Elmer Hess of Erie, Pennsylvania, told of "Hundreds of Boy-Girl Operations." Another doctor claimed to have "performed five operations similar to" Jorgensen's, cases in which "the actual sex had been disguised and was simply released." *Time* magazine soon assessed these reports as the "expert opinion" of doctors who "pooh-poohed the story as anything new . . . far from a medical rarity . . . [with] similar cases in hospitals all over the U.S. right now."[28]

Nonetheless, there was from the beginning a hint that the Jorgensen story might be different. In the first week of publicity, G. B. Lal, the science editor of *American Weekly* (a nationally distributed Sunday newspaper supplement), suggested that Jorgensen "was physically speaking, adequately a male, yet somehow felt the urge to be a woman." Such a situation "would call for drastic alterations—such as no doctor would perform in this country." Lal then referred to Harry Benjamin and cases of "transvestism" but immediately retreated to a discussion of intersexed conditions. "We may assume," Lal wrote, "still without knowing the facts, that Jorgensen was a case of sex confusion—what is known as pseudo-hermaphroditism, in which one's inborn real sex is hidden." As in earlier cases, the muddled reporting attracted transgendered readers who wondered about the journalists' claims. In early December, shortly after the story broke, Louise Lawrence, a full-time male-to-female cross-dresser in San Francisco, wrote to Benjamin: "This case, I think, has received more publicity even than Barbara [Richards Wilcox]'s ten years ago." She could not, though, "make any concrete decision regarding it because there have actually been no absolute facts given." Still, she wondered why Jorgensen would have traveled to Denmark for "a case of hermaphroditism" that "could be handled in this country very easily. . . . From the papers, it seems that such cases are being handled all over the country."[29]

As the publicity continued, the press began to publish new details that gradually undermined the initial reports. In mid-February, *American Weekly* orchestrated Jorgensen's return to New York to coincide with the publication of its exclusive five-part series, Jorgensen's "The Story of My Life," "the only authorized and complete account of the most dramatic transformation of modern times." The series adopted a first-person confessional formula that personalized the coverage and invited readers to sympathize with Jorgensen's ordeal. As *American Weekly* later reported, it saw the story "not as a sensationalized bit of erotica, but as the courageous fight of a desperately unhappy person with the fortitude to overcome a seemingly hopeless obstacle." With the help of a veteran reporter, Jorgensen emphasized the "feminine qualities" she had manifested as the lonely boy George, including a teenage romantic attraction to a male friend. To explain her problem, Jorgensen did not adopt the metaphor, common by the 1960s, of a woman "trapped" in a male body.[30] Instead, she referred to herself as "lost between sexes," a phrase that implied a physical condition as much as a psychological one. As in earlier stories of sex change, she presented her problem as a biological disturbance, in this case a "glandular imbalance," and as a spiritual longing to become "the woman [she] felt sure Nature had intended." But Jorgensen veered away from earlier accounts when she described her doctors, her diagnosis, and what her treatment entailed. In Denmark, endocrinologist

Christian Hamburger (a student of Steinach) had agreed to treat her free of charge. Hamburger had reassured her that she was not, as she feared, a homosexual but rather had a "condition called transvestism" and might (but did not necessarily) have female "body chemistry" and female "body cells." Over the course of two years, she had undergone hormone treatments, psychiatric examination, "removal of sex glands," and plastic surgery."[31]

Before and after the series, entrepreneurial journalists realized that Jorgensen attracted readers. She caught the public imagination in part because her story embodied tensions central to the postwar culture. In the atomic age, Jorgensen's surgery posed the question of whether science had indeed triumphed over nature. In an era of overt cultural contests over changing gender roles, the press stories on Jorgensen enabled a public reinscription of what counted as masculine and what counted as feminine. At the same time, though, they also incited the fantasy of boundary transgression, with convincing evidence of how a person might present a masculine persona on one day and a feminine one on another. As homosexuality became increasingly visible and as homophobic reaction intensified, Jorgensen brought the issue into the mainstream news with the confession of her preoperative longing for a male friend. But she also confounded the category as she distinguished a depathologized version of cross-gender identification (in which she loved a man because she understood herself as a heterosexual woman) from a still-pathologized version of same-sex desire. And all along, she demonstrated an affinity for the media that kept her in the public eye. She reinforced her popularity by adopting a feminine style that played on the postwar cult of "blond bombshell" glamor. At least one author has speculated that Jorgensen, despite her expressed surprise, leaked her own story to the press. Whether she did or not, she eventually courted the attention to boost her career on the stage.[32]

The unremitting interest allowed a public hashing out of what Jorgensen represented, especially after the *American Weekly* series provided a more detailed account. Journalists soon began to question Jorgensen's status as "100 per cent woman." By mid-March, they asserted that Jorgensen was "neither hermaphroditic nor pseudo-hermaphroditic": she had "no vestiges of female organs or female reproductive glands." Following these leads, the *New York Post* ran a six-part exposé, "The Truth about 'Christine' Jorgensen," that was reprinted in other cities. Based on interviews with Danish doctors, reporter Alvin Davis claimed that Jorgensen was "physically . . . a normal male" before her treatment, and now a castrated male, with no added female organs. (Jorgensen did not undergo vaginoplasty until 1954.) Davis classified Jorgensen as a transvestite, hinted at homosexuality, and referred to her disrespectfully with male pronouns. He contrasted American doctors' outrage at what they saw as mutilating surgery with Danish doctors' advocacy of the operations.[33] In the wake of the [alleged] exposé, *Time* declared, "Jorgensen was no girl at all, only an altered male," and *Newsweek* followed suit. In the mainstream American press, an intersexed person had a legitimate claim to female status, but a male-to-female "transvestite," even surgically and hormonally altered, apparently did not. Jorgensen's doctors in Denmark seemed to confirm the exposé in the *Journal of the American Medical Association,* in which they described Jorgensen's case as one of "genuine transvestism." Pulp magazine sensation followed. *Modern Romances,* for example, ran "Christine Jorgensen: Is She *Still* a Man?" Another pulp called the case "Sex-Change Fraud."[34]

Not surprisingly, these reports upset Jorgensen. She had not represented herself as a pseudohermaphrodite, although she clearly preferred organic explanations that presented her problem as a biological disorder, often described as a hormonal imbalance. She followed her Danish doctors who, in accord with Hirschfeld and others, saw cross-gender identification not as psychopathology but as a somatic condition. Her emphasis on biological causes helped cleanse her cross-gender identification of the taint of sin or weakness and underscored how deeply she felt the need for surgery. Mostly, though, she bridled at the insinuation that she "had perpetrated a hoax" when calling herself a woman, and she resented the disrespectful tone and "pseudo-scientific commentary" of some of the reports. Ultimately, the stories did little to damage her popularity. Shortly after the exposés, a crowd of "more than 2000" met her at the Los Angeles airport. Journalists continued to follow her every move—her nightclub tour, her interview with Alfred Kinsey, her romances with men. While occasional reports portrayed her as an oddity or a joke, in general the press continued to treat her as a woman and a star.[35]

In any case, the European version of sex change as treatment for "transvestites" had finally hit America. News reports alerted transgendered readers that transformative surgery might take place without a claim to an intersexed condition. San Francisco cross-dresser Louise Lawrence appreciated the *Post* exposé. "I can see how it would disturb [Jorgensen]," she wrote, "but I still think it is the fairest explanation yet published."[36] Stories of other transsexuals soon established that Jorgensen was not alone. In 1954, the press reported on Americans Charlotte McLeod and Tamara Rees, MTFs who had surgery in Denmark and Holland, respectively, and also on Roberta Cowell in England. The openly gay and wildly eccentric San Francisco millionaire John Cabell ("Bunny") Breckenridge announced that he, too, planned to undergo sex change surgery. In these post-Jorgensen cases, the press rarely claimed that the surgery had any connection to an intersexed condition.

From the beginning, the Jorgensen story had tremendous impact on its readers. Letter writers flooded Jorgensen with requests for advice. In her 1967 autobiography, Jorgensen referred to "some twenty thousand letters" in the first few months of publicity. Because of her celebrity, letters addressed simply to "Christine Jorgensen, United States of America" reached their destination. Some letters came from admirers or critics, but a "briefcase full" came from people who identified with Jorgensen and expressed "a seemingly genuine desire for alteration of sex." In Denmark, Christian Hamburger also reported hundreds of letters requesting surgery. In less than a year after Jorgensen entered the public domain, Hamburger received "765 letters from 465 patients who appear to have a genuine desire for alteration of sex." Of the 465 letter writers, 180 wrote from the United States. Within the United States, other doctors reported themselves "besieged by would-be castrates pleading for the Danish 'cure.'"[37]

As in the 1930s and 1940s, some readers of the popular press saw themselves in the stories about sex change. With Jorgensen, though, the sheer magnitude of coverage, depth of detail, and public accounting of what the surgery entailed provided a more highly informative how-to story. An unprecedented number of readers identified with Jorgensen, who in turn used her access to the media to encourage them. "The letters that say 'Your story is my story; please help,'" she wrote, "make me willing to bare the secrets of my confused childhood and youth in the hope that they will bring courage, as well as understanding, to others." The exposés that provided the diagnosis of transvestism

also helped transgendered readers who were not visibly intersexed to find their own stories within Jorgensen's. In various cities, some of these readers paid homage by collecting press clippings about Jorgensen. Louise Lawrence, for example, compiled a carefully constructed Jorgensen scrapbook, now housed in the archives of the Kinsey Institute. These clipping collections, several of which still exist today, offer tangible testimony to Jorgensen's popularity and the impact of the press on isolated readers.[38]

For some such readers, Jorgensen stood jointly as revelation, role model, and public defender of the cause. One MTF remembered her overwhelming sense of "being a freak." Before reading about Jorgensen, she had understood herself variously (and uncomfortably) as "effeminate, homosexual, a transvestite, a narcissist, a masturbator, ... a would-be castrate, a potential suicide, and a paranoid." Then:

> The Jorgensen case appeared in all the newspapers and changed my life.... Suddenly, like a revelation, I knew WHO and WHAT I was—and something COULD BE DONE ABOUT IT! Christ only knows how much time I spent poring over every last item about Christine I could lay my hands on. Not Christ but Christine, I thought, was my Saviour! Now everything about me made perfect sense, I knew what had to be done, and I had some real HOPE of being able to live a normal life *as a woman*! Talk about your shock of recognition! Man, this was IT![39]

For others, the "shock of recognition" provoked more ambivalent feelings. Stephen Wagner (a pseudonym) ... focused on one sentence in one of the stories in the *Chicago Sun-Times*: "They may have the physical form of one sex and think, act and feel like the opposite." "This seems to describe me to the dot," he wrote. He recognized Jorgensen immediately as "a normal man," not a pseudohermaphrodite, and tortured himself with the thought that he could not gain access to the surgery she had managed to obtain. "When I read about Christine's case," he wrote, "I got terribly upset. I was really very frantic." On the East Coast, Albert Savon (a pseudonym) had a similar reaction: "Life ... was bearable, at least it was until the Jorgensen story came out. From then on, I have suffered, because *her* life parallels mine so closely! It is *me* twenty years younger.... Her story is my story.... I need help, I need relief and I need it soon." On the West Coast, Barbara and Lauren Wilcox were interested in Jorgensen "from the point of view of, 'when and where will the operation be made available to Barbara.'"[40]

In the wake of the Jorgensen story, FTMs were only a small minority of the letter writers seeking surgery, Of the 180 Americans who asked Christian Hamburger about sex change surgery, only thirty-nine sought female-to-male operations. Commentators of the era believed that MTFs far outnumbered FTMs.[41] The lesser response of FTMs might have reflected economic and technological inequities. Those who lived and worked as women were less likely to have the economic means to finance medical intervention, and FTMs in general were less likely to pursue a surgical solution that still could not produce a functioning penis. As Hamburger acknowledged, the media probably had some influence as well. The publicity accorded to Jorgensen helped mark transsexuality as a male-to-female phenomenon, a distinct reversal from the 1930s when stories of female-to-male sex changes predominated in the popular press. . . . Some FTMs, though, did see themselves immediately in Jorgensen's story. In a later account, Mario Martino described his reaction at the age of fifteen when he first read press accounts on Jorgensen: "Over and over I read the news stories I'd secreted in my room. . . . At last I had hope. *There were people like me.*"[42]

The stories of sex change also had wider appeal. Jorgensen, in particular, inspired non-transgendered correspondents. . . . Over and over again, [they] identified with her and sympathized with her struggle. They placed her story in the context of their own lives and their own beliefs. She had overcome obstacles, and so could they. "My problem," one man wrote, "seems so insignificant to the hell you had to wade through . . . You've really made me wake up." Like Helen Keller, she served for some readers as a model of how the human will might triumph over adversity. A number of letters adopted religious language to express the inspirational lessons they drew. No doubt the name Christine, derived from Christ, helped some readers cast Jorgensen in religious form. Jorgensen's story, one woman said, "reminds me of the suffering Christ had to go through so we might have salvation." Others referred to Jorgensen's surgery as an example of miracles. "I have seen in Christine," one man wrote, "a miracle of God." . . . Jorgensen's story also served as a model for struggles for human rights. "I am a Negro," a woman wrote Jorgensen's parents, and "find many obstacles that must be overcome." Jorgensen, too, she said, "belonged to a minority group but she [broke] through its

limitations. If more people would face the brunt of the battle I am sure we would all live in a much more pleasant world." . . . The letters indicate that Jorgensen's attempt to portray her particular battle as a more common story of human striving had struck a resonant chord.[43]

The publicity showered on Jorgensen did not bring direct relief to those who identified with her. Overwhelmed with sex change requests, Danish officials forbade operations for foreigners. Jorgensen and Hamburger began to refer correspondents to Harry Benjamin, who offered paternalist sympathy, hormone treatment, and the diagnosis "transsexual," but not surgery. Benjamin helped a few male-to-female patients arrange operations through [a] urologist . . . in Los Angeles for a brief period in the 1950s, and sent others to Holland and Mexico for surgery. But many avowed transsexuals, especially poorer ones, had no access to surgery.[44]

It was not until the late 1960s that more American surgeons began to perform sex reassignment surgery. Nonetheless, the ground had shifted. By the mid-1950s the mass media were reporting constantly on sex change. Christine Jorgensen had agreed tacitly to serve as an icon for those who wanted to change sex and also for nontransgendered people who looked to her as a model of persistence, faith, and hope. With ambition and a sense of her mission, she perpetuated her popularity and kept herself on stage. Although she could not control the media, she asserted her presence, and she refused to let the press define her. She told a story that humanized her and defended her right to pursue her own happiness, and she pushed the public to acknowledge her status as a woman.[45]

Jorgensen also pushed American doctors and scientists to redefine their terms. By the mid-1950s they began to adopt the term *transsexual* and to enter into heated debates about the merits of surgical intervention. An American scientific literature on transsexuality, which had not existed before Jorgensen made the news, soon engaged the older European literature that had originated in Germany. American doctors and scientists [in coming decades would return over and over again] to the unanswered questions, "What is a woman and what is a man?"

In all of . . . [these developments], Jorgensen could have been the exception that proved the rule, but instead she became the exception that undermined the rules. It could have been said, for example, that we are all distinctly male or female except for a few people like Christine Jorgensen; instead, transsexuals, doctors, and journalists argued repeatedly that no one is one hundred percent male or one hundred percent female. It could have been argued that sex cannot be changed; instead, various observers reconceived sex as the sum of constituent parts, some of which could be altered and some of which could not. It could have been claimed that gender is part of biological sex, except in the case of handful of people like Jorgensen; instead, researchers debated the sources of gender and saw in transsexuality "an opportunity to study the whole problem of how human beings normally get their sense of being a male or a female."[46] It could have been stated (and sometimes it was) that Jorgensen was a gay crossdresser; instead, a prevailing view gradually emerged that transsexuality differed from homosexuality and transvestism. In sum, in the context of her day, with the concepts of sex, gender, and sexuality already in flux, Jorgensen showed her public how sex changed, a process that continues today.

NOTES

1. "Ex-GI becomes Blonde Beauty," New York Daily News, Dec. 1, 1952, 1; "Christine and the News," Newsweek, Dec. 15, 1952, 64.

2. See, for example, John D'Emilio and Estelle B. Freedman, Intimate Matters: A History of Sexuality in America, 2d ed. (Chicago: University of Chicago Press, 1997); Paul Robinson, The Modernization of Sex, 2d ed. (Ithaca: Cornell University Press, 1989); Sharon R. Ullman, Sex Seen: The Emergence of Modern Sexuality in America (Berkeley: University of California Press, 1997); Jonathan Ned Katz, The Invention of Heterosexuality (New York: Dutton, 1995).

3. Magnus Hirschfeld, Transvestites: The Erotic Drive to Cross Dress, trans. Michael A. Lombardi-Nash (1910; reprint, Buffalo: Prometheus, 1991), 219, 226; Gregorio Marañon, The Evolution of Sex and Intersexual Conditions (London: George Allen and Unwin, 1932), 24.

4. Margaret Mead, Male and Female: A Study of the Sexes in a Changing World (New York: William Morrow, 1949); Alfred C. Kinsey, Sexual Behavior in the Human Male (Philadelphia: W. B. Saunders, 1948). For important recent formulations, see, for example, Judith Butler, Gender Trouble: Feminism and the Subversion of Identity (New York: Routledge, 1990); Anne Fausto-Sterling, Sexing the Body: Gender Politics and the Construction of Sexuality (New York: Basic Books, 2000).

5. See Richard Green, "Mythological, Historical, and Cross-Cultural Aspects of Transsexualism," in Transsexualism and Sex Reassignment, ed. Richard Green and John Money (Baltimore: Johns Hopkins Press, 1969), 13–22; Vern L. Bullough, "Transsexualism in History," Archives of Sexual Behavior 4:5 (1975), 561–71; Leslie Feinberg, Transgender Warriors: Making History from Joan of Arc to RuPaul (Boston: Beacon, 1996).

6. Bernice Hausman, Changing Sex: Transsexualism, Technology, and the Idea of Gender (Durham, N.C.: Duke University Press, 1995), 140.

7. In the popular lingo used today, transsexuals are a subset of "transgendered" people, an umbrella term for those with various forms and degrees of crossgender practices and identifications. "Transgendered" includes, among others, some people who identify as "butch" or masculine lesbians, as "fairies," "queens," or feminine gay men, and as heterosexual crossdressers as well as those who identify as transsexual. The categories are not hermetically sealed, and to a certain extent the boundaries are permeable. The same person might identify as a butch lesbian at one point in life and as an FTM (female-to-male) transsexual at another. Transsexuals today are understood to differ from homosexuals, who rarely wish to change their sex. The longing to change the sex of one's body does not necessarily correspond with any set pattern of erotic behavior or sexual desire. Some transsexuals identify themselves as (and engage in behavior recognized as) homosexual, bisexual, or asexual. Transsexuals are also understood to differ from transvestites or crossdressers, who dress in the clothes of the other sex but do not necessarily hope to change the sex of their bodies. By the definitions most commonly used today, transsexuals are not intersexed, a term used to describe the people who used to be called "hermaphrodites" and "pseudohermaphrodites," people with various physical conditions in which the genitals or reproductive organs do not fit into the standard category of female or male. All these terms have histories.

8. Eugen Steinach, Sex and Life: Forty Years of Biological and Medical Experiments (New York: Viking, 1940) 66. On Steinach, see Harry Benjamin, "Eugen Steinach, 1861–1944: A Life of Research," Scientific Monthly 61 (1945): 427–42; Sexual Anomalies and Perversions: A Summary of the Work of the Late Dr. Magnus Hirschfeld, Compiled as a Humble Memorial by His Pupils (London: Francis Aldor, 1944 [1938]), 172–77.

9. J. Allen Gilbert, "Homo-Sexuality and Its Treatment," Journal of Nervous and Mental Disease 52 (October 1920): 297–322, quotations on 321. In Gilbert's article, Hart is referred to as "H." Jonathan Katz's sleuthing uncovered Hart's identity. See Jonathan Katz, Gay American History: Lesbians and Gay Men in the U.S.A.: A Documentary Anthology (New York: Crowell, 1976), 419.

10. Sexual Anomalies and Perversions, 179, 218; Magnus Hirschfeld, Transvestites: The Erotic Drive to Cross Dress (New York: Prometheus Books, 1991[1910]), 235; Felix Abraham, "Genitalumwandlung an zwei männlichen Transvestiten," Zeitschrift für Sexualwissenschaft und Sexualpolitik 18 (10 September 1931): 223–26, quotation on 223.

11. Niels Hoyer, ed., Man into Woman: An Authentic Record of a Change of Sex (New York: Dutton, 1933), 284. On Elbe's death and the involvement of Hirschfeld and the Institute, see Preben Hertoft and Teit Ritzau, Paradiset er ikke til salg: Trangen til at vaere begge koen (Paradise is not for sale: the desire to be both sexes) (Denmark: Lindhardt og Ringhof, 1984), 82–83.

12. S. W. [pseud.], letter to Alfred C. Kinsey, 14 Dec. 1947, Correspondence file: S. W., Kinsey Institute for Research in Sex, Gender, and Reproduction, Indiana University, Bloomington, Ind. (hereafter, KI).

13. Hoyer, *Man into Woman*, 178, xi–xii. The claim to hermaphroditism is hard to believe. By the late 1930s, the reigning expert in the field, Hugh Hampton Young, found only twenty medically confirmed cases of hermaphroditism; not one of them had, as the story of Lili Elbe suggested, two ovaries in the pelvis and two testes in the scrotum. See Hugh Hampton Young, *Genital Abnormalities, Hermaphroditism and Related Adrenal Diseases* (Baltimore: Williams and Wilkins, 1937), 200–201.

14. "Man in Woman's Body," *Your Body*, September 1937, 12–15, quotation on 15. "Boy Prisoner Slowly Changing into a Girl," n.p., n.d. [ca. 1936]; "When Science Changed a Man into a Woman!" n.d. [ca. 1934], 2: both in "Order Book" scrapbook, box 1/1 scrapbooks, Virginia Prince Collection, California State University at Northridge (hereafter, VPC).

15. Gordon Kahn, "['Bad-Old'] Days of Newly-Made Man," *New York Daily Mirror*, n.d. [ca. 1936]; Kahn, "Boy Ex-Girl 'Corsetiere,'" ibid., n.d. [ca. 1936]; "Former Girl Athlete Arrives, Now a Man"; Kahn, "Once Girl, He Talks of Loves," ibid., n.d. [ca. 1936]; and Kahn, "Koubkov Met Love at Track," ibid., n.d. [ca 1936], all in "Order Book" scrapbook, box 1/1 scrapbooks, VPC.

16. See, for example, Brett Riley, "Are Sexual Changes Possible?" n.d. [late 1930s or 1940s], box 1/4 clippings, VPC.

17. Jacob Hubler, "Science Turns Girl into Boy," *Sexology* 2:3 (Nov. 1934): 158.

18. Letter to the editor, "Dissatisfaction with Sex," *Sexology* 1:12 (Aug. 1934), 810; Letter to the editor, "Changing Sex," *Sexology* 5:4 (Dec. 1937), 265; "They Want to Change Sexes," *Sexology* 5:1 (Sept. 1937), 32.

19. "Dissatisfaction with Sex," 810; "Changing Sex," 265. For articles, see "Woman into Man," *Sexology* 10:8 (March 1944), 484–85; David O. Cauldwell, "A Man Becomes a Woman," *Sexology* 13:2 (Sept. 1946), 73–79, and 13:3 (Oct. 1946), 149–52. For letters to the editor, see "Homosexuality," *Sexology* 9:6 (Nov. 1942), 390, 392; "'Man into Woman'?" *Sexology* 13:1 (Aug. 1946), 59–60; "Man into Woman," *Sexology* 13:5 (Dec. 1946), 312; and "Desire to Be of the Opposite Sex," *Sexology* 15:1 (Aug. 1948), 53.

20. David O. Cauldwell, "Psychopathia Transexualis," *Sexology* (Dec. 1949), 276, 278.

21. Ibid., 280, 274; David O. Cauldwell, *Questions and Answers on the Sex Life and Sexual Problems of Trans-Sexuals* (Girard, Kans.: Haldeman-Julius Publicans, 1950), front cover, 11.

22. Jim Kepner, "Excavating Lesbian and Gay History," *ONE/IGLA Bulletin* 2 (spring/summer 1996): 9.

23. Cauldwell, *Questions and Answers*, 13, 24.

24. Gene St. Ledges, "Can Science Switch Sexes?" *Whisper* (Jan. 1950), box 1/4 clippings, VPC; "Would You Change Your Sex?" *Glance* (March 1950), box 1/1 scrapbooks, ibid.

25. Tom Buckley, "Transsexuality Expert, 90, Recalls 'Maverick' Career," *New York Times*, Jan. 11, 1975, B1. On Benjamin's career in the United States, see Harry Benjamin, "Reminiscences," *Journal of Sex Research* 6:1 (Feb. 1970): 3–9.

26. "Medical Report on V. B.," July 19, 1948, pp. 1–3; V. B. to Harry Benjamin, May 19, 1949, both in V.B. folder, box 3, Series IIC, Harry Benjamin Collection, KI (hereafter, HBC). On the mayhem statute, see Robert Veit Sherwin, "The Legal Problem in Transvestism,"

American Journal of Psychotherapy 8 (April 1954), 243–244. By all accounts, no surgeon engaged in sex reassignment was ever prosecuted under the mayhem statute. More generally, surgeons hesitated to engage in sex change surgery for other reasons; they worried, for example, about their reputations in the medical community, and they also feared liability suits. By the late 1960, doctors and lawyers had ceased using the mayhem statutes as an excuse to refuse sex reassignment surgery.

27. Harry Benjamin, letter to V. B., May 31. 1949; Harry Benjamin, letter to Edmund G. Brown, Nov. 22, 1949, both in V. B. folder, box 3, Series IIC, HBC; Berdeen Frankel Meyer, "Case Summary and Closing Note," Oct. 2, 1950, 8, in ibid.

28. Alton Blakeslee, "Thousands Do Not Know True Sex," *New York Daily News*, Dec. 7, 1952, C6; Jack Geiger, "Sex Surgery Specialist Reports Hundreds of Boy-Girl Operations," n.d. [ca. 2 Dec. 1952], Christine Jorgensen scrapbook, Louise Lawrence Collection, KI (hereafter, LLC); "Doctor Tells of Five Sex Operations," *New York Daily News*, Dec. 18, 1952, C4; "The Great Transformation," *Time*, Dec. 15, 1952, 59.

29. G. B. Lal, "MD's and Public to Eagerly Follow Christine's Life," *New York Journal-American*, Dec. 7, 1952, 18L; Louise Lawrence, letter to Harry Benjamin, Dec. 9, 1952, TRNSV notebook, LLC.

30. Christine Jorgensen, "The Story of My Life," *American Weekly*, Feb. 15, 1953, 5, 9; "How AW Got and Prepared Christine Story," *Editor and Publisher*, March 28, 1953, 62. See Gert Hekma, "'A Female Soul in a Male Body': Sexual Inversion as Gender Inversion in Nineteenth-Century Sexology," in *Third Sex, Third Gender: Beyond Sexual Dimorphism in Culture and History*, ed. Gilbert Herdt (New York: Zone Books, 1996), 213–39.

31. Christine Jorgensen, "The Story of My Life," *American Weekly*, Feb. 22, 1953, 4, 6; March 8, 1953, 8, 9.

32. Susan Stryker, "Transsexuality: The Postmodern Body and/as Technology," *Exposure: The Journal of the Society for Photographic Education* 30 (1995): 38–50; Dallas Denny, "Black Telephones, White Refrigerators: Rethinking Christine Jorgensen," in Denny, ed. *Current Concepts in Transgender Identity* (New York: Garland Publishing, 1998), 35–44.

33. "Christine Discounted as 100 Pct. Woman by Her Copenhagen Doctor," *San Francisco Call-Bulletin*, Feb. 18, 1953, Christine Jorgensen scrapbook, Louise Lawrence Collection, KI; "AMA Studies Christine–Some U.S. Doctors Say She's Not a Woman Still," *San Francisco Chronicle*, March 11, 1953, in ibid.; Alvin Davis, "The Truth about 'Christine' Jorgensen," *New York Post*, pt. 1, April 6, 1953.

34. "The Case of Christine," *Time*, April 20, 1953, 82; "Boy or Girl?" *Newsweek*, May 4, 1953, 91; Christian Hamburger, Georg Stürup, and E. Dahl-Iversen, "Transvestism: Hormonal, Psychiatric, and Surgical Treatment," *Journal of the American Medical Association* 152 (May 1953): 396; Robert King, "Christine Jorgensen: Is She *Still* a Man?" *Modern Romances*, Aug. 1953, in ONE/International Gay and Lesbian Archives (ONE/IGLA), University of Southern California, Los Angeles, file: Christine Jorgensen; "Sex-Change Fraud," *Exclusive*, Feb. 1955, vertical file: Christine Jorgensen, KI.

35. Christine Jorgensen, *Christine Jorgensen: A Personal Autobiography* (New York: Paul S. Eriksson, 1967),

207, 209; "2000 in L.A. Greet Christine," *Los Angeles Herald and Express*, May 7, 1953, Christine Jorgensen scrapbook, LLC. For a different interpretation of the media's treatment of Jorgensen, see David Harley Serlin, "Christine Jorgensen and the Cold War Closet," *Radical History Review* 62 (Spring 1995): 136–65.

36. Louise Lawrence to Harry Benjamin, April 22, 1953, TRNSV notebook, LLC.

37. Jorgensen, *Christine Jorgensen*, 189, 217; Christian Hamburger, "The Desire for Change of Sex as Shown by Personal Letters from 465 Men and Women," *Acta Endocrinologica* 14 (1953): 361–76, quotation on 363; Davis, "The Truth about 'Christine' Jorgensen," *New York Post*, April 9, 1953.

38. Jorgensen, "Story of My Life," *American Weekly*, Feb. 15, 1953, 7. In addition to Louise Lawrence's scrapbook, see the various scrapbooks and clipping collections in the Virginia Prince Collection. Special thanks to Joseph Agnew for lending me the "Christine" scrapbook from Chicago in his private possession.

39. R.E.L. Masters, *Sex-Drive People: An Autobiographical Approach to the Problem of the Sex-Dominated Personality* (Los Angeles: Sherbourne, 1966), 229–32.

40. S. W. to Alfred C. Kinsey, Dec. 8, 1952, Correspondence file S. W., KI; S. W. to Harry Benjamin, July 2, 1954, S. W. folder, Box 8, Series IIC, HBC; A. S. [pseud.], letter probably to Harry Benjamin [ca. March 1954], A. D. folder, ibid.; Louise Lawrence to Harry Benjamin, April 6, 1953, TRNSV notebook, LLC.

41. On ratios of MTFs and FTMs, see Ira B. Pauly, "Male Psychosexual Inversion: Transsexualism," *Archives of General Psychiatry* 13 (Aug. 1965): 179. The ratios offered by various doctors in the 1950s and early 1960s ranged from 6:1 to 2:1. In general, the published ratios have declined over time, and some today now posit an equal number of FTMs and MTFs. In the 1950s, though, MTFs clearly predominated in the doctors' estimates, and some mid-century sexologists considered transvestism and transsexualism, like fetishism, largely, if not wholly, "male" conditions. Among the broader population of transgendered people, were there in fact more MTFs than FTMs? If so, why? These larger questions remain unanswered.

42. Hamburger, "The Desire for Change of Sex," 364; Mario Martino, with Harriet, *Emergence: A Transsexual Autobiography* (New York: Crown Publishers, 1979), 40. For a lengthier discussion of the contemporary marking of transsexuality as male to female, see Marjorie Garber, *Vested Interests: Cross-Dressing and Cultural Anxiety* (New York: Routledge, 1992), ch. 4.

43. H. S. to Christine Jorgensen [c. 1953], Christine folder; Barbara Williams to George and Florence Jorgensen, Dec. 1, 1952, loose, both in Letters Box, Christine Jorgensen Papers, Royal Danish Library, Copenhagen.

44. Harry Benjamin, "Transvestism and Transsexualism," *International Journal of Sexology* 7 (Aug. 1953), 13; and see the collected correspondence in HBC.

45. Jorgensen died on May 3, 1989, at the age of sixty-two.

46. Frederic G. Worden and James T. Marsh, "Psychological Factors in Men Seeking Sex Transformation: A Preliminary Report," *Journal of the American Medical Association* 157:15 (April 9, 1955), 1292.

BETH L. BAILEY

Prescribing the Pill: The Coming of the Sexual Revolution in America's Heartland

In this fascinating bit of historical detective work, Beth Bailey explodes the myth that the advent of the oral contraceptive in 1960 ushered in the Sexual Revolution, freeing women—especially those who were unmarried—to engage in sex without fears of unwanted pregnancies. Bailey tells a different story, one in which use of the new contraceptive is closely linked to concerns about overpopulation and poverty. By narrowing her focus to Lawrence, Kansas, home to the University of Kansas, she provides a clear view of the complex process by which college women gained access to the pill.

Why does Bailey refer to this process as "elite-managed, gradual change"? At what point did young women demand access on their own behalf? Why were

Excerpted from "Prescribing the Pill," ch. 4 of *Sex in the Heartland* by Beth L. Bailey (Cambridge, Mass.: Harvard University Press, 1999). Reprinted with permission of the author and publisher. Notes have been renumbered and edited.

their voices virtually mute throughout the 1960s, even though Bailey provides clear evidence that their behavior was changing? Is this silencing on the part of heterosexual young women related in any way to the silencing that Betty Friedan or lesbian athletes imposed on themselves in the postwar era?

American women went "on the pill" in the 1960s. The oral tablets that most Americans called simply "the pill" were approved for contraceptive use by the FDA in 1960. By early 1969, eight and a half million women were using the pill; their numbers had grown by about one million each year from 1961.[1] Every day for three weeks out of their monthly menstrual cycle, millions of women popped the tiny tablet through the foil package that fit into the daisy-wheel container that somewhat resembled a compact—if one didn't know better. The high hormonal doses of the early oral contraceptives had pronounced side effects, which mimicked pregnancy: breast tenderness, weight gain, some nausea. But the pill was more than 99 percent effective, in no way dependent on the direct cooperation of the woman's partner, and completely separate from the act of sexual intercourse. A great many women were willing to accept some side effects in exchange for freedom from fear of pregnancy. By giving women greater control over their sexual and reproductive lives, this new contraceptive technology helped change the meaning and experience of sex in America.

The great majority of the women who went on the pill in its early years, however, were not the young single women who lived "the revolution." Most were married. . . . Nonetheless, by the mid-1960s the pill symbolized the revolution in sex. . . . In America, talk of the sexual revolution inevitably turned to talk of the pill, and discussions of the pill often centered on its possible effects on America's sexual mores.

Largely because of its symbolic role, the pill frequently appears in discussions (both then and now) as a sort of *deus ex machina*, bringing about the sexual revolution. In 1968 a no less distinguished figure than Pearl S. Buck, writing for the mass market in *Reader's Digest*, linked a crisis in sexual morality to the pill: "It is a small object—yet its potential effect upon our society may be even more devastating than the nuclear bomb."[2] . . . [But Buck's analogy to the bomb] overlooks a key fact. The pill was not simply a new technology available in the free marketplace of postwar America. It had to be prescribed by a physician.

Doctors, then as now, controlled access to oral contraceptives. And at that time only a small minority of physicians would prescribe birth control pills to women who were not married. Most believed, along with a large majority of the American public, that it was wrong for unmarried women to have sex. Thus, before the pill could play any significant role in the sexual behavior of America's unmarried youth, something had to change. Unmarried women—in large numbers—had to have access to oral contraceptives. How did single women get the pill?

Once again, revolutionary change in Americans' sexual mores and behavior was made possible inadvertently. . . . The pill did not become available to single women because they raised their voices and demanded the right to sexual freedom and control of their own bodies. Instead, it became available to them as a by-product of two political movements that were at the heart of sixties liberalism and its attempts to ameliorate the difficult social problems that plagued America and the world.

One of these movements was driven by concern about population growth, both international and domestic, which reached near-panic proportions in the United States during the 1960s and early 1970s. The other, Lyndon Johnson's Great Society, used federal funds and programs to attack the causes and consequences of poverty and racism in the United States. Neither set of efforts, by any stretch of the imagination, was intended to foster a sexual revolution. However, these two movements helped make the pill available to single women, in large part by providing rationales for prescribing contraceptives that did not employ a language of morality. . . .

[In Kansas, population control advocates urged the state senate to] vote on legislation allowing public agencies to distribute information about contraceptives to Kansas citizens. Senate Bill 375 stemmed largely from the intense lobbying efforts of Patricia Schloesser, M.D., head of the state division of maternal and child services, who was motivated by a frightening vision of unrestrained world population growth. . . . [T]he senate voted unanimously in favor of the measure. The house vote the following April, however, was close enough to require a roll call. . . . While it was now legal for public institutions to offer birth control and contraceptive information to citizens of Kansas, the legislature had offered no . . . funding. Without money for birth control services, the change in law had little practical impact. . . .

Among the most vocal and vehement advocates of birth control in Kansas was the director of Lawrence's public health department, Dr. Dale Clinton. . . . Like Dr. Schloesser, Clinton believed that the world population explosion was a greater threat to public health than any contagious disease or environmental hazard. . . . In 1959 the professional organization for public health workers, the 20,000-member American Public Health Association (APHA), had adopted a resolution that called for attention, at "all levels of government," to "the impact of population change on health." And in 1963 the APHA called population growth "one of the world's most important health problems" and began lobbying government officials for action.[3]

[While the population advocates pressed for maximum dissemination of both information about contraceptives and the contraceptives themselves, the Johnson administration pursued a similar strategy as part of a very different objective.] President Johnson pledged in his state of the union address "to seek new ways to use our knowledge to help deal with the explosion in world population and the growing scarcity of world resources." In April [1965], Senator Gruening of Alaska introduced a bill that led to the funding of birth control programs through the Department of Health, Education, and Welfare. Earlier, the Office of Economic Opportunity (OEO) had funneled some money to family planning programs under the "local option" policy that allowed community groups to initiate welfare programs. (Initially the OEO did not allow its funds to be used for contraceptives for unmarried women; that restriction was lifted in 1966.)[4] The federal government's decisions to spend taxpayers' money on public family planning programs were not based on concern about women's reproductive health or a wish to promote sexual freedom. Rather, the funding was a result of the confluence of alarm about the "population problem" and increased federal involvement in programs intended to alleviate the effects of poverty in the United States. Limiting the number of children born to poor women (or allowing poor women to avoid unplanned and unwanted pregnancies) was a priority for these programs.

The political implications of linking Johnson's Great Society (with its strong focus on poverty) and population control were as apparent at the time as they are today. In the early twentieth century, many advocates of birth control had worked closely with the eugenics movement, which sought to limit childbearing among people the eugenicists deemed genetically and racially inferior and so preserve the dominance of white, Anglo-Saxon Americans. Those uncomfortably close links between the birth control movement and the eugenics movement were not so far in the past. . . .

The politics of the Johnson administration's "war on poverty" and welfare programs were complicated at best, and those who attempted to implement policies struggled with opposition from widely divergent sources. In the case of birth control, the administration faced both the suspicions of targeted groups such as poor African Americans *and* voters' reservations about the costs of burgeoning social welfare programs. . . . The American Association of Public Health consistently focused on the dangers of world population growth, an argument that was more compelling to Americans who rejected the idea of "benefits" for the poor and underprivileged. But throughout the 1960s, authors also attempted to demonstrate that contraception for America's poor was fully in keeping with "broadly democratic principles of equal opportunity for all." Birth control, one prominent activist wrote in an attempt to shift the grounds for suspicion, should not be the "special privilege" of the "well-to-do."[5]

Many Americans, however, drew connections between birth control and antipoverty programs that were exactly what government agencies had tried to avoid. For example, when *Good Housekeeping* sampled its 20,000-member "consumer panel" in 1967 on the question "Should Birth Control Be Available to Unmarried Women," its editors discovered that the negative responses (significantly, a strong majority) were based on "moral" arguments, while the affirmative responses were "practical." An Arizona woman wrote: "It would eliminate many dollars in child-welfare payments." A more vehement response came from a woman in the Midwest, who supported birth control for unmarried women because "I deeply resent having to deprive my family of privileges I cannot afford because I have to pay support for others not of my choosing."[6] . . .

Once the Kansas legislature made funding available, Dr. Clinton moved quickly and Lawrence's health department began to offer contraceptive services—something fewer than 20 percent of local health departments in the United States did at that time. Clinton, however, was decidedly uninterested in the professional debate about birth control for the indigent and the related directives. Though the framework provided by state (and eventually federal) guidelines indicated an implicit, but clear, association of these programs with services for the poor, Clinton made it equally clear that his birth control clinic was not "indigent-oriented," nor did he consider it the appropriate site for clinical medicine. He did not intend to focus on the poor, and he did not mean to provide women (of any income level) with health care. Instead, he intended to combat the scourge of unrestrained population growth by offering contraceptives to any and all.

. . . Kansas's laws restricting birth control, in effect from 1870 through 1963, had applied only to public agencies. Even before 1963 a married woman in Lawrence had ready access to birth control if she could afford a private doctor. When the pill became available for contraceptive purposes in 1960, Lawrence doctors had begun prescribing it to married women. . . .

As private doctors in Lawrence were already meeting the needs of their patients, the health department, naturally, would draw from a different constituency. Married women who could afford private doctors were more or less out of the pool. Who was left? Those for whom medical fees were too expensive. . . .

There was also another constituency, one that the state and federal governments had not intended to target: unmarried women. And because of the University of Kansas and Haskell Indian Junior College, Lawrence had a disproportionately high number of young, unmarried women. The Kansas legislature had mandated access to contraceptive information and services only for *married* women 18 years and older. Parental permission was required for women under 18, no matter what their marital status. But the legislature also provided a back door to access: Any woman might receive contraceptives at a public clinic if she was "referred to said center by a licensed physician." Clinton interpreted this law in the broadest terms. He was a licensed physician, legally

authorized to make such referrals. Thus, as he made clear in newspaper interviews and public talks, any woman who wanted birth control might receive her referral at the clinic itself, at the time of her appointment. With virtually no exceptions, women seeking contraceptives at the health department came away with the pill.

[At the University of Kansas,] the question was whether the University Health Service should prescribe the pill to unmarried women students. This debate . . . centered [on] issues of morality. It was precipitated by a 1966 forum on the topic: "Should unmarried undergraduates be given birth control information and/or materials through Watkins Hospital [the student health service]?"

The panelists were three: Rev. Simmons, the campus minister who had helped form the family planning clinic [affiliated with Planned Parenthood] and who focused on sexuality counseling and birth control in his ministry at KU; Father Falteisch, chairman of the moral theology department at St. Louis University and a Roman Catholic priest; and Dr. Raymond Schwegler, director of KU's student health service. According to coverage by the *University Daily Kansan,* Simmons argued that population control was desperately needed. Father Falteisch agreed, and suggested that the Church was moving toward accepting the "responsible use" of contraceptives as legitimate, though not for the unmarried. In the context of 1966 America and their respective churches, both men of the cloth took liberal to progressive positions. The hard line, however, came from the man of medicine.

The *Kansan* described Dr. Schwegler, then about 60 years old, as a "small, white-haired man" with a soft voice, but he certainly never minced words. Watkins would not, Schwegler insisted, give contraceptives to unmarried students "under any circumstances." "I know this is old fashioned, mid-Victorian, and the *Kansan* will cut us to ribbons," he is quoted in the *Kansan* as saying, "but I don't want to do it and my staff backs me completely." Rev. Simmons pushed, arguing that unless premarital intercourse was grounds for expulsion, Schwegler's policy was unfair. Schwegler replied: "We'd have trouble keeping the student population up [if we expelled students for premarital intercourse]. But Watkins will not contribute to the recreational activities of the campus." When a student asked about the possibility of a "rebel doctor," Schwegler deemed it impossible: "All the doctors are handpicked—by me." He continued: "If I had somebody over there who I thought was as far out as some of the teaching faculty, I'd fire him. I want a conservative hospital that can be respected."[7]

The 1966 forum on birth control prompted a flood of letters to the *Kansan*. The letters contained no dire predictions about the earth's future if population growth continued uncontrolled. Instead, students used a language of morality to dispute Schwegler's stance. . . .

The first response to Schwegler published in the *Kansan* was . . . from a graduate student from Iola, Kansas. . . . Noting that the health service did provide the pill to married women, he argued that by so doing the administration had defined the issue as moral, not medical. Thus, he said, the question was, "Who should make the moral decision, the university or the students themselves?" Another graduate student (from Gettysburg, South Dakota) questioned "the irresponsible use of the concept 'morality' as employed primarily by the 'anti-pill' proponents." Morality, he insisted, existed only in a situation in which there was "opportunity for choice." Without "free access" to contraceptives, students were not making a moral—or immoral—choice about premarital intercourse. Instead, their choices were constrained by fear or coercion.

The "anti-pill" faction was represented by only one letter. The writer, a male sophomore from Nebraska, argued that because the university was a "public servant," it must follow the "doctrines of the society." He warned that premarital sex would be likely to increase if single women could get the pill, for without fear of pregnancy, "restraining factors would be few and far between." Reaching for an analogy, he asked: "If the possibility of punishment for murder were eliminated," would there not be "a substantial increase in the number of murders committed every year?" . . .

What was largely missing in this flurry of letters was a statement embracing sexual freedom—an affirmative voice. . . . [M]ost of the writers shifted the focus away from sex in making their arguments. . . . While their central claim—that the university should provide contraceptives to unmarried women students—was quite radical, their arguments were not. These were not yet the voices of revolution.

In the forum and in the ensuing debate, there were no arguments centering around the rights of women to control their own bodies. In fact, only two women participated in this public debate, and their names do not appear, effaced in the signatures "Mr. and Mrs. James Cooley" and "Mr. and Mrs. Angus Wright." . . . Why didn't women speak out in the paper? After all, the debate was about women's choices—it was not men who might go "on the pill."

Women did not write because the stakes for them were so high. Discussions about morality and the pill in the larger society did not center on the morality of existential choice, but on the immorality of premarital sex. In the February 1967 *Good Housekeeping* poll on unmarried women and the pill, respondents made comments such as: "I truly pity a generation growing up with the morals of alley cats"; and "Making birth control available to unmarried girls to me would mean lowering our moral standards and destroying our culture." These women were not policymakers or experts. . . . [T]heir voices represent a different sort of authority. These are the voices of mothers—mothers of the sort whose daughters went to state colleges in the Midwest. The *Kansan* was a student paper, but news of a daughter's making public claims about her right to birth control was very likely to travel fast and to travel home.

. . . Writings in the *Journal of the American College Health Association, School and Society,* and the *Journal of School Health* at the time were equally emphatic about the evils of premarital sex. . . . The director of the Princeton health service . . . warned against prescribing contraceptives to unmarried women, as "the student's unconscious mind might interpret such prescriptions as a signal from 'authority' giving permission for sexual freedom."[8] [A] physician at the Ohio State University health service . . . made an unfortunate analogy to sex: "It is all a bit like cars: Some choose a new one and break it in with loving care; others buy from a used car lot—it is just as nice and shiny but you are not sure what problems the previous drivers have left you."[9]

Mass-circulation magazines and professional journals would not have devoted so much space to debates over premarital sex if there had been no audience for them. . . . Nonetheless, these are essentially prescriptive discourses. What of the students themselves?

In the spring semester of 1964 the "Roles of Women" committee of the Associated Women Students (AWS) surveyed its constituency. Presented with descriptions of behavior ("using race as one basis for choosing your associates"; "showing disrespect for those in authority"; "wearing short shorts in town"; "feeling very angry with someone"), students were asked to judge each item. Categories were "morally or ethically right," "generally acceptable," "generally unacceptable," and "morally or ethically wrong." The instructions emphasized that each student should indicate what was right or wrong "for *you*." More than 1,900 women completed the survey.

Questions about sex provoked the strongest responses. Significantly higher percentages of women students disapproved of "mixed swimming parties in the nude" than of using an exam "which has been illegally obtained." . . . [M]ost of the respondents (77 percent of the freshmen and 68 percent of the seniors) rated premarital sex with a fiancé as "morally or ethically wrong," not merely as "generally unacceptable." Even stronger was the students' disapproval of sexual intercourse when the couple was not engaged to be married. A striking 91 percent of both freshmen and seniors labeled it unacceptable or wrong. Only 2 percent of each group deemed premarital sex for those who were not engaged "morally or ethically right."

. . . In 1967 a student union forum offered three professors addressing the question "Is Free Love a Bargain?" . . . This forum was dominated by a professor of English, who accused the audience of coming in search of "some rationalization for the sex you've indulged in." . . . [In] such a climate, with the threat of moral condemnation from peers and authorities alike, few students wished to make public their private decisions about sex.

In 1967, following the "Is Free Love a Bargain?" forum, an unmarried woman finally wrote to the editor of the campus newspaper, claiming her right to both sex and the pill: "I take the pill because I'd rather express my love than repress it. I'm not promiscuous, but once in a while I meet a 'special' guy. I've seen too many girls on campus totally disregard school for several weeks as they suffer anxiety over a missed menstrual period. . . . If a girl takes one chance a year, that's enough to warrant taking the pill." . . . Her letter, which had begun, "I'm a woman and I'm glad," employed a feminist language, emphasizing women's right and capacity to choose. It was a powerful and affirmative statement. But it was unsigned. An editor's note below the letter read: "Contrary to established editorial page policy, we are printing this letter without signature." All letters, no matter how controversial their claims, required signature—except this one. A woman's

claiming her right to sex and the pill was understood as a whole different category of risk.

That this woman remained anonymous and was allowed to do so by the *Kansan* editorial board in violation of its policy, that women's voices were so conspicuously silent in the previous year's debate on the pill, that 91 percent of the women students surveyed *said* they believed premarital sex to be "ethically or morally wrong"—all this is strong evidence that it wasn't only the prescriptive voices of adults denying the legitimacy of the culture of youth. Even within student culture, there was a gulf between public claims and private behavior. For the women of KU were having sex. And they were, in increasing numbers, on the pill.

Actually getting the pill could be complicated, however. When a young, single woman sought a prescription for contraceptives in the 1960s, she was making a statement about her sexual status. Virgins didn't need birth control pills unless they did not plan to remain virgins much longer. . . . When a single woman went to a doctor to request any sort of contraceptive device, she risked refusal, embarrassment, even lectures on morality and appropriate behavior. Some women bought cheap rings and tried to pass them off as wedding bands. Others claimed they were coming in for a "premarital exam," with the wedding pending. Still others complained of menstrual cramps or heavy bleeding and came away with the pill, prescribed to "regulate" their periods. But many doctors, especially those in small towns and university communities, saw through such pretexts and often treated young women with suspicion. Single women were not guaranteed, by law or custom, access to birth control.

As women learned through informal networks, alternative newspapers, and the completely mainstream *Journal World*, the quickest, cheapest, and least complicated place to get birth control pills in Lawrence was the public health department. The university student health service refused to "contribute to the recreational activities of the campus," in its director's colorful words, and many students worried about having such information about their sex lives in what were, after all, official university records at the health service. . . . [The Planned Parenthood–affiliated] clinic was open only two nights a month, and simply could not serve large numbers of women. . . .

The number of women obtaining oral contraceptives at the public health department grew dramatically from year to year, and the vast majority of the new patients each year were KU students. The patient load closely followed the academic year. In 1971, for example, there were only 44 new patients in August, but in September, with the beginning of the fall semester, there were 300. That year the Lawrence-Douglas County health department served 8,529 birth control patients and dispensed or prescribed almost 38,000 months of pills. . . . The pill was a wonder drug not simply because of its effectiveness for women but also because of its possible convenience for those who prescribed it. Women went to the health department and walked out a few minutes later "on the pill." Stories of young women who were offered virtual armloads of free pills and told to pass them on to their friends still circulate today. . . .

The Planned Parenthood–affiliated clinic took a very different approach. Prescription of the pill was contingent upon not only a physical examination but also a time-consuming process of education and counseling. . . . The clinic, which had opened in early 1967, closed its doors permanently on the first day of 1970. Though it had been founded to serve low-income residents of Lawrence, the president of its sponsoring group explained, it had been used almost exclusively by KU students (she did not say whether they were married or single). Many of the volunteers were frustrated by what they saw as a misdirection of resources, and upon closing the clinic the directors sent a letter to Dr. Schwegler at the student health service and to the chancellor arguing that the university must take responsibility for its students' birth control needs instead of allowing students to overwhelm community resources needed by and for a different population.[10]

. . . In 1970, after the closing of the Planned Parenthood clinic, a student group approached top-level administrators about the health service's birth control policies. The administrators responded sympathetically, promising that two upcoming vacancies at Watkins would be filled with doctors who would prescribe the pill without using marital status or "morality" as criteria. This never happened. . . . In 1970, 53 percent of American college health services offered no gynecological care to women students, and 72 percent did not prescribe contraceptives (to single or married students).[11]

Thus far, the story of the pill in Lawrence, Kansas, has been one of elite-managed, gradual change. . . . Until the 1970s, Lawrence's youth also fit into this model. . . . While thousands of young women went on the pill during the 1960s, public acknowledgment of that private behavior lagged behind. [Although the] pill may have been revolutionary in its results, it was not especially revolutionary in its introduction.

In the early 1970s the women's movement captured the pill, in both its symbolic and its physical manifestations. Women in Lawrence—and not only young women—interrupted the process of gradual change within the paradigms of population control and sexual morality and offered, instead, revolutionary claims about gender equality, cultural authority, and sexual freedom.

By 1972 any woman in Lawrence—married or unmarried—could obtain birth control pills, free if necessary. This had been true, and widely known, for at least five years. But it wasn't simply access to the pill that was at stake. It was the nature of the access, and the meaning attributed to it, that angered some women. In 1972 two different groups of women in Lawrence challenged the medical men who controlled access to the pill.[12] Though the two groups used different methods and different vocabularies . . . both made claims based on the rights and needs of women themselves and not on those of the larger society. In so doing they stepped outside the discourses of morality and of the population problem and centered the debate over access to the pill in a discourse on women, rights, and freedom.

. . . KU's dean of women, Emily Taylor, was a NOW-style feminist who lobbied for political legislation and university policies supporting equal rights for women. Her office had supported a form of liberal feminism on campus, including a commission on the status of women, and had served as a center of action for some women students and administrators throughout her tenure.

On the other end of the continuum, women in Lawrence's large and diverse counterculture had begun to draw connections between the oppression of minorities and the oppression of women. The women of *Vortex* (the most important underground newspaper) published a women's issue in 1970, and soon afterward the *Lavender Luminary*, a lesbian paper, appeared. W.I.T.C.H. (Women's International Terrorist Conspiracy from Hell) emerged briefly as a local group. Consciousness-raising groups formed. In Lawrence, women were talking with other women about their lives, and those conversations would have repercussions in the world they inhabited.

[In February 1972,] a lecture by radical feminist Robin Morgan inspired these two groups of women to unite as the February Sisters. They took over a university building to voice their demands for full health care for women students, a federally funded child care center on campus, an end to discriminatory employment practices at KU, more women in high-level administrative positions, an affirmative action program, and a department of women's studies. . . . When the Sisters emerged from the building early the next morning, they had won commitments from the administration on a substantial portion of their demands, including the women's health program.

[The Sisters] couched their argument in language echoing the American tradition of rights and freedoms. "We, the February Sisters," their proposal for a human sexuality clinic began, in an invocation of the U.S. Constitution. Arguing that "control of her reproductive functions is a fundamental right of every woman," the Sisters insisted: "The University cannot view the action proposal . . . as a request for additional privileges, but rather as a demand to recognize right [sic] which have been neglected."[13]

It was not simply the right to access these women claimed. . . . More important, these women were rejecting the frameworks of sexual morality and population control that had governed access to contraceptives for more than a decade. The February Sisters condemned the ways that many Americans used concepts of sexual morality to deny women's autonomy and dignity—a fairly obvious and expected critique—but also criticized the efforts of population control groups. . . . These women understood that rationales for contraception based on population control, no less than those based on morality, left room for comments like the one made by the irritated director of student health, Dr. Schwegler, who said that he did so many pelvic exams he sometimes felt like he worked in a whorehouse. The February Sisters and their allies meant to provide a new framework for prescribing the pill that centered around the needs of women themselves and left no room for such demeaning and disrespectful remarks.[14]

After the actions of the February Sisters in February 1972, Watkins student health center officially began prescribing the pill to unmarried women. Somewhat ironically, the following month the Supreme Court ruled that women could not be denied contraceptives on the basis of marital status.

The struggles over the pill in Lawrence were not yet over, however. Even though Watkins offered contraceptives, students still sought the quick access to birth control and the relative anonymity offered by Dr. Clinton's clinic at the public health department. . . . In August 1972, however, the Kansas State Department of Health cut off funding for Clinton's birth control program. The state agency received its funding from the Department of Health, Education, and Welfare (HEW), and it came with federal mandates [that] committed doctors to follow a specified procedure in prescribing the pill, including performing a complete physical exam, pap smear, visual exam for cancer, tuberculin test, hemoglobin, and urinalysis. Clinton . . . refused to perform these tests. . . . Comprehensive medical services for the indigent were not his mandate, he insisted, and he would continue to provide birth control as before, funding it through donations from patients, not to exceed $1 per woman each month. Dr. Schwegler, the director of KU's student health service, who was also serving as chairman of the public health committee, told the Journal World that he was "irritated as a private citizen" over the state health department's action. Clinton prevailed with Lawrence's Board of Health, and his refusal stood. Though the local clinic lost a $12,000 federal grant, it was soon running a $10,000 surplus from donations by birth control patients.[15]

Young women who took the pill Clinton prescribed had sex without fear of pregnancy. They obtained the pill simply by request, without the demeaning act of lying about an impending marriage or the purchase of a cheap gold ring at a drugstore. They were, by and large, grateful. By prescribing the pill, Dr. Clinton inadvertently facilitated the sexual revolution in Lawrence and changed the lives of thousands of young women and their partners. . . .

Notes

1. Elizabeth Rose Siegel Watkins, in "On the Pill: A Social History of Oral Contraceptives in America, 1950–1970" (Ph.D. diss., Harvard University, 1996), pp. 130–131.

2. Pearl S. Buck, "The Pill and the Teen-Age Girl," *Reader's Digest* 92 (April 1968):111, quoted in Watkins, "On the Pill," p. 138.

3. Donald Harting and Leslie Corsa, "The American Public Health Association and the Population Problem," *American Journal of Public Health* 59 (Oct. 1969):1927–29. For a history of population control initiatives, see James Reed, *From Private Vice to Public Virtue* (New York: Basic Books, 1978).

4. Leslie Corsa, "Public Health Programs in Family Planning," *American Journal of Public Health* 56 (Jan. 1966, supplement); Reed, *From Private Vice,* p. 378; Watkins, "On the Pill," pp. 141–142. For statistics on federal funding see "Family Planning Services," Hearing before the Subcommittee on Public Health and Welfare of the Committee on Interstate and Foreign Commerce, House of Representatives, serial no. 91–70 (Washington: GPO, 1970), pp. 190–193.

5. Mary Calderone, "Health Education for Responsible Parenthood: Preliminary Considerations," *American Journal of Public Health* (Jan. 1964): 1735–40.

6. "Should Birth Control Be Available to Unmarried Women?" *Good Housekeeping,* Feb. 1967, p. 14.

7. Will Hardesty, "Birth Control Practices Debated," *University Daily Kansan (UDK),* Nov. 4, 1966.

8. Willard Dalrymple, M.D., "A Doctor Speaks of College Students and Sex," *Journal of the American College Health Association* 15 (Feb. 1967):286.

9. W. Roy Mason Jr., M.D., "Problems of Married College Students: Health Education Implications," *ibid.,* 14 (April 1966):273–274. Frances K. Harding, M.D., "The College Unmarried Population Explosion," *Journal of School Health* 35 (Dec. 1965):450–457.

10. "Over-Interest Closes County Clinic," *UDK,* Feb. 3, 1970; "Birth Control Clinic Closes," *UDK,* Feb. 5, 1970.

11. The student request was in conjunction with the Commission on the Status of Women at KU, sponsored by the dean of women's office. Information here is from "February Sisters Position Statement on a Health Care Program for Women," Addendum II, in Lorna Zimmer personal files, Lawrence, Kan.; "Women—February First Movement," Women's Studies Program Archives, KU (WSPA); Judy Browder, "Women's Decade of History," WSPA; "Campus Problems for Consideration," Council on Student Affairs files, University of Kansas Archives.

12. There was at least one woman physician in Lawrence, and she had been quoted in the *UDK* refusing to prescribe contraceptives to unmarried women. But in this controversy the divisions that appeared publicly were strictly along gender lines.

13. "February Sisters Position Statement on a Health Care Program for Women," in Zimmer files.

14. Judy Henry, "Groups Urge Birth Control," *UDK,* April 4, 1971. Browder, "Women's Decade," and transcript of "February Sisters Panel Discussion," 1987, statement by Mary Coral, in WSPA.

15. "State Drops Birth Control Funding Here," *Lawrence Daily Journal World (JW),* Sept. 22, 1972; "Birth Control Funding Possible," *JW,* Sept. 27, 1972; Tim Pryor, "Health Agency Says Changes Due," *JW,* Jan. 10, 1973; Toby MacIntosh, "Policy on Pills is Controversial," *JW,* Feb. 9, 1973.

JI-YEON YUH

Korean Military Brides: Cooking American, Eating Korean

How do transnational and multiracial families navigate cultural differences? In the aftermath of the Korean War, U.S. military personnel stationed in Asia married "native" women. These marriages were part of a broader trend. American military men going abroad socialized and sometimes married foreign women in many countries.

Couples who wanted to marry across national borders faced challenges. First, they had to seek permission from the U.S. soldier's senior officer, and the U.S. military generally discouraged these unions. The armed forces promoted commercialized sexual interactions by helping establish red-light districts and rest-and-recreation sites. But marriage was more problematic. Racially discriminatory immigration laws were being reversed in the aftermath of World War II

Excerpted from the introduction and ch. 4 of *Beyond the Shadow of Camptown: Korean Military Brides in America* by Ji-Yeon Yuh (New York: New York University Press, 2002). Reprinted by permission of the author and publisher. Notes have been renumbered and edited.

and during the Cold War and the civil rights movement. Even so, it was not until 1967 that the Supreme Court ruling in *Loving v. Virginia* made antimiscegenation laws unconstitutional. Beyond these regulations and laws, interracial and international couples met with many social and cultural challenges.

Ji-Yeon Yuh's essay explores some of these difficult dynamics in Korean-American families in the United States through an examination of foodways—the social and cultural practices associated with producing, preparing, and consuming food. For Yuh and her interview subjects, food is intimate and symbolic. The culinary desires and practices of a wide range of immigrant families reveal profound longings for cultural connection as well as deep conflicts concerning cultural identity.

A young Asian woman in Western clothing steps off a boat and is greeted with flowers by middle-aged Americans. She is a Korean war bride meeting her in-laws for the first time, announces the narrator, who then intones a platitude about embarking on a new American life.[1]

Images similar to this grainy scene from a Korean War-era government newsreel could also be found in popular American magazines such as *Life* and *Time* during the 1940s and 1950s. For the most part, these numerous depictions of war brides featured smiling young women waving from ships as they arrived in the United States to join their American soldier husbands. At the dawning of the so-called American Century, these women, who had left behind all that was familiar for an American man, were seen by the American public as proof positive of America's superiority. The very term "war brides" emphasizes the women's dependence on men and their link to war, conferring an identity on them as human war booty. There were even "war bride ships" that took entire groups of young women from Europe to America to join their husbands.

But despite the burgeoning sense of American superiority that came with victory in World War II, there was some doubt among the general public as to the wisdom of American men marrying foreign women, and couples were made to jump through quite a few bureaucratic hoops before gaining the necessary permission to marry. It was, however, generally assumed and expected that the women were eager to become Americans, both out of wifely love and admiration for the American way of life.[2]

When the brides in question were Asian, these expectations were simultaneously tempered by a keener suspicion and bolstered by a stronger confidence. The generally held view at the time was that women from such alien cultures would not make suitable wives for American men and would likely have great difficulty really becoming American. Their choice of America, however, validated America's confidence in itself as the greatest country on earth. In the early years, legal barriers to Asian immigration greatly restricted the number of Asian war brides permitted to enter America. A series of laws culminating in the 1924 Immigration Act prohibited [most] Asians from immigrating and the War Brides Act of 1945 made no provision that allowed for an exception in the case of Asian women who married American soldiers. It was not until the immigration laws were revised in 1952 that the prohibition against Asian immigration was lifted. Until then, Asian war brides—primarily those from Japan, but also a few from Korea—were allowed to immigrate only through special acts of Congress that established temporary windows of opportunity through which American soldiers could bring home their Asian wives.[3]

Despite suspicions as to their ability to do so, Asian war brides were fully expected to Americanize as quickly as possible. After all, they were now married to American men. That their new lives as Americans were structured by racial, cultural, and gender ideologies privileging white male authority and mainstream American culture is made explicit in the 1952 movie, *Japanese War Bride*. The heroine's troubles are linked to her friendship with Japanese American neighbors. She achieves happiness only by rejecting Japanese Americans and ensconcing herself within a nuclear family household headed by her white American husband. This kind of cinematic portrayal of the expectations that Asian war brides had to meet was based on real-life experiences. A survey of Korean war brides in the 1970s, for example, revealed that their primary conflict was with in-laws who demanded that they renounce

Korean culture, even restricting their contact with fellow Koreans.[4]

For war brides, then, becoming American meant discarding one's culture and forsaking relationships with ethnic kin in order to cleave to the culture of a husband and serve as housewife and mother within an all-American family. In other words, war brides were expected to fulfill a role defined by others. In the case of Asian war brides this was further complicated by the particular suspicions, stereotypes, and racism that Americans directed at Asians.

Between 1950 and 1989 nearly a hundred thousand Korean war brides immigrated to the United States. . . . Until recently, few Koreans or Americans really knew who these women were. They existed as stereotypes at the fringes of consciousness. For Koreans, they were women of questionable character who had married American soldiers because such marriage was their only escape from poverty. For Americans, they were foreigners whom red-blooded American men had inexplicably married. . . . For second-generation Korean Americans, they were the women sitting alone, without husbands, during church service and fellowship, the ones they'd ignore because everyone else did. Their presence has barely been acknowledged and their histories have been marginalized. But their presence is significant and Korean women continue to marry American soldiers every year.[5]

Korean women met and married American soldiers in the historical context of U.S. military domination over South Korea that preceded the 1950–53 Korean War and extends into the present. Thus for Korean war brides, as well as for most other Asian war brides, the term "war bride" is misleading. The majority of Korean war brides married their soldier husbands during times of suspended armed conflict, that is, during times of relative peace, not war.[6] Their marriages are a direct result of ongoing U.S. military troop deployments in South Korea since 1945. U.S. military domination is what made these marriages possible and it has also had far-ranging effects on the tenor of Korean-American marriages. For this reason, . . . I call these women "military brides."

Korean military brides were born and raised in a country that went from being a Japanese colony to being sundered in two by the superpower rivalry between the United States and the Soviet Union. They come from a nation-state, South Korea, that has served the needs of

U.S. national security in the name of anticommunism and defense against North Korea, often at the expense of its own citizens. South Korea has been politically, militarily, and economically subordinated to the United States since before its inception in 1948. . . .[7]

Military brides, like most South Koreans, are in constant negotiation with American cultural hegemony, accepting some of its demands and constraints while seeking to reject others. The neoimperialist relationship between South Korea and the United States has shaped the ways in which these women have experienced and encountered America, as well as the ways in which they are positioned within their families and American society as a whole. Korean military brides have been on the front line of Korea-U.S. cultural and social contact for the past half-century.

. . . As women, they have been shaped by Korean gender ideology to view marriage and motherhood as the ultimate feminine goals. But as women who have married non-Koreans and as women who—regardless of their social background—are stained by presumed association with U.S. military camptowns and prostitution simply because they married an American soldier, they are left standing outside the bounds of both respectable Korean womanhood and authentic Koreanness. Thus military brides are constantly defending their respectability as well as their Korean identity. . . .

[This essay explores one aspect of] the women's attempts to be both good Korean women and good American wives, highlight[ing] food as a form of cultural expression. The stories presented in these pages are based primarily on oral history interviews and fieldwork conducted over a three-year period. The women and families I interviewed and observed were found through personal contacts throughout the Korean immigrant community. The women I met led me to other women, who led me to three regional associations of military brides and a Korean church composed of military brides and their families. I attended meetings and fund-raising dinners held by the associations and became a member of the church for two years, participating in church life. . . .[8]

Throughout my research, I was acutely aware of my outsider-insider status. I too am a Korean woman but I am not a military bride and I'm usually not of the same generation as the women I interviewed for this book. Like them, I'm an immigrant Korean woman, but unlike them, I came as a child rather than as an adult. I am a racial and ethnic minority in America, as they are, but I'm also fluent in English. That fluency has allowed me many privileges, including an advanced education, higher social status, and greater earning power. . . .

Studying the lives and history of Korean military brides has profound ramifications for American history, Asian history, and Asian American history. The history I tell of Korean military brides reveals a history of American involvement in Korea and Korean involvement with America seen from "way, way, way down below."[9] The linkages I make—between the imperialist nature of Korea-U.S. relations and husband-wife dynamics, between pressures to Americanize and Orientalist images of Asian women and family relations—demonstrate that even the most personal of relationships are deeply rooted in and shaped by historical and social circumstances. In this history, I trace the contours of an everyday resistance not against strangers or social superiors in public spaces, but against family intimates in private spaces. It shows us the hollowness of American multiculturalism even as it shows us the ways in which military brides contest that particular hegemony. And it offers us a glimpse of the transformative potential of imagining and locating community beyond the nation.

In the United States, where people of different cultures, races, and ethnicities have encountered each other since the beginning, food is a signifier of difference and identity. It is a terrain where ethnicity is contested, denigrated, and affirmed. It is an arena of struggle between Americanization and adherence to native cultural ways, where the demands are often either-or, but the lives lived are more often constructed from pieces of both.[10]

The experiences of Korean military brides with food mirror their broader experiences as interculturally and interracially married immigrant women. As military brides learned to cook and eat American foods, they enacted a process of assimilation that was demanded of them by husbands, in-laws, and even children who had the weight of the dominant American culture behind them. The marginalization and stigmatization of Korean food within their households represent their cultural isolation within their own families. The incorporation of "palatable" Korean foods into American meals illustrated their own incorporation into their American families, their Korean culture and identity literally consumed as cultural accessories in a process that cultural critic bell hooks has called "consumer cannibalism."[11] At the same time, their perseverance in cooking and eating Korean food and their insistence on maintaining a Korean identity testifies to the limits of the United States' ongoing project of Americanization.

Historian Donna Gabaccia's study of American foodways, *We Are What We Eat*, celebrates the incorporation of ethnic foods into mainstream American culture, drawing a picture of a harmonious and peaceful America full of what she calls multiethnics, people of different backgrounds who eat foods from different backgrounds. In her picture, conflict between native-born Americans and immigrants as expressed in "food fights"—particularly during the first half of the twentieth century—is a thing of the past. No longer do Americans turn up their noses at different foods and try to Americanize the eating habits of immigrants. Instead, they enthusiastically adopt new foods introduced by new immigrants. Eating a mélange of ethnic foods has become the American thing to do. Marriage across cultural and ethnic boundaries is one way, she suggests, that multiethnic peoples and foods are produced.[12]

The experiences of military brides, however, illustrate that "food fights" are not yet over; they are simply conducted more quietly and with less fanfare than in the past. Military brides' narratives reveal that a matrix of power relations surrounds the choice of what foods are cooked and eaten in the families that have resulted from interracial and intercultural marriages.

The first part of the story is that of the deprivation that began with the physical absence of Korean food. Korean military brides who immigrated to the United States in the decades of the 1950s and 1960s, a time when the proverbial land of plenty was basking in unprecedented economic wealth, told me that "here, there was nothing to eat." For these women, accustomed to the tastes and smells of Korean food, American food was not food at all. Like the overwhelming majority of Korean immigrants—indeed, like most immigrants from any country—they craved the foods of their homeland. Women who immigrated in later decades experienced few of the difficulties of their predecessors, for Korean food could be found relatively easily at stores and restaurants catering to the burgeoning

Korean immigrant population. Many of them had already experienced American food in Korea, where hamburgers and pizza, along with McDonald's and KFC, became well known to urban dwellers beginning in the 1980s. Nevertheless, these women also spoke of missing Korean food, for not everything Korean could be found everywhere in America.

The very absence of Korean food in the midst of a bounty of American food is itself a powerful force for Americanization, for immigrants are faced with a choice between eating the food that is available or starving. The choice is obvious. The women ate American food. But their consumption of American food was not necessarily a sign of their Americanization. Even though they ate it, they did not necessarily like it. The women not only longed for Korean food, they also searched for it, invented ways to replicate it, and gave it an emotional loyalty they never developed for the American food they ate out of necessity. . . .

For the military brides who arrived during the 1950s and 1960s, a time when immigration from Korea and other Asian countries was still legally restricted and Korean communities were small and mostly limited to Hawaii and California, the biggest shock was the food. Suddenly, every meal became a painful reminder of having left home. Not only did the absence of Korean food intensify their feelings of homesickness and loneliness, but it also caused physical problems: American food was so unpalatable that eating was difficult and hunger was a constant companion.

One woman, who arrived by boat in 1951 with her soldier husband, said that the most difficult thing during her first years in the United States was craving Korean food, but having to eat American food. Like many other Koreans, she found American food to be heavy, greasy, and bland. The smell and taste of butter, used in so many American foods, was distasteful. "[A]t that time," said Mrs. Mullen, "I was very homesick, and the most difficult thing was food, eating, yes. It was difficult, back then."

The craving for Korean food was so strong that even her dreams were all about food:

Food, Korean food, very very . . . I think about it, I dream about it, in my dreams there is no Korean food, or I am eating Korean food, or Korean food appears, this is what I dream about. When I first came, what I survived on was, well, rice was, you know, but I survived on *American pickle*. And

spaghetti, that's what I survived on. It was terrible, I wanted so badly to eat [Korean] food, it was terrible. Oh, I suffered very very much.

. . . Pickles and spaghetti, however, weren't enough to sustain her.[13] Mrs. Mullen noted in a later conversation that she lost weight during those first years in America. This appears to [have been] common among military brides of her generation. . . .

Craving for Korean food was accompanied by homesickness and a loneliness that resulted from the absence of other Koreans in their lives. Both Mrs. Mullen and Mrs. Crispin spoke in the same breath about missing Korean food and missing Korean people. . . . For Mrs. Crispin as well, missing Korea and missing Korean food were intertwined:

Back then, I was always thinking about Korea, in Korea this is delicious and that is delicious. . . . So when we [she and other Koreans] sit and talk, the talk starts with food and ends with food. In Korea the pears are delicious and so are the apples, and so are the fried pancakes and so on. We talk about this the whole time and then go home, after just smacking our lips the whole time. We were lonesome for people, very lonesome, but back then eating was a big shock as well. The food just wasn't to our taste.

The opportunity to eat Korean food came with meeting other Korean people, illustrating the connection between food and companionship. For Mrs. Mullen, that opportunity came through the first Korean woman she met in America, a woman from Seoul. The friend would sometimes go shopping in New York—a distance of some four hours by car—for Korean food. The two women would then cook and eat Korean food together. . . .

. . . The lack of Korean food was compounded by the inability to cook Korean food. Like many other military brides I interviewed, both Mrs. Mullen and Mrs. Crispin had never learned to cook Korean food. So even though some of the ingredients necessary to make Korean food, such as soy sauce, soybean curd, and Korean vegetables could be found at grocery stores in urban Chinatowns, many women were unable to duplicate the tastes of home.[14] . . .

Red pepper paste and soybean paste, two crucial seasonings in Korean food, were virtually impossible to find during those early years. Unlike soy sauce, they were not available in Chinatown stores, for they are not part of any tradition of Chinese cooking. But the women were inventive and passed their inventions on to each other. Mrs. Crispin learn[ed]to make imitation red pepper paste, [drying] "the heels from loaves of bread, and pour[ing] soy sauce over it. {laughs} When the bread became all soggy, [you] would sprinkle crushed red pepper and mix it all up. And then you call that red pepper paste and eat it!" The taste was not the same as the real stuff, of course. It could not be used for making stews, only as a condiment for rice. . . .

. . . [M]any of the later arrivals also spoke about food when they talked about missing home and being lonely. . . . One woman noted that no matter how prevalent Korean food has become in America, it can't compare with the prevalence of American food. In Korea, she pointed out, one can find Korean food anywhere and everywhere, and the variety is seemingly endless. But even in the so-called multicultural 1990s in America, one still has to know exactly where to look to find Korean food and the repertoire available in Korean restaurants is depressingly standardized and bland.

. . . Many of the military brides I interviewed stated that Korean food in America just doesn't taste as good as Korean food in Korea. . . . [When] Mrs. Crispin described the pears [she loved in Korea,] it was Korea she was always thinking about, not Korean food. It wasn't Korean food that tastes good and which they missed, it was food in Korea. Location was important.

. . . In short, Korean food in America just isn't the same as Korean food in Korea. . . . The issue here is displacement. Displaced from its home, the food apparently loses a certain something. The women's craving for Korean food is linked to a longing for a return home, to a time before . . . [they became] strangers in a strange land.

Throughout the first half of the twentieth century, immigrant and ethnic women were subject to native-born American women's attempts to Americanize immigrant families by teaching the women how to cook and eat American food. It was an urgent project, for Americans feared that America would be "swallowed by foreigners" unless they were properly Americanized. The fact that America at that time was more a conglomeration of regional cultures than a unified national culture made America seem vulnerable to foreign influence and thus endowed the project with greater urgency. . . .

It was also a zero-sum project, for—in keeping with the prevailing sentiment that immigrants must shed their old identities in order to become American—it was not enough to add American food to one's diet. One also had to subtract or substantially alter the familiar foods of home. It was also an endeavor that disguised its fundamental ethnocentricity and nativism under the progressive banner of good health, science, and economical housekeeping. Asian and southern European women were told to feed their families more milk for proper nutrition. Italian women were told not to cook meat, cheese, beans, and macaroni together because the combination allegedly hindered digestion. Mexican women were told to use less tomato and pepper to make blander foods that were purportedly easier to digest and kinder to the kidneys, and were urged to stop the allegedly unsanitary practice of dipping with tortillas into the same pot at the dinner table. And everyone was urged to eat plain, bland, thrifty foods such as mashed potatoes and baked beans.[15]

In these admonitions to immigrant women by American women home economists, nutritionists, and other professionals can be seen several strong and interconnected ideas about food. One is the gendered conceptualization of food preparation as the women's domain; another is the endowment of food with cultural properties, such that what one eats and how it is eaten become markers of group identity.[16] What one ate clearly marked one as either a backward, ignorant immigrant or an educated, modern American. Furthermore, the belief that educating immigrant women would lead to educating and thus Americanizing their entire immigrant families rests on assumptions about women as the bearers of culture and thus the mediating force for Americanization. Although these Americanization-through-food projects fizzled as fears of immigrant hordes receded during the 1940s and 1950s and disparate regions became increasingly bound within a "national culture" disseminated through the mass media and mass commerce, the underlying assumptions about food, gender, and Americanization have remained very much in force.

Thus Korean military brides found themselves subject to pressures to Americanize . . . primarily from husbands, children, and mothers-in-law—people difficult, even dangerous, to ignore precisely because they were intimate family members. There is remarkable consistency in the women's narratives regardless of the time period in question. A woman who came in the 1990s was just as likely as a woman who came in the 1950s to face demands that she cook primarily, or even only, American food. The one difference is that the husbands and in-laws of women who arrived in later decades seem to have been more open to incorporating selected items of Korean food into the household repertoire. This seems connected to a general revival of interest in ethnic foods, however, and is not related to any desire to allow Korean women to maintain their Korean identity.

Although they married Korean women, most husbands do not seem to have been interested in a Korean wife complete with all the cultural trappings of customs, food, and language. . . . [T]hey were looking for women with the traditional feminine values of submissiveness and deference to male authority, and believed that Asian women had such characteristics. They wanted wives who would serve them roast beef and potatoes, with English and a smile. . . . [17]

Expressed in the language of teaching a new wife or new daughter-in-law how to please her husband and adjust to her new environment, the racial and cultural power dynamics of Americanization were effectively hidden in the gender dynamics of marriage. In this matrix of intersecting and overlapping power relations—between mainstream American culture and a "foreign," minority culture, between a neoimperialist United States and a neocolonial Korea, between American men and Korean women, between husband and wife, between primary breadwinner and dependent—Korean women were almost always at a disadvantage. Their acceptance of gender roles often led them into compliance, making overt expressions of Americanization on the part of husbands or in-laws unnecessary. But in acceding to these pressures, as did most of the women I encountered, they were not necessarily undergoing a willing or total Americanization. Rather, their compliance was part of the complex negotiation in which they alternately resisted and complied. . . .

As married women, they took for granted the expectation that it was their duty to cook for their husbands and that this meant cooking what husbands liked to eat. . . . Learning to cook American food, an experience that one woman described as universal for Korean military brides, was one that set them apart from their other immigrant compatriots in an important way. Most Korean immigrants were not interested in learning how to cook non-Korean foods, but instead focused on recreating Korean dishes in an American immigrant setting.[18] For military brides, however, learning to cook American food became one of their primary tasks as they learned how to become good American wives.

. . . [In] the families of Korean military brides, . . . since most American husbands prefer to eat American food, and some even dislike Korean food intensely, whatever Korean cooking ability the wives may possess is virtually useless. In accordance with the husbands' preferences, family meals are characterized by the presence of American food and the absence of Korean food. The wives must either eat American food with their husbands, or eat Korean food alone. Their biracial children also tend to prefer American food. Her son, Mrs. Peterson reported, doesn't like to eat rice, stating that he is an American boy and therefore must eat bread. This seven-year-old boy has already singled out food as a marker of identity, refusing to eat food that he considers foreign to his sense of self. The male prerogative of the husband coupled with the cultural dominance of America leave little room for Korean food at the dining tables of these intercultural and interracial families. Food is a marker of difference and of the accompanying power inequities of which every meal is a potential reminder. . . . Thus, unlike other immigrant women, military brides become the transmitters not of their own familiar cultures, but of the foreign cultures of their husbands. . . .

. . . Despite their own distaste for most American food, learning to cook it was so important that many women considered this task to be at the center of their adjustment to American life. This was also true of military brides who arrived in later years and had few problems eating American food. None of the women I interviewed had ever cooked American food before they married their American husbands, and they all said that they spent a great deal of time and effort learning how to cook to suit their husbands' tastes. Those who could not cook Korean food, or cooked it poorly by their own estimation, noted regretfully that they had had no chance to learn because they were preoccupied with cooking American food for their families. For these women, learning to cook

American food had the result of blocking their acquisition of Korean cooking skills. An important expression of culture and self, food, thus changed dramatically for these women as a result of intermarriage and subsequent migration to the husband's country.

At the same time, every woman I interviewed expressed pride in her ability to cook American food. Several women, such as Mrs. Goldin, said they cooked American food better than Americans, and many noted that their husbands complimented them on their cooking. This pride in meeting the expectations of their husbands and in acquiring new skills cannot be easily dismissed. It can be read as a partial, if problematic, resistance to the denial of Korean identity that their participation in the daily mealtime rituals of family production entails. They may be suppressing their Korean identity, but they are actively building a new life around their American husbands. By learning to cook American food and fulfilling the roles of mother and wife, they were also living up to the traditional ideal of Korean womanhood, which dictates self-sacrifice for the sake of the family.[19] Thus, learning to cook American food and the denial of ethnic self which that entails can be read as an ironic affirmation of their Korean womanhood, a merger of their struggle to be both good American wives and good Korean women....

... The kitchens of these military brides were filled with food products common to middle-class Americans across the nation, from A-1 steak sauce and Heinz ketchup to Oscar Mayer bologna, Kraft American Cheese, and Quaker Instant Oatmeal. This was true regardless of the specific ethnic background of their husbands. Their comments and their kitchens demonstrate that while America may not have a national cuisine, it certainly has national food habits that are readily discernible by newcomers.... These foodways are closely linked to commercialized, processed, and prepared foods whose brands are household names and can be found everywhere from the supermarket to the neighborhood corner grocery.[20]

In addition to salads, bacon, lettuce, and tomato sandwiches, and steak, many women also learned to cook dishes reflecting their husbands' particular cultural backgrounds. Mrs. Weinberg, who came in 1969 with her Jewish American husband, learned to cook blintzes, potato latkes, and chicken soup, among other dishes. With pride, and some self-conscious laughter for complimenting herself, Mrs. Weinberg said that she had become quite a good cook. Mrs. Goldin, who said she can cook American food better than many Americans, learned to cook soul food for her African American husband. Mrs. Bugelli, who arrived in 1959, learned to cook Italian food, including all kinds of Italian cakes and cookies, for her Italian American husband and his two sons.... Despite the presence of ethnic foods, however, standard or mainstream American food seemed to predominate.... Asked whether American food or Jewish food was eaten more often in her home, Mrs. Weinberg replied that Jewish food was eaten occasionally, especially at Passover, but that most meals were "just American."[21] ...

Based on observations of her own family's eating habits and preferences, sociologist Mary Douglas has aptly observed that meals have structures.... Korean meals are structured around a bowl of rice and several side dishes. There are no courses and everything is served at once. The side dishes usually include a bowl of soup or a pot of stew, and always include *kimchi*. Only rice and soup are served in individual portions; other side dishes are served each in its own dish placed at the center of the table. Diners use their own chopsticks or spoons to take mouthfuls of the side dishes. Many of the side dishes, including different varieties of *kimchi*, are prepared in advance and eaten slowly over a period of several days or even several months. Some side dishes actually require advance preparation, since several days or weeks are needed to produce the desired flavor. Eating the same side dishes meal after meal is common.[22]

The structure of American meals, on the other hand, is [typically] a main dish accompanied by two supporters. Families that put together a full dinner usually have a main course (1a) and a first course and dessert (2b). Soup or salad is often served as the first course. The main course usually consists of meat or fish (1a) accompanied by two side dishes (2a) served on the same plate. If rice is served, not only is it unlikely to be Korean-style rice, but it appears as a side dish, not the meal's center. Everything is individually served, and diners do not dip their eating utensils into the same bowls or plates of food. Eating the same thing twice in a row is usually considered to be eating leftovers. Dessert, a common ending to middle-class American meals, has no equivalent in Korean meals. . . .

[And yet, in some families,] Korean foods [were] incorporated into other American food rituals [besides formal meals]. Mrs. Orellana, who arrived in 1991, expressed surprise that her husband, their preschool son, and her parents-in-law enjoyed eating seasoned *keem,* thin sheets of dried laver. *Keem* is a common side dish at Korean meals, where it is eaten wrapped around a spoonful of rice. She then noted that while they also like rice, they never ate *keem* with rice. . . . Instead, to her surprise, they ate the seasoned *keem* like a snack while talking or watching TV, . . . a snack akin to potato chips. . . . [Here,] a Korean food is accepted by the American family, but on their own terms. . . .

This is not to say, however, that the families do not identify the foods as Korean. They do. They are aware that they are eating Korean *keem* and not American potato chips, [or] Korean barbecued beef and rice, not American steak and potatoes. These Korean foods are incorporated into a larger American structure of meals and food habits so that rather than the foods "Koreanizing" American meals, the [practice] "Americanizes" the foods even as they are labeled "Korean." It is one of the steps toward Americanization that various other ethnic foods—pizza, corn chips, tacos, hot dogs, and bagels come to mind—have taken in the course of American history.[23] The new foods serve to enrich, not transform, American culture, and eating them does not necessarily turn Americans into multiethnics.

The interest in Korean food seems linked to a general surge of interest in ethnic foods that began in the 1960s and soared in the 1980s. Mrs. Orellana's mother-in-law, for example, took an interest in foods from different cultures and bought a Korean cookbook in preparation for meeting her new daughter-in-law in 1991. Another woman, who arrived in 1989, said her sister-in-law commented that having a Korean in the family made life more interesting because it allowed them to be close to a different culture. Although friendly interest is preferable to hostility, this does not necessarily place the Korean cultures of the women on par with the American cultures of the husbands and in-laws. The husbands and in-laws can choose whether or not to learn about Korean culture and eat Korean food, that is, they can choose whether or not to make their lives more interesting, but the women do not have similar freedom of choice regarding American culture. Nor does their acquisition of American culture serve to strip it of context and transform it into a consumer item for pleasure and cultural enrichment. When the husbands, children, and in-laws of military brides consume selected items of Korean food, this is not necessarily evidence of biculturality or multiethnicity. Especially in households that otherwise devalue and stigmatize the Korean culture of the wife and mother, it is just as likely to be a shallow gesture that appropriates bits and pieces of Korean culture for a variety that adds "spice" to American life.[24] . . .

[A] pattern of eating American food with their husbands and Korean food when alone was common among military brides I met. . . . Those who insisted on eating Korean food daily often found themselves cooking two sets of meals, serving one and then eating the other alone. Rather than a family affair eaten together that symbolizes and reaffirms the unity of the family, . . . meals became individual affairs eaten separately that symbolized the internal cultural dissonance within the family. . . .

. . . [Mrs. Peterson reported that her husband] didn't mind her cooking and eating Korean food. He rarely complained about the smell of Korean food, she said, except once in a while when she cooked *doenjang* stew or *kimchi* stew. This was a common refrain among women who cooked Korean food at home: even if he doesn't eat it, at least he doesn't complain much about the smell when I do. The feeling seemed to be that they were among the lucky ones. . . .

Those who were unable to keep Korean food at home spoke of attending Korean functions where food was served, simply to eat some Korean food as well as to see some Korean faces, or of calling up other military brides and getting themselves invited over for a Korean lunch. Some women told me that one of the most enjoyable aspects of going to Korean churches was the food. Gatherings of military brides, such as the monthly meetings of military bride organizations, invariably include Korean food. Even their fund-raising dinners—aimed at a mixed audience of Koreans and Americans—usually feature Korean food. Every military bride who spoke with me about participating in such organizations noted that the chance to eat Korean food was a major attraction. . . .

Although they maintain their families through the cooking and serving of meals that suppresses their Korean culture and identity, and although they live under constant awareness of the marginalization of their cultures, military brides do retain their identities as Korean women. They negotiate through and around the suppression and marginalization, finding ways to express their Korean selves and to eat the foods they crave. Even if, like Mrs. Mullen, they rarely eat these foods, their views of the tastiness of Korean food versus American food tend to favor Korean food. They speak as if it were natural that they should concede the family territory to American food but reserve a slice of personal space for Korean food, for themselves. Eating Korean food is a way of expressing Korean identity, of partaking of ethnic community, of being connected to kin, hometown, and fellow immigrants. The women spoke of a strong need for the comforts of the familiar, for affirmation of self, and for emotional sustenance. Eating Korean food and retaining their loyalties to it appear to be a way of meeting these needs and keeping body and soul together . . .

The women at New York's Rainbow Center, a women's collective of and for Korean military brides, know that food is more than just food. They have experienced its healing powers. Many of the women who come to the Rainbow Center come after suffering years of abuse. As a result, some have emotional and mental problems. When center women know that a new woman is due to arrive, they make sure that the house is redolent with the fragrance of Korean food. The new arrivals are treated to meal after meal of Korean food: *doenjang* stew, *kimchi* stew, *kimchi,* and lots of rice. The dominant language at the center is Korean, the atmosphere is familial, and the kitchen is filled with Korean food and Korean eating utensils. In this deliberately Korean atmosphere, said the center's founder and director, the Rev. Geumhyun Yeo, the women slowly come back to life. During some twenty years of working with military wives, she said, she came to realize that many of the emotional and mental problems that troubled military brides are linked to their deprivation

of Korean food and Korean companionship. Surrounding them with these things is therefore an essential part of the Rainbow Center's program of resuscitating abused military brides, she said.[25]

While preparing our dinner after our formal oral history session, Mrs. Crispin talked about the different ways of cooking seaweed soup, which was on our menu for the evening. Asking me how my mother cooked it, she said that she usually first sautéed the seaweed and dried anchovies in sesame oil, then added hot water and simmered it until done. My aunt, I replied, usually used bits of beef instead of dried anchovies, while my vegetarian mother used neither but added only a different variety of seaweed that is used primarily to make broth. Women from the coastal regions of Korea used fresh clams and other shellfish, Mrs. Crispin noted, recalling her childhood years spent in those regions. She then sighed a little and said, "It's more than just fun to talk about this, don't you think?" Noting that she had lived in the United States for so long that it seemed like home, she said that times like this, cooking and eating Korean food with another Korean woman, even a stranger like myself, gave her an indescribable feeling. Searching for words to express herself, she said, "Maybe something like drinking water after being thirsty for a really long time."

NOTES

1. Seen in the documentary *Women Outside,* by Hye-Jung Park and J. T. Takagi (Third World Newsreel, 1996).

2. For example, "War Brides Arriving in U.S.," *Life,* February 18, 1946, p. 27.

3. Chinese American men in the armed forces also brought home Chinese women as brides. As citizens of China, an American ally during World War II, these women were exempt from immigration restrictions against Asians; about six thousand Chinese war brides came under the War Brides Act. This influx of women helped even skewed gender ratios in Chinese American communities. See Sucheng Chan, *Asian Americans: An Interpretive History* (Philadelphia: Temple University Press, 1991), p. 140. Apparently, few of the Chinese war brides married non-Chinese Americans.

4. *Japanese War Bride,* 91 min., directed by King Vidor.

5. Daniel B. Lee, "Korean Women Married to Servicemen," in *Korean American Women Living in Two Cultures,* ed. Young In Song and Ailee Moon (Los Angeles: Academia Koreana, Keimyung-Baylo University Press, 1997), pp. 94–123.

6. The Korean War ended with a truce, not a peace treaty, and thus the United States remains officially at war on the Korean peninsula despite the absence of outright armed conflict. This is why South Korea is categorized as a combat zone by the U.S. military and soldiers posted there are given hardship pay.

7. See Bruce Cumings, *The Origins of the Korean War*, 2 vols. (Princeton: Princeton University Press, 1981 and 1990), and, Cumings, *Korea's Place in the Sun: A Modern History* (New York: W. W. Norton, 1997).

8. All interviews for this study were conducted in Korean and translated into English by the author. All names of military brides are pseudonyms, and some identifying traits have been changed as necessary to protect confidentiality.

9. I first heard this phrase during a talk Robin D. G. Kelley gave at the University of Pennsylvania in 1993–94 about southern blacks, resistance, and the civil rights movement.

10. Roland Barthes, "Toward a Psychosociology of Contemporary Food Consumption," in *Food and Culture*, ed. Carole Counihan and Penny Van Esterik (New York: Routledge, 1997), p. 21. The ideal of Americanization, one that posits a white America and things white American as superior, has remained strong throughout the twentieth century. One important measure of Americanization has been food.

11. bell hooks, "Eating the Other: Desire and Resistance," in *Eating Culture*, ed. Ron Scapp and Brian Seitz (Albany: State University of New York Press, 1998), 181–200.

12. Donna Gabaccia, *We Are What We Eat* (Cambridge, Mass.: Harvard University Press, 1998).

13. Spaghetti became a popular foreign dish among many Koreans, perhaps because it contains garlic and because noodles topped with sauce is a familiar form of food to Koreans.

14. It is common for Korean women to know only the rudimentary basics of cooking when they marry and to learn how to cook as young wives under the direction of their mothers-in-law. For military brides, marriage to an American can thus mean that they never learn to cook Korean food.

15. Gabaccia, *We Are What We Eat*, pp. 122–48. See also George Sanchez, "'Go after the Women': Americanization and the Mexican Immigrant Woman, 1915–1929," in *Unequal Sisters: A Multicultural Reader in U.S. Women's History*, ed. Vicki L. Ruiz and Ellen Carol Dubois (New York: Routledge, 1990), pp. 284–97.

16. See, for example, Marjorie L. DeVault, *Feeding the Family: The Social Organization of Caring as Gendered Work* (Chicago: University of Chicago Press, 1991); Jacqueline Burgoyne and David Clarke, "You Are What You Eat: Food and Family Reconstitution," in *The Sociology of Food and Eating*, ed. Anne Murcott (Aldershot, England: Gower Publishing House, 1983); and M. Ekstrom, "Class and Gender in the Kitchen," in *Palatable Worlds: Sociocultural Food Studies*, ed. E. L. Furst, R. Prattala, M. Ekstrom, L. Holm, and U. Kjaernes (Oslo: Solum Forlag, 1991).

17. Ji-Yeon Yuh, *Beyond the Shadow of Camptown: Korean Military Brides in America* (New York: New York University Press, 2002), ch. 3.

18. Min Pyong Gap et al., *Migug Sok-eu Hangugin (Koreans in America)* (Seoul: Yurim Munhwa Sa, 1991), pp. 179–80.

19. See Laurel Kendall and Mark Peterson, ed., *Korean Women: View from the Inner Room* (New Haven, Conn.: East Rock Press, 1983) Sandra Mattielli, ed., *Virtues in Conflict: Tradition and the Korean Woman Today* (Seoul: Royal Asiatic Society. Korea Branch, 1977); Yung-Chung Kim, ed. and trans., *Women of Korea*, by the Committee for the Compilation of the History of Korean Women (Seoul: Ewha Women's University Press, 1976); and Alternative Culture, ed., *Jubu: Geu Makhim-gwa Teu-im (Housewife: That Closing and Opening)* (Seoul: Alternative Culture Press, 1990).

20. Sidney Mintz, *Tasting Food, Tasting Freedom* (Boston: Beacon Press, 1996), has observed that America does not have a cuisine per se but a distinctive way of eating characterized by fast food, instant food, frozen food, canned food, and other ready-to-cat and easy-to-prepare edibles.

21. One study of white Americans shows that while eating the foods of one's own ethnic background (Italian, Polish, etc.) is the most common ethnic-related activity (reported by 47 percent of respondents), such foods are eaten less than once a month by the majority of these respondents; Richard D. Alba, *Ethnic Identity: The Transformation of White America* (New Haven, Conn.: Yale University Press, 1990), pp. 79–80, 85–86. See also Mary C. Waters, *Ethnic Options: Choosing Identities in America* (Berkeley: University of California Press, 1990).

22. Mary Douglas, "Deciphering a Meal," in *Food and Culture*, ed. Carole Counihan and Penny Van Esterik (New York: Routledge, 1997), pp. 36–54. My description of the structure of Korean meals is based on my life experience eating meals in middle-class Korean families in Korea and in America, plus discussions with other Korean women about what constitutes a proper Korean meal. Fancy Korean meals served in restaurants vary in structure, and some include courses.

23. Gabaccia, *We Are What We Eat*, discusses the incorporation of ethnic food items into American culture.

24. On the superficial incorporation of aspects of foreign cultures other than food, see Kristin L. Hoganson, *Consumer's Imperium: The Global Production of American Domesticity, 1865–1920* (Chapel Hill: University of North Carolina Press, 2007).

25. Similarly, Indochinese and Hmong immigrant women speak of eating their native foods as a means of healing the illnesses and emotional traumas that come from the stress of cultural change. See Donna Gabaccia, *From the Other Side: Women, Gender, and Immigrant Life in the U.S., 1820–1990* (Bloomington: Indiana University Press, 1994), p. 121.

LISA LEVENSTEIN
Hard Choices at 1801 Vine: African American Women, Child Support, and Domestic Violence in Postwar Philadelphia

Drawing lines between the deserving and the undeserving, the worthy poor and the unworthy poor, the independent and the dependent—along with the stigmatizing of the dependent—has been an enduring part of our history. In this essay, Lisa Levenstein explores the efforts of working-class African American women to claim public protection against domestic violence and to seek economic support in the years after World War II. Examining the records of the Philadelphia Municipal Court, she finds that poverty and domestic violence were inextricably entangled in ways that public officials often found difficult to appreciate. The straightforward claims of women citizens for entitlements that the law provided— Aid to Families with Dependent Children, for example—all too easily were translated by judges and social workers into reproach: blame of fathers who could not support their children, blame of women who could not "hold" a husband, blame of mothers who could not care for their children and simultaneously hold a full- time job. Yet African American women continued to turn to the Philadelphia Municipal Court, where they had some real success in persuading judges to recognize their claims and meet their needs.

For their part, legal officials began with the assumption that the wage levels sufficient to enable a single male earner to support his wife and children—the "family wage"—were universally available. They tended to discount the racial discrimination that excluded many African Americans from the secure work force. What other assumptions does Levenstein find that court officials were likely to make when they assessed the charges made by African American women? What risks did African American women take when they turned to the courts? What did they want court officials to understand?

In a Philadelphia criminal courtroom on November 18, 1947, Judge Gay Gordon called Janice Carson, an African American woman in her early twenties, to testify in an assault and battery case that she had brought against her husband. When questioned, Mrs. Carson told the court that she and Vince Carson had had a rocky marriage with constant domestic vio- lence both before and after he served in the army during World War II. The most recent in- cident had occurred after she told Vince that she was pregnant with their second child: He "beat me and he struck me. . . . He was chok- ing me and he knocked me against a radiator, and the night after that I had a miscarriage."

When Vince Carson took the stand, he ad- mitted that he had beaten Janice. However, he stated that the incident had occurred during an argument "about her allowance" and that he had hit her in self-defense. "She slapped me first," he testified, "and I just lost thy head and slapped her—" "Your Honor, I never struck

Excerpted and slightly revised by the author from ch. 2 of *A Movement Without Marches: African American Women and the Politics of Poverty in Postwar Philadelphia* by Lisa Levenstein (Chapel Hill: University of North Carolina Press, 2009). Reprinted by permission of the author and publisher. Notes have been edited and renumbered.

him first," interrupted Mrs. Carson. "Everyone knows he fights me." At this point, Judge Gordon intervened in the dispute. "You talk too much," he told Mr. Carson. The judge proceeded to call Mr. Carson a "brute," told him that the "seeds of murder" were planted in his home, and warned him that he would end up in the electric chair one day.

After a few more questions, Judge Gordon turned to Mrs. Carson and asked, "Madam, what do you want me to do with him?" Mrs. Carson explained that although she had separated from Mr. Carson, she still needed his financial support because she had been in poor health since the miscarriage and could not seek employment to support herself and her son. She asked for a "peace bond," a type of bail that would give Mr. Carson freedom and allow him to look for a job as long as he did not beat her. The judge told Mrs. Carson that Mr. Carson belonged in jail, but that he would grant the peace bond. The day after his release, Vince Carson attacked his wife, tore her clothing, and beat her up.[1]

In the years after World War II, working-class African American women like Janice Carson turned to the Philadelphia Municipal Court for economic support and protection from domestic violence ... The legal system was geared toward preserving two-parent families and limiting the parent financial support that the government provided to poor single mothers through the Aid to Dependent Children (ADC) program. However since judges strongly believed that men needed to fulfill their roles as breadwinners and owed women physical protection and financial support, women could harness the court's biases to work in their favor. Most women won their cases, often obtaining either a small amount of money or limited protection from domestic violence.

Of all the public institutions in the city, it was in the municipal court that the intimate connections between poverty and domestic abuse became most clearly visible. During years when civil rights activists focused on violence outside the home, and well before middle-class feminists would interpret spousal abuse as a political issue, working-class African American women placed the issue of domestic violence squarely on the public stage. Like Mrs. Carson, many viewed their need for protection from violence as integrally linked to their need for financial assistance and struggled because the municipal court separated charges of assault from charges for support. They had to choose between freedom from violence and freedom from hunger, even though gaining one often meant sacrificing the other.

... Instituted in early twentieth-century cities throughout the country, municipal courts worked under the assumption that common crimes should be addressed in a comprehensive manner that promoted individual and social rehabilitation. The Philadelphia Municipal Court had been created by the state legislature in 1913 in response to agitation by white middle-class social reformers.... Although ... it was a court of record and had the power to imprision offenders, like most twentieth-century municipal courts, it sought not only to punish, but also to assist, educate, and discipline its clients. Legal authorities conducted thorough investigations of their clients' life circumstances and provided medical testing, counseling, and other social services. To provide specialized attention to different types of cases, the court was divided into five divisions: civil, criminal, domestic relations, juvenile, and misdemeanant. ... [2]

African American women's legal dealings usually took place in the courthouse that handled domestic and juvenile cases, which they referred to by its address as "1801 Vine." Marcelle Blackwell, who grew up in postwar Philadelphia, described 1801 Vine as the "most famous address in the city of Philadelphia" because of the frequency of women's visits.[3] Opened in 1940, on the eighteenth block of Vine Street, a wide, central thoroughfare for municipal buildings in Philadelphia, its architecture exuded a formality that distinguished it from most other public institutions in the city. The imposing limestone structure had a colonnaded front. Grand front doors opened onto an expansive main hallway with high ceilings, chandeliers, murals, and terrazzo floors. ... A series of murals throughout the building symbolized the "uplifting" work that the court envisioned itself performing—reuniting families and rehabilitating juvenile delinquents.

... Legal rituals underscored the court's function as an institution that enforced the rule of law. Although most trials were conducted without juries, women had to swear before signing petitions or testifying in front of judges, and their statements were carefully recorded by court employees. They interacted mainly with middle-class, often college-educated, interviewers and probation officers who were the foot soldiers of the court's efforts to collect and

organize personal and demographic information about clients. . . . In the mid-1950s, African
Americans comprised less than one-quarter of
the city's population, but black women were half
of the plaintiffs in nonsupport cases and two-
thirds of the plaintiffs in assault and battery
cases. Although African American and white
women both experienced domestic violence and
nonsupport, black women had less access to alternative resources than did white women and
were more likely to take legal action against men.

Women who pressed charges in the municipal court confronted judges whose outlooks
exemplified some of the limitations of postwar
liberalism in meeting their needs. In the 1950s,
the court had fourteen judges, elected by city
voters to ten-year terms. All of the judges who
worked in the domestic relations court were
white men, usually Democrats from Italian
American, Polish American, or Jewish backgrounds.[4] Although many of them were active
in a range of civic organizations and known for
their humanitarianism, they felt little sympathy
for the plight of struggling African Americans.
Most believed that two-parent families with
male breadwinners were superior to other
family forms. They looked down on unmarried
mothers, particularly those who received welfare, and expressed contempt for fathers who
could not adequately support their wives and
childen.

Most women who approached the municipal court sought child support or protection
from domestic violence. Their suits took three
main forms. Unmarried women's suits against
the fathers of their children for financial support, called fornication and bastardy, were
handled in the women's criminal division,
making it ambiguous exactly who legal officals
believed should be on trial.[5] In the 1950s, on average, nearly two thousand women pressed
these charges each year. The domestic relations
court handled married women's financial support cases, usually in the form of nonsupport
charges against their husbands. These cases
numbered over four thousand each year. . . .
Finally, assault and battery charges brought by
women against violent men were handled in
the criminal division until 1952, when the domestic relations division took control of their
adjudication.[6] The court usually handled over
six hundred of these cases each year. Although
women did not press charges of assault as
often as they pressed charges of nonsupport,
the large number of assault cases challenges

feminist scholarship that has portrayed this
period as a time when women rarely used the
legal system to prosecute domestic violence.[7]

The rulings in women's assault and battery cases varied widely because judges did
not have formal procedures in place for dealing with them. Prior to 1952, the municipal
court sent abused women to the magistrates'
courts for an initial hearing. Some women settled their cases with the magistrates, securing
warnings, peace bonds, and occasionally jail
sentences for their husbands. Those not satisfied with the magistrates' hearings could pay
a $10 fee to obtain a warrant for their hus-
bands' arrest and press assault and battery
charges in the criminal division of the municipal court. During the criminal trials, municipal
court judges almost always tried to reconcile
couples. However, when reconciliation proved
impossible, judges used their own discretion to
settle the disputes, finding some men not guilty
and requiring others to post peace bonds or
go to jail.

. . . The legal system did not address or help
remedy the connections between poverty and
domestic abuse: women who were financially
dependent on their husbands were more vulnerable to abuse, and abuse could reinforce
women's poverty by injuring and isolating
them. If women with abusive husbands chose
to seek support orders, they were left without
protection from violence. If they pressed criminal charges and their husbands ended up in jail,
they were left without financial support. Faced
with this impossible choice, some abused
women who relied on men's financial support
sought a compromise: They pressed assault
charges and then asked judges to give their husbands a warning or put them on probation,
hoping that this would allow men to continue
earning money while helping curb subsequent
episodes of violence. As Mrs. Carson's case illustrates, this strategy could backfire by making
men so furious that they continued the abuse.

Nonsupport . . . cases had far more predictable outcomes. Married women seeking to
press nonsupport charges met with an interviewer, usually a woman, who recorded detailed information about their cases and their
backgrounds. The interviewer then contacted
women's husbands and requested their presence in court. Probation officers investigated
men's places of employment to verify their
wages and sometimes conducted home visits to

inspect couples' living arrangements. Seven to ten days after the women's initial contact with the court, most men came in for their meetings with interviewers. Interviewers spoke individually with the men and then met with the couples together in one or more joint conferences. No matter what interviewers learned about the men's and women's relationships, they tried to convince couples to reconcile. Most women refused and insisted on filing a formal petition for a trial. The cases then joined a line of hundreds of other similar cases waiting for a trial, a backlog caused by the large numbers of women pressing nonsupport charges and the limited number of judges assigned to the cases. On average, it took ten to fourteen weeks before women received hearings. The trials themselves usually lasted less than five minutes because judges were under tremendous pressure to move quickly. Even when men painted unflattering portraits of women's behavior by complaining about their promiscuity, failure to perform domestic chores, or excessive nagging, court policy was formulated so that judges almost always ruled in women's favor and awarded them financial support.[8]

Fornication and bastardy cases, which concerned unmarried couples, involved similar procedures, but were usually settled more quickly. To secure benefits, women had to press charges within two years of the conception of a child. Because the couples were not married, interviewers did not try to persuade them to reconcile. Instead, during the initial meetings and fieldwork inquiries, court workers pressured men to admit paternity and agree to pay child support. Most men recognized that they had a slim chance of winning their cases, acknowledged that they had fathered the child, and agreed to comply with a support order. Fewer than one in ten cases went to trial, and the mothers who testified were usually awarded financial support.

The legal priorities that undergirded the policies favoring reconciliation and men's support of women and children reflected judges' commitment to the family-wage system and to preventing women's dependence on the state. Family-wage ideology envisioned men earning a wage that was sufficient to support a wife and children at home. This ideal was unattainable for most working class African Americans; men could rarely obtain stable, well-paying jobs, and many women with young children were gainfully employed. State authorities recognized that African American women held jobs because African American men's wages were insufficient, but they did not believe that women should be the primary breadwinners for their families or head their own households. Judges claimed that households with married couples and male breadwinners were morally superior to those headed by single mothers. They also preferred two-parent households for fiscal reasons because most married women did not qualify for welfare. The court's Annual Reports noted that interviewers tried to "effect a reconciliation . . . and a reestablishment of wholesome family relationships" to save "the community many millions of dollars" in welfare payments.[9] In cases in which reconciliations proved impossible, judges promoted support orders in order to diminish women's welfare checks. . . .

Women often faulted the court for failing to ensure that they received adequate financial assistance. Many criticized the judges' practice of calculating support orders according to men's wages, which typically awarded them one-third of men's pay. Since most men who came before the court held low-wage jobs, most women received very small stipends. Jessie Redd observed, "When you take a man into court you hardly get enough to pay a babysitter."[10] The fact that the court was notoriously slow and inefficient in delivering support checks on time exacerbated the problem. . . . Even more troubling for many women was the court's failure to compensate them for the high rates of male noncompliance. In 1960, 70 percent of the support orders in effect were not being paid.[11]

To address the problem of noncompliance, judges advocated changing men's behavior, a solution that did not take into account many working-class men's precarious economic circumstances. Annual Reports attributed men's default to willful neglect, charging that men found "devious and sundry" ways to "escape their family obligations." . . . This approach did not take into account how unemployment and low-wage jobs made it difficult for many men—especially African American men—to support families. . . . When there was a sharp increase in the cost of living just after World War II, many men returned to court to get their support orders decreased. That many women returned to have their orders increased for the very same reason illustrates a fundamental problem with court policies that made poor women and children directly dependent on poor men for their livelihood.[12]

Many men charged that they suffered from the court's financial support policies. Those who had remarried, lost their jobs, or had to care for parents or other family members usually found support orders financially burdensome. Particularly in cases involving unmarried mothers, the court's policy of ruling in favor of women was so entrenched that men had little chance of being found innocent even if they did not believe that they had fathered the child. Throughout the postwar period, legal officials engaged in periodic crackdowns on delinquent accounts in which field-workers tracked down men and sometimes even arrested them at their places of employment. Authorities experimented with jail terms and garnished wages; in 1959, 463 men were jailed for nonpayment of support orders. Judges justified the crackdowns by emphasizing that men's avoidance of child support resulted in increased welfare payments to women, claiming that it was "the state and not the wife—who suffers when the husband fails to meet the court order." By laying part of the blame for welfare expenditures on unpaid support orders, judges suggested that African American men contributed to the immorality and fiscal irresponsibility that they associated with ADC.[13]

Working-class African American women insisted that they, not the state, were the victims of men's noncompliance. Thousands of women lived in precarious situations, never assured of receiving financial support because the legal and welfare system forced them to depend on men's irregular contributions. Arlene Starks remarked: "Maybe the next week I'll get a check. Maybe the following week I'll get a check. Now the next two weeks I don't get no check. See, that keeps me off base all the time." Court policies stipulated that men had to default on four consecutive payments before women could issue a complaint at the Department of Accounts. After women reported the nonpayment, probation officers often instructed them to track down men themselves to find the reason for the defaults. . . .

Throughout the 1950s, nearly seven thousand women returned to court each year to complain of men's noncompliance. Many women needed their small support checks so desperately that they returned five to fifteen times over the course of several years when men refused or were unable to pay.[14]

Even when women managed to get their husbands back into court, they did not always receive compensation for missed payments. Several years after Corrine Elkins pressed charges, her husband stopped paying his support order. When she took him back to court, "he was $4,800 in arrears." To Mrs. Elkins's dismay, "The judge dismissed $2,000 of it. He said, 'Well, just get rid of $2,000 of it, and you owe $2,800, and you can pay $5.00 extra each week.'" Knowing that this ruling would have little effect on her husband's behavior, Mrs. Elkins said that she "came to the conclusion, you've got to do things yourself, girl" and started putting in more overtime, working twelve to sixteen hours a day, six or seven days each week. With her arduous schedule and decent city job, Mrs. Elkins could get by without her missed support payments. Most poor mothers could not.[15]

When the court advocated policies that ensured women's financial dependence on men, why did it fail so consistently in enforcing them? First, enforcement procedures were expensive since, as women knew from experience, it could take weeks to track down men and verify their wages. By forcing women to find and discipline men themselves, the court saved money. . . . Second, because welfare administrators decreased women's ADC checks after they pressed nonsupport charges, the state conserved money simply by issuing a support order, regardless of whether or not judges enforced it. Third, as historian Anna R. Igra has argued, in an era in which the "taint of corruption . . . adhered to state spending," the court's financial support policies performed an important symbolic function. By strongly advocating support orders, public authorities . . . could demonstrate both their desire to conserve state monies and their adherence to social norms concerning men's responsibilities to their wives and children.[16]

In most cases, women made carefully calculated decisions about their use of the court. Taking legal action was an ordeal, requiring regular visits to court, several interviews, and a great deal of paperwork. Those with small children found the process particularly difficult. Bell Jackson described a typical visit: "My children and I spent almost six hours in court. I took them at 9:30 that morning and we didn't get out until 3:00 that afternoon . . . I spent my last money getting there, and all that time.

And what happened? Nothing, except we discussed why he wasn't staying with us and how come we broke up, which I've been over a lot of times." Prior to initiating such frustrating procedures, women took stock of their circumstances and tried to decide whether the assistance they could receive from the court was worth the costs.[17] . . .

Most ADC recipients tried to avoid going to court because they risked losing money by pressing charges. The fathers of their children usually could not keep up with support orders, and since welfare caseworkers subtracted the dollar amount of support orders from their ADC checks and rarely provided compensation when men defaulted, taking legal action was a potential financial burden, not a help. Women on decent terms with the fathers of their children generally preferred to receive full welfare grants with no court order, supplemented "under the table" with informal gifts from men.

Some women tried to avoid getting involved with the court because of the humiliation that frequently accompanied the process of taking legal action. Pursuing assistance from the court was never publicly maligned in the way that seeking welfare was, but it was still tarnished by its association with low-income Philadelphians. When Hazel Weinberg, a Jewish woman, went to court to press nonsupport charges, she did not return after her first visit because the interviewers were rude and condescending and she found the process "degrading." Many African American women dreaded testifying in court because the judges were well-known for publicly condemning their reliance on ADC and claiming that they neglected their children. Whether or not they received welfare, all black women felt vulnerable to judges' wrath. Joan Park, a financially secure working-class African American woman, explained that she "wouldn't be caught dead in court" because she considered herself an upstanding member of her community and did not want to subject herself to the indignities involved in pursuing legal action.[18]

The women who decided to press nonsupport charges frequently had financial troubles that led them to believe that even a meager court order would make a positive difference in their lives. . . . Ada Morris, a welfare recipient, explained the importance of her small support check to her livelihood: "I sit down on the first of the month . . . and I count my money

up—to who I owe. . . . My rent comes first. My gas comes next. My food bill . . . comes next. . . . If I don't get nothing from him—well, I can't pay." For women like Mrs. Morris, who struggled each month to make ends meet, even a small stipend made a difference.[19]

Women who pressed domestic abuse charges tended to come from slightly more financially stable homes than those who pursued nonsupport charges and considered their need for physical protection to be their most pressing concern. They were rarely middle-class, but they were often not completely impoverished either. Although some very poor abused women like Mrs. Carson pressed assault charges, others were either deterred by the $10 fee (until 1952, when the fee was waived) or prioritized financial support over protection from violence. . . .

Most abused women decided to avoid legal action completely. Some lived in an acute state of terror with extremely violent and volatile husbands. They were unable or unwilling to leave their marriages and feared that pressing charges would only make the abuse worse. Charlotte Elkins decided to "hang in there" with her husband while "getting my butt beat" for thirteen years because of the "mental abuse" that accompanied his physical violence. She stated that her husband's verbal and physical assaults made her feel worthless and convinced her that she would be unable to survive on her own. Many women who did not go to court resisted the abuse in other ways, escaping to friends' and relatives' houses, attempting to protect their children, and fighting back. Catherine Sanderson recalled standing up to her husband when he beat her. "I sure would . . . hit him back," she explained. "He wasn't my father." Corrine Elkins never fought back until the night that she decided to leave her husband: "He came home . . . and got crazy, and I went for the kitchen knife . . . and . . . really tried" to kill him.[20]

When women made decisions about their pursuit of legal action, they considered their responsibility for children, access to alternative resources, employment opportunities, and experiences of domestic violence. They also took into account a wide range of facts about their husbands and boyfriends: how much money men made, whether they were abusive or unfaithful, and how involved they were with their children. Most women only pressed financial support charges against men who had jobs because they knew that unemployed men did not have any money to give them.

While legal authorities assumed that all African American men who did not provide for their families were irresponsible, African American women had a different and more nuanced definition of nonsupport. Recognizing that racial discrimination made it difficult for the most dedicated husband and father to earn enough to support his wife and children, they did not condemn all men who failed to provide them with financial resources. Instead, most African American women reserved charges of nonsupport for cases in which men deliberately withheld funds from their families, complaining about men squandering their wages on alcohol, other women, or luxury items, instead of rent, food, and clothing for their families. For some married women, the discovery that their husbands had been cheating on them further galvanized them to press nonsupport charges. Unmarried women sometimes responded similarly when they learned that their boyfriends had wives. In other cases, unmarried women may have only had casual contact with the father of their children and pressed charges in court because they had nothing to lose.[21] . . .

Many women who maintained cordial relationships with the fathers of their children found that even the threat of legal action provided them with considerable leverage when negotiating financial support. Because of the strength of their community information networks, women and men who had never set foot in court knew from other people's experiences that women would almost always win financial support cases. Men understood that they would be saddled with a court order and subjected to humiliating treatment from legal authorities, and women knew that men would be angry and would rarely pay regularly. Many women decided that, rather than alienate men by pressing charges, they were better off having men feel indebted to them for not pursuing legal action. The undesirability of legal action gave some leverage to women like Beverly Jordan, who was separated with one child and worked in a coat factory in postwar Philadelphia. Every year, Mrs. Jordan was laid off for two to three months during slow seasons around Christmas and Easter. When this occurred, she would phone her ex-husband and ask for money for food and for her daughter's Christmas present, threatening to take him to court if he did not comply. . . .

In women's dealings with the court, they frequently challenged legal authorities' attempts to collect detailed personal information. Interviewers sought to compile extensive files documenting women's backgrounds and grievances, while field-workers investigated men's earnings and employment records and made home visits to ask about children's school attendance and inspect women's living conditions. Unmarried mothers had to provide detailed descriptions of their relationships with the fathers of their children, the date of the sexual intercourse that produced the child, and accounts of their previous sexual experiences. Many women refused to give court interviewers full access to their private lives, falsifying information or refusing outright to answer questions that they deemed too personal. . . .

One of the only times that interviewers and judges did not attempt to challenge or pry into women's decisions about their private lives was when women withdrew their assault and battery charges against their husbands, which occurred in approximately one-third of all abuse cases. On the witness stand, these women usually minimized the abuse and told judges that they had changed their minds and did not want to press charges. Even when women testified that their husbands had "busted my head open" or stabbed them with knives, if they stated that they wanted to return home with their husbands, judges made no attempt to dissuade them. Most judges feared that if couples separated or the men received jail sentences, the wives would seek public assistance.[23] . . .

. . . Working-class African American women faced problems at every level of the criminal justice system but still refused to give up on the municipal court. Most African Americans in Philadelphia believed that the police department and the courts were racially prejudiced institutions. Yet, building on decades of African American legal assertiveness, women sought to harness a system that they viewed as racist to work on their behalf. Had black women testified against white men, judges' racial prejudices might have served as more of a deterrent to their use of the court. However, since most African American women pressed charges against African American men, they knew that the verdicts would usually be in their favor. Although women did not receive very much money or physical protection from their legal victories, most of them faced such severe problems and had so few alternative sources of support that even the small amount of assistance they secured from the court made a difference. Mrs. Elkins recalled, "In those days, the women didn't really have too much going for them. Except 1801 Vine."

NOTES

1. Case 447, November 18, 1947, Philadelphia City Archives, Philadelphia, PA [hereafter PCA].

2. Clarence B. Shenton, *History and Functions of the Municipal Court of Philadelphia* (Philadelphia: Thomas Skelton Harrison Foundation, 1930), 66, 80–81; *Philadelphia Municipal Court Annual Reports* [hereafter *PMC-AR*], 1949, A19.

3. All interviews were conducted by the author in Philadelphia, PA, between July 1, 1999 and June 27, 2000. Audiotapes are in author's possession. M.B.M. interview.

4. The juvenile division had the court's only black judge, Juanita Kidd Stout, the first African American woman appointed to a court of record in the nation.

5. In the 1940s, Pennsylvania, Maryland, and Massachusetts courts considered fornication and bastardy a criminal action. In eight states, the courts did not allow unmarried women to prosecute the fathers of their children for support at all. Other states heard these cases but dealt with them in civil court. Not until 1963 did the Philadelphia courts begin to hear the cases as civil rather than criminal proceedings.

6. *PMC-AR, 1959,* 318; *PMC-AR, 1964,* 221. Although a few cases of nonsupport each year were brought by husbands against wives, their numbers were very small.

7. Ruth Rosen, *The World Split Open: How the Modern Women's Movement Changed America* (New York: Viking, 2000), 186. Linda Gordon found that poor women's complaints about domestic abuse in social service agencies increased in the 1930s and 1940s, but her account suggests that they rarely approached the legal system; see Linda Gordon, *Heroes of Their Own Lives: The Politics and History of Family Violence: Boston, 1880–1960* (New York: Viking, 1988), 250–60, 280–81.

8. "Municipal Court Judges Decries 'Assembly-Line Justice,'" *Philadelphia Evening Bulletin* [hereafter *PEB*], February 17, 1957, 1, 6; *PMC-AR, 1950,* 132, 135;

"Court Backlog Boosts Aid to Unwed Mothers Here," *PEB*, May 15, 1959, 34.

9. First quotation in *PMC-AR, 1954,* 153; second quotation in *PMC-AR, 1957,* 197.

10. Quoted in "Unwed Mothers Speak Their Piece," *Philadelphia Afro-American*, January 31, 1959, 3.

11. "Court Slashes Backlog in Distributing Support Cases," *Philadelphia Inquirer*, January 4, 1959, 14; "In Municipal Court Holidays Bring Added Work . . . Held-up Checks," *Philadelphia Independent*, December 28, 1958, 3; *PMC-AR, 1960,* 21–211.

12. "Wanted: Solomon with an Adding Machine as HCL Plagues Estranged Couples," *PEB*, August 28, 1946, 14.

13. *PMC-AR, 1959,* 196; "Bonnelly Acts to Clear Up Support Cases," *PEB*, March 8, 1959, 3.

14. Starks quoted in Gail Levy and Judith Shouse, "A Concept of Alienation: A New Approach to Understanding the AFDC Recipient," (Master of Social Service Thesis, Bryn Mawr College, 1965), 54; *PMC-AR, 1960,* 210–211; *PMC-AR, 1961,* 215. Similarly in early twentieth-century New York, see Anna R. Igra, "Likely to Become a Public Charge: Deserted Women and the Family Law of the Poor in New York City," *Journal of Women's History* 11:4 (2000): 59–81.

15. C. E. interview. Similarly, see G.J. interview.

16. Anna R. Igra, *Wives Without Husbands: Marriage, Desertion, and Welfare in New York, 1900–1935* (Chapel Hill: University of North Carolina Press, 2007), 44, 97, 122, quotation on 44; Igra, "Likely to Become a Public Charge," 73. On postwar public assistance policy, see *PMC-AR, 1953,* A23; *PMC-AR, 1957,* 201.

17. Quoted in Levy and Shouse, "Concept of Alienation," 81.

18. H. C. interview; J. P. interview.

19. Quoted in Levy and Shouse, "Concept of Alienation," 23.

20. Sanderson quoted in C. S. interview; Elkins quoted in C. E. interview.

21. *PMC-AR, 1944,* A62–A63; *PMC-AR, 1949,* 261; *PMC-AR, 1934,* 276–77; *PMC-AR, 1939,* 1, 310–12; *PMC-AR, 1950,* 173; *PMC-AR, 1957,* 237.

22. M.B.M. interview; J.E.J, interview; Van Dyke interview.

23. *PMC-AR, 1953,* 166. For "busted my head open," see Case 127, February 18, 1948, PCA. For knife wounds, see Case 631 and Case 632, May 22, 1957, PCA. It is not clear from the records whether these cases involved African Americans or whites.

DOCUMENTS

Kay Weiss, "With doctors like these for friends, who needs enemies?"

Bubbling up in the 1950s and 1960s came critiques of physicians not only from female patients and medical students but also from health care workers at every level. Gynecologists and obstetricians who treated women on matters relating to sexual activity, abortion, and childbirth received the severest scrutiny. Many were patronizing, moralistic, and infantilizing in their treatment of female patients. Critics emphasized that the problem was not just the personal shortcomings of individual doctors. Nor was it merely the result of their training. At the heart of the problem was a fundamental devaluation of women that led physicians to feel that it was their responsibility to make health care decisions for their female patients, since women were simply not competent to participate in informed decisions regarding their own health. Medical scientists under the imprimatur of the National Institutes of Health, operating under their own masculinist bias, tested drugs on men and mistakenly assumed the results would apply to women, whom they didn't bother to include in the tests.

Many of these early critiques, like the one that follows, were published and distributed through women's movement networks. In calling for women to take greater responsibility for their own health care, they were forerunners of the classic *Our Bodies, Ourselves*. The book had its origins in 1969 in the discussion of a small group of Boston women who felt frustrated about doctors whom they considered "condescending, paternalistic, judgmental, and non-informative."* (See if you can find the table of contents of the most recent edition [2011] or an older edition online. Try to imagine what it would have been like to encounter the text and illustrations in the chapters on sexuality and birth control in 1971.)

While these early indictments, including the one that follows, may have verged on exaggeration, they also provide a window into psychotherapy in the age of the feminine mystique. It should come as no surprise that feminists would challenge a sexist psychiatric and psychological establishment that recommended treatment for any woman who displayed mental and physical symptoms suggesting she was not behaving as a "mature adult" who found sexual fulfillment in vaginally induced orgasm and personal fulfillment in marriage and maternity.

In your own experience with the medical community, have most of the problems about which young women complained a quarter of a century ago been remedied as both sexes have come to take greater responsibility for their medical treatment and as more physicians are women? What vestiges linger?

*The Boston Women's Health Book Collective, *The New Our Bodies, Ourselves* (New York: Simon & Schuster, 1984), quoted from the preface of the original edition, xvii.

Kay Weiss, "What Medical Students Learn," KNOW pamphlet #310, Pittsburgh, 1975; reprinted in *Dear Sisters: Dispatches from the Women's Liberation Movement*, ed. Rosalyn Baxandall and Linda Gordon (New York: Basic Books, 2000), pp. 118–120.

One of the cruelest forms of sexism we live with today is the unwillingness of many doctors to diagnose people's diseases with equality. The education of doctors can explain this. [Consider the messages in] the recently revised text *Obstetrics and Gynecology* (1971, 4th edition), which is used this year [1975] in 60 of the nation's medical schools.

SHE'S A CHILD

In *Obstetrics and Gynecology*, women are childlike, helpless creatures with animal-like or "instinctive" natures, who can't get through intercourse, pregnancy, labor or child-raising without "enlightened" physician intervention. The woman in childbirth is just a child herself. Her doctor, even if he is a novice and she is an old pro, is a fount of knowledge while she is "anxious," "fearful," afraid of "getting messy" and may feel "ashamed" and "guilty." The medical student is taught to believe that many symptoms of illness in pregnancy (excessive nausea, headache) are really a result of her "fear of pregnancy" rather than any physical condition he (all medical students and physicians are "he" in *Obstetrics and Gynecology*) need test for. . . .

SHE LOVES RAPE

Many gynecology texts reveal a greater concern with the patient's husband than with the patient herself and tend to maintain sex-role stereotypes in the interest of men and from a male perspective. But *Obstetrics and Gynecology* clearly spells out the attitudes that other texts only imply:

> The normal sexual act . . . entails a masochistic surrender to the man . . . there is always an element of rape.
>
> The traits that compose the core of the female personality are feminine narcissism, masochism, and passivity.
>
> Every phase of a woman's life is influenced by narcissism. Women then love in a different way from men. The woman falls in love with the idea of being loved; whereas the man loves an object for the pleasure it will give. She says, "I am valuable, important, etc. because he loves me. . . . " This type of narcissism finds expression in . . . her interest in clothes, personal appearance, and beauty. Too much feminine narcissism without masochism produces a self-centered woman.

> The idea of suffering is an essential part of her life.

SHE FEELS LIKE AN ANIMAL

Women are described in the text alternately as psychopathic and idiotic: "She is likely to feel that she is animal-like . . . to think of the vagina as a 'dirty cavity.' Black patients will think that the source of sexual desires is in the uterus; white patients think that it is in the ovaries. . . . Orgasm represents the woman's ability to accent her own feminine role in life. . . . Menstruation symbolizes her role in life. . . . "

The medical student is persuaded by the authors that women with dysmenorrhea (menstrual dysfunctions including painful uterine contractions) have no organic disease they need test for; these women simply have "personality disorders," "emotional difficulty in the home," or "neurotic predispositions." They need "sex education" and "mental hygiene" . . . if not "intensive psychotherapy." . . . A brief concession is made to the possible physical causes for menstrual pain, but the authors then quickly return to the problem of diagnosis:

> It is important to ascertain how crippling the symptom and how much emotional gain the patient is deriving from it. For example, does the whole household revolve around whether or not the mother is having menstrual cramps? . . .
>
> The adult woman who presents this symptom very often is resentful of the feminine role. Each succeeding period reminds her of the unpleasant fact that she is a woman. . . .

SHE NEEDS A PSYCHIATRIST

. . . Frigidity is defined as "occasional failure to obtain orgasm," placing 99 percent of women in the category of abnormal. If pleasure is only felt from clitoral stimulation, she may be referred to a psychiatrist. . . . Her frigidity may develop because she "resents her husband's preoccupation with his work or his recreational activities." The physician, a "parental figure," should "discover the problem in the patient's personality" and "encourage her to mature sexually."

Twenty-seven gynecology texts written over the past three decades were reviewed by Diana Scully and Pauline Bart in the *American Journal of Sociology* in January 1973. . . . No text Scully and Bart examined incorporated

Kinsey's 1953 findings that orgasm without stimulation "is a physical and physiological impossibility for nearly all females" or Masters and Johnson's 1966 findings that portions of the vagina have no nerve endings and lack sensation and that although orgasm is felt in the vagina, the feeling derives from stimulation of clitoral nerves.

With doctors like these for friends, who needs enemies?

Roe v. Wade, 1973; Planned Parenthood of Southeastern Pennsylvania v. Casey, 1992; Carhart v. Gonzales, 2007; Recent Developments

---

The Comstock Act of 1873 was echoed by a series of anticontraception and antiabortion laws throughout the country. By 1900, James Mohr observes, "Every state in the Union had an antiabortion law of some kind on its books . . . except Kentucky, where the state courts outlawed the practice anyway."* (See Leslie Reagan's essay, pp. 451–456.)

In 1962 the ethics of abortion became a pressing problem when it was revealed that thalidomide, a drug extensively used in Europe and occasionally in the United States, resulted in the birth of thousands of babies with phocomelia (deformed or missing arms and legs). Sherri Finkbine, an Arizona woman who had taken the drug, demanded a legal abortion. Although her own doctors supported her, the county medical society refused to approve the procedure, and, lacking confidence that she and her doctors would be granted immunity from prosecution, she fled to Sweden, where abortion was legal. Believing that other women should not have to discover the dangers of thalidomide the way she did, Sherri Finkbine told her story to local newspapers, and the news traveled quickly across the nation.

Her plight, and her challenge to hospital practice, helped to shift public opinion, both within the medical profession, which would subsequently be instrumental in advocating liberalization of abortion legislation, and among women's groups, which began to articulate dismay that women were generally denied access to safe abortion services. Estimates of the number of illegal abortions performed each year before 1973 range from 200,000 to 1,200,000; it is estimated that at least 200 women died each year as a result. Abortion was virtually the only medical procedure to which middle-class women did not have access. The issue was less intense for black women's groups; working-class minority women lacked a wide range of medical services, and abortion was only one among many which they needed. Thus, at the beginning of the reinvigorated women's movement of the late 1960s, black and white women were divided about the place that access to legal abortion should hold in their list of priorities for legal change.

Some physicians, like those who had approved Sherri Finkbine's request for a therapeutic abortion, sought to liberalize antiabortion laws, arguing that medical practitioners were best situated to judge when an abortion was appropriate. They were joined by a grassroots movement of women throughout the country who argued that current abortion statutes undermined their own constitutional right to equal protection of the laws. It was not equal protection, they insisted, when women with financial resources—like Sherri Finkbine—could find safe abortions and poor women could not, nor when women could not make their own

---

*James C. Mohr, *Abortion in America: The Origins and Evolution of National Policy, 1800–1900* (New York: Oxford University Press, 1978), pp. 229–30.

fundamental decisions whether to carry and bear a child. The severe social stigma to which unmarried pregnant women were subjected deprived them of dignity.

Before the *Roe* decision was handed down, a number of expansions of reproductive rights were made on the state level. In Connecticut over 800 women, joined as plaintiffs in a case popularly known as "Women versus Connecticut," convinced the state supreme court to declare the state's severe law unconstitutional; in 1969 the California Supreme Court held the California abortion law unconstitutional because it violated "the fundamental right of the woman to choose whether to bear children," citing the U.S. Supreme Court's decisions in *Griswold* (see pp. 671–672) and *Loving* (see pp. 669–670). Women activists also filed lawsuits in New Jersey, Rhode Island, Pennsylvania, and Massachusetts. In Iowa the Young Women's Christian Association supported abortion reform as early as 1966; women legislators took the lead in introducing reform bills, and a statewide organization largely composed of women—the Iowa Association for Medical Control of Abortion—lobbied vigorously for reform.** In 1970, Alaska, Hawaii, the state of Washington, and New York, legalized abortion. (In New York, the measure passed the lower house by a single vote; the Assemblyman who gave it predicted accurately that he would lose his seat.)

Faith groups divided on the issue. For many Catholics, opposition to abortion reform was of a piece with opposition to the death penalty. As members of Americans United for Life put it in 1972, "those who argue for the unborn child's right to life are arguing not only for the unborn child, but for the civil right to life of every human being–the mentally ill, the aged, the genetically incompetent, the idle, the useless." Clergy of a wide range of Protestant denominations and Reform and Conservative Rabbis, on the other hand, organized the Clergy Consultation Service in 1967, a nationwide network providing reliable information for women seeking safe abortions before the procedure was legal. (Recent studies show that close to 30 percent of women now obtaining abortions identify as Catholic; over 35 percent identify as Protestant.)†††

Texas law continued to prohibit abortion except for the purpose of saving the mother's life. In 1970, Norma McCorvey, a single pregnant woman, known as Jane Roe to protect her privacy, brought a class action suit challenging the constitutionality of that law as a violation of her right to liberty as guaranteed by the due process clause of the Fourteenth Amendment.

The Supreme Court's 7–2 decision in *Roe v. Wade* marked a sharp change from long-established practice. As the opening lines of the majority decision make clear, the justices were aware they were making a sensitive and important decision. There were two dissents; one, by Justice William Rehnquist, characterized the desire for abortion by a healthy woman as a matter of her "convenience."

On what constitutional grounds does Justice Blackmun base the Supreme Court's reasoning? Where does he find the right of privacy? (See the Fourteenth

**Amy Kesselman, "Women Versus Connecticut: Conducting a Statewide Hearing on Abortion," in *Abortion Wars: A Half Century of Struggle*, ed. Rickie Solinger (Berkeley: University of California Press, 1998), pp. 42–67; *People v. Dr. Leon Belous*, 458 P.2d 194 (1969); James C. Mohr, "Iowa's Abortion Battles of the Late 1960s and Early 1970s: Long-term Perspectives and Short-term Analyses," *Annals of Iowa* 50, no. 1, 3rd ser. (Summer 1989): 63–89. Selections from Americans United for Life , the Clergy Consultation Service, and many opponents and supporters of reform are included in Linda Greenhouse and Reva B. Siegel, *Before* Roe v. Wade: *Voices that Shaped the Abortion Debate Before the Supreme Court's Ruling* (New York: Kaplan, 2010). The 2nd edition (New Haven: Yale Law School, 2012), with a new afterword, is available free as a downloadable PDF at http://documents.law.yale .edu/sites/default/files/BeforeRoe2ndEd_1.pdf.

†††Fact Sheet: Induced Abortion in the United States, July 2014, Guttmacher Institute http://www.guttmacher .org/pubs/fb_induced_abortion.html.

Amendment, p. 289, and inspect the Bill of Rights—the first ten amendments to the U.S. Constitution, readily available on-line). What limits does the Court place on the exercise of that right?

ROE V. WADE, 1973

MR. JUSTICE HARRY A. BLACKMUN DELIVERED THE OPINION OF THE COURT:

We forthwith acknowledge our awareness of the sensitive and emotional nature of the abortion controversy, of the vigorous opposing views, even among physicians, and of the deep and seemingly absolute convictions that the subject inspires. One's philosophy, one's experiences, one's exposure to the raw edges of human existence, one's religious training, one's attitudes toward life and family and their values, and the moral standards one establishes and seeks to observe, are all likely to influence and to color one's thinking and conclusions about abortion.

In addition, population growth, pollution, poverty, and racial overtones tend to complicate and not to simplify the problem.

Our task, of course, is to resolve the issue by constitutional measurement, free of emotion and of predilection. We seek earnestly to do this. . . .

The principal thrust of the appellant's attack on the Texas statutes is that they improperly invade a right, said to be possessed by the pregnant woman, to choose to terminate her pregnancy. Appellant would discover this right in the concept of personal "liberty" embodied in the Fourteenth Amendment's Due Process Clause; or in personal, marital, familial and sexual privacy said to be protected by the Bill of Rights . . . or among those rights reserved to the people by the Ninth Amendment. . . .

It perhaps is not generally appreciated that the restrictive criminal abortion laws in effect in a majority of States today are of relatively recent vintage. Those laws, generally proscribing abortion or its attempt at any time during pregnancy except when necessary to preserve the pregnant woman's life, are not of ancient or even of common-law origin. Instead, they derive from statutory changes effected, for the most part, in the latter half of the nineteenth century. . . . At common law, at the time of the adoption of our Constitution, and throughout the major portion of the nineteenth century . . . a woman enjoyed a substantially broader right to terminate a pregnancy than she does in most states today. . . .

When most criminal abortion laws were first enacted, the procedure was a hazardous one for the woman. This was particularly true prior to the development of antisepsis. . . . Abortion mortality was high. . . . Modern medical techniques have altered this situation. Appellants . . . refer to medical data indicating that abortion in early pregnancy, that is, prior to the end of the first trimester, although not without its risk, is now relatively safe. Mortality rates for women undergoing early abortions, where the procedure is legal, appear to be as low as or lower than the rates for normal childbirth. Consequently, any interest of the State in protecting the woman from an inherently hazardous procedure . . . has largely disappeared. . . . The State has a legitimate interest in seeing to it that abortion, like any other medical procedure, is performed under circumstances that insure maximum safety for the patient. . . .

The Constitution does not explicitly mention any right of privacy. In a line of decisions, however . . . the Court has recognized that a right of personal privacy, or a guarantee of certain areas or zones of privacy, does exist under the Constitution. . . . This right . . . whether it be founded in the Fourteenth Amendment's concept of personal liberty . . . or . . . in the Ninth Amendment's reservation of rights to the people, is broad enough to encompass a woman's decision whether or not to terminate her pregnancy. . . . We . . . conclude that the right of personal privacy includes the abortion decision, but that this right is not unqualified and must be considered against important state interests in regulation. . . .

. . . the State does have a important and legitimate interest in preserving and protecting the health of the pregnant woman . . . and . . . it has still *another* important and legitimate interest in protecting the potentiality of human life. These interests are separate and distinct. Each grows in substantiality as the woman approaches term, and, at a point during pregnancy, each becomes "compelling."

With respect to the State's important and legitimate interest in the health of the mother, the "compelling" point, in the light of present medical knowledge, is at approximately the end of the first trimester. This is so because of the now-established medical fact . . . that until the end of the first trimester mortality in abortion may be less than mortality in normal childbirth. It follows that . . . for the period of pregnancy prior to this "compelling" point, the attending physician, in consultation with his patient, is free to determine, without regulation by the State, that in his medical judgment, the patient's pregnancy should be terminated.

. . . For the stage subsequent to approximately the end of the first trimester, the State, in promoting its interest in the health of the mother, may, if it chooses, regulate the abortion procedure in ways that are reasonably related to maternal health.

For the stage subsequent to viability, the State in promoting its interest in the potentiality of human life may, if it chooses, regulate, and even proscribe, abortion except where it is necessary, in appropriate medical judgment, for the preservation of the life or health of the mother.

Our conclusion . . . is . . . that the Texas abortion statutes, as a unit, must fall. . . .

Roe v. Wade, 410 U.S. 113 (1973).

In the years before 1973, when abortion was generally illegal, commonly performed in the private offices of doctors and unlicensed practitioners without emergency medical support, and generally without anesthesia, death from abortion was substantial. In 1985, it was estimated that only two deaths occurred from illegal abortion and only six deaths resulted from legal abortion.

Another large question remains: How does "equal protection of the laws" apply to reproductive rights and access to abortion? Justice Blackmun grounded *Roe v. Wade* in a right of privacy, balanced against a compelling state interest in the health of the fetus in the late stages of pregnancy. Because only women become pregnant, and because there is no obvious parallel to pregnancy in male experience, arguments about abortion are less easily made on the simple equal treatment grounds that served women's rights activists so well in *Frontiero v. Richardson* (see pp. 752–753) and other similar cases. It has been left to Justice Ruth Bader Ginsburg (and Justices William Brennan, William O. Douglas, and Thurgood Marshall before her) to give abortion rights an equal-protection context: pregnancy is woman-specific. Is pregnancy leave vacation time? Is it sick leave? Is the denial of insurance benefits for work loss resulting from a normal pregnancy sex discrimination? Or does the commitment to equal protection require the law to make it possible for women to be both parents and workers on the same terms as men? In 1974, dissenting in *Geduldig v. Aiello* (17 U.S. 484), Justices Brennan, Douglas, and Marshall insisted that California's failure to cover pregnancy-related disabilities threatened "to return men and women to a time when 'traditional' equal protection analysis sustained legislative classifications that treated differently members of a particular sex solely because of their sex." They cited three of Ginsburg's benchmark cases: *Muller*, *Goesaert*, and *Hoyt*. They, like Ginsburg in her arguments on behalf of the Women's Rights Project (see pp. 752–753), believed that the thinking that undergirded those earlier rulings was antiquated. (For Muller, see p. 357; for Goesaert, pp. 699–700; and for Hoyt, pp. 741–742.)

In writing the majority decision, Justice Blackmun observed "this right is not unqualified and must be considered against important state interests in regulation." The state, he went on to say, has a "legitimate interest in protecting the health of the pregnant woman . . . and it has still another important and legitimate interest in protecting the potentiality of human life." The interest in protecting the pregnant woman's health is to be balanced against a "compelling state interest" in the health of the fetus in the late stages of pregnancy.

In the 1980s, a number of states tested what boundaries would be considered reasonable limits on the abortion rights sustained in *Roe*. In 1980, the Supreme Court upheld the "Hyde Amendment" by which Congress refused to fund even medically necessary abortions for indigent women (*Harris v. McRae*, 448 U.S. 297). This decision was not the focus of massive public protest, and it was replicated in the laws of many states. An effort to defeat the Hyde Amendment failed in Congress in 1993, but some states did revise their practice, covering some abortions for indigent women, usually in the case of rape or incest.

Missouri legislators developed further the position that the state could deny any form of public support or facilities for the performance of abortions. A 1986 law prohibited the use of public employees and facilities to perform or assist abortions not necessary to save the life of the mother and also prohibited the use of public funds for counseling a woman in abortion decisions not necessary to save her life. It included a preamble that claimed that the life of each human being begins at conception and a provision that required that medical tests of fetal viability—tests whose efficacy was disputed—be performed before any abortion on a fetus estimated to be twenty weeks or more in gestation. Since 97 percent of all late abortions (done at an estimated sixteen-week gestational age) were performed at a single hospital in Kansas City that, although private, received public aid and was located on public property, the practical impact of the law was great.

In deciding *Webster v. Reproductive Health Services* in July 1989, by a 5–3 vote, the Supreme Court majority claimed that the conclusions of *Roe* had not been changed.*** Missouri law left a pregnant woman free to terminate her pregnancy so long as neither public funds nor facilities were used for it; this was, the Court majority said, a "value judgment" favoring childbirth over abortion. But the majority raised a general question about *Roe*. "[T]he rigid Roe framework," wrote Chief Justice Rehnquist in the majority opinion, "is hardly consistent with the notion of a Constitution cast in general terms, as ours is, and usually speaking in general principles, as ours does. The key elements of the *Roe* framework—trimesters and viability—are not found in the text of the Constitution or in any place else one would expect to find a constitutional principle . . . the result has been a web of legal rules that . . . [resemble] a code of regulations rather than a body of constitutional doctrine." Justice Anthony Scalia concurred, adding that in his view, *Roe* should have been overturned; abortion is, he thought, a field in which the Court "has little proper business since the answers to most of the cruel questions posed are political and not juridical." He was appalled at efforts to bring the pressure of public opinion to bear on the decisions of the Court, notably the March on Washington of some 200,000 people that had been sponsored by pro-choice groups shortly before the *Webster* case was argued in April 1989.

Justice Harry A. Blackmun, who had written the Court's opinion in *Roe,* now wrote a bitter dissent for the minority. He denied that Rehnquist's opinion left *Roe* "undisturbed." Rather it challenged a large body of legal precedent that had established a "private sphere of individual liberty," which although not explicitly specified in the Constitution had long been taken to have been implied by the Fourth Amendment guarantee against unreasonable searches. The right to privacy had been invoked in the 1960s when the Court protected the sale and use of birth control devices; the *Webster* decision, Blackmun feared, bypassed "the true jurisprudential debate underlying this case: . . . whether and to what extent . . . a right to privacy extends to matters of childbearing and family life, including abortion." Justice John Paul Stevens argued that the preamble's claim that life begins at conception was a religious view, and to write it into law was to ignore First Amendment requirements for the separation of church and state. Finally, Blackmun argued that the state had a distinct interest in maintaining public health, and that

---

***William L. Webster, Attorney General of Missouri v. Reproductive Health Services, 109 S. Ct. 3040 (1989).

as safe and legal abortions became more difficult to get, an increase in deaths from illegal abortions could be predicted. "For today," he concluded, "the women of this Nation still retain the liberty to control their destinies. But the signs are evident and very ominous, and a chill wind blows."

The Court's decision in *Webster* left many questions open. If states could deny public funds for abortions, what other limitations was it reasonable for state legislatures to impose? Was it reasonable to require a waiting period? Was it reasonable to require minors to get the consent of one parent? of both parents?

In 1988 and 1989 Pennsylvania amended its Abortion Control Act of 1982 extensively, requiring a twenty-four-hour waiting period and the provision of "certain information" twenty-four hours before the abortion is performed. Minors were required to have the consent of one parent, and married women to have notified their husbands, although it was possible for a court to waive that requirement and all requirements could be waived in the event of a "medical emergency." Because most of the justices had made public substantial reservations about the decision in *Roe*, it seemed to many observers not unreasonable to predict that the Court would uphold the entire Pennsylvania statute and, possibly, overturn *Roe v. Wade*. Instead, a plurality organized by Justices Sandra Day O'Connor, Anthony Kennedy, and David Souter, joined by Harry Blackmun and John Paul Stevens, wrote a complex opinion that began with a ringing affirmation of *Roe*. But O'Connor, Kennedy, and Souter also made it clear that they shared Rehnquist's skepticism of the trimester framework of *Roe*. How does the plurality think the principle of equal protection of the laws should be applied in abortion decisions?

Note the comments on coverture at the end of the plurality opinion; why did court find it useful to refer to *Bradwell v. Illinois* (pp. 292–294) and *Hoyt v. Florida* (pp. 741–742)? The final statement in the selection marks the first explicit recognition by the Court of the end of coverture. Why do the dissenting justices think *Roe* should be overturned?

PLANNED PARENTHOOD OF SOUTHEASTERN PENNSYLVANIA V. CASEY, 1992

Justices O'Connor, Kennedy, Souter: (with whom Justices Blackmun and Stevens join)

Liberty finds no refuge in a jurisprudence of doubt. Yet 19 years after our holding that the Constitution protects a woman's right to terminate her pregnancy in its early stages ... that definition of liberty is still questioned. ... After considering the fundamental constitutional questions resolved by *Roe*, principles of institutional integrity, and the rule of *stare decisis* [the principle that decisions of previous courts should be let stand unless there is overwhelming reason to change them], we are led to conclude this: the essential holding of *Roe v. Wade* should be retained and once again reaffirmed. ... Constitutional protection of the woman's decision to terminate her pregnancy derives from the Due Process Clause of the Fourteenth Amendment. It declares that no State shall "deprive any person of life, liberty, or property, without due process of law." ... It is a premise of the Constitution that there is a realm of personal liberty which the government may not enter. We have vindicated this principle before. Marriage is mentioned nowhere in the Bill of Rights and interracial marriage was illegal in most States in the 19th century, but the Court was no doubt correct in finding it to be an aspect of liberty protected against state interference by the substantive component of the Due Process Clause in *Loving v. Virginia* 388 U.S. 1 (1967). ...

Men and women of good conscience can disagree, and we suppose some always shall disagree, about the profound moral and spiritual implications of terminating a pregnancy, even in its earliest stage. Some of us as individuals find abortion offensive to our most basic principles of morality, but that cannot control our decision. Our obligation is to define the liberty of all, not to mandate our own moral code. . . .

Our law affords constitutional protection to personal decisions relating to marriage, procreation, contraception, family relationships, child rearing, and education. . . . These matters, involving the most intimate and personal choices a person may make in a lifetime, choices central to personal dignity and autonomy, are central to the liberty protected by the Fourteenth Amendment. At the heart of liberty is the right to define one's own concept of existence, of meaning, of the universe, and of the mystery of human life. Beliefs about these matters could not define the attributes of personhood were they formed under compulsion of the State. The woman's right to terminate her pregnancy before viability is the most central principle of *Roe* v. *Wade*. It is a rule of law and a component of liberty we cannot renounce.

On the other side of the equation is the interest of the State in the protection of potential life. The *Roe* Court recognized the State's "important and legitimate interest in protecting the potentiality of human life." . . . That portion of the decision in *Roe* has been given too little acknowledgment and implementation by the Court in its subsequent cases. . . . Though the woman has a right to choose to terminate or continue her pregnancy before viability, it does not at all follow that the State is prohibited from taking steps to ensure that this choice is thoughtful and informed. Even in the earliest stages of pregnancy, the State may enact rules and regulations designed to encourage her to know that there are philosophic and social arguments of great weight that can be brought to bear in favor of continuing the pregnancy to full term. . . . We reject the trimester framework, which we do not consider to be part of the essential holding of *Roe*. . . . Measures aimed at ensuring that a woman's choice contemplates the consequences for the fetus do not necessarily interfere with the right recognized in *Roe* . . . not every law which makes a right more difficult to exercise is, ipso facto, an infringement of that right. . . .

. . . We . . . see no reason why the State may not require doctors to inform a woman seeking an abortion of the availability of materials relating to the consequences to the fetus. . . . Whether the mandatory 24-hour waiting period is . . . invalid because in practice it is a substantial obstacle to a woman's choice to terminate her pregnancy is a closer question. [We

do not agree with the District Court] that the waiting period constitutes an undue burden. . . . [From Part D: We have already established the precedent, and] we reaffirm today, that a State may require a minor seeking an abortion to obtain the consent of a parent or guardian, provided that there is an adequate judicial bypass procedure. . . .

. . . Pennsylvania's abortion law provides, except in cases of medical emergency, that no physician shall perform an abortion on a married woman without receiving a signed statement from the woman that she has notified her spouse that she is about to undergo an abortion. The woman has the option of providing an alternative signed statement certifying that her husband is not the man who impregnated her; that her husband could not be located; that the pregnancy is the result of spousal sexual assault which she had reported [or that she fears bodily harm from him]. A physician who performs an abortion on a married woman without receiving the appropriate signed statement will have his or her license revoked, and is liable to the husband for damages.

. . . In well-functioning marriages, spouses discuss important intimate decisions such as whether to bear a child. But there are millions of women in this country who are the victims of regular physical and psychological abuse at the hands of their husbands. . . . Many may have a reasonable fear that notifying their husbands will provoke further instances of child abuse [or psychological abuse]. . . .

. . . [A]s a general matter . . . the father's interest in the welfare of the child and the mother's interest are equal. Before birth, however, the issue takes on a very different cast. It is an inescapable biological fact that state regulation with respect to the child a woman is carrying will have a far greater impact on the mother's liberty than on the father's. [That is why the Court has already ruled that when the wife and husband disagree on the abortion decision, the decision of the wife should prevail.]

. . . There was a time, not so long ago, when a different understanding of the family and of the Constitution prevailed. In *Bradwell* v. *Illinois* [pp. 292–294], three Members of this Court reaffirmed the common-law principle that "a woman had no legal existence separate from her husband." . . . Only one generation has passed since this Court observed that "woman is still regarded as the center of home and family life," with attendant "special responsibilities" that precluded full and independent legal status under the Constitution (*Hoyt v. Florida* [pp. 741–742]). These views, of course, are no longer consistent with our understanding of the family, the individual, or the Constitution. . . . [The Pennsylvania abortion law] embodies a view of marriage consonant with the common-law status of married women but repugnant to our present understanding of marriage and of the nature of the rights secured by the Constitution. Women do not lose their constitutionally protected liberty when they marry.

CHIEF JUSTICE REHNQUIST, WITH WHOM JUSTICE WHITE, JUSTICE SCALIA, AND JUSTICE CLARENCE THOMAS JOIN:

The joint opinion . . . retains the outer shell of *Roe v. Wade* . . . but beats a wholesale retreat from the substance of that case. We believe that *Roe* was wrongly decided, and that it can and should be overruled consistently with our traditional approach to *stare decisis* in constitutional cases. We would . . . uphold the challenged provisions of the Pennsylvania statute in their entirety. . . . [B]y foreclosing all democratic outlet for the deep passions this issue arouses, by banishing the issue from the political forum that gives all participants, even the losers, the satisfaction of a fair hearing and an honest fight, by continuing the imposition of a rigid national rule instead of allowing for regional differences, the Court merely prolongs and intensifies the anguish.

We should get out of this area, where we have no right to be, and where we do neither ourselves nor the country any good by remaining.

The U.S. Supreme Court began its opinion in *Casey* by scorning "a jurisprudence of doubt." In 2000 it reaffirmed its support of the principles of *Roe v. Wade*, and struck down another state abortion statute, this one a Nebraska law forbidding a specific procedure for late term abortion that physicians called "Dillation and Evacuation" and opponents called "partial birth abortion" (*Stenberg v. Carhart*, 530 U.S. 914 [2000]). But within a few years, Congress overrode that decision by passing a federal "partial birth abortion ban." The four Nebraska physicians who had challenged the state statute now challenged the federal version—not least on the grounds that it did not contain an exception for the health of the mother. Now the U.S. Supreme Court denied their challenge despite the strong opposition of the American College of Obstetricians and Gynecologists, which found the procedure necessary and proper in certain cases.

In *Carhart v. Gonzales* (550 U.S. 124 [2007]), the Supreme Court agreed with Congress that the procedure was distinctively "brutal and inhumane," and that Congress and the Court could bar it "in furtherance of its legitimate interests in regulating the medical profession." Although the majority, in an opinion written by Justice Anthony Kennedy, acknowledged that "we find no reliable data to measure the phenomenon," it announced that "it seems unexceptionable to conclude some women come to regret their choice to abort the infant life they once created and sustained. . . . Severe depression and loss of esteem can follow." For the mother's own good, he wrote that "[t]he law need not give abortion doctors unfettered choice in the course of their medical practice. . . . " Justice Kennedy acknowledged early on that "the principles set forth in the joint opinion in *Planned Parenthood of Southeastern Pa. v. Casey* . . . did not find support from all those who join [in this] opinion," but he asserted that they reaffirmed "*Roe*'s essential holding."

The principle of equal protection lurks within every abortion argument. The failure to ground the decriminalization of abortion in equal protection and to specify the end of coverture (married women's legal subordination to husbands) has had major consequences. Nowhere is the argument that access to abortion is a matter of equal protection made more eloquently than in Ruth Bader Ginsburg's

Planned Parenthood of Southeastern Pennsylvania v. Casey, 505 U.S. 833 (1992).

dissent, in which she was joined by justices Stevens, Souter and Breyer. Ginsburg took the unusual step of reading her emphatic dissent from the bench. She began by restating *Roe*'s promise, emphasizing not only "the right of the woman to choose to have an abortion before viability and to obtain it without undue interference from the State," but also that the State's "legitimate interests . . . in protecting . . . the life of the fetus that may become a child" were limited by its interests "in protecting *the health of the woman*" [her emphasis]. The Court, Ginsburg asserted, was now "retreating from prior rulings that abortion restrictions cannot be imposed absent an exception safeguarding a woman's health." She was deeply critical of the reasoning on which Congress had based the "partial birth abortion ban" statute: "Congress claimed that there was a medical consensus that the banned procedure is never necessary . . . and that 'there is no credible medical evidence that partial-birth abortions are safe or are safer than other abortion procedures.' But the congressional record includes . . . statements from nine professional associations, including the American College of Obstetricians and Gynecologists, the American Public Health Association, and the California Medical Association, attesting that intact D&E carries meaningful safety advantages over other methods . . . the physicians who testified that intact D&E is never necessary to preserve the health of a woman had slim authority for their opinions. They had no training for, or personal experience with the intact D&E procedure. . . . " Relying on misleading information, "the Court deprives women of the right to make an autonomous choice, even at the expense of their safety."

As the Court had recognized in *Casey* fifteen years before, Ginsburg observed, "at stake in cases challenging abortion restrictions is a woman's 'control over her [own] destiny.'" She ended by quoting and commenting on the lines from the *Hoyt* decision that had been rejected by the Court in *Casey*:

> "There was a time, not so long ago, when women were regarded as the center of home and family life, with attendant special responsibilities that precluded full and independent legal status under the Constitution." In the *Casey* decision, the Court made clear that these views "are no longer consistent with our understanding of the family, the individual, or the Constitution." Women, it is now acknowledged, have the talent, capacity, and right no participate equally in the economic and social life of the Nation. Their ability to realize their full potential, the Court [had] recognized, is intimately connected to "their ability to control their reproductive lives" Thus, legal challenges to undue restrictions on abortion procedures do not seek to vindicate some generalized notion of privacy; rather they center on a woman's autonomy to determine her life's course, and thus to enjoy equal citizenship stature.

RECENT DEVELOPMENTS

The legalization of abortion improved women's health care. After 1973, states assumed responsibility for ensuring that qualified physicians in licensed facilities performed the procedure. Medical complications from abortions plummeted. But resistance to recognizing access to abortion—a medical procedure that men do not need—as a matter of equal protection (men confront no similar law limiting their choice of medical procedures) continued and strengthened. The decision in *Carhart* was evidence of the success with which opponents of legal abortion reform worked to expand what can be understood as the state's "legitimate interest . . . in regulation." Women who need access to a constitutionally protected medical procedure now face, in state after state, mandatory waiting periods that increase the physical dangers of the procedure; parental consent or notification requirements that constrain young women who have reason to fear their own parents, especially women who are victims of incest; mandatory pre-abortion sonograms accompanied by "counseling" by medical staff who are required to describe the fetus as a "baby." Under the federal Affordable Care Act of 2013, health plans cannot be required to include abortion coverage.

The legalization of abortion was accompanied by a paradox: when the procedure was legitimized and made safer by the state, extremists in the antiabortion movement imperiled the health and safety of abortion providers. Between 1977 and 1993, abortion providers reported 543 cases of vandalism, 113 cases of arson, and 166 death threats to federal authorities.

By 1993, antiabortion violence reached a fevered pitch: clinics across the United States reported a one-hundred percent increase in hate mail and harassing phone calls over the previous year, while the number of bomb threats nearly doubled and death threats against abortion providers increased by nearly tenfold. In March 1993, Dr. David Gunn was shot and killed outside of a Pensacola, Florida, clinic. Five months later, Shelley Shannon, an antiabortion extremist, shot Dr. George Tiller in both arms outside of his Wichita, Kansas, clinic, where he was one of a handful of physicians nationwide who performed third-trimester abortions. In 2009, less than two years after the Supreme Court's decision in *Carhart v. Gonzales,* Tiller became the eighth abortion clinic employee and the fourth physician to be murdered by an antiabortion extremist when Scott Roeder shot and killed the physician inside of his church.

Many women had a harder time finding abortion providers by the first decade of the twenty-first century than they had in the 1970s. Between 1992 and 2000, the number of abortion providers in the United States declined by 11 percent. Rural states, including Georgia, Kansas, Kentucky, and Missouri lost more than 50 percent of their providers during this period. And in 2009, the year Dr. Tiller was murdered, 87 percent of counties in the United States lacked a single abortion provider. One out of every three women lived in a county without abortion services.

Since 2009 there has been a dramatic increase in state-level provisions restricting access to abortion and physicians' ability to provide safe abortion services. Some states now ban abortions starting at 20 weeks—the point at which tests to determine the health of the pregnancy are available—rather than the usual ban at viability, which is about 24 weeks. Some states require abortion providers to have admitting privileges in nearby hospitals. (Generally hospitals require physicians to admit a minimum number of patients in order to maintain these privileges, a requirement that is rarely possible for clinic-based physicians to meet.) Both the American Medical Association and the American Congress of Obstetricians and Gynecologists have opposed these restrictions. In 2013, 27 states had at least four types of major abortion restrictions. The risks associated with abortion increase with the length of pregnancy.[†]

Such restrictions have had major impact. Five states (all of them large, geographically, with significant rural populations) have only one abortion clinic: Arkansas, Mississippi, North Dakota, South Dakota, and Wyoming. In some cases, statutes have passed forcing them to close; these statutes are being appealed. In 2014, a federal district court in North Dakota found unconstitutional a state law that would have banned abortion once a fetal heartbeat could be detected—an event that normally occurs at around six weeks of pregnancy, before some women are even aware of their condition. The decision is being appealed.[††] Women in rural areas have particular difficulty getting abortions. When the last clinic in the Texas Rio Grande Valley closed, women had to travel 250 miles to the nearest city clinic—facing extra costs of gas, lodging, and child care.

In June 2014, the U.S. Supreme Court unanimously overturned a Massachusetts law that prohibited protestors from coming within 35 feet of an abortion clinic; the statute was designed to create a "buffer zone" for patients and staff.[†††] Cities and states had begun to enact buffer zone laws in the 1990s, after it had become commonplace for antiabortion activists to harass patients and after

---

[†]"Fact Sheet: Induced Abortion in the United States, July 2014," Guttmacher Institute, http://www.guttmacher.org/pubs/fb_induced_abortion.html. See the points under "Law and Policy."

[††]For more about women's work in the anti-abortion movement, see Karissa Haugeberg, *Women to the Rescue: Leaders, Martyrs, and Foot Soldiers in the Campaign to End Abortion* (Urbana: University of Illinois Press, forthcoming). A useful and regularly updated guide to state policies on reproductive health is conveniently found on a website maintained by the Guttmacher Institute: http://www.guttmacher.org/statecenter/spibs/index.html.

[†††]*McCullen v. Coakley,* U.S. Sup. Ct. Docket 12-1334, 2014.

extremists had begun to bomb clinics and to shoot physicians. Courts have generally overturned these measures on the grounds that they violate activists' First Amendment right to free speech. Pro-choice activists have countered that patients seeking abortions deserve the types of buffer zone protections afforded to voters, students, and Supreme Court justices as they enter polling sites, schools, and the U.S. Supreme Court.

The Affordable Care Act (ACA) does not require health plans to cover abortion except in the case of rape, incest, or endangerment of life; and forbids the use of federal funding for abortion coverage. It does include all medically authorized forms of contraception, as part of a wide range of essential health benefits, some specific to women's "preventive health" services, such as annual check-ups, pap smears, and mammograms. Religiously affiliated employers—generally understood to be nonprofit institutions like schools and hospitals—who had religious reservations to birth control were permitted to opt-out of coverage, and employees who wished coverage for contraception were assured a route to private or federal coverage. (Most private insurance companies found the prospect of subsidizing contraceptives appealing because it is less expensive to pay for birth control than to provide health care coverage for dependent children.)

Hobby Lobby, a family-owned arts-and-crafts chain, filed suit against the Department of Health and Human Services, charging that the ACA requirement of no-cost access to contraception violated the Religious Freedom Restoration Act of 1993 by forcing them to pay for products that violated their religious beliefs. The corporation objected to contraception, and it claimed that some of the common forms of birth control—the "morning-after" pill and two kinds of intrauterine devices (IUDs)—should be understood not as preventative but as "abortifacients" because they prevent the implantation of a fertilized egg in the uterus. In June 2014, in a 5–4 decision, the U.S. Supreme Court ruled in favor of Hobby Lobby, finding that the birth control requirement was a substantial burden on the owners' religious freedom (*Burwell v. Hobby Lobby Stores*, Docket No. 13-354).

The dissenters—the three women members and Justice Stephen Breyer—joined in a dissent written by Justice Ginsburg, reaching back to the *Casey* decision to stress that "the ability of women to participate equally in the economic and social life of the nation has been facilitated by their ability to control their reproductive lives." Women's need for coverage of their expenses was real: Ginsburg cited a recent Institute of Medicine report that "women are consistently more likely than men to report a wide range of barriers to receiving . . . medical tests and treatments." A few days later, the court temporarily exempted a Christian college from some administrative regulations governing its own employees and students' access to contraception. As we go to press, the line between access to abortion and access to birth control may be blurring.

What difference would it have made if, in 1973, the majority in *Roe* had grounded its defense of women's right to choose not in privacy rights but in equal protection and equal rights claims? Consider that *Roe v. Wade* granted women, in consultation with their physicians, the right to abortion, but did not guarantee women access to the procedure. How might we create policies that ensure that all women have the ability to obtain safe medical care? And how might we protect the health and safety of clinic employees while preserving the First Amendment rights to free speech of anti-abortion activists?

A Challenge for Our Readers: Become an Historian! As the 40th anniversary of Roe passes, activists of the 1960s—on both sides of the debate—are now in their 70s and 80s. Activists of the 1950s are in their 90s. The time available to us is short. Most have never been interviewed; many are hungry to place their experience on the historical record. Some have kept in their possession the records of the small groups of which they were a part, yet they are not aware that their collected materials and their recollections may be welcomed by historical societies and college- and university-based archives. Local newspapers—many now digitized—can be searched. The papers of some state legislators have been archived; often they are filed by topic, and thus one can identify materials by searching under "abortion." Many of these collections include letters from constituents on both sides of the question, urging action. Some of these letters are heartbreaking; all are interesting. (Archivists will generally ask researchers to sign an agreement not to publish the names of the authors.)

Catholic bishops were early to organize challenges to abortion reform; the role of Catholic clergy and of nuns in our towns and counties deserves its own history.

Although the Clergy Consultation Service on Abortion originated in New York City, chapters flourished throughout the country. Identifying participants in these campaigns in your town or county or state—and interviewing them about their memories of their work—could make significant contributions to recapturing the history of the fight over abortion reform. Partisan alignments after *Roe* took longer to develop than many appreciate, and varied greatly from one region or county to another. *Roe*'s 40th anniversary is both a warning about rapidly fading memories and an opportunity to capture a history that still shapes American lives and politics.

Rethinking Marriage: Loving v. Virginia, 1967; Griswold v. Connecticut, 1965; Defense of Marriage Act, 1996; Goodridge v. Massachusetts Department of Public Health, 2003; Recent Developments

---

Although marriage is generally understood to be the most private of matters, it has been subjected to regulation by colonies and the states since the founding era. Even when marriage ceremonies take a religious form, marriage in the United States has always been regulated by civil laws. States rely on marriages to maintain stable households, legitimate and care for children, and minimize public support for the vulnerable. States set and enforce the terms of marriage—including who can and cannot marry, what marital rights and obligations are, and the terms for ending it in divorce. States set the rules of inheritance—that is, the transmission of property from one generation to the next within marital families. Throughout much of American history, states enforced the rules of coverture that gave husbands expansive powers over their wives' bodies, property, and choices.

The national government has also been deeply involved in defining which marriages would be legally recognized. It has enacted laws in areas ranging from polygamy, to immigration policy, to the family structures that would be eligible for social security and aid to dependent children. As World War II ended, pressures for legislative change grew. American military personnel successfully claimed the right to bring spouses into the United States more easily than established quotas permitted. Federal laws that made Asians ineligible for citizenship proved embarrassing when China was a U.S. ally during World War II; the exclusion of Chinese was ended in 1943. American military personnel stationed in Japan during the occupation repeatedly challenged the rule that Asians were ineligible for citizenship. Acts passed in 1945 and 1946, which cautiously facilitated the entry of foreign fiancées and spouses regardless of race, were responses to this situation. And the joint income tax, devised in 1948, offered substantial advantages to married couples that unmarried individuals did not (and still do not) enjoy.*

The democratic, inclusive rhetoric of a war against fascism made American practices of segregation increasingly anomalous and an international embarrassment. Among the civil rights that increasing numbers of citizens claimed was the right to marry the person of their choice despite state laws defining interracial marriage between whites and others as miscegenation. (Generally, these statutes

---

*Carolyn Jones, "Split Income and Separate Spheres: Tax Law and Gender Roles in the 1940s," *Law and History Review*, 6 (Fall 1988): 259–310.

permitted interracial marriage among other groups.) At the close of World War II, the laws of thirty states barred interracial marriage. Challenges built state by state. Although the California Supreme Court struck down that state's miscegenation statute in 1948[†] and thirteen other legislatures repealed their laws, bans continued to be enforced with serious penalties in sixteen other states.

Virginia's law made it illegal for "any white person in the state to marry any save a white person, or a person with no other admixture of blood than white and American Indian." (The link between whiteness and Native Americans was arranged in order to include all those white Virginians who proudly claimed descent from Pocahontas.) In 1958, two Virginians, Mildred Jeter, who was black, and Richard Loving, who was white, married in a ceremony in Washington, D.C. When they returned to Virginia to live, they were indicted for violating Virginia's ban on interracial marriages. They were found guilty and sentenced to one year in jail, which would be suspended if they left the state and did not return for twenty-five years. The aptly named Lovings moved to Washington, D.C., and challenged the conviction; eventually their case reached the U.S. Supreme Court. Richard Loving said to his attorney, "Tell the Court I love my wife, and it is just unfair that I can't live with her in Virginia."

How did the state of Virginia defend its practice? On what grounds did the Supreme Court declare the miscegenation law illegal? How did the Court describe "freedom to marry"?

LOVING V. VIRGINIA, 1967

CHIEF JUSTICE EARL WARREN WROTE THE OPINION FOR A UNANIMOUS COURT:

. . . the State [of Virginia] argues that the meaning of the Equal Protection Clause [of the Fourteenth Amendment, see p. 247] . . . is only that state penal laws containing an interracial element as part of the definition of the offense must apply equally to whites and Negroes in the sense that members of each race are punished to the same degree. Thus the State contends that, because its miscegenation statutes punish equally both the white and the Negro participants in an interracial marriage, these statutes, despite their reliance on racial classifications, do not constitute an invidious discrimination based upon race. . . .

Because we reject the notion that the mere "equal application" of a statute containing racial classifications is enough to remove the classifications from the Fourteenth Amendment's proscription of all invidious racial discriminations, we do not accept the State's contention. . . . There is patently no legitimate overriding purpose independent of invidious racial discrimination which justifies this classification. The

fact that Virginia prohibits only interracial marriages involving white persons demonstrates that the racial classifications must stand on their own justification, as measures designed to maintain White Supremacy. . . . There can be no doubt that restricting the freedom to marry solely because of racial classification violates the central meaning of the Equal Protection Clause.

These statutes also deprive the Lovings of liberty without due process of law in violation of the Due Process Clause of the Fourteenth Amendment. The freedom to marry has long been recognized as one of the vital personal rights essential to the orderly pursuit of happiness by free men.

Marriage is one of the "basic civil rights of man," fundamental to our very existence and survival. To deny this fundamental freedom on so unsupportable a basis as the racial classifications embodied in these statutes . . . is surely to deprive all the State's citizens of liberty without due process of law. . . . Under our Constitution, the freedom to marry or not marry, a person of another race resides with the individual and cannot be infringed by the state.

These convictions must be reversed. It is so ordered.

[†]*Perez v. Sharp*, 32 Cal 2d. 711 (1948).

Loving v. Virginia, 388 U.S. 1 (1967).

Meanwhile, debate over the appropriate limits of contraceptives—dating at least from the Comstock Act (see p. 212)—continued in the postwar era. Long after they were legal in other states, Connecticut continued to forbid their use. Seeking to test the statute, the Planned Parenthood League (PPL) of Connecticut established a center in New Haven where a physician offered counsel and prescriptions to married couples. It opened on November 1, 1961; within 10 days it had served 75 patients. But on the tenth day, detectives arrived to arrest its volunteer physician, Dr. C. Lee Buxton, who was the chairman of the Yale Medical School's department of obstetrics and gynecology, and Estelle Griswold, the executive director of the PPL. They were quickly convicted and fined. They appealed their conviction. When their case reached the U.S. Supreme Court, they won on a 7–2 decision.

Note the discussion of marital privacy in Justice Douglas's opinion. Why did Justice Stewart disagree?

GRISWOLD V. CONNECTICUT, 1965

JUSTICE WILLIAM O. DOUGLAS WROTE THE MAJORITY OPINION:

. . . The association of people is not mentioned in the Constitution nor in the Bill of Rights . . . [but] specific guarantees in the Bill of Rights have penumbras, formed by emanations from those guarantees that help give them life and substance. Various guarantees create zones of privacy.

The right of association contained in the penumbra of the First Amendment is one. . . . The Third Amendment in its prohibition against the quartering of soldiers "in any house" in time of peace without the consent of the owner is another facet of that privacy. The Fourth Amendment explicitly affirms the "right of the people to be secure in their persons, houses, papers, and effects, against unreasonable searches and seizures." . . . We deal with a right of privacy older than the Bill of Rights— older than our political parties, older than our school system. Marriage is a coming together for better or for worse, hopefully enduring, and intimate to the degree of being sacred. It is an association that promotes a way of life, not causes; a harmony in living, not political faiths, a bilateral loyalty, not commercial or social projects. Yet it is an association for as noble a purpose as any involved in our prior decisions.

JUSTICE BYRON WHITE, CONCURRING

In my view this Connecticut law as applied to married couples deprives them of "liberty" without due process of law . . . the liberty entitled to protection under the Fourteenth Amendment includes the right "to marry, establish a home and bring up children." . . . These [prior] decisions affirm that there is a "realm of family life which the state cannot enter" without substantial justification.

JUSTICE POTTER STEWART, DISSENTING

Since 1879 Connecticut has had on its books a law which forbids the use of contraceptives by anyone. I think this is an uncommonly silly law. As a practical matter, the law is obviously unenforceable . . . as a philosophical matter, I believe the use of contraceptives in the relationship of marriage should be left to personal and private choice, based upon each individual's moral, ethical and religious beliefs. . . . But we are not asked in this case to say whether we think this law is unwise, or even asinine. We are asked to hold that it violates the United States Constitution. And that I cannot do. . . .

What provision of the Constitution, then, does make this state law invalid? The Court says it is the right of privacy "created by several fundamental constitutional guarantees." With all deference I can find no such general right of privacy in the Bill of Rights, in any other part of the Constitution. . . . It is the essence of judicial duty to subordinate our own personal views, our own ideas of what legislation is wise and what is not. If, as I should surely hope, the law before us does not reflect the standards of the people of Connecticut, the people of Connecticut can freely exercise their true Ninth and Tenth Amendment rights to persuade their elected representatives to repeal it. That is the constitutional way to take this law off the books.

Griswold v. Connecticut, 381 U.S. 479 (1965). See Mary L. Dudziak, "Just Say No: Birth Control in the Connecticut Supreme Court Before Griswold v. Connecticut," Iowa Law Review 75 (May 1990): 915–39.

Griswold v. Connecticut limited its decision to married couples, recognizing for them a zone of privacy in their intimate relations into which the state could not intrude. Not until 1972 did the Supreme Court rule that unmarried people also have a right to contraceptives. That decision, as historian Nancy F. Cott has observed, "pronounced a historic reversal, since it denied the state's right to distinguish between citizens of differing marital status." The Court recognized "the right of the individual, married or single, to be free from unwarranted governmental intrusion into matters so fundamentally affecting a person as the decision whether to bear or beget a child."* That decision made state practice congruent with the sexual revolution that characterized American society in the 1960s and 1970s, sustained by new developments in contraceptive technology, notably the widely available birth control pill. (See Beth Bailey's essay on the pill, pp. 629–637.) Nearly fifty years later, access to contraception again became a subject for litigation, and new questions were opened by the Supreme Court decision in *Burwell v. Hobby Lobby Companies* (June 2014, see pp. 668.)

But the Supreme Court was not prepared to recognize intimate privacy for same-sex couples. From the 1970s to early twenty-first century, gay men and lesbians challenged criminal sodomy laws, usually written in generic terms but enforced only against gay couples, which denied intimate privacy. In 1986 the Atlanta police, acting on a tip, entered the apartment of Michael Hardwick and found him in bed with another man. When they were arrested for violating Georgia's sodomy statutes, they claimed—unsuccessfully—that their constitutional right to equal protection of the laws had been violated. Chief Justice Warren Burger observed, "Decisions of individuals relating to homosexual conduct have been subject to state intervention throughout the history of Western civilization." The vote in this case (*Bowers v. Hardwick*, 478 U.S. 186 [1986]), was 5-4; voting with the majority was Justice Lewis Powell, who stated publicly several years later that the decision was one he regretted.

In the aftermath of *Bowers v. Hardwick*, gay men and lesbians argued with increasing conviction that they were marked as criminals for behavior covered by the protections of privacy when engaged in by heterosexuals. They argued that they too fulfilled one of the major social reasons for the practice of marriage—the choice of committed relationships rather than transient ones. Lesbians and gay men also identified ways in which the status of marriage gave privileges and rights to heterosexual couples, including tax advantages in the form of joint-income tax returns; the ability to share health insurance coverage (often paid for in part by employers); and rights related to the acquisition and inheritance of property, awards of child custody, and companionship as next of kin when partners were hospitalized or dying. And they resented the stigma of being marked as criminals.

By the late twentieth century, these claims developed a dynamism of their own. The number of states that had laws criminalizing sodomy declined substantially, and virtually none enforced these laws against private, consensual, heterosexual conduct. The European Court of Human Rights sustained the right of homosexual adults to engage in intimate, consensual conduct. As this book goes to press, same-sex marriages are valid in 16 nations, including Argentina, Belgium, Brazil, Canada, Denmark, France, Iceland, Netherlands, New Zealand, Norway, Portugal, Spain, South Africa, Sweden, United Kingdom (including Scotland), and Uruguay.

In 1993, the Hawaii Supreme Court held that although it was not prepared to say that the claim of gay men and lesbians to same-sex marriage was a fundamental

Eisenstadt v. *Baird*, 405 U.S. 438 (1972). Nancy F. Cott, *Public Vows: A History of Marriage and the Nation* (Cambridge, Mass.: Harvard University Press 2000) pp. 198–99.

right "rooted in the traditions and collective conscience of our people," it did agree that by limiting the rights and benefits that were associated with marriage to heterosexual couples, the state had established a sex-based classification, reserving "a multiplicity of rights and benefits" for a single class of people, and therefore presumed to be unconstitutional unless it could be justified by "compelling state interests." The logic of the decision established twenty years before in *Frontiero v. Richardson* (see pp. 752–753) that illegality must turn on the act, not the gender of the actor—opened the door to claims on behalf of same-sex partnerships. In 2000, Vermont extended the rights and protections of marriage to same-sex couples who had established a "civil union."

In 2003, the U.S. Supreme Court heard arguments in *Lawrence v. Texas*, a case with many similarities to *Bowers*. Acting on what turned out to be a false report of a disturbance, Houston police entered John Lawrence's apartment and found him in bed with Tyron Garner. Lawrence and Garner challenged the Texas law that criminalized private homosexual intimacy. Writing for the majority in a sweeping 6–3 decision, Justice Anthony Kennedy placed the matter in the center of constitutional understandings of liberty: "As the Constitution endures, persons in every generation can invoke its principles in their own search for greater freedom." The protection against intrusion should be broadly understood; liberty is traditionally the protection from unwarranted government intrusions into a dwelling or other private places. In our tradition the state is not omnipresent in the home. Liberty is also the right to "an autonomy of self that includes freedom of thought, belief, expression, and certain intimate conduct. [This case] involves liberty of the person both in its spatial and more transcendent dimensions. . . . To say that the issue in *Bowers* was simply the right to engage in certain sexual conduct demeans the claim [of John Lawrence] . . . just as it would demean a married couple were it to be said marriage is simply about the right to have sexual intercourse . . . [this] personal relationship . . . is within the liberty of persons to choose without being punished as criminals."

The Court explicitly overturned *Bowers*. It recognized that the decision in *Bowers* had relied on historical misunderstandings and overstatements. The Court was persuaded that laws directed specifically against homosexual conduct are of a relatively recent vintage; in the nineteenth century, laws against sodomy criminalized heterosexual as well as homosexual conduct and were enforced generally only when the activity was public or involved a minor or the victim of assault. "It was not until the 1970s that any state singled out same-sex relations for criminal prosecution." And the Court pointed to changing international understandings: "the right the petitioners seek has been accepted as an integral part of human freedom in many other countries."*

Many people, however, were deeply dismayed by these moves toward treating marriage as malleable. Polls in 2000 showed strong popular support for the extension of health insurance, Social Security benefits, and insurance rights to same-sex partners. But strong majorities—as high as two-thirds—opposed "marriage." Hawaii voters, who supported the extension of benefits, also overwhelmingly supported a constitutional amendment to bar same-sex marriages. Predicting that once a single state recognized same-sex marriage, gay and lesbian couples would travel there to solemnize their relationship and then return to their home states to live (much as couples had made use of Nevada's "quickie" divorce laws in the 1940s and 1950s), Congress quickly passed the Defense of Marriage Act in 1996. It was a brief statute with two major parts.

Lawrence v. Texas, 539 U.S. 558 (2003).

AN ACT TO DEFINE AND PROTECT THE INSTITUTION OF MARRIAGE, 1996

... No State, territory or possession of the United States, or Indian tribe, shall be required to give effect to any public act, record, or judicial proceeding of any other State, territory possession or tribe respecting a relationship between persons of the same sex that is treated as a marriage under the laws of such other State, territory, possession or tribe, or a right or claim arising from such relationship . . .

In determining the meaning of any Act of Congress, or of any ruling, regulation, or interpretation of the various administrative bureaus and agencies of the United States, the word "marriage" means only a legal union between one man and one woman as husband and wife, and the word "spouse" refers only to a person of the opposite sex who is a husband or a wife.

U.S. Statutes at Large, 110:2419

DOMA, as the Defense of Marriage Act came to be known, was echoed by a successful movement to enact similar state statutes and to amend state constitutions. The movement strengthened over the next decade. Within a decade, 29 states had constitutional provisions that restricted marriage to heterosexuals; another thirteen states had laws that did the same. Supporters argued that restricting marriage to heterosexual couples respected the long history of an unchanging institution. They also argued that such marriages sustain children–both biological and adopted–better than same-sex partnerships. The following paragraphs track the mounting challenges to Defense of Marriage Acts, first at the state level, then in the U.S. Supreme Court.

Challenges to limiting marriage to heterosexuals also grew in number and in intensity. In November 2003, the Supreme Judicial Court of Massachusetts decided by a 4–3 vote that barring same-sex couples from "access to the protections, benefits and obligations of civil marriage" "arbitrarily" deprives them "of membership in one of our community's most rewarding and cherished institutions. That exclusion is incompatible with the constitutional principles of respect for individual autonomy and equality under law" and "violates the Massachusetts Constitution." To those who would offer civil unions as the equivalent of marriage, and who thought that the constitutional claim was merely a semantic quibble over language, Chief Justice Margaret Marshall and her colleagues in the majority invoked the decision of the U.S. Supreme Court in *Brown v. Board of Education*: a separate but equal institution is inherently unequal.

GOODRIDGE V. MASSACHUSETTS DEPARTMENT OF PUBLIC HEALTH, 2003

CHIEF JUSTICE MARSHALL:

Marriage is a vital social institution. The exclusive commitment of two individuals to each other nurtures love and mutual support; it brings stability to our society. For those who choose to marry, and for their children, marriage provides an abundance of legal, financial, and social benefits. In return it imposes weighty legal, financial, and social obligations. The question before us is whether, consistent with the Massachusetts Constitution, the Commonwealth may deny the protections, benefits, and obligations conferred by civil marriage to two individuals of the same sex who wish to marry. We conclude that it may not. The Massachusetts Constitution affirms the dignity and equality of all individuals. It forbids the creation of second-class citizens. In reaching our conclusion we have given full deference to the arguments made by the Commonwealth. But it has failed to identify any constitutionally adequate reason for denying civil marriage to same-sex couples.

We are mindful that our decision marks a change in the history of our marriage law. . . .

In Massachusetts, civil marriage is, and since pre-Colonial days has been, precisely what its name implies: a wholly secular institution. No religious ceremony has ever been required to validate a Massachusetts marriage . . . Civil marriage anchors an ordered society by encouraging stable relationships over transient ones. It is central to the way the Commonwealth identifies individuals, provides for the orderly distribution of property, ensures that children and adults are cared for and supported whenever possible from private rather than public funds, and tracks important epidemiological and demographic data.

Marriage also bestows enormous private and social advantages on those who choose to marry . . . the decision whether and whom to marry is among life's momentous acts of self-definition. . . . The benefits accessible only by way of a marriage license are enormous . . . "hundreds of statutes" are related to marriage and to marital benefits. With no attempt to be comprehensive, we note that some of the statutory benefits conferred by the Legislature on those who enter into civil marriage include, as to property: joint Massachusetts income tax filing; tenancy by the entirety (a form of ownership that provides certain protections against creditors and allows for the automatic descent of property to the surviving spouse without probate); extension of the benefit of the homestead protection (securing up to $300,000 in equity from creditors) to one's spouse and children; automatic rights to inherit the property of a deceased spouse who does not leave a will. . . .

Where a married couple has children, their children are also directly or indirectly, but no less auspiciously, the recipients of the special legal and economic protections obtained by civil marriage . . . [including] the greater ease of access to family-based State and Federal benefits that attend the presumptions of one's parentage.

It is undoubtedly for these concrete reasons, as well as for its intimately personal significance, that civil marriage has long been termed a "civil right." See, e.g., *Loving v. Virginia*. . . .

The Department [of Health] . . . argues that broadening civil marriage to include same-sex couples will trivialize or destroy the institution of marriage as it has historically been fashioned. Certainly our decision today marks a significant change in the definition of marriage as it has been inherited from the common law, and understood by many societies for centuries. But it does not disturb the fundamental value of marriage in our society.

Here, the plaintiffs seek only to be married, not to undermine the institution of civil marriage. They do not want marriage abolished. They do not attack the binary nature of marriage, the consanguinity provisions, or any of the other gate-keeping provisions of the marriage licensing law. Recognizing the right of an individual to marry a person of the same sex will not diminish the validity or dignity of opposite-sex marriage, any more than recognizing the right of an individual to marry a person of a different race devalues the marriage of a person who marries someone of her own race. If anything, extending civil marriage to same-sex couples reinforces the importance of marriage to individuals and communities. That same-sex couples are willing to embrace marriage's solemn obligations of exclusivity, mutual support, and commitment to one another is a testament to the enduring place of marriage in our laws and in the human spirit.

The *Goodridge* decision set off, one historian observed, "a rolling act of civil disobedience" as mayors in San Francisco, Portland, Oregon, and other cities issued marriage licenses. But the decision was also met with a firestorm of protest: every one of these non-Massachusetts marriages was nullified by state courts while at the same time DOMA statutes and constitutional amendments seemed to block same-sex marriage in other jurisdictions. The issue continued to be hotly debated throughout the nation in state and federal elections. Civil unions were embraced in Vermont. Prompted by a 2006 state supreme court ruling in New Jersey that same-sex couples are entitled to the same benefits and protections as opposite-sex couples, the legislature authorized civil unions. New Hampshire, Maine, and Vermont legalized same-sex marriage in 2009.

Goodridge v. Massachusetts Department of Public Health, 798 N.R. 2d 941 (Mass. 2003).

In April 2009, the Iowa Supreme Court became the first court to overturn a DOMA statute unanimously, ruling that limiting marriage to heterosexuals is a violation of the Iowa state constitution's equal protection clause and the constitutional separation of powers.* To rule otherwise, they said, would be a denial of the court's "constitutional mandate to protect the free exercise of religion in Iowa," and also its general responsibility to "proceed as civil judges, far removed from the theological debate of religious clerics." They observed that they were instructed by the Iowa Code § 595A.1 that "provides that 'Marriage is a civil contract' and then regulates that civil contract . . . we give respect to the views of all Iowans on the issue of same-sex marriage—religious or otherwise—by giving respect to our constitutional principles. These principles require that the state recognize both opposite-sex and same-sex civil marriage." The court invoked its own strong history of sustaining civil rights: roughly a century before the U.S. Supreme Court made its rulings, public school segregation, the denial of equal access to public accommodations, and the definition of interracial marriage as miscegenation had all been declared to be denials of equal protection of the laws in Iowa. And the court took note of Iowa's recognition of women's equality: it was the first state to admit a woman to the practice of law and to its public university on the same terms as male students.Whatever position supporters or opponents take, the terms of marriage are now increasingly recognized as not only a private matter but also a civil rights issue. In October 2008, the Connecticut Supreme Court ruled that equal protection of the law requires equal access to marriage. The California Supreme Court had made a similar ruling a few months before, but California voters interrupted with an initiative (Proposition 8 on the fall 2008 state ballot) to add a state constitutional amendment barring such marriage, and in the spring of 2009, the California Supreme Court ruled that the initiative was a valid exercise of the voters' right to amend the Constitution.

Meanwhile, the American Foundation for Equal Rights initiated a challenge to Proposition 8 in the *federal* courts, on behalf of Kristin Perry and Sandra Stier, and another same-sex couple who had been denied marriage licenses, claiming that they had been denied the equal protection of the law promised in the Fourteenth Amendment. The trial in *Perry v. Schwarzenegger* was held in the U.S. District Court for the Northern District of California in January, 2010. The first two witnesses to testify at length against Proposition 8 were historians. Nancy Cott, author of *Public Vows: A History of Marriage and the Nation* (2000), whose essay on equal rights appears on pp. 503–512 of this book, testified that the history of marriage has changed over time and that it has been a secular, not religious, institution in the United States. George Chauncey, author of *Gay New York: Gender, Urban Culture, and the Making of the Gay Male World, 1890–1940* (1994), testified to the long history of discrimination against gay men and lesbians in the United States. It is rare that historians are asked to testify at such length; their testimony can be followed on the transcripts posted by the Equal Rights Foundation (http://www.equalrightsfoundation.org/our-work/hearing-transcripts. Start with page 181 of Day 1 for Cott's testimony; page 356 for Chauncey's).

Arnold Schwarzenegger, the governor of the State of California declined to support Proposition 8; its defense was conducted by private attorneys. In the summer of 2010, Judge Vaughn R. Walker ruled that Proposition 8 was an unconstitutional denial of the equal protection and due process guaranteed by the Fifth and Fourteenth Amendments to the Constitution. The case, now called *Hollingsworth v.*

Varnum v. Brien, 763 N. W. 2d 862 (Iowa 2009).

Perry, was appealed to the U.S. Supreme Court. In June 2013, the Court upheld Judge Walker's decision, on the technical ground that as private citizens, the sponsors of Proposition 8 did not have standing to challenge Judge Walker's decision.

By 2012, same-sex couples could marry in more than a dozen states, among them New York. They were entitled to the benefits offered by state law. But DOMA meant that federal law did not recognize their marriages; they were not entitled to any of the many federal benefits, including the rules of inheritance. Edith Windsor launched the challenge that ended up in the U.S. Supreme Court. She and Thea Spyer had met in New York City in 1966 and had a loving relationship thereafter. When New York gave same sex couples the right to register as domestic partners, in 1993, they did so. When Canada recognized same-sex marriage in 2007, they traveled there to marry. Speyer died in February 2009, leaving her entire estate to Windsor. The Internal Revenue Service ruled that Windsor was not a "surviving spouse" and did not qualify for the marital exemption from the federal estate tax. Windsor paid $363,053 in estate taxes and sued on the grounds that she had been denied the Fifth Amendment's guarantee of due process and therefore equal protection of the laws.

In June 2013–on the same day that it handed down its decision on Proposition 8—the U.S. Supreme Court ruled for Edith Windsor. While deferring to the authority of individual states to set the rules for civil marriage, it held that DOMA "singles out a class of persons . . . , [instructing] all federal officials, and indeed all persons with whom same-sex couples interact, including their own children, that their marriage is less worthy than the marriages of others. . . . [N]o legitimate purpose overcomes the purpose and effect to disparage and to injure those whom the State, by its marriage laws, sought to protect in personhood and dignity."[**]

Technically, the Windsor decision applied only to people in states where same-sex marriage was recognized. There, married same-sex couples would not be subjected to two different tax regimes or excluded from the benefits of the 1,000 federal laws that apply to married couples. But the eloquent decision prompted same-sex couples in many other states to ask: "if marriage is included in the equal protection of the laws in New York or California or Iowa, why isn't it included in my own state?" Many acted on that question, joining in litigation to overturn state bans. Polls show rapidly changing public opinion, especially among people under age 30. A March 2014 Washington Post-ABC News poll found 59 percent to 34 percent in favor—a result that crossed party lines and reversed the results of a poll 10 years earlier.[††]

When we published the previous edition of *Women's America*, same-sex marriage was legal in a half-dozen states. As this book goes to press, same-sex marriage is legal in 31 states and the District of Columbia. The situation remans fluid. For reasonably up-to-date summaries of the rapidly changing marriage laws in the various states, consult the website of the National Conference of State Legislatures: http://www.ncsl.org/research/human-services/same-sex-marriage.aspx.

The impact of striking down DOMA has repercussions beyond marriage law. DOMA was struck down because its purpose, according to the Court, was to "impose inequality" on a class of individuals based on their sexual orientation. This could apply in many contexts.

[**]*U.S. v. Windsor*, 133 S. Ct. 2675 (2013). The vote was 5–4; the majority opinion was delivered by Justice Anthony Kennedy. For an elegant history of marriage laws, see the historians' brief, Brief on the Merits for Historians, Am. Historical Ass'n et al. as Amici Curiae Supporting Respondents, *United States v. Windsor*, 133 S. Ct. 2675 (2013) (No. 12-307).

[††]Dana Milbank, "The Politics of Same-Sex Marriage Are Swiftly Changing," *Washington Post*, May 30, 2014.

GENDER AND THE ARMED FORCES

MARGOT CANADAY
Finding a Home in the Army: Before "Don't Ask, Don't Tell"

The military has traditionally been a male realm. Women's exclusion from arms-bearing on behalf of the state has been a major marker of the ambivalence of their citizenship. Margot Canaday shows that the years in the late 1940s and 1950s when women joined the armed forces as soldiers on a permanent, not temporary, basis coincided with a campaign to identify and target lesbians for exclusion. Yet, given the long-standing cultural acceptance of life-long, intimate friendships between women (see Carroll Smith-Rosenberg's and Leila J. Rupp's essays in this volume), lesbians were more difficult for military officials to detect than gay male soldiers. Canaday tells the story of the lengthy, wide-ranging investigations that ensued, along with the resistance strategies used by women service members. One of her surprising conclusions is that state repression can prompt individuals to "see" and articulate an important, latent aspect of their sense of self, and thus can help produce historically complex identities such as "lesbian."

Why did military leaders seek to exclude lesbians from the armed forces? How did they go about identifying lesbians? Note the wide-ranging impact of these investigations. How do these lesbian witch-hunting campaigns during the Cold War compare with the "Don't Ask, Don't Tell" policy (1993–2011) and with evolving military policies on sexuality?

While Alfred Kinsey's 1953 study of female sexuality is usually remembered for shattering several mid-twentieth-century myths about women's sexual behavior, the volume also contained several important observations about the American state, especially concerning the regulation of homosexuality among women. The relationship between the state and female homosexuality, Kinsey concluded in *Sexual Behavior in the Human Female*, was not a well-developed one. The state had, in fact, a long history of indifference to homosexuality among women. . . . Kinsey's survey of . . . recent enforcement of sex law in New York City revealed three cases from the 1940s or 1950s in which

women had been arrested for homosexuality. "But all of these cases were dismissed, although there were some tens of thousands of arrests and convictions of males charged with homosexual activity" during those same years.[1]

Kinsey's assertion about government indifference to lesbianism is accurate even when applied in contexts beyond the state-level regulation of sexual behavior that he surveyed. In the early years of the twentieth century, . . . the federal government's concern with sexually degenerate aliens included effeminate men and male sodomists, but focused on neither mannishness nor same-sex eroticism among women. While World War I vice investigators

Excerpted from ch. 5 of *The Straight State: Sexuality and Citizenship in Twentieth-Century America* by Margot Canaday (Princeton, N.J.: Princeton University Press, 2009). Reprinted by permission of the author and publisher. Notes have been edited and renumbered.

occasionally identified "female pervertors" in and around military bases, . . . such revelations seemed to have little impact on local, state, or federal policing, which remained directed at men. . . . In his study of gays and lesbians during the Second World War, Allan Bérubé argues that lesbians were often invisible to military authorities and women were rarely discharged for homosexuality. Even during the massive 1950s' purge of homosexuals from the civil service, women (who comprised 40 percent of the federal workforce) were far less likely to be targeted than men. "Of the initial ninety-one homosexuals fired from the State Department," historian David Johnson writes, "only two were women."[2]

Yet while generally true, Kinsey's conclusion about state indifference to lesbianism does not hold in at least one time and place: the early Cold War military. Here one finds a state that did not ignore, conflate, or subsume lesbianism, but was instead focused upon it. Although women made up just 1 percent of the force during the late 1940s and early 1950s, the military's efforts to purge soldiers suspected of homosexuality targeted women especially. Military officials maintained that homosexuality among women was more disruptive to morale and discipline than homosexuality in men, and they attributed a far higher rate of homosexual activity to female than male personnel. . . . [3]

As with earlier moments of increased federal attention to homoerotic practices and desires, the process of state-building itself stimulated growing federal interest in homosexuality among military women. The coming of the Cold War . . . gave an enduring "cast to the transmutations of World War II"—especially the increased size of the bureaucratic state, which remained "intact." The postwar boom in military spending expanded the economy generally, paving the way for greater numbers of women to enter the civilian labor force. Cold War expansion also created a lasting need for women inside the military. When Congress authorized a permanent peacetime force that was at least five times its 1939 size, it simultaneously provided for a stable nucleus of women who would attend to the military's growing clerical, administrative, and other needs. Legislation that permanently integrated women into the regular forces was passed in 1948.[4]

Homosexuality mattered most to state officials in the places where citizenship was defined, and if women's military service was becoming less peripheral, then so was their perversion. The Cold War military thus reveals [a] . . . federal arena in which the increasingly salient opposition between citizenship and homosexuality was forged. . . . Women's proximity to first-class citizenship helps to explain why the focus on lesbianism first became apparent inside the Cold War military, but other factors were at work. The federal regulation of homosexuality among women also depended on the crystallization of a binaristic conception of homosexuality and heterosexuality, which . . . developed gradually in the years before World War II, and then hardened during and immediately after the war. By the late 1940s and early 1950s, many Americans (and certainly most state officials) believed that individuals were either heterosexual or homosexual, and that "normal" men and women were those who had sexual relations with persons of the opposite sex. As a result of this broad-ranging conceptual shift, . . . men and women who were identified as homosexual were seen as fundamentally similar kinds of people, and this paved the way for a military policy that applied to both men and women "irrespective of sex."[5]

In drafting new guidelines after the war, military officials were adamant that a single policy would be used to deal with homosexuality among both sexes. Under that policy, women, like men, could be discharged for either committing homosexual acts or possessing homosexual tendencies. Yet . . . , the policy was implemented in ways that suggested gender difference. Unsure of how to define a homosexual act between women, military authorities often relied on the provision barring soldiers who had homosexual "tendencies" to eliminate women who were physically intimate with other women. Moreover, officials not only believed that sex among women was less easily defined than sex between men, but that women were more private in their sexual lives. As a result, and in contrast to the way that investigations of homosexuality among men often centered around the commission of an act, women's romantic attachments, social networks, and emotional ties were all scrutinized for evidence that a woman possessed homosexual tendencies. . . .

As relationships (rather than relations) became the focus of state policing, antilesbian investigations took on an unprecedented size. Such investigations encompassed not simply the parties to an alleged sexual encounter, but an expansive web of friends and acquaintances that sometimes extended far beyond a single base or unit. These ordeals—which represented a huge expansion of the state's investigatory power—were a manifestation of the military's own ambivalence about the women who served in the military after the war. In contrast to the women whose World War II service was understood as a heroically brief interlude before marriage, this later cohort signed up not to meet a temporary emergency but, rather as part of a permanent nucleus of women within the armed services. Because they were seen as choosing the military (as opposed to marriage) for a career, these soldiers were automatically suspect, considered overly ambitious and unlikely to be satisfied with the things that "normal" women wanted. The way that these soldiers were policed, then, was related to why they were policed: antilesbian investigations aimed not only to remove a few women from the service, but to employ the threat of lesbianism to secure the subordination of women soldiers as a class. Policing this vast network of relationships enabled military officials to touch the lives of virtually every woman in a unit under investigation, warning each not only to monitor her own relationships with other women on her base, but to avoid appearing too driven or exercising too much authority as well. The exclusion of women believed to be lesbians was, in short, closely related to the inclusion of women in the service in general. Lesbianism was constituted by military authorities to help maintain gender hierarchy after women's integration eliminated a historic barrier between male and female service. . . .

Albeit in a temporary capacity, women first served in the U.S. military in significant numbers during the Second World War. Approximately 350,000 women enlisted during those years in the WAC or its equivalent in the other branches of the armed services (the WAVES, WAF, WASP, or SPARS).[6] Women were drawn to the military for a variety of reasons—it offered excitement and independence, as well as a chance to serve the country. A portion of those who enlisted were also attracted by the emotional and perhaps sexual dimensions of working and living with other women. Some of these women continued in the military a lesbian life they had led before the war; some had their first romantic or sexual experiences with women after they enlisted. As long as they did

not attract public attention, the military generally ignored "romantic friendships" among women. But women who drew suspicion of lesbianism to their unit—usually butch, often working-class women—presented a greater problem for military authorities. Such women were only rarely subject to formal regulations barring homosexuality, but . . . they might be discharged for unsuitability (or for such general offenses as public drunkenness or insubordination), if they even made it past the initial screening procedures that "focused on class background, education, personality, and behavior. . . ."[7] "During the war," WAC commander Mary Hallaren remembered, "we skirted the homosexual problem." . . . Similarly, WAC psychiatrist Margaret Craighill described homosexuality as a "serious problem" for men during the war, but "much less of a problem than . . . expected" for women.[8]

Such attitudes stand in stark relief to those expressed in the years after the war. Women's entry into the armed services paralleled a broader movement of women into the labor market overall during these years, and women in the military generally performed the same kind of clerical work as their counterparts in the civil service. But while many working women pushed up against the conservative gender ideology of the era, only women in the service threatened the special relationship between men, soldiering, and martial citizenship. . . . Widespread concern about lesbianism among women in the military actually preceded the 1950s' "lavender scare" in the federal government. What one journalist referred to as the military's "project lesbian" instead coincided with congressional debates on women's integration in 1947 and 1948. During those hearings, military and congressional leaders argued that the services would only be able to meet recruitment goals for female personnel if women were given the opportunity to build a lasting career in the military. Official interest in lesbianism arose in tandem with the military's growing need for women.[9]

It was, for example, as Congress was making plans for women's permanent entry into the service in 1947 that the army drafted instructions for investigating homosexuality among female soldiers. . . . In 1948, as integration was enacted, the military established the WAC Training Center at Fort Lee, and in response to what it then described as an extraordinarily high rate of homosexuality among women, included lectures on homo-sexuality in the curriculum for enlistees. . . . Leadership courses for noncommissioned officers and officer refresher courses introduced around the same time included segments on how to detect and handle abnormal conduct among female personnel. The approach was, the WAC director wrote, to bring homosexuality among women out from "behind a veil of silence and mystery."[10] . . .

Some months later Lieutenant General Lutes reported to WAC director Hallaren that "the indications continue to grow that a condition of homosexuality is widespread in the army." Despite the outbreak of war with Korea—which might have encouraged officials to look the other way—150 enlisted women and officers were implicated, Lutes told Hallaren, in investigations into homosexuality in the Fourth Army. In 1951, a memo from the commanding officer of the Military District of Washington described the situation in more alarming tones. "The number of sexual perverts in the WAC who are assigned to this command is a matter of grave concern to me," he wrote. "This situation is steadily growing worse, although I have been cognizant of it for some time and have used every means at my disposal to cope with it." The command had already separated two officers and transferred four more; nine enlisted women had been undesirably discharged for homosexuality. Beyond that, the general claimed to have conclusive evidence that another thirteen WAC soldiers were perverts and stated that eleven others were under suspicion. The general's memo prompted a high-level meeting with seven other commanders a month later. The numbers themselves were not unusual, but reflected a broader pattern. Investigations conducted at any given base during these years regularly involved up to twenty women and sometimes several times that number.[11]

The army's postwar focus on homosexuality among women existed with equal or greater intensity in the navy, air force, and marines. When he took command of his office, for instance, the head of the air force's special investigations unit did not believe the rumors concerning homosexuality among air force women because they were so incredible. He soon found that the "situation was actually more fantastic than the rumors." . . . A 1952 report on the women's marine detachment at El Toro, California, observed that homosexuality

among the women there was considered to be a "definite problem" that probably existed at other bases as well.[12] Yet it was the navy's 1957 Crittenden report that most clearly articulated that homosexuality was a special problem among women. The report noted that "homosexual activity of female members of the military has appeared to be more disruptive of morale and discipline . . . than similar male activity," and it posited a higher rate of homosexuality for women than men in the navy.[13] . . .

To understand the military's broadest purposes in regulating homosexuality, it is necessary to look at its most precise targets. Antilesbian repression in the military was *broadly* powerful against all women because it was *individually* devastating against a smaller number. How, then, was homosexuality in women defined, how was it policed in specific women, and how did those individuals who were directly targeted resist such policing? . . .

. . . Homosexuality in women might consist of anything, Fort McClellan psychiatrists stated, from the "bus station pick up . . . to a close emotional relationship extending over a period of years with no more than . . . casual physical contact."[14] As this broad range suggests, the ambiguity of homosexuality in women increased its scope.

Part of the confusion as to what comprised female homosexuality resulted from a greater cultural tolerance for homosocial intimacy between women than between men. Acts that were "indicative of homosexuality in the male" were thought "normal [in] the female." Women might, the Crittenden Board reported, "kiss and embrace . . . and live together and occupy the same bed without any connotation of homosexuality," while "similar acts on the part of males would immediately be branding." In a military context, where women had to adapt to male behavioral norms, such circumstances meant that "normal female propensities" might be misinterpreted as homosexual acts. "It is very difficult to know where to draw the line on anything of this kind," commented WAC director Hallaren.[15]

But military officials did not attribute the high rate of homosexuality among women solely to such misinterpretation. Rather, as the WAC director conceded of the women in her branch, there might be "some fact among the fancy." Indeed, widespread acceptance of the expression of affection between women could conceal actual homosexuality in the service. Relationships among women, army psychiatrists wrote, could be "more easily covered" than relationships among men. A homosexual act between two women "leaves no physical evidence of its commission," an army manual on female homosexuality noted, "and seldom if ever is committed in the presence of an innocent person." Relatedly, the Crittenden Board noted that female homosexuality was difficult to detect because women were "more secretive" and "more seclusive" than men.[16] Because women were thought more likely to engage in sex in private, and because military officials were unclear about how to define sexual activity between women even when it was witnessed, the regulation of female homosexuality could not rest primarily on homosexual acts.

. . . The navy acted first to update its guidelines on homosexuality for the postwar period, releasing in July 1949 a policy instructing military officials to consider homosexuality among personnel, whether "male or female." The navy policy then guided the work of a Department of Defense (DOD) committee charged with creating a uniform policy for all branches of the service. The DOD committee—in what was a harbinger of rising homophobia throughout the federal government—firmly broke with World War II policies that permitted some personnel charged with homosexuality to be rehabilitated and returned to the service. "Prompt separation of homosexuals from the military is mandatory," the DOD policy of October 1949 read. The committee, which included a representative from the WAC to cover "women's interests," wrote women into the hardening opposition between homosexuality and martial citizenship. Homosexuals were not to be allowed to serve in any capacity, these officials mandated, and "the character of separation" would be, moreover, "without distinction as to sex."[17]

. . . The new policy established three classes of homosexual offenders. Class I homosexuals, as with the World War II–era policy, were violent offenders who were to be court-martialed. Class II homosexuals, also a carryover from the war years, were to be undesirably discharged for consensual homosexual acts. Finally, the new policy inaugurated the category of the Class III homosexual, who had homosexual "tendencies," and was to be either generally or undesirably discharged.[18]

To be clear, the idea that a person could have homosexual tendencies was not entirely new—during World War II the term referred to a soldier (generally male) who declared himself homosexual but had committed no in-service acts.[19] But the new policy's denotation of such persons as a separate class indicated a growing emphasis on the category of tendencies by the end of the 1940s. "The only major change prescribed by [the DOD policy]," wrote Under Secretary of the Navy Dan Kimball, "is the establishment of the Class III category of personnel."[20]

As deployed by the new guidelines, the concept of tendencies paved the way for more aggressive policing, capturing, as one air force captain put it, "the complexity of the homosexual problem." . . . With women, the category could designate (a physically) unexpressed homosexuality . . . [and it] helped military officials cope with the fact that, despite their best efforts, they still did not understand how homosexuality in women was expressed. The concept of tendencies absolved military officials of the responsibility of drawing a line between sex and what was considered normal female intimacy. In so doing, the designation of the Class III homosexual enabled military officials to extend the apparatus they used to police women far beyond sexual acts. The label of tendencies not only penalized mannish women for "the way they walk[ed], talk[ed], or dress[ed]," but also brought a sprawling web of women's friendships and associations under state surveillance.[21] Military authorities, in short, had begun to identify a new set of attributes as evidence of homosexuality, revealing the power of the state to not only regulate but constitute identity as well. . . .

How, then, did military police and administrative discharge boards enforce the DOD's policy on homosexuality against individual women? Military discharge files for *male* soldiers from the early 1950s follow remarkably clear patterns. Most cases involved two or perhaps four men, who either admitted or were observed in acts of sodomy or fellatio. (Often the admissions followed being caught by other men in their units.) The investigation, while undoubtedly painful to those accused, was a contained and relatively straightforward inquiry: Did two men engage in sexual relations together? How, when, and where? Who saw it?[22] When male soldiers were processed as Class III (for tendencies), the investigation still generally revolved around the commission of acts, albeit ones with fewer witnesses. In one case, for example, . . . a male soldier wrote a letter to the president stating that he was a homosexual and asking for help to cope with his condition. After this admission, the army commenced an investigation into the soldier's homosexual tendencies. . . . The soldier received a general discharge for homosexual tendencies "after the investigation disclosed that [the accused] committed acts."[23]

Policing homosexuality among women was not as clear-cut. While military police sometimes encountered two women hugging and kissing in cars on base, and were aware that many of the women "[went] steady" together, military authorities did not expect to observe acts between women that could clearly be identified as homosexuality. When they did, they were not well equipped to deal with such situations. In one episode from 1952, a military police officer (MP) spotted one WAC member performing oral sex on another in the front seat of a parked car. He watched for about thirty seconds, before the two women (having recognized the MP vehicle behind them) drove off. Although he had identified the two women, he did not make a report because, as he admitted subsequently, "I wouldn't know how." He further explained that "there never were any orders given to me to cover anything like that."[24] . . .

One could conclude, based on the way that these MPs responded to the two WAC soldiers, that military authorities were uninterested in policing sexual activity between women. But that was not the case. Military authorities sought evidence of physical involvement between women suspected of being lesbians. Yet MPs simply did not expect that women would routinely engage in homosexual acts where they could be observed. "It was just one of those things you read about and hear about," declared one of the MPs who had spotted the two women together in the car, "but never *see*."[25] Accordingly, in most cases the policing of women relied more on interrogation, through which investigators induced women to confess and corroborate sexual activity with other women, sometimes quite successfully. . . .

. . . [H]omosexual tendencies were also attributed to women who exhibited gender inversion, or as one military guide to homosexuality among women put it, "the wearing of the clothes and the desire to assume the role of the opposite sex." . . . [For example,] one recruit testified, Williams was a "queer one" . . . who had "masculine ways." She would announce her presence in the barracks by calling out, "There's a man in the house!" She wore mannish clothes, "combed her hair in a mannish way," and women appeared to be drawn to her. She had, the investigation revealed, "magnetism."[26]

The investigator's mention of recruit Williams's apparent ability to attract women demonstrates that in identifying the attributes of homosexuality in women, military officials were attuned to not only sexual activity and gender traits but also women's relationships with one another. Indeed, the bonds between women were commonly scrutinized for evidence of homosexual tendencies—an assessment that rested on intimacy as much as sex. Moreover, including relationships within their scope meant that investigations among women often took on an enormous scale. An investigation that began with evidence of a single homosexual incident might lead to every woman in a unit being called in for questioning. As women were pressured to name their associates, investigations thus expanded to massive proportions involving a complex web of women, sometimes spreading across several bases in different regions of the country. . . .

In contrast to investigations involving male soldiers, then, a focus on relationships and associations could supplement or even supplant questions about sexual activity when women were the subjects of official scrutiny. One such large-scale probe at Fort Meyer, Virginia, began when one woman admitted to her commanding officer that she was a homosexual and had "performed acts of cunnilingus." A comparable admission by a male soldier most likely would have resulted in his discharge and that of his sex partner(s). The scope of the WAC investigation's final report was much broader: "Baker has told Armstrong, that she, Baker, loves Duffy. It is known that Duffy visits Baker at Ft. Meyer, and vice versa." Mitchell and Tracey were "co-owners of a Nash two-door sedan automobile," and the investigating officer explained, "this partnership was consummated to strengthen their friendship." These two women also exchanged Christmas presents; two others, Abel and McNeil, exchanged letters. Hale and Taylor were constantly together, and "Hale wears a ring of Taylor's." Warren and Schneider had also exchanged rings, and so had Baker and Simonides, which "undoubtedly hurt Edwards." Baker knew "Edwards to be extremely jealous of Simonides." But the latter woman also dated Jones. Edwards wanted to exchange rings with Jones, but "Jones denied this offer for fear of consequences which had developed after having exchanged rings with Simonides." And on and on it went.[27]

Military authorities did not just police sexual acts or gender traits; they policed a culture of women. That broad focus involved, despite official "consensus" that one policy on homosexuality govern both sexes, the development of an entirely separate and quite elaborate methodology for investigating homosexuality among women. This methodology borrowed extensively from loyalty and other anticommunist investigations (which also uncovered a network among women, although one allegedly connected by political ideology rather than sexual desire). One manual described army procedure to handle the "widespread condition" of "female homosexuality": in addition to "scientific" interrogation, unit commanders were instructed to set up a cross-reference file (with information from the FBI and civil vice squads as well as military intelligence agencies); "secure a . . . roster of the unit concerned [and] a list of all automobiles owned or operated by suspects"; "secure and maintain informant-informer systems"; "arrange for mail cover"; and finally, that the most valuable information would come "through surveillance, the secretive and continuous watching of persons, vehicles, and places." Should such surveillance reveal female homosexuals, commanders were instructed to "plan and conduct a detailed search of their personal effects, automobiles, and any known 'off post' residences, for the purposes of obtaining correspondence, literature, or pictures of a homosexual nature."[28]

In carrying out their duties, agents went through wastepaper baskets looking for notes. They conducted "shakedowns" of the barracks, searching for letters, photographs, and books with lesbian themes.[29] They set up wiretaps and took polygraphs. Investigators planted informants within units to report on the complicated textures of women's lives together. They uncovered evidence of lesbian weddings, and noted which women had arrived in men's formal wear. Agents recorded the names of women who lived with "notorious homosexuals," as well as those who expressed tolerance for or curiosity about such women. They knew which soldiers did not date the men on base, and they kept a record of which women gave each other gifts, shared a bank account, participated in a business venture, traveled together, or did each other's grocery shopping.[30] "They knew the times I was [with a lover], the buses that I took, how long I stayed, my mode of transportation home, [and] what I wore," one woman in the air force recalled of the painful investigation she experienced. "They knew every damn move I made. It was mind shattering."[31]

Such intensive techniques were in some measure the result of the military's belief that homosexual acts among women were more obscured and less clear-cut than similar acts between men. They were also a result of fierce misogyny. Simply put, there is little evidence in the documentary record that male soldiers went through anything like what their female counterparts did. "The methods used by these investigators," one WAC major wrote in a complaint to the inspector general, were "calculated to embarrass and humiliate the women involved." The major described how investigators searched the belongings of a woman "not even 20 years of age" by opening "the woman's box of Tampax" and going "to the extreme of ripping the tissue paper from each of them." She asked, "What could possibly have been gained by this action except to perpetrate an indignity on this young woman in front of her Commanding Officer?" . . . Women were picked up for questioning at all hours, held under guard, and not allowed telephone calls or visitors. . . . And the interrogation itself was a humiliating experience that could approximate psychological rape. One woman, for example, was asked if she was not "missing a lot of fun" because she had never had intercourse with a man. "You are the same as a little girl that didn't like cake because she had never had any," the investigating officer chided her.[32]

Women investigated for homosexuality went through ordeals that could last months. It was "psychological warfare," one WAF member recalled of her investigation by the air force's Office of Special Intelligence. "They opened my mail . . . they'd look under my mattress . . . they'd get me up in the middle of the night for questioning." She recalled being questioned once or twice each day for four months. "They'd come to the mess hall and get me in the middle of a meal. They knew no bounds." But the worst part was the isolation. "There was no way I could tell [my lover] what was happening and explain to her that my whole relationship with her was something of value, not some tawdry affair." Other women on base avoided this soldier too, "for fear of their own careers."[33] ...

When her discharge finally came—an undesirable, not a general one—it was soul destroying. "I left that base feeling like a real piece of shit." Fired twice when employers learned of her discharge, "for the next six years, I felt like a real loser. . . . I had no ego left, no self-image, no confidence, no surety-of-self." For years, the WAF member "never told a soul about it." Evidence suggests that other women were equally tormented by these witch hunts. . . . "I have steadily lost weight," [one] WAC member stated, "[and] I have had to go on 'sick call' for a nervous condition caused by this aggravation." Some women committed suicide. The scale of these investigations, moreover, made even those who were not targeted feel vulnerable. "If you were so accused, how would you prove your innocence?" one WAC major asked herself, in the midst of a destructive investigation in her unit. She concluded that this was a "precarious and untenable position to occupy. How does one prove the absence of tendencies?"[34] ...

. . . Yet while soldiers rarely fought their discharges in the federal courts, it was not unusual for military women to refuse to be discharged administratively and to demand a court-martial proceeding. Perhaps women did so out of desperation. What better career option than the military existed in the early 1950s for working-class women who wanted to avoid marriage and family, or who did not conform to conventional gender stereotypes? "I went into the service to be a career woman . . . and I'd have stayed there," remembered one woman who was devastated by losing everything "that was air force" right down to her boots. "I request that I be allowed to stay in the army [to] prove that I can be a good soldier," another wrote. Alternatively, women may also have demanded trial by court-martial because they were politically savvy, insisting that the military prove a case that was often based on tenuous evidence regarding emotional ties and loose associations (rather than well-documented accounts of homosexual acts). While military regulations allowed the secretary of each branch to administratively remove a soldier without a court-martial who refused a discharge for homosexuality, in practice a demand for a court-martial could derail the entire process. Officials sometimes just dropped a case, in other words, when a

discharge was refused and conviction by court-martial seemed unlikely.[35] ...

[Some] women refused to pathologize their sexuality during the investigatory process. One soldier, for instance, described her relationship as "beautiful" and told investigators that her "life in the future [would] be centered around [her] relationship." Another woman told investigators that she did not consider her homosexual activity to be unnatural. Perhaps most remarkably, one woman wrote in a detailed confession for the Criminal Investigation Division, "I am not ashamed of what I have done, for it was something which has been born with me."[36]

As such declarations indicate, state repression was productive of identity in complicated ways—women's attempts to manage the antilesbian apparatus within the military frequently led them to articulate a lesbian identity in much sharper terms. "The patient declares that she has been homosexual all her life," one psychiatrist reported, but "did not realize [it] until . . . the investigation into this problem at Ft. Lee stimulated her interest." . . . "Knowing about [homosexuality] now," one woman informed authorities during an investigation at her base, "I look back into my childhood and feel that I have been gay all my life."[37] ...

Here . . . [we see] how involved the conversation was between the regulator and the regulated, how much women themselves worked with the state to produce the category of lesbianism. It was, to be sure, a forced and unpleasant collaboration, but also extremely far-reaching in that it did not just affect the women who had begun to think of themselves as homosexual, the women who literally and figuratively *found themselves* in front of military boards. From the beginning, the lesbian witch hunt had a much broader audience and purpose. . . .

As a few DOD officials pointed out during these years, the most "undesirable" personnel could have been purged—without such intensive and far-reaching investigations. . . . Perhaps the point of the investigation[s] was not removal as much as submission—to train those who survived the purge, in other words, to be junior partners in the military marriage that . . . [leaders] envisioned. Military officials were uneasy not only about . . . lesbians [being] well represented [among the women who chose military careers]. They worried as well about maintaining gender hierarchy as formal barriers separating men's and women's service fell.

Prior to the Women's Integration Act, women's service was always differentiated from men's in such a way as to highlight its lesser character, to set it apart from the kind of sacrifice that produced first-class citizenship. Women's service was auxiliary, quasi-auxiliary, or temporary. After 1948, only the provision keeping women out of combat demarcated women's service as different—a distinction that was becoming less and less meaningful in the nuclear age. . . .

The extent of official concern about maintaining women's subordination in the postintegration period . . . is perhaps nowhere more obvious than in the hostility directed at women officers across the service branches, and the way in which lesbian baiting worked especially to rein in those marked as deviant by their own career ambitions. (The vitriol directed at women officers, usually older women, was also expressed via concerns about the potentially harmful impact of having menopausal women in the service.)[38] So a psychiatrist noted the "drive" of one officer under investigation for homosexuality. She desired independence, the psychiatrist said, positing that her homosexuality was the result of "competitive feelings toward men." Moving up the ranks was itself a sign that an officer bore watching. One navy memo, for instance, noted that female homosexuals achieved "rapid advancement" because they worked hard to "compensate for or to avoid suspicion of [their] sexual weakness."[39]

Women officers were regularly blamed when lesbianism was seen as flourishing within their commands. It was women officers who allegedly opened the floodgates to lesbian recruits, or who turned a blind eye on sexual misconduct because "there but for the grace of God go I." Sometimes such complaints were registered by enlisted women, perhaps as a way of turning the tables on an authority figure.[40] But it was the male command structure that viewed women officers with the most animosity. "I cannot depend on WAC officers to command even a small detachment," one general wrote in a scathing memo on perversion among women. He advocated that both the WAC Training Center and WAC units over a certain size be placed under the control of male officers. It was also proposed that "male officer inspection teams make periodic inspection of all WAC installations," during the course of which enlisted women be granted confidential interviews to discuss their concerns on the subject of "leadership" and "homosexuality."[41]

For enlisted women as well but especially for officers, the closer women moved to power, to first-class citizenship, the more homosexuality seemed to matter.[42] Indeed, the air force was the first service to feature coeducational officer training and a single gender-integrated officer promotion list. It was also "far ahead of the army in investigating and discharging female homosexual personnel." The extent to which the air force carried both gender integration and lesbian persecution only makes clearer their interconnection across the service branches. Women knew at what cost their own ambition came . . . and how carefully they had to manage it. Perhaps this was part of what led the women service directors (all unmarried) to personally fight congressional legislation that would have allowed them each to obtain a rank higher than colonel. "They were afraid of appearing 'grasping.'" It was similarly what motivated these same women to stop saying, as their counterparts had during World War II, that female personnel could "replace" men, and instead talk about how well female soldiers "complemented" male personnel.[43] . . .

The way that women's integration intensified antilesbian repression makes citizenship seem like a zero-sum game: as one group wins, another must lose. A parallel observation may be made with respect to racial integration, which was also occurring as the armed forces adopted increasingly homophobic policies more generally.[44] Yet while this substitutionist logic dominates the rhetoric of citizenship, one need not probe far beneath it to see that every new inclusion was deeply sedimented by past exclusion. Women's integration, in short, did not neuter the tradition of martial citizenship, which remained male. To preserve gender hierarchy in citizenship, though, the state had needed to constitute lesbianism. The incredibly broad way it did so meant that so many women were touched during the course of any given investigation that it was not individual women who were policed, but women in the service as a class.

NOTES

1. Alfred C. Kinsey, *Sexual Behavior in the Human Female* (Philadelphia: Saunders, 1953), 484–85. See also "The Consenting Adult Homosexual and the Law: An Empirical Study of Enforcement and

Administration in Los Angeles County," *UCLA Law Review* 13 (1966): 740.

2. Allan Bérubé, *Coming Out Under Fire: The History of Gay Men and Women in World War II* (New York: Plume, 1991), 28; David K. Johnson, *The Lavender Scare: The Cold War Persecution of Gays and Lesbians in the Federal Government* (Chicago: University of Chicago Press, 2004), 12. Elizabeth Lunbeck notes that male homosexuality has almost always been more condemned by sexologists than lesbianism. See Elizabeth Lunbeck, *The Psychiatric Persuasion: Knowledge, Gender, and Power in Modern America* (Princeton, NJ: Princeton University Press, 2003), 410–11.

3. Crittenden Report, 40, box 16, World War II Project Records, Gay, Lesbian, Bisexual, and Transgender Historical Society, San Francisco.

4. Bruce D. Porter, *War and the Rise of the State: The Military Foundations of Modern Politics* (New York: Free Press, 1994), 286–91; Alice Kessler-Harris, *Out to Work: A History of Wage Earning Women in the United States* (Oxford: Oxford University Press, 1982), 303; Women's Armed Services Act of 1948, Public Law 80-625, *U.S. Statutes at Large* 62 (1948) 368. Two weeks after the enactment of women's integration, Harry S. Truman authorized the nation's first-ever peacetime draft (the Selective Service Act of 1948). Jeanne Holm, *Women in the Military: An Unfinished Revolution* (Novato, CA: Presidio Press, 1992), 129.

5. Hubert E. Howard to the Secretary of the Army, the Secretary of the Navy, the Secretary of the Air Force, "Discharge of Homosexuals from the Armed Services," October 11, 1949, decimal 250.1, box 100, Assistant Secretary of Defense decimal file 1949–1950, Records of the Secretary of Defense, RG 330, National Archives, College Park, MD.

6. Most of the evidence for this chapter is from army records, because records are most available for that branch of the service. The Records of the Secretary of the Air Force at the National Archives, for example, have only been declassified recently. Because all branches were under the DOD after 1947, however, relatively uniform policies guided all branches, and wherever possible, I have included evidence from the air force and navy.

7. Leisa D. Meyer, "The Myth of Lesbian (In)visibility: World War II and the Current Gays in the Military Debate," in *Queer American History*, ed. Alida M. Black (Philadelphia: Temple University Press, 2001), 272; Leisa D. Meyer, *Creating G.I. Jane: Sexuality and Power in the Women's Army Corps* (New York: Columbia University Press, 1996), 156, 161, and chapter 7 generally.

8. Memorandum from Colonel Mary Hallaren to Major General G. E. Byers, "The Homosexual Problem," January–February 1950, box 86, Background Papers, Women's Army Corps 1945–1978, Records of the Army Chief of Staff, RG 319. Margaret Craighill, "Psychiatric Aspects of Women Serving in the Army," *American Journal of Psychiatry* 104 (1947–1948): 228.

9. On women's work in the military, see Holm, *Women in the Military*, especially 113, 175. On domestic ideology during the 1950s, see especially Elaine Tyler May, *Homeward Bound: American Families in the Cold War Era* (New York: Basic Books, 1988). Sam Crown, "Do Lesbians Dominate Our WAC?" *SIR* (March 1956): 20, in vertical file "Homosexuals in the

Military," Kinsey Institute, Indiana University, Bloomington. Janann Sherman, "'They Either Need These Women or They Do Not': Margaret Chase Smith and the Fight for Regular Status for Women in the Military," *Journal of Military History* 54 (January 1990): 72.

10. Memo from R. L. Howze, "Investigation of WAC Personnel," October 14, 1947, decimal 321, box 843, "WAC Project," G-1 (Personnel) decimal file 1946–1948, War Department General Staff, RG 165. Memorandum from Colonel Mary Hallaren to Major General G. E. Byers on "the Homosexual Problem."

11. Lt. General L. Lutes to Colonel Mary A. Hallaren, November 22, 1950, decimal 333.9, "Fourth Army," box 1012, decimal file July 1950–June 1951, Records of the Inspector General, RG 159, National Archives, College Park, MD. Memorandum from Major General Thomas W. Herren, March 26, 1951, "Unsatisfactory Control," decimal 250.1, box 967, G-1 (Personnel) decimal file 1951–1952, Records of the Army Chief of Staff, RG 319; Memorandum from Colonel W. T. Moore, Chief, Personnel Actions Branch, April 24, 1951, "Homosexuality," decimal 250.1, box 967, G-1 (Personnel) decimal file 1951–1952, Records of the Army Chief of Staff, RG 319.

12. Major Robin Elliott to Colonel Lewis and General Lutes, "Air Force Investigation," November 20, 1950, decimal 333.9, "Fourth Army," box 1012, decimal file July 1950–June 1951, Records of the Inspector General, RG 159. Lt. Bowdre L. Carswell to Chief of the Bureau of Medicine and Surgery, October 22, 1952, file no. P13-1, box 503, Administrative Division General Correspondence 1952–1955, Bureau of Medicine and Surgery, RG 52, National Archives, College Park, MD.

13. The Crittenden Board was a special committee assembled by the navy in 1957 to study homosexuality in the military. Crittenden Report, 40–41, box 16, World War II Project Records. Because the services did not break down overall discharge statistics by gender, there is not hard statistical evidence available to back up this claim. Approximately 4,380 cases of perversion were handled by the armed services from January 1947 to October 1950. Another estimated 10,000 cases were handled by the armed services from November 1950 to December 1955. Louis Jolyon West, William T. Doidge, and Robert L. Williams, "An Approach to the Problem of Homosexuality in the Military Service," *American Journal of Psychiatry* 115 (November 1958): 400.

14. M. D. Hogan and R. E. Anderson to CG, Third Army, "Fort McClellan, Mental Hygiene Consultations Service Report," September 14, 1956, box 64, Background Papers, Women's Army Corps 1945–1978, Records of the Army Chief of Staff, RG 319.

15. Crittenden Report, 40–41; Colonel Mary Hallaren, Interview by Colonel Donald Hargrove and Lt. Colonel Milton Little, March 7, 1977, box 86, Background Papers, Women's Army Corps 1945–1978, Records of the Army Chief of Staff, RG 319.

16. Mary Hallaren to Marion B. Kenworthy, April 17, 1950, "WAC Conference June 1950" folder, box 26, Marion Kenworthy Papers, Rare Book and Manuscript Library, Columbia University, New York. Hogan and Anderson to CG, Third Army, "Fort McClellan, Mental Hygiene Consultations Service Report"; "Female Homosexuality," 1950,

decimal 333.9, "Fourth Army," box 1012, decimal file July 1950–June 1951, Records of the Inspector General, RG 159; Crittenden Report, 40–41.

17. Elmer Wohl to Ralph Stohl, "Study to Revise Regulations for the Handling of Homosexuals in the Armed Services for Both Sexes," June 20, 1949, decimal 730, box 153, Assistant Secretary of Defense, decimal file 1949–1950, Records of the Secretary of the Defense, RG 330; Hubert E. Howard to the Secretary of the Army, Secretary of the Navy, and Secretary of the Air Force, "Discharge of Homosexuals from the Armed Services," October 11, 1949, decimal 250.1, box 100, Assistant Secretary of Defense decimal file 1949–1950, Records of the Secretary of Defense, RG 330; file M-46, box 1481, Assistant Secretary of Defense Subcommittee Studies 1948–1951, Records of the Secretary of Defense, RG 330; Manfred S. Guttmacher, *Sex Offenses: The Problem, Causes, and Prevention.*(New York: W. W. Norton, 1951), 132–33; Bérubé, *Coming Out Under Fire*, 260–62.

18. File M-46, box 1481, Assistant Secretary of Defense Subcommittee Studies 1948–1951, Records of the Secretary of Defense, RG 330.

19. Bérubé, *Coming Out Under Fire*, 141–48. From 1945 to 1947, the army made honorable discharges available to soldiers with homosexual tendencies who had committed no homosexual acts in the service. In 1947, the policy changed such that a soldier who had tendencies but had committed no acts would be given either an undesirable discharge or a general discharge.

20. Kimball to Chairman of the Personnel Policy Board, "Discharge of Homosexuals from the Armed Services," December 16, 1949, file M-46, box 1481, Assistant Secretary of Defense Subcommittee Studies 1948–1951, Records of the Secretary of Defense, RG 330.

21. Colonel Robert R. Gideon Jr. to Director of the Staff, "Preliminary Survey of Separation Procedures for Homosexuals in the Armed Forces," March 15, 1949, file M-46, box 1481, Assistant Secretary of Defense Subcommittee Studies 1948–1951, Records of the Secretary of Defense, RG 330. Hogan and Anderson to CG, Third Army, "Fort McClellan, Mental Hygiene Consultations Service Report."

22. See the thirty-two discharge files for homosexuality involving men, decimal 220.8, boxes 3592–93, Classified decimal file 1948–1950, Records of the Adjutant General, RG 407; decimal 220.8, boxes 3776–78, Classified decimal file 1950–1951, Records of the Adjutant General, RG 407.

23. ———Case, decimal 220.8, box 3776, Classified decimal file 1950–1951, Records of the Adjutant General, RG 407. In order to protect the privacy of individuals who may still be living, I have omitted surnames in case file citations. (Most case files involve investigations of multiple women.) The surnames that appear in the text are pseudonyms. I have not changed the names of individuals (in the citations or text) in court cases because of the public nature of those documents.

240. ———Case, decimal 220.8, box 3776, Classified decimal file 1950–1951, Records of the Adjutant General, RG 407.

25. Ibid. (emphasis added).

26. "Female Homosexuality," decimal 333.9, "Fourth Army," box 1012, decimal file July 1950–June 1951, Records of the Inspector General, RG 159.
———Case, decimal 220.8, box 3593, Classified decimal file 1948–1950, Records of the Adjutant General, RG 407.

27. ——— Case, decimal 220.8, box 3776, Classified decimal file 1950–1951, Records of the Adjutant General, RG 407.

28. ——— Case, decimal 220.8, box 3776, Classified decimal file 1950–1951, Records of the Adjutant General, RG 407. On women's networks and the way they were uncovered during loyalty investigations, see Landon R. Y. Storrs, "Red Scare Politics and the Suppression of Popular Front Feminism: The Loyalty Investigation of Mary Dublin Keyserling," *Journal of American History* 90 (September 2003): 508–9.

29. The 1950 pulp novel *Women's Barracks*—which sold three million copies and was singled out during a congressional investigation in 1952 into pornographic materials—must have enjoyed considerable circulation among military women. See Martin Meeker, *Contacts Desired: Gay and Lesbian Communications and Community, 1940s–1970s* (Chicago: University of Chicago Press, 2006), 87, 118.

30. For these investigatory techniques, see cases involving homosexuality among women in decimal 220.8, boxes 3592–93, Classified decimal file 1948–1950, Records of the Adjutant General, RG 407; decimal 220.8, boxes 3776–78, Classified decimal file 1950–1951, Records of the Adjutant General, RG 407.

31. Interview with Loretta "Ret" Coller, in Mary Ann Humphrey, *My Country, My Right to Serve: Experiences of Gay Men and Women in the Military, World War II to the Present* (New Yorker: HarperCollins, 1990), 13.

32. Complaint to Inspector General from Major Florence M. Packard, June 18, 1957, decimal 333, "Ft. McPherson," box 2283, Confidential decimal file July 1957–June 1958, Records of the Inspector General, RG 159. Letter to Senator Wayne Morse, decimal 333.5, "Ft. McClellan," box 2375, Confidential decimal file July 1958–June 1959, Records of the Inspector General, RG 159. ——— Case, decimal 220.8, box 3778, Classified decimal file 1950–1951, Records of the Adjutant General, RG 407.

33. Interview with Coller, in Humphrey, *My Country, My Right to Serve*, 13–14.

34. Ibid., 16–17. B. L. to Senator Spessard L. Holland, decimal 201.23, box 2281, Confidential decimal file July 1957–June 1958, Records of the Inspector General, RG 159. On suicide, see Allan Bérubé and John D'Emilio, "The Military and Lesbians during the McCarthy Years," *Signs: Journal of Women in Culture and Society* 9 (Summer 1984): 775. Complaint to Inspector General from Major Florence M. Packard, June 18, 1957, decimal 333, "Ft. McPherson," box 2283, Confidential decimal file July 1957–June 1958, Records of the Office of the Inspector General, RG 159.

35. It is unclear as to how women knew to do this; it seems plausible that word traveled among women being investigated from base to base. Interview with Coller, in Humphrey, *My Country, My Right to Serve*, 11–12. ———Case, decimal 220.8, box 3592, Classified decimal file, 1948–1950, Records of the Adjutant General, RG 407. *Fannie Mae Clackum v. United States*, 296 F.2d 226 (Ct. Cl. 1960), trial records at the National Archives.

36. "Beautiful," "not ashamed": ———— Case, decimal 220.8, box 3777, Classified decimal file 1950–1951, Records of the Adjutant General, RG 407. ———— Case, decimal 220.8, box 107, decimal file 1953–1954, Records of the Adjutant General, RG 407.

37. ———— Case, decimal 220.8, box 3777, Classified decimal file 1950–1951, Records of the Adjutant General, RG 407.

38. Menopausal women were discussed during hearings on women's integration. See Sherman, "They Either Need These Women or They Do Not," 69. The irony is, of course, that they, along with lesbians, were a perfect solution to the military's pregnancy problem.

39. ———— Case, decimal 220.8, box 3777, Classified decimal file 1950–1951, Records of the Adjutant General, RG 407. Lt. Bowdre L. Carswell to Chief of the Bureau of Medicine and Surgery, "Prophylactic Measures for Control of Homosexuality among Women Personnel of the Armed Services," October 22, 1952, file no. P13-1, box 503.

40. Resume of Proceedings, June 27, 1957, decimal 333, "Ft. McPherson," box 2283, Confidential decimal file July 1958–June 1958, Records of the Inspector General, RG 159; Hogan and Anderson to CG, Third Army, "Fort McClellan, Mental Hygiene Consultations Service Report." ————Case, decimal 201.36, box 52, General Correspondence 1939–1947, Records of the Inspector General, RG 159.

41. Memorandum from Major General Thomas W. Herren, March 26, 1951, "Unsatisfactory Control," and Colonel T. J. Hartford, "Recommendations regarding WAC Enlistment and Utilization," March 29, 1951, decimal 250.1, box 967, G-1 (Personnel) decimal file 1951–1952, Records of the Army Chief of Staff, RG 319; Hogan and Anderson to CG, Third Army, "Fort McClellan, Mental Hygiene Consultations Service Report."

42. This point would not have been lost on Kinsey, whose study of female sexuality attributed overall state indifference to lesbianism to women's lack of social and cultural power. Kinsey, *Sexual Behavior in the Human Female,* 485.

43. Linda Witt, Judith Bellafaire, Britta Granrud, and Mary Jo Binker, *"A Defense Weapon Known to Be of Value": Servicewomen of the Korean War Era* (Hanover, N.H.: University Press of New England, 2005), 36, 8, 93. Lt. General Lutes to Colonel Mary A. Hallaren, Nov. 22, 1950, decimal 333.9, "Fourth Army," box 1012. Colonel Mary A. Hallaren (army), Colonel Mary Jo Shelly (air force), Colonel Katherine Towle (marines), and Captain Joy Bright Hancock (navy) were all unmarried at this time.

44. In 1945, military officials suggested the increasing separation of policies on race and sexuality in a statement that there was "less reported homosexuality among colored troops then [sic] white"; and again, in a claim in 1957 that homosexuality "could not be correlated with any other characteristic." Lt. Colonel Lewis H. Loeser, "The Sexual Psychopath in the Military Service: A Study of 270 Cases," *American Journal of Psychiatry* 102 (July 1945): 100; Crittenden Report, 11, box 16, World War II Project Records. Also intriguing is an enormous witch hunt in 1947 concerning fifty African American WAC soldiers at Camp Beale, California. Because the service feared "probable publicity concerning racial discrimination," the women were "surplused" rather than being given undesirable discharges for lesbianism. ————Case, decimal 201.36, box 52, General Correspondence 1939–1947, Records of the Inspector General, RG 159.

ELIZABETH L. HILLMAN
The Female Shape of the All-Volunteer Force

During the Vietnam War, President Johnson and other officials referred to our "boys in uniform" without apology to the women who also served in that war. By the twenty-first century, however, when President George W. Bush deployed U.S. troops to fight the war on terror in Afghanistan and Iraq, these troops were always referred to by government officials and members of the media as "our brave men and women in uniform." In the span of 30 short years, the participation of women in the military rose dramatically; since early 2009, women have comprised roughly 15 percent of the armed forces. No longer invisible, servicewomen are now consistently acknowledged as critical members of the U.S. military.

"The Female Shape of the All-Volunteer Force" by Elizabeth L. Hillman, ch. 8 of *Iraq and the Lessons of Vietnam, or, How Not to Learn from the Past,* ed. Lloyd C. Gardner and Marilyn B. Young (New York: New Press, 2007). Reprinted by permission of the New Press and the author. Notes have been edited and renumbered. 2014 postscript prepared by the author for this edition of *Women's America,* all rights reserved.

In this essay, Elizabeth Hillman explains how women came to figure crucially in recruitment, and how the military has responded to this dramatic demographic shift within its ranks. What factors account for the "feminization" of the armed services? Why have military leaders supported affirmative action? What have been the benefits and the costs of women's enhanced presence in the U.S. military? Why have many women found military service appealing? What dangers have they experienced from their own colleagues in the U.S. military? How do military policies related to race, gender, and sexual orientation relate to one another?

Because of the numbers and influence of women in the ranks, the U.S. military took on a distinctively female shape in the last decades of the twentieth century. In every service, at nearly every rank and grade, in virtually every unit and at every installation, servicewomen reported for duty alongside men. As early as the 1970s, military and political leaders knew that the military could not meet its personnel needs without drawing on the female labor force. And the need for women in uniform has not let up since. The tremendous demand for military resources in the post-Vietnam era, coupled with women's push for equal opportunity, has drawn women into the military in transformative numbers. In spite of the resistance of military institutions, the post-Vietnam armed forces have become "feminized" in many key respects. "Female" issues such as promoting healthy families, ending sexual harassment, and preventing sexualized torture command the attention of military task forces and congressional committees. "Feminine" skills including compromise, negotiation, and communication are among the skills most critical to successful peacekeeping operations and even to military interrogation. And women themselves are essential cogs in the military manpower machine.

But this new gender balance, this "feminization," has caught military and political leaders off guard. The United States has not reconceived military service as a civic duty of and career opportunity for both women and men, nor has it made the military workplace safe for women. Instead, military and civilian leaders have restricted women's opportunities and reinvented a "warrior" culture of aggression and male coming-of-age.[1] Despite the integration of women and racial minorities into most of the armed forces, the U.S. military remains one of the only American institutions that can legally discriminate on the basis of sex.

In the last three decades, observers in and out of uniform have debated the wisdom and consequences of women's military service. But none can dispute the new gender demographics of the post-Vietnam U.S. military. Those demographics reveal a startling and largely ignored truth: with the end of forcible service for men, women rescued the all-volunteer force from devastating shortfalls in the number and quality of recruits. As the Vietnam War ended, the Selective Service Act was allowed to expire. When the last draft call went out in 1973, women made up less than 2 percent of the U.S. military. Ten years later, the female presence in the ranks had increased five times over. By September 2005, women were 16 percent of the American armed forces.[2] Without them, the military would have suffered not only a shortage of personnel, but also a striking drop in the education levels and test scores of new recruits.

Much as the officials and consultants of the Vietnam era failed to appreciate the degree to which women and racial minorities would become essential military personnel, the architects of the early twenty-first century military transformation have failed to reckon with the consequences of women's heightened military participation. One of the lessons that the military has forgotten since the Vietnam War is that women saved the all-volunteer force. That rescue came at great cost—to servicewomen, to the military, and to the United States.

THE ALL-VOLUNTEER FORCE: WOMEN AS SAVING GRACE

In 2003, the University of Michigan won a battle in the courts to preserve its ability to consider race in student admissions decisions. It won by arguing that diversity was a compelling objective of state educational policy.[3] A turning point in that case was the amicus curiae [friend of the court] brief signed by twenty-nine retired generals and admirals, including notable military leaders such as Admiral William T. Crowe, chairman of the Joint Chiefs of Staff from 1985 to 1989; General Norman Schwarzkopf, commander of allied forces in the Gulf War of 1991; and General Wesley Clark, supreme allied commander in Europe from 1997 to 2000. Their brief, quoted at some length in Justice Sandra Day O'Connor's opinion for the Supreme Court, stressed the negative consequences of racial disparities in the Vietnam-era armed forces and declared that affirmative action was essential to maintaining a diverse, well-qualified military. That amicus brief was a direct outgrowth of the military's role as a model of successful racial integration. Active-duty as well as retired military leaders routinely invoke the rhetoric of equal opportunity in the strongest possible language.[4] The armed forces of the early twenty-first century embrace diversity as a positive good as thoroughly and publicly as any American institution.

But thirty years ago, the experts who were asked to prepare the nation for the end of conscription did not see diversity as a possibility, much less a goal. During the Vietnam War, the Department of Defense had relied on forced service, not volunteers, to fill many of the least desirable and most dangerous military occupations. The risks and hardships of serving in the Army's ground forces rather than in the more technical, less martial forces of the air and sea services persuaded many young men to enlist in the Navy or Air Force rather than wait for a draft notice and end up in the infantry. After the war, military planners and civilian government officials underestimated the degree to which the end of the draft would also end this incentive to volunteer. They also misjudged the extent of American youth's disenchantment with military service. As a result, they anticipated almost no change in the gender or racial demographics of military service in a volunteer military.[5]

The most influential expert assessment was the report prepared by the Gates Commission in 1970. Chartered by President Nixon to develop a plan to end the draft and named for its chair, Thomas S. Gates, a former secretary of defense, the commission unanimously recommended that conscription be ended. The commission's report ignored women entirely, mentioning female service only in the context of alternatives to a volunteer force. Instead, the report stressed the importance of increasing military pay, describing "the first indispensable step" toward a successful volunteer force as removing "the present inequity in the pay" of servicemen. This emphasis on financial incentives reflected the influence of commissioners such as economists Alan Greenspan and Milton Friedman, but the commission's failure to discuss even the possible recruitment of

women was nonetheless a remarkable omission.[6] Military leaders knew—and had known since at least World War II, when more than 350,000 women served in military uniforms—that women could be relied upon to fill gaps in military staffing. A 1966 Pentagon task force had studied the use of women to meet the personnel needs of the war in Vietnam, and in 1967 Congress had lifted the 2 percent ceiling on female enlistments.[7] In addition, the commissioners themselves had identified the structural factors—the evolution in military occupations and the skills that those occupations required—that soon led to many more women in uniform. The commission noted the trend toward more technical and bureaucratic military jobs, documenting how the proportion of military occupations involving ground combat had fallen from 25 percent in 1945 to 10 percent by 1974. This meant that an increasing number of military positions could be filled by servicewomen without even reaching the question as to whether women should be subjected to combat situations. The commission also identified the quality of recruits as a major concern for an all-volunteer force, a problem that could logically be addressed by broadening the potential pool of recruits to include women. But the commission failed to connect the dots when it came to women. The demographics of the commission itself were part of the problem: only one of fifteen commissioners, and none of the thirty-one senior staff and research leads, was a woman.[8]

The experts' botched forecast was apparent almost immediately. As soon as the draft ended, the numbers and quality indicators of male volunteers fell and the Department of Defense scrambled to recruit women. By 1972, Secretary of Defense Melvin R. Laird was establishing a task force, to prepare contingencies for the use of women if the draft ended, and by 1978, the Carter administration was explicitly directing the Pentagon to increase the number of servicewomen.[9] A 1977 Brookings Institution study recommended recruiting women because it was less expensive and would reduce the pressure for more men.[10] Fifteen years after the draft ended, the number of women in uniform had increased from 1.5 percent to more than 9 percent. Women's scores on military aptitude tests shored up the military's quality indicators as well as its overall numbers.[11] In fiscal years 1974 to 1976, for example, 88 percent of the women who joined the Army were high school graduates, as compared to only 52 percent of the men; in the first decade of the volunteer force, 92 percent of all women enlistees had high school diplomas, compared to only 70 percent of male enlistees. One scholar bluntly wrote, "It is widely acknowledged that women were the saving grace of the volunteer concept during the 1970s."[12]

After the 1970s, women continued to enlist in larger numbers than initially expected, spurred in part by changes in military personnel policies. In order to attempt to recruit more men, the military increased pay and benefits and recognized the need to support military families and service members' dependents. These changes in military policy created economic and social incentives that made recruiting and retention of skilled, reliable servicemen possible. But they also made a military career more attractive to women, especially those who lacked significant economic opportunities in the civilian sector. The military eliminated restrictions on assignments that prevented women from serving in many military occupations and relaxed restrictions that forced pregnant women to be discharged and limited the number of dependent children of recruits. These trends combined to make the armed forces a viable career choice for those seeking economic security and educational support. By the late 1990s, the number of military personnel who served for more than four years had increased significantly, one of many indicators of an increasingly career-oriented force.[13]

This sea change in military demographics made women the fastest-growing segment of veterans in the early twenty-first century. In 1983, Congress established a Secretary of Veterans' Affairs Advisory Committee on Women Veterans. In 1994, a Center for Women Veterans was established in the Department of Veterans Affairs after legislation championed by Representative Maxine Waters of California.[14]

In addition to missing the gender implications of the volunteer force, government planners also underestimated the rate at which African Americans would enlist in a volunteer military. The percentage of African Americans in the military nearly doubled in the first decade after the end of the draft. This concurrent increase in minority and female participation led to a dramatic rise in the number of African American women in the service; by 1986, black women were 43 percent of Army enlisted women and 30 percent of the entire female force.[15] In 2005, women constituted 16 percent of the military workforce and 48 percent of the overall civilian workforce. African American women, however, accounted for 28 percent of the female military presence despite being only 13 percent of the female civilian labor force. In the Army, this overrepresentation of African American women was especially pronounced: black women made up 39 percent of female Army personnel on active duty in 2004.[16] In recent years, the Congressional Black Caucus Veterans Braintrust has paid particular attention to the needs of the fast-growing population of African American female veterans. In many respects, African American women were at the center of the demographic transformation triggered by the end of the Vietnam War. Their experience crystallizes the role and treatment of women in the volunteer force: they helped to save the volunteer army by enlisting in disproportionately high numbers but their opportunities for military success were circumscribed by discrimination and harassment.

WOMEN VOLUNTEERS: FITS, STARTS, AND PROGRESS

Once in uniform, women were assigned, evaluated, and promoted in ways that reflected cultural assumptions about female capability. Military laws and policies structured the work environments of servicewomen and reinforced a gender hierarchy that affected civilian as well as military women. Within that hierarchy, sexual harassment and assault became a feature of the military workplace and threatened the lives and health of women around domestic and foreign military bases. Because the volunteer force needed female servicemembers, and because women needed the career stability and economic opportunities that military service offered, the ranks of servicewomen steadily grew. But the emphasis on male authority and aggressiveness that predominated in many quarters of military service left women unprotected from discrimination and abuse. Women made great strides toward becoming full participants in military service. Their success, however, came against a backdrop of continued restrictions and a repetitious debate about whether or not they belonged in the service at all.

When the Vietnam War ended, servicewomen had already won the support of many commanders and political leaders. The Defense Department Advisory Committee on Women in the Services, established by Secretary of Defense George C. Marshall in 1951 to aid in the recruitment of women during the Korean War, monitored the progress of women's service and recommended solutions to recurring problems.[17] The promotion and recruiting restrictions that had prevented women from either attaining high rank or reaching a significant proportion of the force were already gone, and by 1972, the Air Force, Army, and Navy Reserve Officer Training Corps (ROTC) programs were all open to women.[18] Admiral Elmo Zumwalt, the Navy's maverick chief of naval operations from 1970 to 1974, opened many previously closed naval occupational specialties to women during his tenure. The Air Force led the way in accommodating women's reproductive lives by allowing women with children to enlist and permitting waivers of the Department of Defense's automatic discharge policy for pregnant women. Civil courts, responding to new pressure for civil rights and expanding notions of legal equality, had also begun to push the armed forces to treat women fairly. Sharron Frontiero, who served in the Air Force, found that her male colleagues automatically got dependents' benefits for their wives, but in order for her to get dependent's allowances for her husband, she had to prove that she provided more than 50 percent of his financial support. She challenged this practice, and in 1973, the Supreme Court struck down sex discrimination in the distribution of military benefits.[19] Still, in 1972, just before the draft ended, only 42,000 women served in the military, and more than 90 percent were assigned to jobs classified as medical, dental, or clerical in nature.[20]

The advent of the volunteer force brought sharp increases not only in servicewomen's numbers (more than 100,000 women were serving in 1976 and more than 150,000 by 1979) but also in their opportunities. By 1976, the percentage of women in those "feminine" military classifications had dropped to 60 percent, and by 1983, it was down to 55 percent, with increasing numbers of women assigned to fields such as intelligence, supply, and equipment repair.[21] Congress opened the elite national service academies to women in 1976, and the courts continued to nudge the military in the direction of equitable gender policies, holding in 1976 that the Marine Corps' policy of mandatory discharge of pregnant Marines violated the Constitution and ordering the Navy to open additional ships to women in 1978.[22] By

2005, women accounted for about one-sixth of the active and reserve forces. They were most outnumbered in Marine Corps, where female marines were but 5 percent of the force, but they made up nearly a quarter of both Army and Air Force reserves.[23]

Progress toward equal opportunity across gender lines was not a steady march, however. As the number of servicewomen grew, gender-based restrictions on military assignments remained in place. Military leaders limited the changes wrought by women's military presence by preserving some positions as male-only. They argued that the risks involved, the physical capabilities required, or the military facilities available (such as berthing capacity on ships) would make women's presence in these positions a detriment to military effectiveness. This debate centered on the issue of the appropriateness and practicability of assigning women only to noncombat jobs. Proponents of women in combat argued that the restrictions protected masculine privilege, not female bodies, while opponents pointed to the history of male participation in war fighting and the vital importance of bonding ("unit cohesion") in guaranteeing performance under fire. The Supreme Court upheld the all-male Selective Service system in 1981 on the grounds that women were not eligible for combat, demonstrating the importance of this military personnel policy.[24]

The patchwork of combat exclusion rules that evolved as Congress and the president negotiated with the services revealed widespread resistance to the full inclusion of female service members. Identifying combat positions was not a simple task; some military occupational specialties were opened, closed, and reopened to women as opinions shifted about their suitability for women. Lawrence J. Korb, a scholar of military affairs and an assistant secretary of defense from 1981 to 1985, once described the "combat-exclusion policy" as "the worst of all possible worlds for female military personnel" because it limited women's advancement but failed to protect them from the risks of dangerous service. The arguments for and against permitting women to serve in combat positions were endlessly recycled during the first three decades of the volunteer force.[25]

Still, the trend was clearly in the direction of opening doors to women. Most military jobs are now performed by both men and women. In 1988, the Department of Defense opened about 30,000 new positions to service women by setting a single standard (called the "risk rule") to be used in evaluating sex-based restrictions on assignments. The service of military women in the invasion of Panama in 1989 and the Persian Gulf War in 1990 and 1991 led to more pressure to lift sex-based restrictions on assignments. Combat aviation opened to women in 1993, and a 1994 policy change rescinded the "risk rule" in favor of a ban on the assignment of women to units below the brigade level with a primary mission of engaging in direct ground combat. Servicewomen have acted as peacekeepers in Haiti, enforced no-fly zones in Iraq, flown combat missions in Kosovo, died in terrorist attacks on the USS *Cole* in 2000 and at the Pentagon in 2001, and been wounded alongside men in Afghanistan and Iraq in the first U.S. wars of the twenty-first century.[26]

Thirty years into the volunteer force, women shoulder the burdens of military duty but have yet to ascend to the highest ranks of military institutions. In 2005, there were 43 female flag or general officers as compared to 874 male such officers, a female representation of less than five percent, and only one woman stood among the 173 men at the two highest grades. The wide gap between women's representation at the top and the bottom of the military hierarchy reflects more than the time lag between accession to duty and late-career promotions.[27]

The vestiges of the combat exclusion policy keep women off the fastest tracks to military promotion. In 2005, sex-based restrictions on women's assignments placed 15 to 20 percent of military positions off-limits for women, most of them in the infantry and special forces. Women are excluded from 178 enlisted specialties (5 percent of all available specialties) and 17 officer specialties (1 percent of those available). Servicewomen remain concentrated in health care and administrative occupations. Although these combat exclusions cannot eliminate female casualties, they have placed disproportionately more servicemen than women in harm's way. Even in the ongoing war in Iraq, which has brought female military casualties and deaths to the front pages of U.S. newspapers, servicewomen account for only 1 percent of deaths and 2 percent of the wounded.[28] For those who served short terms in the conscript army of the Vietnam War, avoiding combat had been a way to stay alive; for those who make careers in the volunteer military, avoiding combat is still a safer way to

go, but it has also become a professional liability. Women are "underrepresented in tactical operations, the area that yields two-thirds of the general and flag officers of the Services." Women are also a smaller percentage of service academy graduates than men, partly because so many women are directly commissioned as nurses but also because women's presence at the academies has been carefully monitored by officials unwilling to permit too many women to populate the ranks of elite cadets and midshipmen. Women of all races have lower promotion and retention rates than men, though the data vary across race lines. White women tend to leave the military before attaining high rank, while African American women—notwithstanding a widespread perception among white servicemen that minorities are favored in selection for promotions—are promoted at lower rates than the members of any other demographic category. Every service except the Air Force still includes photographs in the packets considered by promotion boards, furthering the perception that race and gender are taken into account—as pluses or minuses in the promotion process.[29]

Family responsibilities also contribute to women's underrepresentation at the highest levels of military service. Although most senior servicemen are married, husbands—and children—are scarce for women at high ranks as compared to men. At the relatively senior ranks of O–5 and O–6 (that is, lieutenant colonels and colonels in the Army, Air Force, and Marine Corps and commanders and captains in the Navy), 90 percent of men but only 55 percent of women are married. Ninety-four percent of military spouses are women. Even with such relatively low rates of marriage, servicewomen routinely identify family issues such as child care among their primary concerns about continued military service.[30]

Women's family responsibilities were of great concern to those who opposed the integration of women into the military infrastructure. But fears about women missing too much time for medical reasons and maternity, including pregnancy-related disabilities, have proven unfounded. Most studies of gender differences in performance point out that men miss more time for disciplinary matters such as drug and alcohol abuse than women miss for medical leave. After all, the demands of family push servicemen as well as women away from the sacrifices that a military career requires.[31]

THE VOLUNTEER FORCE TODAY

Women's military opportunities have opened up dramatically since the Vietnam War, and women were critical in keeping the volunteer army afloat after the draft ended. But women's appearance in the volunteer military was not enough to meet the armed forces' relentless need for more people, more expertise, and more money. Servicewomen mitigated, but did not end, the constant pressure to recruit. The military's failure to promote gender equity in assignment and promotion policies and its inability to build a culture in which women were valued and respected as much as men have created additional problems for the volunteer force. Though the gender transformation of the volunteer military answered the question of whether women should serve, doubts about the proper extent of that service have persisted in American public discourse. In the post-9/11 military, the debate continues over women's military participation, even in the face of rising demands for military personnel and declining success in recruiting.[32]

Thirty years into the volunteer military, the United States has invested enormous resources in recruiting military personnel. In fiscal year 2003, the Department of Defense spent $455 million on special incentives such as enlistment bonuses, college funds, and loan repayments. In addition to these incentive programs, the United States has repeatedly increased military pay since the Vietnam era, responding to studies that stressed higher pay as a primary means of recruiting high-quality personnel. These financial incentives are necessary because current military personnel policies prohibit so many potential recruits from enlisting. According to the Department of Defense, at least half of U.S. youth between the ages of 16 and 21 are not qualified to enlist, mostly because of "physical and mental deficits" such as asthma, obesity, illegal drug use, or the use of prescription antidepressants. Potential recruits are also disqualified for failure to meet educational, aptitude, or moral character standards (measured by criminal convictions and evidence of "asocial behavior"). A recruit can also be disqualified for having too many children; if unmarried, no dependent children are allowed, and if married, a recruit may have no more than two dependent children. Waivers to these requirements are permitted and are more likely during times of greatest need; in 2005, the GAO reported that waivers for physical disabilities appeared to be increasing, while waivers for character failings were declining. The military's policy prohibiting service by men and women who are unable—or refuse—to hide their gay or lesbian sexual orientation also limits the pool of available military recruits. The constant need for more personnel both taxes resources and undermines morale.[33]

The twenty-first-century U.S. military also faces an uphill battle in retaining high-quality personnel because of the conditions under which many service members work and live. One recent study described the strain that the post-9/11 military actions have placed on the volunteer military as "unprecedented" because of lengthy, frequent deployments and "exposure to nontraditional, hostile combat conditions." These conditions have contributed to declining interest among male high school students in military service, a shift that is especially evident among African American young men since fiscal year 2002. As a result of these trends, the military has little choice but to recruit women to help to fill its ranks.[34]

The women who heed the call to join, as well as the civilian women who live or work with service members, must reckon with not only limits on advancement but also a climate of sexual harassment, assault, and violence.[35] Some of the abuse endured by military and civilian women at the hands of servicemen takes place at home, where the stresses of military life can explode into family violence. The pressures of military service are often worst at the bottom of the military hierarchy, where financial pressures are greatest and where the wives of young enlistees often find their career opportunities limited by their husbands' service. Military families often face "separations, serious financial pressures, isolation from family and peer support systems, and frequent moves," all of which increase the risk of family violence. Military training and combat experience may also increase the risk of domestic violence. The Department of Defense has responded to public outcry and congressional mandates by establishing programs to discourage and track spousal and child abuse in military families, but the problem is far from resolved.[36]

Abuse of women also takes place in military workplaces, partly because of continued resistance to the integration of the volunteer force. Women and racial minorities struggle with being excluded, tested, and harassed more often than white men, who still dominate the ranks, constituting 58 percent of the 2005 military. Servicewomen routinely hear denigrating comments about female capabilities, rebuff unwanted sexual advances, are physically harassed, and must face down assumptions that they are promoted because of, not in spite of, their gender and/or race. The parade of military sexual harassment and assault scandals in the 1990s and first few years of the 2000s demonstrated that sexualized abuse had become a part of military service.[37] Servicewomen are also disproportionately censured under the "don't ask/don't tell" policy, and fear of being called a lesbian deters women from reporting unwanted sexual advances and assaults. The military's zero-tolerance response to this epidemic of abuse has led some servicemen to avoid allegations of sexual harassment by avoiding women entirely, a reaction that further isolates servicewomen and limits their advancement. As a 2005 task force on sexual harassment and assault at the U.S. service academies described the situation: "Although progress has been made, hostile attitudes and inappropriate actions toward women, and the toleration of these by some . . . continue to hinder the establishment of a safe and professional environment."[38]

Even with the help of women enlistees, the volunteer force faces constant challenges to meet its personnel needs. Despite their willingness to serve, women have not been able to rescue the U.S. military from the threat posed by the end of conscription, nor have they changed its fundamental nature. Their service has not ended the insular nature of military service, lessened the rigidity of military culture, or restored the luster of military service to attract and keep the best and brightest. They have not transformed the military's social and political order into the entrepreneurial, risk-taking environment that Secretary of Defense Donald Rumsfeld called for. And neither has their presence forestalled the sexual violence so often committed by U.S. service members.

Perhaps the most telling example of the success and limits of the gender integration of the volunteer force is the appearance of women at the center of the first major military scandal of the twenty-first century. Although the sexual harassment and torture of detainees in the post-9/11 wars was perpetrated by both women and men, the public faces of the American torturers indisputably belonged to two Army women, a private and a general: the derisive

smile and dangling cigarette of Specialist Lynndie R. England, a young female enlistee photographed while pointing at naked detainees, and the stern visage of Brigadier General Janis Karpinski, the Army Reserve officer in charge of the prison at Abu Ghraib during the most publicized incidents of prisoner abuse.[39] Other women were also key figures in the debacle, including dozens of enlisted military police and nonmilitary interrogators. Lieutenant Colonel Diane E. Beaver, the staff judge advocate for a joint task force at Guantanamo Bay, wrote a key legal brief recommending the use of more aggressive interrogation techniques in 2002. Major General Barbara Fast, the highest-ranking woman to serve in Iraq, was the intelligence chief for the U.S. military ground commander and oversaw the interrogation centers at Abu Ghraib during 2003 and 2004. Not all of these women were punished for their roles in the scandal, but several were, most notably Karpinski, who was reprimanded and demoted, and England, who was sentenced to three years' confinement and dishonorably discharged. Servicewomen's successful integration into the intelligence, military police, and legal career fields put them at the center of detainee operations in Iraq and made them relatively easy to blame for the military's maltreatment of detainees and mismanagement of detention facilities.[40]

Whoever bears ultimate responsibility for the crimes that took place in American detention facilities in the post-9/11 wars, Lynndie England has joined the rogues' gallery of U.S. service members punished for their failures in wartime. That gallery used to be exclusively male, featuring the troubled Eddie Slovik, executed during World War II for desertion; the unfortunate Claude Batchelor, a trumpet player turned infantryman who was court-martialed after the Korean War for collaborating with Communists while imprisoned in North Korea; and the notorious William Calley, convicted but barely punished for leading the horrifying massacre at My Lai. The addition of women to such a dubious military legacy suggests that women bear the impossible burdens of wartime service no more nobly or easily than men.

POSTSCRIPT, 2014

The U.S. military's policies with respect to gender and sexual orientation continue to evolve, and the military continues to depend on women to perform its missions around the world in the first decades of the twenty-first century. After a long campaign of advocacy and litigation by activists for equal rights, the military's "don't ask, don't tell" regime came to an end in 2011 when Congress, the executive branch, and the military agreed to end sexual orientation discrimination in the military. Meanwhile, women comprised a relatively constant fraction, about 15 percent, of military personnel and continued to be most commonly assigned to medical and administrative specialities. Policy restrictions limit women's participation in "combat" arms, though the Obama administration has promised to lift the ban on women in combat by 2016, and women remained a small fraction of the military's highest ranks. In April 2014, servicewomen were less than 7 percent of the military's generals and admirals, and only one woman appeared among 37 four-star flag officers. In 2008, Ann E. Dunwoody became the first woman nominated to the rank of four-star general. The Air Force's Janet C. Wolfenbarger ascended to four stars in 2012 and the Navy's Michelle J. Howard became the first four-star female admiral in 2014. Hence, women have broken nearly every barrier in the armed forces yet are still far scarcer in the higher ranks compared to their representation among rank-and-file service members.[41]

Sexual assault in the military became a primary concern of Congress in 2012 with the release of reports about high numbers of sexual assaults against service members, several high-profile scandals, and a privately produced and widely distributed documentary about military sexual assault, *The Invisible War*. President Barack Obama spoke out against military sexual assault, and Congress created an independent panel in 2013 to both assess the effectiveness of military responses to sexual assault and consider pending and prospective legislation intended to address the problem. Whether this external pressure for change will hasten the advent of gender equality and an end to sexual violence in the military remains to be seen.[42]

Notes

1. See Judith A. Youngman, "Whatever Happened to the Citizen Soldier?" in *Women in Uniform: Exploding the Myths, Exploring the Facts* (Washington, DC: Women's Research and Education Institute, 1998); Laura Miller, "Not Just Weapons of the Weak: Gender Harassment as a Form of Protest for Army Men," *Social Psychology Quarterly* 60 (1997), pp. 32–51.

2. *Military Personnel: Reporting Additional Service member Demographics Could Enhance Congressional Oversight*, General Accounting Office Report to Congressional Requesters, September 2005 (hereafter GAO report), pp. 10–11; see also chart, p. 38.

3. *Grutter v. Bollinger*, 539 U.S. 306 (2003).

4. Defense Equal Opportunity Council, *Report of the Task Force on Discrimination and Sexual Harassment*, vol. I, Washington, DC, May 1995, p. i.

5. Martin Binkin and Mark J. Eitelberg, "Women and Minorities in the All-Volunteer Force," in *The All-Volunteer Force After a Decade: Retrospect and Prospect*, ed. William Bowman et al. (New York: Pergamon-Brassey's, 1986), p. 74.

6. *The Report of the President's Commission on an All-Volunteer Force* (New York: Collier/Macmillan, 1970).

7. Binkin and Eitelberg, "Women and Minorities in the All-Volunteer Force," p. 82.

8. *The Report of the President's Commission on an All-Volunteer Force*, pp. 43, 18. The only female commissioner was Dr. Jeanne Noble, a professor of education and vice president of the National Council of Negro Women, who in 1962 had become one of the first African American women to receive tenure at New York University.

9. Binkin and Eitelberg, "Women and Minorities in the All-Volunteer Force," p. 83.

10. Carolyn Becraft, "Women and the Military: Bureaucratic Policies and Politics," in *Women in the Military*, ed. E. A. Blacksmith (New York: H. W. Wilson, 1992), p. 9.

11. Lawrence Korb, "The Pentagon's Perspective," in *Who Defends America? Race, Sex, and Class in the Armed Forces*, ed. Edwin Dorn (Washington, DC: Joint Center for Political Studies, 1989), pp. 24–25.

12. Martin Binkin, *America's Volunteer Military: Progress and Prospects* (Washington, DC: Brookings Institution, 1984), pp. 7–8, 48.

13. Office of the Under Secretary of Defense Personnel and Readiness, *Career Progression of Minority and Women Officers* (Washington, DC: 1998) (hereafter *Career Progression* report), p. 10.

14. See the research compiled by the Women's Research and Education Institute, available at www.wrei.org, which uses Bureau of Labor Statistics to document the rising number of women veterans.

15. Binkin and Eitelberg, "Women and Minorities in the All-Volunteer Force," p. 82; *Who Defends America?*, p. 48.

16. GAO report, pp. 3, 42.

17. Laura L. Miller, "Feminism and the Exclusion of Army Women from Combat," in *Women in the Military*, ed. Rita James Simon (New Brunswick, NJ: Transaction, 2001), p. 109. See also the DACOWITS website at http://www.dtic.mil/dacowits (visited July 29, 2006).

18. For a chronology of significant dates, see Captain Lory Manning, *Women in the Military: Where They Stand*, 5th ed. (Washington, DC: Women's Research and Education Institute, 2005), pp. 4–9.

19. *Frontiero v. Richardson*, 411 U.S. 677 (1973). (See pp. 752–753.)

20. Binkin and Eitelberg, "Women and Minorities in the All-Volunteer Force," p. 85.

21. It is important to remember that these aggregate figures describe a volunteer military that was not a monolith but instead a collection of service branches and subcultures. The almost entirely

male Marine Corps shares little in mission or tradition, for instance, with the technocratic Air Force, which is nearly one-fifth female.

22. *Crawford v. Cushman*, 538 F.2d 1114 (1976); *Owens* et al. *v. Brown*, 455 F.Supp. 291 (1978).

23. GAO report, p. 38.

24. *Rostker v. Goldberg*, 453 U.S. 57 (1981).

25. Becraft, "Women and the Military," pp. 11–15; Korb, "The Pentagon's Perspective," p. 25. For a useful overview of the issues surrounding women in combat, see *Female Soldiers: Combatants or Noncombatants*, ed. Nancy Loring Goldman (Westport, CT: Greenwood Press, 1982). In 2005, the arguments looked much the same as in 1982. See, e.g., "G.I. Jane, Again," *National Review* 57, no. 10 (June 6, 2005), pp. 22–24 (Army's restrictions on women in combat and debating the efficacy of such restrictions); "Women Already See Combat," *USA Today*, May 25, 2005; M.C. Devilbiss, *Women and Military Service: A History, Analysis, and Overview* (Maxwell Air Force Base, AL: Air University Press, 1990); Linda Grant DePauw, *Battle Cries and Lullabies* (Norman: University of Oklahoma Press, 1998).

26. On the integration of women into combat aviation, see Captain Alice W. W. Parham, "The Quiet Revolution: Repeal of the Exclusionary Statutes in Combat Aviation—What We Have Learned from a Decade of Integration," 12 *William and Mary Journal of Women and the Law* 377 (2006); Korb, "The Pentagon's Perspective," p. 25.

27. Department of Defense, *Active Duty Military Personnel*, September 30, 2005, available at the Office of the Secretary of Defense (OSD) website, http://www.defenselink.mil/osd/; Susan Hosek et al., *Minority and Gender Differences in Officer Career Progression* (Santa Monica, CA: Rand, 2001), pp. 2–3.

28. GAO report, pp. 38–39, 45, 121.

29. *Career Progression* report, pp. viii, 24, 18, 58, 75–76.

30. Karen Houppert, *Home Fires Burning: Married to the Military—for Better or Worse* (New York: Ballantine, 2005), p. xix.

31. Korb, "The Pentagon's Perspective," p. 25. See also Elizabeth Lutes Hillman, *Defending America: Military Culture and the Cold War Court-Martial* (Princeton, NJ: Princeton University Press, 2005), pp. 70–79.

32. See, e.g., Rowan Scarborough, "Iraq War Muddles Role of Women," *Washington Times*, October 17, 2005, p. A4; Jodi Wilgoren, "A Nation at War: Women in the Military: A New War Brings New Role for Women," *New York Times*, March 28, 2003, p. Bl; Rowan Scarborough, "Army Affirms Its Ban on Women in Combat," *Washington Times*, January 19, 2005, p. A1.

33. The Gates Commission report was the first such study; the most recent is the Government Accounting Office's *Military Personnel: DOD Needs to Improve the Transparency and Reassess the Reasonableness, Appropriateness, Affordability, and Sustainability of Its Military Compensation System*, GAO-05-798 (Washington, DC: July 19, 2005), which points out that military pay is but 70 percent of comparable civilian pay scales; GAO report, pp. 4, 68–76.

34. James Hosek, Jennifer Kavanaugh, and Laura Miller, *How Deployments Affect Service Members* (Santa Monica, CA: Rand, 2006), p. xiii; GAO report, pp. 80, 67, 4; "Problem for Navy: Too Few Hands on Deck," *New York Times*, February 2, 1999, pp. Al, 17.

35. Notwithstanding this grim picture, the primary targets of military sexual violence are civilian rather than military women. Cynthia Enloe's work reveals the stark dimensions of the military's long and tragic history of participating in human sex trafficking and prostitution around the world. Cynthia Enloe, *Does Khaki Become You? The Militarization of Women's Lives* (Boston: South End Press, 1983), pp. 18–45; *Bananas, Beaches, and Bases: Making Feminist Sense of International Politics* (Berkeley: University of California Press, 1990), pp. 81–90; *The Morning After: Sexual Politics at the End of the Cold War* (Berkeley: University of California Press, 1993), pp. 142–160. In the ongoing war in Iraq, the secondary targets of sexual violence seem to be the male enemy, particularly captured irregulars thought to be terrorists and considered "high-value" detainees.

36. See, e.g., Margaret C. Harrell, *Invisible Women: Junior Enlisted Army Wives* (Santa Monica, CA: Rand, 2000); James Hosek et al., *Married to the Military: The Employment and Earnings of Military Wives Compared with Those of Civilian Wives* (Santa Monica, CA: Rand, 2002), and *Battle Cries on the Homefront: Violence in the Military Family*, ed. Peter J. Mercier and Judith D. Mercier (Springfield, IL: Charles C. Thomas, 2000). See also http://www.vva.org/Committees/WomenVeterans/MilesFoundationSAMM.htm Accessed 20 October 2014.

37. GAO report, p. 40; *Career Progression* report, chapter 7; see Linda Bird Francke, *Ground Zero: The Gender Wars in the Military* (New York: Simon & Schuster, 1997).

38. See Aaron Belkin and Geoffrey Bateman, eds., *Don't Ask/Don't Tell: Debating the Gay Ban in the Military* (Boulder.CO: Lynne Rienner, 2003); Human Rights Watch, *Uniform Discrimination: The "Don't Ask, Don't Tell" Policy of the U.S. Military* (January 2003), http://www.hrw.org/reports/2003/usa0103/ (accessed July 24, 2006) (especially the section titled "Impact on Women"); Servicemembers Legal Defense Network statistics on the disproportionately high discharge rate for servicewomen accused of being lesbians, http://www.sldn.org/binarydata/SLDN_ARTICLES/pdf_file/351 .pdf (accessed July 10, 2006); *Report of the Defense Task Force on Sexual Harassment and Violence at the Military Service Academies* (Washington, DC: Department of Defense, June 2005), executive summary.

39. See, e.g., Karen J. Greenberg and Joshua L. Dratel, eds., *The Torture Papers: The Road to Abu Ghraib* (New York: Cambridge University Press, 2005).

40. James W. Smith III, "A Few Good Scapegoats: The Abu Ghraib Courts-Martial and the Failure of the Military Justice System," 27 *Whittier Law Review* 671 (2006).

41. Military personnel statistics for 2014 are drawn from the Defense Manpower Data Center: https://www.dmdc.osd.mil/appj/dwp/dwp_reports.jsp (accessed Jun. 19, 2014).

42. Materials on military sexual assault appear at the website of the Response Systems Panel, http://responsesystemspanel.whs.mil/ and *The Invisible War* is described at http://invisiblewarmovie.com/ (accessed Jun. 19, 2014).

Goesaert v. Cleary, 1948

In response to the worries of returning World War II veterans over finding well-paying jobs in the postwar recession, Michigan's legislature passed a statute prohibiting any woman from serving liquor as a bartender in cities of more than 50,000 unless she was "the wife or daughter of the male owner" of a licensed liquor establishment. (Women could, however, be hired as waitresses.) The statute was justified on the grounds that the presence of a man behind the bar shielded women from drunken violence; we can see it as another version of the protective legislation that had been upheld in *Muller v. Oregon* (1908) (see p. 357).

Valentine Goesaert's husband had recently died. She and her daughter Margaret wanted to continue to operate their family's tavern in Dearborn, Michigan. They were joined by 26 other women bar owners and barmaids who claimed their right to equal protection guaranteed by the Fourteenth Amendment. Their legal expenses were partially paid for by the Michigan Barmaids Association; their attorney, Anne R. Davidow, had graduated from law school in time to vote in 1920, and had represented the leaders of the United Auto Workers Union. The Federal District Court for Michigan denied their claim, observing that the legislature had not been unreasonable: "[T]he legislature may have reasoned that a graver responsibility attaches to the bartender who has control of the liquor supply than to the waitress who merely receives prepared orders of liquor from the bartender for service at a table." The Goesaerts appealed to the U.S. Supreme Court, where they lost again. The decision was 6–3. Note the reasoning of the dissenters as well as the majority.

JUSTICE FELIX FRANKFURTER, WRITING FOR THE MAJORITY:

[The question is: can Michigan forbid females generally] from being barmaids and at the same time make an exception in favor of the wives and daughters of the owners of bars? . . . Beguiling as the subject is, it need not detain us long. To ask whether or not the Equal Protection of the Laws Clause of the Fourteenth Amendment barred Michigan from making the classification the State has made between wives and daughters of owners of liquor places and wives and daughters of non-owners, is one of those rare instances where to state the question is in effect to answer it.

We are to be sure, dealing with a historic calling. We meet the alewife, sprightly and ribald, in Shakespeare, but centuries before him she played a role in the social life in England. . . . The Fourteenth Amendment did not tear history up by the roots, and the regulation of the liquor traffic is one of the oldest and

Goesaert v. Cleary, 335 U.S. 464, 69 S.Ct. 198 (1948). For a history of this case, based in part on oral histories, see Amy Holtman French, "Mixing It Up: Michigan Barmaids Fight for Civil Rights," *Michigan Historical Review* 40 (Spring 2014): 1–20. The principle of *Goesaert* was not undermined until 1971, when the California Supreme Court upheld the right of women to tend bar in *Sail'er Inn, Inc. v. Kirby*, 5 Cal. 3d 1 (1971). *Sail'er Inn* was argued by a very recent law school graduate, Wendy Webster Williams, using a brief written by two law students, Mary Dunlap and Margaret Kemp.

most untrammeled of legislative powers. Michigan could, beyond question, forbid all women from working behind a bar. This is so despite the vast changes in the social and legal position of women. The fact that women may now have achieved the virtues that men have long claimed as their prerogatives and now indulge in vices that men have long practiced, does not preclude the States from drawing a sharp line between the sexes, certainly in such matters as the regulation of the liquor traffic. . . . The Constitution does not require legislatures to reflect sociological insight, or shifting social standards, any more than it requires them to keep abreast of the latest scientific standards.

While Michigan may deny to all women opportunities for bartending, Michigan cannot play favorites among women without rhyme or reason. The Constitution in enjoining the equal protection of the laws upon States precludes irrational discrimination as between persons or groups of persons in the incidence of a law. But the Constitution does not require situations "which are different in fact or opinion to be treated in law as though they were the same." . . . Michigan evidently believes that the oversight assured through ownership of a bar by a barmaid's husband or father minimizes hazards that may confront a barmaid without such protecting oversight. . . . [If it is reasonable,] as we think it is, Michigan has not violated its duty to afford equal protection of the laws. We cannot cross-examine . . . the mind of Michigan legislators nor question their motives . . . we cannot give ear to the suggestion that the real impulse behind this legislation was an unchivalrous desire of male bartenders to try to monopolize the calling. . . .

JUSTICE WILEY RUTLEDGE, DISSENTING:

. . . This statute arbitrarily discriminates between male and female owners of liquor establishments. A male owner, although he himself is always absent from his bar, may employ his wife and daughter as barmaids. A female owner may neither work as a barmaid herself nor employ her daughter in that position, even if a man is always present in the establishment to keep order. This inevitable result. . . . belies the assumption that the statute was motivated by a legislative solicitude for the moral and physical well-being of women who, but for the law, would be employed as barmaids. Since there could be no other conceivable justification for such discrimination against women owners of liquor establishments, the statute should be held invalid as a denial of equal protection.

"We were the first American women sent to live and work in the midst of guerrilla warfare. . ."

The American ships and planes that went to Vietnam carried women as well as men. There were approximately 10,000 military women and more than 13,000 Red Cross women, as well as smaller numbers of women foreign service officers, staff of the U.S. Agency for International Development, and employees of the united service organizations (USO). In 1980, Congress authorized a memorial to be built "in honor and recognition of the men and women of the Armed Forces of the United States who served in Vietnam." The competition for the design of the memorial was won by twenty-one-year-old Maya Lin, an undergraduate architecture student at Yale. The memorial stands today in Washington, visited by millions of people each year. They leave offerings as at a shrine: flowers, photographs, mementos.

The design of the memorial—whose black granite walls bear the names of 58,000 Americans who died, including eight women—was controversial from the

U.S. Senate Committee on Energy and Natural Resources, *Vietnam Women's Memorial.* Hearing before the Subcommittee on Public Lands, National Parks, and Forests to consider S. 2042, February 23, 1988, 100th Cong., 2nd Sess.

beginning. Many veterans groups insisted on a more traditional, representational design. In 1984 an additional statue that depicted three soldiers was placed in a grove of trees nearby. When the additional statue failed to include the figure of a woman, women veterans began to urge the addition of another statue honoring the women who had served.

In 1988 Congress authorized a statue recognizing women, to be constructed on federal property at the Vietnam Veterans Memorial from funds (like those of the other memorials) raised from private donations. The comments that follow were made at hearings conducted by Senator Dale Bumpers of Arkansas, chair of the Senate Subcommittee on Public Lands, National Parks, and Forests.

Each of the veterans had complex memories of their experience in Vietnam, 20 years before. How do the women explain the meaning of their service? How is Robert Doubek's testimony affected by concerns about class, race, and gender?

Karen Johnson's testimony addresses the issue of whether men and women have an equal obligation to serve in the military. Do you think men and women have an equal obligation to serve in the military in time of war, as Karen Johnson believes? Does that obligation extend to service in combat? Does the exclusion of women from combat suggest that American society attaches greater value to women's lives than men's? What other factors might also be relevant in explaining the exclusion of women from combat? (For more on these issues, see Elizabeth Hillman's essay, above. For the perspectives of peace and antiwar activists in both North America and Vietnam, see Judy Tzu-Chun Wu's essay, pp. 719–730.)

STATEMENT OF DONNA-MARIE BOULAY, CHAIRMAN, VIETNAM WOMEN'S MEMORIAL PROJECT

Mr. Chairman, people who serve in wars have unique experiences. War was never meant to be. War makes death. Day after day, even hour after hour, we lived and worked amidst the wounded, the dead, and the dying.

I arrived in Vietnam at the end of February 1967. A few days later I was assigned to triage for the first time. The medevac helicopters brought twelve soldiers into our emergency room. Ten were already dead. Two were bleeding to death.

Mr. Chairman, our daily duty was to care for the badly wounded, the young men whose legs had been blown off, whose arms had been traumatically amputated, whose bodies and faces had been burned beyond recognition.

We eased the agony of a young marine, his legs amputated, his wounds dangerously infected. We worked hard to stop the bleeding of a sailor who had been shot in his liver. He died three days after, in immense pain.

We cared for a young Army lieutenant from New York named Pat who had been admitted with a badly mangled leg and later evacuated to Japan, like many of the other seriously wounded soldiers we treated. I do not know whether Pat's leg was saved. I hope so. Pat was a good soldier.

Mr. Chairman, "Pat" is not short for "Patrick." Pat is a nurse. Patty was a nurse. She was stationed at the 24th Evacuation Hospital in Long Binh.

We were the first American women sent to live and work in the midst of guerrilla warfare. The month-long Tet offensive was especially frightening. The Viet Cong blew up the ammunition dump down the street, causing a wall in our unit to collapse on some patients.

VC snipers shot at us. The North Vietnamese Army artillery roared throughout the nights. Those of us not at work huddled in our bunkers, wondering if we would survive until dawn.

At work, listening to the thundering sounds around us, we tried to keep our hands from shaking, the fear out of our voices and off of our faces, so that the wounded would not see or hear it.

Women served in Vietnam in many capacities. We served as personnel specialists, journalists, clerk-typists, intelligence officers, and nurses. There was no such thing as a generic woman soldier, as there was no such thing as a generic male soldier. Men served as mechanics, engineers, pilots, divers, and infantrymen.

The design of the men's statue at the Veterans Memorial was selected, according to Frederick

Hart, the sculptor, because they "depict the bonds of men at war and because the infantry bore the greatest burden."

Mr. Chairman, we are proposing that the design for the women's statue be that of a nurse who served in Vietnam. The statue of a nurse is so compatible with the existing trio of figures because the nurses' experience so closely parallels the experience of the infantrymen—the intensity, the trauma, the carnage of war.

The statue design which we are proposing is an easily recognizable symbol of healing and hope, consistent with the spirit and the experience of the Vietnam Veterans Memorial. . . .

STATEMENT OF KAREN K. JOHNSON, LITTLE ROCK, AR

I was born in Petersburg, Virginia. My father was in the military. He was killed in France on November the 11th, 1944.

I was raised in Oklahoma. I graduated from college in 1964 and explored the military as a career and joined the Army in 1965.

My family was very patriotic because of the trials and tribulations that we had to go through because of being raised without a father. Considering that everyone in my family had experienced all that patriotism, when I said that I was going to join the Army it was not a new thought, even though I was the first woman to have joined.

My family felt that all Americans owed their country any sacrifice needed for the national good, regardless of their race or sex, that patriotism should be a blind emotion, and it should be accepted by our country without any thought or qualm as to who offered such patriotism.

Consequently, after I served in Germany from 1966 to 1968, when my country asked me to go overseas again to Vietnam, I went. I served in Vietnam from July of 1970 to March of 1972, for a total of 20 months in country.

When I tell people these facts, they always ask me, was I a nurse, that I did not see any combat, and that I must have volunteered. When I tell them that I was awarded a Bronze Star, they ask me what for.

For 18 years I have answered these questions with several long-winded explanations which were really an apology for my Vietnam service, because I was not a nurse and I was not a combat soldier, and there were many others who had served who the public much better understood their service in their traditional roles.

I have kept silent on what I did in Vietnam because it was easier than making the apologies or trying to educate my listener. I know now that I have done many Vietnam veterans a great disservice by my silence. Thanks to the support of the Arkansas Vietnam Veterans, my husband and my grandchildren, I have made my last apology, felt my last twinge of embarrassment, and I will not remain silent to the detriment of my comrades in arms.

I am a veterans' veteran and I am proud of it. I was not a nurse. I saw very little fullfledged combat, and when my country called I went willingly. I see no disgrace in answering such a call or in volunteering to serve in the United States Army.

I served as the Command Information Officer of the United States Army, Vietnam Headquarters, located at Long Binh. However, my job entailed finding out what Army troops were doing, photographing those troops, writing news reports, and printing the internal publications to keep the troops informed.

I could not do that from Long Binh. I traveled all over Vietnam. Wherever there were Army troops, I went, too. I have flown in attack helicopters, been shot at in jeeps, and I went over the Hay Van Pass in several convoys.

Whatever it took to get the news out to the troops is what I and my staff did, and we did it very well. "Uptight Magazine," one of our publications, was awarded the Thomas Jefferson Award for the outstanding military publication in its field, an award that was given to me by "Time Magazine."

Our office published a twice-daily news bulletin, a weekly Long Binh paper, the weekly "Army Reporter," "Uptight Magazine Quarterly"; and "Tour 364," the history of the war, was updated every six months so that troops rotating home had a written history of their service. We were also responsible for the free distribution of "Stars and Stripes" to ensure that every U.S. military personnel serving in Vietnam had daily access to a newspaper.

There were a lot of obstacles to resolve to make all of this happen. My staff made it happen every day for 20 months, in 12 hour shifts, seven days a week, including Christmas, when we worked harder because we were responsible for making Operation Jingle Bells work so that the troops could see Bob Hope.

I am here today to tell you that I am very proud of that staff, and especially of Spec. 5 Steven Henry Warner, who gave his life so the American soldier could be the best informed and most motivated soldier in the world. I do not believe they would want me to apologize for our service or the fact that Steve Warner gave his life as a journalist and not as a combat soldier.

If there is any apology owed, it is the one I owe my staff for not standing up for them for the last 18 years because I did not like the questions my admission to being a Vietnam veteran elicited because I was a woman, something not well understood by the American public.

Their service and mine should be given equal recognition with all who served, not diminished because of the non-traditional position I held.

I come before you today to ask you to legislate equal dignity for the women who served their country by answering the call to arms. The Vietnam Women's Memorial would do much to give women veterans a new sense of self-respect and it will make a strong public statement that bias, prejudice, or ignorance of the sacrifices that women veterans have made for their country will no longer be tolerated.

Today the flag that covered my father's casket when he was put to final rest in 1948 lies in front of me, because I have always wanted him to be proud of me, his only child. And I believe he would be proudest of me today when I say, after 18 long years of silence: I was an American soldier; I answered my country's call to arms; and I am an American veteran, a title I should be able to share with equal dignity with all who have served before me and will serve after me. . . .

STATEMENT OF ROBERT W. DOUBEK . . .

Mr. Chairman, my name is Robert W. Doubek of Washington, D.C. I am a Vietnam veteran. I am employed in the private sector. I was a founder of the Vietnam Veterans Memorial Fund. I served as its Executive Director and Project Director. I was responsible for building the memorial. I did the work. In recognition of my achievement, I was nominated for a Congressional Gold Medal which was a bill passed by the Senate on November 14, 1985.

The fact is that women are not represented by the Vietnam Veterans Memorial. The fact is also that the memorial does not represent anyone. It is not a legislative body. It is a symbol of honor, and as such, it is complete as a tribute to all who served their country in the Vietnam War.

It is a basic rule of common sense that mandates that something which is not broken should not be fixed. The genius of the wall is its equalizing and unifying effect. All veterans are honored, regardless of rank, service branch, commission, sex, or any other category. The names of the eight women casualties take their rightful places of honor. To ensure that this fact is never overlooked, the inscription on the first panel of the wall states that the memorial is in honor of the men and women of the Armed Forces. The reason I know this is because I was instrumental in drafting the inscription.

In 1982, politics required that we add a figurative sculpture as a more specific symbol of the Vietnam veteran. Even with the heroic and dangerous service rendered by other combatants such as Air Force and Navy pilots, Navy swiftboat crews, and the life saving efforts of nurses, helicopter pilots and medics, there was only one possible choice of what category would be literally depicted to symbolize the Vietnam veteran, and that could only be the enlisted infantrymen, grunts. They account for the majority of names on the wall; they bore the brunt of the battle. The fact is all grunts were men.

The addition of a statue of a woman or of any other category, for that matter, would reduce the symbolism of the existing sculpture from honoring or symbolizing the Vietnam veterans community as a whole to symbolizing only enlisted infantrymen. This in turn would open a Pandora's box of proliferating statuary toward the goal of trying to depict every possible category. The National Park Service has already received requests for a statue to literally depict Native Americans and even for scout dogs, and in fact, I want to say that the figure for Native American casualties was 225.

The addition of a statue solely on the basis of gender raises troubling questions about proportion. Is gender of such overriding importance among veterans that we should have a specific statue to women who suffered eight casualties, and none for the Navy which suffered over 2,500, nor for the Air Force which suffered over 2,400? Is gender of such importance to outweigh that some 90 percent of the women who served in Vietnam in the military were officers [nurses were commissioned officers], while over 87 percent of all casualties were enlisted? ... Approval ... would set the precedent that strict literal depiction of both genders is an absolute requirement of all military related memorials. What about the new Navy memorial? Will Congress mandate an additional figure at the Iwo Jima Memorial?

STATEMENT OF COL. MARY EVELYN BANE, USMC (RETIRED), ARLINGTON, VA

Mr. Chairman, my name is Mary Evelyn Bane. I live in Arlington, Virginia, and I have lived in the Washington metropolitan area for a total of almost 19 nonconsecutive years. I retired in 1977 from a 26-year career in the United States Marine Corps in the grade of colonel. I never served in Vietnam, only a few women Marines did, and they were in Saigon, but I was in active service during the entire period of the war there. My career was in personnel management and, like most Marine officers, I had a variety of assignments and experiences, including two tours at our famous or infamous Parris Island training recruits, and an assignment with the Joint Staff in France. All of my male Marine colleagues did serve in Vietnam, many of them more than once, and some of their names are on the Vietnam Veterans Memorial.

I am opposed to the installation of a statue of a woman at the site of the VVM for both artistic and philosophical reasons, artistically, because it is at odds with the design as well as the theme of the memorial ... [and] philosophically simply because I am a woman. This may seem unfathomable to the statue's proponents, but perhaps I can explain. From the beginning of my chosen career in what most will agree is a macho outfit, I tried hard to be the best Marine I was capable of being. When I was commissioned, fewer than 1 percent of the officers in the Marine Corps were female. Women were assigned to women's billets, and restricted to a handful of occupational specialties considered appropriate for women. Over the years, through the combined efforts of many, many people, of which I am happy to say I am one, the concept of how women could and should serve their country has changed. The huge increase in the military's population required by the Vietnam War hastened the changes.

Nevertheless, in 1973 when I, then a lieutenant colonel, was assigned as the Marine Corps member of a Department of Defense ad hoc group studying the recruitment and processing of non-prior service personnel, the Civil Service GS-15 chair of the group complained to the Commandant of the Marine Corps that he had not appointed a real Marine.

My point here is that sex is an accident of birth. I chose to be a Marine and worked hard at it, and spent a career combatting discrimination based on sex. I feel every service person should be recognized for what he or she accomplished as a soldier, sailor, Marine or airman. The Vietnam Veterans Memorial recognizes American military members for their service in Vietnam, irrespective of sex, rank, service, race, or occupational specialty. To single out one of these criteria for special recognition in the form of a statue on the site of the Vietnam Veterans Memorial would not only violate the integrity of the design, but would be discriminatory.

FEMINISMS

ROSALYN BAXANDALL AND LINDA GORDON
The Women's Liberation Movement

How did the women's liberation movement transform American society? Rosalyn Baxandall and Linda Gordon seek to dispel myths about the feminist movement of the 1960s and 1970s and to document what they describe as "the largest social movement in the history" of the United States.

As you read the essay, think about the following questions: What motivated women to become part of the women's liberation movement? What did the movement accomplish—and when? Where do you see evidence of backlash? What challenges remain?

The women's liberation movement, as it was called in the 1960s and 1970s, or feminism, as it is known today, reached into every home, school, and business, into every form of entertainment and sport. Like a river overflowing its banks and seeking a new course, it permanently altered the landscape. Some think its impact has been excessive and others—like us—believe that much more progress toward sex equality is needed. But all agree that it has left an indelible mark on women, men, and children everywhere. Women's liberation was the largest social movement in the history of the U.S. . . .

. . . Widespread misconceptions [exist] about the movement. . . . These exist not because the public is foolish or hostile to feminism. In fact, 1998 Roper polls found that 51 percent of Americans believe feminists have been helpful to women, 53 percent that feminists are "in touch with the average American woman," 65 percent that black feminists help the black community. The misimpressions derive in part from widely published misinformation. Indeed, it is hard to imagine an historical event as widespread and powerful as the women's liberation movement that has been so poorly documented and reported. . . .

Part of this problem is the movement's success. Its achievements—the broad range of work women now do, the equal treatment they expect, the direct way women express themselves—have become the very air we breathe, so taken for granted as to be invisible. . . . Furthermore, the largest grassroots part of the women's movement is difficult to study precisely because it was so big, so decentralized, so varied, and often left few records. It is hardly surprising that most of what has been written has focused on the main national feminist organization, the National Organization for Women, and its leaders, such as Gloria Steinem and Betty Friedan, because this aspect of the movement was more centralized, less outrageous, more focused—and kept better records. . . .

There are deeper reasons, too, for the lack of reliable studies and the perpetuation of false stereotypes. Despite the huge changes in our society brought about by the women's movement, feminism's fundamental ideas are still controversial—indeed, they are at the root of the hottest debates of our times: abortion rights, contraception for teenagers, welfare, women in the armed forces, gay marriage,

Excerpted from the introduction of *Dear Sisters: Dispatches From The Women's Liberation Movement*, by Rosalyn Baxandall and Linda Gordon (New York: Basic Books, 2000; orig. publ. 1995). Reprinted by permission of the authors and publisher.

affirmative action. The media—and not only conservative sources—often portray the women's movement through unrepresentative anecdotes and outright falsehoods. . . . In turn, such poor journalism arises in part from the lack of scholarly research upon which reporters can draw.

Three biases from three different perspectives infuse the misinformation about women's liberation: an overtly hostile, conservative perspective that demonizes the movement as acting against nature, even doing the work of the devil; the perspective of those feminist activists who, disappointed by the movement's incomplete success, consider it a failure; and a trivializing view of the movement as a lifestyle rather than politics, as personal self-transformation rather than social change, as a digression from traditional politics. These biases give rise to widespread myths about women's liberation. Depen-ding on one's particular bias, women's libbers:

- were privileged, white young women who had neither knowledge about nor concern for working-class women or women of color.
- rejected motherhood and considered children only a burden.
- ignored bread-and-butter economic issues and focused only on sex, violence, and personal issues.
- drew energy away from movements aimed at correcting major social and economic problems, such as militarism, racism, and poverty, and prevented the formation of strong coalitions or united efforts.
- hated being women and rejected everything feminine, from bras and long hair to shaved legs and high heels.
- were man-haters who tried to belittle and compete with men, often rejecting them entirely and becoming lesbians.
- were losers, bitter because men rejected them.
- were humorless and prudish, quick to take offense.
- were spoiled, self-centered, and self-pitying women who whined about life's difficulties and exaggerated the discrimination against women.

Like most myths, some of these contain kernels of truth. Yes, feminists did reject confining clothing such as high heels and girdles. (See p. 477.) Many stopped dieting and curling, straightening, processing, dyeing, shaving, plucking their hair. Yes, feminists wanted help raising children—from husbands and organized day care—as more and more women joined the workforce. Yes, feminists were angry at men who beat them, harassed them, belittled them, and kept them in inferior and dead-end jobs. Yes, women's liberation was particularly strong among college-educated young women. Yes, in order to be heard, especially because women had a history of being timid, soft-spoken, and ignored, feminists sometimes shouted and oversimplified.

But some of these myths contain not a grain of truth. Feminists never rejected motherhood; rather, they sought to improve its conditions. . . . All [feminists] had sons, brothers, fathers, male friends, or coworkers whom they loved. Far from being losers, feminists were typically the most achieving and self-confident of women. Feminist humor was so popular it became mainstream—think of Lily Tomlin and Nicole Hollander. Anything but prudes, feminists dedicated themselves to liberating women's sexuality. They were doers, not complainers. They identified discrimination for the purpose of trying to change it.

SOCIAL ROOTS OF WOMEN'S LIBERATION

Women's liberation was a movement long overdue. By the mid-1950s a majority of American women found themselves expected to function as full economic, social, and political participants in the nation while still burdened with handicaps. As wage-earners, as parents, as students, as citizens, women were denied equal opportunity and, often, even minimal rights and respect. Many women experienced sharp conflict among the expectations placed on them—education, employment, wife- and motherhood. Looking back at the beginning of the twenty-first century, we can see feminism as a necessary modernizing force and, not surprisingly, one which rapidly became global. Within the U.S., the movement gained widespread support so quickly because it met real needs, because the great majority of women stood to benefit from reducing discrimination, harassment, and prejudice against them. A movement that might at first have seemed to promise to rationalize the current political and economic system by integrating women into it quickly took off—as many social movements do—into uncharted territory, exposing the degree to which basic social structures had rested on a traditional gender system. . . .

How did an apparently arch-conservative decade like the 1950s produce a movement so radical? To answer that we have to look beneath a veneer that concealed discomforts and discontents. The period between the end of World War II and the birth of women's liberation at the end of the 1960s has usually been described as an era of prosperity, stability, and peace, leading to the conclusion that it was also an era of satisfaction and little change. An intensely controlled and controlling official and commercial culture seemed to provide evidence for that conclusion. The domestic correlate of the Cold War and the Korean War was the hysterical anticommunism that stigmatized nonconformity, including that related to family, sex, and gender. Anxiety about the Soviet threat made family stability seem critical and linked women's domestic roles to the nation's security. . . . Historian Elaine Tyler May [has] observed that the concept of containment, first used to characterize the U.S. policy of preventing Soviet expansion, could characterize equally well the stifling of female ambitions, the endorsement of female subordination, and the promotion of domesticity by Cold War gender culture. Resistance to these norms was un-American, and that label became a heavy club with which to beat misfits and dissidents. . . .

Cold War culture demanded sexual as well as political and gender conformity. The witch hunts targeted not only alleged communists but also homosexuals, and drove many people out of their employment. Films and magazines depicted the lesbian as a moral threat, a symbol of decay, chaos, and predatory evil. Vice control units of local police departments, along with private moral crusade organizations like the American Society for Social Hygiene and public health officials, routinely rounded up those engaged in "immoral" sexual activities. Psychiatrists labeled homosexuals and discontented women alike as sick and in need of rehabilitation.

Girls grew up in this Cold War era barred from wearing blue jeans or sneakers to school, required to sit with their knees together and to set their hair in pin curls. Nothing in the culture encouraged them to become strong or competitive. Girls grew to hate athletics and dread physical education in school, where they were required to wear unfashionable tunics or bloomers. Girls were not encouraged to fantasize about careers, about what they would "become" when they grew up. They were expected to break a date with a girlfriend if a boy asked for a date. They watched movies and TV in which married couples slept in twin beds and mothers were full-time housewives. The people of color on TV were stereotypes, comic or worse: step-and-fetch-it black servants, marauding Apaches, or fat lazy Mexicans. Rape, illegitimacy, abortion—some of women's real problems—were among many tabooed subjects, whispered about but rarely seriously or openly discussed.

But this official feminine-mystique culture obscured an unofficial but probably more widespread reality that was, ironically, designated as deviant. A small band of historians has been uncovering the story of what turns out to be the majority of American women who did not, and often could not, conform. . . . In contrast to official norms, women's labor-force participation climbed rapidly throughout the fifties and by 1954 women's employment had equaled that during World War II. Most women displaced from well-paid, industrial jobs at the war's end did not return to domesticity but found work in traditionally female low-paying jobs in the expanding service and clerical sectors. As has long been true in American history, African American women and poor women of all colors had particularly high rates of employment, so that the domesticity myth was in part a racist assumption that elite white norms were universal. Women in "pink collar" employment swelled the membership of unions, such as the Hotel Employees and Restaurant Employees and the National Federation of Telephone Workers. And these working women were not only young and single: By 1960, 30 percent of married women were employed, and 39 percent of mothers with school-age children were in the labor force. By 1955, 3 million women belonged to unions, constituting 17 percent of union members. In unions in which women made up a significant part of the membership, they wielded considerable power, especially at the local level.

The number of married women seeking employment rose fastest in the middle class. Women benefited from an enormous expansion in higher education after World War II. Government investment in universities after the war had multiplied educational opportunity, especially in public institutions. In 1940, 26 percent of American women completed college; in 1970, 55 percent. These relatively privileged American women faced a particular dilemma: educated with men and often achieving, despite discrimination, the same levels of knowledge, discipline, and sophistication as the men of their social class, they were still expected to forego professional or intellectual pursuits after college to become full-time housewives and mothers. Those who resisted this directive and sought employment, through choice or economic necessity, usually found themselves limited to clerical or low-level administrative jobs.

In part as a response to this restriction, many women . . . defied the limits of domesticity through community and political activism. Even in the suburbs, where women seemed to be conforming to the "feminine mystique" by staying home with small children, many were active in churches, schools, libraries, and parks. New forms of organizing appeared: In 1956, for example, the first all-female La Leche group met to encourage breast feeding. Other groups, alarmed by Rachel Carson's studies of the dangers of pesticides like DDT, had the audacity to challenge official science. Women Strike for Peace, composed largely of left-wing women, attacked military spending priorities, raised an alarm about strontium-90 fallout in milk, and directly challenged the Cold War and American military buildup by contesting U.S. government propaganda about the threat of Soviet expansionism. . . . Conservative women, while paying official homage to the ideal of women's domesticity, were organizing in the Ku Klux Klan, White Citizen's Councils, John Birch Society, and Republican Party.

Some forms of deviance from the official domestic norms were more private. At the edges of mainstream culture a counterculture began to emerge in the early 1950s, reflecting a mood of depression, alienation, and anger at the shallowness of dominant standards. True, the "beat" poets and artists were mainly male, but they attracted female groupies who preferred this alternative masculinity and identified with the rejection of respectability and conformity. Beatnik women, dressed in black with heavy black eye makeup and uncurled hair, hung around coffeehouses in New York and San Francisco. Rebelling against consumerism and conformity, yearning for something more genuine, some embraced Zen Buddhism and existentialism. Even popular commercial culture was riddled with contradictions, ambivalence, competing voices, and transgressions. . . .

Only now, as the women's movement can be seen in historical context, have historians looked back again and noticed the complexity of the cultural messages. In addition to emphasizing femininity and domesticity, many women's magazines featured and honored women who made a mark beyond their homes. Magazine articles glorified housewives, but they also offered tips to women managing wage work along with housework and openly praised participation in community activism and politics. Readers met, for example, Dorothy McCullough Lee, who cultivated the image of a pale, frail housewife but as mayor of Portland single-handedly defeated the heavyweights of organized crime; Louise Williams, mother of two, a great cook but an even better mechanic at American Airlines; and Babe Didrikson Zaharias, a champion golfer and pole vaulter who continued competing despite cancer. *Reader's Digest* placed Mary McLeod Bethune among the world's greatest living women, despite the fact that she was the highest-ranking African American in the New Deal and had been accused of being a communist by McCarthy. Honoring women's work and public activity was especially pronounced in black journalism: magazines like *Ebony* and *Jet* promoted marriage and motherhood but also professional and artistic achievement. . . .

Dissidence in the 1950s was, of course, particularly pronounced in youth culture. . . . Nowhere was the youth rebellion as intense or as contagious as in music, and the transcendence of race segregation was the proximate cause. The officially dominant 1950s white sound (Peggy Lee, Jo Stafford, Rosemary Clooney, and Pat Boone) combined inane lyrics, like "How Much Is That Doggie in the Window," with soothing melodies, bland orchestration, and ballad rhythms. Yet this is the decade that produced rock and roll, a revolution in popular music. The term was first applied to black rhythm and blues by Alan Freed, the white disk jockey who promoted black music to white audiences. The breakthrough singer was Elvis Presley, the "white boy who could sing black." Not only did whites start to buy records by black artists, but they also attended huge concerts where for the first time white and black youth mingled and danced. In Los Angeles, for example, racially mixed rock concerts were busted up by the police. Conservatives considered rock and roll the music of the devil, dangerous, degenerate, mongrel, oversexualized, and in a way they were right: it is difficult to overestimate the impact of rock and roll on the men and women who moved from the inchoate, half-conscious alienation of rebels without a cause to the organized radical movements that began with the civil rights movement.

POLITICAL ROOTS OF WOMEN'S LIBERATION

From the vantage point of the [twenty-first] century, the women's liberation movement appears extravagant, immoderate, impatient, as well as young and naive. It was all those and more, but how one weighs its radicalism, positively or negatively, and how one measures its naivete depend on understanding its historical context. Fifty years later our culture has been so transformed, the expectations of young women so altered, that it is hard to grasp the unique combination of anger and optimism that made second-wave feminism so determined to change so much so fast.

Women coming into adulthood at the end of the 1960s, both middle- and working-class, faced an economy that was producing an ever larger number of jobs; ... [also,] women had unprecedented access to education. But many were disappointed in the jobs they could get. They went from being the equals or even the superiors of men in educational achievement to working as secretaries or "administrative assistants" for the same class of men. Although they faced discrimination in their colleges and universities, they also encountered professors who recognized and challenged their intelligence. Yet their studies, no matter how rigorous, offered them no way to escape the cultural imperative that directed them toward marriage and family as their fundamental and often exclusive source of identity and satisfaction.

If economic and educational abundance opened windows for the women who began women's liberation in 1968, the passionate new social activism of the 1950s and 1960s opened doors and invited women in. But these movements, like the economy as a whole, also sent women a double message. Whenever there have been progressive social change movements in modern history, women's movements have arisen within them, and for similar reasons: in the crucible of activism for civil rights,

for peace, for the environment, for free speech, for social welfare, women have been valued participants who gained skills and self-confidence. At the same time they have been thwarted, treated as subordinates, gophers, even servants, by the men in charge—including men who considered themselves partisans of democracy and equality. Within these movements women learned to think critically about social structures and ideologies, to talk the language of freedom and tyranny, democracy and domination, power and oppression. Then they applied these concepts to question their own secondary status. It is precisely this combination of raised aspirations and frustration that gives rise to rebellion.

... By the 1960s, there was a sense of unity among progressive campaigns for social justice; in fact, they came to be collectively called "the movement," a singular designation. Reflecting the relative prosperity of the period, its mood was optimistic, even utopian. Its members came largely from the middle class, but working-class people also participated. The movement was as critical of commercialization, conformity, and moral hypocrisy as of poverty. Its guiding principle was to challenge received wisdom and hierarchical authority. Quintessentially a movement of young people, it was correspondingly impatient and preferred direct action to political process. In dress, in sexual behavior, in its favorite intoxicants, and above all in its beloved music, it distinguished itself sharply from grown-ups.

By the mid-1960s, the more ideologically Left currents within the movement were called the New Left, because they differed fundamentally from the older Lefts: communism, socialism, and New Deal progressivism. At least a decade earlier, the civil rights movement had been the first to break with conventional politics, helped by its high proportion of student activists, ability to stimulate mass participation, decentralized and pluralist organization, and commitment to direct but nonviolent action. Like all mass movements, the civil rights movement had no defined beginning, although the 1955 Montgomery bus boycott announced to the country that something big was happening. Thousands of African Americans were challenging three hundred years of apartheid, demonstrating unprecedented discipline, solidarity, and bravery against brutal retaliation. Their courage forced racist viciousness into the open; journalists and their cameras then brought into living rooms the high-power water hoses turned on peaceful protesters, the grown men who spat on first-graders, the dogs who charged at protesters singing gospel hymns. The news brought a heightened appreciation of the possibility of making change from the bottom up. In contrast to the bitter liberal-versus-conservative national division in the 1980s and 1990s, the civil rights struggles seemed to galvanize, at least among the most articulate citizenry, broad majority approval for social change in the direction of greater democracy and equality. (There may have been a "silent majority" that did not approve.) While any individual battle might be won or lost, it seemed to supporters that their cause was unstoppable, so great was the groundswell of desire for the long-overdue racial equality and respect.

... Civil rights was, at first, preeminently a black movement, but it was also the first of a series of youth movements that would transform American culture. Civil rights generated youth protest throughout the country, producing a political culture marked by antiauthoritarianism, direct action, and anger at the constraints of respectability. Particularly in the South, many whites from religious backgrounds were drawn into the movement through the student division of the YWCA, which was far more committed to interracial activity than the YMCA. The drama of the attack on segregation drew some northern and western young blacks and whites to the South to help, while others were inspired to contest inequality where they lived. Young whites emulated African American activists in many ways: they adopted the blue jeans that Student Nonviolent Coordinating Committee (SNCC) workers wore in identification with poor southern farmers and workers; their artistic sensibility was permanently revolutionized by black music—blues and rock and roll—and their images of heroism and virtue were modeled after the nonviolent resistance of SNCC volunteers who refused to run or defend themselves from beatings.

In the late 1950s, another kind of rebellion was developing, primarily among the more privileged whites: a cultural rebellion. Discovering and inventing unconventional art, music, and poetry; exploring a variety of intoxicants; and signaling defiance in the way they dressed, adherents of this new cultural revolution soon grew visible enough to draw mainstream media attention. The press created popular icons—"flower children" and "hippies"—whose values resembled those of the earlier 1950s beatnik rebels. The influence of this lifestyle dissent can be measured by how quickly it was picked up by commercial interests and sold back to a broader public: the new fashion included beards, long straight hair, psychedelic design, granny dresses, and beads. Handmade, patched, and embroidered clothing and jeans once bought at Sears Roebuck or Goodwill were soon being mass-produced in Hong Kong and sold in department stores. For its most zealous participants, counterculture iconoclasm and adventurousness meant such an extreme rejection of the work ethic, temperance, and discipline that it horrified many observers, including some in the movement. Excessive use of drugs, promiscuous sexuality, and irresponsibility were sometimes destructive to participants, some of whom later rebounded into conventionality. Women suffered particular exploitation, as the counterculture's gender ideology reaffirmed that of the conventional culture, but now with a twist, lauding "free" and "natural" heterosexual relations between women who were sexually open and "giving" and men who could not be tied down. Women were to be earth mothers, seeking fulfillment by looking after men and children, while guys needed freedom from marital or paternal responsibilities in order to find and express themselves.

This cultural rebellion had transformative potential and gave rise to some serious political challenges. When civil rights and the counterculture intersected on campuses, the result was a college students' movement for free speech that would ultimately create the New Left and women's liberation. The first major student revolt, at the University of California at Berkeley in 1964, arose in reaction to the administration's attempt to prevent students from recruiting civil rights volunteers on campus. This protest movement spread to campuses late in the 1960s throughout the U.S., producing a series of protests against *in loco parentis* rules that treated students like children.

Campus protests soon expanded to include national issues and nonstudents. Sensitized to injustice and convinced of the potential of grassroots activism by what they learned from civil rights, more and more Americans began to see the Vietnam War as immoral and undemocratic. In the name of stopping communism, the U.S. was defending a flagrantly corrupt regime that had canceled elections when it seemed likely to lose to a popular, nationalist liberation movement that promised land reform in the interests of the poor peasantry. The most powerful nation in the world was attacking a tiny nation that had demonstrated not the slightest aggression toward Americans. The U.S. employed some of the cruelest weapons and tactics yet developed: shooting down unarmed peasants because of fear that they might be supporting the liberation movement; bulldozing villages; spraying herbicides from planes to deprive the guerrilla fighters of their jungle cover; dropping napalm, a jellied gasoline antipersonnel weapon that stuck to the skin and burned people alive. . . . Americans routinely witnessed these atrocities on the evening news. American soldiers of color and of the working class were killed and injured in disproportionate numbers. Hundreds of young men began resisting or dodging the draft while scores of soldiers deserted and defied orders. So widespread, vocal, and convincing were the protests at home, including several massive national demonstrations, that by its end the Vietnam War became the only war in U.S. history to be opposed by a majority of the population.

The Vietnamese revolution was part of a wave of nationalist struggles of Third World countries against Western imperial domination, and these also influenced American domestic politics. Many of these emerging nations and movements took socialist forms, as Third World nationalists observed that the introduction of capitalism increased inequality and impoverishment. But many of these newly independent countries fell under Soviet domination as the price of the aid they so desperately needed, and leading parts of the American New Left, already angry at the stultifying domestic culture of the Cold War, neglected to subject Soviet control to the same critique. U.S. interventions against communism, both military and covert, had the ironic effect of making the New Left less critical of Soviet and Chinese communism than it might have been otherwise.

Before Vietnam, the Cuban revolution of 1959 had seized the developing New Left imagination. Cubans overthrew the Batista dictatorship and brought to power a group of daring reformers committed, at first, not only to economic justice but also to educational, cultural, and political democracy. Influential New Leftists, including many future feminists, traveled to Cuba in the 1960s, volunteering to work in the sugar harvests, and their enthusiasm for Cuba's valiant struggle led them to overestimate its independence from the U.S.S.R., just as the anti–Vietnam War movement romanticized Vietnam (and overlooked its lack of democracy). The New Left's increasing identification with anti-imperialist and nationalist struggles around the world caused it to subordinate its early emphasis on freedom and democracy.

. . . In this context of international mobilization, American radicals associated civil rights struggles in the U.S. with anti-imperialism. Blacks and other nonwhite groups identified themselves as a Third World within the U.S., victims of internal colonialism. (Some feminist groups would argue that women were another colonized people.)

Activism spread throughout the U.S., creating civil rights movements among other racial/ ethnic groups, including Chicanos, Asian Americans, Native Americans; movements to protect the environment; a movement for the rights of the disabled; and renewed labor struggles for a fair share of the prosperity. Among whites there soon arose a national student organization that was to become central to the white New Left, Students for a Democratic Society (SDS), established in 1962. With a membership reaching about 100,000 at its peak in the late 1960s, and with many times that number of students—including high school students— who considered themselves a part of the movement, SDS changed the attitudes of a considerable part of a generation. New Leftists and counterculture activists created institutions that spread progressive ideas still further: radical bookstores, a few national magazines, and many local underground newspapers. These were produced by amateurs working in scruffy offices, offering critical perspectives on everything from U.S. foreign policy to the local police to the latest films. Many of these underground newspapers combined words and graphics in innovative ways, inspired in part by the street art of 1968 in France where the *beaux arts* students had considerable influence.

Although the movement (civil rights and the New Left) had no unified ideology—its members included anarchists, social democrats, Marxist-Leninists, black nationalists—it bequeathed identifiable legacies to feminism.

Most important among these were anti-authoritarianism and irreverence. Favorite buttons and T-shirts read "Question Authority" and "Never Trust Anyone Over 30." . . . The movement's message was: look beneath formal legal and political rights to find other kinds of power, the power of wealth, of race, of violence.

. . . Some women began in the mid-1960s to examine power relations in areas that the movement's male leaders had not considered relevant to radical politics. The women's preliminary digging uncovered a buried deposit of grievances about men's power over women within the movement. Women in civil rights and the New Left were on the whole less victimized, more respected, and less romanticized than they were in the mainstream culture or the counterculture. Despite women's passionate and disciplined work for social change, however, they remained far less visible and less powerful than the men who dominated the meetings and the press conferences. Women came into greater prominence wherever there was grassroots organizing, as in voter registration in the South and the SDS community projects in northern cities. Throughout the civil rights and the student movements, women proved themselves typically the better organizers, better able than men to listen, to connect, to reach across class and even race lines, to empower the previously diffident, to persevere despite failure and lack of encouragement. Still, the frustrations and humiliations were galling. In every organization women were responsible for keeping records, producing leaflets, telephoning, cleaning offices, cooking, organizing social events, and catering to the egos of male leaders, while the men wrote manifestos, talked to the press, negotiated with officials, and made speeches. This division of labor did not arise from misogyny or acrimony. It was "natural" and had always been so, until it began to seem not natural at all.

THE RISE OF SECOND-WAVE FEMINISM

Although women's liberation had foremothers, the young feminists of the late 1960s did not usually know about this heritage because so little women's history had been written. Feminist historians have now made us aware that a continuing tradition of activism stretched from "first-wave" feminism, which culminated in winning the right to vote in 1920, to the birth of the "second wave" in 1968. Some women of unusual longevity bridged the two waves. Florence Luscomb, who had traveled the state of Massachusetts speaking for woman suffrage during World War I, also spoke for women's liberation in Boston in the early 1970s. Within many progressive social movements, even at the nadir of the conservative 1950s, there were discontented women agitating against sex discrimination and promoting female leadership. Within the Communist and Socialist Parties there had been women's caucuses and demands to revise classic socialist theory to include sex inequality. . . . Some women spanned the older progressive causes and the new feminism—Ella Baker, Judy Collins, Ruby Dee, Eleanor Flexner, Fanny Lou Hamer, Flo Kennedy, Coretta Scott King, Gerda Lerner, Amy Swerdlow.

Liberal women had continued to be politically active between feminism's two waves. They were mainly Democrats but there were some Republicans, such as Oveta Culp Hobby, who became the first secretary of the Department of Health, Education and Welfare, established in 1953. In 1961 this women's political network persuaded President Kennedy, as payback for their support in the close election of 1960, to establish a Presidential Commission on the Status of Women. It was chaired by Eleanor Roosevelt, embodying continuity with first-wave feminism and the New Deal, and Women's Bureau head Esther Peterson served as vice-chair. Kennedy may have expected this commission to keep the women diverted and out of his hair. But the commission produced substantive recommendations for a legislative agenda and set in motion a continuing process. Its report, issued in 1963, called for equal pay for *comparable* work (understanding that equal pay for *equal* work would not be adequate because women so rarely did the same work as men), as well as child care services, paid maternity leave, and many other measures still not achieved. Determined not to let its momentum stall or its message reach only elite circles, the commission built a network among women's organizations, made special efforts to include black women, and got Kennedy to establish two ongoing federal committees. Most consequentially, it stimulated the creation of state women's commissions, created in every state by 1967. The network that formed through these commissions enabled the creation of the National Organization for Women (NOW) in 1966.

NOW's history has been often misinterpreted, especially by the radical women's liberationists, who denounced it, as the radicals of SNCC criticized their elders and the New Left criticized the Old Left, as stodgy and "bourgeois." At first NOW included more working-class and minority leadership than women's liberation did. Many of its leaders identified strongly with civil rights and defined NOW as pursuing civil rights for women. Former Old Leftist Betty Friedan and black lawyer and poet Pauli Murray were centrally involved in the East, while in the Midwest, labor union women . . . were prime movers. NOW's first headquarters was provided by the UAW. NOW concentrated heavily on employment issues, . . . and NOW's membership was composed largely of employed women. NOW refused to endorse reproductive rights, which the majority considered too controversial, but it rejected the idea that gender was immutable and called for "equitable sharing of responsibilities of home and children and of the economic burdens of their support." This position marked a decisive break with earlier women's rights agitation, which had primarily accepted the traditional division of labor—breadwinner husbands and housewives—as inevitable and desirable. And this position was to give rise to tremendous advances in feminist theory in the next decades.

NOW represented primarily adult professional women and a few male feminists, and at first it did not attempt to build a mass movement open to all women. Although only thirty women had attended its founding conference, and 300 its second conference, NOW demonstrated political savvy in creating the impression that it spoke for a mass power base. It had no central office of its own for three years—networking among a relatively small group did not require one. Its members used their professional and political skills to exert pressure on elected officials.

NOW concentrated on lobbying, using its ties to the few women in influential positions in government; its program focused on governmental action against sex discrimination. Its members met with the attorney general, the secretary of labor, the head of the Civil Service Commission. Its board of directors read like entries from a "Who's Who" of professional women and their male supporters. Its initial impetus was anger that the Equal Employment Opportunity Commission (EEOC) was not enforcing the sex-discrimination provisions of the Civil Rights Act of 1964, and it got immediate results: in 1967 President Johnson issued Executive Order 11375, prohibiting sex discrimination by federal contractors. In the same year NOW forced the EEOC to rule that sex-segregated want ads were discriminatory (although newspapers ignored this ruling with impunity for years). NOW's legal committee, composed of four high-powered Washington lawyers, three of them federal employees, brought suits against protective legislation that in the name of protecting women's fragility in fact kept them out of better jobs. . . .

Women's liberation derided NOW's perspective and tactics as "liberal"—not in the 1990s pejorative sense, coined by the Right, of permissive, but in the 1960s sense, used by the Left, as legalistic and compromising. When a mass women's movement arose, it was not liberal but radical in the sense of seeking out the roots of problems and working for structural change at a level more fundamental than law. It wanted not just to redistribute wealth and power in the existing society, but to challenge the sources of male dominance: the private as well as the public, the psychological as well as the economic, the cultural as well as the legal. Given this radical agenda it was hard for women's liberation to become a player in the political process, and it tended to make purist and moralistic judgments of those who chose to work within the system.

The mass women's movement arose independently of NOW and the government commissions, and its members had a different style: they were younger, typically in their twenties, and less professional. Most importantly, it generated groups consisting of women only. The new women's liberation movement insisted that women needed a woman-only space in which they could explore their grievances and define their own agenda. They observed that women frequently censored not only what they said but even what they thought when men were around. Arriving directly from male-dominated, grassroots social-justice movements, these women longed for a space where they could talk freely with other women. First in Chicago, then in several other cities such as Gainesville, Florida; Chapel Hill, North Carolina; Washington, D.C.; and New York City, women's liberation groups formed in 1967 and 1968. At a 1968 antiwar demonstration in Washington organized by the Jeannette Rankin Brigade, 500 women gathered as a women's liberation counter-conference and then spread the movement to other towns and cities. In August 1968 twenty of them met in Sandy Springs, Maryland, to plan a larger conference. Everyone present was disturbed by the fact that they were all white. But identifying this problem did not mean they could solve it: when over 200 women from thirty-seven states and Canada met in Chicago at Thanksgiving, black women's groups were not represented, because they had not been invited or because they were not interested.

The first women's liberation groups were founded by veteran activists, but soon women with no previous movement experience joined. The decentralization of the movement was so great . . . that different geographic locations developed different agendas and organizational structures. In Iowa City, a university town, the movement began with college students and concentrated much of its energies on publishing a newspaper, *Ain't I a Woman?* In Gainesville, Florida, another university town, the movement originated in civil rights networks. In several large cities—Baltimore, Chicago, Boston, Los Angeles—single citywide organizations brought different groups together; in New York City an original group, New York Radical Women, gave birth to several smaller groups with divergent ideologies. Small-town feminists had to hang together despite their differences, while in big cities there was room to elaborate various political positions. Different cities had different ideological personalities: Washington, D.C., was best known for The Furies, a lesbian separatist group, while Chapel Hill, North Carolina, was noted for its socialist-feminist orientation.

The movement developed so widely and quickly that it is impossible to trace a chronology, impossible to say who led, what came first, who influenced whom. This lack of a clear narrative, and the sense that participants across great distances were making some of the same breakthroughs simultaneously, are characteristic of all mass social movements. . . .

WOMEN'S LIBERATION DEVELOPS

The movement's characteristic form of development was consciousness-raising (CR), a form of structured discussion in which women connected their personal experiences to larger structures of gender. . . . These discussion groups, usually small, sprung up starting in 1968–70 throughout the country among women of all ages and social positions. They were simultaneously supportive and transformative. Women formed these groups by the hundreds, then by the thousands. In Cambridge/Boston where a core group offered to help other women form CR groups, a hundred *new* women attended weekly for several months. The mood was exhilarating. Women came to understand that many of their "personal" problems—insecurity about appearance and intelligence, exhaustion, conflicts with husbands and male employers—were not individual failings but a result of discrimination. The mood became even more electric as women began to create collective ways of challenging that discrimination. At first there was agitprop: spreading the word through leaflets, pamphlets, letters to newspapers; pasting stickers onto sexist advertisements; verbally protesting being called "girl" or "baby" or "chick"; hollering at guys who made vulgar proposals on the streets. Soon action groups supplemented and, in some cases, replaced CR groups. Women pressured employers to provide day care centers; publicized job and school discrimination; organized rape crisis hot lines; opened women's centers, schools, and credit unions; built unions for stewardesses and secretaries; agitated for women's studies courses at colleges; published journals and magazines.

Soon different groups formulated different theoretical/political stands. But the clarity and discreteness of these positions should not be exaggerated; there was cross-fertilization, none was sealed off from others, the borderlines and definitions shifted, and there were heated debates *within* tendencies. Liberal feminists were at first associated with NOW and similar groups, although these tended to merge with women's liberation by the end of the 1970s. Those who remained committed to a broad New Left agenda typically called themselves socialist feminists (to be distinguished from Marxist feminists, who remained convinced that Marxist theory could explain women's oppression and were not committed to an autonomous women's movement). Socialist feminists weighed issues of race and class equally with those of gender and tried to develop an integrated, holistic theory of society. Radical feminists, in contrast, prioritized sexual oppression, but by no means ignored other forms of domination.

Our research suggests that the radical/social-ist opposition was overstated, but small theoretical differences seemed very important at the time because the early feminists were in the process of developing new political theory, not yet making political alliances to achieve concrete objectives. A few separatists, often but not exclusively lesbians, attempted to create self-sustaining female communities and to withdraw as much as possible from contact with men. By the late 1970s, some women had become cultural feminists, celebrating women's specialness and difference from men and retreating from direct challenges to sexist institutions; they believed that change could come about through building new exemplary female communities. But despite this proliferation of ideological groupings, most members of women's liberation did not identify with any of these tendencies and considered themselves simply feminists, unmodified.

Racial/ethnic differences were more significant. Feminists of different racial/ethnic groups established independent organizations from the beginning and within those organizations created different feminisms: black, Chicana, Asian American, Native American. Feminists of color emphasized the problems with universalizing assumptions about women and with identifying gender as a category autonomous from race and class. . . . [F]eminists of color were not more unanimous than white feminists—there were, for example, black liberal feminists, black socialist feminists, black radical feminists, black cultural feminists. These complexities do not negate the fact that feminists of color experienced racism within the women's movement. The majority of feminists, white women from middle-class backgrounds, were often oblivious to the lives of women from minority and working-class families. Feminists of color faced the additional problems that certain women's issues, such as reproductive rights, had been historically tainted by racism; and that feminist criticisms of men were experienced differently, often as betraying racial solidarity when the men were themselves victims of racism.

Lesbians sometimes created separate feminist groups. . . . As lesbians became more open and vocal, they protested the heterosexual assumptions of straight feminists, but they also experienced discrimination from the male-dominated gay movement. For the most part lesbians continued to be active in women's liberation and made important contributions to feminist theory. Lesbians even led campaigns of primary concern to heterosexual women, such as campaigns for reproductive rights.

At the beginning of the movement, feminists tended to create multi-issue organizations, which in turn created committees to focus on single issues, such as day care, rape, or running a women's center. One of the fundamental tenets of early feminist theory was the interconnectedness of all aspects of women's oppression. As political sophistication grew and activists grasped the difficulties of making sweeping changes, feminists settled for piecemeal, fragmented activism. By the mid-1970s feminist politics often occurred in single-issue organizations focused on, for example, reproductive rights, employment discrimination, health, domestic violence, female unions, women's studies. Single-issue politics de-emphasized theory, which reduced divisions; it had the advantage of making coalitions easier but . . . made the movement less radical and more practical. Single-issue politics also lessened the movement's coherence as its activists became specialized and professionalized.

ORGANIZATIONAL PRINCIPLES OF WOMEN'S LIBERATION

In sharp opposition to its liberal feminist sisters in NOW, women's liberation preferred radical decentralization. . . . Women, whose voices had been silenced and whose actions had been directed by others, were loath to have anyone telling them what to think or do. They understood that central organization would produce principles, programs, and priorities they would be required to follow. They also sensed that a movement growing at such velocity could not be contained by central organizations, which would only inhibit creative growth. Without formal rules of membership, any group of women could declare themselves a women's liberation organization, start a newspaper or a women's center, issue a manifesto. The resulting diversity then made it all the harder to keep track of, let alone unify, the many groups.

Not only was there no formal structure bringing groups together, there was very little structure within groups, and this was, again, by choice. Feminists . . . were often hostile in principle to formal procedures, which they saw as arbitrary and not organic. This attitude was part of the feminist critique of the public/private distinction, and it was a way of making the public sphere accessible to women who were traditionally more experienced with a personal, familial form of conversing. In small meetings, especially in the consciousness-raising groups that were the essence of women's liberation, the informal "rapping" style was nurturant, allowing women to speak intimately and risk self-exposure, and therefore to come up with rich new insights into the workings of male dominance. When there were large meetings and/or sharp disagreements, the sessions often became tediously long, unable to reach decisions, and even chaotic. As a result, small groups of women or strong-minded and charismatic individuals sometimes took charge, and others, exhausted by the long aimless discussions, grudgingly relinquished power to these unelected leaders.

Women's liberation faced a major dilemma with respect to leadership. Its search for direct democracy led the movement to revere the principle of "every woman a leader" and to imagine that collectives could speak with one voice. Consequently the movement empowered thousands of women who had never dreamt they could write a leaflet, speak in public, talk to the press, chair a meeting, assert unpopular points of view, or make risky suggestions. The emphasis on group leadership meant that many important statements were unsigned, written anonymously or collectively, or signed with first names only, indicating the degree to which theory and strategy were being developed democratically. But the bias against leadership hindered action, decision-making, and coherent communication beyond small groups. More problematically, the movement did create leaders, but they were frequently unacknowledged and almost always unaccountable because they were essentially self-appointed rather than chosen by the members. This led to widespread, sometimes intense resentment of leaders. The hostility, usually covert, sometimes escalated to stimulate open attacks, as women publicly criticized or "trashed" leaders in meetings. One result was that individuals who had worked hard and made personal sacrifices felt betrayed and embittered. Another was that women's liberation groups became vulnerable to takeovers by highly organized sectarian groups (mainly the Marxist-Leninist sects) or obstruction by

disturbed individuals who could not be silenced. Perhaps the most deleterious result was that many women became reluctant to assert leadership and thus deprived the movement of needed talent. The leadership problem involved the movement's denial of internal inequalities, its refusal to recognize that some women were more articulate and self-confident; had more leisure time, connections, and access to power; or were simply more forceful personalities. These inequalities mainly derived, as the feminists' own analysis showed, from the class and race hierarchy of the larger society. This is an example of utopian hopes becoming wishful thinking: feminists so badly wanted equality that they pretended it was already here.

Despite decentralization and structurelessness, women's liberation created a shared culture, theory, and practice. In an era before e-mail, even before xeroxing, printed publications were vital and feminists spent a significant proportion of their energy, resources, and ingenuity producing them. Mimeographed pages stapled together into pamphlets were the common currency of the early years of the movement, and soon a few feminist publishing houses, such as KNOW in Pittsburgh, Lollipop Inc. in Durham, and the Feminist Press in New York, were printing and selling feminist writings for prices ranging from a nickel to a quarter. These were widely discussed, debated, and answered in further publications. . . . By the mid-1970s over 500 feminist magazines and newspapers appeared throughout the country, such as *Women: A Journal of Liberation* from Baltimore, *It Ain't Me Babe* from the San Francisco Bay Area, *Off Our Backs* from Washington, D.C., *Everywoman* from Los Angeles. . . .

Unlike *Ms.*, a mass-circulation advertisement-supported liberal feminist magazine established in 1972, women's liberation publications struggled along without funds or paid staff. . . . Many articles were signed simply "Susan" or "Randy," or not signed at all, because the movement was hostile to the idea of intellectual private property. The papers sometimes forgot to print dates of publication, addresses, and subscription information. Women worked hard at producing these publications but, unfortunately, less hard at financing and distributing them, so many were irregularly published and short-lived. Nevertheless, it was in these homespun rags that you could find the most creative and cutting-edge theory and commentary.

WHAT WOMEN'S LIBERATION
ACCOMPLISHED

... [Specific] achievements arose from [women's liberation] campaigns, [but] most transformations only revealed themselves later. Social change, after all, happens slowly. Judicial and legislative victories include the legalization of abortion in 1973, federal guidelines against coercive sterilization, rape shield laws that encourage more women to prosecute their attackers, affirmative action programs that aim to correct past discrimination—but not, however, the Equal Rights Amendment, which failed in 1982, just three states short of the required two-thirds. There are many equally important but less obvious accomplishments: not only legal, economic, and political gains, but also changes in the way people live, dress, dream of their future, and make a living. In fact, there are few areas of contemporary life untouched by feminism. As regards health care, for example, many physicians and hospitals have made major improvements in the treatment of women; about 50 percent of medical students are women; women successfully fought their exclusion from medical research; diseases affecting women, such as breast and ovarian cancer, now receive more funding thanks to women's efforts. Feminists insisted that violence against women, previously a well-kept secret, become a public political issue; made rape, incest, battering, and sexual harassment understood as crimes; and got public funding for shelters for battered women. These gains, realized in the 1980s and 1990s, are the fruits of struggles fought in the 1970s.

Feminist pressure generated substantial changes in education: curricula and textbooks have been rewritten to promote equal opportunity for girls, more women are admitted and funded in universities and professional schools, and a new and rich feminist scholarship in many disciplines has won recognition. Title IX, passed in 1972 to mandate equal access to college programs, has worked a revolution in sports. Consider the many women's records broken in track and field, the expanding number of athletic scholarships for women, professional women's basketball, and the massive popularity of girls' and women's soccer.

Campaigning to support families, feminists organized day care centers, developed standards and curricula for early childhood education, demanded day care funding from government and private employers, fought for parental leave from employers and a decent welfare system. They also struggled for new options for women in employment. They won greater access to traditionally male occupations, from construction to professions and business. They joined unions and fought to democratize them, and they succeeded in organizing previously nonunion workers such as secretaries, waitresses, hospital workers, and flight attendants. As the majority of American women increasingly need to work for wages throughout their lives, the feminist movement tried to educate men to share in housework and child raising. Although women still do the bulk of the housework and child rearing, it is common today to see men in the playgrounds, the supermarkets, and at the PTA meetings.

Feminism changed how women look and what is considered attractive, although the original feminist impulse toward simpler, more comfortable, and less overtly sexual clothing is being challenged by another generation of women at the turn of the century. As women's-liberation influence spread in the 1970s, more and more women refused to wear the constricting, uncomfortable clothes that were required in the 1950s—girdles, garter belts, and stockings; tight, flimsy, pointed, and high-heeled shoes; crinolines and cinch belts; tight short skirts. Women wearing pants, loose jackets, walking shoes, and no makeup began to feel attractive and to be recognized by others as attractive. By the 1980s, however, younger women began to feel that feminist beauty standards were repressive, even prudish, and developed a new, more playful, ornate, and multicultural fashion sensibility that may signal a "third wave" of feminism. Women's newfound passion for athletics has made a look of health and strength fashionable, sometimes to an oppressive degree as women feel coerced to reach a firm muscular, spandex thinness. At the same time, a conservative antifeminist backlash is also influencing fashion, trying to reestablish an allegedly lost femininity. The politics of feminism is being fought out on the fashion front.

Other aspects of the culture also reveal feminism's impact. Finally some older movie actresses, such as Susan Sarandon, Olympia Dukakis, and Meryl Streep, are recognized as desirable, and women entertainers in many media and art forms are rejecting simplistic, demeaning, and passive roles, despite the reemergence of misogynist and hypersexualized entertainments. Soap operas, sitcoms, even cop shows now feature plots in which lesbianism, abortion, rape, incest, and battering are portrayed from women's perspectives. . . . The way we speak has been altered: new words have been coined—"sexist" and "Ms." and "gender"; many Americans are now self-conscious about using "he" to mean a human, and text-books and even sacred texts are being rewritten in inclusive language. Women now expect to be called "women" instead of "ladies" or "girls."

Some of the biggest transformations are personal and familial, and they have been hotly contested. Indeed, even from a feminist perspective not all of them are positive. Women's relationships with other women are more publicly valued and celebrated and lesbianism is more accepted. . . . Most women today enter marriage or other romantic relationships with the expectation of equal partnership; since they don't always get this, they seem more willing to live as single people than to put up with domineering or abusive men. Conservatives argue that the growth of divorce, out-of-wedlock childbirth, and single motherhood is a sign of social deterioration, and certainly the growing economic inequality in the U.S. has rendered many women and especially single mothers and their children impoverished, de-pressed, and angry. But, feminists retort, is being poor in a destructive marriage really better than being poor on one's own? Even the growth of single motherhood reflects an ele-ment of women's choice: in different circum-stances both poor and prosperous women are refusing to consider a bad marriage the price of motherhood, and are giving birth to or adopt-ing children without husbands. . . . There is a growing sentiment that families come in a va-riety of forms.

By the mid-1970s an antifeminist backlash was able to command huge funding from right-wing corporate fortunes, fervent support from religious fundamentalists, and considerable media attention. The intensity of the reaction is a measure of how threatened conservatives were by popular backing for women's liberation and the rapid changes it brought about. Even with their billions of dollars, their hundreds of lobbyists and PR men, their foundations and magazines dishing out antifeminist misinfor-mation, as compared to the puny amounts of money and volunteer labor available to wom-en's liberation, the striking fact is that public opinion has not shifted much. Polls show over-whelming support for what feminism stands for: equal rights, respect, opportunity, and access for women.

That there is still a long way to go to reach sexual equality should not prevent us from rec-ognizing what has been achieved. If there is disappointment, it is because women's libera-tion was so utopian, even apocalyptic, emerg-ing as it did in an era of radical social movements and grand optimism. Unrealistic? Perhaps. But without utopian dreams, without anger, with-out reaching for the moon and expecting to get there by express, the movement would have achieved far less. In fact, without taking risks, feminists would never have been able to imag-ine lives of freedom and justice for women.

Feminism is by no means dead. Feminist groups continue to work on specific issues such as reproductive rights, rape, violence against women, sweatshops, sexism in the media, union organizing, and welfare rights. Never-theless, the mass social movement called wom-en's liberation did dissolve by the end of the 1970s. This is not a sign of failure. All social movements are short-lived because of the in-tense personal demands they make; few can sustain the level of energy that they require at their peak of activity. Moreover, as people age, most put more energy into family, employ-ment, and personal life. Equally important, women's liberation could not survive outside the context of the other progressive social movements that nurtured hope and optimism about social change. As the Left declined, the right-wing backlash grew stronger. It did not convert many feminists to conservatism but it moved the mainstream far to the right. Given this change in mainstream politics, it is all the more striking that so few feminist gains have been rolled back and many have continued and even increased their momentum. Al-though the word "feminist" has become a pe-jorative term to some American women, most women (and most men as well) support a femi-nist program: equal education, equal pay, child care, freedom from harassment and violence, shared housework and child rearing, women's right to self-determination. . . .

JUDY TZU-CHUN WU
The Vietnam War and Global Sisterhood

We see some of the complexity of women's activism in the 1960s in the women and peace activists who gathered at the two Indochinese Women's Conferences (IWCs) held in Canada in 1971. (The meetings were held north of the 49th parallel because Canada was officially neutral during the U.S. war in Vietnam. Both U.S. draft resisters and representative of North Vietnam could enter Canada.) Here, an unprecedented number of North American women, many for the first time, encountered female leaders from Southeast Asia. All believed that citizen diplomacy might succeed in advancing peace at a time when governments appeared to balk at substantive negotiations. From Vietnam came representatives of two women's unions, one based in North Vietnam and one in South Vietnam. The westerners were well aware of their guests' deep experience in resisting colonialism and fighting for national liberation. Here were women who had been guerrilla fighters, organized all-women brigades, and endured many losses. Some, like Nguyen Thi Binh, had held high political offices. Their search for self-determination on many fronts held great appeal for North American women who came from different activist strands, including long-time peace advocates whose predecessors are described in Leila J. Rupp's essay (pp. 393–404); recently awakened women's liberationists; and newly empowered Third World women like Marii Hasegawa and Betita Martinez.

What were the differences in experience and in approach to political work between Vietnamese and North American women that emerge from Judy Tzu-Chun Wu's research? As you contemplate political alliances across national borders in today's "globalizing" world, what lessons are found in Wu's conclusions about the global sisterhood achieved in the IWCs?

In April 1971, approximately one thousand female activists from throughout North America gathered in Vancouver and Toronto, Canada, to attend the Indochinese Women's Conferences (IWCs). The U.S. and Canadian women originated from large metropolitan centers, small towns, and even rural communities to meet a delegation of women from North and South Vietnam as well as Laos. . . . The 1971 IWCs, represented the first opportunities for large numbers of North American women to have direct contact with their Asian "sisters."

The IWCs illuminate how women literally and symbolically crossed borders in order to build an international antiwar movement. As such, the organizing of the conferences and the experiences of those who attended shed light on the process of building "global sisterhood." Critics of the idea have argued that the call for female international solidarity represents another form of Western domination, this time by well-intentioned champions of women's rights who see themselves as the saviors of oppressed women in non-Western societies. The IWCs provide an opportunity to rethink global sisterhood in two ways.[1]

First, the conferences highlight the political multiplicity of North American women and the complex process of negotiation that occurred to foster an international peace movement. There were three North American sponsors of the IWCs: "old friends" or more "traditional" women's peace organizations; "new friends" or women's liberation activists;

Excerpted from ch. 7 of *Radicals on the Road: Internationalism, Orientalism, and Feminism During the Vietnam Era* by Judy Tzu-Chun Wu (Ithaca, N.Y.: Cornell University Press, 2013). Reprinted by permission of the author and publisher. Notes have been edited and renumbered.

and "Third World" women or women of color in North America. Within each group, the women ascribed to a variety of political viewpoints. Engaging in an international movement did not unify women in the West. In fact, the IWCs provided a forum to air and accentuate differences between North American women, particularly along the lines of ideology, race, sexuality, and nationality. Fractured by these differences, women from North America did not dominate the political agenda at the IWCs. Instead, they looked to women from Southeast Asia for leadership and inspiration. Thus, the IWCs reveal the political variety among women in the West and how these conflicts can ironically foster the growth of a global women's antiwar movement.

Second, while critics of global sisterhood emphasize the power and misperceptions of Western women, a focus on the Southeast Asian women demonstrates how women from outside the West deployed female internationalism. During the U.S. war in Vietnam, the Women's Union of North Vietnam and the Women's Union for the Liberation of South Vietnam (collectively referred to [here] as the VWUs, Vietnam Women's Unions) played integral roles in fostering a global women's peace movement. Through meetings, correspondence, and the circulation of print as well as visual media, the VWUs actively nurtured American women's interest in U.S. foreign policy and military activity in Southeast Asia. The Vietnamese believed that all human beings, and especially all women, could share a sense of commonality and purpose. To promote an international peace movement, Vietnamese women cultivated a belief in global sisterhood, projecting and cultivating a female universalism that simultaneously critiqued and transcended racial and cultural divides. It was not just an ideology imposed by the West but was promoted by women from the East as well.

The IWCs resulted from a longer history of North American and Southeast Asian women politically engaging with one another. They developed personal and political connections through face-to-face meetings that took place in Eastern and Western Europe, Asia, Cuba, Africa, Australia, and Canada. These conversations and partnerships in turn helped to shape the political content of Vietnamese antiwar appeals, which eventually circulated beyond the individuals involved to influence activist media portrayals of the U.S. war in Vietnam. In this campaign to promote a worldwide antiwar movement, the VWUs established relationships with individual women and with female organizations from a variety of political spectrums and backgrounds. The North American sponsors of the IWC—old friends, new friends, and Third World women—reveal the diversity of individuals engaged in fostering female internationalism.

The term "old friends" referred to the U.S.-based Women Strike for Peace (WSP), the Canadian Voice of Women (VOW), and the Women's International League for Peace and Freedom (WILPF), headquartered in Switzerland but with national sections throughout the world. These organizations were designated old not because of the age of their constituency, although all three did attract largely middle-aged to elderly women. Rather, the organizations were considered old friends because of the history of friendship that these North American women established with Vietnamese women. For example, WSP's contact with the VWU extended back to 1965, when two WSP members were among the first Americans to visit Hanoi after the commencement of U.S. bombing of North Vietnam. That same year, a ten-person delegation from WSP met with representatives from North and South Vietnam in Jakarta, Indonesia, to affirm women's unique abilities to cross Cold War barriers and foster peace.[2] These political and personal relationships continued to develop as WSP sent international delegations to Europe, Canada, Cuba, and North Vietnam throughout the remainder of the war.

Although differences existed among WSP, VOW, and WILPF, they could be characterized as maternalist peace organizations. For example, WSP originated in 1961 from the efforts of predominantly middle-class and middle-raged white women to protect their families from nuclear annihilation. As historian and former WSP activist Amy Swerdlow explained:

On 1 November 1961 an estimated fifty thousand women walked out of their kitchens and off their jobs, in an unprecedented nationwide strike for peace. As a radioactive cloud from a series of Russian atom bomb tests passed over American cities and the United States threatened to retaliate with its own cycle of nuclear explosions, the striking women sent delegations to their elected officials. . . . They demanded that their local officials pressure President John Kennedy on behalf of all the world's children, to end nuclear testing at once and begin negotiations for nuclear disarmament.

This initial strike eventually led committed women to form Women Strike for Peace. The members of the organization ... had "wide-ranging professional identities," yet they chose to publicly identify themselves as "housewives and mothers." These women proclaimed their right to condemn the threat of global and nuclear warfare based on the desire to protect their own and other people's families. They embraced gender difference to define a special role for women on the global stage.[3]

[The Canadian group] VOW, founded just a year before WSP in 1960, was similarly inspired by a belief in women's unique abilities and responsibilities to foster peace. Following the failure of the 1960 Paris summit on disarmament between the United States and the Soviet Union, thousands of women across Canada decided to form VOW. They presented themselves as "respectable" and as maternal, "protectors of the world's children." One of the founding members and an eventual president of the group, Muriel Duckworth, explained that "Voice of Women founders had the idea of women as lifegivers," mothers who could not support acts of aggression and violence.[4]

The roots of this maternalist form of peace politics can be traced back to Victorian and Progressive era notions of gender difference as opposed to more modern beliefs in gender sameness. In fact, WILPF, the third organizational member among the old friends, was founded before American women achieved suffrage and in the context of World War I. Created under the leadership of Jane Addams, WILPF advocated for equal political rights for women because members believed that women had a propensity to promote peace. As suffragist and pacifist Carrie Chapman Catt explained, "War is in the blood of men"; inversely, peace was believed to be in the blood of women.[5]

This maternalist and gender essentialist justification for women's engagement in international politics held particular significance in the early Cold War period. In the midst of the Red Scare, critics of U.S. foreign policies were easily dismissed and ridiculed as communist sympathizers and political ideologues. In fact, members of WSP, VOW, and WILPF all endured anticommunist attacks. By proclaiming the political responsibilities of motherhood, these women presented themselves as "common-sense" or nonideological activists. They sought to defuse global conflict and promote peace in order to protect "all the world's children."[6]

With their similarities, the three organizations frequently collaborated with one another and shared ideas for promoting peace. Representatives of each group corresponded with one another and participated in each other's conferences and activities. The organizations also overlapped in membership. In addition, for all three groups, traveling across geopolitical borders and having face-to-face meetings with their nations' enemies were important strategies for their efforts to defuse global conflict.... Representatives of WSP, following a series of exchanges with Vietnamese women, cosponsored with their Asian counterparts the historic Conference of Concerned Women to End the War. The conference was held in Paris in the spring of 1968, just a few weeks before the formal peace talks began. In attendance were representatives from countries involved in the war, including Japan, Britain, Australia, New Zealand, West Germany, and Canada. One American participant recalled the impact of the meeting: "I have always been convinced that the women who come in contact with the Vietnamese women come back home changed. They seem to march to the beat of another drummer. They have a new sense of urgency. Now I know why. It has happened to me. When you are actually faced with the 'enemy' and realize that American sons and husbands are killing them—it's too much to bear."[7]

After attending the emotionally charged Paris conference, Kay MacPherson, president of VOW, visited Hanoi for the first time. She did so with a sense of trepidation as well as determination. Aware that she would travel in the midst of an ongoing bombing campaign by the United States, MacPherson wrote, "In case I get to Hanoi and end up with a bomb on top of me I want to put down one or two thoughts before hand. ... Not many people are invited to go to Hanoi, though many wish to go. To have earned the trust of the Vietnam women is a very great honour. ... We cannot treat such an honour lightly, nor, however reluctant I felt, would I dream of refusing to go." Following MacPherson's journey to Southeast Asia, VOW sponsored a reciprocal visit by representatives of the North and South Vietnam Women's Unions to Canada in the summer of 1969. Members of WSP, including Jane Spock—wife of Dr. Benjamin Spock—attended this gathering. In fact, they staged a protest against the war on the Fourth of July as they crossed the U.S.-Canada border at Niagara Falls.[8] This

1969 exchange directly inspired the subsequent 1971 IWCs.

The members of WSP, VOW, and WILPF recognized the power of face-to-face communication with Vietnamese women and sought to provide similar opportunities for other individuals. Aware of their own demographic base, they made various attempts to involve younger and nonwhite activists. Cora Weiss, a leader in WSP as well as in the peace movement overall, played arguably the most central role in arranging American delegations to Hanoi during the U.S. war in Vietnam. . . . [Weiss] protested against the Red Scare during her college years at the University of Wisconsin, Madison. While in the home state of Senator Joe McCarthy, she petitioned for his recall of in a campaign called Joe Must Go. She also met her husband in college. Peter Weiss, a survivor of the Holocaust, joined with Cora as they participated in the civil rights movement and in support of African decolonization. During the war, Cora, who is fluent in French, went to Paris several times to meet with Vietnamese representatives. She also helped to organize the 1969 and 1971 women's conferences in Canada. She traveled to Vietnam a total of five times, the first time in December 1969 after the first Canada conference and the last time in 1978. . . . [9]

Weiss traveled to North Vietnam and organized the trips of others because she believed in the power of "citizen diplomacy." On her initial journey in 1969, she discussed with Vietnamese representatives the importance of facilitating communication between American POWs and their families. In keeping with the maternalist outlook of other old friends, Weiss was motivated by a sense of compassion for the soldiers and their families. In addition, she recognized the political impact such humanitarian gestures would have. During the late 1960s and early 1970s, President Nixon and the U.S. administration focused on American POWs and soldiers missing in action to justify extending the war. Weiss and other antiwar activists sought to defuse this issue by facilitating communication for and the release of U.S. POWs. After her first trip in 1969, Weiss established the Committee of Liaison with Servicemen Detained in North Vietnam, which organized monthly visits to Hanoi to serve as mail carriers for American POWs and their families. On her second trip to Hanoi in 1972, Weiss negotiated with the North Vietnamese to release three POWs as a gesture of goodwill.

The regularly scheduled trips, sponsored by the Committee of Liaison, not only delivered mail and packages to U.S. soldiers but also provided an opportunity to expose dedicated peace activists to wartime conditions in Hanoi. In composing the membership of these monthly delegations, Weiss invited individuals from diverse racial, generational, and gender backgrounds to expand the range of people who otherwise would not have the opportunity to travel to North Vietnam. These journeys invariably reaffirmed and further motivated the travelers' engagement in the antiwar movement. [10]

The women from North and South Vietnam who cultivated and encouraged international contact with women from the West also articulated a unique gender role for women in the struggle for peace and national liberation. They represented women's organizations in their respective regions. The Women's Union of North Vietnam, based in Hanoi, traced its history back to the founding of the Indochinese Communist Party in 1930. The Women's Union for the Liberation of South Vietnam was founded in 1960, along with the National Liberation Front (NLF). The phrase "women's liberation" in the Western context referred to activists who sought to identify and subvert the workings of patriarchy. The VWUs conceived of women's liberation primarily through the lens of anticolonial struggles for national liberation. Because of the long history of political repression and anticolonial warfare, Vietnamese women had assumed a variety of political, military, economic and cultural roles. Consequently, they had a wider array of life experiences than did most of their Western counterparts. Yet, interestingly, the Vietnamese women also conveyed the arguments for peace in the name of protecting their families.

Nguyen Thi Binh, who was present at the 1965 Jakarta meeting with WSP as well as the 1968 Paris Women's Conference, became one of the most recognizable Asian female figures in Western women's political circles. Like WSP members, she came from a relatively elite and educated background. The granddaughter of nationalist leader Phan Chu Trinh and the daughter of a civil servant under the French, Binh became a political activist in the 1950s when she led a series of student protests against the French and the United States in Saigon. Imprisoned for three years for these activities, she helped to found the NLF and the Women's Union for the Liberation of South Vietnam after her release. Unlike most WSP members, who were denied formal political power, Binh became an authorized leader as the foreign minister of the Provisional Revolutionary Government. WSP historian Amy Swerdlow noted the unequal status of the American and Asian women who met at international gatherings. While WSP publicly identified itself as consisting of "nonprofessional housewives, . . . the women who represented North and South Vietnam presented themselves as workers, students, professionals, and artists."[11]

Despite the disjuncture in status, Vietnamese women like Binh used a language of sisterhood and motherhood to establish a common connection with their old friends. In a fifteen-minute film produced in 1970 and intended for an American female audience, Binh explained:

> I am so happy as a South Vietnamese woman and mother to have the opportunity to speak to you. . . . May I express my sincere thanks to the Women Strike for Peace for its contribution to the anti-war movements and its sympathy and support to our people, particularly the South Vietnamese women. . . . Our aspirations for peace are all the more ardent for over 25 consecutive years now, our compatriots, we women included, have never enjoyed a single day of peace. Let me tell you that in my own family, several members have been killed while some others are still jailed by the Saigon regime. I myself have had not much time to live with my husband and my children. The moments my son and daughter were allowed to be at my side have become so rare and therefore so precious to them.[12]

Her emphasis on the destructive impact of warfare on family life reflected the actual experiences of women in Vietnam. Her appeal also resonated effectively with maternalist activists in the West who stressed the sanctity of motherhood and home life. . . .

VWU initiated multiple international gatherings to facilitate personal contact with Western women. In addition, VWU circulated print materials to communicate how Vietnamese women both suffered from but also heroically resisted colonialism and military aggression. During the U.S. war in Vietnam, the VWU published a periodical in English and French titled *Women of Viet Nam*. They also shared copies of Vietnamese Studies no. 10, a booklet called *Vietnamese Women* (*VW*). This 1966 English-language publication was presented to U.S. visitors, both at international gatherings and during their travels to Vietnam. The portrayal of Vietnamese women in this work, numbering over three hundred pages, appealed to the political ideologies and sympathies of women from a variety of generations and backgrounds in the West.

[The book] *VW* consisted of eight sections, with chapters having titles such as "The Vietnamese Woman, Yesterday and Today," as well as more intimate and localized portrayals of either individual women or women from particular villages or regions. The overall effect was to personalize and humanize women in North and South Vietnam by providing a narrative of personal and social uplift through four historical stages: (1) Vietnamese women's lives under patriarchal as well as colonial oppression under French rule beginning in the mid- to late nineteenth century; (2) Vietnamese women's efforts to challenge traditional gender roles through involvement in national liberation movements, first against the French and then against the United States; (3) the transformation of Vietnamese women's lives through socialist reconstruction projects in the North after the end of the First Indochina War against the French in 1954; and (4) finally, how the opportunities for improving Vietnamese women's lives continue to be threatened by American imperialism and the Second Indochina War, which was being fought against the United States and the South Vietnamese government. Somewhat predictably, the publication argued that the oppression of Vietnamese women, particularly for the vast majority who were members of the peasantry, was centrally connected to class and national oppression. For Vietnamese women to achieve liberation and equality, then, they had to struggle not only against patriarchal family and societal norms but also for national independence and socialist revolution. The way this political message was conveyed, particularly through intimate portraits, appealed to Western women in various ways.

For maternalist peace activists who subscribed to "traditional" gender roles and justified their political interventions as part of their responsibilities as mothers and housewives, the destructive impact of war on heteronormative family life in Vietnam resonated most strongly. Numerous stories in *VW* emphasize how war separates, sometimes permanently, husbands and wives as well as mothers and children. The tragedy of war, then, was conveyed through heteronormative and maternal loss. One folksong quoted in *VW* expressed this longing of a young woman in North Vietnam and her fiancé who had departed to fight in the South: "Our destinies are bound together, I will wait for you / Even if I should have to wait a thousand years."[13]

Protecting their families and loved ones against colonialism and war required Vietnamese women to engage in or support acts of rebellion and violence. In their publications and in face-to-face meetings, they frequently quoted the traditional saying, "When the enemy comes, even the women must fight." They also cited historic examples of Vietnamese women who battled against foreign invasion, such as the Trung sisters, credited with leading the first national liberation struggle against Chinese domination in 40 AD. This Vietnamese female warrior tradition, which could be regarded as a transgression of traditional gender roles, was framed as a heteronormative or maternalist act of agency. For example, the publication *VW* featured a poem by Minh Khai, a famous revolutionary against the French who wrote on her prison cell before she was executed:

> A rosy-cheeked woman, here I am fighting side by side with you men!
> On my shoulders, weighs that hatred which is common to us.
> The prison is my school, its mates my friends.
> The sword is my child, the gun my husband.[14]

In this poem, instruments of violence are equated with members of a heteronormative family. The evocation of the sword as a child and the gun as a husband justifies the embrace of these objects as a means to fulfill traditional familial responsibilities. Given colonial and wartime conditions that do not allow for peaceful existence of kinship units, the female warrior bears the responsibility of defending her home and homeland in order to become a wife and mother. . . .

Maternalist activists in the West embraced pacifism.[15] However, they could understand the fierce desire to step outside of accepted gender practices in the name of protecting their families. After all, to help end the war and stop nuclear annihilation, members of WSP, VOW, and WILPF also left the confines of the home to travel, lobby, and stage protests. Rather than condemning the Vietnamese women for fighting to save their loved ones, Western women peace activists demanded that the U.S. government end the war. As one slogan adopted by WSP pleaded: "Not Our Sons, Not Their Sons."

The model of revolutionary womanhood that Vietnamese women offered resonated differently for the new friends who cosponsored the IWCs. This designation generally referred to a younger generation of women who became politically active through the civil rights, New Left, and eventually the women's and sexual liberation movements. In contrast to the old friends who claimed their roles as housewives and mothers to justify their political interventions, the new friends sought to fundamentally challenge male domination over women. They demanded equal opportunities and rights for women in the legal and political system as well as the workplace. They identified inequalities in the home, naming the "second shift" that women worked as primary caregivers and housekeepers as well as the limited rights of women in marriage and divorce. They questioned the reproduction of gender roles through child rearing practices and socialization. They protested the sexual objectification and violence directed toward women and their bodies. And they challenged heteronormativity by claiming lesbianism as a sexual and political practice.

Although the individuals referred to as "new friends" differed and disagreed with one another, they collectively constituted members of the so-called second wave of feminism. (The first wave [is said to have] crested with the attainment of suffrage in 1920, while the second wave is associated with women's activism of the 1960s and 1970s.) . . . For them, the experiences of Vietnamese women offered a range of possibilities [for] discover[ing] new political roles and identities.

For liberal feminists seeking access and equality for women in the realm of work and politics, the experiences of Vietnamese women provided insight into the social reconstruction of gender roles. The *VW* booklet notes, "It is easy to inscribe the 'liberation of women' in the programme of a political party, it is much more difficult to get it into legislation, and more difficult still to integrate it into the customs and manners of the time." Significantly, the publication did not regard women in the West as the vanguard of change, stating instead that "at present, women in all Western countries are still asking for equal salary and wages with men. . . . And they are not to get it very soon." Strikingly, the authors regarded women in the West as being engaged in a similar struggle and perhaps even falling behind the so-called

Third World. Because North Vietnam was in the process of constructing a new society, *VW* documented at length the rights and advances women had achieved under the Democratic Republic of Vietnam, such as suffrage, equal pay, and women holding prominent positions of political and economic leadership. At the same time, the publication also frankly acknowledged barriers to greater gender equity, conveying both advances and challenges through individual stories and charts with clear quantitative data.[17]

While the Vietnamese focus on women integrating the public arena might appeal to liberal feminists in the West, other aspects of the Vietnamese analysis resonated more strongly with women's liberation activists in the United States.[18] These individuals sought to identify and subvert the workings of patriarchy in all realms of life, not just in the public sphere of work and politics but also in the private sphere of personal, familial, and sexual relationships. For these women, the Vietnamese provided functioning examples of female communities. They organized all-women economic production teams, guerrilla units, and even regular military battalions, while leading hybridized and improvised family structures in the midst of war. Although products of emergency circumstances, these practices nevertheless offered empowering demonstrations of how women, through separatist institutions, could transform the society around them.

The VWU often used biographical examples of heroic women to offer political instruction. This "emulation campaign" was primarily directed toward the largely peasant constituency in Vietnam. One of the prominently featured women was Nguyen Thi Dinh, a cofounder of the NLF and president of the Women's Union for the Liberation of South Vietnam. Unlike Nguyen Thi Binh, who came from a relatively elite family, Dinh was a peasant. Born in 1920, she began dedicating herself to fighting French colonialism at the age of fifteen. She eventually became a guerrilla fighter and a general in the People's Liberation Army. Like many other women engaged in the struggle for national liberation, described by the Vietnamese as "longhaired warriors," Dinh suffered imprisonment and separation from her husband and child, as well as the death of her loved ones. Dinh's life story as a female revolutionary leader engaged in armed struggle inspired new friends in the West who were trying to understand how they might fundamentally change their society. In addition, the Vietnamese use of the personal to offer political instruction corresponded strongly to one of the key mantras of the U.S. women's liberation movement: the personal is political.[19]

Some "new friend" feminists had the opportunity to learn from Vietnamese women through direct contact. Vivian Rothstein, who was a student activist at Berkeley before her involvement in the women's liberation movement in Chicago, met with Vietnamese women in Eastern Europe and then in North Vietnam in 1967. As a member of Students for a Democratic Society, she had been invited to participate in a significant gathering of antiwar activists in Bratislava, Czechoslovakia, in September 1967. Thirty-eight Americans attended the meeting, including representatives from religious pacifist organizations, the civil rights movement, the liberal and progressive media, and faculty and student antiwar activists. In Bratislava, they met with Vietnamese spokespersons from the North and the South, including Nguyen Thi Binh and other representatives of the VWU.[20]

Rothstein recalled that the Vietnamese women whom she met insisted on having women-only discussions with American representatives. This was unusual for her. She tended to work in mixed-gender settings as a student activist. . . . However, the women from South Vietnam wanted to convey how the war had a unique impact on women. Rothstein recalled that they discussed how militarization fostered the growth of prostitution in South Vietnam. In addition, they provided examples of how American soldiers threatened and utilized rape as well as sexual mutilation as military tactics. Shaken and moved by these meetings, Rothstein requested an audiotape version of their presentation so that she might share their "appeal to the American women."[21]

During the conference in Bratislava, Rothstein received an invitation from the VWU to visit North Vietnam. The trip to Eastern Europe was the first time she had left the United States, so traveling to Hanoi, which was then being bombed, was a "huge, terrifying" experience. Nevertheless, the journey profoundly touched Rothstein. In North Vietnam, she observed how the VWU inspired and mobilized women to protect and transform their society. The VWU had chapters at various levels, ranging from local villages to the national level and operating in schools, workplaces, health clinics, and government units. In all of these settings, the unions trained women for political leadership and advocated for their collective interests. VWU representatives conveyed to Rothstein "how important it was to organize the women ... and how powerful American women could be" as well. When Rothstein returned to the United States, she went back to the "little women's group" that she had participated in before she left. Inspired by her experiences in Czechoslovakia and North Vietnam, Rothstein proposed the formation of the Chicago Women's Liberation Union, a group modeled on the VWU.

Just as American activists learned from the Vietnamese, their hosts were eager to learn from the visitors. Charlotte Bunch-Weeks, a women's liberation activist based in the Washington, DC, area, traveled to Vietnam as part of a multiracial and mixed-sex group in 1970. . . .

Like other travelers to North Vietnam, Bunch-Weeks returned with a deeper commitment to ending the war. She remembers one particularly profound exchange she had with a Buddhist nun [outside of Vinh] south of Hanoi, where the countryside, villages, and towns that had been repeatedly bombed . . . [At] a Buddhist pagoda, which was only partly standing, their host, "a small, thin, quiet Buddhist nun in [a] brown habit," showed them around.

> Suddenly she leaned toward us, grew very intense, and grasped our hands. She said that she had been waiting many years to talk with American women. She was convinced that if the women of the US knew what was really happening in her country, they would make it stop. She told of her experience, of how children came crying to her for their mothers, but she knew their mothers had been killed. Finally she said, "We the women, must unite to stop this war. We must unite to stop the terrible things that are happening in this world. I would like you to take that message back to the women of America."[22]

Accepting this mandate, Bunch-Weeks returned to the United States and shared her experiences through talks and writings, which circulated in women's liberation and antiwar publications. She also cofounded the Women and Imperialism Collective in the Washington, DC, area and proposed to launch the National Women's Anti-War Program. Along with Cora Weiss, Bunch-Weeks served on the steering committee of the New Mobilization Committee to End the War in Vietnam (the new Mobe). The first Mobe or National Mobilization Committee to End the War in Vietnam had organized a series of national protests, including a large rally of over one hundred thousand in Washington, DC, in 1967, the follow-up March on the Pentagon, and the protests at the 1968 Democratic National Convention in Chicago. The new Mobe formed in 1969 and coordinated a series of local and national protests that culminated in two national moratoriums, general strikes to force the Nixon administration to end the war. Held on 15 October and 15 November of that year, the second moratorium attracted over half a million people to Washington, DC. The strong showing sought to challenge Nixon's 3 November appeal to the "silent majority" of Americans whom he believed supported his policies. The new Mobe continued its efforts into the spring of 1970 as Nixon's secret bombings and invasion of Cambodia, a neutral country, were made public.

Although Weiss and Bunch-Weeks played leadership roles in the new Mobe, they both recognized the limited authority and respect that women had within the male-dominated antiwar movement. Even though women performed crucial organizing work, their ideas and voices tended to be marginalized and at times publicly denigrated. To address these issues from within the movement, Bunch-Weeks, Weiss, and other female members on Mobe's national staff and steering committee formed a women's caucus. Their group identified three main goals: (1) "combating male supremacy" in the antiwar movement, (2) developing "ideological and programmatic clarity about how the struggle for the liberation of women is related to the struggles against racism and imperialism," and (3) connecting the "spring actions of the Mobe to their own oppression as women."[23] The Women and Imperialism Collective as well as the Women's Caucus provided opportunities for female activists to organize with other women and to develop a feminist analysis of war and imperialism. . . .

Vivian Rothstein, Charlotte Bunch-Weeks, and other women's liberation activists who met with Vietnamese representatives in Asia and other parts of the world became key organizers of the IWCs. Their face-to-face encounters inspired U.S. women profoundly. Alice Wolfson of the Washington, DC, Women and Imperialism Collective shared her impressions after a 1970 planning meeting for the IWCs that was held in Budapest, Hungary:

We have just had our first formal meeting with the Vietnamese & Cambodians. They are incredible out of sight people. Yesterday, when I first met them, I filled up with tears & wanted to take them in my arms & say "I'm sorry." . . . No matter how much you read & how much you know in your head what a monster imperialism is, it comes home to you with an emotional force that seems physical, meeting women who live under the threat of death. It seems impossible to think that I could ever, even for a minute, contemplate withdrawing or dropping out.[24]

By organizing the IWCs, women's liberation activists had the opportunity to recreate their political intimacy with Southeast Asian women for larger numbers of women who did not have the privilege or opportunity to travel to Asia and other parts of the world.

The final group of cosponsors of the IWCs were Third World women. These individuals from racially oppressed groups in North America identified their status in the West as being akin to the status of Third World peoples globally. Understanding themselves as internal colonial subjects, they expressed solidarity among themselves based on similar experiences of disfranchisement and marginalization within the United States. In addition, they allied with people in the Third World who were fighting for self-determination and national liberation from colonialism and neocolonialism. Given this identification with Third World people both domestically and abroad, women of color tended to distance themselves from the predominantly white old and new friends. Instead, racialized women in the "First World" turned to one another and to women in the Third World for political inspiration.

Both the old and new friends recognized that their groups consisted predominantly of white women. Consequently, they attempted to work with nonwhite women. WSP and WILPF cultivated contacts with Coretta Scott King and other African American women at a time when great pressures were being placed on male civil rights leaders to avoid making public statements about Vietnam.[25] In addition, both organizations also attracted women of Asian ancestry. Aline Berman, a Chinese American, attended the Jakarta and Paris meetings as a WSP representative. . . . In addition, Marii Hasegawa, a Japanese American, served as president of the U.S. Section of WILPF during the late 1960s and early 1970s.

The presence of women of Asian ancestry in mainstream women's peace organizations stemmed from these groups' engagement with domestic racism and international pacifism. Hasegawa explained that WILPF was "one of the few organizations which had passed a resolution against the concentration camps in which Japanese and their citizen children were held in WWII" by the U.S. government.[26] To assist Japanese American internees seeking to resettle outside of the designated internment zones on the West Coast, WILPF supported a hostel in Philadelphia where Hasegawa found a place to stay after she left camp. . . .

The category of Third World women [for the most part was composed of] women who became active during the late 1960s in racially based liberation movements. These activists identified as black, Asian American, Chicana or Mexican American, Puerto Rican, and indigenous or Native. For these individuals, the Vietnamese analysis of women's oppression as resulting from a confluence of patriarchy, colonialism, and capitalism held particular appeal. In the mid- to late 1960s and into the 1970s, women of color in the global North began to articulate an intersectional analysis.[27] Rather than seeing themselves only in terms of their race, gender, or class, they began to understand how multiple systems of social hierarchy operated simultaneously to shape their lives. Consequently, they turned to one another and to women in the Third World for political inspiration.

Like other antiwar activists, women of color also traveled to Vietnam. In 1970, . . . Betita Martinez visited North Vietnam. She believes that she was the first Mexican American to journey there. In fact, she went on the same delegation as Charlotte Bunch-Weeks and was asked to describe the movement that she was engaged in building in New Mexico. Martinez grew up in Washington, DC, a member of an international and multiracial family. Her father, a dark-skinned Mexican, worked for Mexico's embassy, and her mother, a fair-skinned Scotch-Irish, worked for the Swiss embassy. Growing up in the racially polarized, black-white city of Washington, DC, Martinez found it difficult to socially locate herself as a multiracial person of Latino/a heritage. She recalled, "The composition of the neighborhood was either . . . black or white, or both, because that's the way Washington, DC, was. There was no Latinos around the street back then. It was a very lonely thing."[28]

In that environment, Martinez developed both a racial identification with African

Americans and a global consciousness against Western colonialism. She inherited her father's dark skin and was treated as if she was black. Martinez recalled, "The girl next door was not allowed to play with me by her parents because I was too dark ... and we passed for black often on the buses and got sent to the back of the bus." ... During the late 1950s and early 1960s, Martinez became invested in supporting the civil rights movement. As a writer and editor based in New York City at the time, [in reaction to] the 1963 church bombing in Birmingham, Alabama, which killed four black girls, she decided to volunteer for the Student Nonviolent Coordinating Committee (SNCC). [After] work[ing] Mississippi for the 1964 Summer Project, she coordinated the New York office, where she raised funds and mobilized support for civil rights activities in the South. She also edited an important collection of letters about Mississippi Freedom Summer under the name of Elizabeth Sutherland.[29] ...

Martinez's interest in Latino/a issues persisted, though, and her ethnic consciousness eventually emerged. She traveled to Cuba repeatedly, the first time after the 1959 revolution, and eventually published a book in 1967 about her observations of their new society. Also that year, she decided to relocate from New York City to New Mexico.... Eventually, Martinez started an influential Chicano/a newspaper, El Grito del Norte. ...

When Martinez traveled to Vietnam in 1970, her sense of commonality with the Vietnamese, particularly the women, was due not only to gender but also to a comparable colonized status. Because of the heavy bombing campaign ordered by President Nixon at the time, the plane that she and Bunch-Weeks traveled on to Hanoi "landed on a totally dark airstrip in a totally dark airport." Martinez's reflections, though, ... focused on the positive, [indeed indomitable] spirit of the Vietnamese people.... Martinez observed how the vast majority of Vietnamese people were peasants, a status similar to the agricultural background of many Chicano/as of New Mexico. In addition, the Vietnamese were demanding the right to determine their political future, just like what the Chicano/a movement and other liberation movements in the United States and globally were demanding.[30] ...

After returning from Hanoi, Martinez ... focused on sharing her insights with the Chicano/a community. She wrote articles in El

Grito del Norte and also gave public presentations. She was one of the featured speakers at the Chicano National Moratorium. Held in Los Angeles on 29 August 1970, the moratorium was part of a nearly two-year effort to mobilize Chicano/as against the Vietnam War. Similar to African Americans, Mexican Americans tended to have lower socioeconomic status as well as fewer opportunities for career advancement and college admissions. Consequently, Chicanos tended to be overrepresented in the military. Chicano/a activists like Martinez encouraged other members of their communities to question why they were fighting in the war. They formed the only "minority-based antiwar organization, called the National Chicano Moratorium Committee." The National Moratorium attracted an estimated twenty thousand to thirty thousand protesters, including elderly and children; it was the "largest anti-war march by any specific ethnic or racial group in U.S. history." The event was brutally disrupted by the Los Angeles police force. Approximately 150 were injured that day, and three were killed.[31]

Despite this aborted attempt, Martinez found other ways to encourage Chicano/as to understand the issues of the war. She was not able to replicate her own experiences of traveling to Vietnam. The people with whom she interacted in New Mexico lacked the financial means to do so. Also, some expressed reservations that their journey might taint them as communists. However, Chicanas from New Mexico did travel to Vancouver for the IWC. There they met with women from Southeast Asia and other women of color, including other Mexican, Mexican American, and indigenous activists from throughout North America.[32] ...

Maternal peace activists, second-wave feminists, and women of color all developed profound political connections with Southeast Asian women. These alliances across national, cultural, and ideological boundaries provide an opportunity to reexamine global sisterhood in two significant ways. First, rather than regarding women in the Third World as oppressed recipients of Western benevolence and feminist rescue, it is important to emphasize the agency of Vietnamese women in initiating international partnerships and to recognize their role as political mentors for women in the West. In other words, global sisterhood as a political strategy was not just imposed by the West but also crafted and promoted by women in the Global South.

Second, international sisterhood does not depend upon a monolithic, universal analysis of gender oppression that transcends time and space. Rather, the political messages that Vietnamese women conveyed through face-to-face meetings and the circulation of print and visual media suggest that a rich and diverse array of discourses could be transmitted and debated between women of varying backgrounds.... [This message was a balm to North American organizers and attendees of the IWCs in Canada, whose efforts at unity were plagued by volatile factionalism.] In contrast, as Vivian Rothstein noted following her travels to North Vietnam, what impressed her was the emphasis that the VWU placed on organizing a "majoritarian" movement. This approach focused on building broad political agreements and coalitions.[33] Literally engaged in a struggle for life and death, the women of Vietnam cultivated the widest possible range of allies.

Global sisterhood, then, was not intended to propose a rigid universal theory for understanding women's oppression. Rather, the VWU sought to involve women of varying backgrounds and political beliefs to engage in ideas with one another and to learn from each other's life experiences. Vietnamese women did want women from the West to help them end the war. Yet the women from Southeast Asia believed that they had a reciprocal and perhaps even greater ability to inspire the political imagination of women in the First World. The Indochinese Women's Conferences of 1971 represented a continuation of these efforts to build a global antiwar movement among diverse sisters.

NOTES

1. Inderpal Grewal, *Transnational America: Feminisms, Diasporas, Neoliberalisms* (Durham, N.C.: Duke University Press, 2005); Chandra Mohanty, "Under Western Eyes: Feminist Scholarship and Colonial Discourses," *Feminist Review* 30 (Autumn 1988): 61–88; Leila J. Rupp, *Worlds of Women: The Making of an International Women's Movement* (Princeton: Princeton University Press, 1997); and Wu, "Rethinking Global Sisterhood: Peace Activism and Women's Orientalism," *No Permanent Waves: Recasting Histories of U.S. Feminism*, ed. by Nancy A. Hewitt (New Brunswick, N.J.: Rutgers University Press, 2010), pp. 193–220.

2. Amy Swerdlow, *Women Strike for Peace: Traditional Motherhood and Radical Politics in the 1960s* (Chicago: University of Chicago, 1993), pp. 214–215.

3. Ibid., p. 15; Andrea Estepa, "Taking the White Gloves Off: Women Strike for Peace and 'the

Movement,' 1967–73," in Stephanie Gilmore, *Feminist Coalitions: Historical Perspectives on Second-Wave Feminism in the United States* (Urbana: University of Illinois Press, 2008), p. 87.

4. Jill Vickers, "The Intellectual Origins of the Women's Movements in Canada," in *Challenging Times: The Women's Movement in Canada and the United States*, ed. by Constance Backhouse and David H. Flaherty (Montreal: McGill-Queen's University Press, 1992), pp. 53–55; and Candace Loewen, "Making Ourselves Heard: 'Voice of Women' and the Peace Movement in the Early Sixties," in *Framing Our Past: Canadian Women's History in the Twentieth Century*, ed. by Sharon Anne Cook, Lorna R. McLean, and Kate O'Rourke (Montreal: McGill-Queen's University Press, 2001), p. 248. Duckworth: quoted in Judy Rebick, *Ten Thousand Roses: The Making of a Feminist Revolution* (Toronto: Penguin Canada, 2005), p. 3.

5. Quoted in Harriet Hyman Alonso, *Peace as a Women's Issue: A History of the U.S. Movement for World Peace and Women's Rights* (Syracuse, N.Y.: Syracuse University Press, 1993), p. 86. WILPF was officially founded in 1919; the organization evolved from the U.S. Women's Peace Party, which was established in 1915.

6. Estepa, "Taking the White Gloves Off," p. 88.

7. "Paris," *Memo* 6:4 (March 1968): 2;"To Canadian Press Representatives, London," 15 May 1968, Vol. 3, file Hanoi Trip, Voice of Women (VOW) Fonds, MG 28 Series I 218, Library and Archives Canada; Ethel Taylor, "Conference: Paris, April 23–26," *Memo* 6:5 (May–June 1968): 6.

8. Kay MacPherson, "October 9th 1967, Cambridge," Vol. 3, file Hanoi Trip, VOW Fonds; Cora Weiss, "The Face of the Enemy," *Memo* (Fall 1969), pp. 4–7.

9. Swerdlow, *Women Strike for Peace*, p. 222.

10. Mary Hershberger, *Traveling to Vietnam: American Peace Activists and the War* (Syracuse: Syracuse University Press, 1998); Cora Weiss, Interviews with Author, New York City, 7 and 8 April 2006, and 4 May 2006. Also see Swerdlow, *Women Strike for Peace*, and James W. Clinton, "Cora Weiss," in *The Loyal Opposition: Americans in North Vietnam, 1965–1972* (Niwot: University Press of Colorado, 1995).

11. Sandra C. Taylor, *Vietnamese Women at War: Fighting for Ho Chi Minh and the Revolution* (Lawrence: University Press of Kansas, 1999), p. 123; Swerdlow, *Women Strike for Peace*, p. 216.

12. "Madame Nguyen Thi Binh Speaking to American Women," Text of Film, Oct. 1970, p. 1, Series A, 2, Box B, 2, Women Strike for Peace Records, DG 115, Swarthmore College Peace Collection (SCPC), Swarthmore, Penn.

13. *Vietnamese Women*, Vietnam Studies No. 10 (Hanoi: Xunhasaba, 1966) p. 42.

14. Ibid., p. 33.

15. For an analysis of how Women Strike for Peace emphasized a maternalist construction of Vietnamese female identity to foster a common politics based on pacifism, see "Collaborative Efforts to End the War in Viet Nam: The Interactions of Women Strike for Peace, the Vietnamese Women's Union, and the Women's Union of Liberation, 1965–1968," *Peace and Change*, 37, no. 3 (July 2012): 339–365

16. For critiques of the wave metaphor, see Nancy A. Hewitt, ed., *No Permanent Waves: Recasting*

Histories of U.S. Feminism (New Brunswick, N.J.: Rutgers University Press, 2010).

17. *Vietnamese Women*, pp. 3, 307.

18. Agatha Beins examines how women's movement periodicals created political meaning and fostered a sense of community among activists, placing strong emphasis on the representations of Vietnamese women in American women's movement periodicals; Beins, "Free Our Sisters, Free Ourselves! Locating U.S. Feminism through Feminist Publishing" (Ph.D. Dissertation, Rutgers University, 2011); Beins, "Radical Others: Women of Color and Revolutionary Feminism" (unpublished manuscript, 2011).

19. Taylor, *Vietnamese Women at War*.

20. Hershberger, *Traveling to Vietnam*, p. 139.

21. Vivian Rothstein, Telephone Interview with Author, 9 March, 2007 (this paragraph and the next).

22. Charlotte Bunch-Weeks and Frank Joyce, "North Vietnam: A Photo Essay," *Motive* (February 1971): 18, 20.

23. Jan Fenty and Charlotte Bunch-Weeks, "Women and the Anti-War Movement," Box 1, folder 33, Charlotte Bunch Papers, Schlesinger Library, Radcliffe Institute, Harvard University, Cambridge, Mass.

24. Alice Wolfson to "Companeras," n.d., pp. 1–2, Box 1, folder 34, Charlotte Bunch Papers.

25. Hershberger, *Traveling to Vietnam*; and Joyce Blackwell, *No Peace without Freedom: Race and the Women's International League for Peace and Freedom, 1915–1975* (Carbondale: Southern Illinois University Press, 2004).

26. "New President, Board Elected," *Peace and Freedom* 31, no. 7 (July 1971): 1. See also Judy Tzu-Chun Wu, "Journeys for Peace and Liberation: Third World Internationalism and Radical Orientalism during the U.S. War in Viet Nam," *Pacific Historical Review* 76:4 (November 2007): 575–584

27. Frances Beale, "Double Jeopardy: To Be Black and Female," *Sisterhood is Powerful: An Anthology of Writings from the Women's Liberation Movement*, ed. By Robin Morgan (New York: Vintage Books, 1970), pp. 382–396; Benita Roth, *Separate Roads to Feminism: Black, Chicana, and White Feminist Movements in America's Second Wave* (New York: Cambridge University Press, 2003); Cynthia A. Young, *Soul Power: Culture, Radicalism, and the Making of a U.S. Third World Left* (Durham, N.C.: Duke University Press, 2006).

28. Betita Martinez, Telephone Interview with author, 7 Dec. 2006. Also see Lorenza Oropeza, *¡Raza Sí! ¡Guerra No!: Chicano Protest and Patriotism during the Viet Nam War Era* (Berkeley: University of California Press, 2005).

29. Martinez, telephone interview. In the predominantly black-white environment of SNCC, Martinez felt more comfortable using a non-Latino name. In the movement, she was known as "Liz," not Betita. She also chose Sutherland rather than Martinez as her surname, because "in my mother's past there was this Duchess of Sutherland . . . the chief lady in waiting to the queen."

30. "Viet Nam War—Why? Their People . . . Our People . . . ," *El Grito del Norte*, 29 August 1970. Betita Martinez also reported on the treatment of ethnic minorities in Viet Nam, who had the right to bilingual education.

31. Oropeza, *¡Raza Sí! ¡Guerra No!*, p. 6.

32. "Chicanas Meet Indo-Chinese," *El Grito Del Norte*, 5 June 1971, p. K.

33. Rothstein, telephone interview. For more analysis of the IWCs, see Judy Tzu-Chun Wu, *Radicals on the Road: Internationalism, Orientalism, and Feminism During the Vietnam Era* (Ithaca, N.Y.: Cornell University Press, 2013), chs. 8–9.

The Personal Is Political

Many documents—manifestos, handbills, mimeographed newsletters, posters with artwork, meeting minutes—survive, recording the thoughts and actions of groups who identified themselves with the women's liberation or who campaigned for reform. As we urge in our discussion of the abortion wars of recent decades (pp. 658–669), the activism of the 1960s and 1970s is a ripe area for individuals or groups to investigate what happened on your campus and in your town, and to record and preserve materials in concert with librarians, women's centers, and academic programs. Ask your family members, teachers, and friends who came of age in the sixties and seventies what they were reading, debating, and producing in those years! Encourage them to preserve journals, diaries , photographs, programs from concerts and gatherings, and material souvenirs (buttons, hats, t-shirts, etc.).

One good starting point for the broad range of calls-to-action issued in the period are the selected documents we present below. Many others are readily available online. We call your attention to a few "classics":

- "The Redstockings Manifesto," issued in New York City on July 7, 1969, on the Women's Liberation Movement Archives for Action: http://www.redstockings.org/index.php?option=com_content&view=article&id=76&Itemid=59.
- Pat Mainardi, "The Politics of Housework," ca. 1970: a hilarious and powerful critique of many men's learned helplessness, following up on Crystal Eastman's 1920 manifesto, "Now We Can Begin" (pp. 380–382), on the CWLU Herstory website archive: http://www.uic.edu/orgs/cwluherstory/CWLUArchive/polhousework.html.
- Radicalesbians, "The Woman-Identified Woman," 1970, on Documents from the Women's Liberation Movement, Duke University Library: http://library.duke.edu/rubenstein/scriptorium/wlm/womid/.

Carol Hanisch, A Critique of the Miss America Protest, 1968

Women of Betty Friedan's and Phyllis Schlafly's generation were divided as to whether they saw domesticity as sufficient to their personal fulfillment or if there truly was "a problem that had no name," and, if so, what it involved. Many young women, who had joined in the protest movements of the 1960s, had no such doubts. The group who gathered in Atlantic City in 1968 to protest the Miss America Pageant instantly caught the eye of the national and world media. Contrary to myth, no bras were burned. Instead, demonstrators hurled what they called "items of female torture" into a large "Freedom Trash Can," including false

Reprinted by permission of the author, who has condensed the original document—"A Critique of the Miss America Protest" © 1968—especially for *Women's America*. The original document is reproduced online, accompanied by a 2003 radio interview with Hanisch about the protest: www.carolhanisch.org/CHwritings/MissACritique.html.

eyelashes, hair curlers, girdles, high-heel shoes, Toni home permanents (a sponsor of the pageant), *Playboy* and *Good Housekeeping* magazines, and even some bras. The protesters called for the end of beauty competitions, the pressure to conform to false beauty standards and buy related products, and the elevation of appearance over more important human qualities.

Were the concerns of the 1968 protesters valid? Are they relevant to today's women? In what sense are they among the body issues Brumberg introduces in "Fasting Girls" (pp. 420–428)? Why does Hanisch consider some of the actions employed by her sister protesters counterproductive? What was the message of the protest that she believed they failed to get across?

The protest of the Miss America Pageant in Atlantic City told the nation that a new feminist movement is afoot in the land.

Due to the tremendous coverage in the mass media, millions of Americans now know there is a Women's Liberation Movement. The action brought many new members into our group and many requests from women outside the city for literature and information. A recurrent theme was, "I've been waiting so long for something like this."

But no action taken in the Women's Liberation struggle will be all good or all bad. We must analyze each step to see what was effective, what was not, and what was downright destructive.

At this point in our struggle, our actions should be aimed primarily at doing two interrelated things: (1) awakening the latent consciousness of women about our own oppression, and (2) building sisterhood. With these in mind, let us examine the Miss America protest.

The idea for the protest came out of the method used first in New York Radical Women of analyzing women's oppression by analyzing our own experiences, called consciousness-raising. One night at a meeting we were watching *Schmearguntz*, a feminist movie which contains flashes of the Miss America Pageant. I found myself remembering the powerful feelings the pageant had evoked in me as a child, an adolescent, and a college student. When I proposed the action to our group, we decided to go around the room with each woman telling how she felt about the pageant. We discovered that many of us who had always put down the contest still watched it. Others had consciously identified with it.

From our communal thinking came the concrete plans for the action. The original planning group agreed that the main point in the demonstration would be that all women are hurt by beauty competition—Miss America as well as ourselves. We opposed the pageant in our own self-interest, e.g., the self-interest of all women.

Yet one of the biggest mistakes of the whole pageant was our anti-womanism. A spirit of every woman "doing her own thing" began to emerge as women not in the original meetings came to the planning meetings. Some just went ahead and did what they wanted to do, even though it was something we had decided against. Because of this egotistic individualism, a definite strain of anti-womanism was presented to the public to the detriment of the action.

Posters that read "Up against the Wall, Miss America," "Miss America Sells It," and "Miss America Is a Big Falsie" hardly raised any woman's consciousness and really harmed the cause of sisterhood. Miss America and all beautiful women came off as our enemy instead of as our sisters who suffer with us.

A more complex situation developed around the decision of a few women to use an "underground" disruptive tactic. The group approved this activity only after its adherents said they would do it anyway as an individual action. We learned there is no such thing as "individual action" in a movement. There is, at this time, no real need to do "underground" actions anyway. We need to reach as many women as possible as quickly as possible with a clear message that has the power of our person behind it. Women need to see other women standing up together and saying these things. That's why draping a women's liberation banner over the balcony and yelling our message was much clearer than spraying a smelly chemical in the audience. The problem of how to enforce group decisions is one we haven't solved.

Another way we came off as anti-woman was our lack of clarity. We didn't say clearly enough that we women are all *forced* to play the Miss America role—not by beautiful women but by men who we have to act that way for, and by a system that has so well institutionalized male supremacy for its own ends. This was not very clear in our guerrilla theater. Women chained to a replica, red, white, and blue bathing-suited Miss America could have been misinterpreted as our blaming beautiful women. Also, crowning a live sheep Miss America sort of said that beautiful women *are* sheep. However, the action did say to some that women are *viewed as* auction-block, docile animals. The grandmother of one of the participants really began to understand the action when she was told about the sheep, and she ended up joining the protest.

There is as great a need for clarity in our language as there is in our actions. The leaflet that was distributed as a press release and flyer was too long, too wordy, too complex, too hippy-yippee-campy. Instead of an "in" phrase like "Racism with Roses," we could have just called the pageant "racist" and everybody would have understood our opposition on that point.

We should avoid the temptation to say everything there is to say about what is wrong with the world and thereby say nothing that a new person can really dig into and understand. Women's liberation itself is revolutionary dynamite. When other issues are interjected, we should clearly relate them to our oppression as women.

We tried to carry the democratic means we used in planning the action into the actual doing of it. We didn't want leaders or spokesmen. It makes the movement not only *seem* stronger and larger if everyone is a leader, but it actually *is* stronger if not dependent on a few. And, of course, many voices are more powerful than one. We must learn how to fight against the media's desire to make leaders—and some women's desire to appoint themselves spokesmen.

The Miss America protest was a zap action, which means using our presence as a group to make women's oppression into a social issue. In such actions we speak to men as a group as well as to women. It is a rare opportunity to talk to men in a situation where they can't talk back. (Men must learn to listen.) Our power of solidarity, not our individual intellectual exchanges will change men.

The reaction of many of the women we talked to about the protest was, "But I'm not oppressed" or "I don't care about Miss America." If more than half the television viewers in the country watch the pageant, somebody cares! While much of the Left was putting us down for attacking something so "silly and unimportant" or "reformist," the Right saw us as a threat and yelled such things as "Go back to Russia" and "Mothers of Mao" at the picket line. Ironically enough, what the Left/Underground press seemed to like best about our action was what was really our worst mistake—our anti-woman signs.

Surprisingly and fortunately, some of the mass media ignored our mistakes and concentrated on our best points. To quote the *Daily News,* "Some women who think the whole idea of such contests is degrading to femininity, took their case to the people. . . . During boardwalk protest, gals say they're not anti-beauty, just anti-beauty contest." Shana Alexander wrote in a *Life* magazine editorial that she "wished they'd gone farther."

The best slogan for the action came up afterward, when Ros Baxandall blurted out on the David Susskind television show that "Every day in a woman's life is a walking Miss America Contest!" But we shouldn't wait for the perfect slogan; we should go ahead to the best of our understanding.

Jennie V. Chávez, Women of the Mexican American Movement, 1972

Jennie Chávez, like thousands of young women of color, joined liberation movements in the 1960s and 1970s. In this account of her experience in the Chicano movement, Chávez describes the resistance she faced when, recognizing the double oppression of Mexican American women, she organized "Las Chicanas."

What insights does she have into power relationships between Mexican Americans and Anglos as well as between men and women within her own ethnic group? Note her disdain for the consumer goods that signal middle-class status. What evidence is there to suggest that Chávez and her Chicana generation had been affected by the sexual revolution of the 1960s? How did males in the movement respond to women asserting themselves? To what does Chávez attribute their machismo? Note the links between Chávez's La Familia and Vicki Ruiz's insights into the family oligarchy experienced by teenagers in the Southwest earlier in the century (pp. 428–435).

As one of the first members of the United Mexican American Students [UMAS] when it got started in 1969 on the UNM [University of New Mexico] campus, I was given special attention, being fairly attractive and flirtatious. But as soon as I started expounding my own ideas the men who ran the organization would either ignore my statement or make a wisecrack about it and continue their own discussion. This continued for two years until I finally broke away because of being unable to handle the situation. I turned to student government. There I was considered a radical racist Mexican militant, yet with the Chicano radicals I was considered a sellout. I was caught in the middle, wanting to help but with neither side allowing me.

The summer of 1970, after the Cambodia crisis, I traveled extensively, "getting my head together," [and formed] Las Chicanas the following December. [The result was that I] caught more shit than I knew existed from both males and females in the movement. Some felt I was dividing the existing UMAS; some were simply afraid of displeasing the men. Some felt that I was wrong and my ideas were "white," and still others felt that their contribution to La Causa or El Movimiento was in giving the men moral support from the kitchen. It took two months of heartbreak on both sides for the organization to be recognized as valid. Now, however, because a few women were willing to stand strong against some of the macho men who ridiculed them, called them white and avoided them socially, the organization has become one of the strongest and best-known in the state.

It has taken what I consider a long time for [Chicanas] to realize and to speak out about the double oppression of the Mexican-American woman. Chicanas traditionally, have been tortilla-makers, baby-producers, to be touched but not heard. In order to someday obtain those middle-class goods (which in my eyes oppress more people than they liberate from "drudgery")

our women have not only been working at slave jobs for the white society as housemaids, hotel maids and laundry workers, but have tended also to the wants of a husband and many children—many children because contraceptives have been contrary to the ethnic idea of La Familia (with all its socio-political economic implications).

As the social revolution for all people's freedoms has progressed, so Chicanas have caught the essence of freedom in the air. The change occurred slowly. Mexican-American women have been reluctant to speak up, afraid that they might show up the men in front of the white man—afraid that they may think our men not men. Now, however, the Chicana is becoming as well-educated and as aware of oppression, if not more so, as the Mexican-American male.

The women are changing their puritanical mode of dress, entering the professions of law, business, medicine and engineering. They are no longer afraid to show their intellect, their capabilities and their potential. More and more they oppose the Catholic Church, to which a large majority of our ethnic group belongs, challenging its sexual taboos as well as the idea that all Catholic mothers must be baby-producing factories, and that contraceptives are a sin.

Out of the workshop on "Sex and La Chicana" at the first National Mujeres Por la Raza conference in Houston, Texas, [in 1971] came the following resolutions: (1) that Chicanas should develop a more healthy attitude toward sex and get rid of the misconceptions about its "evil," thus allowing ourselves to be as aggressive as men; (2) that we object to the use of sex as a means of exploiting women and for commercial purposes; (3) that no religious institution should have the authority to sanction what is moral or immoral between a man and a woman.

As the new breed of Mexican-American women, we have been, and probably will continue to be, ridiculed by our men for attempting the acrobatics of equality. We may well be ostracized by La Familia for being vendidos, sell-outs to the "white ideas" of late marriage, postponing or not wanting children and desiring a vocation other than tortilla-rolling, but I believe that this new breed of bronze womanhood, as all women today, will be a vanguard for world change.

Naturally, there are liberated Chicanos who respect and treat women as equals, but they are so few that at this point I still have to generalize. Mexican-American men, as other men of oppressed groups, have been very reluctant to give up their machismo [exaggerated assertion of masculinity] because it has been a last retention of power in a society which dehumanizes and mechanizes them. But now they are comprehending the meaning of carnalismo (brotherhood) in the feminine gender as well . . . a new revolution within a revolution has begun.

Editorial Staff of Rodan, Asian Women as Leaders, 1971

L ike their Chicana sisters, Asian American women fought against old stereotypes and encountered new ones when they tried to exercise leadership in the Asian American movement. They too found that male allies were prone to male chauvinism and that as women they had to deal with racism, sexism, and imperialism simultaneously.

On the basis of this document compare the stereotypes that exist about women of both ethnic groups in the larger culture. What vision of the future and what strategies do the anonymous authors advocate?

American society is broken up into different levels based on economic income, education, politics, color, and sex. Each level has a prescribed set of rules for action and interplay—roles that are enforced by the levels above. At the bottom of these varying gradations are women of color. Third World women face domination by both racism and sexism (discrimination based on sex). Both racism and sexism are means by which American society controls and oppresses everyone. Everyone is forced to conform to the values and roles established by the dominant group in order to "succeed." For the Asian movement to progress, it must have a clear understanding of sexism, racism, and imperialism; and deal with them simultaneously.

For Asian women in general, the stereotypes or roles have been of two major kinds: either docile, submissive Oriental dolls who will cater to the whims of any man; or the Suzie Wong, sexpot, exotic bitch-body. Between these two are the efficient secretary, sexy stewardess, the good housekeeper and domestic, the girl any guy would like to marry.

Women in the Asian movement find that these stereotypes are still hovering over their heads. Not only these but new stereotypes, too: i.e., Asian men have tried to define for "their women" what it means to be "heavy." Men in the Asian movement also find themselves tied down to stereotypes. Perhaps they may feel that to be a MAN one must have authority and responsibility. In the same light, they will frown on women who take on a lot of responsibility (and the authority that goes along with it), labelling them as "unfeminine." Women then tend to fear this loss of "femininity" and so they do the clerical work and the cleaning up, activities for which intellect is not essential or expected. Women may also fulfill these jobs because they do them best: And why do they do them the best? Because women are never

"Asian Women as Leaders," by the Editorial Staff, *Rodan: Northern California Asian American Community News* (April 1971), 1–2. Copyright © 1971 by the Regents of the University of California. Used by permission of the UCLA Asian American Studies Center. For an image of the first page, see http://asianamericanactivism .tumblr.com/post/87571581766/asian-women-as-leaders-in-roots-an-asian.

encouraged to do anything else; women's potential abilities as a leader are left untapped and undeveloped. She loses her confidence in being able to handle such responsibility.

The sisters who have achieved a position of authority in the movement are a minority and are still trapped by the stereotypes that society has created. It is a struggle for women to attain the top leadership positions. Women who "make it" into such positions have had to reject the stereotypes already imposed upon them. But because the new definition of "the Asian woman" has not yet evolved, women find themselves in a "limbo." Some find themselves being labelled as Bitches—women who speak out loudly and strongly; who are authoritarian, who boss people around, and command some form of respect. Some must resort to being overly diligent and efficient to prove themselves as worthy of the same leadership positions as the men. Others gain respect by appearing to accomplish work in a multitude of projects but actually only complete a few tasks. And still others attain their leadership positions as token gestures. Some women can gain respect only by putting up with put-downs on other women, i.e., "you're not one of those bird-brained little girls," or "You're as strong as a man!"

Once women do get into leadership positions, they find that their ideas are usurped by the men, who then take credit for the idea as being their own. Women are often heard but not listened to. Many times, the woman must play her old role in order to get things done: "Oh, please, can you help me carry this. It's much too heavy for little old me. . . . "

How can these problems be solved? People must recognize that women are half of the working force in the movement against oppression, exploitation, and imperialism. They are half of the working force in creating the new revolutionary lifestyle. Men and women in the movement must therefore begin to live the ideals and goals they are working for. To do this, they must not let chauvinist acts slide by. People cannot work together effectively if there are hidden tensions or if people let little annoyances build up inside themselves. They must deal with racism or imperialism. They must be able to develop as human beings, not subject to categorizations and stereotypes. Developing as people confident in themselves, in their ideas, they will not be afraid of criticism; they will see the need for criticism, and self-criticism, in order to move forward. The struggle is not men against women nor women against men, but it is a united front striving for a new society, a new way of life.

> If I go forward,
> Follow me.
> Push me if I fall behind.
> If I betray you,
> If they take me,
> Avenge me then in kind.

Combahee River Collective, The Combahee River Collective Statement, 1977

The Combahee River Collective, a black feminist group founded in Boston in 1974, took its name from a guerrilla action planned and led by Harriet Tubman during the Civil War that freed more than 750 South Carolina slaves. The group, which consisted of battle-scarred veterans of the civil rights, New Left, and early women's movements, had done some hard thinking before writing this statement. In it, they stated what they believed to be the limitations of their white feminist sisters as well as their own problems in organizing black feminists.

What were the Collective's specific criticisms of other feminists—radical, liberal, as well as lesbian separatists? Why did they think that black feminism was (and is) so threatening to the black community, especially to black males who identified with black nationalism? What do you regard as their most important insights?

Excerpted from The Combahee River Collective Statement in *Home Girls: A Black Feminist Anthology*, ed. Barbara Smith (Latham, N. Y.: Kitchen Table: Women of Color Press, 1983), pp. 272–82. The original document was dated April 1977. Reprinted by permission of Barbara Smith.

We are a collective of Black feminists who have been meeting together since 1974. During that time we have been involved in the process of defining and clarifying our politics, while at the same time doing political work within our own group and in coalition with other progressive organizations and movements. The most general statement of our politics at the present time would be that we are actively committed to struggling against racial, sexual, heterosexual, and class oppression, and see as our particular task the development of integrated analysis and practice based upon the fact that the major systems of oppression are interlocking. The synthesis of these oppressions creates the conditions of our lives. As Black women we see Black feminism as the logical political movement to combat the manifold and simultaneous oppressions that all women of color face. . . .

1. THE GENESIS OF CONTEMPORARY BLACK FEMINISM

Before looking at the recent development of Black feminism, we would like to affirm that we find our origins in the historical reality of Afro-American women's continuous life-and-death struggle for survival and liberation. Black women's extremely negative relationship to the American political system (a system of white male rule) has always been determined by our membership in two oppressed racial and sexual castes. As Angela Davis points out in "Reflections on the Black Woman's Role in the Community of Slaves," Black women have always embodied, if only in their physical manifestation, an adversary stance to white male rule and have actively resisted its inroads upon them and their communities in both dramatic and subtle ways. There have always been Black women activists—some known, like Sojourner Truth, Harriet Tubman, Frances E. W. Harper, Ida B. Wells Barnett, and Mary Church Terrell, and thousands upon thousands unknown—who have had a shared awareness of how their sexual identity combined with their racial identity to make their whole life situation and the focus of their political struggles unique. Contemporary Black feminism is the outgrowth of countless generations of personal sacrifice, militancy, and work by our mothers and sisters.

A Black feminist presence has evolved most obviously in connection with the second wave of the American women's movement beginning in the late 1960s. Black, other Third World, and working women have been involved in the feminist movement from its start, but both outside reactionary forces and racism and elitism within the movement itself have served to obscure our participation. In 1973, Black feminists, primarily located in New York, felt the necessity of forming a separate Black feminist group. This became the National Black Feminist Organization (NBFO).

Black feminist politics also have an obvious connection to movements for Black liberation, particularly those of the 1960s and 1970s. Many of us were active in those movements (Civil Rights, Black nationalism, the Black Panthers), and all of our lives were greatly affected and changed by their ideologies, their goals, and the tactics used to achieve their goals. It was our experience and disillusionment within these liberation movements, as well as experience on the periphery of the white male left, that led to the need to develop a politics that was anti-racist, unlike those of white women, and anti-sexist, unlike those of Black and white men.

There is also undeniably a personal genesis for Black feminism, that is, the political realization that comes from the seemingly personal experiences of individual Black women's lives. Black feminists and many more Black women who do not define themselves as feminists have all experienced sexual oppression as a constant factor in our day-to-day existence. As children we realized that we were different from boys and that we were treated differently. For example, we were told in the same breath to be quiet both for the sake of being "ladylike" and to make us less objectionable in the eyes of white people. As we grew older we became aware of the threat of physical and sexual abuse by men. However, we had no way of conceptualizing what was so apparent to us, what we *knew* was really happening.

Black feminists often talk about their feelings of craziness before becoming conscious of the concepts of sexual politics, patriarchal rule, and most importantly, feminism, the political analysis and practice that we women use to struggle against our oppression. The fact that racial politics and indeed racism are pervasive factors in our lives did not allow us, and still does not allow most Black women, to look more deeply into our own experiences and, from that sharing and growing consciousness, to build a politics that will change our lives and inevitably end our oppression. Our development must also be tied to the contemporary

738 A TRANSFORMING WORLD 1945–2014

economic and political position of Black people. The post–World War II generation of Black youth was the first to be able to minimally partake of certain educational and employment options, previously closed completely to Black people. Although our economic position is still at the very bottom of the American capitalistic economy, a handful of us have been able to gain certain tools as a result of tokenism in education and employment which potentially enable us to more effectively fight our oppression.

2. WHAT WE BELIEVE

Above all else, our politics initially sprang from the shared belief that Black women are inherently valuable, that our liberation is a necessity not as an adjunct to somebody else's but because of our need as human persons for autonomy. This may seem so obvious as to sound simplistic, but it is apparent that no other ostensibly progressive movement has ever considered our specific oppression as a priority or worked seriously for the ending of that oppression. Merely naming the pejorative stereotypes attributed to Black women (e.g., mammy, matriarch, Sapphire, whore, bulldagger), let alone cataloguing the cruel, often murderous, treatment we receive, indicates how little value has been placed upon our lives during four centuries of bondage in the Western hemisphere. We realize that the only people who care enough about us to work consistently for our liberation are us. Our politics evolve from a healthy love for ourselves, our sisters, and our community, which allows us to continue our struggle and work.

This focusing upon our own oppression is embodied in the concept of identity politics. . . . We reject pedestals, queenhood, and walking ten paces behind. To be recognized as human, levelly human, is enough.

We believe that sexual politics under patriarchy is as pervasive in Black women's lives as are the politics of class and race. We also often find it difficult to separate race from class from sex oppression because in our lives they are most often experienced simultaneously. We know that there is such a thing as racial-sexual oppression which is neither solely racial nor solely sexual, e.g., the history of rape of Black women by white men as a weapon of political repression.

Although we are feminists and Lesbians, we feel solidarity with progressive Black men and do not advocate the fractionalization that

white women who are separatists demand. Our situation as Black people necessitates that we have solidarity around the fact of race, which white women of course do not need to have with white men, unless it is their negative solidarity as racial oppressors. We struggle together with Black men against racism, while we also struggle with Black men about sexism.

We realize that the liberation of all oppressed peoples necessitates the destruction of the political-economic systems of capitalism and imperialism as well as patriarchy. We are socialists because we believe that work must be organized for the collective benefit of those who do the work and create the products, and not for the profit of the bosses. . . .

A political contribution which we feel we have already made is the expansion of the feminist principle that the personal is political. In our consciousness-raising sessions, for example, we have in many ways gone beyond white women's revelations because we are dealing with the implications of race and class as well as sex. Even our Black women's style of talking/ testifying in Black language about what we have experienced has a resonance that is both cultural and political. We have spent a great deal of energy delving into the cultural and experiential nature of our oppression out of necessity because none of these matters has ever been looked at before. . . . An example of this kind of revelation/conceptualization occurred at a meeting as we discussed the ways in which our early intellectual interests had been attacked by our peers, particularly Black males. We discovered that all of us, because we were "smart" had also been considered "ugly," i.e., "smart-ugly." "Smart-ugly" crystallized the way in which most of us had been forced to develop our intellects at great cost to our "social" lives. The sanctions in the Black and white communities against Black women thinkers is comparatively much higher than for white women, particularly ones from the educated middle and upper classes.

As we have already stated, we reject the stance of Lesbian separatism because it is not a viable political analysis or strategy for us. It leaves out far too much and far too many people, particularly Black men, women, and children. We have a great deal of criticism and loathing for what men have been socialized to be in this society: what they support, how they act, and how they oppress. But we do not have the misguided notion that it is their maleness, per se—i.e., their biological maleness—that makes them what they are. As Black women we find any type of biological determinism a particularly dangerous and reactionary basis upon which to build a politic. We must also question whether Lesbian separatism is an adequate and progressive political analysis and strategy, even for those who practice it, since it so completely denies any but the sexual sources of women's oppression, negating the facts of class and race.

3. PROBLEMS IN ORGANIZING BLACK FEMINISTS

During our years together as a Black feminist collective, we have experienced success and defeat, joy and pain, victory and failure. We have found that it is very difficult to organize around Black feminist issues, difficult even to announce in certain contexts that we *are* Black feminists. We have tried to think about the reasons for our difficulties, particularly since the white women's movement continues to be strong and to grow in many directions. In this section we will discuss some of the general reasons for the organizing problems we face and also talk specifically about the stages in organizing our own collective.

The major source of difficulty in our political work is that we are not just trying to fight oppression on one front, or even two, but instead to address a whole range of oppressions. We do not have racial, sexual, heterosexual, or class privilege to rely upon, nor do we have even the minimal access to resources and power that groups who possess any one of these types of privilege have. **No privilege**

The psychological toll of being a Black woman and the difficulties this presents in reaching political consciousness and doing political work can never be underestimated. There is very low value placed upon Black women's psyches in this society, which is both racist and sexist. . . . If Black women were free, it would mean that everyone else would have to be free, since our freedom would necessitate the destruction of all the systems of oppression.

Feminism is, nevertheless, very threatening to the majority of Black people because it calls into question some of the most basic assumptions about our existence, i.e., that sex should be a determinant of power relationships. Here is the way male and female roles were defined in a Black nationalist pamphlet from the early 1970s:

> . . . The man is the head of the house. He is the leader of the house/nation because his knowledge of the world is broader, his awareness is greater, his understanding is fuller and his application of this information is wiser. . . . Women cannot do the same things as men—they are made by nature to function differently. Equality of men and women is something that cannot happen even in the abstract world.[1] . . .

The material conditions of most Black women would hardly lead them to upset both economic and sexual arrangements that seem to represent some stability in their lives. Many Black women have a good understanding of both sexism and racism, but because of the everyday constrictions of their lives, cannot risk struggling against them both.

The reaction of Black men to feminism has been notoriously negative. They are, of course, even more threatened than Black women by the possibility that Black feminists might organize around our own needs. They realize that they might not only lose valuable and hardworking allies in their struggles but that they might also be forced to change their habitually sexist ways of interacting with and oppressing Black women. Accusations that Black feminism divides the Black struggle are powerful deterrents to the growth of an autonomous Black women's movement. . . .

4. BLACK FEMINIST ISSUES AND PROJECTS

During our time together we have identified and worked on many issues of particular relevance to Black women. The inclusiveness of our politics makes us concerned with any situation that impinges upon the lives of women, Third World, and working people. We are of course particularly committed to working on those struggles in which race, sex, and class are simultaneous factors in oppression. We might, for example, become involved in workplace organizing at a factory that employs Third World women or picket a hospital that is cutting back on already inadequate health care to a Third World community, or set up a rape crisis center in a Black neighborhood. Organizing around welfare and daycare concerns might also be a focus. The work to be done and the countless issues that this work represents merely reflect the pervasiveness of our oppression.

Issues and projects that collective members have actually worked on are sterilization abuse, abortion rights, battered women, rape, and health care. We have also done many workshops and educationals on Black feminism on college campuses, at women's conferences, and most <u>recently for high school women.</u>

 younger the better

One issue that is of major concern to us and that we have begun to publicly address is racism in the white women's movement. As Black feminists we are made constantly and painfully aware of how little effort white women have made to understand and combat their racism, which requires among other things that they have a more than superficial comprehension of race, color, and Black history and culture. Eliminating racism in the white women's movement is by definition work for white women to do, but we will continue to speak to and demand accountability on this issue.

In the practice of our politics we do not believe that the end always justifies the means.

Many reactionary and destructive acts have been done in the name of achieving "correct" political goals. As feminists we do not want to mess over people in the name of politics. We believe in collective process and a nonhierarchical distribution of power within our own group and in our vision of a revolutionary society. We are committed to a continual examination of our politics as they develop through criticism and self-criticism as an essential aspect of our practice. . . .

As Black feminists and Lesbians we know that we have a very definite revolutionary task to perform and we are ready for the lifetime of work and struggle before us.

NOTE

1. Mumininas of Committee for Unified Newark, Mwanamke Mwananchi (The Nationalist Woman), Newark, NJ, 1971, pp. 4–5.

Gender Equality and the Law

Hoyt v. Florida, 1961; Taylor v. Louisiana, 1975

Some members of the founding generation had believed that service on juries is a more significant aspect of citizenship than voting; voting, after all, is complete in a moment, while service on juries requires extended periods of time, debate, and deliberation among the jurors, and ultimately the exercise of judgment, which can result in important consequences—including the death sentence—for an accused fellow citizen. The Constitution promises an "impartial" jury drawn from "the district wherein the crime shall have been committed." The conditions of impartiality are not spelled out; the Constitution promises neither "a jury of one's peers," nor one drawn from a "cross-section" of the community. It is tradition that has linked the concept of the jury with "peers," neighbors, and the community in which the crime is committed and from which the jury is chosen.

When women achieved the vote in Wyoming in 1869, it seemed to follow that they could hold office and serve on juries but, after only a few years, the objection of male voters and officeholders was so severe that the law was changed to exclude them.

In some states, the achievement of jury service followed painlessly on the heels of suffrage. In Iowa, Michigan, Nevada, and Pennsylvania, where statutes defined competent jurors as "all qualified electors . . . of good moral character, sound judgment, and in full possession of the senses of hearing and seeing, and who can speak, write and read the English language," the admission of women to the electorate automatically defined them as competent jurors. When these interpretations were tested in state courts, judges usually upheld them. Not all state courts, however, thought it was obvious that "electors" could be properly construed to mean women as well as men. In 1925 the Illinois Supreme Court ruled that because only men had been voters in 1874 when the jury statute had been passed, the terms "legal voters" and "electors" referred only to male persons. Not until 1939 did the Illinois state legislature permit women to serve on juries.

In most states, new statutes were required. By 1923, 18 states and the territory of Alaska had arranged for women to serve on juries. But then the momentum ran out; subsequently the issue had to be debated afresh in each state. A few states continued to exclude women completely, but most developed some form of "voluntary" jury service, in which women could be called to serve but could easily decline. In Florida, no women at all served on juries until 1949, when the legislature passed a law providing that women who wished to be eligible could go to their county courthouses and register their willingness to have their names placed in the *venire*, the randomly selected pool from which jurors are selected.

When Gwendolyn Hoyt came to trial in Tampa in 1957, charged with manslaughter for killing her husband, only 218 women of the more than 46,000 women voters in Hillsborough County had registered to serve; the jury commissioner placed only 10 of those women's names in a pool of 10,000 names. It was no surprise that she was tried—and found guilty—by an all-male jury. It took the six-man jury only 25 minutes to convict Hoyt of second-degree murder; on January 20, 1958, she was sentenced to imprisonment at hard labor for 30 years.

Hoyt appealed, first to the Florida Supreme Court, and then to the U.S. Supreme Court, which heard the case in 1961. Hoyt claimed temporary insanity, brought on by her suspicions of her husband's infidelity, his rejection of her offer of reconciliation, and her own vulnerability to epilepsy. She believed that women would understand her distress better than would men. But with so few women's names in the large jury pool, women had virtually no chance of being chosen.

Hoyt and her lawyers did *not* claim that a fair jury was required to have women as members. Instead, they claimed that a fair jury would have been drawn at random from a list of names from which women had not been excluded. Hoyt believed that in order to enjoy the *right* to a trial by a jury of her peers, other women would have to be *obliged* to serve on juries.

HOYT V. FLORIDA, 1961

MR. JUSTICE JOHN MARSHALL HARLAN:

At the core of appellant's argument is the claim that the nature of the crime of which she was convicted peculiarly demanded the inclusion of persons of her own sex on the jury. She was charged with killing her husband ... in the context of a marital upheaval involving, among other things, the suspected infidelity of appellant's husband, and culminating in the husband's final rejection of his wife's efforts at reconciliation. It is claimed, in substance, that women jurors would have been more understanding or compassionate than men in assessing the quality of appellant's act and her defense of "temporary insanity." No claim is made that the jury as constituted was otherwise afflicted by any elements of supposed unfairness.

... [T]he right to an impartially selected jury assured by the Fourteenth Amendment ... does not entitle one accused of crime to a jury tailored to the circumstances of the particular case, whether relating to the sex or other condition of the defendant, or to the nature of the charges to be tried. It requires only that the jury be indiscriminately drawn from among those eligible in the community for jury service, untrammelled by any arbitrary and systematic exclusions. ... The result of this appeal must therefore depend on whether such an exclusion of women from jury service has been shown.

... Florida's [law] does not purport to exclude women from state jury service. Rather,

the statute "gives to women the privilege to serve but does not impose service as a duty." It accords women an absolute exemption from jury service unless they expressly waive that privilege. ... [W]e [cannot] ... conclude that Florida's statute is ... infected with unconstitutionality. Despite the enlightened emancipation of women from the restrictions and protections of bygone years, and their entry into many parts of community life formerly considered to be reserved to men, woman is still regarded as the center of home and family life. We cannot say that it is constitutionally impermissible for a State, acting in pursuit of the general welfare, to conclude that a woman should be relieved from the civil duty of jury service unless she herself determines that such service is consistent with her own special responsibilities.

II

... Finding no substantial evidence whatever in this record that Florida has arbitrarily undertaken to exclude women from jury service ... we must sustain the judgment of the Supreme Court of Florida.

JUSTICES WARREN, BLACK, AND DOUGLAS, CONCURRING:

We cannot say from this record that Florida is not making a good faith effort to have women perform jury duty without discrimination on the ground of sex. Hence we concur in the result, for reasons set forth in Part II of the Court's opinion.

Hoyt v. Florida, 368 U.S. 57 (1961).

Women line up to register for jury duty at the Hall of Records, New York City, 1937.
When New York State passed a voluntary jury service law for women in 1937, hundreds of women lined up to register. The New York World Telegram *treated the story as cute: "Women jurors registering in the Hall of Records, and do they like it!" The caption—"They augur no good for love slayers"—predicted that women jurors would not join in the common practice of light sentences for men who had wounded or killed their wives' lovers. Dorothy Kenyon, a feminist attorney who had fought for 15 years for mandatory jury service, welcomed the new statute as a first step: "This gives a new lease of life to the jury system." In the 1960s, Kenyon and Pauli Murray would lead the efforts of the American Civil Liberties Union to establish equitable jury service throughout the nation. (Courtesy of the Library of Congress.)*

Note that these three justices are careful to uphold the decision of the lower court only "for reasons set forth in Part II of the Court's opinion." What is the difference between the argument in part I and part II? Did granting women the power to avoid jury duty hurt Hoyt's right to a fair trial? If men and women are equal, does a virtually all-male jury *pool* undermine equality? If men and women are equal, does an all-male *jury* undermine equality? Why do you think Justices Warren, Black, and Douglas wrote a separate concurring opinion? To what extent was the Court's opinion based on arguments from equality? On arguments from difference?

When Ruth Bader Ginsburg began to work on the ACLU's Women's Rights Project (see *Frontiero v. Richardson*, pp. 752–753), she was committed to persuading the Supreme Court to reverse its decisions on several major cases that had sustained sex discrimination; one of those cases was *Hoyt*. Not until 1975, in a case arising in Louisiana, a state in which women were still required to file a written declaration of their desire to be subject to jury service, was *Hoyt* reversed by the Supreme Court. Billy Taylor, convicted of rape and kidnapping, successfully appealed his conviction on the grounds that women had been systematically excluded from the jury pool. His lawyers drew an analogy between his experience and the Court's decision three years before that a white man was entitled to have a jury from which blacks had not been systematically barred. The majority opinion upheld Taylor's claim. It made extensive use of an opinion written by Justice William O. Douglas in 1946, relating to jury selection practices in federal courts. What did Douglas mean when he said that "two sexes are not fungible"? Do you agree?

TAYLOR V. LOUISIANA, 1975

MR. JUSTICE BYRON R. WHITE:

The Louisiana jury-selection system does not disqualify women from jury service, but in operation its conceded systematic impact is that only a few women, grossly disproportionate to the number of eligible women in the community, are called for jury service. In this case, no women were on the venire from which the petit jury was drawn. . . .

The State first insists that Taylor, a male, has no standing to object to the exclusion of women from his jury. . . . Taylor was not a member of the excluded class; but there is no rule that claims such as Taylor presents may be made only by those defendants who are members of the group excluded from jury service. In [1972] . . . a white man [successfully] challenged his conviction on the ground that Negroes had been systematically excluded from jury service. . . .

We are . . . persuaded that the fair-cross-section requirement is violated by the systematic exclusion of women, who in the judicial district involved here amounted to 53 percent of the citizens eligible for jury service. . . . This very matter was debated in *Ballard v. U.S.* [1946]. . . . The . . . view that an all-male panel drawn from various groups in the community would be as truly representative as if women were included, was firmly rejected:

> . . . who would claim that a jury was truly representative of the community if all men were intentionally and systematically excluded from the panel? The truth is that the two sexes are not fungible; a community made up exclusively of one is different from a community composed of both; the subtle interplay of influence one on the other is among the imponderables. . . . The exclusion of one may indeed make the jury less representative of the community than would be true if an economic or racial group were excluded. [Justice William O. Douglas, 1946]

. . . It is untenable to suggest these days that it would be a special hardship for each and every woman to perform jury service . . . it may be burdensome to sort out those who should be exempted from those who should serve. But that task is performed in the case of men, and the administrative convenience in dealing with women as a class is insufficient justification for diluting the quality of community judgment represented by the jury in criminal trials.

Taylor v. Louisiana, 419 U.S. 522 (1975).

The decision in *Taylor* addressed only the problem of who is included in the panels from whom jurors are chosen. Not until 1994 did the Supreme Court rule that the Fourteenth Amendment's equal protection clause prohibits the use of peremptory jury challenges on the basis of gender. Overturning a paternity suit in which a woman challenged virtually all the men in the jury pool, leaving an all-female jury to decide on her claims for child support, the majority held "that gender, like race, is an unconstitutional proxy for juror competence and impartiality."*

J.E.B. v. Alabama, 511 U.S. 127 (1994). For a full treatment of the history of women and jury service, see Linda K. Kerber, *No Constitutional Right to Be Ladies: Women and the Obligations of Citizenship* (New York: Hill & Wang, 1998), ch. 4.

Civil Rights Act, Title VII, 1964

The Civil Rights Act of 1964 was a comprehensive law of enormous significance. It was a complex statute, 28-printed pages long and divided into 11 major sections, or titles. Title I dealt with voting rights; Title III with the desegregation of public facilities; Title V established a Commission on Civil Rights. Title VII defined a long list of practices that would be forbidden to employers and labor unions; obliged the federal government to undertake an "affirmative" program of equal employment opportunity for all employees and job applicants; and created an Equal Employment Opportunity Commission (EEOC) to monitor compliance with the law.

Title VII was notable in that it outlawed discrimination on the basis of sex as well as race. Sex was added to the categories "race, color, religion and national origin" by Congressman Howard Smith, a conservative Democrat from Virginia, who was a vigorous opponent of civil rights legislation. He introduced his motion after urging from Republican supporters of the National Woman's Party, who had been lobbying for an equal rights amendment whether or not it would undermine protective labor legislation, and who wanted to equate discrimination on the basis of race with discrimination on the basis of sex. The debate on Smith's motion was filled with misogyny; Smith joked that his amendment would guarantee the "right" of every woman to a husband. But it passed, supported by conservative members who were more comfortable voting for a civil rights bill if there was something in it for white women.

The EEOC, which began to operate in the summer of 1965, anticipated that virtually all of its complaints would come from blacks. The commission was surprised to discover that 25 percent of the complaints received during the first year were from women from a range of racial and ethnic backgrounds, many African American. In the course of responding to these complaints, both the commission and the courts were driven to a more subtle analysis of female job categories and work patterns. Section 703(e) 1 required that employers wishing to restrict a job category to one sex had to show that being male or female was a "bona fide occupational qualification"; it was not enough to say that men or women had traditionally filled any given job.

In the decade that followed, most states developed their own versions of Title VII, establishing laws that prohibited sex discrimination in employment. The federal statute was amended in 1972 and again in 1978; on both occasions the EEOC was given substantial additional powers and responsibilities. The three major areas of EEOC activity are (1) furnishing assistance to comparable state agencies, (2) furnishing advice to employers and labor unions about compliance, and (3) enforcing compliance by conciliation and legal action. In 1978 Congress passed the Pregnancy Discrimination Act, which amplified the definition of sex to include pregnancy, childbirth, or related medical conditions. EEOC has been willing to view sexual harassment as a form of sex discrimination but has not endorsed the concept of comparable worth.

U.S. *Statutes at Large* 78 (1964): 253–66. For a discussion of the circumstances of the passage of Title VII, see Jo Freeman, "How 'Sex' Got into Title VII: Persistent Opportunism as a Maker of Public Policy," *Law and Inequality* 9 (1991): 163–84.

Sec. 703.(a) It shall be an unlawful employment practice for an employer—

(1) to fail or refuse to hire or to discharge any individual, or otherwise to discriminate against any individual with respect to his compensation, terms, conditions, or privileges of employment, because of such individual's race, color, religion, sex, or national origin; or

(2) to limit, segregate, or classify his employees in any way which would deprive or tend to deprive any individual of employment opportunities or otherwise adversely affect his status as an employee, because of such individual's race, color, religion, sex, or national origin.

(b) It shall be an unlawful employment practice for an employment agency to fail or refuse to refer for employment, or otherwise to discriminate against, any individual because of his race, color, religion, sex, or national origin, or to classify or refer for employment any individual on the basis of his race, color, religion, sex, or national origin.

(c) It shall be an unlawful employment practice for a labor organization—

(1) to exclude or to expel from its membership, or otherwise to discriminate against, any individual because of his race, color, religion, sex, or national origin;

(2) to limit, segregate, or classify its membership, or to classify or fail or refuse to refer for employment any individual, in any way which would deprive or tend to deprive any individual of employment opportunities, or would limit such employment opportunities or otherwise adversely affect his status as an employee or as an applicant for employment, because of such individual's race, color, religion, sex, or national origin; or

(3) to cause or attempt to cause an employer to discriminate against an individual in violation of this section. . . .

(e) Notwithstanding any other provision of this title, (1) it shall not be an unlawful employment practice for an employer to hire and employ employees, for an employment

agency to classify, or refer for employment any individual, for a labor organization to classify its membership or to classify or refer for employment any individual, or for an employer, labor organization, or joint labor-management committee controlling apprenticeship or other training or retraining programs to admit or employ any individual in any such program, on the basis of his religion, sex, or national origin in those certain instances where religion, sex, or national origin is a bona fide occupational qualification reasonably necessary to normal operation of that particular business or enterprise. . . .

Sec. 705.(a) There is hereby created a Commission to be known as the Equal Employment Opportunity Commission, which shall be composed of five members, not more than three of whom shall be members of the same political party, who shall be appointed by the President by and with the advice and consent of the Senate. . . .

(g) The Commission shall have power—

(1) to cooperate with and, with their consent, utilize regional, State, local, and other agencies, both public and private, and individuals; . . .

(3) to furnish to persons subject to this title such technical assistance as they may request to further their compliance with this title or an order issued thereunder;

(4) upon the request of (i) any employer, whose employees or some of them, or (ii) any labor organization, whose members or some of them, refuse or threaten to refuse to cooperate in effectuating the provisions of this title, to assist in such effectuation by conciliation or such other remedial action as is provided by this title;

(5) to make such technical studies as are appropriate to effectuate the purposes and policies of this title and to make the results of such studies available to the public;

(6) to refer matters to the Attorney General with recommendations for intervention in a civil action brought by an aggrieved party under section 706, or for the institution of a civil action by the Attorney General under section 707, and to advise, consult, and assist the Attorney General on such matters. . . .

Equal Rights Amendment, 1972

An equal rights amendment, with wording slightly different from that passed by Congress in 1972, was sponsored in 1923 by the National Woman's Party. It seemed to party members the logical corollary to suffrage. But that amendment was vigorously opposed by the League of Women Voters and other progressive reformers, lest it undermine the protective legislation for which they had fought so hard. A key question raised was what impact the amendment, if passed, would have on a military draft.

An equal rights amendment was introduced regularly in Congress virtually every year thereafter, but it received little attention until after World War II. In 1950 and 1953, it was passed by the Senate but ignored by the House.

By 1970 much protective legislation had been applied to both men and women. It was possible to support an equal rights amendment without risking the undoing of labor law reforms. The hope that the Supreme Court would apply the Fourteenth Amendment's "equal protection of the laws" clause to cases involving discrimination on the basis of sex as firmly as it applied the clause to cases involving racial discrimination had not been fulfilled. When the current Equal Rights Amendment was introduced in 1970, it was endorsed by a wide range of organizations, some of which had once opposed it; these organizations included groups as disparate as the United Automobile Workers and the Woman's Christian Temperance Union. Its main sponsor in the House was Martha Griffiths of Michigan; in the Senate, Birch Bayh of Indiana.

The ERA was passed by Congress on March 22, 1972, and sent to the states for ratification. There was much initial enthusiasm; within two days six states had ratified. But the pace of ratification slowed after 1975, and only 35 of the needed 38 states had ratified it by 1978. (Four state legislatures voted to rescind ratification, although the legality of that move was open to question.) In October 1978 Congress extended the deadline for ratification to June 30, 1982; the extension expired with no additional ratifications. The amendment was reintroduced in Congress in 1983 but has not been passed. Compare the language here to that of the Fifteenth Amendment (p. 289) and Title VII of the 1964 Civil Rights Act (pp. 745–746).

Section 1. Equality of rights under the law shall not be denied or abridged by the United States or by any State on account of sex.

Section 2. The Congress shall have the power to enforce, by appropriate legislation, the provisions of this article.

Section 3. The amendment shall take effect two years after the date of ratification.

Title IX, Education Amendments of 1972

In 1972, women received 9 percent of the M.D. degrees awarded by universities in the United States, 7 percent of the law degrees, and 15 percent of the doctoral degrees. Women were 2 percent of college varsity athletes. It was common practice to encourage women students into specialties marked as appropriate for women: teaching rather than scientific research, for example, or nursing rather than medicine. It was estimated that colleges offered athletic scholarships to 50,000 men, while women athletes received fewer than 50. It was usual practice for the travel expenses of men's athletic teams to be paid for from student fees (paid by both women and men), while women's teams received 0.5 percent of schools' athletic dollars. Women's teams often had to raise their own travel funds, sometimes from bake sales and raffles. Title IX of the Education Amendments to the Civil Rights Act, passed in 1972, was brief but far-reaching.

No person in the United States shall, on the basis of sex, be excluded from participation in, be denied the benefits of, or be subjected to discrimination under any education program or activity receiving Federal financial assistance. . . .

Each Federal department and agency which is empowered to extend Federal financial assistance to any education program or activity, by way of grant, loan, or contract . . . is authorized and directed to effectuate the provisions of . . . this title with respect to such program or activity by issuing rules, regulations, or orders of general applicability which shall be consistent with achievement of the objectives of the statute. . . .

Title IX has proven to be a powerful tool in the fight for gender equity because it affects a wide range of educational opportunities and services. Title IX forbids sex discrimination in admissions policies (outlawing the common practice of using separate standards for men and women); in career training and vocational programs (which had previously been largely segregated by sex); and in employment. Title IX also forbids discrimination against pregnant or parenting students and requires schools to provide an environment that is free of sexual harassment.

Until recently, the most widely discussed consequence of Title IX has been its transformative effect on high school and undergraduate athletic programs. In the years since the passage of Title IX, the number of women participating in National Collegiate Athletic Association (NCAA) intercollegiate athletics has risen from approximately 32,000 in 1971 to roughly 203,600 in 2012–13, an increase of over 600 percent. (The number of men in intercollegiate athletics has also risen at the rate of 53 percent, from 173,000 to 265,600 athletes.) At the high school level, the change is even more striking: over three million girls have participated in high school sports in each of the last seven years, compared with fewer than 300,000 in 1971–72, an increase of nearly 1,000 percent. (During the same time period, high school boys' participation in sports has risen by approximately 15 percent.) Thus, contrary to the widespread misperception that Title IX has decreased the opportunities for males to participate in sports, the number of male athletes has continued to increase and, most significantly, so has the funding for men's sports. At Division I schools (with major football and basketball teams), although the number of men's teams has declined, the amount of money spent on men's athletics is still almost twice as much as the money spent on women's athletics. Between 1995–96 and 2004–5, Division I schools increased their spending on men's football by approximately $2.45 million per team, while the average funding increase for women's teams (except basketball) was about $135,000 per team.

Title IX is enforced by the Department of Education's Office of Civil Rights. Enforcement has been gradual. Not until 1975 were there full federal regulations applying to secondary schools and colleges and universities, and these have continued to evolve over time. The Title IX regulations governing athletic programs require that the total amount of athletic financial assistance awarded to men and women be proportionate to their respective participation rates in intercollegiate athletic programs. They require that male and female athletes receive equivalent— not identical—benefits, treatment, services, and opportunities. Title IX does *not* require that all teams be coeducational, nor that the same number of teams be provided for men and women, nor that men's teams be cut in order for the institution to come into compliance with the law. DEBUNK!

In 2002, the U.S. secretary of education established the Commission on Opportunity in Athletics. At issue were the measures of fairness. After more than a year of intense public debate, the commission announced its wholehearted support for the goal of gender equity in sports, while suggesting that schools be

By the turn of the twenty-first century, diversity in admissions and more equitable funding for women's athletics had made new opportunities for women to hone their skills and overcome challenges, as these players at the University of California attest. (Photo courtesy of the Department of Athletics, University of California, Santa Barbara.)

offered more flexible terms of establishing their compliance with Title IX. The Department of Education relies on a "three-prong test" established in 1979, requiring schools to show either that the ratio of male and female athletes is about equal to the ratio of all male and female undergraduates; that they have a "history and continuing practice" of expanding opportunities for women; or that they are "fully and effectively accommodating the interests and abilities" of women on campus. More than three-quarters of colleges and universities are in comfortable compliance with Title IX, having added women's teams and continued to support men's teams. It is Division I schools, which reserve substantial numbers of slots for revenue-producing sports (even at the expense of cutting men's minor sports), that have found it most difficult to meet Title IX's expectations.

Recent reports confirm several arguments that women have made about Title IX's effects on intercollegiate sports programs. Both men's and women's participation levels in college athletics have increased since the passage of Title IX. College and universities have responded to Title IX by increasing women's participation rather than decreasing men's participation. Men's sports continue to receive funding and athletic opportunities out of proportion to their representation in the college population; 57 percent of undergraduates are women, yet they receive only 43 percent of the athletic participation opportunities. In addition, the NCAA's 2012-13 report on sports participation shows that male athletic participation in intercollegiate sports—both the numbers of athletes and the number of teams—has reached an all-time high.

Argument continues about what constitutes equitable treatment. Is it fair for men to hold the majority of athletic scholarships (an imbalance largely due to the size of men's football and basketball teams)? Is it fair for a university to support a women's varsity rowing team but not a men's varsity rowing team? What is the proper relationship between women's sports and men's sports? Between women's sports and men's "minor" sports? Perhaps most significantly, what is the wise relationship between expenditures on athletics and expenditures on academic programs?

TITLE IX AND SEXUAL ASSAULT

Students and their parents have used Title IX to fight sexual harassment at school and during school-sponsored activities. One of the earliest cases was brought against Yale University in 1977 by a group of female students who argued that harassment of students by professors—and the absence of procedures for students to file effective formal complaints—is a violation of Title IX. In 1999 the Supreme Court responded to the appeal of the fifth-grade girl who had been subjected to explicit sexual teasing by a classmate. He attempted to touch her breasts and genital area, he told her "I want to get into bed with you," and he rubbed his body against her in the hallway. Her grades plummeted as she lost the ability to concentrate on her studies. Although she and her mother complained repeatedly to teachers and the principal, no action was taken. The Court ruled that school districts may be liable for damages when administrators are indifferent to repeated and known acts of student-to-student sexual harassment, during school hours and on school grounds (*Davis v. Monroe County Board of Education*, 119 S.Ct. 1661). The case raised the question of responsibility of schools to provide a harassment-free environment (see *Meritor Savings Bank v. Mechelle Vinson et al.*, pp. 754–756).

In 1990, the Jeanne Clery Act, named for a 19-year old freshman who was raped and murdered in her Lehigh University dormitory room in 1986, required colleges and universities to report crimes committed on campus. In 2010 it was strengthened, requiring institutions to issue timely warnings about crimes that pose an ongoing danger. The law also requires annual public campus security reports that include three years' worth of crime statistics; the statistics must include both forcible and non-forcible sex offenses. The resulting reports were stunning in what they revealed about the frequency of rape and the laxity of punishment. The example of Christy Bronzkala, whose lawsuit against Virginia Tech after her rape by a football player triggered a test of the Violence Against Women Act (VAWA), is exemplary; the players were briefly suspended, but Bronzkala left the university. (For VAWA, see pp. 756–758.) Few schools have expelled violators of campus behavior codes. When victims brought their complaints to police, they regularly encountered disbelief and humiliation. Even today, victims often feel that they have to choose between the dread of facing their assaulters in classes and on campus or transferring to another or dropping out of school.

By 2014, women student activists had forced the question. They organized public protests; they deployed social media to link activists on many campuses; they used student newspapers to publicize the violence they endured; they encouraged one another to file complaints with the Department of Education and the Office of Civil Rights under the Clery Act and Title IX. Through a new organization, "End Rape on Campus," they waged a sophisticated lobbying campaign. They gained the support of members of Congress—among them, Senators Kristin Gillibrand and Claire McCaskill, who had already challenged the military for its weak response to sexual violence. Among the students who filed complaints with the Office of Civil Rights were Annie E. Clark and Andrea Pino of the University of North Carolina and Emma Sulkowicz of Columbia University—all profiled in articles in the *New York Times*. In May 2014 the Department of Education issued a finding that supported a student's complaint that Tufts University had delayed

In 2014, college students organized many public demonstrations addressing sexual violence on campuses, like this one at the University of Iowa on February 24. Photographer: James Soukup. (Courtesy of the Daily Iowan.*)*

investigating her assault and had not protected her from her assailant; the university refused the settlement proposed by the Department of Education and thus risked losing all federal funding.*

As this book goes to press, a White House task force has concluded that one in five female students are assaulted during their college years but only 12 percent of rapes are reported. The Department of Education has announced that it is investigating 55 colleges and universities for their failures to provide a "prompt and equitable response" to complaints of sexual harassment and violence, as Title IX requires. The list included some of the nation's most distinguished public and private institutions. All over the country, women student activists continue to publicize the records of their own universities; at some they are appearing at recruitment tours to warn prospective students about the dangers they face.†

What has been the history of Title IX enforcement and of sexual assault on your campus? Is your college among the 55 singled out for investigation? What programs to increase awareness of sexual violence and to prevent it are in place, and which to your mind are most effective? What have been the responses of students, men as well as women, to the reinvigorated movement for women's safety?**

*See www.endrapeoncampus.org; "Behind Focus on College Assaults, a Steady Drumbeat by Students," *New York Times*, April 29, 2014; "Fight Against Sexual Assaults Holds Colleges to Account," ibid., May 3, 2014.

† See www.notalone.gov.

**This note was prepared with information from reports and press releases issued in 2007, 2008, and 2013 by the National Collegiate Athletic Association (NCAA), the National Federation of State High School Associations (NFHS), the Women's Sports Foundation, the National Coalition for Women and Girls in Education, and the ACLU Women's Rights Projects, which are available on their websites.

Frontiero v. Richardson, 1973

Sharron A. Frontiero was an Air Force officer who was dismayed to discover that she could not claim dependent's benefits for her husband on the same terms that her male colleagues could for their wives. She and her husband brought suit, claiming that statutes requiring spouses of female members of the uniformed services to receive more than half of their support from their wives to be considered dependents, while all spouses of male members were treated as dependents, violated the due process clause of the Fifth Amendment and the equal protection clause of the Fourteenth Amendment.

Until 1971, the Supreme Court had never ruled that discrimination on the basis of sex was a violation of the equal protection clause of the Fourteenth Amendment. So long as a legislature had a "reasonable" basis for making distinctions between men and women, discriminatory laws were upheld. Between 1971 and 1975, in a stunning series of decisions, the Supreme Court placed the burden of proof that discrimination on the basis of sex was reasonable on those who tried to discriminate. Ruth Bader Ginsburg was a thirty-eight-year-old law professor working with the American Civil Liberties Union (ACLU) in 1971 when the Court accepted her argument that an Idaho law requiring that fathers, rather than mothers, always be preferred as executors of their children's estates was unconstitutional (*Reed v. Reed*, 404 U.S. 71 [1971]).

The ACLU set up a Women's Rights Project in 1972 with Ginsburg at its head to follow up on the implications of the *Reed* decision. Ginsburg wrote the brief and managed the argument in *Frontiero*; it was one of a brilliant series of cases that she argued in the early 1970s. With her colleagues, she helped persuade the Court that a wide range of discriminatory practices were illegal. Her career as a litigator would lead to her appointment as a judge on the U.S. Court of Appeals in 1980 and, in 1993, to her appointment to the U.S. Supreme Court.

The Supreme Court ruled in favor of the Frontieros in a complex decision that used statistical information about woman's place in the work force in a manner reminiscent of the Brandeis Brief (see Sklar, p. 357). Speaking for three of his colleagues Justice William J. Brennan, Jr., prepared a historically based argument, explaining the distance American public opinion had traveled since the *Bradwell* case (see pp. 292–294). He drew analogies between discrimination on the basis of race, which the court subjected to strict scrutiny, and discrimination on the basis of sex.

In concurring with Brennan's opinion, three justices observed that although they agreed with the Frontieros in this particular case, they were not yet persuaded that sex ought to be regularly treated as a "suspect category." Only when—or if—the Equal Rights Amendment were passed could the Court be sure that the public agreed that discrimination on the basis of sex ought to be evaluated as critically as discrimination on the basis of race. Note that the facts in *Frontiero* relate to discrimination against the husband of the wage earner, not directly against a woman. It is the family of the wage earner that is discriminated against. A similar case, also argued by Ginsburg, is *Weinberger v. Weisenfeld* (420 U.S. 636 [1975]), in which the husband of a dead woman successfully demanded survivor's benefits equal to those available to widows. Ginsburg and her colleagues stressed that both men and women benefited from gender-blind equal treatment under the law.

MR. JUSTICE WILLIAM J. BRENNAN, JR.,
DELIVERED THE OPINION OF THE COURT:

The question before us concerns the right of a female member of the uniformed services to claim her spouse as a "dependent." . . .

At the outset, appellants contend that classifications based upon sex, like classifications based upon race, alienage, and national origin, are inherently suspect and must therefore be subjected to close judicial scrutiny. We agree. . . .

There can be no doubt that our Nation has had a long and unfortunate history of sex discrimination. Traditionally, such discrimination was rationalized by an attitude of "romantic paternalism" which, in practical effect, put women, not on a pedestal, but in a cage. Indeed, this paternalistic attitude became so firmly rooted in our national consciousness that, 100 years ago, a distinguished Member of this Court was able to proclaim. . . . "The natural and proper timidity and delicacy which belongs to the female sex evidently unfits it for many of the occupations of civil life." . . .

It is true, of course, that the position of women in America has improved markedly in recent decades. Nevertheless, it can hardly be doubted that, in part because of the high visibility of the sex characteristic, women still face pervasive, although at times more subtle, discrimination in our educational institutions, in the job market, and perhaps most conspicuously, in the political arena. . . .

Moreover, since sex, like race and national origin, is an immutable characteristic determined solely by the accident of birth, the imposition of special disabilities upon the member of a particular sex because of their sex would seem to violate "the basic concept of our system that legal burdens should bear some relationship to individual responsibility. . . ." And what differentiates sex from such non-suspect statuses as intelligence or physical disability, and aligns it with the recognized suspect criteria, is that the sex characteristic frequently bears no relation to ability to perform or contribute to society. . . .

. . . over the past decade, Congress has itself manifested an increasing sensitivity to sex-based classification. In Tit[le] VII of the Civil Rights Act of 1964, for example, Congress expressly declared that no employer, labor union, or other organization subject to the provisions of the Act shall discriminate against any individual on the basis of "race, color, religion, *sex*, or national origin." Similarly, the Equal Pay Act of 1963 provides that no employer covered by the Act "shall discriminate . . . between employees on the basis of sex." . . .

With these considerations in mind, we can only conclude that classifications based upon sex, like classifications based upon race, alienage, or national origin, are inherently suspect, and must therefore be subjected to strict judicial scrutiny. Applying the analysis mandated by that stricter standard of review, it is clear that the statutory scheme now before us is constitutionally invalid. . . .

MR. JUSTICE LEWIS F. POWELL, JR.,
WITH WHOM THE CHIEF JUSTICE AND
MR. JUSTICE HARRY A. BLACKMUN JOIN,
CONCURRING IN THE OPINION:

I agree that the challenged statutes constitute an unconstitutional discrimination against servicewomen . . . but I cannot join the opinion of Mr. Justice Brennan, which would hold that all classifications based upon sex . . . are "inherently suspect and must therefore be subjected to close judicial scrutiny." . . . The Equal Rights Amendment, which if adopted will resolve the substance of this precise question, has been approved by the Congress and submitted for ratification by the States. If this Amendment is duly adopted, it will represent the will of the people accomplished in the manner prescribed by the constitution. . . . It seems to me that this reaching out to pre-empt by judicial action a major political decision which is currently in process of resolution does not reflect appropriate respect for duly prescribed legislative processes.

Frontiero v. Richardson, 411 U.S. 677 (1973).

Meritor Savings Bank v. Mechelle Vinson et al., 1986

The term "sexual harassment" was unknown before the mid-1970s. One legal scholar has written, "the term was invented by feminist activists, given legal content by feminist litigators and scholars, and sustained by a wide-ranging body of scholarship generated largely by feminist academics." Another legal scholar observes "[f]or the first time in history, women have defined women's injuries in a law."*

Consider Part 1 of Section 703 of Title VII of the Civil Rights Act of 1964 (p. 746). The authors of the statute were defining economic injuries, and for more than a decade the Equal Employment Opportunity Commission supported only economic claims of sex discrimination. But working women had long put up with behavior that, beginning in the 1970s, they began to say was also sex discrimination: supervisors who referred to all women as "whores," whether or not in joking tones; workplaces that had cheesecake or frankly pornographic calendars on the walls; and, worst of all, covert or explicit pressure to have sex with supervisors or employers for fear of losing their jobs if they refused. *[sex disc. — handwritten margin note]*

Legal scholar Catharine MacKinnon gave names to two forms of sexual harassment: (1) "quid pro quo": when sexual submission to a supervisor becomes, either implicitly or explicitly, a condition of employment; and (2) "offensive working environment": when the conduct of a supervisor, co-employee, or client unreasonably interferes with an individual's work or creates an intimidating and hostile workplace. By the late 1970s, many behaviors that men had described as flirting, and that women had "put up with" because they saw no alternative, could be named and challenged. In 1980, the EEOC published an official set of guidelines describing behavior it would challenge as sexual harassment, even if the actors claimed they were merely flirting or "joking around."

In 1986, a unanimous Supreme Court for the first time formally recognized sexual harassment as a violation of Title VII. Catharine MacKinnon was one of the attorneys for Mechelle Vinson, an African American woman who had been hired in 1974 as a teller-trainee by a vice president of Meritor Savings Bank and was steadily promoted for four years until she became assistant branch manager. During those four years, she had a sexual relationship with the man (Mr. Taylor) who had hired her. . . . (However, when she tried to decline his attentions, he exposed himself to her and forcibly raped her.) *[Black woman — handwritten margin note]*

Vinson claimed that she had been the victim of both "quid pro quo" and offensive environment forms of sexual harassment. Vinson told the court "that because she was afraid of Taylor she never reported his harassment to any of his supervisors and never attempted to use the bank's complaint procedure." But when she was fired for what the bank claimed was excessive use of sick leave, she sued the bank, claiming sexual harassment and asking for punitive damages. The

---

*Martha Chamallas, "Writing About Sexual Harassment: A Guide to the Literature," *UCLA Women's Law Journal* 4 (1993): 37–38; Catharine MacKinnon, *Feminism Unmodified: Discourses on Life and Law* (Cambridge, Mass.: Harvard University Press, 1987), p. 105; Vicki Schultz, "Reconceptualizing Sexual Harassment," *Yale Law Journal* 107 (1998): 1683–1805.

bank claimed that "any sexual harassment by Taylor was unknown to the bank and engaged in without its consent or approval."

A unanimous Court agreed with Vinson. What analogies do they see with race discrimination? Why do they hold Meritor Bank guilty as well as Mr. Taylor? Taylor argued that Vinson wore sexually provocative clothing. How much responsibility do you think the victim of sexual harassment should be expected to take for avoiding the harassment?   ↳ His excuse for raping her

JUSTICE WILLIAM REHNQUIST:

This case presents important questions concerning claims of workplace "sexual harassment" brought under Title VII of the Civil Rights Act of 1964 ... [Vinson] argues ... that unwelcome sexual advances that create an offensive or hostile working environment violate Title VII. Without question, when a supervisor sexually harasses a subordinate because of the subordinate's sex, that supervisor "discriminate[s]" on the basis of sex. [Meritor Bank] does not challenge this proposition. It contends instead that in prohibiting discrimination with respect to "compensation, terms, conditions, or privileges" of employment, Congress was concerned with what petitioner describes as "tangible loss" of "an economic character," not "purely psychological aspects of the workplace environment."

We reject petitioner's view. First, the language of Title VII is not limited to "economic" or "tangible" discrimination. The phrase "terms, conditions, or privileges of employment" evinces a congressional intent "to strike at the entire spectrum of disparate treatment of men and women" in employment. ... As the Court of Appeals for the Eleventh Circuit wrote ... in 1982: "Sexual harassment which creates a hostile or offensive environment for members of one sex is every bit the arbitrary barrier to sexual equality at the workplace that racial harassment is to racial equality. Surely a requirement that a man or woman run a gauntlet of sexual abuse in return for the privilege of being allowed to work and make a living can be as demeaning and disconcerting as the harshest of racial epithets."

... [W]e reject the ... view that the mere existence of a grievance procedure and a policy against discrimination, coupled with respondent's failure to invoke that procedure, must insulate petitioner from liability. ... the bank's grievance procedure apparently required an employee to complain first to her supervisor, in this case Taylor. Since Taylor was the alleged perpetrator, it is not altogether surprising that respondent failed to invoke the procedure and report her grievance to him. ... [W]e hold that a claim of "hostile environment" sex discrimination is actionable under Title VII. ...

Meritor Savings Bank v. Mechelle Vinson et al., 477 U.S. 57 (1986).

A wave of attention to sexual harassment in the workplace took place after the fall of 1991, when hearings on the nomination of Clarence Thomas to the Supreme Court were interrupted by the charges of Anita Hill that he had sexually harassed her a decade earlier. Ironically, their encounter had taken place within the EEOC itself, where Thomas had been director and Hill had been a lawyer on his staff. In response, Thomas charged that he was himself victimized by the media attention. Adrienne Davis and Stephanie Wildman observe, "in a stunning sleight of hand, [Thomas] managed to convince all involved, including the Senate, (that white racism, rather than a Black woman) had accused him of harassment."* Thomas's nomination to the Supreme Court was confirmed by the Senate.

Over the years since the *Meritor* decision, increasing numbers of workers have filed sexual harassment complaints, and a massive body of doctrine has developed on the details of the law's protection. In 1998 the Supreme Court ruled

*Adrienne D. Davis and Stephanie M. Wildman, "The Legacy of Doubt: Treatment of Sex and Race in the Hill-Thomas Hearings," *Southern California Law Review* 65 (1992): 1367.

that harassment based on an employee's homosexuality could constitute sex discrimination, and that male-on-male harassment could be a cause of action (*Oncale v. Sundowner Offshore Services, Inc.*). The definition of an "offensive working environment" remains under debate. Legal theorist Vicki Schultz has proposed:

> Many of the most prevalent forms of harassment are actions that are designed to maintain work—particularly the more highly rewarded lines of work—as bastions of masculine competence and authority. Every day, in workplaces all over the country, men uphold the image that their jobs demand masculine mastery by acting to undermine their female colleagues' perceived (or sometimes even actual) competence to do the work. The forms of such harassment are wide-ranging. They include characterizing the work as appropriate for men only; denigrating women's performance or ability to master the job; providing patronizing forms of help in performing the job; withholding the training, information, or opportunity to learn to do the job well; engaging in deliberate work sabotage; . . . isolating women from the social networks that confer a sense of belonging . . . much of the time, harassment assumes a form that has little or nothing to do with sexuality but everything to do with gender.[†]

Have you or your family members or friends encountered some of these forms of harassment, or others?

Violence Against Women Act, 1994, 2000, 2005, 2013

The Violence Against Women Act (VAWA) was part of the comprehensive Violent Crime Control and Law Enforcement Act, passed in 1994. It was path-breaking in establishing a new right: "All persons within the United States shall have the right to be free from crimes of violence motivated by gender." Congress was persuaded that the states fail to treat violent assaults against women as seriously as they treat other forms of violent assault. As one member of the Senate observed, "Typically we do not ask whether the victim of a barroom brawl is a real victim; we do not comment that the victim deserved to be hit; we do not inquire whether there was resistance or whether the victim said 'no' persistently enough."

VAWA provided funding to states for criminal law enforcement against perpetrators of violence. It also created (based on the commerce clause of the Fourteenth Amendment) a new federal civil rights remedy for victims of violence resulting from "animus based on the victim's gender." It defined domestic violence and sexual assault as potential infractions of the victim's civil rights. It overrode the inadequate remedies that persist in many states (for example, several states exempted cohabiting companions from rape laws). A victim of a violent crime motivated by the victim's gender was permitted to bring a civil lawsuit in federal or state court, seeking money damages or an injunction.

(a) PURPOSE.—Pursuant to the affirmative power of Congress to enact this subtitle under section 5 of the Fourteenth Amendment to the Constitution, as well as under section 8 of Article I of the Constitution, it is the purpose of this subtitle to protect the civil rights of victims of gender motivated violence and to promote public safety, health, and activities affecting interstate commerce by establishing a Federal civil rights cause of action for victims of crimes of violence motivated by gender.

(b) RIGHT TO BE FREE FROM CRIMES OF VIOLENCE.—All persons within the United States shall have the right to be free

[†]Schultz, p. 1687.

from crimes of violence motivated by gender (as defined in subsection (d)).

(c) CAUSE OF ACTION.—A person (including a person who acts under color of any statute, ordinance, regulation, custom, or usage of any State) who commits a crime of violence motivated by gender and thus deprives another of the right declared in subsection (b) shall be liable to the party injured, in an action for the recovery of compensatory and punitive damages, injunctive and declaratory relief, and such other relief as a court may deem appropriate.

(d) DEFINITIONS.—For purposes of this section—

(1) the term "crime of violence motivated by gender" means a crime of violence committed because of gender or on the basis of gender, and due, at least in part, to an animus based on the victim's gender; and

(2) the term "crime of violence" means—

(A) an act or series of acts that would constitute a felony against the person or that would constitute a felony against property if the conduct presents a serious risk of physical injury to another, and that would come within the meaning of State or Federal offenses described in section 16 of title 18, United States Code, whether or not these acts have actually resulted in criminal charges, prosecution, or conviction and whether or not those acts were committed in the special maritime, territorial, or prison jurisdiction of the United States; and

(B) includes an act or series of acts that would constitute a felony described in subparagraph (A) but for the relationship between the person who takes such action and the individual against whom such action is taken.

U.S. Statutes at Large, 110:2419.

Not long after VAWA was passed, Christy Brzonkala charged that she had been raped by two college football players in her dorm during her first semester at Virginia Polytechnic Institute. The athletes were not suspended from school, even though they had boasted about what they'd done and had been found guilty of "abusive conduct" by the university's judicial committee. Virginia Tech sentenced one of the players to two semesters' suspension, but upon appeal the provost set the suspension aside, calling it excessive punishment.

Brzonkala dropped out of school, fearing its dangers, and sued Virginia Tech, claiming damages equal to what the school earned from the Sugar Bowl, in which the athletes played. She lost. In May 2000, the U.S. Supreme Court upheld an appeals court ruling that Congress had reached too far in its interpretation of a right to regulate interstate commerce. The Court invalidated the part of the VAWA that permitted victims of rape, domestic violence, and other crimes "motivated by gender" to sue their attackers in federal court.*

Congress acted quickly: Within a few months it had reauthorized all but the contested section of VAWA. It provided more than $3 billion to fight violence against women: (1) $1 billion over five years to help prosecutors track down domestic abusers; (2) $875 million to expand shelters for battered women; (3) $95 million over two years to protect foreign women brought into the country by the international sex trade; and (4) $140 million to stop violent crimes against women on college campuses. The amount of money required is itself an indictment of the extent to which gender-motivated crimes, international trafficking in women, and the conditions on college campuses are major threats to women. VAWA was reauthorized and expanded in 2013, after a long legislative battle. (Every woman in Congress, regardless of party, voted for it.). The new legislation expands federal programs to assist local communities with law enforcement and it protects gay, bisexual, or transgender victims from domestic and sexual abuse. Recognizing

*U.S. v. Morrison, 529 U.S. 598 (2000).

that Native American women have a higher likelihood of being sexually assaulted than any other group, VAWA 2013 also permits Native American women who are assaulted on reservations to press charges against non-Indians in tribal courts. (Generally tribal courts do not have jurisdiction over defendants who do not live on tribal land.) The White House Task Force to Protect Students from Sexual Assault, established in 2014, is charged with adding teeth—giving force to the safeguards promised not only by VAWA but also by Title IX and the Jeanne Clery Act (see p. 750).

BORDERS AMONG US

PIERRETTE HONDAGNEU-SOTELO
Domésticas Demand Dignity

Anti-immigration rhetoric is pervasive in U.S. political discourse today. In some ways, the arguments against immigrants echo nativist sentiment at the turn of the twentieth century, which culminated in the passage of exclusion and restriction laws. However, there are some differences as well. Over a hundred years ago, the largest number of immigrants came from eastern and southern Europe. In contrast, immigrants in recent decades are more likely to come from Latin America and Asia. In addition, while immigrants during the last century tended to be predominantly male, women are migrating in equal and sometimes even greater numbers. In fact, some of the fears about immigrants center on women, whose existing or future children are thought of as acting as an unwanted drain on the shrinking social services available.

Pierrette Hondagneu-Sotelo examines why women are migrating in greater numbers in the context of a globalized economy in which factories, capital, and workers increasingly cross national borders. She focuses on the mounting demand for service and domestic workers, as more middle-class American women seek paid employment outside their homes, and on the difficulty of recognizing work done inside a home as labor. In Los Angeles, most recently it has been Central American immigrant women whose poorly paid labor has helped maintain affluent homes and communities. The author's interviews with domestic workers and her research on their pay, working conditions, and migration, work, and family histories reveal much about both continuities and variations in the situations of domestic workers over the past three centuries. What are some of the dilemmas facing care and domestic workers that you have witnessed or are aware of?

Today, a substantial number of domestic workers provide care to the increasing numbers of the aged, infirm, and housebound, most of who are also women. Home health care is among the fastest growing and least well paid occupations; more and more have been joining unions. Some successes in organizing domestic workers and enacting legislation have challenged the view that the labor movement in the United States is dying. In fall 2013 and summer 2014, the governors of California and Massachusetts signed Domestic Workers' Bills of Rights into law, following similar statutes in New York and Hawaii. And in September 2013, the Obama administration put into place rules extending the Fair Labor Standards Act (FLSA) to home health workers. The difficulties of implementing these steps

Excerpted from the prefaces and Chaps. 2 and 8 of *Doméstica: Immigrant Workers Cleaning and Caring in the Shadows of Affluence* by Pierrette Hondagneu-Sotelo (Berkeley: University of California Press, 2007; orig. pub. 2001). Reprinted by permission of the author and publisher. Notes have been edited and renumbered.

are illustrated in the continuing legal challenges faced by unions and their state government partners.* Moving forward, what do you think are some solutions to the problems that Hondagneu-Sotelo depicts?

We live in the age of migration. Around the world, at least 185 million people, and perhaps as many as 200 million, reside in countries other than those where they were born. Why are so many people leaving their countries of origin? The legacies of colonialism, neocolonialism, imperialism, civil wars, imperial wars, uneven development, and the contemporary shock effects of neoliberalism [meaning policies such as deregulation, free trade, and government down-sizing] and political shifts have laid the structure for today's global migration. Meanwhile, innovations in technology, particularly in transportation and communications, have facilitated this vast human movement. International migration occurs through legal, quasi-legal, and illegal channels. It is important to recognize, however, that in many cases, deliberate labor-recruitment programs have helped to activate and maintain international labor migration. These are generally inaugurated for employer interests in the receiving society, and they are facilitated by receiving-state government, and sometimes bilateral, agreements. Such programs rely on the state to condone a particular type of legal migration predicated on the denial of migrants' basic human, labor, and civil rights.

Not long ago, migrants were mainly men. In fact, the international labor migration of men was a key feature of industrialization. During peak periods of modernization and industrialization, the industrial state relied on the recruitment and importation of men—usually men from poorer, often colonial societies—to do "men's work." Chinese, Filipino, Japanese, Irish, Italian, and Mexican men, for instance, all took turns as recruits who were brought in to build the infrastructure of an industrializing America. These migrants built canals and railroads, dug deep in mines, stoked factory furnaces, laid irrigation pipes, and provided the labor for large-scale agribusiness. In some

instances, family members were allowed to join them, but in many cases, especially those involving immigrant groups perceived as non-white, dependent family members were denied admission to the migrant-receiving societies. Women and children were perceived as burdens who would consume resources, and they were also seen to be demographically and racially undesirable as permanent members of the society. For these reasons, the reproduction of families and communities was forbidden. In many instances, government legislation enforced these prohibitions on the permanent incorporation of workers and their families. It was labor, not human beings, that was being recruited. The Bracero Program, which issued nearly five million temporary labor contracts to Mexican agricultural laborers in the United States between 1942 and 1964, and the Guest Worker Program, which relied on Turkish and Algerian men to rebuild cities and toil in the factories of Europe after World War II, are the exemplars of these modern systems, in which labor recruitment relied not only on men, but on subordinated men who were subjected to meticulous rules and regulations and to rigorous, dehumanizing bodily inspections.

Today, industry and manufacturing are no longer the primary fulcrums driving labor migration. . . . In a globalized world, factories migrate to places overseas that offer cheaper labor. High-tech and highly educated professionals have now joined the international migration, as have legions of migrant domestic workers. . . . Consequently, in some sites, we are seeing an oversupply of male migrant labor and the saturation of labor markets for working men. . . . In places as diverse as Italy, the Middle East, Taiwan, and Canada, Filipina migrant women working as caregivers and cleaners far out-number Filipino migrant men. . . . In Los Angeles newly arrived Latina

*For example, see the June 2014 U.S. Supreme Court ruling against the fee structure supporting Service Employees International Union (SEIU Illinois) home health care workers, who by unionizing and working as personal assistants in the Illinois Home Services Program were able to nearly double their pay and gain health insurance; *Harris v. Quinn*, decided June 30, 2014. For changes in the home care sector and a history of organizing efforts, see Eileen Boris and Jennifer Klein, *Caring for America: Home Health Workers in the Shadow of the Welfare State* (New York: Oxford University Press, 2012).

immigrant women find jobs much more easily than their husbands and brothers, because of the steady demand for live-in domestic workers.

... Many of the newly industrialized Asian nations, such as Taiwan, Hong Kong, and Singapore, as well as Middle Eastern oil-rich nations, such as Saudi Arabia, Kuwait, and the United Arab Emirates, rely on state-legislated projects to recruit migrant domestic workers. The migrant domestic workers employed in these societies hail from poorer nations that are desperate to capture migrant remittances for foreign exchange, and to diffuse the social and political pressures created by unemployment. Consequently, nations such as the Philippines, Indonesia, Sri Lanka, and Thailand actively promote the out-migration of women into global domestic worker labor markets.

The nation-states from which domestic workers migrate have responded to these pressures in varied ways. The Philippines not only facilitates the out-migration of Filipina women as domestic workers, but it honors the return migrant *domésticas* as "heroes," to emphasize their contributions to building and sustaining the Philippine nation. The Philippines does make some effort to intervene on behalf of the domestic workers, but when Filipino diplomats and labor attachés attempt to impose fair labor standards in the countries where Filipinas go, they often discover that their bargaining power is weak, especially in contexts where migrant women are arriving from other, competing countries. Meanwhile, nations such as Bangladesh act in a more paternalistic, patriarchal way, attempting to thwart abuses by prohibiting the out-migration of women as foreign domestic workers. By contrast, Mexico—the nation that sends by far the most immigrants to the United States, a fair number of whom wind up working as *domésticas*—remains curiously silent on the incorporation of Mexican women as workers in private American homes.

When nation-states collaborate on contract-labor programs for domestic workers, the regulations are usually geared toward the control and submission of these workers, and not toward ensuring their rights. ... [In some countries] migrant domestic workers may be required to remain with one employer for the duration of their contract period, regardless of the treatment they might receive. If they are unhappy with their job, they may not seek out another one, remaining stuck in a feudal-like situation. Some must sign oaths promising

loyalty and docility. Other rules specify how they may dress and wear their hair, and prohibit makeup or lipstick. The confiscation of passports by employers is common. Domestic workers may also be subjected to medical surveillance designed to ensure they are not pregnant, and may be prohibited from leaving the homes where they work except for perhaps a few hours on one afternoon a week. Some are subjected to beatings or sexual abuse, but have no escape or access to legal recourse. ...

Just as slavery produced runaway slaves, many times these conditions result in "runaway maids." In the worst-case scenarios, these sorts of institutional conditions have resulted in the tragic deaths of migrant domestic workers, as in Singapore and Kuwait. Human rights advocates around the globe have raised their voices against such abuses, but the institutionalized violation of domestic workers' human rights has not received as much public attention and action as has been directed toward thwarting the illegal trafficking of women and girls.

In [some] countries, such as the United States, laws and regulations do not tie migrant domestic workers to their.... Moreover, there are labor-protection laws on the books, and legal and community advocates working for enforcement of those rules. For domestic workers and agricultural workers, who were historically excluded from these pacts, the reach of these laws has been limited. Labor activists, legislators, and domestic workers themselves, however, continue to push for change, as they did in 2006, when they tried to change California legislation to allow overtime labor protections for live-in domestic workers and for personal attendants. [The change was enacted in 2013.] Latina immigrant domestic workers in the United States hold a range of legal statuses, from those who are undocumented to those who are naturalized U.S. citizens.... Unlike their global peers working on temporary contract programs, many immigrant domestic workers in the United States already live with their own families in immigrant communities in American cities, but a massive legalization program would allow them to further improve their labor prospects and better support their families....

While the social trends that create the international flow of migrant domestic workers are diverse, the result is the same: families in the wealthy nations get women from poor nations to do the dirty domestic work, while families from the poor nations lose their mothers and wives. Is this simply a continuation of imperialism? As Barbara Ehrenreich and Arlie Hochschild have astutely noted, rich nations increasingly assume "a role like that of the old-fashioned male in the family—pampered, entitled, unable to cook, clean or find his socks." The poor nations, like the traditional woman, remain mired in domestic work and subservience. As for the migrant female domestic workers, who is left at home to do the care for them? This is a big moral question, one with social, political, and economic consequences. . . . [1]

Meanwhile, it is important to listen to the voices and experiences of the domestic workers themselves. Not all immigrant domestic workers are exploited. In fact, many of them remind us that they are valuable contributors to two societies, the one they left behind and the one in which they work. They value their jobs, and when employers and society offer them social recognition and fair labor conditions, they take satisfaction from their work and their earnings.

Can we conceive of a Los Angeles where there is, as the title of a short film puts it, "A Day without a Mexican"?[2] In fact, as I learned while chatting with domestic workers at parks and bus stops, this is an exercise regularly indulged in by Mexican, Salvadoran, and Guatemalan women who work in middle-class and upper-middle-class homes throughout Los Angeles. "If we called a three-day strike," nannies say to their peers, "How many days would it take before we shut it all down?" Not only would households fall into a state of chaos, but professionals, managers, and office workers of all sorts would find themselves unable to perform their own jobs. Latina domestic workers debate this scenario with humor—some arguing that it might take two days, others chiming in with four. They know that in their job, a general strike is unlikely. Yet their strident humor is bolstered by the resurgence of militant unionism among Latino immigrant janitors and hotel and restaurant employees and by collective organizing among gardeners, day laborers, and drywallers in California. Significantly, their running dialogue speaks to a shared recognition of their own indispensability. In their own conversations, they reclaim what their job experiences often deny them: social recognition and dignity. . . .

Private paid domestic work, in which one individual cleans and cares for another individual or family, poses an enormous paradox. In the United States today, these jobs remain effectively unregulated by formal rules and contracts. Consequently, even today they often resemble relations of servitude that prevailed in earlier, precapitalist feudal societies. These contemporary work arrangements contradict American democratic ideals and modern contractual notions of employment. [My research] reveals how these fundamental tensions in American social life are played out in private homes, between the women who do the work and those who employ them.

Paid domestic work is widely recognized as part of the informal "shadow" or "under the table" economy. Although wage and hour regulations do cover the job, scarcely anyone, employee or employer, knows about them. Government regulations remain ineffective, and there are no employee handbooks, unions, or management guidelines to help set wages or job duties or to stipulate how the work should be performed. The jobs are done in isolated, private, widely dispersed households, and typically involve negotiations between two individuals—usually women from radically different backgrounds. . . . Relying on primary information gathered in the mid- to late 1990s from more than two hundred people in Los Angeles (in-depth interviews with 68 individuals, a survey of 153 Latina domestic workers, and ethnographic observations in various settings), I examine how the practices and concerns of both employers and employees shape how paid domestic work occurs today.

There are many lived dramas in America today, and among the least visible and most deeply felt are those that unfold behind carefully manicured lawns and residential facades. [I] highlight the voices, experiences, and views both of the Mexican and Central American women who care for other people's children and homes and of the women in Los Angeles who employ them. The study of paid domestic work thus offers a key window through which we can view contemporary relations between women whose social positions are in stark contrast: between poor women and affluent families; between foreign-born, immigrant women and U.S.-born citizens; and between members of the growing, but still economically and racially subordinate, Latino communities and the shrinking population of white suburban residents, many of whom feel increasingly anxious about these demographic developments. Differences of class, race, nationality, and citizenship characterize the study's participants, yet this is an occupation in which the chasm of social differences plays out in physical proximity. Unlike the working poor who toil in factories and fields, domestic workers see, touch, and breathe the material and emotional world of their employers' homes. They scrub grout, coax reluctant children to nap and eat their vegetables, launder and fold clothes, mop, dust, vacuum, and witness intimate and otherwise private family dynamics. Inside the palatial mansion, the sprawling ranch-style home, or the modest duplex, they do these activities over and over again. . . .

Domestic work was the single largest category of paid employment for all women in the United States during the late nineteenth and early twentieth centuries, in large part because other opportunities were not available. Although the timing of exit varies by race and region, by the mid-twentieth century the doors to retail, clerical, and professional jobs were opening for many working women, and single and married women walked out of their homes and into formal-sector employment. Paid domestic work declined, a trend leading some commentators to predict the occupation's demise. But instead in the late twentieth century new domestic demands arose and new recruits were found, now crossing the southern border to reach the doorstep of domestic work. The work of cleaning houses and caring for children gradually left the hands of wives and mothers and entered the global marketplace. In the process, it has become the domain of disenfranchised immigrant women of color. . . .

I am the daughter of a Latina woman who, like many modestly educated women in mid-twentieth-century Latin America, migrated from the countryside to the city to work as a live-in nanny/house-keeper. Eventually, employment in her native Chile for the American family of an Anaconda copper mining engineer was her ticket to California, bought with indentured labor. When the family that brought her to the United States refused to pay her, she found live-in domestic jobs with other well-to-do American families before eventually marrying my father, a French gardener whom she met on the job. . . .

Today, my husband and I do laundry, cook, and clean daily, but we also pay a Salvadoran woman to clean our house. Every other Thursday she drives from her apartment near downtown Los Angeles to our suburban home to sweep and mop the hardwood floors, vacuum the carpets, dust the furniture, and scrub, wipe, and polish the bathrooms and kitchen to a blinding gleam. I love the way the house looks after she's done her job; but like many of the employers that I interviewed for this study, I remain deeply ambivalent about the glaring inequalities exposed by this arrangement—and exposed in a particularly visible and visceral way. Capitalist manufacturing misery abounds in this world; but when I purchase Nike shoes or Gap jeans, my reliance on child labor in Mauritania or Pakistan, or on Latina garment workers who toil in sweatshops just a stone's throw away from my office at USC, remains conveniently hidden and invisible in the object of consumption. I take possession of a new item, and no one but the cashier stares back at me. By contrast, my privileges and complicity in a worldwide system of inequalities and exploitation are thrown into relief by the face-to-face relations between me and the woman who cleans my house.

When colleagues and students in my classes have discussed these issues, some of them have argued passionately and compellingly that we cannot have a just society until everyone cleans up and picks up after themselves, regardless of their race, sex, or immigration or class status. They might be right (and I'm certainly in favor of men and boys learning to do their fair share), but I think an abolitionist program smacks of the utopian, not the feasible. Domestic work should not fall disproportionately on the shoulders of any one group (such as Filipina, or Latina, or Caribbean immigrant women); but putting an end to domestic employment is not the answer. Upgrading the occupation, a change ushered in by systemic regulation and by public recognition that this seemingly private activity is a job—one that creates particular obligations in both employees and employers—is our best chance for salvaging paid domestic work, for increasing the opportunities of those who do the work and of their families, and for reclaiming the dignity and humanity of both employees and employers.

Since 1990, . . . I have worked toward that end with a group of women under the auspices of the Coalition for Humane Immigrant Rights of Los Angeles (CHIRLA). The project began as an information and outreach program organized by immigrant rights attorneys, community organizers, and myself, but today it is a full-fledged, dues-collecting membership organization called the Domestic Workers' Association (DWA), which is part of CHIRLA. Similar organizations have sprouted up in other cities around the country, and they have long been common in Latin America.... All research is partial, situated and shaped by who we are. My multiple social locations—as the daughter of a former domestic worker, as a current employer, and as an advocate—have certainly shaped my approach and my emphases....

Most Latina immigrant women who do paid domestic work in Los Angeles had no prior experience working as domestics in their countries of origin. Of the 153 Latina domestic workers that I surveyed at bus stops, in ESL classes, and in parks, fewer than 10 percent reported having worked in other people's homes, or taking in laundry for pay, in their countries of origin. This finding is perhaps not surprising, as we know from immigration research that the poorest of the poor rarely migrate to the United States; they simply cannot afford to do so.[3]

Some of the Latina immigrant women who come to Los Angeles grew up in impoverished squatter settlements, others in comfortable homes with servants. In their countries of origin, these women were housewives raising their own children, or college students, factory workers, store clerks, and secretaries; still others came from rural families of very modest means. Regardless of their diverse backgrounds, their transformation into housecleaners and nanny/housekeepers occurs in Los Angeles....

Who are these women who come to the United States in search of jobs, and what are those jobs like? Domestic work is organized in different ways. [Here] I describe live-in [jobs] and housecleaning jobs, and profile some of the Latina immigrants who do them and how they feel about their work.... [I also discuss] why it is that Latina immigrants are the primary recruits to domestic work [and what wage and hour regulations apply. I then offer a short history of efforts to organize domestic workers in the United States, and, finally, suggest some steps forward.] ...

[Live-ins:] It is the rare California home that offers separate maid's quarters, but that doesn't stop families from hiring live-ins; nor

does it stop newly arrived Latina migrant workers from taking jobs they urgently need. When live-ins cannot even retreat to their own rooms, work seeps into their sleep and their dreams. There is no time off from the job, and they say they feel confined, trapped, imprisoned.

"I lose a lot of sleep," said Margarita Gutiérrez, a twenty-four-year-old Mexicana who worked as a live-in nanny/housekeeper. At her job in a modest-sized condominium in Pasadena, she slept in a corner of a three-year-old child's bedroom. Consequently, she found herself on call day and night with the child, who sometimes went several days without seeing her mother because of the latter's schedule at an insurance company. Margarita was obliged to be on her job twenty-four hours a day; and like other live-in nanny/housekeepers I interviewed, she claimed that she could scarcely find time to shower or brush her teeth. "I go to bed fine," she reported, "and then I wake up at two or three in the morning with the girl asking for water, or food." After the child went back to sleep, Margarita would lie awake, thinking about how to leave her job but finding it hard to even walk out into the kitchen. Live-in employees like Margarita literally have no space and no time they can claim as their own.

Working in a larger home or staying in plush, private quarters is no guarantee of privacy or refuge from the job. Forty-four-year-old Elvia Lucero worked as a live-in at a sprawling, canyon-side residence, where she was in charge of looking after twins, two five-year-old girls. On numerous occasions when I visited her there, I saw that she occupied her own bedroom, a beautifully decorated one outfitted with delicate antiques, plush white carpet, and a stenciled border of pink roses painstakingly painted on the wall by the employer. It looked serene and inviting, but it was only three steps away from the twins' room. Every night one of the twins crawled into bed with Elvia. Elvia disliked this, but said she couldn't break the girl of the habit. And the parents' room lay tucked away at the opposite end of the large (more than 3,000 square feet), L-shaped house.

Regardless of the size of the home and the splendor of the accommodations, the boundaries that we might normally take for granted disappear in live-in jobs. They have ... "no clear line between work and non-work time," and the line between job space and private space is similarly blurred.[4] Live-in nanny/

housekeepers are at once socially isolated and surrounded by other people's territory; during the hours they remain on the employers' premises, their space, like their time, belongs to another. The sensation of being among others while remaining invisible, unknown and apart, of never being able to leave the margins, makes many live-in employees sad, lonely, and depressed. Melancholy sets in and doesn't necessarily lift on the weekends.

Rules and regulations may extend around the clock. Some employers restrict the ability-of their live-in employees to receive telephone calls, entertain friends, attend evening ESL classes, or see boyfriends during the workweek. Other employers do not impose these sorts of restrictions, but because their homes are located on remote hillsides, in suburban enclaves, or in gated communities, their live-in nanny/housekeepers are effectively kept away from anything resembling social life or public culture. A Spanish-language radio station, or maybe a *telenovela*, may serve as their only link to the outside world.

Food—the way some employers hoard it, waste it, deny it, or just simply do not even have any of it in their kitchens—is a frequent topic of discussion among Latina live-in nanny/housekeepers. These women are talking not about counting calories but about the social meaning of food on the job. Almost no one works with a written contract, but anyone taking a live-in job that includes "room and board" would assume that adequate meals will be included. But what constitutes an adequate meal? Everyone has a different idea, and using the subject like a secret handshake, Latina domestic workers often greet one another by talking about the problems of managing food and meals on the job. Inevitably, food enters their conversations.

No one feels the indignities of food more deeply than do live-in employees, who may not leave the job for up to six days at a time. For them, the workplace necessarily becomes the place of daily sustenance. In some of the homes where they work, the employers are out all day. When these adults return home, they may only snack, keeping on hand little besides hot dogs, packets of macaroni and cheese, cereal, and peanut butter for the children. Such foods are considered neither nutritious nor appetizing by Latina immigrants, many of whom are accustomed to sitting down to meals prepared with fresh vegetables, rice, beans, and meat. In some employers' homes, the cupboards are literally bare. . . .

Food scarcity is not endemic to all of the households where these women work. In some homes, ample quantities of fresh fruits, cheeses, and chicken stock the kitchens. Some employer families readily share all of their food, but in other households, certain higher-quality, expensive food items may remain off-limits to the live-in employees, who are instructed to eat hot dogs with the children. One Latina live-in nanny/housekeeper told me that in her employers' substantial pantry, little "do not touch" signs signaled which food items were not available to her; and another said that her employer was always defrosting freezer-burned leftovers for her to eat, some of it dating back nearly a decade. . . .

The issue of food captures the essence of how Latina live-in domestic workers feel about their jobs. It symbolizes the extent to which the families they work for draw the boundaries of exclusion or inclusion, and it marks the degree to which those families recognize the live-in nanny/housekeepers as human beings who have basic human needs. When they first take their jobs, most live-in nanny/housekeepers do not anticipate spending any of their meager wages on food to eat while on the job, but in the end, most do—and sometimes the food they buy is eaten by members of the family for whom they work.

Although there is a wide range of pay, many Latina domestic workers in live-in jobs earn less than minimum wage for marathon hours: 93 percent of the live-in workers I surveyed in the mid-1990s were earning less than $5 an hour (79 percent of them below minimum wage, which was then $4.25), and they reported working an average of sixty-four hours a week. Some of the most astoundingly low rates were paid for live-in jobs in the households of other working-class Latino immigrants, which provide some women their first job when they arrive in Los Angeles. Carmen Vasquez, for example, had spent several years working as a live-in for two Mexican families, earning only $50 a week. By comparison, her current salary of $170 a week, which she was earning as a live-in nanny/housekeeper in the hillside home of an attorney and a teacher, seemed a princely sum.[5] . . .

Once they experience it, most women are repelled by live-in jobs. The lack of privacy, the mandated separation from family and friends, the round-the-clock hours, the food issues, the low pay, and especially the constant loneliness prompt most Latina immigrants to seek other job arrangements. Some young, single women who learn to speak English fluently try to move up the ranks into higher-paying live-in jobs. As soon as they can, however, the majority attempt to leave live-in work altogether. Most live-in nanny/housekeepers have been in the United States for five years or less. . . . Like African American women earlier in the century, who tired of what the historian Elizabeth Clark-Lewis has called "the soul-destroying hollowness of live-in domestic work," most Latina immigrants try to find other options.[6]

Until the early 1900s, live-in jobs were the most common form of paid domestic work in the United States, but through the first half of the twentieth century they were gradually supplanted by domestic "day work." Live-in work never completely disappeared, however, and in the last decades of the twentieth century, it revived with vigor, given new life by the needs of American families with working parents and young children—and . . . by the needs of newly arrived Latina immigrants, many of them unmarried and unattached to families. When these women try to move up from live-in domestic work, they see few job alternatives. Often, the best they can do is switch to another form of paid domestic work, either as live-out nanny/housekeeper or as a weekly housecleaner. When they do such day work, they are better able to circumscribe their work hours, and they earn more money in less time.[7] . . .

[House cleaners:] Like many working mothers, every weekday morning Marisela Ramírez awoke to dress and feed her preschooler, Tomás, and drive him to school (actually, a Head Start program) before she herself ventured out to work, navigating the dizzying array of Los Angeles freeways. Each day she set off in a different direction headed for a different workplace. On Mondays she maneuvered her way to Pasadena, where she cleaned the stately home of an elderly couple; on Tuesdays she alternated between cleaning a home in the Hollywood Hills and a more modest-sized duplex in Glendale; and Wednesdays took her to a split-level condominium in Burbank. You had to keep alert, she said, to remember where to go on which days and how to get there!

By nine o'clock she was usually on the job, and because she zoomed through her work she was able to finish, unless the house was extremely dirty, by one or two in the afternoon. After work, there were still plenty of daylight hours left for Marisela to take Tomás to the park . . . before she started dinner. Working as a housecleaner allowed Marisela to be the kind of wife and mother she wanted to be. Her job was something she did, she said, "because I have to"; but unlike her peers who work in live-in jobs, she enjoyed a fairly regular family life of her own, one that included cooking and eating family meals, playing with her son, bathing him, putting him to bed, and then watching *telenovelas* in the evenings with her husband and her sister. On the weekends, family socializing took center stage, with *carne asadas* in the park; informal gatherings with her large Mexican family, which extended throughout Los Angeles; and music from her husband, who worked as a gardener but played guitar in a weekend *ranchera* band.

Some might see Marisela Ramírez as just another low-wage worker doing dirty work, but by her own account—and gauging by her progress from her starting point—she had made remarkable occupational strides. Marisela had begun working as a live-in nanny/housekeeper in Los Angeles when she was only fifteen years old. Ten years later, the move from live-in work to housecleaning had brought her higher hourly wages, a shorter workweek, control over the pace of work, and flexibility in arranging when she worked. Cleaning different houses was also, she said, less boring than working as a nanny/housekeeper, which entailed passing every single day "in just one house, all week long with the same routine, over and over."

For a while she had tried factory work, packaging costume jewelry in a factory warehouse located in the San Fernando Valley, but Marisela saw housecleaning as preferable on just about every count. "In the factory, one has to work very, very fast!" she exclaimed. "And you can't talk to anybody, you can't stop, and you can't rest until it's break time. When you're working in a house, you can take a break at the moment you wish, finish the house when you want, and leave at the hour you decide. And it's better pay. It's harder work, yes," she conceded, "but it's better pay."

"How much were you earning at the factory?" I asked.

"Five dollars an hour; and working in houses now, I make about $11, or even more. Look, in a typical house, I enter at about 9 A.M., and I leave at 1 P.M., and they pay me $60. It's much better [than factory work]." Her income varied, but she could usually count on weekly earnings of about $300. By pooling these together with her husband's and sister's earnings, she was able to rent a one-bedroom bungalow roofed in red tile, with a lawn and a backyard for Tomás's sandbox and plastic swimming pool. In Mexico, Marisela had only studied as far as fifth grade, but she wanted the best for Tomás. Everyone doted on him, and by age four he was already reading simple words. . . .

Breaking into housecleaning is tough, often requiring informal tutelage from friends and relatives. Contrary to the image that all women "naturally" know how to do domestic work, many Latina domestic workers discover that their own housekeeping experiences do not automatically transfer to the homes where they work. As she looked back on her early days in the job, Marisela said, "I didn't know how to clean or anything." . . . Erlinda Castro, a middle-aged woman who had already run her own household and raised five children in Guatemala, . . . recalled . . . : "Learning how to use the chemicals and the liquids" in the different households was confusing, and, as friends and employers instructed her on what to do, she began writing down in a little notebook the names of the products and what they cleaned. Some women learn the job by informally apprenticing with one another, accompanying a friend or perhaps an aunt on her housecleaning jobs. . . .

Housecleaning represents . . . the "modernization" of paid domestic work. Women who clean different houses on different days sell their labor services in much the same way that a vendor sells a product to various customers.[8] The housecleaners themselves see their job as far preferable to that of a live-in or live-out nanny/housekeeper. They typically work alone, during times when their employers are out of the home; and because they are paid "by the job" instead of by the hour, they don't have to remain on the job until 6 or 7 P.M., an advantage much appreciated by women who have families of their own. Moreover, because they work for different employers on different days, they are not solely dependent for their livelihood on one boss whom they see every single day. Consequently, their relationships with their employers are less likely to become highly charged and conflictual; and if problems do arise, they can leave one job without jeopardizing their entire weekly earnings. . . .

Housecleaners also see working independently and informally as more desirable than working for a commercial cleaning company. "The companies pay $5 an hour," said Erlinda Castro, whose neighbor worked for one, "and the women have to work their eight hours, doing up to ten, twenty houses a day! One does the vacuuming, the other does the bathroom and the kitchen, and like that. It's tremendously hard work, and at $5 an hour? Thank God, I don't have to do that." Two of the women I interviewed, one now a live-out nanny/housekeeper and the other a private housecleaner, had previously worked for cleaning services, and both of them complained bitterly about their speeded-up work pace, low pay, and tyrannical bosses.

Private housecleaners take enormous pride in their work. When they finish their job, they can see the shiny results, and they are proud of their job autonomy, their hours, their pay, and, most important, what they are able to do with their pay for themselves and for their families. Yet housecleaning brings its own special problems. Intensive cleaning eventually brings physical pain, and sometimes injury. "Even my bones are tired," said fifty-three-year-old Lupe Vélez; and even a relatively young woman like Celestina Vigil at age thirty-three was already reporting back problems that she attributed to her work. While most of them have only fleeting contact with their employers, and many said they work for "good people," just about everyone has suffered, they said, "inconsiderate persons" who exhort them to work faster, humiliate them, fail to give raises, add extra cleaning tasks without paying extra, or unjustly accuse them of stealing or of ruining a rug or upholstery. And the plain old hard work and stigma of cleaning always remain, as suggested by the answer I got when I asked a housecleaner what she liked least about her job. "The least?" she said, with a wry smile. "Well, that you have to clean." . . .

As Mexican and Central American immigrant women move into live-out and housecleaning jobs, their family lives change. With better pay and fewer hours of work, they become able to live with their own family members. Among those I surveyed, about 45 percent of the women doing [live-out] day work were married, but only 13 percent of the live-ins were married. Most women who have husbands and children with them in Los Angeles do not wish to take live-in jobs; moreover, their application for a live-in job is likely to be rejected if they reveal that they have a husband, a boyfriend, or children living in Los Angeles. . . . Live-out nanny/housekeepers often face this family restriction too, as employers are wary of hiring someone who may not report for work when her own children come down with the flu.

Their subminimum wages and long hours make it impossible for many live-in workers to bring their children to Los Angeles; other live-ins are young women who do not have children of their own. [A] substantial proportion of Latina domestic workers in Los Angeles whose children stay in their countries of origin are in the same position as . . . the Filipinas who predominate in domestic jobs in many cities around the globe. This is what I label "transnational motherhood." . . . Today, international labor migration and the job characteristics of paid domestic work, especially live-in work, virtually impose transnational motherhood on many Mexican and Central American women who have children of their own.[9] . . .

Why today are Central American women hugely overrepresented in these jobs in Los Angeles in comparison with Mexicans (whose immigrant population is of course many times larger)? In the survey I conducted of 153 Westside Latina domestic workers, 75 percent of the respondents were from Central America; of those, most were from El Salvador and Guatemala. And in census counts, Salvadoran and Guatemalan women are, respectively, twelve times and thirteen times more likely than the general population to be engaged in private domestic work in Los Angeles. Numerous studies paint a similar picture in other major U.S. cities, such as Washington, D.C., Houston, and San Francisco; one naturally wonders why this should be so.[10] . . .

Mexican migration to the United States goes back over a hundred years, initially driven by labor recruitment programs designed to bring in men to work in agriculture. Since the late 1960s, it has shifted from a primarily male population of temporary or sojourner workers to one that includes women and entire families; these newcomers have settled in rural areas, cities, and suburbs throughout the United States, but disproportionately in California. Many Mexican women who migrated in the 1970s and 1980s were accompanied by their families and were aided by rich social networks; the latter helped prevent the urgency that leads new immigrants to take live-in jobs. . . . When Mexican women arrive in the United States, many of them enjoy access to well-developed, established communities whose members have long been employed in various industries, particularly agriculture, construction, hotels, food-processing plants, and garment factories. . . . Their social networks give Mexican women greater variety in their employment options; paid domestic work is only one of their alternatives.[11]

Salvadoran and Guatemalan women migrating to the United States have done so under different circumstances than Mexican women. For Central Americans coming to *el norte,* there was no long-standing labor program recruiting men who could then bring, or encourage the migration of, their wives and daughters. . . . More significantly, Salvadoran and Guatemalan women and men left their countries in haste, often leaving their children behind, as they fled the civil wars, political violence, and economic upheaval of the 1980s. Theirs are immigrant communities that subsisted without legal status for nearly two decades, grew rapidly, and remain very poor. . . .

Family structures and marriage patterns may have also contributed to the preponderance of Central American women in paid domestic work. El Salvador has traditionally had one of the lowest marriage rates in the hemisphere, especially among the urban poor, where common-law marriages and legacies of internal and intra–Central America labor migration— mostly for work on coffee plantations—have encouraged the formation of female-headed households. Thus Salvadoran women have been more likely to migrate on their own and accept live-in jobs. . . . [12]

The experience of Central American women might also be compared to that of Asian immigrant women, who have been entering the United States at increasing rates. The latter are an extremely heterogeneous group, but on average—and this is particularly true of Chinese, Indian, and Filipina women—they arrive with much higher levels of education, better English language skills, and more professional credentials than do their Latina peers. They are also more likely to have legal status; and members of some groups, especially Korean immigrant women, enjoy access to jobs in family businesses and ethnic enclaves.[13] At the same time, the generally poorer and less-educated women from Vietnam, Laos, and Cambodia have been able to withstand periods of underemployment and unemployment because they are officially sanctioned political refugees and therefore enjoy access to welfare and resettlement assistance from the federal government. While some individual Asian immigrant women are working in paid domestic work, they have not developed social networks that channel them into this niche.

It is particularly striking that Filipina immigrants predominate in this occupation elsewhere around the globe, but not in the United States. Worldwide, about two-thirds of Filipina migrants in countries as different as Italy, Canada, Hong Kong, Taiwan, Singapore, Saudi Arabia, and Jordan, do paid domestic work; but in the United States, their high levels of education and fluent English enable most of them to enter higher status occupations that require more skills than does domestic work. In 1990, 71 percent of the Filipinas in the United States were working in managerial, professional, technical/sales, and administrative support jobs, and only 17 percent were employed in service jobs. They are disproportionately concentrated in the health professions, the result of formal recruitment programs designed to fill U.S. nursing shortages. Experience in the health professions leads many Filipinas to take jobs in elder care. . . . [14]

During the period that I was researching this book, I attended funerals for three children of Latina domestic workers. Two perished in an apartment blaze with their mother, victims of suspected arson, and another fell to her death from the balcony of a public housing project while her mother was at work. To my mind, the deaths of these three young children were neither accidents of fate nor the result of parental abuse, but rather tragedies of poverty. If their mothers, who worked as domestics, had earned higher wages, they could have afforded safer housing, and these children might still be alive.

These deaths are among the most glaring costs of the way paid domestic work is done today in Los Angeles. The more mundane costs to the domestic workers—the loss of dignity, respect, and self-esteem; the inability to even live with their children; and the daily hardships of raising families on poverty-level wages—do not command the same attention, but they are, nevertheless, social prices. When working people who earn the legal minimum wage cannot bring home enough money to keep a family of three above official poverty levels, Latina domestic workers who earn *below* minimum wage are in big trouble.[15]

As we have seen, the arrangements of paid domestic work give rise to many problems, largely because paid domestic work is not treated as bona fide employment and because the women who do it—in Los Angeles, Latina immigrant women—are among the most disenfranchised members of society. . . . [Are] these problems are remediable? . . .

Most people involved in domestic work, employers as well as employees, still do not know that wage and hour regulations cover paid domestic work. The reason for their ignorance is obvious: virtually no attempt has been made by the government or media to educate domestic workers and employers about these laws. . . . Among the most basic labor protections [on the books] are those regarding wages and hours; these are codified in the federal Fair Labor Standards Act (FLSA), which was enacted in the wake of the Great Depression. Based on a model of industrial wage employment, the FLSA initially excluded private household workers; but in 1974 . . . Congress amended the act to guarantee private domestic workers the right to receive minimum wages and overtime pay.[16] The amendment covered a range of domestic occupations, including the jobs of butlers, cooks, housekeepers, and maids. Accordingly, domestic employees who work more than eight hours in one workweek are entitled to receive the minimum wage. Various legal precedents . . . have established that undocumented immigrant workers are also covered under the FLSA. It would seem, then, that basic legal protection with respect to wages is already in place.

There are two significant limitations in this federal legislation, however. First, domestic employees who work as personal attendants—for example, baby-sitters, caregivers to young children, or companions of the elderly and infirm—are explicitly *excluded* from the right to earn minimum wage and overtime pay; only those domestic employees who can show that they devote at least 20 percent of their work time to housekeeping duties are covered. Thus, while our society may pay great lip service to the value of caring for people, especially for the young, the elderly, and the ill, those who do private care work are not granted the same legal rights as those who clean and care for material possessions. Indeed, this legislative divide suggests that those responsible for caring for other human beings are not recognized as workers at all. . . .

A second and far more serious weakness of the FLSA is that live-in employees are completely exempt from overtime coverage. Accordingly, domestic workers who reside in the households where they work have no right under federal law to overtime pay. The legislation seems to encode the assumption that live-in domestic work is closer to being "just like one of the family" than to wage employment. . . . California laws, however, to some extent remedy the FLSA, regulating deductions for room and board and mandating overtime pay for some domestic workers.

A third weakness of the statutes already on the books lies outside the law itself: when it comes to paid domestic work, there is effectively no enforcement of these laws, or even encouragement of compliance. . . . [For] five Southern California counties, twenty agents are charged with the monumental task of investigating and enforcing labor practices among a population of millions. Given their scarcity of resources, labor investigators naturally focus on work sites such as factories or farms that affect more than one employee. Moreover, investigating infractions of wage and hours in a home raises far more sensitive issues of privacy than does searching a factory.

State wage and hours laws complement the federal Fair Standards Labor Act. Some states (usually those with relatively high costs of living) mandate higher hourly wages than federal law. Others specifically expand the labor rights of paid domestic workers. New York, for example, extends overtime protections to live-in workers. Still other states, among them Alaska, Delaware, Hawaii, Idaho, and Kansas, exclude domestics from state minimum wage laws and from other protections, leaving them only the inadequate protection of the FLSA. More than half the states also exclude paid domestic workers from the protection of civil rights laws, which are intended to guard against discrimination, and some state laws exempt domestic employers from compliance with occupational safety and health regulations. . . .

Formal organizations and collective efforts focused on improving domestic workers' jobs have been rare in the United States, but they are not impossible undertakings. Virtually every Latin American nation has active domestic workers' associations and unions, and since 1988 many of them have met in inter–Latin American congresses.[19] In recent years, as Latina and Caribbean immigrants have swelled the numbers of women in the occupation in the United States, a plethora of innovative, community-based associations for Latina domestic workers, each one slightly different in form and focus, have sprouted on the East and West Coasts.[17]

Efforts to organize domestic workers in the United States began in the first half of the twentieth century, but those early groups were concerned less with advocacy for the domestic workers than with vocational training for them, so they might better serve employers. The most notable exception in this regard is the National Committee on Household Employment (NCHE), which initially grew out of a 1928 Young Women's Christian Association–sponsored conference on domestic workers' wages and job hours, held in Washington, D.C. The white middle-class women of the YWCA were more reformers than union organizers. At one point, Eleanor Roosevelt served as honorary chair. . . . The group at first tried to mediate between white housewives who wanted a supply of well-trained help and black women workers who wanted better wages and limited hours. Although its members sincerely desired to remedy abuses in the occupation, the NCHE remained, in this early phase, a primarily white, middle-class, employers' organization, adamantly opposed to the imposition of written contracts and regulations.[18]

After the NCHE reorganized in 1964 under the leadership of the National Council on Negro Women, it began affiliating with and receiving support from other groups. During this period, the NCHE became a more militant advocate, organized by and for African American paid domestic workers. It worked to publicize the poor working conditions and lack of labor regulations in the occupation, to establish training programs to standardize job skills, and to open contracting centers for job placement. Training programs were implemented in eight cities between 1967 and 1971, assisted by mediators who helped individual domestic employees bargain with individual employers. The NCHE's biggest concrete achievement came in 1974, when domestic workers were finally included in the Fair Labor Standards Act.[19] . . .

Although personal attendants (baby-sitters, nannies, and attendants to the elderly and infirm who do not clean) still lack minimum wage rights, the 1974 victory was significant. The NCHE has faded away, but it had a lasting impact on private domestic work.[20]

Organizing labor is not easy in any industry, and the obstacles to efforts in domestic work are particularly daunting. One of the biggest impediments is that many women who work as housecleaners and housekeeper/nannies find it difficult to see themselves as workers, for reasons that include the stigma attached to the job, its location in a private residence, and the tasks themselves—which are associated with women's "natural" expressions of love and caring. . . . Besides the job's low status, its low pay and the limits on upward mobility within the occupation also persuade many Latina domestic workers, especially young women, that they should leave it altogether. Often these women find that their alternative sources of employment are no more attractive; but regardless of whether they actually leave or not, their ambivalence about staying in domestic work lessens the likelihood that they will put their energy into collective organizing to make the occupation better.

Those who do seek to organize and upgrade domestic work find their efforts hindered by spatial and legal constraints. Because the work sites are spread through residential neighborhoods, there is no obvious place in which to begin organizing—no garment district or factory gates for organizers to target with leaflets and recruitment efforts. Moreover, paid domestic workers are not covered by the National Labor Relations Act of 1935 (NLRA), which declares that "The term employee shall include any employee . . . but shall not include any individual employed . . . in the domestic service of any family or person at his home" (section 152, provision 3). Domestic workers have no legal rights to organize, and therefore no protection from termination if they begin to organize. . . .

[What can be done?] Many wonder why Latina immigrants who are dissatisfied with their jobs don't simply look for other types of work in Los Angeles; or failing that, why they don't just "go home." Aren't they ambitious? Don't they aspire to something better? Some Latina domestic workers do try to leave the occupation, but they find the alternatives scarce. Among the most common and easily accessible jobs for them are informal vending, janitorial work, and factory work, often in the garment sector. But garment industry jobs in Los Angeles have deteriorated in recent years. Of the estimated 120,000 garment workers in Los Angeles, the majority are Latina immigrant women and many of them now earn less than the state minimum wage at jobs that present serious health and safety problems.[21] And as more immigrant women have turned to vending, competition has increased and shaved already slim profits even further. . . . Even Latina domestic workers who have all of their legal papers, who have years of experience in the United States, who have received some higher education, and who are totally bilingual have few options. The kinds of jobs they might get as cosmetologists, secretaries, or bank tellers, they say, would require high investment in work clothes and would still bring in low earnings . . .

The bad news is this: there are no ladders of upward mobility leading out of paid domestic work today, as there were for European immigrant women in the early twentieth century. We live in a society that is increasingly characterized by an occupational hourglass, without a booming industrial sector for Latina domestic workers or their husbands to latch onto in the United States. While some of them hope to retire in El Salvador or Mexico, their possibilities for sustainable employment in their countries of origin have lessened with globalization, the North American Free Trade Agreement, and the economic aftermath of civil wars.

Many Latina domestic workers would like to have better jobs, but their options and their opportunities for advancement are slim. Upgrading their current occupation is one solution to their dilemma. How to achieve that, however, is less clear. . . . Nearly all nanny/housekeepers and housecleaners work without written contracts. States could also take inspiration from New York State, which in 1997 (through the efforts of Latina immigrant workers) passed what is reputed to be the toughest wage enforcement law in the country, the Unpaid Wages Prohibition Act.[22]

Strengthening the formal employment standards is not enough, however. Widespread compliance with those standards will require a program of public education and outreach directed at middle-class and upper-middle-class employers, as well as enforcement of the laws

Cover for the novela graphic, Super Doméstica, *published by the Coalition for Human Immigrant Rights of Los Angeles (CHIRLA), artwork by Kelvin Manzanares. Reprinted with permission of the artist and publisher. The Domestic Workers' Association in Los Angeles had its start in 1990 as an advocacy program under the wing of CHIRLA. Organizers created and distributed free, inexpensive booklets—novelas—with captioned pictures, aimed at informing domestic workers about wage and hour rights, safety issues, and more.* Super Doméstica, *as Pierrette Hondagneu-Sotelo explains, "featured the story of a house-keeper who successfully learns to negotiate with her demanding employer." Domestic workers who were activists embraced the icon, "taking turns dressing" as the superhero "when the group marched together in political rallies or protests or in neighborhood parades. . . . Political marches took on a festive aspect, and the costume—a red cape, a short skirt showing a spray bottle of cleanser and a feather duster attached to her thighs, and yellow rubber gloves on both hands—made the Domestic Workers' Association increasingly visible and drew many inquiries. The Super Doméstica icon was also featured on the organization's first T-shirts" and starred in a community theater work created by organization members. When a few critics charged that the icon "represented an unrealistic, sexist, idealized physical figure," DWA women responded, "She's a Super Hero!" The icon echoes the figure "Super Barrio, a caped and masked priest in Mexico City who organized protests in squatter settlements."*

that apply to them. Employers . . . must learn to act as employers with particular obligations rather than as consumers of domestic services. . . . Improving the occupation will also require collective organizing by and for domestic workers. In spite of the many obstacles that Latina domestic workers face in undertaking such a project, . . . they *are* organizing in major cities around the country. The Domestic Workers' Association in Los Angeles, just one example of these associations, provides a site for domestic workers to give and receive social recognition, to seek job advice, and to pursue new occupational skills (e.g., how to do CPR, serve at a seder, or file income taxes); and when necessary, it helps its members pursue claims for back wages. . . . When the members of the Domestic Workers' Association listed their job demands, dignity and respect topped the list. [These] aspects of the job, unlike wages and hours, cannot be legislated. . . . Organizations aiming at improving the terms of paid domestic work, might take a page from strategies used in the garment organizing campaigns of the 1990s, which targeted consumers and consumers' consciences with their "No Sweat" labels and National Day of Conscience.[23] Domestic workers could similarly target their employers.

Indeed, the employers have good reason to change: they and their family members who are cared for by Latina nannies will benefit greatly if the occupation is upgraded. They stand to gain better child care and other domestic services, greater length of service by those they employ, and perhaps even a fuller sense of humanity. We might ask ourselves what kind of society we wish to create for ourselves and our children. Do we wish to continue current arrangements, whereby many Latina and Caribbean immigrant women in nanny/housekeeper jobs must forfeit their own family and community lives, leaving their own young children in their countries of origin? Is transnational motherhood and a form of domestic apartheid what we want? Should the costs of care be borne so disparately? Or can we imagine and design domestic jobs so that, like other forms of employment, these can accommodate and allow for employees' own social and family lives? While we cannot legislate caring about employees, we can strive for public education and social acknowledgment that paid domestic work is work, that it is an integral part of how our society is organized today, and that the Latina immigrant women who do the work are people with their own families, communities, and concerns.

NOTES

1. Barbara Ehrenreich and Arlie Russell Hochschild, eds., *Global Woman: Nannies, Maids, and Sex Workers in the New Economy* (New York: Henry Holt, 2002), 11.

2. *A Day Without a Mexican* (2004), 100 minutes, directed by Sergio Arau. For a comparison of the economic status of Mexican immigrants and Mexican Americans in Los Angeles, see Vilma Ortiz, "The Mexican-Origin Population: Permanent Working Class or Emerging Middle Class?" in *Ethnic Los Angeles*, ed. Roger Waldinger and Mehdi Bozorgmehr (New York: Russell Sage Foundation, 1996), 247–77.

3. Mary Romero, *Maid in the U.S.A.* (New York: Routledge, 1992).

4. Evelyn Nakano Glenn, *Issei, Nisei, Warbride: Three Generations of Japanese American Women in Domestic Service* (Philadelphia: Temple University Press, 1986), 141. In drawing on my interviews, pseudonyms are used for all employees and employers.

5. Many Latina domestic workers do not know the amount of their hourly wages; and because the lines between their work and nonwork tend to blur, live-in nanny/housekeepers have particular difficulty calculating them. Consider a prototypical live-in who works 5 days a week, from 7 A.M. until 9 P.M., with 1.5 hours off during the children's nap time. Her on-duty work hours would total 64.5 hours per week. The weekly pay of live-in nanny/housekeepers surveyed ranged from $130 to $400, averaging $242. Dividing this figure by 64 yields an hourly wage of $3.80. None of the live-ins were charged for room and board—but 86 percent said they brought food with them to their jobs. The majority reported being paid in cash.

6. Elizabeth Clark-Lewis, *Living In, Living Out: African American Domestics in Washington, D.C., 1910–1940* (Washington, D.C.: Smithsonian Institution Press, 1994), 123.

7. In many urban regions of the United States, the shift to day work accelerated during World War I, so that live-out arrangements eventually became more prevalent. See David M. Katzman, *Seven Days a Week: Women and Domestic Service in Industrializing America* (Urbana: University of Illinois Press, 1981), and Phyllis Palmer, *Domesticity and Dirt: Housewives and Domestic Servants in the United States, 1920–1945* (Philadelphia: Temple University Press, 1989). Elsewhere, and for different groups of domestic workers, these transitions happened later; see Glenn, *Issei, Nisei, Warbride*, 143.

8. Romero, *Maid in the U.S.A.*

9. Pierette Hondagneu-Sotelo and Ernestine Avila, "'I'm Here, But I'm There': The Meanings of Latina Transnational Motherhood," *Gender and Society* 11 (1997), 548–71; Judith Rollins, *Between Women: Domestics and Their Employers* (Philadelphia: Temple University Press, 1985); Glenn, *Issei, Nisei, Warbride*; Romero, *Maid in the U.S.A.*; Mary Romero, "Who Takes Care of the Maid's Children? Exploring the Costs of Domestic Service," in *Feminism and Families,*

ed. Hilde L. Nelson (New York: Routledge, 1997), 63–91.

10. On the census data, see David E. Lopez, Eric Popkin, and Edward Telles, "Central Americans: At the Bottom, Struggling to Get Ahead," in *Ethnic Los Angeles*, 279–304. For other cities, see Terry A. Repak, *Waiting on Washington: Central American Workers in the Nation's Capital* (Philadelphia: Temple University Press, 1995); and Jacqueline Maria Hagan, *Deciding to be Legal: A Maya Community in Houston* (Philadelphia: Temple University Press, 1994).

11. According to the PUMS (Public Use Microdata Sample) Census data, about 70 percent of Central American women between the ages of 24 and 60 in Los Angeles County are in the labor force, while only 56 percent of their Mexican peers are. Among this same group, 71 percent of Mexican immigrant women but only 56 percent of their Central American peers are married and living with a spouse. To put it more starkly, 28 percent of Mexican immigrant women and 43 percent of Central American women report living with family members or adults other than their spouses.

12. Some studies estimate that as many as 50 percent of poor households in San Salvador were formed by "free unions" rather than marriage by law. This pattern is related not just to migration but also to urban poverty, as there is no need to secure inheritance rights when there is no property to share. See Isabel Nieves, "Household Arrangements and Multiple Jobs in San Salvador," *Signs* 5 (1979), 130–50; and Repak, *Waiting on Washington*. For a comparative study, see Katharine Donato, "Understanding U.S. Immigration: Why Some Countries Send Women and Others Send Men," in *Seeking Common Ground: Multidisciplinary Studies of Immigrant Women in the United States*, ed. Donna Gabaccia (Westport, Conn.: Praeger, 1992), 159-84.

13. On Korean immigrant business owners, see Pyong Gap Min, *Caught in the Middle: Korean Communities in New York and Los Angeles* (Berkeley: University of California Press, 1996).

14. D. Mar and M. Kim, "Historical Trends," in *The State of Asian Pacific America: Economic Diversity, Issues, and Policies*, ed. Paul Ong (Los Angeles: LEAP American Pacific American Public Policy Institute and UCLA Asian American Studies Center, 1994). Between 1966 and 1985 nearly 25,000 Filipina nurses came to work in the United States, and another 10,000 came between 1989 and 1991. Filipinas who were formally recruited through government programs then informally recruited their friends and former nursing school classmates; Paul Ong and Tania Azores, "Health Professionals on the Front Line," in ibid., 139–63. Interviews conducted with 26 Filipina domestic workers in Los Angeles reveal that many have college diplomas and [yet] are working in homes because they are older and face age discrimination; they tend to earn more as care providers for the elderly ($425 per week) and as nanny/housekeepers ($350 per week) than do Latina immigrants in these same jobs. See Rhacel Salazar Parreñas, "Migrant Filipina Domestic Workers and the International Division of Reproductive Labor," *Gender and Society* 14:4 (Aug. 2000), 560–80.

15. Robert Pollin, "Living Wage Gives a Boost to Demand," *Los Angeles Times*, April 1, 1999, B9; Pollin, *The Living Wage: Building a Fair Economy* (New York: Free Press, 1998).

16. National Organization for Women, *Out of the Shadows: Strategies for Expanding State Labor and Civil Rights Protections for Domestic Workers* (New York: NOW Legal Defense and Education Fund, 1997), Appendix A: The Fair Labor Standards Act. See also Linda Martin and Kerry Seagrave, *The Servant Problem: Domestic Workers in North America* (Jefferson, N.C.: McFarlands, 1985); Rollins, *Between Women*.

17. Katharine A. Schmidt, "Domestic Workers Note Abuse, Low Pay," *Santa Monica Outlook*, Nov. 5, 1991, A1, A3; Tracy Wilkinson, "To Protect Those Who Must Serve," *Los Angeles Times*, Feb. 2, 1992, A1, A12; Doreen Carvajal, "For Immigrant Maids, Not a Job but Servitude," *New York Times*, Feb. 25, 1995, C1, C19. In 1988 domestic workers belonging to unions in 11 countries met in Bogota, Colombia, to form the Confederation of Household Workers in the Caribbean and Latin America (CONLATRAHO). In March 1999 they held their inter-American meetings in Mexico City with organized domestic workers from the United States, including representatives from the Domestic Workers' Association of CHIRLA. See the essays by Thelma Galvez and Rosalba Todoro, Mary Goldsmith, Magdelena Leon, and Suzana Prates in *Muchachas No More: Household Workers in Latin America and the Caribbean*, ed. Elsa M. Chaney and Mary Garcia Castro (Philadelphia: Temple University Press, 1989).

18. On early organizing efforts and on the NCHE, see Palmer, *Domesticity and Dirt*; Romero, *Maid in the U.S.A.*; and Phyllis Palmer, "Housework and Domestic Labor: Racial and Technological Change," in *My Troubles Are Going to have Trouble with Me*, ed. Karen Brodkin Sacks and Dorothy Remy (New Brunswick, N.J.: Rutgers University Press, 1984), 80–91.

19. The 1974 amendment passed partly because of a vociferous bloc of women representatives in Congress (Shirley Chisholm, Marjorie S. Holt, Leonor K. Sullivan, Yvonne Brathwaite Burke, Patsy T. Mink, Julia Butler Hansen, Edith Green, Martha W. Griffiths, Ella T. Grasso, Bella S. Abzug, Elizabeth Holtzman, Barbara Jordan, and Patrica Schroeder). Their rhetoric framed the amendment as part of a national initiative to fight poverty: they wished to include domestic workers under the FLSA so that domestic workers would be kept above poverty levels and off public assistance; H.R. Res. No. 93-913, 93d Cong., 2d sess. 2842–2844; see their letter quoted in NOW, *Out of the Shadows*, 2.

20. The decline of the NCHE and the entry of Latina and Caribbean immigrant women into U.S. domestic work coincided with the exodus from the occupation of African American women (especially young women) after the civil rights era. Many U.S.-born women of color left private household work for jobs in cafeterias, offices (as janitors), hotels, and restaurants, jobs that one scholar refers to as "public reproductive work"; Evelyn Nakano Glenn, "From Servitude to Service Work: Historical Continuities in the Racial Division of Women's Work," *Signs* 18 (1992), 1–43. The United Domestic Workers Alliance was another important worker-based effort aimed at organizing workers in private homes. It began in San Diego, inspired by César

Chávez and the UFW. Later, it pursued collective bargaining for home care workers who care for the elderly in private homes. [For more on the UDWA, see Eileen Boris and Jennifer Klein, *Caring for America: Home Health Workers in the Shadow of the Welfare State* (New York: Oxford University Press, 2012), 143–48, 207–208, 212.]

21. On wage levels, see Nancy Cleeland, "Garment Jobs: Hard, Bleak, and Vanishing," *Los Angeles Times*, March 11, 1999, A1, A14–16. On the numbers of garment workers and the rise of the sweatshop apparel industry, see Edna Bonacich and Richard P. Appelbaum, *Behind the Label: Inequality in the Los Angeles Apparel Industry* (Berkeley: University of California Press, 2000).

22. Jennifer Gordon, "Immigrants Fight the Power," *The Nation*, Jan. 3, 2000, 16–20.

23. See Andrew Ross, ed., *No Sweat: Fashion, Free Trade, and the Rights of Garment Workers* (New York: Verson, 1997).

ASHRAF ZAHEDI
Muslim American Women After 9/11

The date September 11, 2001, has become a defining moment in U.S. history. On that day, four airplanes crossing U.S. territory were hijacked by al-Qaeda terrorists. Two of the planes flew into and collapsed the twin towers of the World Trade Center. Another targeted the Pentagon, and a fourth was brought down by passengers before it could be used as a weapon. In response, the government launched a global war on terrorism, targeting al-Qaeda, the organization responsible for the attacks.

Critics have noted that the war on terrorism has often been conflated with war on Islam. The term Islamaphobia has been coined to describe this intense fear and hatred of Muslims and Muslim culture. In addition, non-Muslims, such as Sikhs, have been mistaken for Muslims and targeted for violence.

Ashraf Zahedi's essay explores how Muslim women in the United States have navigated this fraught political landscape. Zahedi, a sociologist, interviewed women of diverse ethnic, racial, and national backgrounds as part of her research. She also draws on images of Muslim women in the mainstream media and in political discourse, and she tells us about women's leadership roles in several American Muslim organizations. Skewering the classic European assumption that veiled Muslim women are passive, uneducated, and monolithically oppressed, Zahedi underscores the variability in contemporary veiling practices. More importantly, we see the wide range of issues about which Muslim women are concerned. As with all the essays and documents in this book, think about how you could use her findings to contradict misinformation and spark constructive dialogue.

The events of 11 September 2001 are clearly marked as transformative events in the history of the United States of America. These events shattered Americans' sense of security and heightened their anxiety. While the majority of Americans feared potential future terrorist attacks, Muslim Americans not only feared such attacks but also feared attacks from their fellow Americans.

Unfortunately, this was not an unfounded fear. Many Americans associated Muslim Americans with the attackers who happened to be Muslims. Public frustration and misplaced anger, in many cases, have led to violence against

Excerpted from "Muslim American Women in the Post-11 September Era" by Ashraf Zahedi in *International Feminist Journal of Politics* 13, no. 2 (June 2011): 183–203. Reprinted with permission of the author and publisher. Notes have been edited.

Muslim men and women or those perceived as Muslims, such as Sikh men wearing turbans and beards. They have been chased, attacked verbally and attacked physically, resulting in a number of deaths, Among Muslim women, those wearing headscarves or the hijab were the most identifiable Muslims and got the brunt of the hate and harassment.

Concerned with the negative public perception of Islam and Muslims, some Muslim women have retreated to their own communities. Other women, however, have chosen to engage non-Muslims and serve as public educators. They have used public spaces available to them to explain their religion, affirm their membership in American society, and assert their identities as Muslim, American and women. This has been a major shift from keeping a low socio-political profile, as had been the case before 11 September, to demonstrating their integration in American society and claiming their place in civic and political spaces.

This [essay] seeks to explain the socio-political dimension of "Otherization" of Muslim women and examines the impact of the 11 September events on their lives. These events paradoxically posed challenges to their civil rights as American citizens while serving to present them with opportunities to engage with Americans at large and move from the margin to the mainstream. Their efforts in engaging Americans, however, have been hampered by discriminatory anti-Muslim sentiments including racial profiling and hate crimes. Their efforts have also been eclipsed by two opposing discourses on Muslim women, Orientalism and Islamic fundamentalism, which essentialize the image and meaning of Muslim womanhood. Despite the odds, Muslim American women have been taking an active role in simultaneously challenging and changing the singular image imposed on them by Orientalists and fundamentalists alike and carving a space for themselves as Muslim American women.

Following 11 September, many Muslims and ethnic minorities experienced racial profiling, hatred and hate crimes; however, the focus of this article is hijab-wearing immigrant Muslim American women. Although African-American Muslim women observe the hijab as well, their head covers and style of wearing the hijab draw on African tradition and reflect their African-American identity. Often they do not cover their ears and necks while hijab-wearing immigrant Muslim women do. The difference in style of hijab signifies their different ethnic identity. Hijab-wearing first- and second-generation immigrant Muslim women are more likely to be associated with Islam and foreignness. What is more, African-American Muslims and immigrant Muslims have different ethno-racial histories and are divided on ethnicity, race, social class, and claims of Islamic authenticity and American nativism. While both groups have experienced ethnic, racial and religious discrimination, . . . "after 9/11 it was better to be African Americans than immigrant Muslims." African-Americans were regarded more as Americans and less as Muslims while the opposite was true for immigrant Muslim Americans.[1] Thus the latter have been the subject of mistrust and misplaced anger following 11 September. With these differences in mind, I have chosen to focus on immigrant Muslim women, both the first generation and second generation born in the United States.

. . . I have drawn on different research methods. . . . I have consulted the reports of Muslim civic and community organizations, attended Muslims' public events, reviewed academic literature, and interviewed twenty-four first- and second-generation immigrant Muslim women. The interviews were semi-structured and conducted individually. In conducting this research, I have drawn upon my training as a sociologist, my religious background as a Muslim woman and my relations with Muslim organizations.

I have changed interviewees' names to protect their identities. These women belong to diverse ethnic, racial, and national backgrounds. Their national origins are: Pakistan; India; Bangladesh; Syria; Palestine; Sudan; Eritrea; and Montenegro (former Yugoslavia). The interviewees were mostly middle class and college educated, as these are often the characteristics of the members of formal community and civic organizations. Their age ranged from 23 to 50 and all except two of them wear the hijab. They work for Muslim organizations in different capacities: as staff, attorney and board members. . . .

Muslims have had a long history in the United States. Amber Haque believes that the "first Muslims may have arrived in the Americas as early as 1178, when Chinese Muslim sailors landed on the West Coast." Of the estimated 6 to 10 million African slaves who came to the United States in later centuries, about 30 percent of them were Muslims. Arab Muslims migrated to America between 1870 and World War II. They came from Greater Syria (Syria, Lebanon, the Palestinians, Israel, Jordan and possibly Iraq), which was under Ottoman rule. Since World War II, and particularly after the long-standing national origin quota was repealed and the Immigration Act of 1965 was adopted, Muslim migration to the United States has increased significantly. Political upheavals, wars, and revolutions have expedited Muslims' migration from all over the world.[2]

American Muslims enjoy a great diversity. According to the Council on American-Islamic Relations, "The three major ethnic groups in the Muslim community are South Asian (32 percent), Arabs (26 percent) and African American (20 percent)." The remaining Muslims come from Africa and Europe. Of the estimated 6 to 7 million Muslim Americans, 36 percent were born in the United States and 64 percent were born in eighty different countries around the world. They are indeed a microcosm of the Muslim world. They have higher levels of education than average Americans and thus enjoy higher incomes and are professionally and economically integrated.[3]

Despite Muslims' long presence in the United States and their diversity in terms of ethnicity, race, national origin, social class, and gender, the American public tends to view them as homogenized and as an undifferentiated distinct religious community. Some Muslims have been in the United States for generations but are still viewed as outsiders . . . and as the perpetual "Other."[4]

Much like the Europeans, the Americans' perceptions of the Muslim Other were shaped by the ideology of the Crusades Wars, which promoted the superiority of Christianity. Christian missionaries were important players in shaping these perceptions by providing "the lens through which" people of the West saw Muslims.[5] Americans' views of Muslims had also been influenced by the European colonial constructs of the colonized as less civilized people who led inferior religious and social lives compared to the Europeans: these constructs justified Europe's civilizing mission. . . .

The United States inherited the European Orientalist legacy and over time constructed its own. Scores of scholars have examined this construct and how Orientalism has made its way into American culture. Nineteenth-century American literature (novels, travel books,

missionary reports and books and political writings) has contributed to the making of American Orientalism. These literary works have been, to varying degrees, tainted by the authors' Orientalist views and ideological biases portraying the people of the so-called Orient, including Muslims, as inferior and unworthy others. Many travel writers . . . "focused on the picturesqueness and exoticism of the 'backward' Eastern races." The much-celebrated Mark Twain whose books were widely read viewed Muslims as "a people by nature and training filthy, brutish, ignorant, unprogressive [and] superstitious."[6]

Through text and images, the widely circulated magazine, *National Geographic*, contributed to the construct of American Orientalism by depicting African, Asians, Arabs, and Muslims as backward. The film industry has also been a significant player in the dissemination of Orientalist ideology. . . . Hollywood popular movies and television sitcoms have caricaturized Muslims, continuously casting their Muslim characters as villains, violent and fanatical. . . .[7]

What is more, Orientalist ideology is reflected in political writings and the view of many American political writers and politicians, . . . [often shaping] US foreign policy toward Muslim countries. Sharing this mindset, the American mass media have constructed a negative image of Muslims and justified unfair American policies in the region. Moreover, they have characterized the national aspirations and political struggles of the people of the Muslim world as violent acts of terrorism. In short, they have demonized the political forces critical of the United States.[8]

Unfortunately, the events of 11 September and the religious background of the attackers have intensified negative perceptions about Muslims. Now Muslims are associated with terrorism, and Islam as a belief system is blamed. Islam is generally perceived as archaic, barbaric, irrational and a "religion of violence and aggression that supports terrorism."[9]

Muslim women have shared the sociopolitical characterization of "Other" imposed on them. Yet, the Otherization of Muslim women has had a gender dimension as well. The Muslim female body, covered by the veil, serves as context for Otherization. Western perceptions of the veil and the social meaning they have assigned to it have led westerners to view the veil as symbolic of Muslim women's oppression. They have reduced the multifaceted oppression of women in the Islamic world to the veil and concealment of the female body.

Although the veil is often associated with Islam, research indicates that veiling, as a status symbol, was practiced in Persia and the Byzantine before the advent of Islam. The practice of veiling, as a form of modesty, was observed in some Jewish and Christian communities as well. Early Muslims appropriated the veil as a result of their exposure to the cultures of conquered countries.[10]

In most contemporary Muslim countries, the practice of veiling has limited application and many observant Muslim women wear head scarves along with loose clothing, the hijab. Only two Muslim countries have mandatory veil (Saudi Arabia) and hijab (Iran); yet in the western mind, the image of Muslim women has been tied to the singular image of the veil. Western perceptions of the veil, as will be discussed, continue to essentialize Muslim women. In the veil or hijab, Muslim women are perceived as passive, oppressed and at the mercy of the male members of their family. Like many Muslim women throughout the world, Muslim American women challenge this portrayal.

Muslim American women, like other Americans, were devastated by the human tragedy of 11 September. They joined the search and rescue efforts; they donated money and blood. They mourned the death and destruction. They affirmed their loyalty to America, condemned acts of terror and reached out to other Americans; yet the legal system that was supposed to protect them worked to their disadvantage.

Drawing on public support for civil rights limitations for Muslims and building on the existing feeling of Otherization of Muslims, the House and Senate, without much critical discussion, passed the USA-Patriot Act (Uniting and Strengthening America by Providing Appropriate Tools Required to Intercept and Obstruct Terrorism Act of 2001). The Patriot Act expanded the power of the US government. This expansion of power allowed the government, in the name of security, to wire tap Muslims' conversations, seize their property, and freeze their bank accounts.[11]

In the politically and emotionally charged environment of post-11 September, some directed their frustration and anger toward Muslims. According to the FBI, the number of hate crimes against Muslims rose from twenty-eight in 2000 to 481 in 2001, a seventeen fold increase. Hate crimes caused the deaths of Muslim and

Sikh men. The Council on American-Islamic Relations, a Muslim civil rights organization, reported 1,717 incidents of "backlash discrimination against Muslims" between 11 September 2000 and February 2001. Hate incidents ranged from verbal assault to damage to property to vandalism of mosques and Muslim organizations.[12]

Hijab-wearing women received the brunt of hate incidents in the first few years after 11 September. As a result, some women stayed home, others went out only in groups or in the company of non-Muslims. Muslim organizations and mosques developed safety tips for women and children. . . . While sharing the national pains of 11 September, they also had to endure the pain of being suspects, thereby carrying multiple burdens. Many women's husbands, fathers, brothers and sons were detained based on the Patriot Act.[13] . . . These women had to deal with the emotional, legal, political and financial impacts of their male relatives' detention. In the climate of hyper-patriotism, their troubles did not get much public attention. Rather, the public scene was saturated with images and symbols of American unity: American flags were displayed everywhere— houses, shops, buildings and even cars. Some people wore t-shirts with the American flag on the front and patriotic phrases on the back. Assortments of merchandise with flags or patriotic slogans flooded the market. In that political climate, some Americans did not view Muslim Americans as belonging to America and challenged their American-ness. Many Muslims shared conflicting feelings like those of Noor, one of the interviewees for this research: "I recall particularly the level of anger that existed, and the way in which American patriotism felt like an assault on ethnic and religious minorities. The number of flags waving everywhere was on the one hand reassuring, but on the other felt like a political statement against immigrants and non-Christian Americans."

Ironically, the hijab that was supposed to bring Muslim women anonymity brought unwanted attention. As Noor remarked, "Every day since 9/11 has reminded me vividly that I will never be anonymous again." A large number of the Muslim women I interviewed experienced stares, dirty looks, verbal attack, name-calling, harassment, and hate incidents. In the hijab, they were, as Noor put it, a "moving target." Twenty-two out of twenty-four interviewees indicated that they were yelled at, chased or tail-gated on high-ways, and told to "go back to your country." Some men spat on women's head-scarves or tried to pull them off.... "Some people tried to light the tips of the scarves with a match to set them on fire."[14] Women I interviewed recalled unpleasant experiences: "I was verbally harassed by a car-load of college-aged guys while I was at an ATM machine, and I've been told to go back to my country more times than I can remember," said Noor. "The worse thing for me has been people yelling out of passing cars," ... remarked Sarah....

... [Due to the] many incidents of hate and discrimination target[ing] women in the hijab, discussions ensued in mosques, Islamic organizations, and on the Internet over the viability of wearing the hijab and the safety of Muslim women. A fatwa or religious decree was issued [by the Muslim Women's League] according to which it was permissible for women to remove their hijab: "If a Muslim woman senses a possibility of danger to herself, adjusting her attire to minimize the chances of physical attack is a logical and Islamically permissible precaution that falls squarely within the Fiqh [Islamic jurisprudence] principles of necessity and hardship."Muslim leaders validated "Muslim women wearing non-obvious alternative attire such as hats in public."[15]

Interestingly, the harassment of women wearing the hijab had different outcomes. Some took off the hijab; others, however, were more determined to exert their religious identity. Karima, for example, chose to take off her hijab: "Hijab is supposed to provide you with safety; it no longer did, so I removed my hijab," she remarked. Actually, many did, but with much hesitation and with a sense of being disempowered by the hostile political environment. At the same time, other women chose to wear the hijab. Shabana pointed out, "Other Muslim women felt empowered and started wearing the hijab shortly after 9/11." Mahbooba resisted the temptation to take off her hijab: "Even my husband thought at one point that I should [remove my hijab]; however, I refused to give up my Islamic identity." For women such as Mahbooba, the hijab symbolizes their choice of self-presentation and assertion of their identity.

Fortunately, Muslim Americans' experiences with the American public have not been all negative: many non-Muslim Americans, driven by a strong sense of justice and morality, extended their support to Muslim Americans. One of the highly praised expressions of solidarity with Muslim women was the Scarf Campaign. Jennifer Schock came up with this idea as "a simple gesture of solidarity with Muslim women"; she invited non-Muslim women to wear headscarves for a day. She wanted to convey to Muslim women that they are "not alone." Schock's Scarf Campaign created an opportunity for interaction and dialogue between Muslims and non-Muslims. On 8 October 2001, non-Muslim women donned scarves in many cities through out the United States. They gathered in churches, mosques, community centers, and schools to show their solidarity with Muslim women.[16]

Many Muslim American organizations and individuals shared stories of support and sympathy from their neighbors, community members, and interfaith groups: they have received cards, phone messages, and flowers. Across the county, non-Muslim women volunteered to chaperone Muslim women to shopping, medical appointments, and schools to pick up their children. Zarina echoed the appreciation expressed by many Muslim women: "I was pleasantly surprised by the number of average Americans who reached out to us to let us know they stood with us and they were not falling prey to the climate of fear that was quickly taking over the country."

During these trying times, Muslim women established strong ties with other women with whom they otherwise may not have socialized. These newly found friendships have been very important to Muslim women. Noor put it nicely: "The deep and meaningful and dear friendship I have developed with many Christian and Jews and atheists have had a profound impact on my life, my perception of myself, my community and my faith. I wouldn't trade this enhanced self-awareness for anything."

Yet hate incidents continue to be documented. Although ten years have passed since 11 September 2001, anti-Muslim sentiments remain high due to the American led wars in Afghanistan and Iraq. Displaced anger in the wake of the unsuccessful wars and large numbers of American war casualties has continued to target Muslim Americans. Nevertheless, Muslim American women have continued to speak at interfaith gatherings, appear on television, take part in radio programs, and provide training for corporations, health care providers, and law enforcement authorities. Despite their efforts, a singular, one-dimensional image continues to be projected on them by Orientalists and Islamic fundamentalists. . . .

The predominant image that outsiders have of Muslim women is one swathed in the veil/hijab. This constructed singular image has overshadowed the racial, ethnic, national, and cultural diversity of Muslim women. Their entire existence has been reduced to their public attire. Yet not all Muslims agree on the Islamic mandate of this attire and draw on Quranic verses to support their position. Many Islamic scholars, such as Leila Ahmed Asma Barlas, and Riffat Hassan, contest the universal use of the hijab and thus do not observe it.[17]

Muslim women choosing the hijab or the veil have emotional, socio-political, and religious rationales for this. The hijab can be functional, providing safety and generating respect. Observing the hijab can serve to gain access to resources and opportunities. Some women use the hijab as a means of "negotiating with patriarchy" and appropriate it to their own advantage. Observing the hijab can secure conservative families' consent, allowing their female members to get an education and seek employment, which in turn can lead to the empowerment of Muslim women. Wearing the hijab can serve as a symbol of political and cultural resistance against the West, as has been the case in Egypt, Turkey and Iran. Some women may use the hijab to challenge the tyranny of fashion and the sexualization of the female body. And last, but not least, wearing the hijab can be based on Muslim women's strong beliefs and their piety.[18]

Muslim women challenge the singular meaning that westerners assign to the hijab and their perception of the veil/hijab as a univocal symbol of women's oppression. As Yasmeen remarked, "Muslim women are viewed as illogical for choosing or complying with a religion that is viewed as oppressive towards women." All interviewees expressed their disappointment with many western feminists for their limited understanding of the hijab and Islam and their views of Muslim women as oppressed victims who need to be saved.

Saving Muslim women has served as an integral part of Orientalist/colonial ideologies. Many scholars have therefore challenged the notion of the Christian West saving supposedly oppressed Muslim women. The scholars ask, "do Muslim women need saving?" And what are Muslim women saved from? Inherent to the

concept of saving is the given-ness of the power play: the superiority of the savior and the inferiority of the subjects in need of saving. . . . This form of western "compassion" effectively creates a hierarchy between women and assigns positive meanings to the lives of western women and negative meanings to Muslim ones. Dichotomous notions such as "veiled/unveiled, Islamic/secular, Western/non-Western, and free/unfree" both signify and legitimize this hierarchy.[19]

Despite their criticism of Orientalist feminism and the lack support from American feminists following the tragedy of 11 September, some of the Muslim women I interviewed expressed their willingness to work with American feminists. "While I obviously don't agree with all the premises and goals of western feminism, I do feel there are common challenges. We can stand together against [these challenges] as long as we have clear understanding of Islam's goals for women," Iman remarked. Noor agreed: "I have not worked with [American feminists] nor have they reached out to me . . . I am not opposed to working with them because there is value to exchanging ideas and experiences in order to enhance mutual understanding."

Yet, many interviewees pointed out that they do not share some western feminists' prioritizing of gender over other forms of inequality. Much like other women of color, these women support "the basic premise of universal gender equality but reject the prioritization of gender over race and class." They are engaged in multiple sites of struggle and gender is a part of their struggle. Overall, interviewees expressed a preference for working with third-wave feminists who incorporate the issues of race, ethnicity, nationality, sexuality, and social class in their gender analysis.[20]

. . . Although some Muslim women are inclined to work with western feminists, others have a limited knowledge of western feminism, its struggles, and its achievements. Jahan's statement that "western feminism does not appeal to me" and Fatama's remark that "I have all the rights in Islam and do not need western feminism" . . . [obscure the possibility that there might be] much to be learned from western feminism. It seems that some Muslim women, while objecting to the essentializing of Muslim women by westerners, do not hesitate to essentialize western feminists. . . . Western feminists are viewed as anti-family, anti-men, self-centered, and consumed with sexual liberation. These Muslim women's views are influenced by misinformation propagated by conservative forces, secular and religious, of their own communities.[21] . . .

Mainstream western feminists, for their part, will benefit from jettisoning their notion of saving Muslim women and freeing them from oppression. Women's oppression is not a creation of Islam; it is an aspect of patriarchy shared by other religions that have not completed the process of reformation. Islamic reformation has been truncated as a result of western domination and resistance to it. Resistance to foreign domination has diverted national attention to external threats and effectively masked domestic forms of gender oppression. . . .

Many western feminists are driven by their empathy for Muslim women as oppressed women, yet, . . . empathy "does not necessarily lead to insight."[22] Women's oppression has socio-economic, political, and cultural bases and manifests itself in different forms and degrees. Assigning meaning to the female body, covered or concealed, as a site of liberation or oppression is misleading and serves to prevent Muslim women's alliances with women of the West. Liberation and oppression are multilayered and dynamic. Understanding the complexity, . . . is essential for women's alliances. What is more, western women can make an important contribution to the status of Muslim women by demanding that their own governments pursue fair socio-economic and political policies in Muslim societies. By doing so, they can disarm Muslim forces, secular and religious, that have undermined women's rights in the guise of protecting Muslim women. One such force is Islamic fundamentalists.

Islamic fundamentalists aim to construct a singular image of Muslim women. In line with other forms of religious fundamentalism—whether Jewish, Christian, or Hindu—Islamic fundamentalism's agenda for women is framed in the language of care and protection. Control of women is an important element of fundamentalist movements. This control, fundamentalists claim, is for women's good and they have carefully selected self-serving religious texts to support their claim. Fundamentalists tend to refer to religious texts rigidly and literally and to project their interpretation of religious texts as the sole truth: final and unchangeable. Although Islamic fundamentalists tend to favor "puritan and literalist trends

within the Islamic ideological, social, and political traditions," not all of them adhere to extremism and violence. Nevertheless, all Islamic fundamentalists claim to have a monopoly on the truth about Islam and the status of women in Islam. Their truth, however, has been shaped by a patriarchal mindset and misogynist practices. Islamic fundamentalists have constructed one image of Muslim womanhood that is in sharp contrast with multiple images and identities of Muslim women and their varied life experiences.[23]

Muslim women scholars criticize fundamentalists' vision and definition of women and challenge their interpretation of Islamic texts. Azizah Al-Hibri believes that Muslims are bound only by the Qur'an and not its patriarchal interpretations. These scholars argue in favor of historicizing and contextualizing the religious texts; ijtihad, . . . [or adopting] critical thinking that corresponds to the changing times, is central to their arguments . . . Ijtihad "involves a process of recontextualizing the Qur'an through new modes of reading none of which can exhaust it meanings. Verses of the Qur'an fundamentalists rely on so heavily need to be historicised and contextualized rather than blindly followed." Riffat Hassan makes a similar statement: "In every age the Qur'an had to be reread and recontextualized."[24] Islamic fundamentalists, however, stand firm against reform in Islam and, correspondingly, against any change in the status of Muslim women. They have used harsh words for Muslim women who challenge them, accusing them of being agents of western colonialism and working against Islamic societies. . . . Fundamentalists' ideal of authentic Islamic culture can only exist outside history. As the Islam of the seventh century entered different regions and built on existing cultures and traditions, many Islamic cultures emerged. Muslim women of these varying regions and cultures have different views about their Islamic culture and the notion of authenticity. Yet, this belief in authenticizing Muslim women has been shared by some fundamentalist members of Muslim American communities and has impacted gender relations within Muslim American organizations.[25]

Muslim American organizations have played a major role in reaching out to the American public and presenting a peaceful image of Islam and Muslim communities. Embedded in the image of Islam has been the image of hijab-wearing women. The hijab and the status of Muslim women have been of great interest to the American public and Muslim organizations have created opportunities for Muslim women's engagement with non-Muslims. Although the primary interest of these organizations has been the defense of Islam, the attire of these women has kept gender in the spotlight.

Faced with a barrage of questions about the status of women in Islam, many Muslim women have increased their knowledge of Islam and different interpretations of the Qur'an. Some acknowledge that certain beliefs and attitudes have had a negative impact on the social standing of women in the family and society; they often attribute these negative outcomes to pre-Islamic customs and cultures. These women believe the Qur'an has granted equal status to men and women, but that the male interpretations of the Qur'an and Hadith (the sayings and deeds of Prophet Muhammad) have led to social and economic disadvantages for women. They have been revisiting Islamic laws with a new vigor, analyzing the Qur'an, and extracting verses that support gender equality. With knowledge of Islam and dedication to the faith, Muslim American women have been serving as public educators.

As my interviewees and I have observed, Muslim American organizations have experienced an increase in women's participation after 11 September. These women, moved by their own agency and the desire to depict an accurate picture of a true Islam, have been engaged at every level of civic activity, some becoming the public face of their organizations. However, although there has been a significant increase in Muslim women's civic participation, the majority of these women have been volunteers and not part of a decision-making body. Even those in paid positions often lack organizational authority. Like other organizations, secular and religious, glass ceilings have been at play in Muslim American organizations. The interplay of gender, financial resources, and politics has kept many women out of the boardrooms. Since major donors to Muslim organizations are often men, they tend to support the board membership of men and prefer men for important organizational positions. Some women who have experienced this glass ceiling have chosen to form their own organizations. In small women-run organizations such as the Muslim Women's League and Muslim Women's Lawyers for Human Rights,

women do fill the boardrooms and exercise organizational authority. . . .

. . . The increased number of women board members of local chapters of the Council on American-Islamic Relations (CAIR), and the recent election of Ingrid Mattson, a hijab-wearing Canadian-American Muslim convert, to the presidency of one of the largest Muslim organization in the USA, the Islamic Association of North American (ISNA), testify to changing tides. The glass ceiling may be broken [once] but the question remains: is Mattson in a position to advance gender issues? Wafa, [one interviewee,] believed Mattson "cannot afford to focus on women. She cannot alienate the others [men]. She is the first woman and needs to succeed to be politically effective (given the conservative framework of the ISNA)." . . .

While some smaller organizations such as the Muslim Women's League, Muslim Women Lawyers for Human Rights, and the American Society for Muslim Advancement have both hijab-wearing and non-hijab-wearing women on the board, women in hijab are still the dominant image of Muslim woman in larger Muslim organizations. Although non-hijab-wearing women staff these organizations, the two prominent Muslim organizations, CAIR and ISNA, have only hijab-wearing women officially representing them. Hijab-wearing Noor [commented].

> Who gets to speak for Islam and Muslims with credibility and authority and truth has become only more complex since 9/11, particularly for women. Many mainstream Muslim leaders and organizations have been hesitant at least, and downright oppositional at worst, to the possibility of a non-hijab-wearing Muslim women speaker representing Islam. This symbol of modesty has become more and more a construction of Muslim womanhood—and has therefore placed a difficult question before Muslim women in public roles on behalf of the community . . . women feel obligated to wear hijab because of their public role.

In a way, the hijab, . . . "has become the litmus test of a Muslim women's piety" and those not "covering their hair and throat are judged as women" who have not reached the ideal "level of devotion to God." Some Muslim American organizations have promoted the hijab as an essential aspect of Muslim women's image and identity. Non-hijab-wearing Muslim women are highly critical of this singular image of Muslim women: they believe, as Saba said, that "beliefs are personal and private and should not be publicly displayed. I do not want to wear my beliefs outside. I am a Muslim but hijab does not define me or my beliefs." They would like to see multiple images of Muslim women being allowed to surface at the high levels of Muslim American organizations.[26]

In the post-11 September era, Muslim American women have played an important role in shaping public perception of Islam and women in Islam. They are in a position to redefine the meaning of women in Islam, thereby shaping the meaning of American Islam. American Islam, in turn, has the potential to inspire the quest for reform in Islam worldwide. The amazing diversity of Muslim American women allows them to be culturally connected to all parts of the world and yet be truly Americans. Their unique position as Muslims and as believers in American values—liberty, personal rights, and democracy—provides them with a great opportunity to be agents of change both in the United States and, by extension, the world over.

NOTES

1. Sherman A. Jackson, *Islam and the Blackamerican: Looking toward the Third Resurrection* (Oxford: Oxford University Press, 2005); Jamillah Karim, *American Muslim Women: Negotiating Race and Gender with the Ummah* (New York: New York University Press, 2008), 40.

2. Amber Haque, "Islamophobia in North America: Confronting the Menace," in Barry Van Dreil, ed., *Confronting Islamophobia in Educational Practice* (Oakhill, Va.: Trentham Books, 2004), 1–18, quotation on 4. On post-1870 migration, see Michael W. Suleiman, ed., *Arabs in America: Building a New Future* (Philadelphia, Penn.: Temple University Press, 1999), 2.

3. Council on American-Islamic Relations (CAIR), "Western Muslim Minorities: Integration and Disenfranchisement," Policy Bulletin, April 26, 2–3. Available at http://www.cair.com/Portals/0/pdf/policy_bulletin_integration_in_the_West.pdf (accessed Oct. 19, 2009).

4. Sam Afridi, "Muslims in America: Identity, Diversity, and the Challenge of Understanding," Carnegie Corporation of New York, 2001, 2. Available at http://carnegie.org/fileadmin/Media/Publications/PDF/muslims.pdf.

5. Yvonne Yazeck Haddad, Jane I. Smith, and Kathleen M. Moore, *Muslim Women in America: The Challenge of Islamic Identity Today* (Oxford: Oxford University Press, 2006), 24.

6. Twain quoted in Douglas Little, *American Orientalism* (Chapel Hill: University of North Carolina Press, 2002), 13. On Orientalism in the U.S. and elsewhere, see Edward Said, *Orientalism* (New York: Vintage, 1979); Malini Johar Schueller, "Orientalism," in Janet Gabler-Hover and Robert Sattelmeyer, eds., *American History through Literature, 1820–1920*

(New York: Charles Scribner's Sons, 2006), 839; and Amira Jarmakani, *Imagining Arab Womanhood: The Cultural Mythology of Veils, Harems, and Belly Dancers in the U.S.* (New York: Palgrave Macmillan, 2008).

7. Little, *American Orientalism*, 10; Haddad et al., *Muslim Women in America*, 22. A few examples of popular movies are *The Sheik* (1921), *Aladdin* (1992), *Executive Decision* (1996), *The Siege* (1998), and *Rules of Engagement* (2000).

8. Little, *American Orientalism*; Zachary Lockman, *Contending Visions of the Middle East: The History and Politics of Orientalism* (Cambridge: Cambridge University Press, 2004); Suad Joseph, "Against the Grain of the Nation: The Arab," in Suleiman, *Arabs in America*, 257–71.

9. Haque, "Islamophobia in North America," 3.

10. Practice of veiling: John L. Esposito, ed., *The Oxford Encyclopedia of the Modern Islamic World*, 4 vols. (New York: Oxford University Press, 1995), 2:108; Guity Nashat, "Women in Pre-Islamic and Early Islamic Iran," in Guity Nashat and Lois Beck, eds., *Women in Iran from the Rise of Islam to 1800* (Urbana: University of Illinois Press, 2003), 38.

11. Louise Cainkar, "The Impact of the September 11 Attacks and Their Aftermath on Arab and Muslim Communities in the United States," *Global Security and Cooperation (GSC) Quarterly* 13 (Summer–Fall 2004): 1.

12. Human Rights Watch, "'We Are Not the Enemy': Hate Crimes Against Arabs, Muslims, and Those Perceived to Be Arab or Muslim after September 11" (Nov. 14, 2002), available at http://www.hrw.org/sites/default/files/reports/usa1102.pdf.

13. See the Council on American-Islamic Relations (CAIR) website: http://www.cair.com/american-muslims/67-cair-muslim-community-safety-kit.html.

14. Scarves on fire: Sandy Banks, "Donning Scarves in Solidarity," *Los Angeles Times*, Sept. 25, 2001.

15. Muslim Women's League, "Muslim Dress in Dangerous Times" (2001), available at http://www.mwlusa.org/topics/Sept11/hijab_dangerous_times.htm (accessed 19 Oct. 2009).

16. Chris L. Coryn, James M. Beale, and Krista M. Myers, "Response to September 11: Anxiety, Patriotism, and Prejudice in the Aftermath of Terror," *Current Research in Social Psychology* 9:12 (Dec. 2004): 165–84. Scarf campaign: Banks, "Donning Scarves."

17. Leila Ahmed, *Women and Gender in Islam: Historical Roots of a Modern Debate* (New Haven, Conn.: Yale University Press, 1992); Asma Barlas, *"Believing Women" in Islam: Unreading Patriarchal Interpretations of the Qur'an* (Austin: University of Texas Press, 2002); Riffat Hassan, "Interview with Dawn Newspaper of Pakistan Regarding the Role of Religion and Status of Women in Pakistan, January 2003," in Fawzia Afzah-Khan, ed., *Shattering the Stereotypes: Muslim Women Speak Out* (Northampton, Mass.: Olive Branch Press, 2005), 184–91.

18. Arlene Elowe Macleod, *Accommodating Protest: Working Women, the New Veiling, and Change in Cairo* (New York: Columbia University Press, 1991); Fadwa El Guindi, *Veil: Modesty, Privacy and Resistance* (Oxford: Berg, 1999); Faegheh Shirazi, *The Veil Unveiled: The Hijab in Modern Culture* (Gainesville: University Press of Florida, 2001); Saba Mahmood, *Politics of Piety: The Islamic Revival and the Feminist Subject* (Princeton, N.J.: Princeton University Press,

2004); Ashraf Zahedi, "Contested Meaning of the Veil and Political Ideologies of Iranian Regimes," *Journal of Middle East Women's Studies* 3 (March 2007), 75–98; Deniz Kandiyoti, "Bargaining with Patriarchy," *Gender and Society* 2:3 (Sept. 1988): 274–90; Lila Abu-Lughod, "Do Muslim Women Really Need Saving? Anthropological Reflections on Cultural Relativism and Its Others," *American Anthropologist* 104 (March 2002): 787.

19. Shahnaz Khan, *Muslim Women: Crafting North American Identity* (Gainesville: University Press of Florida, 2000), 5; Abu-Lughod, "Do Muslim Women Really Need Saving?" 783, 788; Mahmood, *Politics of Piety*, 189; Haddad, et al., *Muslim Women in America*, 146; Minoo Moallem, *Between Warrior Brother and Veiled Sister: Islamic Fundamentalism and the Politics of Patriarchy in Iran* (Berkeley: University of California Press, 2005), 16.

20. Carolyn Rouse, *Engaged Surrender: African American Women and Islam* (Berkeley: University of California Press, 2004), 143.

21. Shahrzad Mojab, "The Politics of Theorizing 'Islamic Feminism': Implications for International Feminist Movements," WLUML (Women Living under Muslim Laws) Dossier 23–24 (July 2001), available at http://www.wluml.org/node/344.

22. Corinne Fowler, "Journalists in Feminist Clothing: Men and Women Reporting Afghan Women during Operation Enduring Freedom, 2001" *Journal of International Women's Studies* 8:2 (Jan. 2007): 13.

23. Marie-Aimee Hélie-Lucas, "What Is Your Tribe? Women's Struggles and the Construction of Muslimness," in Courtney W. Howland, ed., *Religious Fundamentalisms and the Human Rights of Women* (New York: Palgrave Macmillan, 2001), 22; Nira Yuval-Davis, "The Personal is Political: Jewish Fundamentalism and Women's Empowerment," in ibid., 34; Lily Zakiyah Munir, "Islamic Fundamentalism and Its Impact on Women" (March 2003), available at http://www.law.emory.edu/ihr/acessay.html; Jasmin Zine, "Between Orientalism and Fundamentalism: Muslim Women a Feminist Engagement," in Krista Hunt and Kim Rygiel, eds., *(En)Gendering the War on Terror: War Stories and Camouflaged Politics* (Aldershot, Eng.: Ashgate, 2006), 28.

24. Azizah Al-Hibri, "Muslim Women's Rights in the Global Village: Challenges and Opportunities," in Afzal-Khan, *Shattering the Stereotypes*, 161; Barlas, *"Believing Women" in Islam*, 60; Hassan, "Interview with Dawn Newspaper," 191.

25. Gwendolyn Zoharah Simmons, "Are We Up to the Challenge? The Need for a Radical Re-Ordering of the Islamic Discourse on Women," in Omid Safi, *Progressive Muslims: On Justice, Gender, Pluralism* (Oxford: Oneworld, 2003), 243.

26. Haddad et al., *Muslim Women in America*, 39, 40.

Wilma Mankiller and Michael Wallis, A Chief and Her People

Wilma Mankiller (1945–2010) served from 1985–1995 as the first female principal chief of the Cherokee Nation, the second-largest indigenous group in the United States. She received *Ms.* magazine's Woman of the Year for 1987, the Presidential Medal of Freedom in 1988, and was inducted in the National Women's Hall of Fame in 1993. In an obituary published by *Ms.* magazine, Mankiller was described as making "great strides to improve health, education, housing, utilities management, and tribal government during her time as chief. She also devoted much of her time to civil rights work, focusing largely on women's rights."*

The introduction to Mankiller's autobiography, written collaboratively by Mankiller and historian-biographer-reporter Michael Wallis provides an overview of Mankiller's life. It introduces the land and the community that inspired her political activism. The excerpt and the rest of the autobiography also highlight how Mankiller's commitments and achievements as a female indigenous political leader were shaped by a longer history. Mankiller felt that her life was intertwined with the forced removal of the Cherokee Nation (through the Trail of Tears) from the U.S. Southeast to the central plains in the 1830s. Mankiller's ownership of land traced back to the 1887 Dawes Severalty Act, which promised allotments of land in exchange for indigenous people giving up sovereignty, communal living, and reservations. The Cherokee were able to prevent tribal termination, but they faced steady pressure to assimilate culturally. These pressures intensified after World War II through the Termination Policy (1953–1968), which sought once again to relocate native people, this time to urban centers such as San Francisco, Los Angeles, and Minneapolis. Mankiller's parents moved the family to San Francisco when she was 10. The ghettoization and poverty that "urban Indians" faced in cities as well as on reservations led to the emergence of an American Indian Movement during the 1960s. Inspired by black liberation and Third World liberation movements of that time, the movement attracted Wilma Mankiller, then a young mother. Her relocation back to Cherokee lands in Oklahoma and her political ascendancy represent the culmination of this longer history of oppression and resistance.

Wilma Mankiller's election to principal chief also resonated with an even longer history of indigenous women. Historian Theda Perdue argues that prior to European contact, Cherokee women held great authority and power. Women farmed, controlling a steady food supply for their communities. Kinship, clans,

---

*"First Woman Cherokee Chief Mankiller Dies," April 13, 2010, http://www.msmagazine.com/news/uswirestory.asp?ID=12346.

Excerpted from the introduction to *Mankiller: A Chief and Her People* by Wilma Mankiller and Michael Wallis (New York: St. Martin's Griffin, 1993), xxvii–xxvi. Reprinted by permission of Michael Wallis and the publisher.

and households were based on female lineage, which meant women were decision-makers and authority figures. Women also held political power. These gender structures were challenged by European and American contact. Anglo-Americans tended to recognize only male-led political systems and patriarchal nuclear family structures. The Cherokee Nation, particularly the women, resisted these western gender norms but some aspects were adopted.[†] The election of Wilma Mankiller resurrects, in some ways, the precontact and eighteenth-century practice of female political leadership. (For more on these issues, see Kathleen M. Brown's essay, pp. 12–23.) How do you see her twentieth-century leadership in comparison with the "public mothers" that Lucy Murphy describes (pp. 161–168)? What are the similarities and differences between Mankiller and a figure like Hillary Clinton?

Dawn arrives in the countryside of northeastern Oklahoma, warm and familiar like an old pal who's come calling. . . . Before too long the front door slowly opens and Wilma Mankiller—the woman of the house—emerges. She is barefoot and wears a brightly colored dress. Her dark hair is still damp from a morning shampoo. She sits on a kitchen chair on the narrow porch and sips a mug of coffee. . . .

The surrounding forests and hills conceal the animal life native to this eastern region of Oklahoma. . . . This is the place on earth that Wilma Mankiller loves best. She is surrounded by 160 acres of ancestral property, allotted to her paternal grandfather, John Mankiller, when Oklahoma became a state in 1907. The land is located in Adair County, within hollerin' distance of the Cherokee County line. Named for a prominent Cherokee family, Adair County is the heart of the area first settled by Cherokees in the late 1830s. The county still claims a higher percentage of Native American population than any other in the United States. . . . Here, a person's wealth and worth are measured in other ways besides bank accounts and worldly goods.

In generations past, the Cherokee people came to this area to rebuild their nation after the westward trek from their beloved homelands in the mountainous South. Herded by federal soldiers, the Cherokees took a path in 1838–39 that became known as the Trail of Tears.

At Tahlequah, the seat of Cherokee County in the eastern foothills of the Ozarks, where their bitter journey ended, the Cherokees built new homes and some of the first schools west of the Mississippi for the education of both men and women. They also reestablished an intricate government in Indian Territory, including a system of courts of law. Although oral historians assert that the tribe possessed a written language long before, the Cherokees put to good use the eighty-five-character syllabary developed by Sequoyah over a twelve-year period prior to the Trail of Tears, to publish Oklahoma's first newspaper in both Cherokee and English.[*]

. . . It is country where conversation centers on farming, hunting, weather, football and, forever and always, politics. Not just mainstream party politics, such as candidates for county commissioner or sheriff or the U.S. Senate, but also tribal politics—the critical issue of Cherokee leadership.

Much of the talk at the gas stations, bait shops, and convenience stores scattered along the country roads is about Wilma Mankiller. This is only natural, since she serves as the principal chief of the Cherokee Nation of Oklahoma. The Cherokees represent the second-largest tribe in the United States, after the Dine (Navajo) Nation. Mankiller is the first female to lead a major Native American tribe. With an enrolled tribal population worldwide of more than 140,000, an annual budget of more than $75 million, and more than 1,200 employees spread across 7,000 square miles, her responsibilities as chief are the same as a head of state and the chief executive officer of a major corporation.

Although it is the land of rugged males who, for the most part, prefer to see fellow "good ol' boys" run for political office, it is difficult to find anyone from the Cherokee ranks, including some of Mankiller's former political foes, who can find fault with the performance of her administration. It was not always that

[†]Theda Perdue, *Cherokee Women: Gender and Cultural Change, 1700–1835* (Lincoln: University of Nebraska Press, 1998).

way. In the beginning, there were many problems and obstacles. Often, those were mean times. There were some Cherokees who didn't wish to be governed by a female. Wilma Mankiller had her share of enemies. Her automobile tires were slashed. There were death threats. Chief Mankiller was admittedly an unlikely politician. But gradually she won acceptance. In time, most of her constituents became quite comfortable with her. Now when disagreements occur, they are based on issues rather than gender.

Wilma Mankiller shares her home and life with her husband, Charlie Soap, and Winterhawk, his son from a former marriage. Her two daughters, Felicia and Gina, and their children often stop by to visit, as do other family members and friends. Mankiller's widowed mother lives just down the road.

In the winter, Mankiller's house is warmed by a stove fed by the constant supply of firewood cut from the surrounding forest. Native American art, including masks, baskets, and pottery as well as Cherokee, Kiowa, and Sioux paintings, adorns the shelves and walls. Colorful blankets drape the chair backs and couches. Framed family photographs are scattered about tabletops. On a living room shelf is a small bust of Sam Houston, the revered Texas statesman and folk hero called "the Raven" by the Cherokees who adopted him. Cases hold Mankiller's beloved books, mostly volumes of poetry, novels, biographies, and histories. The works of her favorite authors, including Gloria Steinem, Alex Haley, and Alice Walker, are mixed with the writings of Vine Deloria, Joy Harjo, Robert Conley, Chaucer, Tolstoy, and Milton.

As comfortable as the house is, Mankiller also loves being outside on the land. She tends to the garden and sometimes she walks, trailed by one or two of the family dogs, to a nearby spring where past generations of Mankillers fetched fresh water and gathered mint and watercress.

The nearest community—with just a small grocery–gas station and a school—is called Rocky Mountain. The land where Mankiller and her family reside is known as Mankiller Flats. Born at Hastings Indian Hospital in Tahlequah in 1945, she was raised at Mankiller Flats from her first days. She spent her early years there, with her parents and eight of her ten brothers and sisters. The land is important to Mankiller. It was allotted to her grandfather, and now she and her family maintain it. The land is an important part of their heritage, and they preserve it for future generations.

But of primary importance to Mankiller— the woman who overcame tremendous personal crises—are the thousands of people she serves and her mission to bring self-sufficiency to them. Mankiller felt honored to become her tribe's chosen leader, but she readily adds that she did not seek the responsibility. Indeed, she thought she had reached her pinnacle in tribal government in 1983, when she became her tribe's first female deputy chief.

"Prior to my election, young Cherokee girls would never have thought that they might grow up to be chief," she says. Mankiller had been asked to run as deputy chief by Ross Swimmer, a quarter-blood Indian lawyer and former bank president, who assumed leadership of the Cherokee Nation in 1975. Swimmer convinced Mankiller that, if elected, she could effect greater change in the rural Cherokee communities where she worked.

When Swimmer, a staunch Republican, resigned in 1985 to go to Washington to head the Bureau of Indian Affairs, it was his deputy, a liberal Democrat, who took over. Mankiller was left with a tribal council which more than likely would not have chosen her to take Swimmer's place had it not been for the Cherokee Constitution mandating that the deputy chief move to the higher post when the chief resigns.

In a historic tribal election in July 1987, Mankiller won the coveted post in her own right, and political success brought an unprecedented worldwide interest in both her and the Cherokee Nation. In 1991—winning with an 83 percent majority—she was reelected for four more years.

"We are a revitalized tribe," says Mankiller. "After every major upheaval, we have been able to gather together as a people and rebuild a community and a government. Individually and collectively, Cherokee people possess an extraordinary ability to face down adversity and continue moving forward. We are able to do that because our culture, though certainly diminished, has sustained us since time immemorial. The Cherokee culture is a well-kept secret."

Since becoming chief of her people, Mankiller has become a visible force in America. Named *Ms.* magazine's Woman of the Year in 1987, she has been awarded many honorary degrees and citations, and makes numerous national media appearances and public presentations on behalf of her tribe. But the hardworking chief is much the same unaffected person she always has been. She is at her best when in the halls of Congress quietly advocating better health care, improved housing, or more jobs for the Cherokee people.

Her father, the late Charley Mankiller, was a full-blooded Cherokee, and her mother, Irene, is of Dutch-Irish descent. "We traced our family name back to the eastern part of the country, where the Cherokees lived in great numbers," says Mankiller. "As best we can tell, our name is an old Cherokee military title. It was usually given to a person who was in a position of safeguarding a Cherokee village."

Cherokee culture thrived for hundreds of years in the southeastern United States until the tribe was pushed westward out of its homelands. Among those who survived the Trail of Tears were some of Mankiller's paternal ancestors. They were part of the tribe that regrouped to make Tahlequah its capital and embarked on what historians today call the Cherokees' "Golden Age." This was, in spite of the removal, a time of prosperity, marked by the development of businesses, schools, and a flourishing culture. In those days, people helped each other more and maintained a greater sense of interdependence.

Nonetheless, this prosperity did not last. The years of good fortune and revival after the shameful removal ended with tribal division over the Civil War. At the war's end in 1865, the Cherokees—many of whom had not taken a side—were treated like defeated southerners. Eventually, poverty replaced affluence as a predominant theme as more and more Cherokee land was taken to make room for other tribes who were also forced to leave their homes and move into Indian Territory.

By 1907, the federal government had dismantled the tribal government, ignored the Cherokee Constitution, and divided up the land in individual allotments. It was at that time that Wilma Mankiller's family received its share of property in the wooded hills. In that remote setting, where she and her siblings were raised, the family grew strawberries and other crops for a living. There was no indoor plumbing, so the Mankiller children hauled water about a quarter of a mile to their home.

"I remember when we bartered with neighbors and ate what we grew," she says. "Those days helped me so much. I was raised with a sense of community that extended beyond my family."

When she was ten years old, Mankiller's entire family was moved to California as participants in the federal government's relocation program. "It was part of the national Indian policy of the 1950s," she explains. "The government wanted to break up tribal communities and 'mainstream' Indians, so it relocated rural families to urban areas. One day I was living in a rural Cherokee community, and a few days later I was living in California and trying to deal with the mysteries of television, neon lights, and elevators. It was total culture shock."

The Mankiller family eventually became acclimated to California. Mankiller attended school and met her first husband, a well-to-do Ecuadoran. They had two daughters, Felicia in 1964 and Gina in 1966 It was during the turbulent 1960s, while starting her family, that Mankiller began to raise her political consciousness. Her concern for Native American issues was fully ignited by 1969 when a band of university students occupied the abandoned prison on Alcatraz Island in San Francisco Bay. They wanted to attract attention to issues affecting them and their tribes. Mankiller answered the call. Out of that historic experience, an activist was born.

"In most ways I was a typical housewife at that time," recalls Wilma, "but when Alcatraz occurred, I became aware of what needed to be done to let the rest of the world know that Indians had rights too. Alcatraz articulated my own feelings about being an Indian. It was a benchmark. After that, I became involved."

She attended sociology classes at San Francisco State College and took on Native American issues with a fervor. Mankiller worked as a volunteer for five grueling years with the Pit River Tribe in California on treaty-rights issues, helping to establish a legal defense fund for the battle to reclaim the tribe's ancestral lands. She also devoted much of her time to Native American preschool and adult education programs and directing a dropout prevention program for Native American youngsters.

In 1974, Mankiller divorced her husband of eleven years. "He wanted a traditional housewife. I had a stronger desire to do things in the community than at home." Two years later, she returned to Oklahoma with her daughters. "I was delighted to be back on our ancestral homelands," she recalls. "I wanted to come home and raise my kids and build a house on my land."

She managed all that and more. In 1979, after almost three years of helping to procure important grants and launch critical rural services for the tribe, Mankiller enrolled in graduate courses at the nearby University of Arkansas. Late one morning in the fall of 1979, while returning home from class on a two-lane country road, Mankiller was seriously injured in a freak automobile accident which resulted in a fatality. An oncoming car, which had pulled into her lane to pass, collided head-on with Mankiller's station wagon. Unbelievably, the young woman driving the other vehicle, who was killed, was Mankiller's close friend. When Mankiller regained consciousness in the hospital, her face was crushed and her ribs and legs were broken. It was one of several brushes with death. After avoiding the amputation of her right leg, she endured seventeen operations and was bedridden for months. During the long healing process, Mankiller never allowed herself to become discouraged or to sink into despair.

"That accident in 1979 changed my life," she says. "I came very close to death, felt its presence and the alluring call to complete the circle of life. I always think of myself as the woman who lived before and the woman who lives afterward. I was at home recovering for almost a year, and I had time to reevaluate." For Mankiller, it proved to be a deep spiritual awakening when she adopted what she referred to as "a very Cherokee approach to life—what our tribal elders call 'being of good mind.'"

Then in November 1980, just a year after the tragic accident, Mankiller was diagnosed with myasthenia gravis, a chronic neuromuscular disease that causes varying weakness in the voluntary muscles of the body. Treatment required surgery to remove the thymus gland and a program of drug therapy. In December 1980—just barely out of the hospital—she was back on the job. She needed only one month to recover from her illness. Although a regimen of drugs followed, work seemed to be the best medicine of all.

"I thought a lot about what I wanted to do with my life during that time," says Mankiller. "The reality of how precious life is enabled me to begin projects I couldn't have otherwise tackled."

In 1981, she spearheaded the tribe's most ambitious and lauded experiment to that date—the Bell Community Revitalization Project. With hundreds of thousands of dollars in federal and private funds and with their own labor, the residents of a poverty-stricken community named Bell in eastern Oklahoma remodeled dilapidated housing, constructed new homes, and laid a sixteen-mile pipeline that brought running water to many homes for the first time. Beyond the physical improvements, the volunteers from the Bell community did the work themselves, while developing a strong bond and gaining a sense of control over their own lives.

The national publicity that followed made the Bell Project a model for other Native American tribes eager for self-sufficiency. This work also established Mankiller as an expert in community development, and brought her to the attention of Cherokee Chief Swimmer.

The election to deputy chief occurred two years later, and in 1985, when Swimmer resigned from office, Mankiller became principal chief. Still, she did not feel she had a mandate until 1987 when she was elected on her own, even though from the very start she never slowed down.

"In order to understand how I operate, it is necessary to remember that I come from an activist family," says Mankiller. "My father was involved in union organizing, community service, and liked to discuss political issues. With a background like that, you naturally get involved in the community."

Her terms of office have produced countless highlights: a dramatic increase in tribal revenue and services; the attraction of new businesses to eastern Oklahoma, where many Cherokees live; the garnering of more than $20 million in construction projects, including new clinics, the procurement of funding for innovative programs to help Cherokee women on welfare develop microenterprises, the establishment of an $8 million Job Corps training center; and dozens of other projects, ranging from an extensive array of services for children to revitalization of the Cherokee judicial system. Other initiatives Mankiller has spearheaded include a new tribal tax commission, an energy-consulting firm, a pilot self-government agreement with the federal government, and an agreement with the Environmental Protection Agency.

In October 1986, Wilma married her old friend Charlie Soap, a full-blooded Cherokee and the former director of the tribal development program. Mankiller and Soap met while working together on the Bell Project. Known as a quiet but effective "Cherokee powerhouse,"

Soap has focused his effort on development projects for several low-income Cherokee communities. . . . When Soap recites his personal heroes, his wife tops the list. When Mankiller names her heroes, Soap is her first choice. "He is the most secure male I have ever met," says Mankiller. "He is not threatened by strong women. He is supportive of women, of women's causes, and of me and my work."

Mankiller's love of family and her people paid off in major dividends again, in 1990, when she was faced with yet another physical dilemma. Recurrent kidney problems resulted in the need for a kidney transplant. Her oldest brother, Don Mankiller, consented to serve as the donor, and the operation was a success. During her convalescence, she had many long talks with Charlie Soap and other members of her family before ultimately deciding to run for yet another term as chief.

"It was a big decision," says Mankiller, who admits that it finally came down to the fact that she believed too much unfinished work remained. Her mission was not completed. With her reelection in 1991, the Cherokee people returned Mankiller to office with a landslide vote.

But all the honorary degrees and successful tribal development projects do not begin to measure the influence that Mankiller has had in so many diverse circles of America. First and foremost are her stewardship of the Cherokees, and the pride she has instilled in thousands of Native American people. She has shown—in her typically ebullient and joyous way—not what Cherokees or other native people can learn from European Americans, but what whites can learn from native people. In fact, without the knowledge of the interconnectedness of all living things and the spirituality that Native American culture so powerfully possesses, many white Americans are beginning to understand that they have much to learn from native wisdom, culture, and spirituality.

Spirituality is then key to the public and private aura of Wilma Mankiller, a leader who has indeed become known as much for her able leadership of the Cherokee Nation as for her spiritual presence among all Americans A woman rabbi who serves as the head of a large synagogue in New York City commented that Mankiller was a significant spiritual force in the nation. One would imagine that a rabbi in Manhattan and an Indian chief in Oklahoma would have little in common, but it is clearly Mankiller's way of life—her religion, so to speak—that has formed bonds with spiritual leaders throughout the country.

No less significant has been Mankiller's reputation among women and women's groups. A woman who proudly describes herself as a feminist, a leader who is concerned with women's issues worldwide, Mankiller is ironically a female leader who has been as comfortably embraced by men as by women. Most of the attacks directed against her in those early days of campaigning because of her gender, because she threatened the male Cherokee status quo, have subsided. She has become a leader who can play easily to a multitude of audiences—from the cover of *Ms.* to the cover of *Parade*—in an effortless way that few others have been able to duplicate. Perhaps it truly is her innate love of all people that breaks down so many doors.

Hillary Clinton, "Women's Rights Are Human Rights," 1995

The United Nations Charter of 1948 committed the UN to promote and encourage respect for human rights "without distinction as to race, sex, language and religion." A Commission on Human Rights, with a Subcommission on the Status

Women's Rights are Human Rights" (speech, First Lady Hillary Clinton, United Nations Fourth World Conference on Women, Plenary Session, Beijing, China, September 5, 1995). A full video and audio file of this speech, along with the unabridge text, is available at http://www.americanrhetoric.com/speeches/hillaryclintonbeijingspeech.htm.

*Sequoyah, who was born in about 1776, was the son of Wut-Teh (the daughter of a Cherokee chief) and a Virginia fur trader, Nathaniel Gist. During the War of 1812, Sequoyah enlisted under Andrew Jackson to fight against the British. In the war's aftermath, he spent 12 years working on a written language for Cherokee, introducing it in 1821. For a chart of the syllabary, see hhttp://www.nlm.nih.gov/nativevoices/timeline/270.html

of Women, was constructed as part of the UN's Economic and Social Council (ECOSOC); shortly afterward, the subcommission broke off to be an independent Commission on the Status of Women (CSW), reporting directly to the Economic and Social Council. Whether constituted as subcommission or commission, members found it almost impossible to get the attention of ECOSOC or to persuade the UN that women's infirmities really deserved international attention. The shrill insistence of the Soviet Union that it had already solved all of women's problems meant that it was almost impossible to make critical assessments of women's status independently of Cold War rivalries.

Yet the CSW did engage in significant advocacy, even though the press paid almost no attention to it and most male politicians, inside and outside the UN, were dismissive. For example, that some of the language of the Universal Declaration of Human Rights is gender-neutral is due to CSW insistence. At the time of its founding, nearly one-third of UN member nations did not allow women to vote; the CSW moved its 1950 meeting to Lebanon to call international attention to the denial of democracy there and elsewhere. French women could not vote until 1945, and women in French Algeria not until 1958, on the eve of their own independence; Swiss women did not get the right to vote or stand for election until 1971. In 2011, King Abdullah of Saudi Arabia granted women the right to vote but only in municipal elections. (As we go to press, they still lack the right to drive.) In Lebanon, where all men over 21—whatever their education—are required to vote, women over 21 may now choose to vote, but only if they have an elementary education, which is not required of men.)* The CSW identified and sought to publicize weaknesses in women's literacy, education, employment, and the integrity of their citizenship. By 1979 the UN adopted—at the CSW's urging—a Convention on the Elimination of All Forms of Discrimination Against Women (CEDAW), which recognizes women's rights in family life—the right to freedom from domestic violence, for example—and in the public sector—rights to equal education, work, and health care. The United States participated in drafting the convention and President Jimmy Carter signed it within its first year. But the Senate has not ratified this convention, and as this volume goes to press, the United States remains one of only seven nations that have refused to do so. (The others include Sudan, Somalia, and Iran.)

Identifying 1975–85 as the UN Decade for Women, the UN convened three major international conferences—1975 in Mexico City, 1980 in Copenhagen, and 1985 in Nairobi. All three generally focused on economic development. A fourth was held a decade later, in 1995 in Beijing, on the heels of the UN Conference on Human Rights held at Vienna in 1993, at which it had been clear that it was not easy to find international consensus on women's entitlements. The declaration that emerged from Vienna specified that "the human rights of women and of the girl-child are an inalienable, integral, and indivisible part of universal human rights"; it named as a target "gender-based violence and all forms of sexual harassment and exploitation, including those resulting from cultural prejudice and international trafficking"; but it omitted provisions on reproductive rights because they had run afoul of religious arguments about what constituted freedom.**

At Beijing, as at the conferences that had preceded it, the number of official delegates was swamped by the enormous numbers of women who surrounded

*Data on women's voting from CIA *World Factbook*, available at https://www.cia.gov/library/publications/the-world-factbook/fields/2123.html.

**Vienna Declaration and Programme of Action, UN World Conference on Human Rights, June 14–25, 1993, A/Conf 157/23, Sec. I, par. 18.

the conference with meetings of their own. These meetings were sponsored by hundreds of women's nongovernmental organizations (NGOs), notably from underdeveloped countries which demanded improvements in the status of women that could be measured by international law. The conference itself was an expression of post–Cold War confidence, and the invitation to Hillary Clinton, wife of the then president of the United States, to offer a major speech recognized the international power of the United states and Clinton's own long-standing commitment to women's rights. The speech was expected to attract international attention.

In her memoir, Clinton describes the care she and her "speech team"—which included Madeleine Albright, then the U.S. permanent representative to the United Nations (President Bill Clinton would appoint her secretary of state in 1997)—lavished on the wording. "Although I had delivered thousands of speeches, I was nervous," Hillary Clinton wrote.

> I felt passionately about the subject, and I was speaking as a representative of my country. . . . If nothing came out of the conference, it would be viewed as another missed opportunity to galvanize global opinion on behalf of . . . the cause of women's rights. . . . I wanted the speech to be simple, accessible and unambiguous in its message that women's rights are not separate from, or a subsidiary of, human rights. . . . Pushing the envelope in this speech meant being clear about the injustice of the Chinese government's behavior. The Chinese leadership had blocked non–governmental organizations from holding their NGO forum at the main conference in Beijing. They forced NGOs devoted to causes ranging from prenatal care to microlending to convene at a makeshift site in the small city of Huairou, forty miles north, where there were few accommodations or facilities. Although I didn't mention China or any other country by name, there was little doubt about the egregious human rights violators to whom I was referring.[†]

Fourteen years later, President Barak Obama would appoint Hilary Clinton Secretary of State. In 2011 she launched the Women's Nationality Initiative, collaborating with the United Nations High Commission on Refugees to encourage change in the laws of the 29 nations that now prevent women from acquiring, retaining, or transmitting citizenship to their children or their foreign spouses, a situation that results in widespread statelessness. (For the existence of similar rules in the United States in the first half of the twentieth century, see *Mackenzie v. Hare*, pp. 413–415.)

As you read this speech, note the women's vulnerabilities that are named. Compare the list that Hillary Clinton constructs with the demands for reform in the 1848 Seneca Falls Declaration of Sentiments. What has changed? What has remained the same? Review the UN Declaration of Human Rights at http://www .un.org/en/documents/udhr/. Do you think it is useful to describe women's rights as human rights? What difference does it make? Does the impact or emphasis of Clinton's speech seem to change in any way when you listen to the audio version?

I would like to thank the Secretary General for inviting me to be part of this important United Nations Fourth World Conference on Women. This is truly a celebration—a celebration of the contributions women make in every aspect of life: in the home, on the job, in the community, as mothers, wives, sisters, daughters, learners, workers, citizens and leaders.

It is also a coming together, much the way women come together every day in every country. . . . Whether it is while playing with our children in the park, or washing clothes in a

†Hillary Rodham Clinton, *Living History* (New York: Simon & Schuster, 2003), pp. 303–5.

river, or taking a break at the office water cooler, we come together and talk about our aspirations and concerns. And time and again, our talk turns to our children and our families. However different we may appear, there is far more that unites us than divides us. We share a common future, and we are here to find common ground so that we may help bring new dignity and respect to women and girls all over the world, and in so doing bring new strength and stability to families as well.

By gathering in Beijing, we are focusing world attention on issues that matter most in our lives—the lives of women and their families: access to education, health care, jobs and credit, the chance to enjoy basic legal and human rights and to participate fully in the political life of our countries.

There are some who question the reason for this conference. . . . There are some who wonder whether the lives of women and girls matter to economic and political progress around the globe. . . .

The great challenge of this conference is to give voice to women everywhere whose experiences go unnoticed, whose words go unheard. Women comprise more than half the world's population, 70% of the world's poor, and two-thirds of those who are not taught to read and write. We are the primary caretakers for most of the world's children and elderly. Yet much of the work we do is not valued—not by economists, not by historians, not by popular culture, not by government leaders.

At this very moment, as we sit here, women around the world are giving birth, raising children, cooking meals, washing clothes, cleaning houses, planting crops, working on assembly lines, running companies, and running countries. Women also are dying from diseases that should have been prevented or treated. They are watching their children succumb to malnutrition caused by poverty and economic deprivation. They are being denied the right to go to school by their own fathers and brothers. They are being forced into prostitution, and they are being barred from the bank lending offices and banned from the ballot box.

Those of us who have the opportunity to be here have the responsibility to speak for those who could not. As an American . . . I want to speak up for mothers who are fighting for good schools, safe neighborhoods, clean air, and clean airwaves; for older women, some of them widows, who find that, after raising their families, their skills and life experiences are not valued in the marketplace; for women who are working all night as nurses, hotel clerks, or fast food chefs so that they can be at home during the day with their children; and for women everywhere who simply don't have time to do everything they are called upon to do each and every day.

Speaking to you today, I speak for them, just as each of us speaks for women around the world who are denied the chance to go to school, or see a doctor, or own property, or have a say about the direction of their lives, simply because they are women. . . . We need to understand there is no one formula for how women should lead our lives. That is why we must respect the choices that each woman makes for herself and her family. Every woman deserves the chance to realize her own God-given potential. But we must recognize that women will never gain full dignity until their human rights are respected and protected.

Our goals for this conference, to strengthen families and societies by empowering women to take greater control over their own destinies, cannot be fully achieved unless all governments— here and around the world—accept their responsibility to protect and promote internationally recognized human rights. The international community has long acknowledged and recently reaffirmed at Vienna that both women and men are entitled to a range of protections and personal freedoms, from the right of personal security to the right to determine freely the number and spacing of the children they bear. No one should be forced to remain silent for fear of religious or political persecution, arrest, abuse, or torture.

Tragically, women are most often the ones whose human rights are violated. Even now, in the late 20th century, the rape of women continues to be used as an instrument of armed conflict. Women and children make up a large majority of the world's refugees. And when women are excluded from the political process, they become even more vulnerable to abuse. I believe that now, on the eve of a new millennium, it is time to break the silence. It is time for us to say here in Beijing, and for the world to hear, that it is no longer acceptable to discuss women's rights as separate from human rights.

These abuses have continued because, for too long, the history of women has been a history of silence. Even today, there are those who are trying to silence our words. But the voices of this conference . . . must be heard loudly and clearly: It is a violation of *human* rights when babies are denied food, or drowned, or suffocated, or their spines broken, simply because they are born girls; . . . when women and girls are sold into the slavery of prostitution for human greed—and the kinds of reasons that are used to justify this practice should no longer be tolerated; . . . when women are doused with gasoline, set on fire, and burned to death because their marriage dowries are deemed too small; . . . when individual women are raped in their own communities and when thousands of women are subjected to rape as a tactic or prize of war; . . . when a leading cause of death worldwide among women ages 14 to 44 is the violence they are subjected to in their own homes by their own relatives; . . . when young girls are brutalized by the painful and degrading practice of genital mutilation; . . . [and] when women are denied the right to plan their own families, and that includes being forced to have abortions or being sterilized against their will.

If there is one message that echoes forth from this conference, let it be that human rights are women's rights and women's rights are human rights once and for all. And among those rights are the right to speak freely—and the right to be heard.

Women must enjoy the rights to participate fully in the social and political lives of their countries, if we want freedom and democracy to thrive and endure. . . .

In my country, we recently celebrated the 75th anniversary of Women's Suffrage. It took 150 years after the signing of our Declaration of Independence for women to win the right to vote. It took 72 years of organized struggle, before that happened, on the part of many courageous women and men. It was one of America's most divisive philosophical wars. But it was a bloodless war. Suffrage was achieved without a shot being fired. . . . We have seen peace prevail in most places for a half century. We have avoided another world war. But we have not solved older, deeply-rooted problems that continue to diminish the potential of half the world's population.

. . . As long as discrimination and inequities remain so commonplace everywhere in the world, as long as girls and women are valued less, fed less, fed last, overworked, underpaid, not schooled, subjected to violence in and outside their homes—the potential of the human family to create a peaceful, prosperous world will not be realized.

Let this conference be our—and the world's—call to action. Let us heed that call so we can create a world in which every woman is treated with respect and dignity, every boy and girl is loved and cared for equally, and every family has the hope of a strong and stable future. . . .

God's blessing on you, your work, and all who will benefit from it.

INDEX

Comstock Act and, 212, 457, 458, 658

Griswold v. Connecticut and, 659, 671–74

Keller, H., and, 315

in marriage, 457, 631–32, 635

poverty and, 631–32

Sanger and, 457–64

sexual revolution and, 629–36

Contracts, marriage and, 120

Contribution history, 4

Convention of American Women Trade Unionists, 370

Convention on the Elimination of All Forms of Discrimination Against Women (CEDAW), 1, 791

Cook, Blanche Wiesen, 523–29

Cooke, Joe, Jr., 595–96

Cooking

by Asian American women, 632–46

as housework, 45, 46–47, 50

by Native American women, 14–15

Cooking Methods (Beals), 389

Coolidge, Calvin, 507

Cooper, Anna Julia, 300

Cooper, Mandy, 154

Cooper Union's Great Hall of the People, 371

"Cordwainers' Song," 133

CORE. *See* Congress of Racial Equality

Corey, Giles, 62

Corey, Martha, 62

Cosmetics

for African Americans, *472*

beauty and, 422

for Mexican-American women, 430–31

Cott, Nancy F., 503–11, 672, 676

Cottrell, Elsie, 144

Coughlin, Charles E., 525

Council of National Defense, 307

Council of Trent, 170

Council on American-Islamic Relations (CAIR), 777, 778, 782

Couper, Mary Black, 199

Coutume de Paris (customary law code), 163

Coverture, 56, 119–24

brothels and, 121

Creoles and, 163

Kendall on, 242–44

Mackenzie v. Hare and, 413–16

slavery and, 145

Supreme Court on, 124

Cowell, Roberta, 625

Cox, Laura, 601

CR. *See* Consciousness-raising

Craighead, Rebeca, 282

Craighill, Margaret, 680

CRC. *See* Community Relations Committee

Creel, George, 494

Creoles, 161–67

coverture and, 163

fornication and, 163

as healers, 165

marriage of, 163, 167

as midwives, 165

St. Louis World's Fair and, 386

Crerar Library, 355

Cress, Becky, 180, 184–86

Cress, William, 180–86

Crisis (NAACP newspaper), 316

Cristero movement, 496

Crittenden Board, 681–82, 687n13

Cromwell, Oliver, 170

Cross, Nora, 555–56

Cross-dressing, 34–42, 110, *120*, 218–19

Crowe, William T., 690–91

Cry the Beloved Country (Paton), 319

CSW. *See* Commission on the Status of Women

Culbreath, Mary, 154

Cultural revolution, 710–12

Cushing, Caleb, 217, 218

Customary law code (*coutume de Paris*), 163

D

Daily Commercial, 326

Daily Kansan, 632

Daily Tulean Dispatch, The, 532

Dall, Caroline, 135, 352

Dances of All Nations (Beals), 389

D'Angelo, Josephine, 556–57

Daniels, Josephus, 528

Daniels, Roger, 412

"Danny Thomas Show, The," 563

Daughters of Bilitis, 550

Davidow, Anne R., 699

Davis, Alvin, 624

Davis, Angela, *475*, 737

Davis, E. M., *257*

Davis, Fred, 602

Davis, Jefferson, 313

Davis, Katharine Bement, 445

Davis, Rachel, 128, 180–88

Davis, Sarah, 73

Davis v. Monroe County Board of Education, 750

Day, Doris, 606, 708

Day, Madison, 283

Dayton, Cornelia Hughes, 1–8

"Day without a Mexican, A" (film), 762

DDT, 708

De Beauvoir, Simone, 579n18, 609

De Bruyne, Elvira, 619

De Bry, Theodor, 28, *29*

Debs, Eugene V., 368

Decade for Women (United Nations), 791

Declaration of Independence, 1

Centennial reading of, 295

Declaration of Sentiments and, 224

Declaration of Sentiments, 221, 224–25, 247–50, 406, 506

Torch Relay and, *265*

Dee, Ruby, 712

Defense Department Advisory Committee on Women in the Services, 692–93

Defense of Marriage Act (DOMA), 673–77

De Forest, Lee, 409

Degler, Carl N., 211n31

De Hart, Jane Sherron, 1–8

Deloria, Vine, 787

Del Rio, Dolores, 431

De Maree, Pieter, 28–30

Democratic National Committee, 586

Democratic National Convention, 593, 726

Democratic Party

ERA and, 511

Ku Klux Klan and, 280

suffrage and, 408

Department of Defense (DOD)

all-volunteer force and, 695

homosexuals and, 682, 685

pregnancy and, 693

risk rule of, 693–94

in Vietnam War, 691

Department of Education, 748, 750

Department of Health, Education, and Welfare (HEW), 522, 636, 712

Department of Health and Human Services, 668

Department of Labor, U.S., 353

De Riencourt, Amaury, 613–14

Description and historicall declaration of the golden Kingedome of Guinea, A (de Maree), 28–30